P9-DCZ-609

Basic Marketing Research

Basic Marketing Research

A Decision-Making Approach

SECOND EDITION

Naresh K. Malhotra
Georgia Institute of Technology

Mark Peterson
University of Texas at Arlington

PEARSON Prentice Hall

Pearson Education International

Acquisitions Editor: Katie Stevens
Editorial Director: Jeff Shelstad
Associate Editor: Wil Mara
Editorial Assistant: Rebecca Lembo
Media Project Manager: Peter Snell
Executive Marketing Manager: Michelle O'Brien
Marketing Assistant: Joanna Sabella
Associate Director Production Editorial: Judy Leale
Production Editor: Kelly Warsak
Permissions Supervisor: Charles Morris
Manufacturing Buyer: Michelle Klein
Design Manager: Maria Lange
Art Director: Pat Smythe
Interior and Cover Designer: Brian Salisbury
Line Art Illustrations: GTS Publishing Services
Director, Image Resource Center: Melinda Reo
Manager, Rights and Permissions: Zina Arabia
Manager, Visual Research: Beth Brenzel
Manager, Cover Visual Research and Permissions: Karen Sanatar
Photo Researcher: Teri Stratford
Image Permission Coordinator: Robert Farrell
Manager, Print Production: Christy Mahon
Composition/Full-Service Project Management: Carlisle Communications/Ann Imhof
Printer/Binder: Courier-Kendallville
Cover Printer: Lehigh Press
Typeface: 10 pt. Janson Text-Roman

Credits and acknowledgments borrowed from other sources and reproduced, with permission, in this textbook appear on page 601.

All software-output illustrations used in this book were created by the authors and based on output from both Microsoft Excel and SPSS. Microsoft Excel® is a trademark of the Microsoft Corporation. SPSS® is a trademark of SPSS, Inc.

If you purchased this book within the United States or Canada you should be aware that is has been wrongfully imported without the approval of the Publisher or the Author.

Copyright © 2006, 2002 by Pearson Education, Inc., Upper Saddle River, New Jersey 07458.
Pearson Prentice Hall. All rights reserved. Printed in the United States of America. This publication is protected by Copyright and permission should be obtained from the publisher prior to any prohibited reproduction, storage in a retrieval system, or transmission in any form or by any means, electronic, mechanical, photocopying, recording, or likewise. For information regarding permission(s), write to: Rights and Permissions Department.

Pearson Prentice Hall™ is a trademark of Pearson Education, Inc.
Pearson® is a registered trademark of Pearson plc
Prentice Hall® is a registered trademark of Pearson Education, Inc.

Pearson Education LTD.
Pearson Education Singapore, Pte. Ltd
Pearson Education, Canada, Ltd
Pearson Education—Japan
Pearson Education Australia PTY, Limited
Pearson Education North Asia Ltd
Pearson Educación de Mexico, S.A. de C.V.
Pearson Education Malaysia, Pte. Ltd
Pearson Education, Upper Saddle River, New Jersey

PEARSON
Prentice Hall

10 9 8 7 6 5 4 3 2
0-13-197121-2

To my wife and best friend, Veena, with love.—Naresh

To my wife and best friend, Cindy, with love.—Mark

"A prudent wife is from the LORD."

PROVERBS 19:14

"Husbands, love your wives, even as Christ also loved the church, and gave himself for it."

EPHESIANS 5:35

BRIEF CONTENTS

Part 1
Introduction and Early Phases of Marketing Research 2

Chapter 1 Introduction to Marketing Research 2
Chapter 2 Defining the Marketing Research Problem and Developing an Approach 30
Cases for Part 1 60
Video Cases for Part 1 62

Part 2
Research Design Formulation 68

Chapter 3 Research Design 68
Chapter 4 Exploratory Research Design: Secondary Data 94
Chapter 5 Exploratory Research Design: Syndicated Sources of Secondary Data 122
Chapter 6 Exploratory Research Design: Qualitative Research 146
Chapter 7 Descriptive Research Design: Survey and Observation 178
Chapter 8 Causal Research Design: Experimentation 208
Chapter 9 Measurement and Scaling: Fundamentals and Comparative Scaling 236
Chapter 10 Measurement and Scaling: Noncomparative Scaling Techniques 258
Chapter 11 Questionnaire and Form Design 284
Chapter 12 Sampling: Design and Procedures 320
Chapter 13 Sampling: Final and Initial Sample Size Determination 352
Cases for Part 2 375
Video Cases for Part 2 383

Part 3
Data Collection, Analysis, and Reporting 386

Chapter 14 Field Work: Data Collection 386
Chapter 15 Data Preparation and Analysis Strategy 402
Chapter 16 Data Analysis: Frequency Distribution, Hypothesis Testing, and Cross-Tabulation 426
Chapter 17 Data Analysis: Hypothesis Testing Related to Differences 460
Chapter 18 Data Analysis: Correlation and Regression 494
Chapter 19 Report Preparation and Presentation 528
Cases for Part 3A: Cases With External Data 549
Cases for Part 3B: Cases Without External Data 555
Video Cases for Part 3 558

Part 4
Comprehensive Cases and Video Cases 562

Cases for Part 4: Cases With External Data 562
Video Cases for Part 4 575

CONTENTS

Foreword xxix

About the Authors xxxix

Part 1
Introduction and Early Phases of Marketing Research 2

Chapter 1
Introduction to Marketing Research 2

Opening Questions 3
How Reebok Fits Shoes 3
Overview 4
Definition of Marketing Research 5
A Classification of Marketing Research 7
Marketing Research Process 9
- Step 1: Defining the Problem 9
- Step 2: Developing an Approach to the Problem 10
- Step 3: Formulating a Research Design 10
- Step 4: Doing Field Work or Collecting Data 10
- Step 5: Preparing and Analyzing Data 10
- Step 6: Preparing and Presenting the Report 10

The Role of Marketing Research in Marketing Decision Making 11
The Information Value Chain for Marketing Research 14
The Decision to Conduct Marketing Research 15
An Overview of the Marketing Research Industry 15
Selecting a Research Supplier 18
Careers in Marketing Research 19
The Role of Marketing Research in MIS and DSS 20
Summary Illustration Using the Opening Vignette 22
Application to Contemporary Issues 23
International Marketing Research 23
Technology and Marketing Research 24
Ethics in Marketing Research 25
SPSS Windows and EXCEL 27
Summary 27
Key Terms and Concepts 27
Suggested Cases and Video Cases 28
Live Research: Conducting a Marketing Research Project 28
Acronyms 28
Review Questions 28
Applied Problems 29
Group Discussion 29

Chapter 2
Defining the Marketing Research Problem and Developing an Approach 30

Opening Questions 31
The World's First Sports-Utility Wagon 31
Overview 32
The Importance of Defining the Problem 33
The Process of Defining the Problem and Developing an Approach 35
Tasks Involved 35
Discussions with Decision Makers 36
Interviews with Industry Experts 39
Secondary Data Analysis 39
Qualitative and Exploratory Research 40
Environmental Context of the Problem 42
Past Information and Forecasts 42
Resource Constraints and Objectives 43
Buyer Behavior 43
Legal, Economic, Marketing, and Technological Environments 44
Management-Decision Problem and Marketing Research Problem 45
Defining the Marketing Research Problem 47
Components of the Approach 49
Analytical Framework and Models 49
Research Questions and Hypotheses 50
Specification of Information Needed 52
Summary Illustration Using the Opening Vignette 53
International Marketing Research 54
Technology and Marketing Research 54
Ethics in Marketing Research 55
SPSS Windows 55
Summary 57
Key Terms and Concepts 57
Suggested Cases and Video Cases 58
Live Research: Conducting a Marketing Research Project 58
Acronyms 58
Review Questions 58
Applied Problems 59
Group Discussion 59

CASES FOR PART 1

Case 1.1 Gillette Has a Razor-Sharp Edge Over Its Competitors 60
Case 1.2 Sears: Meeting the Challenge of the Future 61

VIDEO CASES FOR PART 1

Video Case 1.1 Burke: Learning and Growing Through Marketing Research 62
Video Case 1.2 Accenture: The Accent Is in the Name 66

Part 2
Research Design Formulation 68

Chapter 3
Research Design 68

Opening Questions 69
Marketing Research Helps Spiegel Redesign Its Product Lines 69
Overview 70
What Is a Research Design? 71
Basic Research Designs 72
Exploratory Research 74
Descriptive Research 76
Cross-Sectional Designs 78
Longitudinal Designs 78
Cross-Sectional Versus Longitudinal Designs 79
Causal Research 80
Relationships Among Exploratory, Descriptive, and Causal Research 82
Tasks Involved in Formulating a Research Design 84
Research Design and the Value of Marketing Research 85
Budgeting and Scheduling the Project 85
Marketing Research Proposal 86
Summary Illustration Using the Opening Vignette 87
International Marketing Research 88
Technology and Marketing Research 89
Ethics in Marketing Research 89
Summary 91
Key Terms and Concepts 91
Suggested Cases and Video Cases 92
Live Research: Conducting a Marketing Research Project 92
Acronyms 92
Review Questions 92
Applied Problems 92
Group Discussion 93

Chapter 4
Exploratory Research Design: Secondary Data 94

Opening Questions 95
Secondary Data Vindicate the *Vindicator!* 95
Overview 96
Primary Versus Secondary Data 97
Advantages and Uses of Secondary Data 99
Disadvantages of Secondary Data 100

Criteria for Evaluating Secondary Data 100
Specifications: Methodology Used to Collect the Data 100
Error: Accuracy of the Data 100
Currency: When the Data Were Collected 102
Objective: The Purpose for the Study 102
Nature: The Content of the Data 102
Dependability: How Dependable Are the Data? 103
Classification of Secondary Data 103
Internal Secondary Data 103
Customer Databases 104
Data Mining, Customer Relationship Management Systems, and Database Marketing 104
External Secondary Data: Published Sources 106
General Business Data 106
Guides 106
Indexes and Bibliographies 106
Directories 107
Nongovernmental Statistical Data 107
Government Sources 107
Census Data 108
Other Government Publications 108
Computerized Databases 109
Online Databases 110
Internet Databases 110
Offline Databases 110
Categories of Database Types 111
Bibliographic Databases 111
Numeric Databases 111
Full-Text Databases 111
Directory Databases 111
Special-Purpose Databases 112
Directories of Databases 112
Combining Internal and External Secondary Data 112
Geo-Demographic Coding 113
Geo-Visual Databases 113
Buying Power Index 114
Summary Illustration Using the Opening Vignette 114
International Marketing Research 115
Technology and Marketing Research 116
Ethics in Marketing Research 118
SPSS Windows 118
Summary **120**
Key Terms and Concepts **120**
Suggested Cases and Video Cases **120**
Live Research: Conducting a Marketing Research Project **120**
Acronyms **121**
Review Questions **121**
Applied Problems **121**
Group Discussion **121**

Chapter 5
Exploratory Research Design: Syndicated Sources of Secondary Data 122

Opening Questions 123
A Casual Affair 123
Overview 124
The Nature of Syndicated Data 125
A Classification of Syndicated Services 127
Surveys 127
Periodic Surveys 127
Panel Surveys 127
Shared Surveys 129
Psychographics and Lifestyles 130
Advertising Evaluation 131
General Surveys 131
Uses of Surveys 131
Advantages and Disadvantages of Surveys 131
Purchase and Media Panels 132
Purchase Panels 133
Media Panels 133
Uses of Purchase and Media Panels 134
Advantages and Disadvantages of Purchase and Media Panels 134
Electronic Scanner Services 134
Uses of Scanner Data 136
Advantages and Disadvantages of Scanner Data 137
Syndicated Data from Institutions 137
Retailer and Wholesaler Audits 137
Uses of Audit Data 138
Advantages and Disadvantages of Audit Data 138
Industry Services 138
Uses of Industry Services 139
Advantages and Disadvantages of Industry Services 139
Combining Information from a Variety of Sources: Single-Source Data 140
Summary Illustration Using the Opening Vignette 140
International Market Research 140
Technology and Marketing Research 142
Ethics in Marketing Research 142
Summary **144**
Key Terms and Concepts **144**
Suggested Cases and Video Cases **144**
Live Research: Conducting a Marketing Research Project **145**
Acronyms **145**
Review Questions **145**
Applied Problems **145**
Group Discussion **145**

Chapter 6
Exploratory Research Design: Qualitative Research 146

Opening Questions 147
Gillette Supports Equal Rights for Women: A Close Shave 147
Overview 148
Primary Data: Qualitative Versus Quantitative Research 150
A Classification of Qualitative Research Procedures 152
Focus-Group Interviews 152
Conducting a Focus Group 152
Designing the Environment 153
Recruiting and Selecting Focus-Group Participants 153
Selecting a Moderator 154
Preparing the Discussion Guide 154
Conducting the Group Interview 154
Preparing the Focus-Group Report 154
Advantages and Disadvantages of Focus Groups 157
Online Focus Groups 158
Advantages of Online Focus Groups 158
Disadvantages of Online Focus Groups 159
Applications of Focus Groups 159
In-Depth Interviews 161
Conducting In-Depth Interviews 161
Advantages of In-Depth Interviews 162
Disadvantages of In-Depth Interviews 162
Applications of In-Depth Interviews 162
Projective Techniques 164
Association Techniques 165
Completion Techniques 165
Construction Techniques 166
Expressive Techniques 166
Advantages of Projective Techniques 168
Disadvantages of Projective Techniques 168
Applications of Projective Techniques 168
Analysis of Qualitative Data 169
Summary Illustration Using the Opening Vignette 170
International Marketing Research 170
Technology and Marketing Research 172
Qualitative Research Software 172
Ethics in Marketing Research 173
Summary **175**
Key Terms and Concepts **175**
Suggested Cases and Video Cases **175**
Live Research: Conducting a Marketing Research Project **176**
Acronyms **176**
Review Questions **176**
Applied Problems **177**
Group Discussion **177**

Chapter 7
Descriptive Research Design: Survey and Observation 178

Opening Questions 179

Procter & Gamble's New Marketing Platform: Everyday Low Pricing and Brand Extensions 179

Overview 180

Survey Methods 181
- Advantages and Disadvantages of Survey Research 181

Survey Methods Classified by Mode of Administration 183
- Telephone Methods 183
  - *Traditional Telephone Interviews* 183
  - *Computer-Assisted Telephone Interviewing* 184
  - *Advantages and Disadvantages of Telephone Interviewing* 184
- Personal Methods 186
  - *Personal In-Home Interviews* 186
  - *Advantages and Disadvantages of In-Home Interviewing* 186
  - *Mall Intercept Personal Interviews* 187
  - *Advantages and Disadvantages of Mall Intercepts* 187
  - *Computer-Assisted Personal Interviewing* 187
  - *Advantages and Disadvantages of CAPI* 188
- Mail Methods 188
  - *Mail Interviews* 188
  - *Mail Panels* 190
  - *Advantages and Disadvantages of Mail Surveys* 190
- Electronic Methods 190
  - *E-mail Surveys* 191
  - *Internet Surveys* 191
  - *Advantages and Disadvantages of Electronic Methods* 191

Criteria for Selecting a Survey Method 193

Improving Survey Response Rates 193
- Prior Notification 193
- Incentives 193
- Follow-up 194
- Other Facilitators of Response 195

Observation Methods 195
- Personal Observation 196
- Mechanical Observation 196

A Comparison of Survey and Observation Methods 198
- Relative Advantages of Observation 198
- Relative Disadvantages of Observation 199

Ethnographic Research 200

Other Methods 200

Summary Illustration Using the Opening Vignette 201

International Marketing Research 201

Technology and Marketing Research 202

Ethics in Marketing Research 203

Summary **205**

Key Terms and Concepts **205**

Suggested Cases and Video Cases 206
Live Research: Conducting a Marketing Research Project 206
Acronyms 206
Review Questions 206
Applied Problems 207
Group Discussion 207

Chapter 8
Causal Research Design: Experimentation 208

Opening Questions 209
Muzak: An Uncommon Remedy for the Common Cold 209
Overview 210
Concept of Causality 210
Conditions for Causality 212
Concomitant Variation 212
Time Order of Occurrence of Variables 212
Absence of Other Possible Causal Factors 213
Role of Evidence 213
What Is Experimentation? 214
Independent Variables 214
Test Units 214
Dependent Variables 214
Extraneous Variables 214
Random Assignment to Experimental and Control Groups 215
Experimental Design 215
Definition of Symbols 216
Validity in Experimentation 216
Internal Validity 216
External Validity 216
Extraneous Variables 217
History 217
Maturation 217
Testing Effects 217
Instrumentation 217
Statistical Regression 218
Selection Bias 218
Mortality 218
Controlling Extraneous Variables 218
Randomization 218
Matching 219
Statistical and Design Control 219
A Classification of Experimental Designs 219
Preexperimental Designs 220
One-Shot Case Study 220
One-Group Pretest/Posttest Design 221
Static Group Design 221
True Experimental Designs 222
Pretest/Posttest Control Group Design 222
Posttest-Only Control Group Design 223
Quasi-Experimental Designs 224

Time Series Design 224
Statistical Designs 225
Factorial Design 225
Selecting an Experimental Design 226
Laboratory Versus Field Experiments 226
Limitations of Experimentation 227
Time 227
Cost 228
Administration 228
Application: Test Marketing 228
Summary Illustration Using the Opening Vignette 229
International Marketing Research 229
Technology and Marketing Research 230
Ethics in Marketing Research 231
Summary **233**
Key Terms and Concepts **233**
Suggested Cases and Video Cases **233**
Live Research: Conducting a Marketing Research Project **234**
Acronyms **234**
Review Questions **234**
Applied Problems **234**
Group Discussion **235**

Chapter 9
Measurement and Scaling: Fundamentals and Comparative Scaling 236

Opening Questions 237
Scaling the Olympics 237
Overview 238
Measurement and Scaling 238
Primary Scales and Levels of Measurement 240
Nominal Scale 240
Ordinal Scale 242
Interval Scale 243
Ratio Scale 244
Selecting a Level of Measurement 245
Nominal Scale 245
Ordinal Scale 245
Interval Scale 245
Ratio Scale 245
A Classification of Scaling Techniques 246
Comparative Scaling Techniques 247
Paired Comparison Scaling 247
Rank Order Scaling 248
Constant Sum Scaling 249
Relationship of Measurement and Scaling to the Marketing Research Process 251
Summary Illustration Using the Opening Vignette 251

International Marketing Research 252
Technology and Marketing Research 252
Ethics in Marketing Research 253
SPSS Windows 254
Summary **256**
Key Terms and Concepts **256**
Suggested Cases and Video Cases **256**
Live Research: Conducting a Marketing Research Project **257**
Acronyms **256**
Review Questions **257**
Applied Problems **257**
Group Discussion **257**

Chapter 10
Measurement and Scaling: Noncomparative Scaling Techniques 258

Opening Questions 259
Noncomparative Scaling Techniques Result in an Incomparable Hit Movie 259
Overview 260
Noncomparative Scaling Techniques 260
Continuous Rating Scale 260
Itemized Rating Scales 264
Likert Scale 264
Semantic Differential Scale 265
Stapel Scale 267
Noncomparative Itemized Rating Scale Decisions 268
Number of Scale Categories 268
Balanced Versus Unbalanced Scale 268
Odd or Even Numbers of Categories 269
Forced or Nonforced Choice 269
Nature and Degree of Verbal Description 269
Physical Form or Configuration 270
Multi-Item Scales 271
Scale Evaluation 273
Reliability 273
Test–Retest Reliability 273
Alternative-Forms Reliability 273
Internal-Consistency Reliability 274
Validity 274
Content Validity 274
Criterion Validity 274
Construct Validity 274
Relationship Between Reliability and Validity 276
Choosing a Scaling Technique 276
Summary Illustration Using the Opening Vignette 276
International Marketing Research 277
Technology and Marketing Research 278
Ethics in Marketing Research 278
SPSS Windows 281
Summary **281**

Key Terms and Concepts 281
Suggested Cases and Video Cases 281
Live Research: Conducting a Marketing Research Project 282
Acronyms 282
Review Questions 282
Applied Problems 282
Group Discussion 283

Chapter 11
Questionnaire and Form Design 284

Opening Questions 285
World Vision Imparts Donors a Vision for Caring 285
Overview 286
Importance of the Questionnaire 288
Questionnaire Definition 288
Questionnaire Design Process 288
Specify the Information Needed 289
Specify the Type of Interviewing Method 290
Determine the Content of Individual Questions 292
Is the Question Necessary? 292
Are Several Questions Needed Instead of One? 292
Design the Question to Overcome the Respondent's Inability to Answer 293
Is the Respondent Informed? 293
Can the Respondent Remember? 293
Can the Respondent Articulate? 294
Design the Questionnaire to Overcome the Respondent's Unwillingness to Answer 294
Effort Required of the Respondent 294
Legitimate Purpose 295
Sensitive Information 295
Decide on the Question Structure 296
Unstructured Questions 296
Structured Questions 296
Multiple-Choice Questions 297
Dichotomous Questions 298
Scales 298
Determine the Question Wording 299
Define the Issue 299
Use Simple Words 300
Use Unambiguous Words 300
Avoid Leading or Biasing Questions 301
Balance Dual Statements 302
Arrange the Questions in Proper Order 302
Opening Questions 302
Type of Information 303
Difficult Questions 303
Effect on Subsequent Questions 303
Logical Order 304
Choose the Form and Layout 305
Reproduce the Questionnaire 306
Pretest the Questionnaire 307

Observational Forms 307
Summary Illustration Using the Opening Vignette 310
International Marketing Research 310
Technology and Marketing Research 312
Ethics in Marketing Research 312
Summary 315
Key Terms and Concepts 315
Suggested Cases and Video Cases 315
Live Research: Conducting a Marketing Research Project 315
Acronyms 316
Review Questions 316
Applied Problems 316
Group Discussion 317
Appendix 11A 318

Chapter 12
Sampling: Design and Procedures 320

Opening Questions 321
Gillette Clear Stick Clears the Way for Growth in the Deodorant Market 321
Overview 322
Sample or Census 322
The Sampling Design Process 325
Define the Target Population 326
Determine the Sampling Frame 326
Select a Sampling Technique 327
Determine the Sample Size 328
Execute the Sampling Process 329
A Classification of Sampling Techniques 330
Nonprobability Sampling Techniques 330
Convenience Sampling 330
Judgmental Sampling 331
Quota Sampling 332
Snowball Sampling 333
Probability Sampling Techniques 334
Simple Random Sampling 335
Systematic Sampling 336
Stratified Sampling 337
Cluster Sampling 338
Choosing Nonprobability Versus Probability Sampling 339
Internet Sampling 341
Issues in Online Sampling 341
Online Sampling Techniques 342
Summary Illustration Using the Opening Vignette 344
International Marketing Research 344
Technology and Marketing Research 346
Ethics in Marketing Research 346
Summary 348
Key Terms and Concepts 349

Suggested Cases and Video Cases 349
Live Research: Conducting a Marketing Research Project 349
Acronyms 350
Review Questions 350
Applied Problems 350
Group Discussion 351

Chapter 13
Sampling: Final and Initial Sample Size Determination 352

Opening Questions 353
Sizing the Sample Size Problem 353
Overview 354
Definitions and Symbols 355
The Sampling Distribution 356
Statistical Approach to Determining Sample Size 358
The Confidence Interval Approach 358
Sample Size Determination: Means 360
Sample Size Determination: Proportions 362
Adjusting the Statistically Determined Sample Size 365
Incidence Rate 365
Completion Rate 366
Combined Adjustment 366
Online Sampling Adjustments 367
Summary Illustration Using the Opening Vignette 368
International Marketing Research 368
Technology and Marketing Research 369
Ethics in Marketing Research 369
Summary 371
Key Terms and Concepts 371
Suggested Cases and Video Cases 371
Live Research: Conducting a Marketing Research Project 372
Acronyms 372
Review Questions 372
Applied Problems 372
Group Discussion 373
Appendix 13A 373

CASES FOR PART 2

Case 2.1 Maxfli: Going for the Long Ball 375
Case 2.2 Can the Caddie Make a Comeback? 376
Case 2.3 Research Prompts HCA-Healthcare to Re-evaluate Its Internet Focus 378
Case 2.4 Bloomingdale's: Inviting the Bloom into the Store 379
Case 2.5 Burger King Is Frying to Become Number One in French Fries 381

VIDEO CASES FOR PART 2

Video Case 2.1 Starbucks: Staying Local While Going Global Through Marketing Research 383
Video Case 2.2 Nike: Associating Athletes, Performance, and the Brand 384

Part 3
Data Collection, Analysis, and Reporting 386

Chapter 14
Field Work: Data Collection 386

Opening Questions 387
Gallup's Galloping Field Work 387
Overview 388
The Nature of Field Work 390
Field Work/Data Collection Process 390
Selection of Field Workers 390
Training of Field Workers 391
Supervision of Field Workers 392
Validation of Field Work 394
Evaluation of Field Workers 395
Using the Internet in Field Work 396
Summary Illustration Using the Opening Vignette 396
International Marketing Research 397
Technology and Marketing Research 398
Ethics in Marketing Research 398
Summary 400
Key Terms and Concepts 400
Suggested Cases and Video Cases 400
Live Research: Conducting a Marketing Research Project 401
Acronyms 401
Review Questions 401
Applied Problems 401
Group Discussion 401

Chapter 15
Data Preparation and Analysis Strategy 402

Opening Questions 403
Database Awakens a Sleeping Giant 403
Overview 404
The Data Preparation Process 405
Questionnaire Checking 406
Editing 406
Coding 407
- Coding Structured and Open-Ended Questions 409
- Coding of Open-Ended Question Responses 410

Transcribing 411
Data Cleaning 412
- Consistency Checks 412
- Treatment of Missing Responses 413

Variable Respecification and Recoding 414
Selecting a Data Analysis Strategy 414
Summary Illustration Using the Opening Vignette 415

International Marketing Research 416
Technology and Marketing Research 416
Ethics in Marketing Research 417
Software Applications 417
SPSS Windows 419
EXCEL 420
Summary 423
Key Terms and Concepts 424
Suggested Cases and Video Cases 424
Live Research: Conducting a Marketing Research Project 424
Acronyms 424
Review Questions 424
Applied Problems 424
Group Discussion 425

Chapter 16
Data Analysis: Frequency Distribution, Hypothesis Testing, and Cross-Tabulation 426

Opening Questions 427
Consumers Consume Coupons 427
Overview 428
Frequency Distribution 429
Statistics Associated with Frequency Distribution 432
Measures of Location 433
Mean 434
Mode 434
Median 434
Measures of Variability 435
Range 435
Variance and Standard Deviation 435
Introduction to Hypothesis Testing 436
A General Procedure for Hypothesis Testing 437
Step 1: Formulating the Hypothesis 438
Step 2: Selecting an Appropriate Test 438
Step 3: Choosing Level of Significance 439
Type-I Error 439
Type-II Error 439
Power of a Test 439
Step 4: Data Collection 439
Step 5: Determining the Probability (Critical Value) 440
Steps 6 and 7: Comparing the Probability (Critical Value) and Making the Decision 441
Step 8: Marketing Research Conclusion 441
Cross-Tabulations 442
General Comments on Cross-Tabulation 444
Statistics Associated with Cross-Tabulation 445
Chi-Square 445
Phi Coefficient 447
Contingency Coefficient 447
Cramer's *V* 448

Cross-Tabulation in Practice 448
Summary Illustration Using the Opening Vignette 449
Software Applications 450
SPSS Windows 450
Frequency Distribution 450
Cross-Tabulation 452
EXCEL 452
Frequency Distribution 452
Cross-Tabulation 454
Summary **455**
Key Terms and Concepts **455**
Suggested Cases and Video Cases **455**
Live Research: Conducting a Marketing Research Project **456**
Acronyms **456**
Review Questions **456**
Applied Problems **457**
Group Discussion **458**

Chapter 17
Data Analysis: Hypothesis Testing Related to Differences 460

Opening Questions 461
Loyalty Versus Butterfly and Convenience Versus Price 461
Overview 462
Hypothesis Testing Related to Differences 462
The *t* Distribution 464
Testing Hypothesis Based on the *t* Statistic 464
One-Sample *t*-Tests 465
Test for a Single Mean 465
Test for a Single Proportion 467
Two-Sample *t*-Tests 468
Two Independent Samples 468
Means 468
Proportions 472
Paired Samples 473
Means 474
Proportions 475
Testing Hypotheses for More Than Two Samples 476
Dependent and Independent Variables 477
Decomposition of the Total Variation 477
Measurement of Effects 478
Significance Testing 478
Illustrative Applications of One-Way Analysis of Variance 479
Proportions for More Than Two Samples 480
Summary Illustration Using the Opening Vignette 482
Software Applications 482
SPSS Windows 484
Detailed Steps: One-Sample *t*-Test 485
Detailed Steps: Two-Independent-Samples *t*-Test 485
Detailed Steps: Paired-Samples *t*-Test 485
Detailed Steps: One-Way ANOVA 486

EXCEL 488
Detailed Steps: One-Sample *t*-Test 488
Detailed Steps: Two-Independent-Samples *t*-Test 489
Detailed Steps: Paired-Samples *t*-Test 489
Detailed Steps: One-Way ANOVA 490
Summary **490**
Key Terms and Concepts **490**
Suggested Cases and Video Cases **491**
Live Research: Conducting a Marketing Research Project **491**
Acronyms **491**
Review Questions **491**
Applied Problems **492**
Group Discussion **493**

Chapter 18
Data Analysis: Correlation and Regression 494

Opening Questions 495
Regression Models Model the Marketing Strategy of Adidas 495
Overview 496
Product Moment Correlation 497
Regression Analysis 503
Bivariate Regression 504
Conducting Bivariate Regression Analysis 504
Scatter Diagram 505
Bivariate Regression Model 505
Estimation of Parameters 506
Standardized Regression Coefficients 508
Significance Testing 509
Strength and Significance of Association 509
Prediction Accuracy 512
Examination of Residuals 512
Multiple Regression 513
Conducting Multiple Regression Analysis 514
Partial Regression Coefficients 514
Strength of Association 515
Significance Testing 516
Summary Illustration Using the Opening Vignette 518
Software Applications 520
SPSS Windows 520
Detailed Steps: Correlation 520
Detailed Steps: Bivariate and Multiple Regression 520
EXCEL 522
Detailed Steps: Correlation 522
Detailed Steps: Bivariate and Multiple Regression 523
Summary **523**
Key Terms and Concepts **524**
Suggested Cases and Video Cases **524**
Live Research: Conducting a Marketing Research Project **524**
Acronyms **524**
Review Questions **524**

Applied Problems 525
Group Discussion 526

Chapter 19
Report Preparation and Presentation 528

Opening Questions 529
Research Reports Make United's Friendly Skies Even More Friendly 529
Overview 530
Importance of the Report and Presentation 531
The Report Preparation and Presentation Process 532
Report Preparation 533
Report Format 533
Title Page 534
Letter of Transmittal 534
Letter of Authorization 534
Table of Contents 534
Executive Summary 534
Problem Definition 534
Approach to the Problem 535
Research Design 535
Data Analysis 535
Results 535
Limitations and Caveats 535
Conclusions and Recommendations 535
Report Writing 535
Guidelines for Tables 536
Title and Number 536
Arrangement of Data Items 536
Basis of Measurement 537
Leaders, Rulings, Spaces 537
Explanations and Comments: Headings, Stubs, and Footnotes 537
Sources of the Data 537
Guidelines for Graphs 537
Geographic and Other Maps 538
Pie Charts 538
Line Charts 538
Pictographs 539
Histograms and Bar Charts 539
Schematic Figures and Flow Charts 539
Oral Presentation and Dissemination 540
Research Follow-Up 541
Assisting the Client 541
Evaluating the Research Project 541
Summary Illustration Using the Opening Vignette 542
International Marketing Research 542
Technology and Marketing Research 543
Ethics in Marketing Research 544
Software Applications 544
SPSS Windows 546
Summary 546
Key Terms and Concepts 546

Suggested Cases and Video Cases 547
Live Research: Conducting a Marketing Research Project 547
Acronyms 547
Review Questions 548
Applied Problems 548
Group Discussion 548

CASES FOR PART 3A: CASES WITH EXTERNAL DATA

Case 3.1 Ford Seeks a New Image 549
Case 3.2 A Breeze for Darden Restaurants 551
Case 3.3 Should Microsoft "Soften" Up to Rescue Its Image? 553

CASES FOR PART 3B: CASES WITHOUT EXTERNAL DATA

Case 3.4 Are Catalogs Risky Business? 555
Case 3.5 Does Advertising Subsidize the Price of Consumer Magazines? 556

VIDEO CASES FOR PART 3

Video Case 3.1 AFLAC: Marketing Research Quacks a Duck 558
Video Case 3.2 Honest Tea: Honesty Is the Best Policy 559

Part 4
Comprehensive Cases and Video Cases 562

CASES FOR PART 4: CASES WITH EXTERNAL DATA

Case 4.1 Boeing: Taking Flight 562
Case 4.2 Do Gucci Catalogs Stack Up in Direct Marketing? 568

VIDEO CASES FOR PART 4

Video Case 4.1 Subaru: "Mr. Survey" Monitors Customer Satisfaction 575
Video Case 4.2 Marriott: Marketing Research Leads to Expanded Offerings 577

Appendix of Statistical Tables 581
Notes 593
Photo Credits 601
Subject Index 603
Company and Product Index 611
Name Index 615

FOREWORD

Basic Marketing Research: A Decision-Making Approach, second edition, is yet another outstanding text book from Dr. Naresh K. Malhotra, a very well-known and highly successful author, and Dr. Mark Peterson. Dr. Malhotra's *Marketing Research: An Applied Orientation* has been translated into Chinese, Spanish, Portuguese, French, Russian, Hungarian, and Indonesian and published in several English editions including North American, International, European, and Australian editions.

Basic Marketing Research: A Decision-Making Approach, second edition, carries Dr. Malhotra's pedagogical skills and expertise in marketing research even further. With its focus on contemporary issues like international marketing research, technology, and ethics, the book effectively captures the current environment. The application of Web-based marketing research is integrated in a pervasive way throughout the book, which reflects the state-of-the-art orientation of the material presented in this text.

This book is rich in tangible examples that bring the student closer to the business world and every day realities of the marketplace. The opening vignettes, interwoven throughout the respective chapters, further illustrate the marketing research concepts in real-life settings. The Be an MR! and Be a DM!, What Would *You* Do?, and Experiential Learning exercises provide a rich and hands-on experience. The case studies and video case studies are great learning tools and further reinforce the highly applied and managerial orientation of the text. There are several diagrams and figures in each chapter that truly enhance learning. The lessons are conceptually sound, technically accurate, and communicate the basic research concepts with simplicity and clarity. The book is strong in qualitative concepts and imparts the necessary quantitative knowledge and skills, with the use of SPSS and other statistical software.

Basic Marketing Research: A Decision-Making Approach, second edition, provides a strong foundation that we believe every student should have. This book is unsurpassed as a basis for students to become researchers and intelligent users of marketing research.

Ken Athaide
Executive Manager & Senior VP
TNS

PREFACE

Basic Marketing Research: A Decision-Making Approach, second edition, attempts to build on the success of the first edition and on the success of the four editions of *Marketing Research: An Applied Orientation*. The latter book is the most widely used graduate marketing research book, with more than 144 universities adopting the book in the United States. That book has been translated into Chinese, Spanish, Portuguese, Russian, French, and Hungarian, and several English-language editions, including an international edition, European edition, Indian edition, and Australian and New Zealand editions.

Basic Marketing Research: A Decision-Making Approach, second edition, is current, contemporary, illustrative, and sensitive to the needs of undergraduate students. It has a unique focus on decision making, illustrating the interaction between marketing research decisions and marketing management decisions. It also emphasizes a hands-on approach, affording students several opportunities to experience these interactions through pedagogical tools, such as the Opening Vignette, Be an MR!, Be a DM!, Experiential Learning, What Would *You* Do?, Research in Action, cases, video cases, and extensive review questions, applied problems, and group discussions. The data analysis chapters involve a tight integration of SPSS, illustrating each step in running the program in detail. SPSS files are provided for all datasets; outputs and screen captures are posted on the Web site. Detailed instructions and datasets are also provided for Microsoft EXCEL.

Audience

This book is suitable for use in a basic marketing research course at the undergraduate level. The marketing research concepts and principles are presented at a basic level. The book presents the material in a manner that is easy to read and understand. There is an abundance of diagrams, tables, pictures, illustrations, and examples that help to explain the basic concepts, which are features that typically appeal to undergraduates. The opening questions serve not only to raise interest but also to structure the material in each chapter. This structure is further reinforced by the two opening figures. The first figure illustrates the relationship of the chapter to the previous chapters and to the marketing research process. The second figure presents an overview of the chapter, further reinforcing structure. There is ample evidence suggesting undergraduate students learn structured material more easily.

Organization

The book is organized into main parts, based on a six-step framework for conducting marketing research. Part 1 provides an introduction to marketing research and discusses problem definition, the first and the most important step. It also describes the nature and scope of research undertaken to develop an approach to the problem, the second step in the marketing research process.

Part 2 covers research design, the third step, and describes in detail exploratory, descriptive, and causal research designs. The types of information commonly obtained in marketing research, as well as the appropriate scales for obtaining such information are described. Guidelines for designing questionnaires are presented and the procedures, techniques, and statistical considerations involved in sampling are explained.

Part 3 presents a practical and managerially oriented discussion of field work, the fourth step in the marketing research process. It also covers data preparation and analysis, the fifth step. Basic statistical techniques are discussed in detail, with emphasis on explaining the procedures, interpreting the results, and managerial implications. Four statistical packages, SPSS, SAS, MINITAB, and EXCEL are featured. A student version of SPSS is available with the book, along with SPSS files for all the datasets used. We provide detailed, step-by-step instructions for running SPSS, including illustrations. Detailed instructions and data files are also provided for EXCEL. Communicating the research by preparing and presenting a formal report constitutes the sixth step in the marketing research process, which is also discussed in Part 3.

New for the Second Edition

The addition of Mark Peterson as a coauthor has contributed significantly to the second edition. While retaining the desirable features, the second edition contains major revisions. Several significant changes have been made. These changes were identified by conducting surveys of professors (users and nonusers) and students, and by obtaining critical reviews and detailed evaluations. Major changes include

1. **Chapter modifications.** Each chapter has been modified to present new ideas, update existing materials, or, in some instances, to further clarify concepts. These changes are extensive in most of the chapters.
2. **Be!** Be an MR (marketing researcher)! and Be a DM (decision maker)! scenarios have been added after the key concepts in each chapter. These scenarios show the interaction between marketing research and marketing management and actually require the students to do research and make marketing decisions.

BE a DM!

As the marketing director of the NFL, what marketing strategies would you formulate to target female fans?

BE an MR!

Visit NFL's Web site (www.nfl.com) and search the Internet using a search engine as well as your library's online databases to obtain information on women's attitudes toward the NFL.

The NFL is tickled pink and would like to target female fans, what kind of marketing research would you recommend?

3. **Experiential Learning.** Experiential Learning scenarios have been added in each chapter. These also require the students to do research, which is much more extensive than required in Be an MR! In several instances, the students have to download materials from the Web site for this book. Hence, the students learn by doing.

EXPERIENTIAL LEARNING

The World of Marketing Research on the Internet

The WorldOpinion Web site (www.worldopinion.com) is designed to bring you up-to-date news and comprehensive information on the market research industry. Here's how to find what you're looking for and get the most out of your visit.

If you're job hunting or hiring, the classifieds section lists jobs in research, marketing, advertising, public relations, and allied professions. There are literally thousands of current job openings. You're welcome to submit your resume, or job listing, at no charge.

Looking for the right research company for your project? The directory of researchers lists over 8,500 research locations in 99 countries. Search by company name or search by company type and/or geography.

The news section, updated daily, brings you company, conference, and product news from the world of market research.

If you're thinking of attending a marketing or research event or need more information on research education opportunities, check out the WorldOpinion calendar. Hundreds of events and research courses from throughout the world are listed.

There are many other ways the WorldOpinion Web site brings the world of marketing research to you. Explore it!

4. **What Would *You* Do?** These are managerial situations, featured in each chapter, that require the students to make marketing research decisions and marketing management decisions. The students can check their decisions against what the decision maker featured in the situation did, as well as go to the Web site for the book and see how their decisions compare to those of other students.

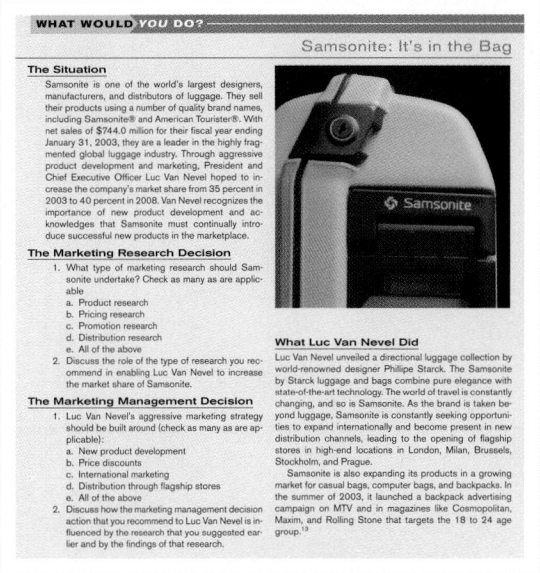

WHAT WOULD *YOU* DO?

Samsonite: It's in the Bag

The Situation

Samsonite is one of the world's largest designers, manufacturers, and distributors of luggage. They sell their products using a number of quality brand names, including Samsonite® and American Tourister®. With net sales of $744.0 million for their fiscal year ending January 31, 2003, they are a leader in the highly fragmented global luggage industry. Through aggressive product development and marketing, President and Chief Executive Officer Luc Van Nevel hoped to increase the company's market share from 35 percent in 2003 to 40 percent in 2008. Van Nevel recognizes the importance of new product development and acknowledges that Samsonite must continually introduce successful new products in the marketplace.

The Marketing Research Decision

1. What type of marketing research should Samsonite undertake? Check as many as are applicable
   a. Product research
   b. Pricing research
   c. Promotion research
   d. Distribution research
   e. All of the above
2. Discuss the role of the type of research you recommend in enabling Luc Van Nevel to increase the market share of Samsonite.

The Marketing Management Decision

1. Luc Van Nevel's aggressive marketing strategy should be built around (check as many as are applicable):
   a. New product development
   b. Price discounts
   c. International marketing
   d. Distribution through flagship stores
   e. All of the above
2. Discuss how the marketing management decision action that you recommend to Luc Van Nevel is influenced by the research that you suggested earlier and by the findings of that research.

What Luc Van Nevel Did

Luc Van Nevel unveiled a directional luggage collection by world-renowned designer Philipe Starck. The Samsonite by Starck luggage and bags combine pure elegance with state-of-the-art technology. The world of travel is constantly changing, and so is Samsonite. As the brand is taken beyond luggage, Samsonite is constantly seeking opportunities to expand internationally and become present in new distribution channels, leading to the opening of flagship stores in high-end locations in London, Milan, Brussels, Stockholm, and Prague.

Samsonite is also expanding its products in a growing market for casual bags, computer bags, and backpacks. In the summer of 2003, it launched a backpack advertising campaign on MTV and in magazines like Cosmopolitan, Maxim, and Rolling Stone that targets the 18 to 24 age group.[13]

5. **Integrated coverage of the Internet.** The section on "Internet Applications;" that appeared in each chapter of the first edition has been eliminated. Instead, this material has been expanded, updated, and integrated throughout each chapter. We discuss and illustrate in a pervasive way how the Internet can be used to implement the concepts in that chapter. Topics, URLs, and examples illustrating the use of the Internet appear throughout each chapter. The Internet and computer exercises that also appear in each chapter have been expanded. The data analysis chapters, Chapters 15 to 18, feature several new computer exercises for which the data have been provided.

6. **SPSS (and EXCEL).** The main emphasis is on SPSS with additional emphasis on EXCEL. While the data analysis chapters feature four statistical packages: SPSS, SAS, MINITAB, and EXCEL, special emphasis has been placed on SPSS. The relevant chapters contain a special section on SPSS Windows that illustrates the relevant SPSS programs and the detailed steps required to run them. SPSS files have been provided for all input datasets that are featured at the beginning of all data analysis chapters (15 through 18), input data sets that appear in "Applied Problems;" input datasets for cases (3.3, 3.4, 3.5, 4.1, and 4.2), as well as the corresponding output files. These datasets are also provided as ASCII and EXCEL files. The SPSS Windows student version contains a tutorial that students can use to learn/refresh their knowledge of SPSS. Detailed steps are also provided for executing the various procedures using EXCEL.
7. **New Video Cases.** Each part of the book contains video cases, all of which are new to the second edition. These cases have been drawn from the Prentice Hall video library but have been written from a marketing research perspective. The questions at the end of each video case are all marketing research questions. The videotapes containing these cases are available to instructors who adopt the book. Solutions to these video cases are provided in the instructor's manual.
8. **New figures, tables, exhibits, and text.** Such additions have been made throughout the text. Where appropriate, new material has been added to present a new idea, update the technology, or clarify the subject.

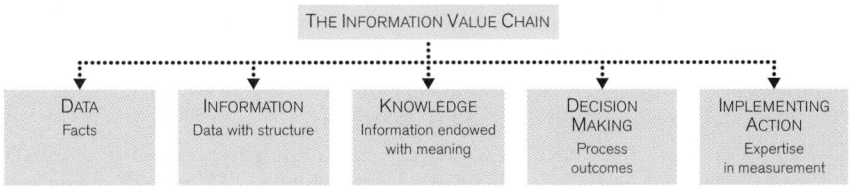

Figure 1.6
The Information Value Chain

Table 1.1
Honomichl Global Top 25

Top 25 Global Research Organizations

Rank 2003	Rank 2002	Organization	Headquarters	Parent Country	Web Site	No. of Countries with Subsidiary Branch Offices[1]	Global Research Revenue[2] (U.S. $ millions)	Percent of Global Revenue from Outside Home Country
1	1	VNU N.V.	Haarlem	Netherlands	www.vnu.com	81	$3,048.3	99.0%*
2	–	Taylor Nelson Sofres plc	London	U.K.	www.tns-global.com	70	1,565.1	83.5
–	4	Taylor Nelson Sofres	London	U.K.	www.tns-global.com	54	1,050.5	78.6
–	8	NFO WorldGroup Inc.	Greenwich, Conn.	U.K.	www.tns-global.com	40	514.6	93.5
3	2	IMS Health Inc.	Fairfield, Conn.	U.S.	www.imshealth.com	75	1,381.8	61.1
4	3	The Kantar Group	Fairfield, Conn.	U.K.	www.kantargroup.com	61	1,002.1	66.1*
5	6	GfK Group	Nuremberg	Germany	www.gfk.com	48	673.6	62.8
6	7	Ipsos Group S.A.	Paris	France	www.ipsos.com	36	644.6	84.1
7	5	Information Resources Inc.	Chicago	U.S.	www.infores.com	18	554.3	30.0
8	9	Westat Inc.	Rockville, Md.	U.S.	www.westat.com	1	381.6	NA
9	11	Synovate	London	U.K.	www.synovate.com	46	357.7	91.3
10	10	NOP World	London	U.K.	www.nopworld.com	6	335.6	80.5
11	12	Arbitron Inc.	New York	U.S.	www.arbitron.com	3	273.6	2.9
12	13	Maritz Research	St. Louis	U.S.	www.maritzresearch.com	4	188.8	34.9
13	14	Video Research Ltd.[3]	Tokyo	Japan	www.videor.co.jp	4	166.7	1.1
14	16	J.D. Power and Associates	Agoura Hills, Calif.	U.S.	www.jdpower.com	6	144.8	17.8
15	17	Harris Interactive Inc.	Rochester, NY	U.S.	www.harrisinteractive.com	4	137.0	19.0
16	15	Opinion Research Corp.	Princeton, NJ	U.S.	www.opinionresearch.com	6	131.2	35.4
17	18[4]	INTAGE Inc.[3]	Tokyo	Japan	www.intage.co.jp	2	122.3	1.0
18	19[4]	The NPD Group Inc.	Port Washington, NY	U.S.	www.npd.com	11	117.6	17.7
19	21	AGB Group	Milan	Italy	www.agb.com	19	81.6	79.0
20	23	Market & Opinion Research Int'l	London	U.K.	www.mori.com	2	64.4	2.8
21	25	Lieberman Research Worldwide	Los Angeles	U.S.	www.lrwonline.com	1	63.2	8.7
22	20	Dentsu Research Inc.	Tokyo	Japan	www.dentsuresearch.co.jp	1	57.0	1.1
23	23	Abt Associates Inc.	Cambridge, Mass.	U.S.	www.abtassociates.com	3	54.0	4.3
24	–	Nikkei Research Inc.	Tokyo	Japan	www.nikkeiresearch.com	4	52.1	3.5
25	22	Wirthlin Worldwide	McLean, Va.	U.S.	www.wirthlin.com	4	52.0	22.9
						Total	$11,651.0	67.3%

* Estimated by Top 25.
[1] Includes countries that have subsidiaries with an equity interest or branch offices, or both.
[2] Total revenue that includes nonresearch activities for some companies are significantly higher. This information is given in the individual company profiles.
[3] For fiscal year ending March 2004.
[4] Reranked based on corrected revenue of the NPD Group Inc. See NPD's profile for details.
Source: Drawn from *Marketing News* with permission from the American Marketing Association.

9. **New and updated examples and cases.** Several new examples have been added, some old ones deleted, and the remaining examples have been updated as appropriate. Some new cases have been added and all the rest updated to reflect the current marketing and marketing research environment. Particularly noteworthy is the addition of the Boeing comprehensives (Case 4.1) that features a real-life dataset. The comprehensive cases (4.1 and 4.2) contain questions on each chapter of the book.
10. **Updated references.** The references have been updated. Each chapter contains many references that are dated 2003 or later. However, some of the classic references have been retained.
11. **Multiple marketing research firms.** Instead of focusing exclusively on one marketing research firm, the second edition presents opening quotes and examples from several different marketing research user companies and the providers of marketing research services.
12. **Deletions.** To conserve space, some materials in the first edition have been deleted, including the section entitled Marketing Research and TQM.

Key Features of the Text

The book has several salient or unique features in terms of both content and pedagogy.

Content Features

1. A chapter is devoted to problem definition and developing an approach. These important steps in the marketing research process are discussed thoroughly and extensively (Chapter 2).
2. A chapter covers secondary data analysis. In addition to the traditional sources, computerized databases are also covered extensively. Use of the Internet for secondary data analysis is discussed in detail (Chapter 4).
3. A chapter is devoted to syndicate research. The types of syndicated data available from firms, such as IRI, ACNielsen, and Scarborough Research, and the applications of such data are described in detail (Chapter 5).
4. A whole chapter is dedicated to qualitative research. Focus groups, in-depth interviews, and projective techniques are discussed in detail with emphasis on the applications of these procedures. Use of the Internet for qualitative research is discussed in detail and the analysis of qualitative data is described (Chapter 6).

5. A chapter presents survey and observation methods (Chapter 7), while another discusses experimentation (Chapter 8). Thus, descriptive and causal designs are covered in detail with due emphasis on the Internet.
6. Two chapters are devoted to scaling techniques. One chapter is devoted to the fundamentals and comparative scaling techniques (Chapter 9). The other chapter covers noncomparative techniques and the basic procedures for assessing their reliability and validity (Chapter 10).
7. A chapter discusses questionnaire design. A step-by-step procedure and several guidelines are provided for constructing questionnaires (Chapter 11).
8. Two chapters cover sampling techniques. One chapter discusses the qualitative issues involved in sampling and the various nonprobability and probability sampling techniques (Chapter 12). The other chapter explains statistical issues, as well as final and initial sample size determination (Chapter 13).
9. A chapter presents field work. We give several guidelines on interviewer training, interviewing, and supervision of field workers (Chapter 14).
10. Four chapters have been devoted to the analysis of marketing research data covering all the basic techniques. Chapters have been devoted to
    a. Data preparation (Chapter 15)
    b. Frequency distribution, hypothesis testing, and cross-tabulations (Chapter 16)
    c. Testing hypotheses related to differences, including the various *t*-tests and analysis of variance (Chapter 17)
    d. Correlation and regression analysis (Chapter 18)

    The dataset used to explain each technique is provided in the beginning of the chapter. Data analysis is illustrated for four statistical packages: SPSS, SAS, MINITAB, and EXCEL. A student version of SPSS and SPSS files for all the datasets, including the output files, can be downloaded for the book. We provide step-by-step instructions for running SPSS, including illustrations. Detailed instructions for running EXCEL are also given.
11. A chapter covers report preparation and presentation (Chapter 19).
12. At the end of each part, there are several cases and video cases. Toward the end of the book, we present comprehensive cases and video cases. Several of the cases contain datasets. Additional cases and video cases are available in the Instructor's Manual and on the Web site.

Pedagogical Features

1. This book is unique in the way it illustrates the interaction between marketing research decisions and marketing management decisions. In a pervasive way, each chapter shows how marketing research decisions influence marketing management decisions and vice versa. This interaction is illustrated through several pedagogical tools, such as the Opening Vignette, Be an MR!, Be a DM!, Experiential Learning, What Would *You* Do?, and Research in Action. Cases, video cases, review questions, applied problems, and group discussions further reinforce this interaction. Thus, the book has a highly applied and managerial orientation. We illustrate in a pervasive manner how marketing researchers apply the various concepts and techniques, and how managers implement the findings in order to improve marketing practice.
2. Be an MR!, Be a DM!, Experiential Learning, and What Would *You* Do? require students to actually do some research and make marketing research and marketing management decisions through a hands-on orientation. In What Would *You* Do? scenarios, the students can go to the Web site for the book and see how their answers compare to those of other students. This hands-on orientation is further reinforced by cases, video cases, review questions, applied problems, and group discussions.
3. Several real-life examples are presented in each chapter and entitled Research in Action. These examples describe in detail the kind of marketing research used to address specific managerial problems and the decisions that were based on the

findings. Where appropriate, the sources cited have been supplemented by additional marketing research information to enhance the usefulness of these examples.

RESEARCH IN ACTION

A CEO's View of Marketing Research

What does a time-pressed senior executive expect from marketing researchers within the firm? Southern Company (www.southerncompany.com) Chairperson, President, and CEO Allen Franklin has some valuable insights on this question. *Fortune* magazine has named Southern Company "most admired" electric and gas utility in America for the last two years.

Addressing the American Marketing Association's Electric Utility Customer Research Conference in Atlanta, Franklin described one manager-researcher exchange of which he was part as follows: Marketing Researcher: "What do you want?"

Franklin (responding slowly and feeling slightly embarrassed for not having a ready answer): "What do you have?"

Marketing Researcher: "I don't have anything, yet. That's why I am here."

Franklin (growing increasingly irritated): "Well, then get out of here! You are keeping me from what I need to be doing!"

The implication of Franklin's exchange is that the researcher needs to understand the current context for decision makers. This comes from scanning the business press, following developing stories, attending conferences within the industry, as well as conducting more focused research projects. In short, the researcher needs to be curious and to be one of the best learners in the firm. Franklin says it this way: "It is not data that are critical, but the people between the data and the management decision maker. Senior managers will tend to work with those who make the managers more comfortable. Comfort is not increased by two-hour presentations that leave management saying to itself, 'What are we going to do with that?'" Here is one way a marketing researcher should approach a senior executive like Allen Franklin:

Marketing Researcher: "We know the firm currently has this problem. We can resolve or minimize it by doing this study and acting upon what we learn."[2]

4. Each part of the book contains short cases. These cases illustrate the concepts discussed. The conciseness of the cases will allow for their use in examinations. Some long cases are also provided including some cases with statistical data. These cases are current and deal with topics of interest to students.
5. Each part of the book contains video cases. These cases have been drawn from the Prentice Hall video library, and have been written from a marketing research perspective. The questions at the end of each video case are all marketing research questions. The videotapes containing these cases are available to instructors who adopt the book.
6. There is extensive Internet coverage. The text discusses how the Internet can be integrated in each step of the marketing research process and how it can be used to implement the concepts discussed in each chapter. The coverage of the Internet is so extensive and pervasive that it has not been singled out. Internet applications are ubiquitous. For example, all the Be an MR! exercises require the students to do Internet research.
7. A contemporary focus has been achieved by integrating the coverage of international marketing research, technology, and ethics in marketing research throughout the text. The text shows how the concepts discussed in each chapter can be applied to address the salient issues in these important and contemporary areas.
8. Each chapter opens with a set of questions to arouse curiosity and to impart structure. Each chapter also contains an Opening Vignette that is used as a running example throughout the chapter. After discussing the main concepts in each chapter, we revert to the Opening Vignette to summarize and illustrate the concepts in a section entitled "Summary Illustration Using the Opening Vignette".
9. Each chapter, except the first, opens with a diagram that gives the focus of that chapter, its relationship to the previous chapter(s), and its relationship to the marketing research process. Also included is a diagram that provides an overview of the chapter, showing the major topics and linking them to figures and tables.
10. Data analysis procedures are illustrated with respect to SPSS, SAS, MINITAB, and EXCEL, along with other popular computer programs. However, the emphasis is on SPSS. Detailed, step-by-step instructions are given for running the various statistical procedures using SPSS. SPSS files are provided for all datasets and outputs. Detailed steps are also given for EXCEL.
11. Each chapter contains one or more helpful acronyms that summarize the salient concepts. Acronyms are the most popular mnemonic technique college students

use. Theoretical and empirical evidence supporting the effectiveness of mnemonic techniques and their usefulness as a pedagogical tool has been discussed in a paper Naresh Malhotra published in the *Journal of the Academy of Marketing Science*, (spring 1991): 141–150.

12. A complete set of learning aids has been provided, including a functional and useful Web site, an instructor's manual, PowerPoint slides, video cases, exercises in marketing research, and test item file.

Instructional Support

The book is supported by a rich set of supplements detailed below.

1. **A functional and useful Web site.** This site can be accessed at *www.prenhall.com/malhotra*. This site contains the following:
   - The entire instructor's manual (password protected).
   - Test item file (password protected).
   - PowerPoint slides containing a chapter outline and all the figures and tables (password protected).
   - Data for Cases 3.1 (Ford Taurus), 3.2 (Darden), 3.3 (Microsoft), 4.1 (Boeing), and 4.2 (Gucci), given in the book.
   - Files for all the Experiential Learning exercises.
   - Data files for all the Applied Problems.
   - Data file for the dataset(s) used in each data analysis chapter.
   - Additional cases and video cases.

   The Web site is being enhanced continually.
2. **Instructor's Manual.** Written by Naresh Malhotra, the entire instructor's manual is very closely tied to the text. Each chapter contains objectives; author's notes; chapter outline; teaching suggestions organized by objective; and answers to all end-of-chapter review questions, applied problems, and group discussions. Answers are also provided for Be an MR!, Be a DM!, Experiential Learning, and What Would *You* Do? scenarios. In addition, solutions are provided for all the cases, including those that involve data analysis. Solutions are also provided for all the video cases.
3. **Test Item File.** Written by Mark Peterson, this valuable test item file contains a wide variety of tests for each chapter that allow you to create your own exams.
4. **Video Cases.** A set of videos containing these cases is available to adopters. The solutions to these cases are provided in the instructor's manual and are also available on the Web site.
5. **PowerPoint slides.** These slides contain the major concepts, all the figures, and all the tables for each chapter of the book.
6. A student version of SPSS and SPSS files for all the datasets used in the book.
7. Microsoft EXCEL files for all the datasets used in the book.

Acknowledgments

Several people have been extremely helpful in writing this textbook. Naresh would like to acknowledge Professor Arun K. Jain (State University of New York at Buffalo) who taught him marketing research in a way he will never forget. His students, especially former doctoral students, particularly Ashutosh Dixit, Charla Mathwick, Rick McFarland, and Cassandra Wells, as well as several research assistants, have been helpful in many ways. The students in his marketing research courses have provided useful feedback, as the material was class-tested for several years. His colleagues at Georgia Tech, especially Fred Allvine, have been very supportive. William D. Neal (founder and senior executive officer of SDR Consulting, Incorporated) has been very helpful and supportive over the years.

Mark would like to echo the acknowledgement of William Neal, his boss at SDR Consulting, Incorporated. In Mark's view, Bill is a "Green Beret" among the ranks of researchers today—freeing managers from the oppression of uncertainty. Mark would also like to acknowledge the inspiration of his highly committed graduate students at the University of Texas at Arlington (UTA), and the motivating example of the UTA MSMR advisory board chaired by Jerry Thomas of Decision Analyst, Incorporated of Arlington. Mark's current and past faculty colleagues in the marketing department at UTA—among them John Bassler, Glen Jarboe, Susan Kleiser, Carl McDaniel, Jim Munch, and Roger Dickinson—have always encouraged his work with the research industry. Many exercises and illustrations added to this edition have come from these endeavors with practicing marketers and researchers.

The reviewers have provided many constructive and valuable suggestions. Among others, the help of the following reviewers is gratefully acknowledged.

Reviewers for the First Edition

Dennis B. Arnett
University of Texas at San Antonio

Jerry Katrichis
University of Hartford

Paul L. Sauer
Canisius College

Alan G. Sawyer
University of Florida

Reviewers for the Second Edition

Ronald E. Goldsmith
Florida State University

Manish Kacker
Tulane University

John S. Kakalik
Western Connecticut State University

Alyse Lancaster
University of Miami

Tom Schmidt
Simpson College

Larry Seibert
University of Central Oklahoma

Donald E. Stem, Jr.
Washington State University

R. Greg Surovick
Lehigh University

The team at Prentice Hall provided outstanding support. Special thanks are due to Jeff Shelstad, editorial director; Katie Stevens, acquisitions editor; Wil Mara, associate editor; Michelle O'Brien, executive marketing manager; Kelly Warsak, production editor; Rebecca Lembo, editorial assistant; and Teri Stratford, photo researcher. Special recognition is due to the several field representatives and sales people who did an outstanding job.

Naresh wants to acknowledge, with great respect, his parents, the late Mr. H. N. Malhotra and Mrs. S. Malhotra. Their love, encouragement, support, and the sacrificial giving of themselves have been exemplary. His heartfelt love and gratitude go to his wife Veena, and his children Ruth and Paul, for their faith, hope, and love.

Mark wants to acknowledge his parents Eugene and Margaret Peterson for the love of life they have shared with family members and so many others through the years. His wife Cindy has been a special encourager, as well as their future researchers—Emily, Angela, and Rachel.

Most of all, we want to acknowledge and thank our Savior and Lord, Jesus Christ, for the abundant grace and favor He has bestowed upon us. This book is, truly, the result of His favor—"For thou, LORD, wilt bless the righteous; with favor wilt thou compass him as with a shield" (Psalms 5:12).

Naresh K. Malhotra

Mark Peterson

ABOUT THE AUTHORS

Dr. Naresh K. Malhotra is regents' professor (highest academic rank in the university system of Georgia), in the College of Management, Georgia Institute of Technology. He has been listed in Marquis *Who's Who in America* continuously since its fifty-first edition in 1997, and in *Who's Who in the World* since 2000. In 2005, he received the Academy of Marketing Science Outstanding Marketing Educator Award.

In an article by Wheatley and Wilson (1987 AMA Educators Proceedings), Professor Malhotra was ranked number one in the country based on articles published in the *Journal of Marketing Research* during 1980 through 1985. He also holds the all-time record for the maximum number of publications in the *Journal of Health Care Marketing*. He is ranked number one based on publications in the *Journal of the Academy of Marketing Science* (JAMS) since its inception through Volume 23, 1995. He is also number one based on publications in JAMS during the 10-year period 1986 through 1995. In an editorial by Schlegelmilch [JIM 11(1), 2003], Dr. Malhotra was ranked number one based on publications in the *International Marketing Review* from 1992 to 2002.

He has published more than 100 papers in major refereed journals, including the *Journal of Marketing Research*, *Journal of Consumer Research*, *Marketing Science*, *Management Science*, *Journal of Marketing*, *Journal of Academy of Marketing Science*, *Journal of Retailing*, *Journal of Health Care Marketing*, and leading journals in statistics, management science, and psychology. He has received seven best-paper awards for articles published in JCR (finalist), JMR, JR, JAMS, IMR (twice), and JIM.

He was chairperson of the Academy of Marketing Science Foundation, 1996 to 1998, was president of the Academy of Marketing Science, 1994 to 1996, and chairperson of the Board of Governors, 1990 to 1992. He is a distinguished fellow of the Academy and Fellow, Decision Sciences Institute. He is the editor of *Review of Marketing Research*. He has served as an associate editor of *Decision Sciences* for 18 years and has served as section editor of "Health Care Marketing Abstracts," *Journal of Health Care Marketing*. He serves on the editorial board of eight journals, including *Journal of Consumer Research*. He has also served on the editorial boards of *Journal of Marketing* and *Journal of Marketing Research*.

His book entitled *Marketing Research: An Applied Orientation*, fourth edition, was published by Prentice Hall in 2004. This book has been translated into Chinese, Spanish, Russian, Portuguese, Hungarian, and French. In addition, this book also has several English-language editions, including North American, international, European, Australian, and New Zealand. The book has received widespread adoption at both the graduate and undergraduate levels, with more than 144 schools using it in the United States. His book, *Basic Marketing Research: Application to Contemporary Issues*, was first published by Prentice Hall in 2002.

Dr. Malhotra has consulted for business, nonprofit, and government organizations in the United States and abroad, and has served as an expert witness in legal and regulatory proceedings. He has special expertise in data analysis and statistical methods. He is the winner of numerous awards and honors for research, teaching, and service to the profession, including the Academy of Marketing Science, Outstanding Marketing Teaching Excellence Award, 2003.

Dr. Malhotra is a member and deacon of First Baptist Church, Atlanta. He lives in the Atlanta area with his wife, Veena, and children Ruth and Paul.

Dr. Mark Peterson is associate professor of marketing in the College of Business at the University of Texas at Arlington (UTA). He is privileged to have the opportunity to teach in one of the few master's programs for marketing research in the world: UTA's Master of Science in Marketing Research (MSMR) program. He teaches marketing research, qualitative research, product management, marketing strategy, and international marketing to these talented and ambitious students committed to developing their careers in the marketing research field.

He has published 18 articles in refereed journals, including the *Journal of the Academy of Marketing Science*, *Journal of Business Research*, *Journal of Small Business Management*, *Journal of Macromarketing*, and the *International Marketing Review*. In addition, he has published four book chapters related to quality of life.

Upon graduating from Georgia Tech with a Ph.D. in marketing, Dr. Peterson joined the marketing research firm SDR Consulting, Incorporated as a consultant for research methods. For two years, he served in a dynamic environment pursuing solutions for client firms in a variety of industries, including services, consulting, biotechnology, and consumer packaged goods. In 1996, Dr. Peterson came to UTA where he has taught undergraduate, masters, and doctoral students.

After completing 25 classroom-business research projects with his students at UTA, Dr. Peterson is excited about the deeper insights into research endeavors offered by experiential learning. He is pleased to join Naresh Malhotra as a coauthor and to share experiential learning lessons he has learned from his time in the field with businesses.

Basic Marketing Research

CHAPTER 1

Introduction to Marketing Research

"As a user of marketing research, I gain so much from a well-crafted research project. You can implement marketing programs so much more vigorously when you are confident you understand what is currently important to the customer."

JUSTIN STEAD, *VP International, Fossil, Inc., Richardson, TX*

OPENING QUESTIONS

1. How do you define marketing research and what are the major classifications of marketing research?
2. What are the six steps in the marketing research process?
3. What role does marketing research play in designing and implementing successful marketing programs?
4. What is the information value chain and how is it related to the decision to conduct marketing research?
5. What is the marketing research industry, and how should a firm select a marketing research supplier?
6. What careers are available in marketing research, and what skills do you need to succeed in them?
7. How is marketing research relevant to decision support systems?
8. Why is international marketing research more complex than domestic marketing research?
9. How can technology improve marketing research?
10. What are the ethical aspects of marketing research? What responsibilities do the marketing research stakeholders have to themselves, each other, and the research project?

How Reebok Fits Shoes

Reebok International designs, markets, and distributes sportswear, footwear, and equipment. According to the Sporting Goods Manufacturers Association, as of 2004 Reebok had 18 percent of the foot and sports apparel market, second to Nike's 35 percent market share in the United States. For the summer Olympic Games of 2004 in Athens, Greece, Reebok outfitted athletes and coaches with their new line of apparel and footwear. The product manager for the Olympic apparel said, "The Olympic Games present a great honor and challenge for both the athletes and those of us who are responsible for ensuring their complete comfort during training and competition." In order to provide "complete comfort" for athletes and consumers, Reebok invested much of their efforts into market research. Although the slogan belongs to Nike, when it comes to marketing research, Reebok just does it!

Reebok uses "time-use" research to determine how consumers spend their spare time. This type of information enables Reebok to identify opportunities for new products and markets and then design its marketing program to take advantage of them, as illustrated by the recently introduced line of footwear, Reebok Classic. The company researches time-use trends using a variety of methods, including analysis of secondary data (data collected for other purposes, for example, data available from publications, Internet, and commercial sources). It also uses qualitative research, such as focus groups (interviews with 8 to 12 people as a group), and survey research by telephone, in the malls, on the Internet, and interviews at consumer homes.

Management was wondering what Reebok should do to increase market share. Time-use research helped shape the development of recent aerobic athletic products, including shoes, videotapes, and home-step products. Analysis of secondary data showed that health club memberships had grown 9 percent in the 1990s and early 2000s. Focus groups indicated that the new popular venue in fitness was step aerobics (standard aerobics courses made more intense by the addition of a three- to seven-inch platform: a step). Reebok then conducted a survey to determine the market potential of step aerobics and found that members of health clubs were spending less time in the clubs by an average of 12 percent.

This research further showed that the percentage of adults who exercised in their homes had grown from 20 percent in 1990 to 30 percent in 2002. Several research questions were framed around exercising at home. Based on these findings, Reebok designed a home-step aerobics line, including home steps, videotapes, aerobic shoes, and body weights. Product research indicated a strong consumer preference for the home-step aerobics line and, therefore, it was launched nationally. This line has been very successful and the popularity of these products has resulted in a Reebok step workout program on ESPN.

In this project, Reebok's in-house marketing research specialists were actively involved in defining and designing the research. However, Reebok contracted fieldwork or data collection and data analysis to external suppliers, who collected and analyzed the data using appropriate statistical techniques. External suppliers may also be used in writing the report, but presentation of the results to the management and assistance in implementation is the primary responsibility of the in-house marketing research department. Reebok makes use of full-service suppliers who provide assistance in all the steps of the marketing research process as well as limited-service suppliers who may handle only one or a few steps of the process. The data and the findings generated by this ongoing research become a part of Reebok's decision support system.[1] •

Overview

Marketing research is one of the most important and fascinating aspects of marketing. As the opening vignette illustrates, marketing research provides a company with valuable information, which guides all of the marketing activities. In this chapter, we define and describe the two broad forms of marketing research: (1) research designed to identify problems and (2) research designed to solve problems. We explain the six steps of the marketing research process and take a look at how marketing research fits into the entire marketing decision-making process. The marketing research industry consists of a variety of firms and the field offers exciting career opportunities. We conclude by describing the contribution of marketing research to marketing information systems (MIS) and decision support systems (DSS).

The use of the Internet is interwoven in a pervasive way in each chapter. Throughout this book, we also discuss applications to contemporary issues that are important in the current marketing and marketing research environment: international marketing research, technology, and ethics. This first chapter provides an introduction to these important application areas; an overview is presented in Figure 1.1. As can be seen in Figure 1.1, the Opening Vignette, and Application to Contemporary Issues encompass all of the topics discussed in each chapter. We encourage a hands-on approach through the use of "Be an MR!" (Be a Marketing Researcher!) and "Be a DM!" (Be a Decision Maker!) boxes also found in each chapter. These hands-on exercises have built in the interaction between marketing research and marketing decision making, integrating the use of the Internet. To further highlight this interaction, sometimes the "Be an MR!" box appears first while at other times "Be a DM!" appears first. The research decision-making interaction that is pervasive throughout the book is also emphasized in each chapter by the "What Would *You* Do?" situation facing a real company. The situation is described and students are required to provide answers to the marketing research and the marketing management decisions facing the company. This orientation provides a better overall understanding of the key concepts and illustrates how applications can be made in other important areas that are discussed throughout the book.

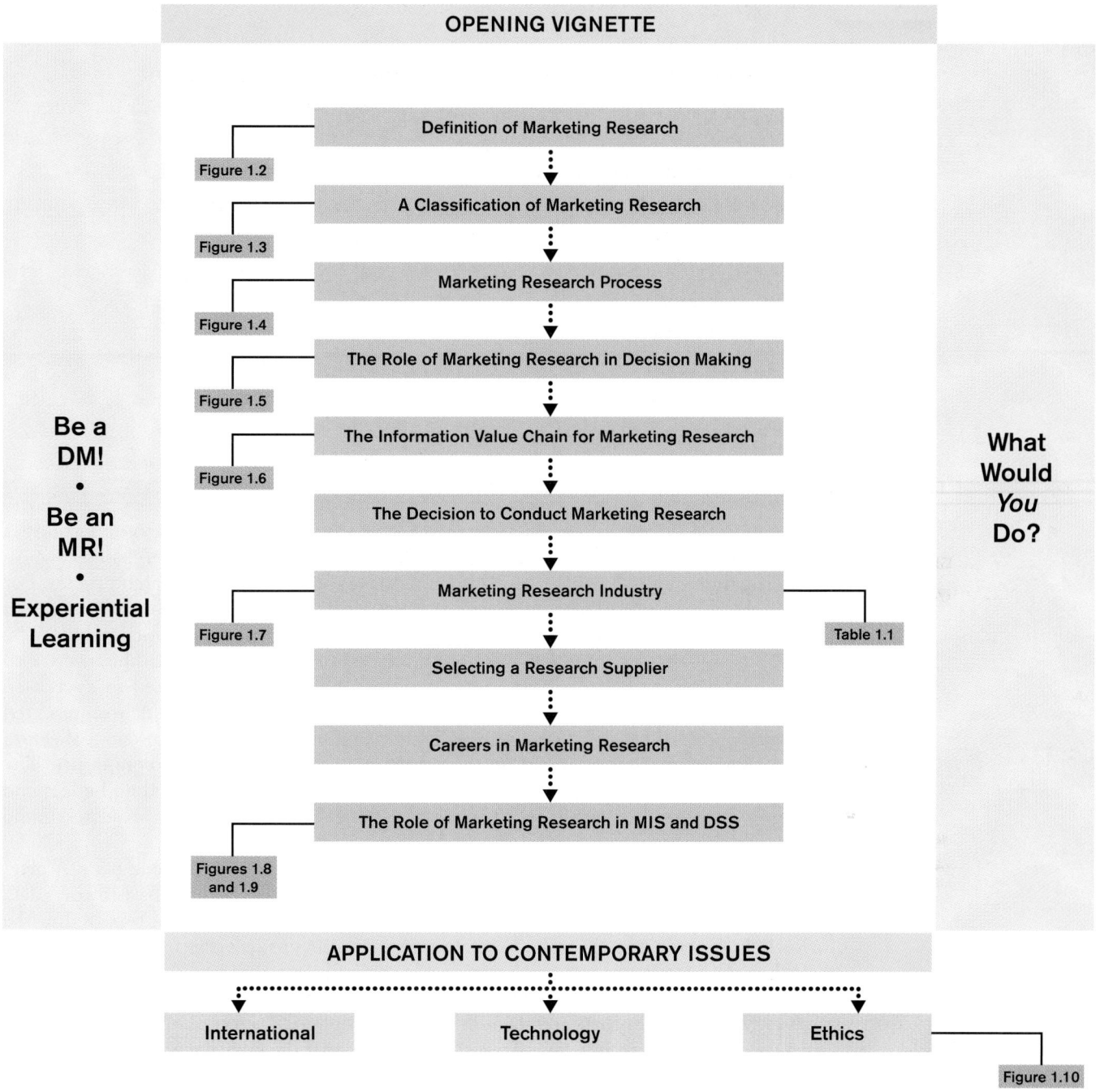

Figure 1.1

Introduction to Marketing Research: An Overview

Definition of Marketing Research

In this book, we emphasize the importance of research in marketing decision making. **Marketing research** is the systematic and objective identification, collection, analysis, dissemination, and use of information that is undertaken to improve decision making related to identifying and solving problems (also known as opportunities) in marketing.

This definition gives marketing research a broad scope that opens up a world of opportunities.

Several aspects of this definition are noteworthy. Marketing research involves the identification, collection, analysis, dissemination, and use of information (Figure 1.2). Each phase of this process is important. Marketing research begins with the identification or

marketing research
The systematic and objective identification, collection, analysis, dissemination, and use of information that is undertaken to improve decision making related to identifying and solving problems (also known as opportunities) in marketing.

Figure 1.2
Defining Marketing Research

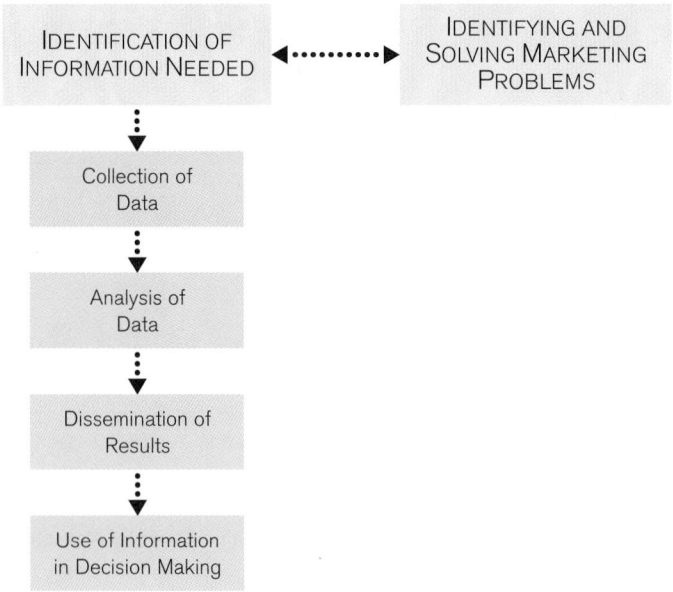

definition of the research problem or opportunity. Problems often lead to opportunities in business, so from a research perspective, the two words are used interchangeably. An investigation of both problems and opportunities follows the same research process. For example, the discovery that adults were spending less time in health clubs and more time exercising at home represented a problem as well as an opportunity for Reebok. The problem was that when people were spending less time in health clubs, they were also using athletic shoes and equipment to a lesser extent, which resulted in decreased demand. The opportunity was more time spent exercising at home, which represented greater potential for shoes and home exercise equipment. The range of data collection methods and the sources to collect the data vary in sophistication and complexity. The methods used depend on the specific requirements of the project, including budget and time constraints. The data are then analyzed and the results are formally presented to the client and used in decision making.

Marketing research is systematic, which means it follows a predictable path. A marketing research project is planned and documented. It has a scientific basis in that data are collected and analyzed to draw conclusions. The time-use research reported in the Reebok vignette is an example. Marketing research obtains its value from its objectivity. It should be conducted impartially, free from the influence of personal or political biases. This is easier said than done because companies sponsoring the research sometimes pressure the researcher or research firm to generate "support" for a certain desired outcome. However, bending to this sort of pressure is a breach of the ethical codes of conduct that guide the profession. The notion of providing an unbiased "outside opinion," or objective opinion, gives marketing research its value. Without that objectivity, results cannot be trusted, and the entire discipline is undermined.

The Internet is fast becoming a useful tool in the identification, collection, analysis, and dissemination of information related to marketing research. The Interactive Marketing Research Organization (www.imro.org) was formed in 2000. The IMRO is a worldwide association of researchers dedicated to providing an open forum for the discussion of best practices and ethical approaches to research being conducted via the Internet.

BE an MR!

Visit the Web site of Coca-Cola (www.cocacola.com) and click on the USA button. In what way does this site collect marketing research information?

How would you improve the Web site of Coca-Cola to collect more/better marketing research information?

BE a DM!

As the brand manager for Coke how would you use information collected at Coca-Cola's Web site to more effectively market your brand?

RESEARCH IN ACTION

A CEO's View of Marketing Research

What does a time-pressed senior executive expect from marketing researchers within the firm? Southern Company (www.southerncompany.com) Chairperson, President, and CEO Allen Franklin has some valuable insights on this question. *Fortune* magazine has named Southern Company "most admired" electric and gas utility in America for the last two years.

Addressing the American Marketing Association's Electric Utility Customer Research Conference in Atlanta, Franklin described one manager-researcher exchange of which he was part as follows: Marketing Researcher: "What do you want?"

Franklin (responding slowly and feeling slightly embarrassed for not having a ready answer): "What do you have?"

Marketing Researcher: "I don't have anything, yet. That's why I am here."

Franklin (growing increasingly irritated): "Well, then get out of here! You are keeping me from what I need to be doing!"

The implication of Franklin's exchange is that the researcher needs to understand the current context for decision makers. This comes from scanning the business press, following developing stories, attending conferences within the industry, as well as conducting more focused research projects. In short, the researcher needs to be curious and to be one of the best learners in the firm. Franklin says it this way: "It is not data that are critical, but the people between the data and the management decision maker. Senior managers will tend to work with those who make the managers more comfortable. Comfort is not increased by two-hour presentations that leave management saying to itself, 'What are we going to do with that?'" Here is one way a marketing researcher should approach a senior executive like Allen Franklin:

Marketing Researcher: "We know the firm currently has this problem. We can resolve or minimize it by doing this study and acting upon what we learn."[2]

The next section elaborates on this definition of marketing research by classifying different types of marketing research.

A Classification of Marketing Research

Our definition states that organizations engage in marketing research for two reasons: to identify and to solve marketing problems. This distinction serves as a basis for classifying marketing research into problem-identification research and problem-solving research, as shown in Figure 1.3.

Figure 1.3
A Classification of Marketing Research

problem-identification research
Research undertaken to help identify problems that are not necessarily apparent on the surface and yet exist or are likely to arise in the future.

Problem-identification research involves going below the surface to identify the true underlying problem that the marketing manager is facing. Often these problems may not be readily apparent or they may be likely to arise in the future. Problem-identification research may be designed to estimate market potential, market share, brand or company image, market characteristics, sales analysis, short-range forecasting, long-range forecasting, or uncover business trends. Polo Ralph Lauren may undertake research to determine the size of the market for men's shirts, the projected growth rate, and the market share of major brands. This research may reveal a problem. Say that while Polo's sales of men's shirts have been increasing, they have not been keeping pace with the growth of the industry. Moreover, Polo has been gradually losing market share to competitors such as Tommy Hilfiger.

Problem identification is the more common of the two forms of research and is undertaken by virtually all marketing firms. This type of research is used to assess the environment and diagnose problems. Information regarding changes in the market provides an initial alert to potential opportunities or problems. A firm that is operating in a growing market but suffering from a declining market share may be dealing with company-specific problems, such as ineffective advertising or high turnover in its salesforce. In other instances, problems, such as declining demand, may be common to all the firms in the industry. Considering the economic, social, cultural, or consumer behavior trends may help identify such problems or opportunities.

problem-solving research
Research undertaken to help solve specific marketing problems.

Once a problem or opportunity has been identified, a firm undertakes **problem-solving research** to address the problem. Most marketing firms conduct problem-solving research as well. Problem-solving research addresses many topics, including segmentation, product, pricing, promotion, and distribution. Problem-identification research and problem-solving research go hand in hand, and a given marketing research project may combine both types of research.

Classifying marketing research into two main types is useful from a conceptual as well as a practical viewpoint. The McDonald's example illustrates that these two types of research often go hand in hand. Marketing research discovered the health consciousness

RESEARCH IN ACTION

The Arch of Marketing Research at the Golden Arches

In the decade of the 1960s, McDonald's (www.mcdonalds.com) earned about $170 million domestically; today the company earns more than that in two days. This growth can be attributed in no small part to marketing research. In 1968, McDonald's formed its marketing research department, which has grown dramatically since its creation. The most prominent aspect of this operation is that 85 percent of all McDonald's are franchises. McDonald's research actively supports these restaurants by conducting problem-identification and problem-solving research.

In 2003, problem-identification research in the form of market characteristics research revealed that the reason for sales decline was increased health consciousness of consumers. Based on subsequent problem-solving (segmentation and product) research, McDonald's introduced a line of premium salads. As a result, sales turned around and increased in the second half of 2003. In 2004, McDonald's advertising was targeting mothers in a special way, hoping that mothers will not only patronize McDonald's, but also buy plenty of Happy Meals for their young children.

As of 2004, the company is the world's leading food service retailer with more than 30,000 restaurants in 119 countries serving 46 million customers each day. While most fast-food restaurants have a ratio of visits to outlets of about 1, for McDonald's that ratio is almost 1.7. It's the feelings the arches evoke. It's the result of problem-identification and problem-solving research that McDonald's undertakes on an ongoing basis.[3]

of the consumer (problem identification), and the solution was the introduction of a line of premium salads (problem solving). The Reebok International vignette also illustrates this point. Problem identification involving analysis of secondary data, focus groups, and a market potential survey revealed that adults were spending less time in health clubs and more time exercising at home. Problem-solving research in the form of product research led to the development and introduction of the successful home-step aerobics line.

BE a DM!

As the marketing director of the NFL, what marketing strategies would you formulate to target female fans?

BE an MR!

Visit the NFL's Web site (www.nfl.com) and search the Internet using a search engine as well as your library's online databases to obtain information on women's attitudes toward the NFL.

The NFL is tickled pink and would like to target female fans, what kind of marketing research would you recommend?

Marketing Research Process

The **marketing research process** consists of six steps (Figure 1.4). This process is a general one and can be followed for conducting research in any functional area, (e.g., marketing, finance, accounting, and so forth). Each of these steps is discussed in great detail in subsequent chapters. We will provide only a brief overview here.

marketing research process
A set of six steps that defines the tasks to be accomplished in conducting a marketing research study: problem definition, developing an approach to the problem, research design formulation, field work, data preparation and analysis, and report preparation and presentation.

Step 1: *Defining the Problem*

The first step in any marketing research project is to define the problem. Researchers accomplish problem definition through discussions with the decision makers, interviews with industry experts, analysis of secondary data, and, perhaps, some qualitative research, such as focus groups. Problem definition involves defining the management decision problem (what should the management do) and the marketing research problem (what information is needed). In the opening vignette, the management decision problem was: What should Reebok do to increase its market share? The marketing research problem for Reebok was assessing the market potential and determining the

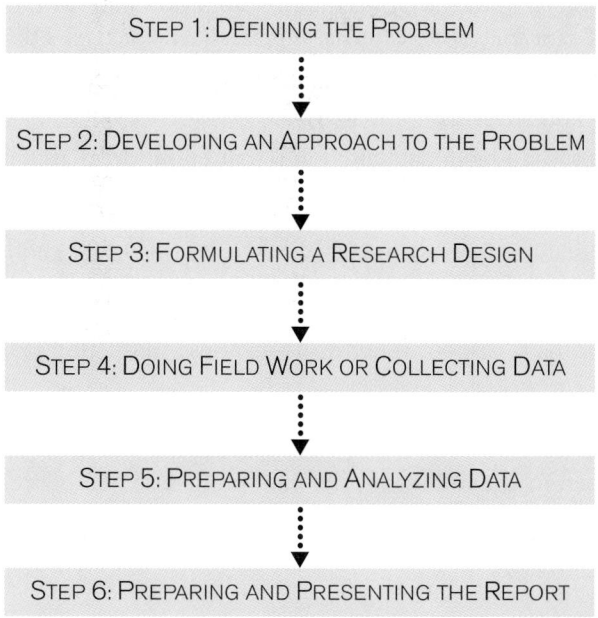

Figure 1.4
The Marketing Research Process

demand for home-step aerobic products. Once the problem has been precisely defined, the research can be designed and conducted properly. (See Chapter 2.)

Step 2: *Developing an Approach to the Problem*

Developing an approach to the problem includes formulating an analytical framework and models, research questions and hypotheses, and the information needed. This process is guided by the same tasks performed to define the problem. (See Chapter 2.) In the opening vignette, several research questions were investigated related to exercising at home.

Step 3: *Formulating a Research Design*

A research design is a framework or blueprint for conducting the marketing research project. It details the procedures needed to obtain the required information. A study may be designed to test hypotheses of interest or determine possible answers to the research questions, both of which contribute to decision making. Conducting preliminary or exploratory research and precisely defining the variables and designing appropriate scales to measure them are also part of the research design. The issue of how the data should be obtained from the respondents (for example, by conducting a survey or an experiment) must be addressed. In the opening vignette, the research design involved analysis of secondary data and focus groups, and a survey was conducted to assess the market potential for home-step aerobic equipment. It is also necessary to design a questionnaire and a sampling plan to select respondents for the study. These steps are discussed in detail in Chapters 3 to 13.

Step 4: *Doing Field Work or Collecting Data*

Data collection is accomplished using a staff that operates in the field. Field work involves personal, telephone, mail, or electronic interviewing. Proper selection, training, supervision, and evaluation of the field force are essential to ensure high-quality data collection. Reebok contracted field work or data collection to external suppliers, who collect the required data. (See Chapter 14.)

Step 5: *Preparing and Analyzing Data*

Data preparation involves data-processing steps leading up to analysis. This includes the editing, coding, and transcribing of collected data. This entire process must then be verified for accuracy. The editing process involves an initial inspection of questionnaires or observation forms for completeness and reasonableness of responses. After this initial inspection, the response to each question is coded to ensure standardized entry into the computer. The data from the questionnaires are transferred onto storage media and then analyzed using different statistical techniques. These results are then interpreted in order to find conclusions related to the marketing research problem. In the opening vignette, Reebok contracted data analysis to external suppliers, who analyzed the data using appropriate statistical techniques. (See Chapters 15 to 18.)

Step 6: *Preparing and Presenting the Report*

The entire project should be documented in a written report that addresses the specific research questions; describes the approach, the research design, data collection, and data analysis procedures; and presents the results and the major findings. The written report is supplemented by tables, figures, and graphs to enhance clarity and impact, and is usually accompanied by a formal presentation. Reebok may use external suppliers in writing the report, but presentation of the results to the management and assistance in implementation is the primary responsibility of its in-house marketing research department. (See Chapter 19.)

Reebok International follows a research process that incorporates all six of these steps. As can be seen in the following, the marketing research process (see Figure 1.4) is very consistent with the definition of marketing research presented earlier (see Figure 1.2).

Definition of Marketing Research (Figure 1.2)	Marketing Research Process (Figure 1.4)
Identification of information needed	Step 1: Defining the problem
Collection of data	Step 2: Developing an approach to the problem
	Step 3: Formulating a research design
	Step 4: Doing field work or collecting data
Analysis of data	Step 5: Preparing and analyzing data
Dissemination of results	Step 6: Preparing and presenting the report
Use of information	

The Internet is very useful for project management. Internet e-mail combined with software such as Lotus Notes are being used for communication by researchers and clients, and for coordinating and managing the six steps of the marketing research process. The Internet is also being used to disseminate marketing research results and reports, which can be posted on the Web and made available to managers on a worldwide basis.

BE a DM!

As the marketing chief for Fossil, you are considering the introduction of a superfunctional, fashionable wristwatch for men and women priced at $99. What kind of information do you need to help you make this decision?

BE an MR!

Visit Fossil's Web site (www.fossil.com) and search the Internet using a search engine as well as your library's online databases to obtain information on consumers' preferences for wristwatches.

Fossil wants to determine consumer preferences for a superfunctional, fashionable wristwatch for men and women priced at $99. Describe the six steps of the marketing research process that should be followed.

The Role of Marketing Research in Marketing Decision Making

The Reebok vignette illustrates only a few applications of marketing research and its role in the marketing decision-making process. Marketing research, indeed, has a broad range of applications and plays a crucial role in the marketing decision-making process. One way to describe the role of marketing research is in light of the basic marketing paradigm given in Figure 1.5.

A major goal of marketing is to identify and then satisfy needs of the various customer groups (e.g., consumers, employees, channel members, suppliers). To do this, marketing managers need information about the various customer groups, competitors, and other forces, such as environmental trends in the marketplace. In recent years, timely market information has become even more valuable. For example, the speed of new products entering the marketplace, domestic and international competition, and the increase in demanding and well-informed consumers all contribute to the importance of this type of market data.

The task of marketing research is to assess the information needs and provide management with relevant, accurate, reliable, valid, and current information to aid marketing decision making (see Figure 1.5). Companies use marketing research to stay competitive and to avoid high costs associated with making poor decisions based on unsound information. Sound decisions are not based on gut feeling, intuition, or even pure judgment; they're based on sound information. Without sound information, management cannot make sound decisions. Reebok's successful introduction of the home-step aerobics line was guided by systematic marketing research.

The following example illustrates how General Motors's (GM's) car design process was improved through the use of marketing research. Due to the new car design, GM has

Figure 1.5
The Role of Marketing Research in Marketing

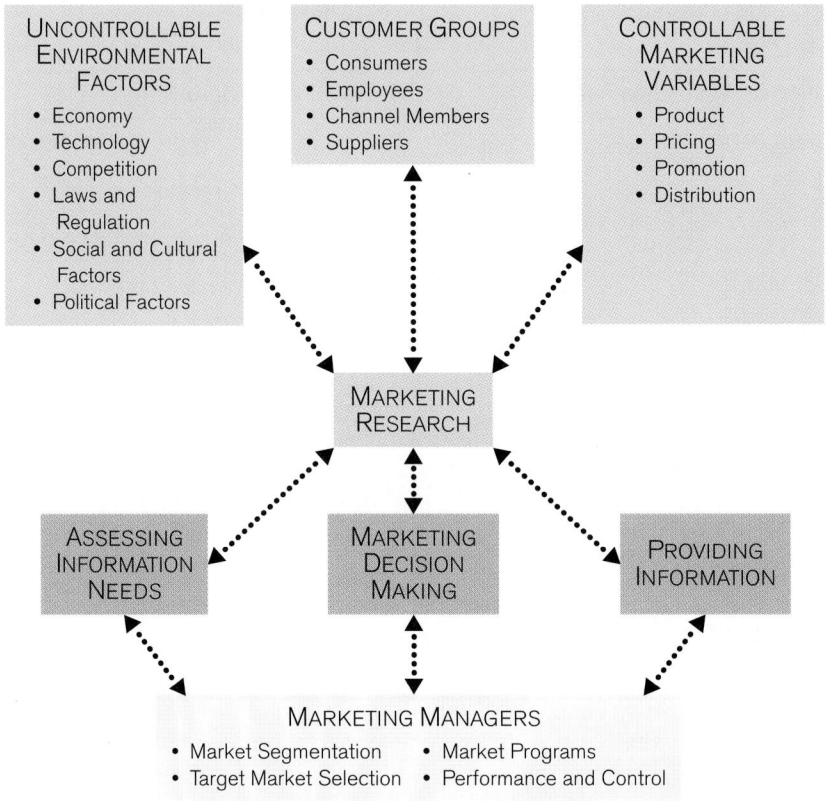

pleased customers who were initially dissatisfied with certain features of the vehicle. GM reinforces the fact that management cannot make sound decisions without sound information provided by marketing research.

This example from GM illustrates the numerous strategic and tactical decisions marketing managers face and how marketing research can be helpful in improving the decision-making process. Identifying and finding solutions to customer needs (a primary goal of marketing) requires the integration of a wide range of factors, not just intuition. Figure 1.5 illustrates this range, which includes decisions about potential opportunities, target market selection, market segmentation, planning and implementing marketing programs, marketing performance, and control. These decisions often result in actions related to product, pricing, promotion, and distribution.

To make the decision process even more complicated, a manager must also consider uncontrollable external factors that influence the marketing process. These include general economic conditions (an economic slow-down or recession), technology (the impact of new technology, such as the Internet), public policies and laws (those related to environmental pollution affect automobile companies), political environment (the Republicans are considered pro-business), competition (many dot-coms have not been able to survive because of competition), and social and cultural changes (the reversal of traditional marital roles). Another factor in this mix is the complexity of the various customer groups: consumers, employees, channel members, and suppliers. The marketing manager must attempt to monitor and incorporate all these considerations. Marketing research removes some of the uncertainty and improves the quality of decision making in this highly complex environment.

The Internet can be useful to marketing researchers in many ways. A variety of marketing research information related to the client company—its competitors, the industry, and relevant marketing, economic, governmental, and environmental information—can be obtained by conducting a search using popular search engines: AltaVista (www.altavista.com), AOL Search (www.search.aol.com), Ask Jeeves (www.askjeeves.com), FAST search (www.alltheweb.com), Google (www.google.com), Lycos (www.lycos.com),

RESEARCH IN ACTION

Marketing Research Makes the Customer GM's Design Chief

General Motors (www.gm.com) historically had little or no regard for marketing research. The company had the attitude that its size and resource base provided it with a technological edge that was sufficient for continued success. Certainly, the company did not need any input from the customer. Indeed, GM did not form a marketing research division until 1985.

As an example of their "know-all" attitude, GM executives were positive that the popular Camaro and Firebird lines sold because of their exterior design. However, in one of the company's first marketing research projects, consumers indicated that while looks were important, performance and quality rated very high in selecting a car. The consumers went on to say that they were very satisfied with the exterior design, but that they were not as satisfied with the performance and quality. The obvious shortcomings of executive assumptions regarding customer values spawned the birth of "needs-based" market research.

General Motors began compiling information from existing and potential customers in 1986. Since then, GM has conducted interviews with millions of consumers, and has amassed a vast portfolio of information on consumer needs in all product segments. Once the information has been gathered, the marketing research team, "can build a model of the entry-level segment showing the market volume and the number of buyers in the various needs categories, and then introduce the factors of incomes and demographics."

Both classes of research are used extensively. In 2003, problem-identification research in the form of market potential study revealed growing demand from minority segments. Based on subsequent problem-solving research (i.e., promotional research) GM decided to increase its multicultural advertising outlay from $40 million annually in 2003 to $140 million annually in 2008.

The real value of this research was improvement of GM's car design process. This research shifted the company's focus from the products of its competitors to the needs of the consumer. According to Chris Cedergren, senior vice president of AutoPacific Group, an automotive marketing and product consultant firm, "With what GM is doing, it can assess what the needs and desires are five to 10 years from now." GM now focuses more on what the consumers say, and less on the gut feelings of its executives. All a result of marketing research.[4]

MSN Search (search.msn.com), Netscape Search (search.netscape.com), WebCrawler (www.webcrawler.com), and Yahoo! (www.yahoo.com).

Traditionally, a clear distinction existed between the responsibilities of the marketing researchers and the marketing manager. However, these roles are beginning to merge as marketing researchers become more involved in decision making and marketing managers are becoming more involved with research. This trend can be attributed to better training of marketing managers, advances in technology, and use of research as an ongoing aspect of the marketing function. In essence, marketing research must add value to marketing decision making and we further illustrate this role of marketing research in our discussion of the information value chain.[5]

BE an MR!

Visit Nokia's Web site (www.nokia.com) and search the Internet using a search engine as well as your library's online databases to obtain information on consumers' preferences for cellular handsets.

What type of marketing research information would you obtain to help Nokia target 15- to 24-year-olds, the heavy users of cellular handsets?

BE a DM!

As the marketing manager for Nokia, what strategies would you formulate to target 15- to 24-year-olds, the heavy users of cellular handsets?

The Information Value Chain for Marketing Research

information value chain
There is a progression in value for the user as data is rendered into information, and then into knowledge, which is used in making and implementing decisions.

An extremely valuable concept for understanding how to increase the impact of marketing research is the information value chain (Figure 1.6). The concept of the **information value chain** is: There is a progression in value for the user as data is rendered into information, and then into knowledge, which is used in making and implementing decisions. An example using the entries in a spreadsheet can help illuminate the information value chain concept. Imagine a one-page spreadsheet with single-digit entries in each cell. In this spreadsheet, each row contains a different customer's answers to a satisfaction survey given by a firm. Each column of the spreadsheet corresponds to a separate question on this satisfaction survey. Keeping such a spreadsheet in mind, "data" would be the individual cell entries of the spreadsheet. "Information" would result from analysis of a more aggregated form of the cell entries, such as inserting a new row at the bottom of the spreadsheet and computing averages for each corresponding column. Now, the user would have data with structure—a measure of central tendency—for the responses to each question. "Knowledge" would result from comparing these average values among themselves. Now, the information would be endowed with meaning, as the generally lowest rating and the highest rating could be identified. Richer knowledge would result from comparing the firm's average ratings with the same ratings for a competing firm.

However, this is not the end of creating value from data. Managers want the implications of new knowledge made clear. Making a concise recommendation to managers is also needed, as well as a justification for this recommended course of action over other possible ones. By doing this, researchers now enter the realm of the decision maker. The outstanding researcher will not only make reasoned recommendations to management, but will position the research team to bring measurement expertise to the evaluation of the unfolding results for implementing decisions. "Implementing action" is the final link in the information value chain for marketing research.

Eastman Kodak is a company that has made changes in the way its marketing research department functioned that showcase the potential value in having marketing researchers involved in each part of the information value chain for marketing research. Eastman Kodak has given its marketing researchers the responsibility for gathering data and then rendering information about consumer trends, as well as insights based on knowledge about consumer motivations. Then, these researchers translate this data, information, and knowledge into product and service ideas for the company.

Recently, Eastman Kodak launched a new disposable camera that uses film, but delivers the pictures digitally on a computer disc.[6] Researchers successfully recommend how to position the new product in the marketplace. Within one year of introduction, this new product brought in more than $80 million in sales. Fran Linnane, director of business insights for Eastman Kodak, summed up this new focus on creating value in the information chain this way: "We have helped teach (our market researchers) how to get engaged (in the marketing mix) and how to have an impact on the company. Now, they are getting awards and special recognition. That wasn't happening before."

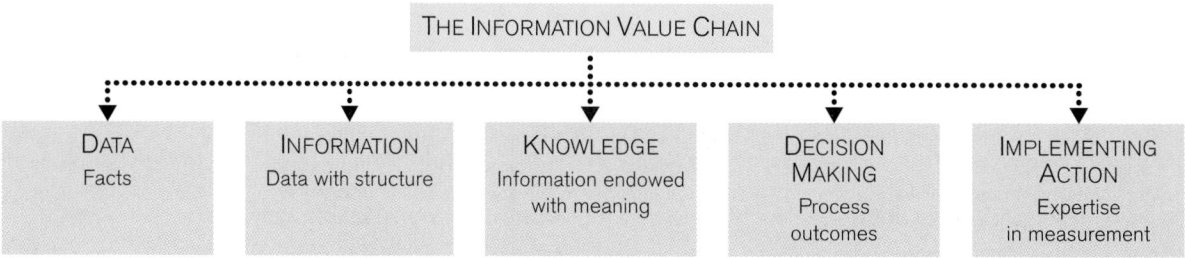

Figure 1.6
The Information Value Chain

The Decision to Conduct Marketing Research

While marketing research can be beneficial in a variety of situations, the decision to conduct research is not automatic. Rather, this decision should be guided by a number of considerations, including the costs versus the benefits, the resources available to conduct the research, the resources available to implement the research findings, and management's attitude toward research. Marketing research should be undertaken when the expected value of information it generates exceeds the costs of conducting the marketing research project. In general, the more important the decision confronting management and the greater the uncertainty or risk facing them, the greater the value of information obtained. Formal procedures are available for quantifying the expected value as well as the costs of a marketing research project. While in most instances the value of information exceeds the costs, there are instances when the reverse may be true. A pie manufacturer wanted to understand the purchase of pies in convenience stores. We advised against a major marketing research project when we discovered that less than one percent of the sales were coming from convenience stores and that this situation was unlikely to change in the next five years.

The resources, especially time and money, are always limited. If either time or money is not available in adequate amounts to conduct a quality project, that project probably should not be undertaken. It is better not do a formal project than undertake one in which the integrity of the research is compromised because of lack of resources. In one instance, we advised Fisher-Price not to undertake a formal research project because a go/no-go decision regarding the introduction of a new toy had to be made in just a few days and time was too limited to conduct quality research. Likewise, a firm may lack the resources to implement the recommendations arising from the findings of marketing research. In that case, spending the resources to conduct the research may not be warranted. If management does not have a positive attitude toward research, then it is likely that the project report will gather dust if the research is conducted. However, there may be exceptions to this guideline. We conducted a project for a retail chain where the chain management was hostile toward the project, but the research was commissioned and funded by the parent organization. While the store management was opposed to the findings that reflected negatively on the store chain, the parent company did implement our recommendations.

There are other instances that may argue against conducting a marketing research project. If the required information is already available within the organization, the decision for which the research is to be conducted has already been made, or the research is going to be used for gaining political ends, then the value of information generated is greatly reduced and the project is generally not warranted.

BE a DM!

As the marketing director of Estée Lauder company, would you conduct a formal marketing research project to determine consumer response to a proposed new line of cosmetics? Why or why not?

BE an MR!

Visit Estée Lauder's Web site (www.esteelauder.com) and search the Internet using a search engine as well as your library's online databases to find information on the marketing strategy of the Estée Lauder company.

What type of problem-solving research would you conduct for the proposed new line of cosmetics?

An Overview of the Marketing Research Industry

The **marketing research industry** consists of suppliers who provide marketing research services. Figure 1.7 broadly categorizes research suppliers as either internal or external. An **internal supplier** is a marketing research department within the firm. Internal research departments can be found in large organizations across a wide range of industries, including automobile companies (GM, Ford), consumer products firms (Procter &

marketing research industry The marketing research industry consists of suppliers who provide marketing research services.

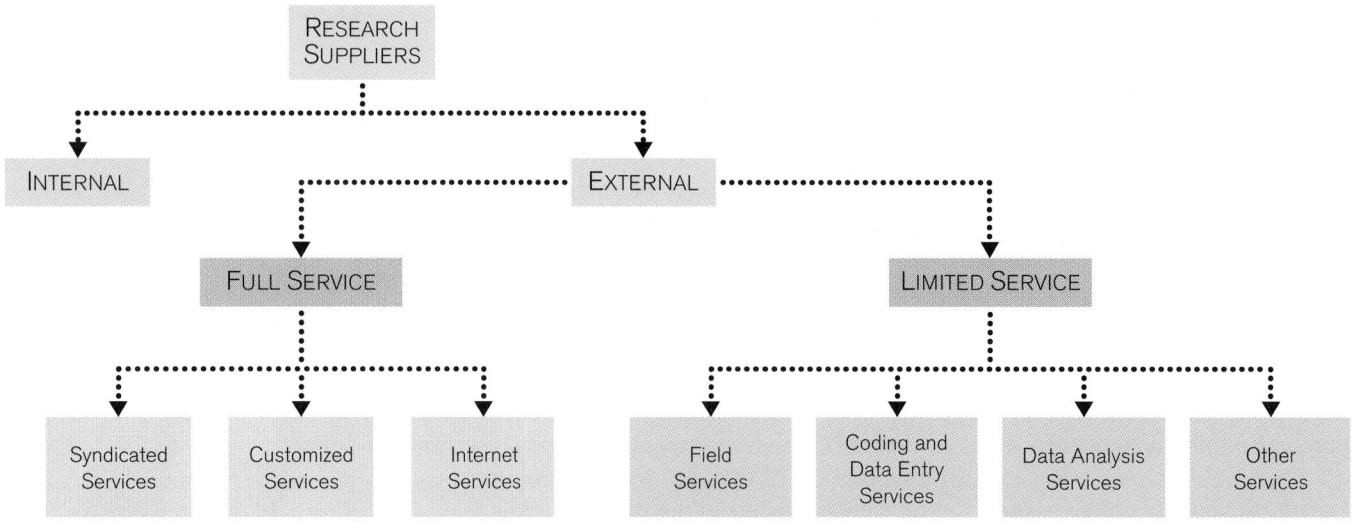

Figure 1.7

Marketing Research Industry: Suppliers and Services

internal suppliers
Marketing research departments located within a firm.

Gamble, Colgate Palmolive, Coca-Cola, Reebok) and banks (Citigroup, JPMorganChase). For these larger companies, the research function is often centrally located at the corporate headquarters. One corporate marketing research department caters to all of the firm's research needs. For smaller or decentralized firms that operate independent divisions, the market research function is distributed among these separate divisions. In decentralized organizations, divisions may be structured around products, customers, or geographical regions, with marketing research personnel assigned across the country. Each division (or group based on product line or geographical region) will have its own marketing research operation. While companies can be found operating under a number of organizational structures, the recent trend has been toward centralization and a trimming of internal marketing research staff.

external suppliers
Outside marketing research companies hired to conduct a complete marketing research project or a part of it.

External suppliers are outside firms hired to supply marketing research data. Even firms such as HP and Reebok (see opening vignette) with in-house marketing research departments make at least some use of external suppliers. External suppliers range in size from one- or two-person shops to multinational corporations. Most of the research suppliers are small operations. Table 1.1 lists the top 25 global marketing research suppliers.[7] Many external suppliers form strategic alliances with other firms in the marketing research industry. These alliances enable participating firms to gain each other's expertise and resources. These are formed through a merger, acquisition, or contractual agreement. For example, Burke, Inc. has a strategic alliance with Infratest Burke AG, Munich, Germany (an NFO WorldGroup company) that owns 50 percent interest in Burke, Inc. This alliance gives Burke, Inc. access to Europe and other international markets. It also gives Infratest Burke AG resources to conduct research in the United States.

full-service suppliers
Companies that offer the full range of marketing research activities.

External suppliers can provide either full service or limited service. **Full-service suppliers** offer the entire range of marketing research services, from problem definition, developing an approach, questionnaire design, sampling, data collection, data analysis, and interpretation, to report preparation and presentation. The services of these suppliers can be further broken down into syndicated services, customized services, and Internet services (see Figure 1.7).

syndicated services
Companies that collect and sell common pools of data designed to serve information needs that a number of clients share.

Syndicated services are companies that collect and sell common pools of data designed to serve information needs that are shared by a number of clients. Surveys, purchase and media panels, scanners, and audits are the main means by which these data are collected. For example, the Nielsen Television Index provides information on audience size and demographic characteristics of households watching specific television programs (www.nielsenmedia.com). The ACNielsen Company (www.acnielsen.com) also provides scanner volume tracking data, such as those generated by electronic scanning at checkout

Table 1.1

Honomichl Global Top 25

Top 25 Global Research Organizations

Rank 2003	Rank 2002	Organization	Headquarters	Parent Country	Web Site	No. of Countries with Subsidiary Branch Offices[1]	Global Research Revenue[2] (U.S. $ millions)	Percent of Global Revenue from Outside Home Country
1	1	VNU N.V.	Haarlem	Netherlands	www.vnu.com	81	$3,048.3	99.0%*
2	–	Taylor Nelson Sofres plc	London	U.K.	www.tns-global.com	70	1,565.1	83.5
–	4	Taylor Nelson Sofres	London	U.K.	www.tns-global.com	54	1,050.5	78.6
–	8	NFO WorldGroup Inc.	Greenwich, CT	U.K.	www.tns-global.com	40	514.6	93.5
3	2	IMS Health Inc.	Fairfield, CT	U.S.	www.imshealth.com	75	1,381.8	61.1
4	3	The Kantar Group	Fairfield, CT	U.K.	www.kantargroup.com	61	1,002.1	66.1*
5	6	GfK Group	Nuremberg	Germany	www.gfk.com	48	673.6	62.8
6	7	Ipsos Group S.A.	Paris	France	www.ipsos.com	36	644.6	84.1
7	5	Information Resources Inc.	Chicago	U.S.	www.infores.com	18	554.3	30.0
8	9	Westat Inc.	Rockville, MD	U.S.	www.westat.com	1	381.6	NA
9	11	Synovate	London	U.K.	www.synovate.com	46	357.7	91.3
10	10	NOP World	London	U.K.	www.nopworld.com	6	335.6	80.5
11	12	Arbitron Inc.	New York	U.S.	www.arbitron.com	3	273.6	2.9
12	13	Maritz Research	St. Louis	U.S.	www.maritzresearch.com	4	188.8	34.9
13	14	Video Research Ltd.[3]	Tokyo	Japan	www.videor.co.jp	4	166.7	1.1
14	16	J.D. Power and Associates	Agoura Hills, CA	U.S.	www.jdpower.com	6	144.8	17.8
15	17	Harris Interactive Inc.	Rochester, NY	U.S.	www.harrisinteractive.com	4	137.0	19.0
16	15	Opinion Research Corp.	Princeton, NJ	U.S.	www.opinionresearch.com	6	131.2	35.4
17	18[4]	INTAGE Inc.[3]	Tokyo	Japan	www.intage.co.jp	2	122.3	1.0
18	19[4]	The NPD Group Inc.	Port Washington, NY	U.S.	www.npd.com	11	117.6	17.7
19	21	AGB Group	Milan	Italy	www.agb.com	19	81.6	79.0
20	23	Market & Opinion Research Int'l	London	U.K.	www.mori.com	2	64.4	2.8
21	25	Lieberman Research Worldwide	Los Angeles	U.S.	www.lrwonline.com	1	63.2	8.7
22	20	Dentsu Research Inc.	Tokyo	Japan	www.dentsuresearch.co.jp	1	57.0	1.1
23	23	Abt Associates Inc.	Cambridge, MA	U.S.	www.abtassociates.com	3	54.0	4.3
24	–	Nikkei Research Inc.	Tokyo	Japan	www.nikkeiresearch.com	4	52.1	3.5
25	22	Wirthlin Worldwide	McLean, VA	U.S.	www.wirthlin.com	4	52.0	22.9
						Total	$11,651.0	67.3%

* Estimated by Top 25.

[1] Includes countries that have subsidiaries with an equity interest or branch offices, or both.

[2] Total revenue that includes nonresearch activities for some companies are significantly higher. This information is given in the individual company profiles.

[3] For fiscal year ending March 2004.

[4] Reranked based on corrected revenue of the NPD Group Inc. See NPD's profile for details.

Source: Drawn from *Marketing News* with permission from the American Marketing Association.

counters in supermarkets. The NPD Group (www.npd.com), another example of a syndicated service, maintains one of the largest panels in the United States. Syndicated services are discussed in more detail in Chapter 5.

customized services
Companies that tailor the research procedures to best meet the needs of each client.

Customized services offer a wide variety of marketing research services customized to suit a client's specific needs. Each marketing research project is designed to meet the unique needs of the client. Some of the marketing research firms that offer these services are Synovate, TNS, and Burke, Inc.

Internet services
Companies that have specialized in conducting marketing research on the Internet.

Several marketing research firms, including some who have specialized in conducting marketing research on the Internet, offer **Internet services**. For example, Greenfield Online Research Center Inc., Westport, CT (www.greenfieldonline.com), a subsidiary of the Greenfield Consulting Group (www.greenfieldgroup.com), offers a broad range of customized qualitative and quantitative online marketing research for consumer, business-to-business, and professional markets. Using large, proprietary databases, studies are conducted within the company's secure Web site.

limited-service suppliers
Companies that specialize in one or a few phases of the marketing research project.

field services
Companies whose primary service offering is their expertise in collecting data for research projects.

Limited-service suppliers specialize in one or a few steps of the marketing research process. Limited-service suppliers can be found specializing in field services, coding and data entry services, data analysis services, and other services. **Field services** collect data. They may use the full range of data collection methods (mail, personal, telephone, or electronic interviewing) or they may specialize in only one method. Some field service organizations maintain extensive interviewing facilities across the country for interviewing shoppers in malls. Many offer qualitative data collection services, such as focus-group interviewing (discussed in Chapter 6). Some firms that offer field services are Field Facts, Inc. (www.fieldfacts.com), Field Work Chicago, Inc. (www.fieldwork.com), Quality Controlled Services division of Maritz (www.Maritz.com), and Survey America (www.survey-america.com).

coding and data entry services
Companies whose primary service offering is their expertise in converting completed surveys or interviews into a usable database for conducting statistical analysis.

data analysis services
Firms whose primary service is to conduct statistical analysis of quantitative data.

Coding and data entry services provide support services after the data have been collected. The services they perform include editing completed questionnaires, developing a coding scheme, and transcribing the data onto diskettes or magnetic tapes for input into the computer. NRC Data Systems provides such services. **Data analysis services** are offered by firms, also known as tab houses, which specialize in computer analysis of quantitative data, such as those obtained in large surveys. Firms such as SDR of Atlanta offer sophisticated data analysis using advanced statistical techniques. Microcomputers and statistical software packages enable firms to perform data analysis in-house. However, the specialized data analysis expertise of outside suppliers is still in demand. Other services include branded marketing research products and services developed to address specific types of marketing research problems.

A firm without an internal marketing research department or specialists will be forced to rely on external, generally full-service suppliers. A firm with an internal marketing research staff will make use of both full-service and limited-service suppliers. The need for external suppliers may arise because the firm may not have the resources or the technical expertise to undertake certain phases of a project. Also, political conflict-of-interest issues may determine that a project be conducted by an outside supplier, as in the case of Reebok in the opening vignette. Data collection in almost every case, and data analysis in most instances, are contracted to external suppliers. Sometimes Reebok also retains full-service suppliers to conduct the entire marketing research project.

Selecting a Research Supplier

When initiating a marketing research study, a firm will often need to hire external suppliers for all or part of the project. The process of selecting an outside supplier can be informal, relying primarily on word-of-mouth endorsements, or it may be very formal, involving a "request for proposal." In the latter case, research suppliers are requested to submit formal proposals for evaluation by the hiring firm. The first step involves compiling a list of prospective suppliers from trade publications, professional directories, Internet sources, and personal contacts. For example, the Green Book (www.greenbook.org) enables you to locate marketing research suppliers by region, specialty, and other criteria.

Regardless of the formality of the process, the hiring firm must develop a checklist detailing its criteria governing the selection of outside suppliers. That checklist should go beyond technical requirements, covering the following areas:

- What is the supplier's reputation?
- Does the firm complete projects on schedule? Is it flexible?
- Is it known for maintaining ethical standards?
- Are its research projects of high quality?
- What kind and how much experience does the supplier have?
- Has the firm had experience with projects similar to this one?
- Do the supplier's personnel have both technical and nontechnical expertise?
- Has the firm formed any strategic alliances? What resources does it have access to?

Reebok International, which subcontracts a great deal of its research to external suppliers, uses a similar checklist. A checklist helps managers examine the working relationships as well as the project requirements. Because of the importance of most research efforts, compatible working relationships and good communication skills can become primary considerations when hiring.

A competitive biding process often is used in selecting external suppliers, particularly for large jobs. However, awarding projects based on lowest price is not a good rule of thumb. The completeness of the research proposal and the criteria discussed above must all be factored into the hiring decision. Moreover, long-term contracts with research suppliers are preferable to selection on a project-by-project basis.

BE an MR!

Visit Green Book's Web site (www.greenbook.org) and identify all the marketing research firms in your local area that conduct Internet-based surveys.

As the research director for Yahoo! you are to select a marketing research firm that specializes in researching consumers who shop on the Internet. Make a list of five such firms. Which one will you select and why?

BE a DM!

As the director of marketing, how would you use information on consumer shopping on the Internet in redesigning the Yahoo! Web site?

Careers in Marketing Research

Promising career opportunities are available with marketing research firms (for example, ACNielsen, TNS, Burke, Inc., M/A/R/C). Equally appealing are careers in business and nonbusiness firms and agencies with in-house marketing research departments (for example, Procter & Gamble, Coca-Cola, Reebok, the Federal Trade Commission, U.S. Census Bureau). Advertising agencies (for example, BBDO International, Ogilvy & Mather, J. Walter Thompson, Young & Rubicam) also conduct substantial marketing research and employ professionals in this field.

A career in research often begins with a supervisory position in field work or data analysis. With experience, the researcher moves up to project-management positions, resulting in director and, eventually, in a vice president–level position. The most common entry-level position in the marketing research industry for people with bachelor's degrees (for example, BBA) is operational supervisor. An operational supervisor is responsible for supervising the day-to-day operations of specific aspects of the marketing research process. These may range from field work, to data editing, to coding for programming and data analysis. Rather than enter the discipline from the operations side, BBAs with strong organizational skills may start as assistant project mangers. An assistant project manager will learn and assist in questionnaire design, review field instructions, and monitor timing and costs of studies. As research techniques become more sophisticated, there is a growing preference for people with master's degrees. Those with MBAs or equivalent degrees are likely to be employed as project managers. In marketing research firms, such as Burke, Inc., the project manager works with the account director in managing the day-to-day operations of a marketing research project.

A researcher entering the profession on the client side would typically begin as a junior research analyst (for BBAs) or research analyst (for MBAs). The junior analyst and the research analyst learn about the particular industry and receive training from a senior staff member, usually the marketing research manager. The junior analyst position includes a training program to prepare individuals for the responsibilities of a research analyst, including coordinating with the marketing department and sales force to develop goals for product exposure. The research analyst responsibilities include checking all data for accuracy, comparing and contrasting new research with established norms, and analyzing data for the purpose of market forecasting.

As these job titles indicate, careers in marketing research can be either highly technical, specializing in the design and the statistical side of the industry, or they can be of a general management nature, with emphasis on client relationships. To prepare for a career in marketing research you should

- Take all the marketing courses you can.
- Take courses in statistics and quantitative methods.
- Acquire computer and Internet skills.
- Take courses in psychology and consumer behavior.
- Acquire effective written and verbal communication skills.
- Think creatively. Creativity and common sense command a premium in marketing research.

It is important for marketing researchers to be liberally educated in order to better understand the problems managers face and then be able to address them from a broad perspective.[8] A career in marketing research will involve working with other bright, energetic people in a fast-paced, dynamic environment. You will get to work on diverse qualitative and quantitative projects with clients in a variety of industries, including e-commerce, travel, telecommunications, pharmaceuticals, government, and nonprofit. The benefits include on-going training and career development, a competitive salary, comprehensive health and dental plans, a 401k, the option to wear business-casual attire, and excellent advancement opportunities.

College graduates' lack of awareness of marketing research as a career and a growing demand for marketing researchers in the fields of information technology, pharmaceuticals, financial services, and other attractive industries has created a shortage of professionals in the field. Marketing research organizations would like to have more incoming talent in order to have a greater presence in senior management in the future. The need for marketing researchers could not be greater. This makes a career worth pursuing for both the short and the long term. For more information on jobs in marketing research, check out the American Marketing Association's career center (www.marketingpower.com) or the WorldOpinion Web site (www.worldopinion.com).

The Role of Marketing Research in MIS and DSS

Earlier, we defined marketing research as the systematic and objective identification, collection, analysis, and dissemination of information for use in marketing decision making. Combining external market information with internal billing, production, and other records results in a powerful marketing information system (MIS; Figure 1.8).

EXPERIENTIAL LEARNING

The World of Marketing Research on the Internet

The WorldOpinion Web site (www.worldopinion.com) is designed to bring you up-to-date news and comprehensive information on the market research industry. Here's how to find what you're looking for and get the most out of your visit.

If you're job hunting or hiring, the classifieds section lists jobs in research, marketing, advertising, public relations, and allied professions. There are literally thousands of current job openings. You're welcome to submit your resume, or job listing, at no charge.

Looking for the right research company for your project? The directory of researchers lists over 8,500 research locations in 99 countries. Search by company name or search by company type and/or geography.

The news section, updated daily, brings you company, conference, and product news from the world of market research.

If you're thinking of attending a marketing or research event or need more information on research education opportunities, check out the WorldOpinion calendar. Hundreds of events and research courses from throughout the world are listed.

There are many other ways the WorldOpinion Web site brings the world of marketing research to you. Explore it!

Marketing information systems (MIS) are a formalized set of procedures for generating, analyzing, storing, and distributing information to marketing decision makers on an ongoing basis. Marketing information systems are differentiated from marketing research in that they are continuously available. Marketing information systems are designed to complement the decision maker's responsibilities, style, and information needs. The power of MIS is in the access it gives managers to vast amounts of information, combining production, invoice, and billing information with marketing intelligence, including marketing research. Marketing information systems offer the potential of much more information than can be obtained from ad hoc marketing research projects. However, that potential is often not achieved when the information is structured so rigidly that it cannot be easily manipulated.

marketing information systems (MIS)
A formalized set of procedures for generating, analyzing, storing, and distributing pertinent information to marketing decision makers on an ongoing basis.

Developed to overcome the limitations of MIS, **decision support systems (DSS)** have built-in flexibility that allow decision makers to interact directly with databases and analysis models. A DSS is an integrated system including hardware, a communications network, database, model base, software base, and the DSS user (decision maker) who collects and interprets information for decision making. Information collected by marketing research becomes a part of the DSS, as in the case of Reebok in the opening vignette. Specifically, marketing research contributes research data to the database, marketing models and analytical techniques to the model base, and specialized programs for analyzing marketing data to the software base. Many firms are building huge internal databases as part of the DSS (see database marketing in

decision support systems (DSS)
An information system that enables decision makers to interact directly with both databases and analysis models. The important components of a DSS include hardware and a communication network, database, model base, software base, and the DSS user (decision maker).

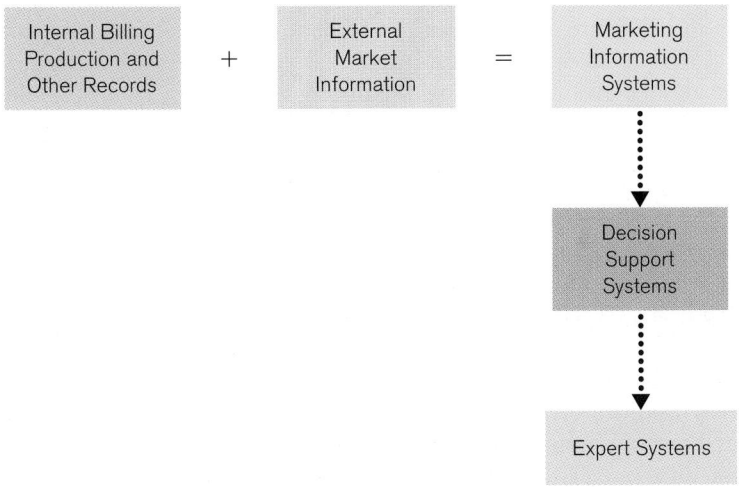

Figure 1.8
The Development of MIS and DSS

Figure 1.9

Marketing Information Systems (MIS) vs. Decision Support Systems (DSS)

MIS	DSS
• Structured problems • Use of reports • Information displaying restricted • Can improve decision making by clarifying new data	• Unstructured problems • Use of models • Adaptability • Can improve decision making by using "what-if" analysis

Chapter 4). The analytical techniques and the software to analyze these data are also discussed later (see Chapters 15 to 18.) Decision support systems differ from MIS in that they combine the models and analytic techniques of traditional marketing research with easy access and retrieval of MIS (Figure 1.9). Well-designed DSS adapt to the decision-making needs of the user with easy interactive processes. In addition to providing easy access to data, DSS can also enhance decision-making effectiveness by using "what-if" analysis. Reebok International makes use of a sophisticated DSS that enables it to assess the impact of introducing new footwear, making a promotional offer, or opening a new facility at a specific location, when these projects are still in the planning stage.

Marketing information systems and DSS can greatly improve decision making by giving management access to a wide range of information. An advanced form of DSS, called expert systems, uses artificial intelligence procedures to incorporate expert judgment. In addition to crunching numbers and storing and retrieving information, these systems are programmed to reason and make inferences. Thus, the expert systems can actually lead to decisions recommending certain courses of action to the management. All these systems can greatly enhance the effectiveness of marketing.

BE a DM!

As the marketing manager for Sony digital cameras your objective is to switch more traditional photographers to the digital camera. What information from the company's DSS would you find helpful in achieving this goal?

BE an MR!

Visit Sony's Web site (www.sony.com) and search the Internet using a search engine as well as your library's online databases to find information on the market for digital cameras.

What kind of marketing research would you undertake to obtain the information identified by the DM?

Summary Illustration Using the Opening Vignette

To summarize and illustrate the concepts in this chapter, let's return to the opening vignette. Marketing research involves the identification, collection, analysis, dissemination, and use of information about consumers, channel members, competitors, changes and trends in the marketplace, and other aspects of the firm's environment. In the opening vignette, Reebok used "time-use" research in an attempt to discover what consumers do with their spare time. Marketing research may be classified as problem-identification research or problem-solving research. Reebok used problem-identification research involving secondary data analysis, focus groups, and a market potential survey to discover that adults were spending less time in health clubs and more time exercising at home. Problem-solving research, in the form of product research, then led to the development of the successful home-step aerobics line.

The marketing research process consists of six steps, which must be followed systematically. Reebok follows a very similar marketing research process and some of these steps were illustrated in the opening vignette. Marketing research may be conducted internally and/or may be purchased from external suppliers. In the case of Reebok, in-house marketing research specialists are actively involved in defining and designing the marketing research project and also have the primary responsibility for presentation of the results to management and providing assistance in implementation. Reebok also makes use of full-service suppliers who provide assistance in all the steps of the marketing research process as well as limited-service suppliers who may handle only data collection and analysis and assist in report writing.

The marketing research industry offers a wide range of careers in both corporate (for example, Reebok) and independent service organizations. Information obtained using marketing research can stand alone or be integrated into an MIS and DSS, as in the case of Reebok.

Application to Contemporary Issues

The use of the Internet is integrated in a pervasive way throughout each chapter. While we also address several contemporary issues throughout each chapter, we focus special attention on international marketing research, technology and marketing research, and ethics in marketing research. Each of these issues receives a separate section in each chapter of the text (except the data analysis chapters, 16 to 18). We show how marketing research principles can be applied when conducting research in an international setting. Since we live in a technological age, the technological developments that impact marketing research are also discussed. Ethical issues in marketing research are described.

International Marketing Research

The United States accounts for only about 40 percent of the marketing research expenditures worldwide. About 40 percent of all marketing research is conducted in Western Europe and about 10 percent in Japan. Most of the research in Europe is done in Germany, the United Kingdom, France, Italy, and Spain.[9] With the globalization of markets, marketing research has assumed a truly international character, a trend that is likely to continue. Several U.S.-based market research firms are equipped to conduct international marketing research. They include IMS Health, Information Resources, and Maritz Research (see Table 1.1). Foreign-based firms include the Kantar Group and TNS (United Kingdom) and the GfK Group (Germany).

International marketing research is much more complex than domestic marketing research. Research of this type should be sensitive to differences in customs, communication, and culture. The environment in the countries or international markets that are being researched influences the way the six steps of the marketing research process should be performed. These environmental factors include marketing, government, legal, economic, structural, informational and technological, and sociocultural. Properly conducted international marketing research can yield high dividends, as demonstrated by the success of Procter & Gamble in China.

BE an MR!

Visit Levi's Web site (www.levis.com) and search the Internet using a search engine as well as your library's online databases to find information on consumer preferences for jeans.

Levi's would like to conduct marketing research to increase its share of the jeans market in the United States and India. How would you conduct marketing research in the two countries?

BE a DM!

As Levi's marketing chief, what information would you need to formulate strategies aimed at increasing market share?

RESEARCH IN ACTION

Head & Shoulders Stands Head and Shoulders above Competition in China

As of 2005, P&G (www.pg.com) markets almost 300 products to more than five billion consumers in 140 countries. Procter & Gamble (P&G) products are the largest daily-use consumer products in China. The company has achieved this status by ignoring popular maxims, instead relying on marketing research.

The success of P&G comes because it ignored the standard practices used in marketing to a Chinese audience. It did not cater to a wealthy audience, although it was told that none other could afford its expensive products. By relying on marketing research, such popular maxims were seen for what they were—misunderstandings. Additionally, by conducting proper cross-cultural research, P&G was able to overcome any Western bias based on erroneous beliefs about China, such as middle-class Chinese could not afford expensive Western products.

Marketing research revealed that dandruff was a major concern as the Chinese have dark hair, where dandruff readily stands out. Furthermore, Chinese shampoos were ineffective in fighting this malady. Research also revealed that most Chinese were willing to pay a premium for a shampoo that addressed this problem.

So P&G decided to establish its foothold in China by fighting dandruff. P&G targeted a broad segment, rather than just the wealthy. P&G introduced Head & Shoulders as a premium brand, and within three years it was China's leading shampoo. P&G then introduced antidandruff versions of Pert and Pantene. Using careful targeting, both brands performed extremely well. Overall, P&G commands 57 percent of the shampoo market in China, even though its products are priced over 300 percent higher than local brands. Its sales of personal-care products rose to over $1 billion for the fiscal year ending in June 2004. These figures show that those who overcome their biases and conduct proper research can stand head and shoulders above the competition.[10]

Technology and Marketing Research

The term third wave, coined from Alvin Toffler's book of the same name, has come to symbolize the contemporary transition from current ways of viewing and doing things to a new age. The third wave of marketing research will shape not only the way information is used but also our fundamental conception of the role of marketing research in assisting management decisions.

In the first wave, we progressed from seat-of-the-pants decision making to data-based decisions. The emphasis was on supporting marketing decisions with data. As more data became available, a large problem arose. Marketers were soon floating in a sea of individual facts about their products and markets with very little in the way of assimilating the data.

In the second wave, the progression was from data-based decisions to information-based decision making. Rather than review a multitude of individual facts, the role of marketing research became one of analyzing data to summarize the underlying patterns. If we could understand the relationships and patterns in the data, so the logic went, this would lead to the insights necessary to make sound marketing decisions.

Now with the third wave, we're moving from information-based decision making to system-based decisions. Computer technology, a major driving force behind the third wave, allows for a better fit of marketing information to the needs of the market planning process. We can create a better interface and information exchange between marketing researchers and marketing managers, resulting in a unique knowledge base that captures the expertise of each group. The third wave involves a number of developments centered on decision support systems and expert systems that put the power of marketing information directly into the hands of nontechnical decision makers.

A major goal of this new, improved technology is to link the customer to the information superhighway through the Internet, interactive telephone, interactive TV, home shopping channels, and integrated call centers. Such a system knows who is calling based on the customer's phone number and can identify information the customer will likely need. This allows researchers to know in real time what is happening in the marketplace. Cyberspace as a data-collection alternative will rival the telephone in the twenty-first century. Researchers will be doing research in an interactive environment. As the leading edge of the third wave begins to emerge, one can imagine many intriguing ways that marketing research will be used in the future.[11]

Ethics in Marketing Research

Business activities are often discussed from the perspective of different stakeholders, those individuals or groups who have an interest in or are directly involved in activities related to business. Marketing research activities affect four stakeholders: (1) the marketing researcher, (2) the client, (3) the respondent, and (4) the public. Ethical questions arise when conflict occurs between these stakeholders (Figure 1.10). In the face of conflict, the behavior of the stakeholders should be guided by codes of conduct. Several organizations, such as the Marketing Research Association and the American Marketing Association, provide codes in the area of ethical research behavior. Each stakeholder has responsibilities. Neglect of these responsibilities may result in hurting another stakeholder or the research project. It will always damage the research process and the integrity of the profession.[12] These issues are discussed in more detail in subsequent chapters.

BE a DM!

As the marketing director of CNN, how would you deal with the situation in which an Internet marketing research firm you hired to determine consumers' usage of your Web site (www.cnn.com) has violated respondents' privacy rights in the course of the project?

BE an MR!

Visit the Marketing Research Association Web site (www.mra-net.org) and describe the Marketing Research Association's ethical guidelines for the use of the Internet for conducting opinion and marketing research.

As a researcher conducting Internet research for CNN, how would you ensure that respondents' privacy rights are not violated?

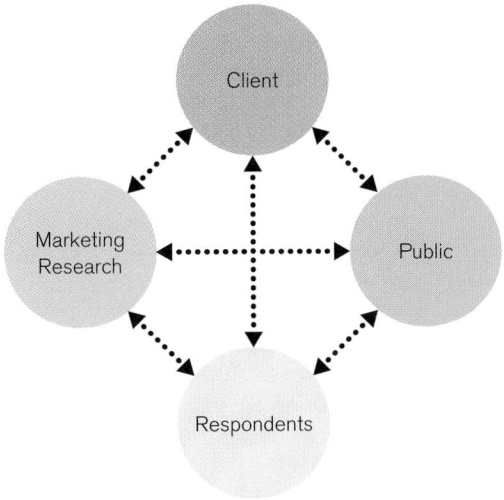

Figure 1.10
Stakeholders in Marketing Research: An Ethical Perspective

EXPERIENTIAL LEARNING

Ethical Guidelines

Compare the ethical guidelines for conducting marketing research posted at the following Web sites: CASRO: The Council of American Survey Research Organizations (www.casro.org), CMOR: Council for Marketing and Opinion Research (www.cmor.org), and ESOMAR: European Society for Opinion and Marketing Research (www.esomar.nl).

Which organization has the most stringent set of guidelines?

Which organization's ethical guidelines are the most complete?

What is missing from the guidelines of all three organizations?

WHAT WOULD *YOU* DO?

Samsonite: It's in the Bag

The Situation

Samsonite is one of the world's largest designers, manufacturers, and distributors of luggage. They sell their products using a number of quality brand names, including Samsonite® and American Tourister®. With net sales of $744.0 million for their fiscal year ending January 31, 2003, they are a leader in the highly fragmented global luggage industry. Through aggressive product development and marketing, President and Chief Executive Officer Luc Van Nevel hoped to increase the company's market share from 35 percent in 2003 to 40 percent in 2008. Van Nevel recognizes the importance of new product development and acknowledges that Samsonite must continually introduce successful new products in the marketplace.

The Marketing Research Decision

1. What type of marketing research should Samsonite undertake? Check as many as are applicable.
   a. Product research
   b. Pricing research
   c. Promotion research
   d. Distribution research
   e. All of the above
2. Discuss the role of the type of research you recommend in enabling Luc Van Nevel to increase the market share of Samsonite.

The Marketing Management Decision

1. Luc Van Nevel's aggressive marketing strategy should be built around (check as many as are applicable):
   a. New product development
   b. Price discounts
   c. International marketing
   d. Distribution through flagship stores
   e. All of the above
2. Discuss how the marketing management decision action that you recommend to Luc Van Nevel is influenced by the research that you suggested earlier and by the findings of that research.

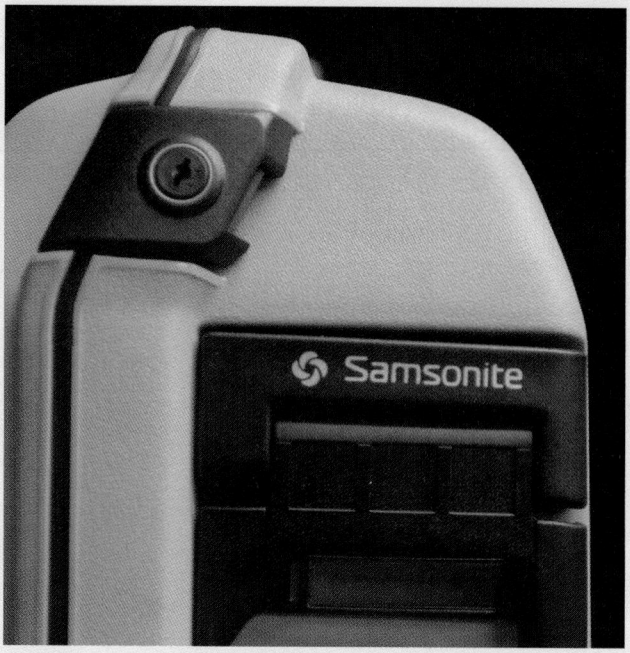

What Luc Van Nevel Did

Luc Van Nevel unveiled a directional luggage collection by world-renowned designer Philippe Starck. The Samsonite by Starck luggage and bags combine pure elegance with state-of-the-art technology. The world of travel is constantly changing, and so is Samsonite. As the brand is taken beyond luggage, Samsonite is constantly seeking opportunities to expand internationally and become present in new distribution channels, leading to the opening of flagship stores in high-end locations in London, Milan, Brussels, Stockholm, and Prague.

Samsonite is also expanding its products in a growing market for casual bags, computer bags, and backpacks. In the summer of 2003, it launched a backpack advertising campaign on MTV and in magazines like *Cosmopolitan, Maxim,* and *Rolling Stone* that targets the 18 to 24 age group.[13]

SPSS Windows and EXCEL

In this book, we feature SPSS programs, not merely as a statistical package, but as an integrative package that can be used in the various stages of the marketing research process. We illustrate the use of SPSS for defining the problem, developing an approach, formulating the research design, data collection, data preparation and analysis, and report preparation and presentation. In addition to the BASE module, we also feature other SPSS® programs, such as Decision Time, What If?, Maps, Data Entry, SamplePower Missing Values, TextSmart, and SmartViewer.

The data analyses are also illustrated with three other software packages: EXCEL, SAS, and MINITAB. Detailed, step-by-step instructions are provided for both SPSS WINDOWS and EXCEL. All the data files are available for both SPSS and EXCEL. The screen captures for these software programs can be downloaded from the Web site for this book.

Summary

Marketing research assesses information needs and provides relevant information in order to improve the marketing decision-making process. It is a systematic and objective process designed to identify and solve marketing problems. Thus, marketing research can be classified as problem-identification research and problem-solving research. The marketing research process consists of six steps that must be followed systematically. Marketing research provides information about consumers, channel members, competitors, changes and trends in the marketplace, and other aspects of the firm's environment.

A firm may conduct its own marketing research or may purchase it from external suppliers. External suppliers can provide full service or they may specialize in one or more aspects of the process. Full-service suppliers provide the entire range of marketing research services, from problem definition to report preparation and presentation. The services provided by these suppliers can be classified as syndicated services or customized services. Limited-service suppliers specialize in one or a few phases of the marketing research project. Services offered by these suppliers can be classified as field services, or other services such as coding and data entry, and data analysis.

The marketing research industry offers a wide range of careers in both corporate and independent service organizations. Marketing research firms, business and nonbusiness firms, and advertising agencies all employ research professionals. Information obtained using marketing research can stand alone or be integrated into an MIS or DSS. Marketing research contributes to the DSS by providing research data to the database, marketing models and analytical techniques to the model base, and specialized marketing research programs to the software base.

International marketing research is much more complex than domestic research because researchers must consider the environment in the international markets they are researching. Technological developments are reshaping the role of marketing research, as well as the way in which it is conducted. The ethical issues in marketing research involve four stakeholders: (1) the marketing researcher, (2) the client, (3) the respondent, and (4) the public.

Key Terms and Concepts

Marketing research, 5
Problem-identification research, 8
Problem-solving research, 8
Marketing research process, 9
Information value chain, 14
Marketing research industry, 15
Internal suppliers, 16
External suppliers, 16
Full-service suppliers, 16
Syndicated services, 16
Customized services, 18
Internet services, 18
Limited-service suppliers, 18
Field services, 18
Coding and data entry services, 18
Data analysis services, 18
Marketing information systems (MIS), 21
Decision support systems (DSS), 21

Suggested Cases and Video Cases

Cases

1.1 Gillette	**1.2 Sears**	**4.1 Boeing**	**4.2 Gucci**

Video Cases

1.1 Burke, Inc.	**1.2 Accenture**	**4.1 Subaru**	**4.2 Marriott**

Additional cases and video cases are available in the Instructor's Manual and on the instructor and student Web sites.

Live Research: Conducting a Marketing Research Project

1. Give a background of the client organization.
2. Discuss the marketing organization and operations of the client.
3. Explain how the project results will help the client make specific marketing decisions.
4. Organize the class. This may require the formation of project teams. The entire class could be working on the same project with each team working on all aspects of the project or each team could be assigned a specific responsibility (e.g., a specific component of the problem or a specific aspect of the project like collection and analysis of secondary data). Each student should participate in primary data collection. Alternatively, the class could be working on multiple projects with specific teams assigned to a specific project. The approach is flexible and can handle a variety of organizations and formats.
5. Develop a project schedule clearly specifying the deadlines for the different steps.
6. Explain how the teams will be evaluated.
7. One or a few students should be selected as project coordinators.

Acronyms

The role and salient characteristics of marketing research may be described by the acronym RESEARCH:

R ecognition of information needs
E ffective decision making
S ystematic and objective
E xodus/dissemination of information
A nalysis of information
R ecommendations for action
C ollection of information
H elpful to managers

Review Questions

1. Define marketing research. What are some of the noteworthy aspects of this definition?
2. Describe a classification of marketing research and give examples.
3. Describe the steps in the marketing research process.
4. Describe the task of marketing research and illustrate with an example.
5. What decisions do marketing managers make? How does marketing research help them to make these decisions?
6. Explain one way to classify marketing research suppliers.
7. What are syndicated services and how do they help a firm undertake marketing research?
8. What is the main difference between a full-service and a limited-service supplier?
9. List five guidelines for selecting an external marketing research supplier.
10. What career opportunities are available in marketing research? Are you interested in pursuing such a career? Why or why not?
11. What is a marketing information system?
12. How is DSS different from MIS?
13. Who are the stakeholders in marketing research?

Applied Problems

1. Visit the Web sites of one of the marketing research firms given in Table 1.1. Write a report on the types of marketing research conducted by this firm. Classify this firm based on the scheme presented in Figure 1.7.
2. Look through recent issues of newspapers and magazines to identify five examples of problem-identification research and five examples of problem-solving research.
3. Describe one marketing research project that would be useful to each of the following organizations:
   a. Your campus bookstore.
   b. The public transportation authority in your city.
   c. A major department store in your area.
   d. A restaurant located near your campus.
   e. A zoo in a major city.
4. Visit Productscan's Web site (www.productscan.com) and click on What's New. Select one innovation on the list, search the Internet using a search engine as well as your library's online databases, and write a report about the marketing research undertaken to develop this product.
5. Visit the Web sites of MRA (www.mra-net.org), ESOMAR (www.esomar.nl), and MRSA (www.mrsa.com.au) and compare and contrast the information available at these sites. Of the three marketing research associations, which has the most useful Web site, and why?
6. Visit the Bureau of Labor Statistic's Web site (www.bls.gov) and search the Internet to obtain information on the employment potential for marketing researchers.

Group Discussion

As a small group of four or five, discuss the following issues.

1. What type of institutional structure is best for a marketing research department in a large business firm?
2. What is the ideal educational background for someone seeking a career in marketing research?
3. Can ethical standards be enforced in marketing research? If so, how?

CHAPTER

2

Defining the Marketing Research Problem and Developing an Approach

"The most challenging part of any research project is defining the problem in the terms management understands and in a way that ensures the desired information is obtained."

Roger Bacik, *Senior Vice President, CMI, Atlanta, GA*

OPENING QUESTIONS

1. What is a marketing research problem, and why is it important to define it correctly?
2. What tasks are involved in problem definition?
3. How do environmental factors affect the definition of the research problem, and what are these factors?
4. What is the distinction between the management-decision problem and the marketing research problem?
5. How should the marketing research problem be defined?
6. What are the various components of the approach to the problem?
7. Why are defining the problem and developing an approach more complex processes in international marketing research?
8. How can technology help define the problem and develop an approach?
9. What ethical issues and conflicts arise in defining the problem and developing the approach?

The World's First Sports Utility-Wagon

The 2005 Outback 2.5 XT Ltd. Wagon was marketed as "the ultimate sports utility wagon." *Financial Times Automotive World* magazine named Subaru the "Most Improved Car Company in the World." How was the Outback born?

Subaru of America was trying to identify new opportunities for penetrating the automobile market in the early 1990s. The marketing research firm they hired undertook a comprehensive examination of this marketing situation (a problem audit). The audit enabled the research firm to identify the real problem confronting management (the management-decision problem) as "What can Subaru do to expand its share of the automobile market?" The marketing research problem was defined broadly as determining the various needs of automobile users and the extent to which current product offerings were satisfying those needs. However, for marketing research to be conducted effectively and efficiently, the problem had to be defined more precisely. The management and the researcher agreed on the following specific components:

1. What needs do buyers of passenger cars, station wagons, and sports-utility vehicles (SUVs) seek to satisfy?
2. How well do existing automobile product offerings meet these needs?
3. Is there a segment of the automobile market whose needs are not being adequately met?
4. What automobile features does the identified segment desire?
5. What is the demographic and psychographic profile of the identified segment?

The approach to the marketing research problem was developed based on the postulate or framework that buyers first decide on the type of car (e.g., station wagon, SUV, passenger car) they want, and then they decide on a particular brand. The researcher also formulated specific research questions and possible answers (hypotheses) to be tested by collecting survey data.

The research indicated a strong market potential for a vehicle that combined the features of a station wagon and a compact sports-utility vehicle.

The needs of a sizable male-dominated segment were not being met by either the station wagon or the SUV, and they wanted a hybrid product.

Based on these findings, Subaru of America introduced the 1996 Outback as "the world's first sports utility wagon." Subaru said in a press release that the Outback fills the niche between the SUV and the passenger car. The Outback has several important features that are missing from most SUVs, including an all-wheel-drive system that operates under all road conditions and vehicle speeds, four-wheel independent suspension, antilock brakes, dual air bags, and a side-intrusion protection system. It also has a low door threshold for easy passenger entry and exit, and a lower center of gravity for road handling and ride comfort. Inside amenities were also upgraded, and several other features were added.

Cars are subject to regulations in terms of emissions control and corporate average fuel economy (CAFÉ). As Subaru makes primarily high-mileage economy cars, the Outback did not negatively influence its CAFÉ ratings. However, the big automakers could not respond to the Outback because such an introduction would have negatively affected their CAFÉ ratings.

A TV campaign for Outback featured *Crocodile Dundee*'s Paul Hogan. Viewers liked the ads, and, of course, the product. Those taking a test-drive were very impressed with the capabilities of the vehicle. The result? Sales were triple what Subaru originally expected. Sales of the Outback continued to be strong through the 2005 model year.[1] •

Overview

This chapter covers the first two of the six steps of the marketing research process described in Chapter 1: defining the marketing research problem and developing an approach to the problem. Figure 2.1 briefly explains the focus of the chapter, the relation of this chapter to the previous one, and the steps of the marketing research process on which this chapter concentrates.

In the opening vignette, Subaru's introduction of the Outback to exploit a new market segment demonstrates the crucial importance of correctly defining the marketing research problem. Subaru correctly defined the marketing research problem as determining the various needs of automobile users and the extent to which current product offerings were satisfying those needs. Defining the research problem is the most important aspect of the research process. Only when a problem has been clearly and accurately identified can a research project be conducted properly. This is because problem definition sets the course for the entire project. In this chapter, we will identify the tasks involved and the factors to be considered at this stage, and will provide guidelines to help the researcher avoid common errors.

The chapter also discusses how to develop an approach to the research problem once it has been identified. The approach lays the foundation for how to conduct the research by specifying the relevant theory and models. It further refines the specific components of the problem by asking more specific questions and formulating the hypotheses that will be tested. The approach also specifies all the information that would need to be collected in the marketing research project. The special considerations involved in defining the problem and developing an approach in international marketing research are discussed. The impact of technology and several ethical issues that arise at this stage of the marketing research process are also considered. Figure 2.2 gives an overview of the topics discussed in this chapter and how they flow from one to the next.

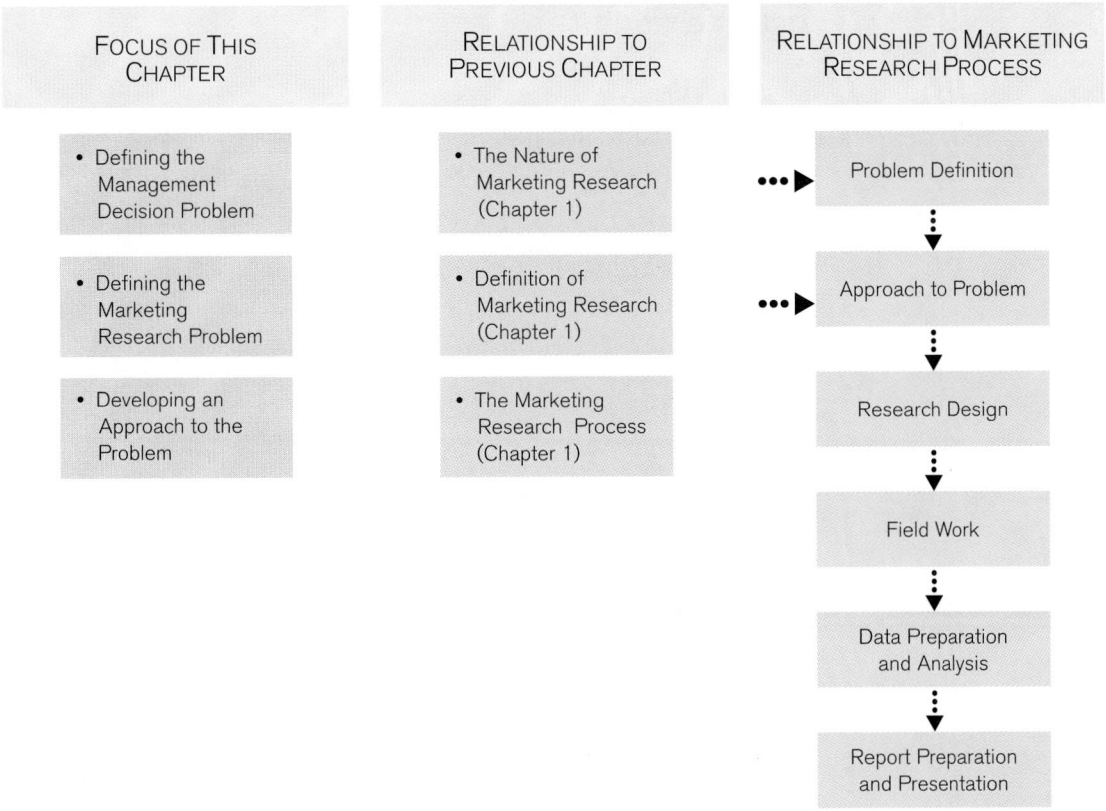

Figure 2.1

Relationship of Problem Definition and Approach to the Previous Chapter and the Marketing Research Process

The Importance of Defining the Problem

While every step in a marketing research project is important, problem definition is the most important step. As mentioned in Chapter 1, marketing researchers consider problems and opportunities confronting management as interchangeable since an investigation of both follows the same research process. **Problem definition** involves stating the general problem and identifying the specific components of the marketing research problem, as illustrated in the opening vignette.

problem definition
A broad statement of the general problem and identification of the specific components of the marketing research problem.

The opening vignette provided a broad statement of the problem confronting Subaru and also identified its five specific components. The researcher and the key decision makers on the client side should agree on the definition of the problem. The client is the individual or organization commissioning the research. The client might be an internal person, as in the case of a research director dealing with a decision maker in her or his own organization. Alternatively, the client might be an external entity if the research is being conducted by a marketing research firm. (See Chapter 1.)

Only when both parties have clearly defined and agreed on the marketing research problem can research be designed and conducted properly. Mistakes made at this stage of the process can only mushroom into larger mistakes as the project progresses. Of all the steps in the marketing research process, none is more vital to the ultimate fulfillment of a client's needs than an accurate and adequate definition of the research problem. All the effort, time, and money spent from this point on will be wasted if the problem is not properly defined.

This point is worth remembering. Inappropriate problem definition is one of the major sources of failure in marketing research. The basic message here is that clear identification and definition of the marketing research problem are critical. This was illustrated in the opening vignette. Subaru defined the problem correctly by determining the various needs of automobile users and the extent to which those needs were being satisfied by the current product offerings. The research resulted in an important finding that a substantial segment of the marketplace desired the features of both a station wagon and

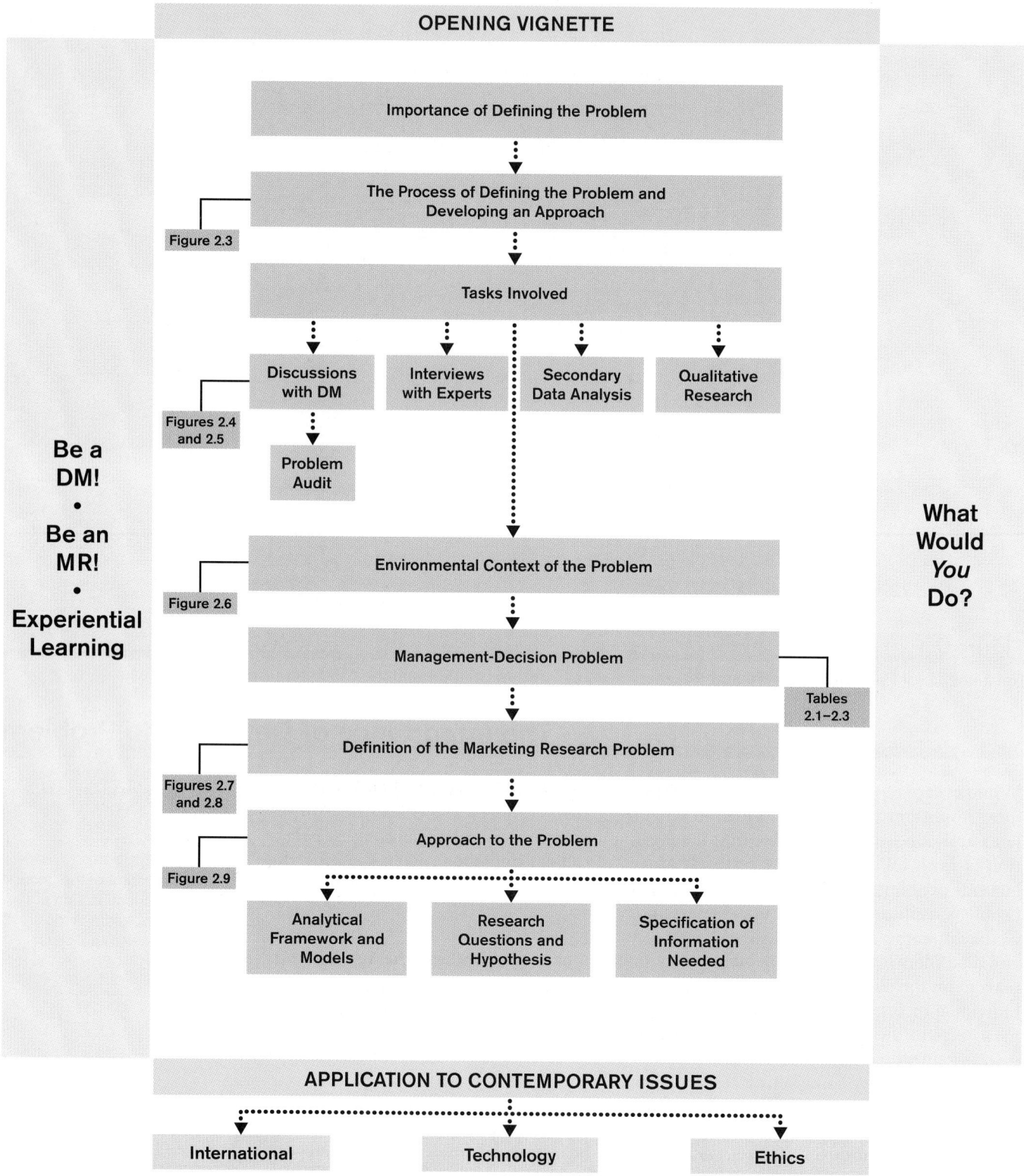

Figure 2.2

Defining the Marketing Research Process and Developing an Approach: An Overview

an SUV, leading to the introduction of a very successful product. Suppose Subaru had incorrectly defined the problem as determining the preferences of the red-hot SUV owners. It is highly likely that the Outback would not have been developed.

The problem definition process provides guidelines on how to correctly define the marketing research problem.

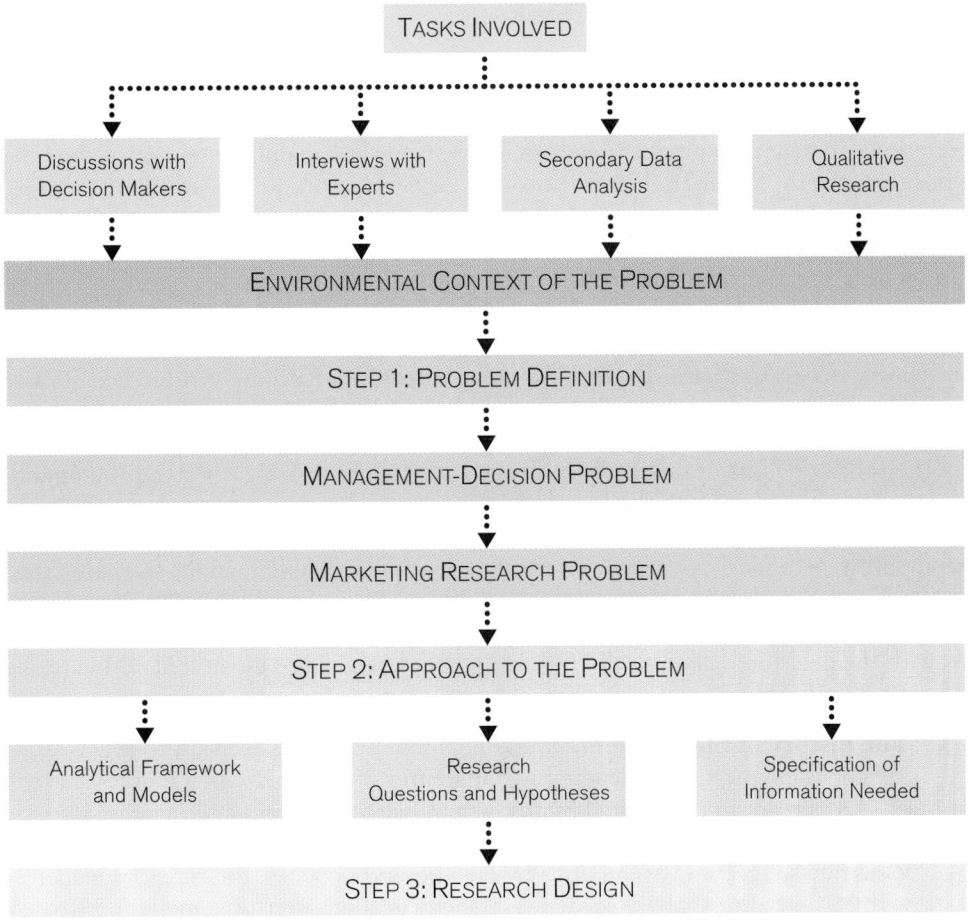

Figure 2.3
The Problem Definition and Approach Development Process

The Process of Defining the Problem and Developing an Approach

The problem definition and approach development process is illustrated in Figure 2.3. To define a research problem correctly, the researcher must perform a number of tasks. The researcher must discuss the problem with the decision makers in the client organization, interview industry experts and other knowledgeable individuals, analyze secondary data, and sometimes conduct qualitative research. This informal data collection helps the researcher understand the context or environment within which the problem has arisen. A clear understanding of the marketing environment also provides a framework for identifying the management-decision problem: What should the management do? The management-decision problem is then translated into a marketing research problem: the problem that researcher must investigate. Based on the definition of the marketing research problem, the researcher develops an appropriate approach. Further explanation of the problem definition process follows with a discussion of the tasks involved.

Tasks Involved

As mentioned earlier, the tasks involved in problem definition include discussions with the decision makers, interviews with industry experts, secondary data analysis, and qualitative research. The purpose of performing these tasks is to obtain information on the factors of the environment and to help define the management-decision problem and the corresponding marketing research problem, as well as develop an approach to the problem. We will discuss and illustrate each of these tasks.

Discussions with Decision Makers

It is essential that the researcher understand the nature of the decision the managers face—the management-decision problem—as well as management's expectations of the research. This discussion gives the researcher an opportunity to establish achievable expectations. The decision maker needs to understand the capabilities as well as the limitations of research. Research does not provide automatic solutions to problems; rather, it serves as an additional source of information that the manager should consider in the decision-making process.

To identify the management problem, the researcher must possess considerable skill in interacting with the decision maker and maneuvering through the organization. When the ultimate decision maker is a senior executive, the researcher may have difficulty gaining access to that individual. To complicate the situation even further, several individuals may be involved in the final decision. All individuals responsible for resolving the marketing problem should be consulted in this early phase of the project. The quality of the project will be dramatically improved when the researcher is given the opportunity to interact directly with the key decision makers.

problem audit
A comprehensive examination of a marketing problem to understand its origin and nature.

Discussions with the decision maker can be structured around the **problem audit** that helps identify the underlying causes of the problem. The problem audit, like any other type of audit, is a comprehensive examination of a marketing problem with the purpose of understanding its origin and nature (Figure 2.4). The problem audit involves discussions with the decision maker on the following issues, which are illustrated with a problem facing M&M/Mars.

1. **The history of the problem.** The events that led to the decision to act. M&M/Mars, the second-leading manufacturer of candies, with a market share of 23.4 percent in the United States, would like to maintain and increase its share of the market at the start of the new century. This problem has come into focus due to recent introductions by Hershey's chocolates, the category leader with 33.0 percent share. Recently, Hershey's product spin-offs, including Reese's FastBreak, Hershey's Kisses filled with caramel, and sugar-free York Peppermint Patties were introduced, threatening M&M/Mars.
2. **The alternative courses of action available to the decision maker.** The set of alternatives may be incomplete at this stage, and qualitative research may be

Figure 2.4
Conducting a Problem Audit

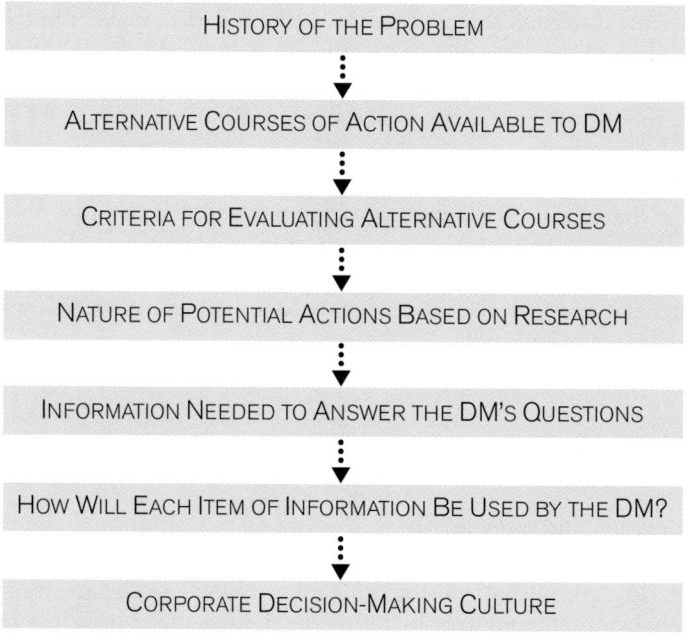

needed to identify the more innovative courses of action. The alternatives available to the management of M&M/Mars include introducing new brands of chocolates, reducing the prices of existing brands, expanding channels of distribution, and increasing advertising expenditures.

3. **The criteria that will be used to evaluate the alternative courses of action.** For example, new product offerings might be evaluated on the basis of sales, market share, profitability, return on investment, and so forth. M&M/Mars will evaluate the alternatives based on contributions to market share and profits.
4. **The nature of potential actions that are likely to be suggested based on the research findings.** The research findings will likely call for a strategic marketing response by M&M/Mars.
5. **The information that is needed to answer the decision maker's questions.** The information needed includes a comparison of Hershey's and M&M/Mars on all the elements of the marketing mix (product, pricing, promotion, and distribution) in order to determine relative strengths and weaknesses.
6. **The manner in which the decision maker will use each item of information in making the decision.** The key decision makers will devise a strategy for M&M/Mars based on the research findings and their intuition and judgment.
7. **The corporate culture as it relates to decision making.** In some firms, the decision-making process is dominant; in others, the personality of the decision maker is more important. A sensitivity to corporate culture in order to identify the individuals who are either responsible for the decision or who have a significant influence over the decision process is essential. In this case, the corporate culture at M&M/Mars calls for a committee approach in which key decision makers make the critical decisions.

Conducting a problem audit is essential in order to clarify the problem for the researcher. Not surprisingly, it may serve the same function for the decision maker. Often, the decision maker has only a vague idea of the real problem. For example, the decision maker may know that the firm is losing market share but may not know why. This is because most decision makers focus on the symptoms of a problem rather than its causes. An inability to meet sales forecasts, loss of market share, and a decline in profits are all symptoms. Research that adds value goes beyond the symptoms to address the underlying causes. For example, loss of market share may be caused by a superior promotion by the competition, inadequate distribution of the company's products, lower product quality, price undercutting by a major competitor, or any number of factors (Figure 2.5). As shown in Table 2.1, a definition of the problem based on symptoms can be misleading. Only when the underlying causes are identified can the problem be successfully addressed, as exemplified by the effort of BellSouth to stop the loss of market share and revenues in its call-collect business in the Research in Action example that follows.

The Internet provides several mechanisms that can help the researcher communicate with decision makers. The first and most obvious is Internet e-mail. This makes it possible

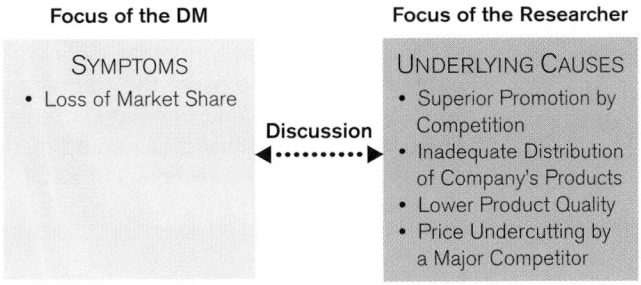

Figure 2.5
Discussion between the Researcher and the DM

Table 2.1

Problem Definition Based on Symptoms Can Be Misleading

Problem Definition			
Firm	Symptoms	Based on Symptoms	Underlying Causes
Manufacturer of orange soft drinks	Consumers say the sugar content is too high	Determine consumer preferences for alternative levels of sugar content	Color. The color of the drink is a dark shade of orange giving the perception that the product is too "sugary."
Manufacturer of machine tools	Customers complain prices are too high	Determine the price elasticity of demand	Channel management. Distributors do not have adequate product knowledge to communicate product benefits to customers.

to reach the decision makers at any place or time. Chat rooms can provide good forums for discussion with the decision makers. For instance, a discussion could be developed around a problem audit with multiple decision makers. The researcher could introduce the audit issues in the chat, and then the decision makers could respond to the issues and to each other's responses. Chat rooms can be secured with a password if there is a need to protect the contents of the discussions.

RESEARCH IN ACTION

"Forget the Code," Not Phone War, Rings the Bells for BellSouth

BellSouth (www.bellsouth.com), headquartered in Atlanta, was losing sales and market share in the collect-calling business. Declining sales and market share resulted in management attention being placed on those two symptoms. Unable to find an easy solution, the management commissioned marketing research. The research firm conducted a problem audit that examined all of the possible underlying causes and looked at each aspect of the marketing mix in order to identify alternative courses of action. The problem audit did not reveal any specific criticism of BellSouth's collect-calling services. It was found that as a Southern phone company, BellSouth was perceived as customer-friendly, civil, and trustworthy.

The real cause of the problem was intense competition from AT&T and MCI. AT&T and MCI had spent $15 million in BellSouth's territory with their 1-800-CALL-ATT and 1-800-COLLECT campaigns, respectively. Their goal was to convince consumers to call them directly and bypass the BellSouth operators. These two companies used the traditional phone wars language of "savings." Their efforts had paid off.

Once the underlying causes were identified, the problem was broadly defined as how to enhance the comparative appeal of BellSouth's collect-calling services, rather than narrowly as retaliating with price cuts and counter-savings claims. Subsequent research revealed that for many consumers the promise of "savings" had proved empty once they found out how many conditions were attached. Furthermore, consumers were willing to pay a premium for simplicity as collect calls are often made under stressful conditions. This led BellSouth to develop a campaign based on the strategic focus of "the simplest way to call collect." Consumers had to simply dial "0" rather than an 11-digit code. BellSouth's new slogan was "Forget the Code," a jab at AT&T's "Know the Code." The campaign was very successful. Determining the underlying causes and appropriately defining the problem enabled BellSouth to avoid the trappings of the phone wars and focus on what consumers really wanted. This approach led to increased sales and market share. The company had operating revenues of $22.635 billion in the year 2003.[2]

BE a DM!

As the brand manager for Sprite, the third-largest soft drink brand, you are concerned about improving the performance of the brand. Identify possible symptoms that indicate to you that the performance of Sprite is below expectations.

BE an MR!

Visit Coca-Cola and Sprite's Web site (www.cocacola.com and www.sprite.com) and obtain as much information about the marketing program of Sprite as you can. Write a brief report.

You are conducting marketing research for Sprite to help improve the performance of the brand. Identify possible underlying causes that might be contributing to the lack of performance.

Interviews with Industry Experts

In addition to discussions with the decision maker, interviews with industry experts—individuals knowledgeable about the firm and the industry—may help researchers formulate the marketing research problem. Experts may be found both inside and outside the firm. If the notion of experts is broadened to include people knowledgeable about the general topic being investigated, then these interviews are also referred to as an **experience survey**. While formal questionnaires are normally not used, a prepared list of topics to be covered during the interview is often helpful. The order in which these topics are covered and the questions to ask should not be predetermined but rather decided as the interview progresses. This allows greater flexibility in capturing the insights of the experts. The purpose of interviews with experts is to help define the marketing research problem rather than to develop a conclusive solution. Expert interviews are more commonly used in industrial rather than consumer research applications. In industrial or highly technical environments, the experts are often more easily identified than they would be in consumer research settings. This is because consumer settings are more broad and diffused than industrial or technical environments. Expert interviews are also helpful in situations where little information is available from other sources, as in the case of radically new products. Experts can provide valuable insights in modifying or repositioning existing products, as illustrated by the repositioning of Sears.

experience survey
Interviews with people knowledgeable about the general topic being investigated.

For years, the sales at this giant retailer floundered and it lost its status as America's number-one retailer to Wal-Mart in 1989. When industry experts were consulted, researchers were able to identify the real problem: lack of image. Traditionally a discount store, Sears had unsuccessfully tried to upgrade its image to a prestigious department store, thereby alienating its loyal customers. Sears finally gave up its attempt to upgrade and re-embraced the image of a discount chain store. Since then, sales and profitability have improved. In 2004, Kmart announced that it was acquiring Sears in a $11.5-billion merger.

Researchers can also use the Internet to enhance their ability to obtain information from experts in a specific industry. One approach to finding experts is to use newsgroups. Due to the large amount of information available, searching through the newsgroups for specific information can be an arduous task. A good place to start is Google Groups (www.groups.google.com), which provides categorized lists of newsgroups. Also, you may have access to newsgroups through your ISP (Internet service provider). After finding a relevant newsgroup, access the newsgroup and search for postings about the topics in which you are interested. Surveying the postings in a newsgroup would provide a good starting point for making contacts with the experts in that industry.

Secondary Data Analysis

The information that researchers obtain from the decision maker and the industry experts should be supplemented with available secondary data. **Secondary data** are data collected for some purpose other than the problem at hand, such as data available

secondary data
Data collected for some purpose other than the problem at hand.

BE an MR!

Visit Wal-Mart's Web site (www.walmart.com) and search the Internet using a search engine as well as your library's online databases to identify the challenges and opportunities facing Wal-Mart, the largest retailer in the United States.

Visit Google Groups Web site (www.groups.google.com), survey the posting in online retailing newsgroups to identify an expert in online retailing. Interview this expert (via telephone or online) to identify the challenges and opportunities facing Wal-Mart.

BE a DM!

As the CEO of Wal-Mart, what marketing strategies would you formulate to overcome these challenges and capitalize on the opportunities?

primary data
Data originated by the researcher specifically to address the research problem.

from trade organizations, the Bureau of Census (www.census.gov), and the Internet. **Primary data**, on the other hand, are originated by the researcher for the specific problem under study, such as survey data. Secondary data include information made available by business and government sources, commercial marketing research firms, and computerized databases. Secondary data are an economical and quick source of background information.

Analyzing available secondary data is an essential step in the problem definition process and should always precede primary data collection. Secondary data can provide valuable insights into the problem situation and lead to the identification of innovative courses of action. For example, the U.S. Department of Labor says that the average age of the American workforce will increase from 35 to 40 by the year 2006. This is, in part, the result of the maturation of the "baby bust" generation (those born between 1965 and 1976), which will cause a decline in the number of young (ages 16 to 24) workers available to fill entry-level positions. This potential shortage of young workers has caused many marketers, particularly those in the service industries, to investigate the problem of consumer response to self-service. Some companies, such as Arby's, have switched from a "high-touch" to a "high-tech" service orientation. By using high-tech equipment, consumers now perform many of the services formerly done by workers, such as placing their own orders by entering them directly into the electronic terminal. Given the tremendous importance of secondary data, this topic will be discussed in detail in Chapters 4 and 5.

BE a DM!

As the marketing director for Wendy's, what significance do you attach to secondary data showing the aging population of the United States? What are the implications of these data for increasing the market share of Wendy's?

BE an MR!

Identify the sources of secondary data that would be helpful in defining the problem of Wendy's increasing its share of the fast-food market.

Visit Wendy's Web site (www.wendys.com) and search the Internet using a search engine as well as your library's online databases to determine the market share of Wendy's for the past three years.

Qualitative and Exploratory Research

qualitative research
An unstructured, exploratory research methodology based on small samples intended to provide insight and understanding of the problem setting.

Information obtained from the decision maker, industry experts, and secondary data may not be sufficient to define the research problem. Sometimes qualitative research must be undertaken to gain a clear understanding of the factors underlying a research problem. **Qualitative research** is unstructured in that the questions asked are formulated as the research proceeds. It is exploratory in nature, based on small samples, and may use popular qualitative techniques such as focus groups (group interviews) or in-depth interviews (one-on-one interviews that probe the respondents' thoughts in detail). Other exploratory research techniques, such as pilot surveys and case studies, may also be undertaken to gain insights into the phenomenon of interest. **Pilot surveys** tend to be less structured than large-scale surveys in that they generally contain more open-ended questions and the sample size is much smaller. **Case studies** involve an intensive examination of a few selected cases of the phenomenon of interest. The cases could be consumers, stores, firms, or a variety of other units, such as markets, Web sites, and so forth. The data are obtained from the company, external secondary sources, and by conducting lengthy unstructured interviews with people knowledgeable about the phenomenon of interest. In a project we conducted for a major department chain store, valuable insights into factors affecting store patronage were obtained in a case study comparing the five best stores with the five worst stores.

pilot surveys
Surveys that tend to be less structured than large-scale surveys in that they generally contain more open-ended questions and the sample size is much smaller.

case studies
Case studies involve an intensive examination of a few selected cases of the phenomenon of interest. Cases could be customers, stores, or other units.

Once the leader in the Caribbean cruise market, Norwegian Cruise Lines, Coral Gables, Florida, had slipped to fourth position. To identify the underlying causes and appropriately define the problem, focus group and pilot (small-scale) surveys were conducted. This qualitative research revealed that one worry that kept people from cruising was the fear of being confined to a boat for a week or more with little to do. This concern was particularly acute among young people. This concern became a major component of the problem and a large survey was conducted to address it. The survey verified the findings of qualitative research.

Based on these research findings, Norwegian Cruise Line's advertising fought this myth by emphasizing that passengers have the flexibility to make their cruise vacation whatever they want it to be. Its provocative, award-winning print and TV campaigns featured close-ups of young people, often on land, having lots of fun. The campaign helped Norwegian attract new and younger customers and improve its market share and penetration. This success was achieved despite the fact that Norwegian was out-spent in advertising two to one by Carnival Cruise Lines and one and one-half to one by Royal Caribbean Cruises.[3] (Exploratory research is discussed in more detail in Chapter 3, and qualitative research techniques are discussed in detail in Chapter 6.)

While research undertaken at this stage may not be conducted in a formal way, it can provide valuable insights. These insights, together with information obtained from discussions with the decision makers, industry experts, and analysis of secondary data, guide the researcher to an appropriate definition of the problem, as illustrated by the Century City Hospital in Los Angeles.

RESEARCH IN ACTION

Century City Hospital Moves into New Century of Health Care

Like most hospitals across the country were doing in the early 2000s, the Century City Hospital (www.centurycityhospital.com) in Los Angeles was considering a course of action that emphasized cost cutting to improve profitability. An external marketing research firm was hired to suggest areas where costs could be cut without alienating consumers. However, the research firm realized that lower profitability was merely a symptom. Based on discussions with key decision makers and industry experts, the underlying cause of low profitability was identified as lack of a clear focus and market positioning by the hospital. Specifically, the hospital did not understand who its target customers were and what their unique needs were.

Secondary data from the Bureau of Census indicated that nearly 50 percent of the local residents had high incomes. Qualitative research in the form of focus groups revealed that this group valued the best in food, accommodations, privacy, and exclusiveness. These people were not price sensitive and were willing to pay for added benefits.

As an outcome of this process, the problem was redefined as to how the Century City Hospital could best meet the medical needs of its high-income residents. Based on the findings of the research undertaken subsequently, the Century City Hospital opened its deluxe Century Pavilion, offering luxurious private accommodations at a premium price. Thus, the Century City Hospital was able to carve a profitable niche and entered the twenty-first century in a strong position. As of 2005, Century City Hospital was owned by Tenet Healthcare Corporation, which is one of the largest hospital chains in the United States.[4]

Figure 2.6

Factors to Be Considered in the Environmental Context of the Problem

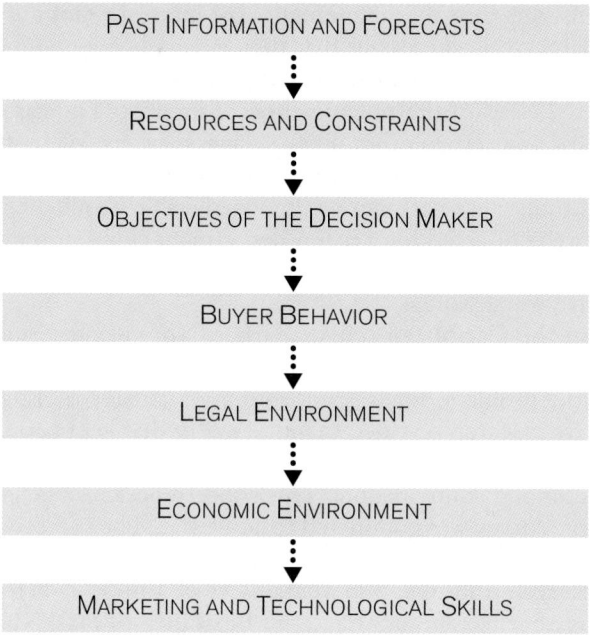

Environmental Context of the Problem

environmental context of the problem
Consists of the factors that have an impact on the definition of the marketing research problem, including past information and forecasts, resources and constraints of the firm, objectives of the decision maker, buyer behavior, legal environment, economic environment, and marketing and technological skills of the firm.

The insights gained from qualitative research, along with discussions with decision makers, interviews with industry experts, and analysis of secondary data, help the researcher understand the environmental context of the problem. The researcher must have a full understanding of the client's firm and industry. Several factors that comprise the **environmental context of the problem** can play an important role in defining the marketing research problem. These factors consist of past information and forecasts pertaining to the industry and the firm, resources and constraints of the firm, objectives of the decision maker, buyer behavior, legal environment, economic environment, and marketing and technological skills of the firm (Figure 2.6). Each of these factors is discussed briefly.

Past Information and Forecasts

Past information and forecasts of trends with respect to sales, market share, profitability, technology, population, demographics, and lifestyle combine to provide the researcher with a fuller picture of the underlying marketing research problem. Not only should the firm's performance and projections be analyzed, but the firm's performance relative to the overall industry should be examined as well. For example, if a firm's sales have decreased but industry sales have increased, the problems will be very different than if the industry sales have also decreased. In the former case, the problems are likely to be specific to the firm.

Past information, forecasts, and trends can be valuable in uncovering potential opportunities and problems. For example, pizza restaurants have sought to exploit potential opportunities in the recent trend toward takeout food and home delivery. Pizza Hut has successfully capitalized on this trend by emphasizing takeout and home-delivery services. It opened several takeout-only (with no dine-in service) outlets to better serve this market. As another illustration, in the Subaru vignette, forecasts of future sales of station wagons and SUVs indicated to management that both these types of automobiles were not tapping the full market potential.

Past information and forecasts can be especially valuable if resources are limited and there are other constraints on the organization.

BE an MR!

Obtain from secondary sources data on the sales of restaurants for the past year and sales forecasts for the next two to five years.

How would you obtain this information using the Internet?

BE a DM!

You are the marketing manager for Houston's restaurants. You come across information stating that more and more people are having lunch on the go and that this trend is expected to continue for the next five years. What kind of problems and opportunities does this information suggest?

Resource Constraints and Objectives

To formulate a marketing research problem of appropriate scope, it is necessary to take into account the resources available, such as money, research skills, and operational capabilities, as well as operational and time constraints. While adjustments in proposed research expenditure levels are common, proposing a large-scale $100,000 project when only $40,000 has been budgeted will put the research firm at a serious competitive disadvantage. Time constraints are also an important factor in many research projects. A project for Fisher-Price, a major toy manufacturer, involving mall-intercept interviews (conducted with shoppers in malls) in six major cities (Chicago, Fresno, Kansas City, New York, Philadelphia, and San Diego) had to be completed in four weeks. Why the rush? The results had to be presented at an upcoming board meeting where a major (go/no-go) decision was to be made about a new product introduction. Time constraint was a major factor that guided the problem definition and the approach adopted in this case.

In formulating the management-decision problem, the researcher must also have a clear understanding of two types of **objectives**: (1) the organizational objectives (the goals of the organization) and (2) the personal objectives of the decision maker. For the project to be successful, it must serve the objectives of the organization and of the decision maker. This may become a challenge when the two are not complementary. For example, the decision maker may wish to undertake research to postpone an awkward decision, to lend credibility to a decision that has already been made, or to get promoted.

objectives
Goals of the organization and of the decision maker must be considered in order to conduct successful marketing research.

It may take skill to get the decision maker to think in terms of objectives that management can act upon (actionable objectives). One effective technique may be to confront the decision maker with a number of possible solutions to a problem and ask whether he or she would follow that course of action. If the answer is no, further probing may be needed to uncover any deeper objectives as to why this solution is unsatisfactory.

Buyer Behavior

Buyer behavior is a central component of the environment. It includes the underlying motives, perceptions, attitudes, buying habits, and demographic and psychographic (psychological and lifestyle) profiles of buyers and potential buyers. Most marketing decisions involve a prediction of the buyers' response to a particular marketing action. An understanding of the underlying buyer behavior can provide valuable insights into the problem. Note that in the Subaru vignette, information on the demographic and psychographic characteristic of the automobile segment whose needs were not being met was an important component of the marketing research problem.

buyer behavior
A body of knowledge that tries to understand and predict consumers' reactions based on an individual's specific characteristics.

BE a DM!

As the marketing manager for Timberland, how would your understanding of the consumers' decision-making process affect your decision to sell outdoor shoes on the Internet?

BE an MR!

Visit Timberland's Web site (www.timberland.com) and conduct an Internet search using a search engine and your library's online database to obtain information on Timberland's marketing program for outdoor shoes.

What decision-making process do consumers follow while deciding on the purchase of outdoor shoes?

In another case, buyer behavior research told ConAgra Frozen Foods that more than 55 percent of Americans pack a lunch and that more and more meals are eaten on the run. However, while consumers increasingly want their food to be portable, they still demand high flavor and good nutrition. Wanting to capitalize on this aspect of buyer behavior, ConAgra further investigated the marketing research problem of consumer preferences for healthy, delicious, and portable food.

The company's answer, based on the findings of this research, was a new entry into the premium-meals category, Healthy Choice Hearty Handfuls frozen sandwiches. As an alternative to many frozen convenience foods, the product targeted an adult taste profile with bakery-style breads, lean meats, and crisp vegetables. True to the name, the sandwiches are both healthy (low in fat and calories) and hearty (at six ounces, an estimated 35 percent larger than most frozen sandwiches). According to ConAgra, the Hearty Handfuls line exceeded sales expectations, becoming the number-three frozen sandwich brand in its first six months.

The increased preference for portable, healthy, and hearty food could be attributed to changes in the sociocultural environment, which includes demographic trends and consumer tastes. The legal, economic, marketing, and technological environments also have a significant impact in some industries.

Legal, Economic, Marketing, and Technological Environments

legal environment
Regulatory policies and norms within which organizations must operate.

The **legal environment** includes public policies, laws, government agencies, and pressure groups that influence and regulate various organizations and individuals in society. Important areas of law include patents, trademarks, royalties, trade agreements, taxes, and tariffs. Federal regulation and deregulation have both had a huge impact on the marketing process in many industries, such as airline, banking, and telecommunication industries. The legal and regulatory considerations relevant to a business must be taken into account by the researcher.

In the opening vignette, it was explained that cars are subject to regulations in terms of emissions control and CAFÉ. As Subaru makes primarily high-mileage economy cars, the Outback did not negatively influence its CAFÉ ratings. However, the big automakers could not respond to the Outback because such an introduction would have negatively affected their CAFÉ ratings.

Another important component of the environmental context is the economic environment, which is comprised of purchasing power, gross income, disposable income, discretionary income, prices, savings, credit availability, and general economic conditions. The general state of the economy (rapid growth, slow growth, recession, or stagflation) influences the willingness of consumers and businesses to take on credit and spend on big-ticket items. Thus, the economic environment can have important implications for marketing research problems.

JC Penney is one of the largest and most well-known department stores in the United States. In the 1980s, JC Penney suffered due to inconsistent sales growth and a drop in company image. In the early 2000s, JC Penney began a massive overhaul toward a higher-quality image to counter these problems. The company courted famous name brands such as Oshkosh B'Gosh, Levi's, and Charles of the Ritz. Unfortunately, JC Penney decided to raise prices and go for the high-end fashion line at a bad time. Price increases coincided with the recession and the economic downturn of 2001 and 2002 and people did not have sufficient money to spend. Its most recent attempt in 2005 to recover its image has been to stick with good brand names, to control prices, and market itself as the store for "middle America." JC Penney's lost image has been found through keeping prices competitive and carrying good brand names.

A firm's marketing and technological skills greatly influence which marketing programs and strategies can be implemented. A company's expertise with each element of the marketing mix as well as its general levels of marketing and production skills affect the nature and scope of the marketing research project. For example, the introduction of a new product that requires retooling of a manufacturing process or presumes sophisticated marketing skills may not be a viable alternative if the firm lacks the skills to manu-

RESEARCH IN ACTION

Satin Care for Women Provides a Satin Touch for Gillette

Analysis of past information indicated that most women continued to pamper themselves with products for their beauty regimen and that this trend is likely to continue. The Gillette Company (www.gillette.com) was willing to devote its tremendous financial resources and its marketing expertise with the objective of capturing a larger share of the women's shaving products market. An examination of the underlying buyer behavior revealed that women had a strong preference for personal-care products that were rich in moisturizers. Economic and marketing analysis indicated that a substantial segment of this market was not price sensitive and was willing to pay a premium for such products. Accordingly, the marketing research problem was formulated as the investigation of women's preferences and purchase intentions for a shaving preparation rich in moisturizers.

Based on the affirmative findings of this research, Gillette introduced Satin Care for Women. The product brought innovation to the category with the first nonsoap-based shaving preparation with seven moisturizers. The product introduction was so successful that Satin Care for Women exceeded all expectations in the launch markets of the United States, Canada, and northern Europe. This success reinforced Gillette's understanding of the shaving environmental factors. Building on its continuous success of Satin Care, Gillette introduced "Anti Nicks & Cuts" shave gel and Floral Passion shave gel in 2002. These products have continued to do well through 2005.[5]

facture or market such a product. On the other hand, if the company can capitalize on its marketing and technological skills, its products and new introductions are likely to succeed, as illustrated in the Subaru vignette.

A good understanding of the environmental context of the problem enables the researcher to appropriately define the problem, as illustrated by the Gillette Company in the introduction of Satin Care for Women.

Many of the factors to be considered in the environmental context of the problem can be researched via the Internet. Past information and forecasts of trends can be found by searching for the appropriate information with search engines. For company-specific information pertaining to the client or a competitor, the researcher can go to the company home page. After clicking on the Netsearch icon on the browser, simply type the company's name and get the information from there.

Gaining an adequate understanding of the environmental context of the problem allows the researcher to define both the management-decision problem and the marketing research problem.

Management-Decision Problem and Marketing Research Problem

The **management-decision problem** asks what the decision maker needs to do, whereas the **marketing research problem** asks what information is needed and how it can best be obtained (Table 2.2). Research is directed at providing the information necessary to make a sound decision. The management-decision problem is action oriented, framed from the perspective of what should be done. How should the loss of market share be arrested? Should the market be segmented differently? Should a new product be introduced? Should the promotional budget be increased?

management-decision problem
The problem confronting the decision maker. It asks what the decision maker needs to do.

marketing research problem
The marketing research problem asks what information is needed and how it can best be obtained.

In contrast, the marketing research problem is information oriented. Research is directed at providing the information necessary to make a sound decision. The

Table 2.2
Management-Decision Problem Versus the Marketing Research Problem

Management-Decision Problem	Marketing Research Problem
Asks what the decision maker needs to do	Asks what information is needed and how it should be obtained
Action oriented	Information oriented
Focuses on symptoms	Focuses on the underlying causes

management-decision problem focuses on the symptoms, whereas the marketing research problem is concerned with the underlying causes (Table 2.2).

In the opening vignette, the management-decision problem was "What can Subaru do to expand its share of the automobile market?" The marketing research problem focused on information about the needs of the buyers of passenger cars, station wagons, and SUVs, and on identifying a segment whose needs were not being met. Also, information was to be obtained on the automobile features desired by the identified segment, and on the demographic and psychographic characteristics of this segment.

To further illustrate the distinction between the two orientations, we will consider an illustrative problem: loss of market share for the Old Spice product line (after-shave, cologne, deodorant). The decision maker is faced with the problem of how to recover this loss (the management-decision problem). Possible responses include modifying existing products, introducing new products, reducing prices, changing other elements in the marketing mix, and segmenting the market. Suppose the decision maker and the researcher believe that the problem can be traced to market segmentation in that Old Spice should be targeted at a specific segment. They decide to conduct research to explore that issue. The marketing research problem would then become the identification and evaluation of different ways to segment or group the market. As the research process progresses, problem definition may be modified to reflect emerging information. Table 2.3 gives additional examples, including that of Subaru in the opening vignette, that may further clarify the distinction between the management-decision problem and the marketing research problem.

A good way to link the broad statement of the marketing research problem with the management-decision problem is by making use of a conceptual map.[6] A conceptual map involves the following three components:

Management wants to (take an action).
Therefore, we should study (topic)
So that we can explain (question).

The first line states the rationale for the question and the project. This is the management-decision problem. The second line of the conceptual map declares what broader topic you are investigating. The third line implies the question you are investigating—the who/how/why that you want to explain. Thus, the second and third lines define the

Table 2.3
Management-Decision Problem and the Corresponding Marketing Research Problem

Management-Decision Problem	Marketing Research Problem
Should the advertising campaign be changed?	To determine the effectiveness of the current advertising campaign.
Should the price of the product be changed?	To determine the impact on sales and profits of various levels of price changes.
What can Subaru do to expand its automobile market?	To determine the various needs of the automobile users and the extent to which those needs were being satisfied by the current product offerings.

EXPERIENTIAL LEARNING

P&G's Conceptual Map

In an attempt to take market share away from arch-rival Kimberly-Clark's Huggies, P&G's baby-care division has developed a diaper designed to remain wet for two minutes prior to drying. Called "Feel 'n Learn Advanced Trainers," these diapers alert toddlers to try tinkling in the toilet once the toddlers partially wet the diaper. The Pampers team has a keen interest in the primary-customer segment they call "30 & Smart." This segment currently accounts for 15 percent of Pampers and 20 percent of Huggies sales. Members of this segment live primarily in metropolitan areas, are between 30 and 39 years of age, and have a high degree of education.[7]

Visit P&G's Web site (www.pg.com) and search the Internet and your library's electronic database to obtain information on P&G's and competing diaper brands. Develop a three-level conceptual map from the elements below:

a. Management wants to overtake Huggies in the diaper wars.
b. Management wants to successfully introduce a new diaper that will capture an 80 percent market share in the 30 & Smart segment within 12 months after introduction.
c. Therefore, we are studying what will make the best diaper.
d. Therefore, we are studying 30 & Smart evaluations of Feel 'n Learns in a test market.
e. So that we can explain preference for competing brands of diapers.
f. So that we can explain the probability of switching to the Feel 'n Learn diapers within this segment.

broad marketing research problem. An example of the conceptual map for Cingular Wireless follows:

> Management wants to (develop retention programs that will retain 90 percent of heavy users and lead to 10 percent higher sales over the next two years).
> Therefore, we should study (heavy-user loyalty)
> So that we can explain (what will be the most important variables in retaining these customers over the next two years).

As can be seen, the preceding example provides valuable definitions of the management-decision problem and the broad marketing research problems that are closely linked. The problem is now focused upon a segment of customers (heavy users) and one behavior of these customers (staying with the company over the next two years). Measurable results, such as "90 percent retention of heavy users" are included, as well as a company goal (10 percent increase in sales over the next two years).

Defining the Marketing Research Problem

A general guideline for defining the research problem is that the definition should (1) allow the researcher to obtain all the information needed to address the management-decision problem, and (2) guide the researcher in proceeding with the project. Researchers can make two common errors by defining the research problem either too broadly or too narrowly (Figure 2.7). A broad definition fails to provide clear guidelines for the subsequent steps involved in the project. Examples of overly broad marketing research problem definition are: developing a marketing strategy for the brand, improving the competitive position of the firm, or improving the company's image. These definitions are not specific enough to suggest an approach to the problem or a research design.

Focusing the problem definition too narrowly can also be a serious flaw. A narrow focus may inhibit a full examination of plausible options, particularly innovative ones. It may also prevent the researcher from addressing important components of the management-decision problem. For example, a problem will be too narrowly defined if it is confined to how a company should adjust its pricing, given that a major competitor has initiated price changes. The narrow focus on pricing alone leaves out other possible

Figure 2.7

Errors in Defining the Market Research Problem

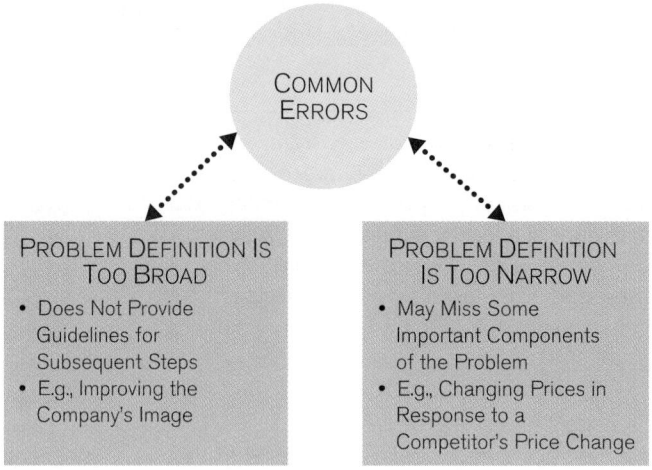

responses (alternative courses of action), such as introducing new brands, changing advertising, or adding new distribution channels.

A narrow definition of the problem could also lead to restrictive sampling resulting in erroneous conclusions. If Revlon is targeting females aged 16 to 29 for its cosmetics line, that's fine for guiding media placement. However, the problem would be too narrowly defined for research measuring advertising effectiveness if the study is restricted to females 16- to 29-years-old. The reason is that TV advertising has a much larger reach. Suppose the advertising turns out to be really effective among women aged 34 to 54 instead of 16 to 29. Revlon might have canceled a very effective campaign because it appeared to be failing among the target audience. On the other hand, it is possible that Revlon's commercials are working among 16- to 29-year-olds but driving all other age groups away. If we were sampling only the 16-to-29 segment, we would have overlooked this critical failing. Remember: Always define the problem broadly enough so as not to overlook any relevant aspects.

broad statement of the problem
The initial statement of the marketing research problem that provides an appropriate perspective on the problem.

specific components of the problem
The second part of the marketing research problem definition. The specific components focus on the key aspects of the problem and provide clear guidelines on how to proceed.

To minimize the possibility of a wrong decision due to an incorrect definition of the marketing research problem, it's a good idea for the researcher to adopt a two-stage process. First, the marketing research problem is stated in broad, general terms; then, it is reduced to its specific components (Figure 2.8). The **broad statement** provides perspective on the problem and acts as a safeguard against committing the second type of error. The **specific components of the problem** focus on the key aspects and provide clear guidelines on how to proceed further, avoiding the first type of error.

This process was illustrated in the opening vignette. The broad statement of the problem was to determine the various needs of automobile users and the extent to which current product offerings were satisfying those needs. In addition, five specific components were identified. The *Tennis* magazine provides another example of an appropriate marketing research problem definition.

Figure 2.8

Proper Definition of the Marketing Research Problem

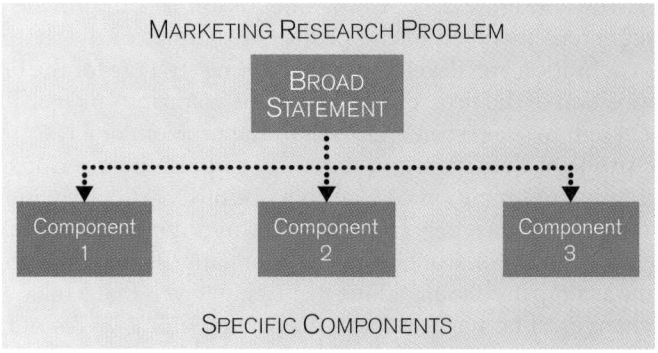

RESEARCH IN ACTION

Research Serves *Tennis* Magazine

Tennis magazine (www.tennis.com), a publication of the New York Times Company, wanted to obtain information about its readers. The broad marketing research problem was defined as gathering information about subscribers. The specific components of the problem were as follows:

1. **Demographics.** Who are the men and women who subscribe to the magazine?
2. **Psychological characteristics and lifestyles.** How do subscribers spend their money and their free time? Lifestyle indicators to be examined were fitness, travel, car rental, apparel, consumer electronics, credit cards, and financial investments.
3. **Tennis activity.** Where and how often do subscribers play tennis? What are their skill levels?
4. **Relationship to *Tennis* magazine.** How much time do subscribers spend with the issues? How long do they keep them? Do they share the magazine with other tennis players?

Because the questions were so clearly defined, the information provided by this research helped management design specific features on tennis instruction, equipment, famous tennis players, and locations to play tennis to meet readers' specific needs. These changes made *Tennis* magazine more appealing to its readers and resulted in increased circulation.

Once the marketing research problem has been broadly stated and its specific components identified, as in the case of *Tennis* magazine, the researcher is in a position to develop a suitable approach.

Be a DM!

A TiVo DVR is like a VCR, but with a hard drive and without the hassle of videotapes or timers. Browse the TiVo Web site (www.tivo.com) to get a better idea of this innovative product/service.

As the marketing manager, you want to increase the market share of TiVo. What information do you need in accomplishing this goal?

Be an MR!

Broadly define and identify the specific components of the marketing research problem facing TiVo.

Components of the Approach

The tasks performed earlier also help in developing an approach. An approach to a marketing research problem should include the following components: analytical framework and models, research questions and hypotheses, and a specification of the information needed (see Figure 2.3). Each of these components is discussed in the following sections.

Analytical Framework and Models

In general, marketing research should be based on objective evidence and supported by theory. **Objective evidence** (evidence that is unbiased and supported by empirical findings) is gathered by compiling relevant findings from secondary sources. A **theory** guides the collection of this data. It is a conceptual framework based on foundational statements, called axioms, which are assumed to be true. Theory may come from academic literature contained in books, journals, and monographs. For example, according to attitude theory, attitude toward a brand, such as Nike sneakers, is determined by an evaluation of the brand on salient attributes (e.g., price, comfort, durability, and style). Relevant theory provides insight regarding which variables should be investigated and which should be treated as dependent variables (those whose values depend on the values of other variables) and which as independent variables (those whose values affect the values of other variables). Thus, attitude toward Nike will be the dependent variable; price, comfort, durability, and style will be independent variables. The approach should be based on some kind of working theory or framework. This is also helpful in developing an appropriate model.

objective evidence
Unbiased evidence that is supported by empirical findings.

theory
A conceptual scheme based on foundational statements, which are assumed to be true.

An **analytical model** consists of a set of variables related in a specified manner to represent all or a part of some real system or process. Models can take many forms. The

analytical model
An explicit specification of a set of variables and their interrelationships designed to represent some real system or process in whole or in part.

verbal models
Analytical models that provide a written representation of the relationships between variables.

graphical models
Analytical models that provide a visual picture of the relationships between variables.

mathematical models
Analytical models that explicitly describe the relationships between variables, usually in equation form.

most common are verbal, graphical, and mathematical structures. In **verbal models**, the variables and their relationships are stated in prose form. These models are often a summary or restatement of the main points of the theory. **Graphical models** are visual and pictorially represent the theory. They are used to isolate variables and to suggest directions of relationships but are not designed to provide numerical results. They are logical, preliminary steps to developing mathematical models. **Mathematical models** explicitly specify the strength and direction of relationships among variables, usually in equation form. Graphical models are particularly helpful in conceptualizing an approach to the problem, as the following jeans purchase model illustrates.

In the opening vignette, the analytical model postulated that buyers first decide on the type of car they want (e.g., station wagon, SUV, passenger car) and then they decide on a specific brand based on their choice criteria (e.g., features, performance, price, repair and maintenance, gas mileage, and so forth). The verbal, graphical, and mathematical models complement each other and help the researcher identify relevant research questions and hypotheses, as shown in Figure 2.9.

BE an MR!

Write a report about GM's automobile brands by visiting GM's Web site (www.gm.com.)

Develop a graphical model explaining consumers' selection of an automobile brand.

BE a DM!

As the marketing chief of GM, how can a graphical model explaining consumers' selection of an automobile brand help you in positioning GM's various brands?

Research Questions and Hypotheses

research questions
Refined statements of the specific components of the problem.

Research questions (RQs) are refined statements of the specific components of the problem. A problem component may break into several RQs. Research questions are designed to ask the specific information required to address each problem component. Research questions that successfully address the problem components will provide valuable information for the decision maker.

RESEARCH IN ACTION

Lee Riveted Rivets Young Consumers with "The Brand That Fits"

According to consumer decision-making theory, the consumer first decides whether to purchase jeans or other casual clothes. If jeans are to be purchased, the consumer will form selection criteria for evaluating alternative brands. The selection criteria consist of factors such as color, price, fit, cut, comfort, and quality. The competing brands of jeans are then evaluated based on the selection criteria to purchase one or more brands. The following graphical model illustrates the decision process for jeans for a consumer considering the purchase of casual clothing. Lee Riveted jeans (www.leejeans.com) are targeted at young people who buy jeans based primarily on fit and cut. Therefore, the marketing theme of Lee Riveted with tag lines "the brand that fits" and "cut to be noticed" was based on this model. In Fall 2003, Lee Jeans expanded its reach among young women with One True Fit, a new style and fit concept based on its popular five-pocket jean.[8]

Graphical Model

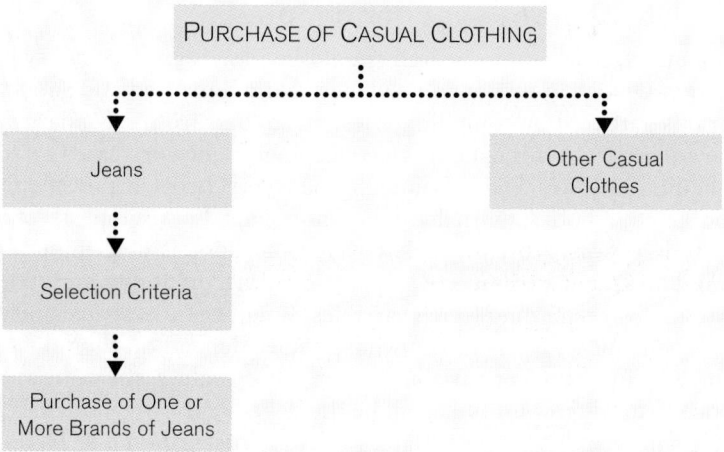

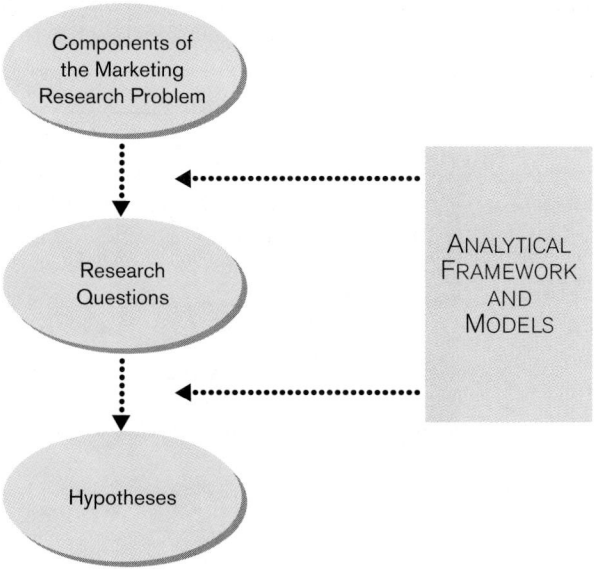

Figure 2.9
Development of Research Questions & Hypothesis

The formulation of the RQs should be guided, not only by the problem definition, but also by the analytical framework and the model adopted. In the Lee Riveted jeans example, the factors of the choice criteria were postulated based on theoretical framework as color, price, fit, cut, comfort, and quality. Several research questions can be posed related to these factors: What is the relative importance of these factors in influencing consumers' selection of jeans? What factor is the most important? What is the least important factor? Does the relative importance of these factors vary across consumers?

A **hypothesis** (H) is an unproven statement or proposition about a factor or phenomenon that is of interest to the researcher. It may be a tentative statement about the relationships discussed in the theoretical framework or represented in the analytical model. The H may also be stated as a possible answer to the research question. Hypotheses are statements about proposed relationships rather than merely questions to be answered. They reflect the researchers' expectation and can be tested empirically. (See Chapter 16.) Hypotheses also play the important role of suggesting variables to be included in the research design. The relationship between the marketing research problem, research questions, and hypotheses, along with the influence of the objective/theoretical framework and analytical models, is described in Figure 2.9.

hypothesis
An unproven statement or proposition about a factor or phenomenon that is of interest to the researcher.

In commercial marketing research, the hypotheses are not formulated as rigorously as they are in academic research. An interesting research question and related hypotheses that could be posed about the need for a hybrid product in the Subaru vignette are as follows.

RQ: Is there an overlap between the features sought by station wagon buyers and buyers of SUVs?

H1: The buyers of station wagons rate certain features of SUVs as important.

H2: The buyers of SUVs rate certain features of station wagons as important.

The "Got Milk?" example on the next page further illustrates RQs and Hs.

BE an MR!

Visit the *Tennis* magazine Web site (www.tennis.com) and write a report about the current editorial content and features of the magazine.

Formulate two research questions with corresponding hypotheses for the third component of the problem in the *Tennis* magazine example.

BE a DM!

As the editor of *Tennis*, how would you change the editorial content of the magazine if the formulated hypotheses were supported by data collected in a survey of readers?

RESEARCH IN ACTION

"Got Milk?"

Milk consumption had steadily declined for 20 years. Qualitative research indicated that people had misconceptions about milk. Hence, survey research was undertaken to address the following RQ and Hs:

RQ: Do people have misconceptions about milk?

H1: Milk is perceived as fat-laden and unhealthy.

H2: Milk is perceived as an old-fashioned drink.

H3: People believe that milk is meant only for kids.

When the survey data supported these hypotheses, the Milk Processor Education Program launched the well-known "milk mustache" campaign with the "Got Milk?" slogan. This creative advertising was a real attention-getter, showing celebrities from Joan Lunden to Rhea Perlman and Danny DeVito sporting the famous white mustache. The result? Humble milk, until a few years before, an also-ran in the advertising race behind soft drinks and juices, catapulted into a key beverage-industry player. The decline in milk consumption was arrested and annual milk consumption among children reached 28 gallons in 2002—the highest level in 10 years. Consumption continued to be stable through 2005 (www.gotmilk.com). In March 2004, "Got Milk?" crossed the Atlantic as Great Britain's Milk Development Council (MDC) began offering the "Got Milk?" trademark throughout England, Wales, and Scotland.[9]

Specification of Information Needed

By focusing on each component of the problem and the analytical framework and models, research questions, and hypotheses, the researcher can determine what information should be obtained. It is helpful to carry out this exercise for each component of the problem and make a list specifying all the information that should be collected. We illustrate this process with respect to the opening vignette.

Component 1

- Needs of buyers of passenger cars operationalized in terms of the attributes or features desired in an automobile.
- Needs of buyers of station wagons operationalized in terms of the attributes or features desired in an automobile.
- Needs of buyers of SUVs operationalized in terms of the attributes or features desired in an automobile.

Component 2

- Evaluation of passenger cars on the desired attributes.
- Evaluation of station wagons on the desired attributes.
- Evaluation of SUVs on the desired attributes.

Component 3

- No new information to be collected. The segment can be identified based on information obtained for the first two components.

EXPERIENTIAL LEARNING

Defining the Problem and Developing an Approach

Visit a local business located near your campus. Interview the business owner or manager and identify some of the marketing challenges facing this business. Also, interview an expert in this industry. Search and analyze secondary data pertaining to this business and the industry and identify the environmental context of the problem.

1. Define the management-decision problem.
2. Define the marketing research problem.
3. Develop a graphical model explaining the consumer-choice process leading to the patronage of this business or its competitors.
4. Develop an appropriate RQ and H.

Component 4

- No new information to be collected. The desired features can be identified based on information obtained for the first two components.

Component 5

- Standard demographic characteristics (e.g., gender, marital status, household size, age, education, occupation, income, and type and number of automobiles owned) and psychographic characteristics. Psychographic characteristics include outdoor and recreational activities, family orientation, and attitude toward daily commuting.

Summary Illustration Using the Opening Vignette

We can summarize and illustrate the major concepts discussed in this chapter by returning to the opening vignette. The Subaru vignette illustrates the importance of correctly defining the problem and showing how a problem audit can help in the process. The tasks involved in formulating the marketing research problem should lead to an understanding of the environmental context of the problem. In the case of Subaru, forecasts of future sales of station wagons and SUVs indicated that these two types of automobiles were not tapping the market potential. Subaru undertook research to understand the underlying behavior of the consumers, their needs, and desires. It capitalized upon its marketing and technological skill to achieve the successful introduction of "the world's first sports utility wagon."

Analysis of the environmental context should help identify the management-decision problem, which should then be translated into a marketing research problem. The management-decision problem focuses on what the decision maker should do, and the marketing research problem asks what information is needed and how it can be obtained effectively and efficiently. In the opening vignette, the management-decision problem was "What can Subaru do to expand its share of the automobile market?" The marketing research problem focused on information about the needs of the buyers of passenger cars, station wagons, and SUVs, and identifying a segment whose needs were not being met. Also, information was to be obtained on the automobile features desired by the members of this segment and on their demographic and psychographic characteristics. A broad statement of the problem was given, and specific components were identified.

Developing an approach to the problem is the second step in the marketing research process. The components of an approach consist of analytical framework and models, RQs, Hs, and specification of the information needed. The analytical model postulated that buyers first decide on the type of vehicle (e.g., station wagon, SUV, passenger car) and then decide on a specific brand. Research questions and Hs related to the overlap between the features sought by station wagon buyers and buyers of SUVs were formulated. In specifying the information required, the researcher operationalized the needs of automobile buyers in terms of the attributes or features desired. Evaluations of passenger cars, station wagons, and SUVs on the desired attributes had to be obtained. Information on standard demographic characteristics and the identified psychographic characteristics was also needed.

International Marketing Research

Conducting research in international markets often means working within unfamiliar environments. This lack of familiarity with the environmental factors of the country in which the research is being conducted can greatly increase the difficulty of appropriately defining the problem, as illustrated by the Heinz Company in Brazil.

Many international marketing efforts fail because a problem audit is not conducted prior to entering the foreign market, and the relevant environmental factors are not taken into account. This leads to an incorrect definition of the marketing research problem and an inappropriate approach, as illustrated in the case of Heinz. While developing theoretical frameworks, models, research questions, and hypotheses, remember that differences in the environmental factors, especially the sociocultural environment, may lead to differences in the formation of perceptions, attitudes, preferences, and choice behavior.

For example, orientation toward time varies considerably across cultures. In Asia, Latin America, and the Middle East, people are not as time conscious as Westerners, which can influence perceptions and preferences for convenience foods, such as frozen foods and prepared dinners. In defining the problem and developing an approach, the researcher must be sensitive to the underlying factors that influence consumption and purchase behavior.

Technology and Marketing Research

Decision support and expert systems (see Chapter 1) can also help identify alternative courses of action and define the marketing research problem and development of an approach. Other specialized software enables the researcher to use a systematic approach to organizing problems in components, resulting in logical problem formulation. These programs, such as MaxThink (www.maxthink.com), can portray graphically the relationship between the many facets of a complex problem and incorporate both quantitative and qualitative information, including managerial experience and intuition. This type of software allows the researcher to structure complex problems into manageable forms and to develop suitable approaches, as illustrated by Marriott.

RESEARCH IN ACTION

Heinz Ketchup Couldn't Catch Up in Brazil

As of 2005, approximately 60 percent of Heinz's (www.heinz.com) total sales came from outside the United States, making it one of the most international U.S.-based food companies. Despite good track records domestically and overseas, H. J. Heinz failed in its initial attempts to penetrate South America's biggest and most promising market. As an entry strategy into Brazil, Heinz entered into a joint venture with Citrosuco Paulista, a giant orange juice exporter, with the future possibility of buying the profitable company. However, the sales of Heinz products, including ketchup, did not take off. Where was the problem?

A post-entry problem audit revealed that the company lacked a strong local distribution system. Heinz had attempted to duplicate a strategy, which had been successful in Mexico: distribution through neighborhood shops. However, the problem audit revealed that 75 percent of the grocery shopping in Sao Paulo is done in supermarkets, not the smaller shops. Although Mexico and Brazil may appear to have similar cultural and demographic characteristics, consumer behavior was found to vary greatly. A problem audit and an examination of the environmental context of the problem prior to entry in Brazil could have prevented this failure.[10]

The Marriott Corporation is faced with the problem of developing an effective marketing strategy for its resorts. Data obtained from in-depth interviews with potential customers are analyzed with an outline processor, such as MaxThink. This analysis reveals that different ideas are associated with different regions of the United States. West Coast cities, such as San Diego, are associated with sand, surf, sun, and palm trees. Midwest cities, such as Chicago, are considered exciting, fun, and big. East Coast cities, such as Buffalo, elicit ideas such as Niagara Falls, friendliness, and neighbors. This suggests an approach that considers different marketing strategies for resorts in different regions. Furthermore, decision support systems can be used to conduct "what-if" analysis and determine the demand for resorts in different regions based on assumed levels of marketing expenditures. Regions can be combined or split so that the demand potential for each region lies in a predetermined range.

Ethics in Marketing Research

The stakeholders involved in ethical conflicts during the process of defining the problem and developing an approach are likely to be the marketing researcher and the client. Personal interests or hidden agendas of either stakeholder may lead to ethical dilemmas. Ethical issues arise when the personal objectives of the decision maker (for example, defending a decision already made) are at variance with the objectives of the client firm. The client should be forthright in disclosing the relevant objectives and the purpose for which the research is being undertaken. Likewise, the researcher should have the best interest of the client at heart.

Suppose that while conducting the problem definition tasks, a researcher discovers that the problem is a lot simpler than both parties originally thought. While the reduced scope of the problem will result in substantial savings for the client, it will also cut the revenues for the research firm. Does the researcher continue with the problem definition given in the proposal? Codes of ethics suggest that this situation should be fully discussed with the client.

Sometimes a client wants to conduct research that, in the opinion of the researcher, is not warranted or needed. Again, the researcher is faced with the ethical dilemma of what to do. Codes of ethics indicate that the researcher should communicate to the client that the research is not necessary. If the client is still insistent, the researcher should feel free to undertake the research.[11]

Likewise, ethical issues may also arise in developing an approach to the problem. Such issues include using models and approaches developed for specific projects for other clients. Researchers who conduct studies for different clients in related industries (e.g. banks and brokerage firms) or in similar research areas (e.g., measuring company image) may be tempted to reuse client-specific models or findings from other projects. However, unless the researcher has obtained client permission, this practice may be unethical.

SPSS Windows

In defining the problem and developing an approach, the researcher can make use of Decision Time and What If? distributed by SPSS. Forecasts of industry and company sales, and other relevant variables, can be aided by the use of Decision Time. Once the data are loaded onto Decision Time, the program's interactive wizard asks you three simple questions. Based on the answers, Decision Time selects the best forecasting method and creates a forecast.

What If? uses the forecast by Decision Time to enable the researcher to explore different options to get a better understating of the problem situation. The researcher can generate answers to questions such as: How will an increase in advertising affect the sales

WHAT WOULD *YOU* DO?

Kellogg's: From Slumping to Thumping

The Situation

Kellogg's is the world's leading producer of cereal and a leading producer of convenience foods, including cookies, crackers, toaster pastries, cereal bars, frozen waffles, meat alternatives, pie crusts, and cones, with projected annual sales of about $10 billion and a market share of more than 30 percent in 2004. Carlos Gutierrez, CEO of Kellogg's, takes pride in being a part of the Kellogg's company because of the consistency of the decisions that are made within the company to promote the long-term growth of their business, as well as serve the needs of their people and communities.

With such a large share of the market, one would think that Kellogg's is untouchable. However, Kellogg's faced a slump in the market. Its cereal sales were declining and it had to face the challenge of getting out of its slump. Kellogg's, therefore, turned to marketing research to identify the problem and develop several solutions to increase cereal sales.

To identify the problem, Kellogg's used several tasks to help them in the process. The researchers spoke to decision makers within the company, interviewed industry experts, conducted analysis of available data, and performed some qualitative research. Several important issues came out of this preliminary research. Current products were being targeted to the kids. Bagels and muffins were winning for favored breakfast foods. High prices were turning consumers to generic brands. Some other information also came to light during the research. Adults want quick foods that require very little or no preparation.

The Marketing Research Decision

1. What do you think is the underlying problem facing Kellogg's? Check as many as are applicable.
   a. Kellogg's is targeting the wrong segment: kids
   b. Competition from bagels and muffins
   c. Kellogg's prices are too high
   d. Kellogg's needs to introduce new products
   e. Kellogg's needs to change its advertising
2. Define an appropriate marketing research problem that Kellogg's needs to address.
3. Discuss the role of the type of marketing research problem you have identified in enabling Carlos Gutierrez to increase the sales of Kellogg's.

The Marketing Management Decision

1. Carlos Gutierrez is wondering what changes Kellogg's should make to increase market share. Should Kellogg's (check as many as are applicable):
   a. Introduce new cereals targeted at adults
   b. Decrease prices
   c. Increase advertising budget and launch a new campaign
   d. Launch a sales promotion campaign
   e. All of the above
2. Discuss how the marketing management decision action that you recommend to Carlos Gutierrez is influenced by the research that you suggested earlier and by the findings of that research.

What Carlos Gutierrez Did

Kellogg's began to introduce flavors more suited to the adult palette, but were not the tasteless varieties of the past. For example, it introduced Honey-flavored Shredded Wheat and Honey Crunch Corn Flakes, both aimed towards the adult market. It also implemented promotions featuring Microsoft software for the entire family instead of the usual toys. Then, it launched an ad campaign aimed at adults called, "Cereal. Eat it for life."[12,13]

of the product? How will a decrease/increase in price affect the demand? How will an increase in the sales force affect the sales by region?

Forecasts and what-if analyses can help the researcher to isolate the underlying causes, identify the relevant variables that should be investigated, and formulate appropriate RQs and Hs.

Summary

The most important step in a research project is defining the marketing research problem. It is frequently made difficult by the tendency of managers to focus on symptoms rather than underlying causes. The researcher's role is to help management identify and isolate the problem.

The tasks involved in formulating the marketing research problem include discussions with management, including the key decision makers; interviews with industry experts; analysis of secondary data; and qualitative research. This data gathering process should lead to an understanding of the environmental context of the problem. Within the environmental context, a number of factors should be analyzed and evaluated. These factors include past information and forecasts about the industry and the firm, objectives of the decision maker, buyer behavior, resources and constraints of the firm, the legal and economic environment, and marketing and technological skills of the firm.

Analysis of the environmental context should help identify the management-decision problem, which should then be translated into a marketing research problem. The management-decision problem focuses on what the decision maker should do, while the marketing research problem asks what information is needed and how it can be obtained effectively and efficiently. The researcher should avoid defining the marketing research problem either too broadly or too narrowly. The researcher can avoid these errors by first defining the research problem using a broad statement and then breaking it down into specific components.

The next step in the marketing research process is to develop an approach to the problem. The components of an approach are the analytical framework and models, RQs, and Hs. In addition, all the information that needs to be obtained in the marketing research project should be specified. The approach developed should be based on objective or empirical evidence and be grounded in theory. Models are useful for portraying the relationships among variables. The most common kinds of models are verbal, graphical, and mathematical. The research questions are refined statements of the components of the problem that ask what specific information is required with respect to each component. Research questions may be further refined into hypotheses. By focusing on each component of the problem and the analytical framework and models, RQs, and Hs, the researcher can determine what information should be obtained.

When defining the problem and developing an approach in international marketing research, the researcher must isolate and examine the impact of cultural factors. Technological advances have produced software in the form of text or idea processors, and outline processors that can process and analyze facts and ideas, restructuring them to facilitate problem definition and the development of an approach. Several ethical issues that have an impact on the client and the researcher can arise at this stage but can be resolved by open and honest communication.

Key Terms and Concepts

Problem definition, 33
Problem audit, 36
Experience survey, 39
Secondary data, 39
Primary data, 40
Qualitative research, 40
Pilot surveys, 41
Case studies, 41
Environmental context of the problem, 42
Objectives, 43
Buyer behavior, 43
Legal environment, 44
Management-decision problem, 45
Marketing research problem, 45
Broad statement of the problem, 48
Specific components of the problem, 48
Objective evidence, 49
Theory, 49
Analytical model, 49
Verbal models, 50
Graphical models, 50
Mathematical models, 50
Research questions, 50
Hypothesis, 51

Suggested Cases and Video Cases

Cases

1.1 Gillette **1.2 Sears** **2.2 Cadillac** **2.5 Burger King**
4.1 Boeing **4.2 Gucci**

Video Cases

1.1 Burke, Inc. **1.2 Accenture** **4.1 Subaru** **4.2 Marriott**

Additional cases and video cases are available in the Instructor's Manual and on the instructor and student Web sites.

Live Research: Conducting a Marketing Research Project

1. Invite the client to discuss the project with the class.
2. Have the class (or different teams) analyze the environmental context of the problem: past information and forecasts, resources and constraints, objectives, buyer behavior, legal environment, economic environment, and marketing and technological skills.
3. Jointly with the client, the instructor should make a presentation to the class discussing the management-decision problem and the marketing research problem. The students should come up with formal definitions of the management-decision problem and the marketing research problem. In conjunction with the client, arrive at consensual definitions.
4. Ask the class or specific teams to develop an approach (analytical framework and models, RQs, Hs, and identify the information needed). Through class discussion, arrive at a consensus.

Acronyms

The factors to be considered while analyzing the environmental context of the problem may be summed up by the acronym PROBLEM:

P ast information and forecasts
R esources and constraints
O bjectives of the decision maker
B uyer behavior
L egal environment
E conomic environment
M arketing and technological skills

Review Questions

1. What is the first step in conducting a marketing research project?
2. Why is it important to correctly define the marketing research problem?
3. What are some reasons that management is often not clear about the real problem?
4. What is the role of the researcher in the problem definition process?
5. What is a problem audit?
6. What is the difference between a symptom and a cause? How can a skillful researcher differentiate between the two and identify a true problem?
7. What are some differences between a management-decision problem and a marketing research problem?
8. What are the common types of errors encountered in defining a marketing research problem? What can be done to reduce the incidence of such errors?
9. How are the RQs related to components of the problem?
10. What are the differences between RQs and Hs?
11. What are the most common forms of analytical models?

Applied Problems

1. Visit the U.S. Census Bureau's Web site (www.census.gov) and obtain data relating to population trends by age groups.
2. State the marketing research problems for each of the following management-decision problems.
   a. Should a new product be introduced?
   b. Should an advertising campaign, which has run for three years, be changed?
   c. Should the in-store promotion for an existing product line be increased?
   d. What pricing strategy should be adopted for a new product?
   e. Should the compensation package be changed to motivate the sales force better?
3. State the management-decision problems for which the following marketing research problems might provide useful information.
   a. Estimate the sales and market share of department stores in a certain metropolitan area.
   b. Determine the design features for a new product, which would result in maximum market share.
   c. Evaluate the effectiveness of alternative TV commercials.
   d. Assess current and proposed sales territories with respect to their sales potential and workload.
   e. Determine the prices for each item in a product line so as to maximize total sales for the product line.
4. Identify five symptoms and a plausible cause for each one.
5. Suppose you are doing a project for American Airlines. Identify, from secondary sources, the attributes or factors passengers consider when selecting an airline.
6. You are a consultant to Coca-Cola USA working on a marketing research project for Diet Coke.
   a. Use the online databases in your library to compile a list of articles related to the Coca-Cola Company, Diet Coke, and the soft-drink industry published during the past year.
   b. Visit the Coca-Cola (www.cocacola.com) and PepsiCo (www.pepsico.com) Web sites and compare the information available at each.
   c. Based on the information collected from the Internet, write a report on the environmental context surrounding Diet Coke.
7. Select any firm. Using secondary sources, obtain information on the annual sales of the firm and the industry for the last five years. Use a spreadsheet package, such as Excel, or any microcomputer or mainframe statistical package, to develop a graphical model relating the firm's sales to the industry sales.
8. Visit the Web sites of competing sneaker brands (Nike, Reebok, and Adidas). The URLs are (www.nike.com), (www.reebok.com), and (www.adidas.com). From an analysis of information available at these sites, determine the factors of the choice criteria used by consumers in selecting a sneaker brand.

Group Discussion

1. Form a group of five or six people to discuss the following statement: "Correct definition of the marketing research problem is more important to the success of a marketing research project than sophisticated research techniques." Did your group arrive at a consensus?
2. We are all aware that the Coca-Cola Company changed its flagship brand of 99 years to New Coke and subsequently returned to the old favorite, Coca-Cola Classic. Working in a group of four, read as much material as you can on this marketing bungle. Identify the decision problem that Coke management faced. As a team of researchers, define the marketing research problem and its specific components.

CASES FOR PART 1

CASE 1.1

Gillette Has a Razor-Sharp Edge Over Its Competitors

Founded in 1901, Gillette is the world leader in male grooming products. This category includes blades, razors, and shaving preparations. Gillette also holds the number-one position worldwide in selected female grooming products, such as wet-shaving products and hair-epilation devices. The company is the world's leader in toothbrushes and oral care appliances under the brand of Oral-B. In addition, this company is the world leader in alkaline batteries with the Duracell brand. Within its powerhouse businesses of grooming, batteries, and oral care, the company has a formidable portfolio of global brands. These seem poised for growth as Gillette products, across a spectrum of product performance and price points, continuously attract new consumers. As of 2005, the company's products are distributed in over 200 countries and territories around the world.

As shown by the above statistics, Gillette has been a very successful consumer-products company. However, its current status was not achieved without some ups and downs along the way. In the late 80s, Gillette found itself in the precarious position of being a victim of a market it helped create. In the 70s and 80s, inexpensive disposable razors became the razor of choice. Gillette helped to foster this by participating in a strategy that de-emphasized brand quality and focused on price. Marketing dollars went to promotions, not to its then-premium shaving system, the Atra Plus. Gillette was guilty of teaching consumers how to not be loyal and how the best razor was the cheapest one at the moment. By employing this strategy, the disposable razor market grew to over 60 percent of total razor sales. Gillette lost some of the quality image and saw its margins shrink, which lead to three failed hostile takeover attempts.

Gillette managers were forced to examine their position in the market or risk losing control of their company. Gillette compiled and analyzed past sales information that uncovered the flaws in its marketing strategy. Marketing research in the form of focus groups and surveys revealed that Gillette could reform its approach to the market by re-emphasizing quality and brand equity in the hopes of reversing the trend. To accomplish this, Gillette discontinued all advertising for its disposable razors and began to heavily market its shaving systems. This effort led to the well-known Gillette catch phrase, "The Best a Man Can Get." Marketing research also revealed the critical importance of developing and introducing new products. Therefore, Gillette began making significant investments in research and development, developing new shaving systems over the coming years (Sensor, Sensor Excel, Mach III, M3Power, Venus, and such). In addition to changing its advertising focus, Gillette has undertaken numerous direct-mail campaigns, giving away free razors in order to further develop its brands. Gillette believes that once men and women try its products and experience the superior quality, they will be willing to pay the premium.

Through its refocused marketing strategy, Gillette was very successful at reversing the trend. Since the launch of its Sensor razor system, 10 percent of men switched from using disposables to using refillable razors. This shift gave refillable razors over 50 percent of the entire razor market. Gillette has continued this aggressive approach to marketing the premium shaving systems and has clearly become the market leader.

In addition to the men's and women's razor market, Gillette has refocused its marketing efforts in other personal-care segments. In each one, the focus is on creating a distinctive brand and differentiating its products. Currently, 1.2 billion people around the world use one or more of Gillette's products. About 700 million consumers use Gillette razor blades. Across the consumer-products industry, Gillette is considered to be one of the most effective companies at translating brand muscle into revenues and profits, with the likes of Coca-Cola and Procter & Gamble.

Gillette's success can be attributed to its willingness to rethink its overall strategy based on marketing research findings. By simply examining internal historical sales information, Gillette realized that the current trends would lead it further away from profit growth and closer to the inevitable hostile takeover. The changes made based on marketing research results throughout the past decade have made Gillette what it is today, much to the delight of its stockholders. The market value of Gillette's outstanding stock increased from $6 billion to $45 billion from 1990 to 2004. In January 2005, it was announced that Proctor & Gamble would buy Gillette for $54 billion. Continued reliance on marketing research should help Gillette maintain a razor-sharp edge over its competitors.

Questions

1. Discuss the role of marketing research in determining consumer preferences for personal-care products.
2. What was the management-decision problem facing Gillette when it realized that its brand equity had eroded?
3. Define the marketing research problem corresponding to the management-decision problem you have identified in Question 2.
4. Develop a graphical model explaining men's choice of a shaving razor.
5. Develop a research question and a corresponding hypothesis about the role of brand loyalty and price in consumers' selection of personal-care products.

References

1. (www.gillette.com/company).
2. William Symonds, "Can Gillette Regain Its Edge? Its New $15 Battery-Powered M3Power Shaver Ups the Arms Race with Schick," *Business Week*, (3867) (January 26, 2004): 46.
3. Charles Forelle, "Gillette's Profit and Sales Jump; Restructuring Starts to Pay Off," *Wall Street Journal*, (April 30, 2004): B2.
4. Nikhik Deogun, Charles Forelle, Dennis K. Berman, and Emily Nelson, "P & G to Buy Gillette for $54 Billion," *Wall Street Journal*, (January 28, 2005): A1, A5.

CASE 1.2

Sears: Meeting the Challenge of the Future

Right behind Wal-Mart, Sears Roebuck and Co. holds the title of the nation's second-largest retailer of apparel, home furnishings, electronics, and automotive products. Sears operates approximately 870 department stores and over 2,000 retail locations throughout the United States. In addition, Sears provides a full line of products through online shopping at the company's Web site (www.sears.com). For many years, consumers have relied on Sears as a one-stop shop for home, auto, and clothing needs. In late 2004, Kmart announced that is was purchasing Sears.

However, in the tough economic environment of 2001 to 2003, Sears faced many challenges. Marketing research showed that many customers believed Sears is overpriced and did not have a wide range of brands, particularly in appliances. Sears, however, believed that its sales prices were competitive but to counter price (mis)perception, dropped prices on select items in 2004. With the appliances, Sears launched a new advertising campaign in 2004 that focused on brands other than its own (Kenmore), such as Maytag and Whirlpool. Other changes were also made.

On the clothing scene, in 2003 Sears made arrangements with Land's End (catalog clothing giant) to sell its apparel in Sears' stores as well as on the Internet. This effort was made to expand the product offering, something the customers wanted, as well as to gain insight on how to effectively sell on the Internet (something Land's End has done successfully).

Furthermore, marketing research revealed that the physical layout of Sears' stores needed changing. Sears is planning on rolling out smaller stores across the country called Sears Grand. With smaller stores, customers shop more often and cross-shop more than in larger stores. In addition, Sears is hoping a larger number of stores will increase incremental revenue and contribute to the bottom line. In the traditional stores, significant remodeling has taken place, along with the expansion of product lines in the home textile department, which includes towels and top-of-bed merchandise.

Retail analysts predicted that Sears would face a challenging environment in 2005 to 2008. As Sears looked to the future, it was clear that, in order to experience continued growth, the company would have to adopt sound marketing strategies based on extensive marketing research. Mr. Alan Lacy, CEO, realized that Sears' marketing strategies should be based on an understanding of how consumers select department stores while shopping for specific needs. He looked to his marketing research department to provide this information.

Questions

1. What role can marketing research play in helping Sears continue to grow sales?
2. Visit Sears' Web site (www.sears.com) and write a report about Sears' marketing program.
3. What is the management-decision problem facing Sears' CEO, Mr. Alan Lacy?
4. Give an appropriate definition of the marketing research problem in this case.
5. Develop a graphical model explaining how consumers select a department store for shopping.

References

1. "Sears Expanding in Grand Style," *Homes Textiles Today*, 35(36) (May 17, 2004): 1.
2. Amy Merrick, "Sears to Sell Clothing on Its Web Site," *Wall Street Journal*, (September 26, 2003): B2.
3. (www.sears.com).

VidEO Cases for Part 1

VIDEO CASE 1.1

Burke: Learning and Growing Through Marketing Research

Alberta Burke who previously worked in the marketing department of Procter & Gamble Company founded Burke, Inc. in 1931. At that time, there were few formalized marketing research companies, not only in the United States but also in the world. As of 2005, Burke, based in Cincinnati, Ohio, is a decision support company involved with helping clients understand their business practices and making them more efficient. This video case traces the evolution of marketing research and how Burke implements the various phases of the marketing research process.

The Evolution of Marketing Research

The first recorded marketing research took place more than a century ago in 1895 or 1896. A professor sent out by telegram, questions to advertising agencies about the future of advertising. He got back about 10 responses and he wrote a paper describing what was happening. In the first years, most of the marketing research done was a spin-off of the Bureau of Census data and the analysis was basically limited to counting. The next wave of marketing research came in the early 1930s and can be described as the ladies with white gloves that were knocking on doors and checking pantries for cake mixes. The methodologies used were primarily door-to-door surveys; telephone was not a very widely utilized service at that time.

Then came World War II, which saw the introduction of the psychological side of marketing research. Through the 1950s and 1960s television became more of an integral part of the public's lives and, with that, came television advertising. Testing advertising commercials became the hot area of marketing research in the 60s and 70s. In the 60s and 70s, there came another fundamental change. The marketing research industry made a shift from just generating and testing new ideas and sharing them with clients to working more with clients on how to use those ideas to make decisions.

The emphasis on generating information to improve decision making increased in the 1980s and 1990s. The marketing research industry started developing processes that generated information to be used as input into management decision making. Thus, the marketing research industry has come a long way from the telegrams of 1895. As of 2005, the industry is trying to find creative ways to research consumers using methods such as telephone interviews, mall intercepts, Web interviews, and multimode methods.

To constantly learn, grow, and stay on the cutting edge, Burke conducts meta-research (research about how to do research). Recently, Burke was concerned whether the length of an online (Internet) survey had an adverse impact on the completion rate. So Burke fielded two Internet surveys. One was brief (10 questions taking an average of five minutes to complete) and the other was longer (20 questions taking about 20 minutes to complete). The completion rate for the short survey was 35 percent whereas it was only 10 percent for the longer survey. Thereafter, Burke designed shorter Internet surveys so as to reduce the proportion of people who drop off without completing the survey.

How Burke Implements the Marketing Research Process

Defining the Marketing Research Problem and Developing an Approach

The simplest way to find when a company needs help is when it has to make a decision. Any time there is a go or no-go, a yes or no, or a decision to be made, it asks what information can help reduce the risk associated with the decision. At this point, Burke likes to talk with the company to develop the information that would help reduce that risk.

The first step is to define the marketing research problem and a lot of discovery takes place here. The account executive (AE) will sit down with a client and try to determine whether or not what the client believes is the problem really is the case or whether Burke needs to change or broaden the scope of the problem. Discussions with the key decision maker (DM) may reveal that the company has been focusing on too narrow an issue, or that it has been focusing on the wrong problem all together.

Burke believes that defining the marketing research problem is critical to a successful research project. The company will find out what the symptoms are and work with the client to identify the underlying causes. Considerable effort is devoted to examining the background or the environmental context of the problem. In at least half the cases, when they go through the process of exploring the problem, the problem will change. It will gain a new scope or direction. This process results in a precise definition of the marketing research problem, including an identification of its specific components.

Once the problem has been defined, Burke develops a suitable approach. The problem definition is refined to generate more specific research questions and sometimes hypotheses. Because of its vast experience, Burke has developed a variety of analytical models that are customized to the identified problem. This process also results in the identification of information that would help the client solve its problem.

Research Design Formulation

Qualitative Research. One of the pitfalls that Burke encounters comes with qualitative research. Qualitative research is nice because it is immediate. The information that you get tends to be extremely rich and in the customer's words. You get a lot of interaction in that you get to see what kinds of answers are being given and what kinds of questions and concerns your customers or potential customers might have. However, one of the dangers comes from thinking that all of your customers or potential customers might view your products or service offering in this manner (i.e., generalize the findings of qualitative research to the population). Burke also has the ability to do focus groups online.

Survey Methods. While Burke uses a variety of methods, telephone studies represent about 70 percent of the surveys. Other methods used include mall intercept, mail, and Internet or Web-based surveys. Burke carefully selects the method that is best suited to the problem. Burke predicts that telephone surveys will decrease and Internet surveys will increase.

If Burke is trying to interview customers around the globe, the company sends an e-mail invitation to respondents to complete the survey via the Web. Burke likes the Internet's ability to show pictures of a particular product or concept to the survey respondents.

Questionnaire Design. In designing the questionnaire, Burke pays particular attention to the content and wording of the questions. There are some questions that are well defined and can be easily framed. Then, there may be other issues that need to be investigated, but the exact questions to ask may not be clear. The simpler the question and the more you know who needs to be asked (i.e., the target respondents), the better the information you are going to get.

Sampling Design. Burke has a sampling department within data collection and it consults with the senior account management team and account executives to determine the proper sample to use. The sampling frame is defined in terms of who the respondents are that can answer the questions that need to be addressed. The target population is defined by the marketing research problem and the research questions. Burke often buys the sampling lists from outside firms that specialize in this area. Burke is concerned about using a representative sample so that the results can be generalized to the target population (e.g., all the target consumers as opposed to only the consumers included in the sample).

Data Collection and Analysis

Once the information has been collected, it will reside either in a computer-related format or a paper format that is entered into a computer format. Essentially, the results are tabulated and analyzed via computers. Through the "Digital Dashboard" product, Burke not only has the ability disseminate the results to clients when the project is finished, but it also has the ability to show them the data as they are being collected. Burke breaks down the data analysis by relevant groups. You might see information by total respondents, and you might see information broken out by gender or business size. Burke looks at different breaks in the data to try to understand what is happening and if there are differences that exist depending on different criteria and how to make decisions based on that. In addition, Burke likes the data to be categorized into usable units such as time, frequency, or location instead of the vague responses that respondents give sometimes.

Report Preparation and Presentation

Clients need information much faster than they have in the past because decisions need to be made much more quickly than they were previously. So the idea of organizing large meetings to present data analysis results is no longer very practical. Most of what Burke is doing in reporting and delivering data is again done over the Web. The report documents the entire research process. It discusses the management-decision problem, the marketing research problem, the approach and research design, the information obtained to help management make the decision, and the recommendations.

The report writing process starts from the first conversation with the client and it is written as the research proceeds, not when the project is almost done. The entire report is written and presented with a focus on improving management's decision making. Burke's goal is to help clients have better decision-making abilities so that the clients are more valuable to their respected companies. Burke emphasizes this focus by reminding the clients, "Recall, here are the management-decision and marketing research problems we agreed upon. Here's the information we gathered. Here's the decision it points to." Burke might even add, "This is what we recommend you do."

Burke believes that a successful research project often leads to a subsequent research project; the research process is more of a cyclical process. It is not one that typically has a finite beginning and end. Once you solve a problem, there is always another one on which to work. Realizing this is what helps Burke and its clients constantly learn and grow.

Questions

1. Describe the evolution of marketing research. How has the role of marketing research changed as this field has evolved?
2. What is Burke's view of the role of marketing research?
3. Visit Burke's Web site (www.burke.com) and write a report about the various marketing research services offered by Burke.
4. What is Burke's view of the importance of defining the marketing research problem? What process does Burke follow and how does it compare to that given in Chapter 2?
5. What is Burke's view of the marketing research process? How does it compare with that given in Chapter 1?
6. If Burke were to offer you a position as an account executive with the responsibility of providing marketing research services to Procter & Gamble would you accept this position? Why or why not?

References

1. (www.burke.com).
2. John Kiska, "Customer Satisfaction Pays Off," *HRMagazine,* 49(2) (February 2004): 87–90.
3. Allen Hog and Jeff Miller, "Watch Out for Dropouts," *Quirk's Marketing Research Review,* (July/August 2003): online at (www.quirks.com).

VIDEO CASE 1.2

Accenture: The Accent Is in the Name

As of 2005, Accenture is the world's leading management- and technology-services organization. Through its network of businesses approach, the company enhances its consulting, technology, and outsourcing expertise through alliances, affiliated companies, venture capital, and other capabilities. Accenture delivers innovations that help clients across all industries quickly realize their visions. With over 110 offices in about 50 countries, Accenture can quickly mobilize its broad and deep global resources to accelerate results for clients. The company has extensive experience in 18 industry groups in key business areas, including customer-relationship management, supply-chain management, business strategy, technology, and outsourcing. Accenture also leverages its affiliates and alliances to help drive innovative solutions. Strong relationships within this network of businesses extend Accenture's knowledge of emerging business models and products, enabling the company to provide its clients with the best possible tools, technologies, and capabilities. Accenture uses these resources as a catalyst, helping clients anticipate and gain value from business and technology change. Accenture's clients include 89 of the *Fortune* Global 100, and more than half of the *Fortune* Global 500.

Accenture was originally named Andersen Consulting and was created in 1989 as a part of Arthur Andersen. In 2000, Andersen Consulting won the right to divorce itself from Arthur Andersen after the parent company broke contractual agreements moving into areas of service where Andersen Consulting was already an established leader. However, this required that it change the company's name from Andersen Consulting to something else. This was an extremely significant event because Andersen Consulting had built up considerable brand equity in its name, partly through the spending of approximately $7 billion over 10 years. In addition, the new name would need to be trademarked in 41 countries as the original name was. Thus, the name change became a top priority and the company focused much of its time and effort on this task.

The first task was to pick a new name. The company challenged its employees to come up with suggestions for a new name by creating an internal contest. The contest resulted in a list of over 2,500 entries. After extensive marketing research on various names, which included surveys of target customers, it decided to go with the name Accenture. Marketing research revealed that the "Acc" in the name connotes accomplishment and accessibility, and the name sounds like "adventure." The company settled on this name because it believed this name conveyed the message that it was focused on the future. It also spent a considerable amount of time creating a new logo. The final version of this was the company's name accented with a greater than (>) symbol, which it believed stressed its focus on the future.

Another task, which occurred simultaneously with the first task, was to get the word out and prepare the target market for the brand change. The company began running ads notifying everyone that its name would change at the beginning of 2001. Accenture has a well-defined group of companies that comprises the target market and it had to focus its efforts on them.

On January 1, 2001, Accenture announced its new name to the world. The initial campaign illustrated the change by the slogan, "Renamed. Redefined. Reborn." Accenture used this opportunity not only to present the new name but also to sell its services and help people understand what it had to offer. In the end, Accenture spent a total of $175 million to rebrand itself, but it did not stop there. In February 2001, it began a new campaign titled, "Now It Gets Interesting." This campaign took the perspective that, despite all the incredible changes that have occurred recently due to technology, there are still even more challenges that lie ahead. The commercials showed how Accenture could help the clients capitalize on these challenges. The success of this campaign was evidenced by the increased traffic on its Web site.

This is very important to Accenture because it believes that if it can get somebody to visit its site, then there is a better opportunity to tell the whole story. This was followed by the "I Am Your Idea" theme. This campaign was followed by "High Performance. Delivered" that was running in 2004. It also featured Tiger Woods with the tag line "Go on. Be a Tiger."

Accenture has been successful in the quest of transferring the brand equity to its new name. Marketing research revealed that it has approximately 50 percent awareness with the public, which is essentially the same number it had under the old name. Accenture's marketing goes far beyond the name as it is constantly challenged because the product it offers is consistently changing. To be successful it must have good marketing research, creative marketing, a big budget, and an understanding of future trends. This will help the company to continue building equity in the Accenture name.

Questions

1. Discuss the role of marketing research in helping Andersen Consulting select a new name (Accenture).
2. Define Accenture's target market. Discuss the role of marketing research in helping Accenture understand the needs of its target customers.
3. Accenture would like to increase preference and loyalty for its services. Describe the management-decision problem.
4. Define a suitable marketing research problem corresponding to the management-decision problem that you have identified in Question 3.
5. Develop a graphical model explaining how a Fortune 500 firm would select a consulting organization.
6. Develop two research questions, each with two hypotheses, based on the marketing research problem you have defined in Question 4.

References

1. (www.accenture.com).
2. "Accenture Wins Homeland Security Contract," *Telecomworldwire*, (June 2, 2004): 1.
3. Todd Wasserman, "Accenture Accents Idea Campaign," *Brandweek*, (September 30, 2002): 4.

stylist advice:

"Each piece you see stands on its own, yet mixes in with your existing wardrobe for a totally new look."
Wayne Scot Lukas celebrity stylist

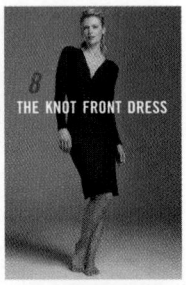

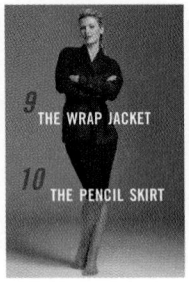

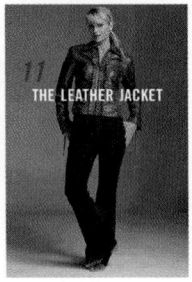

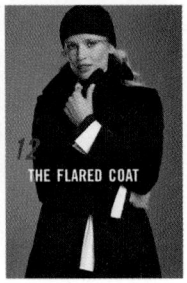

WAYNE'S RULES

Believe in who you are, just as you are right now, in any size or any shape. Then wrap this perfect gift and present yourself to the world.

Better to shop with a body you love than one that you judge. Work with what you have.

Accentuate your positives with jewelry. But don't decorate yourself like a holiday mantle.

I love a monochromatic outfit under a "shock of red" jacket. Monochromatic looks are always slimming.

Lightweight layering can create a myriad of looks. Choose pieces that stand on their own, then mix them up for an exciting wardrobe of outfits.

This fall, accessories are in animal prints and furs, whether faux or real. Let them become your accent pieces. The right shoe and bag can take a pair of jeans to a very polished level.

Go for gorgeous lines and simple tailoring. Remember: you're the star.

Precious metals bring that "summer glow" to the winter months. They radiate an inner light.

www.waynescotlukas.com

4 Order Anytime 1.800.345.4500

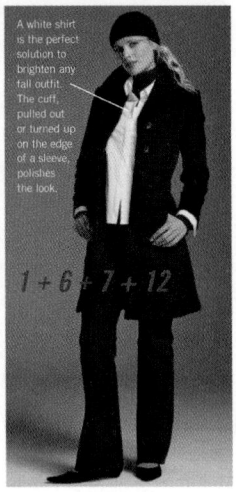

1 THE WOVEN SHIRT
Pintucks with French cuffs. Cotton/nylo
spandex. Machine wash. White. Import
Misses: 4-18. A27 942 0316 **$29**
Women's: 14W-24W. W27 942 0317

2 THE SILK V-NECK
Fine-gauge ribbed knit. Machine wash.
Import. Burgundy, Black, Deep brown,
Misses: S-XXL. B81 942 0292 **$29**

3 THE TROUSER
High-waisted with adjustable tabs. Fron
pockets. Polyester/rayon/spandex. Dry
Import. Black, Deep brown. 32" inseam.
Misses: 4-18. B27 942 4016 **$49**
Women's: 14W-24W. W27 942 4017

4 THE SHORT BLAZER
3/4-length sleeves with flap pockets an
a notched collar. Polyester/rayon/spand
Lined. Dry clean. Import. Deep brown,
Misses: 4-18. B27 942 5014 **$59**
Women's: 14W-24W. W87 942 5016

5 THE SKIRT
Pleated with a clean waist. Invisible sid
Polyester/rayon/spandex. Dry clean. Im
Deep brown, Black. 23½" long.
Misses: 4-18. B27 942 2032 **$49**
Women's: 14W-24W. W87 942 2033

6 THE TURTLENECK
Shirred with a scrunch neckline and bu
along the right side. Rayon/spandex. M
wash. Import. Black, Burgundy, Deep
Ecru. Misses: XS-XXL. B27 942 0314

7 THE JEANS
Bootcut cotton denim with a contour w
carpenter pockets and contrast stitchin
Machine wash. Black wash. Import.
32" inseam. Misses: 4-18. A27 942 363

8 THE KNOT FRONT DRESS
A-line shape with a gathered front and
empire waist. Cotton/spandex. Machine
Import. Black, Deep brown. 37" long.
Misses: XS-XXL. B27 942 3038 **$49**

9 THE WRAP JACKET
Tie front with topstitching, patch pocke
a back vent. Lined. Rayon/wool. Dry cle
Import. Burgundy, Deep brown, Black.
Misses: 4-18. B27 942 5012 **$99**
Women's: 14W-24W. W27 942 5015

10 THE PENCIL SKIRT
A clean waist with an invisible back zip
Polyester/rayon/spandex. Dry clean.
Import. Black, Deep brown. 24" long.
Misses: 4-16. B27 942 2034 **$39**
Women's: 14W-24W. W27 942 3330

11 THE LEATHER JACKET
Ruched zip front with a ruffled placket
and lacing at the sleeves and princess
seams. Lined. Leather care. Tan. Impo
Misses: 4-18. A13 942 7245 **$99**

12 THE FLARED COAT
Slightly flared sleeves and front seam d
Buttonfront. Wool/nylon. Dry clean. Imp
Black, Burgundy, Deep brown. 37½" lo
Misses: 4-18. B13 942 7246 **$149**

13 SHIRRED V-NECK SWEATER
Shirred with tuck detail at the bust and
Silk/rayon/angora/cashmere. Dry clean.
Black, Deep brown, Burgundy. Misses:
B27 942 5821 **$29**

A RUCHED BOOT
Kidsuede with man-made lining, sole
and insole. 3" heel. Black. Import.
B(Medium): 6-10, 11. B33 942 3110

tip To create a longer loo
Monochromatic dress
extends your body. With
same color skirt, hose and s
you'll look taller ever.

CHAPTER 3 Research Design

"Formulating a methodical research design is crucial in every project. It's like making a map for what you will do later in the research project when time is of the essence."

CHRIS WALLACE, *Research Director, VHA, Irving, TX*

OPENING QUESTIONS

1. What is a research design and what are the kinds of basic research designs?
2. How can the basic research designs be compared and contrasted?
3. What are the major sources of errors in a research design?
4. How does the researcher coordinate the budgeting and scheduling aspects of a research project?
5. What elements make up the marketing research proposal?
6. What factors should the researcher consider while formulating a research design in international marketing research?
7. How can technology facilitate the research design process?
8. What ethical issues arise when selecting a research design?

Marketing Research Helps Spiegel Redesign Its Product Lines

Spiegel (www.spiegel.com) is one of the leading direct marketers, offering the benefits of home-based shopping via the catalog and the Internet. However, in March 2003, the company filed for Chapter 11 bankruptcy protection. Spiegel realized a turnaround had to happen to regain profits and customer growth. To achieve this turnaround, the company lowered expenses, reduced inventory, and concentrated on creating an improved Web site to draw in new customers and ultimately boost revenues. Spiegel also wanted to improve its products and marketing programs.

Spiegel conducted extensive marketing research. The marketing research problem was to understand the shopping behavior of its potential and current consumers. Several research questions and hypotheses were formulated to examine the unique aspects of the buying behavior of the consumers. The research design Spiegel used consisted of two phases. The first, the exploratory phase, consisted of analysis of secondary data plus 10 focus groups with Spiegel customers. Secondary data provided good background information on current and potential catalog shoppers and vital statistics, such as the size of this segment. Focus groups helped Spiegel understand the values, attitudes, and behavior of its customers related to clothing, home furnishings, and shopping. The focus groups revealed that these customers wanted variety and quality. They also felt appreciated when a company designed special promotions directed to them. Spiegel came up short on all of these dimensions.

In the second, the descriptive phase, the findings of the exploratory phase were tested with a telephone survey of a sample of 1,000 Spiegel customers selected randomly, that is, selected based on chance, to measure and control random sampling error. Efforts were also undertaken to control the various sources of nonsampling error. For example, the interviewers were carefully selected and thoroughly trained, and close supervision was exercised to minimize interviewing errors. The results of the survey confirmed the demand for more Spiegel product offerings, and also showed that the Spiegel lines needed more promotion. In the fall of 2003, Spiegel spent millions of dollars on a print campaign aimed at revitalizing its product lines. The research results led to more product offerings and an increased amount of promotions across the product lines. Since then, Spiegel has witnessed an increased growth rate, which hopefully will lead to continued success.[1] •

Overview

As we've seen in Chapter 2, defining a marketing research problem and developing a suitable approach are both critical to the success of the entire marketing research project. The next step is to formulate a detailed research design to achieve the defined goals. Figure 3.1 gives the relationship of research design to previous chapters and to the marketing research process.

This chapter classifies and describes the basic research designs. At the broad level, there are two major types of research designs: exploratory and conclusive. Conclusive research designs can be further classified as descriptive or causal. Thus, this classification results in three basic designs: exploratory, descriptive, and causal. These three basic designs are used in different combinations and sequences.

We consider the value of marketing research information within the context of controlling research design errors. We discuss budgeting and scheduling of a proposed research project and present guidelines for writing research proposals. As applications, we consider research design concepts in the context of international marketing research, technology, and ethics in marketing research. Figure 3.2 presents an overview.

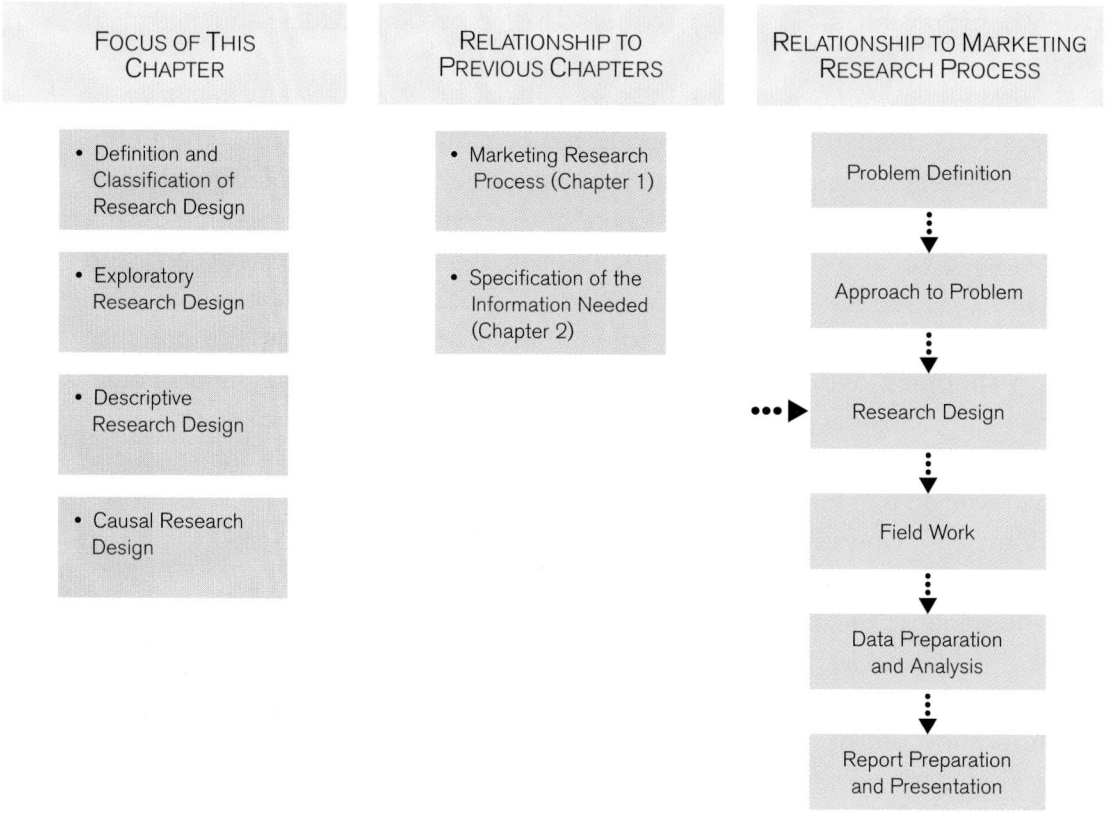

Figure 3.1

Relationship of Research Design to the Previous Chapters and the Marketing Research Process

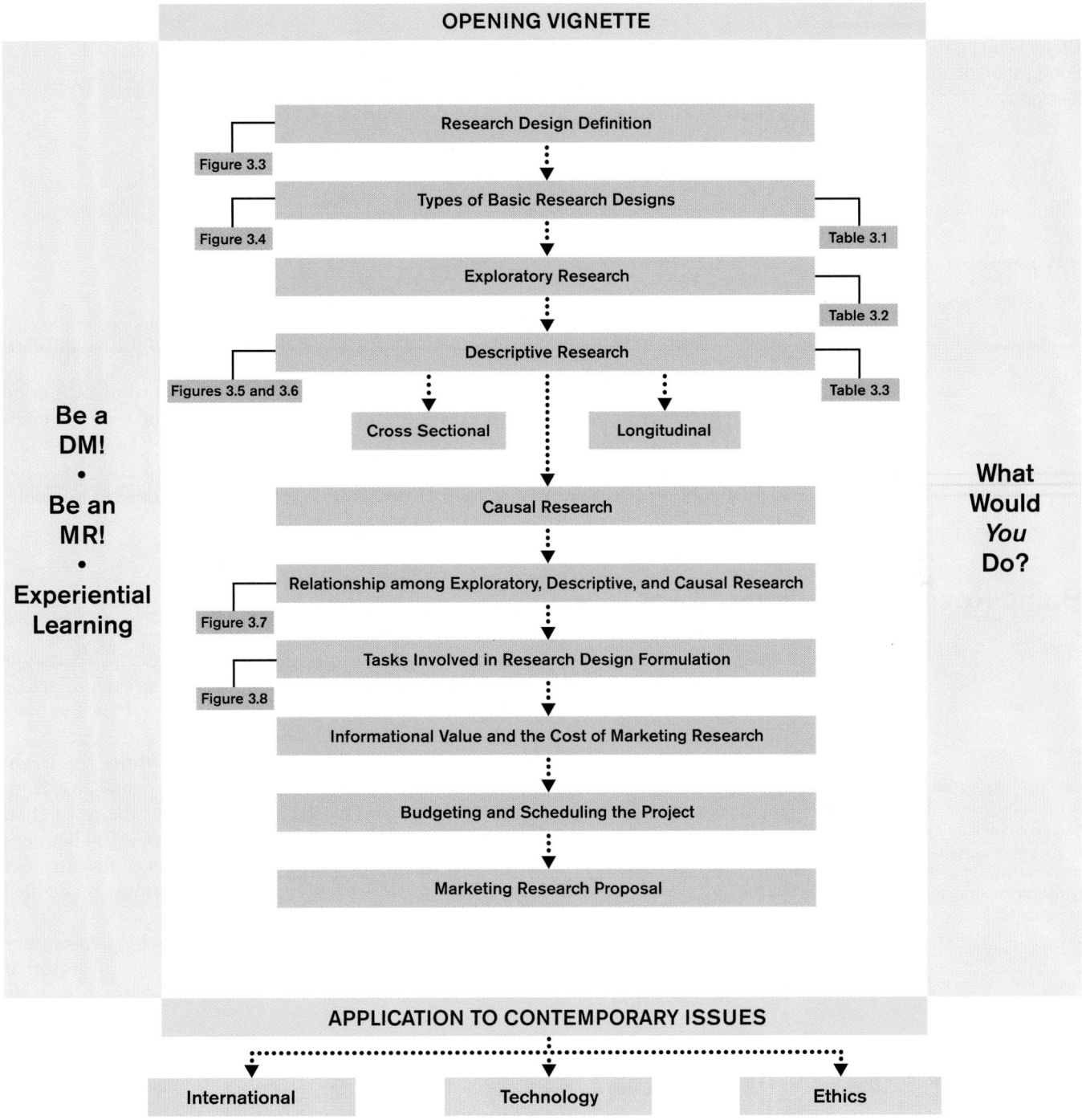

Figure 3.2

Research Design: An Overview

What Is a Research Design?

The **research design** is a roadmap for conducting the marketing research project. It provides details of each step in the marketing research project. Implementation of the research design should result in all the information needed to structure or solve the management-decision problem. The design process begins by defining the marketing research problem. Next comes the approach: a conceptual framework, research questions, hypotheses, and the information needed. (See Chapter 2.) The research design is

research design
A framework or blueprint for conducting the marketing research project that specifies the procedures necessary to obtain the information needed to structure and/or solve the marketing research problem.

Figure 3.3

Steps Leading to the Formulation of a Research Design

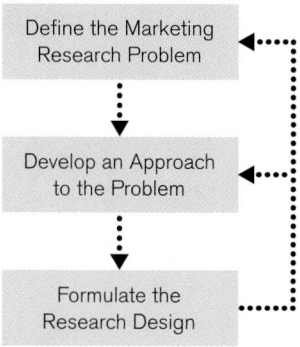

based on the results of these first two steps: the problem definition and the approach (Figure 3.3).

Many designs may be appropriate for a given marketing research problem. A good research design ensures that the information collected will be relevant and useful to management and that all of the necessary information will be obtained. A good design should also help ensure that the marketing research project will be conducted effectively and efficiently. In this chapter, we will consider the basic types of research designs available. These basic designs can be classified in terms of the research objectives.

Basic Research Designs

Research designs are of two broad types: exploratory and conclusive. Conclusive designs may be either descriptive or causal. Descriptive designs may be further categorized as either cross sectional or longitudinal. Exploratory, descriptive, and causal are the basic research designs we examine in this chapter (see Figure 3.4).

exploratory research
A type of research design that has as its primary objective the provision of insights into and comprehension of the problem situation confronting the researcher.

Table 3.1 states the differences between exploratory and descriptive research. **Exploratory research** is research conducted to explore the problem situation, that is, to gain ideas and insight into the problem confronting the management or the researcher. Exploratory research may be used when management realizes a problem exists but does not yet understand why. Perhaps sales are slipping in a particular region, or customer service complaints have increased sharply. As a first step, the problem must be defined and alternate courses of action identified.

Because the information needs are only loosely defined at this stage, exploratory research has to be flexible and unstructured. For example, exploratory research that

Figure 3.4

A Classification of Market Research Designs

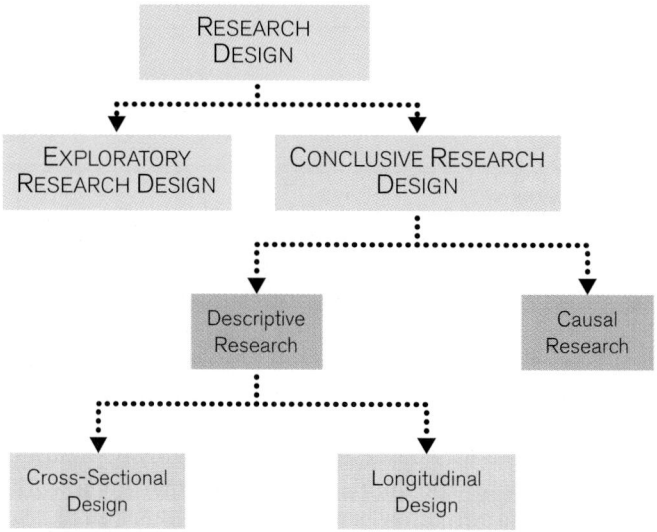

Table 3.1
Differences between Exploratory and Conclusive Research

	Exploratory	Conclusive
Objective:	To provide insights and understanding	To test specific hypotheses and examine relationships
Characteristics:	Information needed is defined only loosely	Information needed is clearly defined
	Research process is flexible and unstructured	Research process is formal and structured
	Sample is small and nonrepresentative	Sample is large and representative
	Analysis of primary data is qualitative	Data analysis is quantitative
Findings/Results:	Tentative	Conclusive
Outcome:	Generally followed by further exploratory or conclusive research	Findings used as input into decision making

investigates why some customers are dissatisfied with Ivory bath soap may begin with an analysis of calls recorded on the consumer hot line regarding the nature of complaints. Then, depending on the nature of the findings, the researcher may decide to conduct focus groups with users of Ivory soap. Suppose six focus groups, each involving 10 respondents, reveal that users are dissatisfied with the lack of lather and moisturizing ability. Should Procter & Gamble (P&G) immediately change the Ivory formula?

No! Exploratory research is conducted on a small and nonrepresentative sample, so the findings should be regarded as tentative and should be used as building blocks for further research. Typically, more formally defined exploratory research or conclusive research follows. There is a danger when exploratory research is the only step taken toward developing a solution. The tendency to overlook the limited usefulness of the information, particularly if it confirms preconceived ideas about a problem, can lead management in the wrong direction. Despite these risks, exploratory research can be valuable when researchers are faced with a problem that is not fully understood, for example, why some customers are dissatisfied with a specific brand of bath soap. Exploratory research in the form of in-depth interviews or focus groups could provide valuable insights.

Conclusive research is research designed to assist the decision maker in determining, evaluating, and selecting the best course of action in a given situation. Conclusive research can be used to verify the insights gained from exploratory research. As illustrated in the opening vignette, the findings from secondary data and focus groups (exploratory research) were further tested in a telephone survey (conclusive research). Conclusive research is based on the assumption that the researcher has an accurate understanding of the problem at hand. The information needed for addressing the management-decision problem has been clearly specified. The objective of conclusive research is to test specific hypotheses and examine specific relationships.

conclusive research
Research designed to assist the decision maker in determining, evaluating, and selecting the best course of action for a given situation.

Conclusive research is typically more formal and structured than exploratory research. The researcher specifies the detailed steps in the research to be conducted prior to initiating the project. Large, representative samples are used to collect data that are analyzed with statistical techniques. In the Ivory soap example, a large national survey involving 1,000 randomly selected respondents could be conducted to verify the findings of the in-depth interviews or focus groups. The survey could be used to obtain consumer evaluations of Ivory soap and competing brands on the important attributes such as mildness, lather, shrinkage, price, fragrance, packaging, moisturizing, and cleaning power.

BE an MR!

Visit Holiday Inn's Web site (www.ichotelsgroup.com/h/d/hi/1/en/home) and write a report about the various hotel brands owned by Holiday Inn.

What type of research would you conduct for determining a coherent marketing strategy for the various hotel brands owned by Holiday Inn?

BE a DM!

As the vice president of marketing for Holiday Inn, discuss the role that exploratory and conclusive research can play in determining a coherent marketing strategy for the various hotel brands owned by Holiday Inn, such as Holiday Inn Hotels and Resorts, Holiday Inn Select, Holiday Inn SunSpree Resorts, and Holiday Inn Family Suites Resorts.

Exploratory Research

As its name implies, the objective of exploratory research is to explore or search through a problem or situation to provide insights and understanding (Tables 3.1 and 3.2). For example, Adidas could make use of exploratory research to understand the reasons for its lower market share in the United States as compared to Nike. Exploratory research could be used for any of the following purposes, which are illustrated using the Adidas example.

1. **To formulate a problem or define a problem more precisely.** Exploratory research may reveal that Adidas has a lower market share because its brand image is not as strong as Nike.
2. **To identify alternative courses of action.** Alternative courses of action to boost the image of Adidas might include improving product quality, increasing the television advertising budget, distributing the product through upscale company-owned stores, increasing the prices of its athletic shoes and apparel, and so forth.
3. **To develop hypotheses.** An interesting hypothesis is that the heavy users of athletic shoes are more brand conscious than the light users. Another is that the heavy users have a weaker image of Adidas as compared to the light users.
4. **To isolate key variables and relationships for further examination.** Celebrity endorsements can have a positive influence on the image of Adidas.
5. **To gain insights for developing an approach to the problem.** Brand image is a composite variable that is influenced by the quality of the product, pricing strategy, image of the outlets through which the product is distributed, and the quality and intensity of advertising and promotion.
6. **To establish priorities for further research.** Adidas might want to examine the purchase and consumption behavior of heavy users of athletic shoes.

Table 3.2

A Comparison of Basic Research Designs

	Exploratory	Descriptive	Causal
Objective:	Discovery of ideas and insights	Describe market characteristics or functions	Determine cause-and-effect relationships
Characteristics:	Flexible Versatile	Marked by the prior formulation of specific hypotheses	Manipulation of one more independent variables
	Often the front end of total research design	Preplanned and structured design	Control of other mediating variables
Methods:	Expert/experience surveys	Secondary data: Quantitative	Experiments
	Pilot surveys	Surveys	
	Case studies	Panels	
	Secondary data: Qualitative	Observational and other data	
	Qualitative research		

Exploratory research is often conducted in the beginning stages of a project, as illustrated in the Spiegel vignette. Secondary data provided good background information on Spiegel's customers while focus groups helped Spiegel understand the values, attitudes, and behavior of this segment concerning clothing and shopping. The results indicated that current and potential customers wanted variety and quality and also appreciated special promotions. However, exploratory research can be used at any point in the research process when the researcher is unclear about the problem situation.

Exploratory research relies heavily on the curiosity and insight of the researcher. It is more like a process of informal discovery. Yet the abilities of the researcher are not the sole determinants of good exploratory research. While the process is highly flexible and relatively informal, exploratory research can benefit from use of the following methods (see Table 3.2):

- Survey of experts/experience surveys (discussed in Chapter 2).
- Pilot surveys (discussed in Chapter 2).
- Case studies (discussed in Chapter 2).
- Qualitative analysis of secondary data, including literature review (discussed in Chapters 4 and 5).
- Qualitative research, such as focus groups and one-on-one in-depth interviews (discussed in Chapter 6).

As discussed in Chapter 2, the Internet can provide many resources for marketing research. Newsgroups list servers and other bulletin board–type services can be very useful in the exploratory phase of research. Messages posted to newsgroups can often direct you to other valid sources of information. Newsgroups can be used to set up more formal focus groups with experts or individuals representing the target audience in order to obtain initial information on a subject. In Chapter 6, we discuss the use of the Internet for conducting focus groups in more detail.

Spiegel analyzed secondary data and conducted 10 focus groups as part of its exploratory research to understand the clothing preferences and shopping behavior of its customers. The use of exploratory research in defining the problem and developing an approach was discussed in Chapter 2. The following Bank of America (BOA) example provides another application of exploratory research.

Note that BOA, like Spiegel, did not rely exclusively on exploratory research. Once new product ideas were identified, they were further tested by descriptive research in the form of surveys.

RESEARCH IN ACTION

Banking on Exploratory Research

Bank of America (BOA; www.bankofamerica.com), formed by merging NationsBank and BankAmerica, is the largest bank in the United States. Assets in 2005 exceeded $700 billion. In order to increase its share of a very competitive market, BOA conducted exploratory research using focus groups of current and potential customers to find out where new branches should be located and what new products to introduce. Many new product ideas were generated through exploratory research. These ideas were further investigated using descriptive research in the form of customer and noncustomer surveys. The research enabled BOA to successfully introduce new products, such as innovative checking, savings, and institutional accounts, and to improve profitability.

Recently, focus groups followed by a telephone survey revealed that a large segment of households wanted interest payment on their checking account balances but were very sensitive to any checking account fees. These consumers maintained large balances in their checking account and were, therefore, open to a reasonable minimum balance requirement. Accordingly, BOA introduced an interest-paying checking with no fees (monthly or per check) but with a minimum balance requirement of $2,500. Exploratory and descriptive research have helped BOA to become the largest bank in the country.[2]

BE an MR!

Visit the Häagen-Dazs Web site (www.haagendazs.com) and search for additional information about the company on the Internet. Write a report about the flavors and products being offered by Häagen-Dazs as well as the marketing strategy of the company.

You are conducting a project for Häagen-Dazs to understand consumers' perceptions and preferences for high-quality ice cream. Would you conduct exploratory research? If yes, which methods would you use and why?

BE a DM!

As the marketing manager for Häagen-Dazs, how would you use information on consumers' perceptions and preferences for high-quality ice cream to penetrate the upper-income households in the United States?

Descriptive Research

descriptive research
A type of conclusive research that has as its major objective the description of something—usually market characteristics or functions.

Descriptive research is a type of conclusive research that has as its major objective the description of something—usually market characteristics or functions. Most commercial market research is descriptive in nature. Descriptive research is particularly useful whenever research questions relate to describing a market phenomenon, such as frequency of purchase, identifying relationships, or making predictions. (See Table 3.2.) Here are some examples of descriptive research goals:

1. **To develop a profile of a target market.** Levi-Strauss would like to know the age, educational level, income, and media habits of heavy users of jeans in order to make advertising placement decisions.
2. **To estimate the frequency of product use as a basis for sales forecasts.** Knowing that a "heavy" perfume user buys 1.8 bottles of perfumes per month can help Mary Kay cosmetics predict potential sales for a new perfume brand.
3. **To determine the relationship between product use and perception of product characteristics.** In developing its marketing platform, Motorola would like to determine if and how heavy users of cellular phones differ from nonusers, in terms of the importance they attach to performance and ease of use.
4. **To determine the degree to which marketing variables are associated.** Microsoft would like to know to what extent Internet usage is related to age, income, and education level.

Descriptive research assumes that the researcher has prior knowledge about the problem situation. This is one of the major differences between descriptive and exploratory research. Thus, descriptive research, in contrast to exploratory research, is based on a clear statement of the problem, specific hypotheses, and specification of the information needed. (See Chapter 2.) The data are collected in a structured fashion, typically using large, representative samples. The findings are then used to make generalizations about an entire customer group or market. Microsoft, for example, could survey a representative sample of Internet users to determine Internet usage and project the findings to the population of Internet users.

Descriptive studies are used to portray market variables. They describe the customer and the market, and measure the frequency of behaviors, such as purchasing. Among the major types of descriptive studies are internally or externally focused sales studies, consumer perception and behavior studies, and market characteristic studies (Figure 3.5).

- Sales studies include market potential studies, which describe the size of the market, the buying power of consumers, and historic growth rates; market share studies, which determine the proportion of total sales a company and its competitors receive; and sales analysis studies, which describe sales by geographic region, product line, and type and size of the account.

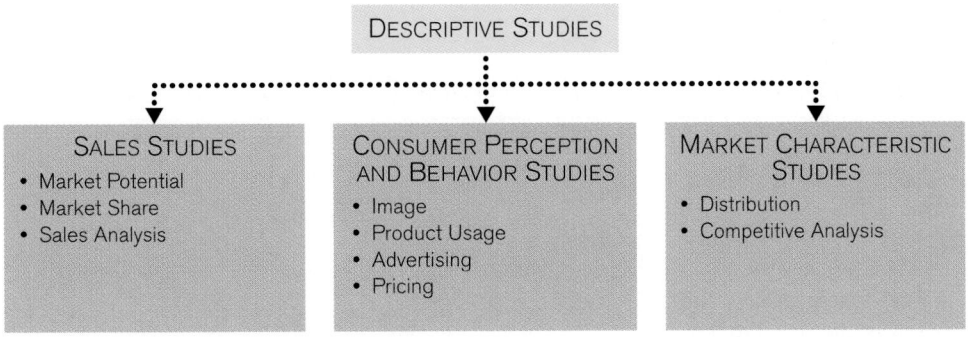

Figure 3.5
Major Types of Descriptive Studies

- Consumer perception and behavior studies include image studies, which determine consumer perceptions of the firm and its products; product usage studies, which describe consumption patterns; advertising studies, which describe media consumption habits and audience profiles for specific television programs and magazines; and pricing studies, which describe the range and frequency of price changes and probable consumer response to proposed price changes.

  Market characteristic studies include distribution studies, which determine traffic flow patterns and the number and location of distributors; and competitive analyses, which compare strengths and weaknesses of industry participants.

Say that Swatch would like to determine the size of the market for sports watches, at what rate the market is growing, and the market shares of the leading brands. It might do an analysis of its own sales of Swatch sport watches by type of outlet—jewelry stores, department stores, sporting-goods stores, specialty stores, catalog, Internet operations, and other outlets. The management might then ask: How do consumers perceive Swatch? Does the image of Swatch vary between owners and nonowners? Which TV programs do people who buy premium sports watches view? How much of a premium are consumers willing to pay for a high-quality sports watch? Swatch would have to undertake consumer perception and behavior studies to provide management with answers to these questions.

Market characteristic studies may examine questions about distributors or competitors, such as: How many distributors does Swatch have for each type of outlet, and how does this compare with other competing brands?

These examples demonstrate the range and diversity of descriptive research studies. Descriptive research also uses a variety of data collection techniques, which we discuss in the following chapters. They include

- Secondary data analyzed quantitatively (Chapters 4 and 5)
- **Surveys** (Interviews with a large number of respondents using a predesigned questionnaire) (Chapter 7)
- Panels (Chapters 5 and 7)
- Observational and other data (Chapter 7)

surveys
Interviews with a large number of respondents using a predesigned questionnaire.

The survey Spiegel conducted in the opening vignette is an example of descriptive research. Descriptive research using these methods can be further classified into cross-sectional and longitudinal research. (See Figure 3.4.)

BE a DM!

As the CEO of American Airlines how would you use information on the image of your airline versus major competitors to improve your competitive positioning?

BE an MR!

Visit the American Airlines Web site (www.americanairlines.com) and search the Internet using a search engine as well as your library's online databases to obtain information on the competitive positioning of American Airlines.

What type of exploratory and descriptive research would you undertake to determine the image of American Airlines versus its major competitors?

RESEARCH IN ACTION

Jergens Body Shampoo Washes Away Consumer Gripes

The Andrew Jergens Company (www.jergens.com) periodically conducts surveys to measure consumers' perceptions, attitudes, and use of soap bars and related personal-care products. A cross-sectional survey involving 600 mall intercept interviews in six major cities showed that many consumers had complaints about the standard soap bar: They didn't like having to pick a mushy bar out of the dish. They didn't like the nasty film it left in their shower or bath. They didn't like the way it dried out their skin. These findings led to the development of an innovative new product. Jergens Body Shampoo was designed to eliminate those woes by providing what the company calls "a creamy lather that rinses away easily for a clean that never felt so good." The product met with instant success upon introduction.

The company credits the product for revolutionizing its category, noting it has spawned more than 10 competitors. Jergens reports that the brand is the number-one seller among body shampoos in food stores and that it helped the category grow to over $500 million by 2004, almost a quarter of the soap category.[3]

Cross-Sectional Designs

cross-sectional design
A type of research design involving the one-time collection of information from any given sample of population elements.

A **cross-sectional design**, sometimes called a sample survey, can be thought of as a snapshot of the marketplace taken at a specific point in time. In this design, the selected group of respondents is measured only once. The cross-sectional survey is the most frequently used descriptive design in marketing research. Spiegel's survey of 1,000 customers is a cross-sectional design, and so is the Jergens Body Shampoo example above.

Longitudinal Designs

longitudinal design
A type of research design involving a fixed sample of population elements that is measured repeatedly on the same variables. The sample remains the same over time, providing a series of pictures, which portray both the situation and the changes that are taking place.

The typical cross-sectional design gives us a snapshot at a single point in time. In contrast, a **longitudinal design** provides a series of pictures, which track the changes that take place over time. In longitudinal designs, a fixed sample from the population is measured repeatedly on the same variables. In other words, two or more measurements on the same variables are obtained from a given group of respondents at different points in time (Figure 3.6). A cross-sectional design would be used to ask the question, "How did the American people rate the performance of George W. Bush immediately following his last

Figure 3.6
Cross-Sectional Versus Longitudinal Designs

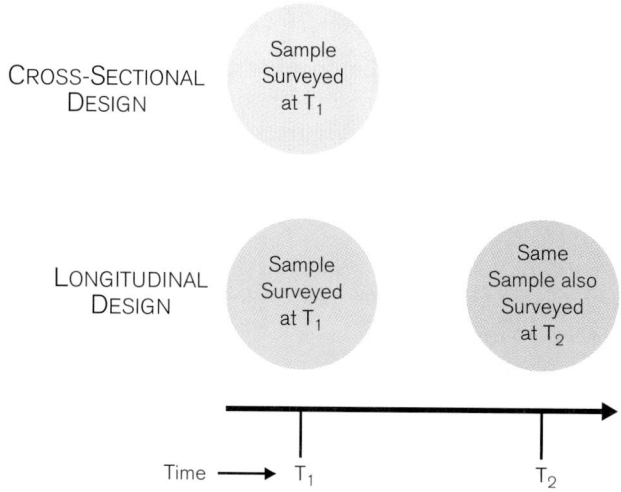

State of the Union address?" A longitudinal design would be used to address the question, "How did the American people change their view of Bush's performance before and after his last State of the Union address?"

Sometimes, the term *panel* is used interchangeably with the term *longitudinal design*. A **panel** consists of a sample of respondents, generally households that have agreed to provide information at specified intervals over an extended period. Because of the long-term commitment needed for participation on a panel, its members are compensated with gifts, coupons, information, or cash. Panel data are typically collected by commercial research organizations known as syndicated firms. The National Purchase Diary (NPD) is one such firm. The NPD tracks changes in consumer purchase patterns and then sells the data to other businesses or interested groups for a flat subscription price. The Mentadent example that follows illustrates longitudinal design. Panels are discussed in more detail in Chapters 5 and 7.

panel
A panel consists of a sample of respondents, generally households, that have agreed to provide information over an extended period.

Cross-Sectional Versus Longitudinal Designs

The relative advantages and disadvantages of longitudinal versus cross-sectional designs are summarized in Table 3.3. Since, in most situations the researcher is interested in obtaining a picture of the marketplace at one point in time, cross-sectional designs are far more commonly used than longitudinal designs. Cross-sectional studies cost less. It is relatively simple to select a representative sample, a group of respondents whose characteristics of interest are a reflection of the entire population. Since different respondents are selected each time a survey is conducted, bias due to the same set of respondents answering multiple surveys is eliminated.

A major advantage of longitudinal designs is the ability to detect change as a result of repeated measurements of the same variables on the same respondents. This is illustrated in the Mentadent example. Since the same individuals provide data on the same variables repeatedly, it is possible to compare the brand of mouthwash an individual purchases at any given time with the brand purchased in the preceding time period. Thus, we can determine whether an individual is engaging in repeat purchase or brand switching.

Panel research also has an advantage over cross-sectional research in terms of the amount of data that can be collected as well as the accuracy of that data. A typical cross-sectional survey requires recall of past purchases and behavior. Panel data, which rely on continuous recording of purchases in a diary, place less reliance on the respondent's memory. A comparison of panel and cross-sectional survey estimates of retail sales indicates that panel data give more accurate estimates.

RESEARCH IN ACTION

Mentadent Toothpaste and Mouthwash: Leveraging Brand Heritage

Longitudinal tracking studies using mail panels indicated that Mentadent toothpaste had developed strong brand loyalty: Many consumers were repeatedly purchasing Mentadent toothpaste. Given a loyal army of users, Chesebrough-Pond's saw an opportunity to leverage the Mentadent brand name. Thus, Mentadent mouthwash was introduced.

Its major selling appeal was that it was the first, and only, mouthwash with baking soda and peroxide. The company said the brand was able to build immediate awareness with strong advertising that capitalized on the successful campaign for Mentadent toothpaste. The introductory advertising campaign showed consumers using the Mentadent mouthwash after a relative recommended it. Chesebrough-Pond's also gave credit to the product's unique packaging: a dual-chambered bottle that not only keeps the reactive ingredients separate but also supports the brand's modern and innovative imagery.

The new product's purchases and repeat purchases were tracked via a mail panel. A sample of panel households provided information on purchases of toothpaste, mouthwash, and other oral hygiene products, every month, for a period of nine months. In its introductory year, Mentadent mouthwash achieved a 3.5 percent dollar share of the category. Analysis of the longitudinal data indicated that repeat purchases continued to build, growing to 39 percent at the end of the introductory year. Mentadent mouthwash has continued to maintain its competitive position through 2005.[4]

Table 3.3
Relative Advantages and Disadvantages of Longitudinal and Cross-Sectional Designs

Evaluation Criteria	Cross-Sectional Design	Longitudinal Design
Detecting change	−	+
Large amount of data collection	−	+
Accuracy	−	+
Representative sampling	+	−
Response bias	+	−

Note: A "+" indicates a relative advantage over the other design.
A "−" indicates a relative disadvantage.

The main disadvantage of panels is that they may not be representative of the population of interest. This may happen because of refusals to participate and because of high dropout rates for panel participants. Bias is also introduced when participants try to give the "right" answer or become bored or fatigued and make incomplete diary or Internet entries. In addition, longitudinal designs are more expensive to implement because of the expenses associated with maintaining a panel. In light of these limitations, longitudinal designs are used only when it is necessary to examine changes over time, such as in studies of repeat purchases, brand switching, and brand loyalty.

Causal Research

causal research
A type of conclusive research whose major objective is to obtain evidence regarding cause-and-effect (causal) relationships.

causal design
A type of conclusive research whose major objective is to obtain evidence regarding cause-and-effect (causal) relationships.

Like descriptive research, **causal research** requires a planned and structured design. Although descriptive research can determine the degree of association between variables, it is generally not very appropriate for examining causal relationships. Causal relations are those that involve cause-and-effect variables.

The hypothesis that a promotional campaign will lead to (cause) an increase in sales is an example. To examine this hypothesis, a researcher would need a **causal design**—a design in which the causal or independent variables are manipulated in a relatively controlled environment. A relatively controlled environment is one in which the other variables that may affect the dependent variable are controlled or checked as much as possible. The effect of this manipulation on one or more dependent variables is then measured to infer causality.

The main method of causal research is an experiment. Experiments can take place either in a laboratory or in a natural setting. An experiment can be designed to test the causal relationship that promotion causes brand sales. Here, the independent variable

EXPERIENTIAL LEARNING

Exploratory and Descriptive Research

Visit Gallup's Web site (www.gallup.com) and examine some of the recent projects conducted by Gallup. Read through some of the reports posted on this Web site.

What type of exploratory research was conducted in these projects? Which methods were used?

What type of descriptive research was conducted in these projects? Which methods were used?

In which project was the research design most appropriate? Why?

that will be manipulated is promotion and the dependent variable is brand sales. Variables other than promotion, which also affect sales, such as product quality, price, and distribution need to be controlled. Participants in a laboratory study may be told to imagine they are on a shopping trip. Various promotional offers, as manipulated by the researcher, will be displayed, with each group of respondents seeing only one offer. The purchases of the respondents in this simulated shopping experience would be measured and compared across groups. The experimenter creates and controls the setting so that product quality, price, and distribution are held constant. In a field experiment, the same study would occur in a natural setting, such as retail stores. Various promotional offers would be displayed in stores, with each group of respondents seeing only one offer. The resulting brand sales would be monitored.

In the opening vignette, Spiegel did not make use of causal research. However, it could have, for example, in testing three alternative depictions of its product lines in its catalog. Each of the three versions of the catalog could be mailed to a distinct group of customers. The purchases of Spiegel products by each group could be monitored and compared to determine the depiction that resulted in the highest sales. Causal research is appropriate for the following purposes, illustrated in the context of examining the effect of a promotional campaign on the sales of BMW cars:

1. **To understand which variables are the causes (independent variables) and which variables are the effects (dependent variables) of a phenomenon.** In other words, if an independent variable is manipulated, a change should be detected in the dependent variable. The independent variables will be the dollar amount spent on advertising and the dollar amount spent on sales promotion during a given time period. The dependent variable will be the sales of BMW (measured in units and dollars).
2. **To determine the extent of the relationship between the predicted effect and the causal variables.** The relationship between sales promotion and advertising expenditures and the sales of BMW is likely to be nonlinear: As more and more is spent on advertising, sales of BMW will increase less and less due to the saturation effect.

The implementation of a causal design is further illustrated by Microsoft's experiment with Windows XP.

In this experiment, the causal (independent) variable was the operating system, which was manipulated to have three levels: Windows XP, Windows 2000, and Windows NT. The effect (dependent) variables were ease of use, power, capabilities, and ability to

A causal design is needed for examining the effect of a promotional campaign on the sales of BMW cars.

RESEARCH IN ACTION

Windows XP: A Window to the Hearts of Computer Users

The key to the success (high awareness and high sales) of Windows XP (www.microsoft.com) was that the product was carefully designed and tested. In a controlled experiment, one group of computer users was asked to work with Windows XP. Two other carefully matched groups worked with the previous versions of Windows: one with Windows 2000 and the other with Windows NT. All three groups rated the operating system on ease of use, power, capabilities, and the ability to enhance a computer user's experience. Windows XP was rated significantly better than the previous versions on all factors, leading to the introduction of this operating system.[5]

enhance a computer user's experience. The influence of the user's background was controlled by carefully matching the three groups on relevant demographic and computer-usage characteristics.

Due to its complexity and importance, the topic of causal designs and experimental research will be fully explained in a separate chapter (Chapter 8). In that chapter, we discuss the conditions for causality, validity in experimentation, and specific types of experimental designs.

BE a DM!

As the advertising manager, how would you determine whether the advertising budget for Taco Bell for the next year should be increased, decreased, or remain the same as the current budget?

BE an MR!

Visit Taco Bell's Web site (www.tacobell.com) and search the Internet using a search engine as well as your library's online databases to obtain information on the advertising for Taco Bell. Write a brief report.

Design an experiment to determine whether the advertising budget for Taco Bell for the next year should be increased, decreased, or remain the same as the current budget. Identify the independent, dependent, and control variables.

Relationships Among Exploratory, Descriptive, and Causal Research

While the preceding example distinguished causal research from other types of research and showed the benefits of causal research, causal research should not be viewed in isolation. Rather, exploratory, descriptive, and causal designs should be used to complement each other. A given problem may lend itself to exploratory, descriptive, or causal research. Consider the loss of market share.

Exploratory Research:	Why are we losing market share?
Descriptive Research:	How do consumers evaluate our brand compared to competing brands?
Causal Research:	By how much will our sales increase if we decrease the price by 5%, 10%, and 15%?

As mentioned earlier, a given project may incorporate more than one basic research design, depending on the nature of the problem and the approach. We offer the following general guidelines for choosing research designs:

1. When little is known about the problem situation, it is desirable to begin with exploratory research. For example, exploratory research is suitable for generating alternative courses of action, research questions, or hypotheses. Exploratory research can then be followed by descriptive or causal research, as in the Spiegel vignette [Figure 3.7(a)].
2. It is not necessary to begin every research design with exploratory research. If the researcher has a good understanding of the problem situation, descriptive or

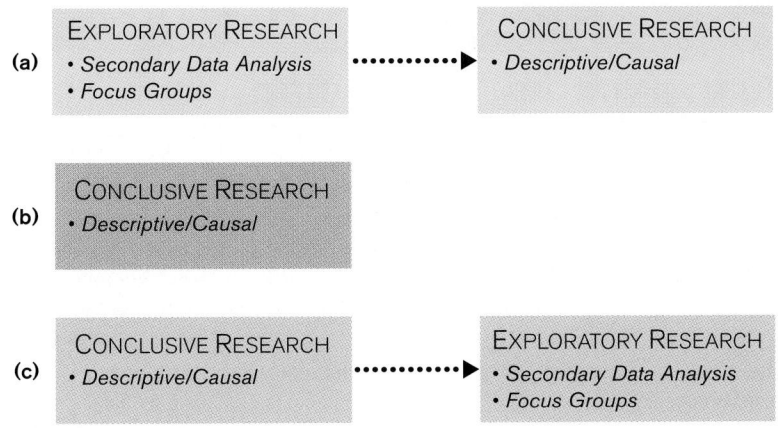

Figure 3.7
Some Alternative Research Designs

causal research may be a more appropriate initial step [see Figure 3.7(b)]. Annual consumer-satisfaction surveys are an example of research that does not need to begin with or include an exploratory phase.

3. Exploratory research can be used at any point in a study. For example, when descriptive or causal research leads to results that are unexpected or difficult to interpret, the researcher may turn to exploratory research for insight [Figure 3.7(c)].

Suppose an image study is conducted for a supermarket chain such as Kroger to identify its strengths and weaknesses relative to competing supermarkets. Exploratory research, including secondary data analysis and focus groups, is first conducted to define the problem and develop a suitable approach. This is followed by a descriptive study consisting of a survey in which a questionnaire is constructed and administered by telephone interviews.

Suppose the image study is to be repeated after two years to determine if any changes had taken place. At that point, exploratory research would probably be unnecessary, and the research design could begin with the descriptive study.

Assume that the survey is repeated two years later and that some unexpected findings are obtained. Kroger management wonders why its supermarkets' ratings on in-store service have declined when the supermarket staff has increased. Exploratory research in the form of focus groups might be undertaken to probe these unexpected findings. The focus groups might reveal that although the store clerks are present, they are not very helpful. This would suggest the need for training the store clerks.

This example illustrates how exploratory and descriptive research can be integrated. Exploratory and descriptive designs are frequently used in commercial marketing research; causal research is not as popular. Many descriptive studies use quantitative secondary data, which we describe in Chapters 4 and 5; surveys, which are discussed in Chapter 7; and panels, which are discussed in Chapters 5 and 7. The use of the Internet for causal research designs is discussed in Chapter 8. The Internet, in its capacity as a source of information, can be useful in uncovering secondary data and collecting primary data needed in conclusive research, as illustrated by E-Valuations.com.

BE an MR!

Visit Wells Fargo's Web site (www.wellsfargo.com) and search the Internet using a search engine as well as your library's online databases to obtain information on consumers' attitudes towards online banking.

The Wells Fargo bank would like to determine consumers' attitudes towards online banking and hopes to repeat this project annually. Which type of research design would you implement and why?

BE a DM!

As the CEO of Wells Fargo, how would you use information about consumers' attitudes towards online banking to improve the competitiveness of your bank?

RESEARCH IN ACTION

E-Valuations.com: Enhancing Value Through Online Marketing Research

E-Valuations.com (www.e-valuations.com), based in Seattle, is a full-service marketing research firm specializing in online marketing research services. E-Valuations.com manages a research site called Questions.net. Questions.net assembles groups of willing research participants by offering them incentives to answer survey questions. Participants are selected from a target group defined by the client, and are best suited for providing the specific information required. E-Valuations.com uses a variety of electronic options when conducting exploratory research, including newsgroup discussions and electronic focus groups. Conclusive research is conducted mainly by using Internet surveys posted at its Web site. The company has conducted exploratory and conclusive research for a wide range of clients and has helped them make successful marketing decisions.

Tasks Involved in Formulating a Research Design

In formulating a research design, typically the researcher must perform the following tasks (Figure 3.8):

1. Specify the information needed (Chapter 2).
2. Design the exploratory, descriptive, and/or causal phases of the research (Chapters 4–8).
3. Specify the measurement and scaling procedures (Chapters 9 and 10).
4. Construct and pretest a questionnaire (interview form) or an appropriate form for data collection (Chapter 11).
5. Specify the sampling process and sample size (Chapters 12 and 13).
6. Develop a plan of data analysis (Chapter 15).

Figure 3.8

Tasks Involved in a Research Design

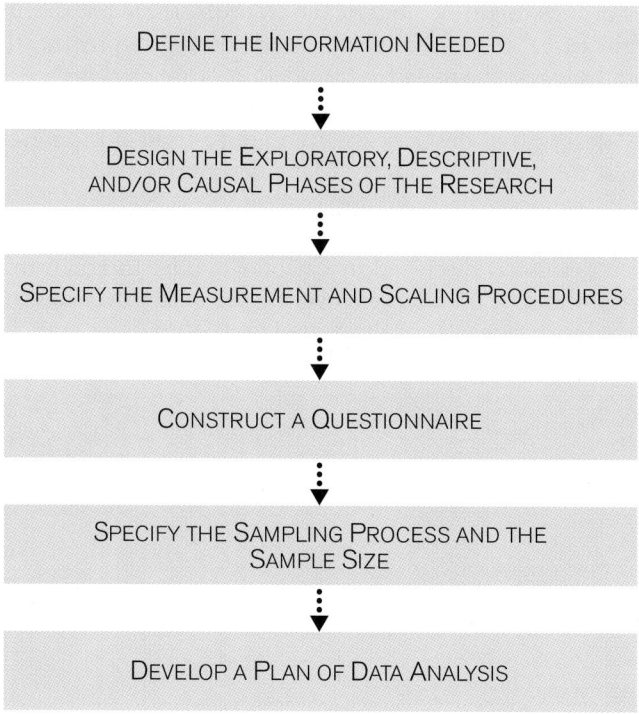

Chapter 2 describes how to specify the necessary information. As noted, we will discuss in detail the rest of the tasks involved in a research design in subsequent chapters.

Research Design and the Value of Marketing Research

Research is conducted to help reduce management error in decision making. The key word here is *reduce.* Research is not designed to "prove" assumptions, but rather to provide management with an assessment of the degree of risk associated with making decisions based on tested assumptions. As the cost of making the wrong decision increases, typically the formality and structure of a study design increases as well. The research design has a major impact on the cost and value of the marketing research project. Ultimately, the cost of any project must be weighted against the reduced risk of making the decision with additional information.

Before committing funds to a study, management must assess, either formally or informally, the value of the additional information obtained by marketing research. For example, suppose the brand manager for Cap'n Crunch cereal is faced with a proposal to spend $50,000 to conduct a causal study regarding the effect of using various promotional offers. The manager must decide whether or not the value of a decision based on current knowledge could be improved by more than $50,000 with the help of research. If the various promotional offers involved couponing versus free trials, the difference in expenses associated with the two approaches (not to mention the difference in consumer response) could far exceed the $50,000 cost of research. In that case, the high cost of making the wrong decision makes it easier to justify the cost of the research.

The information value of research must also be discounted by the degree of error inherent in a study. No research design, no matter how sophisticated, can eliminate all risk from a decision because no research is completely error-free. Several potential sources of error can affect a research design. Estimating the level of error in a study is complicated by the fact that, typically, only random sampling error is quantified. A **random sampling error** is an error resulting from the particular sample selected being an imperfect representation of the population of interest. Total error is made up of both sampling and nonsampling errors. In formulating the research design, the researcher should attempt to control the total error, not just the sampling error.

random sampling error
The error due to the particular sample selected being an imperfect representation of the population of interest.

Nonsampling errors, as would be expected, can be attributed to sources other than sampling. They result from a variety of causes, including errors in problem definition, approach, scales, questionnaire design, survey methods, interviewing techniques, and data preparation and analysis. These nonsampling errors can be attributed to the researcher, the interviewer, or the respondent. A good research design attempts to control the various sources of error, as illustrated in the opening vignette, where Spiegel made an effort to control the sampling and nonsampling errors. Random sampling errors were controlled by having a large sample (1,000) that was randomly selected. Spiegel also controlled various sources of nonsampling errors, including interviewer and respondent errors, by careful selection, training, and supervision of the interviewers. These errors are discussed in great detail in subsequent chapters.

nonsampling error
Errors that can be attributed to sources other than sampling; they can be random or nonrandom.

Budgeting and Scheduling the Project

Once a research design has been specified, the researcher should prepare a detailed budget and schedule. **Budgeting and scheduling** help to ensure that the marketing research project is completed with the available resources: financial, time, personnel, and others. The budget process allows the researcher and the decision maker to compare the estimated value of the information with the projected costs. Additionally, the project schedule will help ensure that the information is obtained in time to address the management-decision problem.

budgeting and scheduling
Management tools needed to help ensure that the marketing research project is completed within the available resources.

Marketing Research Proposal

marketing research proposal
Contains the essence of the project and serves as a contract between the researcher and management.

Once the research design has been formulated, and budgeting and scheduling of the project has been accomplished, the researcher should prepare a written research proposal. The **marketing research proposal** contains the essence of the project and serves as a contract between the researcher and management. The proposal covers all phases of the marketing research process, including cost and time schedules. The format of a research proposal may vary considerably depending on the nature of the problem and the relationship of the client to the research supplier. Most proposals present a detailed research design and contain some or all of the following elements:

1. **Executive Summary.** The proposal should begin with an overview of the entire proposal, a summary of the major points from each of the other sections.
2. **Background.** The background to the problem, including the environmental context, should be described.
3. **Problem Definition/Research Objectives.** Normally, a statement of the problem should be presented. If this statement has not been developed (as in the case of exploratory research), the objectives of the marketing research project should be clearly specified.
4. **Approach to the Problem.** A review of the relevant academic and trade literature, along with some kind of an analytical model, should be included. If research questions and hypotheses have been identified, these should be included in the proposal.
5. **Research Design.** The type of research design, whether exploratory, descriptive, causal, or a combination, should be specified. Information should be provided on the following components: (a) kind of information to be obtained, (b) method of administering the questionnaire (mail, telephone, personal, or electronic interviews), (c) scaling techniques, (d) nature of the questionnaire (i.e., type of questions asked, length, average interviewing time), and (e) sampling plan and sample size. This section often forms the heart of the proposal.
6. **Field Work/Data Collection.** The proposal should discuss how the data will be collected and who will collect it. If the fieldwork is to be subcontracted to another supplier, this should be stated. Control mechanisms to ensure the quality of data collected should be described.
7. **Data Analysis.** The kind of data analysis that will be conducted, and how the results will be interpreted, should be described.
8. **Reporting.** The proposal should specify the nature and number of intermediate reports. The form of the final report, including whether a formal presentation of the results will be made, should also be stated. Industry professionals refer to this part of the report as the "deliverables." The proposal writer must specify what information (specifically, which documents) will be given to the client. Sometimes, the client will want a formal report that is more comprehensive and narrative than the PowerPoint presentation and discussion that may cover many projects. At the least, an executive summary of one to two single-spaced pages should be provided to explain what insights have been gained by the research and what these results mean for the client firm's managers.
9. **Information Investment and Time.** The cost of the project and a time schedule, broken down by phases, should be presented. A payment schedule should also be worked out in advance, especially for large projects. Conventional industry practice would have the project paid in three parts: the first one due after the proposal is accepted, the second due at the project midpoint, and the third due at the conclusion of the project. The time schedule developed for the proposal becomes an important coordinating document between the client and the research agency as the project is conducted.
10. **Project Personnel.** All personnel who will be working on the project should be identified. The job, time duration, responsibility, and authority of each person should be stated.

EXPERIENTIAL LEARNING

Crafting a Research Proposal

Go to the textbook Web site, select "Chapter 3" and download the following file: Meteor Proposal.doc. Meteor Motorcycle Company is one of the industry's leading manufacturers of customized, high-performance bikes in the heavyweight-cruiser class. It is one of the only custom motorcycle makers equipped with full-service design, engineering, manufacturing, paint, polishing and administrative teams.

The company has four different kinds of bikes under production. They are all individually branded under Meteor X, Meteor Y, Meteor Z, and the Comet Chopper brand names, and represent the company's varied product offerings, ranging in price from $23,000 to $100,000 or more. The company has seen a tremendous growth from approximately 27 bikes sold in 2000 to an impressive 2,700 in the year 2004. Comet Chopper, the brainchild of Jeff Branson, the creative force behind Meteor, currently accounts for nearly 55 percent of the annual company sales at approximately $70 million.

1. Open Meteor Proposal.doc and read about an actual study done for one of the exciting heavyweight cruiser motorcycle companies. The names have been changed here. How well does this proposal correspond to the recommendations about proposals just discussed?

If you were the head of the marketing team for the Meteor Motorcycle Company, what would you like to be made clearer in this proposal?

11. **Appendixes.** Any statistical or other information that is of interest to only a few people should be presented in appendixes.

The research proposal represents the contract between management and the researcher. It ensures that there is agreement regarding the objectives of the project, and it helps sell the project to management. Therefore, a research proposal should always be prepared, even when repeating a project for a previous client.

Summary Illustration Using the Opening Vignette

The research design in the opening vignette described how a project was conducted for Spiegel. Research designs may be broadly classified as exploratory or conclusive, while conclusive research may be either descriptive or causal. Typically, the project begins with exploratory research, which is followed by descriptive (or causal) research. As seen in the opening vignette, in order to understand the problem situation, Spiegel analyzed secondary data and conducted 10 focus groups. This exploratory research helped Spiegel to identify and understand the unique aspects of the shopping behavior and clothing needs of its customers. The findings of exploratory research were treated as tentative and were further verified by descriptive research consisting of telephone interviews with a randomly selected sample of 1,000 customers.

Typically, as in the case of Spiegel, a research project begins with exploratory research. However, other combinations of the basic designs are possible. Exploratory research may be conducted at any point in the project or may not be undertaken at all. A well-formulated research design will attempt to control the random sampling as well as the nonsampling errors, as in the opening vignette. A large and randomly selected sample was used to measure and control random sampling error. Efforts were also made to control the various sources of nonsampling error. For example, the interviewers were carefully selected and thoroughly trained, and close supervision was exercised to minimize interviewing errors attributed to the interviewers and respondents.

International Marketing Research

The various methods associated with implementing each step of the research design discussed in this chapter must be reassessed within the context of cultural differences before they can be used internationally. Given environmental and cultural differences, a research design appropriate for one country may not be suitable for another. Consider the problem of determining household attitudes toward major appliances in the United States and Saudi Arabia. When conducting exploratory research in the United States, it is appropriate to conduct focus groups jointly with male and female heads of household. It would not be appropriate to conduct such focus groups in Saudi Arabia. As a result of their traditional culture, wives are unlikely to participate freely in the presence of their husbands. It would be more useful to conduct one-on-one in-depth interviews with both male and female heads of households included in the sample. Procter & Gamble (P&G) encountered a similar situation in Japan.

In developing countries, there are no consumer panels, which makes it difficult to conduct descriptive longitudinal research. In many countries, such as Sierra Leone in Africa, the marketing support infrastructure—retailing, wholesaling, advertising, and promotion development—is often lacking, which makes it difficult to implement a causal design involving a field experiment. In formulating a research design, considerable effort is required to ensure the equivalence and comparability of secondary and primary data obtained from different countries. In the context of collecting primary data, qualitative

RESEARCH IN ACTION

P&G: Exploring and Wooing Japanese Women

The consumer market in Japan is one of the toughest, most competitive, fastest moving markets in the world. Japan represents the cutting edge of worldwide technology in many product categories. When P&G started business in Japan, it conducted a detailed study of market characteristics and market profile. The target market for P&G was homemakers, who were largely responsible for the consumption of several products, such as diapers, household cleaners, soaps, and detergents. Exploratory research followed by descriptive research was undertaken for this purpose. While focus groups are most popular in the United States, one-on-one, in-depth interviews were preferred because of the Japanese cultural tendency to not disagree openly in group settings. The descriptive surveys were fielded using in-home personal interviews.

Results showed that the average Japanese homemaker was uncompromising in her demands for high quality, value, and service. She was a paragon of conservation and efficiency in the management of the household. About half the adult women in Japan were employed, but they generally worked outside of the home only before marriage and after their children were raised. Child rearing was the number-one priority for Japanese mothers.

When it came to foreign versus domestic brands, Japanese women preferred foreign name-brand products that had style and status, such as fashionable clothing, French perfumes, wines, liquors, and designer bags. They did not prefer functional products made in foreign countries since these products usually did not meet their exacting and demanding standards.

Japanese women greatly preferred commercials that conserved traditional social and family values and roles, rather than the typical Western examples. P&G made a few mistakes initially in misjudging nuances of the Japanese culture before this study was conducted. For example, the introduction of Camay bath soap and Pampers diapers were supported with Western-style advertising that was not well received by Japanese women. However, based on the market profile study, the advertising was changed to stress traditional social and family values, thereby increasing its effectiveness.[6]

research, survey methods, scaling techniques, questionnaire design, and sampling considerations are particularly important. We discuss these topics in more detail in subsequent chapters.

BE an MR!

Visit Unilever's Web site (www.unilever.com) and search the Internet using a search engine as well as your library's online databases to find information on consumer preferences for bathing soaps.

Unilever, PLC would like to determine consumer preferences for Lux bath soap in the United States, United Kingdom, and India. Discuss the similarities and differences in the research design that should be adopted in each country.

BE a DM!

As the global marketing manager for Unilever, PLC how would you use information on consumer preferences for Lux in the United States, United Kingdom, and India to formulate the marketing strategy for the brand in each of these countries.

Technology and Marketing Research

"Smart" products have been around for years. Coffee makers and VCRs can be told when to perform their respective duties. Automobiles tell the driver when the lights have been left on or when the door is not fully closed. In the very near future, these products, and others, will become even more "intelligent." Networking subsystems, both hardware and software, will soon be embedded into numerous products, giving them the ability to "talk" and to remember.[7]

These networking subsystems could be added to the production process for new products or easily added to existing products. The necessary technology already exists; it is just a matter of applying it. When triggered, or turned on, by a preprogrammed event, the product would "speak" with the user and record the conversation. The conversation (or data) could then be transmitted to the producer instantly or stored and gathered in batches and transmitted at a later date. Dell Computers uses software installed at the factory to periodically run diagnostic tests on Dell PCs and inform Dell of the status of the PCs via the Internet. This feature becomes valuable during troubleshooting of equipment malfunctions, and also provides useful information for product design. Such data can also be invaluable to marketing managers. Smart products could be used to collect not only exploratory data, but also cross-sectional or longitudinal descriptive data.

In some form, these subsystems are already proving very useful to companies, including software developers such as Microsoft. When added to a software application like Microsoft Office, they are programmed to activate when the user encounters an error message. After interacting with the user, the subsystem stores all the relevant data. Then, the developer can determine what happened and what could be done to prevent that error from recurring. Any user observations or opinions can also be stored for analysis. This information assists Microsoft when producing new products or upgrading versions of Microsoft Office.

Ethics in Marketing Research

The choice of a research design has ethical overtones for both the client and the research firm. For example, if Maxwell House is interested in examining brand switching in coffee purchases, a longitudinal design is the only appropriate way to assess changes in an individual respondent's choice of coffee brands. A research firm that justifies the use of a cross-sectional design simply because it has no experience in conducting longitudinal studies is behaving unethically.

Researchers must ensure that the research design will provide the information needed to address the marketing research problem. The client should have the integrity not to misrepresent the project, should describe the constraints under which the researcher

RESEARCH IN ACTION

Just Business Versus Unethical Concessions

Ethical dilemmas may arise due to the strong desire of marketing research firms to become suppliers to large business firms who are heavy users of marketing research. For example, Visa, Delta Airlines, Coca-Cola, and Ford Motor Company have large marketing research budgets and regularly hire external marketing research suppliers. These large clients can manipulate the price for the current study or demand unreasonable concessions in the research design (e.g., more focus groups, a larger sample, or additional data analyses) by suggesting the potential for the marketing research firm to become a regular supplier. This may be considered just business, but it becomes unethical when there is no intention to follow up with a larger study or to use the research firm in the future. Marketing research firms should be aware of such unethical practices and must discern the intent of the client firms before offering concessions to gain future business.[8]

must operate, and should not make unreasonable demands. If customer contact has to be restricted, or if time is an issue, the client should make these constraints known at the start of the project. It would be unethical for a client to extract details from a proposal submitted by one research firm and pass them to another who actually would do the project for the client. A proposal is the property of the research firm that prepared it, unless the client has paid for it. The client should not take advantage of the research firm by making false promises of future research contracts in order to solicit concessions for the current project, as illustrated in the Just Business Versus Unethical Concessions example.

Equally important, responsibilities to respondents must not be overlooked. The researcher should design the study so as not to violate the respondents' right to safety, privacy, or choice. Furthermore, the client must not violate the anonymity of the respondents. (Respondent-related issues are discussed in more detail in Chapters 4, 5, 6, and 7).

WHAT WOULD *YOU* DO?

NASCAR: Changing the Southern Image

The Situation

The sound of engines roaring, the voices of screaming fans, the beating of hearts pumping ... the excitement of NASCAR! The National Association of Stock Car Auto Racing (NASCAR) is a company unlike any other. While it does generate excitement in fans across the nation, NASCAR has been stereotyped as only appealing to Southerners with lower incomes that work in laborer-type jobs. Mike Helton, CEO of NASCAR, wanted to increase its audience and make over its stereotyped image.

NASCAR conducted exploratory research to identify ways to penetrate the nonrace market, reach younger fans, and build its brand image across the nation. Extensive focus groups revealed that: (1) NASCAR had a rural sports image, (2) this image was not necessarily negative, and (3) companies that supported sports were viewed positively.

The Marketing Research Decision

1. Do you think the research design adopted by NASCAR was appropriate? Why or why not?
2. Which one of the following research designs would you recommend?
   a. Exploratory research: focus groups
   b. Exploratory research: in-depth interviews
   c. Exploratory research followed by a descriptive survey

d. Exploratory research followed by causal research
e. Descriptive survey followed by exploratory research

3. Discuss the role of the type of research design you recommend in enabling Mike Helton to change the image of NASCAR.

The Marketing Management Decision

1. Mike Helton realizes that it is crucial for NASCAR to project the right image. However, he wonders what that image is. Is it (check as many as are applicable):
   a. A rural sports image
   b. An urban sports image
   c. Southern heritage
   d. Blue-collar sports
   e. A national sport for all lifestyles
2. Discuss how the course of action you recommend to Mike Helton is influenced by the research that you suggested earlier and by the findings of that research.

What Mike Helton Did

Mike Helton attempted to position NASCAR as a national sport for all lifestyles. He took several initiatives to involve minorities in the sport, which was expanded both by Nextel's national sponsorship in 2004 and by moving races from the South to speedways across the country. NASCAR also targeted the nontraditional demographic segments, including families, children, and minorities. To further reinforce the national image, Mike Helton appointed nonsoutherners to key positions in the company.[9]

Summary

A research design is the roadmap for conducting the marketing research project. It specifies the details of how the project should be conducted. Research designs may be broadly classified as exploratory or conclusive. The primary purpose of exploratory research is to provide insights into the problem. Conclusive research is used to test hypotheses and examine specific relationships. Conclusive research may be either descriptive or causal and is used as input into managerial decision making.

The major objective of descriptive research is to describe market characteristics or functions. Descriptive research can be further classified into cross-sectional and longitudinal designs. Cross-sectional designs involve the collection of information from a sample drawn from a population at a single point in time. In contrast, longitudinal designs entail repeated measurements on a fixed sample at different points in time. Causal research is designed to obtain evidence about cause-and-effect (causal) relationships via an experiment.

In evaluating a research proposal, management must discount the value of the information by the level of error inherent in the study. Error can be associated with any of the six components of the research design. Managers should prepare a written marketing research proposal that includes all the elements of the marketing research process.

The various methods associated with implementing each step of the research design must be reassessed within the context of cultural differences before they can be used internationally. Technology and the Internet can facilitate the implementation of exploratory, descriptive, or causal research. In addition to ethical aspects that concern researcher and client, the rights of respondents must be respected when formulating the research design.

Key Terms and Concepts

Research design, 71
Exploratory research, 72
Conclusive research, 73
Descriptive research, 76
Surveys, 77
Cross-sectional design, 78
Longitudinal design, 78
Panel, 79
Causal research, 80
Causal design, 80
Random sampling error, 85
Nonsampling error, 85
Budgeting and scheduling, 85
Marketing research proposal, 86

Suggested Cases and Video Cases

Cases

2.1 Maxfli **2.5 Burger King** **4.1 Boeing** **4.2 Gucci**

Video Cases

3.2 Honest Tea **4.1 Subaru** **4.2 Marriott**

Additional cases and video cases are available in the Instructor's Manual and on the instructor and student Web sites.

Live Research: Conducting a Marketing Research Project

1. Each team should present to the class the type of research design they think is appropriate. Normally, the teams will end up with similar research designs, unless they are working on different projects.
2. As a class, discuss and select the research design for this project.
3. It is helpful to invite the client to this session.
4. Prepare a formal proposal, as described in this chapter, and obtain client approval.

Acronyms

The components of a research design may be summarized by the acronym DESIGN:

D ata analysis plan
E xploratory, descriptive, causal design
S caling and measurement
I nterviewing forms: questionnaire design
G enerating the needed information
N umber: sample size and plan

Review Questions

1. Define *research design* in your own words.
2. How does formulating a research design differ from developing an approach to a problem?
3. Differentiate between exploratory and conclusive research.
4. What are the major purposes for which descriptive research is conducted?
5. Compare and contrast cross-sectional and longitudinal designs.
6. Discuss the advantages and disadvantages of panels.
7. What is a causal research design? What is its purpose?
8. What is the relationship between exploratory, descriptive, and causal research?
9. List the major components of a research design.

Applied Problems

1. Sweet Cookies is planning to launch a new line of cookies and wants to assess the market size. The cookies have a mixed chocolate-pineapple flavor and will be targeted at the premium end of the market. Discuss the type of research design that may be used.
2. Welcome, Inc. is a chain of fast-food restaurants located in major metropolitan areas in the South. Sales have been growing very slowly for the last two years. Management has decided to add some new items to the menu; however, first they want to know more about their customers and their preferences.
   a. List two hypotheses.
   b. What kind of research design is appropriate? Why?
3. Visit the Greenfield Online Research Center (www.greenfieldonline.com).

a. What are the surveys currently being conducted by Greenfield?
b. How are the respondents being recruited for these surveys?
c. Discuss the different type of errors likely to arise given the way the respondents are being recruited.

4. Visit the Web page of three of the marketing research firms listed in Table 1.1. What types of research designs have these firms implemented recently?
5. You are conducting an image study for Carnival Cruise Lines. As part of exploratory research, analyze the messages posted to the newsgroup: rec.travel.cruises to determine the factors that consumers use in evaluating cruise companies. This newsgroup can be located at the Google Group Web site (www.groups.google.com).

Group Discussion

1. Discuss the following statement: "If the research budget is limited, exploratory research can be dispensed with."
2. Discuss the following statement: "The researcher should always attempt to develop an optimal design for every marketing research project."
3. "There are many potential sources of error in a research project. It is impossible to control all of them. Hence, marketing research contains many errors and we cannot be confident of the findings." Discuss these statements as a group. Did your group arrive at a consensus?

SUNDAY

October 24, 2004
www.vindy.com

SERVING THE MAHONING AND SHENANGO VALLEYS SINCE 1869

The Vindicator

$

SPORTS

OSU ends skid; YSU falls again

▸ **OHIO STATE** snapped its three-game losing streak with a 30-7 homecoming win over Indiana. Youngstown State wasn't so fortunate, losing 30-24 at Illinois State.

PAGE C1

LOCAL

For a better life

▸ **FOR THE PAST** five years, a computer and specialized button affixed to the wheelchair have made life easier for 12-year-old Justin Malovec of Poland Township.

PAGE B1

Trick-or-treat hours

▸ **TRICK-OR-TREAT** days and hours for communities in the region are listed.

PAGE B2

LIFE&WORK

Body language

▸ **WHY** do we respond certain ways when people get close (or don't)? There's a science

MAHONING VALLEY SCHOOLS

The Vindicator/Bruce Palmer

SCHOOL DAYS: Kayla Theisler, a third-grader from Coitsville, works on a problem in Theresa Iuoiciani's class at Lowellville Elementary. Kayla is one of about 200 pupils from outside Lowellville who attend Lowellville schools through open enrollment. Her father, Jim, waited in line outside the board of education offices to fill out an open enrollment application for her.

MAHONING VALLEY

Force takes on toughest crimes

The leader of the task force is concerned about renewal of a sales tax in Mahoning County.

By PATRICIA MEADE
VINDICATOR CRIME REPORTER

Magnuson

YOUNGSTOWN — You'll find drugs connected to almost every crime — whether you live in a rural farming community, a city fallen on hard times or a township rich with development, says a task force leader.

"If you look at burglaries, thefts, robberies and homicides, the underlying cause is probably drugs," said Bob Magnuson, commander of the Mahoning Valley Law Enforcement Task Force. "No individual [po-

CHAPTER

4

Exploratory Research Design: Secondary Data

"Open source information–also called secondary data–is the foundation for any competitive intelligence effort and can be very significant if properly analyzed."

PAUL DISHMAN, *President, Society of Competitive Intelligence Professionals (SCIP), 2002 to 2003*

OPENING QUESTIONS

1. Why are secondary data important? How do we distinguish secondary data from primary data?
2. What are the advantages and disadvantages of secondary data?
3. How should secondary data be evaluated to determine their usefulness?
4. What are the different sources of secondary data, including internal sources and external sources?
5. What is database marketing? How does it make use of secondary data?
6. How can published secondary data be classified?
7. How can computerized databases be classified?
8. How do we identify and classify the sources of secondary data useful in international marketing research?
9. What is the impact of technology and what ethical issues are involved in the use of secondary data?

Secondary Data Vindicate the *Vindicator!*

The *Vindicator* (www.vindy.com or www.vindicator.com), a medium-sized Youngstown, Ohio, newspaper, wanted to increase its revenues from advertising. Management set forth a one-year goal for its 14 retail and 4 classified salespeople to substantially raise the number of advertisers and thus total ad revenue. To be able to increase ad revenues, the sales force needed to pinpoint what specifically could help them recruit more advertisers to the newspaper or increase the amount that existing advertisers were spending. From past experience, many on the sales force knew that to recruit advertisers required proving to these advertisers, with hard facts, that their money spent in the *Vindicator* would be an excellent investment. For this purpose, the internally available data routinely collected by the *Vindicator* on the number of customers, duration of subscription, renewals/nonrenewals, and so forth would not be sufficient. Additional data would have to be obtained by conducting marketing research.

In this case, the *Vindicator* decided that it needed information on the potential in advertising readership and how these numbers compared to the potential of other advertising media that the advertisers could use instead of the *Vindicator.* While the sales force could commission marketing research to obtain primary data, such a project would be quite expensive and time-consuming. Hence, that course of action was not taken. Instead, the *Vindicator* decided to search for secondary research that could be used to obtain the answers they sought. Because the *Vindicator* is a medium-sized newspaper with limited staff resources, they turned to an outside supplier. Inland Research Corp., a small company in Erie, Pennsylvania, was commissioned to conduct a secondary research study.

The Inland Research Corp. compiles data developed from interviews from about 40 different sources. Half of their data comes from general business sources, such as the Audit Bureau of Circulations (www.accessabc.com), and the other half comes from state and federal agencies, such as the U.S. Census Bureau (www.census.gov) and the Bureau of Labor Statistics (www.bls.gov). In addition to printed publications, Inland Research also searches several online and Internet databases. Inland Research evaluates

The Vindicator

MAHONING VALLEY SCHOOLS

MAHONING VALLEY

Force takes on toughest crimes

funds go with pupils
ss district boundaries

FUNDING THE FUTURE

ABOUT THE SERIES

TERRORISM

all secondary data by examining the methodology, accuracy, timeliness, and nature of the data. Only data from dependable sources are used.

Inland Research receives requests for data from its clients who need to solve a specific problem they face. Inland Research then begins an exhaustive search through its data warehouse to obtain information that is pertinent to the clients' needs. In about 4 to 6 weeks, the corporation produces reports addressing the clients' problems. In the case of smaller firms like the *Vindicator,* this represents a fraction of the time it would take for the client to do the research in-house. Inland's biggest selling point is the low price they charge for their research services. The prices range from $3,595 for a newspaper with circulation up to 14,900 to $8,445 for a newspaper with circulation of 60,000 or more. According to Inland Research President and CEO Jerry Szorek, "No other company produces similar reports for newspapers," which makes the information they provide to firms like the *Vindicator* extremely valuable.

For the *Vindicator,* Inland Research focused on obtaining data reports on topics such as the amount of advertising effectiveness and penetration for different forms of media. For example, information like data on the relationship between advertising frequency in different media and the resulting effectiveness were collected. Using Inland Research results and secondary data available internally within the organization, the *Vindicator* sales representatives were able to persuade some current advertisers to increase the frequency at which their ads were run. They accomplished this in a number of ways utilizing the Inland reports. For instance, one Inland chart demonstrated that advertisement readership grows from 53.5 percent with one ad per week to 81.3 percent with five ads per week. This gave advertisers a reason to increase the frequency of advertising.

In attempting to wean advertisers' dollars away from radio, the *Vindicator* sales representatives were able to use Inland data indicating that each of the city's seven biggest radio stations had fewer than 8,000 listeners during an average quarter hour whereas internal secondary data showed that the *Vindicator* had a circulation of 200,000. To reduce advertising spending on TV, the reps used the following statistics on viewer activity during commercials: 33.6 percent got up and left the viewing room, 29.6 percent talked with others, 9.2 percent switched channels, and 5.9 percent muted the set. It was discovered that only 21.7 percent listened to the TV commercial. Such selling tactics by the sales force were successful. Thus, the *Vindicator* management discovered that using secondary research during sales calls strengthened the sales pitches with hard data that could sway advertisers toward spending more on print advertising.[1] •

Overview

As mentioned in Chapter 2, analysis of secondary data helps to first define the marketing research problem and then to develop an approach to that problem. Also, as part of formulating the research design (Chapter 3), the researcher should analyze the relevant secondary data, as illustrated by the *Vindicator* vignette. The relationship of secondary data to the research issues presented in the previous chapters is shown in Figure 4.1. This chapter discusses the distinction between primary and secondary data as well as the

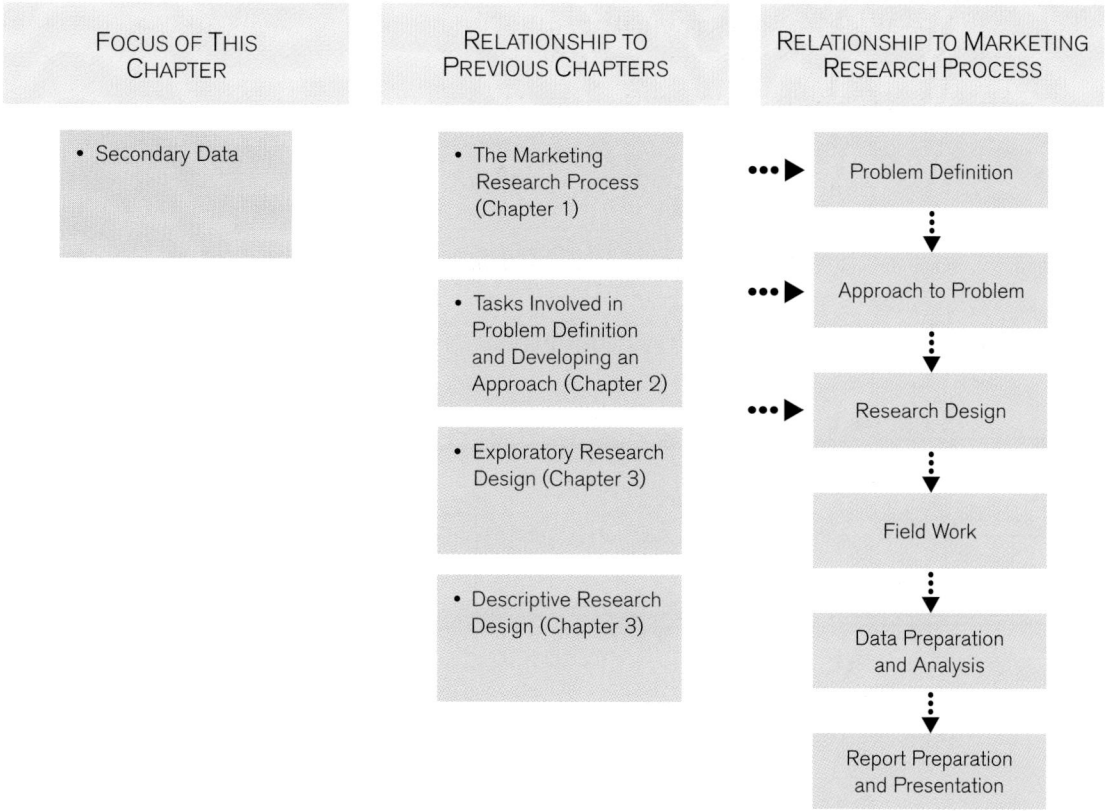

Figure 4.1

Relationship of Secondary Data to the Previous Chapters and the Marketing Research Process

advantages, disadvantages, and criteria for evaluating secondary data, which can be generated both internally and externally. The chapter concludes with a discussion of the practice of merging internal and external secondary data. Additionally, we will discuss applications of secondary data, collecting international secondary data, the impact of technology, ethical questions related to secondary data, and Internet applications. Figure 4.2 presents an overview of this chapter.

Secondary data can best be distinguished from primary data when we consider the purpose of the original data collection.

Primary Versus Secondary Data

An early outcome of the research process is to define the marketing research problem and identify specific research questions and hypotheses (Chapter 2). When data are collected to address a specific marketing research problem, they are referred to as **primary data**. Obtaining primary data can be expensive and time-consuming because it involves all six steps of the marketing research process (Figure 4.1).

primary data
Data originated by the researcher for the specific purpose of addressing the research problem.

Before initiating primary data collection, a researcher should remember that the problem under study might not be unique. It is possible that someone else has investigated the same or a similar marketing research problem. A search through existing data may lead to relevant information. **Secondary data** represent any data that have already been collected for purposes other than the problem at hand. Relative to primary data collection, these data can be located quickly and inexpensively, as in the case of the *Vindicator*. The differences between primary and secondary data are summarized in Table 4.1.

secondary data
Data collected for some purpose other than the problem at hand.

It is easy to overlook the many sources of secondary data while developing a formal research design. Once a secondary data search is initiated, however, the volume of existing information can be overwhelming. In order to cost-effectively browse through this

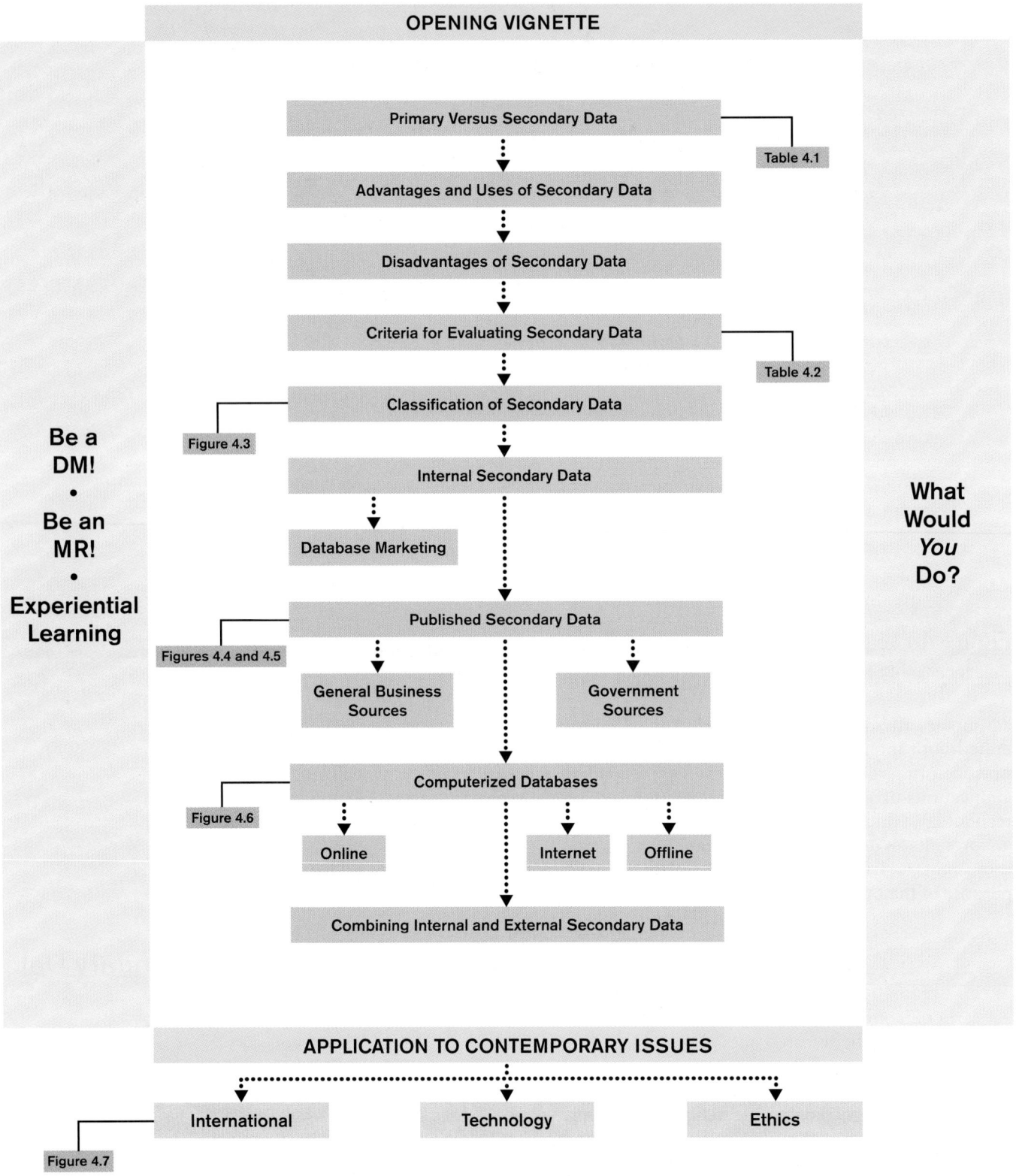

Figure 4.2

Secondary Data: An Overview

mountain of information, it is important that the researcher be familiar with various sources of secondary data, including marketing research firms that specialize in secondary data, such as Inland Research in the opening vignette.

Table 4.1
A Comparison of Primary and Secondary Data

	Primary Data	Secondary Data
Collection purpose	For the problem at hand	For other problems
Collection process	Very involved	Rapid and easy
Collection cost	High	Relatively low
Collection time	Long	Short

Advantages and Uses of Secondary Data

The main advantages of secondary data are the time and money they can save. This was evident from the low-cost secondary research provided by the Inland Research Corp. in the opening vignette. Additionally, the collection of some secondary data, such as those provided by the U.S. Census Bureau, would not be feasible for individual firms like Inland Research or the *Vindicator*. While it is rare for secondary data to provide all the answers to a nonroutine research problem, analysis of secondary data should always be the first step taken toward solving a research problem. Secondary data provided the *Vindicator* with a better understanding of advertising effectiveness and penetration for different forms of media. Such data can help you

1. Identify the problem.
2. Better understand and define the problem.
3. Develop an approach to the problem.
4. Formulate an appropriate research design (e.g., by identifying the key variables).
5. Answer certain research questions and test some hypotheses.
6. Interpret primary data with more insight.

Additionally, secondary data are also useful for demand estimation, monitoring the environment, developing business intelligence systems, segmentation and targeting, and a variety of other applications.

Given these advantages and uses of secondary data, we state a basic rule of research:

> Examine available secondary data first. The research project should proceed to primary data collection only when the secondary data sources have been exhausted or yield marginal returns.

In the opening vignette, the *Vindicator* exemplifies the rich dividends obtained by following this rule. Another example that follows involves Frost Bank.

This example shows that analysis of secondary data can provide valuable insights and lay the foundation for conducting more formal research, such as focus groups and surveys. The researcher should be cautious when using secondary data, however, because there are some disadvantages.

BE an MR!

Search the Internet using a search engine as well as your library's online databases to obtain information on the use of celebrity endorsements in marketing.

You are conducting a marketing research project to determine the effectiveness of celebrity endorsements in Nike advertising. What type of secondary data would you examine?

BE a DM!

As the marketing director of Nike, how would you use secondary data on celebrity endorsements to determine whether you should continue to contract celebrities to endorse the Nike brand?

RESEARCH IN ACTION

Bank "Zips" Up the Market

From its inception as a small downtown San Antonio bank in 1868, Frost Bank (www.frostbank.com) has grown into a multibillion dollar, full-service financial institution with more than $10 billion in assets in 2005. It offers a full range of banking and financial services to retail and commercial customers throughout Texas. The bank was considering modifying its Young Leaders Club (YLC) account to enhance its appeal to San Antonians between the ages of 21 and 35. The YLC offered members a checking account with enhancements such as life insurance, discount movie tickets, store coupons, tours, and social events, all for a monthly membership fee. Extensive analysis of secondary data was conducted. Using internal secondary data on transactions and addresses, club members were evaluated by zip code and account activity. The results of zip-code analysis helped attract advertising and discount coupons from merchants in areas of San Antonio where large numbers of YLC members lived. External secondary data available on this age group provided additional insights for redeveloping the YLC package. Census information related to population, age, and income allowed Frost Bank to estimate the size of the potential market for the YLC. This secondary data analysis was followed by focus groups and survey research. After completing their marketing research, which began with the examination of secondary data, Frost Bank was able to significantly increase the number of YLC accounts in the target market.[2]

Disadvantages of Secondary Data

The value of secondary data is typically limited by their degree of fit with the current research problem and by concerns regarding data accuracy. The objectives, nature, and methods used to collect secondary data may not be compatible with the present situation. Also, secondary data may be lacking in terms of accuracy, compatibility of units of measurement, or time frame. Before using secondary data, it is important to evaluate them using the criteria in Table 4.2. The Inland Research Corp. used similar criteria in the opening vignette.

Criteria for Evaluating Secondary Data

Specifications: Methodology Used to Collect the Data

The research design specifications—that is, the methodology used to collect the data—should be critically examined to identify possible sources of bias. Factors that are all important in identifying potential error as well as relevance of the data include the size and nature of the sample, response rate and quality, questionnaire design and administration, procedures used for field work, and data analysis and reporting procedures. One reason it is advantageous to use data from the originating source is that a description of the research design is typically provided as a part of the original published study.

Error: Accuracy of the Data

Both secondary and primary data can have errors, stemming from the research approach, research design, sampling, data collection, analysis, and reporting stages of the project. Moreover, it is difficult to evaluate the accuracy of secondary data when the researcher has not directly participated in the research.

Secondary data can be obtained either directly from the source that originated the data or from a secondary source that secured the data from someone else. The further removed you are from the originating data source, the greater the possibility of problems with accuracy. An original source is likely to be more accurate and complete than a non-originating source. Always use the originating source if it is available.

One approach to controlling accuracy problems is to find multiple sources of data and compare those using standard statistical procedures. The accuracy of secondary data can

Table 4.2
Criteria for Evaluating Secondary Data

Criteria	Issues	Remarks
Specifications/ Methodology	Data collection method Response rate Quality of data Sampling technique Sample size Questionnaire design Field work Data analysis	Data should be reliable, valid, and generalizable to the problem at hand.
Error/Accuracy	Examine errors in: approach, research design, sampling, data collection, data analysis, reporting	Assess accuracy by comparing data from different sources.
Currency	Time lag between collection and publication Frequency of updates	Census data are periodically updated by syndicated firms.
Objective	Why were the data collected?	The objective will determine the relevance of data.
Nature	Definition of key variables Units of measurement Categories used Relationships examined	Reconfigure the data to increase their usefulness, if possible.
Dependability	Expertise, credibility, reputation, and trustworthiness of the source	Data should be obtained from an original rather than an acquired source.

also be verified by conducting field investigations, as recommended by the International Council of Shopping Centers.

As this example indicates, the accuracy of secondary data can vary, particularly if it relates to highly volatile market conditions. Moreover, data obtained from different sources may not agree. In these cases, the researcher should verify the accuracy of secondary data by conducting pilot studies or by other appropriate methods. With a little creativity, this can often be accomplished with little expense and effort.

RESEARCH IN ACTION

Population Dynamics and the Accuracy of Secondary Data

The International Council of Shopping Centers (www.icsc.org) conducted a study to evaluate the consistency of market profiles provided by private vendors of secondary demographic information. Several vendors (e.g., CACI, www.caci.com; Claritas, www.claritas.com; Donnelley Marketing Information Services, www.donnelleymarketing.com) participated in the research. Three market areas were analyzed: Baltimore, Detroit, and Phoenix. The vendors supplied the Council with statistics and demographic data for each market area. The Council then analyzed the differences among the vendors' reports using standard statistical procedures.

The results indicated that there was little variation in the data from different sources when the population was relatively stable. However, the vendor-supplied demographic data varied considerably in areas with rapidly changing population. In such cases, the Council recommended that users verify vendor data findings with field investigations of their own.[3]

Currency: When the Data Were Collected

Secondary data may not be current. There may be a time lag between data collection and publication, as is the case with census data. Additionally, the data may not be updated frequently enough to answer questions related to the problem at hand. Marketing research requires current data; therefore, the value of secondary data is diminished as they become dated. For instance, while the 2000 Census of Population data are comprehensive, they may not be applicable to a metropolitan area whose population has changed rapidly during the last few years. Thus, such data may not be current enough for use by Home Depot in predicting potential demand for the next year. Fortunately, several marketing research firms update census data periodically and make the current information available for a fee.

Objective: The Purpose for the Study

Understanding why secondary data were originally collected can sensitize the researcher to the limitations of using them for the current marketing problem. Suppose *Sports Illustrated* surveyed its renewing subscriber base regarding readership of its articles and recall of its advertising. One objective of this study was to use the information to sell advertising space. With that in mind, the results of the study would be made available to advertising managers who were likely to be making decisions regarding advertising placement. This type of secondary information may be relevant to the question of where to place future advertising. The results of this survey from *Sports Illustrated* would be biased, however, in that they would reflect the behavior of their renewing subscribers, a group that may be more involved with the magazine than the general subscribers. To accurately interpret this secondary data, the advertising manager would have to understand how closely the *Sports Illustrated* renewing segment represented its total subscribing population.

Nature: The Content of the Data

The nature, or content, of the data should be examined with special attention to the definition of key variables, the units of measurement, categories used, and the relationships examined. One of the most frustrating limitations of secondary data comes from differences in definition, units of measurement, time frame examined, or questionable assumptions regarding the relationships of key variables. If the key variables have not been defined or are defined in a manner inconsistent with the researcher's definition, then the usefulness of the data is limited.

Consider, for example, secondary data related to retail sales. While the researcher interprets the information, questions may arise regarding whether the sales are defined net of returned items or whether they represent cash and credit sales. For example, if Visa decides to investigate the sales of credit-card services, this level of distinction becomes critical. Visa spends millions of dollars in marketing the card to retailers and in advertising the card to consumers. The 2004 Olympic Games marked the 18th year of Visa's sponsorship. Visa was the first sponsor to sign on with the Olympic Games through 2012. In order to determine the effectiveness of its advertising and sponsorships, Visa needs secondary data with relevant content.

Secondary data may be measured in units that are not appropriate for the current problem. For example, income can be measured by individual, family, household, or spending unit, and it can be reported as gross or net after taxes and deductions. If income categories reported in secondary sources are different from those required by the research, the information may not be usable. If Mercedes is interested in high-income consumers with gross annual household incomes of more than $90,000, then secondary data with income categories less than $15,000, $15,001 to $35,000, $35,001 to $50,000, and more than $50,000 will not be of much use.

Finally, we must consider the variables of interest to the researcher. For example, if the researcher is interested in actual purchase behavior, then information on attitudes that only implies behavior may have limited usefulness.

Dependability: How Dependable Are the Data?

An overall indication of the dependability of the data may be obtained by examining the expertise, credibility, reputation, and trustworthiness of the source. This information can be obtained by checking with others who have used information this source provides. Data published to promote sales, to advance specific interests, or to carry on propaganda should be viewed with suspicion. The same may be said of data published anonymously or in a form that attempts to hide the details of the data collection methodology and process. On the other hand, secondary data published by reputable organizations, such as the U.S. Census Bureau, are very dependable and of high quality.

BE a DM!

As the CEO of Home Depot, you come across a Gallup poll reporting that an increasing number of women are shopping for home improvement products and services. How will you use this information to improve the competitiveness of Home Depot?

BE an MR!

Visit Gallup's Web site (www.gallup.com.) Examine the information on how Gallup polls are conducted.

By applying the criteria we have considered, evaluate the quality of Gallup polls.

Classification of Secondary Data

As represented in Figure 4.3 and discussed earlier in this chapter, there are two primary sources of secondary data: internal and external. **Internal data** are data generated within the organization for which the research is being conducted. **External data**, on the other hand, are data generated by sources outside the organization. In the opening vignette, the data on circulation obtained from the records of the *Vindicator* were internal data. However, data obtained from Inland Research on advertising effectiveness and penetration for different forms of media were external data.

internal data
Data available within the organization for which the research is being conducted.

external data
Data that originate external to the organization.

Internal Secondary Data

Before collecting external secondary data, it is always useful to analyze internal secondary data. Internal data are typically generated as part of the ongoing process of doing business. These data can come from accounting records, sales reports, production or operation reports, or internal experts. In the opening vignette, the *Vindicator* routinely collects data on the number of customers, duration each customer has been a subscriber, renewals/nonrenewals, and so on. Although it is possible that internal secondary data may be available in usable form, it is more typical that considerable processing effort will be required before such data can be used. For example, cash register receipts of a department store may contain a wealth of information, such as sales by product line, sales by

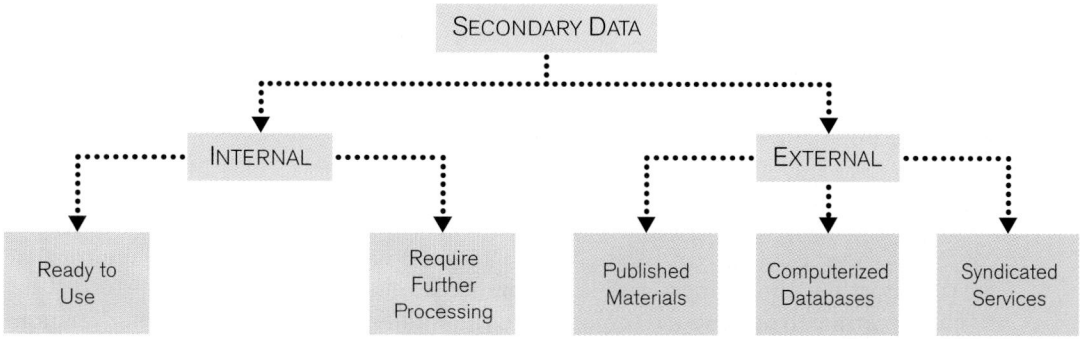

Figure 4.3
A Classification of Secondary Data

specific stores, sales by geographical region, sales by cash versus credit purchases, sales in specific time periods, sales by size of purchase, and so on. To derive this information, however, data must be transcribed from the paper-based sales receipts to a computer database and analyzed extensively. Many organizations are building sophisticated internal databases as platforms for their marketing efforts. A **data warehouse** is a centralized database that consolidates company-wide data from a variety of operational systems. Of special interest to us are customer databases.

data warehouse
Centralized database that consolidates company-wide data from a variety of operational systems.

Customer Databases For many companies, the first step in creating a customer database is to transfer raw sales information, such as that found on sales call reports or invoices, to a personal computer. Customer information is also obtained from other sources, such as warranty cards and loyalty programs (e.g., frequent flier programs of airlines). This is augmented with demographic and psychographic information about the customers obtained from external secondary sources. **Psychographics** refer to quantified psychological profiles of consumers' activities, interests, and opinions. Several companies in this business, including R. R. Donnelley (www.rrdonnelley.com), Experian (www.experian.com), R. L. Polk (www.polk.com), and others, have compiled household lists, which include names, addresses, and a great deal of individual-specific data. The elements of a customer database include the following:

psychographics
Quantified psychological profiles of consumers' activities, interests, and opinions.

- A unique ID or match code
- Name and title of the individual or organization
- Mailing address
- Telephone number(s)
- E-mail address
- Source of referral, inquiry, or order
- Complete transaction history by date, frequency, purchase amounts, and products
- Credit history and rating score
- Demographic and psychographic data for individuals, such as gender, marital status, age, education, occupation, number of children, income, type of residence, geodemographic information, psychographics, and lifestyle data
- Organizational data for institutions, such as North American Industry Classification System (discussed later in this chapter), sales, number of employees, length of time in business, headquarters, international operations, and other relevant data

The size of these customer databases can be staggering. Sears, for example, has more than 75 million households in its customer database. The analysis of such large databases requires special skills and resources and has been termed *data mining*.

Data Mining, Customer Relationship Management Systems, and Database Marketing **Data mining** involves the use of powerful computers with advanced statistical and other software to analyze large databases in order to discover hidden patterns in the data. The term derives its meaning from the exercise of digging through a lot of "coal" (seemingly valueless data) to discover "golden nuggets" (invaluable marketing information). It is a broad term that applies to many different types of data analyses including the use of artificial intelligence procedures that model the way the human brain processes information. The patterns discovered can be very useful for targeting marketing effort. For example, data mining revealed that husbands tend to buy additional life insurance immediately after the birth of their first child. Therefore, Allstate's (www.allstate.com) slogan, "You're in good hands," is particularly appropriate for targeting first-time fathers with life insurance products.

data mining
Involves the use of powerful computers, advanced statistical and other software to analyze large databases in order to discover hidden patterns in the data.

customer relationship management (CRM) system
A decision-support system that is used for managing the interactions between an organization and its customers.

database marketing
Practice of using CRM databases to develop relationships and highly targeted marketing efforts with individuals and customer groups.

Customer databases and data mining are the building blocks for **customer relationship management (CRM) systems**. A CRM is a decision-support system (see Chapter 1) that is used for managing the interactions between an organization and its customers. **Database marketing** is the practice of using CRM databases to develop relationships and highly targeted marketing efforts with individuals and customer groups. The CRM data-

RESEARCH IN ACTION

General Electric: Electrifying Marketing with a Customer Database

As of 2005, General Electric (GE; www.ge.com) operates in more than 100 countries around the world. This includes 250 manufacturing plants in 26 different nations. In the United States, the company has built a huge customer database of more than 50 million households, which it uses effectively for target marketing. GE has combined demographic, psychographic, media consumption, and purchasing data available externally with internal customer transaction records to pinpoint a customer's appliance ownership and history.

Using this database, GE can determine, for example, which customers are typically ready to replace their washing machines: those who bought the washing machine six years ago and have large families. The company can then direct marketing efforts in the form of gift certificates, discounts, and special deals for washing machines at these customers. The database has electrified GE's marketing, resulting in increased market share and profitability.[4]

bases can be analyzed in terms of a customer's activity over the life of the business relationship. Signs of change in the usage relationships (e.g., a heavy user decreases usage) or significant "customer life cycle" events (e.g., anniversaries) can be identified and addressed. These databases provide the essential tool needed to nurture, expand, and protect the customer relationship and can also serve as a foundation for developing marketing programs.

Organizations that bill their customers for services or provide statements of customer activities are in a particularly strong position to use their internal secondary data. Utilities, cable television systems, banks, department stores, and health-care providers are all examples of organizations that use database marketing.

As the GE example illustrates, database marketing can lead to quite sophisticated and targeted marketing programs. Most large organizations have intranets, which greatly facilitate the search for, and access to, internal secondary data. The Procter & Gamble Company, for example, has developed powerful intranet applications that enable its managers worldwide to search for past and current research studies and a wide variety of marketing related information on the basis of keywords. Once located, the information can be accessed online. Sensitive information can be secured electronically with user names and passwords.

BE a DM!

As the marketing director for Apple, how would you use database marketing to increase the penetration of Apple computers in U.S. households?

BE an MR!

Visit Apple Computer's Web site (www.apple.com) and search the Internet to obtain information on the marketing strategy of Apple Computer, Inc.

Identify the variables available internally within Apple as well as from external sources that you would use to build a database to help Apple Computer increase its penetration of U.S. households.

External Secondary Data: Published Sources

Secondary data sources have grown dramatically over the past 20 years. This growth has been stimulated, in part, by the introduction of personal computers into the workplace, which give employees easy access to commercial databases. The following section provides an overview of some of the sources of published external secondary data. Nonprofit organizations (e.g., chambers of commerce), trade and professional organizations, commercial publishers, investment brokerage firms, and professional marketing research firms are just a few of the nongovernmental sources available. To enable you to sort through the overwhelming amount of secondary data, we begin our discussion with a classification of published secondary data (Figure 4.4).

Published external sources may be broadly classified as general business data or government data. General business sources include guides, directories, indexes, and statistical data. Government sources may be broadly categorized as census data and other publications.

General Business Data

Businesses publish a great deal of information in the form of books, periodicals, journals, newspapers, magazines, reports, and trade literature. Audit Bureau of Circulations, cited in the opening vignette, is a general business source that provides data on audits of media, such as newspapers, consumer magazines, trade shows, and the Web. Guides, indexes, and directories can help in locating information available from general business sources. Sources are also available for identifying statistical data. A brief description of each of these resource categories follows.

Guides Standard or recurring information is summarized in guides. Guides provide a path to other sources of secondary data contained in directories or published by professional or trade associations. Because guides can open the door to other sources of data, they are one of the first sources a researcher should consult. Some of the most useful are *Business Information Sources*, *Encyclopedia of Business Information Sources*, and *Monthly Catalog of United States Government Publications.*

Indexes and Bibliographies Bibliographies, which are organized alphabetically by topic, are another good place to start external secondary research. Current or historic discussion of a particular topic of interest will be indexed in these references, leading you to a number of authors.

Several indexes are available for referencing both academic and business topics. Some of the more useful business indexes are *Business Index*, *Business Periodical Index*, *General*

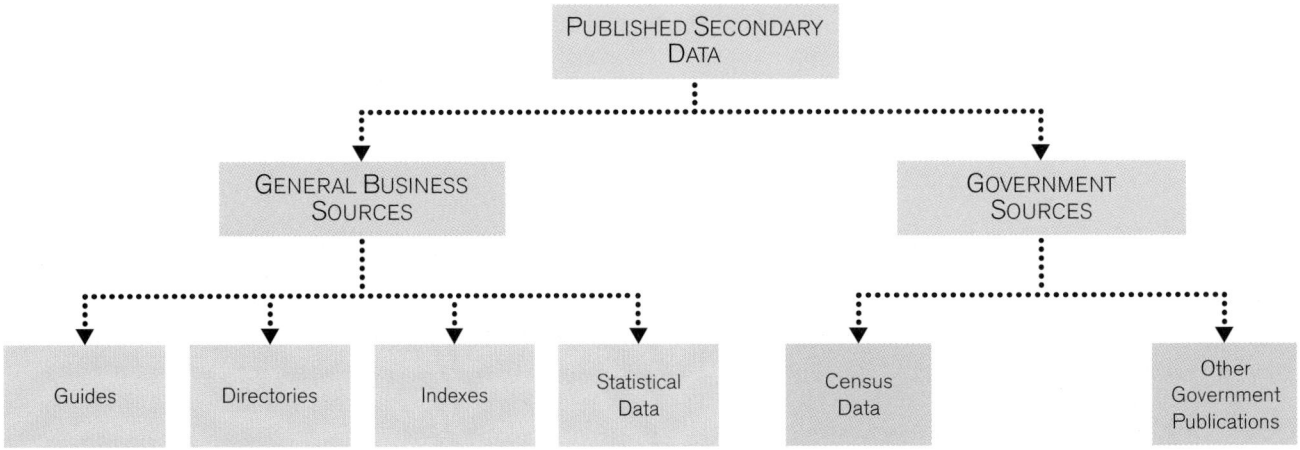

Figure 4.4

A Classification of Published Secondary Sources

Business File, *National Newspaper Index*, *Social Sciences Citation Index*, and the *Wall Street Journal Index*.

Directories Directories provide brief descriptions of companies, organizations, or individuals. They are helpful for identifying manufacturers operating in your market, for compiling names and addresses of associations in your sales territory, or for verifying names and addresses of prospective customers who carry a specific job title. Some of the important directories include *Directories in Print*, *Consultants and Consulting Organizations Directory*, *Encyclopedia of Associations*, *FINDEX: The Directory of Market Research Reports*, *Fortune 500 Directory*, *Million Dollar Directory: Leading Public and Private Companies*, *Standard Directory of Advertisers*, and *Thomas Register of American Manufacturers*.

Nongovernmental Statistical Data

Business research often involves compiling statistical data reflecting market or industry factors. A historic perspective of industry participation and growth rates can provide a context for market share analysis. Market statistics related to population demographics, purchasing levels, television viewership, and product usage are just some of the types of nongovernmental statistics available from secondary sources. Important sources of nongovernmental statistical data include *A Guide to Consumer Markets*, *Predicasts Basebook*, *Predicasts Forecasts*, *Sales and Marketing Management Survey of Buying Power*, *Standard& Poor's Statistical Service*, and *Standard Rate and Data Service*.

A variety of business-related sites can provide sales leads, mailing lists, business profiles, and credit ratings for American businesses. Many sites supply information on businesses within a specific industry. For example, you can gain access to the full text *American Demographics* and *Marketing Tools* publications at (www.marketingtools.com). All of American Marketing Association's publications can be searched by using keywords at (www.marketingpower.com). Encyclopedia Britannica (www.britannica.com) provides free online access to the entire 32 volumes. Data on American manufacturers and key decision makers can be obtained from Harris InfoSource (www.harrisinfo.com). Another good source is USAData.com.

There are several commercial firms, such as FIND/SVP (www.findsvp.com), that specialize in conducting computerized information searches over the Internet and obtaining data from other secondary sources. FIND/SVP provides customized research and analysis related to market and industry profiles, business and competitive intelligence, benchmarking, new business opportunities, and other applications.

Government Sources

The U.S. government is the largest source of secondary data in this country and in the world. The data the government gathers could not feasibly be collected by private industry. Its value ranges from use in developing sales forecasts and market potential estimates to simply locating specific retailers, wholesalers, or manufacturers. The government

RESEARCH IN ACTION

Consumer Information to Go: USAData.com

USAData.com (www.usadata.com) combines business and marketing information from its comprehensive database and distributes it over the Internet. It assembles marketing research information from respected data providers into a searchable format to be purchased by other businesses requiring quick access to information. Using demographic information that has been previously collected, USAData.com can quickly assemble mailing lists that target specific customers. In addition to mailing lists, it provides reports on various industries and companies containing information such as market share, consumer habits, and geographic penetration.

For example, USAData.com can quickly assemble an Internet mailing list targeting middle-aged professionals on the West Coast for a high-class resort seeking to geographically expand its customer base. This approach allows client firms fast access to up-to-date information about consumers and competitors. Thus, USAData.com is a valuable source of secondary data available on the Internet.

sources, because of their breadth and accuracy, provide rich secondary databases. In the opening vignette, Inland Research obtained data from government sources such as the U.S. Census Bureau and the Bureau of Labor Statistics. Government publications can be divided into census data and other types.

Census Data Census data are useful in a variety of marketing research projects. The demographic data collected by the Census Bureau includes information about household types, sex, age, marital status, and race. Consumption detail related to automobile ownership, housing characteristics, work status, and practices as well as occupations are just a few of the categories of information available. What makes this demographic information particularly valuable to marketers is that these data can be geographically categorized at various levels of detail. These data can be summarized at various levels: city block, block group, census tract, metropolitan statistical area (MSA), consolidated metropolitan statistical area (CMSA), region (the Northeast, Midwest, South, and West), or they can be aggregated for the nation as a whole. Figure 4.5 shows the geographic subdivision of an MSA. Census tracts have a population of more than 4,000 and are defined by local communities. In urban areas, the MSAs have a population of at least 50,000 and comprise counties containing a central city. In addition, census data are available by civil divisions, such as wards, cities, counties, and states.

In general, the quality of census data is quite high, and the data are often extremely detailed. To facilitate business analysis, this information is available in multiple forms. One can purchase computer tapes, diskettes, or CD-ROMs from the Census Bureau for a nominal fee and recast this information into the desired format. Important census data include Census of Housing, Census of Manufacturers, Census of Population, Census of Retail Trade, Census of Service Industries, and Census of Wholesale Trade. Claritas is a secondary research company that has created a number of research tools using census and other lifestyle data. Integrating enhanced census data with internal company databases is a useful application of multiple secondary sources. This integration of secondary data is discussed later in the chapter.

Other Government Publications In addition to the census, the federal government collects and publishes a great deal of statistical data, much of it relevant to business. The government developed the Standard Industrial Classification Code (SIC) as the classification scheme used for its Census of Manufacturers. The SIC system classified manufacturing into 20 major groups. Each group was further classified into industry groups and then product categories. The United States, Mexico, and Canada have created a new common classification system to replace the previous classification of each country. The 4-digit

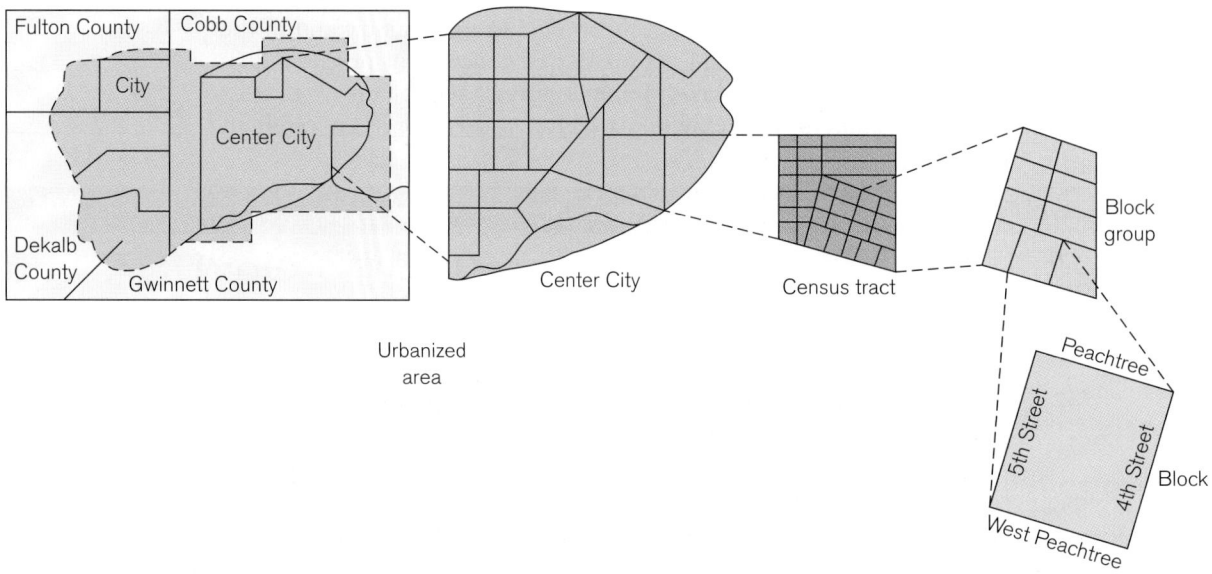

Figure 4.5
The Geographic Subdivision of an MSA

EXPERIENTIAL LEARNING

U.S. Census Bureau

The 2000 Census of the United States provides insight into the demographic profile of not only the United States in full, but also smaller U.S. regions, such as states and metropolitan statistical areas (MSAs). Go to the home page for the U.S. Census Bureau (www.census.gov) and do the following:

1. Find the population clocks on the home page for the U.S. Census Bureau. What is the current population estimate for the United States? For the world?
2. Find "state and county quick facts." Compare your home state's "population percentage change from 1990 to 2000" with that of the United States in full. Which grew faster?
3. Find out how many "singles without children living at home" were counted in your zip code in the 2000 census. Look on the left side of the home page for the U.S. Census Bureau, select "American FactFinder," and follow the steps.

SIC of the United States has been replaced by a 6-digit North American Industry Classification System (NAICS), which was phased in beginning in 1999.

Why was NAICS (www.naics.com) needed? According to statements from the U.S. Department of Commerce, the SIC didn't keep up with rapid changes in U.S. and world economics. The two extra digits in NAICS accommodate the larger number of sectors and allow more flexibility in designating subsections. NAICS is organized in a hierarchical structure, much like the SIC. The new codes will be reviewed every five years.

Other useful government publications include *Business America*, *Business Conditions Digest*, *Business Statistics*, *County Business Patterns*, *County and City Data Book*, *Index to Publications*, *Statistical Abstract of the United States*, and *Survey of Current Business*. Several U.S. government sources can be reached from FedWorld (www.fedworld.gov). Extensive business statistics can be obtained from (www.stat-usa.gov). The U.S. Department of Commerce can be reached at (www.doc.gov). The Bureau of Census information can be reached via the Department of Commerce (www.doc.gov) or directly at (www.census.gov). The Bureau of Labor Statistics (www.bls.gov) provides useful information, especially Consumer Expenditure Surveys. A wide range of economic statistics can be obtained from the Bureau of Economic Analysis (www.bea.doc.gov). These government sites can provide valuable information to the marketing researcher.

Most published information is also available in computerized databases.

Computerized Databases

Computerized databases, accessed directly online or offline or available over the Internet, have made secondary data easily available for organizations of all sizes, as in the opening vignette. A personal computer equipped with a modem linked to relevant telecommunication networks can connect a researcher to vast libraries of information, accessible at any time from any place. Marketing researchers no longer need to leave their offices to monitor changes in their industry, technology, or regulatory environments.

Today there are thousands of databases. Their phenomenal growth is a result of the advantages of electronic dissemination of data over printed data:

1. **Current information.** Because printing is no longer an essential step in information dissemination, data can be updated continuously. Publishers who use computers to edit and publish their periodicals can now electronically transfer those documents to relevant databases, making them available with remarkable speed as compared to the traditional methods of print production and physical distribution.
2. **Faster data search.** Online vendors provide increasing uniformity in the search process, enabling even a relative novice at secondary research to access data more quickly and completely.
3. **Low cost.** The relative cost of accessing computerized databases is low.
4. **Convenience.** This has become perhaps one of the greatest benefits computerized databases have delivered. Information providers now have a direct link to

the end user equipped with a personal computer and modem or otherwise connected to the Internet. They are no longer forced to distribute their products through libraries or retail outlets.

Conducting secondary research via computerized databases, however, is not without limitations. A researcher who doesn't know how to conduct a focused keyword search or who is unsure whether a particular database provides abstracts or articles in their entirety can be buried under a mountain of irrelevant data. However, researchers can overcome these limitations as they gain experience in the computerized search process.

Knowing how computerized databases are classified can help the researcher narrow the search. Database vendors provide a wide array of public information, available to anyone who has computer access to a telecommunications network. Based on how they are distributed, computerized databases are classified as either online, Internet, or offline (Figure 4.6).

Online Databases

online databases
Databases stored in computers that require a telecommunications network to access.

Online databases provide direct, interactive access to data stored remotely on a mainframe computer. A personal computer linked to these mainframes via modem and a telecommunication network is all that is required to initiate a data search and retrieval process. Usage fees are typically based on minutes spent searching a computer file (time online) and on data requests made. A flat monthly access fee may also be charged.

The online database provides an advantage in terms of its currency. Data can be updated and made available for distribution almost simultaneously.

Internet Databases

Internet databases
A specific type of online database compromising information sources available on the World Wide Web (WWW).

Internet databases are a special form of online database. All knowledge workers, and especially market researchers, can benefit from **Internet databases**, which are information sources available on the World Wide Web (WWW). In addition to worldwide e-mail access, the Internet can provide a variety of marketing research documents, as well as both primary and secondary research data. Document access and retrieval via keyword search are of particular interest for secondary data search.

Numerous search utilities and search services can be launched from Internet browsers such as Netscape or Internet Explorer. These packages are general, user-friendly, all-purpose Internet navigation tools that provide access to the WWW, including download and document browsing services. Some of the many Internet search services that are popular include Lycos, YAHOO!, Google, and Webcrawler. The Internet is a very popular option in searching for secondary data, and its use is growing by the day.[5]

Offline Databases

offline databases
Databases that are available on diskette or CD-ROM.

Another way of making information available to users is via **offline databases** that are physically distributed on CD-ROM disks. This type of database service transfers information

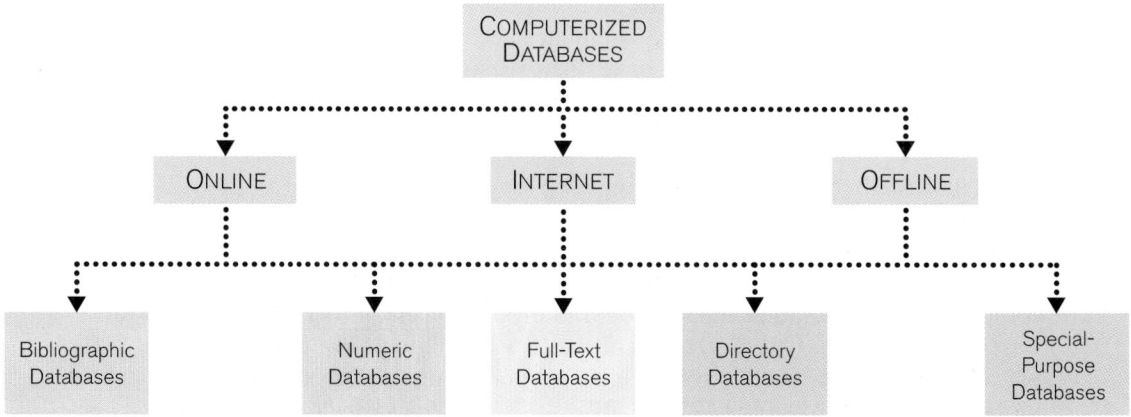

Figure 4.6
A Classification of Computerized Databases

from the mainframe environment to a personal computer. Access to a telecommunication network is not necessary if the researcher is using offline databases. Thus, there are typically no usage fees. However, the potential cost savings must be offset against the time lag inherent in updating offline data. Nevertheless, there is a market for offline databases. The U.S. Census Bureau makes their data files available on CD-ROM disks. These disks contain detailed information organized by census track or zip code. InfoUSA (www.infousa.com) offers a number of databases on CD-ROM, including BusinessUSA, HouseholdsUSA, Physicians & Surgeons, Big Businesses, Manufacturers, and Small Business Owners.

Categories of Database Types

All databases, whether online, Internet, or offline, vary in terms of nature and content. As shown in Figure 4.6, there are five major types of databases: bibliographic, numeric, full-text, directory, or special-purpose databases.

Bibliographic Databases **Bibliographic databases** are indexes of studies and reports published in journals, magazines, and newspapers. They can be on any subject, ranging from marketing research to technical reports and government documents. Summaries of the report findings, known as abstracts, are often provided. An example of a bibliographic database is ABI/INFORM, which contains 200-word abstracts of articles published in more than 1,000 journals and general business publications. It is distributed by ProQuest Information & Learning (www.proquest.com). The Dialog Corp. (www.dialog.com) also distributes a number of databases very useful for marketing research.

bibliographic databases
Databases composed of citations to articles in journals, magazines, newspapers, marketing research studies, technical reports, government documents, and the like. They often provide summaries or abstracts of the material cited.

Numeric Databases **Numeric databases** specialize in disseminating statistical information, such as survey and time series data. Economic and industry data lend themselves to time series presentations, which are developed when the same variables are repeatedly measured over time. This type of data is particularly relevant for assessing market potential, making sales forecasts, or setting sales quotas. The American Statistics Index (ASI) gives abstracts and indexes of federal government statistical publications. The Historical Market Data Center is a database by Dow Jones News Retrieval that gives historical data on securities, dividends, and exchange rates.

numeric databases
Databases that contain numerical and statistical information that may be important sources of secondary data.

Commercially updated census data are another example of numeric databases. Donnelley Marketing Information Services (www.donnelleymarketing.com) provides updated, current-year and five-year projections on population statistics collected in the latest census. A variety of geographic categorization schemes, including census tract, zip code, and ACNielsen's Designated Market Areas or Selling Areas, can be used as keys for searching in this database. The U.S. Census Bureau and CACI (www.caci.com) provide similar services.

Full-Text Databases As the name implies, **full-text databases** contain the complete text of the source documents contained in the database. ABI/Inform Global (www.proquest.com) provides electronic abstracts and full-text delivery and search capabilities for several journals in business and management. One of the most useful full-text business databases is LexisNexis. It provides full-text access to hundreds of business data sources, including selected newspapers, periodicals, company annual reports, and investment firm reports. EBSCO is another valuable full-text database (www.ebsco.com).

full-text databases
Databases containing the complete text of secondary source documents comprising the database.

Directory Databases **Directory databases** provide information on individuals, organizations, and services. Standard & Poor's Corporate Descriptions is an example of a directory database that provides summary data on publicly held U.S. corporations. A secondary researcher wanting to compile information on a competitor or prospective customer can obtain data related to the growth of the organization, the size of its workforce, and its financial performance.

directory databases
Directory databases provide information on individuals, organizations, and services.

Firmographics are the business equivalent of demographics. They include variables such as market share, corporate location, industry classification, and employment size. D&B (formerly Dun and Bradstreet) (www.dnb.com) provides this type of data.

The largest database of companies in this country is contained in the national Electronic Yellow Pages (www.yellowpages.com). This database contains more than 10 million records compiled from the nation's 4,800 telephone books. The names, addresses, phone numbers, and NAIC codes for manufacturers, wholesalers, retailers, professionals, and service organizations are available through this source.

RESEARCH IN ACTION

The LEXISNEXIS Market Research Library

In the LEXISNEXIS Market Research Library (www.lexisnexis.com), customers can purchase report information online by subsection, eliminating the cost of buying an entire report. Users may browse the entire table of contents and study the methodology of most reports as well as view actual tables, minus the data, before purchasing the information. The subsections of the market research reports on the NEXIS Market Research Product have been formatted by the market research providers as complete, stand-alone units of information. The product offers research data from such sources as ACNielsen, Business Trend Analysts, Datamonitor, Euromonitor, FIND/SVP, The Freedonia Group, Leading Edge, and Packaged Facts. For more information, call 800-227-4908 or visit the company's Web site (www.lexisnexis.com).[6]

special-purpose databases Databases that contain information of a specific nature, for example, data on a specialized industry.

Special-Purpose Databases **Special-purpose databases** are more focused in their scope, such as the Profit Impact of Market Strategies (PIMS). The Strategic Planning Institute in Cambridge, Massachusetts, maintains PIMS, which reflects their research and analysis of business strategies from more than 250 companies, representing more than 2,000 businesses. Another relevant database is the Market Research Library by LEXISNEXIS.

The process of locating the database relevant to your specific research problem may seem overwhelming at first. Fortunately, directories of databases have been developed to assist the researcher in narrowing the database search.

Directories of Databases

To avoid being buried under mountains of irrelevant data and to make the process efficient, a search of database directories may be a useful early step in the research process. The following are some useful directories that are periodically updated.

- Directory of Online Databases
  Cuadra Associates, Inc., Santa Monica, California
- Encyclopedia of Information System and Services
  Gale Research Company, Detroit
- Information Industry Marketplace
  R. R. Bowker, New York
- Online Sources of Government Data

About 70 federal agencies regularly publish data. To enable a systematic search of all of these data, the Congressional Information Service, Inc. (CIS) has developed the Statistical Universe that is available as a Web-based service (www.cispubs.com). Statistical Universe is fully indexed and is the most comprehensive source of federal statistics online. Users looking for specific reports or data issued by specific agencies can also consult FEDSTATS (www.fedstats.gov). This site has links to the 70 federal agencies recognized by the Office of Management and Budgets as issuing statistical data, including the U.S. Census Bureau, Department of Commerce, and the Bureau of Labor Statistics.

Combining Internal and External Secondary Data

The usefulness of secondary data can be greatly enhanced when internally generated data are merged with data obtained from external sources. By using both internal and external secondary sources, marketing researchers can overlay demographic, economic, or business statistics on proprietary customer files. These data can then be used to develop market assessments or profiles of various customer groups or simply to educate the sales force. The combination of internal and external data results in inexpensive and valuable information that can be used for a variety of purposes, including database marketing, discussed earlier. In the following sections, we illustrate the merging of internal and external secondary data with applications to geo-demographic coding and geo-visual mapping. We also discuss the buying power index.

Geo-Demographic Coding

Geo-demographic coding involves merging internal customer data with external geographic, demographic, and lifestyle data on the same customers. Some **syndicated services**, which typically offer their information databases by subscription, have developed demographic and psychographic databases at the household level, along with many products based on these data.

geo-demographic coding
Geo-demographic coding involves merging internal customer data with external geographic, demographic, and lifestyle data on the same customers.

syndicated services
Information services offered by marketing research organizations that provide information from a common database to firms that subscribe to their services.

Consider a cable television operator, such as Comcast, which maintains a computerized database of its cable subscribers. This internal database contains customer information on the number of cable services subscribed to, the length of time on service, the changes in subscribed services over time, and the billing history for the past three years. Imagine that the president of the cable company has ambitious plans to increase penetration and market share over the next year. He is looking for a recommendation regarding which geographic markets to target. He wants the geographic market potential, profitability of various customer segments, and current cable operating restrictions to be incorporated in this analysis.

In response to this request, the director of market research decides to supplement the internal customer database with external secondary data. To expand the internal customer file, the director reviews several outside sources of geographic, demographic, and lifestyle data and then selects the Claritas, Inc.

Claritas (www.claritas.com) combines data from a number of sources including the U.S. Census and commercial marketing research firms such as Arbitron, Simmons Marketing Research Bureau, and Mediamark. One of its products, PRIZM (Potential Rating Index for Zip Markets), seems highly appropriate for this research problem. PRIZM is a target marketing system that describes every U.S. neighborhood in terms of 62 distinct lifestyle types called *clusters*. Geographic matching of the internal customer database with PRIZM files begins with a zip-code match followed by street address.

These external data are overlaid on the customer file, in a process called *geo-coding*. The researcher can use the geo-coded information to develop demographic and lifestyle profiles of customer types in terms of cable subscription levels or any other relevant variable. For example, the analysis of geo-coded data may reveal that heavy users of cable television can be described as midscale families with children at home, who fall into the lifestyle cluster PRIZM has named "pools and patios." The PRIZM profiles provide a colorful description of customer segments in terms of income, education, and family size as well as lifestyles. Combining profiles with customer profit history helps the researcher formulate the cable company's expansion plans. Based on this information, the cable company can target direct selling efforts and direct-mail campaigns and also design an appropriate advertising campaign to reach the heavy users of cable television.

BE an MR!

Visit Subway's Web site (www.subway.com) and conduct an Internet search using a search engine and your library's online database to obtain information on SUBWAY's marketing program.

Write a report about the PRIZM product and its appropriateness for determining SUBWAY restaurant locations.

BE a DM!

As the marketing chief of SUBWAY, how will you use geo-demographic information to enhance your market share?

Geo-Visual Databases

Another factor to consider before beginning a marketing campaign for our Comcast example is the physical coverage of the cable system's wire. There is no point in launching a full-scale effort in geographic areas where cable services are not currently available. This pitfall can be avoided by making use of geo-visual databases. **Geo-visual databases** are created by combining internal customer databases with geographic data, as from the Census Bureau,

geo-visual databases
Created by combining internal customer databases with geographic data, as from the Census Bureau, and making use of appropriate computer mapping software.

computer mapping
Maps that solve marketing problems are called thematic maps. They combine geography with demographic information and a company's sales data or other proprietary information and are generated by a computer.

and making use of appropriate computer mapping software. **Computer mapping** generates thematic maps for solving marketing problems by electronically combining geographic and demographic information and a company's sales data or other proprietary information. Such computer mapping is a product of geographic information systems (GIS).

The Census Bureau has introduced a geo-visual product called TIGER (Topologically Integrated Geographic Encoding and Referencing), which provides a digital street map of the entire United States. These mapping files contain data on street locations, highways, railroads, pipeline, power lines, and airports. Overlaying the maps of current neighborhoods wired for cable with customer geo-demographic information results in a powerful targeting tool. Such information is very useful in target-market selection and in micromarketing, which refers to tailoring the marketing mix (the four Ps: product, price, promotion, and place/distribution) to local neighborhoods. Geo-demographic and geo-visual databases can also aid in competitive intelligence, the process of enhancing marketplace competitiveness through a greater—yet unequivocally ethical—understanding of a firm's competitors and the competitive environment as illustrated by Southwestern Bell.

Buying Power Index

Sales & Marketing Management's annual *Survey of Buying Power* (www.mysbp.com) provides data to help in analyzing U.S. markets, whether they are cities, counties, metro areas, or states. It features statistics, rankings, and projections for every county and media market in the United States with demographics broken out by age, race, city, county, and state; information on retail spending; and projections for future growth in these areas. All of the rankings are divided into 323 metro markets (geographic areas established by the Census Bureau) and 210 media markets (television or broadcast markets determined by Nielsen Media Research), all furnished by Claritas Inc.

There are also statistics that are unique to the *Survey*. Effective buying income (EBI) is a measurement of disposable income. The buying power index (BPI), for which the *Survey* is best known, is a unique measure of spending power that takes population, EBI, and retail sales into account to determine a market's ability to buy. The higher the index, the better.

Summary Illustration Using the Opening Vignette

In this section, we summarize and illustrate secondary data by returning to the chapter's opening vignette. In contrast to primary data, which are collected for a specific research problem, secondary data have been generated for reasons other than the current research problem. The data on advertising effectiveness and penetration for different forms of media provided by the Inland Research Corp. and used by the *Vindicator* newspaper are an example of secondary data. The cost and speed advantages of secondary data must be weighed against their limited applicability and accuracy. In evaluating secondary data, factors such as specifications, error, currency, objectivity, nature, and dependability should be considered, as was done by Inland Research.

Internally-generated information can represent a gold mine for a market researcher. Any department that touches the final consumer in some way may be a source of valuable market data. The *Vindicator* generates data on the number of customers, duration of subscription, and renewals/nonrenewals as a normal business operation. The internally-generated data can be supplemented with data available from external sources to produce a rich database that can target customers and guide marketing efforts. In the opening vignette, external data on advertising effectiveness and penetration for different forms of media were combined with internal data on circulation to stress the comparative advantages of the *Vindicator* over other media (i.e., radio and television).

External data are generated by sources outside the organization. These data exist in the form of published (printed) material; online, Internet, and offline databases; or information made available by syndicated services. The Inland Research Corp. obtains secondary data from all of these sources.

RESEARCH IN ACTION

Competitive Intelligence: The Broad Way to Broadband for Southwestern Bell

Southwestern Bell realized that cable TV companies could become its competitors in the emerging field of cable telephony and broadband service. Thus, a competitive intelligence effort was undertaken that combined both primary research as well as both internal and external secondary data. This competitive intelligence task force was called "Project Pronto" and pursued the mission of understanding the extent and capability of potential competition from cable TV companies.

In the primary research stage, members of Project Pronto used tips from Southwestern Bell's sales representatives and outside plant technicians to identify the network components of cable TV companies, such as fiber networks, repeaters, and fiber nodes, that could provide two-way cable services with cable modems. Actual field surveys were then used to validate these reports about cable TV network deployment. Next, the knowledge obtained in the first stage was merged with secondary data. Using geovisual mapping software, routes of these cable TV components were overlaid onto maps with the types and locations of current Southwestern Bell customers. In this way, firm leaders were able to see the extent and capability of potential competition from cable TV companies.

These insights gained by Project Pronto shaped the strategic direction of the firm. Based on this knowledge, Southwestern Bell directed $6 billion to the deployment of broadband services and led the way for its parent company SBC, Inc. to become the largest provider of broadband DSL (digital subscriber line) services today with more than 3.5 million subscribers.[7]

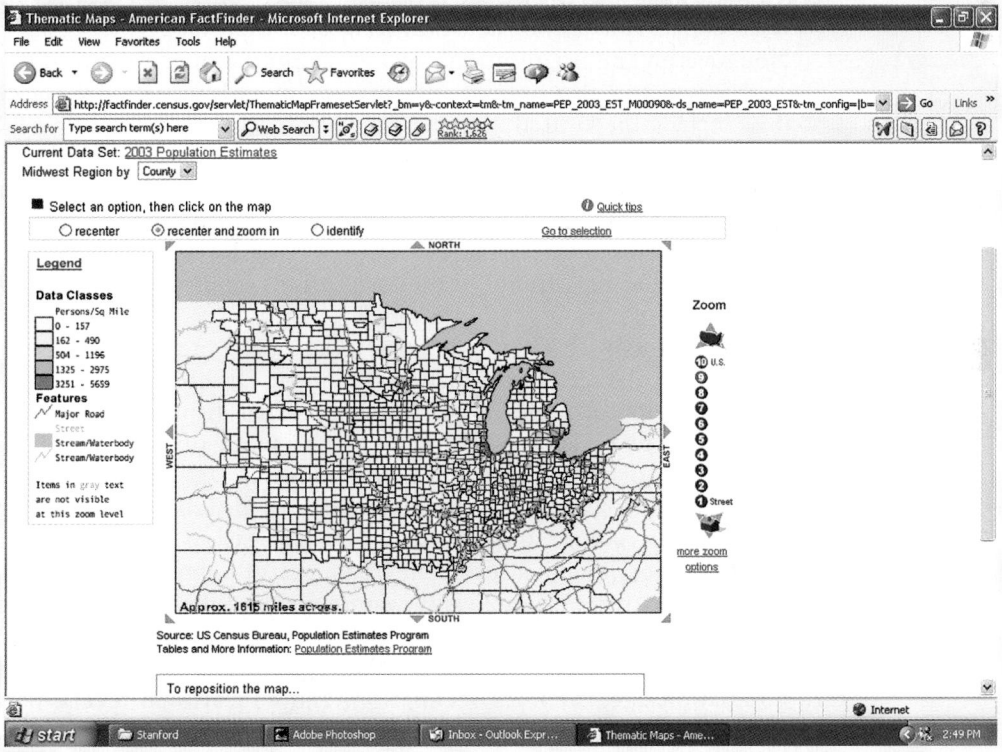

International Marketing Research

Secondary international data are available from both domestic government and nongovernment sources (Figure 4.7). The most important government sources are the Department of Commerce, the Agency for International Development, the Small Business Administration, the Export-Import Bank of the United States, the Department of Agriculture, the Department of State, the Department of Labor, and the Port Authority of New York and New Jersey. The Department of Commerce offers not only a

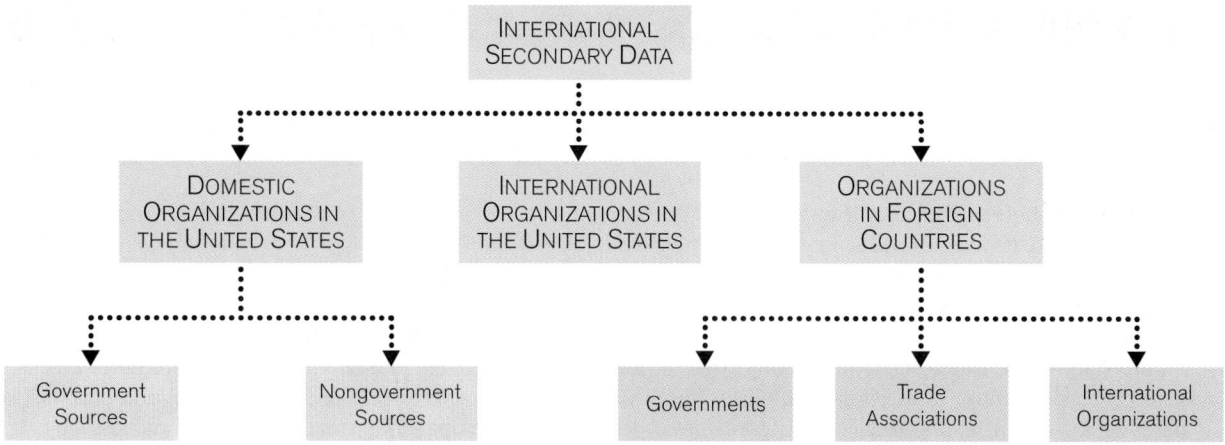

Figure 4.7

Sources of Secondary Data for International Marketing Research

number of publications but also a variety of other services, such as the foreign buyer program, matchmaker events, trade missions, export contact list service, the foreign commercial service, and custom statistical service for exporters.

Nongovernment organizations, including international organizations located in the United States, can also provide information about international markets. These data sources include the United Nations, the Organization for Economic Cooperation and Development (OECD), the International Monetary Fund (IMF), the World Bank, the International Chambers of Commerce, the Commission of the European Community to the United States, and the Japanese External Trade Organization (JETRO). Finally, locally-sourced secondary data are available from foreign governments, international organizations located abroad, trade associations, and private services, such as syndicated firms.

The problems with data compatibility are even more pronounced when dealing with secondary data from international sources. Differences in units of measurement for such common economic statistics as personal disposable income make comparisons between two countries difficult. The accuracy of secondary data may also vary with the level of industrialization in a country. Data from countries such as the United States are likely to be more accurate than those from developing countries. The taxation structure and the extent of tax evasion affect reported business and income statistics. The measurement frequency of population census data varies considerably. An extreme example is the comparison of the U.S. census, conducted every 10 years, to the census conducted in the People's Republic of China, where a 29-year gap occurred between the census of 1953 and 1982. Broad demographic data related to population age, income, occupation, and educational levels, particularly when evaluated over time, can be very useful in providing insight into trends in international markets.

Technology and Marketing Research

New information technologies will continue to revolutionize how marketing research is undertaken. Innovations will change the way both secondary and primary research is conducted. Technological advances have not only facilitated the establishment of sophisticated internal databases, they have enabled firms to collect primary data using creative promotions and automated systems, as illustrated by Pepsi Cola.

EXPERIENTIAL LEARNING

When It Comes to Secondary Data, *Quirk's* Is Not Secondary

One way research professionals stay current with trends and developing techniques of marketing research is by reading *Quirk's Marketing Research Review*. The average issue contains more than 100 pages and is printed in full color on glossy paper.

Go to (www.quirks.com) and click on "Article Archive."

At this Web page for searching the article archives of *Quirk's*, under "Search by Topic," you will find the selection box "Research Topics." Click on the check box to review all of the topics available. Select "International Research Studies." You won't have to make any more selections on this page. Now click the button for "Search Database" at the bottom of this page.

Review the available articles about international research presented here, select one that interests you, and read it by double-clicking on the hyperlink.

1. What interested you in this international research story?
2. What did you learn about international secondary data by reading this article?
3. What does what you learned about this international research topic suggest to you about the complexity of conducting research projects across two or more countries?

RESEARCH IN ACTION

Pepsi Puts Callers in Touch with Ray

In 2004, Diet Pepsi had a 5.1 percent share of the carbonated soft drink market. Pepsi Cola mailed one million cases of Diet Pepsi to Diet Coke consumers drawn from its internal database in a one-time effort to promote its product. Pepsi then decided to follow up its initial promotion with a research-oriented one.

Pepsi wanted an interactive marketing tool, and its direct marketing agency, Tracy-Locke Direct, consulted Modern Media for suggestions on the best available options. The result was an 800-number hotline called "Convert a Million."

Pepsi sent a direct-mail promotion to the same one million households to which it had mailed the Diet Pepsi cases and invited them to "talk" to Ray Charles, the Diet Pepsi pitchman, and potentially win an assortment of prizes. Consumers were required to answer a select group of marketing research questions before they were able to speak to Ray Charles and find out if they had won a prize.

West Interactive, an inbound telemarketing company, was contracted to manage the 800-number and to set up the 3½-minute, touch-tone automated telephone response survey. Pepsi wanted information on the types of soft drinks the consumers drank, how much they purchased, and so on in an effort to probe the mind of the Diet Coke drinker and possibly determine how to best market Diet Pepsi in an effort to convert Diet Coke drinkers.

Pepsi was surprised by the enormity of the response: More than 50 percent of the one million consumers targeted responded to the promotion. The respondents provided information concerning brand preference, consumption rates, and lifestyle activities. The "Convert a Million" survey was so successful, it won a Gold Echo award from the Direct Marketing Association.

According to Jerry Winter, manager of database marketing at Pepsi, the success of the interactive survey convinced Pepsi of the value of technology in marketing research. The company has plans for other interactive surveys/promotions using the database in the future.[8]

Ethics in Marketing Research

Researchers sometimes overlook the disadvantages and advantages of secondary data discussed earlier, which raises ethical issues. The research firm has the ethical responsibility to use only secondary data that are relevant and appropriate to the problem. The data used should be critically evaluated, using the criteria described in this chapter. The researcher should discuss issues surrounding the relevance and accuracy of secondary data with the client.

After a detailed analysis of secondary data has been conducted, the researcher should reexamine the collection of primary data stipulated in the proposal to see if it is still appropriate. Any needed changes in the primary data collection methodology should be discussed with the client. In the extreme case, if primary data are no longer needed, then it is the ethical responsibility of the researcher to disclose this to the client.

In addition to evaluating their quality and completeness, researchers should also evaluate secondary data in terms of moral appropriateness. Data collection may be unethical if the data are generated without the respondents' knowledge or consent and if their use raises ethical questions. While generating secondary data, researchers and syndicate firms should not engage in any questionable or unethical practices, such as abuse of respondents' privacy. Privacy has, indeed, become a burning issue, as illustrated by the following example.

SPSS Windows

SPSS Maps integrates seamlessly with SPSS base menus, enabling you to map a variety of data. The user can choose from six base thematic maps or create other maps by combining map options. Maps can be further customized using the SPSS Syntax Editor. Such maps can be used for a variety of purposes including (1) interpreting sales and other data geographically to determine where the biggest customers are located, (2) displaying sales trends for specific geographic locations, and (3) using buying trend information to determine the ideal location for new company stores.

RESEARCH IN ACTION

Privacy Issue Goes Public

The legal environment is becoming increasingly hostile toward marketing research. Government is considering more legislation that will cover a list of alleged privacy abuses in marketing research. Some 500 bills that cover a list of privacy abuses and protections have been introduced around the United States. The privacy issue has gone public with a wave of consumer complaints against many forms of marketing research.

Two main issues are involved. First, consumers feel they should not have to cope with unsolicited sales pitches that flood their mailboxes, phones, and e-mail addresses. The second issue concerns the sophisticated databases that maintain enormous amounts of information about consumers, ranging from their names to specifics about their lifestyles and product consumption habits. In a privacy survey conducted by Equifax, 78 percent of the respondents said they were concerned about the personal privacy issue. A majority of the respondents said they thought it was reasonable for companies to conduct public record information checks, such as credit checks, auto insurance checks, or job checks, but that consumers should be able to opt out of all other transactions.[9]

WHAT WOULD *YOU* DO?

Tommy Hilfiger: Keeping Abreast of the Market to Remain a High Flyer

The Situation

From the blacktop to the golf course, designer Tommy Hilfiger has the streets covered. His namesake casual wear is worn by rap, rock, teen, and sports stars and fans. These days, many of them are women. Tommy designs, sources, makes, and markets men's and women's sportswear and denim wear, as well as athletic wear, children's wear, and accessories. Through extensive licensing deals (almost 40 product lines), Tommy also offers products such as fragrances, belts, bedding, home furnishings, and cosmetics. The company's clean-cut clothing is sold in major department and specialty stores as well as 165 Tommy Hilfiger shops and outlets. Annual revenue for the 2003 fiscal year was $1.89 billion. With such a large empire, it is no wonder that Tommy Hilfiger Corp. Chairman, CEO, and President Joel J. Horowitz is always kept busy trying to make sure the company does not forget the most important aspect of its business–satisfying consumers' needs!

Selling apparel will never be an easy job. "Just when you think you've figured out exactly what your customers want, everything changes–sometimes overnight," says apparel expert Richard Romer, executive vice president for The CIT Group/Commercial Services, a New York-based credit protection and lending services provider for apparel manufacturers. "Basically, changes in apparel occur every other year: long skirts to short skirts and back to long." The apparel market's constant state of flux forces catalog retailers and other marketers to constantly reevaluate the market they're targeting and then reinvent their companies, their offerings, and their catalogs.

The Marketing Research Decisions

1. What sources of secondary data should Tommy Hilfiger consult to keep informed about apparel fashion trends? Check as many as are applicable.
   a. Apparel industry trade association databases
   b. U.S. Bureau of the Census, census of population
   c. University of Michigan, consumer confidence index
   d. United Nations' international database
   e. All of the above
2. Discuss how the type of research you recommend would enable Joel J. Horowitz and Tommy Hilfiger to keep abreast of the apparel fashion trends.

The Marketing Management Decision

1. In order to enhance the appeal of Tommy Hilfiger clothing to the fashion conscious consumer, Joel J. Horowitz should (check as many as are applicable):
   a. Introduce new lines of designer clothing
   b. Feature supermodels in Tommy Hilfiger's advertising
   c. Increase the distribution of Tommy Hilfiger clothing through fashion boutiques and other specialty channels
   d. Lower the prices of Tommy Hilfiger clothing
   e. Acquire additional brands
2. Discuss how the marketing management decision action that you recommend to Joel J. Horowitz is influenced by the secondary sources of data that you suggested earlier and by the content of information they provide.

What Joel J. Horowitz Did

Tommy Hilfiger Corp. announced on May 8, 2003, that it would begin a search to acquire additional brands. Tommy Hilfiger now says it hopes to develop a multibrand, multichannel business strategy. "While we continue to be focused on improving operations in our existing business, we are aggressively seeking opportunities to further diversify our revenue and earnings base," Horowitz said.

Bold stripes and high contrast were the visual hallmarks of Tommy Hilfiger's newly designed advertising campaign. Fall fashions were mod-inspired and flaunted by a cast of young, sexy models with tousled hair and smoky eyes, all evoking the iconic imagery of the 1960s. The stripes and bold graphic lines reflect the timeless, universal appeal of the classic Hilfiger designs.[10]

Summary

In contrast to primary data that are collected for a specific research problem, secondary data have been generated for reasons other than the current research problem. The cost advantage and speed with which secondary data can be obtained must be weighed against their limited fit to the current research problem and concerns regarding data accuracy. In evaluating secondary data, the researcher should consider factors such as specifications, error, currency, objectivity, nature, and dependability.

Internally-generated information can represent a gold mine for a researcher. Any department that touches the final consumer in some way may be a source of valuable market data. The internally-generated data can be supplemented with demographic and lifestyle data available from external sources to produce a rich database that can target customers and guide marketing effort.

External data are generated by sources outside the organization. These data exist in the form of published (printed) material; online, Internet, and offline databases; or information made available by syndicated services. Published external sources may be broadly classified as general business data or government data. General business sources comprise guides, directories, indexes, and statistical data. Government sources may be broadly categorized as census data and other data. Computerized databases may be online, Internet, or offline, and they may be further classified as bibliographic, numeric, full-text, directory, or specialized databases.

Both internal and external databases yield potentially helpful information. International research is prone to problems of data quality, and thus these data should be carefully evaluated. Technological advances are facilitating the establishment of sophisticated internal databases. The researcher has the ethical responsibility to use only secondary data that are relevant and appropriate to the problem. The Internet is a valuable source of secondary data.

Key Terms and Concepts

Primary data, 97
Secondary data, 97
Internal data, 103
External data, 103
Data warehouse, 104
Psychographics, 104
Data mining, 104
Customer relationship management (CRM) system, 104
Database marketing, 104
Online databases, 110
Internet databases, 110
Offline databases, 110
Bibliographic databases, 111
Numeric databases, 111
Full-text databases, 111
Directory databases, 111
Special-purpose databases, 112
Geo-demographic coding, 113
Syndicated services, 113
Geo-visual databases, 113
Computer mapping, 114

Suggested Cases and Video Cases

Cases

2.1 Maxfli **2.2 Cadillac** **2.4 Bloomingdale's** **2.5 Burger King**
4.1 Boeing **4.2 Gucci**

Video Cases

2.1 Starbucks **4.1 Subaru** **4.2 Marriott**

Additional cases and video cases are available in the Instructor's Manual and on the instructor and student Web sites.

Live Research: Conducting a Marketing Research Project

1. One, some, or all the teams can be assigned the responsibility of collecting and analyzing secondary data.
2. If this work is divided, one or some teams could search the library's electronic database; others could search government sources; and yet other teams could visit the library and work with a reference librarian to identify the relevant sources.

Acronyms

The criteria used for evaluating secondary data may be described by the acronym SECOND:

S pecifications: methodology used to collect the data
E rror: accuracy of the data
C urrency: when the data were collected
O bjective: purpose for which data were collected
N ature: content of the data
D ependability: overall, how dependable are the data

Review Questions

1. What are the differences between primary and secondary data?
2. Why is it important to obtain secondary data before primary data?
3. What are the advantages of secondary data?
4. What are the disadvantages of secondary data?
5. What are the criteria to be used when evaluating secondary data?
6. What is the difference between internal and external secondary data?
7. What are the various sources of published secondary data?
8. What are the different forms of computerized databases?
9. What are the advantages of computerized databases?
10. Is it useful to combine internal and external secondary data? Why?
11. What does geo-coding mean? Give an example.
12. Explain a geo-visual database.
13. What is database marketing?

Applied Problems

1. Select an industry of your choice. Using external published sources, obtain industry sales and the sales of the major firms in that industry for the past year. Estimate the market shares of each major firm. Use a computerized database to obtain information on the market shares of these same firms. Do the two estimates agree? Was it easier to obtain the information from published sources or from a computerized database?
2. Determine the e-commerce sales for the past year from each of the following sources: Forrester Research (www.forrester.com), ComScore (www.comscore.com), Nielsen//Netratings (www.netratings.com), and the U.S. Commerce Department (www.commerce.gov). Do these four estimates agree?
3. You are enhancing Apple's internal household customer data with externally available information. Visit the Experian Web site (www.experian.com) to determine what demographic and psychographic data are available that would be useful to Apple for targeting the household computer market.
4. Visit the NAICS Association Web site (www.naics.com). Find the NAICS codes for "Computers manufacturing" and "Hospitals, general medical and surgical." Discuss the significance and usefulness of these codes.
5. Visit (www.dnb.com) and write a report about the type of information on businesses available from D&B.
6. Visit the Web site of the U.S. Census Bureau (www.census.gov). Write a report about the secondary data available from the Bureau that would be useful to a fast-food firm such as McDonald's for the purpose of formulating a domestic marketing strategy.
7. Visit the U.S. Census Bureau Web site (www.census.gov/statab.) Use State Rankings and Vital Statistics to identify the top six states for marketing products to the elderly.

Group Discussion

1. Discuss the significance and limitations of the government census data as a major source of secondary data.
2. Discuss the growing use of computerized databases.

CHAPTER

5

Exploratory Research Design: Syndicated Sources of Secondary Data

"As competition intensifies, companies increasingly want marketplace metrics to gauge their performance relative to the competition. For many, syndicated data is what they use."

Kris Baker, *Vice President, Group Client Director, ACNielsen, Lewisville, TX*

OPENING QUESTIONS

1. How are syndicated data different from other secondary data? How can such data be classified?
2. What are the major methods of obtaining syndicated data from households/consumers?
3. How are syndicated data collected from institutions?
4. Why should multiple sources of secondary data be used? What is meant by *single-source data*?
5. What syndicated data are available for conducting international marketing research?
6. How does technology enhance the usefulness of syndicated data?
7. What ethical issues are involved in the use of syndicated data?

A Casual Affair

Even though clothing designers seem to be defining fashion as dressy, most Americans seem to be opting for a more casual approach to their fashion needs. Today, companies are saying goodbye to three-piece suits, wingtips, and high heels and are welcoming a more casual dress style. The West Coast dot-com companies have definitely contributed to the casual dress trend. More recently, consulting firms, law firms, and investment companies on the East Coast have joined this trend as well. A recent survey reported that a remarkable 87 percent of responding companies had a casual Friday or an everyday casual policy at their place of business. Companies such as Coca-Cola, Ford, J. P. Morgan, and Accenture have implemented full-time casual dress policies. At many companies today, when someone wears a suit to work, the question asked immediately is, "Are you going on a job interview?"

According to data available from syndicated marketing research firms, there is a growing "business casual" segment. As discussed in Chapter 1, syndicated data are made available for purchase by multiple clients on a subscription basis. For example, according to a recent survey by the NPD Group, a well-known source of syndicated services, almost 90 percent of U.S. workers said they were dressing down at least some of the time. The NPD study revealed that while sales in many categories of tailored clothing, including dresses and men's suits, were down, sales of casual apparel, such as no-iron cotton slacks and sweaters, were on the rise. Several marketers of casual clothing have built their strategies based on these findings.

Haggar Apparel is out to convince its male customers that the company can do everything from tailored to casual. Based on such syndicated data, Haggar realized that the trend is not in the direction of tailored suits, where for years, the company has been the market leader. The company responded by introducing its "City Casuals" line. The wrinkle-free cotton trousers have been the biggest success in this line. Haggar supported all its lines, formal to casual, with its slogan, "Haggar. Stuff You Can Wear," which was developed by Goodby, Silverstein & Partners.

Haggar's internal research showed that Enron and WorldCom weren't the only ones in corporate America allegedly tinkering with numbers. It seems most men don't like to admit their true waist size and end up buying pants that are too small. The product born of this realization was Comfort Fit, a cotton khaki introduced in 2002 that expands up to three inches through hidden elastic embedded in the waistline. Pants also appeal to more economically conservative men who, even if they've gained several pounds, hate to throw out pants in good condition.

Haggar is not the only company offering fashion tips for a more casual appearance. Marshall Field's, one of the premier department stores in the United States, has also tailored its efforts towards the corporate market. Its customer newsletter featured an article on workday dressing down, and the store offered a one-hour seminar on casual fashions, complete with free lunch.

In an effort to capitalize on this trend toward casual clothing, Levi Strauss is pushing both its Dockers and jeans lines. Although 90 percent of U.S. offices permit employees to wear jeans, there is still some reluctance by employees to wear them to work as they are considered too casual. The company has had huge success with the Dockers trouser line that has become standard wear for the casual business dresser. The success of Haggar's Comfort Fit has not been lost on Dockers, which in 2003 introduced its own expandable version, called Individual Fit. This sort of cross-pollination is going on throughout the industry, and the time seems near when consumers will be able to purchase virtually any garment in a stain-free, wrinkle-free, expandable variant.[1]

As this vignette illustrates, even competing firms such as Haggar, Marshall Field's, and Levi Strauss are able to make use of the same data available from syndicate firms such as the NPD Group to formulate their marketing strategies. •

Overview

Chapters 1 and 4 introduced the concept of syndicated sources of information. In this chapter, we explain syndicated data in detail and distinguish them from other external sources of secondary data. As shown in Figure 5.1, this chapter relates to marketing research suppliers and services discussed in Chapter 1, the tasks involved in problem definition and developing an approach covered in Chapter 2, and exploratory and descriptive research designs described in Chapter 3. Thus, it is related to the first three steps of the marketing research process. The three major methods of collecting syndicated data related to consumers and households are surveys, panels, and electronic scanner services. Syndicated data are also collected from institutions. This chapter describes retail and wholesale audits and industrial services used to collect such data. This is followed by a discussion of single-source data. As the name indicates, single-source data combine data from various sources to create a unified database that contains information on consumer purchases, demographic and psychographic variables, and marketing management variables. Finally, the chapter discusses the applications of syndicated data to international marketing research, the impact of technology, ethics, and the use of the Internet. Figure 5.2 gives an overview of the topics discussed in this chapter and how they flow from one to the next.

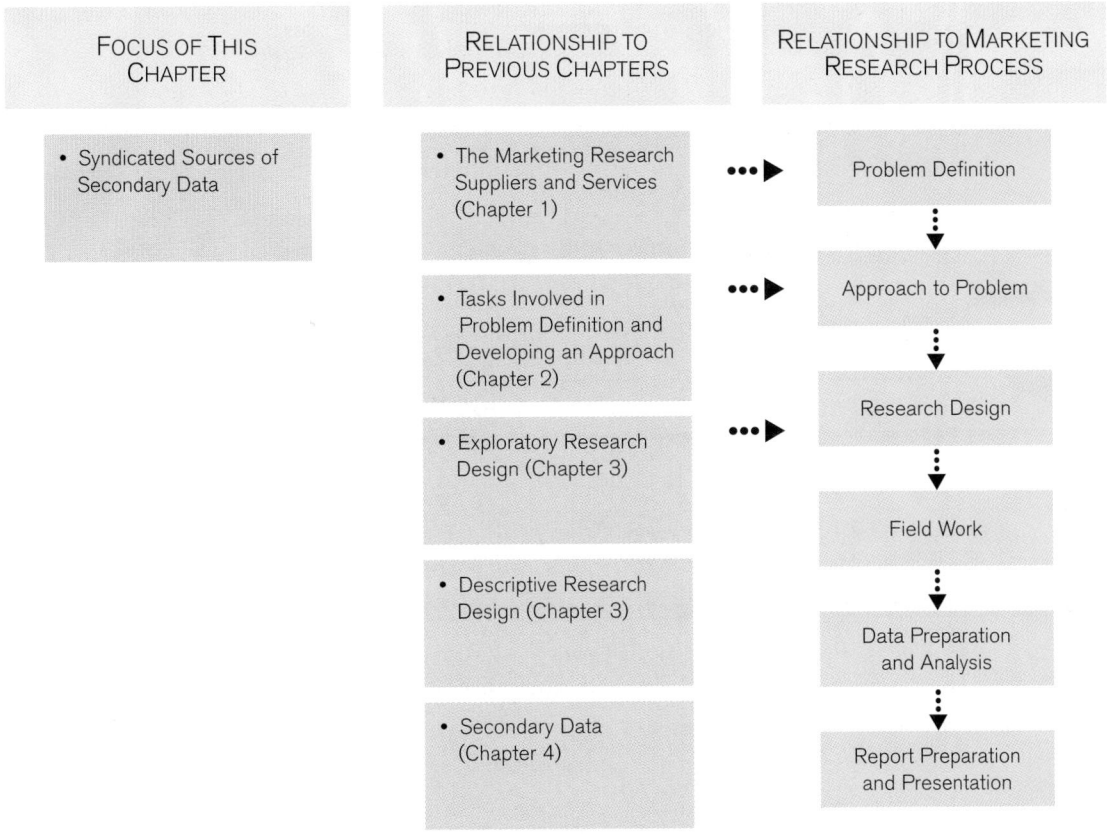

Figure 5.1

Relationship of Syndicated Sources to the Previous Chapters and the Marketing Research Process

The Nature of Syndicated Data

In addition to published data or data available in the form of computerized databases, syndicated sources constitute the other major source of external secondary data. **Syndicated sources**, also referred to as **syndicated services**, are companies that collect and sell common pools of data of known commercial value, designed to serve information needs shared by a number of clients, including competing firms in the same industry. This was illustrated in the opening vignette. Survey data collected by the NPD Group were useful to Haggar Apparel, Marshall Field's, and Levi Strauss. These data differ from primary data in that the research objective guiding the study is common to several client firms. Syndicated firms make their money by collecting data and designing research products that fit the information needs of more than one organization. Often, syndicated data and services are designed for use by multiple clients from multiple industries.

syndicated sources (services)
Companies that collect and sell common pools of data designed to serve information needs shared by a number of clients, including competing firms in the same industry.

Although classified as secondary, syndicated data differ from other sources of secondary data in that syndicated data are collected because they have known commercial value to marketers. Both census data and other externally generated secondary data (Chapter 4) are general data collected for purposes other than the specific marketing research problem a client faces. In contrast, the types of data syndicated services collect have very specific marketing research applications that are of interest to a number of clients.

Any client, even two competitors in the same industry (e.g., Coca-Cola Company and PepsiCo) can purchase the same syndicated data, typically through a subscription process. This process reflects the ongoing nature of many syndicated projects. These projects provide data that enable tracking of change over time as well as point-in-time measurements. The data and reports that syndicate firms supply to client companies can be personalized to fit specific needs. For example, reports could be organized on the basis of the client's sales territories or product lines.

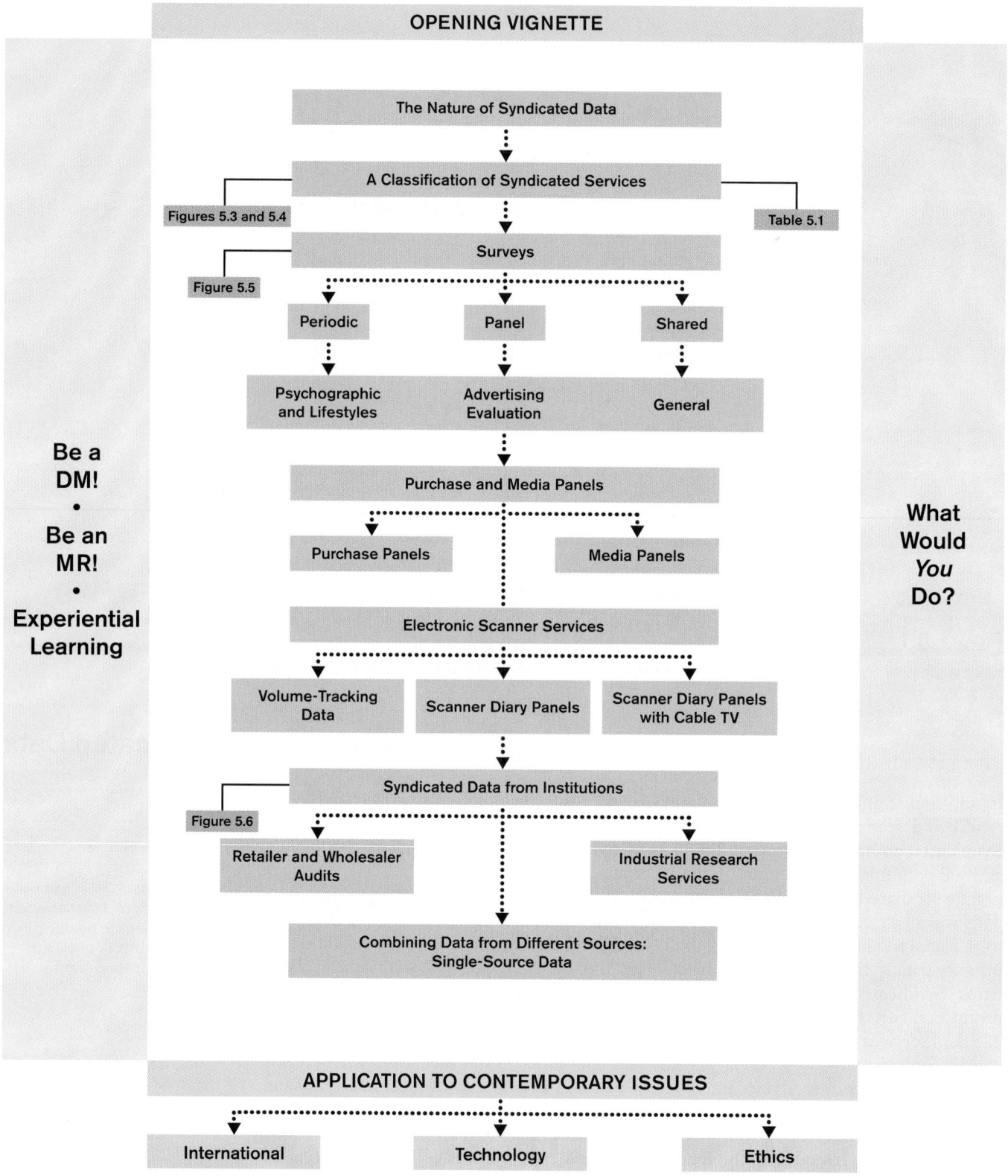

Figure 5.2

Syndicate Sources of Secondary Data: An Overview

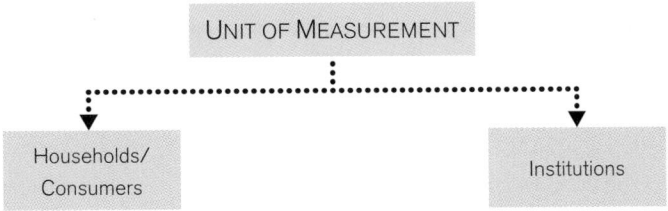

Figure 5.3
A Classification of Syndicated Services

A Classification of Syndicated Services

Figure 5.3 presents a classification of syndicated sources based on either a household/consumer or institutional unit of measurement. Household/consumer data typically relate to general values and lifestyles, media use, or product purchase patterns. Data may be collected through a survey process, recorded manually by the respondent in diaries (paper or electronic), or captured electronically via scanners (Figure 5.4). Consumer surveys are used to obtain information on beliefs, values, attitudes, preferences, and intentions. Panels used in consumer research emphasize information on purchases or media consumption. Electronic scanner services track purchases at the point of sale or in the home through hand-held scanners (Figure 5.4). These data collection techniques may also be integrated, linking electronic scanner data with panels, survey data, or targeted television advertising through cable.

When syndicated services obtain data from institutions rather than households, the primary subjects they track are product movement through the distribution channel (retailers and wholesalers) or corporate statistics. An overview of the various syndicated sources is given in Table 5.1. Each of these sources will be discussed.

Surveys

We will begin our discussion with general surveys. The NPD survey reported in the opening vignette is an example. There are three types of general surveys: periodic, panel, and shared (Figure 5.5).

periodic surveys
Collect data on the same set of variables at regular intervals, each time sampling from a new group of respondents.

panel surveys
Measure the same group of respondents over time but not necessarily on the same variables.

Periodic Surveys **Periodic surveys** collect data on the same set of variables at regular intervals, each time sampling a new group of respondents. Like longitudinal research, periodic surveys track change over time. However, the change due to variation in the respondent pool is not controlled in the way it is for true longitudinal studies. A new sample of respondents is chosen with each survey taken by the syndicate firm. Once analyzed, the data are made available to subscribers.

Panel Surveys Syndicated **panel surveys** measure the same group of respondents over time but not necessarily on the same variables. A large pool of respondents is recruited to

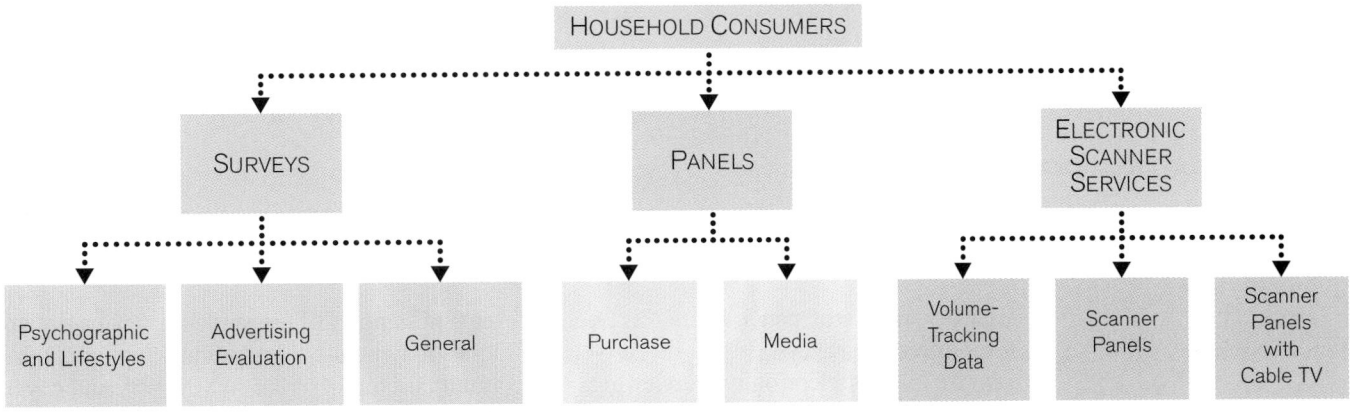

Figure 5.4
A Classification of Syndicated Services: Household Consumers

Table 5.1

Overview of Syndicated Services

Type	Characteristics	Advantages	Disadvantages	Uses
Surveys	Surveys conducted at regular intervals	Most flexible way of obtaining data; information on underlying motives	Interviewer errors; respondent errors	Market segmentation, advertising theme selection, and advertising effectiveness
Purchase Panels	Households provide specific information regularly over an extended period of time; respondents asked to record specific behaviors as they occur	Recorded purchase behavior can be linked to the demographic/ psychographic characteristics	Lack of representativeness; response bias; maturation	Forecasting sales, market share, and trends; establishing consumer profiles and brand loyalty and switching; evaluating test markets, advertising, and distribution
Media Panels	Electronic devices automatically record behavior, supplemented by a diary	Same as purchase panel	Same as purchase panel	Establishing advertising rates; selecting media program or air time; establishing viewer profiles
Scanner Volume-Tracking Data	Household purchases are recorded through electronic scanners in supermarkets	Data reflect actual purchases; timely data less expensive	Data may not be representative; errors in recording purchases; difficult to link purchases to elements of marketing mix other than price	Price tracking, modeling, assessing effectiveness of in-store modeling
Scanner Panels with Cable TV	Scanner panels of households that subscribe to cable TV	Data reflect actual purchases; sample control; ability to link panel data to household characteristics	Data may not be representative; quality of data limited	Promotional-mix analyses, copy testing, new-product testing, positioning
Audit Services	Verification of product movement by examining physical records or performing inventory analysis	Relatively precise information at the retail and wholesale levels	Coverage may be incomplete; matching of data on competitive activity may be difficult	Measuring consumer sales, market share, and competitive activity, analyzing distribution patterns; tracking of new products
Industrial Product Syndicated Services	Data banks on industrial establishments through direct inquiries of companies, clipping services, and corporate reports	Important source of information in industrial firms, particularly useful in initial phases of the marketing research process	Data is lacking in terms of content, quantity, and quality	Determining market potential by geographic area, defining sales territories, allocating advertising budget

participate on the panel. From this pool, different subsamples of respondents may be drawn for different surveys. Any of the survey techniques may be used, including telephone, personal, mail, or electronic interviewing. The content and topics of the surveys vary and cover a wide range. Also known as *omnibus panels*, these panels are different from the panels using longitudinal designs discussed in Chapter 3. It may be recalled that in a longitudinal design, repeated measurements on the same variables are made on the same sample.

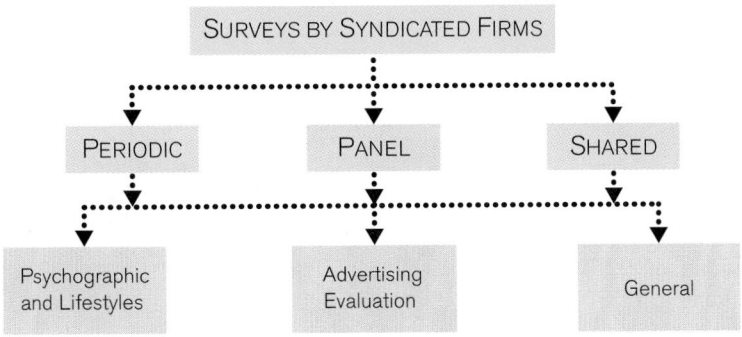

Figure 5.5
Classification of Syndicated Survey Research

Panel surveys are used primarily because of their lower cost compared to random sampling. These savings result due to streamlining of the data collection process, enhanced response rates, and readily available sample frames, which can be precisely targeted. Comprehensive demographic, lifestyle, and product-ownership data are collected only once as each respondent is admitted into the panel. The panel is used as a respondent pool from which the research organization can draw either representative or targeted samples based on the relevant background characteristics of the panel members. Response rates to panel surveys, including mail panels, are substantially improved over the random sampling process because of the commitment panel members make to participate in surveys.

Shared Surveys As the name implies, **shared surveys** are developed and executed for multiple clients, each of whom shares the expenses. The bulk of a shared survey deals with questions of general interest to the client group. These general questions are also typically supplemented with proprietary questions from each participating client. Responses to the general interest questions are available to the entire group, while the answers to proprietary questions are held in confidence and provided only to the appropriate client. This survey may be repeated at regular intervals, or it may be a one-time study. The sample may be drawn from an omnibus panel or randomly from the population of interest. Shared surveys are one way for syndicated research organizations to offer customized reports to their clients.

shared surveys
Developed and executed for multiple clients, each of whom shares the expenses.

The primary advantage of shared surveys, as with all forms of secondary research, is lower cost. The fixed cost of research design and the variable cost of data collection are shared by the participants, making the cost-per-question relatively low for each client. Popular ongoing shared surveys include TeleNation and Data Gage from Synovate (www.synovate.com) and OmniTel Telephone Survey by NOP World (www.nopworld.com). Although a number of clients share these surveys, a certain degree of customization is offered, as illustrated by NOP World.

RESEARCH IN ACTION

NOP World: Customization via Syndication

OmniTel by NOP World (www.nopworld.com) is a syndicated service that offers customization of their survey reports. Their public opinion research service collects data on a broad range of social, economic, political, and consumer issues every week. The organization conducts telephone interviews with a national sample of 1,000 adults aged 18 and older. In addition to the standard questions that are common across clients, clients can add customized questions that are proprietary. Thus, Ford Motor Company can purchase the general survey results related to automobiles. Ford can also request proprietary questions about its models, such as Taurus, to determine why sales are lagging behind major competitors, such as Toyota Camry and Honda Accord.

According to the NOP World, the ability to add proprietary questions along with customized report generation offers a unique combination of frequency, speed of report delivery, quality, low cost, large sample size, and extensive demographic breaks. This ability to customize surveys and reports has been a major factor in the popularity of the OmniTel survey.

RESEARCH IN ACTION

Free at Last

The firm of Yankelovich Research and Consulting Services (www.yankelovich.com) provides the Yankelovich Monitor, a survey that contains data on lifestyles and social trends. The survey is conducted at the same time each year among a nationally projectable sample of 2,500 adults, 16 and older, including a special sample of 300 college students living on campus. The sample is based on the most recent updates of census data. All interviews are conducted in person at each respondent's home and take approximately 2.5 hours to complete.

The Yankelovich Monitor indicated that Americans were becoming more and more health and nutrition conscious. As such, many consumers were giving up hot dogs. Based on these findings, Kraft created a fat-free frank that the company claimed would still offer the expected taste and texture. This marked the introduction of Oscar Mayer FREE Hot Dogs. This little doggie was big news. As the first one to market, the product had news value that generated a lot of coverage.

The company reported that the trial exceeded expectations, with almost 10 percent of households giving the product a shot in the first year. Based on volume, velocity, and distribution, Oscar Mayer FREE is the number-one selling brand among "ultra-healthy" products, which the company believes helped fuel that segment's growth of more than 60 percent.[2]

BE an MR!

Visit NOP World's Web site (www.nopworld.com) and write a brief report about the OmniTel Telephone Survey offered by this firm.

How can you make use of the OmniTel Telephone Survey by NOP World to obtain information that will help Sony increase the penetration of flat-panel television sets in the United States?

BE a DM!

What marketing strategies should Sony adopt to increase the penetration of flat-panel television sets in the United States?

Surveys may also be broadly classified on the basis of their content as psychographics and lifestyles, advertising evaluation, or general surveys (Figures 5.4 and 5.5).

psychographics
Quantified psychological profiles of consumers' activities, interests, and opinions.

lifestyle
A distinctive pattern of living that is described by the activities people engage in, the interests they have, and the opinions they hold of themselves and the world around them (AIOs).

Psychographics and Lifestyles **Psychographics** refer to the quantified psychological profiles of consumers' activities, interests, and opinions. **Lifestyle** refers to the distinctive modes of living within a society or some of its segments, such as the DINKs (Double Income No Kids) lifestyle characterized as being money rich and time poor. Together, these measures are generally referred to as Activities, Interests, and Opinions, or simply as AIOs. The Yankelovich Monitor provides an application.

As another example, SRI Consulting (www.sric-bi.com), partner of SRI International and formerly Stanford Research Institute, conducts an annual survey of consumers that is used to classify persons into VALS (Values and Lifestyles) types for segmentation purposes. Information on specific aspects of consumers' lifestyles is also available. NOP World conducts an annual survey of 5,000 consumers who participate in leisure sports and recreational activities. Several syndicate firms conduct surveys to compile demographic and psychographic information at the household, sub-zip (e.g., 30306-3035), and

RESEARCH IN ACTION

Magazine Impact Research Service (MIRS)

In the MIRS by Gallup and Robinson (www.gallup-robinson.com), ads are tested using an at-home in-magazine context among widely dispersed samples. The system offers standardized measures with flexible design options. Test ads may naturally appear in the magazine or are inserted as tip-ins. It provides strong, validated measures of recall, persuasion, and ad reaction with responsive scheduling. This information is very useful to companies that advertise heavily in print media, such as American Airlines, Gucci, and GM, for evaluating the effectiveness of their advertising. MIRS has become an industry standard for magazine ad testing.[3]

zip-code level, which is then made available on a subscription basis. Such information is particularly valuable for client firms seeking to enhance internally generated customer data for database marketing.

Advertising Evaluation The purpose of these surveys is to measure the size and profile of the advertising audience and to assess the effectiveness of advertising using print and broadcast media. A well-known survey is the Gallup and Robinson Magazine Impact Research Service that is described in the example we have given.

Evaluation of effectiveness is even more critical in the case of television advertising. Television commercials are evaluated using either the recruited audience method or the in-home viewing method. In the recruited audience method, respondents are brought to a theater or mobile viewing laboratory. After viewing a series of advertisements, they are surveyed regarding related product knowledge, attitudes, and preferences as well as reaction to the advertisements. With the in-home viewing method, consumers evaluate commercials in their normal viewing environment. New commercials can be pretested at the network level or in local markets. Audience reaction to the advertisements is recorded along with respondent demographics. Gallup & Robinson, Inc. offers testing of television commercials using both of these methods. These methods are also used for testing the effectiveness of advertising in other media, such as magazines, radio, newspapers, and direct mail.

General Surveys Surveys are also conducted for a variety of other purposes, including examination of purchase and consumption behavior. The Gallup Organization (www.gallup.com) surveys a random sample of 1,000 households by telephone about a variety of topics. The weekly Harris Poll by Harris Interactive (www.harrisinteractive.com) is also based on a nationally representative telephone survey of 1,000 adults aged 18 or over. Again, a wide range of topics is considered.

Uses of Surveys

Surveys that are designed to collect psychographic and lifestyle data can be used for market segmentation, developing consumer profiles, or determining consumer preferences, as for casual clothing in the opening vignette. Surveys are also useful for determining product image or positioning and for conducting price-perception analysis and advertising research.

Advantages and Disadvantages of Surveys

Surveys are the primary means of obtaining information about consumers' motives, attitudes, and preferences. The flexibility of surveys is reflected in the variety of questions that can be asked and the visual aids, packages, products, or other props that can be used during the interviews. Additionally, the sampling process enables targeting of respondents with very specific characteristics.

Because survey researchers have to rely primarily on the respondents' self-reports, there can be serious limitations to data gathered in this way. What people say is not always what they actually do. Errors may occur because respondents remember incorrectly or feel pressured to

EXPERIENTIAL LEARNING

Wal-Mart's Share of the Consumer Market in Chicago

Scarborough Research (www.scarborough.com) is a leader in syndicated consumer market research. Scarborough surveys over 200,000 adults aged 18 and up using a two-phase methodology. Phase I is the telephone interview, and Phase II is a self-administered questionnaire and television diary. A total of 75 leading U.S. markets are measured.

PRIME NExT is Scarborough Research's software that provides a front-end interface to the Scarborough database. It is a Windows-based delivery system that gives users the power to analyze and manipulate local data from all 75 measured markets directly from a subscribing researcher's desktop. Data can be easily exported into spreadsheets, graphic programs, word processors, or mapping and sales-presentation modules for added marketing value.

To understand how a researcher for Wal-Mart could use syndicated data from Scarborough Research to track the share of the consumer market visiting Wal-Mart in the last three months, take the short tutorial about PRIME NExT at (www.library.uiuc.edu/bel/classes/prime_next/). (If this URL has moved, please search the Internet for the new location.) This tutorial will take you through the process of answering the question, "How many individuals between the ages of 18 and 30 shopped at a Wal-Mart in the Chicago area in the last three months?" At the bottom of each page, click the "Next Page >>" link to move forward in the tutorial.

The answers to the following questions can be found in the "View Report" screen in the next to the last row named "Vert %." The number entered in the cell of first column in this row corresponds to the "total group 18–30." The number entered in the cell of the second column corresponds to the "18–20" group, and so on.[4]

1. What is the percentage of Chicago consumers between the ages of 18 and 30 who shopped at Wal-Mart in the last three months?
2. What is the percentage of Chicago consumers between the ages of 18 and 20 who shopped at Wal-Mart in the last three months?
3. What is the percentage of Chicago consumers between the ages of 21 and 24 who shopped at Wal-Mart in the last three months?
4. What is the percentage of Chicago consumers between the ages of 25 and 29 who shopped at Wal-Mart in the last three months?

give the "right" answer. Furthermore, samples may be biased, questions poorly phrased, interviewers not properly instructed or supervised, and results misinterpreted.

Although surveys remain popular for both primary and secondary research, panels do a much better job of tracking consumer behavior.

BE a DM!

As the CEO of Ford Motor Company, what marketing strategies would you adopt to increase the dependability and image of Ford vehicles?

BE an MR!

Visit J. D. Power's Web site (www.jdpower.com) and write a brief report about the latest vehicle-dependability study findings and methodology.

How can you make use of the J. D. Power vehicle-dependability study and other secondary and syndicated data to help Ford Motor Company to increase the dependability and image of its vehicles?

Purchase and Media Panels

A purchase or media panel is made up of a group of individuals, households, or organizations that record their purchases and behavior in a diary or on the Internet over time. Households are continually being recruited and added to the panel as respondents drop out of the study or are removed in order to rotate the panel. The makeup of the panel is designed to be representative of the U.S. population in terms of demographics.

While panels are also maintained for conducting surveys, the distinguishing feature of purchase and media panels is that the respondents record specific behaviors (e.g., product purchases or media usage) as they occur. This makes the information more accurate. Previously, behavior was recorded in a diary, and the diary was returned to the research organization every one to four weeks. Paper diaries have been gradually replaced by electronic diaries. Now, most of the panels are online and the behavior is recorded electronically, either entered online by the respondents or recorded automatically by electronic devices. Panel members are compensated for their participation with gifts, coupons, information, or cash. Based on the content of information recorded, these panels can be classified as either purchase panels or media panels.

Purchase Panels

Survey data can often be complemented with data obtained from **purchase panels**, in which respondents record their purchases in a diary or on the Internet. The NPD Group (www.npd.com) is a leading provider of essential market information collected and delivered online for a wide range of industries and markets and operates in more than 20 countries as of 2005. NPD combines information obtained via surveys with that recorded by respondents about their behaviors to generate reports on consumption behaviors, industry sales, market share, and key demographic trends. NPD consumer information is collected from their Online Panel about a wide range of product categories, including fashion, food, fun, house and home, technology, and automobiles. Respondents provide detailed information regarding the brand and amount purchased, price paid, whether any special deals were involved, the store where purchased, and intended use. The composition of the panel is representative of the U.S. population as a whole. Information provided by the NPD Panel is used by soft drink firms, such as the Coca-Cola Company, to determine brand loyalty and brand switching and to profile heavy users of various brands.

purchase panels
A data gathering technique in which respondents record their purchases in a diary or on the Internet.

Other organizations that maintain purchase panels include the NFO World Group (www.nfow.com). This group maintains a number of panels, including a large interactive one. NFO Special Panels, such as Baby Panel, provide access to highly targeted groups of consumers. Each quarter, approximately 2,000 new mothers and 2,000 expectant mothers join the NFO Baby Panel.

Media Panels

In **media panels**, electronic devices automatically record viewing behavior, thus supplementing a diary. Perhaps the most familiar media panel is Nielsen Television Index (NTI) by Nielsen Media Research (www.nielsenmedia.com). The Index consists of a representative sample of approximately 5,000 households. Each of these households has an electronic device, called a *storage instantaneous peoplemeter*, attached to its television sets. The peoplemeter continuously monitors television viewing behavior, including when the set is turned on, what channels are viewed, and for how long. These data are stored in the peoplemeter and transmitted via telephone lines to a central computer. The data collected by the peoplemeter are supplemented with diary panel records, called *audilogs*. The audilog contains information on who was watching each program, so that audience size and demographic characteristics can be calculated.[5] The Nielsen Television Index is useful to firms such as AT&T, Kellogg, JC Penney, Pillsbury, and Unilever who are looking for advertising media that are reaching their target markets. Nielsen has also developed a passive peoplemeter that recognizes a person entering or leaving the room and keeps track of the person's activities while watching television.

media panels
A data gathering technique that is comprised of samples of respondents whose television viewing behavior is automatically recorded by electronic devices, supplementing the purchase information recorded in a diary.

In addition to the Nielsen Television Index, other services provide media panels. Arbitron maintains local and regional radio and TV diary panels. In the ScanAmerica peoplemeter ratings system, an electronic meter automatically collects continuous detailed measures of television set tuning for every set in the home. TV BehaviorGraphics™ by Simmons Market Research Bureau (www.simmonsresearch.com), is a behavioral targeting system used to identify the best prospects for products and services based on consumers' viewing of broadcast and cable television programs. The system was developed through an integration process that merges the Nielsen National Television Index (NTI) with the

Simmons National Consumer Survey (NCS). It consists of a multisegment cluster system that classifies consumers into distinct groups based on their television viewing behavior. The system, which is used by the top advertising agencies and television media, is available to subscribers. Syndicated services also collect the same type of audience data for radio. Radio audience statistics are typically collected using diaries two to four times per year.

Given the growing popularity of the Internet, syndicated services are also geared to this medium. Nielsen//NetRatings, Inc. (www.netratings.com) tracks and collects Internet usage in real time from home and work users. It reports site and e-commerce activity, including number of visits to properties, domains and unique sites, rankings by site and by category, time and frequency statistics, traffic patterns, and e-commerce transactions. It also reports on banner advertising, including audience response to banners, creative content, frequency, and site placement. This service has been launched in collaboration with ACNielsen. Another leader in the field is ComScore Networks (www.comscore.com). It has built a massive cross section of more than 1.5 million global Internet users who have given ComScore explicit permission to confidentially capture their Web-wide browsing, buying, and other transaction behavior, including offline purchasing. Jupiter Research (www.jupiterresearch.com) focuses on consumer online behavior and interactive technologies for business-to-business and business-to-consumer clients.

Uses of Purchase and Media Panels

Purchase panels provide information useful for forecasting sales, estimating market shares, assessing brand-loyalty and brand-switching behavior, establishing profiles of specific user groups, measuring promotional effectiveness, and conducting controlled store tests. Media panels yield information helpful for establishing advertising rates by radio and TV networks, selecting appropriate programming, and profiling viewer or listener subgroups. Advertisers, media planners, and buyers find panel information to be particularly useful.

Advantages and Disadvantages of Purchase and Media Panels

The advantages of panel data over survey data relate to data accuracy and the generation of longitudinal data. Repeated measurement of the same variables from the same group of respondents classifies this as a form of *longitudinal data*. Longitudinal data enables manufacturers to measure changes in brand loyalty, usage, and price sensitivity over time. Involvement in a purchase panel represents a commitment on the part of the respondent. That commitment is thought to enhance the accuracy and therefore the quality of panel data. Purchase panels, which record information at the time of purchase, also eliminate recall errors. Information recorded by electronic devices is even more accurate because the devices eliminate human errors.

The disadvantage of panel data can be traced to the nonrepresentativeness of panel members and to increased response errors uniquely associated with the process of maintaining a diary. Recruiters for purchase and media panels attempt to mirror the population in the panel makeup. However, they tend to underrepresent certain groups, such as minorities and those with low education levels. The time commitment necessary to participate on panels contributes to the relatively high level of refusal and dropout rates. Additionally, response biases may occur since simply being on the panel may alter behavior. Since purchase or media data are entered by hand, recording errors are also possible.

Electronic Scanner Services

scanner data
Data obtained by passing merchandise over a laser scanner that reads the UPC code from the packages.

Scanner data are obtained by using electronic scanners at the cash register that read the Universal Product Code (UPC) from consumer purchases. Among the largest syndicated firms specializing in this type of data collection are ACNielsen (www.acnielsen.com) and Information Resources (www.infores.com). These companies compile and sell data, which tell subscribers how well their products are selling relative to the competition. This analysis can be conducted for each item with a unique UPC—that is, brand, flavor, and package size. Scanner-based companies represent formidable competition for both

EXPERIENTIAL LEARNING

Nielsen//Net Ratings

Nielsen//Net Ratings reports on nearly 70 percent of the world's Internet usage to give a broad view of the online world. Nielsen//Net Ratings focuses its research on Internet usage in the following countries: Australia, Brazil, France, Germany, Hong Kong, Italy, Japan, the Netherlands, Spain, Sweden, Switzerland, the United Kingdom, and the United States.

Go to Nielsen//Net Ratings' home page (www.netratings.com). On the top menu bar, select "Top Rankings." Next, select "NetView Usage Metrics." To view results for a country, double-click on the country name. For the following exercises, choose "Home Panel" and "Web Usage Data" to view the most recent month's results for each of the countries. Record your findings about each country's "PC Time per Person" in a table.

1. Which country posts the most "PC Time per Person"?
2. Which country posts the least "PC Time per Person"?

For the next part, choose "Global Index" instead of "NetView Usage Metrics" in order to view the latest month's "Global Internet Index: Average Usage."

1. What is the average "PC Time Spent per Month" for the set of countries?
2. Which countries were above the average for "PC Time Spent per Month" for the latest month?
3. Which countries were below the average for "PC Time Spent per Month" for the latest month?

purchase panels and physical audit services. The accuracy and speed with which product movement at the retail level can be recorded using electronic scanners have reshaped the marketing research industry.

Three types of scanner data are available: volume-tracking data, scanner panels, and scanner panels with cable TV. **Volume-tracking data** are data routinely collected by supermarkets and other outlets with electronic checkout counters. When the consumer purchases are scanned, the data are automatically entered into a computer. These data provide information on purchases by brand, size, price, and flavor or formulation, based on sales data collected from the checkout scanner tapes. However, this information cannot be linked to background characteristics of consumers since their identities are not recorded when their purchases are scanned. This information is collected nationally from a sample of supermarkets with electronic scanners. Scanner services providing volume-tracking data include SCANTRACK (ACNielsen) and InfoScan (Information Resources, Inc.). The SCANTRACK service gathers data weekly from a sample of more than 4,800 stores representing more than 800 retailers in 52 major markets. It provides basic tracking information at multiple levels ranging from category-level total U.S. all-outlet sales volume to single-item performance in one market. The InfoScan Syndicated Store Tracking service monitors more than 32,000 stores within supermarket, drugstore, and mass-merchandiser outlets. An example of the type of information available from IRI follows.

volume-tracking data
Scanner data that provides information on purchases by brand, size, price, and flavor or formulation.

For **scanner panels**, each household member is given an ID card that can be read by the electronic scanner at the cash register. Scanner panel members simply present the ID

scanner panels
Scanner data collected from panel members who are issued an ID card allowing panel members' purchases to be linked to their identities.

RESEARCH IN ACTION

Supersizing the Supermarket

Information Resources' (www.infores.com) *Times & Trends,* available at the company's Web site, highlights the consumer packaged goods (CPG) industry's year-end review. *Times & Trends* is a valuable report for busy executives who need a summary insight into today's economic and general business conditions but who also need a detailed insight into CPG trends and retail marketing conditions. For example, a recent report highlighted that at 60 percent household penetration, Wal-Mart supercenters grab 10 percent of shopper spending. Expanding supercenter distribution enables Wal-Mart to grab a larger share of the faster growing dinner solution market. About 25 percent of Wal-Mart supercenters' shopper spending is for the most challenged meal occasion of the day, the dinner meal. Frozen dinners and entrees are the fifth most purchased food and beverage category item by supercenter shoppers at Wal-Mart with frozen poultry at number nine. Such information has enabled Wal-Mart to further expand its line of frozen dinners and entrees.[6]

card at the checkout counter each time they shop. In this way, consumer identity is linked to products purchased as well as the time and day of the shopping trip, and the firm can build a shopping record for that individual. Alternatively, some firms provide hand-held scanners to panel members. These members scan their purchases once they are home.

The ACNielsen (www.acnielsen.com) consumer panel, called Homescan, is used to record the purchases of approximately 125,000 households throughout the world. The consumer scans the bar codes on purchases with a hand-held scanner, which records the price, promotions, and quantity of each item. The information in the hand-held scanner is then transmitted to ACNielsen through telephone lines. ACNielsen uses the information from the scanner and additional information gathered from the consumer to determine such things as consumer demographics, quantity and frequency of purchases, percentage of households purchasing, shopping trips and expenditures, price paid, and usage information. Manufacturers and retailers use this information to better understand the purchasing habits of consumers.

scanner panels with cable TV
The combination of a scanner panel with manipulations of the advertising that is being broadcast by cable TV companies.

An even more advanced use of scanning technology, **scanner panels with cable TV**, combines scanner panels with new technologies that have grown out of the cable TV industry. Households on these panels subscribe to one of the cable TV systems in their market. By means of a cable TV "split," the researcher targets various commercials into the homes of the panel members. For example, half the households may see test commercial A during the 6 o'clock newscast while the other half see test commercial B. Thus, these panels allow researchers to conduct fairly controlled experiments in a relatively natural environment. They also offer a way to target marketing effort. It is possible to transmit a Danon yogurt commercial only to Yoplait consumers to determine if they can be induced to switch brands.

Systems have been developed to allow transmission of advertising into participating households without the use of a cable TV system. Since the panels can be selected from all available TV households, not just those with cable TV, the bias of cable-only testing is eliminated. Using this type of system, General Mills, for example, can test which one of four test commercials for Total cereal results in the highest sales. Four groups of panel members are selected, and each receives a different test commercial. These households are monitored via scanner data to determine which group purchased the most Total cereal. As can be seen, scanner services incorporate advanced marketing research technology, which results in some advantages over survey and purchase-panel data.

Uses of Scanner Data

Scanner data are useful for a variety of purposes. National volume-tracking data can be used for tracking sales, prices, distribution, and for modeling and analyzing early warning signals. Scanner panels with cable TV can be used for testing new products, reposi-

RESEARCH IN ACTION

At Home with Quality via Homescan

The Kellogg Company (www.kelloggs.com) uses ACNielsen's Homescan scanner panel (www.acnielsen.com), discussed earlier in this chapter, to answer a variety of questions:

- In what areas of the country are Kellogg's cereals purchased most frequently?
- What promotions were offered at the time of purchase?
- What is the number and size of the cereal boxes the typical consumer purchases?
- What are the demographic characteristics of the heavy cereal users?

Kellogg uses this information to better target its products to consumers. The information is also used to design sales promotions, such as coupons and point-of-sale displays, to better meet the needs of consumers. For example, larger families of Hispanic origin in California tend to be heavy users of Kellogg's cornflakes. Kellogg's has attempted to cultivate and retain the patronage of these users by directing coupons and promotional offers to them. Thus, the quality of Kellogg's marketing is greatly increased by achieving a greater focus on consumer needs through Homescan.[7]

tioning products, analyzing promotional mix, and making advertising and pricing decisions. These panels provide marketing researchers with a unique controlled environment for the manipulation of marketing variables.

Advantages and Disadvantages of Scanner Data

Given that the large grocery chains have largely completed the conversion to electronic scanning and drug stores are following suit, electronic data collection is likely to continue to grow. The prompt feedback about point-of-sale product activity enables managers to evaluate existing marketing programs as well as to formulate new ones.

Scanner data are not only available more quickly, they are also typically more accurate than data collected through either surveys or purchase panels. The response bias that plagues manual data collection is lessened because the respondents are much less conscious of their role as members of a scanner panel. Errors due to failures in recall are also eliminated with electronic data collection. They also offer the ability to study very short time periods of sales activity.

Another advantage is that in-store variables such as pricing, promotions, and displays are also recorded. Finally, a scanner panel with cable TV provides a highly controlled test environment for alternate promotional messages.

A major weakness of scanner data is found in its lack of representativeness. Only retailers equipped with scanners are included in the research. Entire retail categories, such as food warehouses and mass merchandisers, may be excluded. Likewise, the availability of scanners may be lacking in certain geographical areas.

The quality of scanner data is only as good as the scanning process itself and may be limited by several factors. All products may not be scanned. For example, a clerk may use the register to ring up a heavy item to avoid lifting it. If an item does not scan on the first try, the clerk may key in the price and ignore the bar code. Sometimes a consumer purchases many flavors of the same item, but the clerk scans only one package and then rings in the number of purchases. Thus, the transaction is recorded inaccurately.

With respect to scanner panels, the available technology permits the monitoring of only one TV set per household. Hence, there is a built-in bias if the household has a second or third TV set because the viewing of these additional sets is not considered. Also, the system provides information on TV sets in use rather than actual viewing behavior. Thus, the set may be turned on, but the people may not be really paying any attention to it. While scanner data provide behavioral and sales information, they do not provide information on underlying attitudes, preferences, and reasons for specific choices.

BE a DM!

As the marketing manager for Lay's potato chips, how would you determine the right price?

BE an MR!

Visit ACNielsen's Web site (www.acnielsen.com) and write a brief report about the SCANTRACK service.

How will you make use of SCANTRACK to determine the optimal price that management should charge for Lay's potato chips?

Syndicated Data from Institutions

We have already discussed syndicated data collected from consumers and households. Parallel electronic and manual systems are also used to collect institutional and industrial data. As Figure 5.6 shows, syndicated data are available for retailers and wholesalers as well as industrial firms.

audit
A data collection process derived from physical records or inventory analysis. Data are collected personally by the researcher or by representatives of the researcher, and the data are based upon counts, usually of physical objects other than people.

Retailer and Wholesaler Audits

Collecting product movement data for wholesalers and retailers is referred to as an **audit**. These periodic audits may be a physical count of the inventory, or they may be managed through a link to the scanning process. These audits track inventory flow, current inventory levels, and the impact of both promotional and pricing programs on inventory levels.

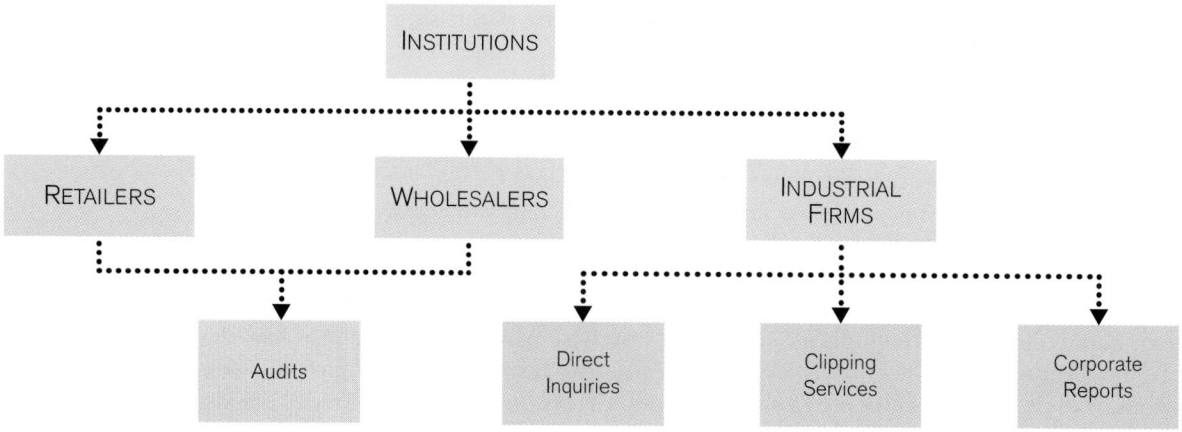

Figure 5.6

Classification of Syndicated Services: Institutions

A physical audit is a formal examination and verification of product movement carried out by examining physical records or analyzing inventory. An example of the traditional audit is the ACNielsen Convenience Track (www.acnielsen.com) which is a retail audit of convenience stores in 30 local markets. For high speed and accuracy, these in-store audits use hand-held computers to capture UPC information electronically. Retail audit data can be useful to consumer product firms. For example, imagine that Colgate-Palmolive is contemplating introducing a new toothpaste brand. A retail audit can help determine the size of the total market and distribution of sales by type of outlet and by different regions.

Wholesale audit services, the counterpart of retail audits, monitor warehouse withdrawals. Participating operators, who include supermarket chains, wholesalers, and frozen-food warehouses, typically account for more than 80 percent of the volume in this area. Audits are now being increasingly conducted by using scanner data and electronic records rather than by physical examination and verification.

Uses of Audit Data

Standardized as well as customized reports are available to help subscribers manage their brands. These reports provide information that can be used to (1) determine market size and share for both categories and brands by type of outlet, region, or city; (2) assess competitive activity; (3) identify distribution problems, including shelf-space allocation and inventory issues; (4) develop sales potentials and forecasts; and (5) develop and monitor promotional allocations based on sales volume. Scanners are now used to collect data that cross the wholesale, retail, and customer levels. The information they offer has had a profound impact on the marketing process.

Advantages and Disadvantages of Audit Data

Audits provide relatively accurate information on the movement of many products at the wholesale and retail levels. Furthermore, this information can be broken down by a number of important variables, such as brand, type of outlet, and size of market.

A major disadvantage of physical audits, however, is the limited retail coverage and delay associated with compiling and reporting inventory data. Typically, there is a two-month gap between the completion of the audit cycle and the publication of reports. Another disadvantage of physical audits is that, unlike scanner data, audit data cannot be linked to consumer characteristics. In fact, there may even be a problem in relating audit data to advertising expenditures and other marketing efforts.

Industry Services

industry services
Secondary data derived from industrial sources and intended for industrial use.

Industry services provide syndicated data about industrial firms, businesses, and other institutions. Financial, operating, and employment data are also collected by these syndicated research services for almost every North American Industry Classification System

RESEARCH IN ACTION

Hispanic Small Food Store Audit

The Hispanic Small Food Store Audit is conducted bimonthly by NOP World (www.nopworld.com). Marketers who target this burgeoning segment in the U. S. can now measure the results of their campaigns through the Hispanic Small Food Store Sales index. A measurement of sales in a channel for which there is little sales data, this study is conducted through personal visits to over 400 stores in high-density Hispanic population markets. The audit tracks:

- Sales and brand shares
- Distribution
- Inventories
- Pricing
- Causal data

Marketers like P&G, attempting to penetrate the Hispanic market, can make use of the audit findings to determine distribution outlets, product mix, inventories, advertising campaigns, and prices.[8]

BE an MR!

Visit NOP World's Web site (www.nopworld.com) and write a brief report about the audit services offered by this firm.

How will you make use of retail audit data to determine the store locations for Paul Stuart Custom Jewelers?

BE a DM!

As the marketing chief for Paul Stuart Custom Jewelers, how would you determine the best store locations?

(NAICS) industrial category. These data are collected by making direct inquiries from clipping services that monitor newspapers, the trade press, or broadcasts, and from corporate reports. The range and sources of syndicated data available for industrial goods firms are more limited than those available to consumer goods firms. D&B can provide reports of businesses located in the United States and abroad.

The D&B International Business Locator (www.dnb.com) provides one-click access to more than 28 million public/private companies in more than 200 countries. After locating a business, the Locator will provide key business data, including full address information, NAIC/line of business details, business size (sales, net worth, employees), names of key principals, and identification of this location's headquarters, domestic parent company, and/or global parent company.

These data are very useful in developing business-to-business sales plans and direct-marketing lists, estimating market potential and share within industries, and developing overall market strategies. Business statistics related to annual sales, geographic coverage, supplier relationships, and distribution channels are just a few of the categories of information available to business-to-business market planners. These secondary sources also serve as a source for sampling frames when conducting business-to-business research.

Uses of Industry Services

Information provided by industrial services is useful for sales management decisions, including identifying prospects, defining territories, setting quotas, and measuring market potential by geographic areas. It can also aid in advertising decisions, such as targeting prospects, allocating advertising budgets, selecting media, and measuring advertising effectiveness. This kind of information is also useful for segmenting the market and designing custom products and services for segments in the target markets.

Advantages and Disadvantages of Industry Services

Published industrial information provides a valuable first step in business-to-business marketing. The information is typically limited to publicly traded firms, however, and dissemination of that data is typically controlled by the reporting firm itself. A researcher has to be wary of the completeness of reported data as well as the bias introduced by this form of respondent self-report. These data are limited in the nature, content, quantity, and quality of information.

Combining Information from a Variety of Sources: Single-Source Data

As we discussed in Chapter 4, combining data from different sources can enhance the value of secondary data. This practice in syndicated services is referred to as *single-source research*. Single-source research tracks the full marketing process from initial advertising communication through product purchase. The process links a person's demographic and psychographic information with TV, reading, and shopping habits. A combination of surveys, diaries, and electronic scanners is used to integrate such information. Manufacturer pricing and promotional activities are overlaid on this consumer data as well. Thus, **single-source data** provide integrated information on household variables, such as media consumption and purchases, and on marketing variables, such as product sales, price, advertising, promotion, and in-store marketing effort.

single-source data
An effort to combine data from different sources by gathering integrated information on household and marketing variables applicable to the same set of respondents.

Information Resources, Inc. (www.infores.com) collects consumer purchase information from a nationally representative household panel of approximately 70,000 recruited households with coverage at the regional, national, and individual market level. It is designed to supply strategic direction to marketers by focusing on the consumer dynamics that drive brand and category performance. Complete multi-outlet purchase information on these households is tracked electronically. Panel households use a simple in-home scanning device, called a ScanKey, to record their purchases from all outlets. Panelists are not required to record any causal information except for manufacturer coupons. Price reductions are recorded by a scanner, and features and displays are captured by IRI's in-store personnel, ensuring an accurate and unbiased record of sales. The Campbell Soup Company example illustrates an application of single-source data.

Summary Illustration Using the Opening Vignette

Syndicated research firms specialize in designing research systems that collect data of commercial interest to multiple users. This was seen in the opening vignette, where the results of the NPD survey were used by multiple firms in the same industry: Haggar, Marshall Field's, and Levi Strauss.

Syndicated sources can be classified based on the unit of measurement (households/consumers or institutions). Syndicated data from households may be obtained via surveys, purchase or media panels, or electronic scanner systems. Although a survey was used in the opening vignette, data on purchases of business casual clothing can also be collected using purchase panels and electronic scanners (or similar systems) installed in department stores. When institutions are the unit of measurement, the data may be obtained from retailers, wholesalers, or industrial firms. It is desirable to combine information obtained from different secondary sources to get a more complete picture of the marketplace. Thus, one could combine data on casual clothing obtained from consumers with data from retailers (e.g., Macy's, Sears, etc.) and manufacturers (e.g., Haggar, Levi Strauss, etc.) to get a better understanding of the casual clothing market.

International Market Research

U.S. syndicated research firms are an important source of information on overseas consumer and industrial markets. For companies considering expansion internationally or managing existing international ventures, one of the first steps toward understanding and monitoring these markets may be through syndicated sources. The need for relatively inexpensive, comprehensive data related to international markets, consumer and social trends, as well as existing market structures creates a built-in demand for international syndicated services. Many of the same major syndicated firms operating in the United States have invested heavily in creating data collection systems to support their internationally operating clients. Gallup International is just one of the U.S. syndicated firms that have expanded their services to include international research, as illustrated in the Euroconsumers example.

RESEARCH IN ACTION

Soaps Shed a "Guiding Light" on V8 Consumption

Still running after more than 65 years, CBS's *Guiding Light* is one of the longest-running television shows airing in 2004. In 2004, *Guiding Light* was nominated for 12 Daytime Emmy Awards and has been inducted into the Soap Opera Hall of Fame. For the week of May 17 through 21, 2004, both *Guiding Light* and ABC's *General Hospital* were in the top 10 ratings in overall soap opera viewership (www.soapzone.com).

The Campbell Soup Company (www.campbell.com) used single-source data to target its advertising for V8 juice (www.v8juice.com). By obtaining single-source data on product consumption, media consumption, and demographic characteristics, Campbell found that demographically similar TV audiences consume vastly different amounts of V8. For example, on an index of 100 for the average household's V8 consumption, *General Hospital* viewers had a below-average 80 index, while *Guiding Light* viewers had an above-average 120 index. These results were surprising, because the *General Hospital* audience actually had a slightly higher percentage of women 25 to 54 years old, the demographic group most predisposed to buy V8, and so would have been expected to be a better medium to reach V8 drinkers. Using this information, Campbell rearranged its advertising schedule to raise the average index.

In 2001, Campbell introduced a juicier version of V8, called V8 Splash, to entice those who want a more fruity-flavored drink. Subsequently, Diet V8 Splash and V8 Splash Smoothies were introduced to spur sales growth. As of 2004, V8 Splash came in nine flavors and Diet V8 Splash came in three flavors.[9]

Like the Gallup organization, ACNielsen has made huge investments in European markets over the past 30-plus years, introducing scanner and tracking services at the retail level. With international operations much larger than that of the United States, more than 70 percent of Nielsen's business is outside the United States. Of that overseas business, 50 percent is in Europe.

RESEARCH IN ACTION

Euroconsumers Go for Spending Splash

The Gallup organization (www.gallup.com), which specializes in survey research obtaining both lifestyle and psychographic data, recently conducted interviews with more than 22,500 adults across the European Community. Their results point to an exploding consumer durable market, particularly for convenience items, such as remote controls TVs, microwave ovens, VCRs, and cellular phones. The educational level and the standard of living among this consumer group are generally improving. Europeans are also displaying higher levels of discretionary purchasing demonstrated in growing demand for travel packages, which continued to be strong through the year 2005. In the personal-care market, the number of European women using perfume is declining, offset by a growing demand for deodorants.

This type of syndicated data are useful to marketers such as Motorola, GE, AT&T, and RCA, which are looking to develop European markets. For example, when renting an apartment in Germany, the renter must install all the major appliances and lighting fixtures. GE has developed value packages offering significant savings on appliances and lighting fixtures that are carefully targeted at apartment renters.[10]

Technology and Marketing Research

As technology develops, syndicated firms will establish newer types of panels using sophisticated data collection methods. One distinct possibility in the near future is panels based on two-way TV and on interactive TV and video services. In fact, such technology has been developed and is being refined and tested.

Verizon (www.verizon.com) has already conducted two market trials of its interactive video service, Stargazer video-on-demand system, in northern Virginia and Toms River, New Jersey. Marketers that participated in the first phase of the Stargazer test included Lands' End, Nordstrom, JC Penney, Nissan Motor Cars USA, and Visa International. Verizon Video Services spokesman told marketing researchers to be prepared because interactive TV will be here much sooner than people expect. "The leaders will establish themselves very fast," he said. "The rest will have trouble ever catching up."[11]

In addition, technology used in existing panels, such as scanner and media panels, is being continuously refined. In 1987, Nielsen Media Research introduced the original "peoplemeter." This system keeps track of which family member is watching television at a given time. It also keeps a record of which program is being watched. The problem with the original system was that viewers must enter the information manually via a keypad whenever they begin and finish watching television. Many viewers do not always log in or out because the system can become very tedious. Others, especially children, simply forget to do it.

To deal with this problem, both Nielsen and their main competitor, Arbitron, have developed new "passive peoplemeters." All that is required of viewers under this system is to turn their TV sets on or off. Using computer-image recognition technology, which is a more advanced version of the scanner technology used in supermarkets, the passive peoplemeter scans the room to identify all preprogrammed viewers. The new system also detects whether or not the viewers are looking at the TV set or are looking at something else in the room.

The new passive systems allow researchers to monitor families at a much cheaper rate than possible with the previous technology. Using the older meters, it costs thousands of dollars to monitor a single family. The cost is expected to decrease to somewhere in the hundreds. With this dramatic reduction in the average cost per household, researchers are able to increase the size of the samples and hence the accuracy of the data, while keeping overall costs at a constant level.[12]

Ethics in Marketing Research

Ethical issues in formulating a research design, discussed in Chapter 3, are also relevant in collecting syndicated data. Respondents' rights, particularly their privacy, are another salient issue. Obtaining data from the respondents without their full knowledge or consent is an invasion of privacy. Consider, for example, the frequent shopper cards that supermarkets issue. These cards provide a variety of services, such as check cashing, special notification of sales, and cash discounts or rebates, at no apparent cost to the cardholders. While this may sound like a good deal, many cardholders are unaware of the hidden costs involved.

When applying for a card, each shopper provides data on demographic and shopping-related variables and is assigned a UPC Code. The shopper's UPC code is scanned first before the grocery purchases are scanned. Thus, a shopper's purchases are linked to that shopper's demographic and shopping-related data collected at the time of card application. This information results in a database that contains rich information on shoppers, including a complete demographic profile, when they shop, how much they spend, how they pay for purchases, and what products they buy. As discussed in Chapter 4, this database can be used to target consumers and formulate effective marketing strategies. Often, these data are sold to syndicated firms, who in turn sell them to multiple clients, resulting in much wider dissemination and use. Most consumers, however, are unaware that the supermarket has all this information about them simply because they are cardholders.

The supermarkets and other firms engaging in this practice of collecting data without the respondent's direct knowledge or consent are violating the ethical principle of informed consent. According to this principle, researchers have the ethical responsibility

RESEARCH IN ACTION

Reaching Kids but Alienating Adults: Ethical Repercussions

According to a recent survey by NOP World, a syndicated marketing research firm, the general public is skeptical about advertising aimed at kids. Eight of ten adults agree that business marketing and advertising exploit children by convincing them to buy things that are bad for them or that they don't need.

Adults don't necessarily object to all advertising, only to advertising they perceive as harmful to kids. Eight of ten adults say it is "alright" to advertise products such as toys, cereal, and clothing on television during children's programming. Adults are more likely to object to commercials that "sell" sex and poor nutrition, as for products such as PG-13 movies and candy bars. Thus, marketers who engage in such practices in an attempt to reach kids run the risk of alienating adults. Several syndicated firms, such as NOP World, are playing a significant role in addressing ethical issues in marketing research by sensitizing researchers, clients, and the general public to such issues.[13]

to avoid both uninformed and misinformed participation by respondents in marketing research projects. On a positive note, syndicate firms are playing a significant role in researching ethical issues and sensitizing marketing firms, the marketing research industry, and the general public about these concerns.

WHAT WOULD *YOU* DO?

Boston Market: Sizing the Market

The Situation

Michel Andres, President and CEO of Boston Market, is well aware of the fact that according to syndicated data, home meal replacement (HMR) will be the family dining business of this century. HMR is portable, high-quality food that's meant for take-out, and it is the fastest growing and most significant opportunity in the food industry today. According to ACNielsen's consumer panel data (www.acnielsen.com), 55 percent of respondents purchased a meal for at-home consumption several times a month. Convenience and type of food were the two most influential factors when purchasing HMR. Also, 77 percent of the respondents preferred their meals ready to eat.

Another recent study by the NPD Group (www.npd.com) projected that between 2005 and 2010, virtually all growth in food sales will come from food service, defined as food prepared at least partially away from home. Estimates of total HMR market size, as well as future potential, vary widely. Numbers ranging from $25 billion to $100 billion have been given for the year 2005. Sara Lee projections show HMR accounting for as much as 80 percent of food-industry growth by 2005. Findings by McKinsey & Company support that premise from two perspectives: (1) the fact that virtually all foods' sales growth by the year 2005 will come from food service and (2) that by 2005, many Americans will never have cooked a meal from scratch. It is the most important trend to hit the food industry since the advent of frozen food.

Boston Market is now the HMR leader. As of 2005, Boston Market had more than 650 restaurants and operated in 30 states. The company is a wholly owned

subsidiary of McDonald's Corp. (www.mcdonalds.com). Michel Andres wants to capitalize upon this HMR trend, and to do so, Boston Market is using such data to test new products that could be introduced in 2005. The products being tested include prepackaged "take and go" lunch boxes, expanded catering services, enhanced drive-through operations, and call-ahead pick-up services.

The Marketing Research Decision

1. Given the wide estimates of $25 billion to $100 billion for HMR potential sales for 2005, how can Boston Market get a more reasonable estimate? What sources of syndicated data should be consulted? Check as many as are applicable.
   a. Information Resources, Inc.
   b. ACNielsen
   c. McKinsey & Company

(continued)

d. NPD Group
e. All of the above

2. Discuss the role of the type of research you recommend in enabling Michel Andres to size the HMR market and determine what new products and services Boston Market should introduce.

The Marketing Management Decision

1. What new products and services should Michel Andres introduce? (check as many as are applicable):
   a. Opening of new restaurant concepts
   b. Expanded catering services
   c. Enhanced drive-through operations
   d. Launching of a new advertising campaign
   e. All of the above
2. Discuss how the marketing management decision action that you recommend to Michel Andres is influenced by the syndicated sources of data that you suggested earlier and by the content of information they provide.

What Michel Andres Did

Boston Market Corp. has also recently opened its newest restaurant concept: Boston Market's Rotisserie Grill in St. Charles, Illinois. The new concept is designed to deliver an engaging dining experience typically associated with that of full-service restaurants but at a more appealing fast-casual value. Incorporating a self-paced ordering process and semi-serve system that enables attentive wait staff, the new concept offers an upscale, diverse menu with more than 50 salads, gourmet sides, desserts, and lunch and dinner entrees.

Boston Market worked with Arnold Worldwide of Boston to produce a new advertising campaign. In an effort to energize its brand, Boston Market reminded consumers that the restaurant fulfills their need for quick, convenient, wholesome meals. Portraying real-life, recognizable situations Americans often encounter concerning dinner, the tagline was "We're Always Cooking."[14]

Summary

Syndicated research firms specialize in designing research systems that collect data of commercial interest to multiple users. Collecting data to serve a known commercial purpose is one of the primary differentiators when comparing syndicated services to other types of secondary data (discussed in Chapter 4). Syndicated data are timely and cost-effective. Given the need for an impartial monitor of marketwide trends, as well as consumer reactions or behaviors, syndicated researchers provide a unique and valuable service.

Syndicated sources can be classified based on the unit of measurement (households/consumers or institutions). Syndicated data from households may be obtained via surveys, purchase or media panels, or electronic scanner systems. When institutions are the unit of measurement, the data may be obtained from retailers, wholesalers, or industrial firms. It is desirable to combine information from different sources.

U.S. syndicated research firms are an important source of information on overseas consumer and industrial markets. As technology develops, syndicated firms will establish newer types of panels that collect data from panel members using sophisticated methods. One distinct possibility in the near future is panels based on two-way TV and interactive TV and video services. A major ethical issue in collecting syndicated data is the invasion of privacy of the respondents by obtaining data without their full knowledge or consent.

Key Terms and Concepts

Syndicated sources, 125
Periodic surveys, 127
Panel surveys, 127
Shared surveys, 129
Psychographics, 130
Lifestyle, 130
Purchase panels, 133
Media panels, 133
Scanner data, 134
Volume-tracking data, 135
Scanner panels, 135
Scanner panels with cable TV, 136
Audit, 137
Industry services, 138
Single-source data, 140

Suggested Cases and Video Cases

Cases

2.4 Bloomingdale's **2.5 Burger King** **4.2 Gucci**

Video Cases

4.1 Subaru **4.2 Marriott**

Additional cases and video cases are available in the Instructor's Manual and on the instructor and student Web sites.

Live Research: Conducting a Marketing Research Project

1. It is worthwhile to visit the Web sites of syndicated firms to identify the relevant information, some of which can be obtained without cost.
2. If the project is supported by a budget, then relevant information can be purchased from syndicated sources.
3. One, a few, or all the teams can be assigned the responsibility of collecting and analyzing data from the Internet.
4. Encourage the students to visit relevant Web sites of the client and its competitors as well to conduct a thorough search using search engines.

Acronyms

The role and salient characteristics of syndicated data may be described by the acronym SYNDICATED:

S urveys
Y ields data of known commercial value
N umber of clients using the data
D iary panels
I ndustrial services
C ost is low
A udits
T imely and current
E lectronic scanner services
D ata combined from different sources: single-source data

Review Questions

1. What are the differences between syndicated data and data available from other secondary sources?
2. List and describe the various syndicated sources of secondary data.
3. What is the nature of information collected by surveys?
4. How can surveys be classified?
5. Explain what a panel is. What is the difference between purchase panels and media panels?
6. What are the relative advantages of purchase panels over surveys?
7. What kinds of data can be gathered through electronic scanner services?
8. Describe the uses of scanner data.
9. What is an audit? Discuss the uses, advantages, and disadvantages of audits.
10. Describe the information provided by industrial services.
11. Why is it desirable to use multiple sources of secondary data?
12. Explain what is meant by single-source data.

Applied Problems

1. Visit NPD Group's Web site (www.npd.com) and write a description of the panel maintained by NPD.
2. Visit ACNielson's Web site (www.acnielsen.com) and write a report about the various services offered by ACNielsen.
3. Visit Information Resources' Web site (www.infores.com) and write a report about the products and services offered by Information Resources, Inc.
4. Visit Gallup's Web site (www.gallup.com) and write a report about the syndicated services offered by the Gallup Organization.
5. Visit Arbitron's Web site (www.arbitron.com) and write a report about the syndicated services offered by Arbitron.
6. Select an industry of your choice. Contact one of the syndicated firms to obtain industry sales and the sales of the major firms in that industry for the past year. Estimate the market shares of each major firm. From a published source, obtain information on the market shares of these same firms. Do the two estimates agree?

Group Discussion

1. Discuss how the Nielsen TV ratings can affect the price that advertisers pay for a commercial broadcast during a particular time.

CHAPTER

6 Exploratory Research Design: Qualitative Research

"I have degrees in mathematics, but have become an enthusiastic user of qualitative research because of the rich insights I have gained with well done qualitative research."

MARY KLUPP, *Director, Ford Credit Global Consumer Insights, Ford Motor Company, Dearborn, MI*

OPENING QUESTIONS

1. How is qualitative research different from quantitative research in terms of the objectives, sampling, data collection, data analysis, and outcomes?
2. What are the various forms of qualitative research, including direct and indirect procedures?
3. How are focus groups conducted? What are their applications? What are their advantages and disadvantages?
4. In what way are in-depth interviews different from focus groups? What are their applications? What are their advantages and disadvantages?
5. What is meant by *projective techniques?* What are their uses?
6. How is conducting qualitative research in an international setting different than doing this research domestically?
7. What is the role of technology, and what qualitative research software is available?
8. What ethical issues are involved in conducting qualitative research?

Gillette Supports Equal Rights for Women: A Close Shave

In 2003, Gillette introduced Pink Passion Venus, an extension of its Venus women's razor introduced in 2001. The sales from Gillette's women's products are expected to increase to more than $1 billion dollars by the year 2005. This new product idea was inspired by the earlier successful introduction of Sensor for Women.

How was Sensor for Women developed? After being given the job of redesigning Gillette's feminine razor, Jill Shurtleff relied heavily on qualitative research. She used one-on-one or individual in-depth interviews with 30 women chosen on the basis of her judgment from different segments of the potential target market. Individual in-depth interviews were selected over focus groups because shaving is a rather personal experience for women. This technique allows for extensive probing of the respondent's feelings in a more personal setting and thus provides deeper insights into the shaving experience.

The in-depth interviews showed that women shave very differently from men. The American woman shaves much more surface area than a man but only shaves two or three times per week. She changes the blade about once a month. While men usually shave in front of a well-lit mirror, women generally prefer to shave in the shower, which is often dimly lit, and must shave areas that they can't see well, such as underarms or backs of legs. The research indicated that shaving was a personal experience for women that evoked feelings of anticipation and acceptance.

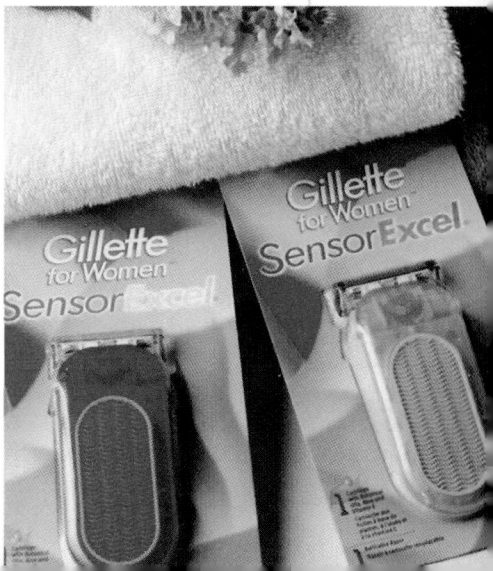

This research also showed that most women did not like so-called women's razors and opted instead for men's razors or cheap disposables. Women preferred razors with a firm grip and those that gave a clean, smooth shave. Typically, men's razors have a much sharper blade than women's. While the chances of a woman nicking herself greatly increase with the use of a man's razor, the shaving quality was better than traditional women's razors. These findings were substantiated in a survey of women using in-home personal interviews. A representative sample of 500 women was selected for this purpose.

With information on the current state of affairs under her belt, Shurtleff began her product design. She first tossed out the T-shaped design used for men's razors, which gives men the sensitive control they need but puts women at risk due to shifting blade angles. Shurtleff settled on a wafer-like design for the handle, white with an aqua insert in the center. The colors were different from the typical pink for women's razors and evoked a clean, watery feeling. The aqua insert was clear plastic and had wavy ridges to help prevent slippage. The razor head was nearly the same as that used by the Sensor (men's razor) and was angled at 46 degrees, a compromise between the ideal underarm and leg-shaving angles.

The finishing touch was the name. The name Lady Sensor was declined because it seemed almost condescending and many women didn't like it. The company settled on the name Sensor for Women since it seemed straightforward, honest, and elicited the most favorable response in a word-association test examining several possible names.

Qualitative research helped to develop a truly successful product. The Sensor for Women quickly and easily displaced the market leader, Personal Touch, and garnered 60 percent of the market share. Moreover, Sensor for Women provided a strong launching pad for Venus and then for Pink Passion Venus.[1] •

Overview

In Chapter 3, we classified marketing research as either exploratory or conclusive. Secondary data analysis, discussed in Chapters 4 and 5, is one aspect of exploratory research. The other major exploratory technique, qualitative research, is the subject of this chapter. Figure 6.1 briefly explains the focus of the chapter, the relation of this chap-

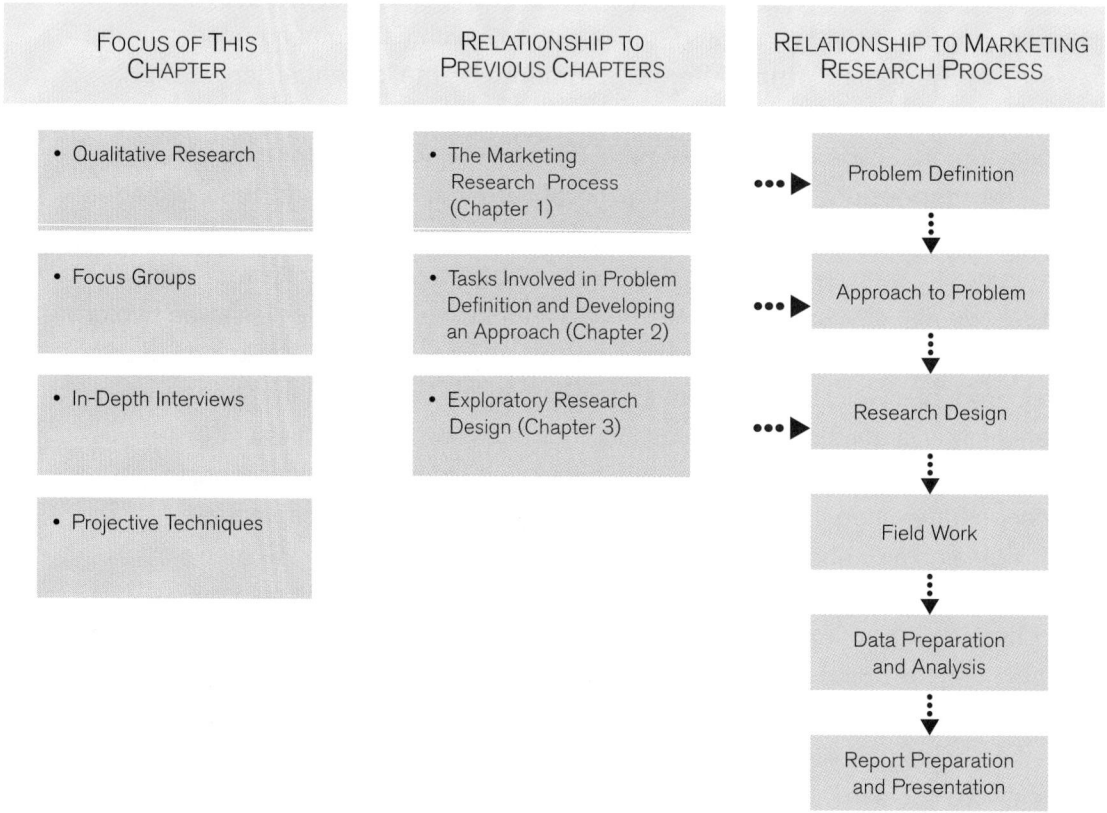

Figure 6.1

Relationship of Qualitative Research to the Previous Chapters and the Marketing Research Process ter to the previous ones, and the steps of the marketing research process on which this chapter concentrates. As can be seen from Figure 6.1, qualitative research is part of the marketing research process presented in Chapter 1, is one of the tasks involved in problem definition and development of an approach covered in Chapter 2, and is one of the techniques of exploratory research design discussed in Chapter 3.

Often, qualitative research follows a review of internal and external sources of secondary data. It is typically used to define the problem more precisely, formulate hypotheses, or identify or clarify key variables to be investigated in the quantitative phase. Our opening vignette illustrated this. The findings of in-depth interviews regarding how women shaved were further investigated by conducting an in-home personal survey (quantitative research).

Unlike secondary data, which are generated for purposes other than the specific marketing research problem at hand, qualitative research generates primary data. The definition of the marketing research problem guides qualitative data collection.

In this chapter, we discuss the differences between qualitative and quantitative research and the role of each in the marketing research project. We present a classification of qualitative research techniques and provide an overview of the major qualitative techniques used in the industry. They include focus groups, in-depth interviews with individuals, and projective techniques. In keeping with the pervasive emphasis of this book, we discuss the application of qualitative research in international marketing research, the impact of technology, and ethical issues. Figure 6.2 gives an overview of the topics discussed in this chapter and how they flow from one to the next.

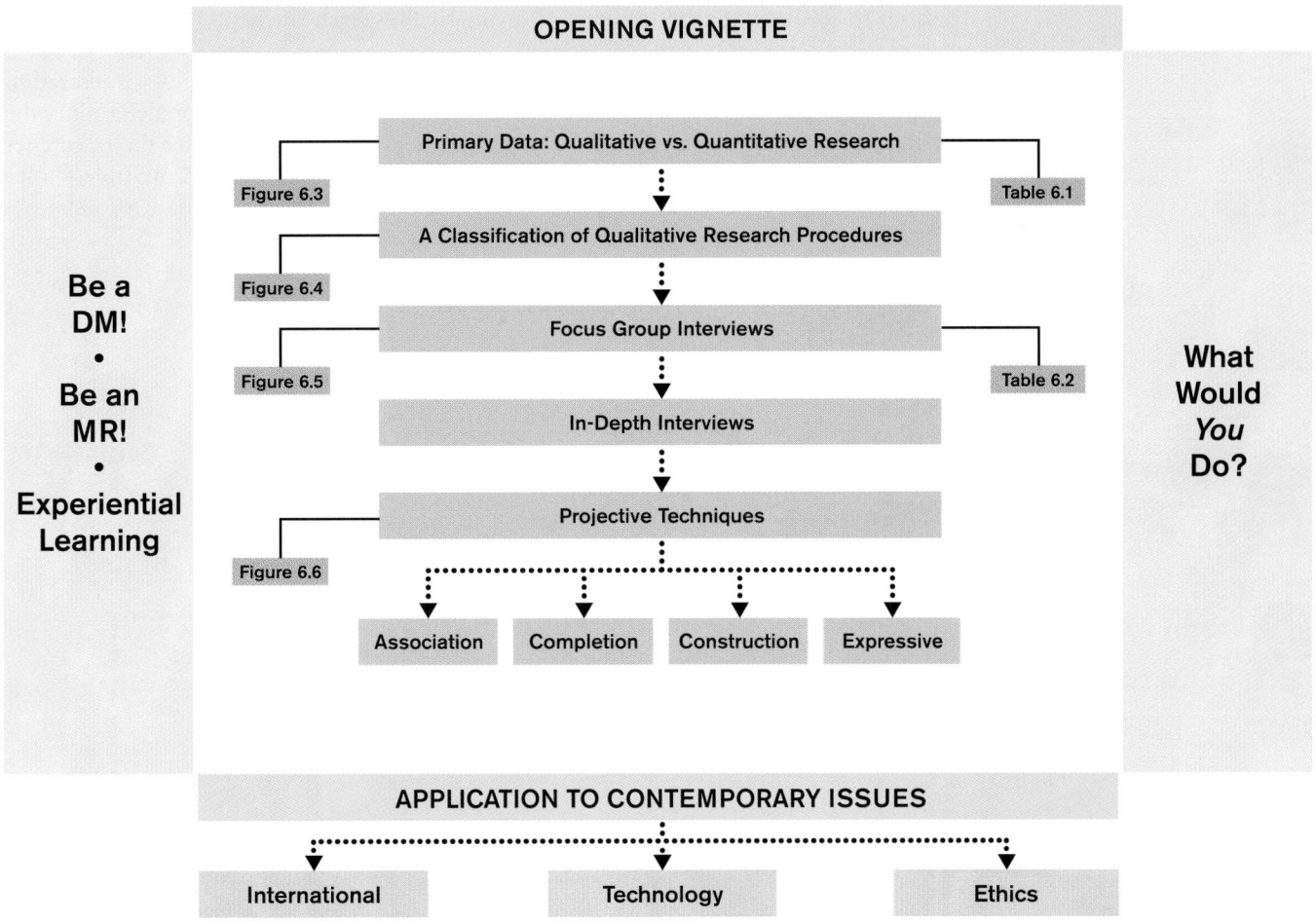

Figure 6.2

Qualitative Research: An Overview

Primary Data: Qualitative Versus Quantitative Research

As mentioned before, even though qualitative research is exploratory in nature, it results in primary data because the research is carried out for the specific purpose of addressing the problem at hand. Therefore, both qualitative and quantitative research may generate primary data, as shown in Figure 6.3. The distinction between qualitative and quantitative research closely parallels the distinction between exploratory and conclusive research discussed in Chapter 3. The differences between the two research methodologies are summarized in Table 6.1.

qualitative research
An unstructured, exploratory research methodology based on small samples that provides insights and understanding of the problem setting.

Qualitative research provides insights and understanding of the problem setting. It explores the problem with few preconceived notions about the outcome of that exploration. In addition to defining the problem and developing an approach, qualitative research is also appropriate when facing a situation of uncertainty, such as when conclusive results differ from expectations. It can provide insight before or after the fact. In the opening vignette, Gillette used qualitative research at the beginning of the project to better understand the shaving needs of women. Qualitative research is based on small, nonrepresentative samples, and the data are analyzed in a nonstatistical way. For in-depth interviews in the Gillette vignette, the researcher chose a sample size of 30 women selected judgmentally from various segments of the target market.

quantitative research
A research methodology that seeks to quantify the data and typically applies some form of statistical analysis.

On the other hand, **quantitative research** seeks to quantify the data. It seeks conclusive evidence, which is based on large, representative samples, and typically applies some form of statistical analysis. In contrast to qualitative research, the findings of quantitative research can be treated as conclusive and used to recommend a final course of action. This was seen in the opening vignette in which Gillette used quantitative (survey) research to substantiate the findings of qualitative research (in-depth interviews) based on a representative sample of 500 women.

The approach to data collection can vary along a continuum from highly structured to completely unstructured. In a highly structured approach, the researcher predetermines the wording of the questions asked and the range of responses available. Thus, the researcher assumes full understanding of the range of possible response options. A multiple-choice question is an example of a highly structured question. Typically, a formal questionnaire is

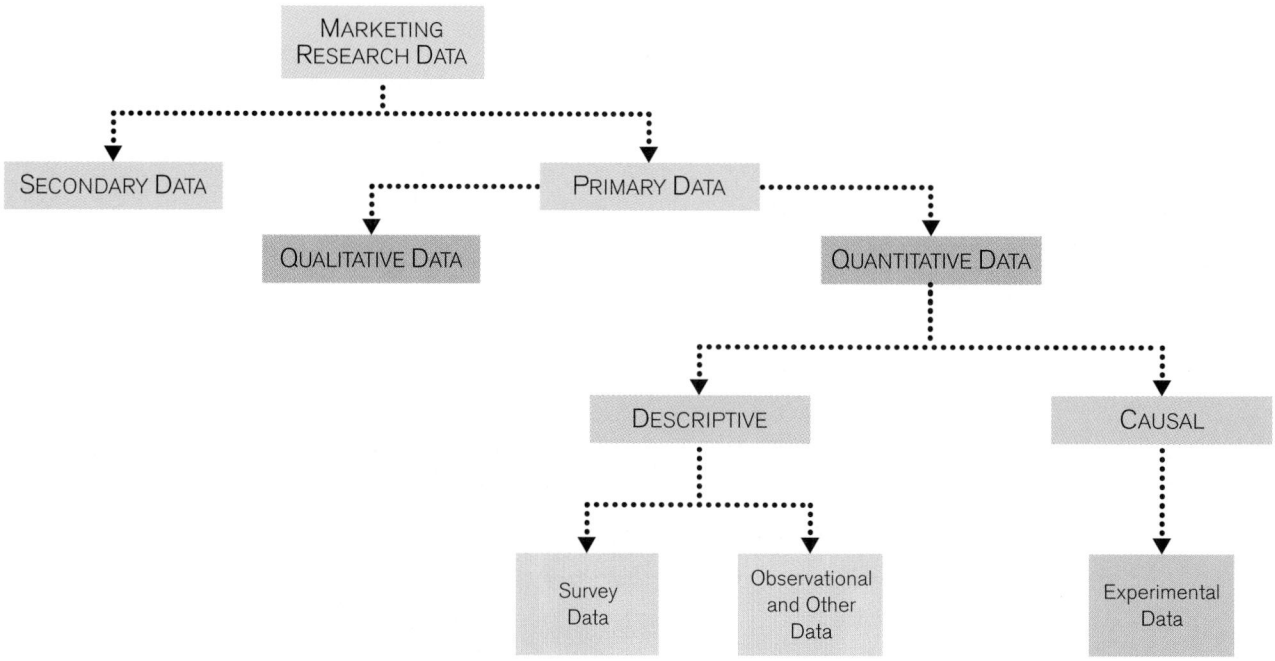

Figure 6.3
A Classification of Marketing Research Data

Table 6.1
Qualitative Versus Quantitative Research

	Qualitative Research	Quantitative Research
Objective	To gain a qualitative understanding of the underlying reasons and motivations	To quantify the data and generalize the results from the sample to the population of interest
Sample	Small number of nonrepresentative cases	Large number of representative cases
Data collection	Unstructured	Structured
Data analysis	Nonstatistical	Statistical
Outcome	Develop a richer understanding	Recommend a final course of action

used. This is in contrast to an unstructured data collection approach in which neither the questions nor the possible responses are predetermined. The respondent is encouraged to talk freely about the subject of interest. Qualitative or exploratory research lies at the unstructured end of this continuum, whereas quantitative research is highly structured.

Whenever a new marketing research problem is addressed, quantitative research must be preceded by appropriate qualitative research, as Gillette did. Sometimes qualitative research is undertaken to explain the findings obtained from quantitative research. The findings of qualitative research are misused, however, when they are regarded as conclusive and are used to make generalizations to the population of interest. For example, if 20 of the 30 women in the in-depth interviews said they preferred men's razors to women's razors, it would not be appropriate to conclude that 66.7 percent of the women in the general population have the same preference. Quantitative data from a large, representative sample should be collected using a survey, as in the opening vignette, if the sample results are to be projected to the population. It is a sound principle of marketing research to view qualitative and quantitative research as complementary rather than competitive parts of the research process.

The danger of ignoring qualitative research when the research problem is not fully understood and directly proceeding to quantitative research is illustrated by Coca Cola's decision to change Coke to New Coke. The decision to change the formulation of the flagship soft drink brand was based on extensive quantitative taste tests without the benefit of appropriate qualitative research. The results clearly indicated that consumers preferred the taste of the new formulation. However, when the change was made and New Coke replaced Coke, there was a strong consumer backlash. The loyal users of Coke reacted because their favorite soft drink had been changed. The quantitative research conducted was misguided because it asked the wrong questions. The researchers were focusing on taste rather than the emotional attachment consumers had forged with the brand, which was actually a more significant variable guiding brand preference and loyalty than taste.

These types of mistakes can be avoided by conducting qualitative research. Had the researchers first used qualitative techniques to explore why people purchased Coke, rather than assuming they knew why, the quantitative research conducted would have been different, leading management to a different decision. This classic marketing mistake also points out that the researcher must obtain an adequate understanding of the problem situation before formulating a research design.

BE a DM!

As the marketing manager, what marketing strategies would you formulate in helping Nine West increase its penetration of the women's shoes market?

BE an MR!

1. Visit Nine West's Web site (www.ninewest.com) and search the Internet using a search engine as well as your library's online databases to obtain information on the marketing strategy of Nine West.
2. How would you use qualitative and quantitative research in helping Nine West increase its penetration of the women's shoes market?

A Classification of Qualitative Research Procedures

direct approach
One type of qualitative research in which the purposes of the project are disclosed to the respondent or are obvious given the nature of the interview.

indirect approach
A type of qualitative research in which the purposes of the project are disguised from the respondents.

A classification of qualitative research procedures is presented in Figure 6.4. These procedures are classified as either direct or indirect, based on whether the respondents know the true purpose of the project. A **direct approach** is not disguised. The purpose of the project is disclosed to the respondents or is otherwise obvious from the questions asked. Focus groups and in-depth interviews are the major direct techniques. In contrast, research that takes an **indirect approach** disguises the true purpose of the project. Projective techniques are the most commonly used indirect approach. A discussion of each of these techniques follows, beginning with focus groups.

Focus-Group Interviews

focus group
An interview conducted by a trained moderator among a small group of respondents in an unstructured and natural manner.

A **focus group** is an interview with a small group of respondents conducted by a trained moderator who leads the discussion in a nonstructured and natural manner. The main purpose of a focus group is to gain insights on issues of interest to the researcher by listening to a group of people from the appropriate target market. The value of the technique lies in the rich findings that can be obtained from a free-flowing group discussion.

Focus groups are the most important qualitative research procedure. They are so popular that many marketing research practitioners consider this technique synonymous with qualitative research. Several hundred facilities around the country now conduct focus groups several times a week. The typical focus group costs the client about $4,000. Given their importance and popularity, the procedure for conducting focus groups is described in detail.

Conducting a Focus Group

The process of conducting a focus group, as with any research effort, involves careful planning. This chapter discusses considerations related to the environment for focus groups, the selection of participants, and the moderator. It also covers the development of a discussion guide, the conducting of a group interview, and the format for summarizing the results (Figure 6.5).

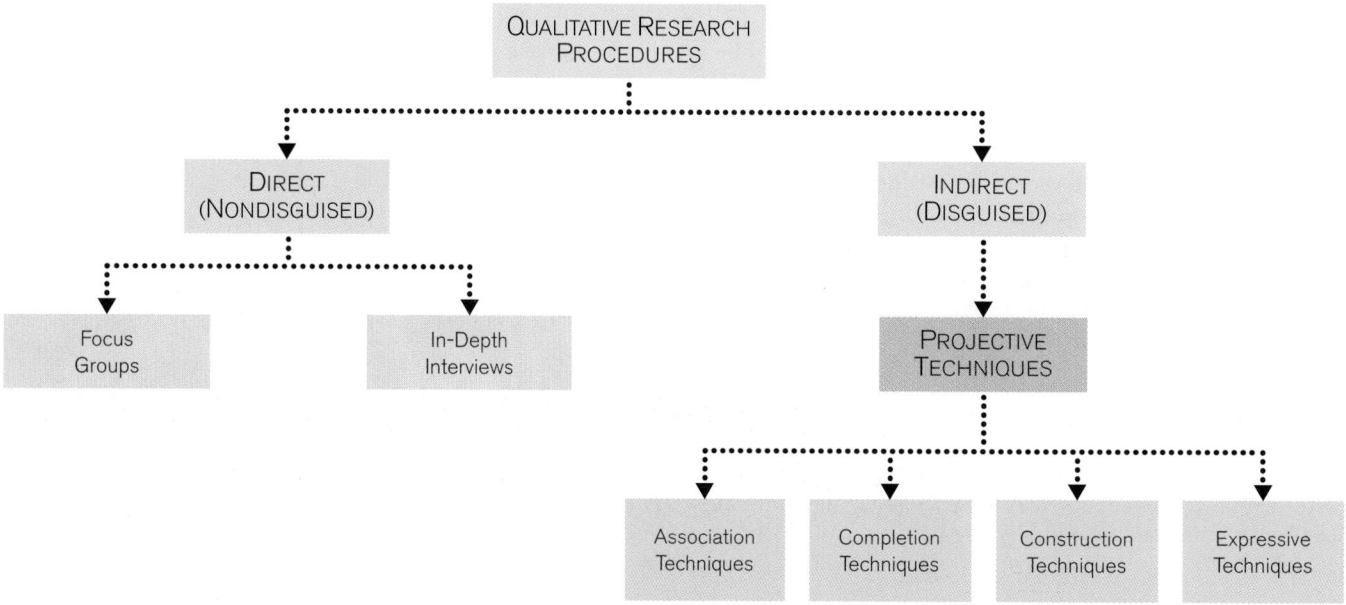

Figure 6.4
A Classification of Qualitative Research Procedures

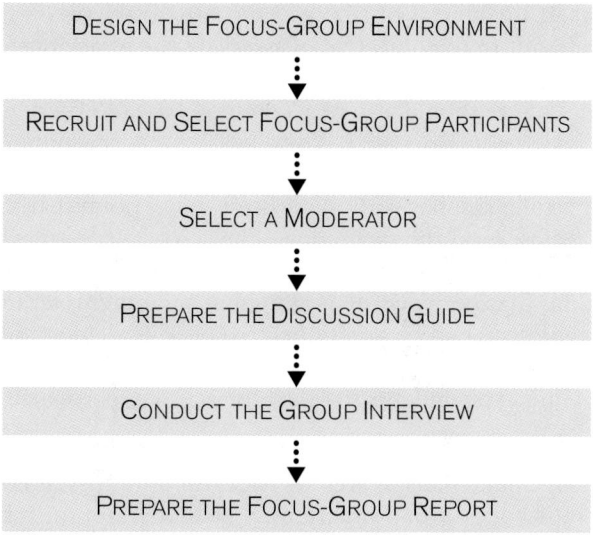

Figure 6.5
Procedure for Conducting a Focus Group

Designing the Environment Focus-group sessions are typically held in facilities specially equipped to comfortably accommodate and record a group discussion. The setting is typically an informal conference room equipped with a one-way mirror and microphones throughout the room. Behind the one-way mirror is a viewing room for management.

Most focus groups are scheduled to last one to three hours (Table 6.2). This amount of time is needed to establish rapport with the participants and to explore in depth their beliefs, feelings, ideas, attitudes, and insights regarding the topics of concern. Focus groups are either audio-recorded or videotaped to preserve the comments for analysis later. Videotaping has the advantage of recording facial expressions and body movements, but it can increase the costs significantly.

Frequently, clients observe the session from an adjacent room using a one-way mirror. Video-transmission technology can also allow the clients to observe the focus-group session live from a remote location.

Recruiting and Selecting Focus-Group Participants The major characteristics of a focus group are summarized in Table 6.2. A focus group is generally made up of 8 to 12 members. The advantages that come from the group dynamics are often lost to groups larger than this. Minigroups of four or five respondents may sometimes be used if the session is highly exploratory and if extensive, unstructured probing is necessary.

A focus group should be homogeneous in terms of product usage, demographics, and socioeconomic characteristics. This commonality among group members avoids interactions and conflicts on side issues. Suppose a focus group is conducted to evaluate the appeal of a line of frozen foods. It may not be desirable to include professional women and homemakers in the same group. It is clear that these two subgroups have strong differences of opinion regarding the role of women in the family. If they are included in the same group, the conversation could deviate into a discussion of the role of women in

Table 6.2
Characteristics of Focus Groups

Group size	8 to12 participants
Group composition	Homogeneous; respondents prescreened
Physical setting	Relaxed, informal atmosphere
Time duration	1 to 3 hours
Recording	Use of audiocassettes and videotapes
Moderator	Observational, interpersonal, and communication skills of the moderator are critical

the family rather than the appeal of the frozen foods. If so, the researcher would not gain any insights relevant to the objective of assessing the basic appeal of the product.

Not only should the group be homogeneous in terms of demographic and socioeconomic characteristics, there should also be a common base of experience or involvement with the object or issue being discussed. Thus, heavy users and nonusers of the product should not be included in the same group. Finally, people who have participated in multiple focus groups become familiar with the process to the point that their responses may be biased by their exposure to the technique. These so-called professional respondents should be screened out of the group. To ensure that the focus-group respondents are homogeneous in terms of experience, demographics, and other relevant variables, potential respondents are prescreened. A questionnaire covering demographic characteristics, attitudes, product use, and experience of the respondent is typically developed and administered to potential respondents to select focus group participants.

Selecting a Moderator The moderator plays a key role and must be well trained. General group management skills as well as background in psychology and marketing typically suffice in most focus-group situations. The moderator must be able to establish rapport with the participants, keep the discussion moving forward, and probe the respondents to elicit insights. In addition, this individual may also play a central role in the analysis and interpretation of the data. Therefore, the moderator should possess knowledge of the discussion topic and an understanding of the nature of group dynamics in order to appropriately interpret focus-group responses. Despite the importance of the moderator, there is no central body that certifies or trains focus-group moderators. This lack of standardization in qualifications is one of the problems to be overcome in this type of research. This limitation can be minimized by preparing a detailed moderator discussion guide.

Preparing the Discussion Guide Regardless of the skills or qualifications of the moderator, any focus group will flounder without an outline of the topics to be covered. The discussion guide should reflect the objectives of qualitative research. The objectives, in turn, should be derived from the definition of the marketing research problem, approach, and the research design adopted. A moderator's discussion guide can reduce some of the reliability problems inherent in focus groups, such as the lack of consistency in topics covered from group to group.

Most group discussions can be broken into three phases, the first being an introduction to establish rapport, relax the group, and describe the process. The bulk of the group session revolves around discussion of the research topic. In the closing phase, the moderator summarizes the comments and attempts to get a final read on the strength of the group's commitment to the statements made. The questions are typically kept fairly general to allow the moderator to pursue important ideas when participants mention them. To be effective, the moderator must understand the client's business, the focus-group objectives, and how the findings will be used. Presented is a sample discussion guide for focus groups of users on purchase motivations and buying process for pocket PCs/hand-held organizers.

Conducting the Group Interview During the interview, the moderator must (1) establish rapport with the group, (2) state the rules of group interaction, (3) set objectives, (4) probe the respondents and provoke intense discussion in the relevant areas, and (5) attempt to summarize the group's response to determine the extent of agreement.

The number of focus groups conducted depends on (1) the nature of the issue, (2) the number of distinct market segments, (3) the number of new ideas generated by each successive group, and (4) time and cost. Ideally, groups should be conducted until the moderator becomes familiar enough with the range of responses and can anticipate what will be said. This usually happens after three or four groups. It is recommended that a minimum of two groups be conducted.[2]

Preparing the Focus-Group Report Following the focus-group session, the moderator and the managers who viewed the session often engage in an instant interpretation.

RESEARCH IN ACTION

Focus-Group Discussion Guide for Pocket PCs

Preamble (5 minutes)

- Thanks and welcome
- Nature of a focus group (informal, multiway, all views acceptable, disagree)
- There are no right or wrong answers—all about finding out what people think
- Audio and video recording
- Colleagues viewing
- Help self to refreshments
- Going to be talking about pocket PCs
- Questions or concerns?

Introductions & Warm-up (5 minutes)

I'd like to go around the room and have you introduce yourselves:

- First name
- Best thing about having a pocket PC
- Worst thing about having a pocket PC

Pocket PC Usage (15 minutes)

I'd like to understand a bit about how you typically use your pocket PC:

- How many times a day do you use it?
- What are some of the most common types of things you use it for?

Briefly Explore

- If we were to take away your pocket PC from you, what difference would that make to your life?

Briefly Explore

Past Pocket-PC Purchase (15 minutes)

Thinking now about your current pocket PC, I'd like to talk about two different things:

- How did you actually go about the process of choosing the pocket PC?
- Did you have any criteria for the pocket PC itself?

Past Pocket-PC Selection Process

- Thinking first only about how you went about choosing your pocket PC, not any features you wanted, how did you go about choosing one?

Explore Process

Past Pocket-PC Criteria

- Now tell me what you actually looked for in a pocket PC.

Explore

Usage of Pocket-PC Features (20 minutes)

- Thinking now about pocket-PC features, I'd like to start by making a list of all the features you can think of—anything the pocket PC can do, any settings you can change, etc.
- We'll talk in a minute about which features you actually use, but I want to start with a list of everything your pocket PC *could* do.

Flipchart

- Which features have you *ever* used, even if only once?

Flipchart

- Are there any settings you only changed once, but are really glad you could change?
- Why?

Explore

- Which features do you use regularly?
- Why?

Explore

Desired Features (10 minutes)

- Are there any features your pocket PC *doesn't* have but that you wish it did?

Explore

Motivations for Buying (20 minutes)

You've all been invited here because you own a pocket PC.

- What motivated you to buy your pocket PC?

Explore

- What do you think are some of the reasons that people would buy pocket PCs?

Explore

- What were ALL the factors involved in that decision?
- What was the single *biggest* reason?

Explore

Closing Exercise (10 minutes)

- Finally, I'd like your creativity for a few minutes in coming up with ideas.
- Don't worry about whether it's a good idea or a bad idea.
- The only word I'm going to ban is "free"!
- Supposing a pocket-PC manufacturer wanted to encourage you to buy tomorrow, what could they do?
- Just call out anything at all that occurs to you—obvious, profound, serious, silly, whatever.

Explore & Refine

- Thank the respondents and close the session.

There is value in this free exchange in that it captures the impressions of the group and may be a good source of information for additional brainstorming. The danger is that the emotional power of the group's comments can cloud important points, which may be lost unless a detailed review of the focus-group tapes is conducted. Hence, no conclusions should be drawn until either the moderator or an analyst reviews and analyzes the results and a complete report has been prepared.

Due to the small number of participants, frequencies and percentages are not usually reported in a focus-group summary. Instead, reports typically include expressions such as "most participants thought" or "participants were divided on this issue." The report should not only present the findings based on the verbal comments but should also analyze consistent responses, new ideas, and concerns suggested by facial expressions and body language. Meticulous documentation and interpretation of the session lays the groundwork for the final step, taking action. This usually means doing additional research, as illustrated in the case involving Mall of the Boondocks (the actual name has been disguised).

RESEARCH IN ACTION

Mall of the Boondocks Focus-Group Topline

Focus-Group Objectives

The latest in the quarterly series, Mall of the Boondocks focus groups were conducted to understand shopping-mall expectations of the student segment, to determine this group's perceptions of a recent weekend visit, and to analyze the perceived brand identity of the mall based on the individuals' experience.

Method and Procedures

Reactions were solicited for the Mall of the Boondocks experience from 20 student visitors (8 males and 12 females) who attended the mall on the weekend prior to the group discussion (i.e., Labor Day Weekend). Two focus groups were conducted, each with 10 respondents. A variety of ages, life stages, and previous work experience was represented within the groups. The current focus groups were conducted at Good Stuff's video-conference facility on September 16, 2004. Students were given $30 and instructed to visit the mall between September 3 and 5; however, no other instructions or explanations were given to the students. They were not aware that they would be participating in a discussion group when they visited the mall.

Summary of Findings

Mall-Visit Experience

- For entertainment, participants typically engage in movies (theater and rental), sports (spectator and participatory), drinks, or just "hanging out" with friends. They typically need only three or four hours to experience the mall and try to hold cost to under $30, except for a special occasion.
- Examples of special occasions include dinner, concerts, theater, museums, and theme malls. Most often, the theme mall is a destination like Mall of America, Universal Studios, or Sea World. Many have visited Mall of the Boondocks more than once, and a few have been Mall of the Boondocks "Crown Customers," who shop at the Mall of the Boondocks loyally.
- Visitors were pleasantly surprised and delighted with the mall's entertainment, the surprisingly short lines in the children's area, the first-class magic show, and winning a large stuffed animal.
- When asked to describe feelings surrounding the experience, most were very positive–*"excited to go," "feel like a kid again," "didn't feel like I should have to go to work tomorrow,"* and *"friendly, fun to share the experience with others in attendance."* The only negatives were *"tired," "hot,"* and *"yucky."*

Advantages and Disadvantages of Focus Groups

Focus groups are popular because of their many advantages. The immediacy and the richness of the comments, which come from real customers, make this technique highly useful. The group interaction produces a wider range of information, insights, and ideas than do individual interviews. The comments of one person can trigger unexpected reactions from others, leading to snowballing with participants responding to each other's comments. The responses are generally spontaneous and candid, providing rich insights. Ideas are more likely to arise out of the blue in a group than in an individual interview and are likely to be unique and potentially creative.[3]

However, some of the qualities that make focus groups so strong also create some of their more serious limitations. The disadvantages of focus groups should not be overlooked. The clarity and conviction with which group members often speak leads to a tendency for researchers and managers to regard findings as conclusive rather than as exploratory. Focus groups are also difficult to moderate. The quality of the results depends heavily on the skills of the moderator; unfortunately, moderators who possess all of the desirable skills are rare. Further, the unstructured nature of the responses makes coding, analysis, and interpretation difficult.

- On the other hand, visitors were frustrated to find a lack of signage and maps, a "deserted" feeling resulting from the lack of hosts or guides and the dry, dirty look of some areas in the mall.
- Visitors were asked to suggest necessary changes in the mall.
  - Crowds. Can be daunting, and there must be a way to make them more palatable, such as drinking fountains, benches, water misters, ceiling fans that work, or entertainment. Made comparisons to Mall of America, which respondents said had more space and better-groomed patrons.
  - Dress code. There were complaints that many people were showing a lot of skin but hardly anyone looked like Britney Spears or Ricky Martin. Who wants the bowling alley crowd to dress this way? Several agreed there should be a "no shirt, no shoes, no service" policy.
  - Information. Booths placed in visible spots throughout the mall would be helpful. Visitors agreed that maps were very hard to find and that handing them out in line at the entrance of the mall might help.

Brand Identity Versus Mall of America

General Personality

- **Mall of the Boondocks.** Definitely male, but surprisingly, not teen-aged. Middle-aged or older, a little tired, moody. Blue-collar worker, not very smart, wearing "gimme" t-shirt and cap, maybe with a beer logo (e.g., Budweiser). Drives a big old American car, may have money problems. A follower rather than a leader.
- **Mall of America.** Both female and male, perhaps that loving, indulgent aunt and uncle who shower you with experiences you don't get at home. Dressed classically in khakis and a polo shirt. Nurturing, approachable, well-rounded, and affluent. Like this person better than the Mall of the Boondocks personality because it's more fun.

Brand Value

To many, Mall of the Boondocks was described as "just a bunch of shops and rides." Other malls, such as Mall of America, encompass a complete entertainment experience. Several "long-timers" remember a time when Mall of the Boondocks included the experience of regional history and of other cultures. What made it unique in the past is gone now, as the specific areas have become less distinct and not associated with as much meaning. As a result, there was a general feeling that the value had declined.

Implications

In general, the results of this latest in the series of focus groups–focusing upon student perceptions–are similar to those from previous focus groups with nonstudents. Respondents view the Mall of the Boondocks as more of a "working person's" mall. The student respondents' perceptions of the Mall of the Boondocks were markedly more negative when compared to the Mall of the America than the perceptions of any other segment of customers included in this series of quarterly focus groups begun two years ago. Perhaps Mall of America's recently completed remodeling has become more salient in the minds of the Mall of the Boondocks student customers because of students' higher use of informal "buzz" (word-of-mouth). More research on this topic using a large sample survey is needed.

Online Focus Groups

Online focus groups are becoming increasingly popular because of greater convenience and cost-effectiveness and faster turnaround as compared to traditional focus groups. Using Internet technologies, marketing research companies have created virtual focus-group facilities consisting of waiting rooms, focus-group rooms, and client rooms. The respondents are prerecruited, generally from an online list of people who have expressed an interest in participating. Some are also recruited by using e-mail lists, Web intercepts, banner ads, or traditional methods (phone or mail). A screening questionnaire is administered online to qualify the respondents. Those who qualify are invited to participate in a focus group and receive a time, a URL, a room name, and a password via e-mail. Generally, four to six people participate in the online group. There are fewer people in an online focus group than in a face-to-face meeting because too many respondents can cause confusion.

Before the focus group begins, participants receive information about the focus group that covers such things as how to express emotions when typing. Electronic emotion indicators are produced using keyboard characters and are standard in their use on the Internet. For example, :-) and :-(are examples of smiling and sad faces. The emotion indicators are usually inserted in the text at the point where the emotion is meant. Emotions can also be expressed using a different font or color. The participants can also preview information about the focus-group topic by visiting a Web site and reading information or downloading and viewing an actual TV ad on their PCs. Then, just before the focus group begins, participants visit a Web site where they log on and get some last-minute instructions.

When it is time for the group, they move into a Web-based chat room. They go to the focus-group location (URL) and click on the "Enter Focus Room" item. To enter, they must supply the room name, user name, and password that was e-mailed to them earlier. The moderator signs on early and administers the rescreening questionnaire as the respondents enter the waiting room to verify their identities. Once in the focus-group chatroom, the moderator and the participants type to each other in real time. The general practice is for the moderators to always pose their questions in all capital letters, and the respondents are asked to use upper- and lowercase. The respondents are also asked to always start their response with the question number, so the moderator can quickly tie the response to the proper question. This makes it fast and easy to transcribe a focus-group session. The group interaction lasts for about 60 to 90 minutes. A raw transcript is available as soon as the group is completed, and a formatted transcript is available within 48 hours. The whole process is much faster than the traditional method. An example of companies that provide online focus groups is SurveySite (www.surveysite.com).

New forms of online focus groups continue to emerge. For example, online bulletin board focus groups involve the moderator and the respondents over an extended period of time, from a few days to a few weeks. Thus, respondents can think and respond at their own convenience.

Advantages of Online Focus Groups

People from all over the country or even the world can participate in online focus groups, and the client can observe the group from the convenience of home or office.

EXPERIENTIAL LEARNING

Gatorade: From a Sports Drink to a Lifestyle Drink

Management would like to transform Gatorade from a sports drink to a lifestyle drink. Visit Gatorade's Web site (www.gatorade.com) and search the Internet using a search engine as well as your library's online databases to obtain information on the marketing strategy of Gatorade energy drinks.

1. Prepare a focus-group discussion guide for determining the reasons why people consume Gatorade drinks and what would lead them to consume more Gatorade.
2. Conduct a focus group of 8 to 12 students using your discussion guide.
3. Prepare a focus-group topline report for Gatorade management.

Geographical constraints are removed and time constraints are lessened. Unlike traditional focus groups, online groups offer the unique opportunity for recontacting group participants at a later date to either revisit issues or to introduce them to modifications in material presented in the original focus group. The Internet enables the researcher to reach segments that are usually hard to survey, such as doctors, lawyers, other professional people, working mothers, and others who lead busy lives and are typically not interested in taking part in traditional focus groups.

Moderators may also be able to carry on side conversations with individual respondents, probing deeper into interesting areas. People are generally less inhibited in their responses and are more likely to fully express their thoughts online. A lot of online focus groups go well past their allotted time since so many responses are expressed. Finally, as there is no travel, videotaping, or facilities to arrange, the cost is much lower than for traditional focus groups. Firms are able to keep costs between one-fifth and one-half the costs of traditional focus groups. Online groups are also faster to conduct.

Disadvantages of Online Focus Groups

Only people that have and know how to use a computer can be surveyed online. Since the name of an individual on the Internet is often private, actually verifying that a respondent is a member of a target group is difficult. This is illustrated in a cartoon in the *New Yorker*, where two dogs are seated at a computer and one says to the other "On the Internet, nobody knows you are a dog!" To overcome this limitation, other traditional methods such as telephone calls are used for recruitment and verification of respondents. Body language, facial expressions, and tone of voice cannot be obtained, and electronic emotion indicators obviously do not capture as full a breadth of emotion as does videotaping.

Another factor that must be considered is the lack of general control over the respondent's environment and their potential exposure to distracting external stimuli. Since online focus groups could potentially have respondents scattered all over the world, the researchers and moderators have no idea what else the respondents may be doing while participating in the group. Only audio and visual stimuli can be tested. Products cannot be touched (e.g., clothing) or smelled (e.g., perfumes). Table 6.3 presents a comparison of online and traditional focus groups.

Applications of Focus Groups

Focus groups, whether traditional or online, can be used in almost any situation that requires preliminary understanding or insight into the problem. The range of research topics relevant for focus-group investigation includes research designed to do any of the following:

1. Understand consumer perceptions, preferences, and behavior concerning a product category (e.g., how consumers select a long-distance telephone company and their perceptions of AT&T, MCI, and Sprint).
2. Obtain impressions of new product concepts (e.g., consumer response to the high-definition one-time-use cameras by Kodak).
3. Generate new ideas about older products (e.g., new packaging and positioning for Cheer detergent).
4. Develop creative concepts and copy material for advertisements (e.g., a new campaign for Diet Pepsi).
5. Secure price impressions (e.g., the role of price in consumer selection of luxury cars, such as Cadillac, Lexus, Mercedes, BMW, and Infiniti).
6. Obtain preliminary consumer reaction to specific marketing programs (e.g., General Mills' instant coupons for Cheerios).
7. Interpret previously obtained quantitative results (e.g., the reasons for the 5.6 percent sales decline of Vanderbilt perfume).

Despite broad applicability, focus-group interviewing is only one of the personal interviewing techniques used to collect qualitative data. One-on-one in-depth interviewing is another technique.

Table 6.3
Online Versus Traditional Focus Groups

Characteristic	Online Focus Groups	Traditional Focus Groups
Group size	4 to 6 participants	8 to 12 participants
Group composition	Anywhere in the world	Drawn from the local area
Time duration	1 to 1.5 hours	1 to 3 hours
Physical setting	Researcher has little control	Under the control of the researcher
Respondent identity	Difficult to verify	Can be easily verified
Respondent attentiveness	Respondents can engage in other tasks	Attentiveness can be monitored
Respondent recruiting	Easier. Can be recruited online, by e-mail, panel, or by traditional means	Recruited by traditional means (telephone, mail, mail panel)
Group dynamics	Limited	Synergistic, snowballing (bandwagon) effect
Openness of respondents	Respondents are more candid due to lack of face-to-face contact	Respondents are candid, except for sensitive topics
Nonverbal communication	Body language cannot be observed Emotions expressed by using symbols	Easy to observe body language and emotions
Use of physical stimuli	Limited to those that can be displayed on the Internet	A variety of stimuli (products, advertising, demonstrations, and so on) can be used
Transcripts	Available immediately	Time-consuming and expensive to obtain
Observers' communication with moderator	Observers can communicate with the moderator on a split-screen	Observers can manually send notes to the focus-group room
Unique moderator skills	Typing, computer usage, familiarity with chat-room slang	Observational
Turnaround time	Can be set up and completed in a few days	Takes many days for set up and completion
Client travel costs	None	Can be expensive
Basic focus-group costs	Much less expensive	More expensive due to facility rental, food, video/audiotaping, and transcript preparation

RESEARCH IN ACTION

Online Focus–E*TRADE Canada

E*TRADE Canada (www.canada.etrade.com) is a premiere online securities trading company. Due to the growing number of firms participating in online trading, E*TRADE Canada recently developed a comprehensive research plan to evaluate and improve its trading Web site to maintain market leadership. E*TRADE Canada decided to partner with SurveySite (www.surveysite.com), a marketing research firm specializing in online research, to conduct this project.

The research began with online focus groups including current E*TRADE Canada customers. The objective of the focus groups was to develop insights into key areas of satisfaction, including reactions to customer service, product fees, product quality, technical support, and so on. The focus groups were followed up by a quantitative online survey using respondents recruited through various Internet resources and e-mail invitations. The result of the focus groups and survey information was a new and improved E*TRADE Canada Web site that improved customer satisfaction and provided a significant boost in subscriptions.

RESEARCH IN ACTION

Focus (Groups) on Quality: The ABC of TV Programming

ABC television relies heavily on qualitative research to determine how consumers define quality TV programming. Focus groups conducted by the company have revealed that the characters, plots, and punch lines determine the quality of most TV programs. Therefore, ABC pays close attention to these features while developing its shows. Once the pilot shows are developed, focus groups are conducted to assess consumer reaction and to undertake refinement. ABC has recently decided to schedule only the shows that test well.

ABC used focus groups to test the TV show *Super Millionaire*. The focus groups revealed that the show appealed to parents because of its educational value and that they would encourage their children to watch it. When this was confirmed by survey research, the educational content of the show was strengthened, and the program was launched. The show was a hit with the TV viewers and because of the consistently high ratings, the show continues to remain in the line-up. ABC's customer focus and involvement, achieved via focus groups and survey research, demonstrates the network's commitment to viewers. The whole organization is run for the customer.[4]

In-Depth Interviews

In-depth interviews are loosely structured conversations with individuals drawn from the target audience. Like focus groups, in-depth interviews are an unstructured and direct way of obtaining information. Unlike focus groups, however, in-depth interviews are conducted on a one-on-one basis. These interviews typically last from 30 minutes to more than an hour. They attempt to uncover underlying motives, prejudices, or attitudes toward sensitive issues.

in-depth interviews
Unstructured, direct personal interviews in which a single respondent is probed by a highly skilled interviewer to uncover underlying motivations, beliefs, attitudes, and feelings on a topic.

Conducting In-Depth Interviews

As with focus groups, the interviewer prepares a discussion outline to guide the interview. However, the purpose of in-depth interviews is to uncover hidden issues that may not be shared in a group setting. Therefore, substantial probing is done to surface underlying motives, beliefs, and attitudes. This was illustrated in the opening vignette in which Gillette used in-depth interviews to understand the underlying motives and attitudes of women toward shaving. The in-depth interviews showed that women shave much more surface area than men do, they do this only two or three times a week, they often shave in a dimly lit shower, and they must shave areas they can't see well. Furthermore, shaving tends to be a personal experience for women that evokes feelings of anticipation and acceptance. Probing is necessary to understand these findings and feelings. Probing is done by asking such questions as "Why do you say that?" "That's interesting, can you tell me more?" or "Would you like to add anything else?" (Probing is further discussed in Chapter 14.) As the interview progresses, the type of questions asked, the probes used, and the wording of the questions depend on the answers received.

To illustrate the technique, suppose an interviewer is conducting in-depth interviews with working men and women who are frequent catalog shoppers. The objective is to understand how these shoppers view the catalog-shopping experience. The interview may go something like this:

Interviewer: "Tell me about shopping through catalogs." The interviewer then encourages the subject to talk freely about attitudes and feelings about catalog shopping. After asking the initial question, the direction of the interview is determined by the respondent's initial reply.

Respondent: "I sometimes like to relax with a cup of coffee, flipping through a catalog at the end of the day. It's fun and relaxing."

Interviewer: "Why is it fun and relaxing?"

If the answer is not very revealing (e.g., "It lets my mind wander."), the interviewer may ask further probing questions (e.g., "Why is it fun to let your mind wander?").

Respondent: "I have to think logically all day long. When I sit down with a catalog, I can fantasize about how I will look in certain clothing or how my living room will look with a piece of furniture. And, there is no pressure to do anything!"

Interviewer: "Why is it important to have no pressure to do anything?"

Respondent: "My whole day is pressure. In my job, I have to constantly react to pressure someone else is putting on me. Home is the one place where I can control the pressure, even eliminate it."

As this example indicates, probing is effective in uncovering underlying or hidden information. In this case, the respondent finds catalog shopping relaxing and a form of low-stress escape (the need to feel "no pressure to do anything").

As with focus groups, the success of in-depth interviews rests with the skill of the interviewer. The interviewer should (1) avoid appearing superior and put the respondent at ease; (2) be detached and objective, yet personable; (3) ask questions in an informative manner; (4) not accept brief "yes" or "no" answers; and (5) probe the respondent.

In-depth interviews can be used to create an environment that fosters a more candid and comprehensive discussion of an issue than can be done in a group. The resulting data provide insight into motivation, beliefs, attitudes, and perceived consequences of behavior. Also, because in-depth interviews are conducted one-on-one, the comments can be traced directly to individual respondents. This may be particularly relevant in business-to-business research where a decision maker's comments can be evaluated within the context of that individual's personal and corporate background.

Advantages of In-Depth Interviews

In-depth interviews can uncover deeper insights about underlying motives than focus groups can. Also, in-depth interviews attribute the responses directly to the respondent unlike focus groups where it is often difficult to determine which respondent made a particular response. In-depth interviews result in a free exchange of information that may not be possible in focus groups where there is sometimes social pressure to conform. As a result of probing, it is possible to get at real issues when the topic is complex. This was illustrated in the opening vignette in which Gillette used in-depth interviews to understand the shaving needs of women.

Disadvantages of In-Depth Interviews

The disadvantages of focus groups are magnified in individual in-depth interviews. Skilled interviewers capable of conducting in-depth interviews are expensive and difficult to find. The lack of structure makes the results susceptible to the interviewer's influence, and the quality and completeness of the results depend heavily on the interviewer's skills. The data obtained are difficult to analyze and interpret; the services of skilled psychologists are typically required for this purpose. The length of the interview combined with high costs means that only a small number of in-depth interviews can be conducted in a project.

Despite these disadvantages, in-depth interviews do have applications, particularly in business-to-business marketing where it is often difficult to assemble a group of executives for a focus-group session. They are also useful in advertising research where it is important to understand the feelings and emotions the advertisement evokes. A relative comparison of focus groups and in-depth interviews is given in Table 6.4.

Applications of In-Depth Interviews

As with focus groups, the primary use of in-depth interviews is for exploratory research to gain insight and understanding. Unlike focus groups, however, in-depth interviews are used infrequently in marketing research. Nevertheless, in-depth interviews can be effectively employed in special problem situations, such as those requiring the following:

Table 6.4
Focus Groups Versus In-Depth Interviews

Characteristic	Focus Groups	In-Depth Interviews
Group synergy and dynamics	+	−
Peer pressure/group influence	−	+
Client involvement	+	−
Generation of innovative ideas	+	−
In-depth probing of individuals	−	+
Uncovering of hidden motives	−	+
Discussion of sensitive topics	−	+
Interviews with respondents who are competitors	−	+
Interviews with respondents who are professionals	−	+
Scheduling of respondents	−	+
Amount of information	+	−
Bias in moderation and interpretation	+	−
Cost per respondent	+	−

+ indicates a relative advantage over the other procedure

− indicates a relative disadvantage over the other procedure

1. Detailed probing of the respondent (e.g., automobile purchase).
2. Discussion of confidential, sensitive, or embarrassing topics (e.g., personal finances, loose dentures).
3. Situations where strong social norms exist and the respondent may be easily swayed by the group's response (e.g., attitude of college students toward sports).
4. Detailed understanding of complicated behavior (e.g., department-store shopping).
5. Interviews with professional people (e.g., industrial marketing research).
6. Interviews with a competitor's customers, who are unlikely to reveal the information in a group setting (e.g., travel agents' perceptions of airline package travel programs).
7. Situations where the product consumption experience is sensory in nature, affecting mood states and emotions (e.g., shaving experience, as in the opening vignette).

Research with children is an example for which in-depth interviews may be productive. M&M/Mars used in-depth interviews to uncover an effective advertising approach. This example illustrates the value of in-depth interviews in uncovering the hidden responses that underlie the clichés elicited in ordinary questioning (e.g., "It's good" or "I like it"). Like focus groups, in-depth interviews can also be conducted online.

BE an MR!

Search the Internet using a search engine as well as your library's online databases to obtain information on why people use credit cards.

Conduct two in-depth interviews for determining the reasons why people use credit cards.

BE a DM!

As the marketing manager for Visa, how would you use information about why people use credit cards to increase your market share?

RESEARCH IN ACTION

Mission from Mars

As of 2005, Mars (www.mars.com or www.mmmars.com) was a $14 billion business operating in more than 100 countries. Most children have a very active and colorful fantasy life. Recognizing this characteristic in their target audience, M&M/Mars decided to use in-depth interviews to uncover childhood fantasies that might be relevant to the company's promotional efforts. Mars conducted in-depth interviews with schoolchildren and found that a majority of these fantasies revolves around extraterrestrial beings, wars, and exciting action. Previously, the candy manufacturer had never fully developed its extraterrestrial images, although they seemed natural given product names like Mars and Milky Way. In response to the in-depth interview findings, they decided to introduce extraterrestrial characters from the planet Mars.

The company developed an imaginative story involving the Mars' Minister of Candy. He directed four Martians to bring back the "best candy in the universe," in order to eliminate the suffering Martians had endured for many years. Moreover, this advertising was linked to a promotional campaign that included back-to-school sweepstakes offering a grand prize of $100,000, 50 trips to Disney World, and other prizes. The four extraterrestrial heroes made appearances at malls and children's hospitals across the country. This successful multimillion dollar campaign was shaped by the fantasies of children, uncovered by using in-depth interviews.[5]

Projective Techniques

projective techniques
Unstructured and indirect form of questioning that encourages respondents to project their underlying motivations, beliefs, attitudes, or feelings regarding the issues of concern.

Both focus groups and in-depth interviews are direct approaches in which the true purpose of the research is disclosed to the respondents or is otherwise obvious to them. **Projective techniques** are different from these techniques in that they attempt to disguise the purpose of the research. They are used in market research situations in which the respondent is unable or unwilling to answer a question directly. To get around this problem, the interviewer presents the respondent with a series of vague or incomplete pictures, statements, or scenarios. The underlying assumption is that when asked to respond to these prompts, the individual will be revealing personal information that is perhaps held subconsciously.

Projective techniques are unstructured, indirect forms of questioning that require respondents to describe vague and ambiguous stimulus situations. In describing these situations, respondents indirectly project their own motivations, beliefs, attitudes, or feelings into the situation. The underlying information about respondents is uncovered by analyzing their responses. As an example, respondents may be asked to interpret the behavior of others rather than describe their own behavior. In doing so, respondents indirectly project their own motivations, beliefs, attitudes or feelings into the situation. In a landmark study, the U.S. Postal Service (USPS) made use of this technique to determine why most boys aged 8 to 13 years did not collect stamps as a hobby. A sample of boys was shown a picture on a screen of a 10-year-old boy fixing stamps in his album and asked to describe the scene and characterize the boy. Most respondents described the boy in the picture as a "sissy." Thereafter, the Postal Service undertook a successful advertising campaign directed at 8- to 13-year-olds to dispel the belief that stamp collecting was for "sissies."

Projective techniques used in marketing research may be classified as association, completion, construction, or expressive techniques.

Association Techniques

In **association techniques**, the individual is presented with a list of words or images and asked to respond with the first thing that comes to mind. Word association is the best known of these techniques. In **word association**, respondents are presented with a list of words, one at a time, and asked to respond to each with the first word that comes to mind. The words of interest, called *test words*, are interspersed throughout the list, which also contains some neutral, or filler, words to disguise the purpose of the study. For example, in a retailing study, some of the test words might be: *location*, *parking*, *shopping*, *quality*, and *price*. The subject's response to each word is recorded verbatim, and responses are timed. Respondents who hesitate or reason out (defined as taking longer than three seconds to reply) are identified.

In analyzing these data, the researcher looks at the frequency with which a response is given, the amount of hesitation before responding, and the number of instances when no response is given. Patterns in responses are analyzed, as are the response times. It is often possible to classify the associations as favorable, unfavorable, or neutral. The longer an individual hesitates before answering, the higher the assumed level of involvement with the subject. A nonresponse is thought to indicate the highest level of emotional involvement, as these people are too involved to be able to respond in a short time. Gillette used word association to help them name the Sensor for Women shaver (see opening vignette). A group of women was presented with several different names for the new feminine razor, including Sensor for Women and Lady Sensor, and asked to write down the first word that came to mind. Because Sensor for Women elicited the most favorable responses, the company selected this name.

association techniques
Type of projective technique in which the respondent is presented with a stimulus and asked to respond with the first thing that comes to mind.

word association
A projective technique in which respondents are presented with a list of words, one at a time. After each word is presented, respondents are asked to give the first word that comes to mind.

Completion Techniques

Completion techniques are a natural extension of association techniques, generating more detail about the individual's underlying feelings and beliefs. The respondent is asked to complete a sentence, a paragraph, or a story. In **sentence completion**, respondents are given incomplete sentences and asked to finish them. Generally, they are asked to use the first word or phrase that comes to mind, as in the following example.

A variation of sentence completion is *paragraph completion*, in which the respondent finishes a paragraph that begins with the stimulus phrase. A further expanded version of sentence completion and paragraph completion is **story completion**. In story completion, respondents are given part of a story, enough to direct attention to a particular topic but not enough to hint at the ending. They are required to give the conclusion in their own words.

completion techniques
Projective techniques that require the respondent to complete an incomplete stimulus situation.

sentence completion
A projective technique in which respondents are presented with a number of incomplete sentences and asked to complete them.

story completion
A projective technique in which respondents are provided with part of a story and required to give the conclusion in their own words.

RESEARCH IN ACTION

Tommy Hilfiger Is a High Flyer in Men's Shirts

In order to determine men's underlying attitudes toward Tommy Hilfiger shirts, sentence completion could be used as follows:

A person who wears Tommy Hilfiger shirts is _____

As compared to Polo, Gant, and Eddie Bauer, Tommy Hilfiger shirts are _____

Tommy Hilfiger shirts are most liked by _____

When I think of Tommy Hilfiger shirts, I _____

Using such techniques, Tommy Hilfiger (www.tommy.com) discovered that men preferred shirts that were less formal with a nontraditional cut. Men preferred to buy these shirts at upscale department stores, such as Macy's. These findings, after they were confirmed by survey research, formed the platform for Tommy Hilfiger's successful marketing strategy. The New York-based lifestyle brand had plenty of good news to report in August 2003 when it reported better-than-expected profits and rolled out its men's and women's premium sportswear line, H Hilfiger, at top Federated stores in Spring 2004.

Construction Techniques

construction techniques
Projective techniques in which the respondent is required to construct a response in the form of a story, dialogue, or description.

picture-response techniques
Projective techniques in which the respondent is shown a picture and asked to tell a story describing it.

Construction techniques follow the same logic as other projective techniques, requiring the respondent to construct a response to a picture or cartoon. These techniques provide even less initial structure than verbally oriented association or completion techniques. In **picture-response techniques**, persons or objects are depicted in pictures, and respondents are asked to write a descriptive story, dialogue, or description. The responses are analyzed in an attempt to identify themes reflecting the individual's perceptual interpretation of the pictures. In a variation of this technique, the respondents are asked to bring 12 to 15 pictures of their choice to the interview and then asked to describe the salient content of each picture. The picture descriptions reveal the underlying values, attitudes, and beliefs of the respondents. In another variation, respondents are provided with a photo deck portraying different types of people. Respondents sort the photos to connect the people in the photos with the brands that they would use. A photo sort for Visa revealed that the credit card had a middle-of-the road, female image. Therefore, Visa renewed its relationship with the National Football League through 2010 to attract more males. Another variation of this technique requires the respondents to draw pictures or drawings to express their feelings about the brand or object being investigated.

cartoon tests
Cartoon characters are shown in a specific situation related to the problem. The respondents are asked to indicate the dialogue that one cartoon character might make in response to the comment(s) of another character.

In **cartoon tests**, highly stylized stick characters are used to eliminate references to clothing, facial expressions, and even gender. The respondents are asked to complete the conversation they would attribute to the cartoon characters. These techniques typically ask for verbal responses from the cartoon characters and for unspoken thoughts. This tends to maximize the candid nature of the response. Since cartoon tests are simpler to administer and analyze than picture-response techniques, they are the most commonly used construction technique. An example is shown in Figure 6.6.

In marketing research applications, construction techniques are used to evaluate attitudes toward the topic under study and to build psychological profiles of the respondents, as illustrated by Porsche.

Expressive Techniques

expressive techniques
Projective techniques in which the respondent is presented with a verbal or visual situation and asked to relate the feelings and attitudes of other people to the situation.

role playing
Respondents are asked to play the role or assume the behavior of someone else.

In **expressive techniques**, respondents are presented with a verbal or visual situation and asked to relate, not their own feelings or attitudes, but those of others. The two main expressive techniques are role playing and the third-person technique. In **role playing**,

Figure 6.6
A Cartoon Test

RESEARCH IN ACTION

Taxonomy of a Porsche Buyer

Porsche (www.porsche.com) sells sports cars, the lowest-priced unit costing more than $40,000. The demographics of the Porsche owner are well known: male, mid-40s, college graduate, with average earnings exceeding $200,000 per year. Traditional advertising had focused on the car's performance and how good the car makes the owner look.

Not knowing their customers' motivations and psychological profile, Porsche hired a group of researchers to find out why its buyers bought the car. Among other techniques, the researchers used picture responses. Current and potential buyers were shown pictures of Porsche owners with their cars and asked to describe the owners. The results were surprising and revealed that Porsche had been using the wrong advertising approach.

According to the results, most of the Porsche owners couldn't care less if people saw them in their Porsche. So that advertising could be better directed to potential buyers, researchers produced five psychographic profiles: (1) "Top Guns." Driven, ambitious types. Power and control matter to these people, and they expect to be noticed. (2) "Elitists." Old money, blue bloods. To them a car is just a car, not an extension of their personality; (3) "Proud Patrons." Their car is a trophy earned for hard work, and they are not concerned with whether they are seen in it or not. (4) "Bon Vivants." Worldly jet setters and thrill seekers.

Their car adds excitement to their passionate lives. (5) "Fantasists." Their car is a fantasy escape. They are not trying to impress anyone and, in fact, are a little embarrassed about owning a Porsche.

After survey research confirmed these findings, marketing and advertising were directed at these psychographic segments. As a result of this research and after years of poor sales, Porsche's sales in the United States increased by 48 percent. In mid-March of 2003, Porsche introduced the Cayenne, the sporty off-road vehicle, and sales continue to be strong through at least 2005.[6]

respondents are asked to play the role or assume the behavior of someone else. The researcher assumes that the respondents will project their own feelings into the role.

In the **third-person technique**, the respondent is presented with a verbal or visual situation and asked to relate the beliefs and attitudes of a third person rather than directly expressing personal beliefs and attitudes. This third person may be a friend, a neighbor, a colleague, or a "typical" person. Again, the researcher assumes that the respondent will reveal personal beliefs and attitudes while describing the reactions of a third party. Asking the individual to respond in the third person reduces the social pressure to give an acceptable answer, as the following example shows.

third-person technique
A projective technique in which the respondent is presented with a verbal or visual situation and asked to relate the beliefs and attitudes of a third person to the situation.

In the Research in Action example that follows, asking the question in the first person ("Are you afraid to fly?") did not elicit the true response. Phrasing the same question in the third person ("Do you think your neighbor is afraid to fly?") lowered the

RESEARCH IN ACTION

What Will the Neighbors Say?

A study was performed for a commercial airline to understand why some people do not fly. When the respondents were asked, "Are you afraid to fly?" very few people said "yes." The major reasons given for not flying were cost, inconvenience, and delays caused by bad weather. It was suspected, however, that the answers were heavily influenced by the need to give socially desirable responses. Therefore, a follow-up study was done using the third-person technique. In the second study, the respondents were asked, "Do you think your neighbor is afraid to fly?" The answers indicated that most of the neighbors who traveled by some other means of transportation were afraid to fly. Thus, the third-person technique was able to uncover the true reason for not flying: fear of flying.[7]

respondents' defenses and resulted in truthful answers. In another popular version of the third-person technique, the researcher presents the respondent with a description of a shopping list and asks for a characterization of the purchaser, thus gaining data on shopping behavior.

Suppose the researcher is interested in determining attitudes toward prepared dinners. Two otherwise identical grocery shopping lists are prepared, except that one list contains prepared dinners. Respondents would be asked to characterize the purchaser identified with each list. The differences in the characteristics of the two purchasers reveal attitudes toward prepared dinners. For example, as compared to the other purchaser, the purchaser of prepared dinners may be described as lazy and disorganized. This would reveal that respondents think that lazy and disorganized people purchase prepared dinners.

We conclude our discussion of projective techniques by describing their advantages, disadvantages, and applications.

Advantages of Projective Techniques

Projective techniques have a major advantage over the unstructured direct techniques (i.e., focus groups and in-depth interviews): They may elicit responses that subjects would be unwilling or unable to give if they knew the purpose of the study. At times, in direct questioning, the respondent may intentionally or unintentionally misunderstand, misinterpret, or mislead the researcher. In these cases, projective techniques can increase the validity of responses by disguising the purpose. This is particularly true when the issues to be addressed are personal, sensitive, or subject to strong social norms. Projective techniques are also helpful when underlying motivations, beliefs, and attitudes are operating at a subconscious level.

Disadvantages of Projective Techniques

Projective techniques suffer from many of the disadvantages of unstructured direct techniques but to a greater extent. These techniques generally require personal interviews with highly trained interviewers and require skilled interpreters to analyze the responses. Hence, they tend to be expensive. Furthermore, there is a serious risk of interpretation bias. With the exception of word association, all techniques are open-ended, making analysis and interpretation difficult and subjective.

Some projective techniques, such as role playing, require respondents to engage in unusual behavior. For example, to assess a company's image, respondents may be asked to play the role of a person that best describes the company. It is possible that respondents who agree to participate are themselves unusual in some way. Therefore, they may not be representative of the population of interest. As a result, it is desirable to compare findings generated by projective techniques with the findings of the other techniques that permit a more representative sample.

Application of Projective Techniques

With the exception of word association, projective techniques are used much less frequently than either focus groups or in-depth interviews. Word association is commonly used for testing brand names and occasionally to measure attitudes about particular products, brands, packages, or advertisements. Like focus groups, in-depth interviews and virtually all the projective techniques discussed can be implemented over the Internet. For example, various companies and marketing researchers are using the picture-response technique effectively. Coca-Cola can provide a picture on a Web site and ask respondents to write a story about it. The demographic data of the person coupled with the story can provide valuable insights into the psychographic profile and the consumption motives and attitudes of the respondent. The success of conducting qualitative research over the Internet lies in the respondents having access to and being comfortable with the Internet.

As the examples have shown, projective techniques can be used in a variety of situations. The usefulness of these techniques is enhanced when the following guidelines are observed:

EXPERIENTIAL LEARNING

Online Qualitative Research

The following Web sites illustrate the types of qualitative research that can be conducted online.

1. To experience the steps involved in designing and analyzing online bulletin board research, go to (www.2020research.com/Online/index.htm) and at the bottom of the page, select "View a Flash Overview of QualBoards." To advance this overview, use the buttons at the bottom of the screen.
2. If you would like to join a panel of respondents who would earn prizes and other rewards for participating in online discussions you can (a) go to SurveySite's Web page for those volunteering to join online discussions in the future at (www.surveysite.com/about.html) and follow the instructions or (b) go to 20/20 Research Inc's Web page (www.2020research.com/JoinOurPanel.asp) and select "How do I join your panel (opt-in)." Then, follow the instructions.
3. To experience how a sponsor of an online focus group can monitor the actual focus group as if one was behind the one-way mirror in the back room of the focus-group facility, go to (www.activegroup.net/) and select "Focus Group Demo." You will have to provide an e-mail address and a one-word user name to activate the streaming video.
4. If you would like to understand how the National Institutes of Health recommends designing and executing online focus groups, go to (www.oirm.nih.gov/itmra/weptest/app_a7.htm).

1. Projective techniques are used when the sensitivity of the subject matter is such that respondents may not be willing or able to answer honestly to direct questions.
2. Projective techniques are used to uncover subconscious motives, beliefs, or values, providing deeper insights and understanding as part of exploratory research.
3. Projective techniques are administered and interpreted by trained interviewers who understand their advantages and limitations.

Given these guidelines, projective techniques, along with other qualitative techniques, can yield valuable information.

BE a DM!

As the brand manager for Clinique, how would you use information about the reasons why women use cosmetics to formulate marketing strategies that would increase your market share?

BE an MR!

Visit Clinique's Web site (www.clinique.com) and search the Internet using a search engine as well as your library's online databases to obtain information on the underlying reasons why women use cosmetics.

Which, if any, of the projective techniques would you use to determine the reasons why women use cosmetics?

Analysis of Qualitative Data

Sophisticated computer programs are available for processing large volumes of qualitative data and conducting complex analysis efficiently. The data are transmitted into text using a word processor and then converted into ASCII format. The ASCII format is imported into the computer program. The data have to then be coded. *Codes* are labels assigned by the researcher to data segments to facilitate organization of the data. Thus, the computer can recall and print all the material belonging to a particular code. The source of each data segment is identified so that the researcher can see from where it was extracted. The computer program can perform complex searches, such as listing data segments pertaining to code "scary rides in theme parks" as described by teenagers. The program also enables the researcher to examine relationships between data segments such as the relationship between "scary rides in theme parks" and "fun and excitement in the park." Popular programs include Atlas/Ti, Hyper Research, and NUD.IST.

Summary Illustration Using the Opening Vignette

Qualitative research is appropriate when a company is faced with an uncertain situation or is presented with conclusive results that differ from expectations. This type of research can provide insight either before or after the fact. Qualitative research methods tend to be much less structured than quantitative methods and are based on small, nonrepresentative samples. In the opening vignette, Gillette used qualitative research at the beginning of the project to understand the shaving needs of women by conducting in-depth interviews with 30 respondents.

On the other hand, quantitative research seeks conclusive evidence that is based on large, representative samples and typically applies some form of statistical analysis. This was seen in the opening vignette in which Gillette used quantitative research involving a survey of a representative sample of 500 women to substantiate the findings of qualitative research (in-depth interviews).

Focus groups, the most frequently used qualitative technique, are conducted in a group setting, whereas in-depth interviews are conducted one-on-one. In the opening vignette, Gillette chose in-depth interview over focus groups because shaving is a rather personal experience for women, and their personal feelings could be tapped much better in a one-on-one setting than in a group environment.

Projective techniques aim to project the respondent's motivations, beliefs, attitudes, and feelings onto ambiguous situations. The projective techniques may be classified as association, completion, construction, or expressive techniques. Gillette used word association to select an appropriate name for the new razor. Using word association to select names for new products is quite common.

International Marketing Research

When a company is unfamiliar with the nuances of foreign markets, decisions that appear on the surface to be harmless and logical from a strategic business perspective may fail because the company did not fully understand the culture. This is why quali-

EXPERIENTIAL LEARNING

Galaxy of Rides: A Joy Ride?

One type of qualitative research involves participation. Here, researchers actually involve themselves in the consumer behavior of interest. For example, a set of researchers was hired to better understand the experience of consumers visiting the Galaxy of Rides amusement park. Go to the textbook Web site, select "Chapter 6," and download "Five Narratives.doc." Read the narratives provided by the five participant observers.

1. Which participant helped you understand the consumer experience at Galaxy of Rides the best? Why?
2. Which participant helped you understand the consumer experience at Galaxy of Rides the least? Why?

These narratives could serve as the foundation for a thematic analysis.

3. What themes appear to emerge across the narratives?
4. How do these themes help organize your insights about what could be done by the owners and managers of Galaxy of Rides to improve the consumer experience there?

tative research is crucial in international marketing research. In the initial stages, qualitative research can provide insights into the problem and help in developing an approach by generating relevant models, research questions, and hypotheses. Thus, qualitative research may reveal the differences between foreign and domestic markets.

Focus groups can be used in many settings, particularly in industrialized countries. The moderator should not only be trained in focus-group methodology but should also be familiar with the language, culture, and patterns of social interaction prevailing in that country. The focus-group findings should be derived not only from the verbal contents but also from nonverbal cues, such as voice intonations, inflections, expressions, and gestures. In some countries, such as in the Middle or Far East, people are hesitant to discuss their feelings in a group setting. In these cases, in-depth interviews should be used. The use of projective techniques should be carefully considered because the responses that these techniques generate may reflect deeply rooted cultural influences. When used appropriately, however, as in the Spanish airline example that follows, qualitative techniques can play a crucial role in the success of the marketing research project.

BE an MR!

Visit Johnson & Johnson's Web site (www.jnj.com) and search the Internet using a search engine as well as your library's online databases to obtain information on how consumers select baby-product brands in the United States. Obtain similar information for France.

What qualitative research techniques would you use to determine how consumers select baby-product brands in France?

BE a DM!

As the brand manager for Johnson & Johnson, how would you use information on how consumers select baby-product brands to formulate marketing strategies that would increase your market share in France?

RESEARCH IN ACTION

Spanish Expansion

The Spanish airline Iberia (www.iberia.com) was faced with the problem of expanding the number of routes from Europe to South and Central America in the late 1990s. Amidst a multitude of airliners operating over the Atlantic, the question was how to differentiate Iberia from its many competitors. Focus groups provided some initial answers by revealing several insights: (1) International travelers saw Iberia as "the gateway to South America;" (2) providing several days' layover in Miami would attract a number of passengers, particularly tourists; and (3) the pairing of destinations, such as Miami and Cancun, in travel packages would promote more business. When subsequent survey research confirmed the focus-group findings, Iberia chose to make Miami a hub for its flights to South America. These findings were also used to design travel packages, make changes in services, and differentiate the airline. In 2004, Iberia started offering free additional services, such as hotels, lunches, and tours, at transfer destinations for customers using new transatlantic routes between Europe and destinations in the Americas and vice versa, further strengthening the position of the airline.[8]

Technology and Marketing Research

Researchers are using remote data collection techniques for qualitative research. The availability of videoconferencing links, remote-control cameras, and digital-transmission equipment has boosted the amount of research that can be conducted long distance. While videoconferencing may never replace direct interaction with focus groups, it does offer time and cost savings. Firms offering such services include VideoFocus Direct, Direct Windows, FocusVision, and VideoConferencing Alliance Network.

Qualitative Research Software

The objective of qualitative research is to perform induction—to go from the specific details to the general organizing idea explaining the data. In other words, qualitative researchers must sift and resift data in order to perceive important patterns in the data and make an interpretation, if possible. This is difficult mental work. The process is lengthy, and it is easy to become "lost" in the details of the project.

Once interviews begin, qualitative researchers begin to accumulate an enormous amount of textual data when transcripts of interviews are made. In today's media-rich environment, researchers can also collect photo images, vocal recordings, illustrations, drawings by respondents, as well as artifacts, such as physical prototypes of improved products created by respondents in model form. With any data that can be put in digital form, software is now available for archiving, hyperlinking, and analyzing all such data from qualitative research endeavors.

One of the new tools to allow qualitative researchers to obtain more powerful perspectives on their data is QSR International's XSight software. XSight allows project artifacts and transcripts to be imported and coded. Simple frequency counts can be made of words. Queries can be made about where words are located in the text and what demographic variables are associated with respondents using such focal words. For example, in an extensive qualitative research project about cell-phone usage, researchers could use XSight to query about how many times the word "security" occurs. Because XSight allows researchers to list the respondents' demographic profiles, researchers could also use XSight to query about what percentage of those mentioning "security" comprises teenage girls. In this way, analysis can continue so that meaningful patterns can be identified.

The accompanying screen capture is from an actual marketing research project focused on cell-phone usage. The Project Explorer in XSight comprises the far left-side of the screen. This Project Explorer acts like a frame for a Web page that is always accessible to the user as subsequent navigation using hyperlinks occurs. In this way, the Project Explorer offers an overview of the project structure. Such a structure is developed interactively between the user and XSight. This Project Explorer offers nine frameworks for accessing the data under the heading "Analysis Frameworks." Among these frameworks are "Relationship with Cell Phones," "Core Values of NX (a brand)," and "Response to Mission Impossible Ad" among others. Additionally, seven navigational buttons underneath the analysis frameworks are hyperlinked to important parts of the investigator's notes, such as "Documents" and "Interpretations."

In this example, "Relationship with Cell Phones" is the analysis framework selected, so the details of this analysis framework are presented to the right of the Project Explorer. Here, the "Group1 CF 18–22 (Chicago Females 18–22 years old)" sample is chosen as well as the "Availability" heading. On the right side of the screen, one can see the commentaries in the data about availability for this sample. The first and third commentaries represent notes made by the investigator at an earlier stage in the analysis of the data. The rest of the commentaries are actual quotes from the respondents. In this way, the investigator is able to select different samples and make comparison of the raw data that the investigator has previously coded as being related to availability. Thus, the XSight software allows powerful movement back and forth through the hyperlinked data. This provides the investigator with the ability to make comparisons across samples in pursuit of identifying new themes (headings).

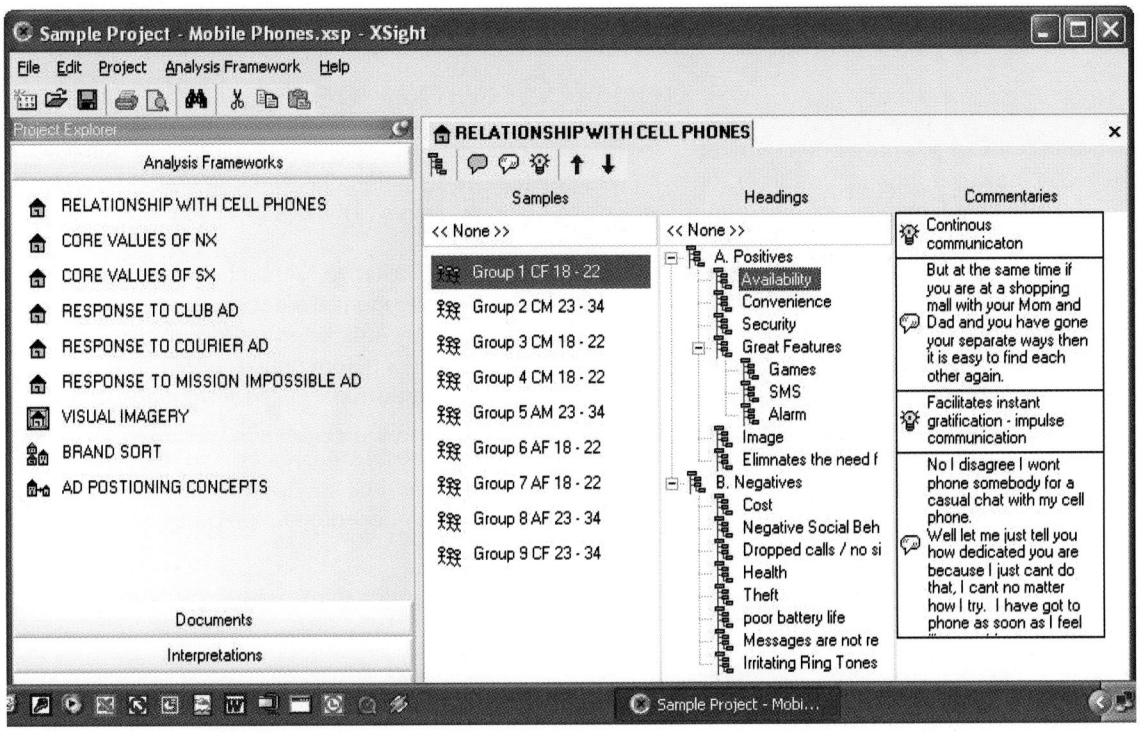

Software, such as QSR International's XSight, enable researchers to identify important patterns in qualitative data.

For a Web-based product tour of QSR International's XSight software, go to (www.qsr.com.au/products/productoverview/XSight.htm).

Ethics in Marketing Research

Respondents' rights and privileges must be respected when conducting qualitative research. Some of the salient ethical issues relate to misleading or deceiving respondents, not maintaining their anonymity, and embarrassing or harming the respondents. An additional issue with wider ramifications is the use of research results in an unethical manner.

Some qualitative researchers allow their clients to be present at focus-group discussions by introducing them as co-researchers. Nonetheless, many participants are able to discern that the co-researcher is in fact the client. This deception raises ethical concerns and generates mistrust that has an adverse impact on the quality of the data and the integrity of marketing research.

As mentioned earlier, focus-group discussions are often recorded using hidden video cameras. Whether or not they are initially told of the hidden camera, the respondents should be informed about the recording at the end of the meeting. The purpose of the video, including who will be able to view it, should be disclosed. In particular, if the client will have access to it, this should be made known as well. Each respondent should be asked to sign a written statement granting permission to use the recording. Participants should be given the opportunity to refuse signing, in which case the tapes should be edited to completely omit the identity and comments of the respondents who refuse.

The researcher has an obligation to make the respondents feel comfortable. If a respondent is experiencing discomfort or stress, the interviewer should show restraint and should not aggressively probe any further. At the end of the interview, respondents should be allowed to reflect on all they have said and be allowed to ask questions. This helps reduce their stress and return them to their preinterview emotional state. A final issue relates to the ethics of using qualitative research results for questionable purposes, as in the mud-slinging presidential campaigns profiled in the Research in Action example that follows.

RESEARCH IN ACTION

Focus (Groups) on Mudslinging

The ethics of negative or "attack" ads have been debated for some time. The focus, however, has shifted from the ads themselves to the ethics of employing marketing research techniques to design the ad message. Nowhere is this phenomenon more prevalent than in political "mudslinging" campaigns. The Bush campaign against Dukakis in the 1988 U.S. presidential election is one example.

Before designing negative ads about Dukakis, Bush campaign leaders tested negative information about Dukakis in focus groups. The idea was to develop some insight into how the American public would react if this negative information was released in the form of advertisements. Negative issues that elicited very negative emotions about Dukakis from the focus groups were chosen for Bush's political advertising. The result? Partly because he was painted "as an ineffectual, weak, liberal, do-gooder lacking in common sense," Dukakis lost the election by a wide margin.

Similar misuse of qualitative research was observed in the 1992 and 1996 presidential elections that Bill Clinton won in part by negatively attacking the Republicans. In the 2000 presidential election, Gore unfairly attacked Bush as lacking in experience after data culled from focus groups and surveys revealing that experience was an important criterion for voters. The 2004 presidential election was also cited for negative attacks by both parties, particularly by Kerry on Bush, again based on focus-group and survey findings.[9]

WHAT WOULD *YOU* DO?

Lotus Development Corporation: Developing Its Web Site

The Situation

Al Zollar is the president and CEO of Lotus Development Corporation (www.lotus.com), which is one of the brands of the IBM Software group. Lotus is a company that recognizes the need for individuals and businesses to work together. Therefore, it redefines the concept of conducting business through practical knowledge management, e-business, and other groundbreaking ways of connecting the world's ideas, thinkers, buyers, sellers, and communities via the Internet. As of 2005, Lotus marketed its products in more than 80 countries worldwide through direct and extensive business partner channels. The company also provides numerous professional consulting, support, and education services through the Lotus Professional Services organization. To help Lotus stay ahead of its competitors, Zollar wishes to increase their Web site's number of hits and wants Lotus to maintain a Web site that is going to best meet the needs of its customers.

Lotus conducts focus groups of customers and business partners every four months to determine users' reactions to its Web site. This routine of focus groups recognizes the fact that Web sites are products with very short lifecycles and need ongoing attention to keep them up to date. The focus groups evaluate Lotus's Web site and the sites of other companies. Some objectives for the focus groups include identifying factors that lead Internet users to visit a Web site, identifying what factors entice visitors to return often to a Web site, and identifying users' technological capabilities.

The use of focus groups allows Lotus to actively collect some information that is not collected passively. Passive counters can keep track of the number of visitors to a Web site as well as the number of visitors who actually use the site. For example, Lotus can monitor the number of visitors who use its chat rooms that pertain to specific products. Just knowing that the number of visitors is changing, however, does not provide a company with insights concerning why there is a decrease or increase in visitors. Focus groups are ways to gain those insights.

From focus groups, Lotus learned that customers wanted improved navigation and a higher level of consistency. In the past, the emphasis was on making sure that information was delivered quickly to customers. Focus groups revealed that the company needed to further develop the site to make it easier for Web site visitors to navigate through all of the information.

The Marketing Research Decision

1. Do you think that Lotus adopted the right research design? Which one of the following types of research designs would you recommend and why?
   a. Focus groups
   b. In-depth interviews
   c. Survey research
   d. Projective techniques
   e. Focus groups followed by survey research
2. Discuss the role of the type of research you recommend in enabling Al Zollar to design an effective Web site.

The Marketing Management Decision

1. What should Al Zollar do to increase the traffic and enhance the experience of visitors to its Web site? Check as many as are applicable.
   a. Redesign the Web site completely.
   b. Upgrade the existing Web site, making only the necessary changes.
   c. Engage in aggressive banner advertising.
   d. Engage in aggressive print advertising.
   e. Offer price discounts to customers on the Web site.
2. Discuss how the marketing management-decision action that you recommend to Al Zollar is influenced by the research design that you suggested earlier and by the findings of that research.

What Al Zollar Did

Al Zollar redesigned the Lotus Web site completely to improve navigation and enhance the efficiency with which visitors could search and download the information they wanted. He also engaged in aggressive print and banner advertising. On June 6, 2003, IBM debuted Lotus Workplace with print advertising in the *Wall Street Journal, New York Times,* and *The Boston Globe.* In addition, banner advertising was launched on a wide variety of Web sites, such as eWeek, Information Week, Business Week, and Forbes. These ads were all part of the "Can You See It" ad campaign that demonstrated how IBM Software enables on-demand business and invited readers to the Web site.[10]

Summary

Qualitative and quantitative research should be viewed as complementary. Qualitative research methods tend to be much less structured and are based on small, nonrepresentative samples. The various qualitative options vary in terms of how directly they ask questions of the respondent. Direct methods, such as focus groups and in-depth interviews, do not attempt to disguise the purpose of the research. Focus groups, the most frequently used qualitative technique, are conducted in a group setting, whereas in-depth interviews are done one-on-one.

The indirect techniques make a deliberate attempt to disguise the true purpose of the research. They are called projective techniques because they aim to project the respondent's motivations, beliefs, attitudes, and feelings onto ambiguous situations. The projective techniques may be classified as association, completion, construction, or expressive techniques. Projective techniques are particularly useful when respondents are unwilling or unable to provide the required information by direct methods.

In the international context, qualitative research may reveal the differences between the foreign and domestic markets. Technological advances, such as the availability of videoconferencing links, remote-control cameras, and digital-transmission equipment, have boosted the amount of research that can be conducted long distance. Ethical issues in qualitative research relate to respecting respondents' rights and privileges. Focus groups and other qualitative procedures can be conducted using the Internet.

Key Terms and Concepts

Qualitative research, 150
Quantitative research, 150
Direct approach, 152
Indirect approach, 152
Focus group, 152
In-depth interviews, 161
Projective techniques, 164
Association techniques, 165
Word association, 165
Completion techniques, 165
Sentence completion, 165
Story completion, 165
Construction techniques, 166
Picture-response techniques, 166
Cartoon tests, 166
Expressive techniques, 166
Role playing, 166
Third-person technique, 167

Suggested Cases and Video Cases

Cases

2.1 Maxfli **2.2 Cadillac** **2.4 Bloomingdale's** **2.5 Burger King**
4.1 Boeing **4.2 Gucci**

Video Cases

2.1 Starbucks **2.2 Nike** **4.1 Subaru** **4.2 Marriott**

Additional cases and video cases are available in the Instructor's Manual and on the instructor and student Web sites.

Live Research: Conducting a Marketing Research Project

1. In most projects, it would be important to conduct some form of qualitative research.
2. Different teams can be assigned different responsibilities (e.g., interviewing key decision makers, interviewing industry experts, conducting in-depth interviews with consumers, doing a focus group, and so forth). Alternatively, all the teams can work on these tasks.
3. If possible, have at least one team use the qualitative research software discussed in this chapter and make a presentation to the class.

Acronyms

The key characteristics of a focus group may be described by the acronym FOCUS GROUPS:

F ocused on a particular topic
O utline prepared for discussion
C haracteristics of the moderator
U nstructured
S ize: 8 to 12 participants
G roup composition: homogeneous
R ecorded: audiocassettes and videotapes
O bservation: one-way mirror
U ndisguised
P hysical setting: relaxed
S everal sessions needed: one to three hours each

The main features of a (in-)depth interview may be summarized by the acronym DEPTH:

D epth of coverage
E ach respondent individually interviewed
P robe the respondent
T alented interviewer required
H idden motives may be uncovered

Review Questions

1. What are the primary differences between qualitative and quantitative research techniques?
2. What is qualitative research, and how is it conducted?
3. What are the differences between direct and indirect qualitative research? Give an example of each.
4. Why is the focus group the most popular qualitative research technique?
5. Why is the focus-group moderator so important in obtaining quality results?
6. What are some key qualifications of focus-group moderators?
7. Why should one safeguard against professional respondents?
8. What are two ways in which focus groups can be misused?
9. What is an in-depth interview? Under what circumstances is it preferable to focus groups?
10. What are the major advantages of in-depth interviews?
11. What are projective techniques? What are the four types of projective techniques?
12. What is the word-association technique? Give an example of a situation in which this technique is especially useful.
13. When should projective techniques be employed?

Applied Problems

1. Following the methods outlined in the text, develop a plan for conducting a focus group to determine consumers' attitudes toward and preferences for imported automobiles. Specify the objectives of the focus group and write a screening questionnaire.
2. Suppose Baskin Robbins wants to know why some people do not eat ice cream regularly. Develop a cartoon test for this purpose.
3. The Coca-Cola Company has asked you to conduct online focus groups with heavy users of soft drinks. Explain how you would identify and recruit such respondents.
4. Could an in-depth interview be conducted via the Internet? What are the advantages and disadvantages of this procedure over conventional in-depth interviews?
5. Visit the Web site of Qualitative Research Consultants Association (www.qrca.org). Write a report about the current state of the art in qualitative research.
6. *Tennis* magazine would like to recruit participants for online focus groups. How would you make use of a newsgroup to recruit participants? Visit (www.groups.google.com) and then select "rec.sport.tennis".

Group Discussion

1. In a group of five or six, discuss whether qualitative research is scientific.
2. Discuss the following statement in a small group: "If the focus-group findings confirm prior expectations, the client should dispense with quantitative research."
3. Discuss the following statement in a small group: "Quantitative research is more important than qualitative research because it results in statistical information and conclusive findings."

CHAPTER

7

Descriptive Research Design: Survey and Observation

"Many of the insights about consumers' future behavior are gained by simply asking consumers about their attitudes and intentions."

Surjya Roy, *Senior Research Manager, Lieberman Research Worldwide, Los Angeles, CA*

OPENING QUESTIONS

1. What survey methods are available to marketing researchers, and how can these methods be classified?
2. What are the criteria for evaluating survey methods and comparing them to determine which is best suited for a particular research project?
3. How can survey response rates be improved?
4. How is observation different than the survey method? What procedures are available for observing people and objects?
5. What are the relative advantages and disadvantages of observational methods as compared to the survey methods?
6. How can survey and observation methods be implemented in an international setting?
7. How can technology improve survey and observation methods?
8. What ethical issues are involved in conducting survey and observation research?
9. What is the role of the Internet in implementing survey and observation methods?

Procter & Gamble's New Marketing Platform: Everyday Low Pricing and Brand Extensions

As part of its ongoing marketing research, Procter & Gamble (P&G) routinely analyzes scanner data and conducts consumer surveys. Scanner-panel data from ACNielsen revealed that a typical family that was brand-loyal spent $725 for a year's worth of P&G products. In comparison, a family that bought similar products as private-label or low-priced brands spent less than $500. In a time when value-consciousness dominated, this premium-pricing strategy presented a problem to P&G. This led P&G to create a new marketing platform for its products.

At the base of the new platform was the concept of value. The platform was designed to fully recognize that P&G had been overcharging for many of its products, including Tide detergent, Crest toothpaste, Pampers disposable diapers, Vick's cough syrup, and Head & Shoulders shampoo. Focus groups and in-depth interviews conducted by P&G revealed that customers were no longer willing to pay for non–value-added costs. Furthermore, surveys using mail panels indicated that customers loyal to P&G preferred prices that were consistently low rather than price discounts and special deals. A computer-assisted telephone survey of a randomly selected representative sample resulted in similar findings for the general population. The concept developed from these findings is known as everyday low pricing (EDLP). This concept was the exact opposite of P&G's previous platform of maintaining high list prices offset by frequent and irregular discounts.

Another problem that led P&G to reformulate its platform had to do with new product development. Previous research indicated that P&G brands enjoyed considerable equity in that they were well known and preferred by a large segment of the market. In 2000, P&G decided to drop the word Oil from Oil of Olay, the line of skin-care products and cosmetics, in an effort to make the line more appealing to younger women. This led to the strategy of brand extensions (BE), the practice of using a successful brand name to launch a new or modified product. An example is Olay Beauty Bar, a brand extension of Olay lotion. The beauty bar was developed as a response to the growing consumer demand for a product that would keep skin feeling soft and young, not only on the face but all over. The bar was specially engineered with a synthetic cleansing system and light Olay moisturizers that help the skin to hold moisture better than soap does. In addition to the special formulation, the bar was designed to stay firm during use and not to melt away like most other beauty bars.

Prior to introduction, the Olay Beauty Bar was tested in mall intercept interviews. In these interviews, respondents actually washed their hands and face with the bar in a test area located in the mall before responding to a survey. Because the results of these mall intercept interviews were quite positive, three types of bars were introduced: pink and white with different scents and an unscented hypoallergenic version for sensitive skin. The Beauty Bar has been a great success and won one of *Marketing News*' Edison Best New Products Awards.

Procter & Gamble is gaining momentum in the U.S. market and abroad. Domestic unit volumes and market shares are once again increasing in 22 out of 32 categories. The strategies of EDLP and BE continue to pay dividends for the company. The company's sales and market share continued to improve through 2005, strengthening its position as a world leader in consumer products.[1] •

Overview

The market research process begins by defining the research problem and then formulating an approach and a research design. As discussed in Chapter 3, the major types of research designs are exploratory and conclusive. Exploratory designs rely primarily on secondary data analysis (Chapters 4 and 5) and qualitative research (Chapter 6). Conclusive research designs may be classified as causal or descriptive. Causal designs are explained in Chapter 8. This chapter discusses survey and observation methods, the quantitative techniques typically used to collect descriptive research data. Figure 7.1 briefly explains the focus of the chapter, the relation of this chapter to the previous ones, and the steps of the marketing research process on which this chapter concentrates.

Survey data do much more than merely report behavior. Surveys can provide insights into who the consumers are, how they behave, and why they behave in certain ways. Respondents' reports of their conscious motives, values, or beliefs provide some insight into consumer behavior. This was illustrated in the opening vignette in which P&G used different types of surveys to understand consumers' preferences for everyday low prices versus discounts and special sales. (Qualitative techniques, discussed in Chapter 6, are more useful in understanding behaviors driven by unconscious motives.)

Surveys can be classified in terms of how the data are collected: telephone interviews, computer-assisted telephone interviews, in-home interviews, mall intercept interviews, computer-assisted personal interviews, mail interviews, mail panels, and electronic surveys (e-mail and Internet). In this chapter, each of these methods is described and the criteria used to select an appropriate method for a particular project are discussed.

We will consider the major observational methods—personal observation and mechanical observation—and discuss the advantages and disadvantages of observation compared to survey methods as well as the role of survey and observation methods in international marketing research. The impact of technology and Internet applications is discussed, and several ethical issues that arise in survey research and observation methods are identified. Figure 7.2 gives an overview of the topics discussed in this chapter and how they flow from one to the next.

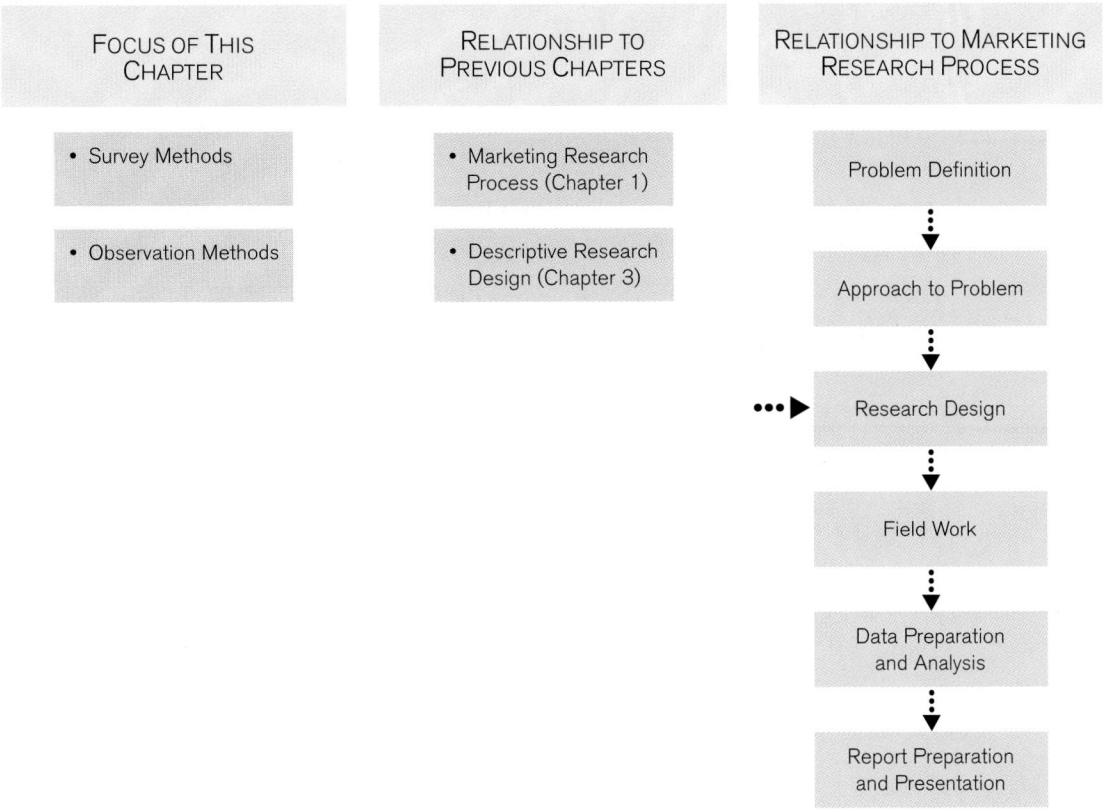

Figure 7.1

Relationship of Survey and Observation to the Previous Chapters and the Marketing Research Process

Survey Methods

The **survey method** of obtaining information is based on questioning respondents. Surveys are used when the research involves sampling a large number of people and asking them a series of questions (Figure 7.3). Surveys may be conducted in person, by telephone, through a mailed questionnaire, or electronically via the computer. Perhaps the biggest issue researchers face is how to motivate respondents to candidly answer their questions. The uninvited intrusion of telemarketers and direct marketers into the home has resulted in an increasing number of consumers shutting the door to anyone trying to make contact. The challenges of controlling this nonresponse problem are discussed later in the chapter.

survey method
A structured questionnaire given to a sample of a population and designed to elicit specific information from respondents.

The range of topics that can be investigated using surveys is as varied as the research problems business face. Questions regarding behavior, intentions, attitudes, beliefs, awareness, motivations, and both demographic and lifestyle characteristics all lend themselves to survey research.

Advantages and Disadvantages of Survey Research

The survey method has the advantages of ease, reliability, and simplicity. Questionnaires are relatively easy to administer. Using fixed-response (multiple-choice) questions reduces variability in the results that may be caused by differences in interviewers and enhances reliability of the responses. It also simplifies coding, analysis, and interpretation of data.

Disadvantages of the survey method are that respondents may be unable or unwilling to provide the desired information. For example, consider questions about motivational factors. Respondents may not be consciously aware of the real reasons they prefer one brand to another. The subconscious nature of their motives may make it impossible for

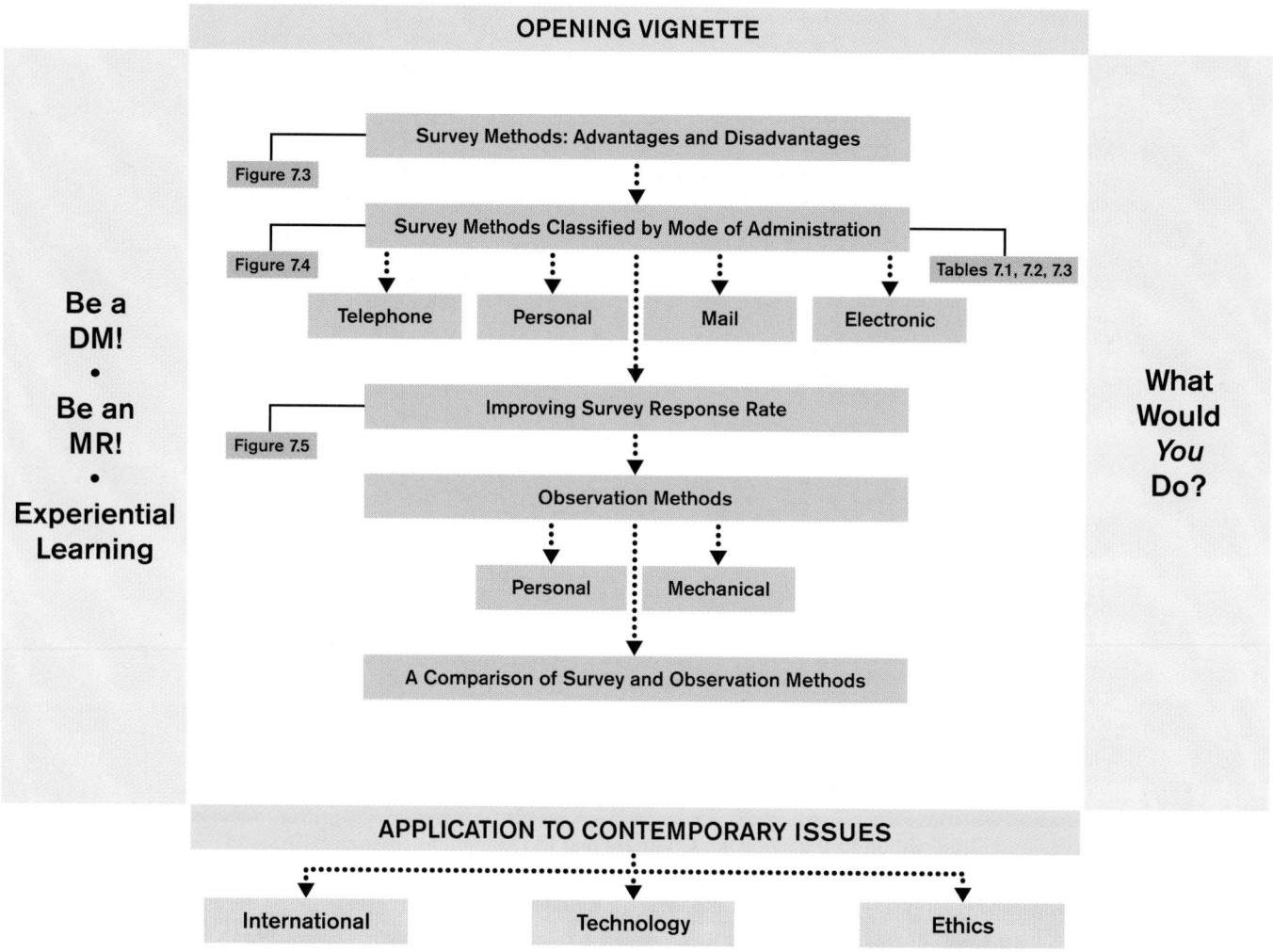

Figure 7.2

Survey and Observation: An Overview

them to answer questions accurately. Respondents may be unwilling to respond if the information requested is sensitive or personal. For example, consider questions about religious beliefs. Respondents may view this topic as very personal and may be unwilling to answer any questions related to it.

structured data collection
Use of a formal questionnaire that presents questions in a prearranged order.

Also, **structured data collection** involving a questionnaire with fixed-response choices may result in loss of validity for certain types of data, such as beliefs and feelings. Finally, properly wording questions is not easy (see Chapter 11 on questionnaire design). Yet, despite these disadvantages, the survey approach is by far the most common method of primary data collection in marketing research.

Figure 7.3

Methods of Obtaining Quantitative Data in Descriptive Research

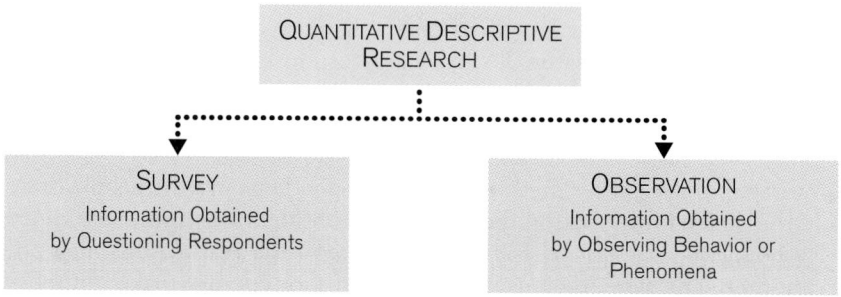

EXPERIENTIAL LEARNING

Surveys and You

The Council of American Survey Research Organizations (CASRO) is the trade association of survey-research businesses, representing over 200 companies and research operations in the United States, Canada, and Mexico. CASRO communicates the importance of survey research in the public realm and helps educate those in the research industry about standards for ethics and performance. Go to the CASRO Web site (www.casro.org) and click on "Surveys and You" under EDUCATION & EVENTS. Here, CASRO has prepared a user-friendly overview to survey research entitled "Surveys and You." Read this short overview and then answer these questions:

1. Of the 12 questions posed in "Surveys and You," which one helped you learn the most?
2. What did you learn as a result of this question?
3. What did you learn about the importance of surveys?

Survey Methods Classified by Mode of Administration

Figure 7.4 illustrates the various methods of collecting survey data, broadly classified as telephone, personal, mail, or electronic interviews. Telephone interviewing can be further broken down in terms of whether or not computers are being used in the interviewing process. Personal interviews may be conducted in-home, as mall intercept interviews, or as computer-assisted personal interviews (CAPI). The third major method, mail interviewing, takes the form of ordinary mail surveys or surveys conducted using mail panels. Electronic interviews are generally administered over the Internet or by using e-mail. Of these methods, telephone interviews are the most popular in the United States, followed by personal interviews. The popularity of electronic surveys is increasing quickly. Mail interviews are the least popular.

Telephone Methods

As stated earlier, telephone interviews vary in terms of the degree of computer assistance supporting the interview.

Traditional Telephone Interviews Traditional telephone interviews involve phoning a sample of respondents and asking them a series of questions. The interviewer

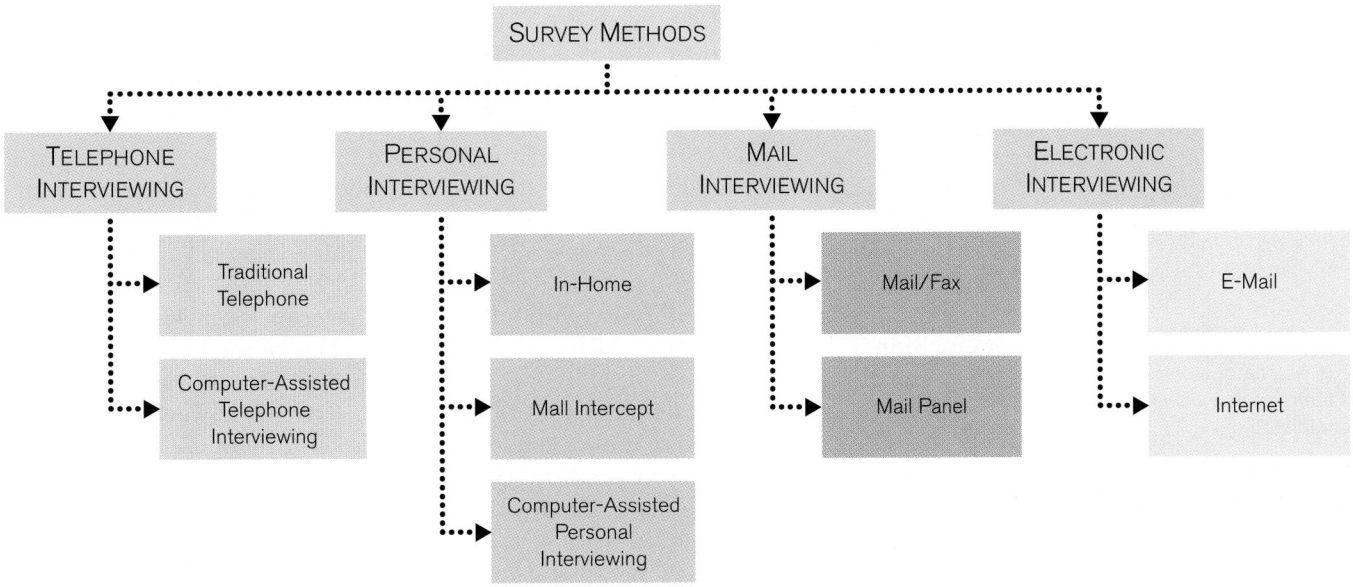

Figure 7.4
Classification of Survey Methods

uses a paper questionnaire and records the responses with a pencil. Telephone interviews are generally conducted from centrally-located research facilities. Telephone research centers are specifically equipped to accommodate large groups of interviewers. These facilities have proliferated because of the cost and control advantages they offer. The low cost of telecommunication services has made nationwide telephone interviewing from a central location practical.

Additionally, field service supervisors can closely monitor the telephone conversations. This monitoring helps to control interviewer bias that results from variation in the way in which the questions are asked and the responses are recorded. Data quality is also enhanced with on-the-spot reviews of completed questionnaires. Finally, the research budget, both in terms of labor costs and time restrictions, can be more easily managed when the interviewers are assembled in one location.

Computer-Assisted Telephone Interviewing Computer-assisted telephone interviewing (CATI) uses a computerized questionnaire administered to respondents over the telephone. The interviewer sits in front of a computer screen and wears a mini-headset. The computer screen replaces a paper-and-pencil questionnaire, and the mini-headset substitutes for a telephone. Computer-assisted telephone interviewing from a central location is now much more popular than the traditional telephone method. More than 90 percent of all telephone interviews in the United States are conducted using a CATI system.

Upon command, the computer dials the telephone number to be called. When contact is made, the interviewer reads the questions posed on the computer screen and records the respondent's answers directly into the computer memory bank. CATI combines the interview with the editing and data entry steps to produce a highly efficient and accurate survey process. Because the responses are entered directly into the computer, interim and update reports can be compiled instantaneously as the data are being collected.

CATI software has built-in logic, which also enhances data accuracy. The program will personalize questions and control for logically incorrect answers, such as percentage answers that don't add up to 100 percent. The software has built-in branching logic, which will skip questions that are not applicable or will probe for more detail when warranted. For example, if a respondent answered "yes" to the question, "Have you ever purchased Nike athletic shoes?" an entire series of questions related to the experience with Nike shoes would follow. If, however, the respondent answered "no," that line of questioning would be skipped. An application of CATI was illustrated in the opening vignette where P&G used this method to survey a randomly selected sample, asking questions related to pricing preferences.

Advantages and Disadvantages of Telephone Interviewing Telephone interviewing, whether conducted with pen and paper or in a computer-assisted format, remains one of the most popular survey methods. This popularity can be traced to several factors. Interviews can be completed quickly since the travel time associated with personal interviews is completely eliminated. **Sample control**, or the ability to reach the units specified in the sample, is good when proper sampling and callback procedures are followed. The control of field force is good because the interviewers can be supervised from a central location. The control is even better in CATI, as these systems allow the supervisor to monitor an interview without the interviewer or the respondent being aware of it. The **response rate**, which refers to the percentage of total attempted interviews that are completed, is good. Moreover, telephone surveys are not very expensive.

sample control
The ability of the survey mode to effectively and efficiently reach the units specified in the sample.

response rate
The percentage of the total attempted interviews that are completed.

There are some inherent disadvantages to telephone interviews, however (Table 7.1). The questioning is restricted to the spoken word. Interviewers cannot use physical stimuli, such as visual illustrations or product demonstrations unless these are pre-delivered to respondents, and they cannot ask complex questions. This limits the applicability of telephone techniques for certain types of research, such as new product or advertising research.

Personal rapport and commitment are difficult to establish due to lack of face-to-face interaction between the interviewer and the respondent. Respondents can easily escape the interview process, either by cutting the interview short or simply hanging up the

Table 7.1

Relative Advantages of Different Survey Methods

Method	Advantatages	Disadvantages
Telephone	Fast	No use of physical stimuli
	Good sample control	Limited to simple questions
	Good control of field force	Low quantity of data
	Good response rate	
	Moderate cost	
In-Home	Complex questions can be asked	Low control of field force
	Good for physical stimuli	High social desirability
	Very good sample control	Potential for interviewer bias
	High quantity of data	Most expensive
	Very good response rate	Some samples (e.g., high-crime areas) may be difficult to access
	Longer interviews can be done	May take long to collect the data
Mall Intercept	Complex questions can be asked	High social desirability
	Very good for physical stimuli	Potential for interviewer bias
	Very good control of environment	Moderate quantity of data
	Very good response rate	High cost
CAPI	Complex questions can be asked	High social desirability
	Very good for physical stimuli	Moderate quantity of data
	Very good control of environment	High cost
	Very good response rate	
	Low potential for interviewer bias	
Mail	No field-force problems	Limited to simple questions
	No interviewer bias	Low sample control for cold mail
	Moderate/high quantity of data	No control of environment
	Low social desirability	Low response rate for cold mail
	Low cost	Low speed
Mail Panel	No field-force problems	Limited to simple questions
	No interviewer bias	Not suitable for household surveys
	High quantity of data	No control of environment
	Low social desirability	Low/moderate speed
	Low/moderate cost	
	Good sample control	
Electronic: E-mail	No interviewer bias	Low sample control
	Low cost	No control of environment
	Low social desirability	Low response rate
	High speed	Moderate quantity of data
	Contact hard-to-reach respondents	Security concerns
Electronic: Internet	No interviewer bias	Low sample control
	Low cost	No control of environment
	Low social desirability	Low response rate
	Very high speed	Moderate quantity of data
	Visual appeal and interactivity	
	Personalized, flexible questioning	
	Contact hard-to-reach respondents	

RESEARCH IN ACTION

Telephone Calling Makes Pizza Hut the One to Call

As of 2005, Pizza Hut was the largest pizza restaurant company in the world. It had 12,000 outlets in 90 countries and served more than 1.3 million pizzas every day to approximately 4 million customers worldwide. Pizza Hut, which initiated the customer satisfaction survey in January 1995, currently conducts 50,000 interviews a week. Data are collected through an outbound telephone survey (which means that Pizza Hut initiates the telephone call). Selected customers in Pizza Hut's delivery and carryout database are called within 24 hours of their purchases. The outbound interviews are limited to four minutes, and customers are given a 60-day breather before they are called again.

The company also has an interactive 800-number inbound survey of randomly selected dine-in customers (the customer initiates the call). One of every 20 to 30 dine-in customers receives a coupon at the bottom of the receipt and a toll-free number to call to participate in the interactive survey. Tracking results show that 67 percent of the surveys are completed within one day of the visit, fulfilling a desire by management for the inbound survey results to be fresh.

The survey focuses only on issues that unit managers can control. The questions deal with service, food, and problems during the customer's latest visit. The survey results have been very useful. For example, customers

rushed to buy the new Stuffed Crust Pizza, but there was no subsequent rise in loyalty. Survey results showed that because of service problems, new customers were not making return trips. The survey helped Pizza Hut identify problems, and it now has a better understanding of how to handle the next major product launch. Half of the unit manager's quarterly bonus is linked to the survey results. As a result, customer satisfaction is at an all-time high. [2]

phone. This results in less tolerance for lengthy interviews over the phone and limits the quantity of data that can be collected.

BE a DM!

As the marketing manager for Delta Airlines, how would you use information on consumers' airline preferences for domestic travel to formulate marketing strategies that would increase your market share?

BE an MR!

Visit Delta's Web site (www.delta.com) and search the Internet using a search engine as well as your library's online databases to obtain information on consumers' preferences for selecting an airline for domestic travel.

What are the advantages and disadvantages of telephone interviewing in conducting a survey to obtain information on consumers' airline preferences for domestic travel? Would you recommend this method for administering a survey for Delta Airlines?

Personal Methods

Personal interviewing methods may be categorized as in-home, mall intercept, or computer-assisted.

Personal In-Home Interviews In personal in-home interviews, respondents are interviewed face-to-face in their homes. The interviewer's task is to contact the respondents, ask the questions, and record the responses. In recent years, the use of personal in-home interviews has declined. Nevertheless, they are still used, particularly by syndicate firms (see Chapter 5).

Advantages and Disadvantages of In-Home Interviewing In-home interviewing offers many advantages. It enables the interviewer to provide clarifications to the respondent, allowing for complex questions. It permits the use of physical stimuli, such as visual aids, charts, and maps, and it allows the interviewer to display or demonstrate the product. It provides very good sample control as well since homes can be selected without generating a list of all the homes in a given area. The homes can be selected by instructing the interviewer to start at a given location, travel in a certain direction and select every n^{th} (e.g., 8th) home. A large quantity of data can be collected because the respondents are interviewed in their own homes, and therefore, they're more willing to participate for a longer period of time. The response rate is very good, particularly if the respondents have been prenotified.

In-home interviewing has lost favor due to social, labor, control, and cost factors. Change in the family, particularly related to the dominance of two-income earners, leaves few people at home during the day. Interviewer supervision and control is difficult, as the interviewers are traveling door-to-door. Consequently, problems with the questionnaire or with the style of the interviewer become more difficult to detect and correct. **Social desirability**, the tendency of respondents to give answers that are socially desirable but incorrect, is high when there is face-to-face contact between the interviewer and the respondent. This factor also leads to a high potential for **interviewer bias**. Interviewers can influence the answers by facial expressions, intonations, or simply by the way they ask the questions. This method is also the most expensive.

social desirability
The tendency of the respondents to give answers that may not be accurate but that may be desirable from a social standpoint.

interviewer bias
The error due to the interviewer not following the correct interviewing procedures.

Despite their value, personal in-home interviews are being largely replaced by mall intercepts.

Mall Intercept Personal Interviews In mall intercept personal interviews, respondents are approached and interviewed in shopping malls. The process involves stopping the shoppers, screening them for appropriateness, and either administering the survey on the spot or inviting them to a research facility located in the mall to complete the interview. For example, in a survey for a cellular phone manufacturer, a shopper is intercepted and asked about age, education, and income. If these characteristics match the client's target population, the individual is then questioned on product usage. Some usage of cellular phones is a prerequisite for inclusion in the sample. Only those who have experience with cellular phones are invited to a test facility located in the mall to evaluate several new prototype designs under consideration.

Although the sample is composed only of individuals who shop in that retail mall, this is not a serious limitation. While not representative of the population in general, shopping mall customers do constitute a major share of the market for many products.

Advantages and Disadvantages of Mall Intercepts A major advantage of mall intercept interviews is that it is more efficient for the respondent to come to the interviewer than for the interviewer to go to the respondent. The popularity of this method is evidenced by the several hundred permanent mall research facilities located across the country. Complex questions can be asked when there is face-to-face contact. Mall intercepts are especially appropriate when the respondents need to see, handle, or consume the product before they can provide meaningful information. This was illustrated in the opening vignette when P&G used this technique to determine consumers' responses to Olay Beauty Bar prior to introduction. Mall intercept interviewing was chosen because it conveniently allowed the respondents to use the beauty bar in a test area in the mall before they responded to the survey. Another example that follows is the testing of IncrediBagel Stuffed Bagels. The researcher has very good control of the environment in which the data are being collected, and the response rate is very good.

The main disadvantages are the potential for social desirability and interviewer bias due to face-to-face contact in the interviewing process. The quantity of data that can be collected is only moderate, as people are generally in a hurry while shopping. The cost of mall intercept interviewing is high.

Computer-Assisted Personal Interviewing In computer-assisted personal interviewing (CAPI), the third form of personal interviewing, the respondent sits in front of a computer terminal and answers a questionnaire on the screen by using the keyboard or a mouse. Several user-friendly electronic packages can aid in designing easy and understandable questions. Help screens and courteous error messages are also provided.

RESEARCH IN ACTION

The Incredible IncrediBagel Stuffed Bagels

Today's increased time demands mean that breakfast (if it's not skipped) may be eaten behind the wheel of a car, and lunch may be consumed at a cluttered office desk. Dallas-based State Fair Foods has created the perfect meal for "stuffed schedules" with its IncrediBagel Stuffed Bagels. Providing a no-mess way to eat on the run, the center of each of these bagels is filled with breakfast or lunch foods for a convenient meal.

The development of Stuffed Bagels was guided by mall intercept interviews conducted in 10 cities across the United States. Shoppers were intercepted and taken to a test kitchen located in the mall. After tasting a stuffed bagel, they responded to a detailed questionnaire. The survey indicated a strong preference for stuffed bagels and pointed out favorite varieties: pizza; ham and cheese; sausage, egg, and cheese; and bacon, egg, and cheese. The company then introduced these varieties with great success.[3]

The colorful screens and on- and off-screen stimuli add to the respondent's interest and involvement in the task. This method has been classified as a personal-interview technique since an interviewer is usually present to serve as a host and to guide the respondent as needed.

This approach is used in shopping malls, preceded by the intercept and screening process described earlier. It is also used to conduct business-to-business research at trade shows or conventions. For example, UPS could measure its image and test the effectiveness of its slogan, "What can Brown do for you?" by administering a CAPI survey at the expedited package delivery trade show. The process of interacting with the computer is simplified to minimize respondent effort and stress. Thus, the use of open-ended questions that require typing is minimized.

Advantages and Disadvantages of CAPI CAPI seems to hold respondent interest and has several advantages. Complex questions can be asked, and the computer automatically performs skip patterns and conducts logic checks. Interviewer bias is reduced since the computer administers the interview. Like mall intercepts, CAPI can be useful when the survey requires the use of physical stimuli. It also offers excellent control of the data collection environment and results in a very good response rate.

Its main disadvantages are the same for mall intercepts–high social desirability, only a moderate quantity of data, and high cost.

BE an MR!

Visit ESPN's Web site (www.espn.com) and search the Internet using a search engine as well as your library's online databases to obtain information on consumers' perceptions of ESPN.

What are the advantages and disadvantages of personal interviews in conducting a survey to obtain information on consumers' perceptions of ESPN? Which, if any, method of personal interviewing would you recommend for administering the survey?

BE a DM!

As the marketing manager for ESPN, how would you use information on consumers' perceptions of ESPN to formulate marketing strategies that would increase your audience?

Mail Methods

Mail interviews, the third major form of survey administration, can be conducted with independently-compiled mailing lists or by using a mail panel.

Mail Interviews The traditional mail interview is a "cold" mail survey that is sent to individuals who meet a specified demographic profile but who have not been precontacted to participate in the survey. A typical mail interview package consists of the outgoing envelope, cover letter, questionnaire, postage-paid return envelope, and possibly, an incentive. Those individuals motivated to do so complete and return the questionnaire through the

Table 7.2
Some Decisions Related to the Mail Interview Package

Outgoing Envelope
Size, color, and return address for envelope
Postage
Method of addressing
Cover Letter
Sponsorship
Signature
Personalization
Postscript
Type of appeal
Questionnaire
Length
Layout
Content
Color
Size
Format
Reproduction
Respondent anonymity
Return Envelope
Type of envelope
Postage
Incentives
Monetary vs. Nonmonetary
Prepaid vs. Promised

mail. There is no verbal interaction between the researcher and the respondent. Individuals are selected for cold surveys through mailing lists the client maintains internally or has purchased commercially. Commercial mailing lists typically contain some demographic and psychographic information that assists in the targeting process. Regardless of its source, a mailing list should be current and closely related to the population of interest.

The researcher must also make decisions about the various elements of the mail interview package (Table 7.2). The type of envelope, the cover letter, the length of the questionnaire, and the incentive, if one is offered, all affect response rates.

The time involved and the response rate can be improved by faxing the questionnaire instead of mailing it. In **fax surveys**, the questionnaire is transmitted by a fax machine to respondents. The respondents can than return the completed questionnaire by faxing it to a designated (toll-free) number or, sometimes, by mail. Fax surveys share many characteristics with mail surveys; however, they can provide faster, and often higher, response rates. Greater urgency is associated with fax correspondence, and people are more likely to respond and do so sooner than they would to mail correspondence. While the image quality of the fax transmission does not match that of a mailed questionnaire, this does not reduce the quality of the data. Fax numbers can be programmed into computers and the documents (cover letter and questionnaire) sent directly by the computer to the fax machine. This not only saves paper and printing costs but labor as well because there is no need to type addresses, print labels, stuff envelopes, and so on. Since many households do not have fax machines, this method is not suitable for household surveys. It can

fax surveys
Surveys for which the questionnaire is transmitted by a fax machine to respondents. The respondents can than return the completed questionnaire by faxing it to a designated (toll-free) number or, sometimes, by mail.

be used in a variety of surveys with commercial and other institutional respondents, however.

mail panels
A large and nationally representative sample of households that have agreed to periodically participate in mail questionnaires, product tests, and telephone surveys.

Mail Panels In contrast to cold mail interviews, **mail panels** consist of a large and nationally representative sample of individuals who have agreed to participate in periodic survey research (see Chapters 3 and 5). Incentives in the form of cash or gifts are often offered to the individuals who agree to participate. Once the individuals have been admitted to the panel, detailed demographic and lifestyle data are collected on each household. The researcher uses this information to select targeted mailing lists within the panel based on client needs.

TNS (www.tns-global.com) is an example of a marketing research organization that maintains mail panels. Mail panels can be used to reach a general as well as a targeted sample. In the opening vignette, P&G used mail-panel surveys to target consumers loyal to P&G and determine their pricing preferences. In a longitudinal design, the purchases of these customers for P&G and competing brands were monitored over time to identify the loyal customers.

Advantages and Disadvantages of Mail Surveys Mail surveys are an economical and efficient way to reach consumers. Cold mail surveys have a low cost, and the cost of mail panels is only moderately higher. The problems of interviewer bias and the expense of field staff management are eliminated. Social desirability is low, as there is no personal contact with the respondent during data collection. A moderate amount of data can be collected through cold mail surveys, whereas mail panels permit the collection of large quantities of data.

These clear advantages are offset, however, by problems regarding lack of control of the interviewing process. Unlike telephone and personal interviewing, there is no personal contact, and the respondent may feel less compelled to either participate or candidly complete the questionnaire. This problem is particularly acute with cold mail interviews. There is little control over who answers the questionnaire, how they answer it, and how quickly they return it. This results in low sample control, low speed, and no control over the data collection environment. Thus, it is difficult to assess the quality and validity of the data.

Finally, response rates to cold mail surveys are low, and nonresponse introduces a serious bias in the data. Those individuals who choose not to participate in mail interviews may have very different demographic and psychographic profiles than responders, resulting in **nonresponse bias**. Individuals with higher income and educational levels, or individuals inexperienced or uninterested in the research topic, all tend to have lower response rates. Mail panels are successful in boosting response rates, and the problem of nonresponse bias is also reduced.

nonresponse bias
Bias that arises when actual respondents differ from those who refuse to participate in ways that affect the survey results.

Despite its shortcomings, the relative ease and low cost of mail interviews continue to make this a viable research option as in the soup example that follows.

BE a DM!

As the marketing manager for Outback Steakhouse, how would you use information on consumers' preferences for casual restaurants to formulate marketing strategies that would increase your sales and market share?

BE an MR!

Visit Outback's Web site (www.outback.com) and search the Internet using a search engine as well as your library's online databases to obtain information on consumers' preferences for casual restaurants.

What are the advantages and disadvantages of using mail, a mail panel, or fax in conducting a survey to obtain information on consumers' preferences for casual restaurants? Which, if any, of these methods would you recommend for conducting a survey for Outback Steakhouse?

Electronic Methods

Electronic surveys can be conducted via electronic mail (e-mail), if the respondents' addresses are known, or by posting the survey to a Web site.

RESEARCH IN ACTION

Kick the Can: Canned Soup, That Is

In a mail survey, respondents were asked to make canned or dry soups at home and then respond to a questionnaire. The findings indicated a strong desire for a fresh alternative to canned and dry soups. Guided by these results, Stockpot Soups (www.stockpot.com), a subsidiary of Campbell Soup based in Redmond, Washington, developed Stockpot Classic Soups Soup Concentrate. Packed in resealable pouches, these soups are sold in the refrigerated dairy case as an alternative to canned and dry soups. Each 10-ounce pouch makes four bowls of hearty home-style soup with ingredients like fresh-cut vegetables, real dairy products, and premium meats and seafoods. This new product has been a success as it was born of consumer desire discovered via a mail survey. As of 2005, StockPot was the leader in fresh-refrigerated soups, and the food-service industry leader, with a 44 percent market share nationwide.[4]

E-mail Surveys E-mail surveys are questionnaires distributed through electronic mail. If the addresses are known, the survey can simply be mailed electronically to respondents included in the sample. E-mail usage in the United States is very high, particularly in business firms where virtually everyone has access to e-mail. Using batch-type electronic mail, researchers send e-mail surveys to potential respondents who use electronic mail. Respondents key in their answers and send an e-mail reply. Typically, a computer program is used to prepare the questionnaire and the e-mail address list and to prepare the data for analysis.

E-mail surveys are simple to prepare and can be distributed very fast. They are also convenient for the respondent as they show up in the e-mail box and catch the attention of the respondent. As compared to regular mail (snail-mail) surveys, e-mail surveys offer time and cost advantages and more flexibility. However, unsolicited e-mails are often treated as "spam" by the screening programs of e-mail hosting services and e-mail recipients.

Some e-mail systems can handle color and graphics, whereas others are limited to plain text. Respondent anonymity is difficult to maintain because a reply to an e-mail message includes the sender's address. Security and privacy issues can also be a concern.

E-mail surveys are especially suited to projects for which the e-mail lists are readily available, such as surveys of employees, institutional buyers, and consumers who frequently contact the organization via e-mail (e.g., frequent fliers of an airline). E-mail letters can also be used to ask respondents to participate in an Internet survey and provide them with a link and password to the Web site where the survey is posted.

Internet Surveys An Internet survey is a questionnaire posted on a Web site that is self-administered by the respondent. The questions are displayed on the screen, and the respondents provide answers by clicking an icon, keying in an answer, or highlighting a phrase. Web survey systems are available for constructing and posting Internet surveys. They consist of a questionnaire designer, Web server, database, and data delivery program. The questionnaire is constructed with a user-friendly editor that uses a visual interface. The Web server distributes the questionnaire and files responses in a database. At any time, the researcher can obtain survey completion statistics, descriptive statistics of the responses, and graphical display of the data. As compared to e-mail surveys, Internet surveys offer more flexibility, greater interactivity, personalization, automatic skip patterns and visual appeal. Several Web sites, such as WebSurveyor (www.websurveyor.com) allow users to design surveys online without downloading the software. The survey is administered on the design site's server. Some sites offer data tabulation services as well. The advantages and disadvantages of electronic surveys relative to the other methods are discussed in more detail in the next section.

Advantages and Disadvantages of Electronic Methods Both e-mail and Internet methods survey thousands of potential respondents simultaneously and quickly, with the Internet surveys being faster. The data collected can be analyzed speedily, almost in real time, with Internet surveys. The incremental cost of reaching additional respondents is marginal, and hence, much larger samples can be accommodated as compared to the other methods.

Both methods are cost-effective. The cost savings as compared to the other methods can be dramatic for large samples. Moreover, both methods are good for contacting hard-to-reach respondents as the survey can be answered at a time and place convenient to each respondent. Thus, high-income professionals, such as doctors, lawyers, and CEOs, can be reached. These groups are well represented online.

Internet surveys, and to some extent e-mail surveys, can be readily personalized. In addition to personalizing the name, the questions themselves can be personalized based on the respondent's answers to the previous questions. For example, if your favorite brand of toothpaste, Crest, was not available, which brand would you buy? Internet surveys can be programmed to automatically perform skip patterns (if the answer to Question 3 is "no," go to Question 9). Internet surveys are also interactive and utilize color, sound, graphics, and animation, much like computer-assisted personal interviewing.

Callbacks are easier to make in e-mail surveys and Internet surveys that draw respondents from a panel. The computer software can automatically send e-mail reminders to respondents who have not answered the survey. The electronic method shares many of the advantages of the mail method, including no field-force problems, no interviewer bias, and low social desirability.

Both methods have some disadvantages as well. They suffer from respondent selection bias in that only people with access to electronic mail or the Internet can be included in the sampling frame. This bias is further accentuated by the fact that heavy users of these media have a higher probability of being actually included in the sample. These individuals may differ from the target population in ways that can seriously bias the results. In fact, it has been shown that Internet users have lower age and higher incomes and also overrepresent households with children. If Internet surfers are intercepted and given an opportunity to participate and no controls are imposed, the same respondent can answer over and over again. Until usage of electronic media becomes more widespread, these methods may be more appropriate for specialized applications, such as IBM surveying heavy computer users.

The electronic methods also share many of the disadvantages of mail surveys. Only simple questions can be asked; there is low sample control and no control of the data collection environment; and there is a low response rate. Only moderate quantities of data can be obtained. Even though these disadvantages exist, the Internet holds tremendous promise.

EXPERIENTIAL LEARNING

Internet Surveys

The following Web sites illustrate the online surveying for respondents as well as researchers.

1. To experience what an Internet survey is like, go to Web Online Surveys at (www.web-online-surveys.com). Select "Sample," and take the short "Website Survey."
2. If you would like to join a panel of respondents who would earn prizes and other rewards for completing online surveys you can (1) go to Lightspeed's home page and volunteer to respond to Lightspeed's surveys in the future at (www.us.lightspeedpanel.com) then follow the instructions or (2) go to (www.zoomerang.com) and select "Become a Panelist," then follow the instructions.
3. To experience how a sponsor of an Internet survey can monitor results during the field portion of the project, go to (www.us.lightspeedpanel.com), read the Lightspeed mini-poll question, and select "View Results."
4. If you would like to examine actual Internet surveys (and some results) fielded by firms in their research programs go to (www.createsurvey.com), and click on any of the hyperlinks under "Real Life Surveys by Customers."

Criteria for Selecting a Survey Method

When evaluating the various survey methods within the context of a specific research project, one has to consider the salient factors relevant to data collection. Often, certain factors dominate, leading to a particular survey method as the natural choice. For example, if a new perishable food product has to be tested, respondents would have to taste the product before answering the questionnaire. This would involve interviewing at central locations, leading to mall intercept or CAPI as the natural choices. If no method is clearly superior, the choice must be based on an overall consideration of the advantages and disadvantages of the various methods. We offer the following guidelines.

- If complex and diverse questions have to be asked, one of the personal methods (in-home, mall intercept, or CAPI) is preferable. Internet surveys may be an option as well.
- From the perspective of the use of physical stimuli, the personal methods (in-home, mall intercept, or CAPI) are preferable.
- If sample control is an issue, cold mail (but not mail panel), fax, and electronic methods may not be appropriate.
- Control of the data collection environment favors the use of central location (mall intercept and CAPI) interviewing.
- High quantity of data favors the use of in-home and mail panels and makes the use of telephone interviewing inappropriate.
- Low response rates make the use of cold mail and electronic methods disadvantageous.
- If social desirability is an issue, mail, mail-panel, fax, and Internet surveys are the best.
- If interviewer bias is an issue, the use of mail (cold and panels), fax, and electronic interviewing (e-mail and Internet) is favored.
- Speed favors Internet, e-mail, telephone, and fax methods.
- Costs favor cold mail, fax, electronic (e-mail and Internet), mail panels, telephone, mall intercept, CAPI, and in-home methods, in that order (most favorable to least favorable).

Often, these methods are combined to enhance the quality of data in a cost-effective manner. This is likely when the research project is large in scope, as in the case of P&G formulating its new marketing platform in the opening vignette. Note that P&G used scanner panels to monitor household expenses of P&G and competing brands and used mail panels to target consumers loyal to P&G. It used CATI to reach a representative sample of all households and used mall intercepts to determine consumer response to the Olay Beauty Bar prior to introduction. The Compaq example that follows illustrates the selection of survey modes.

Improving Survey Response Rates

Regardless of the survey method chosen, researchers should attempt to improve response rates. This can be done by prior notification, incentives, follow-up, and implementing other facilitators of response (Figure 7.5).

Prior Notification

Prior notification consists of sending a letter or e-mail or making a telephone call to potential respondents, notifying them of the imminent mail, telephone, personal, or electronic survey. Prior notification increases response rates for samples of the general public because it reduces surprise and uncertainty and creates a more cooperative atmosphere.

prepaid incentive
Coupons, money, or some other incentive to participate that is included with the survey or questionnaire.

promised incentive
Coupons, money, or some other incentive to participate that is sent only to those respondents who complete the survey.

Incentives

Offering monetary as well as nonmonetary incentives to potential respondents can increase response rates. Monetary incentives can be prepaid or promised. The **prepaid incentive** is included with the survey or questionnaire. The **promised incentive** is sent to

RESEARCH IN ACTION

Good Things Come in Small Packages—and Diskettes

Since its merger with Hewlett Packard on May 3, 2002, Compaq is number two in the personal computer segment with 14 percent of the market share in the first quarter of 2004. Compaq (www.compaq.com) was sorting through survey options, attempting to identify the best method for conducting product research. The complexity of the questions eliminated telephone interviewing as an option. Personal interviews would have been ideal, but costs were prohibitive. Historically low response rates associated with mail surveys also raised concerns about that technique. Compaq knew they could boost response rates with incentives, but the response bias associated with that technique, as well as the cost, were concerns. As the sample was composed entirely of household computer users, Compaq adopted the innovative option of computer interviewing by mail—mailing the questionnaire on a diskette. The electronic option was not used because the e-mail addresses were not available and it was believed that respondents' access to the Internet would be limited.

Using a computer interviewing system, the researchers converted the survey to a series of questions related to various product scenarios, which displayed various product benefits. They mailed the questionnaire, in diskette form, to the respondent group. The researchers thought that the uniqueness of a questionnaire on diskette would motivate this targeted group, eliminating the need for costly incentives. A plastic diskette holder served as an inexpensive alternative to a monetary incentive.

To the researchers' pleasant surprise, the response rate exceeded 55 percent, higher than any mail survey Compaq had ever conducted. The company obtained the relevant information at a low cost and was able to design a successful new product.[5]

only those respondents who complete the survey. The most commonly used nonmonetary incentives are premiums and rewards, such as pens, pencils, books, and offers of survey results.

Prepaid incentives have been shown to increase response rates to a greater extent than promised incentives. The amount of incentive can vary from $1.00 to $50.00 or more. The amount of incentive has a positive relationship with response rate, but the cost of large monetary incentives may outweigh the value of the additional information obtained.

Follow-up

Follow-up, or contacting the nonrespondents periodically after the initial contact, is particularly effective in decreasing refusals in mail surveys. The researcher might send a postcard or letter to remind nonrespondents to complete and return the questionnaire. Two or three mailings are needed in addition to the original one. With proper follow-up, the response rate in mail surveys can be increased to 80 percent or more. Follow-up can also be done by telephone, e-mail, or personal contact.

Figure 7.5

Improving Response Rates

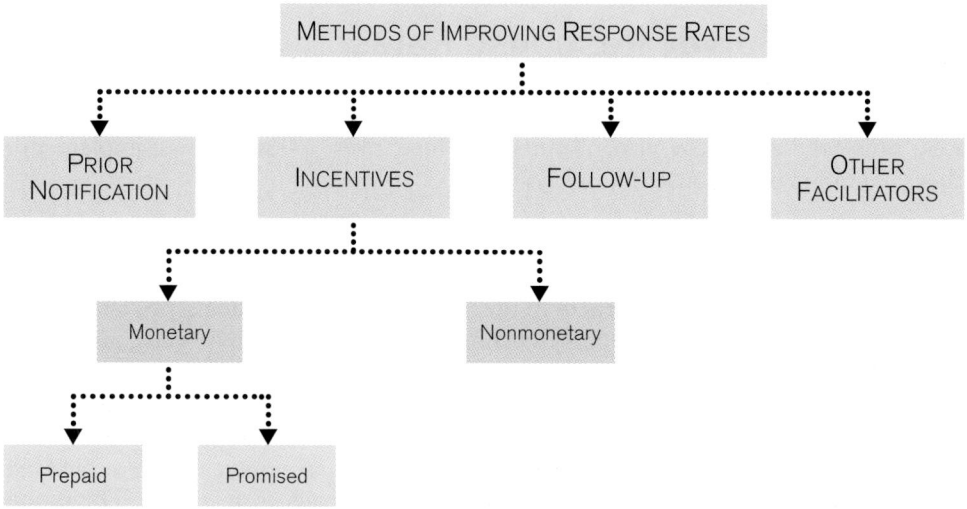

RESEARCH IN ACTION

Bicycling Magazine's Procedure for Increasing Response to Mail Surveys

As of 2005, *Bicycling* magazine (www.bicycling.com) had 2 million readers in the United States with a circulation of more than 400,000. *Bicycling* magazine conducts a semiannual survey of individual bicycle dealers throughout the United States. The following procedure is used to increase the response to the survey.

1. An "alert" letter is sent to advise the respondent that a questionnaire is coming.
2. A questionnaire package is mailed five days after the alert letter. The package contains a cover letter, a five-page questionnaire, a new $1 bill, and a stamped return envelope.
3. A second package, containing a reminder letter, a questionnaire, and a stamped return envelope, is mailed five days after the first package.
4. A follow-up postcard is mailed a week after the second package.
5. A second follow-up postcard is mailed a week after the first.

In a recent survey, 1,000 questionnaires were mailed to bicycle dealers, and 68 percent of these were returned after follow-up. This represents a good response rate for a mail survey.

Other Facilitators of Response

Personalization, or sending letters addressed to specific individuals, is effective in increasing response rates. As illustrated in the *Bicycling* magazine example, multiple methods can be used to increase response rate.

BE a DM!

As the marketing manager for Harley Davidson, how would you use information on consumers' image for motorcycle brands to formulate marketing strategies that would increase your sales and market share?

BE an MR!

Visit Harley Davidson's Web site (www.harleydavidson.com) and search the Internet using a search engine as well as your library's online databases to obtain information on consumers' images for motorcycle brands.

If a survey is to be conducted for Harley Davidson to determine consumers' image for motorcycle brands, which method do you recommend for administering the survey and why? How would you improve the response rate?

Observation Methods

Observation methods are the second type of methodology used in descriptive research. **Observation** involves recording the behavioral patterns of people as well as data on objects and events in a systematic manner to obtain information about the phenomenon of interest. The observer does not question or communicate with the people being observed. Information may be recorded as the events occur or from records of past events. The major methods are personal observation and mechanical observation.

observation
The recording of behavioral patterns of people, objects, and events in a systematic manner to obtain information about the phenomenon of interest.

Personal Observation

personal observation
An observational research strategy in which human observers record the phenomenon being observed as it occurs.

humanistic inquiry
A variation of personal observation in which the researcher is immersed in the system under study.

In **personal observation**, a trained observer collects the data by recording behavior exactly as it occurs. The observer does not attempt to control or manipulate the phenomenon being observed but simply records what takes place. For example, a researcher might record traffic counts and observe traffic flows in a department store. This information could aid in determining store layouts, location of individual departments, shelf locations, and merchandise displays. **Humanistic inquiry** is a variation of personal observation in which the researcher is immersed in the system under study. This is in contrast to the traditional scientific method in which the researcher is a dispassionate observer. In yet another application called *on-site observation*, observers are positioned in supermarkets and presented as shoppers who need advice from another shopper in making purchase decisions.

The main advantage of personal observation is that it is a highly flexible method, as the observer can record a wide variety of phenomena (Table 7.3). It is also highly suitable for use in natural settings. For example, the sales manager of General Motors can observe the attitudes of dealers toward a new inventory policy at one of the regular sales meetings.

The main disadvantage is that the method is unstructured in that an observation form is generally not used for recording the behavior as it occurs. Rather, the observer records the phenomenon after completing the observation in a free, unstructured format. This can lead to high observation bias. Also the data and their interpretation are highly subjective, leading to high analysis bias.

Mechanical Observation

mechanical observation
An observational research strategy in which mechanical devices, rather than human observers, record the phenomenon being observed.

Mechanical observation, as one would expect, involves the use of a mechanical device to record behavior. These devices may or may not require the respondents' direct participation. They are particularly useful for recording continuous behavior, such as traffic flow in a grocery store. ACNielsen's peoplemeter (Chapter 5) is an example of indirect observational devices in use today. Respondents do not need to change their behavior in any way to be involved in this type of observational study. The peoplemeter is attached to a television set to continually record not only the channels a set is tuned to but also who is watching.

Other common examples of indirect mechanical observation include turnstiles that record the number of people entering or leaving a building and traffic counters placed across streets to determine the number of vehicles passing certain locations. On-site cameras (still, motion picture, or video) are increasingly used by retailers to assess the impact of package designs, counter space, floor displays, and traffic-flow patterns. The Universal Product Code (UPC) is also a built-in source for mechanical observation. For those retailers equipped with optical scanners, the UPC system allows for the automatic collection of consumer purchase information, classifying it by product category, brand, store type, price, and quantity (see Chapter 5).

The scanner data that P&G used in the opening vignette is an example of mechanical observation. These data revealed that a typical family that was brand-loyal spent $725 for

Table 7.3
Relative Advantages and Disadvantages of Observation Methods

Method	Advantages	Disadvantages
Personal observation	Most flexible	High observation bias
	Highly suitable in natural settings	High analysis bias
Mechanical observation	Low observation bias	Can be intrusive
	Low-to-medium analysis bias	Not always suitable in natural settings

EXPERIENTIAL LEARNING

Observing Customers' Movements in Retail Stores

Observation of customers' movements in retail stores can provide marketers with valuable insights about improving store layouts. In one study done by IntegralGIS of Seattle, Washington, research teams followed 150 customers through four different retail stores and noted what the customers examined, rejected, and bought. Go to ESRI's case study for Mapping Movement through Retail Stores at (www.esri.com/mapmuseum/mapbook_gallery/volume18/business3.html).

If this URL has changed, search ESRI's Web site (www.esri.com) to locate Mapping Movement through Retail Stores. Make sure you download the plug-in that will allow you to readily zoom in and zoom out on the map, as well as move the map on your screen. This will allow you to read the legends of the maps and better understand the information these maps contain.

1. Can you tell where most of the visual examinations occur that don't result in placing items in a shopper's cart?
2. In what parts of the store might shoplifting be greatest?
3. Which cash registers appear to be most used? How would the use of other cash registers affect the flow of customers at the front of the store? How would it affect where displays could be placed to take advantage of this new movement within the store?
4. What are the ethical issues of employing such personal observations in retail stores?
5. What steps would need to be taken to collect these personal observations in an ethical manner?

a year's worth of P&G products. In comparison, a family that bought similar products as private-label or low-priced brands spent less than $500.

Web-based tracking of Internet users is one exciting and controversial electronic observation technique. Web surfers are served cookies. The cookie is a group of letters and numbers stored in a Web surfer's browser which identify the user. It is a sophisticated means by which a Web site can collect information on visitors. Often, this process takes place without the Web surfer's knowledge. Companies and individuals that host Web sites use cookies to collect marketing research information on visitors. Cookies follow the traveler through the Web site and record the pages accessed by the visitor and the number of minutes spent on each page. Your name, address, phone number, and access site can be collected by the cookie and saved into a database if the visitor enters any information. During a follow-up visit, the cookie accesses this information and has the ability to repeat it to the visitor. In essence, the cookie collects data on the user during every visit to the site. The online advertising company DoubleClick (www.doubleclick.com) uses the information obtained from cookies to target advertising. For example, if a user visits an airline site and then a hotel site, that individual will be targeted with Delta Airlines and Marriott advertisements. Such practices are controversial because they raise privacy concerns amongst individuals and policy makers.

When it comes to developing new products, some smart companies like HP, Motorola, and Steelcase (see example that follows) are observing their customers rather than just listening to what they say. Traditional research, relying exclusively on questioning, can produce bland products. New Coke test marketed well, yet was a dismal failure. People wanted low-calorie burgers but wouldn't buy McDonald's McLean. The movie *Junior* did great in screenings, but made only $36 million. Baseball players loved the pump baseball glove but wouldn't pay the increased cost. This is why it is important to combine questioning with observation methods and why mechanical observation is gaining ground.

Although the Steelcase study did not require direct involvement of the participants, many mechanical observation devices do. Physical responses to sights, sounds, smells, or any sensory stimuli are an important area of observational research. Advertising or other promotional changes, such as special sales, can elicit a physical response in consumers

RESEARCH IN ACTION

Steelcase Makes the Case for Mechanical Observation

Steelcase (www.steelcase.com), a major national furniture manufacturer, won nine Best of Neocon 2003 awards. The company used mechanical observation when it designed a furniture line for work teams. It set up hidden video cameras at various companies to observe what really goes on during the workday, looking for information on behavior and routines people might not even know they exhibited.

The company found that teams function best when members can work collectively some of the time and independently at other times. The results of this study led to the very successful introduction of modular office furniture called Personal Harbor. This furniture can be quickly and easily assembled or reassembled to allow office workers to work in a large team area or in individual work spaces.[6]

that cannot be observed by merely looking at them. Specialized equipment designed to monitor heart and breathing rates, skin temperature, and other physiological changes is used in these situations. Since these measurements cost more than verbal reports of the respondent's reaction, they are only used when it is assumed that the respondent cannot or will not respond accurately to questioning. All of the physiological measurement devices operate on the assumption that the cognitive and emotional responses to stimuli elicit predictable differences in physical response. This assumption has not yet been clearly demonstrated, however.

The main advantage of mechanical observation is low observation bias, as the behavior is recorded mechanically and not by an observer. Likewise, the data are analyzed according to prespecified norms and guidelines, resulting in low analysis bias. The main disadvantages are that some of these methods can be intrusive or expensive and may not be suitable in natural settings such as the marketplace.

BE an MR!

Visit Disney's Web site (www.disney.com) and search the Internet using a search engine as well as your library's online databases to obtain information on the criteria that consumers use for selecting theme parks.

If Disney World wants to determine how many people visit its theme parks on a daily basis and which are the most popular exhibits, can the observation method be used? If yes, which observation method would you use?

BE a DM!

As the marketing manager for Disney World, how would you use information on criteria that consumers use for selecting theme parks to formulate marketing strategies that would increase your attendance and market share?

A Comparison of Survey and Observation Methods

With the exception of scanner data, marketing research is seldom conducted solely with observational methods. There are some unique advantages, however, to collecting data in this fashion. When combined with survey techniques, observation can deliver excellent results.

Relative Advantages of Observation

There are several advantages to using observational data collection methods. First, they do not require conscious respondent participation, which minimizes nonresponse errors. Although ethical questions surround the practice of observation without consent, even conscious participation requires less effort from the respondent than that required with other research techniques.

RESEARCH IN ACTION

Hefty OneZip Bag: Customer Satisfaction Is in the Bag

Mechanical observation coupled with mall intercept interviewing provided rich information on consumers' needs for food storage bags. Shoppers intercepted in malls were led to an observation facility in the mall. They were asked to use food storage bags, and their behavior was recorded using video cameras. They were then administered a survey in an adjoining room. This methodology provided rich insights into needs of consumers, such as the desire for bags that can be closed easily and more securely.

This finding was the impetus behind the development of Hefty OneZip food storage and freezer bags. Looking more like an actual zipper than the closures on most zipper bags, the OneZip Slider promised to eliminate the bothersome tasks of alignment, pinching, and double-checking needed to close conventional zipper bags.

On introduction, Hefty OneZip averaged a 21 percent dollar-share of the storage and freezer segments of the zipper-bag market, where available. With Hefty name recognition, broader distribution, and an aggressive advertising and sampling campaign, OneZip's popularity grew quickly. Within one year of introduction, the product became America's number-two zipper bag. Hundreds of customer compliments thanking the company for making their lives "a little easier" have made Hefty feel as if the OneZip customer satisfaction is securely in the bag. As of 2005, this product line commanded more than 60 percent market share in the slider food bag segment.[7]

Interviewer bias resulting from interaction with the respondent or subjective interpretation of the questionnaire is minimized because the observer only has to record what is occurring. Additionally, the errors inherent in self-reported behavior are eliminated given that the observer records only actual behavior without asking any questions of the respondent.

Data regarding product preferences or reactions to marketing materials from children or pets can best be collected using observational techniques. Observation is also useful in situations investigating unconscious behavior patterns or behaviors that individuals may be unwilling to discuss honestly.

Observational techniques are best applied to phenomena that occur frequently or are of short duration. In these types of applications, observational methods may cost less and be faster than survey methods.

Relative Disadvantages of Observation

Observational data provide insight into what behavior is occurring, but not why. Attitudes, motivations, and values are all lost to the observational method. Additionally, highly personal behaviors related to personal hygiene or intimate family interactions are not available for observation.

Individuals have a tendency to selectively observe only what they want to, and that may cause an observer to overlook important aspects of behavior. This perceptual difference among observers threatens the integrity of the approach.

Finally, observational techniques can be adopted for only frequent behaviors of short duration. Behaviors occurring infrequently or spanning a long period of time (e.g., individual car purchases over time) are too expensive to record using this technique.

To sum up, observation can potentially provide valuable information when properly used. From a practical standpoint, it is best to view observation as a complement to survey methods rather than as being in competition with them, as illustrated by the Hefty OneZip Bag example.

RESEARCH IN ACTION

PortiCo Documents with Documentaries

PortiCo Research (www.porticoresearch.com) specializes in observing individuals, questioning them in depth, recording them on videos, and selling these tapes for tens of thousands of dollars to its major clients, such as Honda, Delta, Lipton, and Procter & Gamble. They have fine-tuned the method of collecting ethnographic data and have made it into a very profitable business.

"PortiCo's specialty is total immersion in the lives of consumers in an effort to document how they make purchasing decisions." Research teams of anthropologists, social psychologists, and ethnographers (professionals who comparatively study people) go into the subjects' homes with videographers. The teams tape the subjects in their homes and also take shopping trips with them to watch what they buy and to get feedback on the reasons for their purchases. After filming, employees of PortiCo transcribe the findings of the videos and analyze them for their clients. The analysis is based on the research problem that the client must gather more information about or solve. For example, PortiCo did a large study for Lipton to find out people's attitudes towards tea. With the results of the study, Lipton would find out whether or not to invest more in advertising, develop new flavors, or market more iced tea instead of hot tea. The findings showed that Americans don't drink very much hot tea, especially because of the presence of caffeinated coffee in the marketplace. If and when they do drink hot tea, it is normally flavored herbal tea. Most of Lipton's hot tea is not in special flavors. They have recently begun to bring herbal teas to market, however. The study did find that American consumers like iced tea. As a result of the findings, Lipton has initiated a lot of creative developments in the area of iced tea. They pushed the marketing of Brisk Iced Tea in the can, which is now the number-one selling brand of ready-to-drink iced tea. Lipton also created a Cold Brew Blend tea bag in both family size to make a whole pitcher and single-glass size for one serving. This tea bag allows iced tea to be brewed with cold water instead of boiling water. Therefore, consumers can enjoy their tea faster with much less hassle. These marketing efforts, guided by the findings of PortiCo Research, have resulted in increased sales and market share for Lipton.[8]

Ethnographic Research

Ethnographic research is the study of human behavior in its natural context and involves observation of behavior and setting along with in-depth interviews. Sometimes, audio and visual recordings are also obtained. Thus, both the questioning and observation methods are combined to understand the behavior of consumers. The PortiCo example illustrates this method.

Other Methods

In addition to ethnographic research, there are also a variety of other methods that combine the use of questioning and observation. One such method that is commonly used is mystery shopping. Trained observers pose as consumers and shop at company or competitor owned stores to collect data about customer–employee interaction and other marketing variables, such as prices, displays, layout, and so forth. The mystery shoppers question the store employees, mentally take note of the answers, and observe the variables of interest.

BE a DM!

As the marketing manager for Kroger, how would you use information on consumer behavior related to supermarket shopping to formulate marketing strategies that would increase your market share?

BE an MR!

Visit Kroger's Web site (www.kroger.com) and search the Internet using a search engine as well as your library's online databases to obtain information on consumer behavior related to supermarket shopping.

Kroger wants to determine to what extent consumers plan their product and brand purchases before entering the store. How will you combine the survey and observation methods to obtain this information?

Summary Illustration Using the Opening Vignette

Surveys involve the administration of a questionnaire and may be classified as traditional telephone interviews, computer-assisted telephone interviews (CATI), in-home personal interviews, mall intercept interviews, computer-assisted personal interviews (CAPI), mail surveys, mail panels, or electronic surveys administered by e-mail or Internet. These data collection methods should not be considered mutually exclusive. Often, it is possible to employ them productively in combination, as illustrated in the opening vignette. P&G used the CATI method to survey the general population, a mail panel to determine the pricing preferences of consumers loyal to P&G brands, and mall intercept interviews to assess reaction to the Olay Beauty Bar prior to introduction.

CATI is very suitable for surveying a representative sample of households, as telephone numbers can be randomly generated using efficient computer programs. A mail panel allows repeated measurements on the same respondents; thus brand-loyal users can be identified (respondents who purchased P&G brands repeatedly). Mall intercept interviews are very conducive to showing a new product to respondents before questioning them. Thus, this method was appropriate for assessing consumer response to P&G's brand extension (Olay Beauty Bar). Electronic methods, especially Internet surveys, can obtain information from large samples of respondents quickly and at a low cost.

In contrast to direct questioning in surveys, observation methods simply observe people and objects. The major observational methods are personal observation and mechanical observation. Certain types of data can be obtained best by observation. An example would be consumers' purchases of various brands in supermarkets. P&G used scanner data (mechanical observation) to determine that a typical family that was brand-loyal spent $725 for a year's worth of P&G products. In comparison, a family that bought similar products as private-label or low-priced brands spent less than $500.

International Marketing Research

Selecting appropriate interviewing methods for international marketing research is much more difficult because of the challenges of conducting research in foreign countries. Given the differences in the economic, structural, informational and technological, and sociocultural environments, the feasibility and popularity of the different interviewing methods vary widely. In the United States and Canada, nearly all households have telephones. As a result, telephone interviewing is the dominant mode of administering questionnaires. This is also true in some European countries, such as Sweden. In many other European countries, however, not all households have telephones. In some developing countries only a few households have them.

In-home personal interviews are the dominant mode of collecting survey data in many European countries, such as Switzerland, and in newly industrialized countries (NICs) or developing countries. While mall intercepts are being conducted in some European countries, such as Sweden, they are not popular in other European countries or in developing countries. In contrast, central location/street interviews constitute the dominant method of collecting survey data in France and the Netherlands.

Due to their low cost, mail interviews continue to be used in most developed countries where literacy is high and the postal system is well developed. Some examples are the United States, Canada, Denmark, Finland, Iceland, Norway, Sweden, and the Netherlands. In Africa, Asia, and South America, however, the use of mail surveys and mail panels is low because of illiteracy and the large proportion of the population living in rural areas. Mail panels are used extensively only in a few countries outside the United States, such as Canada, the United Kingdom, France, Germany, and the

RESEARCH IN ACTION

Nike: Using Dominant Survey Methods to Gain Dominant Market Share

As of 2005, Nike (www.nike.com) was deriving more revenue from outside the United States than domestically. The company, with a 37 percent share of the athletic shoe market in the United States, is seeking to expand in Europe with the goal of significantly improving its competitive position by 2008. Rather than strictly competing with Adidas and Puma in the European premier sport-shoes market, Nike is considering strong marketing programs to sell street sneakers for daily wear to the large European market. A survey of consumer preferences for sneakers is to be undertaken in three countries: Sweden, France, and Switzerland. Comparability of results can best be achieved by using the dominant mode of interviewing in each country: telephone interviews in Sweden, central location/street interviews in France, and in-home personal interviews in Switzerland. The findings of this survey would help Nike to understand the factors that Europeans consider important when purchasing sneakers for daily wear (e.g., comfort, style, and color) and whether the importance attached to these factors varies across Sweden, France, and Switzerland. Nike will then be able to determine whether a uniform marketing strategy should be adopted across these countries or whether marketing effort should be customized for each.[9]

Netherlands. However, the use of panels may increase with the advent of new technology. Likewise, although a Web site can be accessed from anywhere in the world, access to the Web or e-mail is limited in many countries, particularly developing countries. Hence, the use of electronic surveys is not feasible, especially for interviewing households.

Various methods may be reliable in some countries but not others. When collecting data from different countries, it is desirable to use survey methods with equivalent levels of reliability rather than necessarily using the identical method, as illustrated in the Nike example.

As in the case of surveys, the selection of an appropriate observation method in international marketing research should also take into account the differences in the economic, structural, informational and technological, and sociocultural environment.

Technology and Marketing Research

New information technologies will continue to revolutionize the ways in which both primary and secondary data are collected. In earlier chapters, we talked about the role of automated databases in secondary research. Primary data collection and analysis is also changing due to advances in information technology. The researcher can use a computer to automatically dial the telephone numbers of potential respondents' fax machines and electronically send a survey. New software allows fax machines to read and store incoming text and data using "optical character recognition" technology. This makes it possible to conduct and tabulate surveys on a computer. This technology could replace the traditional mail survey, especially in researching business customers since it can gather the same type of information with much greater speed.

Field workers are gathering information in various locations with the aid of notebook computers and electronic hand-held devices. These computers have built-in, wireless modems, allowing for transmission of data to and from virtually anywhere in the world. Another technological innovation is the use of interactive kiosks to collect data in central-location interviews conducted at malls and trade shows.

Marketing researchers now have access to a new form of survey data: interactive phone technology. These systems are called Completely Automated Telephone Surveys (CATS) and use the interactive voice-response (IVR) technology to circumvent the need for the human interviewer. The CATS system uses interactive voice-response technology to conduct interviews. The recorded voice of a professional interviewer asks the questions. The individual simply keys in the corresponding push button to log an answer. For surveys requiring more detailed consumer responses, individual answers can be recorded and later transcribed. This can be very beneficial because managers can learn what customers said and also hear how they said it.

CATS systems can be of the outbound or inbound format. With the outbound format, a computer dials from a sample of phone numbers, the interactive voice asks questions, and the responses are automatically recorded. This method is not very successful because it is very easy for the respondent to hang up. The inbound format has better results because the consumer initiates the call, so the likelihood of a completed call is far greater. Generally, some added incentive is attached to influence the individual to participate. Identification codes can help limit multiple call-ins (to hoard the incentives). These codes can also help to determine the characteristics of the individual who calls in (i.e., if the incentive card/letter is mailed, the code can be used as a tag for the person's location, sex, income, and so on), which aids in the examination of the data.[10]

All of these innovations, as well as future advances in information technology, will continue to improve the way in which researchers collect data.

Ethics in Marketing Research

Surveys are often used as a cover for a targeted sales effort. The real purpose is not to obtain information to address a marketing research problem but to sell a product. This practice, called "sugging" in the trade language, is unethical. A similar unethical practice is "frugging" and involves fund-raising under the guise of research. To illustrate, assume you get a call from a company stating that they are conducting research on consumer attitudes. After asking a few diagnostic questions, the company tries to sell you one of its products (sugging) or asks for a donation (frugging).

Respondents' anonymity, discussed in the context of qualitative research in Chapter 6, is an important issue in both survey and observational search. Researchers have an ethical obligation to not disclose the identities of respondents to anyone outside the research organization, including the client. Only when researchers notify respondents in advance and obtain their consent prior to administering the survey can an exception be made and the respondents' identities revealed to the client. Even in such cases, prior to disclosing identification information, the researcher should obtain an assurance from the client that the respondents' trust will be kept and their identities will not be used for sales effort or misused in other ways. Ethical lapses in this respect by unscrupulous researchers and marketers have resulted in a serious backlash for marketing research.

The researcher has the responsibility to use an appropriate survey method in an ethical and legal way. For instance, federal legislation prohibits unsolicited faxed surveys. In many states, totally automated outgoing (initiated by the researcher) telephoning is illegal.

Often, researchers observe people's behavior without their consent, arguing that informing the respondents may alter their behavior. This can be considered an invasion of the respondents' privacy. One guideline proposed to resolve this problem is that research observation should only be conducted in places where people would expect to be observed by the public. Public places such as malls or grocery aisles, places where people observe other people routinely, are fair game. Nonetheless, notices stating that these areas are under observation for marketing research purposes should be posted at the sites. After observing their behavior, the researcher is still obligated to obtain the necessary permission from the subjects.[11]

It should also be mentioned that the common practice of serving cookies on the Internet raises ethical concerns. Many users do not realize it, but they have been served a cookie or two while on the Internet. A cookie is not a culinary delight in this case. It is a sophisticated means by which a Web site can collect information on visitors. Often this process takes place without the Web surfers' knowledge and is an invasion of their privacy and right to consent, as in the Hotwired example.

RESEARCH IN ACTION

Hotwired? Have a Cookie!

Hotwired (www.hotwired.com), a Web site devoted to technology and culture, offers dynamic online tools, such as search engines, that provide people with important information. Hotwired uses cookies to collect information about Web-site traffic by tracking an individual's preference for hotel choice, airline travel, and other interests. Hotwired uses this information to target customers with advertisements by promoting discounts and specials using the individual's preferred choices. In addition, the information helps marketing personnel at the electronic and print magazine collect demographics on the reader. Also, the company can monitor "hits" on particular topics and gain valuable feedback on user interest. For example, using cookies, Hotwired may find out that after visiting its Web site, a particular respondent then visits Travelocity (www.travelocity.com) for flight and hotel information pertaining to Jamaica. The next time that same visitor visits Hotwired.com, a pop-up Web advertisement will alert that visitor of special airfare and hotel packages to Jamaica offered by Hotwired.

Thus, this disguised technique enables Hotwired to monitor use patterns and to eliminate socially acceptable response bias. Information collected in this manner has been used to modify editorial content and format to make the site more appealing. While this information is helpful to Hotwired, the use of cookies in this way raises several ethical issues.[12]

WHAT WOULD *YOU* DO?

Microsoft: Small Businesses Represent a Big Market

The Situation

Statistics from the U.S. Small Business Administration show that in 2004, small businesses generated about 50 percent of all U.S. sales and also contributed about 50 percent of the private gross domestic product. They also employed about 50 percent of the U.S. workforce. Microsoft Corp. is impressed with these statistics because they indicate that small businesses may represent a big market for its products. It wonders whether the needs of small businesses are different than those of large businesses. Steve Ballmer, Microsoft CEO, would like to develop specialized products for the small businesses. Some of these products could include the following: a Web site just for small businesses; the Microsoft Small Business Council (which provides information to help small businesses use technology); the Microsoft Small Business Technology Partnership Board (an educational resource); the BackOffice Small Business Server (for a more direct route to small businesses through VARs); and a small business edition of Microsoft Works.

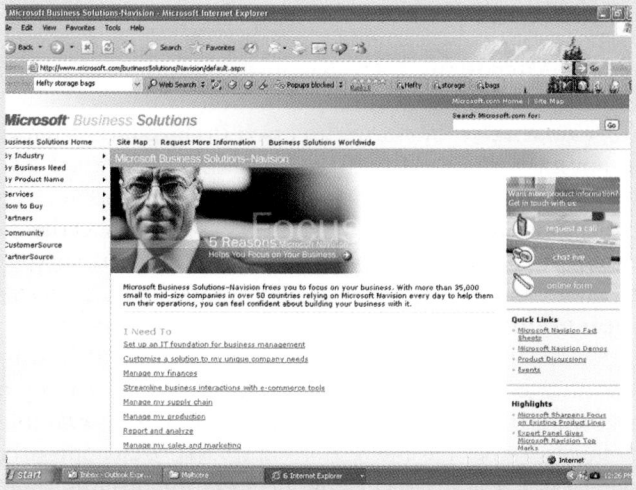

The Marketing Research Decision

1. If a survey is to be conducted to determine small businesses' preferences for software products, which survey method would you recommend and why?
   a. CATI
   b. On-site personal interviews
   c. Mail
   d. Internet
   e. E-mail
2. Discuss the role of the type of research you recommend in enabling Steve Ballmer to determine small businesses' preferences for software products.

The Marketing Management Decision

1. Steve Ballmer is wondering what Microsoft should do to effectively meet the needs of small businesses. Should it (check as many as are applicable):
   a. Develop a specific Web site for small businesses
   b. Develop new products for small businesses
   c. Customize existing products (e.g., Microsoft Office)

d. Give price discounts to small businesses
e. Develop an advertising campaign specifically directed at small businesses

2. Discuss how the marketing management-decision action that you recommend to Steve Ballmer is influenced by the type of survey that you suggested earlier and by the findings of that survey.

What Steve Ballmer Did

Steve Ballmer decided to develop new products for small businesses. Microsoft Corp. aimed to streamline back-office processes for small and midsize companies with business automation software upgrades. Microsoft Business Solutions–Navision 3.7 offers enhancements in financial management, supply-chain management, customer-relationship management, and e-business. In an effort to serve some vertical industries, Navision 3.7 provides flexible warehousing functionality with four new modules and also two new, less complex versions of the current Warehouse Systems Management module. Some application interfaces have been redesigned to make them simpler to use, and forms have been updated to make them more logical.[13]

Summary

Surveys and observations are the two primary methods of conducting quantitative, descriptive research. Surveys involve the direct questioning of respondents, whereas respondent behavior is simply recorded in observation.

Surveys involve the administration of a questionnaire and may be classified based on the method or mode of administration as traditional telephone interviews, computer-assisted telephone interviews (CATI), in-home personal interviews, mall intercept interviews, computer-assisted personal interviews (CAPI), mail surveys, mail panels, or electronic surveys administered by e-mail or Internet. Of these methods, telephone interviews (traditional and CATI) are the most popular in the United States. However, each method has some general advantages and disadvantages. Although these data collection methods are usually thought of as distinct and competitive, they should not be considered mutually exclusive. It is possible to employ them productively in combination.

The major observational methods are personal observation and mechanical observation. As compared to surveys, the relative advantages of observational methods are (1) they permit measurement of actual behavior; (2) there is no reporting bias; and (3) there is less potential for interviewer bias. Also, certain types of data can be obtained best, or only, by observation. The relative disadvantages of observation are (1) very little can be inferred about motives, beliefs, attitudes, and preferences; (2) there is potential for observer bias; (3) most methods are time-consuming and expensive; (4) it is difficult to observe some forms of behavior; and (5) there is potential for unethical behavior. With the exception of scanner data, observation is rarely used as the sole method of obtaining primary data, but it can be usefully employed in conjunction with survey methods.

An important consideration in selecting the methods of administering surveys internationally is to ensure equivalence and comparability across countries. New technologies such as computerized fax machines and Completely Automated Telephone Surveys (CATS) are revolutionizing survey administration. Misuse of surveys as a guise for selling, failing to maintain the anonymity of respondents, and observing behavior without respondents' knowledge or consent are major ethical issues in implementing survey and observation methods.

Key Terms and Concepts

Survey method, 181
Structured data collection, 182
Sample control, 184
Response rate, 184
Social desirability, 187
Interviewer bias, 187
Fax surveys, 189
Mail panels, 190
Nonresponse bias, 190
Prepaid incentive, 193
Promised incentive, 193
Observation, 195
Personal observation, 196
Humanistic inquiry, 196
Mechanical observation, 196

Suggested Cases and Video Cases

Cases

2.1 Maxfli	**2.2 Cadillac**	**2.3 HCA**	**2.4 Bloomingdale's**
2.5 Burger King	**4.1 Boeing**	**4.2 Gucci**	

Video Cases

2.1 Starbucks	**2.2 Nike**	**4.1 Subaru**	**4.2 Marriott**

Additional cases and video cases are available in the Instructor's Manual and on the instructor and student Web sites.

Live Research: Conducting a Marketing Research Project

As a class, discuss the various survey methods, and select one that is appropriate for the project. In addition to the criteria given in this chapter, certain practical constraints may have to be considered if the students must collect data. Examples include the following:

1. There should be a budget for making long-distance calls if a telephone survey is to be done beyond the local calling area.
2. If a CATI system is not available, the telephone method may be limited to traditional telephone.
3. Students will not be allowed to conduct mall intercept interviews unless permission is obtained from the mall management. Some malls have signed exclusive contracts with marketing research firms for data collection.
4. It may not be practical to do in-home personal interviews covering a large geographic area even in the local region.
5. There may not be enough time for a mail survey, and a mail panel may be prohibitively expensive.
6. E-mail addresses may not be available or may be very difficult to get.
7. Mechanical observation devices may be impractical to obtain and use.

The survey method selected should be discussed and approved by the client.

Acronyms

The classification of survey methods by mode of administration may be described by the acronym METHODS:

M ail panels
E lectronic interviews
T elephone interviews
H ome (in-home personal) interviewing
O n-site mall interviews
D irect-mail interviews
S oftware for CATI/CAPI

Review Questions

1. Explain briefly how the topics covered in this chapter fit into the framework of the marketing research process.
2. Name the major modes for obtaining information via a survey.
3. What are the relevant factors for evaluating which survey method is best suited to a particular research project?
4. What would be the most appropriate survey method for a project in which control of field force and cost are critical factors?
5. Name the types of mechanical observation, and explain how they work.
6. What are the relative advantages and disadvantages of observation?

Applied Problems

1. Describe a marketing research problem in which both survey and observation methods could be used for obtaining the information needed.
2. The campus food service would like to determine how many people eat in the student cafeteria. List the ways in which this information could be obtained. Which method is best?
3. Locate and answer an Internet survey for which you would qualify as a respondent. How would you evaluate this survey based on the discussion in this chapter?
4. Locate an Internet survey and examine the content of the questionnaire carefully. What are relative advantages and disadvantages of administering the same survey using CATI or mall intercept interviewing?
5. Design an e-mail survey to measure students' attitudes toward credit cards. E-mail the survey to 10 students. Summarize, in a qualitative way, the responses received. Are student attitudes toward credit cards positive or negative?

Group Discussion

1. As a small group, discuss the ethical issues involved in disguised observation. How can such issues be addressed?
2. "With advances in technology, observation methods are likely to become popular." Discuss this statement as a small group.

CHAPTER

8

Causal Research Design: Experimentation

"Marketing research—and marketing—would be much better off if researchers conducted more experiments. Well-done experiments are and have always been the 'gold standard' of evidence in science."

LARRY GIBSON, *Senior Associate, Eric Marder and Associates, Minneapolis, MN*

OPENING QUESTIONS

1. How is the concept of causality defined in marketing research, and how do we distinguish between the ordinary meaning and the scientific meaning of causality?
2. What are the conditions for causality? Can a causal relationship be demonstrated conclusively?
3. How do we define and differentiate the two types of validity (internal and external)?
4. What are the various types of experimental designs, and what are the differences among preexperimental, true experimental, quasi-experimental, and statistical designs?
5. How can we compare and contrast the use of laboratory versus field experimentation and experimental versus nonexperimental designs in marketing research?
6. What is test marketing, and how does it involve experimentation?
7. Why are the internal and external validity of field experiments conducted overseas generally lower than in the United States?
8. How does technology facilitate causal research?
9. What ethical issues are involved in conducting causal research, and how can debriefing address some of these issues?

Muzak: An Uncommon Remedy for the Common Cold

Once referred to as "background music," Muzak is now referred to as "audio architecture" in the business world. As of 2005, Muzak provided products to more than 300,000 businesses, and more than 100 million people a day heard its harmonic convergences. The company offered music, sound systems, videos, and messaging at 200 sales and service locations across the United States.

Muzak has now moved into audio marketing in supermarkets. In a time of increasing competition, more store advertising at the point of purchase may be just what is needed. Research shows that few customers come to the grocery store with a specific brand in mind. Most consumers know what items they need and choose brands or sizes when they reach the store. So audio advertising, such as Muzak provides, seems to hold promise.

An experiment was designed to test the effectiveness of Muzak advertising. Twenty randomly selected supermarkets were assigned to one of two groups, each group containing 10 supermarkets. One group of supermarkets, randomly selected, was the experimental group and the other the control group. Muzak ads for selected products were run in the experimental group supermarkets for a period of 10 weeks. These ads were informational, telling consumers of the benefits of the advertised products. The price and other factors (e.g., shelf space) affecting the sale of these items were kept the same in both the experimental and control group stores. The sales of the advertised products were monitored for both the experimental and control groups. The results showed an increase in the sales of advertised items, with cold/allergy/sinus-relief products recording the highest increase of 29.8 percent (see chart that follows). Thus, there may be an expanding market for Muzak in the near future.[1] •

Product	Percent of Sales Increase in Experimental Stores
Potato Chips	3.5
Condensed Milk	7.1
Tea Bags	13.7
Cold Cereal	12.2
Juice	14.5
Laundry Detergent	27.4
Toothpaste	28.9
Cold/Allergy/Sinus Relief	29.8

Overview

In Chapter 3, we introduced the two broad categories of conclusive research: causal and descriptive research designs. We discussed descriptive designs in Chapter 7. In this chapter, we will concentrate our discussion on causal research designs. Figure 8.1 briefly explains the focus of the chapter, its relation to the previous ones, and the steps of the marketing research process on which this chapter concentrates. Experimentation is the primary method employed to collect data in causal research designs. The opening vignette illustrates an experiment conducted to determine the effect of in-store Muzak advertising on the sales of selected items.

In this chapter, we will discuss experimentation in detail. We will explain the concept of research validity and threats to that validity. We will present a classification of experimental designs and consider specific designs, along with the relative merits of laboratory versus field experiments. We will consider applications in international marketing research and discuss the impact of technology and ethical issues in experimentation. Figure 8.2 gives an overview of the different topics discussed in this chapter and how they flow from one to the next.

Concept of Causality

A causal inference relates to whether a change in one marketing variable produces a change in another variable. Marketing managers are often faced with decisions in which they attempt to infer causal relationships. For example, will a 10 percent price reduction in Maxwell House coffee result in an increase in sales to a level that will at least cover the revenues lost due to the price reduction? In evaluating this question, the marketing manager is

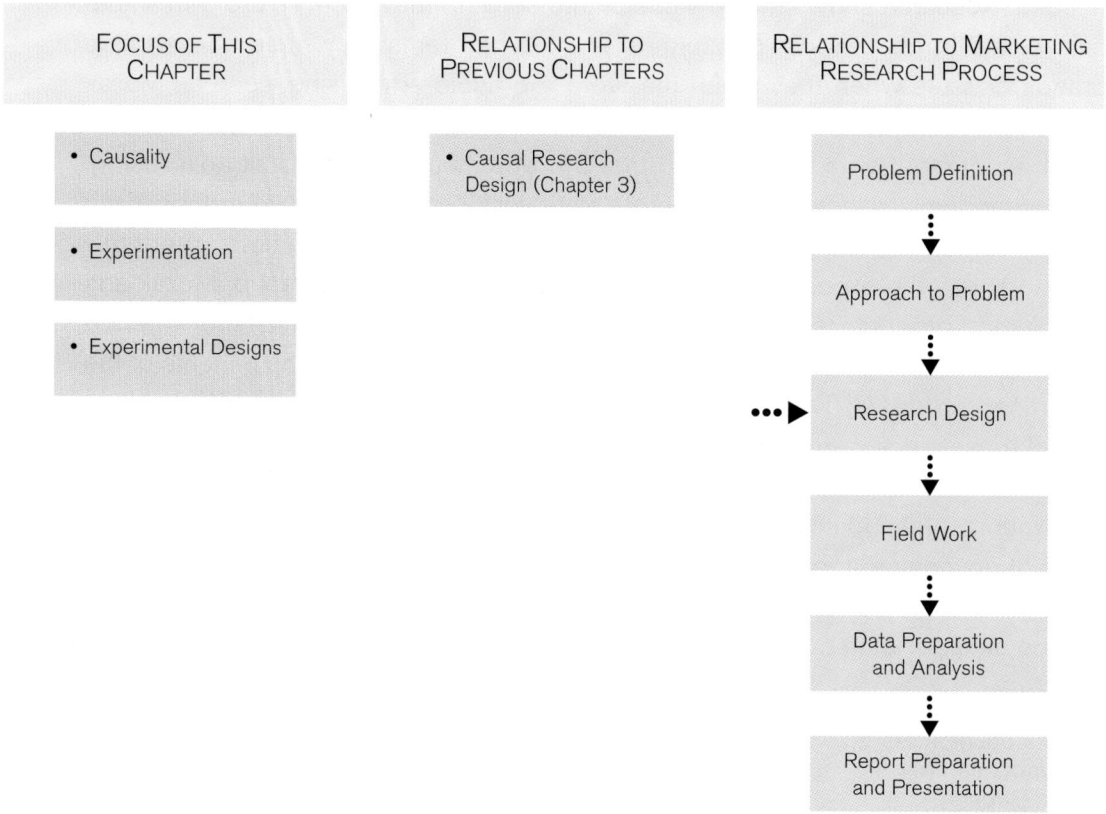

Figure 8.1

Relationship of Experimentation to the Previous Chapters and the Marketing Research Process

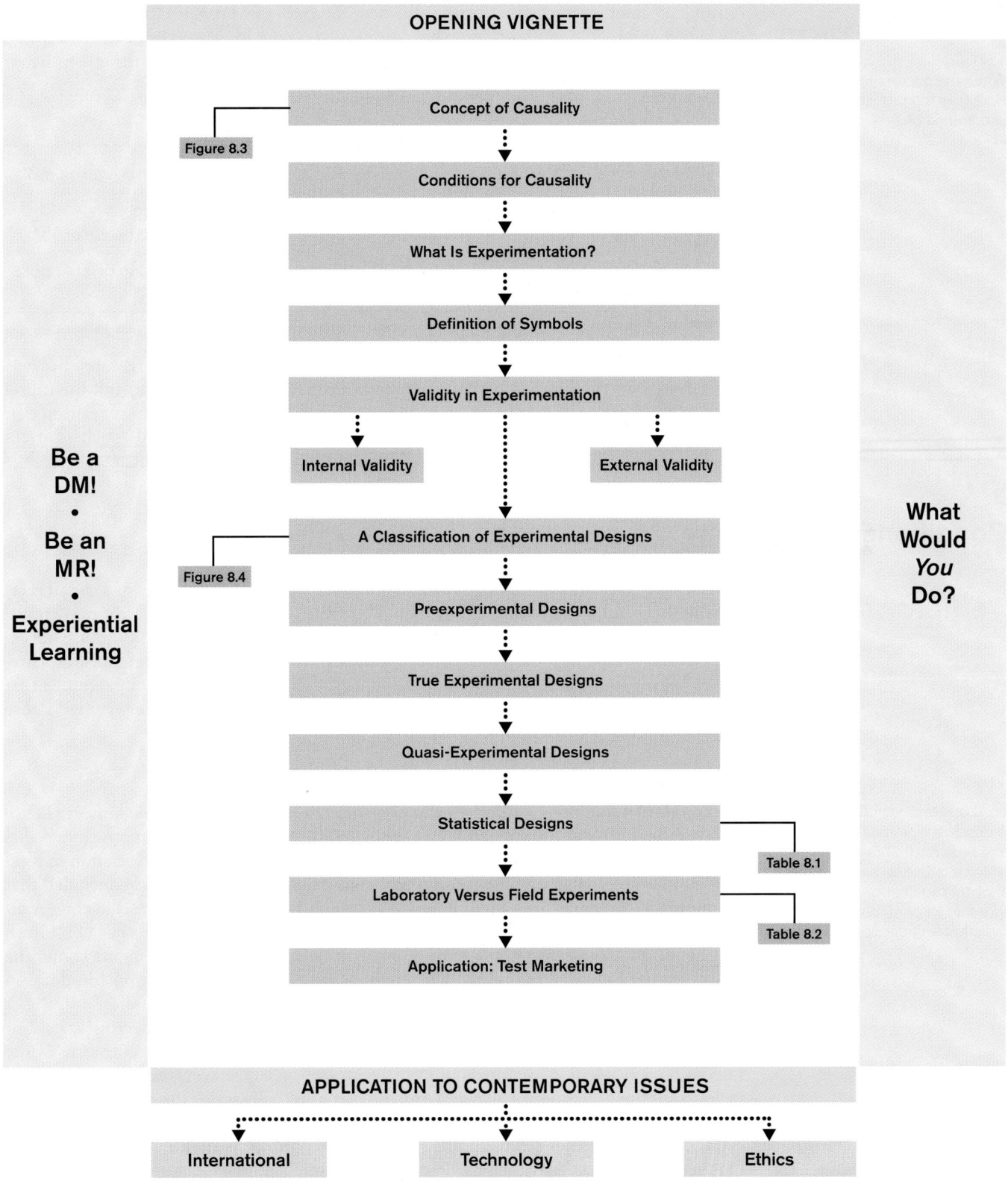

Figure 8.2

Experimentation: An Overview

drawing a causal inference that price influences the sales of Maxwell House coffee. In the opening vignette, the inference was that Muzak advertising leads to (i.e., causes) increased sales. **Causality** means something very different to the average person on the street than it means to a scientist. Take, for example, the statement "*X* causes *Y*."

causality
When the occurrence of X increases the probability of the occurrence of Y.

Ordinary Meaning	Scientific Meaning
X is the only cause of *Y*.	*X* is only one of a number of possible causes of *Y*.
X must always lead to *Y*. (*X* is a deterministic cause of *Y*.)	The occurrence of *X* makes the occurrence of *Y* more probable. (*X* is a probabilistic cause of *Y*.)
It is possible to prove that *X* is a cause of *Y*.	We can never prove that *X* is a cause of *Y*. At best, we can infer that *X* is a cause of *Y*.

The scientific meaning of causality is more appropriate to marketing research because it is sensitive to the limitations that surround our data collection process and the causal inferences we can legitimately draw. In the opening vignette, experimenters realized that in-store advertising was only one cause of sales. There were other causes, such as prices and shelf displays, that affected sales and consequently had to be controlled.

Conditions for Causality

At least three conditions must be satisfied in order to justify the inference of a causal relationship between two variables: (1) concomitant variation, (2) time order of occurrence of variables, and (3) absence of other possible causal factors. These conditions are necessary but not sufficient to demonstrate causality. By that we mean that they must be satisfied to justify drawing a causal inference; however, their presence does not guarantee that we have isolated the true variables responsible for the effects we are observing. These conditions are explained in more detail in the following sections.

Concomitant Variation

concomitant variation
A condition for inferring causality that requires that the extent to which a cause, *X*, and an effect, *Y*, occur together or vary together as predicted by the hypothesis under consideration.

Concomitant variation occurs when the presumed cause (*X*) and presumed effect (*Y*) are both present and both vary in a manner predicted by our hypothesis. Suppose a regional marketing manager for a fast-food outlet wants to identify the causes of variation in food sales across the 20 outlets in her region. After visiting all 20 sites, she has concluded that the monthly outlet performance scores (*X*)—which reflect factors such as average wait time during peak hours, cleanliness, and food quality—directly impact sales (*Y*). Given that hypothesis, outlets that are scoring high on performance measurements should be recording the highest sales levels. Her analysis indicates that this relationship does, in fact, hold. Can she conclude that high performance scores "cause" high sales?

The answer to that question is "no." Many other factors may be impacting sales. For example, the outlet location, the presence of competition, and the concentration of the surrounding residential area may all have an impact on sales, even though they are not included in the outlet performance score. This example illustrates the limitations associated with drawing causal inferences. We cannot conclude that we have identified the cause of fast-food sales from this research. All we can say is that an association exists between performance scores and sales.

Time Order of Occurrence of Variables

Another requirement in determining a causal relationship relates to when the variables occur, that is, the occurrence in time of the presumed cause relative to the presumed effect. For one variable to hypothetically cause another, it must precede or occur simultaneously with the effect. This is referred to as the time order of variables.

Although time order of variables seems like an intuitively obvious requirement, it is not always easy to determine time order in a marketing situation. For example, customers who shop frequently in a department store are more likely to have the charge card for that store. Also, customers who have a department store's charge card are likely to shop there frequently. The time order of these variables—charge card ownership and frequent shopping—is not obvious. Did charge card ownership precede frequent shopping or did frequent shopping precede charge card ownership? An understanding of the underlying phenomena associated with department store shopping may be necessary to accurately identify time order.

Absence of Other Possible Causal Factors

As can be seen in the above examples, both time order and concurrent variation conditions may be satisfied, yet we may not have identified the relevant cause/effect relationship. The presence of additional or extraneous variables that impact the effect (i.e., dependent) variable must be controlled in order to draw causal inferences. In-store service may be a cause of sales if we can be sure that changes in all other factors that affect sales—such as pricing, advertising, level of distribution, product quality, competition, and so on—were held constant or otherwise controlled. Ruling out other possible causal factors is seldom an easy task. The POP Buys example illustrates the difficulty of establishing a causal relationship. If, as the POP Buys example indicates, it is difficult to establish cause/effect relationships, what is the role of evidence obtained in experimentation?

Role of Evidence

The combination of evidence of causality in the form of concomitant variation, time order of occurrence of variables, and elimination of other possible causal factors does not guarantee that a causal relationship exists. However, an accumulation of consistent evidence increases our confidence that a causal relationship exists. Controlled experiments can provide strong evidence of all three conditions.

BE a DM!

As the head of the Federal Trade Commission, what are your concerns about the increased availability of information on the Internet?

BE an MR!

Search the Internet using a search engine as well as your library's online databases to obtain information on Internet usage by consumers.

What conditions are necessary for you to conclude that consumer use is causing greater availability of information on the Internet?

RESEARCH IN ACTION

POP Buys

Recent statistical data show that consumers make as much as 80 percent of their buying decisions at the point of purchase (POP). Point-of-purchase buying decisions have increased concurrently with increased advertising efforts in stores. These include radio advertisements as well as ads on shopping carts, floor space, grocery bags, ceiling signs, and shelf displays. It is difficult to separate the cause from the effect of POP advertising and POP buying. It is possible that these variables may be both causes and effects in this relationship. In other words, there is more POP advertising because there is more POP buying, and there is more POP buying because there is more POP advertising.[2]

What Is Experimentation?

Experimentation is the research technique used in causal research, which is a form of conclusive research (Figure 8.3). It is the primary method for establishing cause-and-effect relationships in marketing (see Chapter 3). Experiments can be described in terms of independent, dependent, and extraneous variables, test units, and random assignment to experimental and control groups. To conduct an **experiment**, the researcher manipulates and controls one or more independent variables and then observes the effects that those manipulated variables have on the dependent variables, while controlling the influence of outside or extraneous variables. In this section, we define these concepts and illustrate them using the example in the opening vignette.

experiment
The process of manipulating one or more independent variables and measuring their effect on one or more dependent variables, while controlling for the extraneous variables.

Independent Variables

Independent variables are variables or alternatives that are manipulated (i.e., the researcher changes their levels) and whose effects are measured and compared. These variables, also known as treatments, may include price levels, package designs, and advertising themes. In the opening vignette, the independent variable was Muzak advertising, and the treatments consisted of Muzak advertising versus no advertising.

independent variables
Variables that are manipulated by the researcher and whose effects are measured and compared.

Test Units

Test units are individuals, organizations, or other entities whose response to the independent variables or treatments is being examined. Test units may include consumers, stores, or geographic areas. The test units were supermarkets in the opening vignette.

test units
Individuals, organizations, or other entities whose response to independent variables or treatments is being studied.

Dependent Variables

Dependent variables are the variables that measure the effect of the independent variables on the test units. These variables may include sales, profits, and market shares. The dependent variables, in the opening vignette, were the sales of specific products.

dependent variables
Variables that measure the effect of the independent variables on the test units.

Extraneous Variables

Extraneous variables are all variables other than the independent variables that affect the response of the test units. These variables can confound the dependent variable measures in a way that weakens or invalidates the results of the experiment. Extraneous variables include store size, store location, and competitive effort. In the Muzak vignette, the extraneous variables would be other variables—such as price, amount of shelf space, and so on—that would affect the sales of the selected products.

extraneous variables
Variables, other than the independent variables, that influence the response of the test units.

Figure 8.3
Experimentation as Conclusive Research

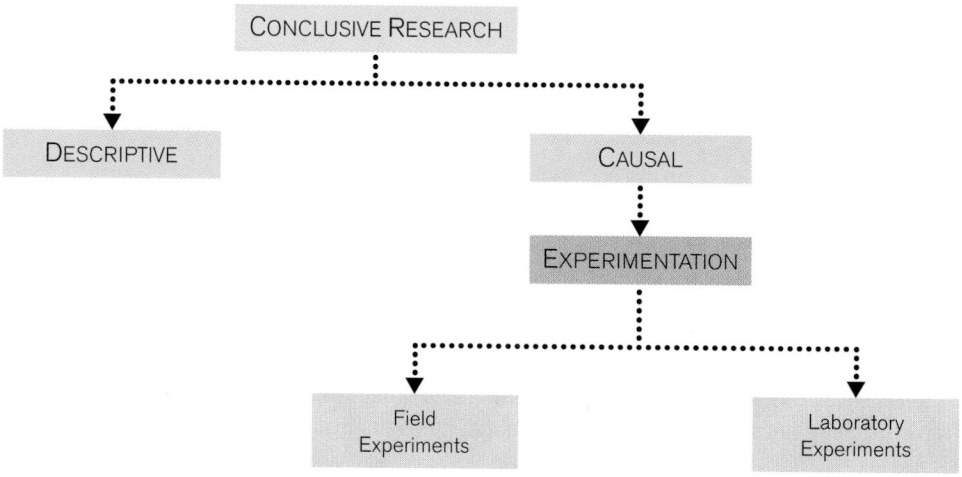

Random Assignment to Experimental and Control Groups

Random assignment involves randomly assigning test units to the experimental and control groups and is one of the most common techniques used to control for the effect of extraneous variables on the dependent variable. Random assignment to experimental and control groups attempts to minimize the influence of extraneous factors such as age, income, or brand preference by spreading them equally across the groups under study.

When an experiment is being conducted, at least one group will be exposed to the manipulated independent variable. This is called the **experimental group**. The results of this experimental group may be compared to another experimental group at a differing level of manipulation or to a control group. The **control group** is not exposed to the independent-variable manipulation. It provides a point of comparison when examining the effects of these manipulations on the dependent variable. In the opening vignette, the supermarket stores were randomly assigned to the two groups. One of the groups was randomly chosen to be the experimental group (that was exposed to Muzak advertising), and the other served as the control group (that received no advertising).

random assignment
Involves randomly assigning test units to the experimental and control groups and is one of the most common techniques used to control for the effect of extraneous variables on the dependent variable.

experimental group
The group exposed to the manipulated independent variable.

control group
This group is not exposed to the independent variable manipulation. It provides a point of comparison when examining the effects of these manipulations on the dependent variable.

Experimental Design

An **experimental design** is a set of procedures specifying (1) the test units and how these units are to be divided into homogeneous subsamples, (2) what independent variables or treatments are to be manipulated, (3) what dependent variables are to be measured, and (4) how the extraneous variables are to be controlled.

In the Muzak vignette, the test units were stores that were randomly assigned to two groups. The independent variable to be manipulated was Muzak advertising versus no advertising, and the dependent variables were the sales of specific products. Extraneous variables such as price and shelf space were kept at the same levels in both the experimental and control group supermarkets by exercising managerial control.

As a further illustration of these definitions, consider the following example.

experimental design
The set of experimental procedures specifying (1) the test units and sampling procedures, (2) independent variables, (3) dependent variables, and (4) how to control the extraneous variables.

RESEARCH IN ACTION

Taking Coupons at Face Value

An experiment was conducted to test the effects of coupon value on redemption. Personal interviews were conducted in New York with 280 shoppers who were entering or leaving a supermarket. Two levels of the independent variable (coupon value) were used, one offering 15¢ off and the other 50¢ off. Shoppers were randomly assigned to these two coupon-value levels.

Brand usage was presumed to be an extraneous variable. Four brands—Tide detergent, Kellogg's Corn Flakes, Aim toothpaste, and Joy liquid dishwashing detergent—were used. The respondents answered questions about which brands they used so that the effect of this extraneous variable could be controlled during analysis. Respondents were also asked how likely they were to cash coupons of the given face value the next time they shopped. An interesting finding was that higher face-value coupons produced a greater likelihood of redemption among infrequent or nonbuyers of the promoted brand but had little effect on regular buyers.[3]

In the preceding experiment, the independent variable that was manipulated was the value of the coupon (15¢ versus 50¢). The dependent variable was the likelihood of cashing the coupon. The extraneous variable that was controlled was brand usage. The experimental design required the random assignment of shoppers to two experimental groups. A control group was not used in this design.

Definition of Symbols

To help in our discussion of extraneous variables and specific experimental designs, we will use a set of symbols commonly used in marketing research.

X = the exposure of a group to an independent variable, treatment, or event, the effects of which are to be determined

O = the process of observation or measurement of the dependent variable on the test units or group of units

R = the random assignment of test units or groups to separate treatments

In addition, the following conventions are adopted:

- Movement from left to right indicates movement through time.
- Horizontal alignment of symbols implies that those symbols refer to a specific treatment group.
- Vertical alignment of symbols implies that those symbols refer to activities or events that occur simultaneously.

For example, the symbolic arrangement

$$X \quad O_1 \quad O_2$$

means that a given group of test units was exposed to the treatment variable (X), and the response was measured at two different points in time O_1 and O_2.

Likewise, the symbolic arrangement

$$\begin{array}{lll} R & X_1 & O_1 \\ R & X_2 & O_2 \end{array}$$

means that two groups of test units were randomly assigned (R) to two different treatment groups at the same time (X_1 and X_2), and the dependent variable was measured in the two groups simultaneously (O_1 and O_2).

Validity in Experimentation

In conducting an experiment, a researcher has two goals. The first is to draw valid conclusions about the effect of the independent variables on the dependent variables. This is referred to as internal validity. The second goal is to make valid generalizations from the specific experimental environment to a larger population. This goal is satisfied when external validity is achieved.

Internal Validity

internal validity
A measure of accuracy of an experiment. It measures if the manipulation of the independent variables, or treatments, actually caused the effects on the dependent variable(s).

Internal validity refers to whether the manipulation of the independent variables or treatments actually caused the observed effects on the dependent variables. Internal validity is threatened when the influences of extraneous variables are mixed with the independent variables. Without proper control of the extraneous variables, the researcher is unable to isolate the effect of the independent variable and thus cannot establish internal validity. In the opening vignette, to claim internal validity the researcher had to show that the increase in sales of the products in the experimental group supermarkets was in fact due to (i.e., caused by) Muzak advertising. Thus, the researcher had to show that price and other extraneous variables (e.g., shelf space) affecting the sale of these products were kept the same in both the experimental and control group stores.

External Validity

external validity
A determination of whether the cause/effect relationships found in the experiment can be generalized.

External validity refers to whether the cause/effect relationships found in the experiment remain the same when replicated in a larger population. In other words, can the results be generalized beyond the experimental situation? If so, to what populations, settings, times, independent variables, and dependent variables can the results be projected? In the opening vignette, to claim external validity the researcher must show that the sample of 20 supermarkets was representative, no peculiar conditions were encountered, and the results are generalizable to all supermarkets.

Threats to external validity arise when the experiment is conducted in an unrealistic manner, limiting the ability to generalize. This occurs when the experimental conditions do not account for factors likely to be encountered in the real world. Experiments conducted in a laboratory environment are more likely to lack external validity than field experiments. This is because laboratory experiments are conducted in artificial, highly controlled environments.

Market researchers often have to make decisions to trade off one form of validity in order to gain another. However, internal validity must be protected in order to produce results that are meaningful enough to generalize. Extraneous variables threaten both the internal and external validity.

Extraneous Variables

The need to control extraneous variables in order to establish internal and external validity has already been discussed. In this section we classify extraneous variables in the following categories: history, maturation, testing, instrumentation, statistical regression, selection bias, and mortality.

History

Contrary to what the name implies, **history** (*H*) does not refer to the occurrence of events before the experiment. Rather, history refers to specific events that are external to the experiment but occur at the same time as the experiment. For example, general economic conditions may decline during the experiment, thereby contaminating the post-treatment observation. The longer the time interval between observations, the greater the possibility that history will confound an experiment.

history
Specific events that are external to the experiment but occur at the same time as the experiment.

Maturation

Maturation (*MA*) is similar to history except that it refers to changes in the test units themselves. These changes are not caused by the impact of independent variables or treatments but occur with the passage of time. In an experiment involving people, maturation takes place as people become older, more experienced, tired, bored, or uninterested. Tracking and market studies that span several months are vulnerable to maturation, since it is difficult to know how respondents are changing over time.

maturation
An extraneous variable attributable to changes in the test units themselves that occur with the passage of time.

Testing Effects

Testing effects are caused by the process of experimentation. Typically, these are the effects on the experiment of taking a measure on the dependent variable before and after the presentation of the treatment. For example, the respondents try to maintain consistency between their pre- and post-treatment attitudes. As a result of the testing effect, post-treatment attitudes may be influenced more by pretreatment attitudes than by the treatment itself.

testing effects
The influence on respondent behavior of taking a measure on the dependent variable before and after the presentation of the treatment.

Instrumentation

Instrumentation (*I*) refers to changes in the measuring instrument, in the observers, or in the scores themselves. Sometimes, measuring instruments are modified during the course of an experiment. Consider an experiment in which dollar sales are being measured before and after exposure to an in-store display (treatment). If there is a nonexperimental price change between measurements, this results in a change in instrumentation because dollar sales will be measured using different unit prices. Instrumentation effects

instrumentation
An extraneous variable involving changes in the measuring instrument, in the observers, or scores themselves.

are likely when interviewers make pre- and post-treatment measurements. The effectiveness of interviewers can differ at different times.

Statistical Regression

statistical regression
An extraneous variable that occurs when test units with extreme scores move closer to the average score during the course of the experiment.

Statistical regression (*SR*) effects occur when test units with extreme scores move closer to the average score during the course of the experiment. In the advertising experiment, suppose that some respondents had either very favorable or very unfavorable attitudes. On post-treatment measurement, their attitudes might have moved toward the average. People's attitudes change continuously. Those with extreme attitudes have more room for change, so variation is more likely. This has a confounding effect on the experimental results, because the observed effect (change in attitude) may be attributable to statistical regression rather than to the treatment (test commercial).

Selection Bias

selection bias
An extraneous variable attributable to the improper assignment of test units to treatment conditions.

Selection bias (*SB*) refers to the improper assignment of test units to treatment conditions. This bias occurs when selection or assignment of test units results in treatment groups that differ on the dependent variable before the exposure to the treatment condition. If test units self-select their own groups or are assigned to groups on the basis of the researchers' judgment, selection bias is possible. For example, consider a merchandising experiment in which two different merchandising displays (old and new) are assigned to different department stores. The stores in the two groups may not be equivalent to begin with. They may vary with respect to a key characteristic, such as store size. Store size is likely to affect sales regardless of which merchandising display was assigned to a store.

Mortality

mortality
An extraneous variable attributable to the loss of test units while the experiment is in progress.

Mortality (*MO*) refers to the loss of test units while the experiment is in progress. This happens for many reasons, such as test units refusing to continue in the experiment. Mortality confounds results because it is difficult to determine if the lost test units would respond to the treatments in the same manner as those that remain. Consider again the merchandising display experiment. Suppose that during the course of the experiment three stores in the new display treatment condition drop out. The researcher could not determine whether the average sales for the new display stores would have been higher or lower if these three stores had continued in the experiment.

Controlling Extraneous Variables

Extraneous variables represent alternative explanations of experimental results. They pose a serious threat to the internal and external validity of an experiment. Unless they are controlled, they affect the dependent variable and thus confound the results. For this reason, they are also called confounding variables. There are four ways of controlling extraneous variables: randomization, matching, statistical control, and design control.

Randomization

randomization
One method of controlling extraneous variables that involves randomly assigning test units to experimental groups by using random numbers. Treatment conditions are also randomly assigned to experimental groups.

Randomization refers to the random assignment of test units to experimental groups by using random numbers. Treatment conditions are also randomly assigned to experimental groups. For example, respondents are randomly assigned to one of three experimental groups. One of the three versions of a test commercial, selected at random, is administered to each group. As a result of random assignment, extraneous factors can be represented equally in each treatment condition. It is possible to check whether randomization has been effective by measuring the possible extraneous variables and comparing them across the experimental groups. Therefore, randomization is the preferred method for controlling extraneous variables.

Matching

Matching involves comparing test units on a set of key background variables before assigning them to the treatment conditions. In the merchandising display experiment, stores could be matched on the basis of annual sales, size, or location. Then one store from each matched pair would be assigned to each experimental group. Matching has two drawbacks. First, test units can be matched on only a few characteristics, so the test units may be similar on the variables selected but unequal on others. Second, if the matched characteristics are irrelevant to the dependent variable, then the matching effort has been futile.

matching
One method of controlling extraneous variables that involves matching test units on a set of key background variables before assigning them to the treatment conditions.

Statistical and Design Control

Statistical control involves measuring the extraneous variables and adjusting for their effects through statistical analysis. **Design control** involves the use of experiments designed to control specific extraneous variables. A classification of experimental designs is described in the next section.

statistical control
One method of controlling extraneous variables by measuring the extraneous variables and adjusting for their effects through statistical methods.

design control
One method of controlling extraneous variables that involves using specific experimental designs.

A Classification of Experimental Designs

There are four broad categories of experimental designs: preexperimental, true experimental, quasi-experimental, and statistical designs (Figure 8.4). **Preexperimental designs** do not use randomization to control for extraneous factors. Thus, they suffer from many threats to internal and external validity. However, with a proper note of their limitations, they can add value when used in an exploratory fashion. Three examples of this design are the one-shot case study, the one-group pretest/posttest design, and the static group. These designs, along with the others that follow, are discussed in detail later.

preexperimental designs
Designs that do not control for extraneous factors by randomization.

In **true experimental designs,** the researcher can randomly assign subjects and experimental groups. Therefore, these designs provide a larger degree of control over extraneous variables. Included in this category are the pretest/posttest control group design and the posttest-only control group design.

true experimental designs
Experimental designs distinguished by the fact that the researcher can randomly assign test units to experimental groups and also randomly assign treatments to experimental groups.

Quasi-experimental designs result when the researcher is unable to fully manipulate the independent variables or treatments but can still apply part of the apparatus of true experimentation. These designs are typically employed in natural environments, enabling some degree of experimental control in a natural setting. Two such designs are time series and multiple time series designs.

quasi-experimental designs
Designs that apply part of the procedures of true experimentation, while lacking full experimental control.

A **statistical design** is a series of basic experiments that allows for statistical control and analysis of external variables. Statistical designs are classified on the basis of their characteristics and use. The important statistical designs include factorial designs.

statistical design
Design that allows for the statistical control and analysis of external variables.

We will illustrate the various experimental designs in the context of measuring the effectiveness of PepsiCo advertising. Pepsi makes heavy use of celebrities in its advertising. To capture the teenage market, Pepsi ads highlighted superstars Michael Jackson and

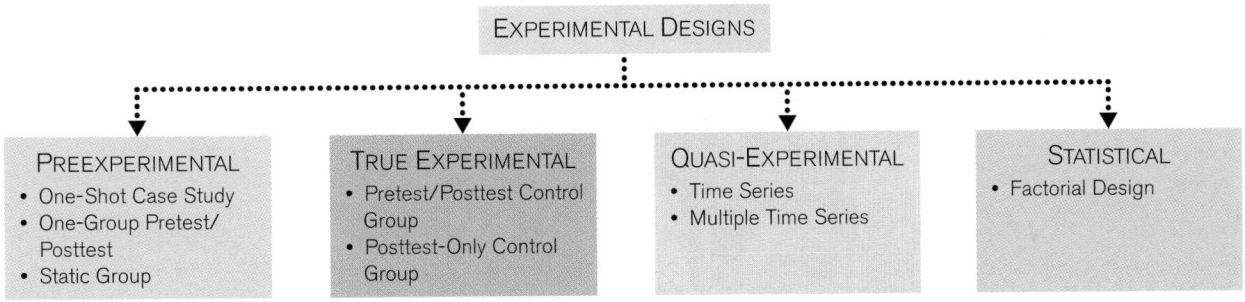

Figure 8.4
A Classification of Experimental Designs

Lionel Richie with the theme "Choice of a New Generation." Other "New Generation" stars featured in Pepsi ads included Don Johnson (of *Miami Vice* fame), Michael J. Fox (star of *Back to the Future)*, and comedian Billy Crystal. The "You've Got the Right One Baby, Uh-Huh!" campaign for Diet Pepsi featured the late Ray Charles. Pepsi struck the right chord when it launched the much-lauded "Joy of Pepsi" campaign, featuring appearances by dimpled Hallie Eisenberg and the comedian television show host Tom Green. Other stars Pepsi has featured include Beyonce Knowles, lead singer of pop group Destiny's Child; the Osbourne's, reality TV's first family; Shakira; and Enrique Iglesias.

Should Pepsi continue to feature celebrities in its advertising? Is this advertising effective? Experimental research that measures advertising effectiveness can provide useful information. We begin our discussion with the preexperimental designs.

Preexperimental Designs

Preexperimental designs are characterized by an absence of randomization. We will describe three specific designs: the one-shot case study, the one-group pretest/posttest design, and the static group.

One-Shot Case Study

one-shot case study
A preexperimental design in which a single group of test units is exposed to a treatment *X*, and then a single measurement on the dependent variable is taken.

Also known as the after-only design, the **one-shot case study** may be symbolically represented as

$$X \quad O_1$$

A single group of subjects is exposed to a treatment (X), and then a single measurement on the dependent variable is taken (O_1). This type of design is constructed using a nonrandom sampling process in which the subjects are self-selected or selected arbitrarily by the researcher. Without randomization, the observed dependent variables are subject to the influences of several extraneous variables.

The effectiveness of Pepsi advertising that makes use of celebrities can be assessed by using appropriate experimental designs.

RESEARCH IN ACTION

One Shot at Pepsi Advertising

To assess the effectiveness of Pepsi advertising featuring celebrities, telephone interviews would be conducted with respondents who report watching the particular TV program on which the commercial was aired the previous night (*X*). The dependent variables (Os) are unaided and aided recall, and attitudes toward the advertisement, the brand, and the celebrity. First, unaided recall would be measured by asking the respondents whether they recall seeing a commercial for a soft drink. If they recall the Pepsi commercial, details about commercial content and execution would be solicited. Respondents who do not recall the test commercial would be asked if they saw a Pepsi commercial (aided recall). For those who have an unaided or aided recall of the commercial, attitudes toward the commercial, the brand advertised, and the celebrity featured would be measured. The results of these experimental measures can be compared with normal scores for these types of questions in order to assess the effectiveness of the advertising and the celebrity featured.

Additionally, the design lacks a control group. Without a control group, there is no point of comparison for the results. Due to lack of randomization and the absence of a control group, this design is clearly weak in terms of internal validity. There is no control for history, maturation, selection, and mortality. For these reasons, the one-shot case study is more appropriate for exploratory rather than conclusive research.

One-Group Pretest/Posttest Design

The **one-group pretest/posttest design** may be symbolized as

$$O_1 \quad X \quad O_2$$

In this design, a group of subjects is measured once before the experimental treatment (O_1) and once after (O_2). Again, there is no control group for comparison. The treatment effect is computed as $O_2 - O_1$. Although this design is considered better than a case study, the validity of conclusions is questionable since extraneous variables are largely uncontrolled due to lack of randomization and lack of a control group. History, maturation, testing, instrumentation, selection, mortality, and regression could possibly be present. The following Can Pepsi Perform in a Theater? example shows how this design is used.

one-group pretest/posttest design
A preexperimental design in which a group of test units is measured twice.

Static Group Design

The **static group** is a two-group experimental design in which one of the groups acts as a control group (CG). Only one group, the experimental group (EG), receives the experimental treatment. The subjects are not assigned randomly, and measurements are made on both groups following the treatment (posttest). This design is expressed symbolically as

$$\begin{array}{lll} \text{EG:} & X & O_1 \\ \text{CG:} & & O_2 \end{array}$$

static group
A preexperimental design in which there are two groups: the experimental group (EG), which is exposed to the treatment, and the control group (CG). Measurements on both groups are made only after the treatment, and test units are not assigned at random.

RESEARCH IN ACTION

Can Pepsi Perform in a Theater?

Firms such as NOP World (www.nopworld.com) commonly use the one-group pretest/posttest design to measure the effectiveness of test commercials. Respondents are recruited to central theater locations in various test cities. The respondents are interviewed, and their attitudes toward Pepsi advertising, brand, and celebrity (O_1) are measured. Then they watch a TV program containing the Pepsi commercial (*X*) and other filler commercials. After viewing the TV program, the respondents are again interviewed regarding their attitudes toward Pepsi advertising, brand, and celebrity (O_2). The effectiveness of the test commercial is determined by the difference between O_2 and O_1.

RESEARCH IN ACTION

Is Pepsi Advertising Static?

A static group comparison to measure the effectiveness of a Pepsi commercial would be conducted as follows. Two groups of respondents would be recruited on the basis of convenience. Only the experimental group would be exposed to the TV program that contains the Pepsi commercial (X). Attitudes toward Pepsi advertising, brand, and celebrity would then be measured in both the experimental (O_1) and the control group (O_2). The effectiveness of the Pepsi commercial would be measured as the difference between the test and control group ($O_1 - O_2$).

The treatment effect would be measured as the difference between the control and experimental groups ($O_1 - O_2$). The lack of randomization leaves the experiment open to some extraneous effects. The two groups may differ before the treatment, leading to selection bias. Mortality effects may be present, as more test units may withdraw from the experimental group than the control group. This design is illustrated by the Is Pepsi Advertising Static? example.

In practice, the control group is often defined as the group receiving the current level of marketing activity, rather than as a group that receives no treatment at all. In many cases, it is impossible to reduce marketing input (e.g., price) to zero.

BE an MR!

Visit Fox News' Web site (www.foxnews.com) and search the Internet using a search engine as well as your library's online databases to obtain information on consumers' preferences for network news channels.

Fox News wants to determine which one of three new formats it should implement. Would you recommend a preexperimental design? If yes, which one?

BE a DM!

As the marketing manager of Fox News, how would you use information on consumers' preferences for network news channels to formulate marketing strategies that would increase your audience and market share?

True Experimental Designs

True experimental designs are differentiated from preexperimental designs by the fact that subjects are randomly assigned to groups. Treatment conditions are also randomly assigned to groups. For example, respondents are randomly assigned to one of three experimental groups. One of the three versions of a test commercial, selected at random, is administered to each group. As a result of random assignment, extraneous factors can be represented equally in each group or treatment condition. Randomization is the preferred procedure for ensuring the prior equality of experimental groups. However, randomization may not be effective when the sample size is small because it merely produces groups that are equal on average. It is possible, though, to check whether randomization has been effective by measuring the possible extraneous variables and comparing them across the experimental groups.

True experimental designs include the pretest/posttest control group design and the posttest-only control group design.

pretest/posttest control group design
A true experimental design in which the experimental group is exposed to the treatment but the control group is not. Pretest and posttest measures are taken on both groups. Test units are randomly assigned.

Pretest/Posttest Control Group Design

In the **pretest/posttest control group design**, subjects are randomly assigned to either the experimental or the control group. A pretreatment measure is taken on each group. Thus, each group is measured prior to administering the treatment to the experimental group. This design is symbolized as

RESEARCH IN ACTION

Pepsi Pre- and Postmortem

An experiment for measuring the effectiveness of Pepsi's advertising using a pretest/posttest control group design would be designed as follows. A sample of respondents would be distributed randomly, half to the experimental group and half to the control group. A pretest questionnaire would be administered to the respondents in both groups to obtain a measurement on attitudes toward Pepsi advertising, brand, and celebrity. Only the respondents in the experimental group would be exposed to the TV program containing the Pepsi commercial. Then, a questionnaire would be administered to respondents in both groups to obtain posttest measures on attitudes toward Pepsi advertising, brand, and celebrity.

EG:	R	O_1	X	O_2
CG:	R	O_3		O_4

The treatment effect (TE) is measured as

$$(O_2 - O_1) - (O_4 - O_3)$$

The use of a control group and randomization in this design controls for most extraneous variables. The extraneous effects are presumed to be equally represented in both the control and experimental groups. The difference between the control and experimental groups is thought to reflect only the treatment. With the use of a pretest measure in this design, the posttest measurement is susceptible to **interactive testing effects**, which means that a prior measurement affects the test unit's response to the independent variable.

interactive testing effects
Effects in which a prior measurement affects the test unit's response to the independent variable.

As this example shows, the pretest/posttest control group design involves two groups and two measurements on each group. A simpler design is the posttest-only control group design.

Posttest-Only Control Group Design

The **posttest-only control group design** does not involve any premeasurement. It may be symbolized as

posttest-only control group design
A true experimental design in which the experimental group is exposed to the treatment but the control group is not and no pretest measure is taken. Test units are randomly assigned.

EG:	R	X	O_1
CG:	R		O_2

The treatment effect is the difference between the experimental and control group measurements.

$$\text{TE} = O_1 - O_2$$

The simplicity of this design offers time, cost, and sample-size advantages. For these reasons, it is the most popular experimental design in marketing research. However, this design is not without limitations. Although randomization is used to equalize groups, without a pretest, there is no way to verify group similarity. Selection bias and mortality may be present. Without a pretest, researchers are also unable to examine changes in individual subjects over the course of the study. Note that, except for premeasurement, the implementation of this design is very similar to that of the pretest/posttest control group design. The opening vignette provided an application. The supermarket stores were randomly assigned to the experimental group and the control group. No premeasurements were taken. Only the stores in the experimental group were exposed to Muzak advertising. Measurements on the sales of advertised items were obtained in the experimental group (O_1) and control group (O_2) stores. The increase in sales due to Muzak advertising was determined as ($O_1 - O_2$).

EXPERIENTIAL LEARNING

Canon

Canon wants to determine consumers' price sensitivity for its new advanced digital camera and hires you as a consultant.

1. Visit BestBuys Web site (www.bestbuys.com) and identify the price ranges of the digital cameras by Canon and other brands.
2. Search the Internet using a search engine as well as your library's online databases to obtain information on consumers' price sensitivity for digital cameras.
3. Canon wants to determine consumers' price sensitivity for its new advanced digital camera. Design an appropriate experiment. Would you recommend a true experimental design? If yes, which one?
4. As the marketing manager of Canon cameras, how would you use information on consumers' price sensitivity for digital cameras to formulate pricing strategies that would increase your market share?

Quasi-Experimental Designs

Quasi-experimental designs are appropriate when researchers are faced with situations where they are unable to randomize or control the scheduling of experimental treatments. The experimenters may, however, be able to control when and on whom experimental measurements are taken. Quasi-experimental designs are faster and less expensive than other experimental designs and, in some natural research settings, may be the only avenue open for data collection. However, because full experimental control is lacking, researchers must take into account the specific variables that are not controlled. Popular forms of quasi-experimental designs are time series and multiple time series designs.

Time Series Design

time series design
A quasi-experimental design that involves periodic measurements on the dependent variable for a group of test units. Then, the treatment is administered by the researcher or occurs naturally. After the treatment, periodic measurements are continued in order to determine the treatment effect.

The **time series design** involves the use of periodic measurements of a group or individuals. At some point during the measurement, an experimental manipulation occurs naturally or is artificially introduced. Additional measurement follows. A time series experiment may be symbolized as

$$O_1\ O_2\ O_3\ O_4\ O_5\ X\ O_6\ O_7\ O_8\ O_9\ O_{10}$$

This is a quasi experiment because of the lack of control the researcher has in terms of randomization of the subjects to treatments. Additionally, the researcher may have no control over the timing of treatment presentation, as well as which subjects are exposed to the treatment. Multiple measurements may create a testing effect, causing a change in measured behavior simply because the respondents know they are being measured. History is not controlled. Nevertheless, time series designs are useful, particularly when evaluating behavior occurring in a natural setting.

multiple time series design
A time series design that includes another group of test units to serve as a control group.

The **multiple time series design** is similar to time series except that it adds a control group that is also repeatedly measured. This group is not subject to the experimental treatment. If the control group is carefully selected, this design can be an improvement over the simple time series experiment.

RESEARCH IN ACTION

Time Will Tell the Effectiveness of Pepsi Advertising: Time Series Design

The effectiveness of a Pepsi commercial (X) may be examined by broadcasting the commercial into a series of markets a predetermined number of times. The test units or respondents are members of a panel. Although the marketer can control the scheduling of the test commercial, it is not possible to control when or if panel members are exposed to it. The marketer will examine panel members' attitudes toward Pepsi advertising, brand, and the celebrity, as well as purchases before, during, and after the campaign to determine whether the test commercial had a short-term effect, a long-term effect, or no effect.

Statistical Designs

Statistical designs consist of a series of basic experiments that allow for statistical control and analysis of external variables. In other words, several basic experiments are conducted simultaneously. Thus, statistical designs are influenced by the same sources of invalidity that affect the basic designs being used. Statistical designs offer the following advantages:

1. The effects of more than one independent variable can be measured.
2. Specific extraneous variables can be statistically controlled.
3. Economical designs can be formulated when each subject is measured more than once.

The most common statistical designs are the factorial designs.

Factorial Design

A **factorial design** is used to measure the effects of two or more independent variables at various levels. It allows for the measurement of interactions between variables. An interaction is said to take place when the simultaneous effect of two or more variables is different from the sum of their separate effects. For example, an individual's favorite drink might be coffee and her favorite temperature level might be cold, but this individual might not prefer cold coffee, leading to an interaction.

factorial design
A statistical experimental design used to measure the effects of two or more independent variables at various levels and to allow for interactions between variables.

A factorial design may also be thought of as a table. In a two-factor design, each level of one variable represents a row, and each level of another variable represents a column. Factorial designs involve a cell for every possible combination of treatment variables, as in the example that follows.

Statistical procedures such as analysis of variance (discussed in Chapter 17) are used to analyze the treatment effects and interactions. The main disadvantage of a factorial design is that the number of treatment combinations increases multiplicatively with an increase in the number of variables or levels. However, this is often not a serious limitation as the researcher can control both the number of variables and the levels.

RESEARCH IN ACTION

Factoring Humor and Information in Pepsi Commercials

Suppose that in the Pepsi case the researcher is interested in examining the effect of humor and the effect of various levels of brand information on advertising effectiveness. Three levels of humor (no humor, medium humor, and high humor) are to be examined. Likewise, brand information is to be manipulated at three levels (low, medium, and high). The resulting table would be three rows (levels of information) by three columns (levels of humor), producing nine possible combinations or cells, as laid out in Table 8.1. The respondents would be randomly assigned to one of the nine cells. Respondents in each cell would receive a specific treatment combination. For example, respondents in the upper left-hand corner cell would view a commercial that had no humor and low brand information. After exposure to a treatment combination, measures would be obtained on attitudes toward Pepsi advertising, brand, and the celebrity from respondents in each cell.

Table 8.1
An Example of a Factorial Design

Amount of Brand Information	Amount of Humor		
	No Humor	Medium Humor	High Humor
Low			
Medium			
High			

EXPERIENTIAL LEARNING

Factorial Experimental Design

A local pizza maker is considering changing its cheese from mozzarella to a provolone/mozzarella cheese mix in a 1:2 ratio, or a 2:1 ratio. This pizza maker is also considering holding the price for pizza the same, increasing price 10 percent, or reducing price 10 percent.

1. Search the Internet using a search engine as well as your library's online databases to obtain information on consumers' preferences for, and consumption of, pizza.
2. Design a marketing experiment that will determine which formulation customers prefer. Your experimental design and format should consist of the following parts:
   a. Independent variables: The things that you changed
   b. Dependent variable(s): What changed as a result of the manipulated variables, such as rating the formulation of cheese and price, or intention to purchase the formulation of cheese and price
   c. Extraneous variables: Everything else that didn't change during the experiment, such as location of the test, the crust, and so forth
   d. Control group: Did you use one? Why or why not?
3. Would it be better to use a laboratory or a field experiment to conduct your research? Why?
4. Use Table 8.1 as a guide. Thirty respondents would be needed in each cell to accurately test your results. If each respondent would be paid $20 for his or her participation, how much would the incentives cost in your experiment?
5. Describe how you would change your experiment to make it less costly. How might these changes affect your results?
6. How can Pizza Hut use this information to increase its market share?

Selecting an Experimental Design

Selecting an experimental design often involves a trade-off in terms of control. Designs that offer the greatest degree of internal validity, typically, are conducted in highly artificial environments that can threaten the generalizability or external validity of the experimental results.

One solution to finding the optimum combination of internal and external validity may be to use differing experimental designs at differing points in the study. For example, designs that offer tight internal validity may be used during the early stages of the research effort. In this way, a more reliable measure of the true treatment effect may be secured. During later stages of the study, more natural settings may be used to enable generalization of results.

In the following section, we will discuss the distinction between laboratory and field experimentation in more detail.

Laboratory Versus Field Experiments

laboratory environment
An artificial setting for experimentation in which the researcher constructs the desired conditions.

demand artifacts
Responses given because the respondents attempt to guess the purpose of the experiment and respond accordingly.

A **laboratory environment** is an artificial one, which affords the greatest amount of control over the crucial factors involved in the study. Advertising testing and test kitchens in central-location theaters are examples of laboratory experiments used in marketing research. Because the environments are highly contrived, questions of external validity are raised. Compared to field experiments, the artificial nature of laboratory environments may cause reactive error in that the respondents react to the situation itself rather than to the independent variable. Also, laboratory environments may cause **demand artifacts**, a phenomenon in which the respondents attempt to guess the purpose of the experiment, modifying their responses accordingly. On the positive side, laboratory experiments do allow for more complex designs than field experiments. Hence, the researcher can control for more factors or variables in the laboratory setting, which increases internal validity.

Table 8.2
Laboratory Versus Field Experiments

Factor	Laboratory	Field
Environment	Artificial	Realistic
Control	High	Low
Reactive error	High	Low
Demand artifacts	High	Low
Internal validity	High	Low
External validity	Low	High
Time	Short	Long
Number of units	Small	Large
Ease of implementation	High	Low
Cost	Low	High

A **field environment** involves measurement of behavior, attitudes, or perceptions in the environment in which they occur. The researcher has much less control over extraneous variables that may impact internal validity. However, if internal validity can be maintained, the results may generalize more easily than those obtained in a laboratory setting. The opening vignette presents an example of a field experiment. The use of scanner panels to conduct field experiments was discussed in Chapter 5. The differences between the two environments are summarized in Table 8.2.

field environment
An experimental location set in actual market conditions.

The Internet can provide a mechanism for controlled experimentation in a laboratory-type environment. Let us continue with the example of testing the effectiveness of Pepsi's advertising. Various Pepsi advertisements or commercials can be posted at various Web sites. Matched or randomly selected respondents can be recruited to visit these sites, with each group visiting only one site. If any pretreatment measures have to be obtained, the respondents answer a questionnaire posted on the site. They are then exposed to a particular Pepsi advertisement or a commercial at that site. After viewing the advertisement or commercial, the respondents answer additional questions providing posttreatment measures. Control groups can be implemented in a similar way. Thus, all types of experimental designs that we have considered can be implemented in this manner.

Internet experiments can also be used to test the effectiveness of alternative Web designs. Visitors are randomly exposed to different Web designs and their purchases are tracked over time while keeping the other marketing variables constant. Thus, the most effective design can be determined and implemented on the company's Web site.

Limitations of Experimentation

Although experimentation is becoming increasingly important in marketing research, it does have limitations: time, cost, and administration of an experiment.

Time

Many types of field experiments become increasingly accurate with time. For example, to observe the long-term effect of a promotional campaign or a new product introduction, purchase behavior must be observed over multiple purchase cycles. The accuracy of such behavioral information tends to increase with the passage of time. This added precision must be weighted against the costs of delaying a product rollout or the launch of a new advertising campaign.

Cost

New product research in field environments can be extremely expensive. It is much more expensive than laboratory experiments, which typically occur on a small scale and use a limited number of subjects. In order to field test a new product, management must consider more than just the direct costs of data collection and analysis. Production must be initiated on a limited scale; point-of-sale promotional campaigns as well as mass advertising must be developed and introduced on a limited basis. Limited distribution channels may also have to be opened. Test market experiments can easily cost millions of dollars.

Administration

Controlling the effects of extraneous variables is an essential aspect of experimental research. Achieving the desired level of control becomes increasingly difficult as the research moves from the laboratory to the field. Field experiments often interfere with a company's ongoing operations, and obtaining cooperation from the retailers, wholesalers, and others involved can be difficult. Also, competitors may deliberately contaminate the results of a field experiment.

Application: Test Marketing

test marketing
An application of a controlled experiment done in limited, but carefully selected, test markets. It involves replicating the planned national marketing program for a product in the test markets.

test markets
A carefully selected part of the marketplace that is particularly suitable for test marketing.

Test marketing is an example of a controlled field experiment conducted in limited but representative parts of a market. The research sites are called **test markets**. In a test market experiment, a national marketing program is replicated on a small scale. The two major objectives of test marketing are (1) to determine market acceptance of the product and (2) to test alternative levels of marketing mix variables. The independent variables being manipulated in such studies typically include elements of the marketing mix. Promotional investments, pricing, product modifications, or distribution elements are all factors that the researcher can manipulate. Observed consumer reactions represent the dependent variables, measured in terms of purchase behavior (i.e., sales) and/or attitudes or reactions to the marketing manipulations being studied.

Designing a standard market test involves deciding what criteria to use for selecting test markets, how many test markets to use, and the duration of the test. Among all of the criteria considered in selecting a test market, representativeness of that market is perhaps the most important. For example, information gathered from a new product test can be used to predict ultimate market acceptance of that product and will govern the go/no-go decision regarding full market rollout. The test market must also be self-contained in terms of media coverage if mass-market advertising is planned to support the test. This prevents wasting promotional dollars. Additionally, the promotion of new products that are available in only a limited area can create negative consumer reaction toward future rollouts.

Test marketing runs the risk of revealing strategies, new product developments, or modified product positioning to the competition. Therefore, the strength of competition in a particular test site is another important consideration. Some commonly used test markets are Charlotte, North Carolina; Fort Wayne, Indiana; Kansas City, Missouri; Knoxville, Tennessee; Rochester, New York; and Sacramento and Stockton, California. These cities are desirable test markets because each is considered to be fairly representative of a large segment of the U.S. population.

In general, the more test markets that can be used, the better. If resources are limited, at least two test markets should be used for each program variation to be tested. However, where external validity is important, at least four test markets should be used. Despite its limitations in terms of time demands, costs, and competitive responses, test marketing can be very beneficial to a product's successful introduction.

Summary Illustration Using the Opening Vignette

Three conditions must be satisfied before causal inferences can be made that *X* is a cause of *Y*: (1) concomitant variation, which implies that *X* and *Y* must vary together in a hypothesized way; (2) time order of occurrence of variables, which implies that *X* must precede or occur simultaneously with *Y*; and (3) elimination of other possible causal factors, which implies that competing explanations must be ruled out. Thus, for Muzak advertising to be a cause of sales, sales of advertised products must be higher in stores with Muzak than in stores without Muzak, Muzak advertising must occur before or simultaneously with an increase in sales (it cannot occur afterwards), and the sales increase must not be attributable to other factors, such as price, shelf space, and so forth.

Experiments provide the most convincing evidence of all three conditions. An experiment is formed when the researcher manipulates one or more independent variables (presence or absence of Muzak advertising) and measures their effect on one or more dependent variables (sales of advertised products), controlling for the effect of extraneous variables (price, shelf space, and so forth).

In designing an experiment, it is important to consider internal and external validity. Internal validity refers to whether the manipulation of the independent variables actually caused the effects on the dependent variables. External validity refers to the generalizability of experimental results. In the opening vignette, to claim internal validity, the researcher must show that Muzak advertising was, in fact, the cause of the increase in sales of the products in the experimental group of supermarkets. Thus, the researcher must show that price and other extraneous variables (e.g., shelf space) affecting the sale of these products were kept the same in both the experimental and control group stores. To claim external validity, the researcher must show that the sample of 20 supermarkets selected was representative, that no peculiar conditions were encountered, and that the results are generalizable to all supermarkets.

Experimental designs may be classified as preexperimental, true experimental, quasi-experimental, and statistical designs. The design selected in the opening vignette was a true experimental design because the supermarkets were randomly selected and assigned to the two groups, and one of the groups was randomly chosen as the experimental group. The specific design adopted was the posttest-only control group. An experiment may be conducted in a laboratory environment or under actual market conditions in a real-life setting, as in the opening vignette.

International Marketing Research

Field experiments pose even greater challenges in international markets than those faced in the United States. The researcher may be faced with market differences in terms of marketing support systems, economics, structural differences, information availability, and technological environment. For example, in many countries, television stations are owned and operated by the government, with severe restrictions on television advertising. This makes field experiments manipulating advertising levels extremely difficult because the researcher may lack the flexibility to vary advertising content and expenditures.

Differential levels of infrastructure development and differing practices associated with retailing also plague test market feasibility. In the Baltic States, for example, the limited availability of supermarkets makes it difficult for Procter & Gamble to conduct experiments to determine the effect of in-store promotions on the sales of its detergents. In emerging countries in Asia, Africa, and South America, achieving adequate distribution of products to the rural populations is difficult because of the lack of basic infrastructures, such as roads, transportation, and warehouse facilities.

Thus, the internal and external validity of field experiments conducted overseas is generally lower than in the United States. While pointing to the difficulties of conducting field experiments in other countries, we do not wish to imply that such causal research cannot or should not be conducted. To the contrary, as the following example indicates, creatively-designed field experiments can result in rich findings.

RESEARCH IN ACTION

French Cola Wars

When putting together their strategy to fight Coca-Cola in France, PepsiCo abandoned a strategy of using singers and celebrities, such as Rod Stewart, Tina Turner, Gloria Estefan, and M. C. Hammer in their commercials. Marketing research in France had revealed that overplaying American celebrities could be detrimental in that market. Coca-Cola had used a similar strategy, and PepsiCo felt they had an opportunity to attack this weakness. Research told them that Europeans in general considered Coca-Cola's marketing effort as "too American." Pepsi, therefore, decided to use taste as a competitive tool. The French, however, prohibited direct competitive advertising. PepsiCo responded by communicating their taste advantage through music. How did this work?

PepsiCo used sweet and melodious music as the backdrop for their product. They found that the music transferred good feelings to the Pepsi brand. As an indirect, competitive attack, they used repugnant and undesirable music as a backdrop for a visual of Coke, with the hope that a negative connotation would also transfer from the music to the Coke brand. This mechanism is called classical conditioning. Test market experimentation confirmed that positive attitudes were transferred from good music and negative attitudes from bad music. Pepsi designed its advertising based on these findings. Subsequently, retail sales in France increased although they still lag behind Coke.[4]

Technology and Marketing Research

Virtual reality (VR) is a real-time, 3-D environment made to represent either reality or an environment out of someone's imagination. These environments are created by high-powered computer systems. As with many of the technological innovations used in marketing research, VR was not developed specifically with research in mind. But VR is finding its way into the field of marketing research and holds great promise for conducting causal research. Using VR, the researcher can create an environment that represents the field (marketplace) and yet exercise the degree of control possible only in a laboratory setting.

IFOP-CMR (www.ifop.com) has developed a program, Visionary Shopper, which allows respondents to shop in a VR store. The goal of the program is to give the user as real, or as close to lifelike, a shopping experience as possible. It does not use all of the "space-age" gadgetry normally associated with VR. The respondents do not have to wear helmets or gloves, and they are not hooked up to a machine with an inordinate number of wires. The system uses a video screen that has high resolution, color, and 3-D images. The screen shows the user a shelf filled with products, just as they would see in the actual store. The image is complete with brand names, price tags, and special displays.

The respondents use either a track-ball or more advanced touch-screen technology to go "shopping" in the VR store. They are able to choose the aisle and the product category. For example, the user can "walk" to the cereal aisle and see the multitude of choices that would be in any grocery store, including Cap'n Crunch, Cheerios, and Frosted Flakes. The shopper can select a specific item, which is then displayed more prominently on the screen. The shopper can turn the box and read any of the labels on the product. The price of an item is also displayed when that item is selected. After the shopper is done looking at the item, he or she can put it back on the shelf or place it in the cart to be "purchased."

Visionary Shopper allows marketing researchers to manipulate almost any variable that they would be able to change in a store in the real world. They can experiment with prices, special displays, labeling, shelf location, and/or packaging. The system even allows researchers to test new product concepts. These new items can be placed near goods that researchers believe will be the main competition if and when the item is introduced. Again, the "Four Ps" of marketing—product, price, promotion, and place—can be tested to come up with the best alternative for the concept.

The system is being used at malls throughout the United States. Respondents are selected as they are in any other mall intercept survey. Each volunteer participates in a session that lasts 20 minutes. In contrast to the typical questionnaire survey, which is often quite daunting, this new method of researching consumer goods is described as enjoyable or fun. In addition, it is much more realistic.[5]

Ethics in Marketing Research

In experimentation, often there is a deliberate attempt by the researcher to disguise the purpose of the research, arguing that disguise is needed to produce valid results. Consider the earlier example of determining the effectiveness of Pepsi commercials. The respondents are recruited and brought to a central facility. They are told that they will be watching a television program on food and then will be asked some questions. Interspersed in the program is the commercial for Pepsi (test commercial) as well as commercials for some other products (filler commercials). After viewing the program and the commercials, the respondents are administered a questionnaire. The questionnaire obtains evaluations on the program content, the test commercial, and some of the filler commercials. Note, the evaluations of the program content and the filler commercials are not of interest but are obtained to reinforce the nature of the disguise. If the respondents knew the true purpose was to determine the effectiveness of the Pepsi commercial, their responses might be biased. However, disguising the purpose of the research does not have to, and should not, lead to deception.

One solution to this problem would be to tell respondents about the possible existence of deception at the start of the experiment and allow them to inquire about it at the conclusion of the experiment. Thus, at the beginning, the researcher should explain the general nature of the experiment, including that the purpose of the experiment will be disguised but will be fully explained at the end, and the role of the respondents. The respondents should know that they are free to discontinue the experiment at any time and withdraw the information they have provided.

Explaining the purpose and details at the conclusion of the experiment is called **debriefing**. Debriefing should include procedures for reducing experimental stress. In the Pepsi example, the respondents could find it discouraging that they'd spent their time evaluating a soft drink commercial. The researcher should address this issue and ease the respondents' discomfort by explaining the true purpose and importance of the experiment, as well as the experimental procedures.

debriefing
After the experiment, the process of informing test subjects what the experiment was about and how the experimental manipulations were performed.

It is the researcher's responsibility to use the most appropriate experimental design for the problem at hand. The researcher should disclose to the client any problems that arise during the course of the experiment, and the research firm and the client should jointly work out a solution, as in the following example.

RESEARCH IN ACTION

Pepsi Advertising: Is the Celebrity Right?

The effectiveness of Pepsi advertising featuring Britney Spears is investigated using a one-group pretest/posttest design. Respondents' attitudes toward Pepsi advertising, Pepsi, and Britney Spears are obtained prior to respondents being exposed to a food program and several commercials, including the one for Pepsi. Attitudes are again measured after respondents have viewed the program and the commercials. By observing the first few subjects, it is discovered that strongly held prior attitudes about Britney Spears are affecting the measurement of attitudes toward Pepsi and Pepsi advertising. This problem should be disclosed immediately to the client and corrective action should be taken jointly. For example, the client and the researcher may decide a more sophisticated statistical design is needed that explicitly controls for attitude toward Britney Spears. If the researcher chooses to ignore this problem and continue with the experiment, a serious ethical breach takes place. In this case, the researcher discovers that the research design adopted is inadequate, but this knowledge is withheld from the client.

WHAT WOULD *YOU* DO?

Levi's: Fading Jeans and Market Share

The Situation

Levi's has been a longstanding company, with over 150 years of being in the clothing business. While one may think this long history can only result in good things, Levi's heritage has been its worst enemy. Philip Marineau, the president and chief executive officer for Levi Strauss & Company, had to work to revamp Levi's antique image and make the brand appealing to younger generations in efforts to boost its declining sales. In the last five years, Marineau saw worldwide sales drop 40 percent, losing market share to competitors like the Gap, and trendier ones, such as Calvin Klein, Tommy Hilfiger, and Diesel. Another problem for Marineau came from store-brand jeans, such as JC Penney's Arizona brand jeans or the Gap's in-house brand, which have changed their image and launched an assault on big brand names like Levi's. These store-brand jeans, along with other store-label jeans, now target the teenage market with "cutting edge" advertising. American trade publication *Brand Strategy* estimated that the brand has lost about 50 percent of the younger consumer market share worldwide between1997 and 2003.

To compete with these brands and maintain leadership, Levi's, the market leader, is considering introducing their own line of private-label jeans to capture a larger portion of the teenage market. Philip Marineau wonders how powerful a national brand like Levi's is when compared to an in-house brand like Gap or a store brand like JC Penney's Arizona jeans.

The Marketing Research Decision

1. If you were Philip Marineau, what type of research would you want to be conducted to help arrive at an answer? Which of the following types of research would be most appropriate? Check as many as are applicable.
   a. Secondary data analysis
   b. Focus groups
   c. Descriptive cross-sectional survey
   d. Descriptive longitudinal survey
   e. Causal research
2. Please explain how you would implement the type of research you have recommended.

3. Discuss the role of the type of research you recommend in enabling Philip Marineau to determine the power of a national brand like Levi's compared to an in-house brand like Gap or a store brand like JC Penney's Arizona jeans.

The Marketing Management Decision

1. What should Philip Marineau do to compete with in-house and store brands of jeans? (check as many as are applicable):
   a. Discount the price of Levi's
   b. Introduce another brand of lower-priced jeans
   c. Sell Levi's through discount stores like Wal-Mart and Target
   d. Increase the advertising budget for Levi's
   e. Aggressively sell Levi's over the Internet
2. Discuss how the marketing management-decision action that you recommend to Philip Marineau is influenced by the research that you suggested earlier and by the findings of that research.

What Philip Marineau Did

Marineau introduced a new line of cheaper jeans and clothing to mark its first foray into the discount market. The new Signature brand was made available through Wal-Mart stores in the United States beginning July 2003, and is a key feature in Levi's drive to reverse years of declining market share.[6]

Summary

The scientific notion of causality implies that we can never prove that *X* causes *Y*. At best, we can only infer that *X* is one of the causes of *Y* in that it makes the occurrence of *Y* probable. Three conditions must be satisfied before causal inferences can be made: (1) concomitant variation, which implies that *X* and *Y* must vary together in a hypothesized way; (2) time order of occurrence of variables, which implies that *X* must precede or occur simultaneously with *Y*; and (3) elimination of other possible causal factors, which implies that competing explanations must be ruled out. Experiments provide the most convincing evidence of all three conditions. An experiment is formed when the researcher manipulates or controls one or more independent variables and measures their effect on one or more dependent variables.

In designing an experiment, it is important to consider internal and external validity. Internal validity refers to whether the manipulation of the independent variables actually caused the effects on the dependent variables. External validity refers to the generalizability of experimental results. For the experiment to be valid, the researcher must control the threats posed by extraneous variables.

Experimental designs may be classified as preexperimental, true experimental, quasi-experimental, and statistical designs. An experiment may be conducted in a laboratory environment or under actual market conditions in a real-life setting.

Although experiments have limitations in terms of time, cost, and administration, they are becoming increasingly popular in marketing. Test marketing is an important application of experimental design. Field experiments pose even greater challenges in international markets than those faced in the United States. Using technological advances, such as virtual reality, the researcher can create an environment that represents the field (marketplace) and yet exercise the degree of control possible only in a laboratory setting. Disguising the purpose of the research should not lead to deception, and debriefing should be used to reduce experimental stress.

Key Terms and Concepts

Causality, 212
Concomitant variation, 212
Experiment, 214
Independent variables, 214
Test units, 214
Dependent variables, 214
Extraneous variables, 214
Random assignment, 215
Experimental group, 215
Control group, 215
Experimental design, 215
Internal validity, 216
External validity, 216
History, 217
Maturation, 217
Testing effects, 217
Instrumentation, 217
Statistical regression, 218
Selection bias, 218
Mortality, 218
Randomization, 218
Matching, 219
Statistical control, 219
Design control, 219
Preexperimental designs, 219
True experimental designs, 219
Quasi-experimental designs, 219
Statistical design, 219
One-shot case study, 220
One-group pretest/posttest design, 221
Static group, 221
Pretest/posttest control group design, 222
Interactive testing effects, 223
Posttest-only control group design, 223
Time series design, 224
Multiple time series design 224
Factorial design, 225
Laboratory environment, 226
Demand artifacts, 226
Field environment, 227
Test marketing, 228
Test markets, 228
Debriefing, 231

Suggested Cases and Video Cases

Cases

2.4 Bloomingdale's **2.5 Burger King** **4.1 Boeing** **4.2 Gucci**

Video Cases

3.1 AFLAC **3.2 Honest Tea**

Additional cases and video cases are available in the Instructor's Manual and on the instructor and student Web sites.

Live Research: Conducting a Marketing Research Project

If an experiment is to be conducted, an experimental design should be chosen based on class discussion. The choice of an experimental design may have to be tempered by several considerations:

1. It may not be possible to control for certain extraneous variables.
2. There may be only limited flexibility to manipulate the independent variables (e.g., advertising or sales effort cannot be reduced to the zero level).
3. Random assignment of test units to the treatment conditions may not be possible.
4. The choice of dependent variables may be limited by measurement considerations.

The experimental design selected should be discussed and approved by the client.

Acronyms

The salient characteristics of experiments may be described by the acronym EXPERIMENT:

E xtraneous variables
X independent variable or treatment
P reexperimental, true experimental, quasi-experimental, and statistical designs
E ffect or dependent variable
R andom assignment
I nternal validity
M easurement or observation
E xternal validity
N eutral or control group
T est units

Review Questions

1. What are the requirements for inferring a causal relationship between two variables?
2. Differentiate between internal and external validity.
3. What key characteristic distinguishes true experimental designs from preexperimental designs?
4. List the steps involved in implementing the posttest-only control group design. Describe the design symbolically.
5. What is a time series experiment? When is it used?
6. How is a multiple time series design different from a basic time series design?
7. What advantages do statistical designs have over basic designs?
8. Compare laboratory and field experimentation.
9. What is test marketing?

Applied Problems

1. An advocacy group wants to test the effectiveness of an abstinence education commercial. Two random samples, each of 250 respondents, are recruited in Chicago. One group is shown the abstinence education commercial. Then, attitudes toward abortion are measured for respondents in both groups.
   a. Identify the independent and dependent variables in this experiment.
   b. What type of design was used?
2. In the experiment just described, suppose the respondents had been selected by convenience rather than randomly. What type of design would result?
3. State the type of experiment being conducted in the following situations.
   a. A major distributor of office equipment is considering a new sales presentation program for its salespeople. The largest sales territory is

selected, the new program is implemented, and the effect on sales is measured.

b. Procter & Gamble wants to determine if a new package design for Tide detergent is more effective than the current design. Twelve supermarkets are randomly selected in Denver. In six of them, Tide is sold in the new packaging. In the other six, the detergent is sold in the old package. Sales for both groups of supermarkets are monitored for three months.

4. Describe a specific situation for which each of the following experimental designs is appropriate. Defend your reasoning.
   a. One-group pretest/posttest design
   b. Pretest/posttest control group design
   c. Posttest-only control group design
   d. Time series design
   e. Factorial design
5. Design an experiment for determining the effectiveness of online coupons based on relevant information obtained from (www.coupons-online.com).
6. Coca-Cola has developed three alternative package designs for its flagship product, Coke. Design an Internet-based experiment to determine which, if any, of these new package designs is superior to the current one.
7. Microsoft has developed a new version of its spreadsheet EXCEL but is not sure what the user reaction will be. Design an Internet-based experiment to determine user reaction to the new and previous versions of EXCEL.
8. Explain how you would implement a posttest-only control group design on the Internet to measure the effectiveness of a new print ad for Toyota Camry.

Group Discussion

1. "Since one cannot prove a causal relationship by conducting an experiment, experimentation is unscientific for examining cause-and-effect relationships." Discuss this statement as a small group.

CHAPTER

9

Measurement and Scaling: Fundamentals and Comparative Scaling

"In every survey project, researchers have to decide what type of scales will be used to measure the variables. You really have to know what these scale types can give you."

James C. Fink, *Ph.D., CEO, Worldwide Marketing Research, Opinion Research Corporation, Princeton, NJ*

OPENING QUESTIONS

1. What is meant by measurement and scaling? Can scaling be considered a part of measurement?
2. What are the primary scales of measurement, and how do we differentiate among them?
3. How can scaling techniques be classified, and what are the various comparative scaling techniques?
4. How do measurement and scaling relate to the various steps of the marketing research process?
5. What considerations are involved in implementing the primary scales of measurement in an international setting?
6. How does technology improve measurement and scaling?
7. What ethical issues are involved in selecting scales of measurement?

Scaling the Olympics

Even as thousands swarmed Athens, Greece, to witness the 2004 Olympics, the games are very popular among teen television watchers. In fact, the Olympic games are the single most popular televised sporting venue (ranked number one) among teenage boys (71 percent) and girls (62 percent), according to The New World Teen Study. The BrainWaves Group, a New York global consulting and trends company, conducted this survey of 6,500 teens in 26 countries. Elissa Moses, managing director of The BrainWaves Group, says, "The Olympics are young people's favorite athletic package because in the global teen culture sport is a dominant theme, with both boys and girls being active participants and spectators."

Globally, the Olympics enjoys its highest popularity rating in the Middle East where it is the favorite televised sporting event of 85 percent of teen boys and girls. Australia, host of the 2000 Olympic games, is third, where the games are the favorite of 84 percent of teen males and 80 percent of teen females. The United States is lower in the ranking: Only 71 percent of teen girls and 68 percent of teen boys named the Olympics their favorite televised sports competition.

However, any similarity between the tastes of teen boys and girls ends with the Olympics. A majority of teen boys (63 percent) cite basketball as their favorite sport, followed by soccer (58 percent). Teen girls voted gymnastics their most popular sport (57 percent), followed by basketball (51 percent). Only 17 percent of the boys voted gymnastics their favorite spectator sport. In fact, on a global basis, teens' favorite spectator sport is basketball.

The BrainWaves Group developed a complete ranking of the popularity of all sports in terms of the percentage of teenagers who indicated each sport as their favorite. Information of this type can be used by marketers of global brands, such as Levi's, in their attempts to penetrate the teenage segment. For example, Levi's would do well to air its commercials on televised basketball and soccer games in order to reach teenage boys. However, to reach teenage girls, Levi's should replace soccer advertising with gymnastics.[1] •

Overview

After developing the type of research design to be implemented (Chapters 3 through 8), the researcher is ready to move to the next phase of research. The researcher must decide how to measure information and which types of scales to use. In the opening vignette, scales had to be designed to measure the popularity of various sports and sporting events.

This chapter describes the concepts of scaling and measurement. Figure 9.1 briefly explains the focus of the chapter, the relation of this chapter to the previous ones, and the steps of the marketing research process on which this chapter concentrates. In this chapter, we review four primary scales of measurement: nominal, ordinal, interval, and ratio. We then discuss both comparative and noncomparative scaling techniques and explain comparative techniques in detail. (Noncomparative techniques are discussed in more depth in Chapter 10.) We discuss the applications of primary scales and comparative scaling in total quality management and international marketing research, as well as the impact of technology on scaling and ethical issues that arise in measurement and scaling. Figure 9.2 gives an overview of the topics discussed in this chapter and how they flow from one to the next.

Measurement and Scaling

measurement
The assignment of numbers or other symbols to characteristics of objects according to certain prespecified rules.

Measurement means assigning numbers or other symbols to characteristics of objects being measured, according to predetermined rules. We are measuring characteristics of the item, rather than the item directly. Thus, we do not measure consumers—only their perceptions, attitudes, preferences, or other relevant characteristics. In the opening vignette, we measured teenagers' preferences for various sports and sporting events.

In marketing research, numbers are usually assigned for one of two reasons:

- To permit statistical analysis of the generated data.
- To help communicate information about the results.

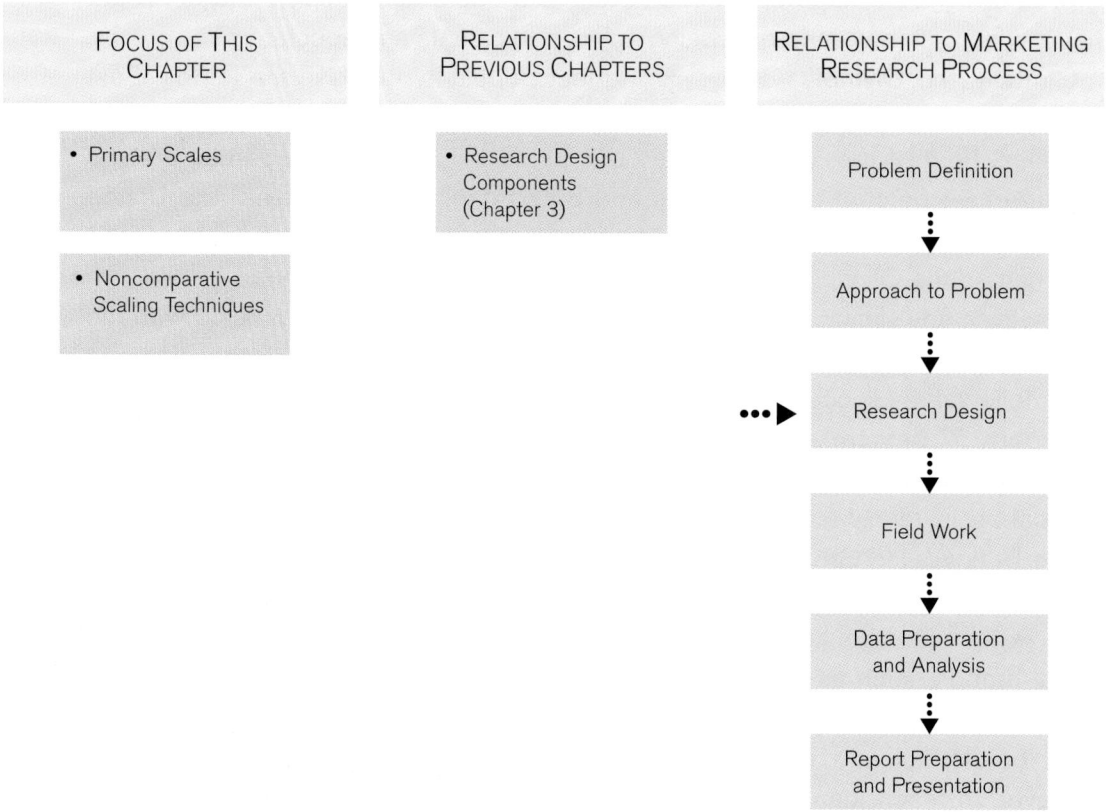

Figure 9.1
Relationship of Comparative Scaling to Previous Chapters and the Marketing Research Process

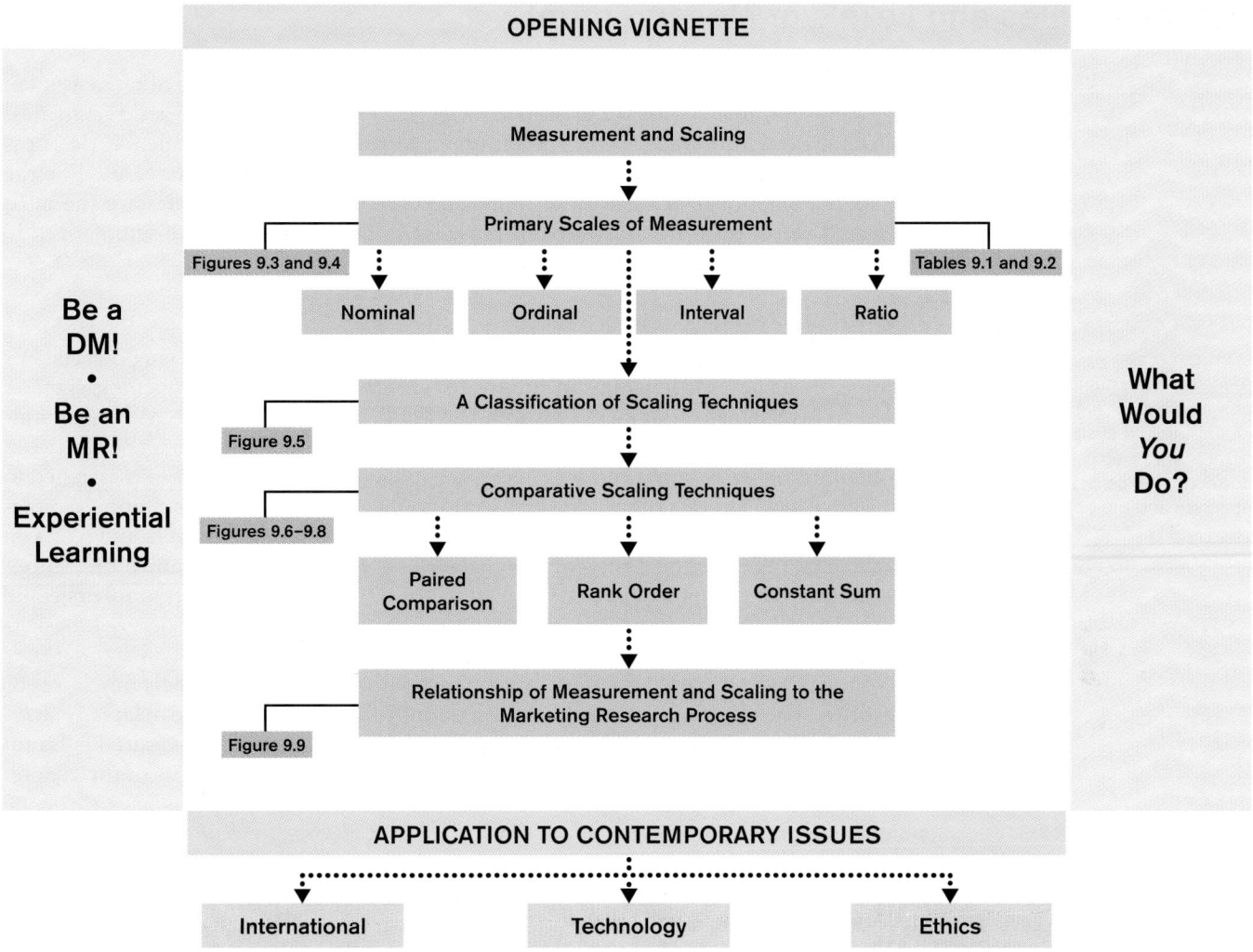

Figure 9.2

Fundamentals and Comparative Scaling: An Overview

The most important aspect of measurement is deciding how to assign numbers to the characteristics being studied. In the opening vignette, numbers had to be assigned to measure the popularity of different sports in terms of the percentage of respondents who mentioned each sport as their favorite (most preferred). In developing the assignment process, there must be a one-to-one correspondence between the numbers and the characteristics being measured. Only then can the numbers be associated with specific characteristics of the object being measured. For example, the same dollar figures are assigned to products that are priced the same. In addition, the rules for assigning numbers should be applied in a standard way. They must not change over objects or time.

Scaling may be considered a part of measurement. Scales place the objects being measured along a continuum. To illustrate, suppose we wanted to measure consumers in terms of their attitude toward Wrigley's chewing gum. Based on the response, each consumer would be assigned a number indicating an unfavorable attitude (measured as 1), a neutral attitude (measured as 2), or a favorable attitude (measured as 3). Measurement is the actual assignment of 1, 2, or 3 to each respondent using a scale that ranges from one to three. In this example, scaling is the process of placing consumer response along an attitudinal continuum from unfavorable, to neutral, to favorable. The scale is the set of values ranging from one to three. In the opening vignette, scaling was the process of placing each sport along a preference continuum from 0 to 100 percent.

scaling
The generation of a continuum upon which measured objects are located.

Primary Scales and Levels of Measurement

The word *primary* means basic or fundamental. The four primary scales of measurement are nominal, ordinal, interval, and ratio scales (Figure 9.3). The nominal scale is the most basic or limited, followed by the ordinal, the interval, and the ratio scale. As the measurement level increases from nominal to ratio, scale complexity increases. For the respondents, nominal scales are the simplest to use, whereas ratio scales are the most complex. These scales are illustrated in Figure 9.4. Their properties are summarized in Table 9.1 and are discussed in the following sections.

Nominal Scale

nominal scale
A scale whose numbers serve only as labels or tags for identifying and classifying objects with a strict one-to-one correspondence between the numbers and the objects.

A **nominal scale** uses numbers as labels or tags for identifying and classifying objects. For example, teenagers participating in the sports survey discussed in the opening vignette may each be assigned a number. This number would be a nominal scale. When a nominal scale is used for identification, there is a strict one-to-one correspondence between the numbers being assigned and the objects being measured. Each number is assigned to only one object, and each object has only one number assigned to it. Common examples include Social Security numbers and numbers assigned to football players and worn on their jerseys. In marketing research, nominal scales are used for brands, attributes, stores, objects, and identifying participants in a study. In the opening vignette, numbers could be used to denote the various spectator sports: 1. tennis, 2. hockey, 3. soccer, 4. basketball, and so on, resulting in a nominal scale.

Nominal scales are used for classification purposes. They serve as labels for classes or categories. The classes are mutually exclusive and collectively exhaustive. *Mutually exclusive* means that there is no overlap between classes; every object being measured falls into only one class. The objects in each class are viewed as equivalent in terms of the characteristic represented by the nominal scale. All objects in the same class have the same number, and no two classes have the same number. *Collectively exhaustive* means that all the objects fall into one of the classes. For example, the numbers 1 and 2 can be used to classify survey respondents based on gender, with 1 denoting female and 2 denoting male. Each respondent will fall into one of these two categories.

The numbers assigned in a nominal scale do not reflect relative amounts of the characteristic being measured. For example, a high Social Security number does not imply that the person is in some way superior to those with lower Social Security numbers or vice versa. The same applies to numbers assigned to classes. By assigning 1 to female and 2 to male, we do not imply that either sex is superior to the other in any way. The numbers in a nominal scale can only be counted. Therefore, the only statistics that are useful

Figure 9.3
Primary Scales of Measurement

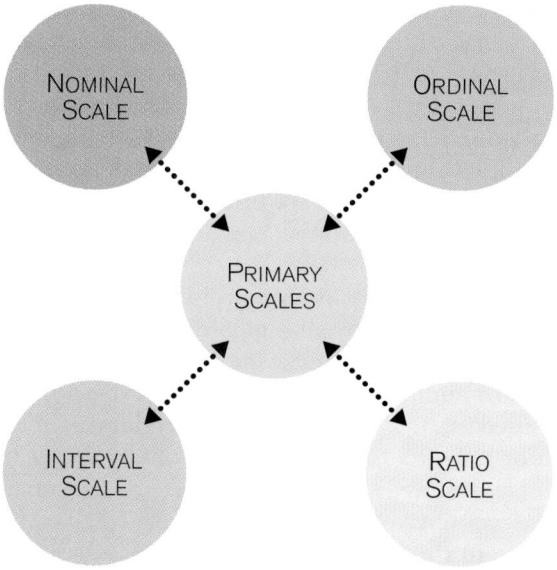

Figure 9.4

Primary Scales Measurement

SCALE					
Nominal	Numbers Assigned to Runners	17	21	13	Finish
Ordinal	Rank Order of Winners	Third Place	Second Place	First Place	
Interval	Performance Rating on a 0 to 100 Scale	74	90	97	
Ratio	Time to Finish, in Seconds	16.1	14.0	13.2	

when using a nominal scale are those based on frequency counts. These include percentage, mode, and chi-square (see Chapter 16). It is not meaningful to compute an average Social Security number or the average gender of the respondents in a survey. The following nominal scale Research in Action example illustrates this limitation.

RESEARCH IN ACTION

Nominal Scale

In a study to measure consumer preferences for jeans, numbers 1 through 10 were assigned to the 10 brands being considered (Table 9.2). Thus, brand number 9 referred to Old Navy. Brand number 6 was assigned to Jordache. This did not imply that Old Navy was in any way superior or inferior to Jordache. Any reassignment of the numbers, such as switching the numbers assigned to Old Navy and Jordache, would have no effect on the results. The numbers did not reflect any characteristics of the brands.

It is meaningful to make statements such as, "Thirty-five percent of the respondents had purchased Levi jeans." The mode, defined as the number with the highest frequency, denotes the brand preferred by the largest number of respondents, for example, Guess?. However, while the average of all the assigned numbers, 1 to 10, is 5.5, it is not meaningful to state that the number of the average brand of jeans is 5.5.

A common example of a nominal scale is numbers assigned to football players.

Table 9.1

Primary Scales of Measurement

Primary Scale	Basics Characteristics	Common Examples	Marketing Examples	Permissible Statistics
Nominal	Numbers identify and classify objects	Social Security numbers, numbering of football players	Brand numbers, store types, gender classification	Percentages, mode
Ordinal	Numbers indicate the relative positions of the objects but not the magnitude of differences between them	Quality rankings, rankings of teams in a tournament	Preference rankings, market position, social class	Percentile, median
Interval	Differences between objects can be compared; zero point is arbitrary	Temperature (Fahrenheit, Celsius)	Attitudes, opinions, index numbers	Range, mean, standard deviation
Ratio	Zero point is fixed; ratios of scale values can be computed	Length, weight	Age, income, costs, sales, market shares	Geometric mean, (All)

Ordinal Scale

ordinal scale
A ranking scale in which numbers are assigned to objects to indicate the relative extent to which some characteristic is possessed. Thus, it is possible to determine whether an object has more or less of a characteristic than some other object.

An **ordinal scale** is a ranking scale. In an ordinal scale, numbers are assigned to objects, which allows researchers to determine whether an object has more or less of a characteristic than some other object. However, we cannot determine how much more or less from this type of scale. Objects ranked first have more of the characteristic being measured than objects ranked second; however, we have no way of knowing whether the object ranked second is a close second or a distant second. Common examples of ordinal scales include quality rankings, rankings of teams in a tournament, and educational levels (less than high school, high school, some college, and so on).

In marketing research, ordinal scales are used to measure relative attitudes, opinions, perceptions, and preferences. Measurements of this type ask the respondent to make "greater than'" or "less than'" judgments. Asking respondents to rank order the various sports in terms of their preference, as in the opening vignette, is an example of an ordinal scale.

Ordinal scales are like nominal scales in that equivalent objects receive the same rank. Any series of numbers can be assigned as long as they preserve the ordered relationships between the objects. Because of this quality, ordinal scales can be transformed in any way as long as the basic ordering of the objects is maintained. In ordinal scales, numbers differ only in terms of their order, not in terms of their magnitude (see the ordinal scale Research in Action example). For these reasons, in addition to the counting operation allowable for nominal scale data, ordinal scales also permit the use of statistics based on centiles. This means that it is meaningful to calculate percentile, median, or other summary statistics from ordinal data (see Chapter 16).

Note that the ordinal scale does not replace the nominal scale but merely supplements it. We could say that brand number 5 receives the highest preference ranking—rank 1 on the first ordinal scale—and identify it as Guess?.

RESEARCH IN ACTION

Ordinal Scale

Table 9.2 gives one respondent's preference rankings. Respondents ranked 10 brands of jeans in order of preference by assigning a 1 to the most preferred brand, a 2 to the second most preferred brand, and so forth. Note that Guess? (ranked 1), is preferred to Calvin Klein (ranked 2). However, we have no way of knowing how much more it is preferred. Also, it is not necessary that we assign numbers from 1 to 10 to obtain a preference ranking. The second ordinal scale, which assigns a number 10 to Guess?, 25 to Calvin Klein, 30 to Gap, and so on, is an equivalent scale. The two scales result in the same ordering of the brands according to preference. This illustrates an important property of ordinal scales: Any series of numbers can be assigned as long as they preserve the ordered relationships between the objects.

BE a DM!

As the marketing director for Home Depot, what marketing strategies would you formulate to enhance satisfaction with Home Depot?

BE an MR!

Visit the Home Depot Web site (www.homedepot.com) and search the Internet using a search engine as well as your library's online databases to obtain information on customer satisfaction with home improvement stores.

How would you use nominal and ordinal scales to measure customer satisfaction with the major home improvement stores, such as Home Depot?

Interval Scale

In an **interval scale,** numerically equal distances on the scale represent equal values in the characteristic being measured. An interval scale contains all the information of an ordinal scale. In addition, it allows you to compare the differences between objects. The difference between 1 and 2 is same as the difference between 2 and 3, which is the same as the difference between 5 and 6. In marketing research, data on attitudes (e.g., attitude toward sports) obtained from rating scales (1 = do not like at all, 7 = like very much) are often treated as interval data. In the opening vignette, interval data would be obtained if the respondents were asked to rate each sport in terms of preference using a seven-point scale with ratings of 1 = not at all preferred and 7 = greatly preferred. Note that, in an interval scale, two objects can be assigned the same number if they each contain the characteristic being measured to the same extent. Scales of this type are discussed further in Chapter 10 on noncomparative scaling.

interval scale
A scale in which the numbers are used to rank objects such that numerically equal distances on the scale represent equal distances in the characteristic being measured.

In an interval scale, the location of the zero point is not fixed. Both the zero point and the units of measurement are arbitrary. This is illustrated in the measurement of temperature. The Fahrenheit scale uses different zero points and smaller units of measurement than the Celsius scale. However, both are used to measure the same characteristic: temperature. Any positive linear transformation of the form $y = a + bx$ will preserve the properties of the scale. Here, x is the original scale value, y is the transformed scale value, b is a positive constant, and a is any constant. Two interval scales that rate women's handbag brands Coach, Dooney and Burke, Vende, and Gucci as 1, 3, 3, and 5, or as 22, 26, 26, and 30 are equivalent. Note that the latter scale can be derived from the former by using $a = 20$ and $b = 2$ in the transforming equation. Their equivalence can also be seen as follows.

Poor	1	2	3	4	5	Excellent

or

Poor	22	24	26	28	30	Excellent

Because the zero point is not fixed, it is not meaningful to take ratios of scale values. Thus, it is not meaningful to say that it is 1.5 times as hot in Phoenix (temperature = 90 degrees Fahrenheit) as it is in Buffalo (temperature = 60 degrees Fahrenheit). When the temperatures are converted to a Celsius scale, the ratio is no longer 1.5 to 1. In the handbag example, the ratio of Gucci to Dooney and Burke is 5:3 using the first scale. It becomes 15:13 when the scale is transformed.

All the statistical techniques and measures of central tendency (mode and median) that apply to nominal and ordinal data can also be applied to interval scale data. In addition, the arithmetic mean, standard deviation (see Chapter 16), and other statistics commonly used in marketing research are permitted. However, certain specialized statistics, such as geometric means, are not meaningful on interval scale data. The following interval scale Research in Action example gives a further illustration of an interval scale.

RESEARCH IN ACTION

Interval Scale

In Table 9.2, a respondent's preferences for the 10 brands in the jeans study are expressed on a seven-point rating scale. We can see that, although Gap received a preference rating of 6 and Wrangler a rating of 2, this does not mean that Gap is preferred three times as much as Wrangler. When the ratings are transformed to an equivalent 11- to 17-scale (next column), the ratings for these brands become 16 and 12, and the ratio is no longer 3 to 1. This example becomes clearer when you realize that an interval scale has an arbitrary origin or zero point.

Ratio Scale

ratio scale
This is the highest level of measurement. It allows the researcher to identify or classify objects, rank order the objects, and compare intervals or differences. It is also meaningful to compute ratios of scale values.

A **ratio scale** possesses all the properties of the nominal, ordinal, and interval scales. In addition, an absolute zero point is specified; that is, the origin of the scale is fixed. When measurement is taken using ratio scales, we can identify or classify objects, rank the objects, and compare intervals or differences. Unlike interval data, it is meaningful to compute ratios of scale values. Not only is the difference between 2 and 5 the same as the difference between 14 and 17, but 14 is seven times as large as 2 in an absolute sense. Common examples of ratio scales include height, weight, age, and income. In marketing, sales, costs, market share, and number of customers are variables measured on a ratio scale. In the opening vignette, ratio data would be obtained if the teenagers were asked to state the amount of time they spent watching each sport on TV during the Olympics.

Ratio scales can be transformed using proportions. The transformation formula is $y = bx$, where b is a positive constant. Note that the a of the interval scale transformation formula is missing here. One cannot transform a ratio scale by adding an arbitrary constant (a), unlike the case of an interval scale. An example of a ratio transformation is provided by the conversion of yards to feet ($b = 3$). Comparisons between measurements are identical, whether made in yards or feet.

All statistical techniques can be applied to ratio data. These include specialized statistics, such as the geometric mean. An illustration of the use of a ratio scale in the context of the jeans is provided in the ratio scale Research in Action example.

Table 9.2
Illustration of Primary Scales of Measurement

Nominal Scale		Ordinal Scale		Interval Scale		Ratio Scale
No.	**Jean Brand**	**Preference Rankings**		**Preference Ratings 1–7**	**11–17**	**Price in Dollars**
1.	Bugle Boy	7	79	5	15	30
2.	Calvin Klein	2	25	7	17	48
3.	Diesel	8	82	7	17	27
4.	Gap	3	30	6	16	32
5.	Guess?	1	10	7	17	34
6.	Jordache	5	53	5	15	35
7.	Lee	9	95	4	14	30
8.	Levi	6	61	5	15	33
9.	Old Navy	4	45	6	16	29
10.	Wrangler	10	115	2	12	24

BE an MR!

Visit Coach's Web site (www.coach.com) and search the Internet using a search engine as well as your library's online databases to obtain information on consumer preferences for leather goods.

How would you use interval and ratio scales to measure consumer preferences for leather goods?

BE a DM!

As the marketing director for Coach, how would you use information on consumer preferences for leather goods to increase your market share?

RESEARCH IN ACTION

Ratio Scale

The ratio scale illustrated in Table 9.2 gives the prices of the 10 brands of jeans. Note that since the price of Calvin Klein is $48 and the price of Wrangler is $24, Calvin Klein costs the buyer twice as much as Wrangler. In dollar terms, the zero point is fixed. A price of zero dollars means that the item is free. Additionally, multiplying these prices by 100 to convert dollars to cents results in an equivalent scale, thus, illustrating the fact that the ratio scale has an absolute zero or a fixed origin.

Selecting a Level of Measurement

A variable of interest may be measured using different types of primary scales. We illustrate this in the context of measuring annual household income.

Nominal Scale

In the past year, who made a contribution to your household income?

1. Male head of the household
2. Female head of the household
3. Both male and female head of the household
4. Other

Ordinal Scale

In the past year, what was your annual household income before taxes?

1. Less than $20,001
2. $20,001 to $50,000
3. $50,001 to $100,000
4. $100,001 to $150,000
5. More than $150,000

Interval Scale

In the past year, what was your annual household income before taxes?

Much Below Average			Average		Much Above Average	
1	2	3	4	5	6	7

Ratio Scale

In the past year, what was your annual household income before taxes?

$ _____

So which type of primary scale should be selected to measure the variable of interest (e.g., income)? The amount of information obtained increases from nominal to ordinal to interval to ratio scale. However, the cognitive load imposed on the respondents while obtaining information also increases in that order. So a trade-off has to be made. The general rule is to select the lowest level of measurement that will enable the researcher to obtain the needed information and conduct the appropriate statistical analyses. Suppose the researcher is merely interested in cross-tabulating the level of income with consumer purchases to see if the level of income has an effect on the amount purchased. To meet this objective, measuring income at an ordinal level would be sufficient. More than one type of primary scale is used in a typical survey, as the Primary Scales in Online Surveys example illustrates.

RESEARCH IN ACTION

Primary Scales in Online Surveys

Oxy-Gen.com (www.oxy-gen.com) is a host service and provider of software used to create online surveys. Its service is provided to anyone who needs to administer a survey through the Internet. Oxy-Gen's software, the Survey Administrator, guides users through the creation of surveys and allows for the use of all of the scales of measurement. Surveys can easily be designed for employee or customer satisfaction, group feedback, organizational effectiveness, and various other applications.

A sample employee satisfaction survey includes questions using the following measurement scales:

1. Job Function–nominal scale
2. Employee Level–nominal scale
3. Years of Service–ratio scale
4. Empowerment Assessment–interval scale
5. Compensation Assessment–interval scale
6. Ranking of Management Efficiency–ordinal scale

Surveys of this type have been used to develop better human resource programs to attract and retain the best employees.

A Classification of Scaling Techniques

comparative scales
One of two types of scaling techniques in which there is direct comparison of stimulus objects with one another.

The scaling techniques commonly used in marketing research can be classified into comparative and noncomparative scales (Figure 9.5). **Comparative scales** involve the direct comparison of two or more objects. For example, respondents might be asked whether they prefer Coke or Pepsi. A comparative scale gives the marketer data that measure relative differences. It has only ordinal or rank order properties.

Comparative scaling is sometimes referred to as nonmetric scaling. The opening vignette presented an example of comparative scaling when the different sports were ranked in terms of the percentage of respondents mentioning each sport as their favorite. The resulting scale presented a relative comparison of all the sports. As Figure 9.5 illustrates, comparative scales include paired comparisons, rank order, and constant sum scales.

The major benefit of comparative scaling is that small differences between objects under study can be detected. The comparison process forces respondents to choose between two objects. Respondents asked to perform a ranking task bring the same point of reference to the task. This makes comparative scales easy to understand and apply. They also tend to reduce halo or carryover effects in which early judgments

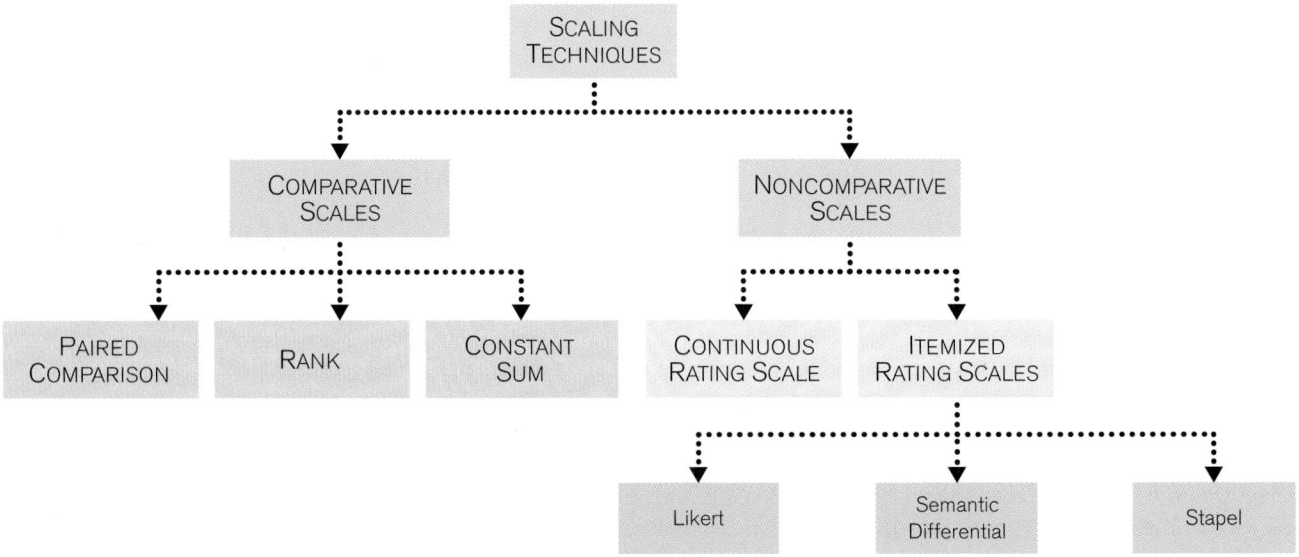

Figure 9.5
A Classification of Scaling Techniques

influence later judgments. The major disadvantage of comparative scales is the limitation in terms of analyzing ordinal data. We are also unable to generalize beyond the objects under study. For instance, say a study was done to compare Coke and Pepsi. If later these brands were to be compared to RC Cola, the researcher would have to do a new study. These disadvantages are substantially overcome by the noncomparative scaling techniques.

In **noncomparative scales**, also referred to as monadic or metric scales, objects are scaled independently of each other. The resulting data are generally assumed to be interval scaled. For example, respondents may be asked to evaluate Coke on a 1 to 7 preference scale (1 = not at all preferred, 7 = greatly preferred). Similar evaluations would be obtained for Pepsi and RC Cola. In the opening vignette, the use of noncomparative scaling would involve respondents rating each sport, taken by itself, on a 1-to-7 preference scale. As Figure 9.5 illustrates, noncomparative scales comprise continuous rating or itemized rating scales. The itemized rating scales can be further classified as Likert, semantic differential, or Stapel scales.

noncomparative scales
One of two types of scaling techniques in which each stimulus object is scaled independently of the others.

Noncomparative scaling is the most widely-used scaling technique in marketing research. Chapter 10 is devoted entirely to noncomparative scaling. The rest of this chapter focuses on comparative scaling techniques.

Comparative Scaling Techniques

Paired Comparison Scaling

As its name implies, in **paired comparison scaling** a respondent is presented with a pair of alternatives and asked to select one according to some criterion. Data obtained in this way are ordinal in nature. A consumer involved in a paired comparison study may state that she shops in JC Penney more than in Sears, likes Total cereal better than Kellogg's Product 19, or likes Crest toothpaste more than Colgate. Paired comparison scales are frequently used when the research involves physical products. Coca-Cola is reported to have conducted more than 190,000 paired comparisons before introducing New Coke. Paired comparison scaling is the most widely used comparative scaling technique (Figure 9.6).

paired comparison scaling
A comparative scaling technique in which a respondent is presented with two objects at a time and asked to select one object in the pair according to some criterion. The data obtained are ordinal in nature.

INSTRUCTIONS

We are going to present you with 10 pairs of shampoo brands. For each pair, please indicate which one of the two brands of shampoo in the pair you would prefer for personal use.

RECORDING FORM

	Jhirmack	Finesse	Vidal Sassoon	Head & Shoulders	Pert
Jhirmack		0	0	1	0
Finesse	1[a]		0	1	0
Vidal Sassoon	1	1		1	1
Head & Shoulders	0	0	0		0
Pert	1	1	0	1	
Number of times preferred	3[b]	2	0	4	1

[a] A "1" in a particular box means that the brand in that column was preferred over the brand in the corresponding row. A "0" means that the row brand was preferred over the column brand.
[b] The number of times a brand was preferred is obtained by summing the 1s in each column.

Figure 9.6
Paired Comparison Scaling

EXPERIENTIAL LEARNING

Which Is It? Coke or Pepsi

Which cola drink would be the most popular among your friends in a taste test? Download the KitKat Taste Test from the Web site of this textbook and, using it as a guide, develop a script for testing for preference between two cola drinks: Coke and Pepsi. Make sure the drinks are chilled to the same temperature, and poured in three groups of identical cups. Each person will select a cup from the first group, taste the cola, eat a cracker, and take a swallow of water. This will be repeated for each person when tasting from the second, and the third groups, also. (The first group might be Pepsi, the second group Coke, and the third group Pepsi.) After tasting from each of the three cola sample groups, have the respondents complete the survey form you created similar to that in the KitKat document that you have downloaded. To avoid a biasing effect from the order of presentation of the samples, it will be important for half of the respondents to have a rotated order of presentation: (The first group Coke, the second group Pepsi, and the third group Coke). Conduct the taste test on 30 respondents/students.

1. How many correctly identified the two identical samples of cola?
2. Of those who correctly identified the two identical samples of cola, which cola was preferred: Coke or Pepsi?
3. Of those who correctly identified the two identical samples of cola, how many had no preference between Coke and Pepsi?
4. In sum, who would you say is the winner in your taste test: Coke or Pepsi? Or, is it too close to tell?

Paired comparison scaling is useful when the number of brands under consideration is limited to no more than five. When a large number of brands are involved, the number of comparisons becomes unwieldy. For example, to evaluate the 10 brands of jeans in Table 9.2, 45 paired comparisons would be involved. The order in which the alternatives are presented may bias the results. Also problematic is the fact that paired comparisons bear little resemblance to the marketplace situation, which involves selection from multiple alternatives. Respondents may prefer one alternative to another; however, that does not imply that they like it in an absolute sense. The following example provides further insights into paired comparison scaling.

rank order scaling
A comparative scaling technique in which respondents are presented with several objects simultaneously and asked to order or rank them according to some criterion.

Rank Order Scaling

After paired comparisons, the most popular comparative scaling technique is rank order scaling. In **rank order scaling,** respondents are simultaneously presented with several alternatives and are asked to rank them according to some criterion (Figure 9.7). For example, consumers may be asked to rank brands of jeans according to overall preference,

Figure 9.7
Rank Order Scaling

INSTRUCTIONS

Rank the various brands of toothpaste in order of preference. Begin by picking out the one brand that you like most and assign it a number "1." Then, find the second most preferred brand and assign it a number "2." Continue this procedure until you have ranked all the brands of toothpaste in order of preference. The least preferred brand should be assigned a rank of "10."

No two brands should receive the same rank number.

The criterion of preference is entirely up to you. There is no right or wrong answer. Just try to be consistent.

BRAND	RANK ORDER
1. Crest	_____
2. Colgate	_____
3. Aim	_____
4. Mentadent	_____
5. Macleans	_____
6. Ultra Brite	_____
7. Close Up	_____
8. Pepsodent	_____
9. Plus White	_____
10. Stripe	_____

as in Table 9.2. These rankings are typically obtained by asking the respondents to assign a rank of 1 to the most preferred brand, 2 to the second most preferred, and so on, until each alternative is ranked down to the least preferred brand. Like paired comparison, this approach is also comparative in nature. However it is possible that even the brand ranked 1 is not liked in an absolute sense; that is, it may be the least disliked. Rank order scaling also results in ordinal data. See Table 9.2, which uses rank order data to derive an ordinal scale.

Rank order scaling is commonly used to measure preferences among brands as well as among brand attributes. Rank order scaling forces the respondent to discriminate among alternatives. This type of scaling process comes closer to resembling the shopping environment. It also takes less time than paired comparisons. Another advantage is that it is easily understood, and the results are easy to communicate. The opening vignette showed that the Olympic games are the single most popular (ranked number one) sporting venue among teenage boys and girls, with basketball as teens' overall favorite spectator sport around the globe. These results are easy to communicate. The major disadvantage of this technique is that it produces only ordinal level data.

RESEARCH IN ACTION

Winning Votes with Marketing Research

For years, Gallup (www.gallup.com) and many other research firms have been asking Americans what they believe is the most important problem facing this country today. These surveys are used to determine the voters' concerns and to guide politicians in developing their election platforms. According to a survey taken in 2004, the five most important issues, in order of importance, were (1) the Iraq war, (2) economy, (3) outsourcing/job losses, (4) terrorism, and (5) abortion/same-sex marriages. This order of importance reflects a rank order scale. These issues turned out to be crucial in the 2004 presidential election and were hotly debated by the Democratic and Republican candidates. By attacking the Democrats on these issues, and by developing a platform for a more prosperous, safer, and more moral America, George W. Bush was able to win over enough votes to make it to the White House.[2]

Constant Sum Scaling

In **constant sum scaling**, respondents allocate a constant sum of units, such as points, dollars, or chips, among a set of alternatives according to some specified criterion. Respondents may be asked, for example, to allocate 100 points to eight attributes of a bath soap (Figure 9.8). The points are allocated to represent the importance attached to each attribute. If an attribute is unimportant, the respondent assigns it zero points. If an attribute is twice as

constant sum scaling
A comparative scaling technique in which respondents are required to allocate a constant sum of units, such as points, dollars, chits, stickers, or chips, among a set of stimulus objects with respect to some criterion.

Figure 9.8
Constant Sum Scaling

INSTRUCTIONS

Below are eight attributes of bathing soaps. Please allocate 100 points among the attributes so that your allocation reflects the relative importance you attach to each attribute. The more points an attribute receives, the more important the attribute is. If an attribute is not at all important, assign it zero points. If an attribute is twice as important as some other attribute, it should receive twice as many points.

FORM

AVERAGE RESPONSES OF THREE SEGMENTS

Attribute	Segment I	Segment II	Segment III
1. Mildness	8	2	4
2. Lather	2	4	17
3. Shrinkage	3	9	7
4. Price	53	17	9
5. Fragrance	9	0	19
6. Packaging	7	5	9
7. Moisturizing	5	3	20
8. Cleaning Power	13	60	15
Sum	100	100	100

BE a DM!

As the marketing manager for Lexus, how would you feel about Jaguar increasing purchase intention 5 percent in the upscale consumer market while Lexus drops the same amount? What other information would you want to know now?

BE an MR!

Visit Lexus' Web site (www.lexus.com) and search the Internet using a search engine as well as your library's online databases to obtain information on consumer purchase intentions for luxury cars.

Would you use a comparative scaling technique to measure consumer purchase intentions for luxury cars? If yes, which technique?

important as some other attribute, the respondent assigns it twice as many points. All the points a respondent assigns must total 100. Hence, the name of the scale: constant sum. A constant sum scale also results whenever percentages are calculated, as in the opening vignette.

Note that the constant sum scale has an absolute zero—10 points are twice as many as 5 points, and the difference between 5 and 2 points is the same as the difference between 57 and 54 points. For this reason, constant sum scale data are sometimes treated as metric. While this may be appropriate in the limited context of the objects scaled, these results are not generalizable or applicable to other objects not included in the study. Hence, strictly speaking, the constant sum should be considered an ordinal scale.

The main advantages of the constant sum scale are that it allows for fine discrimination among alternatives and does not require too much time. However, it has one major disadvantage. Respondents may allocate more or fewer units than those specified. For example, a respondent may allocate 108 or 94 points. If this occurs, the researcher must adjust the data to sum to 100 points or eliminate that respondent from analysis.

Constant sum scales in the form of percentages are often used to present research results. In the opening vignette, the popularity of a spectator sport was measured in terms of the percentage of respondents who reported it as their favorite. As another example, consider the following.

RESEARCH IN ACTION

The Malling of America

The number of malls and shopping centers dotting the U.S. landscape in 2005 exceeded 45,000. California had the highest number of shopping centers, followed by Florida, Texas, and Illinois. According to a recent Maritz Ameri-Poll, visiting the local mall has become part of the American lifestyle. The results of this poll indicated that, on average, 40 percent of adults shop at a mall one or two times per month. Another 20 percent shop three or four times per month, and 10 percent make five to seven trips. "Born to shop" is the description applied to people who average eight or more trips each month. According to this poll, seven percent of the population is "born to shop."

Information conveyed as percentages is an illustration of a constant sum scale. Department store chains use this type of information in planning the number of store locations in malls. The 23 percent who shop less than once per month represent a segment that needs to be penetrated.[3]

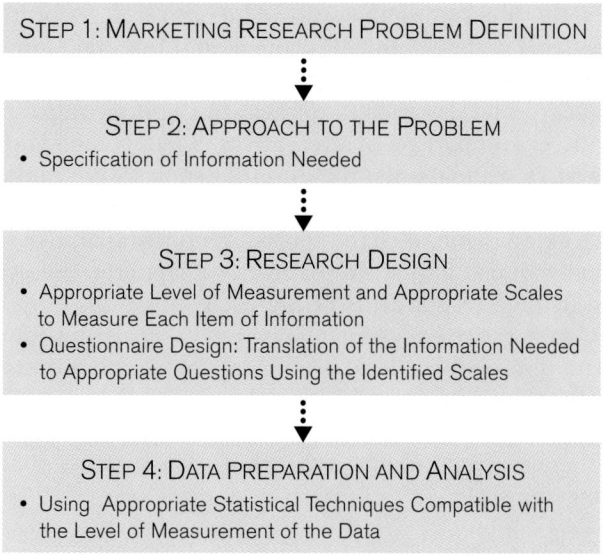

Figure 9.9
Relationship of Measurement and Scaling to the Marketing Research Process

Relationship of Measurement and Scaling to the Marketing Research Process

The relationship of measurement and scaling to the previous and subsequent steps of the marketing research process is described in Figure 9.9. The marketing research problem is defined in Step 1. Based on this definition, an approach to the problem is developed (Step 2). An important component of the approach is specifying the information needed to address the marketing research problem. Measurement and scaling are part of the research design (Step 3). The researcher must identify an appropriate level of measurement (nominal, ordinal, interval, or ratio) for each item of information needed. If the measurement level is ordinal, the researcher generally selects one of the comparative techniques (paired comparison, rank order, or constant sum). If the data are interval, the researcher selects one of the noncomparative techniques (continuous or itemized rating scale: Likert, semantic differential, or Stapel).

Likewise, the researcher must select an appropriate scale for an information item that is to be measured on a nominal or ordinal level. When designing a questionnaire, also part of the research design, the researcher must translate the information needed to appropriate questions using the identified scales. When analyzing the data (Step 4), the researcher should only use those statistical techniques that are compatible with the measurement level of the data. For example, regression analysis, discussed in Chapter 18, assumes that the dependent variable is measured using an interval or ratio scale. Thus, regression analysis should not be used when the data have been measured on an ordinal level.

Summary Illustration Using the Opening Vignette

The four primary scales of measurement are nominal, ordinal, interval, and ratio. Of these, the nominal scale is the most basic. The numbers are used only for identifying or classifying objects under study. In the opening vignette, numbers could be used to denote the various spectator sports: 1. tennis, 2. hockey, 3. soccer, 4. basketball, and so forth. Although soccer is identified by the number 3 and basketball by the number 4, this does not mean that soccer is either more or less preferred to basketball. In the ordinal scale, the numbers indicate the relative position of the objects but not the magnitude of difference between them. The ranking of the various sports, with basketball at the top, constitutes an ordinal scale. The interval scale permits a comparison of the differences between the objects. However, it has an arbitrary zero point. Therefore, it is not meaningful to calculate ratios of scale values on an interval scale. Preference ratings for the various spectator sports on a seven-point scale (1 = not so preferred, 7 = greatly preferred) would be an interval scale.

Alternatively, this preference scale could go from –3 to +3. The latter scale can be derived from the former by subtracting 4 from each scale unit. The ratio scale in which the zero point is fixed represents the highest level of measurement. The researcher can compute ratios of scale values using this scale. The ratio scale incorporates all the properties of the lower-level scales: nominal, ordinal, and interval. Time or money spent watching each sport would be examples of ratio scales.

Scaling techniques can be classified as comparative or noncomparative. Comparative scaling involves a direct comparison of alternatives. The opening vignette presented an example of comparative scaling when the different sports were ranked in terms of the percentage of respondents mentioning each sport as their favorite. The resulting scale presented a relative comparison of all the sports. In noncomparative scaling, objects are evaluated individually, one at a time. In the opening vignette, the use of noncomparative scaling would involve respondents rating each sport, taken by itself, on a 1-to-7 preference scale. Comparative scales include paired comparisons, rank order, and constant sum. The data obtained by these procedures have only ordinal properties. The opening vignette illustrates the use of rank order scaling by ranking basketball at the top. The respondents indicate which sport is their favorite. From these data, we can derive the percentage of respondents indicating each sport as their favorite, which would be a constant sum scale.

International Marketing Research

The higher levels of education and product experience of respondents in many developed countries enable them to provide responses on interval and ratio scales. In some developing countries, the respondents may have difficulty expressing their opinions in a fashion required by interval and ratio scales. Therefore, consumer preferences in these types of countries are best measured with ordinal scales. In particular, dichotomous scales (such as preferred/not preferred), the simplest type of ordinal scale, are recommended. For example, while measuring preferences for jeans in the United States, Levi Strauss could ask consumers to rate their preferences for wearing jeans on specified occasions using a seven-point interval scale. Consumers in the United States have experience with jeans, which should lead to a wide range of preference levels. However, consumers in Papua New Guinea, could be shown a pair of jeans and simply asked whether or not they would prefer to wear it for a specific occasion (e.g., when shopping, working, relaxing on a holiday, and so on). The advantage of matching the primary scales to the profile of the target respondents is well illustrated by the Japanese survey of automobile preferences in Europe.

BE an MR!

Visit Gap's Web site (www.gap.com) and search the Internet using a search engine as well as your library's online databases to obtain information on consumer preferences for casual clothing.

Which comparative scaling technique(s) would you use to measure consumer preferences for casual clothing in the United States and in rural Nigeria?

BE a DM!

As the marketing manager for Gap, what kind of information would you want when selecting summer styles from garment manufacturer's six months in advance of summer?

Technology and Marketing Research

Database managers allow researchers to develop and test several different scales to determine their appropriateness for a particular application. Several questionnaire design and survey programs are available to design basic types of scales and comparative and noncomparative scales. Surveyz! is an online survey-building and survey software provider. Surveyz!'s online survey-building site allows one to build, enhance, and analyze surveys, forms, and databases instantly and online. More than 30 million survey forms have been collected through the online capabilities of Surveyz!.

RESEARCH IN ACTION

Car War–Japan Making a Spearhead

Nissan formed an alliance with Renault, SA and was 44.4 percent owned by Renault as of 2004. Recently, European journalists gave their car-of-the-year award to a Japanese model–Nissan's new British-made Micra, a $10,000 subcompact. This came as a blow to European automakers, who had have been trying to keep the Japanese off the continent. "They will change the competitive balance," warned Bruce Blythe, Ford of Europe's head of business strategy.

How did the Japanese do it?

Nissan conducted a survey of European consumers' preferences for automobiles. They used interval scales to capture the range of differences in preference. For instance, consumers were asked to rate the popular automobile brands and features in terms of preference, using a seven-point scale, with 1 = not at all preferred, and 7 = greatly preferred. The data derived from these interval scales enabled Nissan to compare the differences between automobile brands and features, and determine which features were preferred for what brands. The findings revealed distinct consumer preferences. The cars were redesigned to meet consumer preferences and needs.

The Japanese also benefited by setting up production plants in Europe to customize their cars to local styling tastes and preferences. By 2005, the Japanese were producing more than one million cars a year in Europe, 75 percent of them in Britain. With a strong focus on consumer preferences measured via interval scales, the Japanese are taking away market share from European manufacturers in the European markets.[4]

Ethics in Marketing Research

It is the researcher's responsibility to use the appropriate scales to obtain the necessary data to answer the research questions and test the hypotheses. Take, for example, a study IBM initiated to measure and explain consumer preferences for different brands of computers (IBM, HP, Acer, Gateway, NEC, Apple, Compaq, and Dell). One way to gain information on the preferences of these consumers would be to give each respondent several cards, each listing one computer brand. The respondent rank orders the brands (cards) in order of preference. The respondent selects the card for the most preferred brand first, followed by the card for the second most preferred brand, third most preferred brand, and so on until, last of all, the card for the least preferred brand is selected. This results in ordinal data. Although it will provide rich insight into brand preference by

EXPERIENTIAL LEARNING

Surveyz!'s Question Types and Corresponding Scales

Go to the Surveyz! Web site (www.surveyz.com). In the bottom right quadrant of the Surveyz! homepage, you will see "Build Your Own Survey." Click on "Question Types." Here you will see a "v" that will activate a drop-down list when clicked. Using this drop-down list feature, select the following four question types and categorize each according to the type of scale that is featured with the question type (nominal, ordinal, interval, or ratio):

1. Spreadsheet
2. Select to Add a Question: Single/Multiple Answer
3. Side-by-Side Matrix Question
4. Rank Order

To take the tour of what Surveyz! offers its clients, go to (www.surveyz.com/tour/) and under "Build Your Own Online Survey!" select "Three Minute Tour."

1. What types of question formats are available using Surveyz.com?
2. What types of analyses are available using Surveyz.com?
3. In what types of formats can results be exported?

allowing respondents to compare the cards, shuffle them, compare again, and reshuffle, these data cannot be analyzed using popular statistical techniques. To explain preferences for computer brands in terms of the relevant attributes, interval scale data are needed.

Knowingly using inappropriate scales raises ethical questions. It is the obligation of the researcher to obtain the data that are most appropriate given the research questions, as the following example illustrates.

RESEARCH IN ACTION

Scaling Ethical Dilemmas

In a study designed to measure ethical judgments of male and female marketing researchers, scale items from a previously developed and tested scale were used. However, after a pretest was conducted on a convenience sample of 65 marketing professionals, it became apparent that some original scale items were worded in a way that did not reflect current usage. Therefore, these items were updated. For example, an item that was gender specific, such as, "He pointed out that . . ." was altered to read, "The project manager pointed out that . . ." Respondents were asked to show their approval or disapproval of the stated action of a marketing research director with regard to specific scenarios. Realizing that a binary or dichotomous scale (disapprove/approve) would be too restrictive, approval or disapproval was indicated by having respondents supply interval level data via five-point scales with descriptive labels of 1 = disapprove, 2 = disapprove somewhat, 3 = neither approve or disapprove, 4 = approve somewhat, and 5 = approve. The results revealed some differences, and female marketing researchers were found to be more ethical than their male counterparts. These differences probably would not have been discovered if the original dichotomous scale (approve/disapprove) had been used. However, the finer discrimination afforded by the five-point interval scale enabled the researcher to discover these differences. This example illustrates the use of appropriate scaling techniques in examining ethical issues in marketing research.[5]

SPSS Windows

Using SPSS Data Entry, the researcher can design any of the primary type of scales: nominal, ordinal, interval, or ratio. Either the question library can be used or customized scales can be designed. Moreover, paired comparison, rank order, and constant sum scales can be easily implemented. We show the use of SPSS Data Entry to design ordinal scales to measure education and income. This software is not included but may be purchased separately from SPSS.

Use of SPSS Data Entry to design ordinal scales to measure education and income.

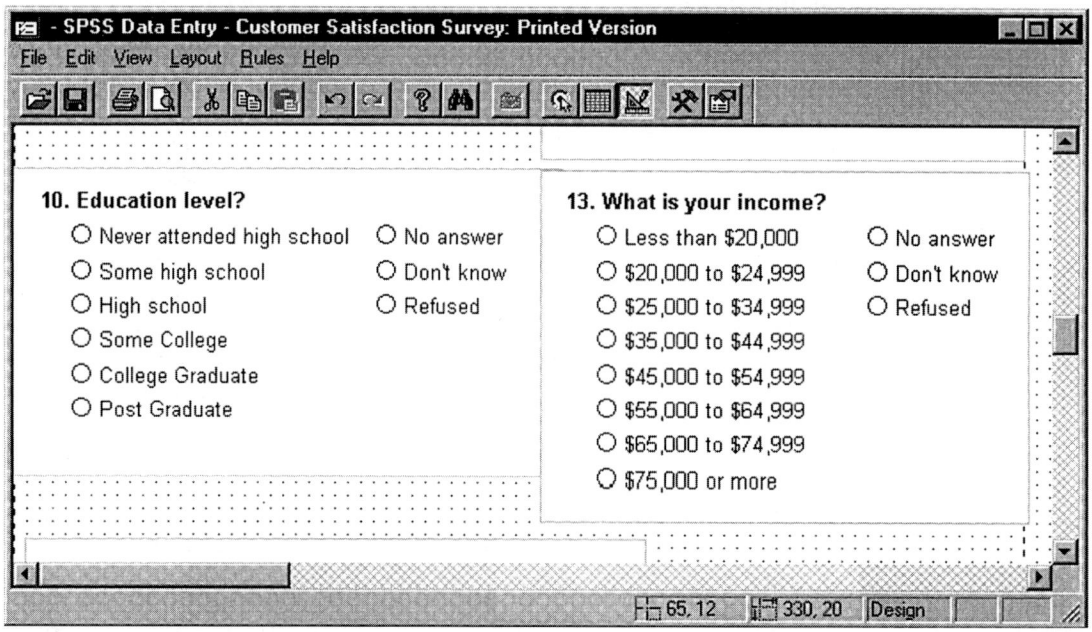

New Balance: Attaining a Balance in Marketing Strategy

The Situation

The U.S. athletic footwear market is likely to grow slowly during 2004 to 2007, characterized by good volume sales and falling prices according to a recently published report from Mintel International. It projects annual growth of 2 percent, before inflation, rising from $13.5 billion in 2002 to $15 billion in 2007. This is due to factors such as overly complex manufacturer/retailer relationships that sap brand loyalty and foster excessive bargain hunting, a slow-growth economy, and competition from brown shoe manufacturers as the previously distinct line between athletic and brown shoes becomes blurred. Alongside this, weak retail pricing is likely to lead to more of a two-tier market—an upscale shoe market for those most dedicated to athletic shoes (young males) and those with higher levels of discretionary income, and a mass market for the rest of the nation. One bright spot revealed by Mintel's consumer research is that respondents overwhelmingly agree that they are willing to "spend money on good sneakers."

Jim Davis, CEO of New Balance Athletic Shoe, Inc., is trying to appeal to those consumers about whom Mintel's research is talking. New Balance rose quickly starting in the mid-1990s to be the third-largest seller of athletic shoes. Its strategy mirrored Nike's in launching the largest possible number of shoe styles and selling primarily through specialty athletic shoe stores and sporting goods stores. A big difference, however, was that New Balance created an upscale brand image that aimed to attract a greater number of 35- to 64-year-olds. Times are changing, however, and New Balance is learning that it must also change to keep improving its market growth and profits.

The Marketing Research Decision

1. New Balance would like to determine consumer preferences for its brand as compared to Nike, Reebok, and Adidas. Which scaling technique should be used? Check as many as are applicable.
   a. Paired comparison
   b. Rank order
   c. Constant sum
   d. Continuous rating scales
   e. Itemized rating scales
2. Discuss the role of the type of scaling technique you recommend in enabling Jim Davis to determine consumer preferences for New Balance as compared to Nike, Reebok, and Adidas and increase the market share of New Balance.

The Marketing Management Decision

1. In order to increase the market share of New Balance, Jim Davis should (check as many as are applicable):
   a. Use celebrity endorsements
   b. Introduce lower-priced shoes
   c. Enhance the style and color of shoes
   d. Increase the promotional budget
   e. Sell New Balance shoes on the Internet
2. Discuss how the marketing management-decision action that you recommend to Jim Davis is influenced by the scaling technique that you suggested earlier and by the findings of that research.

What Jim Davis Did

Rather than use endorsements, New Balance looked at sponsorships and promotions as a way to gain notoriety for their product. Some of the events include the Chicago Marathon, the title sponsorship for the national indoor track and field championships in New York, various walking organizations, and the U.S. modern pentathlon team. Along the promotional aspect, the company offered The Million Dollar Challenge, a seven-figure prize to the man or woman who broke existing U.S. marathon records. Also, their sponsorship of the Race for the Cure has raised money and awareness of New Balance among women.

To continue its success, New Balance added style and color to its already available models, but not enough to lose integrity with old customers. This helped them attract new consumers while maintaining the old ones. New Balance is also planning to boost media spending from $13 million to $20 million next year. Most of the increase is allotted for television advertising of men's running and cross-training shoes. New Balance will also run print ads accenting men's and women's running shoes and women's walking shoes, focusing on the baby-boomer crowd. New Balance is also looking at other market opportunities, such as lower price points, which would best be accomplished under a different brand name.[6]

Summary

Measurement is the assignment of numbers or other symbols to characteristics of objects according to set rules. Scaling involves the generation of a continuum upon which measured objects are located. The four primary scales of measurement are nominal, ordinal, interval, and ratio. Of these, the nominal scale is the most basic. The numbers are used only for identifying or classifying objects under study. In the ordinal scale, the numbers indicate the relative position of the objects but not the magnitude of difference between them. The interval scale permits a comparison of the differences between the objects. However, because it has an arbitrary zero point, it is not meaningful to calculate ratios of scale values on an interval scale. The ratio scale, in which the zero point is fixed, represents the highest level of measurement. The researcher can compute ratios of scale values using this scale. The ratio scale incorporates all the properties of the lower-level scales.

Scaling techniques can be classified as comparative or noncomparative. Comparative scaling involves a direct comparison of alternatives. Comparative scales include paired comparisons, rank order, and constant sum. The data obtained by these procedures have only ordinal properties.

Comparative scaling can yield information vital to improving quality and determining which attributes have the greatest impact on quality. In developed countries, respondents are quite used to providing responses on interval and ratio scales. However, in developing countries, responses can be best measured by using simple ordinal scales. Software is available to enable researchers to construct a variety of comparative scales. Ethical considerations require that the appropriate type of scales be used in order to get the data needed to answer the research questions and test the hypotheses. All of the primary scales can be implemented on the Internet.

Key Terms and Concepts

Measurement, 238
Scaling, 239
Nominal scale, 240
Ordinal scale, 242
Interval scale, 243
Ratio scale, 244
Comparative scales, 246
Noncomparative scales, 247
Paired comparison scaling, 247
Rank order scaling, 248
Constant sum scaling, 249

Suggested Cases and Video Cases

Cases

2.4 Bloomingdale's **2.5 Burger King** **4.1 Boeing** **4.2 Gucci**

Video Cases

3.2 Honest Tea **4.1 Subaru**

Additional cases and video cases are available in the Instructor's Manual and on the instructor and student Web sites.

Live Research: Conducting a Marketing Research Project

1. As a class, discuss the level of measurement (nominal, ordinal, interval, or ratio) that is appropriate for the key variables.
2. Discuss which, if any, of the comparative techniques are appropriate.
3. Consider the practical constraints. For example, if a certain level of measurement has been used to measure a variable in the past (e.g., ordinal preference), the same may have to be used again in the project to allow a comparison of the findings with past results.

Acronyms

The four primary types of scales may be described by the acronym FOUR:

F igurative: nominal scale
O rdinal scale
U nconstrained zero point: interval scale
R atio scale

The different comparative and noncomparative scales may be represented by the acronym SCALES:

S emantic differential scale
C onstant sum scale
A rranged in order: rank order scale
L ikert scale
E ngaged: paired comparison scale
S tapel scale

Review Questions

1. What is measurement?
2. What are the primary scales of measurement?
3. Describe the differences between a nominal and an ordinal scale.
4. What are the implications of having an arbitrary zero point in an interval scale?
5. What are the advantages of a ratio scale over an interval scale? Are these advantages significant?
6. What is a comparative rating scale?
7. What is a paired comparison?
8. What are the advantages and disadvantages of paired comparison scaling?
9. Describe the constant sum scale. How is it different from the other comparative rating scales?

Applied Problems

1. Identify the type of scale (nominal, ordinal, interval, or ratio) being used in each of the following. Please explain your reasoning.
   a. I like to solve crossword puzzles.

Disagree				Agree
1	2	3	4	5

   b. How old are you? _____
   c. Please rank the following activities in terms of your preference by assigning ranks 1 to 5, with 1 being most preferred and 5 being least preferred.
      i. Reading magazines _____
      ii. Watching television _____
      iii. Dating _____
      iv. Shopping _____
      v. Eating out _____
   d. What is your Social Security number? _____
   e. On an average weekday, how much time do you spend doing your homework and class assignments?
      i. Less than 15 minutes _____
      ii. 15 to 30 minutes _____
      iii. 31 to 60 minutes _____
      iv. 61 to 120 minutes _____
      v. More than 120 minutes _____
   f. How much money did you spend last month on entertainment? _____
2. Show how intentions to purchase four brands of soft drinks (Coke, Pepsi, Dr. Pepper, and 7-Up) can be measured using ordinal, interval, and ratio scales.
3. Visit the Web sites of two marketing research firms conducting surveys. Analyze one survey from each firm to critically evaluate the primary type of scales being used.
4. Surf the Internet to find two examples of each of the four primary types of scales. Write a report describing the context in which these scales are being used.
5. Search the Internet to identify the top five selling automobile brands during the last calendar year. Rank order these brands according to sales.
6. Target and Wal-Mart are two of the major department stores. Develop a series of paired comparison scales comparing these two stores on store image characteristics. Identify the relevant store image characteristics by visiting the Web sites of these two stores (www.target.com, www.walmart.com).

Group Discussion

1. "A brand could receive the highest median rank on a rank order scale of all the brands considered and still have poor sales." Discuss.
2. Select one of the readings from the notes in this chapter and lead a class discussion.

CHAPTER

10 Measurement and Scaling: Noncomparative Scaling Techniques

"Different cultures use scales in different ways. For example, in Mexico no one bothers to use points 1 through 4 on a 10-point scale because they learned in school that a grade of '5' on a 10-point scale means you already flunk the test."

MANUEL BARBERENA, *President, Mexico Subsidiary, Pearson Research, Col. Polanco, Mexico*

OPENING QUESTIONS

1. How are noncomparative scaling techniques different from comparative scaling, and what is the distinction between continuous and itemized rating scales?
2. What are the differences between Likert, semantic differential, and Stapel scales?
3. What are the decisions involved in constructing itemized rating scales, and what options should be considered?
4. How are scales evaluated, and what is the relationship between reliability and validity?
5. In what way can noncomparative scaling contribute to total quality management?
6. What considerations are important in implementing noncomparative scales in an international setting?
7. How does technology impact noncomparative scaling?
8. What ethical issues are involved in developing noncomparative scales?
9. How can the Internet be used to construct noncomparative scales?

Noncomparative Scaling Techniques Result in an Incomparable Hit Movie

The entertainment industry regularly conducts market research to determine audience response to its new offerings. For example, film studios routinely conduct prerelease screenings in order to gauge audience reaction. One method of measuring audience reaction is electronic continuous measurement. Audience members are each given a dial and are told to continuously rate their reaction to the film while watching it. They simply turn the dial from positive to negative to record their reactions. Since the recording is continuous, audience reaction to all the scenes can be measured. This method is particularly useful when the size of the audience is 100 or less, that is, when the sample size is relatively small.

When the size of the audience is large, a survey questionnaire is administered at the end of each segment of the movie. These surveys generally employ Likert-type scales that are five-point scales measuring respondents' degree of agreement or disagreement with the specified statements. For example, the following is a statement designed to measure the response to ending scenes:

	Strongly disagree	Disagree	Neither agree nor disagree	Agree	Strongly agree
I like the ending of the movie.	1	2	3	4	5

The scales are balanced so that they have an equal number of agree and disagree categories. Moreover, the scales have an odd number of categories, generally five, to allow neutral responses, such as neither agree nor disagree, since many respondents may not like or dislike specific scenes. All the scale categories are labeled to reduce ambiguity. A "no opinion" option is not provided because it is believed that all respondents should be able to express an opinion having just seen the movie. Sometimes, both electronic continuous measurement and Likert scales are used to allow an assessment of the validity of the scales by comparing responses from the two methods.

Audience reaction and response to the original ending of the movie *Fatal Attraction* was the primary reason its original ending was changed. Although the audience liked the movie in general, electronic continuous measurement and survey responses indicated that the ending was poorly received. With the changes, the movie went on to become one of the blockbuster hits of the last two decades. How was the ending changed?

Fatal Attraction has gone down in history as a major romantic/thriller/slasher-style movie. Michael Douglas stars as a caring husband and father who has a very brief affair with his colleague (Glenn Close). Douglas thinks nothing of the affair, but Close becomes obsessed with Douglas and eventually turns into a psychotic. The original ending of this movie made Douglas out as the villain, and Close as the victim. However, test audiences despised Close's character so much that Paramount spent $1.3 million to switch the ending of the movie to make Close the villain and Douglas the victim. *The Lord of the Rings–The Return of the King* also made extensive use of continuous measurement and Likert-type scales to adapt the movie to audience reactions, and it won 11 Academy awards in 2004. These scaling techniques were also employed in other movies in this sequel such as *The Lord of the Rings–The Fellowship of the Ring.*[1] •

Overview

As discussed in Chapter 9, scaling techniques are classified as either comparative or noncomparative. The comparative techniques discussed in the last chapter consisted of paired comparison, rank order, and constant sum scaling. The subject of this chapter is noncomparative techniques. Figure 10.1 briefly explains the focus of the chapter, the relation of this chapter to the previous ones, and the steps in the marketing research process on which this chapter concentrates.

As discussed in Chapter 9, noncomparative scales are broadly classified as either continuous or itemized. The most popular itemized scales are Likert, semantic differential, and Stapel (see Figure 9.5). The opening vignette illustrated the use of both continuous and itemized rating scales to measure audience response to movies prior to release. Continuous scaling was illustrated by the use of hand-held dials that the respondents turn continuously while watching the movie. The five-point Likert scale that was used to measure response to the ending of the movie was an example of an itemized rating scale.

In this chapter, the multi-item rating scales and the importance and meaning of a scale's reliability and validity are briefly described. It also discusses the applications of these scaling techniques in international marketing research, the impact of technology, and several ethical issues that arise in rating-scale construction. Figure 10.2 gives an overview of the topics discussed in this chapter and how they flow from one to the next.

Noncomparative Scaling Techniques

noncomparative scales
One of two types of scaling techniques in which each stimulus object is scaled independently of the other objects in the stimulus set.

continuous rating scale
A measurement scale in which respondents rate the objects by placing a mark at the appropriate position on a line that runs from one extreme of the criterion variable to the other.

Noncomparative scales are often called *monadic scales* because only one object is evaluated at a time. There is no comparison to another object or to some specified ideal, such as "the perfect brand." Respondents using a noncomparative scale apply their own rating standard. This was illustrated in the opening vignette in which the movie *Fatal Attraction* was evaluated by itself, without comparison to any other movie. The range of noncomparative techniques and their relationship to each other is illustrated in Figure 10.3. The basic characteristics of each scale are summarized in Table 10.1 and are discussed later in this chapter.

Continuous Rating Scale

A **continuous rating scale** allows the respondent to place a mark at any point along a line running between two extreme points rather than selecting from among a set of predetermined response categories. Thus, a score on a continuous scale could be 28.637,

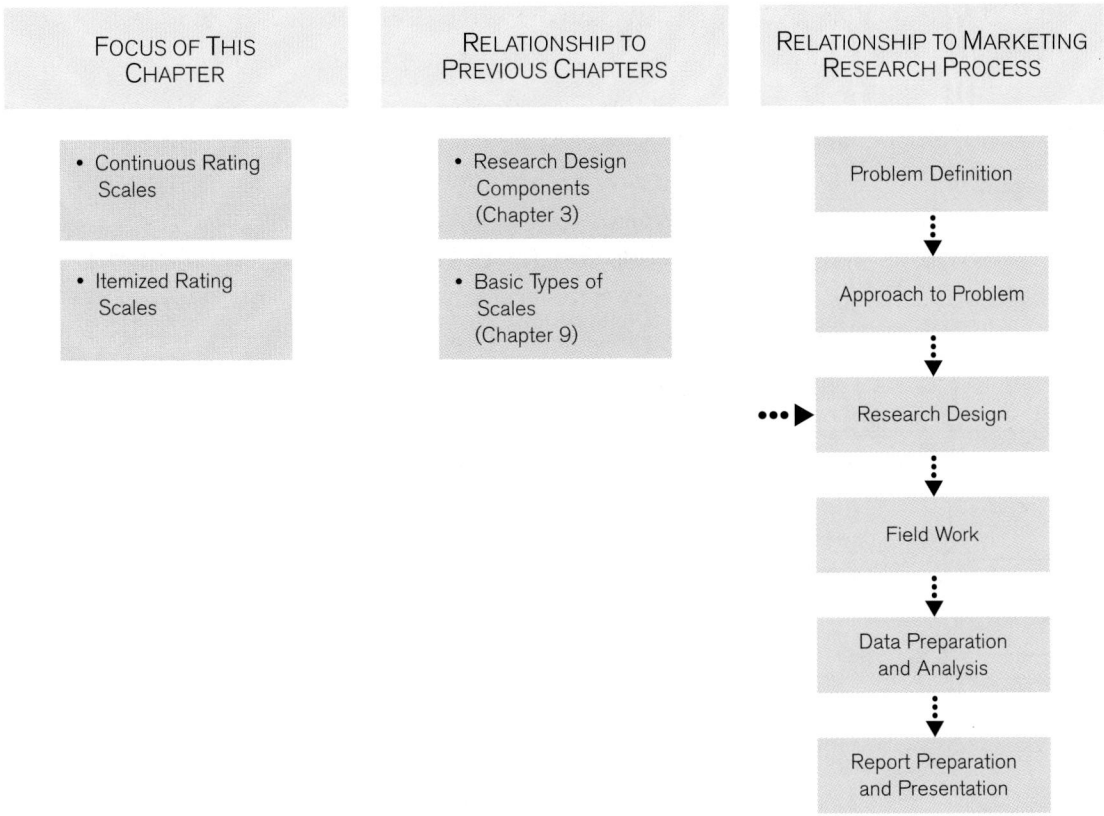

Figure 10.1

Relationship of Noncomparative Scaling to the Previous Chapters and the Marketing Research Process

whereas an itemized rating scale would require the respondent to circle one of the numbers (1, 10, 20, and so on up to 100). The form of the continuous scale may be vertical or horizontal. The scale points may be brief descriptions or numbers. Continuous rating scales are sometimes referred to as *graphic rating scales*. Three versions of a continuous rating scale are illustrated here.

Survey Question

How would you rate Dial bath soap? The cursor/tick mark may be placed at any point along the line.

Version 1

Poor - - - - - - -I - Excellent

Version 2

Poor - - - - - - -I - Excellent

1 10 20 30 40 50 60 70 80 90 100

Version 3

Very bad Neither good nor bad Very good

Poor - - - - - - -I - Excellent

1 10 20 30 40 50 60 70 80 90 100

Once the respondent has provided the ratings or markings on the continuous line, the researcher divides the line into as many categories as desired and assigns scores based on the categories into which the ratings fall. Because the distance between categories is constant and the zero point is arbitrary, this type of scale produces interval data.

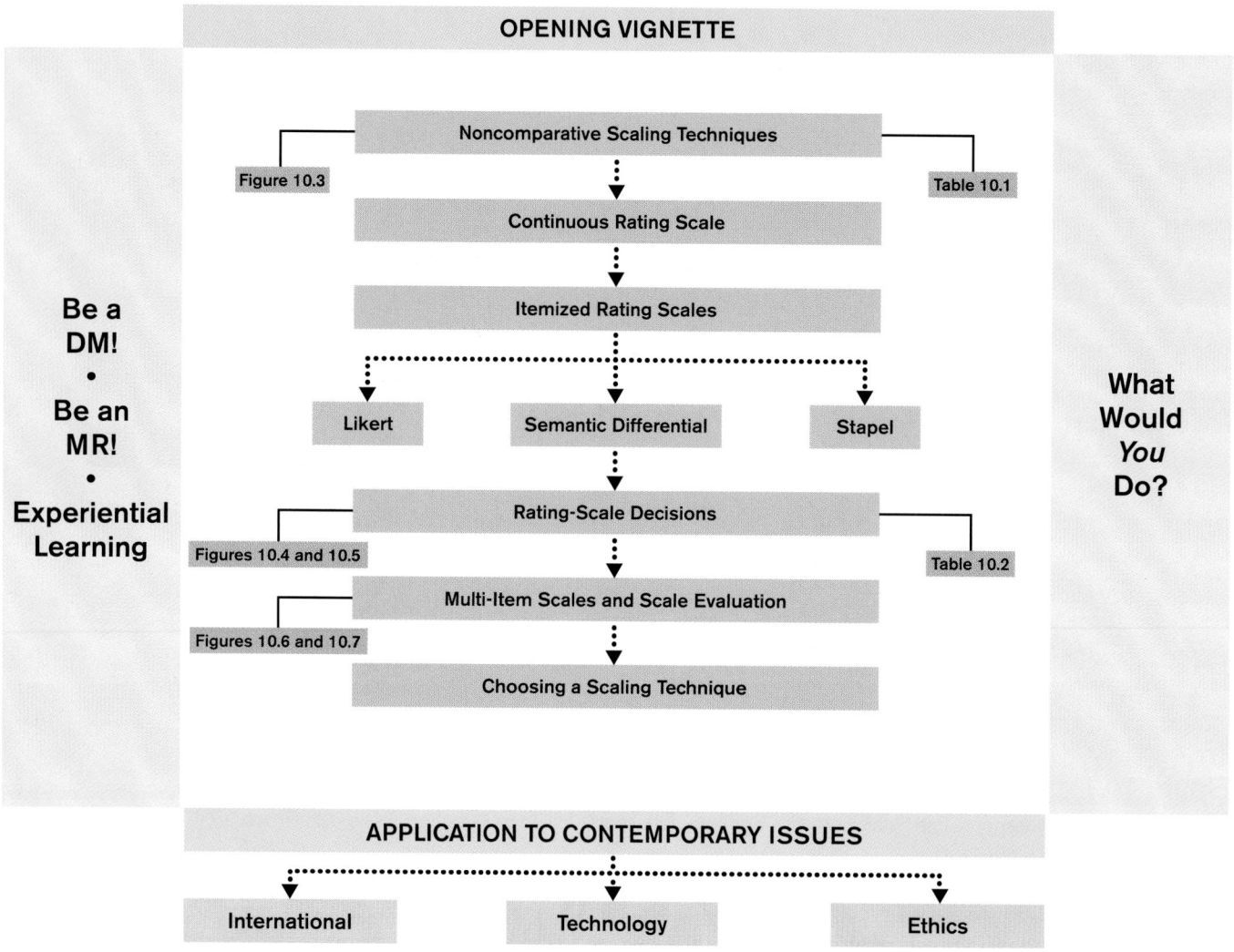

Figure 10.2

Noncomparative Scaling Techniques: An Overview

Continuous scales are easy to construct. However, scoring them can be difficult and unreliable unless they are presented on a computer screen, as in computer-assisted personal interviewing discussed in Chapter 7, or using computerized equipment, as in the opening vignette (see Table 10.1). Continuous rating scales may be easily implemented on the Internet. The cursor can be moved on the screen in a continuous fashion to select the exact position on the scale that best describes the respondent's evaluation. The computer can automatically score the scale values, increasing the speed and accuracy of processing the data.

Figure 10.3

A Classification of Noncomparative Rating Scales

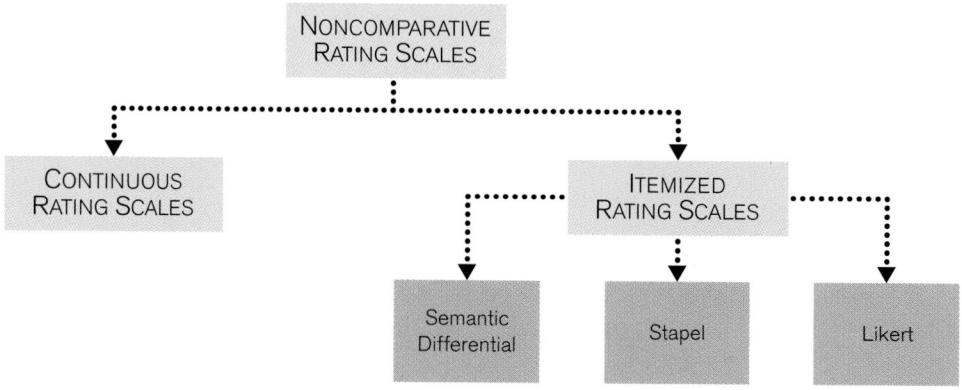

Table 10.1

Basic Noncomparative Scales

Scale	Basic Characteristics	Examples	Advantages	Disadvantages
Continuous Rating Scale	Place a mark on a continuous line	Reaction to TV commercials	Easy to construct	Scoring can be cumbersome unless computerized
Itemized Rating Scales				
Likert Scale	Degree of agreement on a 1 (strongly disagree) to 5 (strongly agree) scale	Measurement of attitudes	Easy to construct, administer, and understand	More time-consuming
Semantic Differential	Seven-point scale with bipolar labels	Brand, product, and company images	Versatile	Difficult to construct appropriate bipolar adjectives
Stapel Scale	Unipolar 10-point scale, −5 to +5, without a neutral point (zero)	Measurement of attitudes and images	Easy to construct and administered over telephone	Confusing and difficult to apply

Continuous scales are being used more frequently as computers, the Internet, and other technologies are used more often in surveys, as illustrated by the opening vignette. Continuous scales are particularly useful for evaluating objects and things, such as movies and TV commercials, continuously over time. You've already seen an example of evaluating a movie; an illustration of a commercial is given in the Research in Action example that follows.

BE an MR!

Visit Disney's Web site (www.disney.com) and search the Internet using a search engine as well as your library's online databases to obtain information on consumer movie-viewing habits and preferences.

How would you measure audience reaction to a new movie slated for release by the Walt Disney Company?

BE a DM!

As the marketing director for Touchstone Pictures—a Disney subsidiary, how would you go about convincing a producer/director of a movie in production that viewer research could be used to develop this movie without compromising the artistic integrity of the entire effort?

RESEARCH IN ACTION

Scaling Emotional Peaks

The Perception Analyzer (www.perceptionanalyzer.com) by MSInteractive is a computer-supported, interactive feedback system composed of wireless or wired hand-held dials for each participant, a console (computer interface), and special software which edits questions, collects data, and analyzes participant responses. Members of focus groups use it to record their emotional response to television commercials, instantly and continuously. Each participant is given a dial and instructed to continuously record his or her reaction to the material being tested. As the respondents turn the dials, the information is fed to a computer. Thus, the researcher can determine the second-by-second response of the respondents as the commercial is run. Furthermore, this response can be superimposed on the commercial to see the respondents' reactions to the various frames and parts of the commercial.

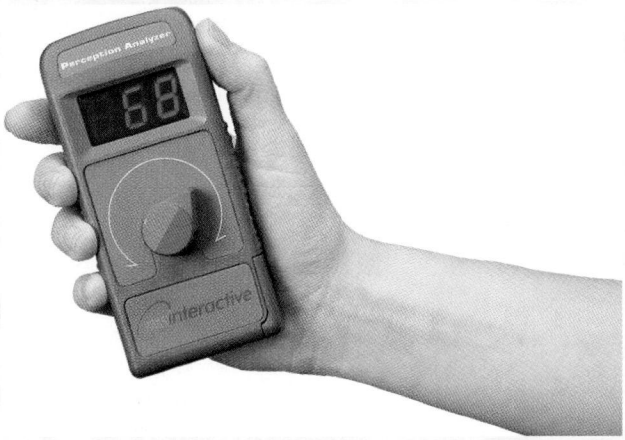

The computer was recently used to measure responses to a series of "slice of life" commercials for McDonald's. The researchers found that mothers and daughters had different responses to different aspects of the commercial. Using the emotional-response data, the researchers could determine which commercial had the greatest emotional appeal across mother–daughter segments.[2]

Itemized Rating Scales

itemized rating scale
A measurement scale that has numbers and/or brief descriptions associated with each category. The categories are ordered in terms of scale position.

An **itemized rating scale** has a number of brief descriptions associated with each response category. The categories are typically arranged in some logical order, and the respondents are required to select the categories that best describe their reactions to whatever is being rated, as illustrated in the opening vignette. Itemized rating scales are the most widely used scales in marketing. This chapter begins by describing the commonly used itemized rating scales—the Likert, semantic differential, and Stapel scales—and then examines the major issues surrounding the use of itemized rating scales.

Likert Scale

Likert scale
A measurement scale with five response categories ranging from "strongly disagree" to "strongly agree," which requires the respondents to indicate a degree of agreement or disagreement with each of a series of statements related to the stimulus object.

Named after its developer, Rensis Likert, the Likert scale is one of the most widely used itemized scales. The end points of a **Likert scale** are typically "strongly disagree" and "strongly agree." The respondents are asked to indicate their degree of agreement by checking one of five response categories. The following example shows how a Likert scale was used in a retailing study.

Instructions

Listed below are different opinions about Target. Please indicate how strongly you agree or disagree with each statement by placing an X beside a number from 1 to 5, where

1 = Strongly disagree
2 = Disagree
3 = Neither agree nor disagree
4 = Agree
5 = Strongly agree

Form

	Strongly disagree	Disagree	Neither agree nor disagree	Agree	Strongly agree
1. Target sells high-quality merchandise.	1	2X	3	4	5
2. Target has poor in-store service.	1	2X	3	4	5
3. I like to shop at Target.	1	2	3X	4	5
4. Target does not offer a good mix of different brands within a product category.	1	2	3	4X	5
5. The credit policies at Target are terrible.	1	2	3	4X	5
6. Target is where America shops.	1X	2	3	4	5
7. I do not like the advertising done by Target.	1	2	3	4X	5
8. Target sells a wide variety of merchandise.	1	2	3	4X	5
9. Target charges fair prices.	1	2X	3	4	5

The data are typically treated as interval. When using this approach to determine the total score for each respondent regarding each store, it is important to use a consistent scoring procedure so that a high (or low) score consistently reflects a favorable response. This requires that the categories assigned to the negative statements by the respondents be scored by reversing the scale. Note that for a negative statement, an agreement reflects an unfavorable response, whereas for a positive statement, agreement represents a favorable response. Accordingly, a "strongly agree" response to a favorable statement and a "strongly disagree" response to an unfavorable statement would both receive scores of five.

In the scale shown above, if a higher score is to denote a more favorable attitude, the scoring of items 2, 4, 5, and 7 will be reversed. This can be easily done by subtracting the original scale value from a number that is the highest scale value plus one. Thus, the second item will be scored as follows: $(5 + 1) - 2 = 4$. The respondent in our example has an attitude score of 22. This equals the sum of all nine item scores after scores for the negative items (2, 4, 5, and 7) are reversed. Each respondent's total score for each store is calculated. A respondent will have the most favorable attitude toward the store with the highest score.

The Likert scale has several advantages (Table 10.1). It is easy for the researcher to construct and administer, and it is easy for the respondent to understand. Therefore, it is suitable for mail, telephone, personal, or electronic interviews. Several variants of the Likert scale are commonly used in marketing which vary the number of scale points (e.g., 7 or 9 points) as well as the descriptors (e.g., importance, familiarity) and other characteristics discussed later. Consider, for example, a seven-point scale designed to measure the importance of attributes, where 1 = not at all important and 7 = very important.

The major disadvantage of the Likert scale is that it takes longer to complete than other itemized rating scales. Respondents have to read the entire statement rather than a short phrase. The following example shows another use of a Likert scale in marketing research.

Semantic Differential Scale

The **semantic differential scale** is a seven-point rating scale on which the end points are adjectives representing opposites. When using a semantic differential, the respondent is typically asked to rate a brand, store, or some other object in terms of these bipolar adjectives, such as "cold" and "warm." This scale is illustrated here by presenting a respondent's evaluation of Target on five attributes.

semantic differential scale
A seven-point rating scale with end points associated with bipolar labels that have semantic meaning.

RESEARCH IN ACTION

The APEAL of Likert Scales

J. D. Power and Associates' (www.jdpa.com) "Automotive Performance, Execution and Layout" (APEAL) survey is based on responses from more than 110,000 new-vehicle owners and measures what excites and delights them with their vehicle's features and design. It comprises eight specific areas of vehicle performance and design, including more than 110 attributes that identify what consumers like and dislike about their new vehicles during the first 90 days of ownership by using Likert-type scales. These areas include the following: vehicle exterior styling; engine and transmission; comfort and convenience; ride, handling, and braking; seats; heating, ventilation, and cooling; cockpit and instrument panel; and sound system.

Carmakers use the results of the J. D. Power survey in advertisements and to check their own results of consumer satisfaction surveys as well as those of competitors. Thus, they can benchmark their performance.

In a recent survey, Lexus models swept all three luxury car segments. The Lexus ES300 was the most appealing entry luxury car, followed closely by its high-performance sibling, the IS300. The GS Sedan topped the mid-luxury car segment, and the LS430 ranked highest among premium luxury cars. Lexus used these results in its advertising to convince consumers that its cars are more appealing to own and operate.[3]

Instructions

This part of the study measures what certain department stores mean to you. We want you to judge the department stores in terms of the following questions. Each question is bounded by bipolar adjectives, which are opposite in meaning. Please mark (X) at the point along the scale that best describes what the store means to you.
Please be sure to mark every scale; do not omit any scale.

Form

Target is

Powerful	–:–:–:–:-X-:–:–:	Weak
Unreliable	–:–:–:–:–:-X-:–:	Reliable
Modern	–:–:–:–:–:–:-X-:	Old-Fashioned
Cold	–:–:–:–:–:-X-:–:	Warm
Careful	–:-X-:–:–:–:–:–:	Careless

The respondents mark the blanks that best indicate how they would describe the object being rated. Thus, in our example, Target is evaluated as somewhat weak, reliable, very old-fashioned, warm, and careful. To encourage careful consideration of each question, the negative adjective or phrase sometimes appears on the left side of the scale and sometimes on the right. This helps to control the tendency of some respondents, particularly those with very positive or very negative attitudes, to mark the right- or left-hand sides without reading the labels. For an expanded discussion of how to select labels for semantic differential scales, see the referenced work by one of the authors describing the application of this scaling technique to the measurement of self-concepts, person concepts, and product concepts.[4] That scale is described in the following Research in Action example.

Individual items on a semantic differential scale may be scored on either a –3 to +3 or a 1 to 7 scale. The resulting data are typically treated as interval data and analyzed using profile analysis. In profile analysis, means or median values for each item are calculated, plotted, and statistically analyzed. By plotting the results, the researcher can see overall differences and similarities among the objects measured. Differences across respondent groups can also be compared. When the researcher requires an overall comparison of objects, such as to determine store preference, the individual item scores can also be summed to arrive at a total score, as with the Likert scale.

RESEARCH IN ACTION

A Semantic Differential Scale for Measuring Self-Concepts, Person Concepts, and Product Concepts

1. Rugged	–:–:–:–:–:–:–:	Delicate
2. Excitable	–:–:–:–:–:–:–:	Calm
3. Uncomfortable	–:–:–:–:–:–:–:	Comfortable
4. Dominating	–:–:–:–:–:–:–:	Submissive
5. Thrifty	–:–:–:–:–:–:–:	Indulgent
6. Pleasant	–:–:–:–:–:–:–:	Unpleasant
7. Contemporary	–:–:–:–:–:–:–:	Noncontemporary
8. Organized	–:–:–:–:–:–:–:	Unorganized
9. Rational	–:–:–:–:–:–:–:	Emotional
10. Youthful	–:–:–:–:–:–:–:	Mature
11. Formal	–:–:–:–:–:–:–:	Informal
12. Orthodox	–:–:–:–:–:–:–:	Liberal
13. Complex	–:–:–:–:–:–:–:	Simple
14. Colorless	–:–:–:–:–:–:–:	Colorful
15. Modest	–:–:–:–:–:–:–:	Vain

PepsiCo, for example, can make use of such a scale for measuring the self-concept of target consumers, the concept or image of selected celebrities, as well as the concept or image of the Pepsi brand (see Chapter 8 examples). This analysis will help Pepsi determine the brand image that will have the greatest appeal to target consumers. It will also help Pepsi select the right celebrities to endorse the brand so as to achieve the desired image and positioning.

The semantic differential is a highly popular scale in market research because of its versatility (Table 10.1). It is used to compare brand, product, and company images; to develop advertising and promotion strategies; and in new product development studies. The major disadvantage is the difficulty in determining the appropriate bipolar adjectives required to construct the scale. Several modifications of the basic scale have been proposed.

Stapel Scale

Stapel scale
A scale for measuring attitudes that consists of a single adjective in the middle of an even-numbered range of values.

The **Stapel scale** was named after its developer, Jan Stapel, and is typically presented vertically, with one adjective appearing at the midpoint of a scale ranging from plus five to minus five. The respondent is not allowed a neutral response, as no zero point is offered. Respondents are asked to indicate how accurately or inaccurately each term describes the object by selecting the appropriate number. The higher the number, the more accurately the adjective describes the object. In the retailing study, evaluations of Target would be obtained as follows.

Instructions

Please evaluate how accurately each word or phrase describes each of the department stores. Select a plus number by placing an (X) beside it for the phrases you think describe the store accurately. The more accurately you think the phrase describes the store, the larger the positive number you should choose. You should select a negative number for phrases you think do not describe the store accurately. A large negative number indicates that the phrase does not describe the store at all. You can select any number, from +5 for phrases you think are very accurate, to −5 for phrases you think are very inaccurate.

Form

	Target	
+5	+5	+5
+4	+4	+4X
+3	+3	+3
+2	+2	+2
+1	+1	+1
High Quality	Poor Service	Wide Variety
−1	−1X	−1
−2X	−2	−2
−3	−3	−3
−4	−4	−4
−5	−5	−5

The data obtained by using a Stapel scale are also treated as interval data, analyzed in much the same way as semantic differential data. Using only one adjective in the Stapel scale has an advantage over semantic differentials, in that no pretest is needed to assure that the adjectives chosen are indeed opposites. The simplicity of the scale also lends itself to telephone interviewing. Some researchers believe the Stapel scale is confusing and difficult to apply, however. It is therefore used the least of the three itemized rating scales discussed here (Table 10.1). The advantages of this scale warrant wider applications than have been made in the past. For instance, it could be used more widely in telephone interviewing, which is currently the most popular method of administering consumer surveys.

BE a DM!

As the brand manager for Diet Coke, how would you use information on consumer attitudes to segment the market?

BE an MR!

Visit Diet Coke's Web site (www.dietcoke.com) and search the Internet using a search engine as well as your library's online databases to obtain information on consumers' attitudes toward diet drinks.

How would you use each of the three itemized scales to measure consumers' attitudes toward Diet Coke and other diet soft drinks? Which scale do you recommend?

Noncomparative Itemized Rating Scale Decisions

One of the advantages of using noncomparative scales is the flexibility of adapting them to a specific research project. When constructing the itemized scales discussed in this chapter, six factors can be adjusted. These factors, along with recommended guidelines, are described in Table 10.2 and briefly reviewed here.

Number of Scale Categories

sensitivity
The sensitivity of a scale is closely related to reliability and is the ability to detect subtle differences in the attitude or the characteristic being measured.

From the researcher's perspective, the larger the number of categories contained in a scale, the finer the discrimination between the brands, alternatives, or other objects under study. The **sensitivity** of a scale is the ability to detect subtle differences in the attitude or the characteristic being measured. Increasing the number of scale categories increases sensitivity. The larger the number of categories, however, the greater the information-processing demands imposed on the respondents. Thus, the desire for more information must be balanced against the demands on the respondent. There is a limit to how much information a respondent can process when answering a question. Another important factor is the mode of data collection. Telephone interviews, in which the respondent cannot see the questionnaire, can become very confusing if the number of scale categories is too large. Space limitations on the survey form itself represent another constraint.

While there is no optimal number, the researcher should strive to balance the need for information with consideration of the demands placed on the respondent and the nature of the data collection task. Traditional guidelines suggest that no fewer than five and no more than nine categories of information should be used. With fewer than five scale categories, we do not get enough information to make the research useful. Beyond nine scale categories, the respondents become confused and fatigued, and the quality of data suffers. The opening vignette illustrated the use of five- and seven-point scales to measure reaction to new films.

Balanced Versus Unbalanced Scale

balanced scale
A scale with an equal number of favorable and unfavorable categories.

In a **balanced scale**, the number of favorable and unfavorable categories or scale points is equal. In an unbalanced scale, they are unequal. Examples of balanced and unbalanced scales are given in Figure 10.4. Generally, balanced scales are desirable, ensuring the data collected is objective, as in the opening vignette. If the researcher suspects that the responses are likely to skew either negatively (that is, most of the responses will be negative or unfavorable) or positively, an unbalanced scale may be appropriate. Under these conditions, more categories are included in the direction of the skew. For example, customer satisfaction is typically positively skewed because

Table 10.2
Summary of Itemized Rating Scale Decisions

Decision Factor	Guidelines
Number of categories	While there is no single optimal number, traditional guidelines suggest there should be between five and nine categories.
Balanced vs. unbalanced	In general, the scale should be balanced to obtain objective data.
Odd vs. even number of categories	If a neutral or indifferent scale response is possible for at least some of the respondents, an odd number of categories should be used.
Forced vs. nonforced	In situations where the respondents are expected to have no opinion, the accuracy of data may be improved by a nonforced scale.
Verbal description	An argument can be made for labeling all or many scale categories. The category descriptions should be located as close to the response categories as possible.
Physical form	A number of options should be tried and the best one selected.

Figure 10.4
Balanced and Unbalanced Scales

Balanced Scale

SURFING THE INTERNET IS
_____ Extremely Good
_____ Very Good
_____ Good
_____ Bad
_____ Very Bad
_____ Extremely Bad

Unbalanced Scale

SURFING THE INTERNET IS
_____ Extremely Good
_____ Very Good
_____ Good
_____ Somewhat Good
_____ Bad
_____ Very Bad

most of the customers are satisfied with the company and its products. Therefore, many researchers prefer to use an unbalanced scale with a larger number of satisfied categories and fewer unsatisfied categories when measuring customer satisfaction. When unbalanced scales are used, the nature and degree of unbalance in the scale should be taken into account in data analysis.

Odd or Even Numbers of Categories

When an odd number of categories are used in a scale, the midpoint typically represents a neutral category. The decision to use a neutral category and its labeling has a significant influence on the response. The Likert scale is an example of a balanced rating scale with an odd number of categories and a neutral point.

The scale should have an odd number of categories if the researcher has reason to believe that a portion of the respondent population is actually neutral on a particular subject. This was illustrated in the opening vignette in which a neutral response was allowed for measuring audience response. It was recognized that many respondents may not like or dislike specific scenes in movies. On the other hand, if the researcher wants to force a response or believes that no neutral or indifferent response exists, a rating scale with an even number of categories should be used. A related issue is whether the choice should be forced or nonforced.

Forced or Nonforced Choice

In a **forced rating scale**, the respondents are forced or required to express an opinion, because a "no opinion" option is not provided. When forced rating scales are applied to situations where a significant portion of the response population holds no opinion, the respondents will tend to select an option at the midpoint of the scale. Marking a middle position when in fact, "no opinion" is the desired response will distort measures of central tendency and variance. In situations where the respondent holds no opinion rather than simply being reluctant to disclose that opinion, a nonforced scale that includes a "no opinion" category may improve the accuracy of data. For example, respondents may not be familiar with some of the brands in a study comparing multiple brands and, therefore, be unable to express an opinion. Otherwise, the use of a "no opinion" category should be avoided, as in the opening vignette. While the neutral point would be the midpoint of the scale, a "no opinion" option may be better placed at the far right or left of the scale, as shown:

forced rating scale
A rating scale that forces the respondents to express an opinion because a "no opinion" option is not provided.

Strongly disagree				Strongly agree	
1	2	3	4	5	No opinion

Nature and Degree of Verbal Description

The way a scale category is described can have a considerable effect on the response. Scale categories may have verbal, numerical, or even pictorial descriptions. They may be provided for each category or only at the end points of the scale. Surprisingly, providing a verbal description for each category may not improve the accuracy or reliability of the data. Yet, an argument can be made for labeling all or many scale categories to reduce scale ambiguity. The category descriptions or labels should be located as close to the response categories (that is, the scale point numbers) as possible, as illustrated by the Likert scale in the opening vignette.

The strength of the adjectives used to anchor the scale also influences the responses. Suppose respondents are asked to indicate their degree of (dis)agreement with the statement, "The moral values in America are declining." Strong anchors (1 = completely disagree, 7 = completely agree) will result in more responses toward the midpoint of the scale because respondents are hesitant to check extreme responses (1 or 7). By contrast, weak anchors (1 = generally disagree, 7 = generally agree) produce uniform or flat distributions. In such cases, the respondents feel more comfortable in checking the scale endpoints (1 or 7) because these responses are not that extreme. Knowledge of the distribution of the characteristic being measured along with the objectives of the study can help the researcher select appropriate anchors.

Physical Form or Configuration

The way a scale is presented can vary quite dramatically. Scales can be presented vertically or horizontally. Categories can be expressed by boxes, discrete lines, or units on a continuum and may or may not have numbers assigned to them. If numerical values are used, they may be positive, negative, or both. Several possible configurations are presented in Figure 10.5. Before selecting a configuration, the researcher should try a number of options. Table 10.3 presents some commonly used scales. While these particular scales have five categories, the number of categories can be varied depending upon the researcher's judgment.

Finally, different types of itemized rating scales may be used in a single questionnaire, as the Advanced Micro Devices example illustrates.

Figure 10.5

Rating-Scale Configurations

A variety of scale configurations may be employed to measure the comfort of Nike shoes. Some examples follow:

Nike shoes are

1) PLACE AN "X" ON THE APPLICABLE BLANK SPACE:

Very Uncomfortable _____ _____ _____ _____ _____ _____ Very Comfortable

2) CIRCLE A NUMBER:

Very Uncomfortable 1 2 3 4 5 6 7 Very Comfortable

3) PLACE AN "X" ON THE APPLICABLE BLANK SPACE:

_____ Very Uncomfortable
_____
_____
_____ Neither Uncomfortable nor Comfortable
_____
_____
_____ Comfortable

4) PLACE AN "X" ON THE APPLICABLE BLANK SPACE:

_____	_____	_____	_____	_____	_____	_____
Very Uncomfortable	Uncomfortable	Somewhat Uncomfortable	Neither Comfortable nor Uncomfortable	Somewhat Comfortable	Comfortable	Very Comfortable

5) CIRCLE A NUMBER:

−3	−2	−1	0	1	2	3
Very Comfortable			Neither Comfortable nor Uncomfortable			Very Comfortable

Table 10.3

Some Commonly Used Scales in Marketing

Construct	Scale Descriptors				
Attitude	Very Bad	Bad	Neither Bad nor Good	Good	Very Good
Importance	Not at All Important	Not Important	Neutral	Important	Very Important
Satisfaction	Very Dissatisfied	Dissatisfied	Neither Dissatisfied nor Satisfied	Satisfied	Very Satisfied
Purchase Intent	Definitely Will Not Buy	Probably Will Not Buy	Might or Might Not Buy	Probably Will Buy	Definitely Will Buy
Purchase Frequency	Never	Rarely	Sometimes	Often	Very Often

BE an MR!

Visit Rockport's Web site (www.rockport.com) and search the Internet using a search engine as well as your library's online databases to obtain information on consumers' preferences for dress shoes.

Develop an itemized scale to measure consumers' preferences for dress shoes and to justify your rating-scale decisions.

BE a DM!

As the marketing manager for Rockport, how would you use information on consumers' preferences for dress shoes to increase your sales?

RESEARCH IN ACTION

Unbalanced Scales Help Advanced Micro Devices Achieve Balance in Customer Satisfaction

CustomerSat (www.customersat.com) is a premier provider of Internet-survey research services. It conducted an Internet-based customer satisfaction survey for Advanced Micro Devices (AMD), a leading manufacturer of integrated circuits (www.amd.com). Various types of itemized rating scales were employed. The importance of attributes used to evaluate AMD was measured on seven-point balanced scales (Extremely Important, Very Important, Important, Neutral, Unimportant, Very Unimportant, Extremely Unimportant). However, satisfaction was measured using five-point unbalanced scales (Excellent, Very Good, Good, Fair, Poor). The use of unbalanced scales to measure satisfaction was justified as satisfaction levels tend to be positively skewed.

Furthermore, a "Not Applicable (N/A)" option was also allowed when measuring satisfaction with AMD on specific attributes, as not all attributes may be relevant for a particular respondent. The results of this survey helped AMD identify customer concerns affecting satisfaction levels and to take corrective actions. For example, filling the orders accurately and in a timely manner had a very important impact on customer satisfaction. Yet, this was an area where AMD was not up to par. Accordingly, AMD reorganized this function, resulting in improved performance and increased customer satisfaction.

Multi-Item Scales

A **multi-item scale** consists of multiple items, where an item is a single question or statement to be evaluated. The Likert, semantic differential, and Stapel scales presented earlier to measure attitudes toward Target are examples of multi-item scales. Note that each of these scales has multiple items. Developing multi-item rating scales requires considerable technical expertise. The steps involved in constructing a multi-item scale are described in Figure 10.6. The researcher begins by developing the construct of interest. A **construct** is a specific type of concept that exists at a higher level of abstraction than do everyday concepts, such as brand loyalty, product involvement, attitude, satisfaction, and so forth. Next, the researcher must develop a theoretical definition of the construct that states the meaning of the central

multi-item scale
A scale consisting of multiple items, where an item is a single question or statement to be evaluated.

construct
A specific type of concept that exists at a higher level of abstraction than do everyday concepts.

Figure 10.6
Developing a Multi-Item Scale

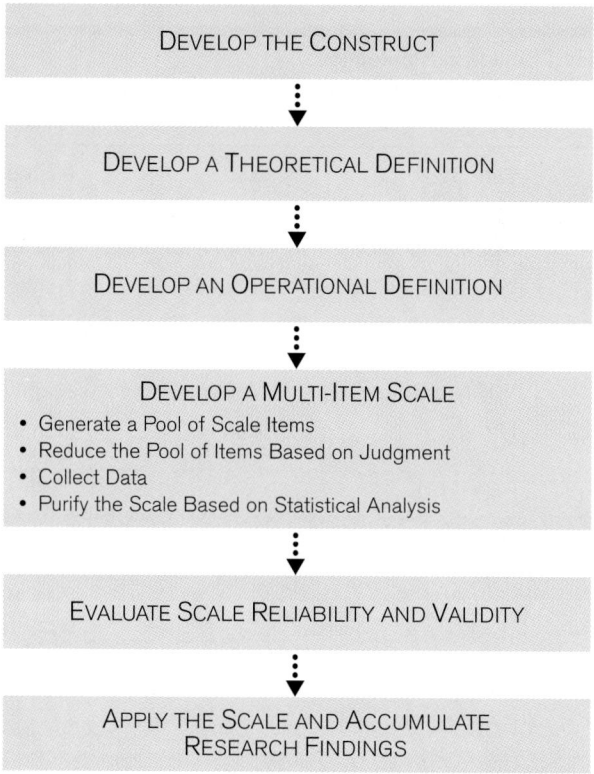

idea or concept of interest. For example, brand loyalty may be defined as the consistent repurchase of a brand prompted by a favorable attitude toward the brand. The construct must be operationalized in a way that is consistent with the theoretical definition. The operational definition specifies the observable characteristics to be measured and the process of assigning value to the construct. For example, in the context of toothpaste purchases, consumers will be characterized as brand loyal if they exhibit a highly favorable attitude (top quartile) and have purchased the same brand on four of the last five purchase occasions. Then, the multi-item scale should be developed. The researcher begins by generating a set of questions based on theory, analysis of secondary data, and qualitative research. This initial pool is repeatedly reduced using input from experts and the researcher's qualitative judgment. If the reduced set of items is still too large, quantitative techniques are available for further reduction and "purification." The researcher evaluates the purified scale for reliability and validity and selects a final set of scale items. The final scale is used in a variety of applications so that a wealth of research findings can accumulate.

EXPERIENTIAL LEARNING

Identifying Comparative and Noncomparative Scales Using Surveyz!

Using Surveyz! (www.surveyz.com), the online survey-building Web site service, can you identify the comparative and noncomparative scales Surveyz! can include in a survey built online?

Go to the Surveyz! home page (www.surveyz.com). On the bottom left of the Web page, select "Question Types" under "Build Your Survey Online." On the new page, click on the checkmark icon under "Choose a Question Type from the drop down list." This will allow you to view the different options for scales and question formats. Starting at the top of the list, view each example presented and record the type of scale that is used. (There is no need to press the "Add Question" button on this page.)

1. How many types of comparative scales are available in Surveyz!?
2. How many format options are available for these comparative scales?
3. How many types of noncomparative scales are available in Surveyz!?
4. How many format options are available for these noncomparative scales?

Scale Evaluation

A multi-item scale should be evaluated for reliability and validity, as shown in Figure 10.7. To understand these concepts, it is useful to think of total measurement error as the sum of systematic error and random error. **Systematic error** affects the measurement in a constant way, that is, in the same way each time the measurement is made. **Random error**, on the other hand, arises from random changes and has a different effect each time the measurement is made. Thus,

Total measurement error = Systematic error + Random error

systematic error
Affects the measurement in a constant way and represents stable factors that affect the observed score in the same way each time the measurement is made.

random error
Measurement error that arises from random changes that have a different effect each time the measurement is made.

Reliability

Reliability refers to the extent to which a scale produces consistent results if repeated measurements are made. Therefore, reliability can be defined as the extent to which measures are free from random error.

Reliability is determined by repeatedly measuring the construct or variable of interest. The higher the degree of association between the scores derived through this repeated measurement, the more reliable the scale. Popular approaches for assessing reliability are test–retest, alternative-forms, and internal-consistency methods.

reliability
The extent to which a scale produces consistent results if repeated measurements are made on the characteristic.

Test–Retest Reliability

In **test–retest reliability**, respondents are administered scales at two different times under as nearly equivalent conditions as possible. The retest typically follows the original measurement by two to four weeks. The degree of similarity between the two measurements is determined by computing a correlation coefficient (see Chapter 18). The higher the correlation coefficient, the greater the reliability.

test–retest reliability
An approach for assessing reliability in which respondents are administered identical sets of scale items at two different times under as nearly equivalent conditions as possible.

Alternative-Forms Reliability

In order to test **alternative-forms reliability**, two equivalent forms of the scale are constructed. The same respondents are measured using alternative scale forms. Correlation between the responses to the two equivalent forms of the scale provides a measure of reliability.

alternative-forms reliability
An approach for assessing reliability which requires two equivalent forms of the scale to be constructed and then measures the same respondents at two different times using the alternate forms.

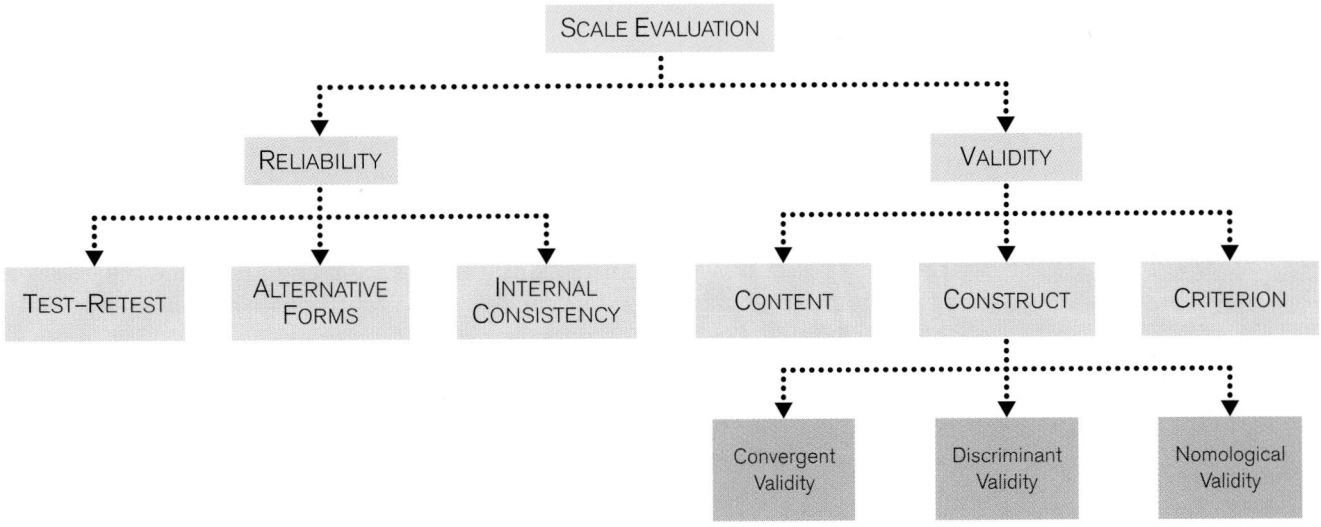

Figure 10.7
Scale Evaluation

Internal-Consistency Reliability

internal-consistency reliability
An approach used to assess the reliability of a summated scale and refers to the consistency with which each item represents the construct of interest.

Internal-consistency reliability is used to assess the reliability of a summated scale, or subscale, where scores for several items are summed to form a total score for a construct (e.g., attitude). In a scale of this type, each item measures some aspect of the construct measured by the entire scale. The items should be consistent in what they indicate about the characteristic. This measure of reliability refers to the consistency with which each item represents the construct of interest. Consider the nine-item Likert scale used to measure attitudes toward Target as discussed earlier in this chapter. How consistently do items, such as "Target sells high-quality merchandise" or "I like to shop at Target," measure attitudes toward Target?

split-half reliability
A form of internal-consistency reliability in which the items constituting the scale are divided into two halves, and the resulting half scores are correlated.

The simplest measure of internal consistency is **split-half reliability**. In applying this procedure, the scale items are randomly divided into halves, and the resulting half scores are correlated. High correlations between the halves indicate high internal consistency. The correlation between the halves will be affected by how the groups are split.

coefficient alpha
A measure of internal-consistency reliability that is the average of all possible split-half coefficients resulting from different splittings of the scale items.

A popular approach to overcoming this problem is to use the coefficient alpha. The **coefficient alpha**, or Cronbach's alpha, is calculated by averaging the coefficients that result from all possible combinations of split halves.[5] This coefficient varies from 0 to 1, and a value of 0.6 or less generally indicates unsatisfactory internal-consistency reliability.

Validity

validity
The extent to which differences in observed scale scores reflect true differences among objects on the characteristic being measured, rather than systematic or random errors.

The **validity** of a scale may be defined as the extent to which differences in observed scale scores reflect true differences in what is being measured, rather than systematic or random error. A scale with perfect validity would contain no measurement error, that is, no systematic error and no random error. Researchers may assess validity in different ways: content validity, criterion validity, or construct validity.

content validity
A type of validity, sometimes called face validity, that consists of a subjective but systematic evaluation of the representativeness of the content of a scale for the measuring task at hand.

Content Validity **Content validity** involves a systematic but subjective assessment of how well a scale measures the construct or variable of interest. For a scale to be content valid, it must address all dimensions of the construct. This is a common-sense evaluation of the scale. For example, a scale designed to measure the construct store image would be considered inadequate if it omitted any of the major dimensions of image (quality, variety and assortment of merchandise, and so on). Content validity alone is not a sufficient measure of the validity of a scale. It must be supplemented with a more formal evaluation of the scale's validity, namely criterion validity and construct validity.

criterion validity
A type of validity that examines whether the measurement scale performs as expected in relation to other variables selected as meaningful criteria.

Criterion Validity **Criterion validity** reflects whether a scale performs as expected given other variables considered relevant to the construct. These variables are called *criterion variables*. They may include demographic and psychographic characteristics, attitudinal and behavioral measures, or scores obtained from other scales. For example, the researcher may measure attitudes toward cereal brands using a multi-item scale administered to members of a scanner panel. Based on attitude levels, future purchases of cereal (criterion variable) are predicted. Scanner data are used to track the actual cereal purchases of the panel members. The predicted and actual purchases are compared to assess criterion validity of the attitudinal scale.

construct validity
A type of validity that addresses the question of what construct or characteristic the scale is measuring. An attempt is made to answer theoretical questions of why a scale works and what deductions can be made concerning the theory underlying the scale.

Construct Validity **Construct validity** addresses the question of what construct or characteristic the scale is, in fact, measuring. In order to assess construct validity, the researcher must have a strong understanding of the theory that provided the basis for constructing the scale. The researcher uses theory to explain why the scale works and what deductions can be drawn from it. As Figure 10.7 shows, construct validity includes convergent, discriminant, and nomological validity. **Convergent validity** is the

convergent validity
A measure of construct validity that measures the extent to which the scale correlates positively with other measures of the same construct.

EXPERIENTIAL LEARNING

McCann Erickson and Ad Promises

As of 2005, McCann Erickson Worldwide Advertising is the world's largest advertising agency network with offices in more than 130 countries. Joe Plummer, Executive Vice-President and Director of Research & Insight Development for McCann Erickson, has become concerned that viewers may be overcome with the "dazzle" of television ads at the expense of actually learning about the brands featured in them. To address the need for improved measures of viewer response to ads, researchers have developed a set of multi-item scales called Ad Promises.[6] Eight-point Likert type scales were used to measure each of the eight sub-scales of Ad Promises.

Go to the Web site for this book and download the following files: (10a) McCann Erickson Experiential learning (Word file); (10b) Ad promises not reversed (Excel file); (10c) Ad promises reversed (SPSS file).

1. Read the Word file (10a) to understand the context of Ad Promises.
2. Using the Excel file (10b), perform the following operations: (See detailed instructions in the Word file (10a).)
   a. Reverse-code the original eight variables into these eight new variables.
   b. Save your Excel file as "Ad Promises Reversed Coded.xls" and then import its contents into SPSS.
3. Using the SPSS file that you have created, perform the following operations (See detailed instructions in the Word file (10a).)
   a. Create a composite variable representing each of the eight Ad Promise constructs.
   b. Compute Cronbach's Alpha for each of these eight sets of items.

extent to which the scale correlates positively with other measures of the same construct. **Discriminant validity** is the extent to which a measure does not correlate with other constructs from which it is supposed to differ. **Nomological validity** is the extent to which the scale correlates in theoretically predicted ways with measures of different but related constructs.

In the opening vignette, construct validity is assessed by measuring audience reaction via continuous measurement using a dial and Likert scales and correlating the measures. In the To Thine Own Self Be True example, we illustrate construct validity in the context of a multi-item scale designed to measure self-concept, the image that consumers have of themselves. This construct is of interest to marketers because consumers prefer products and brands that are consistent with and reinforce their self-concept.

Notice that a high level of reliability was included as evidence of construct validity in this example. This illustrates the relationship between reliability and validity.

discriminant validity
A type of construct validity that assesses the extent to which a measure does not correlate with other constructs from which it is supposed to differ.

nomological validity
A type of validity that assesses the relationship between theoretical constructs. It seeks to confirm significant correlations between the constructs as predicted by theory.

RESEARCH IN ACTION

To Thine Own Self Be True

Following are findings that provide evidence of validity for a multi-item scale to measure self-concept.

- Three experts agree that all the items in the scale are relevant for measuring self-concept (content validity).
- High correlations exist between scales designed to measure self-concept and personality assessments of the same person by their friends (criterion validity).
- High correlations exist with other scales designed to measure self-concepts (convergent validity).
- Low correlations exist with unrelated constructs of brand loyalty and variety seeking (discriminant validity).
- Brands that are congruent with the individual's self-concept are more preferred, as postulated by the theory (nomological validity).
- There is a high level of reliability.

Relationship Between Reliability and Validity

If a measure is perfectly valid, it is also perfectly reliable. In this case, neither systematic nor random error is present. Thus, perfect validity implies perfect reliability. (No measurement error implies no random error.) If a measure is unreliable, it cannot be perfectly valid since at a minimum, random error is present. (If random error is present, measurement error is present.) Furthermore, systematic error may also be present. Thus, unreliability implies invalidity. If a measure is perfectly reliable, it may or may not be perfectly valid because systematic error may still be present. (If there is no random error, measurement error may still be present due to systematic error.) While lack of reliability constitutes negative evidence for validity, reliability does not in itself imply validity. Reliability is a necessary, but not sufficient, condition for validity.

Choosing a Scaling Technique

In addition to theoretical considerations and evaluation of reliability and validity, the researcher should consider certain practical factors in selecting scaling techniques for a particular marketing research problem. These include the level of measurement desired (nominal, ordinal, interval, or ratio), the experience of the respondents with the research topic, the difficulty of administering the scales, and the context. Additionally, using multiple scale items to measure the same characteristic will improve the accuracy of results. In many situations, it is desirable to use more than one scaling technique, as illustrated in the opening vignette.

Summary Illustration Using the Opening Vignette

Noncomparative rating scales can be either continuous or itemized. Both types were illustrated in the opening vignette. Audience members viewing a movie are each given a dial and are told to continuously rate their reactions to the film from positive to negative by turning the dial in the desired direction, thus recording their response on a continuous scale. The itemized rating scales are further classified as Likert, semantic differential, or Stapel scales. Large-scale surveys conducted to assess respondents' reactions to movies make use of Likert scales.

When using noncomparative itemized rating scales, the researcher must decide on the number of scale categories, balanced versus unbalanced scales, odd or even number of categories, forced versus nonforced scales, nature and degree of verbal description, and the physical form or configuration. The Likert scales in the opening vignette make use of five or seven categories following the traditional guidelines and are balanced to avoid bias in any direction. A neutral response (3 or 4) is allowed as it is recognized that many respondents may not like or dislike specific scenes in movies. All the scale categories are labeled in order to reduce ambiguity. A forced scale is used, without a "no opinion" category, as people generally express opinions on movies they have seen.

Multi-item scales consist of a number of rating-scale items. These scales should be evaluated in terms of reliability and validity. Reliability refers to the extent to which a scale produces consistent results if repeated measurements are made. Approaches to assessing reliability include test–retest, alternative forms, and internal consistency. Validity, or accuracy of measurement, may be assessed by evaluating content validity, criterion validity, and construct validity. In the opening vignette, construct validity is assessed by measuring audience reaction using different methods (continuous measurement using a dial and Likert scales) and then correlating the measures.

The choice of particular scaling techniques in a given situation should be based on theoretical and practical considerations. As a general rule, the scaling technique used should be the one that will yield the highest level of measurement feasible. Also, multiple measures should be obtained, as in the opening vignette.

RESEARCH IN ACTION

Copying the Name Xerox

For nearly 30 years, Xerox (www.xerox.com) had been building a solid reputation and market in the Soviet Union. The name Xerox had become synonymous with the act of copying documents and was a brand name people equated with quality. With the disintegration of the Soviet Union into the Commonwealth of Independent States (CIS), sales of Xerox began to fall. The problem was initially attributed to competition from Canon, Ricoh Company, Mitsubishi Electric Corp., and Minolta Camera Company. When Xerox's attempts to improve the competitiveness of their product failed, the company undertook marketing research. The researchers used semantic differential scales to measure Xerox's image. The bipolar labels used were carefully tested to eliminate cultural bias. For example, good–bad was used as a scale item, as these concepts were well understood in the CIS.

The results of the study revealed that the real problem was a growing negative perception among Russian customers towards Xerox products. Xerox management finally traced the explanation for this negative perception to growing trademark infringement by illegal counterfeiters. Some dealers were selling machines with counterfeit Xerox labels. With the disintegration of Soviet Union, government protection from trademark infringement went unchecked. The low quality of the counterfeits was damaging the entire Xerox image. After registering its trademark separately in each republic, Xerox began an extensive corporate image campaign emphasizing its commitment to quality. This was a definite step in removing some of the misconceptions Russian consumers had begun to develop about Xerox. Xerox sponsored the 2004 Olympic Games in Athens, very popular with the Russians, and had more than 60,000 employees worldwide.[7]

International Marketing Research

Pan-cultural scales, designed to be free of cultural biases, are used in international research. In addition to eliminating cultural biases, it is also essential to accommodate differing levels of education and experience. Of the scaling techniques we have considered, the semantic differential has been applied with the greatest consistency in results across countries, as in the Xerox example.

An alternative approach to developing pan-cultural scales is to use descriptors the respondents create themselves. For example, respondents may be asked to indicate the verbal descriptors for the extreme scale categories (anchors) before positioning an object along the scale. This approach is useful when conducting attitude research related to cultural norms (e.g., attitude towards friends). Suppose the researcher is interested in measuring the influence of friends on the purchase of personal clothing in a cross-cultural study involving students in the United States and India. The question asked is "To what extent should your friends influence your purchase of personal clothing?" The responses are obtained on a seven-point scale. Respondents in India may provide the anchors as 1 = little and 7 = much. Respondents in the United States may provide different anchors: 1 = not at all and 7 = a great deal. Such scales have proven to be universally adaptable because they are relatively insensitive to differences in educational level across countries. On the other hand, if the researchers specify the anchors, they should pay special attention to determining equivalent verbal descriptors in different languages and cultures. The end descriptors used to anchor the scale are particularly prone to different interpretations.

Additionally, the scale numbering may have different meanings. In some cultures, 1 may be interpreted as best, while in others it may be interpreted as worst regardless of how it is scaled (1 = best and 7 = worst or 1 = worst and 7 = best). In such cases, it may be desirable to avoid numbers and to just use boxes that respondent can check (worst ☐☐☐☐☐☐☐ best). It is important that the scale end-points and the verbal descriptors be employed in a manner that is consistent with the culture. Finally, in international marketing research it is critical to establish the equivalence of scales and measures used to obtain data from different countries. This topic is complex and is discussed elsewhere by the senior author.[8]

Technology and Marketing Research

Software programs, such as SURVENT by Computers for Marketing Corp. (CfMC) of San Francisco (www.cfmc.com), can customize scales for printed questionnaires or for use by telephone interviewers at computer screens in a fraction of the time this would take without automation. For each new scale, the researcher is presented a screen asking for information about the intended scale. For example, if the question is a noncomparatively scaled question, the researcher would indicate that a "number" response is sought. The researcher would then indicate the valid range of the numbers. After this, a second screen would allow formatting of the scale on the screen as interviewers would see it during data collection.

Another technological development is "smart" instruments that can constantly monitor their own condition and the quality of the information they provide. They can also "talk" directly to the other components of the measurement process, making the integration and processing of information quick and reliable. One such instrument is Option Finder (www.optionfinder.com) from Option Technologies of Minnesota. This system allows for instantaneous feedback. It is designed for use in gathering information from groups as large as 250 persons rather than single individuals. Respondents read a question and then input their responses into the system using a keypad. Since the keypad is the method of data entry, questions are limited to a fixed response, including paired comparisons, Likert-type scales, and discrete-labeled points. The feedback from Option Finder is immediate. The answers to the questions are tallied and processed into graphical form as the respondents enter them.

Ethics in Marketing Research

Since scale construction can influence scale responses and hence the results of the study, several ethical issues are pertinent. Of particular concern is the researcher's attempt to deliberately bias the results by building that bias into noncomparative scales. This can be done, for example, by using scale descriptors that can be manipulated to bias results in a desired direction (e.g., to generate a positive view of the client's brand or a negative view of a competitor's brand). To project the client's brand favorably, the respondents can be asked to indicate their opinion of the brand on several attributes using seven-point scales anchored by the descriptors "extremely poor" to "good." Note that this scale has a strongly negative descriptor with only a mildly positive one. Respondents will be reluctant to rate the product extremely negatively by rating it as "extremely poor." In fact, respondents who believe the product to be only mediocre will end up responding favorably. Try this yourself. How would you rate Chevrolet automobiles on the following attributes?

Reliability:	Horrible	1	2	3	4	5	6	7	Good
Performance:	Very poor	1	2	3	4	5	6	7	Good
Quality:	One of the worst	1	2	3	4	5	6	7	Good
Prestige:	Very low	1	2	3	4	5	6	7	Good

RESEARCH IN ACTION

An Ethical Scale for Measuring Ethics

The theory of moral philosophy was used to develop a scale for measuring ethical evaluations of marketing activities. The resulting scale had 29 seven-point bipolar items ranging from fair to unfair and efficient to inefficient. Evaluations of this scale, through their use in evaluating various ethical scenarios, indicated high internal consistency, reliability (measured via Cronbach's alpha), and a strong degree of construct (convergent, discriminant, and nomological) validity. Accordingly, this scale has been useful in a variety of contexts for investigating ethical issues in marketing. In a recent study, this scale was used to classify the firms as ethical or unethical and to examine the variables that differentiated the two groups. It was found that in ethical firms, ethics were considered more important, the leadership was committed to ethical practices, and codes of ethical conduct were enforced. Also, smaller firms tended to be more ethical than larger firms.[9]

Did you find yourself rating Chevrolet cars positively? The same technique can also be used to negatively bias evaluations of competitors' products by providing a mildly negative descriptor against a strongly positive descriptor.

Thus, it is clearly important to use scales with comparable positive and negative descriptors. This problem emphasizes the need to adequately establish the reliability and validity of scales so that we can be confident that the variables have been accurately measured. The researcher has a responsibility to both the client and respondents to ensure the applicability and usefulness of the scale, as illustrated by the Research in Action example.

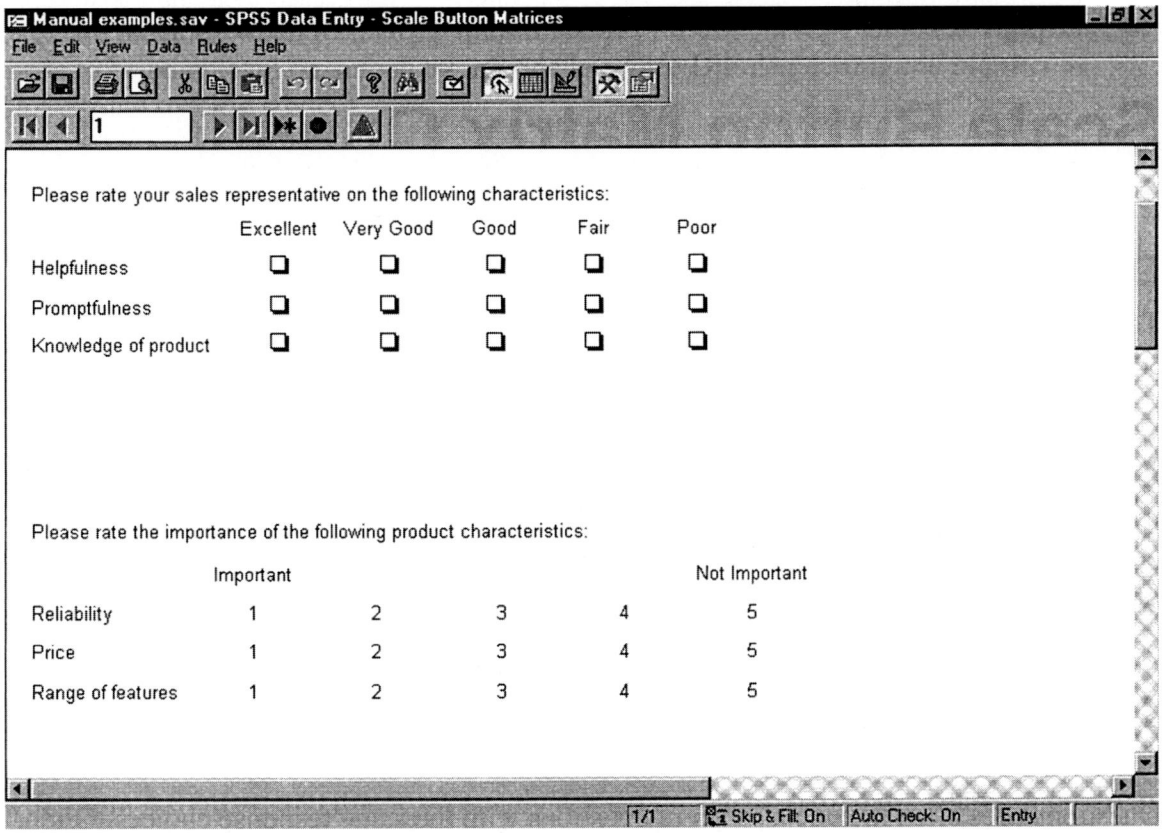

Examples of Likert-type scales designed using SPSS Data Entry.

WHAT WOULD *YOU* DO?

Monster: The Monster of Career Networks

The Situation

When you think of the word "monster," what do you think? Scary creatures under your bed? Elmo and Grover from Sesame Street? The Walt Disney Movie entitled *Monsters, Inc.*? These days, when one hears the word "monster," the person is apt to think of the so-named online job-search company that has connected millions of job searchers with employers. Monster (www.monster.com) was founded in 1994 by Chairman Jeff Taylor. It is the leading online global careers network and the world's number-one hiring management resource. As of 2005, the company's clients included more than 90 of the Fortune 100 and approximately 490 of the Fortune 500 companies. The company had sites in 21 countries around the world. It is no wonder this company has added a whole new meaning to the word "monster."

Monster makes heavy use of marketing research techniques in a unique way. Instead of companies like ACNielsen who conduct marketing research for different companies, Monster researches companies that are in need of employees to fill their positions and provides the service of matching job searchers to these companies. While Monster is doing well, more and more companies have followed in the company's footsteps and have entered the arena of providing online job-search services. Such companies' competitors include HotJobs, Kforce, eJobs, and eCareers. With all of these different services available, the market is becoming saturated with Internet recruiting Web sites. It is important for Monster now more than ever to differentiate themselves from the competition.

The Marketing Research Decision

1. The success of Monster lies in matching their client companies' job specifications with the skills and qualifications of job applicants. What scaling techniques should Monster use to measure companies' job specifications and job applicants' skills and qualifications? Check as many as are applicable.
   a. Ordinal
   b. Likert
   c. Semantic differential
   d. Stapel
   e. Paired comparison
2. Discuss the role of the type of scaling technique you recommend in enabling Jeff Taylor to match companies' job specifications and job applicants' skills and qualifications and thereby increase the market share of Monster.

The Marketing Management Decision

1. What should Jeff Taylor do to gain market share over competitors? Check as many as are applicable.
   a. Give price discounts to their client companies
   b. Aggressively recruit job applicants
   c. Develop a more efficient system to match their client companies' job specifications with the skills and qualifications of job applicants
   d. Increase the quality of job applicants
   e. Promote Monster more aggressively
2. Discuss how the marketing management-decision action that you recommend to Jeff Taylor is influenced by the scaling technique you suggested earlier and by the findings of that research.

What Jeff Taylor Did

Jeff Taylor decided to promote Monster more aggressively. Monster planned to invest about $50 million a year into directly marketing itself to consumers. Monster earns money when employers post job openings on its site and when they hire for those openings. Monster wants to make itself a household name in cities across the country; therefore, the more resumés it has on its site, the more willing corporate human-resource departments will be to spend money advertising job openings there. As part of raising awareness of Monster in locations across the country, Taylor said he is open to doing something extremely bold to build buzz, such as sitting on a billboard for a month. "I am very comfortable putting myself out in front of the brand, and that means different things at different times," he explained.[10]

SPSS Windows

Using SPSS Data Entry, the researcher can design any of the three noncomparative scales: Likert, semantic differential or Stapel. Moreover, multi-item scales can be easily accommodated. Either the question library can be used or customized scales can be designed. We have shown the use of SPSS Data Entry to design Likert-type scales for rating sales people and product characteristics.

Summary

In noncomparative scaling, each object is scaled independent of the other objects in the stimulus set. Noncomparative rating scales can be either continuous or itemized. The itemized rating scales are further classified as Likert, semantic differential, or Stapel scales. When using noncomparative itemized rating scales, the researcher must decide on the number of scale categories, balanced versus unbalanced scales, odd or even number of categories, forced versus nonforced scales, nature and degree of verbal description, and the physical form or configuration.

Multi-item scales consist of a number of rating-scale items. These scales should be evaluated in terms of reliability and validity. Reliability refers to the extent to which a scale produces consistent results if repeated measurements are made. Approaches to assessing reliability include test–retest, alternative forms, and internal consistency. Validity, or accuracy of measurement, may be assessed by evaluating content validity, criterion validity, and construct validity. The choice of particular scaling techniques for a given situation should be based on theoretical and practical considerations. As a general rule, multiple measures should be taken.

In international marketing research, special attention should be devoted to determining equivalent verbal descriptors in different languages and cultures. Software is available for developing and testing continuous and itemized rating scales, particularly multi-item scales. The misuse of scale descriptors also raises serious ethical concerns. Ethically, the researcher has the responsibility to both the client and respondents to ensure the applicability, usefulness, and honesty of the scales.

Key Terms and Concepts

Noncomparative scales, 260
Continuous rating scale, 260
Itemized rating scale, 264
Likert scale, 264
Semantic differential scale, 265
Stapel scale, 267
Sensitivity, 268
Balanced scale, 268
Forced rating scale, 269
Multi-item scale, 271
Construct, 271
Systematic error, 273
Random error, 273
Reliability, 273
Test–retest reliability, 273
Alternative-forms reliability, 273
Internal-consistency reliability, 274
Split-half reliability, 274
Coefficient alpha, 274
Validity, 274
Content validity, 274
Criterion validity, 274
Construct validity, 274
Convergent validity, 274
Discriminant validity, 275
Nomological validity, 275

Suggested Cases and Video Cases

Cases

2.2 Cadillac **2.3 HCA** **4.1 Boeing** **4.2 Gucci**

Video Cases

2.1 Starbucks **2.2 Nike** **4.2 Marriott**

Additional cases and video cases are available in the Instructor's Manual and on the instructor and student Web sites.

Live Research: Conducting a Marketing Research Project

1. Continuous measures are generally more difficult to implement.
2. As a class, discuss the type of itemized rating scales (Likert, semantic differential, or Stapel) that are appropriate for the key variables.
3. Discuss multi-item scales and the issues of reliability and validity.
4. Consider the practical constraints. For example, if a certain type of scale has been used to measure a variable in the past (e.g., a 10-point Likert-type scale to measure customer satisfaction), the same may have to be used again in the project to allow a comparison of the findings with past results or industry norms (e.g., the American Customer Satisfaction Index).

Acronyms

The rating-scale decisions may be described by the acronym RATING:

R esponse option: forced versus nonforced
A ttractive vs. unattractive number of categories: balanced versus unbalanced
T otal number of categories
I mpartial or neutral category: odd versus even number of categories
N ature and degree of verbal description
G raphics: physical form and configuration

Review Questions

1. What is a semantic differential scale? For what purposes is this scale used? Give an example.
2. Describe the Likert scale. Give an example.
3. What are the differences between the Stapel scale and the semantic differential scale? Which scale is more popular?
4. What are the major decisions involved in constructing an itemized rating scale?
5. How many scale categories should be used in an itemized rating scale? Why?
6. What is the difference between balanced and unbalanced scales? Give an example of each.
7. Should an odd or even number of categories be used in an itemized rating scale? Why? When?
8. What is the difference between forced and nonforced scales? Give an example of each.
9. How does the nature and degree of verbal description affect the response to itemized rating scales?
10. What are multi-item scales? Give an example.
11. What is reliability?
12. What are the differences between test–retest and alternative-forms reliability?
13. Describe the notion of internal-consistency reliability.
14. What is validity?
15. What is criterion validity? How is it assessed?
16. What is the relationship between reliability and validity?
17. How would you select a particular scaling technique?

Applied Problems

1. Develop a Likert, semantic differential, and a Stapel scale for measuring store loyalty.
2. Develop a multi-item scale to measure students' attitudes toward internationalization of the management curriculum. How would you assess the reliability and validity of this scale?
3. Construct a Likert scale for measuring Internet usage. Show how the rating-scale decisions were made.
4. Design Likert scales to measure the usefulness of Ford Motor Company's Web site. Visit the site (www.ford.com) and rate it on the scales that you have developed.
5. Design semantic differential scales to measure the perception of FedEx overnight delivery service, and compare it to that offered by UPS. Relevant information may be obtained by visiting the Web sites of these two companies (www.fedex.com, www.ups.com).
6. Visit the QuestionPro.com Web site (www.questionpro.com). Identify one application of the Likert scale and one application of the semantic differential. Write a report describing the context in which you would use these scales.

7. Visit the Web sites of two marketing research firms conducting surveys. Analyze one survey of each firm to critically evaluate the itemized rating scales being used.
8. Surf the Internet to find two examples each of Likert, semantic differential, and Stapel scales. Write a report describing the context in which these scales are being used.

Group Discussion

1. "It really does not matter which scaling technique you use. As long as your measure is reliable, you will get the right results." Discuss this statement as a small group.
2. "One need not be concerned with reliability and validity in applied marketing research." Discuss this statement as a small group.
3. As a small group or as a class, discuss one of the articles listed in the notes to this chapter.

CHAPTER

11

Questionnaire and Form Design

"Pretesting a questionnaire is absolutely essential for success. All legitimate researchers understand this and won't dare waste the public's time or their own effort with a questionnaire that hasn't been pretested."

Diane Bowers, *President, Council of American Survey Research Organizations (CASRO), Port Jefferson, NY*

OPENING QUESTIONS

1. What is the purpose of a questionnaire, and what are its objectives?
2. What is the process of designing a questionnaire, what steps are involved, and what are the guidelines for each step?
3. How are observational forms designed to most effectively observe behavior?
4. What considerations are involved in designing questionnaires for international marketing research?
5. How does technology interface with questionnaire design?
6. What ethical issues are involved in questionnaire design?

World Vision Imparts Donors a Vision for Caring

World Vision (WV), one of the leading charities in 2005, is a Christian-based organization that helps relief victims and needy children in nearly 100 countries around the world. World Vision needed at least $800,000 to continue caring for unsponsored children in developing countries. The children, who needed food, shelter, and medical care, had either never been sponsored or had lost their sponsors for various reasons. World Vision designed a questionnaire to determine donors' motivations for giving. The information obtained, and the order in which it was obtained, follows:

1. Priorities and motivations for giving
2. Awareness of the WV organization
3. Perceptions of the organization
4. Communication with donors
5. Demographic information

To increase the willingness of donors and potential donors to participate and complete the questionnaire, the researchers made the context of the survey clear, and minimized the effort required of the respondents by asking them questions that were easy to answer. Only necessary questions were asked, and combined questions were avoided. Most of the questions were structured; the respondents simply had to circle a number on the scale. However, a few unstructured or open-ended questions were included where it was felt that the respondents needed the freedom to express underlying motivations for giving.

In deciding on question wording, words with unequivocal meaning but familiar to the donors were used. Special effort was made to be objective so as not to bias the responses in any direction. The questionnaire was kept simple and detailed, and clear instructions were given because it had to be administered by mail. The questionnaire was divided into parts, with a separate part devoted to each type of information sought. The names and addresses of the respondents were optional and obtained at the end of the questionnaire. The questionnaire was professionally reproduced to have a neat appearance and was thoroughly pretested.

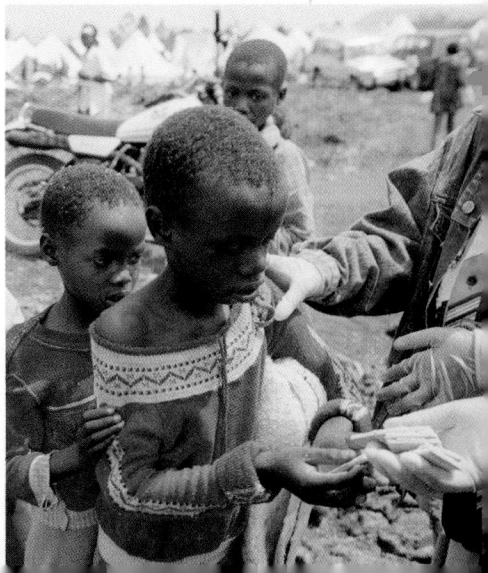

The results of the mail survey showed that the most important factors motivating donors to sponsor a child were the feelings of warmth and contact with the child they were sponsoring. Based on these findings, the charity decided to target its own house list of current sponsors to see if they would consider sponsoring additional children. To motivate these already generous supporters, WV designed a warm, interactive mail package to increase the donor's involvement with the organization. The package included a letter from the WV president, a sticker with the sponsored child's name on it, and a small notebook. The letter explained that in developing nations, paper for schoolchildren is extremely scarce. The recipient was then asked to affix the sticker to the cover of the notebook, sign the inside cover, and mail the book back in an enclosed, postage-paid envelope. The organization would then deliver the notebook to the sponsored child, along with another rarity—a pencil.

With a total budget of $117,796, WV sent 240,893 pieces of direct mail. The response rate in terms of donations received was 46.1 percent, beating the previous campaign by 25.95 percent. The cost per response was a low $0.95. The total income exceeded the goal by $197,000 (23 percent). Beyond the 46.1 percent who responded by making a donation, more than 80 percent of the respondents returned their notebooks, signifying a much higher level of donor involvement than suggested by the donations.[1] •

Overview

The opening vignette illustrates the questionnaire's importance to the research process. The findings obtained by using a questionnaire can assist in the formulation of effective marketing strategies. A well-designed questionnaire enabled WV to discover donors' underlying motivation and design a successful campaign to solicit funds for children in developing countries.

The development of a questionnaire or observational form follows problem definition and approach (see Chapter 2), specification of the type of research design (see Chapters 3 through 8), and selection of the scaling procedures (see Chapters 9 and 10). Figure 11.1 briefly explains the focus of this chapter, the relation of this chapter to the previous ones, and the steps of the marketing research process on which this chapter concentrates.

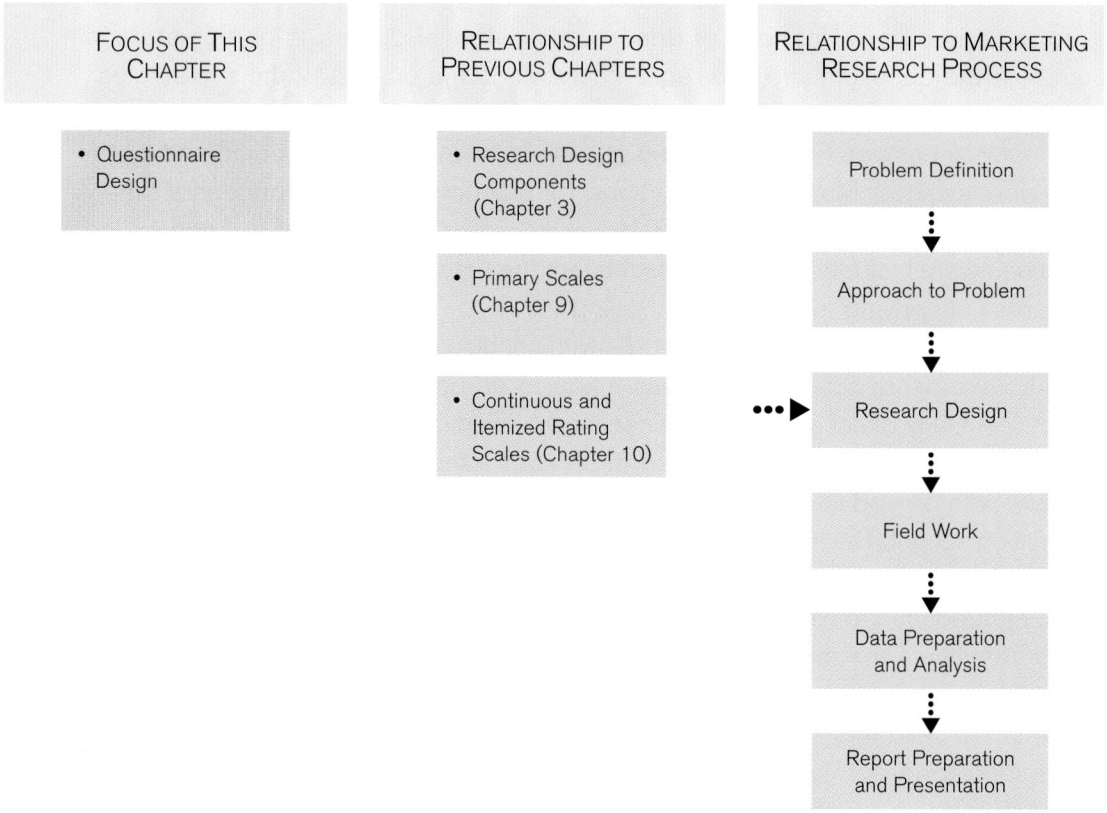

Figure 11.1

Relationship of Questionnaire Design to Previous Chapters and the Marketing Research Process

This chapter describes the importance of a questionnaire and presents the process for developing questionnaires and observational forms. We provide guidelines for questionnaire construction at each stage of the process. We also discuss applications to international marketing, technology, and ethics. Figure 11.2 gives an overview of the topics discussed in this chapter and how they flow from one to the next.

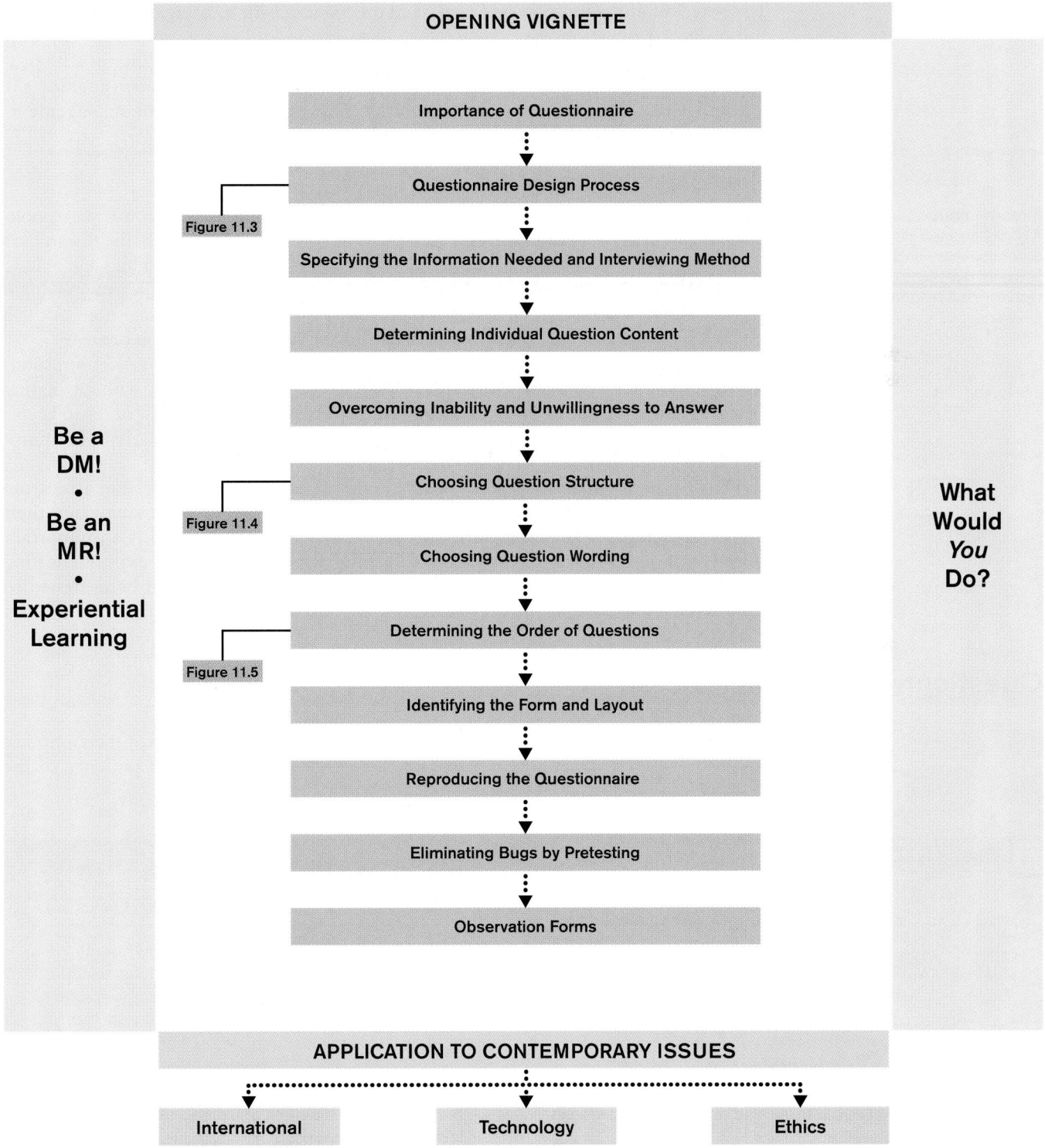

Figure 11.2

Questionnaire and Form Design

Importance of the Questionnaire

As discussed in Chapter 6, researchers can collect quantitative primary data for descriptive research by using either surveys or observation. Standardization of the data collection process is essential to ensure internally consistent and coherent data for analysis. Imagine how difficult it would be to analyze the results of a national survey conducted by 40 different interviewers if the questions had not been asked in a standard way (i.e., if the interviewers had asked different questions using different wording and order). A questionnaire ensures standardization and comparability of the data across interviewers, increases speed and accuracy of recording, and facilitates data processing. As illustrated in the opening vignette, a questionnaire also enables the researcher to collect the relevant information necessary to address the management-decision problem.

Questionnaire Definition

questionnaire
A structured technique for data collection that consists of a series of questions, written or verbal, that a respondent answers.

A **questionnaire** is a formalized set of questions for obtaining information from respondents. It has three specific objectives. The overriding objective is to translate the researcher's information needs into a set of specific questions that respondents are willing and able to answer. While this may seem straightforward, questions may yield very different and unanticipated responses. For example, how would you answer the following question: "Which state is larger, California or Texas?" Would you answer based on population or area?

Second, a questionnaire should be written to minimize demands imposed on respondents. It should encourage them to participate in the entire interview, without biasing their responses. Incomplete interviews have limited usefulness, at best. In order to keep a respondent involved throughout a questionnaire, the researcher should attempt to minimize fatigue and boredom.

Third, a questionnaire should minimize response error. These errors can arise from respondents who give inaccurate answers or from misrecording or misanalyzing their answers. Minimizing the error introduced by the questionnaire itself is an important objective of questionnaire design. The following Research in Action example dealing with young respondents is an illustration of how questionnaires can be designed to achieve these objectives.

Questionnaire Design Process

No scientific principles guarantee an optimal or ideal questionnaire. Questionnaire design is as much an art as it is a science. The creativity, skill, and experience of the

EXPERIENTIAL LEARNING

How Important Is a Questionnaire?

Sprite is the number-three soft drink brand behind Coke and Pepsi. College students are heavy users of soft drinks.

1. As the brand manager for Sprite, what information do you need to target this segment?
2. Conduct an Internet search using a search engine and your library's online database to obtain information that will assist the brand manager of Sprite in targeting the student segment.
3. You and a fellow student each interview one different respondent (another student) to determine preferences for soft drinks, without constructing a questionnaire. How comparable are the data each of you obtained? Develop a formal questionnaire jointly and each of you administer it to another respondent. Are the data obtained now more comparable than before? What does this teach you about the importance of a questionnaire?

RESEARCH IN ACTION

An Old Fashioned Approach with Young Respondents

Just Kid, Inc. (www.justkidinc.com) of Stamford, Connecticut, surveys two age categories of children–6- to 8-year-olds and 9- to 12-year-olds–on a quarterly basis. The objective is to record children's views on favorite snack foods, television shows, commercials, radio, magazines, buzzwords, and movies. The one-on-one interviews conducted in malls are kept short, typically lasting only eight to ten minutes.

Just Kid attempts to make questions as clear and meaningful as possible so that kids can understand and answer them. This is done by establishing a context for questions. For example, when asking about their radio listening habits, they ask, "What about when you're in Mom's car, do you listen to the radio?" rather than, "How often do you listen to radio? More than once a day, once a day, more than once a week?" The latter are kind of big questions for little children.

A tradeoff is made between attempting to cover all possible areas of interest in one study and ensuring that the most important information is of high quality. Given children's limited attention span, minimizing boredom and being sensitive to fatigue becomes more important than asking all possible questions. Thus, Just Kid motivates the kids to complete the questionnaire.

Some clients attempt to meet all of their research objectives with one study. The questionnaires keep going through the approval process and people keep adding questions, "Well, let's ask this question, let's add that question, and why don't we talk about this also?" This results in keeping children 25 minutes in a central mall location, which makes them kind of "itchy." The response error increases and the quality of data suffers. By keeping the questionnaire short and clear, Just Kid also tries to reduce response error. While conducting research on children is not easy, Just Kid has been successful in designing questionnaires that meet their stated objectives.[2]

researcher play a major role in the end design. However, several guidelines are available to assist researchers in the questionnaire development process and to help them avoid major mistakes.

The guidelines to support questionnaire design are shown as a series of 10 steps (Figure 11.3): (1) specify the information needed, (2) specify the type of interviewing method, (3) determine the content of individual questions, (4) design the questions to overcome the respondent's inability and unwillingness to answer, (5) decide on the question structure, (6) determine the question wording, (7) arrange the questions in proper order, (8) choose the form and layout, (9) reproduce the questionnaire, and (10) pretest the questionnaire. In practice, questionnaire design is an iterative rather than a sequential process. For example, pretesting of a question may reveal that respondents misunderstand the wording, sending the designer back to an earlier step.

Specify the Information Needed

The first step in questionnaire design is to specify the information needed. A continual review of the earlier stages of the research project—particularly the specific components of the problem, the research questions, and the hypotheses—will help keep the questionnaire focused. This was illustrated in the WV study in the opening vignette, which clearly specified the information the questionnaire was to obtain.

Questionnaires should also be designed with the target respondents in mind, taking into account their educational level and experience. The language used and the context of the questions must all be familiar to the respondents. Questions that are appropriate for college students may not be appropriate for those with only a high school education. Questionnaires that fail to keep in mind the characteristics of the respondents, particularly their educational level and experience, lead to a high incidence of "uncertain" or "no opinion" responses.

Figure 11.3
Questionnaire Design Process

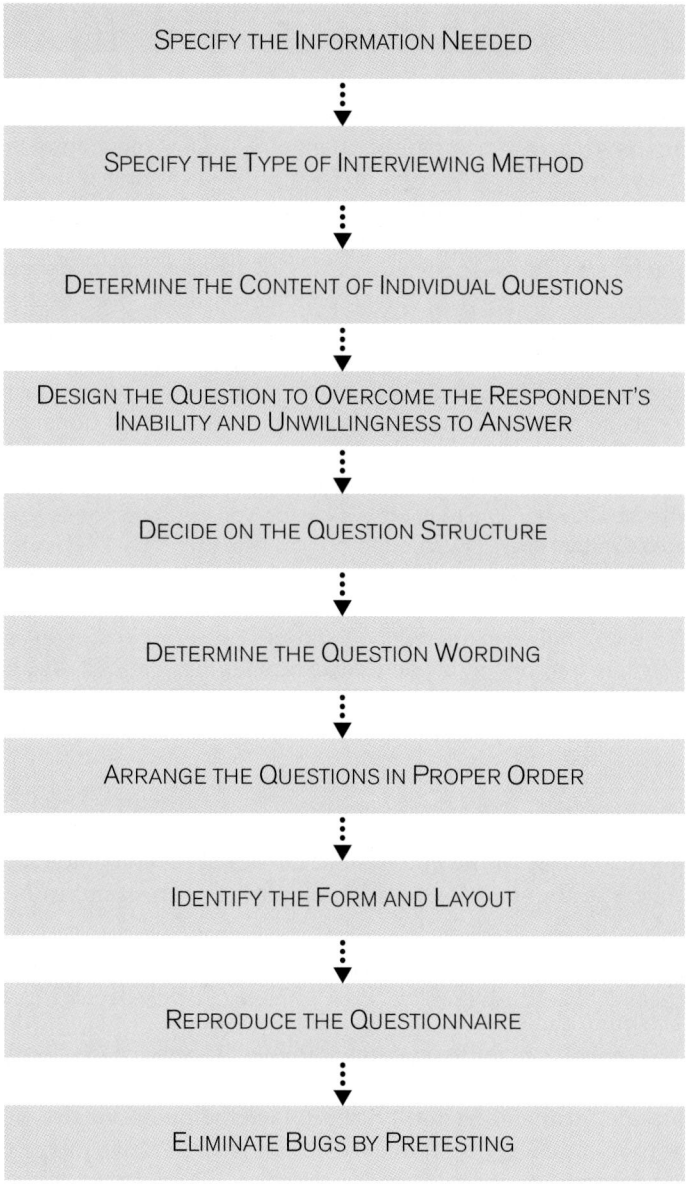

Specify the Type of Interviewing Method

Another important consideration in questionnaire design relates to how the data will be collected. An understanding of the various methods of conducting interviews provides guidance for questionnaire design (see Chapter 7). For example, personal interviews use face-to-face interaction. Due to the opportunity for feedback and clarification, questionnaires can be lengthy, complex, and incorporate visual aids. Since a respondent cannot see the questionnaire in telephone interviews, the questions must be short and simple.

Any type of interviewer-administered questionnaire should be written in a conversational style. Mail and electronic questionnaires are self-administered, involving no personal interaction between the researcher and the respondent. Therefore, both questions and instructions must be kept simple and thorough, as in the WV study in the opening vignette. In computer-assisted interviewing (computer-assisted telephone interviewing, CATI, computer-assisted personal interviewing, CAPI, or Internet; see Chapter 7), the computer guides the respondent through complex skip patterns and can incorporate randomization of questions to eliminate order bias. The impact of the type of interviewing

RESEARCH IN ACTION

Effect of Interviewing Method on Questionnaire Design

Mail, E-mail, or Internet Questionnaire

Please rank the following luxury cars in order of your preference. Begin by picking out the one car brand that you like most and assign it a number 1. Then find the second most-preferred car brand and assign it a number 2. Continue this procedure until you have ranked all the cars in order of preference. The least-preferred car brand should be assigned a rank of 7. No two brands should receive the same rank number. The criterion of preference is entirely up to you. There is no right or wrong answer. Just try to be consistent.

Car Brand	Rank Order
1. Acura	_____
2. Cadillac	_____
3. Lexus	_____
4. Lincoln	_____
5. Infiniti	_____
6. Mercedes	_____
7. BMW	_____

Telephone Questionnaire

I will read to you the names of some luxury cars. Please rate them in terms of your preference. Use a six-point scale, where 1 denotes "not so preferred" and 6 denotes "greatly preferred." Numbers between 1 and 6 reflect intermediate degrees of preference. Remember that the higher the number, the greater the degree of preference. Now, please tell me your preference for (READ ONE CAR BRAND AT A TIME.)

Car Brand	Not So Preferred					Greatly Preferred
1. Acura	1	2	3	4	5	6
2. Cadillac	1	2	3	4	5	6
3. Lexus	1	2	3	4	5	6
4. Lincoln	1	2	3	4	5	6
5. Infiniti	1	2	3	4	5	6
6. Mercedes	1	2	3	4	5	6
7. BMW	1	2	3	4	5	6

Personal Questionnaire

(HAND CAR BRAND CARDS TO THE RESPONDENT.) Here is a set of luxury car names, each written on a separate card. Please examine these cards carefully. (GIVE RESPONDENT TIME.) Now, examine these cards again and pull out the card that has the name of the car brand you like the most, that is, your most-preferred car. (RECORD THE CAR NAME AND KEEP THIS CARD WITH YOU.) Now, please examine the remaining six cards. Of these remaining six names, what is your most-preferred car brand? (REPEAT THIS PROCEDUE SEQUENTIALLY UNTIL THE RESPONDENT HAS ONLY ONE CARD LEFT.)

Car Rank	Name of the Car
1. 1	_____
2. 2	_____
3. 3	_____
4. 4	_____
5. 5	_____
6. 6	_____
7. 7	_____

method on the nature of questions is illustrated in the context of obtaining consumer preferences for luxury cars.

In the luxury car example, you can see how a ranking question changes as the method of interviewing changes. In mail, e-mail, or Internet questionnaires, the respondent records the rank orders. Ranking seven car brands is too complex a task to be administered over the telephone. Therefore, the simpler rating task in which brands are rated one at a time was used. In personal interviewing, the ranking task can be simplified by giving the respondent cards imprinted with the car brand name, and the interviewer is provided with special instructions (in capital letters). The interviewer records the brand names.

Internet questionnaires share many of the features of CAPI questionnaires. The questionnaire can be designed using a wide variety of stimuli, such as graphics, pictures, advertisements, animations, sound clips, and full-motion video. The researcher can control the amount of time that the stimuli are available to the respondents and the number of times a respondent can access each stimulus. This greatly increases the range and complexity of questionnaires that can be administered over the Internet. As in the case of CATI and CAPI, complicated skip patterns can be programmed into the questionnaire. The questions can be personalized, and answers to previous questions can be inserted into subsequent questions, a process called variable piping.

The type of interviewing method also influences the content of individual questions.

Determine the Content of Individual Questions

Once the information needed is specified and the type of interviewing method is decided, the next step is to determine question content. In other words, the researcher must determine what should be included in each question.

Is the Question Necessary?

Before including a question, the researcher should ask, "How will I use these data?" Questions that may be nice to know, but that don't directly address the research problem, should be eliminated. There are exceptions to this rule. Filler questions may be added to disguise the purpose or sponsorship of the project. For example, in brand studies, a researcher may include questions about the full range of competing brands so the respondents won't know who is sponsoring the study. Early in the interviewing process when the researcher is attempting to build a relationship with respondents and capture their attention, a few easy-to-answer neutral questions may be helpful. At times, certain questions may also be repeated for the purpose of assessing reliability or validity.

Are Several Questions Needed Instead of One?

In some cases, two questions are better than one. However, asking two questions in one is not the solution. Consider the following question:

Do you think Nike Town offers better variety and prices than other Nike stores?

(Incorrect)

A "yes" answer will presumably be clear; however, what if the answer is "no"? Does this mean that the respondent thinks that Nike Town does not offer better variety, that it does not offer better prices, or that it neither offers better variety nor better prices? Such a question is called a **double-barreled question** because two or more questions are combined into one. To avoid confusion, these questions should be asked separately, as follows:

double-barreled question
A single question that attempts to cover two issues. Such questions can be confusing to respondents and can result in ambiguous responses.

Do you think Nike Town offers better variety than other Nike stores?
Do you think Nike Town offers better prices than other Nike stores?

(Correct)

Another example of multiple questions embedded in a single question is the "why" question. In marketing research, a primary question of interest to researchers concerns

More than one question is needed to measure the respondents' evaluations of Nike Town.

brand selection. This is a "why" question in actuality. In other words, the researcher can be tempted to ask the question this way: "Why did you choose the Ford Explorer?" A typical answer to this question will likely be short. Answers such as "It was the best buy," or "I liked it" don't help the researchers understand much about this brand choice decision. Instead, a series of questions are needed. For example, "What was your main motivation in choosing the Ford Explorer? How does the Ford Explorer compare to other SUV brands? What features of the Ford Explorer appealed to you?"

BE a DM!

As the CEO of Old Navy, what would you do to improve consumers' perceptions of the quality of your brand?

BE an MR!

Visit Old Navy's Web site (www.oldnavy.com) and conduct an Internet search using a search engine and your library's online database to obtain information on Old Navy's marketing program.

Formulate a double-barreled question to determine consumer perceptions of the quality and style of Old Navy clothing. Then, reformulate this question to obtain unambiguous answers.

Design the Question to Overcome the Respondent's Inability to Answer

Respondents may not always be able to answer the questions posed to them. Researchers can help them overcome this limitation by keeping in mind the reasons people typically cannot answer a question: They may not be informed, may not remember, or may be unable to articulate certain types of responses.

Is the Respondent Informed?

Respondents are often asked to answer questions they are uninformed about. A husband may not be informed about monthly expenses for groceries and department store purchases if it is the wife who makes these purchases, or vice versa. Despite the fact that they are uninformed, respondents may provide answers, as the following Research in Action example shows.

When the research topic requires specialized experience or knowledge, **filter questions**, measuring familiarity, product use, and past experience, should be asked before questions about the topics themselves. Filter questions enable the researcher to eliminate from the analysis those respondents who are not adequately informed.

filter questions
Initial questions in a questionnaire that screen potential respondents to ensure they meet the requirements of the sample.

In addition to filter questions, a "don't know" option to a question is helpful. This option has been found to reduce the number of uninformed responses without reducing overall response rate. If it is suspected that many respondents may be uninformed about the topic, "don't know" should be added to the list of response alternatives.

Can the Respondent Remember?

Many common experiences or practices are difficult to remember. Can you remember the brand name of the shirt you are wearing, what you had for lunch a week ago, or what you were doing a month ago today? Further, do you know how many gallons of soft drinks you

RESEARCH IN ACTION

Unknown Question Elicits Known Answers

In one study, respondents were asked to express their degree of agreement or disagreement with the following statement: "The National Bureau of Consumer Complaints provides an effective means for consumers who have purchased a defective product to obtain relief." Even with a "don't know" option available, 51.9 percent of the lawyers and 75.0 percent of the general public still expressed an opinion about the National Bureau of Consumer Complaints. Why should this high response rate be problematic? Because there is no such entity as the National Bureau of Consumer Complaints![3]

consumed during the last four weeks? When making estimates about product consumption levels, in particular, research has found that consumers dramatically overestimate usage.

We tend to remember events that are personally relevant or unusual, or that occur frequently. People remember their wedding anniversary and birthday or the day Ronald W. Regan died. Likewise, the more recently the event occurred, the more readily an event will be recalled. For example, you are more likely to remember the purchases you made on your last trip to the grocery store than the purchases you made three shopping trips ago.

Questions can be designed to aid recall or they can be unaided, depending on the research objectives. For example, unaided recall of soft drink commercials could be measured by questions such as, "What brands of soft drinks do you remember being advertised last night on TV?" A question that employs aided recall attempts to stimulate the respondent's memory by providing cues related to the event of interest. The aided recall approach would list a number of soft drink brands and then ask, "Which of these brands were advertised last night on TV?" One of the risks of presenting cues is that they may bias responses and make a respondent unduly sensitive to a topic, thus, distorting their answers.

Can the Respondent Articulate?

Respondents may be unable to articulate certain types of responses. This does not mean, however, that they do not have an opinion on that topic. For example, it is difficult to describe the ideal atmosphere of a department store. On the other hand, if the respondents are provided with alternative descriptions of store atmosphere, they will be able to indicate the one they like best. When asked to provide answers that are difficult to articulate, respondents are likely to ignore that question and may refuse to complete the questionnaire. Visual aids in the form of pictures, diagrams, or maps, as well as verbal descriptions, can help respondents articulate responses.

BE an MR!

Conduct an Internet search using a search engine and your library's online database to obtain information on factors that influence the atmosphere of a department store.

Develop four alternative descriptions of store atmosphere. Also, write a description about the ideal atmosphere of a department store.

BE a DM!

As the CEO of Nordstrom, what type of atmosphere do you desire to have in your stores? Why?

Design the Questionnaire to Overcome the Respondent's Unwillingness to Answer

Even if respondents are able to answer a particular question, they may be unwilling to do so. Refusal to answer a question may be due to a variety of circumstances. The respondent may feel that there's simply too much effort involved, that the question serves no legitimate purpose, or that the information requested is too sensitive.

Effort Required of the Respondent

While most individuals are willing to participate in a survey, this sense of cooperation may vanish if the questions require too much effort to answer. Suppose the researcher is interested in determining from which departments in a store the respondent purchased merchandise on their most recent shopping trip. This information can be obtained in at least two ways. The researcher could ask the respondent to list all the items purchased on his or her most recent shopping trip, or the researcher could provide a list of departments and ask the respondent to check the applicable ones.

> Please list all the departments from which you purchased merchandise on your most recent shopping trip to a department store.
>
> (Incorrect)

In the list that follows, please check all the departments from which you purchased merchandise on your most recent shopping trip to a department store.

1. Women's dresses _____
2. Men's apparel _____
3. Children's apparel _____
4. Cosmetics _____

.
.
.

16. Jewelry _____
17. Other (please specify) _____

(Correct)

The second option is preferable because it requires less effort from respondents. In the WV questionnaire in the opening vignette, the effort required of the respondents was reduced by asking easy questions for which the respondents merely had to check one of the response options.

Legitimate Purpose

Respondents also object to questions that do not seem to serve a legitimate purpose. Why should a firm marketing cereals want to know their age, income, and occupation? The researcher should anticipate these types of objections and attempt to overcome them by explaining why the data are needed. A statement such as, "To determine how the consumption of cereal and preferences for cereal brands vary among people of different ages, incomes, and occupations, we need information on . . . " can make the request for information seem legitimate. Moreover, the context of the survey should be clearly explained, as in the WV project.

Sensitive Information

Information of a personal or highly sensitive nature may be difficult to obtain from respondents. Examples of sensitive topics include money, family life, political and religious beliefs, and involvement in accidents or crimes. The respondents may be embarrassed to answer such questions because accurate responses may threaten their prestige or self-image. To increase the likelihood of obtaining sensitive information, such topics should be placed at the end of the questionnaire. By then, rapport has been created and legitimacy of the project established, making respondents more willing to give information. Where appropriate, sensitive information should be obtained in the form of response categories rather than asking for specific figures. While respondents may refuse to answer the question,

What is your household's exact annual income?

(Incorrect)

they may be willing to check the appropriate income category. A better way of obtaining information on income is to ask

Which one of the following categories best describes your household's annual income?

_____ under $25,000
_____ $25,001–$50,000
_____ $50,001–$75,000
_____ over $75,000

Decide on the Question Structure

A question may be unstructured or structured. In the following sections, we define unstructured questions and discuss their advantages and limitations. This is followed by a discussion of the popular forms of structured questions: multiple-choice, dichotomous, and scales (Figure 11.4).

Unstructured Questions

unstructured questions
Open-ended questions that respondents answer in their own words.

Unstructured questions are open-ended questions that respondents answer in their own words. They are also referred to as free-response or free-answer questions. The following are examples of unstructured questions:

- What is your favorite pastime?
- How would you describe the typical user of Land Rover SUVs?
- Do you intend to travel overseas within the next six months?

Open-ended questions are good as first questions on a topic. They enable the respondents to express general attitudes and opinions that can help the researcher interpret their responses to structured questions. Open-ended questions allow the respondent to express their attitudes or opinions without the bias associated with restricting responses to predefined alternatives. Thus, they can be useful in identifying underlying motivations, beliefs, and attitudes, as in the WV vignette. Analysis of the verbatim comments provides a rich context for interpreting later questions. Unstructured questions are useful in exploratory research (Table 11.1).

The disadvantages of unstructured questions relate to recording error, data coding, and the added complexity of analysis. In personal or telephone interviews, successfully recording verbatim comments depends entirely on the recording skills of the interviewer. Interviewer bias is introduced as decisions are made regarding whether to record answers verbatim or write down only the main points. Tape recorders should be used if verbatim reporting is important.

Categorizing the recorded comments to open-ended questions introduces the second source of bias and another major disadvantage. Implicitly, unstructured or open-ended questions give extra weight to respondents who are more talkative or articulate. The process of summarizing comments into a format that can be analyzed is both time-consuming and expensive. Unstructured questions are also of limited value in self-administered questionnaires (mail, CAPI, or electronic) because respondents tend to be more brief in writing than in speaking.

In general, open-ended questions are useful in exploratory research and as opening questions. However, in a large survey, the complexity of recording, tabulation, and analysis outweighs their advantages.

structured questions
Questions that prespecify the set of response alternatives and the response format. A structured question could be multiple-choice, dichotomous, or a scale.

Structured Questions

Structured questions specify the set of responses as well as their format. A structured question may offer multiple choices, only two choices (dichotomous question), or a scale (see Figure 11.4).

Figure 11.4
Types of Questions

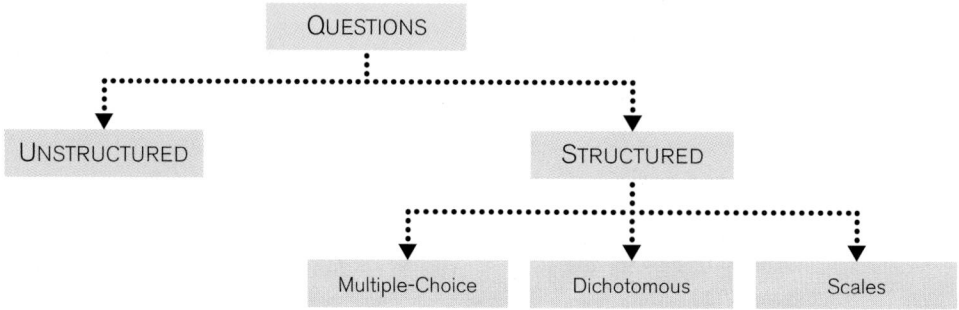

Table 11.1

Advantages and Disadvantages of Unstructured and Structured Questions

Question Type	Advantages	Disadvantages	Comments
Unstructured	Good as first questions Responses are less biased Can provide rich insights	Potential for interviewer bias Coding is costly and time-consuming Greater weight to articulate respondents Unsuitable for self-administered questionnaires	Useful for exploratory research
Multiple-Choice	Interviewer bias is reduced Easy to code and analyze Improved respondent cooperation	Order or position bias Difficult to design response options	Responses should be mutually exclusive and collectively exhaustive Useful in large surveys
Dichotomous	Same as multiple-choice	Wording can bias the responses	Use split-ballot technique
Scales	Same as multiple-choice	Difficult to design multi-item scales	Scales should be evaluated for reliability, validity, and generalizability

RESEARCH IN ACTION

Open-Ended Questions Open the Way to a New Opportunity for Nabisco

In an exploratory survey, ConAgra Foods asked a series of open-ended questions related to cookies with a view to identifying any consumer needs they were not satisfactorily meeting. Included in the survey were questions like these: What do you like about cookies? What do you dislike about cookies? What are the health benefits of cookies? What are health disadvantages of cookies?

The findings revealed that the needs of a subset of specialty cookie consumers were not being met by existing "wellness specialty offerings," cookies that offered health benefits. These consumers wanted great taste combined with health benefits, so that they could enjoy the cookies without feeling guilty. Seeing this opportunity, Nabisco and ConAgra joined to create and market Healthy Choice (www.healthychoice.com), an adult specialty cookie with an indulgent yet healthful profile. Healthy Choice cookies rank among the top-100 specialty cookie/cracker category. The Raspberry Tart ranks 33, the Apricot Tart 92. According to the company, both were outselling all of key competitor Pepperidge Farms' wellness cookies. This success is attributed to a focus on unsatisfied consumer needs identified through open-ended questions. As of 2004, Healthy Choice was a fully owned brand of ConAgra Foods and is one of its 27 $100-million-plus brands.[4]

Multiple-Choice Questions In multiple-choice questions, the researcher provides a choice of answers, and respondents are asked to select one or more of the alternatives given. Consider the following question.

Do you intend to travel overseas within the next six months?

_____ Definitely will not travel
_____ Probably will not travel
_____ Undecided
_____ Probably will travel
_____ Definitely will travel

Many of the issues associated with constructing itemized rating scales (see Chapter 10) also apply to multiple-choice questions. Two additional concerns in designing multiple-choice questions are (1) the number of alternatives that should be included and (2) order or position bias.

Multiple-choice questions should include choices that cover the full range of possible alternatives. The alternatives should be mutually exclusive and collectively exhaustive. An "other (please specify)" category should be included where appropriate. Instructions should clearly indicate whether the respondent is to choose only one alternative or select all that apply. (For example, "Please indicate all the brands of soft drinks that you have consumed in the past week.") As the list of choices increases, the questions become more difficult to answer. When the alternative list becomes long, the researcher should consider using more than one question to simplify the workload for respondents.

order or position bias
A respondent's tendency to choose an alternative merely because it occupies a certain position on the page or in a list.

Order or position bias is the respondents' tendency to check an alternative merely because it occupies a certain position in a list. Alternatives that appear at the beginning and, to a lesser degree, at the end of a list have a tendency to be selected most often. When questions relate to numeric values (quantities or prices), there is a tendency to select the central value on the list. Order bias can be controlled by preparing several forms of the questionnaire with changes in the order of the alternatives from form to form. Each alternative should appear once in each of the extreme positions, once in the middle, and once somewhere in between.

Multiple-choice questions are easier for respondents to answer. They are also easier to analyze and tabulate than open-ended questions. Interviewer bias is also reduced, given that these types of questions work very well in self-administered conditions. Respondent cooperation in general is improved if the majority of the questions are structured.

Multiple-choice questions are not without disadvantages. It is difficult to develop effective multiple-choice options. Often, exploratory research must be conducted using open-ended questions to identify the appropriate response options. When large numbers of respondents check the "other (please specify)" category, it indicates that the alternative list may be seriously flawed. The list of options itself also introduces bias.

dichotomous question
A structured question with only two response alternatives, such as yes and no.

Dichotomous Questions A **dichotomous question** has only two response alternatives: yes or no, agree or disagree, and so forth. Sometimes, multiple-choice questions can alternatively be framed as dichotomous, as in the overseas travel question asked earlier:

Do you intend to travel overseas within the next six months?

_____ Yes

_____ No

Dichotomous questions should be used when the researcher has reason to believe that the respondent thinks of the topic in yes/no terms. When the respondent is highly involved in a subject or has a great deal of knowledge related to the topic, a multiple-choice question or scale may be more appropriate.

Dichotomous questions have many of the strengths and weaknesses of multiple-choice questions. They are among the easiest type of questions to code and analyze. They have one serious flaw, however. The direction of question wording can have a significant effect on the responses given. To illustrate, the statement, "Individuals are more to blame than social conditions for crime and lawlessness in this country," produced agreement from 59.6 percent of the respondents. However, on a matched sample that responded to the opposite statement, "Social conditions are more to blame than individuals for crime and lawlessness in this country," 43.2 percent (as opposed to 40.4 percent) agreed. To overcome this problem, the question should be framed in one way on one-half of the questionnaires and in the opposite way on the other half. This is referred to as the split-ballot technique.

Scales Scales were discussed in detail in Chapters 9 and 10. Sometimes, multiple-choice questions can alternatively be framed as scales, as in the overseas travel question asked earlier.

Do you intend to travel overseas within the next six months?

Definitely Will Not Travel	**Probably Will Not Travel**	**Undecided**	**Probably Will Travel**	**Definitely Will Travel**
1	2	3	4	5

Questions making use of scales are easy to answer and, therefore, are popular, as in the WV vignette.

BE a DM!	BE an MR!
As the marketing chief for Estée Lauder perfumes, how would you instill positive consumer attitudes toward your brands?	Conduct an Internet search using a search engine and your library's online database to obtain information on consumers' attitudes toward perfumes. Obtain information on consumers' attitudes toward Estée Lauder perfumes using an unstructured, multichotomous, dichotomous, and a scaling question.

Determine the Question Wording

Translating the information needed into clearly worded questions that are easily understood is the most difficult aspect of questionnaire development. Poorly worded questions can confuse or mislead respondents, leading to nonresponse or response error. Poorly worded questions can also frustrate the respondents to the point that they refuse to answer those questions or items. This is referred to as item nonresponse and leads to nonresponse error. If respondents interpret questions differently than intended by the researcher, serious bias can occur, leading to response error.

To avoid problems in question wording, we offer five guidelines: (1) define the issue, (2) use ordinary words, (3) avoid ambiguous words, (4) avoid leading questions, and (5) use positive and negative statements.

Define the Issue

Questions should always clearly define the issue being addressed. Beginning journalists are told to define the issue in terms of *who*, *what*, *when*, *where*, *why*, and *way* (the six Ws). These—particularly *who*, *what*, *when*, and *where*—can also serve as guidelines for defining the issue in a question. Consider the following question.

Which brand of toothpaste do you use?

(Incorrect)

On the surface, this may seem to be a well-defined question, but we may reach a different conclusion when we examine it under the microscope of *who*, *what*, *when*, and *where*.

The Ws	Defining the Question
Who	**The Respondent**
	It is not clear whether this question relates to the individual respondent or the respondent's total household.
What	**The Brand of Toothpaste**
	It is unclear how the respondent is to answer this question if more than one brand is used.
When	**Unclear**
	The time frame is not specified in this question. The respondent could interpret it as meaning the toothpaste used this morning, this week, or over the past year.
Where	**Not Specified**
	At home, at the gym, on the road?

A well-defined question is needed to determine which brand of toothpaste a person uses.

A more clearly defined question might read

> Which brand or brands of toothpaste have you personally used at home during the past month? In case of more than one brand, please list all the brands that apply.
>
> (Correct)

Use Simple Words

Simple, ordinary words that match the vocabulary level of the respondent should be used in a questionnaire. When choosing words, keep in mind that the average person in the United States has a high school, not a college, education. For certain respondent groups, the education level is even lower. Simplicity in wording and a conscious effort to avoid technical jargon should guide questionnaire development. As marketing professionals, it is also important to remember that most respondents do not understand marketing terminology. For example, instead of asking,

> Is the distribution of snack foods adequate?
>
> (Incorrect)

ask,

> Are snack foods readily available when you want to buy them?
>
> (Correct)

Use Unambiguous Words

When selecting words for a questionnaire, the questionnaire designer should choose words with only one meaning. This is not an easy task given that a number of words that appear unambiguous can have different meanings to different people. These include *usually*, *normally*, *frequently*, *often*, *regularly*, *occasionally*, and *sometimes*. Consider the following question.

> In a typical month, how often do you go to a movie theater to see a movie?
>
> _____ Never
> _____ Occasionally
> _____ Sometimes
> _____ Often
> _____ Regularly
>
> (Incorrect)

Assessing the distribution of snack foods requires the use of words as ordinary and commmonplace as snack foods themselves.

The categories of this multiple-choice question can have different meanings to different people, leading to response bias. Three respondents who go to movie theaters once a month may check three different categories: occasionally, sometimes, and often. The following is a much better worded question.

In a typical month, how often do you go to a movie theater to see a movie?

_____ Less than once
_____ 1 or 2 times
_____ 3 or 4 times
_____ More than 4 times

(Correct)

This question is less ambiguous because each respondent is answering it from a consistent frame of reference. Response categories have been objectively defined, and respondents are no longer free to interpret them in their own way.

Avoid Leading or Biasing Questions

A **leading question** is one that clues the respondent to what the answer should be, as in the following:

leading question
A question that gives the respondent a clue as to what the answer should be.

Do you think that America should provide financial aid to poor foreign countries when it is not our responsibility to do so?

_____ Yes
_____ No
_____ Don't know

(Incorrect)

This question would lead respondents to a "no" answer. The answer would be unduly biased by the phrase "it is not our responsibility to do so." Therefore, this question would not help determine the preferences of Americans for providing aid to poor foreign countries. A better question would be:

Do you think that America should provide financial aid to poor foreign countries?

_____ Yes
_____ No
_____ Don't know

(Correct)

Words can lead respondents in a particular direction. Identification of the research sponsor can have the same effect. When respondents are made aware of the sponsor, they tend to answer questions about that sponsor in a positive manner. The question,

Is Colgate your favorite toothpaste?

(Incorrect)

is likely to bias the responses in favor of Colgate. A more unbiased way of obtaining this information would be to ask,

What is your favorite brand of toothpaste?

(Correct)

Likewise, the mention of a prestigious or nonprestigious name can bias the response, as in, "Do you agree with the American Dental Association that Colgate is effective in preventing cavities?" Question wording should be objective, as in the WV vignette.

Balance Dual Statements

Many questions, particularly those measuring attitudes and lifestyles, are worded as statements to which respondents indicate their degree of agreement or disagreement using Likert scales. The statements in these types of questions can be worded either positively or negatively. Evidence shows that the responses obtained often depend on the direction of the wording of the questions: whether they are stated positively or negatively. Questions of this type should be balanced by using dual statements, some of which are positive and some negative. Two different questionnaires, which reverse the direction of the questions, could also be used to control for any bias introduced by the positive or negative nature of the statements. An example of dual statements was provided in the summated Likert scale in Chapter 10 that was designed to measure attitudes toward Target.

BE a DM!

As the marketing director for FedEx, how would you penetrate the important small business market for overnight package delivery?

BE an MR!

Visit FedEx's Web site (www.fedex.com) and conduct an Internet search using a search engine and your library's online database to obtain information on the overnight package delivery market. Write a brief report.

Evaluate the wording of the following question asked of small business owners/CEOs: If FedEx were to introduce a new overnight delivery service for small businesses, how likely are you to adopt it?

Arrange the Questions in Proper Order

When arranging questions in a proper order, the researcher should consider the opening questions, the type of information sought, difficult questions, and the effect on subsequent questions. Questions should be arranged in a logical order, organized around topic areas.

Opening Questions

Opening questions set the stage for the remainder of the questionnaire. They serve a variety of purposes. They can introduce the topic, attempt to gain the confidence and cooperation of respondents, or establish the legitimacy of the study. The opening questions should be interesting, simple, and nonthreatening. Questions that ask respondents for their opinions are always good openers because most people like to express their opinions.

Sometimes opening questions may be asked to simply establish rapport. Some studies require a prescreening of the respondents to ensure that they are eligible to participate in the interview. In these cases, qualifying questions are used as opening questions.

RESEARCH IN ACTION

Qualifying Respondents Leads to Unqualified Success for Kellogg's

Looking to expand its share of the ready-to-eat cereal category, Kellogg's conducted a telephone survey of users. The nonusers of ready-to-eat cereals were not relevant for this study and, thus, not part of the target population. The first question was

How often do you have ready-to-eat cereal for breakfast?

___ Less than twice a week

___ Two or three times per week

___ Four or five times per week

___ More than five times per week

If the answer was "less than twice a week," that respondent was thanked and the interview terminated. Such respondents were operationally classified as nonusers and excluded from the study.

The results of the survey indicated that consumers were looking for a crunchy, tasty, yet low-fat and healthy cereal. Based on the findings of this survey, Kellogg's introduced Honey Crunch Corn Flakes. The oven-baked flake is 20 percent thicker than other flakes, offering a crunchier texture. It is low in fat, cholesterol-free, and a source of nine essential vitamins and minerals. The bright yellow package features Cornelius the Rooster, which has been on the Kellogg's Corn Flakes box since 1957. To support the product launch, Kellogg's ran a national TV spot emphasizing the cereal's "Taste of Honey, Heart of Gold." This new brand has been a great success in a very competitive cereal market.[5]

Type of Information

Three types of information are obtained from a questionnaire: (1) basic information, (2) classification information, and (3) identification information. **Basic information** relates directly to the research problem. **Classification information** consists of socioeconomic and demographic characteristics. It is used to classify the respondents in order to analyze results across different groups. **Identification information** includes name, address, and telephone number. Identification information may be obtained for a variety of purposes, including verifying that the respondents listed were actually interviewed, remitting promised incentives, and so forth. Because basic information is the most important aspect of a study, it should be obtained first, followed by classification and then identification information. Classification and identification information is of a more personal nature. Respondents may resist answering a series of personal questions. Therefore, these types of questions should appear at the end of the questionnaire, as in the WV vignette.

basic information
Information that relates directly to the marketing research problem.

classification information
Socioeconomic and demographic characteristics used to classify respondents.

identification information
A type of information obtained in a questionnaire that includes name, address, and phone number.

Difficult Questions

Respondents can perceive questions as difficult for a variety of reasons. They may relate to sensitive issues, or be embarrassing, complex, or dull. Questions that could be perceived as difficult should be placed late in the sequence after a relationship has been established and the respondent is involved in the process. The last question of the classification section is typically income information. The respondent's telephone number is the final item in the identification section for the same reasons.

Effect on Subsequent Questions

Initial questions can influence questions asked later in a questionnaire. As a rule, a series of questions should start with a general introduction to a topic, followed by specific questions related to the topic. This prevents specific questions from biasing responses to the general questions. Consider the following sequence of questions.

Q1: What considerations are important to you in selecting a department store?
Q2: In selecting a department store, how important is convenience of location?

(Correct)

Figure 11.5
The Funnel Approach to Ordering Questions

funnel approach
A strategy for ordering questions in a questionnaire in which the sequence starts with the general questions, which are followed by progressively specific questions, in order to prevent specific questions from biasing general questions.

The first question is general while the second is specific. If these questions were reversed, respondents would be more likely to cite convenience of location as the response to the general question. Going from general to specific is called the **funnel approach** because you begin with broader (more general) questions and then ask narrower (more specific) questions, reflecting the shape of a funnel (Figure 11.5).[6] The funnel approach was illustrated in the opening vignette when general information about motivations for giving was obtained before measuring awareness and perceptions of World Vision. Although the funnel approach is more commonly used, sometimes the inverted funnel approach may be used when the respondents do not have clearly formulated views about a topic or when they lack a common frame of reference in responding to general questions on the topic. In this approach, the specific questions are asked first followed by more general questions.

Logical Order

Questions should be asked in a logical order, organized around topic areas. This was illustrated in the WV vignette. The order in which the questions were asked was as follows: (1) priorities and motivations for giving, (2) awareness of the organization (WV), (3) perceptions of the organization, (4) communication with donors, and (5) demographic information. When switching topics, brief transitional phrases or sentences should be used to help respondents switch their train of thought; for example, "In this section, we ask questions related to your purchase of a new car in the last six months."

branching questions
Questions used to guide an interviewer through a survey by directing the interviewer to different spots on the questionnaire depending on the answers given.

Branching questions direct respondents to different places in the questionnaire based on their response to the question at hand. To avoid confusion, they should be designed carefully. Here is an example of a well-designed question: "If the answer to Question 4 (Have you purchased a new car in the last six months?) is "no," go to Question 10; skip Questions 5 through 9 related to a new car purchase." Branches enable respondents to skip irrelevant questions or elaborate in areas of specific interest. Skip patterns can become quite complex to the point that they are best administered in computer-aided interviewing environments (CATI, CAPI, or Internet; see Chapter 7). The general order of questions is outlined in Table 11.2.

Table 11.2

The General Ordering of Questions in a Questionnaire

Question Type	Nature	Function	Example
Qualifying/Screening Questions	Focus on respondent inclusion criteria	To determine if a respondent is eligible to participate in the survey	Who in your household does most of the shopping for groceries?
Introductory Questions/Warm-Ups	Broad, easy questions	To break the ice and put the respondent at ease	How often do you shop for groceries?
Main Questions: Easy	Related to the information needed but easy to answer	To focus on the survey topic and reassure the respondent that survey is easy	How important is each of the following factors in selecting a supermarket?
Main Questions: More Difficult	Related to the information needed but may be difficult be to answer	To obtain the rest of the information needed	How would you rank order the following eight supermarkets in terms of your preference to shop?
Psychographics/ Lifestyles	Not relevant in all surveys	To obtain personality-related information	Please indicate your degree of dis/agreement with the following statements.
Demographics	Personal information	To classify the respondents	What was your household's total annual income last year?
Identification Information	Name, address, telephone	To identify the respondent	Name:_____

BE an MR!

Conduct an Internet search using a search engine and your library's online database to obtain information on consumers' perceptions, preferences, and purchase intentions for flat-panel television sets.

Specify the information needed and the order in which you would obtain information on consumers' perceptions, preferences, and purchase intentions for Sony flat-panel television sets.

BE a DM!

As the vice president of marketing, what marketing strategies would you formulate to increase Sony's penetration of the flat-panel television market?

Choose the Form and Layout

The physical characteristics of a questionnaire, such as the format, spacing, and positioning can have a significant effect on the results. This is particularly important for self-administered questionnaires. Experiments on mail questionnaires for the 2000 and earlier census revealed that questions at the top of the page received more attention than those at the bottom. Instructions printed in red made little difference except that they made the questionnaire appear more complicated to the respondents.

Dividing a questionnaire into sections with separate topic areas for each section is a good practice, as illustrated in the WV project. Several parts may be needed for questions pertaining to the basic information. The questions in each part should be numbered, particularly when branching questions are used. Numbering also makes coding the responses easier. Preferably, the questionnaires should be precoded. In **precoding**, the codes to enter in the computer are printed on the questionnaire. Typically, the code identifies the line number and the column numbers in which a particular response will be

precoding
In questionnaire design, assigning a code to every conceivable response before data collection.

RESEARCH IN ACTION

Precoding a Questionnaire

Residential Carpeting Survey

(1–3)

(Please ignore the numbers alongside the answers. They are only to help us in data processing.)

Please answer the following questions pertaining to household carpeting by following the specified directions.

Part A

Q1. Does your household currently own carpeting?

1. _____Yes (5)
2. _____No

(IF YES, GO TO QUESTION Q2; IF NO, GO TO QUESTION Q7.)

Q2. Which of the following styles of carpeting do you have in your home? Please check as many as apply.

a. _____One Color; Traditional Style (6)
b. _____Multicolor; Traditional Style (7)
c. _____One Color; Contemporary Style (8)
d. _____Multicolor; Contemporary Style (9)
e. _____Other (10)

Please indicate your agreement with each of the following statements (Q3 and Q4).

Q3. Carpeting is an important part of my home.

Strongly Disagree			Neutral			Strongly Agree	
1	2	3	4	5	6	7	(11)

Q4. Carpeting is a fashion item for the home.

Strongly Disagree			Neutral			Strongly Agree	
1	2	3	4	5	6	7	(12)

entered. Note that when CATI or CAPI (Computer Assisted Telephone Interviewing or Computer Assisted Personal Interviewing) are used, the precoding is built into the software. Coding of questionnaires is explained in more detail in Chapter 15 on data preparation. An example of the process in a questionnaire is shown above.

In the preceding example, the first precoding value (1–3) indicates that the first three columns are used for the questionnaire ID. In general, the questionnaires themselves should be numbered serially as this enhances control of questionnaires in the field, as well as the coding and analysis. This numbering system alerts the researcher if questionnaires are misplaced or lost. A possible exception to this rule is mail questionnaires. Respondents are promised anonymity, and the presence of a questionnaire identifier may be interpreted as a breach of that promise. Some respondents may refuse to participate or answer differently if they believe the answers can be traced to them. However, recent research suggests that this loss of anonymity has little, if any, influence on the results.

Reproduce the Questionnaire

The quality of the paper and print process used for the questionnaire also influences response. For example, if the questionnaire is reproduced on poor-quality paper or is otherwise shabby in appearance, the respondents may conclude that the project is unimportant, and this perception will be reflected in the quality of the responses. Therefore, the questionnaire should be reproduced on good-quality paper and have a professional appearance, as illustrated in the WV study. Multipage questionnaires should be presented in booklet form rather than simply stapled or clipped. This format is easier for the interviewer to handle and it also enhances the overall appearance.

Questions should not be continued from one page to the next. In other words, researchers should avoid splitting a question, including its response categories. Respondents may be mislead into thinking that a split question has ended at the bottom of a page and base their answers on the incomplete question.

The tendency to crowd questions together to make the questionnaire look shorter should be avoided. Overcrowding leaves little space for responses, which results in shorter answers. It also increases errors in data tabulation. In addition, crowded questionnaires appear more complex, resulting in lower cooperation and completion rates. While shorter questionnaires are more desirable than longer ones, reduction in size should not be obtained at the expense of crowding.

EXPERIENTIAL LEARNING

Designing a Survey Questionnaire

Meteor Motorcycle Company is one of the industry's leading manufacturers of customized, high-performance bikes in the luxury cruiser class. Return to Chapter 3's Experiential Learning, "Crafting a Research Proposal," to review the proposal presented to this company. Go to the textbook Web site, select "Chapter 11," and download the following file: Meteor Survey A.doc. This is the draft version of the survey used to fulfill the research objectives listed in the research proposal for the Meteor Motorcycle Company presented in Chapter 3 as Meteor Proposal.doc. Open Meteor Survey A.doc and read the actual draft versions of the survey questionnaire done after this proposal was accepted by Meteor.

1a. How would you improve this draft of the questionnaire? Hints: Think about what was promised in the proposal. Think also about the guidelines presented in this chapter.

1b. Create an electronic copy of Meteor Survey A.doc entitled Meteor Survey A2.doc. Make your proposed revisions in this new document now.

2a. How would you make this draft of the survey appear more appealing to the respondent? Hint: Think about "Form and Layout" and "Reproduce the Questionnaire" sections.

2b. Make your proposed revisions in this new document, Meteor Survey A2.doc, now.

Pretest the Questionnaire

Pretesting refers to testing the questionnaire on a small sample of respondents, usually 15 to 30, to identify and eliminate potential problems. Even the best questionnaire can be improved by pretesting. As a general rule, a questionnaire should not be used in the field study without extensive pretesting, as in the WV vignette. All aspects of the questionnaire, including question content, wording, sequence, form and layout, question difficulty, and instructions should be tested. Additionally, pretesting should be conducted with a subset of the respondent group. The pretest groups should be similar to the respondents in terms of their background characteristics, familiarity with the topic, and attitudes and behaviors of interest.[7]

pretesting
The testing of the questionnaire on a small sample of respondents for the purpose of improving the questionnaire by identifying and eliminating potential problems before using it in the actual survey.

Pretests are best done by personal interviews, even if the actual survey is to be conducted by telephone, mail, or electronically, so that interviewers can observe respondent reactions and attitudes. After the necessary changes have been made, another pretest could be administered using the actual data collection approach, if it is mail, telephone, or electronic. This stage of the pretest will reveal any potential problems in the interviewing method to be used in the actual survey. The pretest should be conducted in an environment and context similar to that of the actual survey.

Based on feedback from the pretest, the questionnaire should be edited, and the identified problems corrected. After each significant revision of the questionnaire, another pretest should be conducted, using a different sample of respondents. Pretesting should be continued until no further changes are needed. As a final step, the responses obtained during the pretest should be coded and analyzed. The analysis of pretest responses can serve as a check on the adequacy of the problem definition, and provide insight into the nature of the data as well as analytic techniques that will be required. Table 11.3 outlines the questionnaire design process in the form of a checklist.

Observational Forms

Observational forms are designed to record respondent reaction to new products, advertising, packaging, or some other marketing stimuli. Since there is no questioning of the respondents, the researcher does not need to be concerned with the psychological impact of the questions and the way they are asked. Observational forms are designed primarily

Table 11.3
Questionnaire Design Checklist

Step 1 Specify the Information Needed

1. Ensure that the information obtained fully addresses all the components of the problem.
2. Have a clear idea of the target population.

Step 2 Type of Interviewing Method

1. Review the type of interviewing method determined based on considerations discussed in Chapter 7.

Step 3 Individual Question Content

1. Is the question necessary?
2. Are several questions needed instead of one to obtain the required information in an unambiguous manner?
3. Do not use double-barreled questions.

Step 4 Overcoming Inability and Unwillingness to Answer

1. Is the respondent informed?
2. If respondents are not likely to be informed, filter questions that measure familiarity, product use, and past experience should be asked before questions about the topics themselves.
3. Can the respondent remember?
4. Questions that do not provide the respondent with cues can underestimate the actual occurrence of an event.
5. Can the respondent articulate?
6. Minimize the effort required by the respondents.
7. Make the request for information seem legitimate.
8. Is the information sensitive?

Step 5 Choosing Question Structure

1. Open-ended questions are useful in exploratory research and as opening questions.
2. Use structured questions whenever possible.
3. In multiple-choice questions, the response alternatives should include the set of all possible choices and should be mutually exclusive.
4. In a dichotomous question, if a substantial proportion of the respondents can be expected to be neutral, include a neutral alternative.
5. Consider the use of the split-ballot technique to reduce order bias in dichotomous and multiple-choice questions.
6. If the response alternatives are numerous, consider using more than one question.

Step 6 Choosing Question Wording

1. Define the issue in terms of *who*, *what*, *when*, *where*, *why*, and *way* (the six Ws).
2. Use ordinary words. Words should match the vocabulary level of the respondents.
3. Avoid ambiguous words: *usually, normally, frequently, often, regularly, occasionally, sometimes,* and so forth.
4. Avoid leading questions that clue the respondent to what the answer should be.
5. Use positive and negative statements.

Table 11.3 *(continued)*

Step 7 Determine the Order of Questions

1. The opening questions should be interesting, simple, and nonthreatening.
2. Qualifying questions should serve as the opening questions.
3. Basic information should be obtained first, followed by classification, and, finally, identification information.
4. Difficult, sensitive, or complex questions should be placed late in the sequence.
5. General questions should precede specific questions.
6. Questions should be asked in a logical order.

Step 8 Form and Layout

1. Divide a questionnaire into several parts.
2. Number the questions in each part.
3. Precode the questionnaire.
4. Serially number the questionnaires themselves.

Step 9 Reproduction of the Questionnaire

1. The questionnaire should have a professional appearance.
2. Use a booklet format for long questionnaires.
3. Reproduce each question on a single page (or double-page spread).
4. Avoid the tendency to crowd questions to make the questionnaire look shorter. Place directions or instructions for individual questions as close as possible to the questions.

Step 10 Pretesting

1. Always pretest.
2. Test all aspects of the questionnaire, including question content, wording, sequence, form and layout, question difficulty, and instructions.
3. Use respondents in the pretest that are similar to those who will be included in the actual survey.
4. Begin the pretest by using personal interviews.
5. Conduct the pretest by mail, telephone, or electronically if those methods are to be used in the actual survey.
6. Use a variety of interviewers for pretests.
7. The pretest sample size should be small, varying from 15 to 30 respondents for the initial testing.
8. After each significant revision of the questionnaire, conduct another pretest, using a different sample of respondents.
9. Code and analyze the responses obtained from the pretest.

for the field work and the tabulation phase, providing a guide for recording information accurately and to simplify coding, entry, and analysis of data.

Observational forms should specify the *who*, *what*, *when*, *where*, *why*, and *way* of behavior to be observed. Please refer to the discussion on descriptive research in Chapter 3 for a similar analysis. Suppose, McDonald's wants to observe consumers' reaction to the deluxe sandwiches to be introduced in 2008. An observational form to record customer reaction would include space for all of the following information.

RESEARCH IN ACTION

Are McDonald's Deluxe Sandwiches Truly Deluxe?

Who: Purchasers, adults, parents with children, teenagers

What: Deluxe sandwiches, other sandwiches and menu items considered/purchased, influence of children or other family members

When: Day, hour, and date of observation

Where: At checkout counter, inside the store in the eating area, outside the store upon exit

Why: Influence of promotion or family members on the purchase

Way: Hidden camera at a McDonald's used to record respondents who were properly rewarded and previously notified of the possibility of such observation.

The same physical design considerations of layout and reproduction apply to both questionnaires and observational forms. A well-designed form guides the observer to appropriately record the details of the observation rather than merely summarize them. Finally, like questionnaires, observational forms also require adequate pretesting.

BE a DM!

As the marketing director for Neiman Marcus, develop marketing programs to capitalize upon consumers' Christmas retail shopping for the upcoming season.

BE an MR!

Conduct an Internet search using a search engine and your library's online database to obtain information on consumers' Christmas retail shopping behavior.

Specify the method and design an observation form to observe the consumers' Christmas retail shopping behavior.

Summary Illustration Using the Opening Vignette

We summarize and illustrate the questionnaire design process by returning to the opening vignette. Notice that the information obtained for WV and the order in which it was obtained were clearly specified. The questionnaire was kept simple, and detailed instructions were provided, because it had to be administered by mail. Only necessary questions were asked, and combined questions were avoided. To increase the willingness of the donors and potential donors to participate and complete the questionnaire, the context of the survey was made clear, and the effort required of the respondents was minimized. Most of the questions were structured questions, requiring the respondents to simply circle a number on the scale. However, a few unstructured or open-ended questions were included, where it was felt that the respondents needed the freedom to express underlying motivations for giving to charity.

Words with unequivocal meaning, but familiar to the donors, were used. Special effort was made to not bias the responses in any direction. The ordering of the questions was logical, and the funnel approach was used. General questions about priorities and motivations for giving were asked first; questions about awareness and perceptions of WV followed. The questionnaire was divided into parts, with a separate part devoted to each type of information sought. Information on name and address was optional, and obtained at the end of the questionnaire. The questionnaire was professionally reproduced and thoroughly pretested.

International Marketing Research

The questionnaire or research instrument should be designed to be sensitive to cultural differences encountered in international research. Differences in underlying consumer behavior, decision-making processes, psychographics, lifestyles, and demographic variables should all be considered. Questions related to marital status, education, household size, occupation, income, and dwelling unit might have to be modified to be comparable across countries, requiring rewording. For example, household definition and size varies greatly, given the extended family structure in some countries and the practice of two or even three families living under the same roof.

While personal interviewing is the dominant survey method in international marketing research, different interviewing methods may be used in different countries. Therefore, the questionnaire must be adaptable to a variety of administration methods. In countries with lower levels of education or product experience, two or more simple questions rather than a single complex question should be used. The researcher should realize that respondents in some countries, for example, in the Far East and the Commonwealth of Independent States (former Soviet Union), might not be as well informed about the subject matter of the survey as respondents in the United States.

Using unstructured or open-ended questions may be necessary if the researcher does not fully understand the range of alternatives associated with a response. Using unstructured questions can also minimize the risk of cultural bias. However, unstructured questions are more sensitive to differences in educational levels than are structured questions. They should be used with caution in countries with high illiteracy rates.

In addition to design considerations, the researcher must also pay close attention to translation issues. Pretesting of the questionnaire is complicated in international research because the linguistic equivalence must be pretested. Two sets of pretests are recommended. The translated questionnaire should be pretested on respondents who speak only their native language, as well as on bilingual subjects. The pretest data from administering the questionnaire in different countries or cultures should be analyzed, and the pattern of responses compared, to detect any cultural biases.

RESEARCH IN ACTION

Engaging Respondents about Engagement

A questionnaire dealing with engagement rings was administered to women in seven European countries. The first set of questions used in England was

1. Are you married?
   If yes, in what year were you married?
   If no, are you engaged to be married?

   If married or engaged:
2. Do you own an engagement ring, or did you obtain one or more rings at the time of your engagement?

   If "yes":
3. What type of ring is it/was it?
   ___ No stones
   ___ Single diamond only
   ___ Several diamonds, no other stones
   ___ Diamonds and other stones
   ___ Other stones only

This looks like a very simple list of questions, involving no difficulty of direct or literal translation. Yet, if the questionnaire were literally translated for use in the other countries, the results would have been meaningless. The question, "Do you own an engagement ring?" would not have worked in Germany since many German women receive a plain gold band at the time of engagement, which they later transfer to the other hand and use as a wedding ring. Instead of a single question, a whole battery of questions was needed to obtain information from Germany that was equivalent to that of the other six countries. Thus, the researcher had to translate the meaning rather than do a literal translation (transliteration).

Another modification to ensure comparability concerned the list of precoded ring types. Although pearl rings were relatively unimportant in most countries covered, they were a high proportion of engagement rings in Spain and France. To include pearl rings as a separate category in most of the countries would have unnecessarily complicated the list. However, to exclude them in Spain or France would have resulted not only in the loss of information but also in confusion arising from the list of type of rings being incomplete.[8] Therefore, the pearl ring was included as a ring type in only the Spanish and French questionnaires.

Technology and Marketing Research

Software is available for designing questionnaires administered over the Internet or other modes (e.g., telephone, personal interviews, or mail). Although we describe the use of the software for constructing Internet questionnaires, the functions are essentially similar for questionnaires constructed by other modes. The software will help develop and disseminate the questionnaire, and, in many cases, retrieve and analyze the collected data, and prepare a report. These software have a variety of features that facilitate questionnaire construction.

Question List. The user can select a variety of formats from a menu of question types such as open-ended, multiple-choice, scales, dichotomous questions, and so forth. Moreover, one can use buttons, drop-down boxes (closed position or open position), check boxes, or open-ended scrolling text boxes.

Question Libraries. The user can select predefined questions or save questions used often in the question library. For example, the question library may contain predefined questions for measuring satisfaction, purchase intention, and other commonly used constructs in marketing.

Questionnaire Appearance. The user can select the background color and graphics of the questionnaire from a range of available templates or create a customized template using the template manager.

Preview. The user can preview the questionnaire as it is being developed to examine the content, interactivity, type of questions, and background design and make any changes that may be needed.

Publish. This user can create the HTML questionnaire, post it to a unique Web page, create a database to collect the data on the hosting server, and obtain a unique URL to which respondents can be directed.

Notification. The user can create, personalize, send, and track e-mail-based invitations to participate in the survey.

As each respondent completes the survey, the data are transferred over the Web to the data file on the host server. The data can be downloaded and analyzed at any time, when the survey is running. Thus, results can be examined in real time. Some commonly used software are SurveyTime (www.surveytime.com), SurveyPro (www.surveypro.com), Surveyz! (www.surveyz.com), and PerfectSurveys (www.perfectsurveys.com). Another popular package is WebSurveyor (www.websurveyor.com).

Several Web sites allow users to create and field their own questionnaires for free. CreateSurvey (www.createsurvey.com) is an online company that allows anyone to create and administer online surveys to whomever they want. It distributes the survey, monitors participation and participants, and then collects and analyzes the data, all for free because it is sponsored by Web advertising. However, CreateSurvey does not provide respondents. Users do this at their discretion. For instance, they may create a Web page and have the survey as a link from the Web page, or they may send out an e-mail with the link requesting people to participate in the survey. Another Web-based service that also lets you create your own surveys is Zoomerang (www.zoomerang.com) by MarketTools, an Internet-based, technology-enabled, full-service marketing research company (www.markettools.com).

The following Research in Action example illustrates the guidelines a marketing research firm follows in order to design good online questionnaires.

Ethics in Marketing Research

Administering the questionnaire is a substantial intrusion by the researcher. Therefore, several ethical concerns arise pertaining to the researcher/respondent relationship. Ethical issues pertinent to the researcher/client relationship may also have to be addressed.

RESEARCH IN ACTION

Designing Internet Survey Questionnaires: The DSS Research Way

DSS Research (www.dssresearch.com), a full-service marketing research firm specializing in research using the Internet, has developed the following guidelines for designing good online questionnaires.

- To ensure that the questionnaire provides the necessary decision-making information for management, DSS includes the responsible managers in the design process and also requires them to sign off on the questionnaire.
- The questionnaires are specifically designed for the intended respondents. Thus, marketing jargon and business terminology that respondents might not understand are not used.
- DSS uses the multimedia capabilities of the Internet to design a questionnaire that is appealing and interesting to the respondents.
- The questionnaire is personalized for each respondent by inserting the name and answers to previous questions, as appropriate. This increases the respondent's involvement.

In consideration of the respondents, questions that are confusing, exceed the respondents' ability, are difficult, or are otherwise improperly worded should be avoided. When asking sensitive questions, researchers should attempt to minimize the respondents' discomfort. It should be made clear at the beginning of the questionnaire that respondents are not obligated to answer any question that makes them uncomfortable. Similarly, overly long questionnaires should be avoided. As a general guideline, the following are considered overly long: a personal, in-home interview lasting over 60 minutes, a telephone interview over 30 minutes, a mall intercept interview over 30 minutes, or a mail or electronic interview over 30 minutes. Overly long questionnaires are burdensome on the respondents and adversely affect the quality of responses.

The researcher has the ethical responsibility to design a questionnaire that obtains the required data in an unbiased manner. Deliberately biasing the questionnaire in a desired direction—for example, by asking leading questions—cannot be condoned. In deciding the question structure, the most appropriate rather than the most convenient option should be adopted, as illustrated by the Research in Action example dealing with International Marketing Ethics. If the questionnaire is not thoroughly pretested, an ethical breach has occurred.

RESEARCH IN ACTION

Questioning International Marketing Ethics

One way to avoid biased questions in the international arena is to use open-ended questions. This is particularly appropriate if the response categories are not known. In a study designed to identify ethical problems in international marketing, a series of open-ended questions were used. The objective of the survey, directed at Australian firms engaged in international marketing activities, was to find the three most frequently encountered ethical problems, in order of priority. After reviewing the results, the researcher tabulated and categorized them into 10 categories that occurred most often: traditional small-scale bribery, large-scale bribery, gifts/favors/entertainment, pricing, inappropriate products/technology, tax evasion practices, illegal/immoral activities, questionable commissions to channel members, cultural differences, and involvement in political affairs. The sheer number of categories indicates that international marketing ethics should probably be questioned more closely! The use of structured questions in this case, although more convenient, would have been inappropriate, raising ethical concerns as the researcher lacked knowledge of the set of possible response options required for multiple-choice questions.[9]

WHAT WOULD *YOU* DO?

Does Delta Stack Up to the Competition?

The Situation

Gerald Grinstein has been chief executive officer of Delta Air Lines since January 1, 2004. Delta is the third-largest U.S. airline in terms of operating revenue and the world's second-largest air carrier in terms of passengers carried. The airline's innovative developments in the areas of technology and e-commerce have also been widely noted. Delta was named the number-one airline, according to the annual Wichita State University Airline Quality Rating study. In addition, *Forbes* magazine ranked Delta number one based on five important customer service criteria.

Since 2000, the Global Airline Performance (GAP) study teamed up with P. Robert and Partners and the London-based Aviation Information and Research unit of the International Air Transport Association (IATA) to perform a two-part syndicated survey for measuring passenger satisfaction on 22 different airlines in 30 different countries. It samples 240,000 passengers each year and is conducted in seven languages. The interviewers catch the respondent's at a most opportune time: while waiting to board the plane. The first part of the survey consists of 20 questions about the airline staff and their willingness to assist; the second part, one that must be sent by mail or fax, asks questions of the boarding process, service on the plane, and comfort.

Delta General Manager of Marketing Research, Paul Lai, agrees that keeping the information fresh in the respondent's mind helps get a clearer view of how the airline can increase customer satisfaction. Another benefit of the survey is that it is ongoing so responses can be tracked over time. Lai also enjoys receiving the data for other airlines so they can put researchers on areas in which Delta lags. The survey revealed to Delta and other airlines that two service issues are most important. One is the operational service such as arrival/departure times without delays. The second is more subjective and cannot be controlled as easily–airline employee and customer relations. If Paul Lai remains in tune with the surveys performed by GAP, Delta should be able to stay ahead of the flight competition.

The Marketing Research Decision

1. Paul Lai would like to improve the effectiveness of Part 2 of the GAP questionnaire given in Appendix 11A. This can be done best by (check as many as are applicable):
   a. Eliminating double-barreled questions
   b. Eliminating leading questions
   c. Rearranging the order of questions
   d. Using unstructured questions
   e. Reducing the length of the questionnaire

2. Discuss the role of the questionnaire you recommend in enabling Paul Lai to determine consumer preferences for airlines and increase the market share of Delta.

The Marketing Management Decision

1. Gerald Grinstein would like to improve Delta's in-flight services. Should he improve? Check as many as are applicable.
   a. The cabin features
   b. The cabin crew
   c. Food and beverages
   d. Onboard amenities/entertainment
   e. All of the above
2. Discuss how the marketing management-decision action that you recommend to Gerald Grinstein is influenced by the questionnaire that you suggested earlier and by the findings of that research.

What Gerald Grinstein Did

Gerald Grinstein significantly stepped up the level of food and drinks and in-flight amenities Delta offers. In particular, he sought to overcome the bad connotations associated with the generally subpar "airplane food." Delta provided "real" food from popular restaurants and bakeries. Therefore, it is now possible to purchase a quality lunch from Gate Gourmet, or one's favorite sandwich from the Atlanta Bread Company, not to mention the continued availability of kosher and vegetarian meals.

Delta, in order to meet the needs of the new technologically savvy business class, has also added e-mail access and hopes to soon have full broadband Internet service. With all BusinessElite seats, there also comes a personal telephone and increased console space to serve as a desk. However, if strict work ethic does not appeal while onboard the fleet's newest member, the Boeing 777, have no fear–there are television screens at every seat offering your choice of movies and an array of programming.[10]

Summary

To collect quantitative primary data, a researcher must design a questionnaire or an observation form. A questionnaire has three objectives. It must (1) translate the information needed into a set of specific questions, (2) motivate respondents to complete the interview, and (3) minimize response error.

Designing a questionnaire is as much an art as it is a science. We can provide guidelines for development, but no one optimal questionnaire design fits every research need. The process begins by specifying the information needed and the type of interviewing method. The next step is to decide on the content of individual questions.

Questions must be written to overcome the respondents' inability to answer. Respondents may be unable to answer if they are not informed, cannot remember, or cannot articulate the response. When too much effort is required, or the research context seems inappropriate, respondents will be unwilling to participate. Questions that attempt to collect sensitive information may also be met with resistance. Questions can be unstructured (open-ended) or structured to a varying degree. Structured questions include multiple-choice, dichotomous questions, and scales.

Determining the wording of each question involves defining the issue, using ordinary words, using unambiguous words, and using dual statements. The issue should be clearly defined in terms of *who*, *what*, *when*, and *where*. The *why* and *way* may not be relevant always. The researcher should avoid leading questions. Once the questions have been worded, the order in which they will appear in the questionnaire must be decided. Special consideration should be given to opening questions, type of information, difficult questions, and the effect on subsequent questions. The questions should be arranged in a logical order.

The stage is now set for determining the form and layout of the questions. The physical considerations in reproducing the questionnaire include: appearance, use of booklets, fitting all the questions on a page, response category format, avoiding overcrowding, placement of directions, color coding, and cost. The effectiveness of all these design decisions must be assessed in a pretest.

The design of observational forms requires explicit decisions about what is to be observed and how that behavior is to be recorded. It is useful to specify the *who*, *what*, *when*, *where*, *why*, and *way* of the behavior to be observed.

The questionnaire or research instrument should be adapted to the specific cultural environment and should not be biased in terms of any one culture. Several software packages are available to facilitate questionnaire design. Several firms provide software and services for designing Internet questionnaires. In consideration of the respondents, overly long questionnaires or questions that exceed the respondents' willingness or ability to respond should be avoided. The questionnaire should be designed to obtain information in an unbiased manner.

Key Terms and Concepts

Questionnaire, 288
Double-barreled question, 292
Filter questions, 293
Unstructured questions, 296
Structured questions, 296
Order or position bias, 298
Dichotomous question, 298
Leading question, 301
Basic information, 303
Classification information, 303
Identification information, 303
Funnel approach, 304
Branching questions, 304
Precoding, 305
Pretesting, 307

Suggested Cases and Video Cases

Cases

2.2 Cadillac
2.4 Bloomingdale's
2.5 Burger King
4.1 Boeing
4.2 Gucci

Video Cases

2.2 Nike
4.1 Subaru
4.2 Marriott

Additional cases and video cases are available in the Instructor's Manual and on the instructor and student Web sites.

Live Research: Conducting a Marketing Research Project

1. Each team can develop a questionnaire following the principles discussed in the chapter. The best features of each questionnaire can be combined to develop the project questionnaire.
2. Each team should be assigned a few pretest interviews.
3. If a questionnaire has already been prepared, it should be critically evaluated in the class.
4. The resulting questionnaire should be discussed and approved by the client.

Acronyms

The objectives and steps involved in developing a questionnaire may be defined by the acronym QUESTIONNAIRE:

Objectives
- **Q** uestions that respondents can answer
- **U** plift the respondent
- **E** rror elimination

Steps
- **S** pecify the information needed
- **T** ype of interviewing method
- **I** ndividual question content
- **O** vercoming inability and unwillingness to answer
- **N** onstructured versus structured questions
- **N** onbiased question wording
- **A** rrange the questions in proper order
- **I** dentify form and layout
- **R** eproduction of the questionnaire
- **E** liminate bugs by pretesting

The guidelines for question wording may be summarized by the acronym WORDS:

- **W** ho, what, when, where, why, and way
- **O** bjective questions: Avoid leading questions
- **R** egularly, normally, usually, etc., should be avoided
- **D** ual statements (positive and negative)
- **S** imple, ordinary words

The guidelines for deciding on the order of questions may be summarized by the acronym ORDER:

- **O** pening questions: simple
- **R** udimentary or basic information should be obtained first
- **D** ifficult questions toward the end
- **E** xamine the influence on subsequent questions
- **R** eview the sequence to ensure a logical order

Review Questions

1. What is the purpose of questionnaires and observation forms?
2. Explain how the mode of administration affects questionnaire design.
3. How would you determine whether a specific question should be included in a questionnaire?
4. What is a double-barreled question?
5. What are the reasons that respondents are unable to answer the question asked?
6. Explain the concepts of aided and unaided recall.
7. What are the reasons that respondents are unwilling to answer specific questions?
8. What can a researcher do to make the request for information seem legitimate?
9. What are the advantages and disadvantages of unstructured questions?
10. What are the issues involved in designing multiple-choice questions?
11. What are the guidelines available for deciding on question wording?
12. What is a leading question? Give an example.
13. What is the proper order for questions intended to obtain basic, classification, and identification information?
14. What guidelines are available for deciding on the form and layout of a questionnaire?
15. Describe the issues involved in pretesting a questionnaire.
16. What are the major decisions involved in designing observational forms?

Applied Problems

1. Develop three double-barreled questions related to flying and passengers' airline preferences. Also, develop corrected versions of each question.
2. List at least 10 ambiguous words that should not be used in framing questions.
3. Do the following questions define the issue? Why or why not?
   a. What is your favorite brand of shampoo?
   b. How often do you go on a vacation?
   c. Do you consume orange juice?
      1. Yes
      2. No
4. Design an open-ended question to determine whether households engage in gardening. Also, develop a multiple-choice and a dichotomous ques-

tion to obtain the same information. Which form is the most desirable?

5. A new graduate hired by the marketing research department of a major telephone company is asked to prepare a questionnaire to determine household preferences for telephone calling cards. The questionnaire is to be administered in mall intercept interviews. Using the principles of questionnaire design, critically evaluate this questionnaire.

HOUSEHOLD TELEPHONE CALLING CARD SURVEY

1. Your name _____
2. Age _____
3. Marital status _____
4. Income_____
5. Which, if any, of the following telephone calling cards do you have?

   1. AT&T____ 2. MCI__ 3. Sprint____ 4. Others____

6. How frequently do you use a telephone calling card?

   Infrequently — Very Frequently

   1 2 3 4 5 6 7

7. What do you think of the telephone calling card offered by AT&T?

   _____

8. Suppose your household were to select a telephone calling card. Please rate the importance of the following factors in selecting a card.

	Not Important				Very Important
a. Cost per call	1	2	3	4	5
b. Ease of use	1	2	3	4	5
c. Local and long-distance charges included in the same bill	1	2	3	4	5
d. Rebates and discounts on calls	1	2	3	4	5
e. Quality of telephone service	1	2	3	4	5
f. Quality of customer service	1	2	3	4	5

9. How important is it for a telephone company to offer a calling card?

   Not important — Very Important

   1 2 3 4 5 6 7

10. Do you have children living at home? _____

Thank You for Your Help!

6. IBM would like to conduct an Internet survey to determine the image of IBM PCs and the image of its major competitors (Sony, Dell, and Hewlett Packard). Develop such a questionnaire. Relevant information may be obtained by visiting the Web sites of these companies (www.ibm.com, www.sony.com, www.dell.com, www.hp.com).
7. Using an electronic questionnaire design package, design a questionnaire to measure consumer preferences for sneakers. Then, develop the same questionnaire manually. Compare your experiences in designing this questionnaire electronically and manually.
8. Visit the Web site of one of the online marketing research firms (e.g., Greenfield Online Research Center, Inc. at www.greenfieldonline.com). Locate a survey being currently administered at this site. Critically analyze the questionnaire using the principles discussed in this chapter.

Group Discussion

1. "Because questionnaire design is an art, it is useless to follow a rigid set of guidelines. Rather, the process should be left entirely to the creativity and ingenuity of the researcher." Discuss in a small group.
2. In a small group, discuss the role of questionnaire design in minimizing total research error.
3. Discuss the importance of form and layout in questionnaire construction.

APPENDIX 11A Global Airline Performance Questionnaire Part 2–English–211

Welcome on Board

Thank you for agreeing to complete this questionnaire.

Your opinion on today's flight performance is **essential**, because it will allow the airline to improve its performance according to your needs.

Please answer Part 2 after you have landed and collected your luggage (if any). Then mail/fax it back to us.

Thank You for Your Help

Unless stated otherwise, all ratings should be provided using the following scale:

5 = Excellent
4 = Very good
3 = Good
2 = Fair
1 = Poor
DN = Did not notice/use

1. Please rate this flight on the following items.

Boarding and Departure

1 Efficiency of aircraft boarding
2 Punctuality of flight departure
3 Information given if flight delayed
Overall rating for boarding and departure

Your Comfort and the Cabin Features

4 Space to store carry-on hand luggage
5 Condition of cabin interior
6 Comfort of seat
7 Sleeping comfort
8 Amount of legroom
9 Cleanliness of your seat and table on departure
10 Cleanliness of toilets/lavatories
Overall rating for comfort and cabin features

The Cabin Crew

11 Professional appearance of cabin crew
12 Responsiveness of cabin crew in serving your needs
13 Courtesy/helpfulness of cabin crew
14 Availability of cabin crew throughout the flight
15 Ability to speak your language
16 Information provided by cabin crew and pilots
Overall rating for cabin crew

Food and Beverages

17 Quality of the meal(s) and/or snack(s)
18 Quantity/sufficiency of the meal(s) and/or snack(s)
19 Choice of beverages available on board
Overall rating for food and beverages

Onboard Amenities/Entertainment

20 Choice of newspapers and magazines
21 Telecommunications services (phone, fax, PC port)
22 Choice of movies shown
23 Choice of other video programming
24 Quality of the video system (sound, vision)
25 Choice of audio programming
26 Quality of the audio programs (sound)
Overall rating for onboard amenities/entertainment

2. After leaving this flight, please rate the following items. (Please tick.)

27 Punctuality of flight arrival
28 Efficiency of leaving aircraft
29 Speed of luggage delivery
30 Arrival lounge
Overall rating for postflight

3. From the specific items you have just rated in Sections 1 and 2, could you please indicate which three items (numbered 1–30) are most in need of improvement for this airline:

The three items in their order of need of improvement:
1st
2nd
3rd

4. Your overall judgment of today's flight:

31 Value for money you received from this flight
32 Your overall rating of this airline's performance today, taking everything into account
33 The airline's performance compared with your expectations
Much better
Little better
Much as expected
Little worse
Much worse

5. Based on your experience of today's flight, would you select this airline for your next trip on this route?

Definitely would
Probably would
Might/might not
Probably not
Definitely not

6. Based on your experience of today's flight, how likely would you be to recommend this airline to a friend or colleague?

Extremely likely
Very likely
Somewhat likely
Not very likely
Not at all likely

7. Approximately how many of the seats were occupied in your section of the aircraft?

Up to half full
Half to three-quarters full
Over three-quarters to nearly full
Full
Completely full

8. In which class did you sit on this flight?

First
Business
Economy/coach
Special economy (which)

9. Flight Date: DD MM YY Airline:
Flight No.: LETTERS NUMBERS Name: Mr./Ms.:

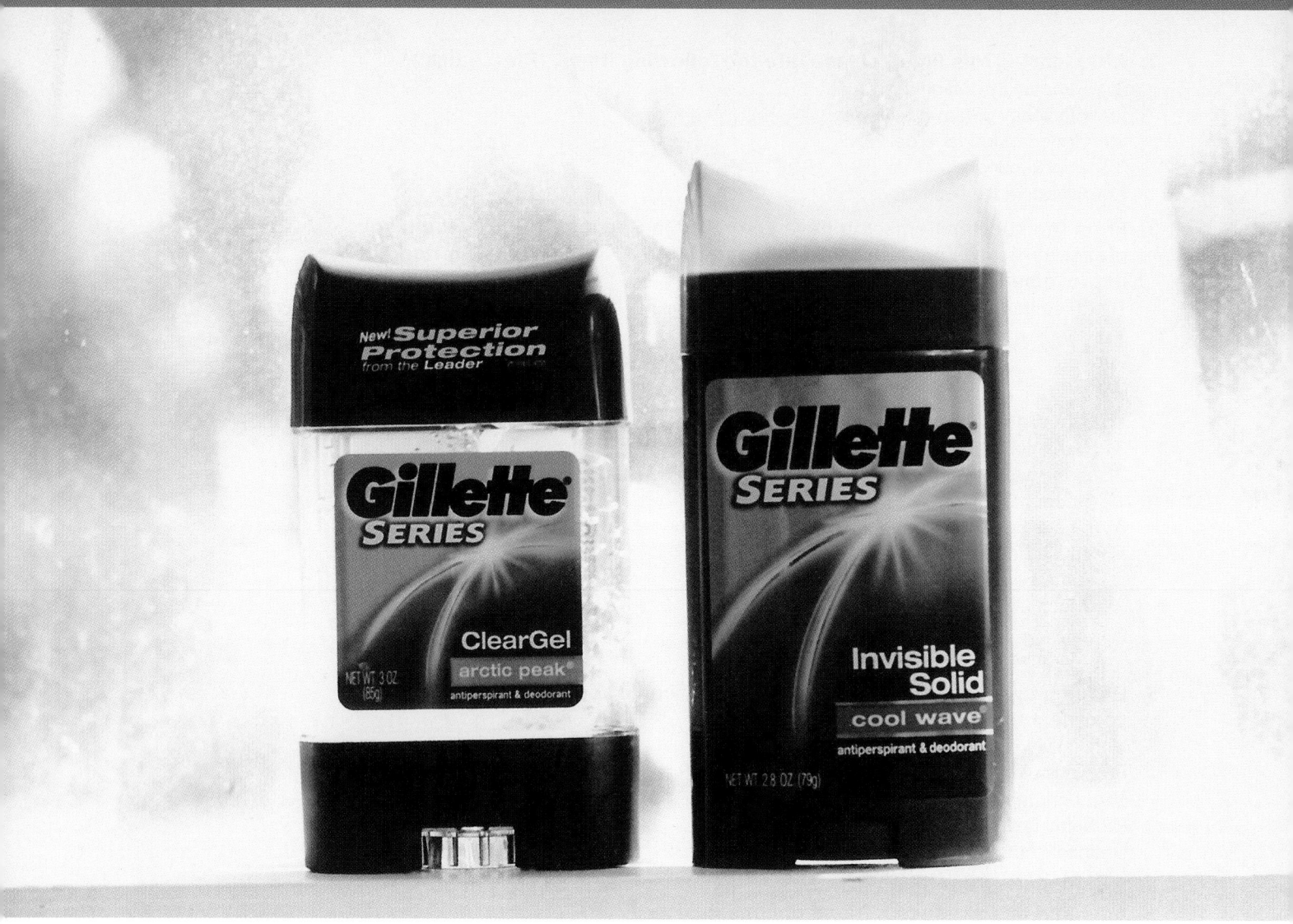

CHAPTER

12 Sampling: Design and Procedures

"A good sampling design, carefully executed, is a key to obtaining high-quality data. Too often this is taken for granted, and the results can be profound."

DAVID FRUEND, *Director and Manager, Market Research, Progress Energy, Inc., Raleigh, NC*

OPENING QUESTIONS

1. How do we differentiate a sample from a census, and what conditions favor the use of a sample versus a census?
2. What steps are involved in the sampling design process?
3. How can sampling techniques be classified, and what is the difference between nonprobability and probability sampling techniques?
4. What are the various nonprobability sampling techniques, and when are they used?
5. What are the various probability sampling techniques, and when are they used?
6. What conditions favor the use of nonprobability sampling versus probability sampling?
7. How should online samples be selected?
8. How are sampling techniques used in international marketing research?
9. How does technology interface with sampling, and what ethical issues relate to the sampling design process?

Gillette Clear Stick Clears the Way for Growth in the Deodorant Market

In August 2004, Gillette decided to focus on three core product areas–razors and blades, grooming products, and Duracell batteries–to cut costs and increase profits. New product development and introduction have always been the backbone of Gillette's marketing strategy, as illustrated by the introduction of their Clear Stick deodorant.

After spending over $30 million to develop the Clear Stick technology, Gillette undertook consumer research to introduce a successful new antiperspirant/deodorant based on this technology. The sampling procedures played a critical role in revealing important findings that guided new product development and introduction. The company defined the population of interest, which is the *target population*, as male heads of households. Then it developed a questionnaire to measure preferences for stick deodorants versus other forms, such as sprays and roll-ons, and to compare the clear stick to conventional sticks. The questionnaire was administered via computer-assisted telephone interviewing.

Given the large size of the target population and limited time and money, it was clearly not feasible to interview the entire population, that is, to take a *census*. So a sample was taken and a subgroup of the population was selected for participation in the research. The basic units sampled were households and within the selected households the male heads of households were interviewed. Probability sampling, where each element of the population has a fixed chance of being selected, was chosen because the results had to be generalizable, that is, projectable to all male heads of households in the United States. Simple random sampling was used to select 1,000 households. This sample size was selected based on qualitative considerations, such as the importance of the decision, nature of the research, statistical analyses that would be required, resource constraint, and the sample sizes used in similar studies Gillette had conducted on new product development. The technique of simple random sampling was selected because efficient computer programs were

available to randomly generate household telephone numbers and minimize wastage due to nonexisting household telephone numbers. An initial call was made to recruit the respondents and explain the study. Those who qualified and agreed to participate were mailed a sample of the new clear stick deodorant with instructions to use it for two weeks. Then a follow-up telephone interview was conducted.

The results indicated that 56 percent of men preferred stick deodorants. Moreover, clear sticks were preferred to conventional sticks on a variety of attributes: gliding on without dragging, ease of application, and no white residue on the skin or clothing. Based on these findings, Gillette introduced Clear Stick. The product packaging was designed to create a high-tech dispensing system. Inspired by the mouse control on most personal computers, Gillette designers created a powerball to replace the dial mechanism found on conventional sticks and solids. The launch was successful, and Clear Stick accelerated the retail value growth of the entire antiperspirant/deodorant market. Sound sampling procedures adopted in this research resulted in clear-cut findings that aided in the development and launch of a successful product.[1] •

Overview

Sampling design issues are a part of the research design process. By this point in the research process, the researcher has identified the information needs of the study as well as the nature of the research design (exploratory, descriptive, or casual; Chapters 3 through 8). Furthermore, the researcher has specified the scaling and measurement procedures (Chapters 9 and 10) and has designed the questionnaire (Chapter 11). The next step is to design suitable sampling procedures. Figure 12.1 briefly explains the focus of the chapter, the relation of this chapter to the previous ones, and the steps of the marketing research process on which this chapter concentrates.

Five basic questions are addressed in the sample design phase: (1) Should a sample be taken? (2) If so, what process should be followed? (3) What kind of sample should be taken? (4) How large should it be? (5) What can be done to adjust for incidence—the rate of occurrence of eligible respondents—and completion rates?

This chapter addresses the first three questions of the sample design. Chapter 13 addresses the last two questions. We will discuss sampling in terms of the qualitative considerations underlying the sampling design process. We first address the question of whether or not to sample and describe the steps involved in sampling. Next, we present nonprobability and probability sampling techniques. These issues were introduced in the opening vignette, in which Gillette used a probability sampling scheme to select the respondents. The use of sampling techniques in international marketing research is described. We also discuss the interface of technology with sampling and identify the relevant ethical issues and Internet applications. Figure 12.2 gives an overview of the topics discussed in this chapter and how they flow from one to the next.

Sample or Census

element
Objects that possess the information the researcher seeks and about which the researcher will make inferences.

In sampling, an **element** is the object (or person) about which or from which the information is desired. In survey research, the element is usually the respondent. A **population** is the total of all the elements that share some common set of characteristics. Each marketing research project has a uniquely defined population that is described in terms of its parameters. The objective of most marketing research projects is to obtain information about the characteristics or parameters of a population. The proportion of consumers

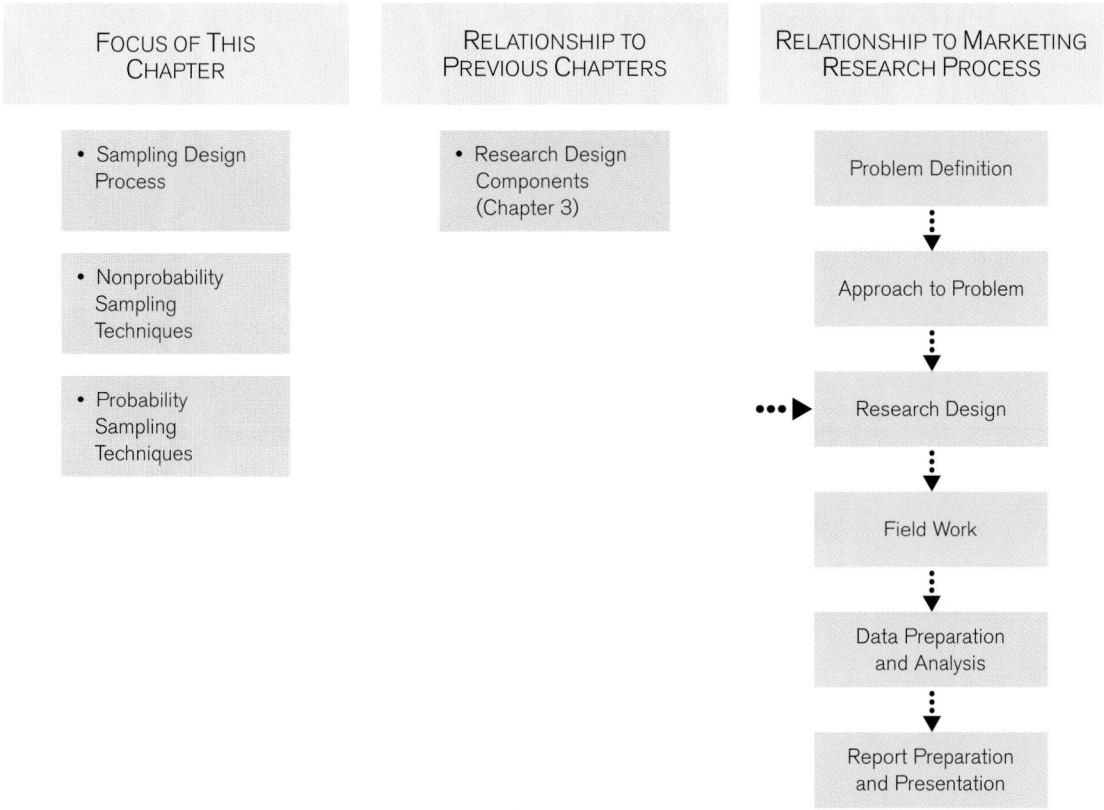

Figure 12.1

Relationship of Sampling Design to the Previous Chapters and the Marketing Research Process

loyal to a particular brand of toothpaste is an example of a population parameter. In the opening vignette, the percentage of male heads of household that preferred a stick deodorant was a population parameter. This parameter was estimated, via sampling, to be 56 percent. The researcher can obtain information about population parameters by taking either a census or a sample. A **census** involves a complete count of each element in a population. On the other hand, a **sample** is a subgroup of the population.

population
The aggregate of all the elements, sharing some common set of characteristics, which comprise the universe for the purpose of the marketing research problem.

census
A complete enumeration of the elements of a population or study objects.

sample
A subgroup of the elements of the population selected for participation in the study.

Table 12.1 summarizes the conditions favoring the use of a sample versus a census. The primary considerations favoring a sample are budget and time limits. A census is both costly and time-consuming to conduct. In research studies involving large populations, such as users of consumer products, it is generally not feasible to take a census, as illustrated in the opening vignette. Therefore, a sample is the only viable option. On the other hand, business-to-business research involving industrial products typically involves a much smaller population. A census becomes not only possible but often also desirable in such situations. For example, while investigating the use of certain machine tools by U.S. automobile manufacturers, a census would be preferable to a sample since the population of automobile manufacturers is small. A census also becomes more attractive when large variations exist in the population. For example, large differences in machine-tool usage from Ford to Honda would suggest the need for taking a census instead of sampling. In this case, if a sample was taken, it is unlikely to be representative of the population because the machine-tool usage of automobile manufacturers not included in the sample is likely to be substantially different than those in the sample. Small populations, which vary widely in terms of the characteristics of interest to the researcher, lend themselves to a census.

The cost of sampling error (e.g., omitting a major manufacturer such as Ford from the machine-tool study above) must be weighed against nonsampling error (e.g., interviewer errors). In many business-to-business studies, concerns involving sampling error support the use of a census. In most other studies, however, nonsampling errors are found to be

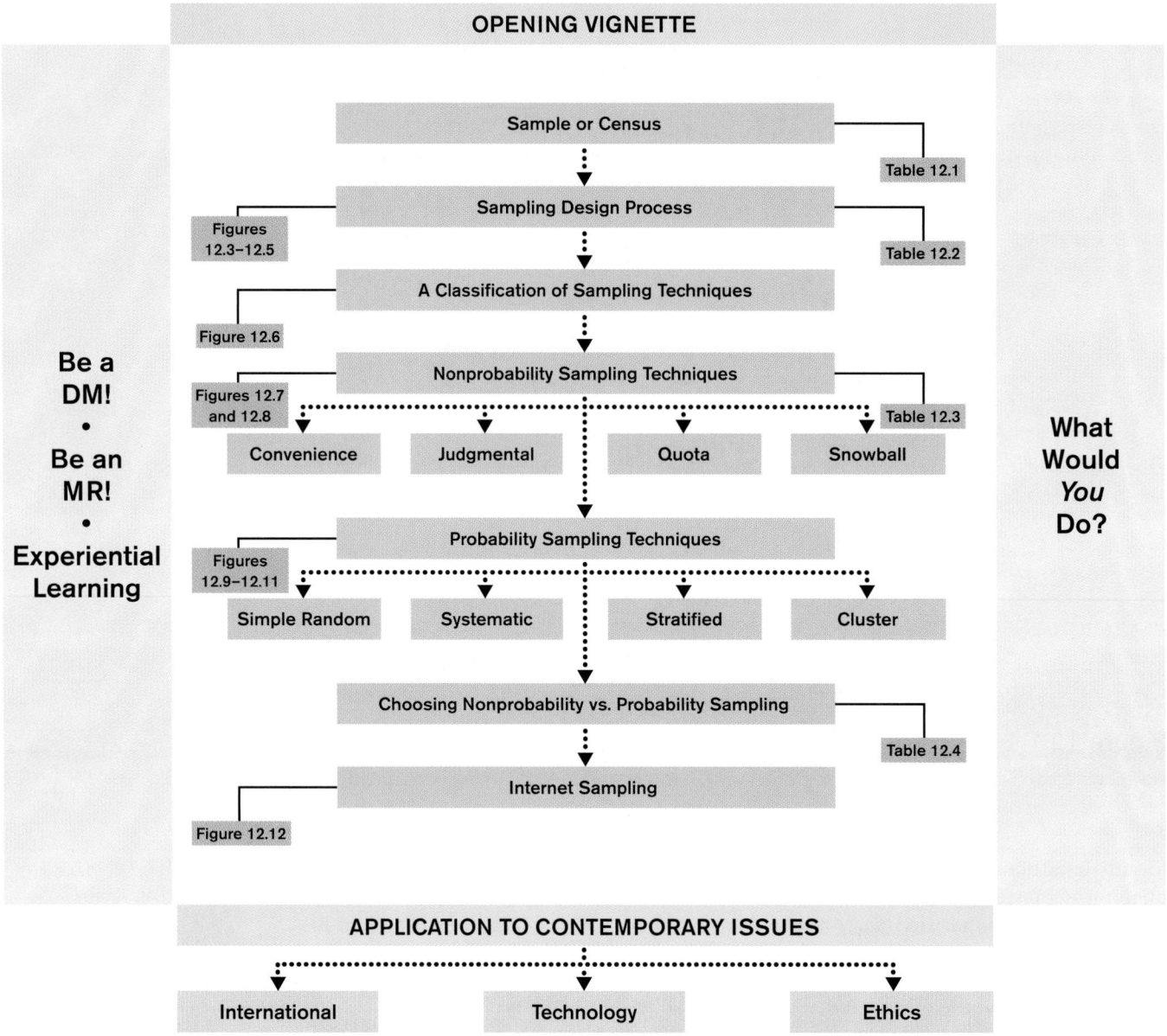

Figure 12.2

Sampling Design Procedures: An Overview

Table 12.1

Choosing a Sample Versus a Census

	Conditions Favoring the Use Of	
Factors	Sample	Census
Budget	Small	Large
Time available	Short	Long
Population size	Large	Small
Variance in the characteristic	Small	Large
Cost of sampling error	Low	High
Cost of nonsampling errors	High	Low
Nature of measurement	Destructive	Nondestructive
Attention to individual cases	Yes	No

the major contributor to total error. While a census eliminates sampling errors, the resulting nonsampling errors may increase to the point that total error in the study becomes unacceptably high. In these instances, sampling would be favored over a census. This is one of the reasons the U.S. Bureau of the Census checks the accuracy of its census by conducting sample surveys.[2]

Sampling is also preferable if the measurement process results in the destruction or consumption of the product. In this case, a census would mean that a large quantity of the product would have to be destroyed or consumed, greatly increasing the cost. An example would be product usage tests that result in the consumption of the product, such as a new brand of cereal. Sampling may also be necessary to focus attention on individual cases, as in the case of in-depth interviews. Finally, other pragmatic considerations, such as the need to keep the study secret (an important consideration for firms such as Coca-Cola), may favor a sample over a census. In the opening vignette, Gillette chose sampling over a census, as the size of the population of male heads of households in the United States is too large to make a census feasible, particularly given limited time and money. Also, as is generally the case in consumer research, the cost of sampling errors was small as compared to the cost of nonsampling errors. As explained in Chapter 3, sampling error is the error due to the particular sample selected being an imperfect representation of the population of interest. On the other hand, nonsampling errors result from a variety of causes, including errors in problem definition, approach, scales, questionnaire design, survey methods, interviewing techniques, and data preparation and analysis. Evidence shows that in consumer research the cost of sampling error is small as compared to the cost of nonsampling errors.

BE an MR!

Conduct an Internet search using a search engine and your library's online database to determine the population of all airlines operating in the United States.

If a survey of airlines is to be conducted to determine their future plans to purchase/lease airplanes, would you take a sample or a census? Why?

BE a DM!

As the CEO of Boeing, how would you use information about the future plans of airlines to purchase/lease airplanes to formulate your marketing strategy?

The Sampling Design Process

The sampling design process includes five steps, which are shown sequentially in Figure 12.3. Each step is closely related to all aspects of the marketing research project, from problem definition to presentation of the results. Therefore, sample design decisions should be integrated with all other decisions in a research project.

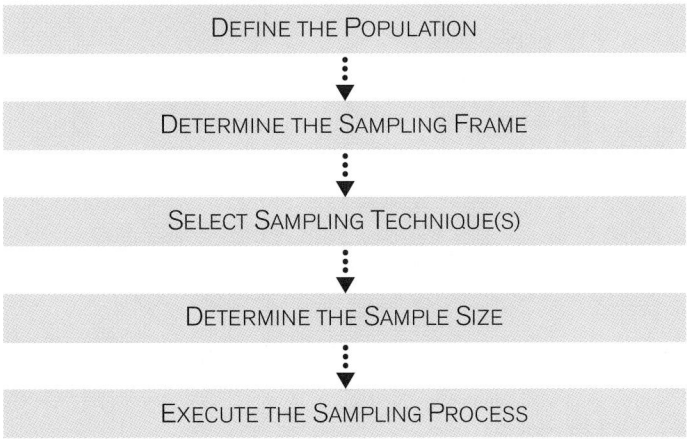

Figure 12.3
Sampling Design Process

Define the Target Population

target population
The collection of elements or objects that possess the information the researcher seeks and about which the researcher will make inferences.

Sampling design begins by specifying the target population. The **target population** is the collection of elements or objects that possess the information the researcher is seeking. It is essential that the researcher precisely define the target population if the data generated are to address the marketing research problem. Defining the target population involves translating the research problem into a precise statement of who should and should not be included in the sample. In the opening vignette, the target population was defined as all male heads of households in the United States.

sampling unit
The basic unit containing the elements of the population to be sampled.

The target population should be defined in terms of elements, sampling units, extent, and time frame. As stated earlier, an element is the object (or person) about which or from which the information is desired. The respondent is an example. A **sampling unit** may be the element itself, or it may be a more readily available entity containing the element. Suppose that Revlon wanted to assess consumer response to a new line of lipsticks and wanted to sample women over 18 years of age. In this study, Revlon's sampling element would be women over 18 years of age. It may be possible to sample them directly, in which case the sampling unit will be the same as an element. More typically, Revlon would use a sampling unit such as households, interviewing one woman over 18 years old in each selected household. Here, the sampling unit and the population element are different. As another illustration, in the opening vignette, the sampling element was male heads of households, and the sampling unit was a household.

Extent refers to geographical boundaries. In our example, Revlon is interested only in the domestic U.S. market. The time frame is the time period of interest. Revlon may be interested in studying lipstick demand for the upcoming summer market. This target population is defined in Figure 12.4.

Determine the Sampling Frame

sampling frame
A representation of the elements of the target population. It consists of a list or set of directions for identifying the target population.

A **sampling frame** is a representation of the elements of the target population. It consists of a list or set of directions for identifying the target population. A sampling frame can come from the telephone book, a computer program for generating telephone numbers, an association directory listing the firms in an industry, a mailing list purchased from a commercial organization, a city directory, or a map. If a listing is not readily available, it must be compiled. Specific instructions for identifying the target population should be developed, such as procedures for generating random telephone numbers of households mentioned in the opening vignette.

Figure 12.4
Defining the Target Population

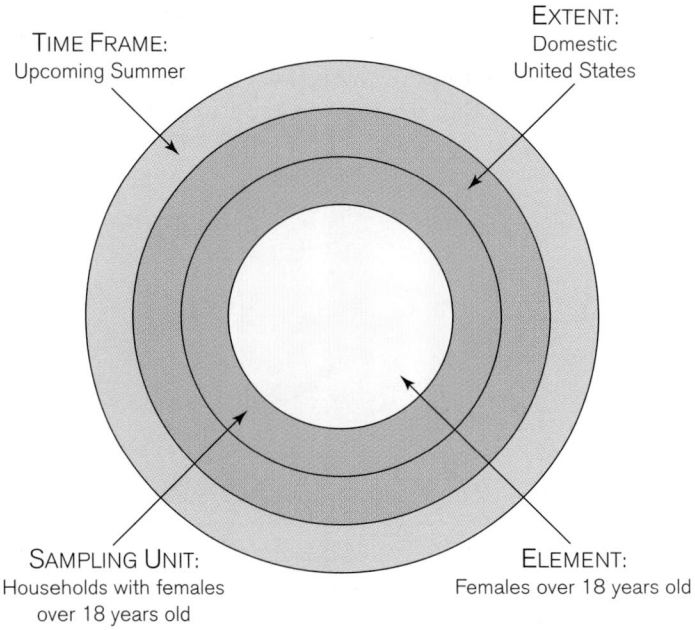

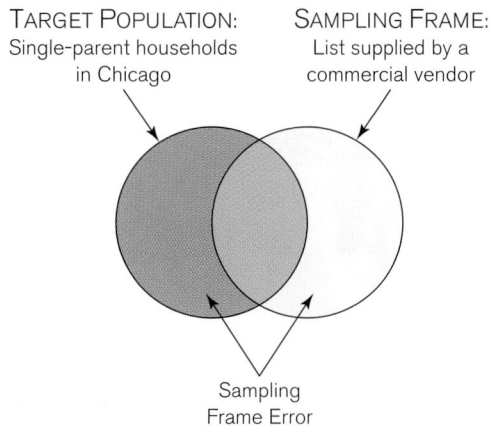

Figure 12.5
Sampling Frame Error

The process of compiling a list of population elements is often difficult and imperfect, leading to sampling frame error. Elements may be omitted, or the list may contain more than the desired population (Figure 12.5). For example, the telephone book is often used as a sampling frame for telephone surveys. However, at least three sources of sampling frame error are present in the telephone book: (1) it does not contain unlisted numbers, (2) it does not contain the telephone numbers of people who have moved into the area after the telephone book was published, and (3) it lists the inactive telephone numbers of people who have moved out of the area since the telephone book was published. Small differences between the sample frame and the population can be ignored. In most cases, however, the researcher should recognize and treat the sampling frame error. The researcher has three options:

1. The population can be redefined in terms of the sampling frame. When the telephone book is used as the sampling frame, the population may be defined as households with a correct listing in the telephone book in a given area. This approach is quite simple and eliminates any misinterpretation of the definition of the population under study.[3]
2. The representativeness of the research frame can be verified during the data collection process. Basic demographic, product familiarity, product usage, and other relevant information can be collected to ensure that the elements of the sampling frame satisfy the criteria for the target population. While inappropriate elements can be identified and eliminated from the sample in this way, this procedure does not correct for elements that have been omitted.
3. The data can be statistically adjusted by weighting under- or overrepresented segments to achieve a more representative sample. While sample frame error can be minimized through this type of adjustment, it assumes the researcher has accurate knowledge of the makeup of the target population.

The researcher can adopt any combination of these adjustments. The important point is to recognize and attempt to eliminate sampling frame error, so that inappropriate population inferences can be avoided.

Select a Sampling Technique

Selecting a sampling technique involves choosing nonprobability or probability sampling (Figure 12.6). **Nonprobability sampling** relies on the personal judgment of the researcher, rather than chance, in selecting sample elements. The researcher may select the sample arbitrarily, based on convenience, or make a conscious decision about which elements to include in the sample. Examples of nonprobability sampling include interviewing people at street corners, in retail stores, or in malls. While nonprobability sampling produces good estimates of population characteristic, these techniques are limited. There is no way to objectively evaluate the **precision** of the sample results. Precision

nonprobability sampling
Sampling technique that does not use chance selection procedures but instead, relies on the personal judgment of the researcher.

precision
The level of uncertainty about the characteristic being measured. Greater precision implies smaller sampling error.

Figure 12.6
Classification of Sampling Techniques

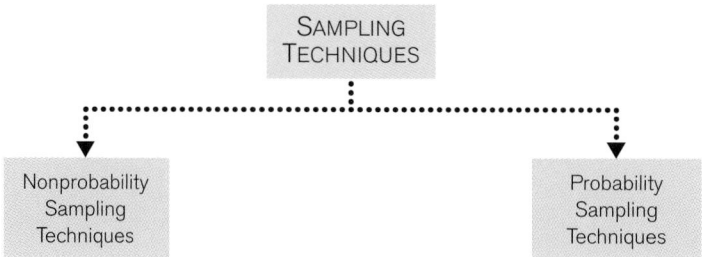

refers to the level of uncertainty about the characteristic being measured. Suppose the researcher wanted to determine how much an average household spends on Christmas shopping and surveyed people in the malls. Due to the convenience nature of the sample, there would be no way of knowing how precise the results of this survey are. The greater the precision, the smaller the sampling error. The probability of selecting one element over another is unknown. Therefore, the estimates obtained cannot be projected to the population with any specified level of confidence.

probability sampling
A sampling procedure in which each element of the population has a fixed probabilistic chance of being selected for the sample.

In **probability sampling**, sampling elements are selected by chance, that is, randomly. The probability of selecting each potential sample from a population can be prespecified. While every potential sample need not have the same probability of selection, it is possible to specify the probability of selecting a particular sample of a given size. Confidence intervals can be calculated around the sample estimates, and it is meaningful to statistically project the sample results to the population, that is, to draw inferences about the target population. Since projectability of the sample results to the population of all male heads of households was important, Gillette used probability rather than nonprobability sampling in the opening vignette. We will discuss the various nonprobability and probability sampling techniques later in this chapter.

Determine the Sample Size

sample size
The number of elements to be included in a study.

Sample size refers to the number of elements to be included in the study. Determining the sample size involves both qualitative and quantitative considerations. We discuss the qualitative factors in this section and the quantitative factors in Chapter 13. Important qualitative factors that the researcher should consider in determining the sample size are (1) the importance of the decision, (2) the nature of the research, (3) the number of variables, (4) the nature of the analysis, (5) sample sizes used in similar studies, and (6) resource constraints.

As a general rule, the more important the decision, the more precise the information must be. This implies the need for larger samples. The need for greater precision must be weighed against the increase in cost that comes with the collection of information from each additional element.

The nature of the research also has an impact on the sample size. Exploratory research, such as a focus group, employs qualitative techniques that are typically based on small samples. Conclusive research, such as a descriptive survey, requires large samples. As the number of variables in a study increases, the sample size must grow accordingly. For example, problem identification surveys that measure a large number of variables typically require large samples of 1,000 to 2,500 (Table 12.2).

The type of analysis planned also influences the sample size requirements. Sophisticated analysis of the data using advanced techniques, or analysis at the subgroup rather than the total population level, requires larger samples, as in the case of Gillette in the opening vignette.

Prior studies can serve as a guide for estimating sample sizes. Table 12.2 gives an idea of sample sizes used in different marketing research studies. These sample sizes have been determined based on experience and can serve as rough guidelines, particularly when nonprobability sampling techniques are used, but they should be applied with caution. Finally, the sample size decisions are guided by money, personnel, and time limitations. In any marketing research project, resources are limited, in turn limiting the sam-

Table 12.2
Sample Sizes Used in Marketing Research Studies

Type of Study	Minimum Size	Typical Range
Problem-identification research (e.g., market potential)	500	1000–2500
Problem-solving research (e.g., pricing)	200	300–500
Product tests	200	300–500
Test-marketing studies	200	300–500
TV/radio/print advertising (per commercial or ad tested)	150	200–300
Test-market audits	10 stores	10–20 stores
Focus groups	2 groups	10–15 groups

ple size. In the opening vignette, the sample size of 1,000 was based on the following considerations: Gillette would use the results to make an important decision involving the introduction of clear stick deodorants, quantitative analysis would be conducted, and this sample size had been adequate in similar studies conducted by Gillette in the past.

Execute the Sampling Process

Execution of the sampling process refers to implementing the various details of the sample design. The population is defined, the sampling frame is compiled, and the sampling units are drawn using the appropriate sampling technique needed to achieve the required sample size. If households are the sampling unit, an operational definition of a household is needed. Procedures should be specified for vacant housing units and for call-backs in case no one is home. Sometimes it is necessary to qualify the potential respondents to make sure they belong to the target population. In such a case, the criteria used to qualify the respondents should be specified, and the qualifying questions should be asked at the beginning of the interview (see Chapter 11). In a survey of heavy users of online services at home, a criterion for identifying heavy users is needed (e.g., those using online services for more than 20 hours per week at home). Detailed information must be provided for all sampling design decisions. This is illustrated by a survey done for the Florida Department of Tourism.

RESEARCH IN ACTION

Tourism Department Telephones Birthday Boys and Girls

A telephone survey was conducted for the Florida Department of Tourism related to the travel behavior of in-state residents. The sampling unit was the household. Probability sampling was used. Data were collected using a stratified random sample from three regions: north, central, and south Florida. To participate in the study, respondents had to meet the following qualifying criteria:

- Age 25 years or older
- Live in Florida at least seven months of the year
- Have lived in Florida for at least two years
- Have a Florida driver's license

All household members meeting these four qualifications were eligible to participate in the study. The person with the next birthday in the household was selected. Repeated call-backs were made to reach that person. Each step in this sampling design process is listed here:

1. **Target population:** Adults meeting the four qualifications (element) in a household with a working telephone number (sampling unit) in the state of Florida (extent) during the survey period (time)
2. **Sampling frame:** Computer program for generating random telephone numbers
3. **Sampling technique:** Probability sampling
4. **Sample size:** 868
5. **Execution:** Allocate the sample among the north, central, and southern strata. Use the probability sampling technique of computerized random-digit dialing. List all members in the household who meet the four qualifications. Select one member of the household using the next-birthday method.[4]

EXPERIENTIAL LEARNING

Yankees Fever

The N.Y. Yankees baseball club is one of America's favorite baseball teams.

1. As the marketing manager of the N.Y. Yankees, what marketing programs will you design to target families?
2. Conduct an Internet search using a search engine and your library's online database to obtain information that will assist the marketing manager of the N.Y. Yankees to target families.
3. The N.Y. Yankees want to conduct a telephone survey to determine how they could attract more families to the Yankees' games. Design the sampling process.

A Classification of Sampling Techniques

Sampling techniques may be broadly classified as nonprobability or probability (Figure 12.6). Commonly used nonprobability sampling techniques include convenience sampling, judgmental sampling, quota sampling, and snowball sampling (Figure 12.7). The important probability sampling techniques are simple random sampling, systematic sampling, stratified sampling, and cluster sampling.

Nonprobabilty Sampling Techniques

Figure 12.8 presents a graphical illustration of the various nonprobability sampling techniques. The population consists of 25 elements and we have to select a sample of size five. A, B, C, D, and E represent groups and can also be viewed as strata or clusters.

Convenience Sampling

convenience sampling
A nonprobability sampling technique that attempts to obtain a sample of convenient elements. The selection of sampling units is left primarily to the interviewer.

Convenience sampling, as the name implies, involves obtaining a sample of elements based on the convenience of the researcher. The selection of sampling units is left primarily to the interviewer. Often, respondents are selected because they happen to be in the right place at the right time. Examples of convenience sampling are (1) use of students, church groups, and members of social organizations; (2) mall intercept interviews conducted without qualifying the respondents; (3) department stores using charge account lists; (4) tear-out questionnaires included in a magazine; (5) "people on the street" interviews; and (6) Internet browsers.

Convenience sampling has the advantages of being both inexpensive and fast. Additionally, the sampling units tend to be accessible, easy to measure, and cooperative. In spite of these advantages, this form of sampling has serious limitations. Primary among them is that the resulting sample is not representative of any definable target population. This sampling process suffers from selection bias, which means the individuals who participate in a convenience sample may have characteristics that are systematically different than the characteristics that define the target population. Because of these limitations, it is not theoretically meaningful to generalize to any population from a convenience sample.

Convenience samples are not appropriate for descriptive or causal research where the aim is to draw population inferences. Convenience samples are useful, however, in

Figure 12.7
Nonprobability Sampling Techniques

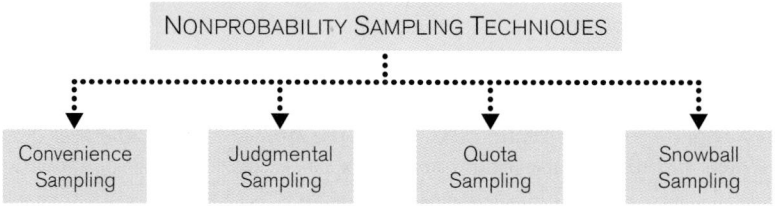

Figure 12.8

A Graphical Illustration of Nonprobability Sampling Techniques

1. CONVENIENCE SAMPLING

A	B	C	D	E
1	6	11	16	21
2	7	12	17	22
3	8	13	18	23
4	9	14	19	24
5	10	15	20	25

Group D happens to assemble at a convenient time and place. So all the elements in this group are selected. The resulting sample consists of elements 16, 17, 18, 19, and 20.
NOTE: No elements are selected from groups A, B, C, and E.

2. JUDGMENTAL SAMPLING

A	B	C	D	E
1	6	11	16	21
2	7	12	17	22
3	8	13	18	23
4	9	14	19	24
5	10	15	20	25

The researcher considers groups B, C, and E to be typical and convenient. Within each of these groups one or two elements are selected based on typicality and convenience. The resulting sample consists of elements 8, 10, 11, 13, 22, and 24.
NOTE: No elements are selected from groups A and D.

3. QUOTA SAMPLING

A	B	C	D	E
1	6	11	16	21
2	7	12	17	22
3	8	13	18	23
4	9	14	19	24
5	10	15	20	25

A quota of one element from each group, A to E, is imposed. Within each group, one element is selected based on judgment or convenience. The resulting sample consists of elements 3, 6, 13, 20, and 22.
NOTE: One element is selected from each column or group.

4. SNOWBALL SAMPLING

RANDOM SELECTION — REFERRALS

A	B	C	D	E
1	6	11	16	21
2	7	12	17	22
3	8	13	18	23
4	9	14	19	24
5	10	15	20	25

Elements 2 and 9 are selected randomly from groups A and B. Element 2 refers to elements 12 and 13. Element 9 refers to element 18. The resulting sample consists of elements 2, 9, 12, 13, and 18.
NOTE: No element is from group E.

exploratory research where the objective is to generate ideas, gain insights, or develop hypotheses. They can be used for focus groups, pretesting questionnaires, or pilot studies. Even in these cases, caution should be exercised in interpreting the results. Despite these limitations, this technique is sometimes used even in large surveys, as in the Starbucks example that follows.

Judgmental Sampling

Judgmental sampling is a form of convenience sampling in which the population elements are selected based on the researcher's judgment. The researcher chooses the sampling elements because she or he believes they represent the population of interest.

judgmental sampling
A form of convenience sampling in which the population elements are purposively selected based on the judgment of the researcher.

RESEARCH IN ACTION

Starbucks Bucks Up on Ice Cream

When Starbucks wanted to assess the brand equity behind its name in order to consider widening its product mix, researchers used convenience sampling to select a group of people patronizing its various coffee shops and retail outlets. Using convenience sampling in this manner was justified because the core market for the line extensions would consist of existing Starbucks customers.

A survey was administered that obtained information on the respondents' preference and loyalty for Starbucks coffee and for other products they would like to see branded with the Starbucks name. Results of this survey revealed a tremendous potential to extend the Starbucks name to ice creams. Accordingly, Starbucks leveraged the strong equity of its coffee and loyal customer base to create a line of ice cream based on its coffee. The product is a rich, creamy ice cream that delivers on the intense flavor of Starbucks coffee. According to Information Resources, Inc. data, it became the nation's number-one brand of coffee ice cream three months after it was introduced.[5]

Common examples of judgmental sampling include (1) test markets selected to determine the potential of a new product, (2) purchase engineers selected in industrial marketing research because they are considered to be representative of the company, (3) bellwether precincts selected in voting behavior research, (4) expert witnesses used in court, and (5) department stores selected to test a new merchandising display system.

Judgment sampling has appeal because it is low cost, convenient, and quick. It is subjective, however, relying largely on the expertise and creativity of the researcher. Therefore, generalizations to a specific population cannot be made, usually because the population is not defined explicitly. This sampling technique is most appropriate in research when broad population generalizations are not required. For example, Frito-Lay test marketed the WOW line of Ruffles, Lays, and Doritos chips, all made with Olestra, in Indianapolis, Indiana. Indianapolis was selected because the researcher felt it would provide a good general indicator of initial response to the new line. Note that Frito-Lay was only looking to evaluate the initial response to WOW, not make projections of how much WOW would sell nationally.

An extension of judgment sampling involves the use of quotas.

Quota Sampling

quota sampling
A nonprobability sampling technique that is a two-stage restricted judgmental sampling. The first stage consists of developing control categories or quotas of population elements. In the second stage, sample elements are selected based on convenience or judgment.

Quota sampling introduces two stages to the judgmental sampling process. The first stage consists of developing control categories, or *quotas*, of population elements. Using judgment to identify relevant categories such as age, sex, or race, the researcher estimates the distribution of these characteristics in the target population. For example, white women aged 18 to 35 years may be considered the relevant control category for a study involving cosmetic purchases. The researcher would then estimate the proportion of the target population falling into this category based on past experience or secondary information sources. Sampling would then be done to ensure that the proportion of white women, aged 18 to 35 years in the target population would be reflected in the sample. Quotas are used to ensure that the composition of the sample is the same as the composition of the population with respect to the characteristics of interest.

Once the quotas have been assigned, the second stage of the sampling process takes place. Elements are selected using a convenience or judgment process. There is consid-

RESEARCH IN ACTION

How "Metro" Is *Metropolitan Home* Magazine's Readership?

A readership study was conducted for *Metropolitan Home* magazine using a quota sample. One thousand adults living in a metropolitan area of 500,000 people were selected. Age, sex, and race were used to define the makeup of the sample. Based on the composition of the adult population in that community, the quotas were assigned as follows:

Control Characteristic	POPULATION COMPOSITION Percentage	SAMPLE COMPOSITION Percentage	SAMPLE COMPOSITION Number
Sex			
Male	48	48	480
Female	52	52	520
	100	100	1,000

Control Characteristic	POPULATION COMPOSITION Percentage	SAMPLE COMPOSITION Percentage	SAMPLE COMPOSITION Number
Age (years)			
18–30	27	27	270
31–45	39	39	390
46–60	16	16	160
Over 60	18	18	180
	100	100	1,000
Race			
White	59	59	590
Black	35	35	350
Other	6	6	60
	100	100	1,000

Note: By imposing quotas proportionate to the population distribution, the researcher was able to select a sample that reflected the composition of the metropolitan area fairly well.

erable freedom in selecting the elements to be included in the sample. The only requirement is that the elements that are selected fit the control characteristics. This technique is illustrated in the following example.

In the preceding example, proportionate quotas are assigned so that the composition of the population in the community is reflected in the sample. In certain situations, however, it is desirable either to under- or oversample elements with certain characteristics. For example, heavy users of a product may be oversampled in order to examine their behavior in greater detail. While this type of sample is not representative, it may nevertheless be quite relevant.

A number of potential problems are associated with this sampling technique. Relevant characteristics may be overlooked in the quota-setting process, resulting in a sample that does not mirror the population on relevant control characteristics. Because the elements within each quota are selected based on convenience or judgment, many sources of selection bias are potentially present. Interviewers may be tempted to select areas where they believe they will have success in soliciting participants. They may avoid people who look unfriendly, who are not well dressed, or who live in undesirable locations. Quota sampling is also limited in that it does not permit assessment of sampling error.

Quota sampling attempts to obtain representative samples at a relatively low cost. Quota samples are also relatively convenient to draw. With adequate controls, quota sampling obtains results close to those for conventional probability sampling.

Snowball Sampling

In **snowball sampling**, an initial group of respondents is selected, usually at random. After being interviewed, these respondents are asked to identify others who belong to the target population of interest. This process is continued, resulting in a snowball effect as one referral is obtained from another. Thus, the referral process effectively produces the sampling frame from which respondents are selected. Although this sampling technique begins with a probability sample, it results in a nonprobability sample. This is because referred respondents tend to have demographic and psychographic characteristics that are more similar to the person referring them than would occur by chance.

snowball sampling
A nonprobability sampling technique in which an initial group of respondents is selected, usually at random. Subsequent respondents are selected based on the referrals or information provided by the initial respondents. This process may be carried out in waves by obtaining referrals from referrals.

Snowball sampling is used when studying characteristics that are relatively rare or difficult to identify in the population. For example, the names of users of some government

RESEARCH IN ACTION

Survey Snowball

To study the demographic profile of marketing research interviewers in Ohio, a sample of interviewers was generated using a variation of snowball sampling. Interviewers were initially contacted by placing classified advertisements in the newspapers of seven major metropolitan areas. These notices asked experienced marketing research interviewers willing to answer 25 questions about their job to write to the author. These responses were increased through a referral system. Each responding interviewer was asked for the names and addresses of other interviewers. Eventually, this process identified interviewers from many communities throughout the state who had not seen the original newspaper notices. Only 27 percent of returned questionnaires resulted from the classified notices; the remainder could be traced to referrals and to referrals from referrals.[6]

or social services, such as food stamps, are kept confidential. Groups with special characteristics such as widowed men under 35 years old or members of a scattered minority population may be impossible to locate without referrals. In industrial research, snowball sampling is used to identify buyer/seller pairs.

The major advantage of snowball sampling is that it substantially increases the likelihood of locating the desired characteristic in the population. It also results in relatively low sampling variance and costs. Snowball sampling is illustrated by the Survey Snowball example.

In this example, the initial groups of respondents were contacted using a nonrandom selection technique, through classified advertisements. In this instance, this procedure was more efficient than random selection. In other cases, random selection of respondents through probability sampling techniques is more appropriate.

BE a DM!

As the vice president of marketing for Polo Ralph Lauren, what information would you need to determine whether the company should launch nationally a new line of unisex shirts it has developed?

BE an MR!

Visit Polo Ralph Lauren's Web site (www.polo.com) and conduct an Internet search using a search engine and your library's online database to obtain information on the marketing strategy of Polo Ralph Lauren.

Polo Ralph Lauren would like to determine initial consumer reaction to a new line of unisex shirts it has developed. If nonprobability sampling is to be used, which sampling technique would you recommend and why?

Probability Sampling Techniques

The probability sampling techniques consist of simple random, systematic, stratified, and cluster sampling (Figure 12.9). Probability sampling techniques vary in terms of sampling efficiency. *Sampling efficiency* is a concept that reflects a trade-off between sampling cost and precision. Costs increase with improved precision. The trade-off comes into play as researchers balance the need for greater precision with higher sampling costs. The efficiency of a probability sampling technique may be assessed by

Figure 12.9
Probability Sampling Techniques

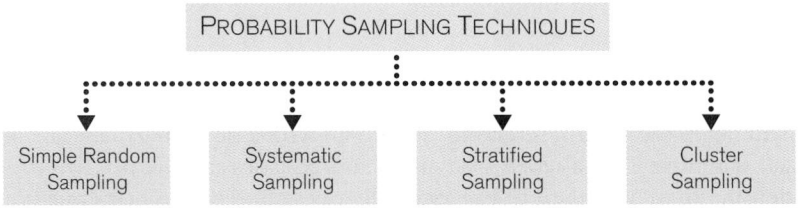

Figure 12.10

A Graphical Illustration of Probability Sampling Techniques

1. SIMPLE RANDOM SAMPLING

A	B	C	D	E
1	6	11	16	21
2	7	12	17	22
3	8	13	18	23
4	9	14	19	24
5	10	15	20	25

Select five random numbers from 1 to 25. The resulting sample consists of population elements 3, 7, 9, 16, and 24.
NOTE: There is no element from group C.

2. SYSTEMATIC SAMPLING

A	B	C	D	E
1	6	11	16	21
2	7	12	17	22
3	8	13	18	23
4	9	14	19	24
5	10	15	20	25

Select a random number between 1 to 5, say 2. The resulting sample consists of population 2, (2 + 5 =) 7, (2 + (5 × 2) =) 12, (2 + (5 × 3) =) 17, and (2 + (5 × 4) =) 22.
NOTE: All the elements are selected from a single row.

3. STRATIFIED SAMPLING

A	B	C	D	E
1	6	11	16	21
2	7	12	17	22
3	8	13	18	23
4	9	14	19	24
5	10	15	20	25

Randomly select a number from 1 to 5 for each stratum, A to E. The resulting sample consists of population elements 4, 7, 13, 19, and 21.
NOTE: One element is selected from each column.

4. CLUSTER SAMPLING (TWO-STAGE)

A	B	C	D	E
1	6	11	16	21
2	7	12	17	22
3	8	13	18	23
4	9	14	19	24
5	10	15	20	25

Randomly select 3 clusters, B , D, and E. Within each cluster, randomly select one or two elements. The resulting sample consists of population elements 7, 18, 20, 21, and 23.
NOTE: No elements are selected from clusters A and C.

comparing it to that of simple random sampling. Figure 12.10 presents a graphical illustration of the various probability sampling techniques. As in the case of nonprobability sampling, the population consists of 25 elements, and we must select a sample of size five. A, B, C, D, and E represent groups and can also be viewed as strata or clusters.

Simple Random Sampling

In **simple random sampling** (SRS), each element in the population has a known and equal probability of selection. Furthermore, each possible sample of a given size *(n)* has a known and equal probability of being the sample actually selected. The implication in a random sampling procedure is that each element is selected independently of every other

simple random sampling
A probability sampling technique in which each element in the population has a known and equal probability of selection. Every element is selected independently of every other element, and the sample is drawn by a random procedure from a sampling frame.

element. Placing the names in a container, shaking the container, and selecting the names in a lottery-style drawing is an example of a random sampling procedure. To draw a simple random sample, the research frame is compiled by assigning each element a unique identification number. Random numbers, generated using a computer routine or random number table (see Table 1 shown in the Appendix of Statistical Tables), are then used to determine which element to select.

In telephone surveys, the random-digit dialing (RDD) technique is often used to generate a random sample of telephone numbers. RDD consists of randomly selecting all 10 digits of a telephone number (area code, prefix or exchange, suffix). While this approach gives all households with telephones an approximately equal chance of being included in the sample, not all the numbers generated in this way are working telephone numbers. Several modifications have been proposed to identify and eliminate the nonworking numbers. This makes the use of SRS in telephone surveys quite attractive, as illustrated in the case of Gillette in the opening vignette.

SRS has many benefits. It is easily understood and is used for producing data that are representative of a target population. Most statistical inference approaches assume that random sampling was used. SRS suffers from at least four significant limitations: (1) constructing a sampling frame for SRS is difficult; (2) SRS can be expensive and time-consuming because the sampling frame may be widely spread over a large geographical area; (3) SRS often results in lower precision, producing samples with large standard error; and (4) samples generated by this technique may not be representative of the target population, particularly if the sample size is small. Although samples drawn will represent the population well on average, a given simple random sample may grossly misrepresent the target population. For these reasons, SRS is not widely used in marketing research. Procedures such as systematic sampling are more popular.

Systematic Sampling

systematic sampling
A probability sampling technique in which the sample is chosen by selecting a random starting point and then picking every *i*th element in succession from the sampling frame.

In **systematic sampling**, the sample is chosen by selecting a random starting point and then picking every *i*th element in succession from the sampling frame. The frequency with which the elements are drawn, i, is called the *sampling interval*. It is determined by dividing the population size N by the sample size n and rounding to the nearest integer. For example, suppose there are 100,000 elements in the population and a sample of 1,000 is desired. In this case, the sampling interval, i, is 100. A random number between 1 and 100 is selected. If, for example, this number is 23, the sample consists of elements 23, 123, 223, 323, 423, 523, and so on.[7]

The population elements used in systematic sampling are typically organized in some fashion. If the telephone book is used as the sampling frame, the elements are alphabetically organized. In some cases, this order may be related to some characteristic of interest to the researcher. For example, credit-card customers may be listed in order of outstanding balance, or firms in a given industry may be ordered according to annual sales. When the population elements are organized in a manner related to the characteristics under study, systematic sampling may produce results quite different from SRS. Systematic sampling from a list of industrial firms, organized in increasing order by sales, will produce a sample that includes small and large firms. A simple random sample may be less representative. For example, only small firms or a disproportionate number of small firms may be drawn. Sampling frames that are organized in a cyclical pattern tend to be less representative when systematic sampling is used.

To illustrate, consider the use of systematic sampling to generate a sample of monthly department store sales from a sampling frame containing monthly sales for the last 60 years. If a sampling interval of 12 is chosen, the resulting sample would not reflect the month-to-month variation in sales.

Systematic sampling is less costly and easier than SRS because random selection is done only once. Systematic sampling can also be applied without knowledge of the makeup of the sampling frame. For example, every *i*th person leaving a department store or mall can be intercepted. For these reasons, systematic sampling is often employed in consumer mail, telephone, and mall intercept interviews, as illustrated by the *Tennis* magazine example.

RESEARCH IN ACTION

Tennis Magazine's Systematic Sampling Returns a Smash

Tennis magazine conducted a mail survey of its subscribers to gain a better understanding of its market. A systematic sample was drawn from the subscription list to produce a sample of 1,472 subscribers. The list was ordered according to the duration of subscription to ensure that recent as well as long-time subscribers would be included. If we assume that the subscriber list had 1,472,000 names, the sampling interval would be 1,000 (1,472,000/1,472). A starting point was selected between 1 and 1,000. Suppose this was 589. The sample would then be collected by selecting every 1,000th subscriber, that is, subscribers numbered 589, 1589, 2589, 3589, and so on. Systematic sampling was chosen because a sampling frame was conveniently available and this procedure is easier to implement than SRS.

An incentive in the form of a brand-new dollar bill was included in the mail survey to boost participation in the study. The respondents were sent an alert postcard one week before the survey. A second, follow-up questionnaire was sent to the whole sample 10 days after the initial questionnaire. Of the 1,472 questionnaires mailed, 76 were returned with no forwarding address, so the net effective mailing was 1,396. Six weeks after the first mailing, 778 completed questionnaires were returned, yielding a response rate of 56 percent.[8]

BE an MR!

Visit *Fortune's* Web site (www.fortune.com) and identify the list of Fortune 500 companies.

A systematic random sample of 25 firms is to be selected from a list of Fortune 500 firms, numbered from 1 to 500. Determine the sampling interval, and specify the firms that should be selected.

BE a DM!

As the marketing director for Dell, how would you target the Fortune 500 companies for computers, servers, storage, and networking equipment?

Stratified Sampling

Stratified sampling involves a two-step sampling process, producing a probability rather than a convenience or judgment sample. First, the population is divided into subgroups called *strata*. Every population element should be assigned to one and only one stratum, and no population elements should be omitted. Second, elements of each stratum are then randomly selected. Ideally, SRS should be used to select elements from each stratum. In practice, however, systematic sampling and other probability sampling procedures may be used.

stratified sampling
A probability sampling technique that uses a two-step process to partition the population into subpopulations, or strata. Elements are selected from each stratum by a random procedure.

A major objective of stratified sampling is to increase precision without increasing cost. The population is partitioned using stratification variables. The strata are formed based on four criteria: (1) homogeneity, (2) heterogeneity, (3) relatedness, and (4) cost. The following guidelines should be observed:

- Elements within strata must be similar or homogeneous.
- Elements between strata must differ or be heterogeneous.
- The stratification variables must be related to the characteristic of interest.
- The number of strata usually varies between two and six. Beyond six strata, any gain in precision is more than offset by the increased costs.

Stratification offers two advantages. Sampling variation is reduced when the research follows these listed criteria. Sampling costs can also be reduced when the stratification

RESEARCH IN ACTION

Stratifying the Success of BMW 5-Series

Extensive marketing research went into the design of the BMW 5-Series models (www.bmwusa.com). When a survey of luxury car buyers was conducted to project preferences for specific luxury car features, stratified random sampling was used. This procedure was selected because it includes all the important subpopulations and results in good precision. The variables chosen for stratification were age and income, variables known to correlate with the purchase of luxury cars. The results indicated that the luxury car buyers put a premium on performance, handling, engineering, and, of course, luxury.

Based on this feedback, the new 5-Series advanced the concept of a four-door sedan that embodies performance, easy handling, active and passive safety engineering, and luxury. In the U.S. models, the six-cylinder 525i and 530i, and the V-8 545i, the engine was larger, delivering greater torque for more effortless performance. For the first time, automatic climate control was standard in 5-Series models offered in the United States. There were extensive innovations and new features in virtually every area of the vehicle

(e.g., Dynamic Stability Control and Dynamic Brake Control). The results? The models were a roaring success. As of 2005, the 5-Series was being marketed with the theme, "Part Athlete. Part Genius. All BMW."[9]

variables are selected in a way that is easy to measure and apply. Variables commonly used for stratification include demographic characteristics (as illustrated in the example for quota sampling), type of customer (credit card versus non–credit card), size of firm, or type of industry. Stratified sampling improves the precision of SRS. Therefore, it is a popular sampling technique, as illustrated in the BMW 5-Series survey.

cluster sampling
A two-step probability sampling technique. First, the target population is divided into mutually exclusive and collectively exhaustive subpopulations called clusters. Then, a random sample of clusters is selected based on a probability sampling technique, such as simple random sampling. For each selected cluster, either all the elements are included in the sample or a sample of elements is drawn probabilistically.

Cluster Sampling

In **cluster sampling**, the target population is first divided into mutually exclusive and collectively exhaustive subpopulations, or *clusters*. Then a random sample of clusters is selected based on a probability sampling technique, such as SRS. For each selected cluster, either all the elements are included in the sample or a sample of elements is drawn probabilistically. If all the elements in each selected cluster are included in the sample, the procedure is called *one-stage cluster sampling*. If a sample of elements is drawn probabilistically from each selected cluster, the procedure is *two-stage cluster sampling* (Figure 12.11). Cluster sampling increases sampling efficiency by decreasing cost.

Figure 12.11
Types of Cluster Sampling

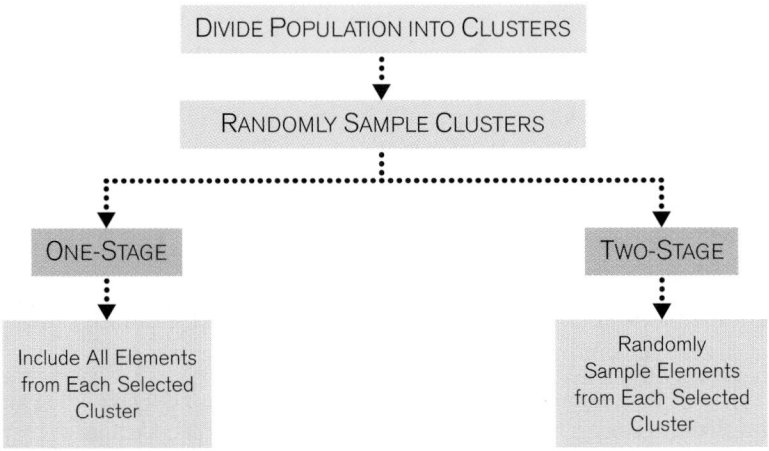

There are a number of key differences and objectives between cluster and stratified sampling. They are summarized in the following table.

Cluster Sampling	Stratified Sampling
• Only a sample of the subpopulations (clusters) is selected for sampling.	• All of the subpopulations (strata) are selected for sampling.
• Within a cluster, elements should be different (heterogeneous), whereas homogeneity or similarity is maintained between different clusters.	• Within a strata, elements should be homogeneous with clear differences (heterogeneity) between the strata.
• A sampling frame is needed only for the clusters selected for the sample.	• A complete sampling frame for the entire stratified subpopulations should be drawn.
• Increases sample efficiency by decreasing cost.	• Increases precision.

One common form of cluster sampling is area sampling. **Area sampling** relies on clustering based on geographic areas, such as counties, housing tracts, or blocks. Sampling can be achieved using either one or more stages. *Single-stage area sampling* involves sampling all the elements within a particular cluster. For example, if city blocks were used as the clusters, then all the households within the selected blocks would be included within a single-stage sample. In the case of *two-stage area sampling*, only a portion of the households within each block would be sampled.

area sampling
A common form of cluster sampling in which the clusters consist of geographic areas, such as counties, housing tracts, blocks, and so forth.

Cluster sampling has two major advantages: feasibility and low cost. Since sampling frames are often available in terms of clusters rather than population elements, cluster sampling may be the only feasible approach. Given the resources and constraints of the research project, it may be extremely expensive and perhaps infeasible to compile a list of all consumers in a population. Lists of geographical areas, telephone exchanges, and other clusters of consumers can be constructed relatively easily. Cluster sampling is the most cost-effective probability sampling technique. This advantage must be weighed against several limitations. Cluster sampling produces imprecise samples in which distinct, heterogeneous clusters are difficult to form. For example, households in a block tend to be similar rather than dissimilar. It can be difficult to compute and interpret statistics based on clusters. The strengths and weaknesses of cluster sampling and the other basic sampling techniques are summarized in Table 12.3.

BE a DM!

As the marketing chief of Herbal Essences, how would you determine which new shampoos should be introduced into the market?

BE an MR!

Conduct an Internet search using a search engine and your library's online database to determine the size of the shampoo market in the United States.

Herbal Essences would like to determine the demand for a new shampoo. If a survey is to be conducted using probability sampling, which sampling technique should be used and why?

Choosing Nonprobability Versus Probability Sampling

Choosing between nonprobability and probability samples is based on considerations such as the nature of the research, the error contributed by the sampling process relative to nonsampling error, variability in the population, and statistical and operational considerations

Table 12.3
Strengths and Weaknesses of Basic Sampling Techniques

Technique	Strengths	Weaknesses
Nonprobability Sampling		
Convenience sampling	Least expensive, least time-consuming, most convenient	Selection bias, sample not representative, not recommended for descriptive or causal research
Judgmental sampling	Low cost, convenient, not time-consuming	Does not allow generalization, subjective
Quota sampling	Sample can be controlled for certain characteristics	Selection bias, no assurance of representativeness
Snowball sampling	Can estimate rare characteristics	Time-consuming
Probability Sampling		
Simple random sampling (SRS)	Easily understood, results projectable	Difficult to construct sampling frame, expensive, lower precision, no assurance of representativeness
Systematic sampling	Can increase representativeness, easier to implement than SRS, sampling frame not necessary	Can decrease representativeness
Stratified sampling	Includes all important subpopulations, precision	Difficult to select relevant stratification variables, not feasible to stratify on many variables, expensive
Cluster sampling	Easy to implement, cost-effective	Imprecise, difficult to compute and interpret results

(Table 12.4). For example, in exploratory research, the findings are treated as preliminary and the use of probability sampling may not be warranted. On the other hand, in conclusive research where the researcher wishes to generalize results to the target population, as in estimating market shares, probability sampling is favored. Probability samples allow statistical projection of the results to a target population. For these reasons, Gillette decided to use probability sampling as described in the opening vignette.

Table 12.4
Choosing Nonprobability Versus Probability Sampling

	Conditions Favoring the Use Of	
Factors	Nonprobability Sampling	Probability Sampling
Nature of research	Exploratory	Conclusive
Relative magnitude of sampling and nonsampling errors	Nonsampling errors are larger	Sampling errors are larger
Variability in the population	Homogeneous (low)	Heterogeneous (high)
Statistical considerations	Unfavorable	Favorable
Operational considerations	Favorable	Unfavorable

When high levels of sampling accuracy are required, as is the case when estimates of population characteristics are made, probability sampling is preferred. In these situations, the researcher needs to eliminate selection bias and calculate the effect of sampling error. To do this, probability sampling is required. Even with this added sampling precision, probability sampling will not always result in more accurate results. Nonsampling error, for example, cannot be controlled with probability sampling. If nonsampling error is likely to be a problem, then nonprobability sampling techniques such as judgment samples may be preferable, allowing greater control over the sampling process.

When choosing between sampling techniques, the researcher must also consider the similarity or homogeneity of the population with respect to the characteristics of interest. For example, probability sampling is more appropriate in highly heterogeneous populations, in which it becomes important to draw a representative sample. Probability sampling is also preferable from a statistical viewpoint, as it is the basis of the most common statistical techniques.

While probability sampling has many advantages, it is sophisticated and requires statistically trained researchers. It generally costs more and takes longer than nonprobability sampling. In many marketing research projects, it is difficult to justify the additional time and expense. Therefore, in practice, the objectives of the study dictate which sampling method will be used, as illustrated in the Allure fragrance example.

Internet Sampling

Issues in Online Sampling

As discussed in Chapter 7, Internet surveys (and sampling) offer many advantages. The respondents can complete the survey at their convenience. The data collection can be fast and inexpensive. A major issue related to Internet sampling is representativeness because of lack of computer ownership and Internet access in many households in the United States. Internet access is even more restricted in foreign countries. Furthermore, heavy users of the Internet may have a disproportionately higher probability of being included. Unrestricted Internet samples in which any visitor can participate are convenience samples and suffer from self-selection bias in that the respondents can initiate their own selection.

Sampling potential respondents who are surfing the Internet is meaningful if the sample that is generated is representative of the target population. More and more industries

RESEARCH IN ACTION

The Alluring Charm of Allure Fragrance

Chanel, Inc. wanted to launch a major new fragrance in department and specialty stores that would reach and sustain at least the sales volume of Chanel No. 5. The target population was defined as women 18 years and older who would appreciate a unique and broadly appealing fragrance. In conducting a survey to determine women's preferences for perfumes, a nonprobability sampling scheme making use of quota sampling was adopted in conjunction with mall intercept interviews. Quotas were assigned for age, income, and marital status. A nonprobability sampling scheme was chosen because the main objective of this exploratory research was qualitative: to understand what constituted a desirable, classic, yet contemporary fragrance that women would choose to wear.

The results of the survey indicated a strong preference for a perfume that was fresh, clean, warm, and sexy. Moreover, women were looking for a perfume that would enable them to express themselves uniquely. Based on these findings, the company launched Allure, a unique and innovative fragrance created by Chanel perfumer Jacques Polge and packaged in a signature beige carton and sleek bottle. Diversity and individuality were successfully communicated through multi-image ads in a breakthrough print and TV campaign. The advertising portrayed many different women because every woman expresses Allure in her own way. After being launched, Allure achieved top-10 ranking in major retail accounts and sales volume equivalent to Chanel No. 5. The success of Allure could be attributed in no small part to the carefully designed sampling procedures that resulted in important survey findings on which the new perfume was developed and marketed.[10]

EXPERIENTIAL LEARNING

U.S. Department of Transportation Survey

Enlightened U.S. public policymakers seek citizen input to the development of the country's infrastructure. One example of this is the requirement for the U.S. Department of Transportation (DOT) to conduct an annual survey about citizen satisfaction with all transportation modes in the country. The Bureau of Transportation Statistics (BTS) is charged with conducting this survey in order to provide insights about citizen satisfaction with travel and transportation to members of Congress, to employees of the U.S. DOT, as well as to U.S. citizens themselves.

Go to the textbook's Web site and download the file U.S. DOT Survey from Chapter 12. This is the actual record of how the BTS and Battelle (a research organization hired to assist in the survey) designed and administered a nationally representative study called the Summer 2000 Omnibus Survey. Read the first two pages of the Introduction and Background (pages 3 and 4), and then Appendix F: The Final Sampling Plan (pages 124–131 or F1–F8).

1. What was the target population in this study?
2. How was the sampling frame derived in this study?
3. Was a nonprobability or probability sampling technique used?
4. What were the two variables used for stratifying the sample?
5. How many implicit strata were employed in the design of the sample?
6. The study designers wanted to secure 2,000 completed interviews. To obtain this number of completed interviews, how many phone numbers will need to be screened to determine if the phone number is a working residential phone number?
7. What do users of the survey results gain from the BTS using this sampling design instead of using a convenience sample of 2,000?

are meeting this criterion. In software, computers, networking, technical publishing, semiconductors, and graduate education, it is rapidly becoming feasible to use the Internet for sampling respondents for quantitative research, such as surveys. For internal customer surveys, where the client's employees share a corporate e-mail system, an intranet survey is practical even if workers have no access to the external Internet. Sampling on the Internet is not yet practical for many noncomputer-oriented consumer products.

To avoid sampling errors, the researcher must be able to control the pool from which the respondents are selected. Also, steps must be taken to ensure that the respondents do not respond multiple times ("stuff the ballot box"). These requirements are met by e-mail surveys, for which the researcher selects specific respondents. Furthermore, the surveys can be encoded to match the returned surveys with their corresponding outbound e-mailings. This can also be accomplished with Web surveys by e-mailing invitations to selected respondents and asking them to visit the Web site where the survey is posted. In this case, the survey is posted in a hidden location on the Web, which is protected by a password. Hence, uninvited Web surfers are unable to access it.

Online Sampling Techniques

The sampling techniques commonly used on the Internet may be classified as online intercept (nonrandom and random), online recruited, and so on as shown in Figure 12.12. Online recruited sampling can be further classified as panel (recruited or opt-in) or nonpanel (list rentals).

In online-intercept sampling, visitors to a Web site are intercepted and given an opportunity to participate in the survey. The interception can be made at one or more Web sites, including high-traffic sites such as Yahoo!. In nonrandom sampling, every visitor is intercepted. This may be meaningful if the Web site traffic is low, the survey has to be completed in a short time, and no incentive is being offered. This results in a convenience sample, however. Quotas can be imposed to improve representativeness. In random-intercept sampling, the software selects visitors at random and a "pop-up" window asks whether the person wants to participate in the survey. The selection can be

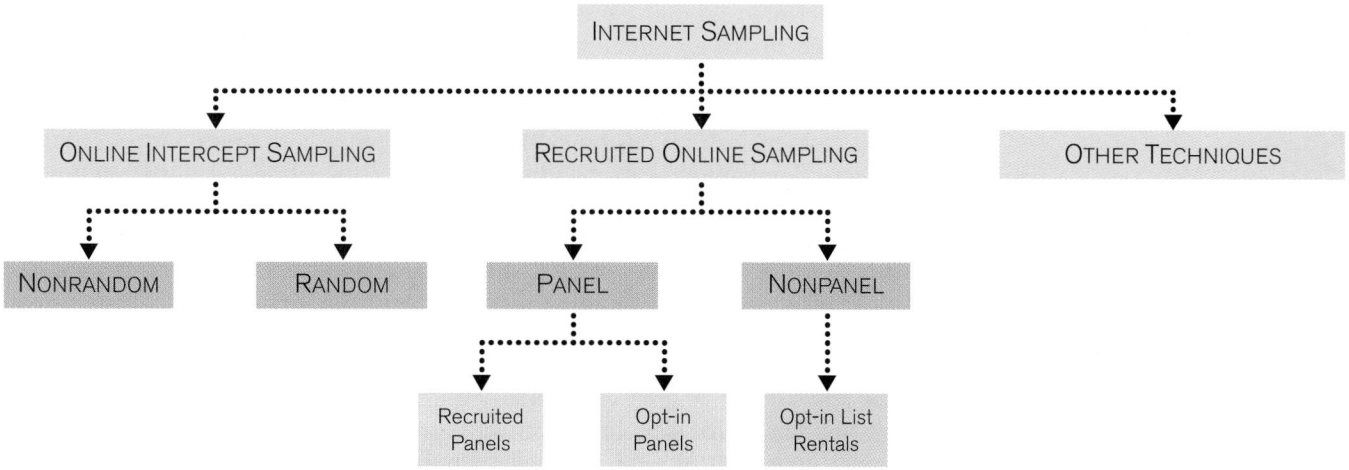

Figure 12.12
A Classification of Internet Sampling

made based on simple random or systematic random sampling. If the population is defined as Web site visitors, then this procedure results in a probability sample (simple random or systematic, as the case may be). If the population is other than Web site visitors, then the resulting sample is more similar to a nonprobability sample. Nevertheless, randomization improves representativeness and discourages multiple responses from the same respondent.

Internet panels function in ways similar to non-Internet panels discussed in Chapters 3 and 5, and they share many of the same advantages and disadvantages. In recruited panels, members can be recruited online or even by traditional means (mail, telephone). Based on the researcher's judgment, certain qualifying criteria can be introduced to prescreen the respondents. They are offered incentives for participation, such as sweepstake prizes, redeemable points, and other types of Internet currencies. Members typically provide detailed psychographic, demographic, Internet usage, and product consumption information at the time of joining. Opt-in panels operate similarly except that members choose to opt in as opposed to being recruited. To select a sample, the online company sends an e-mail message to those panelists who qualify based on sample specifications given by the researcher. All of the sampling techniques can be implemented using both types of Internet panels. The success of probability sampling techniques depends upon the extent to which the panel is representative of the target population. Highly targeted samples can be achieved (e.g., teenage girls who shop in malls more than twice a month). For example, respondents for Harris Poll Online (HPOL) surveys are drawn from the multimillion member HPOL database (www.harrisinteractive.com). E-mail addresses for respondents in the database have been obtained from a number of sources, including the HPOL registration site, HPOL banner advertisements, and Epinion registrations. To maintain the reliability and integrity in the sample, the following procedures are used:

- **Password protection**. Each invitation contains a password that is uniquely assigned to that e-mail address. A respondent is required to enter the password at the beginning of the survey to gain access into the survey. Password protection ensures that a respondent completes the survey only one time.
- **Reminder invitations.** To increase the number of respondents in the survey and to improve overall response rates, up to two additional reminder invitations are typically mailed at 2- to 4-day intervals to those respondents who have not yet participated in the survey.
- **Summary of the survey findings.** To increase the number of respondents in the survey and to improve overall response rates, respondents are often provided with a summary of some of the survey responses via the Internet.

Nonpanel recruited sampling methods can also be used, which involves requesting potential respondents to go online to answer a survey. To illustrate, a computer store, such as CompUSA, may hand its customers a flier that directs them to a specific password-protected site to respond to a questionnaire. If the population is defined as the company's customers, as in a customer satisfaction survey, and a random procedure is used to select respondents, a probability sample will be obtained. Other nonpanel approaches involve the use of e-mail lists that have been rented from suppliers. Presumably, these respondents opted in or gave permission for their e-mail addresses to be circulated. Offline techniques such as short telephone-screening interviews are also used for recruiting Internet samples. Several companies routinely collect e-mail addresses in their customer relationship databases by obtaining that information from customer telephone interactions, product registration cards, on-site registrations, special promotions, and so on.

A variety of other online sampling approaches are also possible. For example, a survey invitation pops up every time a visitor makes a purchase. Furthermore, the Internet can be used to order and access samples generated by marketing research suppliers, such as Survey Samples, Inc. (SSI; www.ssisamples.com).

BE an MR!

Visit Amazon's Web site (www.amazon.com) and conduct an Internet search using a search engine and your library's online database to obtain information on consumer Internet shopping behavior.

Amazon wants you to conduct an Internet survey to determine customer satisfaction. How would you select the sample?

BE a DM!

As the marketing chief for Amazon, what marketing strategies would you adopt to enhance customer satisfaction and loyalty?

Summary Illustration Using the Opening Vignette

In the Gillette Clear Stick antiperspirant/deodorant survey, the target population was defined as male heads of households. Given the large size of the target population and the limited time and money, the company decided to take a sample rather than a census. The sampling unit was households, and the sampling element, or the respondent group, was male heads of households. The sampling frame consisted of telephone numbers of all U.S. households, randomly generated by efficient computer programs. The researchers chose probability sampling because the results had to be generalizable, that is, projectable to all male heads of households. The technique of simple random sampling was selected because efficient computer programs were available to randomly generate household telephone numbers and to minimize wastage due to nonexisting household telephone numbers. Simple random sampling was used to select 1,000 households. This sample size was selected based on qualitative considerations, such as the importance of the decision, the nature of the research, resource constraints, and the sample sizes used in similar studies conducted by Gillette.

International Marketing Research

Implementing the sampling design process in international marketing research is seldom an easy task. Several factors should be considered in defining the target population. Identification and access to the relevant sampling elements may vary widely across countries. Additionally, a reliable sampling frame may not be available. In many studies, the researcher is interested in analyzing the attitudes and behaviors of the household decision maker. This individual responsible for making or influencing decisions may vary across countries. For example, in the United States, children play an important role in the purchase of children's cereals. In countries with authoritarian child-rearing practices, the mother may be the dominant decision maker for that purchase. For an international researcher, this means the mother, rather than the child, would be the sampling element of interest. Identification of the decision maker and the relevant respondent may have to be done on a country-by-country basis.

Developing an appropriate sampling frame is also a difficult task. In the United States, researchers can rely on government census data or commercially available lists for their sampling frames. These types of high-quality secondary data, however, are often not available in international markets. Government data in many developing countries may be unavailable or highly biased. Population lists may not be available commercially. For example, elections are not held in Saudi Arabia, and there is no officially recognized census of population. Hence, there are no voter registration records or accurate maps of population centers. The time and money required to compile this information may be prohibitive. Alternate sampling techniques, such as instructing the interviewers to begin at specified starting points and to sample every *n*th dwelling, may be used until the specified number of units has been sampled.

Equivalence of samples is a key issue in marketing research studies extending beyond the home country. Researchers must minimize the effects of sample differences that are not relevant to the main purposes of the study. For example, if Citibank wanted to compare cultural differences in consumer attitudes toward saving in the United States and Mexico, differences in saving behavior could not be attributed to cultural differences alone if the U.S. respondents averaged 55 years of age while the Mexican respondents averaged 30 years of age. Here, life-stage would be much different for these two groups. The U.S. group would likely be saving for retirement years, while the Mexican group would be saving little in order to establish their households and to pay for the upbringing of their kids. Thus, in order to compare the effects of cultural differences, it would be necessary to hold the other variables constant across the two countries.

Given the lack of suitable sampling frames, the inaccessibility of certain respondents, such as women in some cultures, and the dominance of personal interviewing over other survey methods, probability sampling techniques are uncommon in international marketing research. These constraints have led to a reliance on quota sampling for both consumer and industrial surveys.

RESEARCH IN ACTION

Achieving Sample Comparability Through Diversity

Research in the United States has shown that most consumers feel that a purchase is accompanied by a degree of risk when they choose among alternative brands. A study was conducted to compare the U.S. results with those from Mexico, Thailand, and Saudi Arabia. The targeted respondent in each culture was an upper-middle-income woman residing in a major city. Reaching that target respondent presented challenges that required an adjustment in the sampling process across the countries in this study.

In the United States, random sampling from the telephone directory was used. In Mexico, judgmental sampling was used by having experts identify neighborhoods where the target respondents lived. Homes were then randomly selected for personal interviews. In Thailand, judgmental sampling was also used, but the survey took place in major urban centers, and a store-intercept technique was used to select respondents. Finally, in Saudi Arabia, convenience sampling employing the snowball procedure was used since there were no lists from which sampling frames could be drawn, and social customs prohibited spontaneous personal interviews. Comparability in sample composition and representativeness was achieved by adapting the sampling procedures to suit the social customs and information gathering restrictions of each country.[11]

Sampling techniques and procedures vary in accuracy, reliability, and cost from country to country. If the same sampling procedures are used in each country, the results may not be comparable.[12] To achieve comparability in sample composition and representativeness, it may be desirable to use different sampling techniques in different countries, as the Achieving Sample Comparability Through Diversity example illustrates.

BE a DM!

As the global marketing manager for Intel, the computer microprocessor manufacturer, would you adopt the same or different marketing strategies in the United States and India?

BE an MR!

Conduct an Internet search using a search engine and your library's online database to obtain information on the usage or nonusage of personal computers by households in the United States and India.

Intel wants to conduct cross-cultural research to determine the similarities and differences in the usage or nonusage of personal computers by households in the United States and India. Should the same or different sampling techniques be used in the two countries, and which technique(s) should be used?

Technology and Marketing Research

Computer-based systems can make the sampling design process more effective and efficient. Computers can be used for specifying the sampling frame because they can handle lists of population elements as well as geographical maps. Microcomputers and mainframes may be employed to select the sample needed, using either nonprobability or probability techniques. Once the sampling frame has been determined, the system generates random numbers and selects the sample directly from the database.

These systems are particularly suited for sample generation and control in telephone interviewing. In a typical application, all telephone prefixes in a geographical area (area codes and exchanges) are preprogrammed, and the system selects random numbers. The user can also exclude certain numbers or blocks of numbers. The samples thus generated are called random-digit dialing samples (RDD) and their use is illustrated in the Levi's Research in Action example. The computer can keep track of successfully completed interviews, schedule call-backs, control the interval for redialing busy numbers, and control the number of times a call is attempted by using software such as Survey Sampler. The software then produces lists of numbers to be included in the sample in any customized format.

Firms such as Survey Sampling and Maritz Sampling System have developed proprietary sampling systems to generate samples using a variety of sampling techniques. For example, Survey Sampling has developed software for a range of random-digit dialing samples, clustered samples, and directory-listed samples. They have also developed software to screen and predetermine nonworking telephone numbers. This greatly increases the efficiency of the sample and saves time and money.

Ethics in Marketing Research

The researcher has the ethical responsibility to formulate a sampling design that is consistent with the objectives of the research and adequately controls the sampling error. Probability sampling techniques should be used whenever the results are to be projected to the population. Projecting findings based on nonprobability sampling to the population is misleading and therefore unethical. As the Systematic Sampling Reveals Systematic Gender Differences in Ethical Judgments example demonstrates, appropriate definitions of the population, sampling frame, and sampling technique are essential if the research is to be conducted and the findings are to be used ethically.

RESEARCH IN ACTION

Sampling Design Aids Levi's in Designing Quality Jeans

Levi's 501 faced a challenging task when a new generation of consumers changed its style from the traditional close-fitting 501 button-fly jeans to loose-fitting jeans. Obviously, the consumers' definition of quality jeans had changed, and Levi's wanted to capture this shift by conducting a survey. The Levi's marketing research team adopted the following sampling design.

Target Population

The target population is consumers, male and female, between the ages of 13 and 25 years. The sampling unit is households, and the extent is the United States. The time frame is 2001.

Sampling Frame

The sampling frame is a computer program for random-digit dialing.

Sampling Technique

Use a computer program that provides an accurate random-digit dialing (RDD) sample. This technique will avoid wasting time and money by eliminating nonproductive numbers during the Levi's survey. This method is easy and efficient, and the results can be applied to the target population.

Sample Size

The sample size, based on statistical and nonstatistical considerations, will be 3,000 with 500 interviews conducted in each of six cities to include Atlanta, Boston, Chicago, Los Angeles, Miami, and Seattle.

Execution of the Sampling Process

Use the RDD technique to select a random sample. Use the next-birthday method to choose if more than one person in the selected household is between 13 and 25 years of age. In this case, the person with the next birthday in the household is selected. If no persons between these ages reside in the house, a new random number should be selected.

Results

The results of this survey indicated a shift to innovative fashion looks. Thus, Levi's introduced the popular Levi's® Engineered Jeans™, a reinvention of the classic five-pocket jean. As of 2004, Levi's apparel products were sold under the Levi's®, Dockers®, and Levi Strauss Signature™ brands.[13]

When conducting research with small populations, as in business-to-business marketing or employee research, researchers must be sensitive to preserving the respondents' anonymity. The results should be presented in such a way that respondents cannot be identified or linked to specific comments and findings.

RESEARCH IN ACTION

Systematic Sampling Reveals Systematic Gender Differences in Ethical Judgments

In an attempt to explore differences in research ethics judgments between male and female marketing professionals, data were obtained from 420 respondents. The population was defined as marketing professionals, and the sampling frame was the American Marketing Association directory. The respondents were selected based on a systematic sampling plan from the directory. Systematic random sampling was chosen over simple random sampling because it is easier to implement. Respondents were asked to indicate the degree of ethicalness of various ethical scenarios and promised a copy of the results in an attempt to boost response rates.

The study revealed that female marketing professionals, in general, demonstrated higher levels of research ethical judgments than did their male counterparts. Similar findings have been obtained in other studies. Thus, the systematic random sampling plan was not only efficient but resulted in findings that were generalizable to the target population.[14]

WHAT WOULD *YOU* DO?

MTV: The World's Most Widely Distributed TV Network

The Situation

MTV Networks, which includes MTV, Nickelodeon, and VHI, have earned big profits for parent Viacom. The company used a free-flowing corporate culture and a group of power brands to grow profits by 25 percent annually during the 1990s. As of 2004, MTV was the world's most widely distributed television network, reaching more than 400 million households in 164 countries and territories.

Tom Freston, CEO of MTV, actually took MTV as a small start-up company and turned it into a cultural behemoth. While MTV has become an icon all over the world, with millions of viewers all over the world glued to its programming, MTV is constantly trying to keep up with what's popular and keep its viewers watching.

MTV is always trying to find new ways to engage its target audience, which is 18- to 24-year-olds. This has not always been an easy task. For example, the channel had fading hits with shows like *Beavis & Butt-head* and *The Real World*. Ratings began to slip as users complained that there was no longer music on MTV. Telephone surveys were conducted with the 18- to 24-year-old group. The sample was selected by choosing households based on computerized random-digit dialing. If the household had 18- to 24-year-olds, one person was selected using the next-birthday method. The results of this survey showed that MTV needed a makeover.

The Marketing Research Decision

1. As trends come and go, it is important for MTV to stay in touch with its audience members and know their wants. Tom Freston especially wants to keep in touch with the 18- to 24-year-olds through periodic surveys. What sampling technique would you recommend?
   a. Convenience sampling
   b. Quota sampling
   c. Systematic sampling
   d. Stratified sampling
   e. Simple random sampling
2. Discuss the role of the type of sampling technique you recommend in enabling Tom Freston to keep in touch with the 18- to 24-year-olds.

The Marketing Management Decision

1. What should Tom Freston do to attract the 18- to 24-year-old audience group to MTV? Check as many as are applicable.
   a. Launch music hours shown live from popular places (e.g., Times Square)
   b. Make VeeJays more authentic
   c. Feature more celebrities
   d. Focus more on music programming
   e. All of the above
2. Discuss how the marketing management-decision action that you recommend to Tom Freston is influenced by the sampling technique suggested earlier and by the findings of that research.

What Tom Freston Did

MTV launched music hours shown live from Times Square. New shows like the animated *Daria* were created, and the *Video Music Awards* were revamped. VeeJays became more authentic, and not TV-pretty. The objective was to give MTV a cleaner, more pensive image to keep its viewers happy. The 18- to 24-year-old crowd is important to the network because this is the group that younger teens and the 25- to 35-year-old crowd looks to for image and style ideas.

Currently, MTV is still continuing to make its programming fresh and hip. Programs such as *The Osbournes* and *Punk'd* have gotten great reviews. Also, MTV's detailed Web site (www.mtv.com) lets its viewers do everything from putting in requests for music videos to chatting with fellow MTV fans. MTV is continuing to grow and expand, and with the help of marketing research, MTV should be able to stay hip for generations to come.[15]

Summary

Researchers can obtain information about the characteristics of a population by conducting either a sample or a census. Samples tend to be preferred because of budget and time limits, large population sizes, and small variances in the characteristics of interest. Sampling is also preferred when the cost of sampling error is low, the cost of nonsampling error is high, the nature of measurement is destructive, and attention must be focused on individual cases. The opposite conditions favor the use of a census.

Sampling design begins by defining the target population in terms of elements, sampling units, extent, and time. Then the sampling frame should be determined. A sampling frame is a list of the elements of the target population. Directions for constructing the sampling frame should also be included. Sampling techniques are applied to the sample frame to develop the eventual sample. The sample size is determined based on both quantitative and qualitative considerations. Finally, execution of the sampling process requires detailed specifications for each step in the process.

Sampling techniques may be classified as nonprobability and probability techniques. Nonprobability sampling techniques rely on the researcher's judgment. Consequently, they do not permit an objective evaluation of the precision of the sample results, and the estimates obtained are not statistically projectable to the population. The commonly used nonprobability sampling techniques include convenience sampling, judgmental sampling, quota sampling, and snowball sampling.

In probability sampling techniques, sampling units are selected by chance. Each sampling unit has a nonzero chance of being selected, and the researcher can prespecify every potential sample of a given size that could be drawn from the population, as well as the probability of selecting each sample. It is also possible to determine the precision of the sample estimates and inferences and make projections to the target population. Probability sampling techniques include simple random sampling, systematic sampling, stratified sampling, and cluster sampling. The choice between probability and nonprobability sampling should be based on the nature of the research, degree of error tolerance, relative magnitude of sampling and nonsampling errors, variability in the population, and statistical and operational considerations. Nonprobability as well as probability sampling techniques can be implemented on the Internet, with the respondents being prerecruited or tapped online.

When conducting international marketing research, it is desirable to achieve comparability in sample composition and representativeness even though this may require using different sampling techniques in different countries. Several computer programs are available for implementing nonprobability and probability sampling schemes. It is unethical and misleading to treat nonprobability samples as probability samples and project the results to a target population.

Key Terms and Concepts

Element, 322
Population, 323
Census, 323
Sample, 323
Target population, 326
Sampling unit, 326
Sampling frame, 326
Nonprobability sampling, 327
Precision, 327
Probability sampling, 328
Sample size, 328
Convenience sampling, 330
Judgmental sampling, 331
Quota sampling, 332
Snowball sampling, 333
Simple random sampling, 335
Systematic sampling, 336
Stratified sampling, 337
Cluster sampling, 338
Area sampling, 339

Suggested Cases and Video Cases

Cases

2.2 Cadillac **2.3 HCA** **2.4 Bloomingdale's** **2.5 Burger King**
4.1 Boeing **4.2 Gucci**

Video Cases

2.1 Starbucks **2.2 Nike** **4.1 Subaru** **4.2 Marriott**

Additional cases and video cases are available in the Instructor's Manual and on the instructor and student Web sites.

Live Research: Conducting a Marketing Research Project

1. A census may be feasible in a business-to-business project where the size of the population is small, but it is infeasible in most consumer projects.
2. Define the target population (element, sampling unit, extent, and time), and discuss a suitable sampling frame.
3. Probability sampling techniques are more difficult and time-consuming to implement, and their use may not be warranted unless the results are being projected to a population of interest.

Acronyms

The sampling design process and the steps involved may be represented by the acronym SAMPLE:

S ampling design process
A mount: sample size determination
M ethod: sampling technique selection
P opulation definition
L ist: sampling frame determination
E xecution of the sampling process

Review Questions

1. What is the major difference between a sample and a census?
2. Under what conditions is a sample preferable to a census? When is a census preferable to a sample?
3. Describe the sampling design process.
4. How should the target population be defined?
5. What is a sampling unit? How is it different from the population element?
6. What qualitative factors should be considered in determining the sample size?
7. How do probability sampling techniques differ from nonprobability sampling techniques?
8. What is the least expensive and least time-consuming of all sampling techniques? What are the major limitations of this technique?
9. What is the major difference between judgmental and convenience sampling?
10. What is the relationship between quota sampling and judgmental sampling?
11. What are the distinguishing features of simple random sampling?
12. Describe the procedure for selecting a systematic random sample.
13. Describe stratified sampling. What are the criteria for the selection of stratification variables?
14. Describe the cluster sampling procedure. What is the key distinction between cluster sampling and stratified sampling?
15. What factors should be considered in choosing between probability and nonprobability sampling?

Applied Problems

1. Define the appropriate target population and the sampling frame in each of the following situations:
   a. The manufacturer of a new cereal brand wants to conduct in-home product usage tests in Chicago.
   b. A national chain store wants to determine the shopping behavior of customers who have its store charge card.
   c. A local TV station wants to determine households' viewing habits and programming preferences.
   d. The local chapter of the American Marketing Association wants to test the effectiveness of its new-member drive in Atlanta.
2. A manufacturer would like to survey users to determine the demand potential for a new power press. The new press has a capacity of 500 tons and costs $225,000. It is used for forming products from light- and heavy-weight steel and can be used by automobile, construction equipment, and major appliance manufacturers.
   a. Identify the population and sampling frame that could be used.
   b. Describe how a simple random sample can be drawn using the identified sampling frame.
   c. Could a stratified sample be used? If so, how?
   d. Could a cluster sample be used? If so, how?
   e. Which sampling technique would you recommend? Why?
3. Procter & Gamble would like to conduct a survey of consumer preferences for premium ice cream brands in Los Angeles. Stratified random sampling will be used. Visit the U.S. Census Bureau Web site (www.census.gov) to identify information that will be relevant in determining income and age strata.
4. Using the RAND function in Microsoft Excel, or the random variable function in the SPSS statistical software package, generate a set of 1,000 random numbers for selecting a simple random sample.
5. Visit the SurveySite Web site (www.surveysite.com). Examine the Internet surveys being conducted. Write a report about the sampling plans being used.

Group Discussion

1. "Given that the U.S. Bureau of the Census uses sampling to check on the accuracy of various censuses, a constitutional amendment should be passed replacing the decennial census with a sample." Discuss as a small group.

2. "Because nonsampling errors are greater in magnitude than sampling errors, it really does not matter which sampling technique is used." Discuss this statement.

CHAPTER

13 Sampling: Final and Initial Sample Size Determination

"Sample size not only is determined by statistical considerations, but also real pressures, such as time and cost."

Chris Bonbright, *Manager, Research & Market Analysis, Tracker Marine Group, Springfield, MO*

OPENING QUESTIONS

1. What key concepts and symbols are pertinent to sampling?
2. How are the sampling distribution, statistical inference, and standard error relevant to sampling?
3. What is the statistical approach to determining sample size based on simple random sampling and the construction of confidence intervals?
4. How can we derive the formulas to statistically determine the sample size for estimating means and proportions?
5. How should the sample size be adjusted to account for incidence and completion rates?
6. Why is it difficult to statistically determine the sample size in international marketing research?
7. What is the interface of technology with sample size determination?
8. What ethical issues are related to sample size determination, particularly the estimation of population variance?
9. What role does the Internet play in determining the sample size?

Sizing the Sample Size Problem

A recent article in the *Chicago Tribune* suggested that just as the introduction of television reduced the audiences for both theater and radio, so have online services reduced the audience for television. To support his claim, the author offered up survey data about America Online, Inc., which found that online subscribers watch less television than the average U.S. household. An executive at the research company that performed the survey said, "It doesn't matter why people watch less television. It only matters that they do."

The general reader and the general businessperson might read this piece and walk away with the notion that, indeed, increasing online use is directly related to decreasing television viewing. You can almost imagine the buzzing of such discussions at breakfast tables, water coolers, and in car pools: "Hey, I just read in the paper this morning that. . . "

A more skeptical reader would rightly question much of the study's findings and its application to everyday consumer media preferences. A closer look at the report reveals that the sample size comprised only 262 members of the online service's subscribers. Is this enough to mitigate random sampling error? Is this sample large enough to make such bold claims about TV viewing? To make decisions and set policy and strategy? The *confidence level*, which is the level of certainty, is not reported. Only the margin of error as "probably" about five percentage points is estimated. Was it five or not? How confident are we that this conclusion is accurate? What is the confidence level and what is the *confidence interval*, that is, the range likely to contain the true population parameter? Moreover, the completion rate was not reported. Without considering the appropriate sampling specifications, it is not appropriate to draw inferences from the sample about the population. Therefore, based on this study it is not appropriate to conclude that users of online services, in general, watch less television.[1] •

Overview

In Chapter 12, we considered the role of sampling in research design formulation, described the sampling process, and presented the various nonprobability and probability sampling techniques. This chapter focuses on the determination of sample size in simple random sampling. Figure 13.1 briefly explains the focus of the chapter, the relation of this chapter to the previous ones, and the steps of the marketing research process this chapter describes.

The opening vignette illustrates the importance of statistically determining the sample size and the random sampling error before generalizing the sample findings to the population. In order to understand and appreciate these issues, we will define various concepts and symbols and discuss the properties of the sampling distribution. We will describe statistical approaches to sample size determination based on confidence intervals. We will present the formulas for calculating the sample size with these approaches and illustrate their use.

The sample size determined statistically is the final or net sample size that represents the number of interviews or observations that need to be completed. For example, a sample size of 1,000 for a telephone survey means that the interviewers must complete 1,000 interviews. To obtain this final sample size, however, a much larger number of potential respondents must be contacted initially. Thus, to complete 1,000 interviews, it may be necessary to initially contact as many as 3,000 respondents, for example, as only some of the potential respondents may qualify to participate. That is, the incidence rate is generally less than 100 percent. Furthermore, some of those who do qualify may refuse to participate or complete the survey. The completion rate is also less than 100 percent. This chapter will describe the adjustments that need to be made to the statistically determined sample size to account for incidence and completion rates and to calculate the initial

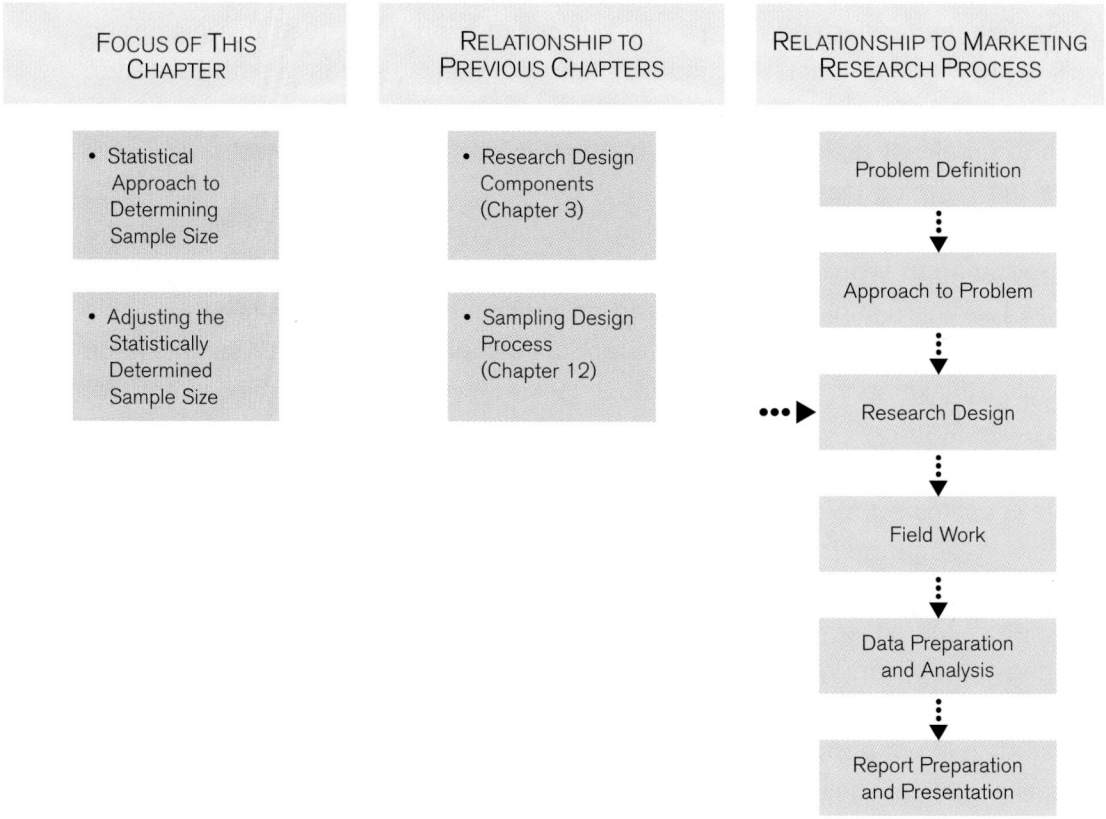

Figure 13.1

Relationship of Sample Size Determination to the Previous Chapters and the Marketing Research Process

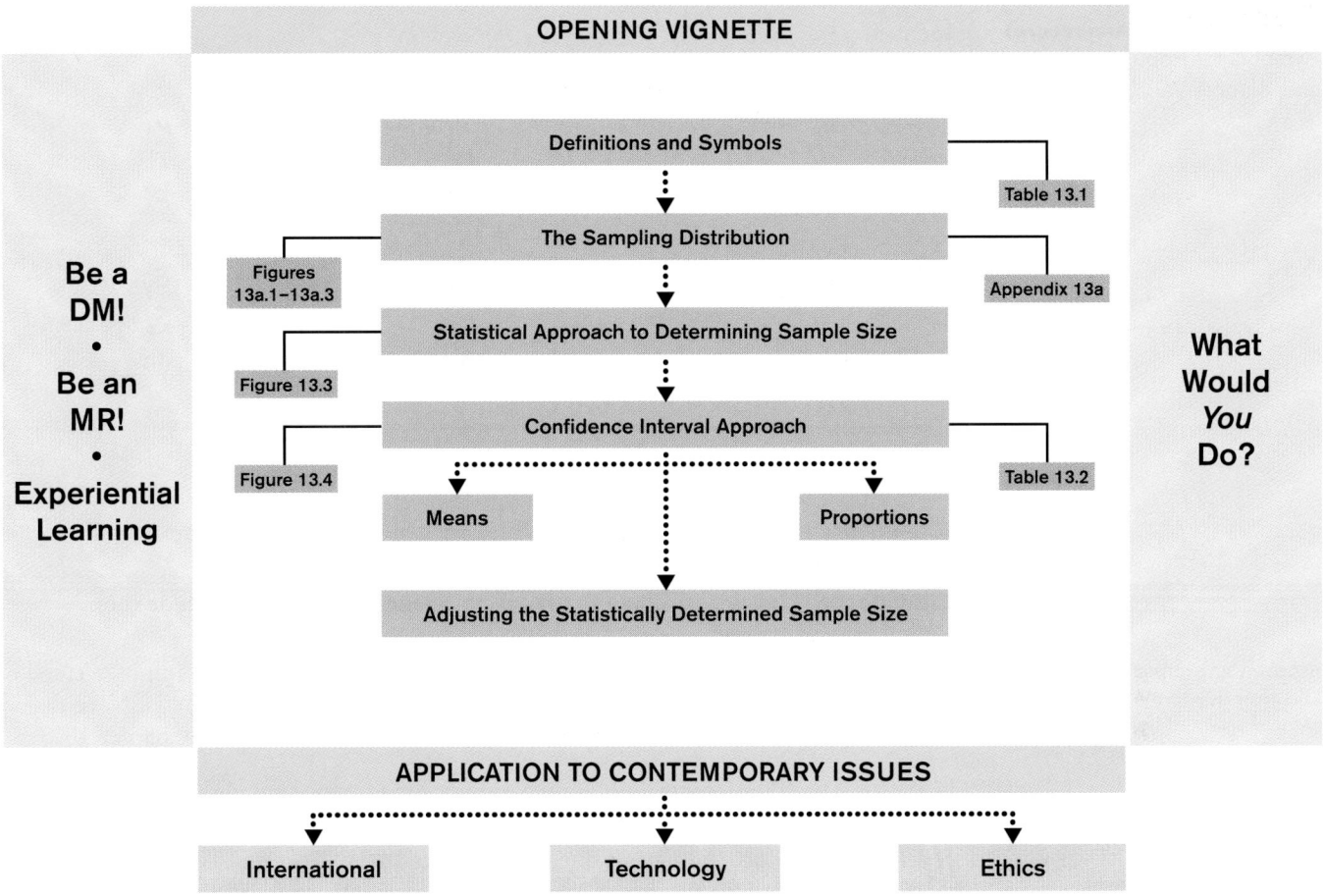

Figure 13.2

Final and Initial Sample Size Determination: An Overview

sample size. The chapter will also discuss the difficulty of statistically determining the sample size in international marketing research, applications of technology, and the relevant ethical issues. Figure 13.2 gives an overview of the topics discussed in this chapter and how they flow from one to the next.

Statistical determination of sample size requires knowledge of the normal distribution and the use of normal probability tables. The **normal distribution** is bell-shaped and symmetrical. Its mean, median, and mode are identical (see Chapter 16). Information on the normal distribution and the use of normal probability tables is presented in Appendix 13A. Reviewing a statistics textbook is also recommended.

normal distribution
A basis for classical statistical inference that is bell-shaped and symmetrical in appearance. Its measures of central tendency are all identical.

Definitions and Symbols

The statistical concepts used in sample size determination are defined in the following list.

Parameter: A summary description of a fixed characteristic or measure of the target population. A parameter denotes the true value that would be obtained if a census (a survey of the complete population), rather than a sample, was undertaken.

Statistic: A summary description of a characteristic or measure of the sample. The sample statistic is used as an estimate of the population parameter.

Precision level: When estimating a population parameter by using a sample statistic, the precision level is the desired size of the estimating interval. This is the maximum permissible difference between the sample statistic and the population parameter.

Table 13.1
Symbols for Population and Sample Variables

Variable	Population	Sample
Mean	μ	$\bar{X}$
Proportion	π	p
Variance	σ^2	s^2
Standard deviation	σ	s
Size	N	n
Standard error of the mean	$\sigma_{\bar{x}}$	$S_{\bar{x}}$
Standard error of the proportion	σ_p	S_p
Standardized variate *(z)*	$\frac{X-\mu}{\sigma}$	$\frac{X-\bar{X}}{s}$

Confidence interval: The range into which the true population parameter will fall, assuming a given level of confidence.

Confidence level: The probability that a confidence interval will include the population parameter.

random sampling error
The error due to the particular sample selected being an imperfect representation of the population of interest.

Random sampling error: The error that results when the particular sample selected is an imperfect representation of the population of interest (see Chapter 3). Note that this is different from the random error in measurement discussed in Chapter 10.

The symbols used in statistical notation for describing population and sample characteristics are summarized in Table 13.1.

The Sampling Distribution

sampling distribution
The distribution of the values of a sample statistic computed for each possible sample that could be drawn from the target population under a specified sampling plan.

The **sampling distribution** is the distribution of the values of a sample statistic, for example, the sample mean. These values are computed for each possible sample of a given size. Under a specified sampling plan, it is possible to draw several different samples of a given size from the target population.[2] The sampling distribution should not be confused with the distribution of the values of the elements in a sample. Suppose a simple random sample of five steel mills is to be drawn from a population of 20 steel mills. There are $(20 \times 19 \times 18 \times 17 \times 16)/(1 \times 2 \times 3 \times 4 \times 5)$, or 15,504 different samples of five steel mills that can be drawn from this population. If the values of the means for annual steel production (in tons) associated with these 15,504 samples were assembled, they would form the sampling distribution of the mean.

statistical inference
The process of generalizing the sample results to the population results.

central limit theorem
As the sample size increases, the distribution of the sample mean of a randomly selected sample approaches the normal distribution.

An important task in marketing research is to calculate statistics, such as the sample mean and sample proportion, and to use them to estimate the corresponding true population values. This process of generalizing the sample results to the population results is referred to as **statistical inference.** In practice, a single sample of predetermined size is selected, and the sample statistics (such as means or proportions) are computed. The sample statistics become the basis for making inferences about the population values. This inferential process is possible because sampling distribution enables us to use probability theory to make inferences about the population values. Of direct relevance is the **central limit theorem,** which states that as the sample size increases, the distribution of the sample mean of a randomly selected sample approaches the normal distribution. This holds true regardless of the shape of the original population distribution from which the sample is drawn.

We now describe the important properties of the sampling distribution of the mean, and the corresponding properties for the proportion, for large samples (30 or more). Please refer to Table 13.1 for a definition of the symbols used in these formulas.

1. The sampling distribution of the mean is a normal distribution (see Appendix 13A). Strictly speaking, the sampling distribution of a proportion is a binomial that approximates the normal distribution in large samples (n = 30 or more).

2. The mean (the average) of the sampling distribution of the mean

$$\left(\bar{X} = \left(\sum_{i=1}^{n} X_i\right) \Big/ n\right)$$

or of the proportion (p) equals the corresponding population parameter value, μ or π, respectively.

3. The standard deviation of the sampling distribution is called the **standard error** of the mean or the proportion. This distinction is made to clarify the point that we are talking about a sampling distribution of the mean or the proportion, not about a distribution of elements in a sample or a population.

   The formula for the mean is

$$\sigma_{\bar{X}} = \frac{\sigma}{\sqrt{n}}$$

   The formula for the proportion is

$$\sigma_p = \sqrt{\frac{\pi(1-\pi)}{n}}$$

4. Often the population standard deviation, σ, is not known. In these cases, it can be estimated from the sample by using the following formula:

$$s = \sqrt{\frac{\sum_{i=1}^{n}(X_i - \bar{X})^2}{n-1}}$$

   or

$$s = \sqrt{\frac{\sum_{i=1}^{n} X_i^2 - \frac{\left(\sum_{i=1}^{n} X_i\right)^2}{n}}{n-1}}$$

   In cases where σ is estimated by s, the standard error of the mean becomes

$$\text{est. } \sigma_{\bar{X}} = \frac{s}{\sqrt{n}}$$

   The "est." denotes the fact that s has been used as an estimate of σ.

5. Likewise, the standard error of the proportion can be estimated by using the sample proportion p as an estimator of the population proportion, π, as

$$\text{est. } s_p = \sqrt{\frac{p\,(1-p)}{n}}$$

6. The area under the sampling distribution (normal distribution) curve between any two points can be calculated in terms of z values. The ***z* value** for a point is the number of standard errors that point is away from the mean. The z values may be computed as follows:

$$z = \frac{\bar{X} - \mu}{\sigma_{\bar{X}}}$$

standard error
The standard deviation of the sampling distribution of the mean or proportion.

***z* value**
The number of standard errors that a point is away from the mean.

For example, 34.13 percent of the area under one side of the curve lies between the mean and a z value of 1.0. The area from the mean to z value of 2.0 and 3.0 is equal to 0.4772 and 0.4986, respectively. (See Table 2 in the Appendix of Statistical Tables.) The same percentages of the area under the sampling distribution curve lie between the mean and z values of –1.0, –2.0, and –3.0. This is because the sampling distribution curve is symmetric around the mean. In the case of proportion, the computation of z values is similar.

Statistical Approach to Determining Sample Size

In addition to statistical considerations, several qualitative factors should be considered when determining the sample size (see Chapter 12). These include the importance of the decision, the nature of the research, the number of variables, the nature of the analysis, sample sizes used in similar studies, incidence rates, completion rates, and resource constraints. The statistically determined sample size is the net or final sample size—the sample remaining after eliminating potential respondents who do not qualify or who do not complete the interview. Depending on incidence and completion rates, the initial sample may need to be much larger than the net or final sample requirements. In commercial marketing research, limits on time, money, and expert resources can exert an overriding influence on sample size determination.

The statistical approach to determining sample size is based on traditional statistical inference using the formulas (equations) presented in the previous section. In this approach, the precision level is specified in advance. This approach is based on the construction of confidence intervals around sample means or proportions (Figure 13.3).

The Confidence Interval Approach

Confidence intervals around sample means or proportions are estimated using the standard error formula. As an example, suppose that a researcher has taken a simple random sample of 300 households to estimate the monthly expenses on department store shopping and has found that the mean household monthly expense for the sample is $182. Past studies indicate that the population standard deviation σ can be assumed to be $55.

We want to find an interval within which a fixed proportion of the sample means would fall. Suppose we want to determine an interval around the population mean that will include 95 percent of the sample means, based on samples of 300 households. That is, we choose 95 percent as the confidence level. The 95 percent could be divided into two equal parts, half below and half above the mean, as shown in Figure 13.4. Calculation of the confidence interval involves determining a distance below ($\bar{X}_L$) and above ($\bar{X}_U$) the population mean μ, which contains a specified area of the normal curve.

Figure 13.3

The Confidence Interval Approach and Determining Sample Size

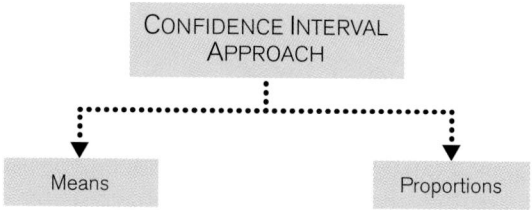

Figure 13.4
95% Confidence Interval

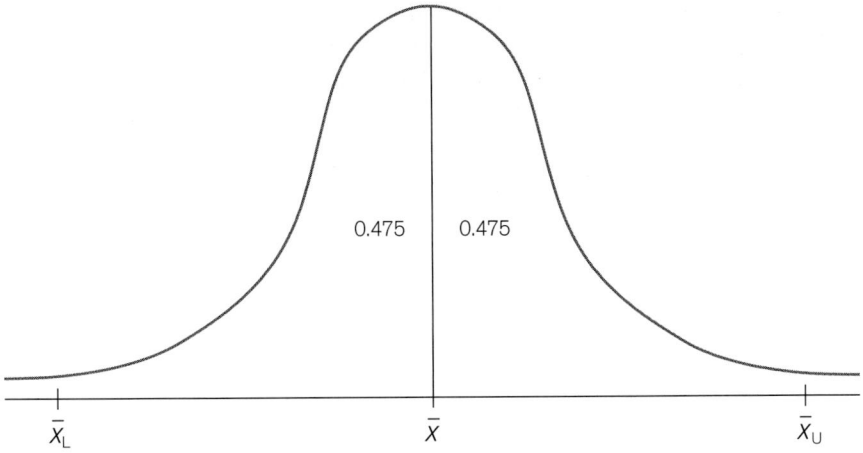

The z values corresponding to $\bar{X}_L$ and $\bar{X}_U$ may be calculated as

$$z_L = \frac{\bar{X}_L - \mu}{\sigma_{\bar{x}}}$$

$$z_U = \frac{\bar{X}_U - \mu}{\sigma_{\bar{x}}}$$

where $z_L = -z$ and $z_U = +z$. Therefore, the lower value of $\bar{X}$ is

$$\bar{X}_L = \mu - z\sigma_{\bar{x}}$$

and the upper value of $\bar{X}$ is

$$\bar{X}_U = \mu + z\sigma_{\bar{x}}$$

Note that μ is estimated by $\bar{X}$. The confidence interval is given by

$$\bar{X} \pm z\sigma_{\bar{x}}$$

We can now set a 95 percent confidence interval around the sample mean of \$182. As a first step, we compute the standard error of the mean:

$$\sigma_{\bar{x}} = \frac{\sigma}{\sqrt{n}} = 55/\sqrt{300} = 3.18$$

From Table 2 in the Appendix of Statistical Tables, we can see that the central 95 percent of the normal distribution lies within $\pm$ 1.96 z values. The 95 percent confidence interval is given by

$$\begin{aligned}
&\bar{X} \pm 1.96\ \sigma_{\bar{x}} \\
&= 182.00 \pm 1.96(3.18) \\
&= 182.00 \pm 6.23
\end{aligned}$$

Thus, the 95 percent confidence interval ranges from \$175.77 to \$188.23. The probability of finding the true population mean to be within \$175.77 and \$188.23 is 95 percent. If the confidence interval is not reported, or cannot otherwise be calculated from the information given, we have no way of knowing how precise the sample estimates are.

RESEARCH IN ACTION

The American Customer Satisfaction Index

The American Customer Satisfaction Index (ACSI) is a national measure of satisfaction with quality that provides a resource for examining the differences in satisfaction among customers of different industries by their demographic and socioeconomic characteristics. The ACSI is based on 42,149 customer interviews and is converted to a 0–100 scale.

The first national measure of ACSI gave an index reading of 74.5 with a 95 percent confidence interval of 74.3 to 74.7. This narrow confidence interval is due to a large sample size and indicates that customer satisfaction was measured with a high degree of precision. The ACSI is also broken down by economic sectors and industries. The ACSI is a useful new tool for companies to benchmark their customer satisfaction scores against those of other companies in their own and other industries.[3]

This was illustrated in the opening vignette, in which it was difficult to evaluate the precision of the results of the America Online survey.

Confidence intervals are often associated with scales used to measure customer satisfaction, as illustrated by the American Customer Satisfaction Index.

Sample Size Determination: Means

Confidence interval estimation formulas can be used to determine the sample size that will result in a desired confidence interval. In this case, we use the same formulas but have a different unknown, namely the sample size, n. Suppose the researcher wants to estimate the monthly household expense on department store shopping so that the estimate will be within ±$5 of the true population value. What should the size of the sample be? The following steps, summarized in Table 13.2, will lead to an answer.

1. **Specify the level of precision.** This is the maximum permissible difference (D) between the sample mean and the population mean. In our example, $D = \pm\$5$.
2. **Specify the level of confidence.** Suppose that a 95 percent confidence level is desired.

Table 13.2

Sample Size Determination for Means and Proportions

Steps	Means	Proportions
1. Specify the level of precision.	$D = \pm\ \$5.00$	$D = p - \pi = \pm\ 0.05$
2. Specify the confidence level (CL).	CL = 95%	CL = 95%
3. Determine the z value associated with the CL.	z value = 1.96	z value = 1.96
4. Determine the standard deviation of the population.	Estimate σ	Estimate π
	$\sigma = 55$	$\pi = 0.64$
5. Determine the sample size using the formula for the standard error.	$n = \frac{\sigma^2 z^2}{D^2}$	$n = \frac{\pi(1-\pi)z^2}{D^2}$
	$n = \frac{55^2(1.96)^2}{5^2}$	$n = \frac{0.64(1-0.64)(1.96)^2}{(0.05)^2}$
	$n = 465$	$n = 355$
6. If necessary, re-estimate the confidence interval by employing s to estimate σ.	$= \bar{X} \pm z s_{\bar{x}}$	$p \pm z s_p$

3. **Determine the z value associated with the confidence level using Table 2 in the Appendix of Statistical Tables.** For a 95 percent confidence level, the probability that the population mean will fall outside one end of the interval is 0.025 (0.05/2) with an associated z value of 1.96.
4. **Determine the standard deviation of the population.** The standard deviation of the population may be available from secondary sources, estimated from pilot-study data, or based on the researcher's judgment. For example, the range of a normally distributed variable is approximately equal to plus or minus three standard deviations. The standard deviation of sample data can therefore be estimated by dividing the range of that data by six. The researcher can often estimate the range based on knowledge of the phenomenon or knowledge of the scale used. For example, the traditional Likert scale has a range of 4 (5 – 1).
5. **Determine the sample size using the formula for the standard error of the mean.** Let us use the formula for z and derive the formula for the sample size, n. Recall that

$$z = \frac{\bar{X} - \mu}{\sigma_{\bar{x}}}$$

because $D = \bar{X} - \mu$

$$z = \frac{D}{\sigma_{\bar{x}}}$$

Solving for $\sigma_{\bar{x}}$

$$\sigma_{\bar{x}} = \frac{D}{z}$$

But

$$\sigma_{\bar{x}} = \frac{\sigma}{\sqrt{n}}$$

Therefore,

$$\frac{\sigma}{\sqrt{n}} = \frac{D}{z}$$

Solving for n

$$n = \frac{\sigma^2 z^2}{D^2}$$

In our example,

$$n = \frac{55^2\ (1.96)^2}{5^2}$$
$$= 464.83$$
$$= 465 \text{ (rounded to the next higher integer)}$$

It can be seen from the preceding formulas that sample size is influenced by three factors. It increases as population variability increases, as greater confidence is required (that is, as confidence level increases), and as the precision level required of the estimate increases.

6. **If the population standard deviation, σ, is unknown and an estimate is used, it should be re-estimated once the sample has been drawn.** The sample standard deviation, s, is used as an estimate of σ. A revised confidence interval should then be calculated to determine the precision level actually obtained.

Suppose that the value of 55 used for σ was an estimate because the true value was unknown. A sample size (n) of 465 is drawn, and these observations generate a mean ($\bar{X}$) of 180 and a sample standard deviation s of 50. The revised confidence interval then is

$$= \bar{X} \pm z s_{\bar{x}}$$
$$= 180 \pm 1.96\ (50/\sqrt{465})$$
$$= 180 \pm 4.55$$

or

$$175.45 \leq \mu \leq 184.55$$

Note that the confidence interval obtained is narrower than planned because the population standard deviation was overestimated to be 55 compared to the sample standard deviation of only 50.

It is very important to note that the population size, N, does not directly affect the size of the sample. An example will make this point more obvious. Suppose all the population elements are identical on a characteristic of interest. A sample size of one would then be sufficient to estimate the mean perfectly. This would be true regardless of whether there were 50, 500, 5,000, or 50,000 elements in the population. The sample size is directly affected by the variability of the characteristic in the population. This variability enters into the sample size calculation by way of population variance σ^2 or sample variance s^2.

BE an MR!

Visit T-Mobile's Web site (www.t-mobile.com) and conduct an Internet search using a search engine and your library's online database to obtain information on the average monthly amount U.S. households spend on cellular (cell phone) services.

Assuming a confidence level of 95 percent, precision level of $10, and a standard deviation of $100, what should be the sample to determine the average monthly household expenditure on cellular services?

BE a DM!

As the vice president of marketing for T-Mobile, how would you use information on the average monthly household expenditure for cellular services to expand your revenues?

Sample Size Determination: Proportions

Proportions are estimated when the choice is dichotomous, meaning there are only two categories (e.g., yes or no). The researcher is examining the percentage of elements that is in one of the two categories. If the statistic of interest is a proportion, rather than a mean, the approach to sample size determination is similar. Suppose that the researcher is interested in estimating the proportion of households possessing a department store credit card. The researcher should follow these six steps:

1. **Specify the level of precision.** Suppose the desired precision is such that the allowable interval is set as $D = p - \pi = \pm 0.05$ (that is, 5 percent expressed as a decimal equivalent).
2. **Specify the level of confidence.** Suppose that a 95 percent confidence level is desired.
3. **Determine the z value associated with the confidence level.** As explained in the case of estimating the mean, this will be $z = 1.96$.
4. **Estimate the population proportion, π.** As explained earlier, the population proportion may be estimated from secondary sources or from a pilot study or be based on the judgment of the researcher. Suppose that based on secondary data the researcher estimates that 64 percent of the households in the target population possess a department store credit card. In this case, $\pi = 0.64$.

5. **Determine the sample size using the formula for the standard error of the proportion.** The derivation of the formula for sample size is similar to that used for means. We know that

$$z = \frac{p - \pi}{\sigma_p}$$

Hence,

$$\sigma_p = \frac{p - \pi}{z}$$

Substituting D for $p - \pi$ we get

$$\sigma_p = \frac{D}{z}$$

We also know that

$$\sigma_p = \sqrt{\frac{\pi(1-\pi)}{n}}$$

Therefore, setting

$$\frac{D}{z} = \sqrt{\frac{\pi(1-\pi)}{n}}$$

and solving for n, we get

$$n = \frac{\pi(1-\pi)z^2}{D^2}$$

In our example,

$$\begin{aligned} n &= \frac{0.64(1-0.64)(1.96)^2}{(0.05)^2} \\ &= 354.04 \\ &= 355 \text{ (rounded to the next higher integer)} \end{aligned}$$

6. **If the estimate of π turns out to be poor, the confidence interval will be more or less precise than desired.** Suppose that after the sample has been taken, the proportion p is calculated to have a value of 0.55. The confidence interval is then re-estimated by employing s_p to estimate the unknown σ_p as

$$p \pm z\, s_p$$

where

$$s_p = \sqrt{\frac{p\,(1-p)}{n}}$$

In our example,

$$\begin{aligned} s_p &= \sqrt{\frac{0.55\,(1-0.55)}{355}} \\ &= 0.0264 \end{aligned}$$

The confidence interval, then, is

$$\begin{aligned} &= 0.55 \pm 1.96\,(0.0264) \\ &= 0.55 \pm 0.052 \end{aligned}$$

which is wider than that specified. This could be attributed to the fact that the sample standard deviation determined from our actual sample was based on

$p = 0.55$. This was larger than our original estimate of the population standard deviation determined from researcher's judgment and based on $\pi = 0.64$.

If the resulting confidence interval is too wide, the sample size can be recalculated using the maximum possible variation in the population. Maximum variation occurs when the product $\pi(1 - \pi)$ is at a maximum. This occurs when π is set at 0.5. This result can also be seen intuitively. If a population was evenly divided in terms of one value of a characteristic, more evidence would be required to obtain a valid inference than if the majority of the population possessed that characteristic. In our example, this leads to a sample size of

$$
\begin{aligned}
n &= \frac{0.5(0.5)(1.96)^2}{(0.05)^2} \\
&= 384.16 \\
&= 385 \text{ (rounded to the next higher integer)}
\end{aligned}
$$

A sample size of 385 is enough to represent India's more than 1 billion people or the more than 275 million American people. The sample size is independent of the population size for large populations.

Thus, in our opening vignette, if the proportion of online users is to be estimated with 95 percent confidence level and with a margin of error (allowable interval) not to exceed plus or minus 5 percent, the sample size should have been at least 385. The sample size was only 262, however, falling substantially short of the required size.

BE an MR!

Visit Wells Fargo's Web site (www.wellsfargo.com) and conduct an Internet search using a search engine and your library's online database to obtain information on the proportion of consumers who use online banking.

If about 15 percent of the people in a given area are expected to use Internet banking, what should be the sample size for 95 percent confidence level and 5 percent precision level?

BE a DM!

As the vice president of marketing for Wells Fargo, what information would you want to determine whether the bank should expand its online services?

Adjusting the Statistically Determined Sample Size

The sample size specified by these statistical methods is a final, or net, sample size. It represents the number of returned mail questionnaires or the number of completed interviews. Initial oversampling, in which a much larger number of respondents are originally contacted, is required to achieve the desired net sample. This is due to two factors, incidence rates and completion rates.

Incidence Rate

Incidence rate refers to the rate of occurrence. It is influenced by the proportion of people in the population with the characteristics under study. When studying a characteristic with a low incident rate, the researcher must initially contact many more people than if the characteristic has a high incidence rate, screening out those who do not meet the study requirements. Suppose a study of jewelry calls for a sample of female heads of households aged 25 to 55 years. Of the women between the ages of 20 and 60 years who might reasonably be approached to see if they qualify, approximately 75 percent are heads of households between ages 25 and 55 years. That is, the incidence rate or the rate of occurrence is 0.75. This means that, on average, 1.33 (1.00/0.75) women must be approached in order to obtain one qualified respondent.

incidence rate
The rate of occurrence of persons eligible to participate in the study expressed as a percentage.

EXPERIENTIAL LEARNING

How the Poll Was Conducted

Credible media sources today, such as the *New York Times* (www.nytimes.com), attempt to make their research methods as transparent as possible to their readers. For example, the *New York Times* routinely runs a sidebar column explaining how a poll was conducted when an accompanying story draws heavily upon the results of such a poll. In one sidebar column entitled "How the Poll Was Conducted," the following was used as part of the details describing the research methods:

> In theory, in 19 cases out of 20 the results based on such samples will differ by no more than three percentage points in either direction from what would have been obtained by seeking out all American adults.

In other words, "19 cases out of 20" would correspond to a 95 percent confidence level. (Remember that the value for z associated with a 95 percent confidence interval would be 1.96.) Also, remember results showing 50 percent "for" and 50 percent "against" would have the highest amount of variance. Therefore, computations using 0.50 as the proportion (π) would account for the most challenging scenario when designing a sample.

1. Using the equations presented in this chapter, estimate the size of the sample used in this national poll if the most challenging scenario existed.
2. What would the size of the sample have to be if researchers wanted a precision level of 1 percent?
3. If the original poll had used a 90 percent confidence interval, what would the sample size have to be?

Additional criteria for qualifying respondents (e.g., they must be using a specific product brand) will further decrease the incidence rate and therefore increase the number of contacts. Suppose it is decided that respondents must have worn jewelry in the past week in order to be eligible to participate in the study. It is estimated that 60 percent of the women contacted would meet this criterion of wearing jewelry. Then the incidence rate drops from 75 percent to 45 percent (0.75 × 0.60). To deliver one qualified respondent to the sample, 2.22 individuals (1.00/0.45) must be initially contacted.

Completion Rate

completion rate
The percentage of qualified respondents who complete the interview. It enables researchers to take into account anticipated refusals by people who qualify.

The number of initial contacts must also be increased in anticipation of refusals coming from people qualified to participate. The **completion rate** denotes the percentage of qualified respondents who complete the interview. For example, if the researcher expects an interview completion rate of 80 percent of eligible respondents, the number of contacts should be increased by a factor of 1.25 (1.00/0.80).

Combined Adjustment

Combining the expected incident and completion rates results in a contacted sample that is 2.77 (2.22 × 1.25) times the final sample size requirement. In general,

$$\text{Initial sample size} = \frac{\text{Final sample size}}{\text{Incidence rate} \times \text{Completion rate}}$$

The number of units that must be sampled is equal to the initial sample size. The following example illustrates a variety of variables that can be used to qualify potential respondents. It also shows that as the number of qualifying variables increases, the incidence rate will fall.

response rate
It is the number of completed interviews divided by the number of eligible respondents in the sample.

Another rate that is of interest in surveys is the **response rate,** which is the number of completed interviews divided by the number of eligible respondents in the sample. Thus, it is calculated as follows:

$$\text{Response rate} = \frac{\text{Number of completed interviews}}{\text{Number of eligible respondents in the sample}}$$

Tools such as Answers Research's (www.answersresearch.com/calculators/response.htm) response-rate calculator are available to determine the completion rate for studies in

RESEARCH IN ACTION

Targeting Women's Lips

When Lancôme, Paris (www.lancome.com) was conducting a survey to determine women's preferences for lip color, they defined the target population very precisely. The screening criteria for a respondent to be included in the survey were: (1) female, (2) age 25 to 55 years, and (3) annual household income of at least $30,000. Having three qualifying factors resulted in a highly targeted sample, although it boosted the sample size because of a much lower incidence rate. Survey results showed that these women were looking for a lipstick that provided more moisturizing comfort, a more even application and coverage, and less caking and feathering.

Based on these findings, Lancôme developed and introduced Rouge Attraction. It was a transfer-resistant lipstick that won't smudge off when you eat, drink, or kiss, and it filled a large gap in consumer product needs. Rouge Attraction was positioned for women who want an ultra long-wearing lipstick with improved comfort and was well received in the marketplace. This success led to the introduction of Rouge Sensation, a multi-sensation lip color.[4]

Estimating monthly household expenses on department store shopping can be done only with a certain degree of confidence.

which data is still being collected. Surveysite (www.surveysite.com) offers response rate statistics for its online surveys. In this manner, clients of Surveysite can readily monitor the progress of research in the field, as the example below illustrates.

Online Sampling Adjustments

The sample size for online surveys generally exceeds that determined statistically. The reason for this is that the marginal cost of collecting and analyzing larger samples is low.

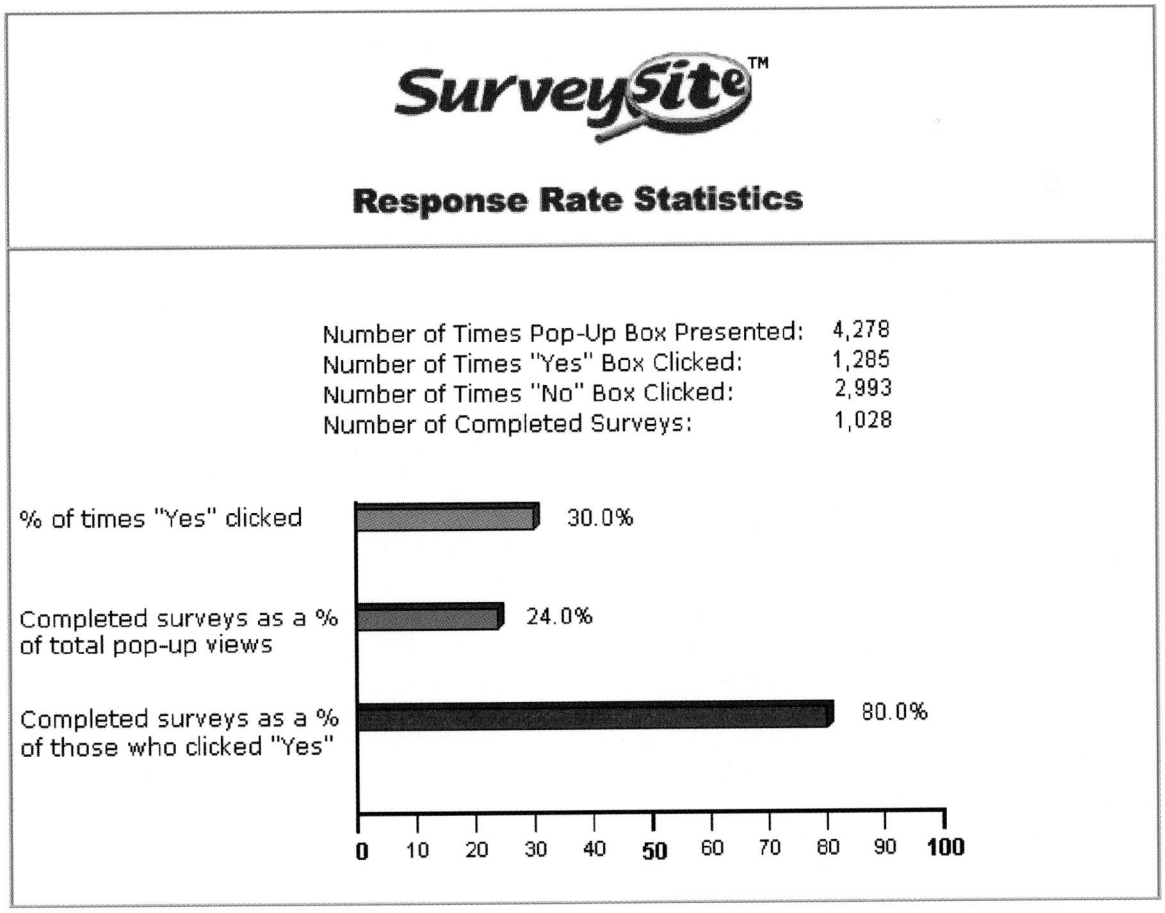

RESEARCH IN ACTION

The (Data)World of Sampling for Online Research

DataWorld Research Inc. (www.surveys-online.com) is a marketing firm specializing in online marketing research and surveying. Other services include traditional telephone surveys and face-to-face interviews.

When possible, the firm uses much larger sample sizes than those determined by statistical methods. It has developed an innovative way for clients to control respondent selection when conducting an online business-to-business survey. Through the use of an "alert postcard," which includes a respondent password, DataWorld can limit the distribution of the survey to a select group of respondents within the client's target group. In essence, the firm has complete control over who will participate, which is normally difficult to achieve when conducting online surveys. This allows traditional sampling techniques to be implemented in the Internet environment. In addition to sample control, DataWorld provides incentives to respondents, such as gift certificates or product giveaways, to improve the response rate.

Moreover, larger samples permit a more detailed level of analysis at the subgroup or segment level. Some of the biggest challenges in online research are the abilities to generate a truly random sample that is representative of the target population and to increase the response rate. This is more problematic when conducting a consumer survey. In the case of business surveys, however, these sampling limitations can be overcome, as illustrated by DataWorld Research.

Summary Illustration Using the Opening Vignette

The statistical approaches to determining sample size based on confidence intervals may involve estimation of the mean (e.g., mean hours spent watching TV or using online services) or proportion (e.g., proportion of respondents using online services). Statistical calculation of sample size requires specification of precision level, confidence level, and population standard deviation. In the opening vignette, only the precision level (about 5 percent) was disclosed. Therefore, we could not determine whether the sample size of 262 in the America Online survey was adequate and whether the conclusion reached was warranted. However, we know that the sample size required to estimate a proportion near 0.5 with 95 percent confidence level and 5 percent precision level is 385. The sample size in the opening vignette falls substantially short of this mark.

International Marketing Research

When conducting marketing research in foreign countries, statistical estimation of sample size may be difficult because estimates of the population variance may be unavailable.

EXPERIENTIAL LEARNING

The Ultimate Rocky Mountain Destination

Skiing is a popular winter sport in the United States.

1. Visit Ski.Com's Web site (www.ski.com) and conduct an Internet search using a search engine and your library's online database to obtain information on the incidence (proportion) of people who ski every season.
2. In a survey of the general population on skiing, what should be the sample size for 95 percent confidence level and 5 percent precision level? As an estimate of the population proportion, use the proportion you have determined in Step 1.
3. Using the incidence rate you have determined and a completion rate of 50 percent, what should be the number of initial contacts to achieve a final sample size of 500 skiers using random-digit dialing?
4. As the director of marketing for Vail Cascade Resort in Colorado, "the ultimate Rocky Mountain destination," what information would you want for formulating marketing strategies to increase your sales?

RESEARCH IN ACTION

The Chinese Take to the Sky

The airline industry seems to have a strong and promising market in China. Spending billions of dollars, China is trying to satisfy a surging demand for air travel and catch up with the rest of the world. The domestic airline traffic is growing as much as 30 percent a year in some markets. Strong economic growth, surging foreign trade, and a revival in tourism have helped to fuel this boom. China is making rapid progress in increasing its fleet and training pilots. While in 1984, the country had only 15 commercial aircraft–mostly outdated Soviet-made models–the fleet is now many times as large, with aircraft from Boeing, McDonnell Douglas, and Airbus. The Civil Aviation Administration of China (once dubbed the "Chinese Airlines Always Cancel") has granted much flexibility to the individual airlines.

Yet, for millions of Chinese, air travel is a relatively new experience, and many more millions have never flown. Hence, Chinese preferences for air travel are likely to exhibit much more variability as compared to those of Americans. In a survey by American Airlines to compare the attitudes toward air travel in China and the United States, the sample size of the Chinese survey would have to be larger than the American survey in order for the two survey estimates to have comparable precision.[5]

Hence, the sample size is often determined by qualitative considerations, as discussed in Chapter 12. When statistical estimation of sample size is attempted, the differences in estimates of population variance should be recognized and factored in if possible. For example, consumer preferences for certain products may be relatively heterogeneous in markets where those products have been newly introduced. Thus, it may be a mistake to assume that the population variance is the same or to use the same sample size across countries as the Chinese Take to the Sky example shows.

Technology and Marketing Research

Computer-based systems are available to determine the sample size for various sampling techniques. For simple applications, appropriate sample size formulas can be programmed using spreadsheet programs. The researcher specifies the desired precision level, confidence level, and population variance. The program then determines the appropriate sample size for the study. By incorporating the cost of each sampling unit, the sample size can be adjusted based on budget considerations.

Several marketing research firms supply sample design software and services, including statistical determination of sample sizes and estimation of sample statistics. Survey Sampling, Inc. (www.ssisamples.com) has a line of sampling products. Their Contact and Cooperation Rate Adjustment software statistically adjusts sample sizes by taking into account the expected contact and cooperation rates.

Ethics in Marketing Research

The sample size is one of the major determinants of cost in a marketing research project. It may seem that if the sample size is statistically determined, this procedure is free from ethical conflicts. This may not be true, however. As this chapter has emphasized, the sample size is directly proportional to the variance of the variable. Estimates of the population variance are based on small pilot studies, related research, and the judgment of the researcher. Because judgment is involved, the researcher has the ethical responsibility to not use large estimates of the population variance simply to increase the cost of the project by

RESEARCH IN ACTION

Surveys Serve Up Elections

The release of political polling results during an election has been strongly criticized as manipulative and unethical. Critics have claimed that the general public is mislead by these results. Polling results released before an election are thought to discourage voters from casting votes for candidates that are clearly trailing. Prediction of election results on election night has come under even harsher criticism. For example in the Bush versus Kerry 2004 presidential election, polls by NBC and the Associated Press had projected the winner in some states when polling was still open in several West Coast states. Opponents of this practice feel that this predisposes voters to vote for the projected winner or that it may even discourage voter turnout if a race appears to be decided. Not only are the effects of such projections criticized, but frequently, the accuracy of the projections is questionable as well. Although voters may be told a candidate has a certain percentage of the votes within plus or minus 1 percent, the confidence interval may be much larger, depending on the sample size.[6]

inflating the sample size. Using the sample size formula, we can see that increasing the standard deviation by 20 percent, for example, will increase the sample size by 44 percent. This practice is clearly unethical.

Furthermore, the researcher may be faced with ethical dilemmas when the sample standard deviation varies widely from that assumed. In this case, the confidence interval will be larger than required if the actual sample standard deviation turns out to be much larger than that used to estimate the sample size. If this happens, the researcher should disclose the larger confidence interval to the client and jointly arrive at a corrective action. The ethical ramifications of miscommunicating the confidence intervals of survey estimates based on statistical samples are underscored in the case of political polling.

WHAT WOULD *YOU* DO?

Procter & Gamble: Taking a Gamble on Core Brands

The Situation

A. G. Lafley, CEO of Procter & Gamble (P&G), turned around the consumer goods giant after taking the top job in 2000. He has refocused P&G on its big brands, including Tide, Pampers, and Crest. Lafley believes there is still tremendous growth in the core brands. He has made one thing clear: P&G's stodgy corporate culture is gone for good.

In May of 2001, Procter & Gamble, Inc. acquired Moist Mates, "America's first moist bath tissue on a roll." Holding the market for the past 20 years with their Charmin bath tissue, P&G found that a significant number of consumers already try to use some type of wet cleaning system. "In fact, Charmin's research reveals that more than 60 percent of adult consumers have tried some alternative form of moist cleaning including: sprinkling water on dry toilet paper, using baby wipes, or wetting a washcloth." With that in mind, the purchase of Moist Mates became a strategic move in the market. P&G took the product and changed the name to Charmin Fresh Mates on a roll to go hand-in-hand with the popular Charmin dry tissue. The biggest problem consumers had felt was that their makeshift cleaning methods were inconvenient. P&G's marketing research showed that the familiarity of brand name, convenience, and easy-to-use wet tissue on a roll appealed to the consumer. "Together, these products offer consumers a convenient way to choose dry, choose moist, or choose both," said Wayne Randall, global franchise manager for Charmin. Charmin Fresh Mates helped bring in more than $40 million in 2004 for P&G, and sales keep increasing. As of 2005, Charmin and other P&G products were available in 140 countries around the world, and the company knows its products are "fresh."

Yet, there is some question as to whether Charmin and Charmin Fresh Mates are perceived as complementary or competing products.

The Marketing Research Decision

1. P&G would like to conduct periodic surveys to determine consumer perceptions and preferences for bath tissues, including Charmin and Charmin Fresh Mates. How should the sample size be determined? Check as many as are applicable.
   a. Using the confidence interval approach: means
   b. Using the confidence interval approach: proportions
   c. Based on sample size used in similar studies
   d. Guided by budget constraints
   e. Set at 500
2. Discuss the role of the sample size you recommend in enabling A. G. Lafley to determine consumer perceptions and preferences for bath tissues, including Charmin and Charmin Fresh Mates.

The Marketing Management Decision

1. To further increase the market share of Charmin and Charmin Fresh Mates, A. G. Lafley should (check as many as are applicable):
   a. Package Charmin and Charmin Fresh Mates together
   b. Lower the prices of Charmin and Charmin Fresh Mates
   c. Increase advertising expenditures on Charmin and Charmin Fresh Mates
   d. Offer "buy one, get the other at half price" promotion
   e. Promote Charmin products aggressively
2. Discuss how the marketing management-decision action that you recommend to A. G. Lafley is influenced by the sample size that you suggested earlier and by the findings of that research.

What A. G. Lafley Did

Lafley decided to promote Charmin products aggressively. P&G introduced the Charmin Pottypalooza tour, which provides bathroom facilities with Charmin products. Charmin's in-bathroom marketing reached 30 million consumers in 2002. Research also shows a 14 percent increase in Charmin sales among those consumers who have used the P&G facilities, leading the company to roll out a second Pottypalooza unit for 2003. This event has given Charmin the ultimate captive audience and integrated marketing opportunity. People lined up outside the bathrooms are entertained by a Charmin bear, and inside, they see a nonstop loop of TV ads featuring the iconic bear.[7]

Summary

The statistical approaches to determining sample size are based on confidence intervals. These approaches may involve the estimation of the mean or proportion. When estimating the mean or the proportion, determination of sample size using the confidence interval approach requires the specification of precision level, confidence level, and population standard deviation. The sample size determined statistically represents the final or net sample size that must be achieved. The initial sample size must be much larger to account for incidence rates and completion rates in order to deliver the final sample size.

The statistical estimation of sample size is even more complicated in international marketing research as the population variance may differ from one country to the next. Several computer programs are available for statistically estimating the sample size and making adjustments for incidence and completion rates. The preliminary estimation of population variance for the purpose of determining the sample size also has ethical ramifications.

Key Terms and Concepts

Normal distribution, 355
Parameter, 355
Statistic, 355
Precision level, 355
Confidence interval, 356
Confidence level, 356
Random sampling error, 356
Sampling distribution, 356
Statistical inference, 356
Central limit theorem, 356
Standard error, 357
***z* value,** 357
Incidence rate, 365
Completion rate, 366
Response rate, 366

Suggested Cases and Video Cases

Cases

2.4 Bloomingdale's **2.5 Burger King** **4.1 Boeing** **4.2 Gucci**

Video Cases

3.1 AFLAC **4.1 Subaru** **4.2 Marriott**

Additional cases and video cases are available in the Instructor's Manual and on the instructor and student Web sites.

Live Research: Conducting a Marketing Research Project

1. Discuss the qualitative and statistical considerations involved in determining the sample size.
2. Illustrate the confidence interval approach (mean or proportion) to calculate the sample size of the project, even though the sample size may have been determined based on qualitative considerations.
3. Discuss the expected incidence and completion rates and the initial sample size.
4. The sampling technique and the sample size should be discussed and approved by the client.

Acronyms

The statistical considerations involved in determining the sample size may be summarized by the acronym SIZE:

S ampling distribution
I nterval (confidence)
Z value
E stimation of population standard deviation

Review Questions

1. Define the sampling distribution.
2. What is the standard error of the mean?
3. Define a confidence interval.
4. What is the procedure for constructing a confidence interval around a mean?
5. How do the degree of confidence and the degree of precision differ?
6. Describe the procedure for determining the sample size necessary to estimate a population mean given the degree of precision and confidence and a known population variance. After the sample is selected, how is the confidence interval generated?
7. Describe the procedure for determining the sample size necessary to estimate a population mean when the degree of precision and confidence level are known but the population variance is unknown. After the sample is selected, how is the confidence interval generated?
8. How is the sample size affected when the absolute precision with which a population mean is estimated is doubled?
9. How is the sample size affected when the degree of confidence with which a population mean is estimated is increased from 95 percent to 99 percent?
10. Describe the procedure for determining the sample size necessary to estimate a population proportion given the degree of precision and confidence. After the sample is selected, how is the confidence interval generated?
11. How can the researcher ensure that the generated confidence interval will be no larger than the desired interval when estimating a population proportion?

Applied Problems

1. Using Table 2 of the Appendix of Statistical Tables, calculate the probability that
   a. z is less than 1.48
   b. z is greater than 1.90
   c. z is between 1.48 and 1.90
   d. z is between −1.48 and 1.90
2. What is the value of z if
   a. 60% of all values of z are larger
   b. 10% of all values of z are larger
   c. 68.26% of all possible z values (symmetrically distributed around the mean) are to be contained in this interval
3. The management of a local restaurant wants to determine the average monthly amount spent by households in fancy restaurants. Management wants to be 95 percent confident of the findings and does not want the error to exceed plus or minus $5.
   a. After the survey was conducted, the average expenditure was found to be $90.30 and the standard deviation was $45. Construct a 95 percent confidence interval.
   b. What sample size would have resulted in a standard deviation of $45?
4. To determine the effectiveness of the advertising campaign for a new videocassette recorder, management would like to know what percentage of the households are aware of the new brand. The advertising agency thinks that this figure is as high as 70 percent. Management would like a 95 percent

confidence interval and a margin of error no greater than plus or minus 2 percent.

a. What sample size should be used for this study?

b. Suppose that management wanted to be 99 percent confident but could tolerate an error of plus or minus 3 percent. How would the sample size change?

5. Assuming that $n = 100$ and $\sigma = 5$, compute the standard error of the mean.

6. Using a spread sheet (*e.g.*, EXCEL) software package, program the formulas for determining the sample size under the various approaches.

7. Solve Problems 3 through 5 using the programs that you have developed.

8. Visit the Gallup organization Web site (www.gallup.com). Identify some of the surveys recently completed by the Gallup organization. What were the sample sizes, and how were they determined in these surveys?

Group Discussion

1. "Quantitative considerations are more important than qualitative considerations in determining the sample size." Discuss this statement as a small group. Alternatively, split a group into two smaller subgroups. One subgroup develops arguments for this statement, the other against.

2. Discuss the various options available for estimating incidence rates.

APPENDIX 13A The Normal Distribution

In this appendix, we provide a brief overview of the normal distribution and the use of the normal distribution table. The normal distribution is used in calculating the sample size, and it serves as the basis for classical statistical inference. Many continuous phenomena follow the normal distribution or can be approximated by it. The normal distribution can, likewise, be used to approximate many discrete probability distributions.[1]

The normal distribution has some important theoretical properties. It is bell-shaped and symmetrical in appearance. Its measures of central tendency (mean, median, and mode) are all identical. Its associated random variable has an infinite range ($-\infty < x < +\infty$).

The normal distribution is defined by the population mean μ and population standard deviation σ. Since an infinite number of combinations of μ and σ exist, an infinite number of normal distributions exist and an infinite number of tables would be required. By standardizing the data, we need only one table, such as Table 2 given in the Appendix of Statistical Tables. Standardization is the process of rescaling data to have a mean of 0 and a standard deviation of 1. Any normal random variable X can be converted to a standardized normal random variable z by the formula:

$$z = \frac{X - \mu}{\sigma}$$

Note that the random variable z is always normally distributed with a mean of 0 and a standard deviation of 1. The normal probability tables are generally used for two purposes: (1) finding probabilities corresponding to known values of X or z and (2) finding values of X or z corresponding to known probabilities. We will discuss each of these uses.

Finding Probabilities Corresponding to Known Values

Suppose Figure 13A.1 represents the distribution of the number of engineering contracts an engineering firm receives per year. Because the data span the entire history of the firm, Figure 13A.1 represents the population. Therefore, the probabilities or proportion of area under the curve must add up to 1.0. The vice president of marketing wishes to determine the probability that the number of contracts received next year will be between 50 and 55. The answer can be determined by using Table 2 of the Appendix of Statistical Tables.

[1] This material is drawn from Mark L. Berenson, David M. Levine, and Timothy Krehbiel, *Basic Business Statistics: Concepts and Applications,* 8th ed. (Upper Saddle River, NJ: Prentice Hall, 2002).

Figure 13A.1

Finding Probabilities Corresponding to Known Values

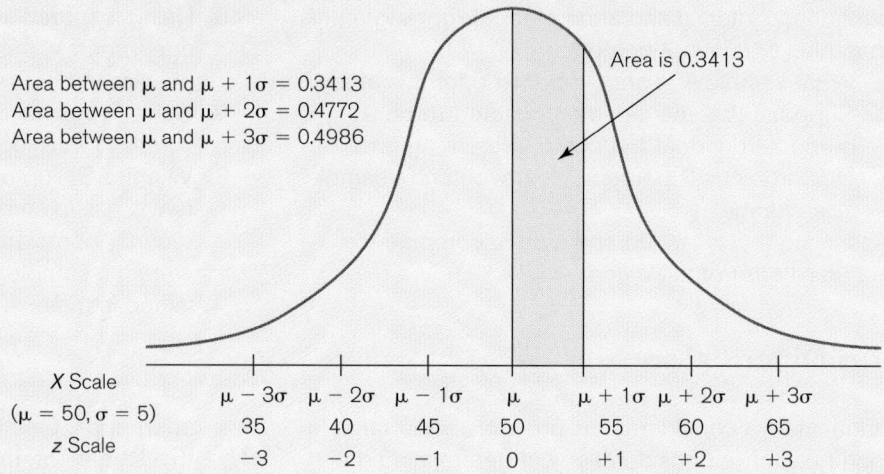

Table 2 of the Appendix of Statistical Tables gives the probability or area under the standardized normal curve from the mean (zero) to the standardized value of interest (z). Only positive entries of z are listed in the table. For a symmetrical distribution with zero mean, the area from the mean to $+z$ (that is, z standard deviations above the mean) is identical to the area from the mean to $-z$ (z standard deviations below the mean).

Note that the difference between 50 and 55, which is 5, corresponds to a difference in z values of 1.00 (1.00 – 0.00). Note that to use Table 2, all z values must be recorded to two decimal places. To read the probability or area under the curve from the mean to $z = +1.00$, scan down the z column of Table 2 until the z value of interest (in tenths) is located. In this case, stop in the row $z = 1.00$. Then, read across this row until you intersect the column containing the hundredth place of the z value. Thus, in Table 2, the tabulated probability for $z = 1.00$ corresponds to the intersection of the row $z = 1.00$ with the column $z = 0.00$. This probability is 0.3413. As shown in Figure 13A.1, the probability is 0.3413 that the number of contracts received by the firm next year will be between 50 and 55. It can also be concluded that the probability is 0.6826 (2×0.3413) or 68.26 percent that the number of contracts received next year will be between 45 and 55.

This result could be generalized to show that for any normal distribution, the probability is 0.6826 that a randomly selected item will fall within ± 1 standard deviation above or below the mean. Also, it can be verified from Table 2 that there is a 0.9544 probability that any randomly selected normally distributed observation will fall within 2 standard deviations above or below the mean and that there is a 0.9973 probability the observation will fall within ± 3 standard deviations above or below the mean.

Finding Values Corresponding to Known Probabilities

Suppose the vice president of marketing wishes to determine how many contracts must come in so that this number represents 5 percent of the contracts expected for the year. If 5 percent of the contracts have come in, 95 percent of the contracts have yet to come. As shown in Figure 13A.2, this 95 percent can be broken down into two parts: contracts above the mean (that is, 50 percent) and contracts between the mean and the desired z value (that is, 45 percent). The desired z value can be determined from Table 2 since the area under the normal curve from the standardized mean, zero, to this z must be 0.4500. From Table 2, we search for the area or probability 0.4500. The closest value is 0.4495 or 0.4505. For 0.4495, we see that the z value corresponding to the particular z row (1.6) and z column (0.04) is 1.64. However, the z value must be recorded as negative (that is, $z = -1.64$) because it is below the standardized mean of zero. Similarly, the z value corresponding to the area of 0.4505 is −1.65. Because 0.4500 is midway between 0.4495 and 0.4505, the appropriate z value could be midway between the two z values and estimated as −1.645. The corresponding X value can then be calculated from the standardization formula as follows:

$$X = \mu + z\sigma$$

or $$X = 50 + (-1.645) \times 5 = 41.775$$

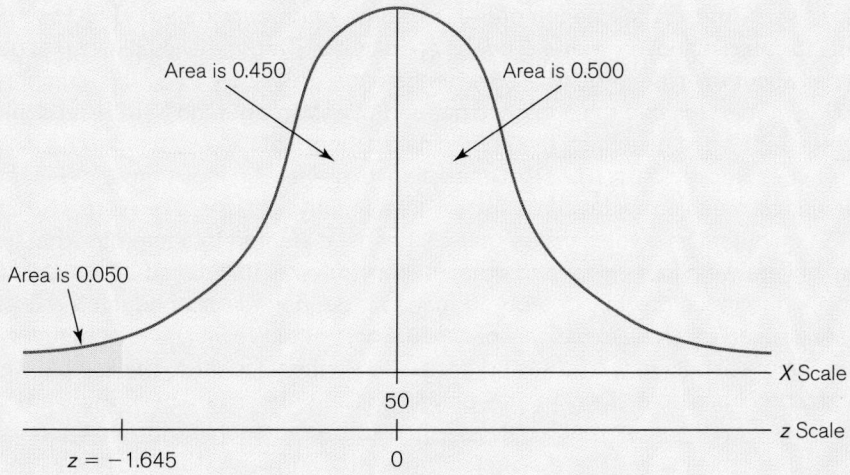

Figure 13A.2
Finding Values Corresponding to Known Probabilities

Suppose the vice president wanted to determine the interval in which 95 percent of the contracts for next year are expected to lie. As can be seen from Figure 13A.3, the corresponding z values are 1.96. This corresponds to X values of 50 ± (1.96) 5, or 40.2 and 59.8. This range represents the 95 percent confidence interval.

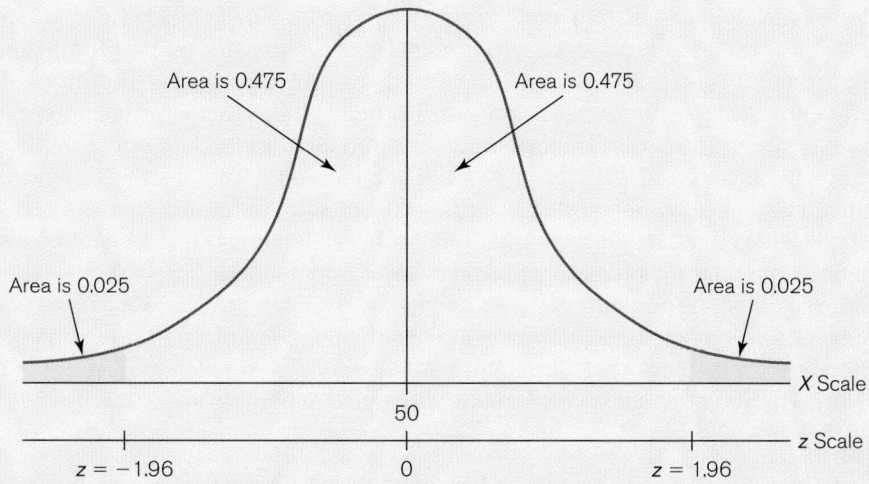

Figure 13A.3
Finding Values Corresponding to Known Probabilities: Confidence Interval

CASES FOR PART 2

CASE 2.1

Maxfli: Going for the Long Ball

For decades, Maxfli (www.maxfli.com) has been one of the top names in quality golf equipment. On December 31, 2002, TaylorMade-Adidas Golf acquired Maxfli to boost its market share in the golf ball segment from less than 1 percent to 7.5 percent. Maxfli produces golf balls, clubs, and other golf accessories. In its early stages, Maxfli's approach to the industry was similar to others: produce good products marketed through the traditional channels (e.g., pro shops, golf specialty stores) and use PGA professionals to market its products. This was a standard formula, but one that was challenged in the 1990s as more and more companies entered the industry. By 1998, Maxfli discovered that its growth in market share dropped below par. It lost sight of its target markets and the understanding of what people in those markets needed. Maxfli began conducting exploratory research because it was unclear as to what direction to steer the company.

Maxfli began exploratory research by conducting focus groups to uncover the motivations behind golf ball purchases. It wanted to understand how consumers identified golf balls (e.g., by brand name, manufacturer, or some unique identifier). The focus-group research indicated that every golf ball needs an identifier. This identifier allows one golfer to tell another about the type of golf balls he or she uses. The ability to do this is important to most golfers. "This signaled to us that we needed to not only get the Maxfli brand into people's minds but also to give them the nomenclature hook that allows them to be inside the games," Dennis Rooke, Maxfli's head of marketing, explains. The focus groups also revealed that golf was as much a mental challenge as it was a physical one. Therefore, Maxfli's goal became to quiet that little voice inside golfer's heads. It wanted to figure out what types of products golfers were looking for and present them in a way that eased their state of mind.

Following the focus groups, in order to research deeper, Maxfli conducted a telephone survey. Maxfli used a Synovate national panel as a cost-effective means to generate a representative sample of golfers who could be accessed via the telephone. The sample was then stratified by purchase points, where they played golf, and other variables. There are several different types of golfers and each category had to be represented for the findings to be meaningful and conclusive. "The research showed that although many golfers were quality oriented, there was an even bigger segment that could be called the fashion crowd of golf." Maxfli then wanted to find out if its brand fit the needs of the so-called "fashion crowd."

Based on the research findings, Maxfli determined that it should offer all levels of golf balls and position its products with a youthful attitude. Each ball had its own identity so that it could be discussed among golfers. In golf, "the ball you choose says a lot about you." Maxfli used exploratory research in the form of focus groups and descriptive research in the form of a telephone survey to make sure its line of golf balls met consumer needs.

In 2004, Maxfli undertook focus groups and surveys and found that the market for high-performance golf balls consisted of two distinct segments. Therefore, Maxfli decided to split its high-performance golf ball portfolio into two lines with different prices and target market segments. Revolution, with three SKUs (stock keeping units) has a price range of $35 to $40 per dozen. Noodle (it's long and soft), also with three SKUs, has a manufacturer suggested retail price (MSRP) of $25. D-Tec with two SKUs rounds the golf ball lines. The balls, targeting different skill levels, are sure to be a success with the reliance on marketing research to which Maxfli is committed.

For Maxfli, creating products that met consumer needs is the first step in maintaining a leadership position in the golf industry. Maxfli is continually looking for the edge that will pull customers to its products. Maxfli has been successful at solidifying its place in the market through good consumer research and creative marketing approaches.

Questions

1. What was the research design adopted by Maxfli in determining a direction for the company? Was it appropriate?
2. Discuss the role of qualitative research in uncovering the motivations behind golf ball purchases. Are focus groups the most appropriate technique for this purpose?
3. Is a telephone survey the most appropriate method for determining the preferences of golfers for golf balls? If not, what survey method would you recommend for this purpose?
4. Can the observation method be used? If yes, which observation method would you recommend and why?
5. Discuss the role of the Internet in Maxfli's future research efforts.

References

1. "News: Newswire," *Brandweek*, (March 8, 2004): 7.
2. Ross Kerber, "Adidas-Salomon Ups Ante for Sports Equipment Maker Top-Flite Golf," *Knight Ridder Tribune Business News*, (July 22, 2003): 1.

CASE 2.2

Can the Caddie Make a Comeback?

At one time, the Cadillac was the ultimate representation of American affluence and success. Unfortunately for General Motors (GM), Cadillac's customer base is aging. With the aging of its customer base, Cadillac sales are slipping. Record sales of over 350,000

Cadillacs in 1978 slipped to just 155,000 cars in 1999. However, the Caddie launched a comeback. After losing ground to imports every year for at least a decade, Cadillac sales were up 16 percent in 2002 from the year before, to 199,748 vehicles, according to WardsAuto.com. BMW sales rose only 8 percent, while Lexus was up 4.5 percent and Mercedes climbed 3 percent. Although Cadillac improved in quality, it was still lagging behind competitors like Lexus. In 2004, Lexus won top honors for the 10th consecutive year in the annual J. D. Power and Associates survey of long-term vehicle dependability. Cadillac faced many other challenges in trying to regain lost market share.

The average age of a Cadillac buyer is 64. The average age of the entry-level luxury-car owner, someone who is buying an upscale car for the first time, with a starting price of approximately $30,000, is 46. Cadillac is traditionally not an entry-level automobile. One reason Cadillac has faltered is because it can't make cars that appeal to anyone under 60. When drivers think Cadillac, they inevitably think "old," not "with it." In order to combat the loss of the Cadillac division, GM is trying to attract younger buyers, including women and minorities. One effort to do this is focused on producing smaller, sleeker cars; however, this effort must be tailored so as not to alienate the established customers. The first efforts set forth to attract a younger clientele failed miserably with the introduction of the Cadillac Cimarron. In order to prevent a repeat of this, Cadillac hired 35-year-old Joe Kennedy as general director of marketing and product planning.

Kennedy's new plans formally began when Cadillac unveiled the Catera, a small (by Cadillac standards) luxury car. The Catera is a clone of the European Opel Omega MV6, which is produced by GM's Adam Opel AG unit. The Catera is priced as an entry-level luxury car, ranging between $30,000 and $40,000. With the Catera, Cadillac hoped to build a new identity. Even the name, Catera, is new, which was coined by a GM employee.

Cadillac attempted to emphasize the benefits of the vehicle itself, rather than focus on the name of Cadillac alone. Once the car is established, GM hopes to more closely associate it with Cadillac. The difference between the Cimarron and the Catera is that the Catera is based on a luxury model, while the Cimarron was basically an up-scaled pedestrian car. Even so, the success of Cadillac may be a thing of the past. In its hay days, Cadillac stood for the "American Dream."

The decline of the Cadillac can be directly linked to two incidents in the recent past. The first is the oil embargo of the early 1970s. As gas prices rose, the Cadillac became less and less popular with cost-conscious consumers. The small car became king, and the large car became out of vogue. However, the real blow came in 1981 when U.S. automakers persuaded the U.S. government to limit the number of vehicles Japan could sell in the United States. The result was that Japan shifted exports to the United States from low-cost models, to higher-profit, higher-cost luxury models. The invasion of the Japanese luxury car had begun. Additionally, BMW became the symbol for yuppie success during the 80s, causing Cadillac's market share to dip from 32.3 percent in 1978 to 16.5 percent in 1999.

One reason for Cadillac's slide is that during the 60s and 70s there was little direct foreign competition. As small cars became popular, GM failed to respond to these changing values. Meanwhile, younger customers were enticed by the sleek engineering of the European luxury cars and the new Japanese models. Luxury brands, such as Mercedes and BMW, started at the high side and used their success to spin off smaller, less pricey models. They had a distinct advantage: just one brand to carry the flag. Cadillac's problem is that it has too many brothers and sisters. If Cadillac spun off smaller models, it would rob from Buick and Pontiac. One point still in GM's favor is that customer satisfaction for new Cadillacs is high. Cadillac consistently scores high marks for quality and power.

The goal of GM is to reincarnate the Cadillac division by tearing it down and rebuilding it. Additionally, Cadillac plans to make its cars even more luxurious, hoping to rival top-of-the-line Mercedes' models. There is also a push to gain more sales in the women's market. Currently, Cadillac sells 30 percent of its cars to women; however, they hope to get that figure up to at least 37 percent. To this end, Cadillac is more actively targeting the female consumer in its advertising and marketing. In addition, Cadillac is employing more top-level female executives in the development of new models. Women want smaller cars, with more safety devices and more comfortable interiors. Cadillac also plans on exporting more cars to European, Chinese, and Japanese markets.

On June 29, 2004, it was announced by a company official that Cadillac, a global symbol of big American cars, will add a British touch by offering models with the steering wheel on the right side as the GM brand tries to break into new markets. Right-hand drive versions of Cadillac's cars are a key for the luxury brand to crack the markets of Britain, Hong Kong, South Africa, Japan, and Australia, John Howell, Cadillac's director of global brand development, said in an interview. Cadillac plans to increase sales in Europe to 10,000 vehicles annually by the end of 2010, up from 791 in 2003. While doubts remain about the Cadillac division, the management hopes that putting the steering wheel on the right side will right the sales and market share and help the Caddie make a comeback.

Questions

1. Identify the management-decision problem facing Cadillac as it seeks to revive the division and regain market share.
2. Define the marketing research problem.
3. Identify sources of secondary data for luxury cars.
4. Search the Internet to determine the total number of cars sold for each year for the past five years by Cadillac, Lincoln, Lexus, Mercedes, and BMW. Do you discover any trends?
5. What role can qualitative research play in helping Cadillac revive its sales and market share? Which qualitative research techniques would you recommend and why?
6. If a survey is to be conducted to determine consumer preferences for luxury cars, which survey method should be used and why?
7. What role can observation methods play in helping Cadillac redesign its models? Which observation method, if any, should be used?
8. Would you use Likert, semantic differential, or Stapel scales to obtain consumers' evaluations of Cadillac and competing brands on important attributes?
9. Design a questionnaire to obtain consumers' evaluations of Cadillac and competing brands on important attributes.
10. What sampling technique should be used to select survey respondents?

References

1. (www.generalmotors.com).
2. "GM Takes Cadillac to Britain Asia. With Eye on Hong Kong, England and Eventually China, Cadillac Puts a Steering Wheel On the Right," (www.money.cnn.com) (June 29, 2004).
3. "Lexus Nets Quality Award—Again," (www.money.cnn.com) (June 29, 2004).

CASE 2.3

Research Prompts HCA-Healthcare to Re-evaluate Its Internet Focus

As of 2005, HCA-Healthcare Corp., formerly known as Columbia-HCA Healthcare Corp., is the largest U.S. hospital chain. HCA owns and operates approximately 200 hospitals and other health-care facilities in 24 states, England, and Switzerland. In addition, it operates more than 80 freestanding surgery centers. HCA's Internet site was created in May 1995 as a channel to promote the company and its health-care information. It averaged 400 hits per month the first few months it was online. However, a change in the company's Internet focus led to a much greater emphasis on Web-based information. As of 2005, in addition to HCA's main Web site (www.hcahealthcare.com), each of HCA's hospitals had its own Web site with content that included local information about services, technologies, and health programs through an agreement with HealthGate Data Corporation.

The change in focus was spurred by secondary research initiatives conducted to determine the demand for information over the Internet. For example, a study by FIND/SVP using focus groups, Internet users, and a national telephone survey revealed that health-care information was the seventh-largest category of information requested by Internet users. FIND/SVP is a consulting and research company that annually produces a large number of syndicated research reports. Organizations in the health-care industry can access studies like these from FIND/SVP, order market and industry studies done by FIND/SVP, or order customized research.

Based upon the information in an Internet survey that FIND/SVP did soon after HCA set up its homepage, HCA saw the opportunity to be more than just an advertising or messaging site. The company reevaluated its Internet strategy and decided to create a health-information resource with a focus on the Internet user's health-information needs.

Centering its consumer Internet strategy on the theory that the best brand in health care is the local hospital, HCA is steering clear of the drkoop.coms of the world. Instead, the Nashville-based company is equipping its local hospitals with World Wide Web site content tailored to meet the needs of each community. By working to connect clinical content to localized information and hospital services, HCA is attempting to make information more useful. According to HCA's Web guru, executing this strategy is what will make the hospital giant a winner in the Internet game. "The winner in this space will combine world-class health care content from the Web and integrate it with local information about services, technologies, and health programs," says Marty Paslick, HCA's vice president of Internet strategy.

Users of the Web site include patients, consumers, physicians, vendors, employers, and clinicians. The site allows HCA to provide high-quality interactive content for the users. This interaction is in line with the organization's mission to provide a continuum of cost-effective, high-quality health care. The HCA homepage includes interactive opportunities, information about the organization, contests and games, announcements of special programs and events, gifts and products (such as flowers that users can order), information on the latest medical research, health tips, e-mail links for comments and questions, and a survey that users can complete concerning their information needs.

E-mail and surveys are means of ongoing data collection. Tracking and measurement of the Web site provides additional data related to hits, time of day, day of week, domains seeking access, and so forth. This information allows HCA to offer online products and services targeted and customized to users. By researching and responding to market needs, HCA has been able to expand its original Internet project into a national information resource.

Questions

1. What data can HCA collect from visitors to its Web site?
2. Are surveys posted to an Internet Web site, such as HCA's, the best method of obtaining information about consumers' health-care needs? Why or why not?
3. Devise the following scales to measure users' overall satisfaction with the health-care services provided by HCA:
   a. Likert scale
   b. Semantic differential scale
   c. Stapel scale
   d. Binary or dichotomous scale
4. Discuss the sampling problems associated with recruiting visitors to HCA's Web site as respondents to a health-care survey.

References

1. (www.hcahealthcare.com) and (www.findsvp.com).
2. "The Tech 20: Marty Paslick," *Nashville Business Journal*, 20(17), (April 23, 2004): A10.

CASE 2.4

Bloomingdale's: Inviting the Bloom into the Store

Federated Department Stores, Inc. operates full-line department stores under the names of Macy's (East and West), Bloomingdale's, Bon-Macy's, Burdines-Macy's, Goldsmith's-Macy's, Lazarus-Macy's, Macy's Home Store, and Rich's-Macy's. As of 2004, the company operates more than 450 stores in 34 states, Guam, and Puerto Rico and sells a wide range of merchandise including apparel and accessories for men, women, and children; cosmetics; home furnishings; and other consumer goods. The company also operates direct-mail catalog businesses under the name Bloomingdale's by Mail and an electronic commerce business, which provides goods and services online under the name macys.com.

It is no secret that marketing emphasis should focus on satisfying customers' needs, but it is important to note that when it comes to customers, wants are considered needs. This is exactly why it is vital to the success of any business today to research and find out precisely what customers want. Bloomingdale's took these issues to heart when it developed its new customer-friendly design philosophy.

As part of the new philosophy, when planning the design of its new department store in Miami, Florida, Bloomingdale's looked to focus groups for input on the needs of customers. The focus groups revealed that the most frequent complaint focuses on the lack of lighting in Bloomingdale's department stores. The groups also brought to the design committee's attention the potential benefit of having natural light and artificial light in the store. Their claim was that when buying clothing it is very beneficial to be able to see what the articles of clothing will look like in both types of lighting, because different lighting can affect the way colors look.

The design committee took the suggestions of the focus groups into consideration and designed the new Miami location accordingly. This was accomplished through the use of a 220-foot facade made entirely out of glass. The glass is covered by a steel screen for protection, complying with the building codes of the area. Fortunately, the light gets through the metal because it is cloven and is, therefore, effective in letting light through the glass dome. As explained by architect Kevin Kennon, "The perforations are very small, like a fine sieve, and create a sense of transparency so that light can penetrate into the building." Not only does the steel screen protect the glass, but it also combats the glare from the southern sun, which protects the clothes from sun damage and creates a more efficient cooling environment.

Since the steel screen was required, artificial light was also necessary. This was not a setback since focus groups suggested both types of light. The control of the steel screen allowed the two types of lighting to blend. The final product was excellent. The glass windows and facade more than doubled the lighting of the other Bloomingdale's department stores, and the design committee was thrilled with the results. In fact, Creative Director Michael Wilkins said, "It's the first new Bloomingdale's store designed so that the introduction of natural light represents a logical progression for the customer from the outside into the store environment."

It is vital for businesses today to keep their customers' interests close in mind in almost every aspect of the business. Bloomingdale's took a big step forward by establishing the new customer-friendly design philosophy. By using the input of focus groups, the department store was able to address a problem it has faced for years: bad lighting. With the new design, Bloomingdale's created a user-friendly environment, inviting the bloom into the store.

Questions

1. Was Bloomingdale's correct in making changes in the store architecture and design based solely on the findings of focus groups? If not, what type of research design should have been adopted?
2. Identify possible sources of secondary data for information on department store sales.
3. What type of information available from syndicated firms would be useful for understanding consumer preferences for department stores?
4. Discuss the role of projective techniques in understanding consumers' preference for department stores.
5. If a survey is to be conducted for determining consumer preferences for department stores, which survey method should be used and why?
6. Design an experiment to measure the effectiveness of lighting in the newly designed Bloomingdale's store. Justify your selection of the experimental design you recommend.
7. Which primary type of scales would you use to measure preference for department stores? State your reasoning.

8. Design a questionnaire to determine consumer preferences and evaluations of the various department store chains operated by Federal Department Stores, Inc. as mentioned in this case.
9. Given the survey method you have selected in Question 5, what sampling technique should be used and why? Would a sample size of 500 be appropriate? Why or why not?

References

1. (www.bloomingdales.com) and (www.federated-fds.com).
2. "Bloomingdale's in 'Playful' Mood," *Home Textiles Today*, 25(37), (May 24, 2004): 2.
3. Emily Scardino, "Bloomies Fans Now 'Do Lunch' Downtown," *DSN Retailing Today*, 43(10), (May 17, 2004):4–6.

CASE 2.5

Burger King Is Frying to Become Number One in French Fries

As of 2005, the Burger King system operates more than 11,350 restaurants in all 50 states and in 58 countries and territories around the world. Ninety-one percent of Burger King restaurants are owned and operated by independent franchisees, many of them family-owned operations that have been in business for decades. For many years in a row, the number-two hamburger chain Burger King, beat out number-one McDonald's in taste tests of hamburgers, but has continuously finished second when it comes to French fries. McDonald's has a firm grasp on the best-tasting fry, and with French fries returning 80 cents on the dollar, McDonald's is not going to give up the spot easily. However, Burger King wants to become the French fry king and is willing to do whatever it takes to win over the fast-food customers.

Burger King began developing its new fry in 1996. Their market research showed that people wanted a fry that was crispy and would remain hot. Burger King envisioned that a crunchy fry would differentiate its fry from McDonald's and would help develop a loyal customer base in a price-sensitive market. The development team came up with 19 pages worth of fry specifications. These new fries were to each produce seven audible crunches and remain hot for more than 10 minutes (average previous time was seven minutes). At this time, a team of marketing executives was formed to investigate a starch-coated fry. While fries were cooked and tasted in test-kitchen conditions, most testers agreed that the coated fries held up to the specifications. Before introducing this fry to the market, each fry supplier had to be equipped with new equipment, and, at the same time, 300,000 Burger King managers had to be comfortable with the new operations and frying techniques.

Burger King introduced this new version of its fry to the market in 1998. Burger King spent a lot of money on the development of this product and set forth $70 million for ad campaigns featuring the new fry. Mr. Potato Head became the new spokesman for the fry and on Friday, January 2, 1998, Burger King introduced the new fry by handing out 15 million free orders of fries to the public. This day was declared "Free Fryday."

How did the new fry taste? "It tasted terrible," said the managers and customers across the country. Fast food thrives on consistency, and this fry was too complex to get right under anything less than perfect conditions. The fry also seemed to get a little too crunchy and lacked in potato taste. This led to a large decrease in fry sales at Burger King, and convinced a large percentage of customers to completely avoid Burger King because of its fries. Managers across the franchise were getting very frustrated with the loss of sales. This new product was considered a flop. Blame was placed on the potato suppliers, a lack of marketing research, an overengineered product, and poor fry cookers. Whatever the problem was, Burger King would have to put forth enormous effort in order to regain the sales that were lost.

Thirty months after the launch of this new fry, Burger King executives finally agreed that something needed to be done. A "new" fry was developed and introduced in 2001. This fry contained less coating and more potato taste. The supply chain and the 19 pages of specifications were simplified. Burger King said that they had it all under control. With fry-taste scores higher than they were three years ago, Burger King believed that it was in a good position to challenge McDonald's again with this newer fry. Alas, objective tests pointed otherwise.

The November 2003 issue of *Consumer Reports* compared the three largest burger chains' French fries and claimed that Burger King's fries had a higher combined level of trans-fatty acids and saturated fats than did those from McDonald's or Wendy's. A medium-size serving of Wendy's fries contained 7.5 combined grams of the two fats, while McDonald's had 10 grams and Burger King's had 11 grams, the magazine claimed. *Consumer Reports* asserted that "It's not much of a stretch to say that fast-food fries are still swimming in 'bad' fat." Health authorities say both trans and saturated fats raise blood cholesterol levels and increase the risk of heart disease.

In 2004, both McDonald's and Wendy's experienced strong sales while Burger King continued to lag. By 2005, industry-leader McDonald's phased out its Super Size fry-and-drink option as part of a move to simplify U.S. operations and implement a consistent and relevant menu, with a range of choices that support a balanced lifestyle. Although lagging behind, Burger King has not given up and is still frying to become number one in French fries. It will have to rely on marketing research if it is to succeed.

Questions

1. Define the management-decision problem facing Burger King regarding its French fries.
2. Define the marketing research problem corresponding to the management-decision problem you have identified in Question 1.
3. What type of research design would be appropriate for investigating consumer preferences for French fries?
4. Use the Internet to determine the annual U.S. sales for McDonald's, Burger King, and Wendy's for the past five years. Interpret the data.
5. What type of syndicated data can be useful to Burger King? Discuss the sources of such data.
6. Do consumers have deeply felt emotions about French fries? If so, what are these emotions? How can Burger King find an answer to these questions?
7. If a survey is to be conducted to determine consumers' preference for French fries, which survey method should be used and why?
8. Design an experiment to compare the preference for French fries made by McDonald's, Burger King, and Wendy's. Justify your selection of the experimental design you recommend.
9. Which primary type of scales would you use to measure preference for French fries made by McDonald's, Burger King, and Wendy's? Develop the appropriate scales.
10. Design a questionnaire that will obtain the information needed to address the marketing research problem defined in Question 2.
11. Develop a sampling plan to conduct the survey specified in Question 7. How would you determine the sample size?
12. If Burger King were to conduct the survey specified in Question 7 in the United Kingdom, how would the research process be different?
13. Discuss the ethical issues involved in researching people's emotions, as in Question 6.

References

1. Amy Garber, "BK Seeks to Flush King-Size Problems as Red-Hot McD Scales Down Portions," *Nation's Restaurant News*, 38(11), (March 15, 2004): 1–2.
2. "Report: 'Bad' Fat Still Weighs Down QSR Fries," *Nation's Restaurant News*, 37(46), (November 17, 2003): 60.

VideO CASES FOR PART 2

VIDEO CASE 2.1

Starbucks: Staying Local While Going Global Through Marketing Research

The Starbucks Corporation purchases and roasts high-quality whole coffee beans and sells them, along with fresh, rich-brewed coffees, Italian-style espresso beverages, cold blended beverages, a variety of pastries and confections, coffee-related accessories and equipment, a selection of premium teas, and a line of compact discs, primarily through company-operated retail stores. In addition to sales through its company-operated retail stores, Starbucks sells coffee and tea products through other channels of distribution, including its Business Alliances business unit and other specialty operations (collectively, Specialty Operations). Starbucks, through its joint venture partnerships, also produces and sells bottled Frappuccino coffee drinks and a line of premium ice creams. For instance, the idea of Frappuccino as iced coffee came from the customers. This would not have been possible without a store staff that opened its arms to the customers and the community. In 2004, Starbucks International Coffee opened in Paris, and the company operated a total of 7,569 retail stores worldwide.

The company's objective is to establish Starbucks as the most recognized and respected brand in the world. It expects to achieve this by continuing with rapid expansion of retail stores and growing its specialty sales and other operations. It will also continually pursue other opportunities to leverage the Starbucks brand through new products and new distribution channels that meet consumer needs as determined by marketing research.

Over the last two decades, Starbucks has revitalized the coffee industry. The inspiration behind Starbucks was conceived when CEO Howard Schultz visited Italy. He noticed the atmosphere of the coffee shops there and wanted to recreate that experience in the United States. Starbucks has shown tremendous growth over recent years. New store locations are determined based on marketing research. Approximately 84 percent of net revenues come from company-operated retail stores. Specialty operations accounted for the remaining 16 percent. Currently, one-third of all the coffee sold in coffee shops comes from either a corporate-owned or licensed Starbucks store. These stores account for 26.5 percent of the coffee shops in the United States.

The major challenge for Starbucks in achieving massive growth goals was to capture the essence of the European coffee-house culture while appealing to a broad range of Americans. Marketing research determined four strategic pillars for expressing the Starbucks brand. The four pillars are coffee, coffee-related products, environment, and experience rooted in involvement with the local community. Even though the coffee and the products are important, the key to its success has been the latter two. It has designed an environment that is warm and welcoming, and provides an experience that makes the company a part of the community or local culture. It has been able to achieve this success by emphasizing the Starbucks culture.

Marketing research has shown that it is important for Starbucks to stay connected to the local community. As it has grown, Starbuck's biggest concern has been that its stores would not stay locally relevant. It was and is important that the company has consistency among its stores in order to maintain the brand quality. It does this by maintaining tight connections with employees within each of these coffee shops. In turn, these employees strive to keep their connections with the clientele. To help preserve connections with local employees, the company treats them as partners and makes them feel like a vital part of the company.

Starbucks uses experience and culture as the key sources of marketing. Thus, it is extremely important to develop, train, and appease their employees because these people help provide this experience and they add to the Starbucks culture. Starbucks has spent much more money on developing its employees than it has on traditional marketing methods. Therefore, its strategy has been to grow by word of mouth, and this has proven extremely successful. Starbucks also draws upon customers for ideas by conducting extensive marketing research. Many of its products and services are a direct result of suggestions from patrons or local employees.

Due to the success of its brand building with the coffee houses, Starbucks has been able to move into other important markets. Syndicated data from ACNielson show that grocery stores sell two-thirds of the coffee in the United States and Starbucks has been able to enter this lucrative market. It has also used partnerships in other industries to increase revenues.

Starbucks has been extremely successful in achieving its objectives. It has been able to maintain a local feel despite massive growth around the globe. Even more surprising, it has been able to achieve this despite the lack of a widespread marketing campaign and without a technology component that would make it unique. It has done this by stressing its culture and placing the focus on its employees and customers through marketing research. Starbucks hopes to continue staying local while going global through marketing research.

Questions

1. Using the Internet, identify secondary sources of information pertaining to coffee consumption in the United States.
2. What are consumers looking for in a coffee-house experience? How do they view the Starbucks coffee-shop experience? How can Starbucks determine answers to these questions?
3. A survey is to be conducted to determine the image coffee drinkers have of Starbucks and other coffee-shop chains. Which survey method should be used and why?
4. Starbucks is thinking of introducing a new gourmet coffee with a strong aroma. Can the observation method be used to determine the consumer reaction to this coffee prior to national introduction? If so, which observation method should be used?
5. What type of scale would be appropriate for measuring the image of Starbucks? Design such a scale.
6. Design a sampling plan for administering the survey in Question 3.

References

1. (www.starbucks.com).
2. Bob Keefe, "Starbucks to Offer CD-Burning Capabilities at Stores in Future," *Knight Rider Tribune Business News*, (June 28, 2004): 1.
3. Dina ElBoghdady, "Pouring It On: The Starbucks Strategy? Locations, Locations, Locations," *The Washington Post*, (August 25, 2002): H01.

VIDEO CASE 2.2

Nike: Associating Athletes, Performance, and the Brand

Nike Inc. designs, develops, and markets footwear, apparel, equipment, and accessory products. Nike is the world's largest seller of athletic footwear, athletic apparel, and other athletic gear, with 30 percent market share worldwide. As of 2005, it sells its products to approximately 18,000 retail accounts in the United States and through a mix of independent distributors, licensees, and subsidiaries in nearly 200 countries. Nike has grown from an $8,000 company in 1963 to a more than $9 billion company in 2005.

In 2004, Nike spent an enormous amount of money, more than $1 billion, on advertising, endorsements, and sales promotion. In order to make sure that this money is being spent properly, Nike relies on marketing research. It has shown a history of innovation and inspiration in its marketing and is quick to adapt to the changing consumer and the world of sports. Nike has used marketing research in understanding where the future growth lies. A recent example is Nike's shift from marketing in the more traditional sports (basketball and running) to other sports (golf and soccer) where it has not been as strong traditionally. Marketing research revealed that awareness of Nike among soccer and golf players was low and it decided to work on increasing these numbers. Nike decided that the money needed for licenses in its strong areas can be better spent in other areas where Nike does not have the brand awareness.

Today, the Nike swoosh symbol is recognized around the world. This is the result of more than 40 years of work and innovation. It signed the first athletes to wear its shoes in 1973. Early on, Nike realized the importance of associating athletes with its products. The partnership helps relate the excellence of the athlete with the perception of the brand. Nike discovered, through marketing research, the pyramid influence, which shows that the mass market can be influenced by the preference of a small group of top athletes. After it realized this effect, Nike began to spend millions on celebrity endorsements. The association with the athlete also helps dimensionalize who the company is and in what it believes. With Nike, this was and is extremely important. It wants to convey a message that the company's goal is to bring innovation to every athlete in the world. Nike also uses the athletes to design new products by attempting to meet their individual needs.

The company also realized that in order to achieve its lofty growth goals it must appeal to multiple market segments. Based on marketing research, Nike divided the market into three different groups. There is the ultimate athlete, the athletics participant, and the consumer who is influenced by the sports culture.

Nike has always been an aggressive user of marketing research and this has been shown in its attack on the European market. It decided to concentrate on different sports in order to reach European consumers. Americans love baseball, football, and basketball. However, Europe's favorite game is soccer. Nike placed its focus on major sporting events (World Cup and Olympics) and celebrity athletes that are relevant to the European consumer. Marketing research in the form of focus groups and survey research revealed that the best positioning for Nike shoes was one that enhanced performance in the sport. Through massive advertising campaigns, it has been able to change the perception of its products from fashion to performance, and in the process increase sales dramatically.

Another technique it has used is to specifically design a product line for a certain market. Nike uses marketing research to determine the lifestyles and product usage characteristics of a particular market segment and then designs products for that segment. An example is the Presto line, which was designed for a certain lifestyle of youths. It put this lifestyle first and designed the products around this group hoping to reach them. It also used marketing research to determine the most effective mediums to communicate with the target market.

All of these methods have allowed Nike to become recognizable by 97 percent of U.S. citizens and its sales have soared in the process. However, it faces a new concern. This concern is that it has gotten away from the traditional image of a smaller innovative company. It also faces future obstacles in maintaining brand equity and brand meaning. Continued reliance on marketing research will help Nike to meet these challenges, associate its brand with top athletes and performance, and enhance its image.

Questions

1. Nike would like to increase its share of the athletic shoe market. Define the management-decision problem.
2. Define an appropriate marketing research problem corresponding to the management-decision problem you have identified.
3. Develop a graphical model explaining consumers' selection of a brand of athletic shoes.
4. How can qualitative research be used to strengthen the image of Nike? Which qualitative research technique(s) should be used and why?
5. Should Nike invest by opening more upscale company retail stores, such as Nike Town? Management is wondering if survey research can provide an answer. How should such a survey be administered?
6. Develop Likert, semantic differential, and Stapel scales for evaluating the durability of Nike running shoes.
7. Develop a questionnaire for measuring the image of Nike, Reebok, and Adidas.
8. Develop a sampling plan for administering the survey in Question 5.

References

1. (www.nike.com).
2. Helen Jung, "Nike Ends Fiscal Year with Muscle," *Knight Rider Tribune Business News*, (June 25, 2004): 1.
3. Leah Beth Ward, "Private Sector: At Nike, Function Over Fashion," *The New York Times,* (April 28, 2002), Section 3: 2.

CHAPTER

14

Field Work: Data Collection

"I make my living interviewing senior executives in firms. I always arrive 30 minutes early for each appointment and always write a thank you note to anyone at the firm who helped me that day. In short, your Mom was right. Courtesy is indispensable to success."

Robert J. Berrier, *Ph.D., Founder and President, Berrier Associates, Narberth, PA*

OPENING QUESTIONS

1. What is meant by field work and what is the field work process?
2. In what aspects of interviewing should field workers be trained?
3. How should the field workers be supervised to enhance their effectiveness and efficiency?
4. How should field workers be evaluated?
5. How should field work be conducted in international marketing research?
6. How does technology facilitate field work?
7. What ethical issues are involved in field work?

Gallup's Galloping Field Work

Now more than ever, Americans are hanging up on interviewers. The primary difficulty of telephone interviewing is declining response rates and, more specifically, increasing refusal rates. Many techniques and procedures have been used to combat this problem, including incentives, aggressive call designs, shorter interviews, and special introductory statements. The most critical variable, however, may be the interviewers themselves.

Refusals are largely a function of interviewing skill. Top interviewers are rarely turned down. The Gallup Organization (www.gallup.com), a prestigious marketing research and consulting firm that specializes in survey research, has identified the following characteristics of an outstanding interviewer:

- **Work Orientation.** Works hard and sees work as more than a job, but as an expression of oneself.
- **Teamwork.** Forms good team relationships with others.
- **Aptitude.** Has a natural affinity for telephone research—enjoys collecting opinions via the telephone.
- **Pride.** Is positive, quality-conscious, and likes being recognized for a job well done.
- **Discipline.** Stays focused on a task and completes it.
- **Third Ear.** Empathizes with a respondent and tailors presentation accordingly.
- **Command.** "Takes charge"—can turn refusals around by conveying the purpose of the survey and its importance.
- **Woo.** Gets people to like him or her quickly; convinces people to cooperate who might not otherwise respond.
- **Ethics.** Is honest and behaves ethically at all times.

Using this theme, the hiring process for interviewers at The Gallup Organization has become very selective, hiring only 1 out of every 16 candidates. The selected interviewers are carefully trained in all aspects of interviewing, from making the initial contact to terminating the interview. The

Council of American Survey Research Organizations' guidelines for effective interviewing are followed. Experienced and qualified supervisors closely monitor the interviewers' work, making sure appropriate procedures are followed and the interviews are being properly conducted.

Validation of field work and the evaluation of interviewers are continuous activities. As a result, The Gallup Organization has not only increased the retention rate of its field workers but has significantly increased the productivity and quality of its data collection. Gallup interviews more than three million people every year in the United States and has built a worldwide reputation for the high quality of its data collection process. As of 2004, Gallup had subsidiary operations in 20 countries, covering 75 percent of the world's GNP.[1] •

Overview

Field work is the fourth step in the marketing research process. It follows problem definition and development of the approach (see Chapter 2), and formulation of the research design (see Chapters 3 through 13). Figure 14.1 briefly explains the focus of the chapter, the relationship of this chapter to the previous ones, and the steps of the marketing research process on which this chapter concentrates.

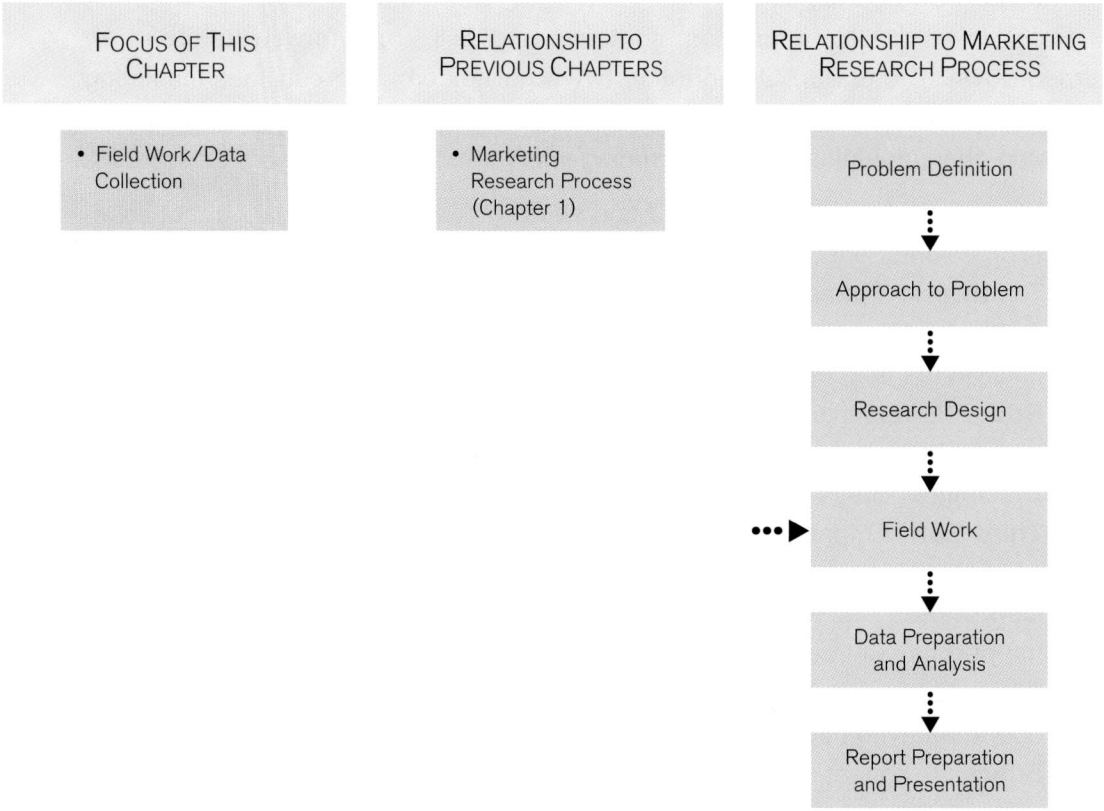

Figure 14.1

Relationship of Field Work to the Previous Chapters and the Marketing Research Process

During this phase, the field workers make contact with the respondents, administer the questionnaires or observation forms, record the data, and turn in the completed forms for processing. Field workers include a personal interviewer administering questionnaires door-to-door, an interviewer intercepting shoppers in a mall, a telephone interviewer calling from a central location, a worker mailing questionnaires from an office, an observer counting customers in a particular section of a store, and others involved in data collection and supervision of the process. The opening vignette gives the characteristics of outstanding interviewers, who form the backbone of field work.

This chapter describes the nature of field work and the field work/data collection process. This process involves the selection, training, and supervision of field workers, the validation of field work, and the evaluation of field workers. Care taken at each of these stages of the field work process can pay big dividends, as illustrated by The Gallup Organization in the opening vignette. We also discuss field work in the context of international marketing research, and technology and marketing research, and identify the relevant ethical issues and Internet applications. Figure 14.2 gives an overview of the topics discussed in this chapter and how they flow from one to the next.

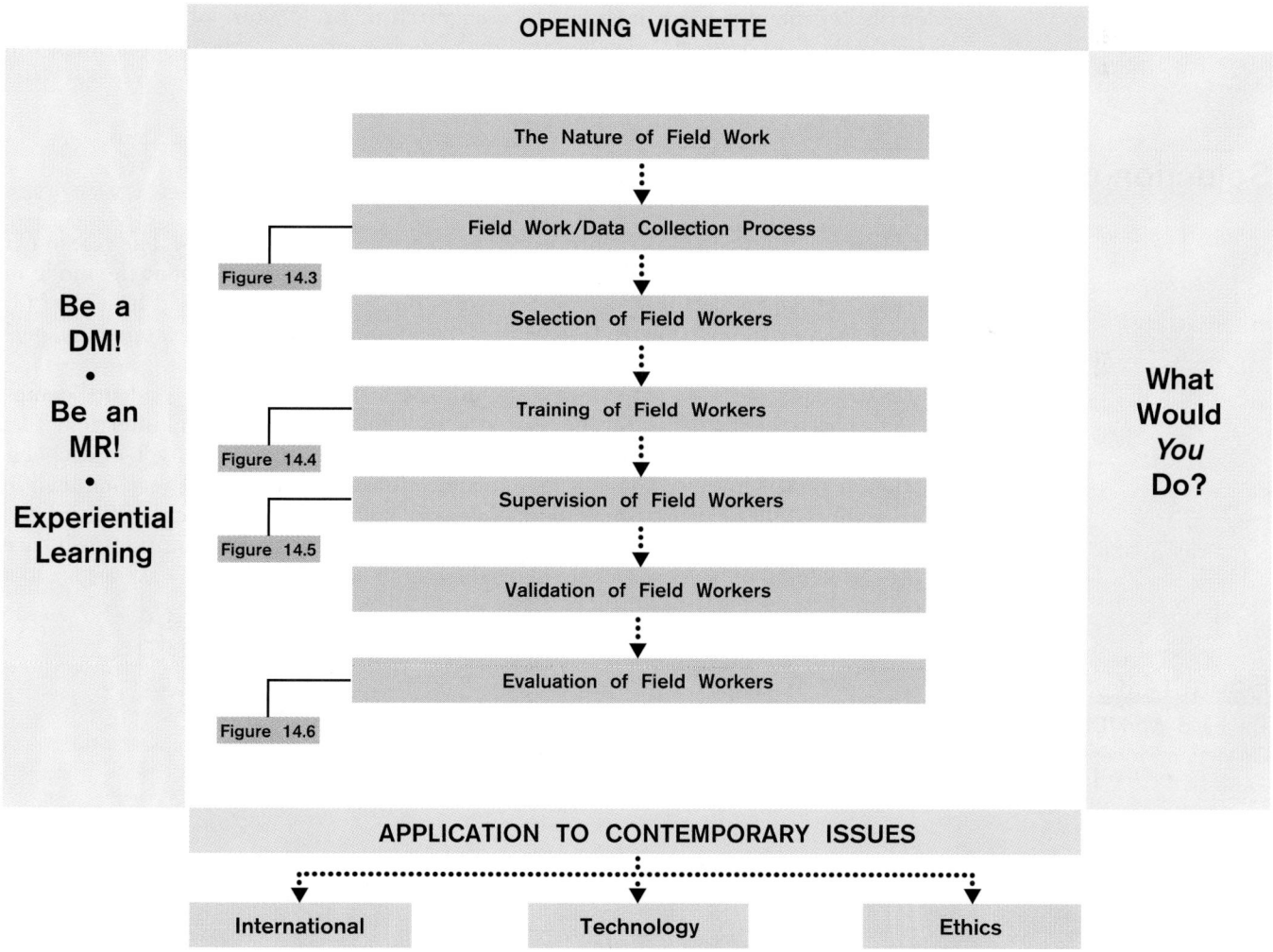

Figure 14.2

Field Work: An Overview

The Nature of Field Work

Those who design the research rarely collect marketing research data. Researchers have two major options for collecting their data: They can develop their own organizations, or they can contract with a field work agency. In either case, data collection involves using some kind of field force. This field force may operate either in the field (personal in-home, mall intercept, computer-assisted personal interviewing, and observation) or from an office (telephone/computer-assisted telephone interviewing, mail/mail panel, and electronic surveys). The field workers who collect the data typically have little research background or training. Therefore, to ensure high quality, the field work/data collection process should be streamlined and well controlled, as discussed in the following section.

Field Work/Data Collection Process

All field work involves the selection, training, and supervision of those who collect the data. The validation of field work and the evaluation of field workers are also parts of the process. All of these aspects were seen in the opening vignette, which described how Gallup selected, trained, supervised, monitored, and evaluated its field workers. Figure 14.3 represents a general framework for the field work/data collection process. While we describe a general process, it should be recognized that the nature of field work varies with the mode of data collection and that the relative emphasis on the different steps will vary for telephone, personal, mail, and electronic interviews.

Selection of Field Workers

The first step in the field work process is the selection of field workers. The researcher should: (1) develop job specifications for the project, taking into account the mode of data collection; (2) decide what characteristics the field workers should have; and (3) recruit appropriate individuals. Interviewers' background characteristics, opinions, perceptions, expectations, and attitudes can affect the responses they elicit.

To the extent possible, interviewers should be selected to match respondents' demographic characteristics since this increases the probability of a successful interview. The job requirements will also vary with the nature of the problem and the type of data collection method. However, some general qualifications of field workers were outlined in the opening vignette: work orientation, teamwork, aptitude, pride, discipline, third ear, command, the ability to woo, and ethics. Interviewers with these qualifications will have a high likelihood of being successful in conducting the field work.

Figure 14.3

The Field Work/Data Collection Process

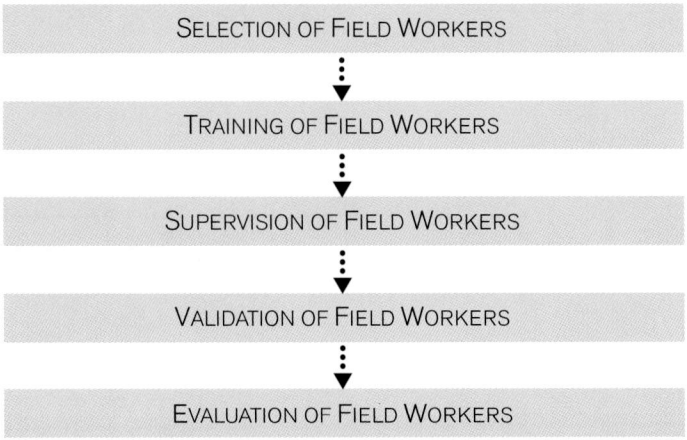

RESEARCH IN ACTION

The Four Faces of Interviewers

Interviewers can be segmented into four distinct psychographic groups, based on an analysis made by M/A/R/C for Marketing Research Association.

Dedicated Debbie: To the Dedicated Debbie, interviewing is not just a job but something much more important. She interviews because she enjoys it.

Independent Inez: Independent Inez interviews because of the independence it gives her. Interviewing gives her freedom to choose when she wants to work and some freedom on the job as well.

Social Sara: This interviewer enjoys interviewing almost as much as Dedicated Debbie, but she does not feel that interviewing is important. What attracts her is the chance to socialize, meet interesting people, and to interact.

Professional Pat: This is the career-oriented interviewer. She sees the job not only as a means to earn her living, but also as a market research career opportunity. Professional Pat considers the two most important attributes of an interviewer to be a detailed mind and exceptional intelligence.

Such an understanding of the psychographic profile of interviewers, along with their demographic characteristics, can greatly assist in identifying and selecting the right interviewers.[2]

Field workers are generally paid an hourly rate or on a per-interview basis. The typical interviewer is a married woman, age 35 to 54, with an above-average education and an above-average household income. The Four Faces of Interviewers example illustrates a psychographic breakdown of interviewers.

Training of Field Workers

Training field workers is critical to the quality of data collected. Training may be conducted in person at a central location, or, if the interviewers are geographically dispersed, by mail. Training ensures that all interviewers administer the questionnaire in the same manner so that the data can be collected uniformly. Training should cover all phases of the interviewing process (see opening vignette): making the initial contact, asking questions, probing, recording answers, and terminating the interview (Figure 14.4).

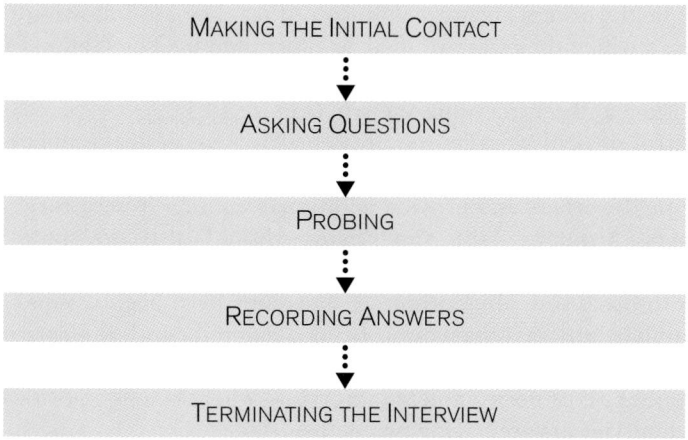

Figure 14.4
Training Field Workers

The initial contact can result in the cooperation or the loss of potential respondents. Interviewers should be trained to make opening remarks that will convince potential respondents that their participation is important. Questions that directly ask permission, such as "May I have some of your valuable time?" or "Would you like to answer a few questions?" should be avoided because people can answer "no." Interviewers should also be instructed on handling objections and refusals. For example, if the respondent says, "This is not a convenient time for me," the interviewer should respond, "What would be a more convenient time for you? I will call back then."

Asking questions is an art. Even a slight change in the wording, sequence, or manner in which a question is asked can distort its meaning and bias the response. Training in asking questions can yield high dividends by eliminating potential sources of bias. One method used to reduce response bias is to probe respondents. **Probing** is intended to motivate respondents to elaborate, clarify, or explain their answers. Probing also helps respondents focus on the specific content of the interview and provide only relevant information. Probing should not introduce any bias. Commonly used probes include questions such as: "Any others?" "Anything else?" "Could you tell me more about your thinking on that?"

probing
A motivational technique used when asking survey questions to induce the respondents to enlarge on, clarify, or explain their answers and to help the respondents focus on the specific content of the interview.

Although recording respondent answers seems simple, several mistakes are common. All interviewers should use the same format and conventions to record the interviews and edit completed interviews. While the rules for recording answers to structured questions vary with each questionnaire, the general rule is to check the box that reflects the respondent's answer. The general rule for recording answers to unstructured questions is to record the responses verbatim.

Before terminating, the interviewer should answer the respondent's questions about the project. The respondent should be left with a positive feeling about the interview. It is important to thank the respondent and express appreciation for their participation. The Mentadent toothbrush example shows the importance of well-trained interviewers in the data collection process and the effect that has on new product development research.

BE a DM!

As the brand manager for Clinique, what information would help you the most in formulating marketing strategies for increasing sales of Clinique's moisturizing lotion for men, called M lotion?

BE an MR!

Visit Clinique's Web site (www.clinique.com) and conduct an Internet search using a search engine and your library's online database to obtain information on women's cosmetics usage.

How would you select and train field workers to conduct a mall intercept survey to determine women's cosmetics usage in a project for Clinique?

Supervision of Field Workers

Supervision of field workers means making sure that they are following the procedures and techniques in which they were trained, as illustrated by The Gallup Organization in the opening vignette. Supervision involves quality control and editing, sampling control, control of cheating, and central office control (Figure 14.5).

Quality control of field workers requires checking to see if the field procedures are being properly implemented. If any problems are detected, the supervisor should discuss them with the field workers and provide additional training if necessary. To understand the interviewers' problems, the supervisors should also do some interviewing. Supervisors should collect questionnaires and edit them daily. They should examine the questionnaires to make sure all appropriate questions have been completed, unsatisfactory or incomplete answers have not been accepted, and the writing is legible. Supervisors should also keep a record of hours worked and expenses. This will make it easy to determine the cost per completed interview, whether the job is moving on schedule, and if any interviewers are having problems.

RESEARCH IN ACTION

Brushing Interviewers Results in a Successful New Toothbrush

When Unilever USA was conducting a survey to determine the market potential for a new toothbrush, the company realized that this research would be crucial to the development and introduction of a new product. To obtain high-quality data, the interviewers were carefully trained in all aspects of interviewing. Training in making the initial contact resulted in a much lower refusal rate. The interviewers were instructed to ask the questions as written, to diligently probe the respondents for open-ended questions, and to record the answers fully and accurately. Probing was crucial for questions, such as, "Why are you (dis)satisfied with the brands of toothbrush currently available in the market?" Probing and recording answers to open-ended questions were particularly important since the company was seeking to identify some creative solutions to the oral-care problems consumers faced.

One innovative idea that emerged from the survey findings was a toothbrush that not only cleaned teeth but also offered an additional benefit of gum care. Based on this finding, Unilever developed and launched the Mentadent Oral Care toothbrush (www.mentadent.com). This was the first toothbrush to offer an additional therapeutic benefit of gum care, thereby pioneering the advanced therapeutic segment of the category. The toothbrush was designed with multilevel interior bristles to clean teeth effectively and with flared side bristles to gently massage and stimulate gums. It was positioned as the state-of-the-art choice for people who were serious about oral care.

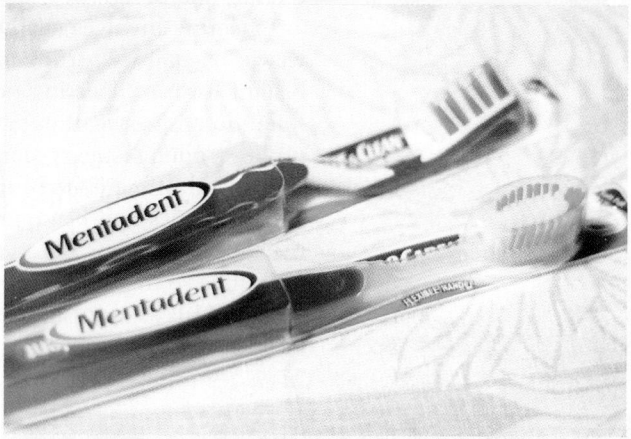

The launch was a strong success because the product addressed an unmet consumer need: care for both teeth and gums. In 2003, the company introduced Mentadent Inter-Sweep, the first toothbrush to integrate Flexible Picks with Micro Fiber Cleaning Bristles. The Inter-Sweep toothbrush is uniquely designed with soft flexible picks, and multilevel and fan-shaped bristles, to clean hard-to-reach areas between teeth, gently and effectively "sweeping" away plaque. A major factor contributing to these successes was the careful training of the interviewers that was instrumental in discovering the need for these innovative toothbrushes.[3]

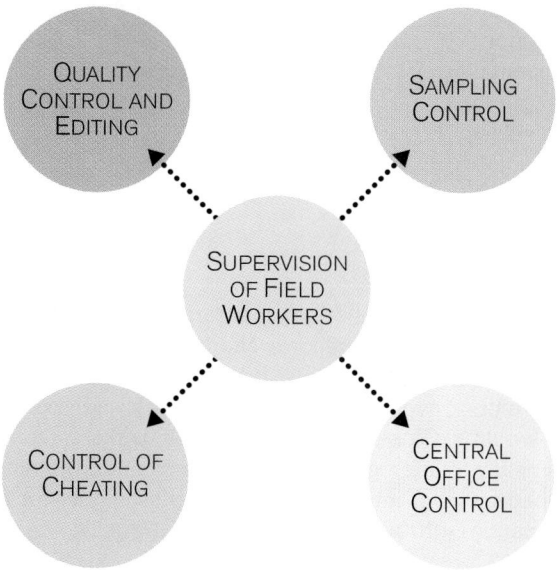

Figure 14.5
Supervising Field Workers

sampling control
An aspect of supervision that ensures that the interviewers strictly follow the sampling plan rather than select sampling units based on convenience or accessibility.

An important aspect of supervision is **sampling control,** which attempts to ensure that the interviewers are strictly following the sampling plan rather than selecting sampling units based on convenience or accessibility. To control these problems, supervisors should keep daily records of the number of calls made, the number of not-at-homes, the number of refusals, the number of completed interviews for each interviewer, and the total for all interviewers under their control.

Cheating involves falsifying part of a question or the entire questionnaire. An interviewer may falsify part of an answer to make it acceptable or may fake answers. The most blatant form of cheating occurs when the interviewer falsifies the entire questionnaire, filling in answers without contacting a respondent. Cheating can be minimized through proper training, supervision, and validation of field work.

Central office control involves tabulating the responses to important demographic characteristics and key questions. It also includes checking on the quotas to make sure they are being met. Supervisors provide quality and cost-control information to the central office so that a progress report can be maintained.

The Milky Way Lite example illustrates the importance of close supervision in collecting high-quality data.

Validation of Field Work

Validation of field work means verifying that field workers are submitting authentic interviews. To validate the study, the supervisors call 10 to 25 percent of the respondents to inquire whether the field workers actually conducted the interviews. The supervisors ask about the length and quality of the interview, reaction to the interviewer, and basic demographic data. The demographic information is cross-checked against the information reported by the interviewers on the questionnaires.

RESEARCH IN ACTION

Lite Bar Is from Mars

M&M/Mars (www.mmmars.com), a division of Mars, Inc. (www.mars.com), frequently conducts mall intercept interviews to identify and test new product concepts. Shoppers are intercepted at various locations in the mall and taken to a central facility where they can taste candy bars under development and then respond to surveys. The surveys contain a fair number of open-ended or unstructured questions that require interviewers to probe respondents. Probing provides rich insights into respondents' underlying values, attitudes, and beliefs. Since all such interviews are conducted at a central location, supervision of the interviewers is greatly facilitated. Completed questionnaires are available to the supervisors immediately after the interview for editing and quality control. Sampling control is easily exercised and cheating is eliminated, eliminating the need for validation. This procedure is also good for implementing quota sampling, which is often used, and also facilitates other aspects of central office control, such as tabulation of responses to key questions.

A recent mall intercept survey indicated a strong preference for a low-fat candy bar, as such a product would allow people to indulge without feeling guilty. Accordingly, M&M/Mars introduced Milky Way Lite Bar, a reduced-fat candy bar. This was the first nationally advertised candy

bar labeled to meet regulations of the U.S. Food and Drug Administration's Nutrition Labeling and Education Act for "lite" products. It has five grams of fat, half the fat of the average leading chocolate brands per 44.5 gram-serving. Close supervision of field workers, made possible by mall intercept interviewing, facilitated the research responsible for introducing yet another winner for M&M/Mars. As of 2005, Milky Way is a top-10 selling candy bar.[4]

EXPERIENTIAL LEARNING

Feeding Interviewers Chips and Snacks

The consumption patterns for chips and snacks change often. The brand manager for Lay's chips would like to conduct a telephone survey to determine the consumption of chips and snacks.

1. Visit Lays Web site (www.lays.com) and conduct an Internet search using a search engine and your library's online database to obtain information on the consumption of chips and snacks. Design an appropriate questionnaire.
2. Train an interviewer (a fellow student) and have her or him conduct the telephone interview with a respondent (another student).
3. How would you supervise this interviewer?
4. As the brand manager for Lay's chips, what information would you like to formulate marketing strategies for increasing your sales?

Evaluation of Field Workers

It is important to evaluate field workers to provide them with feedback on their performance. Evaluation helps identify the more effective field workers in order to build a better, higher-quality field force. As in the case of The Gallup Organization in the opening vignette, the evaluation of field workers should be an ongoing process. The evaluation criteria should be clearly communicated to the field workers during their training. The evaluation of field workers should be based on the criteria of quantity (cost and time, response rates) and quality (quality of interviewing, quality of data), as shown in Figure 14.6.

Interviewers can be compared in terms of the total cost (salary and expenses) per completed interview. Field workers should also be evaluated on how they spend their time. Time should be broken down into categories, such as actual interviewing, travel, and administration. It is important to monitor response rates on a timely basis so that corrective action can be taken if these rates are too low. Supervisors can help interviewers with an inordinate number of refusals by listening to the introductions they use and providing immediate feedback. When all the interviews are over, different field workers' percentage of refusals can be compared to identify the better workers.

To evaluate interviewers on the quality of interviewing, the supervisor must directly observe the interviewing process. The supervisor can do this in person, or the field worker can tape-record the interview. The completed questionnaires of each interviewer should be evaluated for the quality of data. Some indicators of quality data are: (1) the recorded data are legible; (2) all instructions, including skip patterns (discussed in Chapter 11), are followed; (3) the answers to unstructured questions are recorded verbatim; (4) the answers to unstructured questions are meaningful and complete enough to be coded (discussed in Chapter 11); and (5) for structured questions, item nonresponse occurs infrequently.

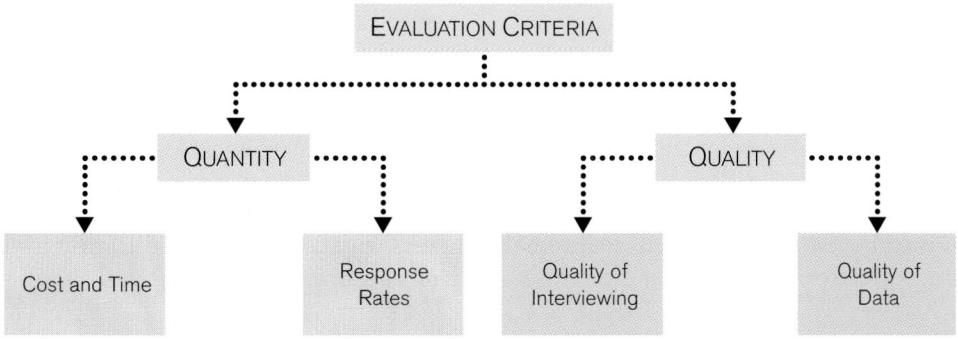

Figure 14.6
Evaluating Field Workers

EXPERIENTIAL LEARNING

Vending Field Work

What is it like to conduct field work? Go to the textbook Web site, select Chapter 14, and download the following file: Vending Machine Survey.doc. Print five copies of this survey, select a building on campus with vending machines, go there and conduct separate survey interviews with five different people from that building.

1. How did you feel approaching these respondents?
2. What seemed to be the most challenging part of the survey for the respondents?
3. If other students were employed to collect the data for this survey project, how should they be trained?
4. If other students were employed to collect the data for this survey project, how should the field work be supervised?
5. If other students were employed to collect the data for this survey project, how should the conduct of the field work be evaluated?

Using the Internet in Field Work

The Internet can play a valuable role in all the phases of field work, including the selection, training, supervision, validation, and evaluation of field workers. As far as selection is concerned, interviewers can be located, interviewed, and hired via the Internet. This process can be initiated, for example, by posting job vacancies notices for interviewers at the company Web site, bulletin boards, and other suitable locations. While this would confine the search to only Internet-savvy interviewers, this may well be a qualification for the job.

Similarly, the Internet, with its multimedia capabilities, can be a good supplementary tool for training the field workers in all aspects of interviewing. Training in this manner can complement personal training programs and add value to the process. Facilitating communication between the supervisors and the interviewers via e-mail and secured chat rooms enhances supervision. By posting progress reports and quality and cost-control information on a secured location at a Web site, it is easily available to all the relevant parties and can strengthen central office control.

Validation of field work, especially for personal and telephone interviews, can be easily accomplished for those respondents who have an e-mail address or access to the Internet. These respondents can be sent a short verification survey by e-mail or be asked to visit a Web site where the survey is posted. The evaluation criteria can be communicated to field workers during the training stage by using the Internet, and performance feedback can also be provided to them using this medium.

Summary Illustration Using the Opening Vignette

Notice the care The Gallup Organization took in selecting its interviewers, choosing only 1 out of every 16 possible candidates. In selecting interviewers, Gallup looks for the following qualities: work orientation, teamwork, aptitude, pride, discipline, third ear, command, and the ability to woo. These interviewers are thoroughly trained by following the guidelines on interviewing by the Council of American Survey Research Organizations. Experienced and qualified supervisors closely supervise the interviewers. The interviewers' work is validated and evaluated, and they are continuously provided with feedback on performance. As a result, Gallup has been very successful in cultivating and retaining high-quality field workers who contribute significantly to the data collection process and the reputation of the organization. The Council of

American Survey Research Organizations has provided the following guidelines for effective interviewing:

1. Provide his or her full name, if asked by the respondent, as well as a phone number for the research firm.
2. Read each question exactly as written. Report any problems to the supervisor as soon as possible.
3. Read the questions in the order indicated on the questionnaire, following the proper skip sequences.
4. Clarify any question by the respondent in a neutral way.
5. Do not mislead respondents as to the length of the interview.
6. Do not reveal the identity of the ultimate client unless instructed to do so.
7. Keep a tally on each terminated interview and the reason for each termination.
8. Remain neutral in interviewing. Do not indicate agreement or disagreement with the respondent.
9. Speak slowly and distinctly so that words will be understood.
10. Record all replies verbatim, not paraphrased.
11. Avoid unnecessary conversations with the respondent.
12. Probe and clarify for additional comments on all open-end questions, unless otherwise instructed. Probe and clarify in a neutral way.
13. Write neatly and legibly.
14. Check all work for thoroughness before turning it in to the supervisor.
15. When terminating a respondent, do so in a neutral way, such as, "Thank you," or "Our quota has already been filled in this area, but thank you anyway."
16. Keep all studies, materials, and findings confidential.
17. Do not falsify any interviews or any answers to any question.
18. Thank the respondent for participating in the study.

International Marketing Research

The selection, training, supervision, and evaluation of field workers are critical in international marketing research. Local field work agencies are unavailable in many countries, therefore, it may be necessary to recruit and train local field workers or import trained foreign workers. Using local field workers is preferable, however, since they are familiar with the local language and culture and can create an appropriate climate for the interview, being sensitive to the concerns of the respondents.

Extensive training of field workers may be required, and close supervision may be necessary. In many countries, interviewers tend to help respondents with the answers and select households or sampling units based on personal considerations rather than the sampling plan. Also, interviewer cheating may be more of a problem in many foreign countries than in the United States because of the lax ethical culture in these countries. For these reasons, validation of field work is critical. Proper application of field work procedures can greatly reduce these difficulties and result in consistent and useful findings, as the following example demonstrates.

BE a DM!

As the international marketing manager for GM, what information would help you the most in formulating marketing strategies for increasing sales in China?

BE an MR!

Visit GM's Web site (www.gm.com) and conduct an Internet search using a search engine and your library's online database to obtain information on Chinese consumers' preferences for cars.

How would you select, train, and supervise field workers conducting an in-home survey in China to determine consumers' preferences for cars?

RESEARCH IN ACTION

American Products Favored in Europe

An image study recently conducted by Research International, a U.K. market research company, showed that, despite unification of the European market, European consumers still increasingly favor U.S. products. The survey was conducted in Germany, the United Kingdom, Italy, and the Netherlands. In each country, local interviewers and supervisors were used, as it was felt they would be better able to identify with the respondents. However, the field workers were trained extensively and supervised closely to ensure that appropriate procedures were followed. The validation efforts were doubled: 20 percent, rather than the minimum 10 percent, of the interviews were validated. These procedures ensured quality results and minimized the variability in country-to-country results due to differences in field work.

A total of 6,724 personal interviews were conducted. Europeans gave U.S. products high marks for being innovative; some countries also regarded them as fashionable and of high quality. Interestingly, France, often considered anti-American, also emerged as pro-American. Among the 1,034 French consumers surveyed, 40 percent considered U.S. products fashionable and 38 percent believed they were innovative, although only 15 percent said U.S. products were of high quality. In addition, when asked what nationality they preferred for a new company in their area, a U.S. company was the first choice. These findings were comparable and consistent across the four countries. A key to the discovery of these findings was the use of local field workers and extensive training and supervision that resulted in uniformly high-quality data across the different countries.

These findings are very useful for U.S. firms marketing in Europe. "Rather than trying to hide the fact that they are American, we think companies ought to stress or try to exploit their American heritage," says Eric Salaam, director of European operations for the Henley Center, the U.K. economic forecasting consultancy. U.S. firms have, in fact, capitalized on the "made in America" equity. As a result, exports to Europe have been soaring in recent years. As of 2004, transatlantic flows of trade and investment between the United States and European Union amount to around $1 billion a day, and jointly, their global trade accounts for almost 40 percent of world trade.[5]

Technology and Marketing Research

A new computer technology, predictive dialing, is allowing marketing research companies using telephone surveys to double their call attempts. A computer accesses a file of phone numbers and does the dialing. When a call is answered, it is instantly sent to an interviewer. The interviewer 's computer terminal displays the caller's name and the appropriate survey to use for the caller. If the computer dials a number that is not answered, it will recycle that number. The computer selects the telephone numbers in such a way as to maximize the probability of contact by predicting that a respondent will be at home and will participate at that time. These systems also include provisions for long, complicated questionnaires with computer-assisted quota control, telephone number management, interviewer monitoring and supervision, and management reports. Computer technology has also made personal interviewing more efficient. Many field workers now use Palmtop personal computers to collect data that are then transmitted to a central computer using a wireless system.

New technology makes it possible for companies to conduct telephone interviews without the use of a live interviewer. As discussed earlier (see Chapter 7), interviews can be conducted using Completely Automated Telephone Surveys (CATS). These systems use "interactive voice response technology." Because no human interviewer is used, CATS greatly reduces interviewer biases by conducting standardized interviews.

Ethics in Marketing Research

High ethical standards should be used when collecting data. Researchers and field workers should make the respondents feel comfortable by addressing their apprehensions and concerns. This can be done by providing respondents with adequate information about the project, addressing their questions, and clearly stating the responsibilities and expectations of both the field workers and the respondents at the beginning of the interview. Otherwise, respondents may be unsure about how their answers will be used and may not

RESEARCH IN ACTION

An Ethical Code for Data Collection and Coding

On May 12, 2003, the Marketing Research Association (www.mra-net.org) adopted a new code of marketing research standards that clarifies expectations by delineating specific acceptable practices. Some of the salient ethical responsibilities of field work firms pertaining to respondents are as follows:

- Companies engaged in data collection . . .
  - will treat the respondent with respect and not influence a respondent's opinion or attitude.
  - will conduct themselves in a professional manner and ensure privacy and confidentiality.
  - will make factually correct statements to secure cooperation and will honor promises made to respondents.
  - will not use information to identify respondents without the permission of the respondent, except to those who check the data or are involved in processing the data.
- will adhere to and follow these principles when conducting online research:
  - Respondents' rights to anonymity must be safeguarded.
  - Unsolicited e-mail must not be sent to those requesting not to receive any further e-mail.
  - Researchers interviewing minors must adhere to the Children's Online Privacy Protection Act (COPPA).
  - Data will not be used in any way contrary to the provider's published privacy statement without permission from the respondent.
- will respect the respondent's right to withdraw or to refuse to cooperate at any stage of the study.
- will obtain and document respondent consent when personally identifiable information of the respondent may be passed to a third party for legal or other purposes.

respond candidly. Researchers and field workers should respect respondents' time, feelings, privacy, and right to self-determination.

Researchers and the field work agencies are also responsible to the clients for following the accepted procedures for the selection, training, supervision, validation, and evaluation of field workers. Field work procedures should be carefully documented and made available to clients. As illustrated by the Research in Action example, ethical codes are available for guiding field work/data collection.

WHAT WOULD *YOU* DO?

Nissan: Taking Xterra to the (E)Xtreme

The Situation

Carlos Ghosn, president of Nissan Motor Company, is known as the "Icebreaker" for his skill at ignoring local business practices that stand in the way of making money. Ghosn is the troubleshooter charged with reviving Nissan Motor Company. Ghosn is not afraid to take different paths and knows that taking risks to meet consumer demand is what business is all about.

Ghosn was faced with a new dilemma. When Nissan considered launching a new SUV model, the marketers wanted to appeal to the Generation "X"er. Hence, the Xterra was born. However, Ghosn did not want the Xterra to just be another SUV. He wanted it to fully meet the needs of drivers.

Ghosn decided to let Nissan partner with The Designory Team to help discover to whom they should advertise this new product. The Designory Team put together a design team for the Xterra to conduct some observational research "trying to get to the heart of what it means to be a hardcore SUV owner." The team headed to the woods to observe how these hardcore SUV owners bungee, kayak, and mountain bike. Nissan wanted to know how to market to this younger Generation "X" market.

Nissan set their goal to have one million additional sales worldwide by the end of fiscal year 2004, measured between October 2004 and September 2005, and compared to fiscal year 2001.

Nissan would like to conduct mall intercept interviews with consumers to determine the type of positioning for Xterra that will appeal to Generation "X"ers. The questionnaire is a mix of unstructured and structured questions. Some of the questions require substantial probing of the respondents, and the supervision of the interviewers will be critical to collecting good quality data.

The Marketing Research Decision

1. In what areas should the supervisors be trained to closely monitor the interviewers? Check as many as are applicable.

(continued)

a. Quality control and editing
b. Sampling control
c. Control of cheating
d. Central office control
e. All of the above

2. Discuss the role of supervisor training you recommend in enabling Carlos Ghosn to identify the needs of Generation "X"ers.

The Marketing Management Decision

1. Carlos Ghosn wants to enhance the appeal of the Xterra to Generation "X"ers. What changes should be made? Check as many as are applicable.
   a. Change the image of Xterra
   b. Change the features of Xterra
   c. Lower the price to make it more affordable
   d. Promote Xterra over the Internet
   e. All of the above
2. Discuss how the marketing management-decision action that you recommend to Carlos Ghosn is influenced by the supervisor training that you suggested earlier and by the findings of mall intercept interviews.

What Carlos Ghosn Did

Carlos Ghosn made tremendous adaptations to the 2002 model of the Xterra in order to enhance its appeal to Generation "X"ers. It includes the availability of a supercharged V6, new front-end styling, a new hood, 17-inch wheels and off-road tires, three new exterior colors, new trim colors, a radically revised interior, new dual-stage airbags, new rear child seat anchors, an optional "Enthusiast Package" for dyed-in-the-wool off-roaders, and some changes to option packages in general. Nissan opted for an Eaton M62 roots-type supercharger, which is a first in a compact SUV. This is the same setup offered as part of an option package in Nissan's Frontier pickup truck. However, unlike the Frontier, Nissan offers Xterra drivers supercharger a la carte, very much in keeping with Xterra's motto, "Everything You Need, Nothing You Don't." The new model really does have more of what you need. Whether it is more power, more style, more interior, or more amenities, this Xterra builds upon an already great compact SUV.[6]

Summary

Researchers have two major options for collecting data: developing their own organizations or contracting with field work agencies. In either case, data collection involves the use of a field force. Field workers should be carefully selected and trained in important aspects of field work, including making the initial contact, asking the questions, probing, recording the answers, and terminating the interview. Supervision of field workers involves quality control and editing, sampling control, control of cheating, and central office control. Validation of field work can be accomplished by calling 10 to 25 percent of those who have been identified as respondents and inquiring whether the interviews actually took place. Field workers should be evaluated on the basis of cost and time, response rates, quality of interviewing, and quality of data collection.

Field work can contribute to, and benefit from, quality-control procedures. The selection, training, supervision, and evaluation of field workers is even more critical in international marketing research, as local field work agencies are not available in many countries. Computer technology is available to facilitate and even completely automate data collection. Ethical issues include making the respondents feel comfortable in the data collection process so that their experience is positive. Every effort must be undertaken to ensure that the data are of high quality. The Internet can greatly facilitate the field work/data collection process.

Key Terms and Concepts

Probing, 392

Sampling control, 394

Suggested Cases and Video Cases

Cases

4.1 Boeing

4.2 Gucci

Video Cases

4.1 Subaru

4.2 Marriott

Additional cases and video cases are available in the Instructor's Manual and on the instructor and student Web sites.

Live Research: Conducting a Marketing Research Project

1. The students conducting field work should be appropriately trained. Follow the guidelines in the chapter.
2. The team leaders can conduct fewer interviews but also act as supervisors. They should be trained in supervision.
3. The callback procedures should be specified (e.g., abandon a telephone number after three callback attempts).
4. If in-home interviews are to be conducted in the local area, each interviewer (student) can be assigned a specific part of a census track.

Acronyms

In the field work/data collection process, the organization VESTS in the field workers:

V alidation of field work
E valuation of field workers
S election of field workers
T raining of field workers
S upervision of field workers

The areas in which field workers should be trained may be summarized by the acronym TRAIN:

T erminating the interview
R ecording the answers
A sking the questions
I nitial contact development
N osy behavior: probing

Review Questions

1. What options are available to researchers for collecting data?
2. Describe the field work/data collection process.
3. What qualifications should field workers possess?
4. What are the guidelines for asking questions?
5. What is probing?
6. How should the answers to unstructured questions be recorded?
7. How should the field worker terminate the interview?
8. What aspects are involved in the supervision of field workers?
9. How can respondent selection problems be controlled?
10. What is validation of field work? How is this done?
11. Describe the criteria that should be used for evaluating field workers.

Applied Problems

1. Write interviewer instructions for in-home personal interviews to be conducted by students.
2. Comment on the following field situations, making recommendations for corrective action.
   a. One of the interviewers has an excessive rate of refusals in in-home personal interviewing.
   b. In a CATI situation, many phone numbers are giving a busy signal during the first dialing attempt.
   c. An interviewer reports that, at the end of the interviews, many respondents asked if they had answered the questions correctly.
   d. While validating the field work, a respondent reports that she cannot remember being interviewed over the telephone, but the interviewer insists that the interview was conducted.
3. Visit the Web sites of some marketing research suppliers. Make a report of what you have learned about important aspects of field work from the information posted on these sites.
4. Visit the Marketing Research Association Web site (www.mra-net.org) and examine the ethical codes relating to data collection. Write a brief report.

Group Discussion

1. Discuss the impact of women's changing lifestyles on field work during the last decade.
2. Discuss the notion of interviewer cheating. Why do interviewers cheat? How can cheating be detected and prevented?

CHAPTER

15 Data Preparation and Analysis Strategy

"In many projects, editing, coding, cleaning, and preparing the data for analysis accounts for the majority of the time an analyst will spend with the data."

JIM MCGEE, *Global Mapping International, Colorado Springs, CO*

OPENING QUESTIONS

1. What is the nature and scope of data preparation, and how can the data preparation process be described?
2. What is involved in questionnaire checking and editing?
3. How should questionnaires be coded to prepare the data for analysis?
4. What methods are available for cleaning the data and treating missing responses?
5. How do we select a data analysis strategy?
6. How should data collected in international marketing research projects be prepared?
7. What is the role of technology in facilitating data preparation?
8. Which ethical issues are important in data preparation and analysis?

Database Awakens a Sleeping Giant

Since its introduction, Sears, Roebuck and Company has been a leading department store retailer of apparel, home products, and automobile products and services. In the late 1990s, Sears tried to lose its reputation as a "hardware and tools" store in order to create a trendier and modern store image for customers. Once held up as a textbook example of a mighty marketer failing to adapt to changing consumer demands, Sears, Roebuck and Company has since become an innovator in the retail world, pulling off a comeback that has even the retailer's harshest critics gushing.

One crucial element in its success was building a high-quality database about its customers and potential customers. By 2004, Sears had built a massive database of more than 70 percent of U.S. households. The data are collected from a variety of primary and secondary sources. One hallmark is the care taken to prepare the data before they become a part of the database. In the case of primary data, the completed questionnaires returned from the field are carefully checked and edited for incomplete responses (e.g., questions that are incorrectly skipped) or inconsistent responses (e.g., a respondent reports purchases made on Sears credit card but does not have one). Any questionnaires with unsatisfactory responses are simply discarded, as the proportion of such respondents is small, and the sample size is large. The data are coded by following appropriate procedures. To ensure uniformity in coding, Sears has prepared a codebook containing the coding instructions and the necessary information about the variables in the data set. The data are then transcribed from the questionnaires into the computer, using state-of-the art technology.

Further checks are performed on the data to ascertain their consistency and accuracy. An effort is made to identify data that are out of range (e.g., a response of 8 on a 1-to-7 scale), logically inconsistent (e.g., sum of percentages totaling more than 100 percent), or have extreme values (e.g., household size of 11). Missing values are kept to a minimum by proper selection, training, and supervision of field workers, and are treated by following a variety of methods to determine the impact on the results. A similar process is followed for data collected from secondary sources.

This superior database enables Sears to identify the needs of the marketplace and target its marketing efforts accordingly. Based on the findings of a random survey of 3,000 households from its database, Sears spent $4 billion renovating its stores. It markedly improved store layout, design, cleanliness, and merchandising mix. The move is clearly paying off, with Sears reporting higher sales and revenue per selling square foot than it did prior to the renovation. In late 2004, Kmart announced that it was acquiring Sears in a $11.5 billion merger.[1] •

Overview

After the researcher has defined the research problem and developed a suitable approach (see Chapter 2), formulated an appropriate research design (see Chapters 3 to 13), and conducted field work (see Chapter 14), she or he can move on to data preparation and analysis, the fifth step of the marketing research process. Figure 15.1 briefly explains the focus of the chapter, the relationship of this chapter to the previous ones, and the steps of the marketing research process on which this chapter concentrates.

Before the raw data contained in the questionnaires can be subjected to statistical analysis, they must be converted into a suitable form. Care exercised in the data preparation phase can substantially improve the quality of the findings, resulting in better managerial decisions, as explained in the Sears opening vignette. On the other hand, inadequate attention to data preparation can seriously compromise statistical results, leading to biased findings and incorrect interpretation.

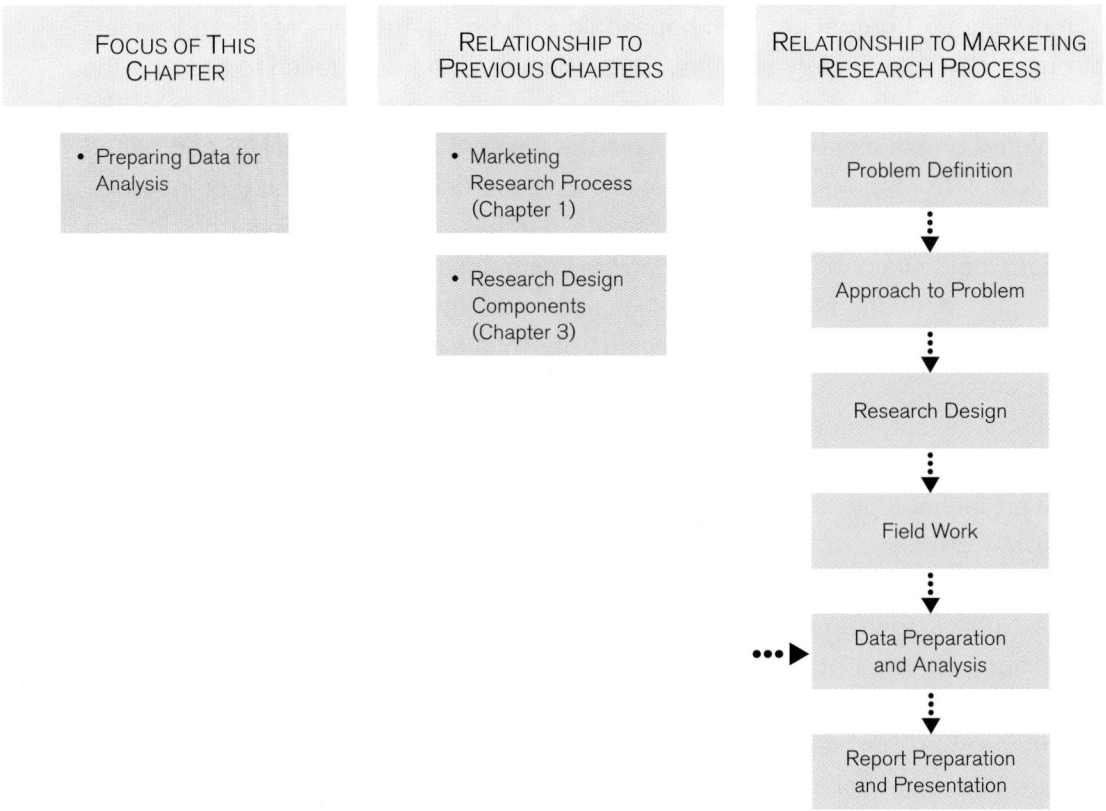

Figure 15.1

Relationship of Data Preparation to the Previous Chapters and the Marketing Research Process

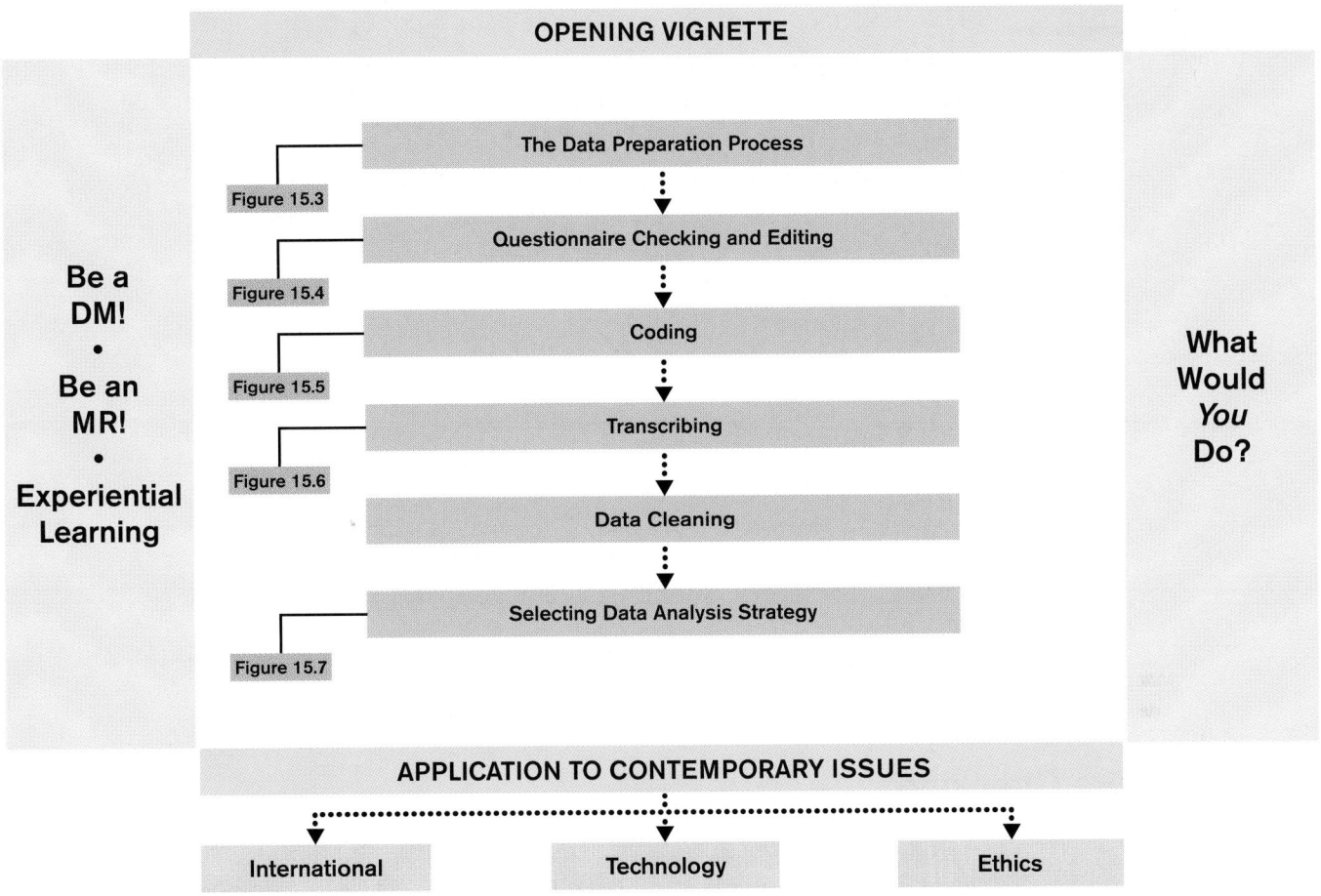

Figure 15.2

Data Preparation: An Overview

This chapter describes the data preparation process, which begins with checking the questionnaires for completeness. Then, we discuss the editing of data and provide guidelines for handling illegible, incomplete, inconsistent, ambiguous, or otherwise unsatisfactory responses. We also describe coding, transcribing, and data cleaning, emphasizing the treatment of missing responses. We then discuss selecting a data analysis strategy, the role of technology, and the ethical issues and Internet applications related to data processing. Figure 15.2 gives an overview of the topics discussed in this chapter and how they flow from one to the next.

The Data Preparation Process

The data preparation process is shown in Figure 15.3. Sears followed a similar process, as explained in the opening vignette. The entire process is guided by the preliminary plan of data analysis that was formulated in the research design phase (see Chapter 3). As the first step, the field work supervisor checks for acceptable questionnaires. This is followed by editing, coding, and transcribing the data, all done by the data collection agency as part of field work (see Chapter 14). The researcher cleans the data, then performs further checks for consistency and specifies how missing responses will be treated. The researcher then selects an appropriate data analysis strategy. The final data analysis strategy differs from the preliminary plan of data analysis due to the information and insights gained since the preliminary plan was formulated. Data preparation should begin as soon as the first batch of questionnaires is received from the field, while the field work is still transpiring. Thus, if any problems are detected, the field work can be modified to incorporate corrective action.

Figure 15.3
Data Preparation Process

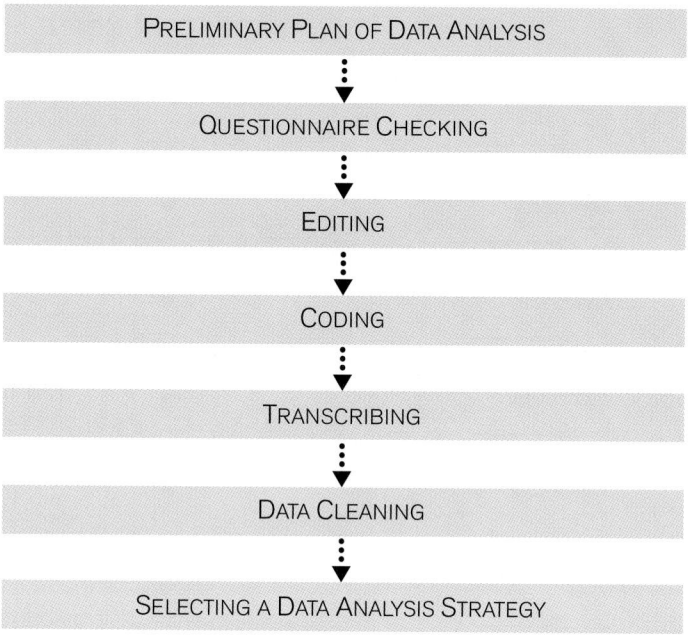

Questionnaire Checking

The initial step in questionnaire checking involves checking for completeness and interviewing quality. This is a continuous process and begins as soon as the first set of questionnaires is returned, while field work is still underway. Therefore, any problems can be detected early on and corrective action can be taken before too many surveys have been completed. A questionnaire returned from the field may be unacceptable for several reasons. For example, parts of the questionnaire may be incomplete, skip patterns may not have been followed (see Chapter 11), one or more pages may be missing, and so forth.

If quotas or cell group sizes have been imposed (see Chapter 12), the acceptable questionnaires should be classified and counted accordingly. Any problems in meeting the sampling requirements should be identified and corrective action taken, such as conducting additional interviews in the underrepresented cells.

Editing

editing
A review of the questionnaires with the objective of increasing accuracy and precision.

Editing involves reviewing questionnaires to increase accuracy and precision. It consists of screening questionnaires to identify illegible, incomplete, inconsistent, or ambiguous responses, as in the opening vignette.

Responses may be illegible if they have been poorly recorded, such as answers to unstructured or open-ended questions. Likewise, questionnaires may be incomplete to varying degrees. A few or many questions may be unanswered. At this stage, the researcher makes a preliminary check for consistency. Certain obvious inconsistencies can be easily detected. For example, a respondent reports an annual income of less than $20,000, yet indicates frequent shopping at prestigious department stores, such as Saks Fifth Avenue and Neiman Marcus. A response is ambiguous, for example, if the respondent has circled both four and five on a seven-point scale.

Unsatisfactory responses are commonly handled by returning to the field to get better data, by assigning missing values, or by discarding unsatisfactory respondents (Figure 15.4).

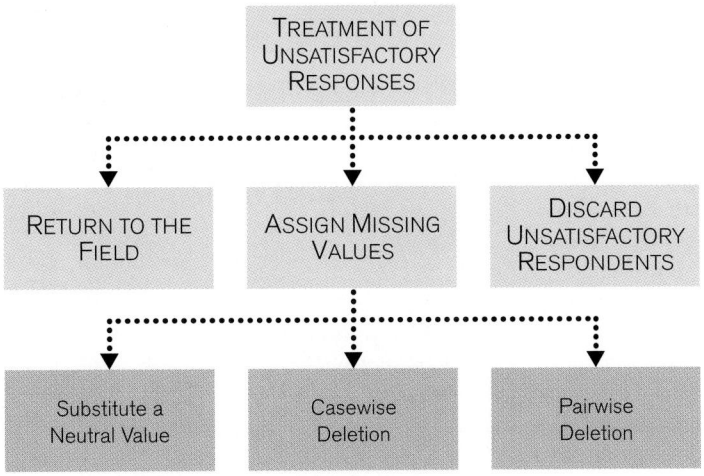

Figure 15.4
Treatment of Unsatisfactory Responses

The questionnaires with unsatisfactory responses may be returned to the field so that the interviewers may recontact the respondents to get better/complete data. This approach is particularly attractive for business and industrial marketing surveys, where the sample sizes are small and the respondents are easily identifiable. If returning the questionnaires to the field is not feasible, the editor may assign missing values to unsatisfactory responses. This approach may be desirable if (1) the number of respondents with unsatisfactory responses is small, (2) the proportion of unsatisfactory responses for each of these respondents is small, or (3) the variables with unsatisfactory responses are not the key variables.

Alternatively, the respondents with unsatisfactory responses are simply discarded. This approach may have merit when (1) the proportion of unsatisfactory respondents is small (less than 10 percent), (2) the sample size is large, (3) the unsatisfactory respondents do not differ from satisfactory respondents in obvious ways (e.g., demographics, product usage characteristics), (4) the proportion of unsatisfactory responses for each of these respondents is large, or (5) responses on key variables are missing (see the opening vignette). However, unsatisfactory respondents may differ from satisfactory respondents in systematic ways, and the decision to designate a respondent as unsatisfactory may be subjective. Both these factors related to unsatisfactory respondents may bias the results. If the researcher decides to discard unsatisfactory respondents, the procedure adopted to identify these respondents and the number of unsatisfactory respondents should be reported by the researcher in the project report, as in the following example.

Coding

Coding means assigning a code, usually a number, to each possible response to each question. The code includes an indication of the column position (field) and data record it will occupy. For example, gender of respondents may be coded as one for females and two for males. A field represents a single item of data, such as the gender of the respondent. A record consists of related fields, such as sex, marital status, age, household size, occupation, and so forth. Thus, each record can have several columns. Generally, all the data for a respondent will be stored on a single record, although a number of records may be used for each respondent. It is often helpful to prepare a **codebook** containing the coding instructions and the necessary information about the variables in the data set (see opening vignette).

coding
The assignment of a code to represent a specific response to a specific question along with the data record and column position that code will occupy.

codebook
A book containing coding instructions and the necessary information about variables in the data set.

The data (all the records) for all the respondents are stored in a computer file, as illustrated in Table 15.1. In this table, the columns represent the fields, and the rows represent the records or respondents, as there is one record per respondent. Table 15.1 presents coded data for part of the record. These data have been coded according to

RESEARCH IN ACTION

A Complaint against Consumer Complaints

In a study examining consumer complaints, 1,000 questionnaires were mailed to households in each of three service categories: automotive repair, medical care, and banking services. The numbers of responses received were automotive repair, 155; medical care, 166; and banking services, 172. The returned questionnaires were carefully checked and edited. Those respondents who did not meet the qualifying criteria (being able to recall a recent dissatisfying experience), and those with a large number of missing values or missing values on key variables were discarded. The usable samples that remained were: automotive repair, 116; medical care, 125; and banking services, 104.

The researchers complained that a large number of respondents had to be discarded because of failure to meet the qualifying criteria or a high incidence of missing values. These complaints are justified because discarding such a high proportion of returned questionnaires (25.2 percent for automotive repair, 24.7 percent for medical care, and 39.5 percent for banking services) is not a good research practice. According to the general guidelines, no more than 10 percent of the returned questionnaires should be discarded.[2]

the coding scheme specified in Figure 15.5. Columns 1 to 3 represent a single field and contain the respondent numbers coded 001 to 271. Column 4 contains the record number. This column has a value of 1 for all the rows since only one record is used for each respondent. Columns 5 and 6 contain the project code, which is 31. The next two columns, 7 and 8, display the interviewer code, which varies from 01 to 55 for respondent number 271. Columns 26 to 35, each representing one field, contain familiarity ratings for the 10 stores, with values ranging from 1 to 6. Column 77 represents the rating of store 10 on prices. There are 271 rows, indicating that data for 271 respondents are stored in this file. One can also use a spreadsheet program, such as EXCEL, to enter the data, as most analysis programs can import data from a spreadsheet. In this case, the data for each respondent for each field is a cell. Typically, each row of the (EXCEL) spreadsheet contains the data of one respondent or case. The columns will contain the variables, with one column for each variable or response. The use of EXCEL can be complicated if there are more than 256 variables. Later in this chapter, in an Experiential Learning situation, we show how the data from an EXCEL file can be converted to an SPSS file.

If the questionnaire contains only structured questions or very few unstructured questions, it is precoded. This means that codes are assigned before field work is conducted.

Table 15.1

Illustrative Computer File: Department Store Patronage Project

	Fields Column Numbers					
Respondent	1–3	4	5–6	7–8.....	26..... 35	77
1	001	1	31	01	6544234553	5
2	002	1	31	01	5564435433	4
3	003	1	31	01	4655243324	4
4	004	1	31	01	5463244645	6
Record #271	271	1	31	55	6652354435	5

Figure 15.5
A Codebook Excerpt

Column Number	Variable Number	Variable Name	Question Number	Coding Instructions
1–3	1	Respondent ID		001 to 890 add leading zeros as necessary
4	2	Record Number		1 (same for all respondents)
5–6	3	Project Code		31 (same for all respondents)
7–8	4	Interview Code		As coded on the questionnaire
9–14	5	Date Code		As coded on the questionnaire
15–20	6	Time Code		As coded on the questionnaire
21–22	7	Validation Code		As coded on the questionnaire
23–24		Blank		Leave these columns blank
25	8	Who shops	I	Male head =1
				Female head =2
				Other =3
				PUNCH THE NUMBER CIRCLED
				Missing values =9
26	9	Familiarity with store 1	IIa	For question II parts "a" through "j" PUNCH THE NUMBER CIRCLED
27	10	Familiarity with store 2	IIb	Not so familiar =1
				Very familiar =6
				Missing values =9
28	11	Familiarity with store 3	IIc	
35	18	Familiarity with store 10	IIj	

If the questionnaire contains unstructured questions, codes are assigned after the questionnaires have been returned from the field (postcoding). While precoding was briefly discussed in Chapter 11 on questionnaire design, we provide further guidelines in the next section.

Coding Structured and Open-Ended Questions

The respondent code and the record number should appear on each record in the data. The following additional codes should be included for each respondent: project code, interviewer code, date and time codes, and validation code. **Fixed-field codes** are highly desirable. This means that the number of records for each respondent is the same and the same data appear in the same column(s) for all respondents. If possible, standard codes should be used for missing data. For example, a code of 9 (or -9) could be used for a single-column variable (responses coded on a 1-to-7 scale), 99 or for a double-column variable (responses coded on a 1-to-11 scale), and so forth. The missing value codes should be distinct from the codes assigned to the legitimate responses.

fixed-field codes
Codes in which the number of records for each respondent are the same, and the same data appear in the same columns for all respondents.

Coding structured questions is relatively simple since the response options are predetermined. The researcher assigns a code for each response to each question and specifies the appropriate record and columns in which the response codes are to appear. For example,

> In the last month, have you bought a product or service over the Internet?
> 1. Yes 2. No (94)

For this question, a "yes" response is coded 1 and a "no" response receives a 2. The number in parentheses indicates that the code assigned will appear in column 94 for this respondent. Because only one response is allowed and there are only two possible responses (1 or 2), a single column is sufficient. In general, a single column is sufficient to code a structured question with a single response if there are less than nine possible responses.

In questions that permit multiple responses, each possible response option should be assigned a separate column. Such questions include those about brand ownership or usage, television viewing, and magazine readership, as in the following example.

Coding unstructured or open-ended questions is more complex. Respondents' verbatim responses are recorded on the questionnaire. Codes are then developed and assigned

RESEARCH IN ACTION

Reading Magazine Readership

Which magazines have you read during the last two months? ("X" as many as apply.)

Time	❑	(102)
Newsweek	❑	(103)
Business Week	❑	(104)
Forbes	❑	(105)
Fortune	❑	(106)
The Economist	❑	(107)
Other Magazines	❑	(108)

Suppose a respondent checked *Time, Newsweek,* and other magazines. On the record for this respondent, a 1 will be entered in the column numbers 102, 103, and 108. All the other columns (104, 105, 106, and 107) will receive a 0.

to these responses by analyzing the data of a few respondents. The following guidelines are suggested for coding unstructured questions and questionnaires in general.

Category codes should be mutually exclusive and collectively exhaustive. Categories are mutually exclusive if each response fits into one, and only one, category code. Categories should not overlap. Categories are collectively exhaustive if every response fits into one of the assigned category codes. This can be achieved by adding an additional category code of "other" or "none of the above." However, only a few (10 percent or less) of the responses should fall into this category. The vast majority of the responses should be classified into meaningful categories.

Data should be coded to retain as much detail as possible. For example, if data on the exact number of trips made on commercial airlines by business travelers have been obtained, they should be coded as such, rather than grouped into two category codes of "infrequent fliers" and "frequent fliers." Obtaining information on the exact number of trips allows the researcher to later define categories of business travelers in several different ways (e.g., less than 3 trips per month, 4- to 6-trips per month, 7- to 10-trips per month, 11- to 15-trips per month, and more than 15 trips per month). If the categories were predefined (e.g., infrequent fliers and frequent fliers), the subsequent analysis of data would be limited by those categories. The following illustrates the coding of responses to open-ended questions.

Coding of Open-Ended Question Responses

Question: Why do you prefer Colgate to Crest toothpaste?
Sample Responses

1. It is a better value
2. It has a lower price
3. Tastes better
4. I like the packaging better
5. Better buy for my money
6. I don't like the taste of Crest
7. It prevents tooth decay
8. It gives me fresh breath
9. It has a better-looking package
10. I like the smell of Colgate
11. I like Colgate advertising
12. Crest has a taste disadvantage

13. Colgate's advertising is creative
14. Colgate is more effective in fighting cavities
15. It is better for your health

Similar responses are grouped, and category codes are developed, as follows.

Category Descriptors	Sample Responses	Category Code
Better value/lower price/better buy	1, 2, 5	1
Tastes better/don't like taste of Crest/Crest's taste disadvantage	3, 6, 12	2
Better packaging/better-looking package	4, 9	3
Prevents tooth decay/fights cavities/better for health	7, 14, 15	4
Fresh breath/like smell	8, 10	5
Like advertising/creative advertising	11, 13	6
Other		7

BE a DM!

As the marketing director for the New England Patriots, what information would you like to formulate marketing strategies to increase the attendance at the Patriots' home games and increase the sales of Patriots' merchandise?

BE an MR!

Visit the NFL Web site (www.nfl.com) and conduct an Internet search using a search engine and your library's online database to obtain information on why people attend professional football games.

A survey was administered to attendees at a Patriots' home game to determine why they were attending. What principle will you follow in checking the questionnaire, editing, and coding?

Transcribing

Transcribing data involves transferring the coded data from the questionnaires or coding sheets onto disks or directly into computers by keypunching or other means, as in the opening vignette. If the data have been collected via computer-assisted telephone interviewing (CATI) or computer-assisted personal interviewing (CAPI), this step is unnecessary since the data are entered directly into the computer as they are collected. Besides keypunching, the data can be transferred by using mark-sense forms, optical scanning, or computerized sensory analysis (Figure 15.6). Mark-sense forms require responses to be recorded with a special pencil in a predesignated area coded for that response. A machine can then read the data. Optical scanning involves direct machine reading of the codes and simultaneous transcription. A familiar example of optical scanning is the transcription of universal product code (UPC) data at supermarket checkout counters. Technological advances have resulted in computerized sensory analysis systems, which automate the data collection process. The questions appear on a computerized grid pad, and responses are recorded directly into the computer using a sensing device.

When CATI, CAPI, or electronic methods are used, data are verified as they are collected. In the case of inadmissible responses, the computer will prompt the interviewer or respondent. In case of admissible responses, the interviewer or the respondent can see the recorded response on the screen and verify it before proceeding.

The selection of a data transcription method is guided by the type of interviewing method used and the availability of equipment. If CATI, CAPI, or electronic methods are used, the data are entered directly into the computer. Keypunching into a computer

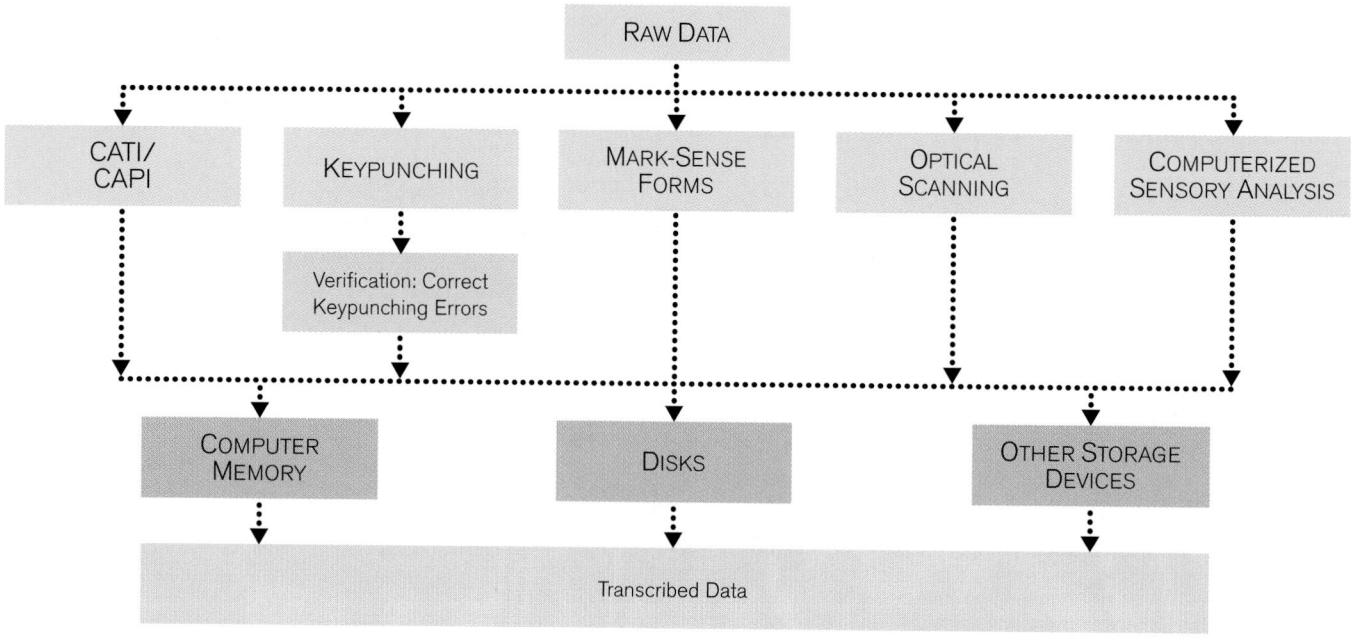

Figure 15.6
Data Transcription

is most frequently used for ordinary telephone, in-home, mall intercept, and mail interviews. However, the use of computerized sensory analysis systems in personal interviews is growing with the increasing use of grid pads and hand-held computers. Optical scanning can be used in structured and repetitive surveys, and mark-sense forms are used in special cases.

Data Cleaning

data cleaning
Thorough and extensive checks for consistency and treatment of missing responses.

Data cleaning includes consistency checks and treatment of missing responses. While preliminary consistency checks have been made during editing, the checks at this stage are more thorough and extensive since they are made by computer.

Consistency Checks

consistency checks
A part of the data cleaning process that identifies data that are out of range or logically inconsistent, or that have extreme values. Data with values not defined by the coding scheme are inadmissible.

Consistency checks identify data that are out of range, logically inconsistent, or have extreme values (see opening vignette). Out-of-range data values are inadmissible and must be corrected. For example, respondents have been asked to express their degree of agreement with a series of lifestyle statements on a 1-to-5 scale. Assuming that 9 has been designated for missing values, data values of 0, 6, 7, and 8 are out of range. These out-of-range responses can arise due to respondent or interviewer errors. Computer packages such as SPSS, SAS, MINITAB, and EXCEL can be programmed to identify out-of-range values for each variable and print out the respondent code, variable code, variable name, record number, column number, and out-of-range value.[3] This makes it easy to check each variable systematically for out-of-range values. The correct responses can be determined by going back to the edited and coded questionnaire.

Responses can be logically inconsistent in various ways. For example, a respondent may indicate that she charges long-distance calls to a calling card, even though she does not have one. Or a respondent might report both unfamiliarity with, and frequent use of, the same product. The necessary information (respondent code, variable code, variable name, record number, column number, and inconsistent values) can be printed to locate these responses and take corrective action.

RESEARCH IN ACTION

Customer Satisfaction Research Links American Cancer Society to the Society

The American Cancer Society (ACS) has instituted ongoing customer satisfaction research. These surveys ask the donors and the general public what is most important to them in the fight against cancer and what role they expect the ACS to play.

Before any analysis is done, the data are thoroughly checked for quality. Any unsatisfactory questionnaires discovered during checking or editing are sent back to the field, as the response of every single respondent is considered important. A standard coding scheme is used and, since most of the data are collected using CATI, subsequent transcription is unnecessary. Several procedural and logical checks are built into the CATI system so that inconsistencies can be identified and rectified while the data are being collected during the course of the interview. These high-quality data provide ACS with an accurate measurement of what is important to donors and the public, enabling it to effectively address those issues in its marketing campaigns and charitable programs. As a result, contributions are at an all-time high, and the ACS is well connected to the society at large.[4]

Extreme values should be closely examined. Not all extreme values result from errors; however, they may point to problems with the data. For example, an extremely low evaluation of a brand may be the result of the respondent indiscriminately circling 1s (on a 1-to-7 rating scale) on all attributes of this brand.

Treatment of Missing Responses

Missing responses represent values of a variable that are unknown, either because respondents provided ambiguous answers or their answers were not properly recorded. The incidence of missing responses should be minimized by proper selection, training, and supervision of field workers (see Chapter 14), as illustrated by Sears in the opening vignette. Treatment of missing responses poses problems, particularly if the proportion of missing responses is more than 10 percent. The following options are available for the treatment of missing responses (see Figure 15.4):

missing responses
Values of a variable that are unknown as these respondents did not provide unambiguous answers to the question.

1. **Substitute a Neutral Value.** A neutral value, typically the mean response to the variable, is substituted for missing responses. Thus, the mean of the variable remains unchanged and other statistics, such as correlations, may not be affected much if the proportion of missing values is small. While this approach has some merit, the logic of substituting a mean value (say 4) for respondents who, if they had answered, might have used either high ratings (6 or 7) or low ratings (1 or 2) is questionable.
2. **Casewise Deletion.** In casewise deletion, cases or respondents with any missing responses are discarded from the analysis. Suppose 20 percent of the respondents do not respond to the income questions. All of these respondents will be excluded from analysis that involves the income variable, thus reducing the sample size by 20 percent. If several variables are involved in the analysis (e.g., income, education, occupation), respondents with missing values on any of those variables will be excluded. Since many respondents may have missing responses on different variables, this approach could result in a small sample. Throwing away large amounts of data is undesirable because it is costly and time-consuming to collect data. Furthermore, respondents with missing responses could differ from respondents with complete responses in systematic ways. If so, casewise deletion could seriously bias the results.
3. **Pairwise Deletion.** In pairwise deletion, instead of discarding all cases with any missing values, the researcher uses only the cases or respondents with complete responses for each calculation. Suppose the researcher is interested in calculating all possible correlations between a set of variables—say awareness, attitude, preference, and purchase intention—all measured on a 1-to-7 scale (see Chapter 18).

casewise deletion
A method for handling missing responses in which cases or respondents with any missing responses are discarded from the analysis.

pairwise deletion
A method of handling missing values in which for each calculation or analysis, only the cases or respondents with complete responses are considered.

Then, in calculating the correlation between attitude and preference, all respondents with legitimate responses on the two variables will be included in the analysis, even though these respondents may have missing values on the other two variables, namely awareness and purchase intentions. In contrast, in casewise deletion, respondents with missing values on any of the four variables would be excluded from the analysis.

Pairwise deletion may be appropriate when: (1) the sample size is large, (2) there are few missing responses, and (3) the variables are not highly related. Yet, this procedure can produce results that are unappealing or even infeasible as different calculations in an analysis may be based on different sample sizes. For example, statistics, such as pairwise correlations, may be based on different sample sizes, making comparisons more difficult.

The different procedures for the treatment of missing responses may yield different results, particularly when the responses are not missing at random and the variables are related. The researcher should carefully consider the implications of the various procedures before selecting a particular method for the treatment of nonresponse. It is also recommended that the data be analyzed using different options for handling missing responses to determine the impact on the results, as illustrated by Sears in the opening vignette.

Variable Respecification and Recoding

variable respecification
Involves the transformation of data to create new variables or modify existing variables.

Variable respecification involves the transformation of data to create new variables or modify existing variables. The purpose of respecification is to create variables that are consistent with the objectives of the study. Often respecification involves summing the items of a Likert-type scale to create a summated score. For example, in Chapter 10 we showed a Likert scale consisting of nine statements designed to measure attitude toward Target. These nine statements need to be summed, after reversing the scoring of the negative statements, to arrive at a total attitudinal score. The process of reversing the scoring for the negative statements, as well as the process of summing, involves variable respecification.

Once the data have been coded, transcribed, and cleaned, it may be necessary to redefine the categories of a categorical variable, such as income. For example, if there are too few respondents in the lowest income category, this category may be combined or merged with the next lowest category. This is referred to as recoding.

BE an MR!

Visit Lexus' Web site (www.lexus.com) and conduct an Internet search using a search engine and your library's online database to obtain information on the criteria buyers use in selecting a luxury car brand.

Demographic and psychographic data were obtained in a survey designed to explain the choice of a luxury car brand. What kind of consistency checks, treatment of missing responses, and variable respecification should be conducted?

BE a DM!

As the marketing manager for Lexus, what information would you like in formulating marketing strategies to increase market share among female executives and professionals earning more than $100,000 per year?

Selecting a Data Analysis Strategy

Selecting a data analysis strategy should be based on the earlier steps of the marketing research process, known characteristics of the data, properties of statistical techniques, and the background and philosophy of the researcher (Figure 15.7).

When selecting a data analysis strategy, the researcher must begin by considering the earlier steps in the process: problem definition (Step 1), development of an approach (Step 2), and research design (Step 3). The researcher should use as a springboard the preliminary plan of data analysis that was prepared as part of the research design. It may be necessary to make changes to the preliminary plan in light of additional information generated in subsequent stages of the research process.

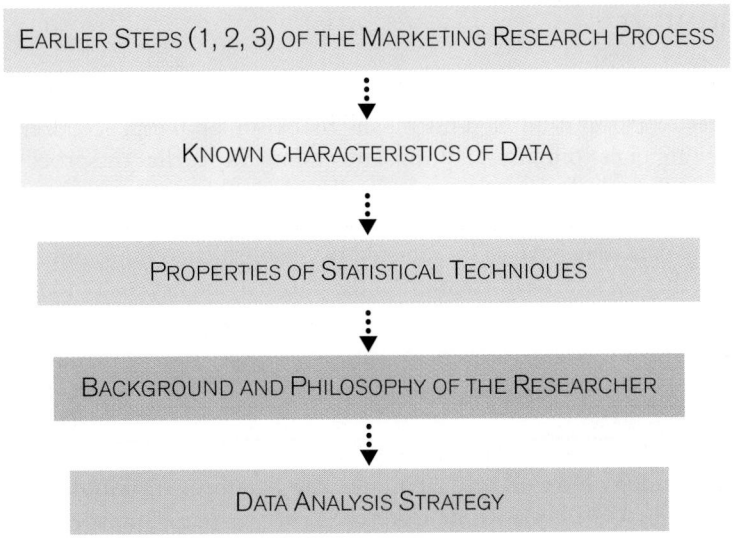

Figure 15.7
Selecting a Data Analysis Strategy

The next step is to consider the known characteristics of the data. The measurement scales used exert a strong influence on the choice of statistical techniques (see Chapter 9). In addition, the research design may favor certain techniques. The insights into the data obtained during data preparation can be valuable in selecting a strategy for analysis.

It is also important to take into account the properties of the statistical techniques, particularly their purpose and underlying assumptions. Some statistical techniques are appropriate for examining differences in variables, others for assessing the magnitudes of the relationships between variables, and others are appropriate for making predictions (see Chapters 16, 17, and 18). The techniques also involve different assumptions, and some techniques can withstand violations of the underlying assumptions better than others. The statistical techniques may be broadly classified as univariate or multivariate. **Univariate techniques** are used for analyzing data when there is a single measurement of each element or unit in the sample; or, if there are several measurements of each element, each variable is analyzed in isolation. On the other hand, **multivariate techniques** are used for analyzing data when there are two or more measurements on each element and the variables are analyzed simultaneously.

The researcher's background and philosophy affect the choice of a data analysis strategy. The experienced, statistically trained researcher will employ a range of techniques.

univariate techniques
Statistical techniques appropriate for analyzing data when there is a single measurement of each element in the sample; or, if there are several measurements of each element, each variable is analyzed in isolation.

multivariate techniques
Statistical techniques suitable for analyzing data when there are two or more measurements on each element and the variables are analyzed simultaneously. Multivariate techniques are concerned with the simultaneous relationships among two or more phenomena.

Summary Illustration Using the Opening Vignette

While collecting primary data, the completed questionnaires returned from the field are carefully checked and edited for incomplete (e.g., questions that are incorrectly skipped) or inconsistent responses (e.g., a respondent reports purchases made on a Sears credit card but does not have one). Any respondents with unsatisfactory responses are simply discarded as the proportion of such respondents is small, the sample size is large, and research by Sears has shown that the unsatisfactory respondents do not differ from satisfactory respondents on the key variables. The data are coded by following the standard procedures given in Sears' codebook. Then, the data are transcribed from the questionnaires into the computer using state-of-the art technology. As part of data cleaning, Sears performs further checks on the data to ascertain their consistency and accuracy. An effort is made to identify data that are out of range (e.g., a response of 8 on a 1-to-7 scale) or logically inconsistent (e.g., sum of percentages adding to more or less than 100 percent), or have extreme values (e.g., household size of 11). Missing values are kept to a minimum by proper selection, training, and supervision of field workers. In addition, Sears analyzes the data by different procedures for treating missing values, including casewise and pairwise deletion, to determine the impact on the results. A similar process is followed for data collected from secondary sources. This care taken in preparing the data has resulted in a high-quality database that enables Sears to identify the needs of the marketplace and target its marketing efforts accordingly.

International Marketing Research

The researcher should ensure that the data have been prepared in a comparable manner across countries or cultural units. This means that comparable procedures must be followed for checking questionnaires, editing, and coding. Note that the procedures must be comparable even though the questionnaire itself and, therefore, the coding scheme, could vary. Certain adjustments may be necessary to make the data comparable across countries. For example, the data may have to be adjusted to establish currency equivalents or metric equivalents. Furthermore, transformation of the data may be necessary to make meaningful comparisons and achieve consistent results, as in the Acer example that follows.

Technology and Marketing Research

Advances in technology have greatly facilitated the data preparation process. When the data are collected by CATI, CAPI, or electronic surveys (e.g., Internet, e-mail), several error checks can be programmed into the questionnaire administration process, and the data are transcribed directly into the computer.

Other advances have also been made. For example, Pearson NCS (www.pearsonncs.com) has released a new data capture system designed to automatically read handwritten information from documents or faxes and process it for a variety of applications. Called NCS Accra, the system verifies and corrects inaccurate information and stores it on optical media. The NCS Accra system features high-production scanners; proven recognition engines for accurate data capture; advanced contextual editing, including address validation and correction; remote fax input capabilities; and robust image archive storage and retrieval options. The system can read hand-printed, machine-printed, and bar-coded data as well as optical marks, including check marks, X's, and tick marks, from documents and images. Once the data have been validated and verified, the ASCII record is transferred to a database or user-application file.[6]

RESEARCH IN ACTION

Acer Pulls Out an Ace

In just a few years, Taiwan-based Acer has transformed itself from a no-name cloner into the seventh-largest personal computer (PC) manufacturer in the world. In 2003, for the fifth year running, Acer was rated by *Reader's Digest* as the Gold Award-winning computer SuperBrand in Asia and was, therefore, inducted into the Hall of Fame. Acer's Ferrari 3200 notebook received the Best Choice Award of Computex Taipei 2004. A crucial factor in Acer's success has been the knowledge of consumer preferences for PCs obtained by conducting surveys in different countries. Great pains are taken at the data preparation stage to ensure that the data are comparable. For example, the price of PCs in each country is transformed to a common unit. This transformation is necessary as the prices are specified in different local currencies, and a common basis is needed for comparison across countries. Also, in each country, the premium price is defined in relation to the prices of competing brands in that country.

The care taken at the data preparation stage has resulted in rich findings. For example, Acer found that, even though the relative importance varies from country to country, eight product attributes contribute to brand preference for desktop PCs on a worldwide basis: price, ease of installation and use, service and support, features, performance, reliability, scope of usage, and compatibility on a network. Such findings have enabled Acer to launch global marketing strategies that are responsive to variations in local preferences.[5]

Ethics in Marketing Research

Ethical issues can arise during the data preparation and analysis step, particularly in areas where the researcher has to exercise judgment. While checking, editing coding, transcribing, and cleaning, the researcher can get some idea about the quality of the data. Sometimes it is easy to identify respondents who did not take the questionnaire seriously or who otherwise provided data of questionable quality. Consider, for example, a respondent who checks the "neither agree nor disagree" response to all the 30 items measuring attitude toward spectator sports. Decisions about whether such respondents should be discarded, that is, not included in the analysis, can raise ethical concerns. A good rule of thumb is to make such decisions during the data preparation phase before conducting any analysis. Discarding respondents after analyzing the data raises ethical concerns, particularly if this information is not fully disclosed in the written report. Moreover, the procedure used to identify unsatisfactory respondents and the number of respondents discarded should be clearly disclosed, as in the following Research in Action example.

Another ethical concern relates to interpretation of the results, drawing conclusions, and making recommendations. Although interpretations, conclusions, and recommendations necessarily involve the subjective judgment of the researcher, this judgment must be exercised honestly, free from any personal biases or agendas of the researcher or the client. Suppose a survey reveals that 31 percent of the respondents preferred the client's brand, while 30.8 percent preferred the closest competing brand, with all the other brands being preferred to a much lesser extent. For the researcher to state that the client's brand is the most preferred brand in the marketplace, without disclosing that a competing brand is a very close second, may be misleading if it conveys the false impression that the client's brand is the dominant brand.

Software Applications

Major statistical packages, such as SPSS (www.spss.com), SAS (www.sas.com), MINITAB (www.minitab.com), and EXCEL (www.microsoft.com/office/excel/) have Internet sites that can be accessed for a variety of information. Exhibit 15.1 details how to use these packages to make consistency checks. These packages also contain options for handling missing responses and for statistically adjusting the data. In addition, a number of statistical packages can now be found on the Internet. While some of these programs may not offer integrated data analysis and management, they can be very useful for conducting specific statistical analyses.

RESEARCH IN ACTION

Ethical Editing of Data

In a study of MBAs' responses to marketing ethics dilemmas, respondents were required to respond to 14 questions regarding ethically ambiguous scenarios by writing a simple sentence regarding what action they would take if they were the manager in those situations. The responses were then analyzed to determine if they were indicative of ethical behavior. However, in the data preparation phase, six respondents out of the 561 total respondents were eliminated from further analysis because their responses indicated that they did not follow the directions that told them to clearly state their choice of action. This is an example of ethical editing of the data. The criterion for unsatisfactory responses is clearly stated, the unsatisfactory respondents are identified before the analysis, and the number of respondents eliminated is disclosed.[7]

WHAT WOULD *YOU* DO?

Banana Republic: Going Bananas Over a Makeover

The Situation

For most of the time as a leading retailer, Gap, Inc. has carefully honed its image through its in-house resources, starting from the design of its clothing to the look of its ads. However, that changed as soon as Jack Calhoun, Banana Republic's new chief marketing officer, took over. Calhoun was one of the first marketing hires by former Walt Disney executive Paul Pressler, who took over as Gap, Inc. president-CEO, succeeding Millard "Mickey" Drexler. One of Pressler's first acts was to hire Publias Groupe's Leo Burnett USA, Chicago, as the agency to oversee segmentation studies of the three Gap brands, including Banana Republic and Old Navy. Calhoun reported to newly hired Banana Republic President Mark Hansen, most recently Gap's head of adult merchandising.

The Banana Republic makeover will be the second in the history of the chain, which started out as a travel catalog and opened safari-themed stores with beat-up jeeps in its storefronts. After the chain was purchased by Gap, Inc., Drexler, known for his ability to spot fashion trends, remade it into an upscale version of Gap.

In recent months, Banana Republic's buzz has quieted and sales have not recovered at a pace that's up to speed with siblings Old Navy and Gap. "The challenge for Banana is the repetition of the fashion lines and marginal quality for the price," said Burt Flickinger, managing director, Strategic Resource Group/Flickinger Consulting, New York.

Calhoun said he and Gap management are carefully building a new positioning for Banana Republic, which traditionally had advertising echoing that of the lower-priced Gap. "We want to build an architecturally sound and beautiful house," said Calhoun of the makeover. "We don't want a Cape Cod with a lot of additions."

A telephone survey was conducted to determine consumers' perceptions of the Banana Republic brand and how the brand could be positioned to offer more value to the consumers.

The Marketing Research Decision

1. The telephone survey resulted in a sample size of 1,008. As the data were being prepared for analysis, it was realized that 132 respondents had missing values. However, the variables with unsatisfactory responses were not the key variables. How should the missing values be treated? Check as many as are applicable.
   a. Return the questionnaires with missing values to the field
   b. Assign missing values: substitute a neutral value
   c. Casewise deletion
   d. Pairwise deletion
   e. Discard respondents with missing values

2. Discuss how the treatment of missing values you recommend influences Jack Calhoun's decision to enhance the image of Banana Republic.

The Marketing Management Decision

1. What should Jack Calhoun do to enhance the perceived value of the Banana Republic brand? Check as many as are applicable.
   a. Launch new product lines
   b. Lower the price
   c. Change advertising
   d. Make the clothing more trendy and fashionable
   e. Make the clothing more functional
2. Discuss how the marketing management-decision action that you recommend to Jack Calhoun is influenced by the treatment of missing values that you suggested earlier and by the findings of the telephone survey.

What Jack Calhoun Did

Jack Calhoun launched new product lines. For women, he introduced a new feminine collection with art-deco-inspired details that brought a soft, romantic touch to the more structured fall looks, and the men's collection conveyed a sense of confidence. He also changed the advertising. What the change meant in terms of ads and marketing was a shift from narrowly defined, single-concept campaigns like "work" and "suede" to those that represented a range of sensibilities in dress. The campaign was comprised of black-and-white photos, along with more vibrant color shots, all with a family album feel. The aim of the new campaign was to express the idea of diversity, age, family, and expressions of the customers. The new personality-focused approach also appealed to a more mature customer than Banana Republic has courted in the past; yet, Banana Republic was not targeting a new audience but rather refocusing on its customers.[8]

SPSS Windows

Using the base module of SPSS, out-of-range values can be selected using the SELECT IF sequence of choices—Menu, Data, Select Cases, If (and then specify the values to be out-of-range). These cases, with the identifying information (subject ID, record number, variable name, and variable value) can then be printed using the LIST or PRINT commands. The PRINT command will save active cases to an external file. If a formatted list is required, the SUMMARIZE sequence of choices can be used—Menu, Analyze, Reports, Case Summaries.

SPSS Data Entry can facilitate data preparation. You can verify respondents have answered completely by setting rules. These rules can be used on existing datasets to validate and check the data, whether or not the questionnaire used to collect the data was constructed in Data Entry. Data Entry allows you to control and check the entry of data through three type of rules: validation, checking, and skip and fill rules.

Although the missing values can be treated within the context of the base module, SPSS Missing Values Analysis can assist in diagnosing missing values and replacing missing values with estimates. TextSmart by SPSS can help in the coding and analysis of open-ended responses.

We illustrate the use of the base module in creating new variables and recoding existing ones using the data of Table 15.2. This table gives the data from a pretest sample of 20 respondents on preferences for restaurants. Each respondent was asked to rate preference to eat in a familiar restaurant (1 = Weak Preference, 7 = Strong Preference), and to rate the restaurant in terms of quality of food, quantity of portions, value, and service (1= Poor, 7 = Excellent). Annual household income was also obtained and coded as: 1 = Less than $20,000, 2 = $20,000 to 34,999, 3 = $35,000 to 49,999, 4 = $50,000 to 74,999, 5 = $75,000 to 99,999, 6 = $100,000 or more.

Table 15.2

Restaurant Preference

ID	PREFERENCE	QUALITY	QUANTITY	VALUE	SERVICE	INCOME	OVERALL	INCOME
1	2	2	3	1	3	6	9	4
2	6	5	6	5	7	2	23	1
3	4	4	3	4	5	3	16	2
4	1	2	1	1	2	5	6	4
5	7	6	6	5	4	1	21	1
6	5	4	4	5	4	3	17	2
7	2	2	3	2	3	5	10	4
8	3	3	4	2	3	4	12	3
9	7	6	7	6	5	2	24	1
10	2	3	2	2	2	5	9	4
11	2	3	2	1	3	6	9	4
12	6	6	6	6	7	2	25	1
13	4	4	3	3	4	3	14	2
14	1	1	3	1	2	4	7	3
15	7	7	5	5	4	2	21	1
16	5	5	4	5	5	3	19	2
17	2	3	1	2	3	4	9	3
18	4	4	3	3	3	3	13	2
19	7	5	5	7	5	5	22	4
20	3	2	2	3	3	3	10	2

We want to create a variable called overall evaluation of the restaurant (Overall) that is the sum of the ratings on quality, quantity, value, and service. Thus,

Overall = Quality + Quantity + Value + Service

The screen captures using SPSS Windows for these steps can be downloaded from the Web site for this book. These steps are as follows.

1. Select TRANSFORM.
2. Click on COMPUTE.
3. Type "overall" in the TARGET VARIABLE box.
4. Click on "quality" and move it to the NUMERIC EXPRESSIONS box.
5. Click on the "+" sign.
6. Click on "quantity" and move it to the NUMERIC EXPRESSIONS box.
7. Click on the "+" sign.
8. Click on "value" and move it to the NUMERIC EXPRESSIONS box.
9. Click on the "+" sign.
10. Click on "service" and move it to the NUMERIC EXPRESSIONS box.
11. Click on TYPE & LABEL under the TARGET VARIABLE box and type "Overall Evaluation." Click on CONTINUE.
12. Click OK.

We also want to illustrate the recoding of variables to create new variables. Income category 1 occurs only once and income category 6 occurs only twice. Therefore, we want to combine income categories 1 and 2, and categories 5 and 6, and create a new income variable "rincome" labeled "Recoded Income." Note that rincome has only four categories that are coded as 1 to 4.

This can be done in SPSS Windows (download screen captures from the Web site for this book) as follows.

1. Select TRANSFORM.
2. Click on RECODE and select INTO DIFFERENT VARIABLES.
3. Click on income and move it to NUMERIC VARIABLE → OUTPUT VARIABLE box.
4. Type "rincome" in OUTPUT VARIABLE NAME box.
5. Type "Recode Income" in OUTPUT VARIABLE LABEL box.
6. Click OLD AND NEW VAULES box.
7. Under OLD VALUES, on the left click RANGE. Type 1 and 2 in the range boxes. Under NEW VALUES, on the right click VALUE and type 1 in the value box. Click ADD.
8. Under OLD VALUES, on the left click VALUE. Type 3 in the value box. Under NEW VALUES, on the right click VALUE and type 2 in the value box. Click ADD.
9. Under OLD VALUES, on the left click VALUE. Type 4 in the value box. Under NEW VALUES, on the right click VALUE and type 3 in the value box. Click ADD.
10. Under OLD VALUES, on the left click RANGE. Type 5 and 6 in the range boxes. Under NEW VALUES, on the right click VALUE and type 4 in the value box. Click ADD.
11. Click CONTINUE.
12. Click CHANGE.
13. Click OK.

EXCEL

Although EXCEL is an effective spreadsheet program, it lacks the qualities of a relational database that SPSS offers. As a result, distributions of variables cannot be directly produced and data recoding must be done through if-then statements. To illustrate the data recoding features of EXCEL, the following example is provided using the same

EXPERIENTIAL LEARNING

Data Conversion and Preparation

Go to the textbook Web site and download the following comma-delimited file: Hotelsat. This is an EXCEL file. You will read in this file in to the SPSS program, and then use the power of the SPSS program to (1) substitute mean values for variables into cells with missing values, and (2) clean the file for out-of-range values.

• Import into SPSS

Open SPSS
FILE
OPEN
DATA
OPEN FILE window
FILES OF TYPE window (All Files)
Select Hotelsat
Text Import Wizard Step 1– accept default settings–NEXT.
Text Import Wizard Step 2–variables arranged delimited–YES;
–variable names at top of file–YES.
Note: Variable names will be taken from the first row of the spreadsheet.
Text Import Wizard Step 3–accept default settings–NEXT.
Text Import Wizard Step 4–accept default settings–NEXT.
Text Import Wizard Step 5–accept default settings–NEXT.
Text Import Wizard Step 6–accept default settings–FINISH.
To view data, click on the DATA VIEW tab at the bottom of the SPSS window.
Note: Variable names will be at the top of the columns. Click VARIABLE VIEW. In the DECIMALS column, set decimals for all variables to 0, one at a time.

• Clean Data

1. Count how many cases have complete sets of responses.
TRANSFORM
COMPUTE
COMPUTE VARIABLE window
(TARGET VARIABLE = numval)
(NUMERIC EXPRESSION = NVALID(Q3 to Q5)
numval = NVALID(Q3 to Q5)
Note: Select NVALID(variable,...) under FUNCTIONS. Replace the "?" with "Q3 to Q5". Click OK.
Note: A new variable "numval" is created. Five of 200 cases have a value of "2," instead of "3," meaning 5 have one missing value.
2. Mean substitution.
TRANSFORM
REPLACE MISSING VALUES
NEW VARIABLE(S) window
Double click on Q3
Q3_1 = SMEAN(Q3) appears as new variable.
Double click on Q4
Q4_1 = SMEAN(Q4) appears as new variable.
Double click on Q5
Q5_1 = SMEAN(Q5) appears as new variable.
Click OK.
Note: Output will show 5 values were replaced for variable Q4_1.
3. Check distributions of the new variables with substituted means for out-of-range values.
ANALYZE
DESCRIPTIVES STATISTICS
FREQUENCIES
FREQUENCIES window: Select (Q3_1 to Q5_1)

(continued)

(Note: These variables will appear as SMEAN(Q3)[Q3_1], SMEAN(Q4)[Q4_1], and SMEAN(Q5)[Q5_1].)
STATISTICS
Select MINIMUM, MAXIMUM, MEAN
STD. DEVIATION
Click OK.

Note: Q4_1 has 5 cases that received the mean value of 5.8.

Q5_1 has 13 cases with the "-9" value. In some data entry plans, such an entry as "-9" is intended to represent a missing value.

4. Convert missing value entries of Q5_1 (Those cases with a "-9" represent a missing value during the data entry phase.) into SYSMIS values.
TRANSFORM
RECODE INTO DIFFERENT VARIABLES
RECODE INTO DIFFERENT VARIABLES window
Select Q5_1. This appears as SMEAN(Q5)(Q5_1)
OUTPUT VARIABLE = Q5new
Select CHANGE
Select OLD AND NEW VALUE
Under OLD VALUE
Select -9
Under NEW VALUE
Select SYSTEM-MISSING (SYSMIS)
Then, select ADD

Note: You are recoding "-9" to have a system missing value so that "-9" will now be recognized by SPSS to be "SYSMIS" –a placeholder, for all practical purposes.

Under OLD VALUE
Select RANGE 1 thru 7
Under NEW VALUE
Select COPY OLD VALUE(S)
Then, select ADD

Note: You are directing SPSS to copy the old values for any entries with a value of 1 through 7.

Then select CONTINUE
Back at the RECODE INTO DIFFERENT VARIABLES window
Click OK.
Check distribution for Q5new by replicating Step 3 above and replacing Q5new for Q3_1, Q4_1, and Q5_1 in the FREQUENCIES window step.
(Note: You will see Q5new has no cases with "-9" now, but Q5new now has 13 cases with missing values.)

5. Check work.
ANALYZE
DESCRIPTIVE STATISTICS
FREQUENCIES
FREQUENCIES window: Select Q3_1, Q4_1, and Q5new

Note: Output for variables Q3_1 and Q5new, should now have only values of 1–7 (Q5new will also have its mean value included), as can be seen for SMEAN(Q3) and Q5new. Q4_1 should have 5 cases with 5.8 with the rest being integers from 1– 7, as can be seen for SMEAN(Q4).

6. Save your new SPSS system file as follows.
FILE
SAVE AS…
(Note: You will now select the location to save this SPSS system file.)
In FILE NAME block of SAVE DATA AS window
Type in "Hotelsat New."
In SAVE AS TYPE block
Select "SPSS(*.sav)"
Click on SAVE.
(Note: Your new SPSS system file will be named in "Hotelsat New.")

hotelsat dataset used to begin the SPSS demonstration in the Experiential Learning exercise. For both Q4 and Q5, the next higher digit to the mean value of each variable will be inserted into any missing or out-of-range value. In this case, the value of 6 will be inserted. The screen captures using EXCEL for these steps can be downloaded from the Web site for this book.

Open Hotelsat
In column F, type in the variable name "q4new"
In cell F2, type in the following if-then statement:
= IF(D2<1,6, IF(D2>7,6,D2))

This if-then statement directs EXCEL to evaluate the current entry in cell D2 in the following manner. If this entry in D2 is less than 1, then enter a value of 6 in cell F2; if this entry in D2 is greater than 7, then enter a value of 6 in cell F2. Otherwise, just enter the current value in D2 in F2.

Click on the lower-right corner of cell F2, and drag to cell F201 in order to copy the F2 cell to all cells from F3 to F201. In this way, you have inserted the value of 6 into any cells with missing or out-of-range values, or simply copied the original values if the cell entries were okay.

In column G, type in the variable name "q5new"
In cell G2, type in the following if-then statement:
= IF(E2<1,6, IF(E2>7,6,E2))

This if-then statement directs EXCEL to evaluate the current entry in cell E2 in the following manner. If this entry in E2 is less than 1, then enter a value of 6 in cell G2; if this entry in E2 is greater than 7, then enter a value of 6 in cell G2. Otherwise, just enter the current value of E2 in G2.

Click on the lower-right corner of cell G2, and drag to cell G201 in order to copy the G2 cell to all cells from G3 to G201. In this way, you have inserted the value of 6 into any cells with missing or out-of-range values, or simply copied the original values if the cell entries were okay.

Summary

Data preparation begins with a preliminary check of all questionnaires for completeness and interviewing quality. Then, more thorough editing takes place. Editing consists of screening questionnaires to identify illegible, incomplete, inconsistent, or ambiguous responses. Such responses may be handled by returning questionnaires to the field, assigning missing values, or discarding the unsatisfactory respondents.

The next step is coding. A numerical or alphanumeric code is assigned to represent a specific response to a specific question, along with the column position that code will occupy. It is often helpful to prepare a codebook containing the coding instructions and the necessary information about the variables in the data set. The coded data are transcribed onto disks or entered into computers via keypunching. Mark-sense forms, optical scanning, or computerized sensory analysis may also be used.

Cleaning the data requires consistency checks and treatment of missing responses. Options available for treating missing responses include substitution of a neutral value, such as the mean, casewise deletion, and pairwise deletion. The selection of a data analysis strategy should be based on the earlier steps of the marketing research process, known characteristics of the data, properties of statistical techniques, and the background and philosophy of the researcher.

Proper data preparation is essential before analyzing data for quality-management programs, such as customer satisfaction. While analyzing the data in international marketing research, the researcher should ensure that the units of measurement are comparable across countries or cultural units. Technological advances are resulting in new ways to capture, edit, code, and prepare data. Several ethical issues are related to data processing, particularly the discarding of unsatisfactory respondents, and evaluation and interpretation of results. Major statistical packages, such as SPSS, SAS, MINITAB, and EXCEL, have Internet sites that can be accessed for useful information.

Key Terms and Concepts

Editing, 406
Coding, 407
Codebook, 407
Fixed-field codes, 409
Data cleaning, 412
Consistency checks, 412
Missing responses, 413
Casewise deletion, 413
Pairwise deletion, 413
Variable respecification, 414
Univariate techniques, 415
Multivariate techniques, 415

Suggested Cases and Video Cases

Cases

4.1 Boeing
4.2 Gucci

Video Cases

3.1 AFLAC
4.2 Marriott

Additional cases and video cases are available in the Instructor's Manual and on the instructor and student Web sites.

Live Research: Conducting a Marketing Research Project

1. The project coordinators should number the questionnaires and keep track of any quotas.
2. The team leaders should be responsible for initial editing of the questionnaires.
3. Each student should be responsible for coding her or his questionnaires and for data entry. It is recommended that the data be entered into an EXCEL spreadsheet using the coding scheme developed by the instructor or one of the teams.
4. The projector coordinators should assemble all the student files into one data file, conduct the computer checks, and clean up the data.
5. The data analysis strategy should be specified by the instructor and discussed in the class.

Acronyms

The data preparation process may be summarized by the acronym DATA PREP:

D ata consistency checks
A djusting the data for missing values
T ranscribing
A nalysis strategy
P ost field work questionnaire checking
R ecording numerical or alphanumerical values: coding
E diting
P reliminary plan of data analysis

Review Questions

1. Describe the data preparation process.
2. What activities are involved in the preliminary checking of questionnaires that have been returned from the field?
3. What does editing a questionnaire mean?
4. How are unsatisfactory responses discovered in editing treated?
5. What is the difference between precoding and postcoding?
6. Describe the guidelines for the coding of unstructured questions.
7. What does transcribing the data involve?
8. What kinds of consistency checks are made in cleaning the data?
9. What options are available for the treatment of missing data?
10. What considerations are involved in selecting a data analysis strategy?

Applied Problems

1. Shown below is part of a questionnaire used to determine consumer preferences for cameras. Set up a coding scheme for the following three questions (Q9, Q10, and Q11). (Note: The first eight questions of the camera survey are not included.)

9. Please rate the importance of the following features you would consider when shopping for a new camera.

	Not so important				Very important
a. DX film speed setting	1	2	3	4	5
b. Auto-film advance	1	2	3	4	5
c. Autofocus	1	2	3	4	5
d. Autoloading	1	2	3	4	5

10. If you were to buy a new camera, which of the following outlets would you visit? Please check as many as apply.
    a. ____ Drugstore
    b. ____ Camera store
    c. ____ Discount/mass merchandiser
    d. ____ Supermarket
    e. ____ Internet stores/shopping sites
    f. ____ Other

11. Where do you get most of your photo processing done? Please check only one option.
    a. ____ Drugstore
    b. ____ Mini labs
    c. ____ Camera stores
    d. ____ Discount/mass merchandiser
    e. ____ Supermarkets
    f. ____ Mail order
    g. ____ Kiosk/other

2. Explain how you would make consistency checks for the part of the questionnaire given in Applied Problem number 1 using SPSS, SAS, MINITAB, or EXCEL.
3. Use an electronic questionnaire design and administration package such as Ci3 (www.sawtoothsoftware.com) to program the camera preference questionnaire given in Applied Problem number 1. Add one or two questions of your own. Administer the questionnaire to five students and prepare the data for analysis. Does computer administration of the questionnaire facilitate data preparation?

Group Discussion

As a small group, discuss the following statements:

1. Data preparation is a time-consuming process. In projects with severe time constraints, data preparation should be circumvented.
2. The researcher should always use computer-assisted interviewing (CATI or CAPI) to collect the data, as these methods greatly facilitate data preparation.

EXHIBIT 15.1 Computer Programs for Data Preparation

SPSS

Out-of-range values can be selected using the SELECT IF or PROCESS IF statements. These cases, with the identifying information (subject ID, record number, variable name, and variable value) can then be printed using the PRINT or WRITE commands. As a further check, the LIST command can be used to display the values of variables for each case. SPSS Data Entry II simplifies the process of entering new data files. It facilitates data cleaning and checking for logical inconsistencies.

SAS

The IF, IF-THEN, and IF-THEN/ELSE statements can be used to select cases with missing or out-of-range values. The select statement executes one of several statements or groups of statements. The LIST statement is useful for printing suspicious input lines. The LOSTCARD statement can be used to identify missing records in the data. The PRINT and PRINTTO procedures can be used to identify cases and print variable names and variable values. In addition, the OUTPUT and PUT statements can be used to write the values of variables.

MINITAB

There are control statements that permit the control of the order of commands in a macro. The IF command allows implementation of different blocks of commands. This includes IF, ELSEIF, ELSE, and ENDIF.

EXCEL

The IF statement can be used to make logical checks and check out-of-range values. The IF statement can be accessed under the Insert>Function>All>IF.

CHAPTER

16

Data Analysis: Frequency Distribution, Hypothesis Testing, and Cross-Tabulation

"Cross-tabulation still remains the most frequently used data analysis technique for marketers. However, cross-tabulation alone leaves a lot of information unexplored and does not exploit the predictive value of research. For that, you need to go beyond cross-tabulation to much more complex and sophisticated multivariate models."

WILLIAM NEAL, *Senior Executive Officer, SDR Consulting, Atlanta, GA*

OPENING QUESTIONS

1. Why is preliminary data analysis desirable, and what insights can be obtained from such an analysis?
2. What is meant by frequency counts, and what measures are associated with such an analysis?
3. What is the general procedure for hypothesis testing, and what steps are involved?
4. How should cross-tabulation analysis be conducted, and what are the associated statistics?
5. How is the chi-square statistic calculated and for what purpose is it used? What other statistics are used to test association between two variables, and when are they used?
6. What computer programs are available for conducting frequency and cross-tabulation analyses?

Consumers Consume Coupons

About 4.5 billion coupons were redeemed in 2003. A recent Promotional Attitudes and Practices Study surveyed 682 female primary grocery shoppers who were members of the Synovate (www.synovate.com) panel. The survey data were analyzed by calculating frequency counts, percentages, and means. This survey found that 93 percent of the respondents liked coupons, 99 percent had used coupons in the last year, and 95 percent had used a coupon within the last 30 days. The survey also reported that 642 respondents (94 percent) said coupons were helpful in reducing the cost of groceries, 593 of them (87 percent) used coupons for brands they normally bought, and 212 of them (31 percent) used coupons to try new products. Despite the growing influence of frequent-customer clubs, frequency counts indicated that most of the respondents did not limit their shopping to a single store. Of the 44 percent who are club members, 19 percent said their membership makes them more likely to shop at that store, while 51 percent shop other stores for specials. The average number of stores shopped was 2.9 per household.

As illustrated here, survey data are often analyzed to obtain frequency counts (593 respondents used coupons for brands they normally bought), percentages (95 percent had used a coupon within the last 30 days), and means (the average number of stores shopped was 2.9 per household). A cross-tabulation of coupon usage with income indicated that households at all income levels were cashing coupons. Furthermore, lower-income households had higher coupon usage as compared to middle- and higher-income households, and this association was statistically significant. Supermarkets can use such findings to target their coupon and promotional strategies. It is clear that supermarkets cannot rely exclusively on frequent-customer clubs. Coupons and price specials also play a major role in attracting shoppers. That is why supermarkets like Kroger make heavy use of coupons and price specials in addition to the Kroger Plus Shoppers' card.[1] •

Overview

Once the data have been prepared for analysis (Chapter 15), the researcher should conduct some basic analyses. Often, this involves computing frequency counts, percentages, and averages, as in the opening vignette. This chapter describes basic data analysis, including frequency distribution, hypothesis testing, and cross-tabulation. Figure 16.1 briefly explains the focus of the chapter, the relation of this chapter to the previous ones, and the steps of the marketing research process on which this chapter concentrates.

First, we describe the frequency distribution of a single variable and explain how it provides both an indication of the number of out-of-range, missing, or extreme values, as well as insights into the central tendency and variability of the underlying distribution. Next, we discuss hypothesis testing and present a general procedure. Then, we consider the use of cross-tabulation for understanding the associations between variables taken two at a time. While the nature of the association can be observed from tables, statistics are available for testing the significance and strength of the association. Figure 16.2 gives an overview of the topics discussed in this chapter and how they flow from one to the next.

Many commercial marketing research projects do not go beyond basic data analysis. These findings are often displayed using tables and graphs, as discussed further in Chapter 19. While the findings of basic analysis are valuable in their own right, the insights gained from the basic analysis are also invaluable in interpreting the results obtained from more sophisticated statistical techniques. Therefore, before conducting more advanced statistical analysis, it is useful to examine the frequency distributions of the relevant variables.

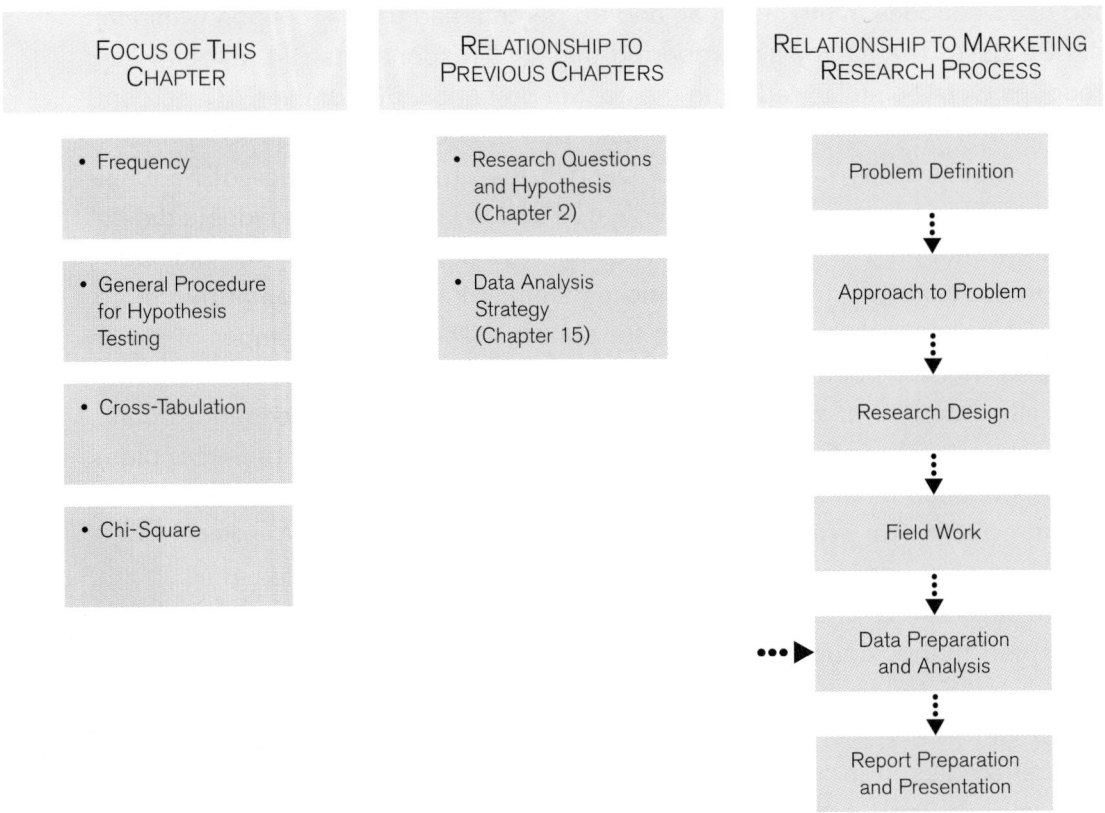

Figure 16.1

Relationship of Frequency Distribution, Hypothesis Testing, and Cross-Tabulation to Previous Chapters and the Marketing Research Process

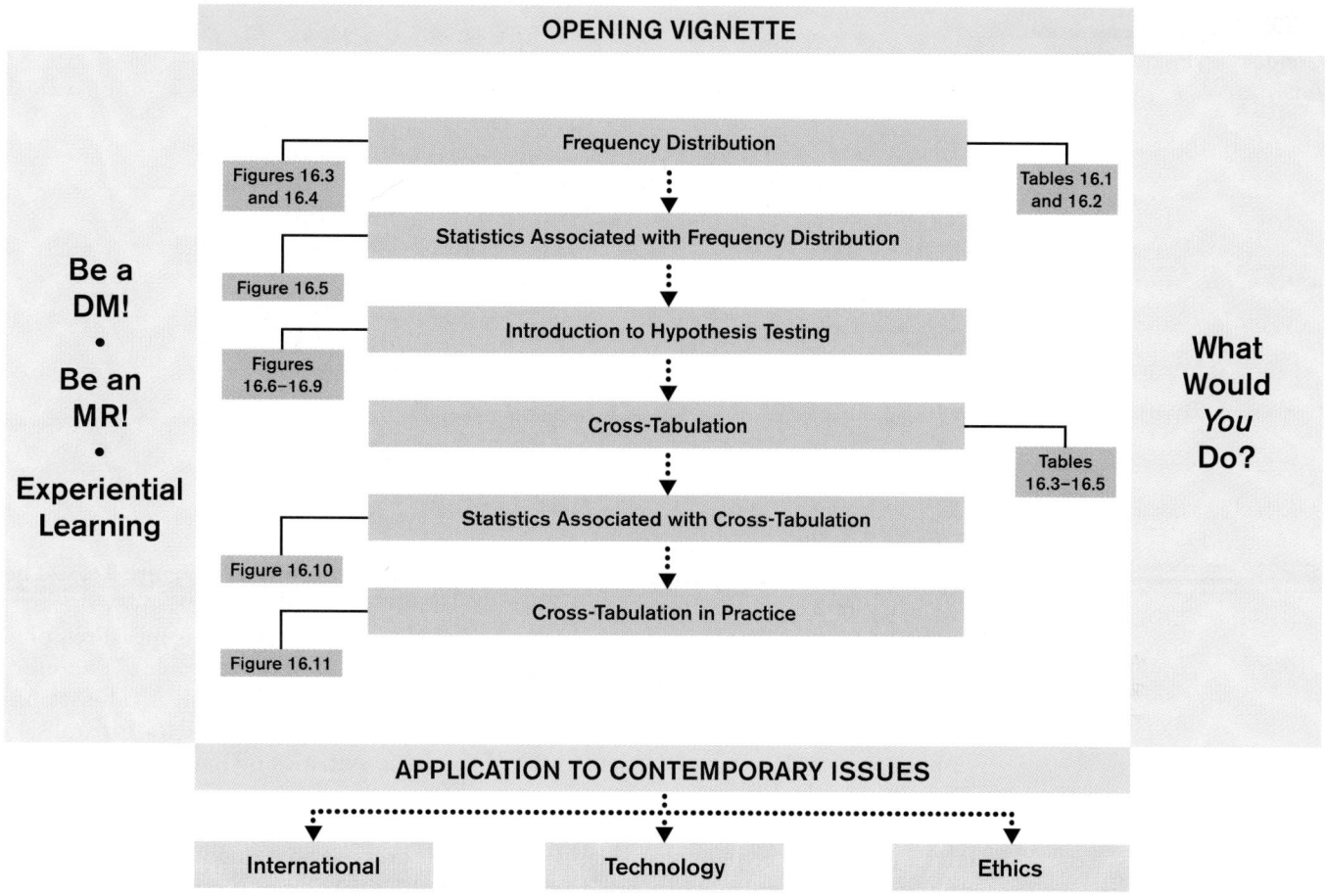

Figure 16.2

Frequency Distribution, Hypothesis Testing, and Cross-Tabulation: An Overview

Frequency Distribution

Marketing researchers often need to answer questions about a single variable. For example,

- What is the percentage of shoppers using coupons? (See opening vignette.)
- What percentage of the market consists of heavy users, medium users, light users, and nonusers?
- How many customers are very familiar with a new product offering? How many are familiar, somewhat familiar, and unfamiliar with the brand? What is the mean rating on familiarity with the brand? Is there much variance in the extent to which customers are familiar with the new product?
- What is the income distribution of brand users? Is this distribution skewed toward low-income brackets?

The answers to these kinds of questions can be determined by examining frequency distributions. In a **frequency distribution**, one variable is considered at a time. The objective is to obtain a count of the number of responses associated with different values of the variable. The relative occurrence, or relative frequency, of different values of the variable is expressed in percentages, as in the opening vignette. A frequency distribution for a variable produces a table of frequency counts, percentages, and cumulative percentages for all the values associated with that variable.

frequency distribution
A mathematical distribution with the objective of obtaining a count of the number of responses associated with different values of one variable and to express these counts in percentage terms.

Figure 16.3
Conducting Frequency Analysis

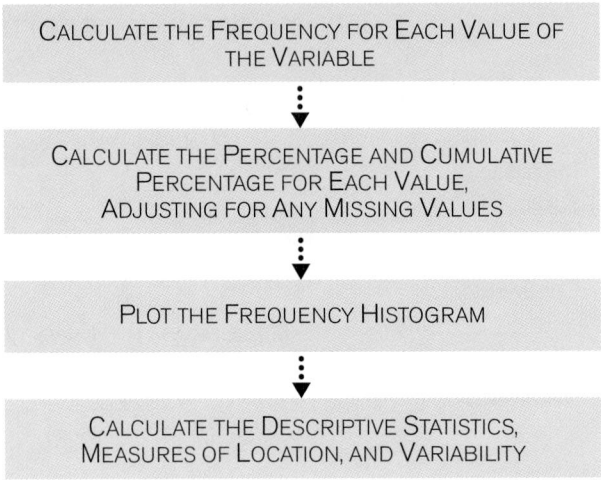

The steps involved in conducting frequency analysis are given in Figure 16.3. The frequency procedure is illustrated using the data of Table 16.1, which gives the attitude toward Nike, usage, and sex of a sample of Nike users. Attitude is measured on a seven-point Likert-type scale (1 = very unfavorable, 7 = very favorable). The users have been coded as 1, 2, or 3, representing light, medium, or heavy users. The sex has been coded as 1 for females and 2 for males. This table gives the data for only 45 respondents so that that the calculations of the basic statistics by hand can be shown. These hand calculations provide the reader a better idea of the basic concepts. In practice, the sample size is much larger. The analysis of such large datasets is illustrated later in the chapter in an Experiential Learning exercise that analyzes the taste-test data for 648 respondents regarding a new reduced-fat version of Nestlé's KitKat candy bar.

Table 16.2 provides the frequency distribution of attitude of Table 16.1. In the table, the first column contains the labels assigned to the different categories of the variable. The second column indicates the code or value assigned to each label or category. The third column gives the number of respondents for each value, including the missing value. For example, of the 45 respondents who participated in the survey, six respondents have a value of 2 denoting an unfavorable attitude. One respondent did not answer and has a missing value denoted by 9. The fourth column displays the percentage of respondents checking each value. These percentages are obtained by dividing the frequencies in column 3 by 45. The next column shows percentages calculated by excluding the cases with missing values, that is, by dividing the frequencies in column 3 by 44 (45 −1). As can be seen, eight respondents (18.2 percent) have an attitude value of 5. If there are no missing values, columns 4 and 5 are identical. The last column represents cumulative percentages after adjusting for missing cases. The cumulative percentage for a value denotes the percentage of responses that are less than or equal to that value. The cumulative percentage corresponding to the value of 5 is 70.5 percent. In other words, 70.5 percent of the respondents have a value of 5 or less. The SPSS and EXCEL outputs along with explanatory notes can be downloaded from the Web site for this book.

A frequency distribution helps determine the extent of illegitimate responses. Values of 0 and 8 would be illegitimate responses, or errors. The cases with these values can be identified and corrective action taken. The presence of *outliers*, or cases with extreme values, can also be detected. In the case of a frequency distribution of household size, a few isolated families with household sizes of 9 or more might be considered outliers. A frequency distribution also indicates the shape of the empirical distribution of the variable. The frequency data may be used to construct a histogram or a vertical bar chart in which the values of the variable are portrayed along the X-axis and the absolute or relative frequencies of the values are placed along the Y-axis.

Table 16.1

Usage and Attitude toward Nike Shoes

Number	User Group	Gender	Attitude
1	3.00	2.00	7.00
2	1.00	1.00	2.00
3	1.00	1.00	3.00
4	3.00	2.00	6.00
5	3.00	2.00	5.00
6	2.00	2.00	4.00
7	2.00	1.00	5.00
8	1.00	1.00	2.00
9	2.00	2.00	4.00
10	1.00	1.00	3.00
11	3.00	2.00	6.00
12	3.00	2.00	6.00
13	1.00	1.00	2.00
14	3.00	2.00	6.00
15	1.00	2.00	4.00
16	1.00	2.00	3.00
17	3.00	1.00	7.00
18	2.00	1.00	6.00
19	1.00	1.00	1.00
20	3.00	1.00	5.00
21	3.00	2.00	6.00
22	2.00	2.00	2.00
23	1.00	1.00	1.00
24	3.00	1.00	6.00
25	1.00	2.00	3.00
26	2.00	2.00	5.00
27	3.00	2.00	7.00
28	2.00	1.00	5.00
29	1.00	1.00	9.00
30	2.00	2.00	5.00
31	1.00	2.00	1.00
32	1.00	2.00	4.00
33	2.00	1.00	3.00
34	2.00	1.00	4.00
35	3.00	1.00	5.00
36	3.00	1.00	6.00
37	3.00	2.00	6.00
38	3.00	2.00	5.00
39	3.00	2.00	7.00
40	1.00	1.00	4.00
41	1.00	1.00	2.00
42	1.00	1.00	1.00
43	1.00	1.00	2.00
44	1.00	1.00	3.00
45	1.00	1.00	1.00

Table 16.2

Frequency Distribution of Attitude toward Nike

Value Label	Value	Frequency	Percentage	Valid Percentage	Cumulative Percentage
Very unfavorable	1	5	11.1	11.4	11.4
	2	6	13.3	13.6	25.0
	3	6	13.3	13.6	38.6
	4	6	13.3	13.6	52.3
	5	8	17.8	18.2	70.5
	6	9	20.0	20.5	90.9
Very favorable	7	4	8.9	9.1	100.0
	9	1	2.2	Missing	
	Total	**45**	**100.0**	**100.0**	

Figure 16.4 is a histogram of the attitude data in Table 16.2. From the histogram, one could examine whether the observed distribution is consistent with an expected or assumed distribution. Note, in this case the observed distribution does not look like the standard normal distribution. This may be important in determining what type of statistical test is appropriate. For further illustration, consider the Yellow Pages Advertising by Physicians example.

Note that the numbers and percentages in the preceding example indicate the extent of advertising. Because numbers are involved, a frequency distribution can be used to calculate descriptive or summary statistics. Some of the statistics associated with frequency distribution are discussed in the next section.

Statistics Associated with Frequency Distribution

As illustrated in the previous section, a frequency distribution is a convenient way of looking at the values of a variable. A frequency table is easy to read and provides basic information, but sometimes, this information may be too detailed and the researcher

A frequency distribution of responses can help in understanding attitude toward Nike.

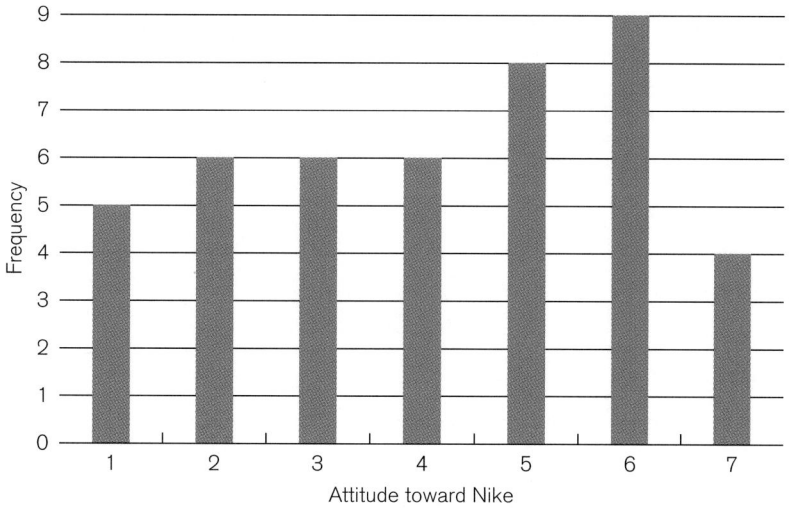

Figure 16.4
Frequency Histogram

must summarize it by the use of descriptive statistics. The most commonly used statistics associated with frequencies are measures of location (mean, mode, and median) and measures of variability (range and standard deviation).

Measures of Location

The **measures of location** that we discuss are measures of central tendency because they tend to describe the center of the distribution (see Chapter 13). If the entire sample is changed by adding a fixed constant to each observation, then the mean, mode, and median change by the same fixed amount. Suppose we added the number 10 to the attitude ratings of all the 44 respondents (45 − 1) who expressed their attitudes toward Nike in Table 16.1. Then the mean, mode, and median will all increase by 10.

measures of location
Statistics that describe locations within a data set. Measures of central tendency describe the center of the distribution.

RESEARCH IN ACTION

The Signal Is Green for Yellow Pages Advertising by Physicians

A census was conducted of every physician's Yellow Pages listing in Atlanta, Georgia; Chicago, Illinois; and Charlotte, North Carolina, and the contents of these listings were analyzed to determine the types of ads. The various types of Yellow Pages ads were as follows:

Type of Yellow Pages Ad	Frequency	Percentage
Nondisplay listings: light face	5,454	46.0
Nondisplay listings: face	1,656	14.0
Display ads	4,694	40.0
Total advertisements	11,804	100.0

Based on the frequency counts, the study concluded that Yellow Pages listings are a widely used form of physician advertising: 11,804 ads were located in the three areas. The majority of the physicians (46 + 14 = 60 percent), however, were using nondisplay (light face/face) listings, which are more appropriate for physicians with established practices who have all the patients they want. Only 40 percent were using the larger display ads that have a much higher likelihood of being seen by potential patients who consult Yellow Pages when looking for a physician. Because a majority of the physicians were looking for new patients, the study concluded that more physicians should use the display rather than nondisplay ads in the Yellow Pages.[2]

mean
The average; that value obtained by summing all elements in a set and dividing by the number of elements.

Mean The **mean**, or average value, is the most commonly used measure of central tendency or center of a distribution (see opening vignette). It is used to estimate the average when the data have been collected using an interval or ratio scale (see Chapter 9). The data should display some central tendency, with most of the responses distributed around the mean.

The mean, $\bar{X}$ is given by

$$\bar{X} = \sum_{i=1}^{n} X_i / n$$

Where

X_i = Observed values of the variable X

n = Number of observations (sample size)

Generally, the mean is a robust measure and does not change markedly as data values are added or deleted. For the frequency counts given in Table 16.2, the mean value is calculated as follows:

$$\begin{aligned}\bar{X} &= (5\times1)+(6\times2)+(6\times3)+(6\times4)+(8\times5)+(9\times6)+(4\times7)/44\\ &= (5+12+18+24+40+54+28)/44\\ &= 181/44\\ &= 4.11\end{aligned}$$

mode
A measure of central tendency given as the value that occurs the most in a sample distribution.

Mode The **mode** is the value that occurs most frequently. It represents the highest peak of the distribution. The mode is a good measure of location when the variable is inherently categorical or has otherwise been grouped into categories. The mode in Table 16.2 is 6 as this value occurs with the highest frequency, that is, 9 times (see also the histogram in Figure 16.4).

median
A measure of central tendency given as the value above which half of the values fall and below which half of the values fall.

Median The **median** of a sample is the middle value when the data are arranged in ascending or descending rank order (see Chapter 9). If the number of data points is even, the median is usually estimated as the midpoint between the two middle values—by adding the two middle values and dividing their sum by 2. The middle value is the value where 50 percent of the values are greater than that value, and 50 percent are less. Thus, the median is the 50th percentile. The median is an appropriate measure of central tendency for ordinal data. In Table 16.2, the middle value is the average of the 22nd and 23rd observations when the data are arranged in ascending or descending order. This average is 4, and so the median is 4. The median can be easily determined by using cumulative percentages in the frequency table. Note that at a value of 4, the cumulative percentage is only 52.3 percent, but for a value of 5, it is 70.5 percent, and for a value of 3 it is 38.6 percent. Therefore, the 50 percent point occurs at the value of 4.

As can be seen from Table 16.2, the three measures of central tendency for this distribution are different (mean = 4.11, mode = 6, median = 4). This is not surprising since each measure defines central tendency in a different way. The three values are equal only when the distribution is symmetric. In a symmetric distribution, the values on either side of the center of the distribution are the same, and the mean, mode, and median are equal (Figure 16.5). The normal distribution discussed earlier in Chapter 13 is a symmetric distribution, and the three measures of central tendency are equal. An advantage of calculating all three measures of central tendency is that we can determine whether the distribution is symmetric or asymmetric. The asymmetry of the distribution of Table 16.2 can also be seen from the histogram of Figure 16.4.

If the distribution is asymmetric, which measure should be used? If the variable is measured on a nominal scale, the mode should be used. If the variable is measured on an ordinal scale, the median is appropriate. If the variable is measured on an interval or ratio scale, the mode is a poor measure of central tendency. This can be seen from Table 16.2. While the modal value of 6 has the highest frequency of 9, it represents only 20.5 percent of the sample. In general, for interval or ratio data, the median is a

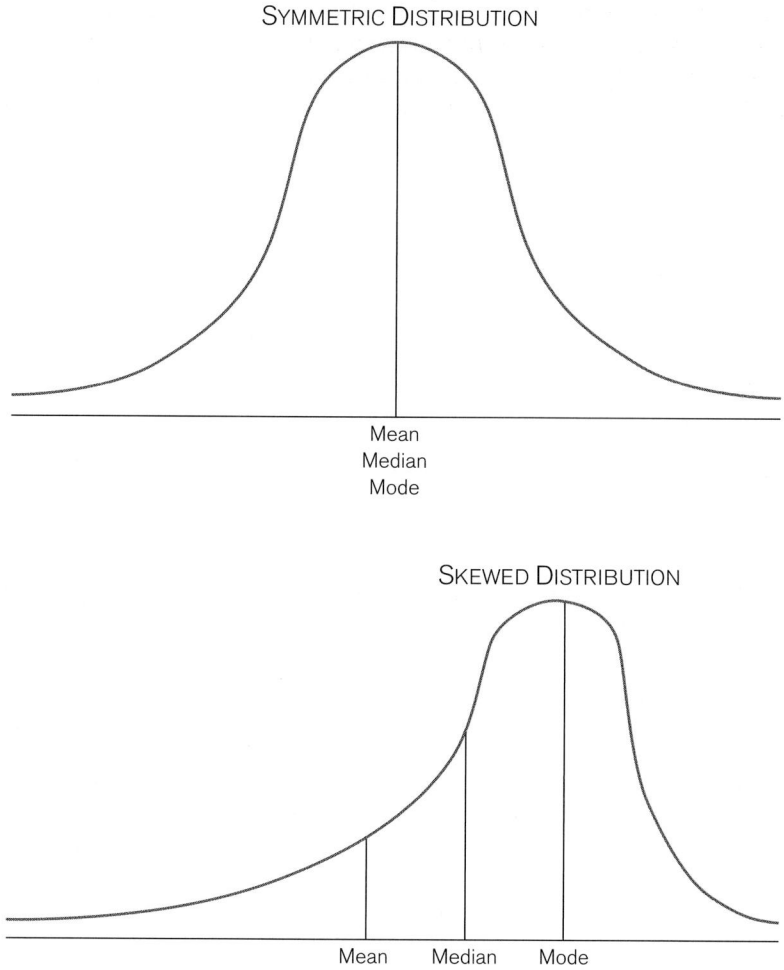

Figure 16.5
Skewness of a Distribution

better measure of central tendency, although it too ignores available information about the variable. The actual values of the variable above and below the median are ignored. The mean is the most appropriate measure of central tendency for interval or ratio data. The mean makes use of all the information available since all of the values are used in computing it. However, the mean is sensitive to isolated cases with outliers, that is, extremely small or extremely large values. When there are outliers in the data, the mean is not a good measure of central tendency, and it is useful to consider both the mean and the median.

Measures of Variability

The most common **measures of variability**, which are calculated on interval or ratio data, are the range and variance or standard deviation.

measures of variability
Statistics that indicate the distribution's dispersion.

Range The **range** measures the spread of the data. It is simply the difference between the largest and smallest values in the sample. As such, the range is directly affected by outliers.

range
The difference between the smallest and largest values of a distribution.

$$\text{Range} = X_{\text{largest}} - X_{\text{smallest}}$$

If all the values in the data are multiplied by a constant, the range is multiplied by the same constant. The range in Table 2 is $7 - 1 = 6$.

Variance and Standard Deviation The difference between the mean and an observed value is called the deviation from the mean. The **variance** is the mean squared deviation from the mean, that is, the average of the square of the deviations from the

variance
The mean squared deviation of all the values from the mean.

mean for all the values. The variance can never be negative. When the data points are clustered around the mean, the variance is small. When the data points are scattered, the variance is large. The variance helps us to understand how similar or different the data points are. If the data points are similar, the variance is small and their distribution is clustered tightly around the mean. If the data points are very different in value, the variance is large and their distribution is spread more widely around the mean. If all the data values are multiplied by a constant, the variance is multiplied by the square of the constant. The **standard deviation** is the square root of the variance. Thus, the standard deviation is expressed in the same units as the data, whereas the variance is expressed in squared units. The standard deviation serves the same purpose as the variance in helping us to understand how clustered or spread the distribution is around the mean value.

standard deviation
The square root of the variance.

The standard deviation of a sample, s_x, is calculated as

$$s_x = \sqrt{\sum_{i=1}^{n} \frac{(X_i - \bar{X})^2}{n-1}}$$

We divide by $n - 1$ instead of n because the sample is drawn from a population and we are trying to determine how much the responses vary from the mean of the entire population. However, the population mean is unknown; therefore, the sample mean is used instead. The use of the sample mean makes the sample seem less variable than it actually is. By dividing by $n - 1$, instead of n, we compensate for the smaller variability observed in the sample. For the data given in Table 16.2, the variance is calculated as follows:

$$\begin{aligned}\text{Variance} = s_x^2 &= \{5\times(1-4.11)^2 + 6\times(2-4.11)^2 + 6\times(3-4.11)^2 \\ &\quad + 6\times(4-4.11)^2 + 8\times(5-4.11)^2 + 9\times(6-4.11)^2 \\ &\quad + 4\times(7-4.11)^2\}/43 \\ &= \{48.36 + 26.71 + 7.39 + 0.07 + 6.34 + 32.15 + 33.41\}/43 \\ &= 154.43/43 \\ &= 3.59\end{aligned}$$

The standard deviation, therefore, is calculated as

$$\begin{aligned}\text{Standard deviation} = s_x &= \sqrt{3.59} \\ &= 1.90\end{aligned}$$

BE a DM!

As the marketing director for Wendy's, how would you target the heavy users of fast-food restaurants?

BE an MR!

Visit Wendy's Web site (www.wendys.com) and conduct an Internet search using a search engine and your library's online database to obtain information on the heavy users of fast-food restaurants.

In a survey for Wendy's, information was obtained on the number of visits to Wendy's per month. How would you identify the heavy users of Wendy's and what statistics would you compute to summarize the number of visits to Wendy's per month?

Introduction to Hypothesis Testing

Hypotheses were defined and illustrated in Chapter 2. It may be recalled that hypotheses are unproven statements or propositions that are of interest to the researcher. Hypotheses are declarative and can be tested statistically. Often, hypotheses are possible answers to research questions. Basic analysis invariably involves some hypothesis testing. Examples of hypotheses generated in marketing research follow:

- The average number of stores shopped for groceries is 3.0 per household (see opening vignette).
- The department store is being patronized by more than 10 percent of the households.
- The heavy and light users of a brand differ in terms of psychographic characteristics.
- One hotel has a more upscale image than its close competitor.
- Familiarity with a restaurant results in greater preference for that restaurant.

Chapter 13 covered the concepts of the sampling distribution, standard error of the mean or the proportion, and the confidence interval.[3] Because all of these concepts are relevant to hypothesis testing, it would be wise to review them. The next section describes a general procedure for hypothesis testing that can be applied to test a wide range of hypotheses.

A General Procedure for Hypothesis Testing

The following steps are involved in hypothesis testing (Figure 16.6).

1. Formulate the null hypothesis H_0 and the alternative hypothesis H_1.
2. Select an appropriate statistical technique and the corresponding test statistic.
3. Choose the level of significance (α).
4. Determine the sample size and collect the data. Calculate the value of the test statistic.
5. Determine the probability associated with the test statistic calculated from the sample data under the null hypothesis, using the sampling distribution of the

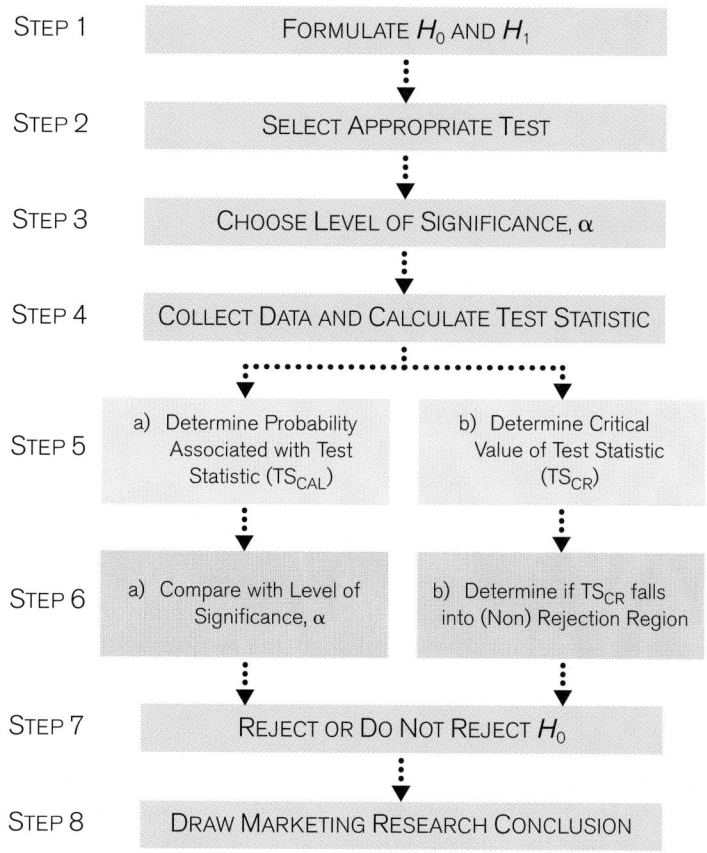

Figure 16.6
A General Procedure for Hypothesis Testing

test statistic. Alternatively, determine the critical value associated with the test statistic that divides the rejection and nonrejection regions, given the level of significance (α).

6. Compare the probability associated with the test statistic with the level of significance specified. Alternatively, determine whether the test statistic calculated from the sample data falls into the rejection or the nonrejection region.
7. Make the statistical decision to reject or not reject the null hypothesis.
8. Arrive at a conclusion. Express the statistical decision in terms of the marketing research problem.

Step 1: Formulating the Hypothesis

null hypothesis
A statement suggesting no expected difference or effect. If the null hypothesis is not rejected, no changes will be made.

alternative hypothesis
A statement suggesting some difference or effect is expected. Accepting the alternative hypothesis will lead to changes in opinions or actions.

The first step is to formulate the null and alternative hypothesis. A **null hypothesis** is a statement of the status quo, one of no difference or no effect. If the null hypothesis is not rejected, no changes will be made. An **alternative hypothesis** is one in which some difference or effect is expected. Accepting the alternative hypothesis will lead to changes in opinions or actions. Thus, the alternative hypothesis is the opposite of the null hypothesis.

The null hypothesis is always the hypothesis that is tested. The null hypothesis refers to a specified value of the population parameter (e.g., μ, σ, π), not a sample statistic (e.g., $\overline{X}$). A null hypothesis may be rejected, but it can never be accepted based on a single test. A statistical test can have one of two outcomes. One is that the null hypothesis is rejected and the alternative hypothesis accepted. The other outcome is that the null hypothesis is not rejected based on the evidence. However, it would be incorrect to conclude that since the null hypothesis is not rejected, it can be accepted as valid. In classical hypothesis testing, there is no way to determine whether the null hypothesis is true.[4]

In marketing research, the null hypothesis is formulated in such a way that its rejection leads to the acceptance of the desired conclusion. The alternative hypothesis represents the conclusion for which evidence is sought. For example, America Online (AOL) is considering the introduction of a new servicing plan. The plan will be introduced if it is preferred by more than 40 percent of customers. The appropriate way to formulate the hypotheses is as follows:

$$H_0: \pi \leq 0.40$$
$$H_1: \pi > 0.40$$

If the null hypothesis H_0 is rejected, then the alternative hypothesis H_1 will be accepted and the new service plan introduced. On the other hand, if H_0 is not rejected, the new service plan should not be introduced unless additional evidence is obtained.

one-tailed test
A test of the null hypothesis where the alternative hypothesis is expressed directionally.

two-tailed test
A test of the null hypothesis where the alternative hypothesis is not expressed directionally.

The test of the null hypothesis is a **one-tailed test** because the alternative hypothesis is expressed directionally: The proportion of customers who express a preference is greater than 0.40. On the other hand, suppose the researcher wanted to determine whether the new service plan is different (superior or inferior) from the current plan, which is preferred by 40 percent of customers. Then a **two-tailed test** would be required, and the hypotheses would be expressed as

$$H_0: \pi = 0.40$$
$$H_1: \pi \neq 0.40$$

In commercial marketing research, the one-tailed test is used more often than a two-tailed test. Typically, there is some preferred direction for the conclusion for which evidence is sought. For example, the higher the profits, sales, and product quality, the better. The one-tailed test is more powerful than the two-tailed test. The power of a statistical test is discussed further in Step 3.

test statistic
A measure of how close the sample has come to the null hypothesis. It often follows a well-known distribution, such as the normal, *t*, or chi-square distribution.

Step 2: Selecting an Appropriate Test

To test the null hypothesis, it is necessary to select an appropriate statistical technique. The researcher should take into consideration how the test statistic is computed and the sampling distribution that the sample statistic (e.g., the mean) follows. The **test statistic** measures how close the sample has come to the null hypothesis. The test statistic often follows a well-known distribution, such as the normal, t, or chi-square distribution. Guidelines for selecting an appropriate test or statistical technique are discussed later in this chapter as well as in Chapter 17.

In our AOL example, the z statistic, which follows the standard normal distribution, would be appropriate. This statistic would be computed as follows for proportions (see Chapter 13):

$$z = \frac{p - \pi}{\sigma_p}$$

Where

$$\sigma_p = \sqrt{\frac{\pi(1-\pi)}{n}}$$

Step 3: Choosing Level of Significance

Whenever we draw inferences about a population, there is a risk that an incorrect conclusion will be reached. Two types of error can occur.

Type-I Error **Type-I error** occurs when the sample results lead to the rejection of the null hypothesis when it is in fact true. In our example, a type-I error would occur if we concluded, based on the sample data, that the proportion of customers preferring the new service plan was greater than 0.40, when in fact it was less than or equal to 0.40. The probability of type-I error (α) is also called the **level of significance**. The type-I error is controlled by establishing the tolerable level of risk of rejecting a true null hypothesis. The selection of a particular risk level should depend on the cost of making a type-I error. The level of significance (α), when expressed as a percentage, is equal to 100 percent minus the confidence level (see Chapter 13).

type-I error
Also known as *alpha error,* it occurs when the sample results lead to the rejection of a null hypothesis that is in fact true.

level of significance
The probability of making a type-I error.

Type-II Error **Type-II error** occurs when, based on the sample results, the null hypothesis is not rejected when it is in fact false. In our example, the type-II error would occur if we concluded, based on sample data, that the proportion of customers preferring the new service plan was less than or equal to 0.40 when, in fact, it was greater than 0.40. The probability of type-II error is denoted by β. Unlike α, which is specified by the researcher, the magnitude of β depends on the actual value of the population parameter (that is, mean or proportion). The probability of type-I error (α) and the probability of type-II error (β) are shown in Figure 16.7. The complement ($1 - \beta$) of the probability of a type-II error is called the *power of a statistical test.*

type-II error
Also known as *beta error,* occurs when the sample results lead to nonrejection of a null hypothesis that is in fact false.

Power of a Test The **power of a test** is the probability ($1 - \beta$) of rejecting the null hypothesis when it is false and should be rejected. Although β is unknown, it is related to α. An extremely low value of α (e.g., 0.001) will result in intolerably high β errors. So, it is necessary to balance the two types of errors. As a compromise, α is often set at 0.05; sometimes it is 0.01; other values of α are rare. The level of α, along with the sample size, will determine the level of β for a particular research design. The risk of both α and β can be controlled by increasing the sample size. For a given level of α, increasing the sample size will decrease β, thereby increasing the power of the test.

power of a test
The probability of rejecting the null hypothesis when it is in fact false and should be rejected.

Step 4: Data Collection

Sample size is determined after taking into account the desired α and β errors, incidence and completion rates, and other qualitative considerations, such as budget constraints (see Chapter 13). Then, the required data are collected and the value of the test statistic computed. In our example, suppose 500 customers were surveyed and 220 expressed a preference for the new service plan. Thus, the value of the sample proportion is $p = 220 / 500 = 0.44$.

Figure 16.7

Type I-Error (Alpha) and Type-II Error (Beta)

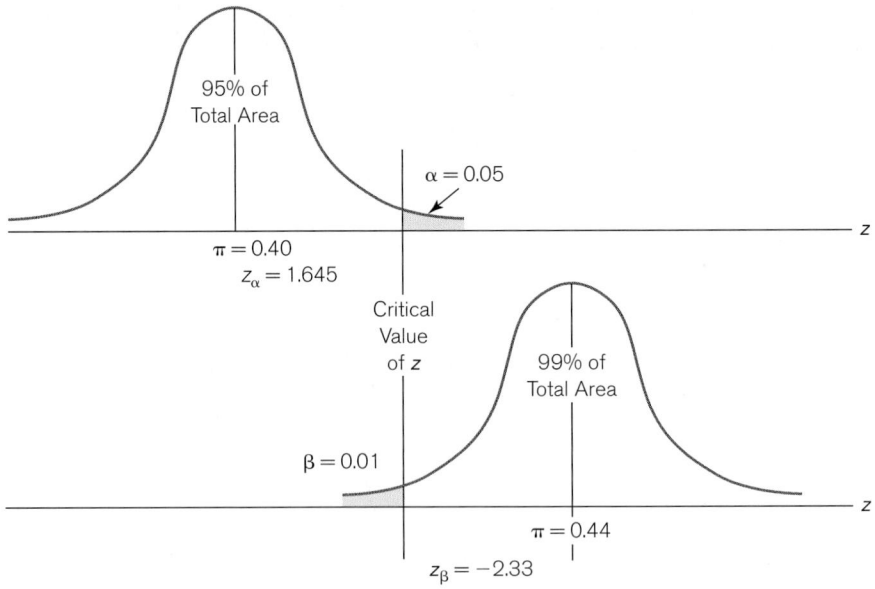

The value of σ_p can be determined as follows:

$$\sigma_p = \sqrt{\frac{\pi(1-\pi)}{n}}$$

$$= \sqrt{\frac{(0.40)(0.6)}{500}}$$

$$= 0.0219$$

The test statistic z can be calculated as follows:

$$z = \frac{p-\pi}{\sigma_p}$$

$$= \frac{0.44-0.40}{0.0219}$$

$$= 1.83$$

Step 5: Determining the Probability (Critical Value)

Using standard normal tables (Table 2 of the Appendix of Statistical Tables), the probability of obtaining a z value of 1.83 can be calculated (Figure 16.8). The shaded area between $-\infty$ and 1.83 is 0.9664. Therefore, the area to the right of $z = 1.83$ is $1.0000 - 0.9664 = 0.0336$. Most computer programs automatically calculate this value.

Figure 16.8

Probability of z Value with a One-Tailed Test

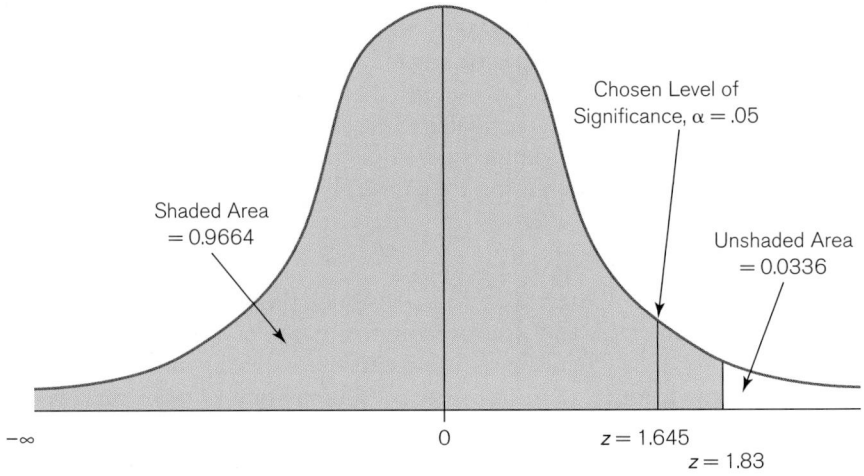

Alternatively, the critical value of z, which will give an area to the right side of the critical value of 0.05, is between 1.64 and 1.65 and equals 1.645. Note that in determining the critical value of the test statistic, the area to the right of the critical value is either α or $\alpha/2$. It is α for a one-tail test and $\alpha/2$ for a two-tail test.

Steps 6 and 7: Comparing the Probability (Critical Value) and Making the Decision

a. The probability associated with the calculated or observed value of the test statistic calculated from the sample data is 0.0336. This is the probability of getting a p value of 0.44 when $\pi = 0.40$. This is less than the level of significance of 0.05. Hence, the null hypothesis is rejected.

b. Alternatively, the calculated value of the test statistic $z = 1.83$ lies in the rejection region, beyond the value of 1.645. Again, the same conclusion to reject the null hypothesis is reached.

Note that the two ways of testing the null hypothesis are equivalent but mathematically opposite in the direction of comparison. If the probability associated with the calculated or observed value of the test statistic (TS_{CAL}) is *less than* the level of significance (α), the null hypothesis is rejected. However, if the calculated value of the test statistic (TS_{CAL}) is *greater than* the critical value of the test statistic (TS_{CR}), the null hypothesis is rejected. The **critical value** is the value of the test statistic that divides the rejection and nonrejection regions. The reason for this sign shift is that the larger the value of TS_{CAL}, the smaller the probability of obtaining a more extreme value of the test statistic under the null hypothesis. This sign shift can be easily illustrated as follows:

critical value
The value of the test statistic that divides the rejection and nonrejection regions. If the calculated value of the test statistic is greater than the critical value of the test statistic, the null hypothesis is rejected.

Under (a),

if probability of TS_{CAL} < significance level (α), then reject H_0

Under (b),

if $TS_{CAL} > TS_{CR}$, then reject H_0

Step 8: Marketing Research Conclusion

The conclusion reached by hypothesis testing must be expressed in terms of the marketing research problem and managerial action that should be taken. In our example, we conclude that there is evidence that the proportion of customers preferring the new service plan is significantly greater than 0.40. Hence, the recommendation would be to introduce the new service plan. Another illustration of hypothesis testing is provided by the International Brand Equity example.

Hypotheses testing can be related to either an examination of associations or an examination of differences (Figure 16.9). In tests of associations, the null hypothesis is that there is no association between the variables (H_0: . . . is NOT related to . . .). In tests of differences, the null hypothesis is that there is no difference (H_0: . . . is NOT different than . . .). Tests of differences could relate to means or proportions. First, we discuss hypotheses related to associations in the context of cross-tabulations.

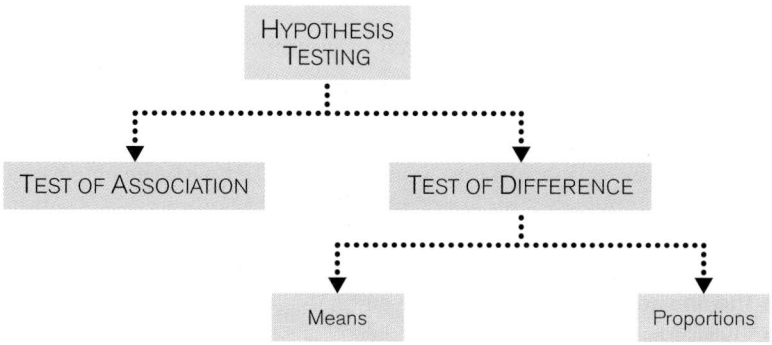

Figure 16.9
A Broad Classification of Hypothesis Testing Procedures

RESEARCH IN ACTION

International Brand Equity—the Name of the Game

In the 21st century, the trend is toward global marketing. How can marketers market a brand abroad where there are diverse historical and cultural differences? According to Bob Kroll, the former president of Del Monte International, uniform packaging may be an asset, yet catering to individual countries' culinary taste preferences is more important. Marketing executives now believe it's best to think globally, but act locally.

A suitable research question might be: Do consumers in different countries prefer to buy global name brands with different packaging customized to suit their local needs? Based on this research question, one can frame the hypothesis that, other factors being constant, standardized branding with customized packaging for a well-established name brand will result in greater market share. The hypotheses may be formulated as follows:

H_0: Standardized branding with customized packaging for a well-established name brand will not lead to greater market share in the international market.

H_1: Other factors remaining equal, standardized branding with customized packaging for a well-established name brand will lead to greater market share in the international market.

To test the null hypothesis, a well-established brand such as Colgate toothpaste, which has followed a mixed strategy, can be selected. The market share in countries with standardized branding and standardized packaging can be compared with market share in countries with standardized branding and customized packaging, after controlling for the effect of other factors. Note that this is a one-tail test.

Cross-Tabulations

While answers to questions related to a single variable are interesting, they often raise additional questions about how to link that variable to other variables. To introduce the frequency distribution, we posed several representative marketing research questions. For each of these, a researcher might pose additional questions to relate these variables to other variables. For example,

- What percentage of coupon users have annual household incomes of more than $35,000? (See opening vignette.)
- Is product use (measured in terms of heavy users, medium users, light users, and nonusers) related to interest in outdoor activities (high, medium, and low)?
- Is familiarity with a new product (unfamiliar, familiar) related to education levels (high school or less, some college, college degree)?
- Is the income (high, medium, and low) of brand users related to the geographic region in which they live (north, south, east, and west)?

cross-tabulation
A statistical technique that describes two or more variables simultaneously and results in tables that reflect the joint distribution of two or more variables that have a limited number of categories or distinct values.

The answers to such questions can be determined by examining cross-tabulations. While a frequency distribution describes one variable at a time, a **cross-tabulation** describes two or more variables simultaneously. Cross-tabulation results in tables that reflect the joint distribution of two or more variables with a limited number of categories or distinct values. The categories of one variable are cross-classified with the categories of one or more other variables. Thus, the frequency distribution of one variable is subdivided according to the values or categories of the other variables. This was illustrated in the opening vignette in which coupon usage was cross-classified with income. The analysis revealed that lower-income households had higher coupon usage as compared to middle- and higher-income households.

Table 16.3

A Cross-Tabulation of Gender and Usage of Nike Shoes

USAGE	Gender: Female	Gender: Male	ROW TOTAL
Light Users	14	5	19
Medium Users	5	5	10
Heavy Users	5	11	16
Column Total	**24**	**21**	**45**

Suppose Nike was interested in determining whether sex was associated with the degree of usage for Nike shoes. In Table 16.1, the respondents were divided into three categories of light (denoted by 1), medium (2), or heavy users (3) based on reported wear-time per week. There were 19 light users, 10 medium users, and 16 heavy users. While data on attitude were missing for one respondent, information on usage and gender was available for all. Gender was coded as 1 for females and 2 for males. There were 24 females and 21 males.

The cross-tabulation is shown in Table 16.3. A cross-tabulation includes a cell for every combination of the categories of the two variables. The number in each cell shows how many respondents gave that combination of responses. In Table 16.3, 14 respondents were females and light users. The marginal totals (column totals and row totals) in this table indicate that, of the 45 respondents with valid responses on both the variables, 19 were light users, 10 were medium users, and 16 were heavy users, confirming the classification procedure adopted.

Furthermore, 21 respondents were males, and 24 were females. Note that this information could have been obtained from a separate frequency distribution for each variable. In general, the margins of a cross-tabulation show the same information as the frequency tables for each of the variables. Cross-tabulation tables are also called **contingency tables**.

contingency tables
Cross-tabulation tables; contain a cell for every combination of categories of the two variables.

Cross-tabulation is widely used in commercial marketing research because (1) cross-tabulation analysis and results can be easily interpreted and understood by managers who are not statistically oriented; (2) the clarity of interpretation provides a stronger link between research results and managerial action; and (3) cross-tabulation analysis is simple to conduct and more appealing to less-sophisticated researchers. We will discuss cross-tabulation for two variables, the most common form in which this procedure is used.

Cross-tabulation with two variables is also known as *bivariate cross-tabulation*. Consider again the cross-classification of sex and usage of Nike shoes given in Table 16.3. Is usage of Nike shoes related to gender? It might be. We see from Table 16.3 that disproportionately more of the males are heavy users and disproportionately more of the females are light users. Computation of percentages can provide more insights.

Since two variables have been cross-classified, percentages could be computed either column-wise, based on column totals (Table 16.4), or row-wise, based on row totals

Table 16.4

Usage of Nike Shoes by Gender

USAGE	Gender: Female	Gender: Male
Light Users	58.4%	23.8%
Medium Users	20.8%	23.8%
Heavy Users	20.8%	52.4%
Column Total	**100.0%**	**100.0%**

Table 16.5

Gender by Usage of Nike Shoes

	Gender		
USAGE	Female	Male	ROW TOTAL
Light Users	73.7%	26.3%	100.0%
Medium Users	50.0%	50.0%	100.0%
Heavy Users	31.2%	68.8%	100.0%

(Table 16.5). Which of these tables is more useful? The answer depends on which variable will be considered as the independent variable and which as the dependent variable. The general rule is to compute the percentages in the direction of the independent variable, across the dependent variable. In our analysis, gender would be considered as the independent variable and usage as the dependent variable. Therefore, the correct way of calculating percentages is as shown in Table 16.4. Note that while 52.4 percent of the males are heavy users, only 20.8 percent of females are heavy users. This seems to indicate that as compared to females, males are more likely to be heavy users of Nike shoes. The recommendation to management may be to promote more heavily to women to increase their usage rate or to promote more heavily to men to prevent brand loyalty erosion. Obviously, additional variables would need to be analyzed before management would act upon such variables. Nevertheless, this illustrates how hypotheses tests should be linked to recommended managerial actions.

Note that computing percentages in the direction of the dependent variable across the independent variable, as shown in Table 16.5, is not meaningful in this case. Table 16.5 implies that heavy usage of Nike shoes causes people to be males. This latter finding is not meaningful. The corresponding SPSS and EXCEL outputs for this cross-tabulation with explanatory notes can be downloaded from the Web site for this book. As another illustration, see Old is Gold Research in Action example.

General Comments on Cross-Tabulation

While three or more variables can be cross-tabulated, the interpretation can be quite complex. Also, because the number of cells increases multiplicatively, maintaining an adequate number of respondents or cases in each cell can be problematic. As a general

RESEARCH IN ACTION

Old Is Gold but Some Marketers Treat It as Dust

A study examined whether older models are depicted in a negative light in TV commercials. Television commercials emanating from the three major networks, one local station, and five cable companies were analyzed by the researchers. The results were as follows in terms of the number and percentage of models of different age groups that were depicted in a positive or negative light:

Age of the Model (yrs)	Positive Depiction		Negative Depiction		Total	
	No.	%	No.	%	No.	%
Under 45	415	83.1	85	16.9	500	100
45–64	64	66.0	33	34.0	97	100
65 and over	28	54.0	24	46.0	52	100

Note that as the age of the model increases, the percentages in the negative depiction column increase. Therefore, the study concluded that older models do tend to be depicted in a negative manner. Sadly, some marketers may be pursuing self-defeating strategies by depicting older consumers unfavorably. Marketers should note that older consumers represent a large and growing segment that controls substantial income and wealth.[5]

rule, there should be at least five expected observations in each cell for the chi-square statistic used for testing cross-tabulation hypothesis to be reliable. Thus, cross-tabulation is an inefficient way of examining relationships when there are several variables. Note that cross-tabulation examines association between variables, not causation. To examine causation, the causal research design framework should be adopted (see Chapter 8).

Statistics Associated with Cross-Tabulation

This section focuses on the statistics commonly used for assessing the statistical significance and strength of association of cross-tabulated variables. The statistical significance of the observed association is commonly measured by the chi-square statistic. The strength of association, or degree of association, is important from a practical or managerial perspective. Generally, the strength of an association is of interest only if the association is statistically significant. The strength of the association can be measured by the phi correlation coefficient, the contingency coefficient, Cramer's V, and the lambda coefficient.

Chi-Square

The **chi-square statistic** (x^2) is used to test the statistical significance of the observed association in a cross-tabulation. It assists us in determining whether a systematic association exists between two variables. This is illustrated in the opening vignette where a systematic association exists between coupon usage and income, with lower-income households consuming more coupons than middle- or higher-income households. The null hypothesis, H_0, is that there is no association between the variables. The test is conducted by computing the cell frequencies that would be expected if no association was present between the variables, given the existing row and column totals. These expected cell frequencies, denoted f_e, are then compared to the actual observed frequencies, f_o, found in the cross-tabulation to calculate the chi-square statistic. The greater the discrepancies between the expected and actual frequencies, the larger the value of the statistic. Assume that a cross-tabulation has r rows and c columns and a random sample of n observations. The expected frequency under the null hypothesis for each cell can be calculated by using a simple formula as follows:

chi-square statistic
The statistic used to test the statistical significance of the observed association in a cross-tabulation. It assists in determining whether a systematic association exists between the two variables.

$$f_e = \frac{n_r n_c}{n}$$

Where

n_r = total number in the row
n_c = total number in the column
n = total sample size

For the data in Table 16.3, the total number in the row, n_r, is 19 for light users, 10 for medium users, and 16 for heavy users. The total number in each column, n_c, is 24 for females and 21 for males. Therefore, the expected cell frequencies for the six cells from left to right and top to bottom are

$f_e = (24 \times 19)/45 = 10.1$ $\quad$ $f_e = (21 \times 19)/45 = 8.9$
$f_e = (24 \times 10)/45 = 5.3$ $\quad$ $f_e = (21 \times 10)/45 = 4.7$
$f_e = (24 \times 16)/45 = 8.5$ $\quad$ $f_e = (21 \times 16)/45 = 7.5$

Generally, the expected cell frequency will be different for each cell, as is the case here. Only when all row totals are the same and all column totals are the same will the expected cell frequency be the same for each cell.

Once the expected cell frequencies are calculated, the value of χ^2 is calculated as follows:

$$\chi^2 = \sum_{\substack{\text{all}\\ \text{cells}}} \frac{(f_o - f_e)^2}{f_e}$$

For the data in Table 16.3, in which there are six cells, the value of χ^2 is calculated as

$$\begin{aligned}\chi^2 &= \frac{(14-10.1)^2}{10.1} + \frac{(5-8.9)^2}{8.9} \\ &\quad + \frac{(5-5.3)^2}{5.3} + \frac{(5-4.7)^2}{4.7} + \\ &\quad \frac{(5-8.5)^2}{8.5} + \frac{(11-7.5)^2}{7.5} \\ &= 1.51 + 1.71 + 0.02 + 0.02 + 1.44 + 1.63 \\ &= 6.33\end{aligned}$$

To determine whether a systematic association exists, the probability of obtaining a value of chi-square as large as or larger than the one calculated from the cross-tabulation is estimated (see Figure 16.6, Step 5). An important characteristic of the chi-square statistic is the number of degrees of freedom (*df*) associated with it. In general, the number of degrees of freedom is equal to the number of observations less the number of constraints needed to calculate a statistical term. In the case of a chi-square statistic associated with a cross-tabulation, the number of degrees of freedom is equal to the product of number of rows (r) less one and the number of columns (c) less one. That is, $df = (r - 1) \times (c - 1)$. The null hypothesis ($H_0$) of no association between the two variables will be rejected only when the calculated value of the test statistic is greater than the critical value of the chi-square distribution with the appropriate degrees of freedom, as shown in Figure 16.10 (see Figure 16.6, Step 6).

chi-square distribution
A skewed distribution whose shape depends solely on the number of degrees of freedom. As the number of degrees of freedom increases, the chi-square distribution becomes more symmetrical.

Unlike the normal distribution, the **chi-square distribution** is a skewed distribution, the shape of which depends solely on the number of degrees of freedom. As the number of degrees of freedom increases, the chi-square distribution becomes more symmetrical. Table 3 in the Appendix of Statistical Tables contains upper-tail areas of the chi-square distribution for different degrees of freedom. In this table, the value at the top of each column indicates the area in the upper portion (the right side, as shown in Figure 16.10) of the chi-square distribution. To illustrate, for 2 degrees of freedom, the critical value of chi-square (χ^2_{CR}) for an upper-tail area of 0.05 is 5.991. This indicates that for 2 degrees of freedom the probability of exceeding a chi-square value of 5.991 is 0.05. In other words, at the 0.05 level of significance with 2 degrees of freedom, the critical value of the chi-square statistic is 5.991.

For the cross-tabulation given in Table 16.3, there are $(3-1) \times (2-1) = 2$ degrees of freedom. The calculated chi-square statistic had a value of 6.33. Because this is greater

Figure 16.10
Chi-Square Test of Association

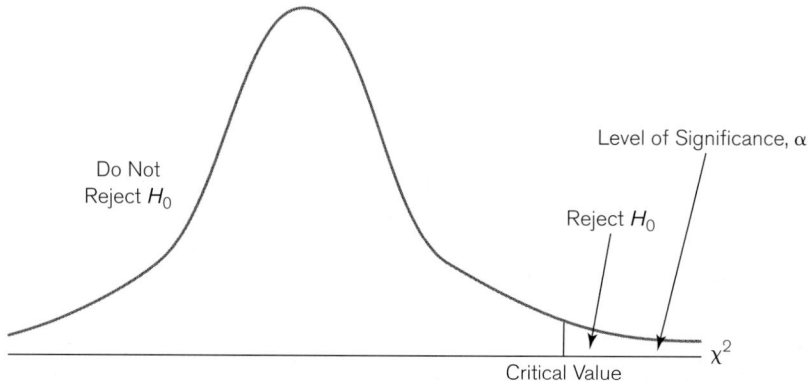

than the critical value of 5.991, the null hypothesis of no association is rejected, indicating that the association is statistically significant at the 0.05 level.

The chi-square statistic can also be used in *goodness-of-fit tests* to determine whether certain models fit the observed data. These tests are conducted by calculating the significance of sample deviations from assumed theoretical (expected) distributions and can be performed on cross-tabulations as well as on frequencies (one-way tabulations). The calculation of the chi-square statistic and the determination of its significance is the same as illustrated earlier.

The chi-square statistic should be estimated only on counts of data. When the data are in percentage form, they should first be converted to absolute counts or numbers. In addition, an underlying assumption of the chi-square test is that the observations are drawn independently. This means that respondents do not influence each other's responses in any way. As a general rule, chi-square analysis should not be conducted when the expected or theoretical frequency in any of the cells is less than five. Low expected frequencies would cause the calculated value of chi-square to be higher than it should be (bias it upward) and make it more likely to commit a type-I error. The issue of cell sizes is directly related to statistical determination of sample size discussed in Chapter 13. When the frequency in any of the cells is low, it is often possible to reduce the size of the table (i.e., reduce the number of rows and/or columns) by combining categories. This was illustrated in Chapter 15 where the RECODE procedure in SPSS Windows was employed to reduce the number of income categories from six to four. In the case of a 2×2 table, the chi-square is related to the phi coefficient.

Phi Coefficient

The **phi coefficient** (ϕ) is used as a measure of the strength of association in the special case of a table with two rows and two columns (a 2×2 table). The phi coefficient is proportional to the square root of the chi-square statistic. For a sample of size n, this statistic is calculated as

phi coefficient
A measure of the strength of association in the special case of a table with two rows and two columns (a 2×2 table).

$$\phi = \sqrt{\frac{\chi^2}{n}}$$

It takes the value of 0 when there is no association, which would be indicated by a chi-square value of 0 as well. When the variables are perfectly associated, phi assumes the value of 1 and all the observations fall just on the main or minor diagonal. (In some computer programs, phi assumes a value of -1 rather than 1 when there is perfect negative association.) In the more general case involving a table of any size, the strength of association can be assessed by using the contingency coefficient.

Contingency Coefficient

While the phi coefficient is specific to a 2×2 table, the **contingency coefficient** (C) can be used to assess the strength of association in a table of any size. This index is also related to chi-square, as follows:

contingency coefficient
A measure of the strength of association in a table of any size.

$$C = \sqrt{\frac{\chi^2}{\chi^2 + n}}$$

The contingency coefficient varies between 0 and 1. The 0 value occurs in the case of no association (that is, the variables are statistically independent) but the maximum value of 1 is never achieved. Rather, the maximum value of the contingency coefficient depends on the size of the table (number of rows and number of columns). For this reason, it should be used only to compare tables of the same size.

Normally, the strength of association is not meaningful and, hence, not calculated when the null hypothesis of no association is not rejected. If there is no relationship between the two variables, there can be no strength. In our case, the null hypothesis was rejected, and thus, it is meaningful to calculate the contingency coefficient. The value of the contingency coefficient for Table 16.3 is

$$C = \sqrt{\frac{6.33}{6.33+45}}$$
$$= \sqrt{.1235}$$
$$= 0.351$$

This value of C indicates that the association is low to moderate.

Cramer's V

Cramer's V
A measure of the strength of association used in tables larger than 2×2.

Cramer's V is a modified version of the phi correlation coefficient, ϕ, and is used in tables larger than 2×2. When phi is calculated for a table larger than 2×2, it has no upper limit. Cramer's V is obtained by adjusting phi for either the number of rows or the number of columns in the table, based on which of the two is smaller. The adjustment is such that V will range from 0 to 1. A large value of V merely indicates a high degree of association. It does not indicate how the variables are associated. As a rule of thumb, values of V below 0.3 indicate low association, values between 0.3 and 0.6 indicate low-to-moderate association, and values above 0.6 indicate strong association. For a table with r rows and c columns, the relationship between Cramer's V and the phi correlation coefficient is expressed as

$$V = \sqrt{\frac{\phi^2}{\min\,(r-1),\ (c-1)}}$$

or

$$V = \sqrt{\frac{\chi^2 / n}{\min\,(r-1),\ (c-1)}}$$

The value of Cramer's V for Table 16.3 is

$$V = \sqrt{\frac{6.33/45}{1}}$$

or

$$V = \sqrt{.01409}$$
$$= 0.375$$

Thus, the association is low to moderate.

Given that the null hypothesis was rejected and we have determined the strength of association as low to moderate, we can interpret the pattern of relation by looking at the percentages in Table 16.4. There is a low-to-moderate association between gender and usage of Nike shoes. Males tend to be heavy users, whereas females tend to be light users.

Cross-Tabulation in Practice

While conducting cross-tabulation analysis in practice, it is useful to proceed following these steps (Figure 16.11):

1. Construct the cross-tabulation table.
2. Test the null hypothesis that there is no association between the variables using the chi-square statistic (see the procedure described in Figure 16.6).
3. If you fail to reject the null hypothesis, there is no relationship.

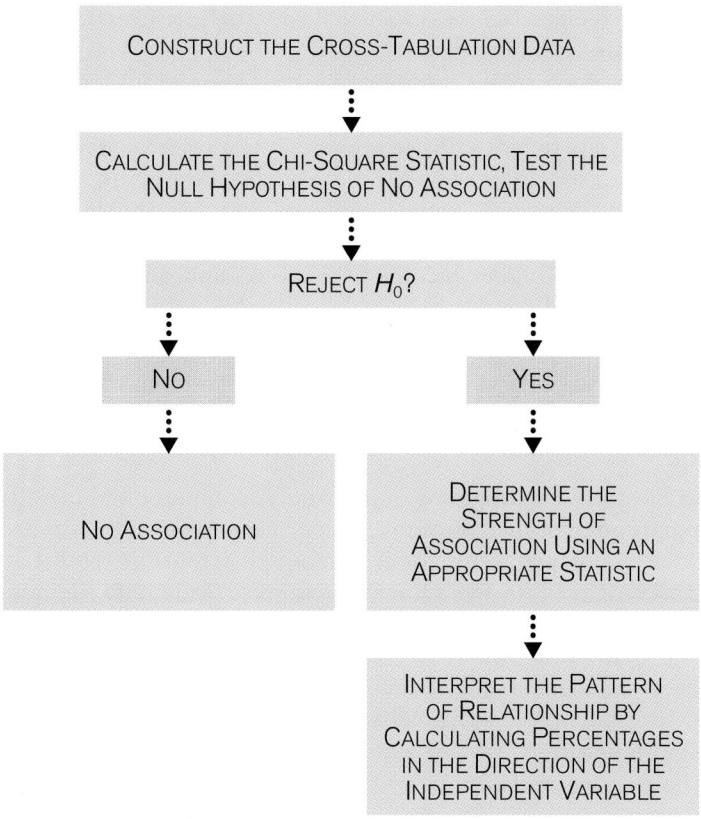

Figure 16.11
Conducting Cross-Tabulation Analysis

4. If H_0 is rejected, determine the strength of the association using an appropriate statistic (phi coefficient, contingency coefficient, or Cramer's *V*) as discussed earlier in this chapter.
5. If H_0 is rejected, interpret the pattern of the relationship by computing the percentages in the direction of the independent variable, across the dependent variable. Draw marketing conclusions.

BE an MR!

Visit L'Oreal's Web site (www.loreal.com) and conduct an Internet search using a search engine and your library's online database to obtain information on the heavy users, light users, and nonusers of cosmetics.

How would you analyze the data to determine whether the heavy users, light users, and nonusers of cosmetics differ in terms of demographic characteristics?

BE a DM!

As the marketing director for L'Oreal, what marketing strategies would you adopt to reach the heavy users, light users, and nonusers of cosmetics?

Summary Illustration Using the Opening Vignette

Basic data analysis provides valuable insights, as in the case of the coupon usage study presented in the opening vignette. A frequency distribution produces a table of frequency counts, percentages, and cumulative percentages for all the values associated with that variable. The mean, mode, and median of a frequency distribution are measures of central tendency. Some of the important statistics and the insights they provided in the opening vignette included frequency counts (593 respondents used coupons for brands they normally bought), percentages (95 percent had used a coupon within the last 30 days), and means (the average number of stores shopped was 2.9 per household).

Hypotheses are declarative statements. Basic analysis invariably involves some hypothesis testing. Based on the data collected in the opening vignette, one could test the hypothesis that the average number of stores shopped for groceries is 3.0 per household. Cross-tabulations are tables that reflect the joint distribution of two or more variables. The chi-square statistic provides a test of the statistical significance of the observed association in a cross-tabulation. In the opening vignette, a cross-tabulation of coupon usage with income indicated that households at all income levels were cashing coupons. Yet, lower-income households had higher coupon usage as compared to middle- and higher-income households, and this association was statistically significant. Such findings can be used by supermarkets to target their coupon and promotional strategies.

Software Applications

SPSS and SAS have similar programs in their microcomputer and mainframe versions for computing frequency distributions, performing cross-tabulations, and testing hypotheses. The major programs for frequency distribution are FREQUENCIES (SPSS) and UNIVARIATE (SAS). Other programs provide only the frequency distribution (FREQ in SAS) or only some of the associated statistics (see Exhibit 16.1). In MINITAB, the main function is Stats>Descriptive Statistics. The output values include the mean, median, standard deviation, minimum, maximum, and quartiles. A histogram in the form of a bar chart or graph can be produced from the Graph>Histogram selection. Several of the spreadsheets can also be used to obtain frequencies and descriptive statistics. In EXCEL, the Tools>Data Analysis function computes the descriptive statistics. The output produces the mean, standard error, median, mode, standard deviation, variance, range, minimum, maximum, sum, count, and confidence level. Frequencies can be selected under the histogram function. A histogram can be produced in bar format.

The major cross-tabulation programs are CROSSTABS (Menu, Analyze, Descriptive Statistics, Crosstabs) (SPSS) and FREQ (SAS). These programs display the cross-classification tables and provide cell counts, row and column percentages, the chi-square test for significance, and all the measures of the strength of the association that have been discussed. In addition, the TABULATE (SAS) program can be used for obtaining cell counts and row and column percentages, although it does not provide any of the associated statistics. In MINITAB, cross-tabulations and chi-squares are under the Stats>Tables function. Each of these features must be selected separately under the Tables function. The Data>Pivot Table function performs cross-tabulations in EXCEL. To do additional analysis or customize data, select a different summary function such as maximum, minimum, average, or standard deviation. ChiTest can be assessed under the Insert>Function>Statistical>ChiTest function (see Exhibit 16.2).

SPSS Windows

Frequency Distribution

The main program in SPSS is FREQUENCIES. It produces a table of frequency counts, percentages, and cumulative percentages for the values of each variable. It gives all of the associated statistics. If the data are interval-scaled and only the summary statistics are desired, the DESCRIPTIVES procedure can be used. All of the statistics computed by DESCRIPTIVES are available in FREQUENCIES. DESCRIPTIVES is more efficient, however, because it does not sort values into a frequency table. Moreover, the DESCRIPTIVES procedure displays summary statistics for several variables in a single table and can also calculate standardized values (z scores). The EXPLORE procedure produces summary statistics and graphical displays, either for all cases or separately for groups of cases. Mean, median, variance, standard deviation, minimum, maximum, and range are some of the statistics that can be calculated.

WHAT WOULD *YOU* DO?

General Mills' Harmony: Helping Women Achieve Nutritional Harmony

The Situation

Stephen W. Sanger, CEO of General Mills, is constantly faced with the challenge of how to keep up with the changing tastes and preferences of consumers. General Mills recently conducted thorough focus-group research on the most important consumers in grocery stores today: women. It is a known fact that three out of every four grocery shoppers in the United States are women, and many of these females are focusing more on their health and the nutritious value of foods. Although there are many cereals on the market with the same amount of valuable vitamins and minerals, such as Total or Kellogg's Smart Start, General Mills decided to design a product specifically engendered for a woman. Harmony would be its name.

Dietician Roberta Duyff claims that women do not get enough nutrients like calcium or folic acid from day to day. "It is great that a woman can now increase her intake of these important nutrients with a simple bowl of cereal for breakfast, and if you add milk, the vitamin D in milk makes the calcium in both the fortified cereal and milk itself more absorbable." This is one way in which General Mills saw an advantage–convenience for the woman. She can grab a bowl in the morning and start off her day with the nutrients she needs. Not only is the convenience of the product an incentive to market it but also the fact that the focus-group findings indicated women like to have a product of their own. According to Megan Nightingale, Assistant Marketing Manager at General Mills, "Our research has shown that women are looking for something that's nutritious, fast, convenient, and has a good taste." Women even enjoy the calming effect of the box with its pale yellow background and blue female figure.

General Mills' success in targeting women with the Harmony cereal suggests women recognize Harmony's benefits. Since January 2001 with its nationwide release, Harmony cereal has helped increase total sales to $7.08 billion for 2001, and sales keep increasing. In fact, annual net sales increased 32 percent over 2002 to $10.5 billion for 2003. Researching and customizing the market for women was the right way to go for General Mills.

A telephone survey was conducted to determine the preference for and consumption of Harmony and the relative importance that women attached to a cereal being nutritious, fast, convenient, and good tasting.

The Marketing Research Decision

1. What is the relative importance of the four variables (nutritious, fast, convenient, and good taste) in influencing women to buy Harmony? What type of analysis should be conducted? Check as many as are applicable.

   a. Frequency distribution of the importance attached to the four factors
   b. Mean levels of importance of the four variables
   c. Cross-tabulation of Harmony purchases with the importance of the four variables: chi-square analysis
   d. Cross-tabulation of Harmony purchases with the importance of the four variables: Cramer's *V*
   e. All of the above
2. Discuss the role of the type of data analysis you recommend in enabling Stephen W. Sanger to understand women's preference for and consumption of Harmony.

The Marketing Management Decision

1. The advertising for Harmony should stress which of the four factors? Check as many as are applicable.
   a. Nutrition
   b. Quick consumption
   c. Convenience
   d. Good taste
   e. All of the above
2. Discuss how the marketing management-decision action that you recommend to Stephen W. Sanger is influenced by the type of data analysis you suggested earlier and by the findings of that analysis.

What Stephen W. Sanger Did

Stephen W. Sanger decided to focus on nutrition, quick consumption, and convenience. General Mills markets Harmony cereal by using the idea that women don't have the time or patience to remember all the vitamins and minerals they need each day to stay healthy. Harmony makes it convenient. Simply pour yourself a bowl of cereal, and you'll get many of the important nutrients you need. On the back of the package, in elegant italics, is the cereal's catch phrase: "Meeting the nutritional needs of women is what Harmony cereal is all about."[6]

To select these procedures, click on the following:

ANALYZE > DESCRIPTIVE STATISTICS > FREQUENCIES. . .
Or ANALYZE > DESCRIPTIVE STATISTICS > DESCRIPTIVES. . .
Or ANALYZE > DESCRIPTIVE STATISTICS > EXPLORE. . .

Detailed steps are presented for running frequencies on attitude toward Nike (Table 16.1) and for plotting the histogram (Figure 16.4). The corresponding screen captures for these steps can be downloaded from the Web site for this book.

1. Select ANALYZE on the SPSS menu bar.
2. Click DESCRIPTIVE STATISTICS, and select FREQUENCIES.
3. Move the variable "Attitude toward Nike [attitude]" to the VARIABLE(S) box.
4. Click STATISTICS.
5. Select MEAN, MEDIAN, MODE, STD. DEVIATION, VARIANCE, and RANGE.
6. Click CONTINUE.
7. Click CHARTS.
8. Click HISTOGRAMS, then click CONTINUE.
9. Click OK.

Cross-Tabulation

The major cross-tabulation program is CROSSTABS. This program will display the cross-classification tables and provide cell counts, row and column percentages, the chi-square test for significance, and all the measures of the strength of the association that have been discussed.

To select these procedures click on the following:

ANALYZE > DESCRIPTIVE STATISTICS > CROSSTABS . . .

We give detailed steps for running the cross-tabulation of gender and usage of Nike shoes given in Table 16.3 and calculating the chi-square, contingency coefficient, and Cramer's *V*. The corresponding screen captures for these steps can be downloaded from the Web site for this book.

1. Select ANALYZE on the SPSS menu bar.
2. Click on DESCRIPTIVE STATISTICS, and select CROSSTABS.
3. Move the variable "User Group [usergr]" to the ROW(S) box.
4. Move the variable "Sex [sex]" to the COLUMN(S) box.
5. Click on CELLS.
6. Select OBSERVED under COUNTS, and select COLUMN under PERCENTAGES.
7. Click CONTINUE.
8. Click STATISTICS.
9. Click on CHI-SQUARE, PHI, AND CRAMER'S *V*.
10. Click CONTINUE.
11. Click OK.

EXCEL

Frequency Distribution

We give detailed steps for running frequencies on attitude toward Nike (Table 16.1) using EXCEL. The screen captures for these steps can be downloaded from the Web site for this book.

1. Select **Tools** (Alt + T).
2. Select **Data Analysis** under Tools.
3. Data Analysis window pops up.
4. Select **Histogram** from Data Analysis window.
5. Click **OK.**

EXPERIENTIAL LEARNING

Categorical Data Analysis

In this experiential exercise you will learn to run frequencies and cross-tabulations using SPSS. Go to the textbook Web site and download the following SPSS system file: KitKat. Also, download the actual taste-test instructions to customers in Nestlé's research: TasteTest. These files refer to the Nestlé taste test presented in Chapter 9. Here, respondents were asked to taste three different samples of the KitKat candy bar. Two of the samples were the currently marketed version of KitKat. One of the samples was a new reduced-fat version of the KitKat candy bar that had not been put into the market yet. In order to minimize an effect from the presentation order (e.g., respondents might tend to prefer the first or the last one presented), the order of presentation was changed for the different respondents.

- **Read the taste-test instructions of TasteTest.**
- **Open KitKat.**
  Double click on icon.
- **Check data by running frequencies.**
  Check distributions for the following variables:
  rotation, sex, age, differen, and prefer.
  Menu Bar
  ANALYZE
  DESCRIPTIVE STATISTICS
  FREQUENCIES
  Transfer each of the five variables in the FREQUENCIES window.
  Click OK.
  Check the distribution of the following variable: state
  Menu Bar
  ANALYZE
  DESCRIPTIVE STATISTICS
  FREQUENCIES
  Select "State" in the FREQUENCIES window.
  CHARTS
  BAR CHARTS
  CONTINUE
  OK
- **Analyze results for the taste test using SPSS.**
  Refer to the frequency distributions you just created in the preceding check data section to answer the following questions.

1. Which of these three demographic variables (sex, age, and state) did the designers of this taste test want to have equal representation across the possible values of the demographic variables?
2. What is the mode in the distribution of "state"?
3. What percent of the respondents preferred the new reduced-fat version of KitKat (the "different sample," in this case)? What percent preferred the currently marketed version of KitKat? What percent expressed no preference between the two versions? Use the variable "prefer" in your analyses for question 3.

- **Do cross-tabulation analysis to determine if a relationship exists between one's sex and preference for the new version of the KitKat candy bar.**

4. Before your analysis, write down what the H_0 and H_1 are for cross-tabbing "sex" and "prefer."

- **Conduct the first cross-tabulation analysis as follows:**
  Menu Bar
  DATA
  SELECT CASES

(continued)

ALL CASES
Click OK.
Menu Bar
ANALYZE
DESCRIPTIVE STATISTICS
CROSSTABS
Select "prefer" for ROW(S) and "sex" for COLUMN(S).
Click STATISTICS. Select CHI-SQUARE.
Click CELLS. Under PERCENTAGES, check COLUMN.
Click CONTINUE. Then click OK.

5. After examining your results, what decision do you make regarding H_0 and H_1 now?
6. What are the H_0 and H_1 for cross-tabulating "sex" and "prefer" when only those stating a preference are considered?

- **Conduct the second cross-tabulation analysis as follows:**

Menu Bar
DATA
SELECT CASES
If
Prefer <= 2
CONTINUE
Menu Bar
ANALYZE
DESCRIPTIVE STATISTICS
CROSSTABS
Select "prefer" for ROWS(S) and "sex" for COLUMN(S).
Click STATISTICS. Select CHI-SQUARE.
Click CELLS. Under PERCENTAGES, check COLUMN.
Click CONTINUE. Then click OK.

7. What decision do you make regarding H_0 and H_1 now?

6. Histogram pop-up window appears on screen.
7. Histogram window has two portions:
   a. Input
   b. Output Options
8. Input portion asks for two inputs.
   a. Click in the **Input Range** box and select (highlight) all the 45 rows under ATTITUDE. $D$2:$D$46 should appear in the input range box.
   b. In the **Bin Range** (Please note that this input is **optional**, if you won't provide reference the system will take values based on range of the data set), leave this box empty.
9. In the Output portion of the pop-up window, select the following Options:
   a. **New Workbook**
   b. **Cumulative Percentage**
   c. **Chart Output**
10. Click **OK.**
11. Please note that Default Chart Output size will be very small. Click on the Histogram Diagram, and drag it on the corners to view better.

Cross-Tabulation

We show the detailed steps for running the cross-tabulation of sex and usage of Nike shoes given in Table 16.3. The screen captures using EXCEL for these steps can be downloaded from the Web site for this book.

1. Select **Data** (Alt 1 D).
2. Select **Pivot Table and Pivot Chart Wizard** under Data.
3. **Pivot Table and Pivot Chart Report** window pops up.

4. Step 1 of 3: **Pivot Table and Pivot Chart Wizard, leave as it is.**
5. Click **Next.**
6. Step 2 of 3: **Pivot Table and Pivot Chart Wizard**. In the **Range Box** select **Data** under the columns CASENO, USERGR, SEX, ATTITUDE. $A$1:$D$46 should appear in the range box. Click **Next.**
7. Step 3 of 3: **Pivot Table and Pivot Chart Wizard,** select **New Worksheet** in this window. Click **Layout** and drag the variables in this format.

```
                    SEX
                ----------------
                |
USERGR          |     CASENO (Double click CASENO and select Count)
                |
```

8. Click **OK** and then **Finish.**

Summary

Basic data analysis provides valuable insights and guides the rest of the data analysis as well as the interpretation of the results. A frequency distribution should be obtained for each variable in the data. This analysis produces a table of frequency counts, percentages, and cumulative percentages for all the values associated with that variable. It indicates the extent of out-of-range, missing, or extreme values. The mean, mode, and median of a frequency distribution are measures of central tendency. The variability of the distribution is described by the range and the variance or standard deviation.

Cross-tabulations are tables that reflect the joint frequency distribution of two or more variables. In cross-tabulation, the cell percentages can be computed either column-wise, based on column totals, or row-wise, based on row totals. The general rule is to compute the percentages in the direction of the independent variable, across the dependent variable. The chi-square statistic provides a test of the statistical significance of the observed association in a cross-tabulation. The phi coefficient, contingency coefficient, and Cramer's *V* provide measures of the strength of association between the variables.

Key Terms and Concepts

Frequency distribution, 429
Measures of location, 433
Mean, 434
Mode, 434
Median, 434
Measures of variability, 435
Range, 435
Variance, 435
Standard deviation, 436
Null hypothesis, 438
Alternative hypothesis, 438
One-tailed test, 438
Two-tailed test, 438
Test statistic, 438
Type-I error, 439
Level of significance, 439
Type-II error, 439
Power of a test, 439
Critical value, 441
Cross-tabulation, 442
Contingency tables, 443
Chi-square statistic, 445
Chi-square distribution, 446
Phi coefficient, 447
Contingency coefficient, 447
Cramer's *V*, 448

Suggested Cases and Video Cases

Cases

3.1 Ford **3.2 Darden** **3.3 Microsoft** **4.1 Boeing**
4.2 Gucci

Video Cases

3.1 AFLAC **3.2 Honest Tea** **4.1 Subaru**

Additional cases and video cases are available in the Instructor's Manual and on the instructor and student Web sites.

Live Research: Conducting a Marketing Research Project

1. Each team can conduct the entire analysis, or the data analysis can be split between teams with different teams conducting a different type of analysis. It is helpful to run a frequency count for every variable. This gives a good feel for the data.
2. Calculate the measures of location (mean, median, and mode), measures of variability (range and standard deviation) for each variable.
3. Relevant associations can be examined by conducting cross-tabulations. Procedures should be specified for categorizing interval- or ratio-scaled variables. In this process, it is helpful to examine the frequency distributions.

Acronyms

The statistics associated with frequencies may be summarized by the acronym FREQUENCIES:

F requency histogram
R ange
E stimate of location: mean
Quotients: percentages
U ndulation: variance
E stimate of location: mode
N umbers or counts
C umulative percentage
I ncorrect and missing values
E stimate of location: median
S hape of the distribution

The salient characteristics of cross-tabulations may be summarized by the acronym TABULATE:

T wo variables at a time
A ssociation and not causation is measured
B ased on cell count of at least five
U derstood easily by managers
L imited number of categories
A ssociated statistics
T wo ways to calculate percentages
E xpected cell frequencies

Review Questions

1. Describe the procedure for computing frequencies.
2. What measures of location are commonly computed for frequencies?
3. What measures of variability are commonly computed for frequencies?
4. What is the major difference between cross-tabulation and frequency distribution?
5. What is the general rule for computing percentages in cross-tabulation?
6. Describe the chi-square distribution.
7. What is meant by the expected cell frequency?
8. How is the chi-square statistic calculated?
9. When is it meaningful to determine the strength of association in a cross-tabulation?
10. What statistics are available for determining the strength of association in cross-tabulation.
11. Discuss the reasons for the frequent use of cross-tabulations. What are some of its limitations?

Applied Problems

1. In each of the following situations, indicate the statistical analysis you would conduct and the appropriate test or test statistic that should be used.
   a. Respondents in a survey of 1,000 households were classified as heavy, medium, light, or nonusers of ice cream. They were also classified as being in high-, medium-, or low-income categories. Is the consumption of ice cream related to income level?
   b. In a survey using a representative sample of 2,000 households from the Synovate consumer panel, the respondents were asked whether or not they preferred to shop at Sears. The sample was divided into small and large households based on a median split of the household size. Does preference for shopping in Sears vary by household size?
2. The current advertising campaign for a major soft drink brand would be changed if less than 30 percent of the consumers like it.
   a. Formulate the null and alternative hypotheses.
   b. Discuss the type-I and type-II errors that could occur in hypothesis testing.
3. A major department store chain is having an end-of-season sale on refrigerators. The number of refrigerators sold during this sale at a sample of 10 stores was

   80 110 0 40 70 80 100 50 80 30

   a. Compute the mean, mode, and median. Which measure of central tendency is most appropriate in this case and why?
   b. Compute the variance and the standard deviation.
   c. Construct a histogram, and discuss whether this variable is normally distributed.
4. In a study measuring households' familiarity with downloading pictures from the Internet, the following results were obtained (1 = not at all familiar, 7 = very familiar).

Level of Familiarity	Number of Households
1	22
2	26
3	34
4	40
5	32
6	28
7	18

   a. Convert the number of households into percentages.
   b. Calculate the cumulative percentages.
   c. Construct a histogram with familiarity on the X-axis and frequency on the Y-axis.
   d. Calculate the mean, median, and mode of the distribution.
5. A research project examining the impact of income on the consumption of gourmet foods was conducted. Each variable was classified into three levels of high, medium, and low. The following results were obtained.

		Income		
		Low	Medium	High
Consumption of Gourmet Foods	**Low**	25	15	10
	Medium	10	25	15
	High	15	10	25

   a. Is the relationship between income and consumption of gourmet food significant?
   b. Is the relationship between income and consumption of gourmet food strong?
   c. What is the pattern of the relationship between income and consumption of gourmet food?
6. A pilot survey was conducted with 30 respondents to examine Internet usage for personal (nonprofessional) reasons. The following table contains the resulting data giving each respondent's sex (1 = male, 2 = female), familiarity with the Internet (1 = very unfamiliar, 7 = very familiar), Internet usage in hours per week, attitude toward Internet and toward technology, both measured on a seven-point scale (1 = very unfavorable, 7 = very favorable), whether the respondents have done shopping or banking on the Internet (1 = yes, 2 = no).
   a. Obtain the frequency distribution of familiarity with the Internet. Calculate the relevant statistics.
   b. For the purpose of cross-tabulation, classify respondents as light or heavy users. Those reporting 5 hours or less usage should be classified as light users and the remaining as heavy users. Run a cross-tabulation of sex and Internet usage. Interpret the results. Is Internet usage related to one's sex?

INTERNET USAGE DATA

Respondent Number	Sex	Familiarity	Internet Usage	Attitude toward Internet	Attitude toward Technology	Usage of Internet: Shopping	Usage of Internet: Banking
1	1.00	7.00	14.00	7.00	6.00	1.00	1.00
2	2.00	2.00	2.00	3.00	3.00	2.00	2.00
3	2.00	3.00	3.00	4.00	3.00	1.00	2.00
4	2.00	3.00	3.00	7.00	5.00	1.00	2.00
5	1.00	7.00	13.00	7.00	7.00	1.00	1.00
6	2.00	4.00	6.00	5.00	4.00	1.00	2.00
7	2.00	2.00	2.00	4.00	5.00	2.00	2.00
8	2.00	3.00	6.00	5.00	4.00	2.00	2.00
9	2.00	3.00	6.00	6.00	4.00	1.00	2.00
10	1.00	9.00	15.00	7.00	6.00	1.00	2.00
11	2.00	4.00	3.00	4.00	3.00	2.00	2.00
12	2.00	5.00	4.00	6.00	4.00	2.00	2.00
13	1.00	6.00	9.00	6.00	5.00	2.00	1.00
14	1.00	6.00	8.00	3.00	2.00	2.00	2.00
15	1.00	6.00	5.00	5.00	4.00	1.00	2.00
16	2.00	4.00	3.00	4.00	3.00	2.00	2.00
17	1.00	6.00	9.00	5.00	3.00	1.00	1.00
18	1.00	4.00	4.00	5.00	4.00	1.00	2.00
19	1.00	7.00	14.00	6.00	6.00	1.00	1.00
20	2.00	6.00	6.00	6.00	4.00	2.00	2.00
21	1.00	6.00	9.00	4.00	2.00	2.00	2.00
22	1.00	5.00	5.00	5.00	4.00	2.00	1.00
23	2.00	3.00	2.00	4.00	2.00	2.00	2.00
24	1.00	7.00	15.00	6.00	6.00	1.00	1.00
25	2.00	6.00	6.00	5.00	3.00	1.00	2.00
26	1.00	6.00	13.00	6.00	6.00	1.00	1.00
27	2.00	5.00	4.00	5.00	5.00	1.00	1.00
28	2.00	4.00	2.00	3.00	2.00	2.00	2.00
29	1.00	4.00	4.00	5.00	3.00	1.00	2.00
30	1.00	3.00	3.00	7.00	5.00	1.00	2.00

Group Discussion

1. "Because cross-tabulation has certain basic limitations, this technique should not be used extensively in commercial marketing research." Discuss as a small group.
2. "Why waste time doing basic data analysis? Why not just conduct sophisticated multivariate data analysis (see Chapter 15)?" Discuss.

EXHIBIT 16.1 Computer Programs for Frequencies

SPSS

The main program in SPSS is FREQUENCIES. It produces a table of frequency counts, percentages, and cumulative percentages for the values of each variable. It gives all of the associated statistics. If the data are interval-scaled and only the summary statistics are desired, the DESCRIPTIVES procedure can be used. All of the statistics computed by DESCRIPTIVES are available in FREQUENCIES. However, DESCRIPTIVES is more efficient because it does not sort values into a frequency table. An additional program, MEANS, computes means and standard deviations for a dependent variable over subgroups of cases defined by independent variables.

SAS

The main program in SAS is UNIVARIATE. In addition to providing a frequency table, this program provides all of the associated statistics. Another procedure available is FREQ. For one-way frequency distribution, FREQ does not provide any associated statistics. If only summary statistics are desired, procedures such as MEANS, SUMMARY, and TABULATE can be used. It should be noted that FREQ is not available as an independent program in the microcomputer version.

MINITAB

The main function is Stats>Descriptive Statistics. The output values include the mean, median, mode, standard deviation, minimum, maximum, and quartiles. A histogram in a bar chart or graph can be produced from the Graph>Histogram selection.

EXCEL

The Tools>Data Analysis function computes the descriptive statistics. The output produces the mean, standard error, median, mode, standard deviation, variance, range, minimum, maximum, sum, count, and confidence level. Frequencies can be selected under the histogram function. A histogram can be produced in bar format.

EXHIBIT 16.2 Computer Programs for Cross-Tabulation

SPSS

The major cross-tabulation program is CROSSTABS. This program will display the cross-classification tables and provide cell counts, row and column percentages, the chi-square test for significance, and all the measures of the strength of the association that have been discussed.

SAS

Cross-tabulation can be done by using FREQ. This program will display the cross-classification tables and provide cell counts as well as row and column percentages. In addition, the TABULATE (SAS) program can be used for obtaining cell counts and row and column percentages, although it does not provide any of the associated statistics.

MINITAB

In MINITAB, cross-tabulations and chi-squares are under the Stats>Tables function. Each of these features must be selected separately under the Tables function.

Excel

The Data>Pivot Table function performs cross-tabulations in EXCEL. To do additional analysis or customize data, select a different summary function such as maximum, minimum, average, or standard deviation. In addition, a custom calculation can be selected to analyze values based on other cells in the data plane. ChiTest can be assessed under the Insert>Function>Statistical>ChiTest function.

CHAPTER

17

Data Analysis: Hypothesis Testing Related to Differences

"While groups such as users or nonusers of a brand are similar in many ways, making statistical comparisons between such groups on their attitude toward a brand can be very revealing."

JENNIFER GARVEY, *Director, Marketing Services, Verizon Information Services, Dallas-Ft. Worth, TX*

OPENING QUESTIONS

1. What is the role of the t distribution in testing hypotheses that are related to differences?
2. How would you test the hypothesis related to one sample?
3. How does hypothesis testing change when there are two independent samples rather than one? Does the hypothesis testing procedure change when testing for difference in proportions rather than means?
4. What about hypothesis testing for paired samples? How is it done?
5. How can the analysis of variance procedure be used for testing a hypothesis related to more than two samples?

Loyalty Versus Butterfly and Convenience Versus Price

As of 2005, grocery-store shoppers have actually been able to save money by spending more. How is this possible? Through the Internet, consumers now have access to a rewards and rebate program offered by grocery stores and other merchants. The program, Microrebate Investing, moves a percentage of loyal consumers' purchases directly into an investment account. The program is designed for customers at all income levels, with no prequalifications to membership. This is only one of many ways in which supermarkets and grocery stores are attempting to build customer loyalty.

A recent study examined the differences between 138 loyal shoppers (LS) and 110 butterfly (disloyal) shoppers (BS) of a major supermarket. Both groups of shoppers were asked to indicate the importance of 15 shopping attributes on a seven-point scale (1 = not important, 7 = very important). Based on the two-independent-samples t-tests, which are used to test the hypothesis of differences between means of two samples, significant differences were identified on five of the 15 attributes as indicated in the following.

	Mean Importance Rating		
Attribute	BS	LS	Significance Level
Low prices	6.30	6.14	0.044
Convenient access	6.24	6.49	0.045
Convenient parking	6.17	6.63	0.030
Convenient opening hours	5.99	6.46	0.001
Attractive displays and decor	4.67	5.14	0.026

While the butterfly shoppers were motivated by the low prices, the loyal shoppers gave significantly greater importance to convenience (access, parking, and opening hours) and displays and decor. Thus, even supermarkets such as Winn-Dixie with its SaveRite Grocery Warehouses, cannot compete on the basis of price alone. To attract loyal shoppers, they must offer convenience, good aisle displays, and attractive internal decor.[1] •

Overview

Chapter 16 described basic data analysis, including frequency distribution, cross-tabulation, and the general procedure for hypothesis testing. As was explained, hypothesis testing procedures are classified as tests of associations or tests of differences. We also discussed statistics for examining the significance and strength of association. This chapter presents tests for examining hypotheses related to differences, as in the opening vignette. Figure 17.1 briefly explains the focus of the chapter, the relation of this chapter to the previous ones, and the steps of the marketing research process on which this chapter concentrates.

The parametric tests that we discuss assume that the data are at least interval-scaled. We first discuss the case for difference in means for one sample followed by hypothesis testing for two samples. We then make the extension to more than two samples and also examine hypothesis testing associated with differences in proportions. Figure 17.2 provides an overview of the topics discussed in this chapter and how they flow from one to the next.

Hypothesis Testing Related to Differences

In Chapter 16, we considered hypotheses testing related to associations. These hypotheses are of the form that two variables are associated with or related to each other. For example, the values of homes purchased are related to the buyers' incomes. We now focus on hypotheses testing related to differences. These hypotheses are of the form that two variables are different from each other. For example, people living in the suburbs have higher incomes than people living in the downtown areas. A classification of hypothesis testing procedures for examining differences is presented in

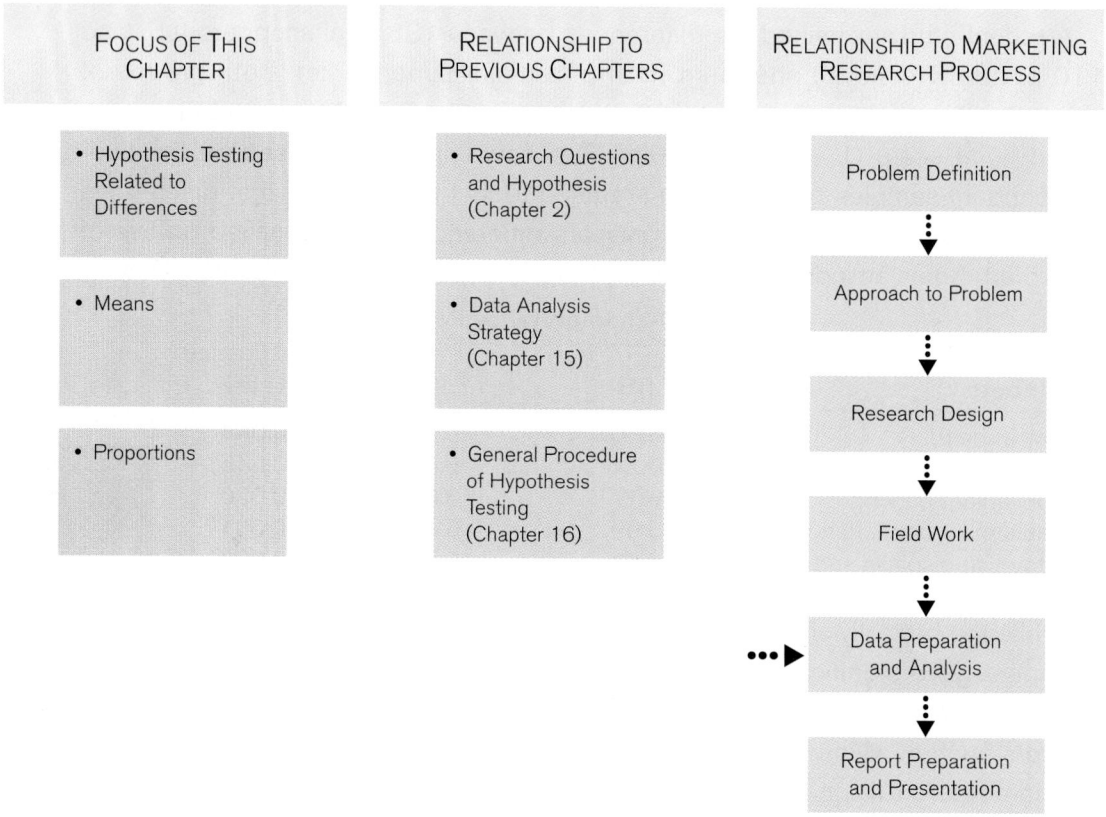

Figure 17.1

Relationship of Hypothesis Testing Related to Differences to Previous Chapters and the Marketing Research Process

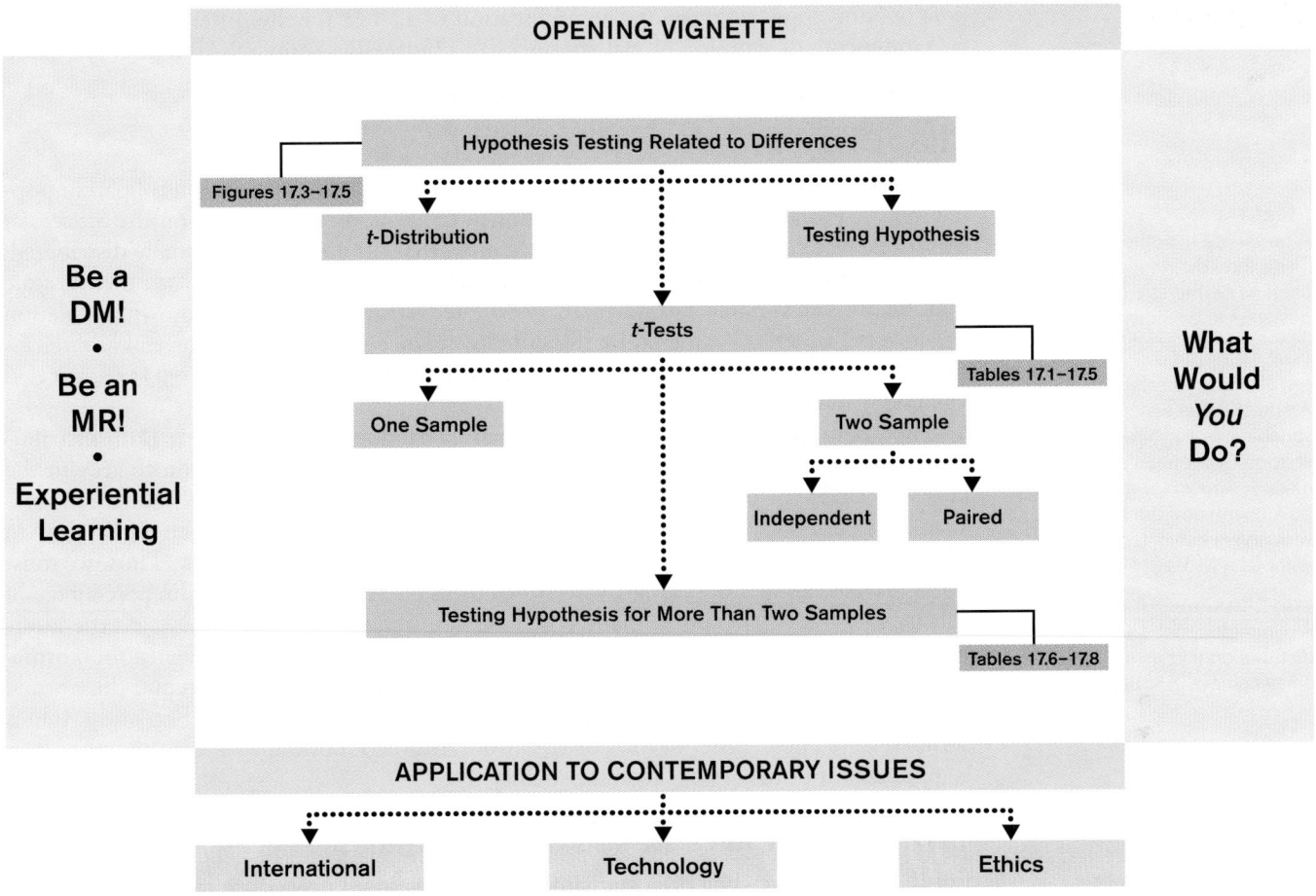

Figure 17.2

Hypothesis Testing Related to Differences: An Overview

Figure 17.3. These procedures are related to examining differences in means or proportions. First, we focus on hypothesis testing procedures examining differences in means. These procedures are also called **parametric tests** because they assume that the variables of interest are measured on at least an interval scale. For example, the average household spends less than $30 per month on long-distance telephone calls. Here, the monthly expenditure on long-distance telephone calls is measured on a ratio scale. The most popular parametric test is the *t*-test conducted for examining hypotheses about means. The *t*-test can be conducted on the means of one sample or two samples of observations. In the case of two samples, the samples can be independent or paired.

parametric tests
Hypothesis testing procedures that assume the variables of interest are measured on at least an interval scale.

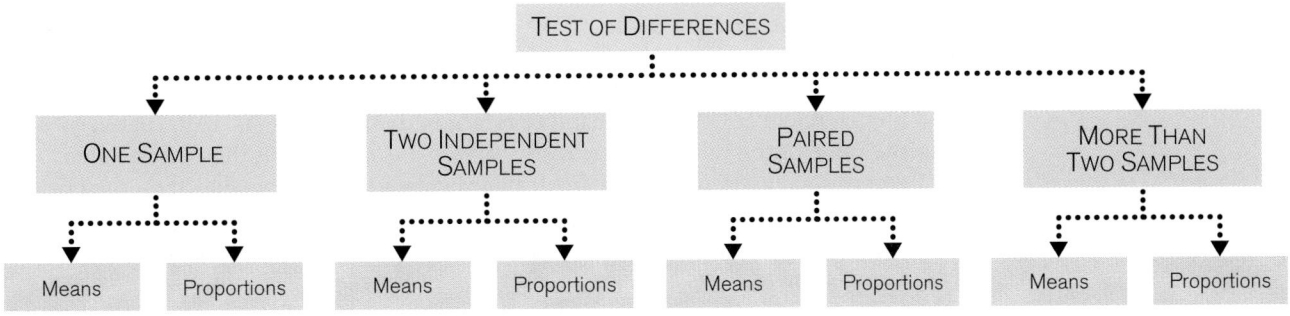

Figure 17.3

Hypothesis Tests Related to Differences

The opening vignette provided an application of a t-test for the difference in means of two independent samples—loyal shoppers and butterfly shoppers. All t-tests are based on the t distribution.

The *t* Distribution

t-test
A univariate hypothesis test using the t distribution, which is used when the standard deviation is unknown and the sample size is small.

t statistic
A statistic that assumes the variable has a symmetric bell-shaped distribution and the mean is known (or assumed to be known), and the population variance is estimated from the sample.

t distribution
A symmetric, bell-shaped distribution that is useful for small sample ($n < 30$) testing.

Parametric tests provide inferences for making statements about the means of parent populations. A ***t*-test** is commonly used for this purpose. This test is based on the *Student's t* statistic. The ***t* statistic** is calculated by assuming that the variable is normally distributed, the mean is known, and the population variance is estimated from the sample. Assume that the random variable X is normally distributed, with mean μ and unknown population variance σ^2, which is estimated by the sample variance s^2. Recall that the standard deviation of the sample mean, $\bar{X}$, is estimated as $s_{\bar{X}} = s / \sqrt{n}$. Then, $t = (\bar{X} - \mu) / s_{\bar{X}}$ is t distributed with $n - 1$ degrees of freedom.

The ***t* distribution** is similar to the normal distribution in appearance. Both distributions are bell-shaped and symmetric. However, the t distribution has more area in the tails and less in the center than the normal distribution. This is because population variance σ^2 is unknown and is estimated by the sample variance s^2. Given the uncertainty in the value of s^2, the observed values of t are more variable than those of z. Thus, we must go to a larger number of standard deviations from 0 to encompass a certain percentage of values from the t distribution than is the case with the normal distribution. As the number of degrees of freedom increases, however, the t distribution approaches the normal distribution. In fact, for large samples of 120 or more, the t distribution and the normal distribution are virtually indistinguishable. Table 4 in the Appendix of Statistical Tables shows selected percentiles of the t distribution. Although normality is assumed, the t-test is quite robust to departures from normality.

Testing Hypothesis Based on the *t* Statistic

For the special case when the t statistic is used, the general procedure for hypothesis testing discussed in the previous chapter is applied as follows (Figure 17.4).

1. Formulate the null (H_0) and the alternative (H_1) hypotheses.
2. Select the appropriate formula for the t statistic.
3. Select a significance level, α, for testing H_0. Typically, the 0.05 level is selected.
4. Take one or two samples and compute the mean and standard deviation for each sample. Calculate the t statistic assuming H_0 is true. Calculate the degrees of freedom.
5. Estimate the probability of getting a more extreme value of the statistic from Table 4 in the Appendix of Statistical Tables. Alternatively, calculate the critical value of the t statistic. Note that in determining the critical value of the test statistic, the area to the right of the critical value is either α or $\alpha/2$. It is α for a one-tail test and $\alpha/2$ for a two-tail test.
6. Compare the probability computed in Step 5 with the significance level selected in Step 3. (Alternatively, compare the calculated t statistic in Step 4 with the critical value determined in Step 5.)
7. Make the statistical decision to reject or not reject the null hypotheses. If the probability computed in Step 5 is smaller than the significance level selected in Step 3, reject H_0. If the probability is larger, do not reject H_0. (Alternatively, if the value of the calculated t statistic in Step 4 is larger than the critical value determined in Step 5, reject H_0. If the calculated value is smaller than the critical value, do not reject H_0.) Failure to reject H_0 does not necessarily imply that H_0 is true. It only means that the true state is not significantly different than that assumed by H_0.[2]
8. Express the conclusion reached by the t-test in terms of the marketing research problem.

The general procedure for conducting t-tests is illustrated in the following sections, beginning with the one-sample case.

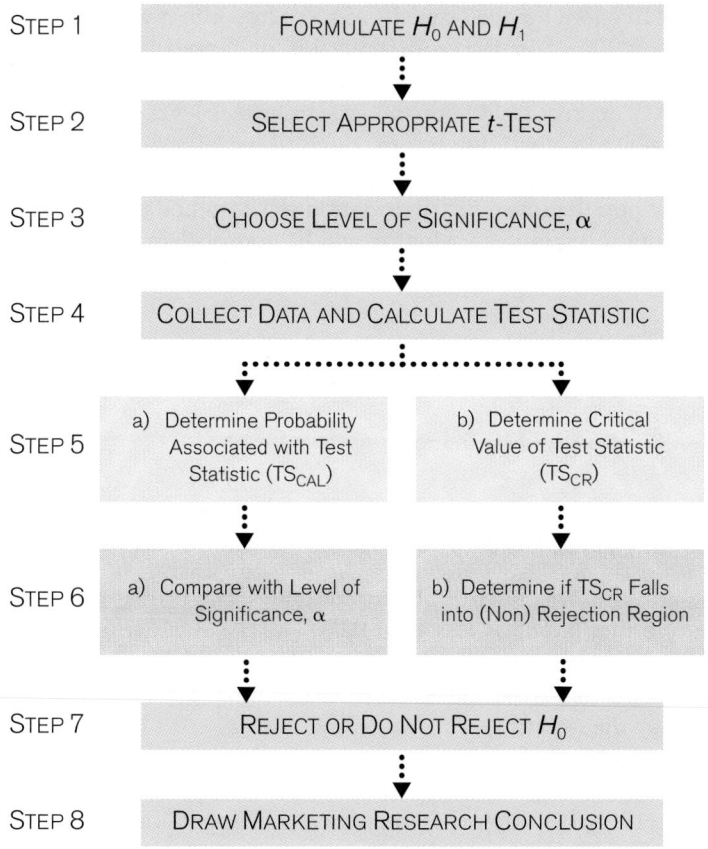

Figure 17.4
Conducting *t*-Tests

One-Sample *t*-Tests

In marketing research, the researcher is often interested in making statements about a single variable against a known or given standard. The following are examples of such statements:

- The market share for the new product will exceed 15 percent.
- At least 65 percent of customers will like the new package design.
- The average monthly household expenditure on groceries exceeds $500.
- The new service plan will be preferred by at least 70 percent of the customers.

These statements can be translated to null hypotheses that can be tested using a one-sample test, such as the *z*-test or the *t*-test. In the case of a *t*-test for a single mean, the researcher is interested in testing whether the population mean conforms to a given hypothesis (H_0). In the opening vignette, the hypothesis that the mean rating of each attribute for the overall sample (loyal shoppers and butterfly shoppers combined) exceeded 5.0 would be tested using the one-sample *t*-test.

Test for a Single Mean

Suppose a new machine attachment would be introduced if it receives a mean of at least 7 on a 10-point scale. A sample of 20 purchase engineers is shown the attachment and asked to evaluate it. The results indicate a mean rating of 7.9 with a standard deviation of 1.6. A significance level of $\alpha = 0.05$ is selected. Should the part be introduced?

$$H_0: \mu \leq 7.0$$
$$H_1: \mu > 7.0$$
$$t = (\bar{X} - \mu) / s_{\bar{X}}$$
$$s_{\bar{X}} = s / \sqrt{n}$$
$$s_{\bar{X}} = 1.6 / \sqrt{20} = 1.6 / 4.472 = 0.358$$
$$t = (7.9 - 7.0) / 0.358 = 0.9 / 0.358 = 2.514$$

The degrees of freedom for the t statistic to test a hypothesis about one mean are $n - 1$. In this case, $n - 1 = 20 - 1$ or 19. From Table 4 in the Appendix of Statistical Tables, the probability of getting a more extreme value than 2.514 is less than 0.05. (Alternatively, the critical t value for 19 degrees of freedom and a significance level of 0.05 is 1.7291, which is less than the calculated value.) Therefore, the null hypothesis is rejected, favoring the introduction of the part.

z-test
A univariate hypothesis test using the standard normal distribution.

Note that if the population standard deviation was assumed to be known as 1.5, rather than estimated from the sample, a ***z*-test** would be appropriate. In this case, the value of the z statistic would be

$$z = (\bar{X} - \mu) / \sigma_{\bar{X}}$$

Where

$$\sigma_{\bar{X}} = 1.5 / \sqrt{20} = 1.5 / 4.472 = 0.335$$

and

$$z = (7.9 - 7.0)/0.335 = 0.9/0.335 = 2.687$$

From Table 2 in the Appendix of Statistical Tables, the probability of getting a more extreme value of z than 2.687 is less than 0.05. (Alternatively, the critical z value for a one-tailed test and a significance level of 0.05 is 1.645, which is less than the calculated value.) Therefore, the null hypothesis is rejected, and we can reach the same conclusion arrived at earlier by the t-test.

The one-sample t-test is further illustrated using the data of Table 17.1. This table contains data from two samples, each consisting of 10 respondents. Sample one consists of teenagers (ages 13 to 19), whereas sample two consists of adults 20 years old or older. The respondents were asked to indicate their preferences for Disney theme parks, immediately before and immediately after their visits, using a 10-point scale. This table gives the data for only 20 respondents because we want to show the calculations of the basic statistics by hand. These hand calculations are shown to provide a better idea of the basic concepts. In practice, the sample size is much larger. The analysis of such large datasets is illustrated later in the chapter in the Experiential Learning exercise that analyzes the data for 146 respondents in a survey for Musial University.

The null hypothesis for Table 17.1, based on a previous survey, is that the preference for sample one before entering the theme park (PREFERENCE 11) will be 5.0. It is possible that the preference for Disney parks could have increased or decreased since the last survey. Hence, the hypotheses are as follows:

$$H_0: \mu = 5.0$$
$$H_1: \mu \neq 5.0$$

We show the calculations for a one-sample t-test by hand. It can be seen that the mean preference of sample one before entering the park is 5.5 with a standard deviation of 1.08. These calculations are as follows:

$$\begin{aligned}
\bar{X}_1 &= (7+6+5+6+4+6+5+4+7+5)/10 \\
&= 55/10 \\
&= 5.5 \\
\Sigma(X_i - \bar{X}_1)^2 &= (7-5.5)^2 + (6-5.5)^2 + (5-5.5)^2 + (6-5.5)^2 + (4-5.5)^2 \\
&\quad + (6-5.5)^2 + (5-5.5)^2 + (4-5.5)^2 + (7-5.5)^2 + (5-5.5)^2 \\
&= 2.25 + 0.25 + 0.25 + 0.25 + 2.25 \\
&\quad + 0.25 + 0.25 + 2.25 + 2.25 + 0.25 \\
&= 10.50 \\
S^2_{x1} &= 10.50/(10-1) \\
S_{x1} &= \sqrt{(10.5)/(10-1)} \\
&= 1.08
\end{aligned}$$

Table 17.1

Preference for Disney Before and After Visiting the Resort

Respondent Number	Sample	Preference for Disney	
		Before	After
1	1.00	7.00	9.00
2	1.00	6.00	8.00
3	1.00	5.00	8.00
4	1.00	6.00	9.00
5	1.00	4.00	7.00
6	1.00	6.00	8.00
7	1.00	5.00	7.00
8	1.00	4.00	7.00
9	1.00	7.00	9.00
10	1.00	5.00	7.00
11	2.00	3.00	7.00
12	2.00	4.00	8.00
13	2.00	4.00	7.00
14	2.00	3.00	6.00
15	2.00	6.00	8.00
16	2.00	5.00	8.00
17	2.00	4.00	9.00
18	2.00	3.00	6.00
19	2.00	3.00	7.00
20	2.00	5.00	9.00

Therefore,

$$t = (\bar{X} - \mu) / s_{\bar{X}}$$
$$s_{\bar{X}} = s / \sqrt{n}$$
$$s_{\bar{X}} = 1.08 / \sqrt{10} = 1.08 / 3.16 = 0.342$$
$$t = (5.5 - 5.0) / 0.342 = 0.5 / 0.342 = 1.46$$

With 9 degrees of freedom, the probability of getting a more extreme value of t exceeds 0.10 (see Table 4 in the Appendix of Statistical Tables). Hence, the null hypothesis cannot be rejected. In other words, the mean preference of sample one before entering the theme park is no different than 5.0. Thus, based on the results, there has been no change in the preference of teenagers since the last survey. This one-sample t-test was also conducted using a statistical program. The results are described in Table 17.2. The corresponding SPSS and EXCEL outputs with explanatory remarks can be downloaded from the Web site for this book.

Test for a Single Proportion

Such hypotheses relate to the proportion or percentage pertaining to a single population. Examples might be "the proportion of brand-loyal users of Coca-Cola exceeds 0.2" or "70 percent of the households eat out at least once a week." The procedure for testing a hypothesis associated with a proportion for one sample was illustrated in Chapter 16 in the section entitled "A General Procedure for Hypothesis Testing."

Table 17.2

One-Sample *t*-Test: Teenagers' Preference Before Visiting

Variable	Number of Cases	Mean	Standard Deviation	Standard Error of Mean
Preference Before Visiting	10	5.5000	1.080	0.342

Test Value = 5

Mean Difference	95% Confidence Interval		*t* Value	Degrees of Freedom	Two-Tailed Significance
	Lower	Upper			
0.50	−0.273	1.273	1.46	9	0.177

Two-Sample *t*-Tests

As can be seen from Figure 17.3, the two samples can be either independent or paired. Furthermore, the hypotheses and the related tests could pertain to examining differences in means or proportions.

Two Independent Samples

independent samples Two samples that are not experimentally related. The measurement of one sample has no effect on the values of the other sample.

Samples drawn randomly from different populations are termed **independent samples**. Several hypotheses in marketing relate to parameters from two different populations:

- The populations of users and nonusers of a brand differ in terms of their perceptions of the brand.
- The high-income consumers spend more on entertainment than low-income consumers.
- The proportion of brand loyal users in Segment I is more than the proportion in Segment II.
- The proportion of households with an Internet connection in the United States exceeds that in Germany.

In each of the foregoing hypotheses, we have two different populations: users and nonusers, high-income and low-income consumers, Segment I and Segment II, and United States and Germany. Samples drawn randomly from these populations will be independent samples. In the opening vignette, the loyal shoppers (LS) and the butterfly shoppers (BS) constituted two independent samples. For the purpose of analysis, data pertaining to different groups of respondents (e.g., males and females) are generally treated as independent samples even though the data may pertain to the same survey. As in the case for one sample, the hypotheses can relate to means or proportions. The first two hypotheses in the introduction to this section relate to means, whereas the latter two relate to proportions.

Means In the case of means for two independent samples, the hypotheses take the following form:

$$H_0: \mu_1 = \mu_2$$
$$H_1: \mu_1 \neq \mu_2$$

In the opening vignette, the hypotheses tested for the importance of each attribute by the loyal shoppers (LS) and the butterfly shoppers (BS) were

$$H_0: \mu_{LS} = \mu_{BS}$$
$$H_1: \mu_{LS} \neq \mu_{BS}$$

The two populations are sampled and the means and variances computed based on samples of sizes n_1 and n_2. If both populations are found to have the same variance, a pooled variance estimate is computed from the two sample variances as follows:

$$s^2 = \frac{\sum_{i=1}^{n_1}(X_{i_1} - \bar{X}_1)^2 + \sum_{i=1}^{n_2}(X_{i_2} - \bar{X}_2)^2}{n_1 + n_2 - 2}$$

or

$$s^2 = \frac{(n_1 - 1)s_1^2 + (n_2 - 1)s_2^2}{n_1 + n_2 - 2}$$

The standard deviation of the test statistic can be estimated as

$$s_{\bar{X}_1 - \bar{X}_2} = \sqrt{s^2\left(\frac{1}{n_1} + \frac{1}{n_2}\right)}$$

The appropriate value of t can be calculated as

$$t = \frac{(\bar{X}_1 - \bar{X}_2) - (\mu_1 - \mu_2)}{s_{\bar{X}_1 - \bar{X}_2}}$$

The degrees of freedom in this case are $(n_1 + n_2 - 2)$.

If the two populations have unequal variances, an exact t cannot be computed for the difference in sample means. For example, consumers in the United States have well-developed preferences for brands, whereas such preference formation seems to be weak for consumers in developing countries. Thus, preferences for shampoo brands in the United States are expected to exhibit lower variance as compared to preferences in the developing country of Sierra Leone in West Africa. In these cases, an approximation to t is computed. The number of degrees of freedom in this case is usually not an integer, but a reasonably accurate probability can be obtained by rounding to the nearest integer.[3] In this case, the standard deviation of the test statistic can be estimated as follows:

$$s_{\bar{X}_1 - \bar{X}_2} = \sqrt{\left(\frac{s_1^2}{n_1} + \frac{s_2^2}{n_2}\right)}$$

An ***F*-test** of sample variance may be performed if it is not known whether the two populations have equal variance. In this case the hypotheses are

F-test
A statistical test of the equality of the variances of two populations.

$$H_0 : \sigma_1^2 = \sigma_2^2$$
$$H_1 : \sigma_1^2 \neq \sigma_2^2$$

The ***F* statistic** is computed from the sample variances as follows:

F statistic
The *F* statistic is computed as the ratio of two sample variances.

$$F_{(n_1-1),(n_2-1)} = \frac{s_1^2}{s_2^2}$$

Where

n_1 = size of sample 1
n_2 = size of sample 2
$n_1 - 1$ = degrees of freedom for sample 1
$n_2 - 1$ = degrees of freedom for sample 2
s_1^2 = sample variance for sample 1
s_2^2 = sample variance for sample 2

***F* distribution**
A frequency distribution that depends upon two sets of degrees of freedom: the degrees of freedom in the numerator and the degrees of freedom in the denominator.

As can be seen, the critical value of the ***F* distribution** depends upon two sets of degrees of freedom—those in the numerator and those in the denominator. The critical values of F for various degrees of freedom for the numerator and denominator are given in Table 5 of the Appendix of Statistical Tables. If the probability of F is greater than the significance level α, H_0 is not rejected and t based on the pooled variance estimate can be used. On the other hand, if the probability of F is less than or equal to α, H_0 is rejected and t based on a separate variance estimate is used.

Using the data of Table 17.1, we can examine whether the teenagers have a different preference (PREFERENCE 11) than adults (PREFERENCE 21) before entering the park. A two-independent-samples t-test is conducted. Since the difference could be in either direction, a two-tailed test is used.

First, we show the calculations by hand. It can be seen that sample one has a mean of 5.5 with a standard deviation of 1.080 or a variance of $(1.080)^2 = 1.166$. These calculations were illustrated earlier for the one-sample test. Similar calculations will show that sample two has a mean of 4.0 and a standard deviation of 1.054 or a variance of 1.111.

$$\begin{aligned}
\bar{x}_2 &= (3+4+4+3+6+5+4+3+3+5)/10 \\
&= 40/10 \\
&= 4.0 \\
\Sigma(X_i - \bar{X}_2)^2 &= (3-4)^2 + (4-4)^2 + (4-4)^2 + (3-4)^2 + (6-4)^2 \\
&\quad + (5-4)^2 + (4-4)^2 + (3-4)^2 + (3-4)^2 + (5-4)^2 \\
&= 1+0+0+1+4+1+0+1+1+1 \\
&= 10
\end{aligned}$$

Therefore,

$$\begin{aligned}
S_x^2 &= 10/(10-1) \\
&= 1.111
\end{aligned}$$

The value of the F statistic for testing the equality of variances is

$$F_{9,9} = (1.166/1.111) = 1.05$$

Note that the F-test of sample variances has a probability that exceeds 0.05. Alternatively, the critical value of $F_{9,9}$ is 3.18 (see Table 5 in the Appendix of Statistical Tables). Accordingly, the null hypothesis of equal variances cannot be rejected, and the t-test based on the pooled variance estimate should be used.

The pooled variance estimate may be calculated as

$$\begin{aligned}
s^2 &= \frac{(10-1)\,1.166 + (10-1)\,1.111}{10+10-2} \\
&= 1.139
\end{aligned}$$

Thus,

$$\begin{aligned}
s_{\bar{X}_1 - \bar{X}_2} &= \sqrt{1.139\left(\frac{1}{10} + \frac{1}{10}\right)} \\
&= 0.477
\end{aligned}$$

Under the null hypothesis, the value of the t statistic is

$$\begin{aligned}
t &= (5.5 - 4.0)/0.477 \\
&= 3.14
\end{aligned}$$

The t value is 3.14, and with $20 - 2 = 18$ degrees of freedom, this gives us a probability of 0.006, which is less than the significance level of $0.05/2 = 0.025$. Alternatively, the critical value of t is 2.1009 (see Table 4 in the Appendix of Statistical Tables). Note that in determining the critical value of the test statistic (TS_{CR}), the area to the right of the critical value is $\alpha/2$ for the two-tail test being conducted. Since the calculated value of t

Table 17.3

t-Tests for Independent Samples: Preference Before Visiting

Variable Sample	Number of Cases	Mean	Standard Deviation	Standard Error of Mean
Teenagers	10	5.5000	1.080	0.342
Adults	10	4.0000	1.054	0.333

Mean Difference = 1.5000
Test for Equality of Variances: $F = 1.05$; $P = 0.472$

***t*-Test for Equality of Means**

Variances	*t* Value	Degrees of Freedom	Two-Tailed Significance	Standard Error of Difference	95% CI for Difference
Equal	3.14	18	0.006	0.477	(0.497, 2.503)
Unequal	3.14	17.99	0.006	0.477	(0.497, 2.503)

exceeds the critical value, the null hypothesis of equal means is rejected. Thus, the conclusion is that the teenagers and adults differ in their preferences for Disney theme parks before entering the park. This two-sample *t*-test was also conducted using statistical software and the results are presented in Table 17.3; the corresponding SPSS and EXCEL outputs can be downloaded from the Web site. Table 17.3 also shows the *t*-test using separate variance estimates since most computer programs automatically conduct the *t*-test both ways.

Suppose we wanted to determine whether teenagers have a higher preference for Disney parks as compared to adults. In this case, a one-tailed rather than a two-tailed test should be used. The hypotheses are as follows:

H_0: $\mu_1 \leq \mu_2$
H_1: $\mu_1 > \mu_2$

The *t* statistic is calculated in exactly the same way as in the two-tailed test. In determining the critical value of the test statistic (TS_{CR}), however, the area to the right of the critical value is α for a one-tail test (Figure 17.5). In this case the critical value of *t* is 1.7341, leading to the same conclusion as arrived at earlier. A two-tailed test is more conservative

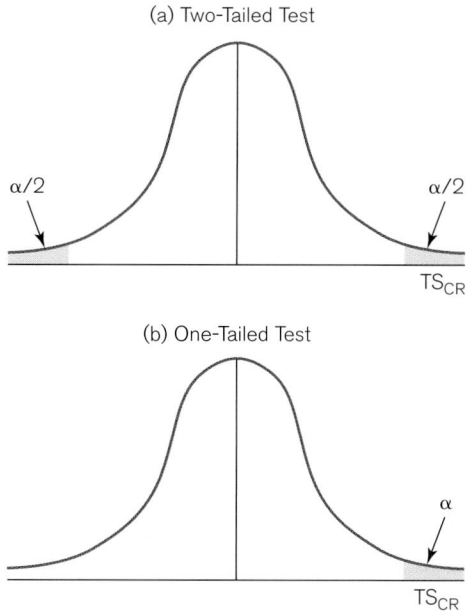

Figure 17.5

Calculating the Critical Value of the Test Statistic: TS_{CR} for Two-Tailed and One-Tailed Tests

RESEARCH IN ACTION

Ethics in Marketing Education: Private Versus Public Schools

A survey of undergraduate marketing students at private and public business schools was undertaken to determine their perceptions of the coverage of ethical topics in marketing courses. There were 101 respondents from private schools and 171 from public schools. Respondents were asked to indicate their degree of (dis)agreement with three statements using a five-point scale (1 = strongly disagree, 5 = strongly agree). Based on two-independent-samples *t*-tests, students from private schools indicated a greater emphasis on ethics than students from public schools.

Statement	Mean Ratings Private	Mean Ratings Public	Level of Significance
In the marketing program at my school, there is a substantial emphasis on teaching ethics.	2.88	2.62	0.02
In my marketing courses, I have the opportunity to initiate discussion of ethical issues.	3.50	3.09	0.00
My professor seems to be concerned about ethical issues.	3.50	3.30	0.06

The mean responses also suggest that schools are merely doing an adequate job of covering ethical issues in marketing courses. Given the importance of the topic, both private and public business schools need to improve the emphasis on ethical issues in marketing courses.[4]

than the corresponding one-tailed test. If a hypothesis is rejected using a two-tailed test then it will also be rejected using the corresponding one-tailed test. As explained in Chapter 16, the area to the right of the critical value is α for a one-tail test and $\alpha/2$ for a two-tail test. In other words, the critical value is larger for a two-tailed test than it is for a one-tailed test.

As another application of *t*-test, consider the Ethics in Marketing Education Research in Action example. In this example, we tested the difference between means. A similar test is available for testing the difference between proportions for two independent samples.

Proportions A case involving proportions for two independent samples is illustrated in Table 17.4, which gives the number (and percentage) of users and nonusers of jeans in the United States and Hong Kong. Is the proportion of users the same in the United States and Hong Kong samples? The null and alternative hypotheses are

$$H_0: \pi_1 = \pi_2$$
$$H_1: \pi_1 \neq \pi_2$$

Table 17.4

Comparing the Proportions of Jeans Users for the United States and Hong Kong

Sample	Usage of Jeans: Users	Usage of Jeans: Nonusers	Row Totals
United States	160	40	200
Hong Kong	120	80	200
Column Totals	**280**	**120**	

A z-test is used as in testing the proportion for one sample. This is a large sample problem. The samples from each population must be large so that the binomial distribution of sample proportions can be approximated by the normal distribution. As a rule of thumb, both np and $n(1 - p)$ must be greater than 10 for each sample. In this case, the test statistic is given by

$$z = \frac{P_1 - P_2}{S_{P_1 - P_2}}$$

In the test statistic, the numerator is the difference between the proportions in the two samples, P_1 and P_2. The denominator is the standard error of the difference in the two proportions and is given by

$$S_{P_1 - P_2} = \sqrt{P(1-P)\left[\frac{1}{n_1} + \frac{1}{n_2}\right]}$$

Where

$$P = \frac{n_1 P_1 + n_2 P_2}{n_1 + n_2}$$

A significance level of $\alpha = 0.05$ is selected. Given the data of Table 17.4, the test statistic can be calculated as

$$P_1 = 160/200 = 0.8$$

$$P_2 = 120/200 = 0.6$$

$$P_1 - P_2 = 0.8 - 0.6 = 0.20$$

$$P = (200 \times 0.8 + 200 \times 0.6)/(200 + 200) = 0.7$$

$$s_{P_1 - P_2} = \sqrt{0.7 \times 0.3\left[\frac{1}{200} + \frac{1}{200}\right]} = 0.0458$$

$$z = 0.2/0.04583 = 4.36$$

Given a two-tail test, the area to the right of the critical value is $\alpha/2$ or 0.025. Hence, the critical value of the test statistic is 1.96. Since the calculated value exceeds the critical value, the null hypothesis is rejected. Thus, the proportion of users (0.80 for the United States and 0.60 for Hong Kong) is significantly different for the two samples.

As an alternative to the parametric z-test considered earlier, one could also use the cross-tabulation procedure to conduct a chi-square test. In this case, we will have a 2×2 table. One variable will be used to denote the sample and will assume the value 1 for sample one and the value of 2 for sample two. The other variable will be the dichotomous variable of interest. The t-test in this case is equivalent to a chi-square test for independence in a 2×2 contingency table. The relationship is

$$\chi^2_{(1)} = t^2_{(n_1 + n_2 - 2)}$$

For large samples, the t distribution approaches the normal distribution, thus the t-test and the z-test are equivalent.

Paired Samples

In many marketing research applications, the observations for the two groups are not selected from independent samples. Rather, the observations relate to **paired samples** in that the two sets of observations relate to the same respondents. Examples of hypotheses related to paired samples include the following:

paired samples
In hypothesis testing, the observations are paired so that the two sets of observations relate to the same respondents.

- Shoppers consider brand name to be more important than price when purchasing fashion clothing.
- Households spend more money on pizza than on hamburgers.
- The proportion of households who subscribe to a daily newspaper exceeds the proportion subscribing to magazines.
- The proportion of a bank's customers who have a checking account exceeds the proportion who have a savings account.

Each of the foregoing hypotheses relates to the same set of people. Furthermore, the first two hypotheses relate to means, whereas the latter two relate to proportions.

Means A sample of respondents may rate two competing brands, indicate the relative importance of two attributes of a product, or evaluate a brand at two different times. The difference in these cases is examined by a **paired-samples *t*-test**. In the opening vignette, the hypothesis that the loyal shoppers (LS) consider convenient parking more important than low prices would be tested by using a paired-samples *t*-test. To compute *t* for paired samples, the paired-difference variable (*D*) is formed and its mean and variance calculated. Then, the *t* statistic is computed. The degrees of freedom are $n - 1$, where n is the number of pairs. The relevant formulas are as follows:

paired-samples *t*-test
A test for differences in the means of paired samples.

$$H_0: \mu_D = 0$$
$$H_1: \mu_D \neq 0$$
$$t_{n-1} = \frac{\bar{D} - \mu_D}{s_{\bar{D}}}$$
$$t_{n-1} = \frac{\bar{D} - \mu_D}{\frac{s_D}{\sqrt{n}}}$$

Where

$$\bar{D} = \frac{\sum_{i=1}^{n} D_i}{n}$$
$$s_D = \sqrt{\frac{\sum_{i=1}^{n} (D_i - \bar{D})^2}{n-1}}$$
$$s_{\bar{D}} = \frac{s_D}{\sqrt{n}}$$

For the data given in Table 17.1, imagine the data in sample 2 represents the same respondents in sample 1 at a later point in time. A paired *t*-test could be used to determine if there is a difference in the preference before (PREFERENCE 11) and after visiting the Disney theme park (PREFERENCE 12) for respondents in sample one. First, the hand calculations are shown. The mean difference between the variables is 2.4, with a standard deviation of 0.516 and a standard error of 0.163. These calculations are as follows:

$$\begin{aligned}\bar{D} &= ((9-7)+(8-6)+(8-5)+(9-6)+(7-4)+\\ &\quad (8-6)+(7-5)+(7-4)+(9-7)+(7-5))/10\\ &= (2+2+3+3+3+2+2+3+2+2)/10\\ &= 2.4\end{aligned}$$

$$\begin{aligned}S_D^2 &= ((2-2.4)^2+(2-2.4)^2+(3-2.4)^2+(3-2.4)^2+(3-2.4)^2+\\ &\quad (2-2.4)^2+(2-2.4)^2+(3-2.4)^2+(2-2.4)^2+(2-2.4)^2)/(10-1)\\ &= (0.16+0.16+0.36+0.36+0.36+\\ &\quad 0.16+0.16+0.36+0.16+0.16)/9\\ &= 0.2667\end{aligned}$$

Thus,

$$S_D = \sqrt{0.2667}$$
$$= 0.516$$

and

$$S_{\bar{D}} = \frac{0.516}{\sqrt{10}}$$
$$= 0.516 / 3.162$$
$$= 0.163$$

This results in a t value of

$$2.4/0.163$$
$$= 14.7$$

With $10 - 1 = 9$ degrees of freedom, this has a probability of less than 0.001. Alternatively, the critical value of t for the two-tailed test is 2.2622 (see Table 4 in the Appendix of Statistical Tables). Therefore, the preferences of teenagers before and after visiting the Disney theme parks are significantly different. This paired-samples t-test was also conducted using statistical software, and the resulting output is shown in Table 17.5. The corresponding SPSS and EXCEL outputs can be downloaded from the Web site for this book. A one-tailed test would have the same value for the t statistic except that the level of significance will be α, rather than $\alpha/2$ (Figure 17.5). Thus, if we wanted to test whether the preferences after visiting the theme park were significantly greater than before the visit, a one-tailed test would also lead to the rejection of the null hypothesis:

$$H_0: \mu_D \leq 0$$
$$H_1: \mu_D > 0$$

Where

D = preference after the visit − preference before the visit.

Another application is provided in the context of determining the effectiveness of advertising.

Proportions The difference in proportions for paired samples can be tested by the chi-square test explained in the previous chapter.

Table 17.5

t-Tests for Paired Samples: Teenagers

Variable	Number of Pairs	Correlation	Two-Tailed Significance	Mean	Standard Deviation	Standard Error of Mean
Preference Before Visiting				5.5000	1.080	0.342
	10	0.881	0.001			
Preference After Visiting				7.9000	0.876	0.277

Paired Differences

Mean	Standard Deviation	Standard Error of Mean	*t* Value	Degrees of Freedom	Two-Tailed Significance	95% Confidence Interval
−2.4000	0.516	0.163	−14.70	9	0.000	(−2.769, −2.031)

RESEARCH IN ACTION

Rockport Rocks the Shoe Market with Comfort Appeal

In 2004, Rockport's advertising slogan was "Move in comfort. Arrive in style." This slogan was rendered differently for men and women, however. The TV commercials, as well as the print ads, were carefully tested before they were released to the media. A group of 200 men were asked to respond to a series of 10 scales designed to measure attitude toward Rockport shoes. They were then exposed to the TV commercial as part of an entertaining program. After the program, attitude toward Rockport shoes was again measured using the same 10 scales (see the one-group pretest/posttest design in Chapter 8). A paired *t*-test indicated a significant increase in attitude after exposure to the commercial. Similar testing was done for commercials and print ads geared to women.

Rockport spent about $10 million on this campaign in 2004. The TV commercials and the print ads not only fared well in the test but also were successful in achieving sales growth.[5]

BE a DM!

As the marketing director for Nike, how would you improve the image and competitive positioning of your brand among golfers?

BE an MR!

Visit Nike's Web site (www.nike.com) and conduct an Internet search using a search engine and your library's online database to obtain information on the factors consumers use to evaluate competing brands of athletic shoes.

The users and nonusers of Nike evaluated the brand on five factors using Likert-type scales. How would you analyze these data using two-independent-samples and paired-samples *t*-test?

Testing Hypotheses for More Than Two Samples

analysis of variance
A statistical technique for examining the differences among means for two or more populations.

Procedures for examining differences between more than two means are called **analysis of variance** (ANOVA). The typical null hypothesis is that all means are equal. Marketing researchers are often interested in examining the differences in the mean values of more than two groups. For example,

- Do the various segments differ in terms of their volumes of product consumption?
- Do the brand evaluations of groups exposed to different commercials vary?
- Do retailers, wholesalers, and agents differ in their attitudes toward the firm's distribution policies?
- Do the users, nonusers, and former users of a brand differ in their attitudes toward the brand?

The answers to these and similar questions can be determined by conducting ANOVA. To further explain this procedure, suppose the researcher was interested in examining whether heavy users, medium users, light users, and nonusers of shampoo differed in their preferences for Pert shampoo, measured on a nine-point Likert scale. The null hypothesis that the four groups were not different in their preference for Pert could be tested using analysis of variance. When conducting ANOVA, it is necessary to distinguish between dependent and independent variables.

Dependent and Independent Variables

In its simplest form, ANOVA must have a dependent variable (preference for Pert shampoo) that is metric (measured using an interval or ratio scale). There must also be one or more independent variables (product use: heavy, medium, light, and nonusers). The independent variables must be all categorical (nonmetric). The differences in preference of heavy users, medium users, light users, and nonusers would be examined by one-way analysis of variance. **One-way analysis of variance** involves only one categorical variable, or a single **factor** that defines the different samples or groups. These groups are also called **treatment** conditions. Thus, the different independent samples are treated as categories of a single independent variable. In this case, heavy users, medium users, light users, and nonusers of shampoo would constitute different samples or groups and would be treated as categories of a single independent variable called "shampoo usage."

one-way analysis of variance
An ANOVA technique in which there is only one factor.

factor
Categorical independent variable; the independent variable must be categorical (nonmetric) to use ANOVA.

treatment
In ANOVA, a particular combination of factor levels or categories.

In the opening vignette, suppose the respondents were classified into three groups: loyal shoppers (LS2—loyal to only one supermarket), multiloyal shoppers (MS2—loyal to two or three supermarkets), and butterfly shoppers (BS2—nonloyal shoppers). The differences in the mean importance ratings attached to each attribute by the LS2, MS2, and BS2 groups would be tested using one-way ANOVA.

The dependent variable is denoted by Y and the independent variable by X. X is a categorical variable having c categories. There are n observations on Y for each category of X. Thus, the sample size in each category of X is n, and the total sample size $N = n \times c$. While the sample sizes in the categories of X (the group sizes) are assumed to be equal for the sake of simplicity, this is not a requirement.

Decomposition of the Total Variation

In examining the differences among means, one-way ANOVA involves the **decomposition of the total variation** observed in the dependent variable. This variation is measured by the sums of squares corrected for the mean (SS). Analysis of variance is so-named because it examines the variability or variation in the sample (dependent variable) and, based on the variability, determines whether there is reason to believe that the population means differ.

decomposition of the total variation
In one-way ANOVA, separation of the variation observed in the dependent variable into the variation due to the independent variables plus the variation due to error.

The total variation in Y, denoted by $\boldsymbol{SS_y}$, can be decomposed into two components:

$$SS_y = SS_{between} + SS_{within}$$

SS_y
The total variation in Y.

where the subscripts *between* and *within* refer to the categories of X. $\boldsymbol{SS_{between}}$ is the variation in Y related to the variation in the means of the categories of X. It represents variation between the categories of X. In other words, $SS_{between}$ is the portion of the sum of squares in Y related to the independent variable or factor X. For this reason, $SS_{between}$ is also denoted as SS_x. $\boldsymbol{SS_{within}}$ is the variation in Y related to the variation within each category of X. SS_{within} is not accounted for by X. Therefore, it is referred to as SS_{error}. The total variation in Y may be decomposed as

$SS_{between}$
Also denoted as SS_x, the variation in Y related to the variation in the means of the categories of X. This represents variation between the categories of X, or the portion of the sum of squares in Y related to X.

SS_{within}
Also referred to as SS_{error}, the variation in Y due to the variation within each of the categories of X. This variation is not accounted for by X.

$$SS_y = SS_x + SS_{error}$$

Where

$$SS_y = \sum_{j=1}^{c} \sum_{i=1}^{n} (Y_{ij} - \bar{Y})^2$$

or

$$SS_y = \sum_{i=1}^{N} (Y_i - \bar{Y})^2$$

$$SS_x = \sum_{j=1}^{c} \sum_{i=1}^{n} (\bar{Y}_j - \bar{Y})^2$$

or

$$SS_x = \sum_{j=1}^{c} n\,(\bar{Y}_j - \bar{Y})^2$$

$$SS_{error} = \sum_{j=1}^{c} \sum_{i=1}^{n} (Y_{ij} - \bar{Y}_j)^2$$

Y_i = individual observation
$\bar{Y}_j$ = mean for category j
$\bar{Y}$ = mean over the whole sample, or grand mean
Y_{ij} = ith observation in the jth category

Measurement of Effects

The effects of X on Y are measured by SS_x. Since SS_x is related to the variation in the means of the categories of X, the relative magnitude of SS_x increases as the differences among the means of Y in the categories of X increase. The relative magnitude of SS_x also increases as the variations in Y within the categories of X decrease. The strength of the effects of X on Y are measured as follows:

$$\eta^2 = SS_x/SS_y = (SS_y - SS_{error})/SS_y$$

The value of eta^2 (η^2) varies between 0 and 1. It assumes a value of 0 when all the category means are equal, indicating that X has no effect on Y. The value of η^2 will be 1 when there is no variability within each category of X but there is some variability between categories. Thus, **eta^2** (η^2) is a measure of the variation in Y that is explained by the independent variable X. Not only can we measure the effects of X on Y, but we can also test for their significance.

eta^2 (η^2)
The strength of the effects of X (independent variable or factor) on Y (dependent variable) is measured by eta^2 (η^2). The value of η^2 varies between 0 and 1.

Significance Testing

In one-way ANOVA, the interest lies in testing the null hypothesis that the category means are equal in the population. In other words,

$$H_0: \mu_1 = \mu_2 = \mu_3 = \ldots = \mu_c$$

Under the null hypothesis, SS_x and SS_{error} come from the same source of variation. In such a case, the estimate of the population variance of Y can be based on either between-category variation or within-category variation. In other words,

the estimate of the population variance of Y

$$S_y^2 = SS_x/(c - 1)$$
$$= \text{Mean square due to } X$$
$$= MS_x$$

or

$$S_y^2 = SS_{error}/(N - c)$$
$$= \textbf{Mean square} \text{ due to error}$$
$$= MS_{error}$$

mean square
The sum of squares divided by the appropriate degrees of freedom.

The **significance of the overall effect** in terms of the null hypothesis may be tested by the F statistic based on the ratio between these two estimates:

significance of the overall effect
A test to determine whether some differences exist between some of the treatment groups.

$$F = \frac{SS_x/(c-1)}{SS_{error}/(N-c)} = \frac{MS_x}{MS_{error}}$$

This statistic follows the F distribution, with $(c - 1)$ and $(N - c)$ degrees of freedom (df). A table of the F distribution is given as Table 5 in the Appendix of Statistical Tables at the end of the book. As mentioned earlier, the F distribution is a probability distribution of the ratios of sample variances. It is characterized by degrees of freedom for the numerator and degrees of freedom for the denominator.[6]

Illustrative Applications of One-Way Analysis of Variance

These concepts are first illustrated with an example showing calculations done by hand followed by calculations using computer analysis. Suppose that a major supermarket is attempting to determine the effect of in-store advertising (X) on sales (Y). In-store advertising is varied at three levels: high, medium, and low. Fifteen stores are randomly selected, and five stores are randomly assigned to each treatment condition. The experiment lasts for four weeks. Sales are monitored, normalized to account for extraneous factors (store size, traffic, and so on) and converted to a 0-to-10 scale. The data obtained (Y_{ij}) are reported in Table 17.6. Again, the sample size (n = 15 stores) is limited so that the hand calculations do not become unwieldy.

The null hypothesis is that the category means are equal:

$$H_0: \mu_1 = \mu_2 = \mu_3$$

To test the null hypothesis, the various means and sums of squares are computed as follows:

$$\begin{aligned}
&\text{Category means: } \bar{Y}_j && 45/5 \quad 25/5 \quad 20/5 \\
& && = 9 \quad = 5 \quad = 4 \\
&\text{Grand mean: } \bar{Y} && = (45+25+20)/15 = 6
\end{aligned}$$

$$\begin{aligned}
SS_y &= (10-6)^2 + (9-6)^2 + (10-6)^2 + (8-6)^2 + (8-6)^2 \\
&\quad + (6-6)^2 + (4-6)^2 + (7-6)^2 + (3-6)^2 + (5-6)^2 \\
&\quad + (5-6)^2 + (6-6)^2 + (5-6)^2 + (2-6)^2 + (2-6)^2 \\
&= 16+9+16+4+4 \\
&\quad +0+4+1+9+1 \\
&\quad +1+0+1+16+16 \\
&= 98 \\
SS_x &= 5(9-6)^2 + 5(5-6)^2 + 5(4-6)^2 \\
&= 45+5+20 \\
&= 70
\end{aligned}$$

Table 17.6
Effect of In-Store Promotion on Sales

Store No.	Level of In-Store Promotion: High	Medium	Low
		Normalized Sales	
1	10	6	5
2	9	4	6
3	10	7	5
4	8	3	2
5	8	5	2

$$
\begin{aligned}
SS_{error} &= (10-9)^2 + (9-9)^2 + (10-9)^2 + (8-9)^2 + (8-9)^2 \\
&\quad + (6-5)^2 + (4-5)^2 + (7-5)^2 + (3-5)^2 + (5-5)^2 \\
&\quad + (5-4)^2 + (6-4)^2 + (5-4)^2 + (2-4)^2 + (2-4)^2 \\
&= 1+0+1+1+1 \\
&\quad +1+1+4+4+0 \\
&\quad +1+4+1+4+4 \\
&= 28
\end{aligned}
$$

It can be verified that

$$SS_y = SS_x + SS_{error}$$

as follows:

$$98 = 70 + 28$$

The strength of the effects of X on Y are measured as follows:

$$
\begin{aligned}
\eta^2 &= SS_x / SS_y \\
&= 70/98 \\
&= 0.714
\end{aligned}
$$

In other words, 71.4 percent of the variation in sales (Y) is accounted for by in-store advertising (X), indicating a strong effect. The null hypothesis may now be tested.

$$F = \frac{SS_x / (c-1)}{SS_{error} / (N-c)} = \frac{MS_X}{MS_{error}}$$

$$
\begin{aligned}
F &= \frac{70/(3-1)}{28/(15-3)} \\
&= 15.0
\end{aligned}
$$

From Table 5 in the Appendix of Statistical Tables, we see that for 2 and 12 degrees of freedom and $\alpha = 0.05$, the critical value of F is 3.89. Since the calculated value of F is greater than the critical value, we reject the null hypothesis. Therefore, we can conclude that the population means for the three levels of in-store advertising are indeed different. The relative magnitudes of the means for the three categories indicate that a high level of in-store advertising leads to significantly higher sales. This one-way ANOVA was also conducted using statistical software and the output is shown in Table 17.7. The corresponding SPSS and EXCEL outputs can be downloaded from the Web site for this book.

Proportions for More Than Two Samples

To test differences in proportions for more than two samples, one could also use the cross-tabulation procedure to conduct a chi-square test (see Chapter 16). In this case, we

Table 17.7

One-Way Analysis of Variance

Source of Variation	Sum of Squares	Degrees of Freedom	Mean Square	*F*	Significance of *F*
Main effects	70.00	2	35.00	15.00	.001
In-store promotion	70.00	2	35.00	15.00	.001
Explained (between groups)	70.00	2	35.00	15.00	.001
Residual (within groups)	28.00	12	2.33		
Total	**98.00**	**14**	**7.00**		

Table 17.8

A Summary of Hypothesis Testing

Sample	Test/Comments
One sample	
Means	*t*-test, if variance is unknown
	z-test, if variance is known
Proportions	*z*-test
Two independent samples	
Means	Two-group *t*-test
	F-test for equality of variances
Proportions	*z*-test
	Chi-square test
Paired samples	
Means	Paired *t*-test
Proportions	Chi-square test
More than two samples	
Means	One-way analysis of variance
Proportions	Chi-square test

will have a $2 \times c$ table. One variable will be used to denote the sample and will assume the value 1 for sample one, the value of 2 for sample two, and the value of c for sample c. The other variable will be the dichotomous variable of interest. The various hypothesis testing procedures for examining differences in means and proportions are summarized in Table 17.8.

RESEARCH IN ACTION

One-Way Analysis of Variance Favors "A Style for Every Story."

Levi Strauss & Company was battling competition from designer labels and private-label brands. Designers such as Polo Ralph Lauren, Calvin Klein, Guess?, and Tommy Hilfiger, as well as traditional competitors such as Gap, had launched substantial marketing and advertising campaigns. At the same time, JCPenney Company and Sears, Roebuck & Company had in place strong national branding efforts for their own private-label jeans.

In response to such stiff competition, Levi Strauss developed three alternative image themes: "Levi's. They go on"; "They're not Levi's jeans until we say they are"; and "A style for every story." The three themes were tested. Three groups of 150 respondents each were recruited. Each group was asked to evaluate one theme by rating it on a 10-point scale. A one-way ANOVA was conducted to examine the differences in the ratings provided by the three groups. "A style for every story" received significantly higher ratings than the other two alternatives. Thus, this campaign was chosen for roll-out on the national media in 2004. Levi Strauss & Company spent millions of dollars on this campaign in an attempt to ward off competition and capture a larger share of the jeans market that was estimated at $11.2 billion in 2004.[7]

BE a DM!

As the marketing director for Dell, how would you segment the home computer market based on the primary purpose for using the computer?

BE an MR!

Visit Dell's Web site (www.dell.com) and conduct an Internet search using a search engine and your library's online database to obtain information on computer usage in U.S. households.

As a marketing research analyst working for Dell, how would you determine whether the three home-computer usage segments (experts, novices, and nonusers) differ in terms of 10 psychographic characteristics, each measured on a seven-point scale?

Summary Illustration Using the Opening Vignette

Hypotheses about means of one or two populations are commonly examined by using a *t*-test. Different forms of the *t*-test are suitable for testing hypotheses based on one sample, two independent samples, or paired samples. In the opening vignette, the hypothesis that the mean rating of each attribute for the overall sample (LS and BS combined) exceeded 5.0 would be tested using the one-sample *t*-test. The hypotheses related to differences in the mean importance ratings attached to each attribute by the loyal shoppers (LS) and the butterfly shoppers (BS) would be tested using the two-independent-samples *t*-test. The hypothesis that the LS consider convenient parking to be more important than low prices would be tested by using a paired-samples *t*-test. Similar tests could be used for testing differences in proportions.

One-way ANOVA involves tests of differences in the means of more than two independent samples. The samples are treated as categories of a single independent variable. The null hypothesis of equal means is tested by an *F* statistic, which is the ratio of the mean square related to the independent variable to the mean square related to error. In the opening vignette, suppose the respondents were classified into three groups: loyal shoppers (LS2—loyal to only one supermarket), multiloyal shoppers (MS2—loyal to two or three supermarkets), and butterfly shoppers (BS2—nonloyal shoppers). The differences in the mean importance ratings attached to each attribute by the LS2, MS2, and BS2 groups would be tested using one-way ANOVA. The differences in the proportion of females among the LS2, MS2, and BS2 could be tested using the cross-tabulation procedure to conduct a chi-square test (see Chapter 16).

Software Applications

The major program for conducting *t*-tests in SPSS is *T*-TEST. This program can be used to conduct *t*-tests on independent as well as paired samples. In SAS, the program *T*-TEST can be used. Parametric tests available in MINITAB in descriptive stat function are *z*-test mean, *t*-test of the mean, and two-sample *t*-test. The available parametric tests in EXCEL and other spreadsheets include the *t*-test: paired two sample for means, *t*-test: two independent samples assuming equal variances, *t*-test: two independent samples assuming unequal variances, *z*-test: two samples for means, and *F*-test: two samples for variances (Exhibit 17.1).

SPSS and SAS also have programs for conducting analysis of variance. In addition to the basic analysis that we have considered, these programs can also perform more complex analysis. MINITAB and EXCEL also offer programs. Exhibit 17.2 contains a description of the relevant programs for conducting analysis of variance. Refer to the user manuals for these packages for more details.

WHAT WOULD *YOU* DO?

Marriott: Luring Business Travelers

The Situation

Marriott International, Inc. is a leading worldwide hospitality company. Its heritage can be traced to a small root beer stand opened in Washington, D.C. in 1927 by J. Willard and Alice S. Marriott. Today, Marriott International has more than 2,600 lodging properties located in the United States and 63 other countries and territories. Among the Marriott's most frequent visitors are its business-travel customers. For many years, business travelers have faced a fundamental problem in figuring out a comfortable and convenient way to get their jobs accomplished in hotel rooms without a functional workspace. Though many were not very productive, they did hone important skills such as writing legibly on top of a comforter, stretching arms beyond maximum length to reach hidden outlets behind or underneath furniture, and squinting to make documents readable by bedside-lamp light.

Marriott recognized these unmet needs of its business travelers and wanted to do something about it. Susan Hodapp, brand director for Marriott Hotels, Resorts and Suites commissioned a survey to determine business travelers' preferences for hotels and the factors that are important in their hotel selection process. Part of the questionnaire focused on the features of the hotel room. Each respondent rated the relative importance of the following factors on a seven-point scale (1 = not at all important, 7 = extremely important): Room décor, room lighting, room furniture, voice and data access in the room, and price of the room per night.

The Marketing Research Decision

1. Marriott would like to determine what features of a hotel room are most important in business travelers' choice of a hotel. What analysis should be conducted? Check as many as are applicable.
   a. Two-independent-samples *t*-test: means
   b. Two-independent-samples *t*-test: proportions
   c. Paired-samples *t*-test: means
   d. Paired-samples *t*-test: proportions
   e. One-way analysis of variance
2. Discuss how the type of data analysis you recommend to Susan Hodapp would enable her to understand business travelers' preferences for hotel rooms.

The Marketing Management Decision

1. To lure business travelers, what should Marriott focus on (check as many as are applicable):
   a. Room décor
   b. Room lighting
   c. Room furniture
   d. Voice and data access in the room
   e. Price of the room per night

2. Discuss how the marketing management-decision action that you recommend to Susan Hodapp is influenced by the type of data analysis you suggested earlier and by the findings of that analysis.

What Susan Hodapp Did

The survey revealed various features business travelers wanted most in their rooms. In response, Marriott introduced their "Room That Works" program, creating a modern-day Renaissance of workspace design. Today, many guest rooms are furnished with upgraded workstations with standard features such as,

- Roomy, oversized desks with plenty of space to spread out papers
- Lighting fixtures that not only produce adequate work-area light, but also feature desk-level outlets and data ports for laptops or other productivity devices
- An ergonomic, adjustable chair that swivels
- Multiple-line telephones with call-waiting feature so guests can use the Internet and receive calls simultaneously

At Marriott, Hodapp said she felt the company's customers wanted added flexibility in a workstation. "Our guests have a compressed time frame to get things done, so we wanted them to be able to modify the work environment for personalized comfort," she said. Therefore, Marriott's workstations feature desks on casters and an arm that swings out of the guest room desk for additional workspace.[8]

EXHIBIT 17.1 Computer Programs for *t*-Tests

SPSS

The major program for conducting *t*-tests in SPSS is *T*-TEST. This program can be used to conduct *t*-tests on independent as well as paired samples.

SAS

In SAS, the program *T*-TEST can be used to conduct *t*-tests on independent as well as paired samples.

MINITAB

Parametric tests available in MINITAB in descriptive stat function are *z*-test mean, *t*-test of the mean, and two-sample *t*-test.

EXCEL

The available parametric tests in EXCEL and other spreadsheets include the *t*-test: paired sample for means, *t*-test: two independent samples assuming equal variances, *t*-test: two independent samples assuming unequal variances, *z*-test: two samples for means, and *F*-test: two samples for variances.

EXHIBIT 17.2 Computer Programs for Anova

SPSS

One-way ANOVA can be efficiently performed using the program ONEWAY. For performing more complex analysis of variance, the program ANOVA can be used.

SAS

The main program for performing analysis of variance is ANOVA. This program can handle data from a wide variety of experimental designs.

MINITAB

Analysis of Variance can be assessed from the Stats>ANOVA function. This function performs one-way ANOVA and can also handle more complex designs. In order to compute the mean and standard deviation, the cross-tabulation function must be used. To obtain *F* and *p* values, use the balanced ANOVA.

EXCEL

Both a one-way ANOVA and more complex designs can be analyzed under the Tools>Data Analysis function.

SPSS Windows

The major program for conducting *t*-tests in SPSS is *T*-TEST. This program can be used to conduct *t*-tests on one sample or independent or paired samples. One-way ANOVA can be efficiently performed using the program ONEWAY. To select these procedures using SPSS for Windows, click

ANALYZE > COMPARE MEANS > MEANS . . .
ANALYZE > COMPARE MEANS > ONE-SAMPLE *T*-TEST . . .

ANALYZE > COMPARE MEANS > INDEPENDENT-SAMPLES *T*-TEST . . .
ANALYZE > COMPARE MEANS > PAIRED-SAMPLES *T*-TEST . . .
ANALYZE > COMPARE MEANS > ONE-WAY ANOVA . . .

Detailed Steps: One-Sample *t*-Test

Provided here are the detailed steps for running a one-sample test on the data of Table 17.1. The corresponding screen captures for these steps can be downloaded from the Web site for this book. The null hypothesis is that the mean preference for sample one before entering the theme park is 5.0.

1. Select DATA from the SPSS menu bar.
2. Click SELECT CASES.
3. Check IF CONDITION IS SATISFIED. Then click the IF button.
4. Move SAMPLE [sample] into the SELECT CASES: IF box. Click "=" and then click "1."
5. Click CONTINUE.
6. Check UNSELECTED CASES ARE FILTERED.
7. Click OK.
8. Select ANALYZE from the SPSS menu bar.
9. Click COMPARE MEANS and then ONE-SAMPLE *T*-TEST.
10. Move "Preference Before Visiting [pref1]" into the TEST VARIABLE(S) box.
11. Type "5" in the TEST VALUE box.
12. Click OK.

Detailed Steps: Two-Independent-Samples *t*-Test

Next are the detailed steps for running a two-independent-samples *t*-test on the data of Table 17.1. The null hypothesis is that the mean preference for adults and teenagers before visiting Disney theme parks is the same. First, make sure all cases will be included in the analysis.

Menu Bar
    DATA
        Select CASES.
            Choose ALL CASES.

Now, begin the analysis as follows:

1. Select ANALYZE from the SPSS menu bar.
2. Click COMPARE MEANS and then INDEPENDENT-SAMPLES *T*-TEST.
3. Move "Preference Before Visiting [pref1]" into the TEST VARIABLE(S) box.
4. Move "Sample [sample]" to GROUPING VARIABLE box.
5. Click DEFINE GROUPS.
6. Type "1" in GROUP 1 box and "2" in GROUP 2 box.
7. Click CONTINUE.
8. Click OK.

Detailed Steps: Paired-Samples *t*-Test

Next are the detailed steps for running a paired-samples *t*-test on the data of Table 17.1. The null hypothesis is that there is no difference in the mean preference of teenagers before and after visiting Disney theme parks.

1. Select DATA from the SPSS menu bar.
2. Click SELECT CASES.
3. Check IF CONDITION IS SATISFIED. Then click the IF button.
4. Move "SAMPLE[sample]" into the SELECT CASES: IF box. Click "=" and then click "1."
5. Click CONTINUE.
6. Check "UNSELECTED CASES ARE FILTERED."
7. Click OK.
8. Select ANALYZE from the SPSS menu bar.

9. Click COMPARE MEANS and then PAIRED-SAMPLES *T*-TEST.
10. Select "Preference Before Visiting [pref1]" and then select "Preference After Visiting [pref2]." Move these variables into the PAIRED VARIABLE(S) box.
11. Click OK.

Detailed Steps: One-Way ANOVA

The following are the detailed steps for running a one-way ANOVA on the data of Table 17.6. The corresponding screen captures for these steps can be downloaded from the Web site for this book. The null hypothesis is that there is no difference in mean normalized sales for the three levels of in-store promotion.

1. Select ANALYZE from the SPSS menu bar.
2. Click COMPARE MEANS and then ONE-WAY ANOVA.
3. Move "Normalized Sales [sales]" into the DEPENDENT LIST box.
4. Move "In-Store Promotion [promotio]" to the FACTOR box.
5. Click OPTIONS.
6. Click DESCRIPTIVE.
7. Click CONTINUE.
8. Click OK.

EXPERIENTIAL LEARNING

Testing Differences

Go to the textbook Web site and download the survey used in interviewing recently nonreturning students at Musial University (MU), an urban public university in the mid-sized city of Musial. While the actual name of the university has been disguised, the research project and the accompanying data are real. The administrators at MU were interested in obtaining the perspectives of "drop-out" or "stop-out" students so that the administrators at MU could enhance the programs, facilities, and services at MU. Download the actual survey used in this study (Musial Retention Survey) as well as the relevant SPSS system file (Musial Retention Data).

- **Read the survey Musial Retention Survey.**
- **Open SPSS and the SPSS system file Musial Retention Data.**
- **At the bottom of the SPSS window, click on the tab VARIABLE VIEW.**
- **Enter LABELS.**

Enter abbreviated forms of the names for the questions. For example, Q1 could be "enrolled elsewhere," Q2 could be "educational plans," and so forth. Do this for Q3, Q4, and Q5a through Q5bb. Enter these names directly into each corresponding cell in the LABEL column.

- **Enter VALUES for the LABELS.**

Enter labels for the possible values for each question. For example, for Q1, a value of "1" should receive a label of "Yes," a value of "2" should receive a label of "No," and so forth. Do this for all questions. For Q5a through Q5bb, the value of "1" should receive a label of "Strongly Disagree," and the value of "10" should receive a label of "Strongly Agree." Enter these names directly into each corresponding cell in the "Values" column by first clicking on each cell (now with "None" entered), then clicking on the gray box with three dots that appears in the cell. In the Values window, enter the value (e.g., "1"), enter the label (e.g., "Yes"), and then click on the ADD button before clicking on the OK button that closes the Values window for the cell.

- **Clean the data for all questions except the ID question.**

As was done in the Data Prep Experiential Learning Exercise of Chapter 15, "−9" must be recoded to SYSMIS. An alternative method for doing this would be to enter "−9" into each cell in the column MISSING after clicking on the VARIABLE VIEW tab at the bottom of the SPSS window. Likewise, the range "11 to highest" must be recoded to SYSMIS.

- ***t*-Tests**

Conduct three *t*-tests comparing the subgroups of Q1 (those enrolled at another institution this semester vs. those that are not) on the following dependent variables:

Q5j: MU encourages students to participate in extracurricular activities.

Q5k: MU offers good recreational facilities to students.

Q5l: The social environment at MU is great.

What is your null hypothesis (H_0) and alternative hypothesis (H_1) for each of these *t*-tests?

In SPSS, take the following steps to examine the means and standard deviations for these three variables:

```
ANALYZE
   COMPARE MEANS
      MEANS
         MEANS window
            DEPENDENT LIST, enter Q5j, Q5k, Q5l.
            INDEPENDENT LIST, enter Q1.
            Click OK.
```

In SPSS, take the following steps to conduct *t*-tests comparing the subgroups of Q1 on the three dependent variables Q5j, Q5k, and Q5l:

```
ANALYZE
   COMPARE MEANS
      INDEPENDENT-SAMPLES T-TEST
      INDEPENDENT-SAMPLES T-TEST window
         TEST VARIABLE(S), enter Q5j, Q5k, and Q5l.
         GROUPING VARIABLE, enter Q1.
               DEFINE GROUPS
                  GROUP 1 = 1
                  GROUP 2 = 2
                  Click CONTINUE.
                     Click OK.
```

Examine your results by assuming the variance among the groups is equal, and viewing the corresponding cells for each of the three variables under the columns labeled "t" and "Sig (2-tailed)."

- **One-Way ANOVA**

Compare the subgroups of Q2 "educational plans for the future" on the dependent variable of Q5n "I would have very much enjoyed having a football team at MU." First, collapse some of the categories to avoid splintering of the subgroups for Q2 with too few cases to allow statistically meaningful comparisons. Do this in the following way:

```
Recode Grouping Variable Q2
TRANSFORM
   RECODE INTO DIFFERENT VARIABLES
         RECODE INTO DIFFERENT VARIABLES window
            Select Q2.
               OUTPUT VARIABLE = Q2new
            Select OLD AND NEW VALUE.
               Under OLD VALUE
                  RANGE
                     1 through 2
               Under NEW VALUE
                  COPY OLD VALUE
               Then select ADD.
               Under OLD VALUE
                  VALUE
                     3
```

(continued)

Under NEW VALUE
NEW VALUE
2
Then select ADD.
Under OLD VALUE
RANGE
4 through 5
Under NEW VALUE
NEW VALUE
3
Select ADD, then CONTINUE.
Click CHANGE and then OK on the RECODE INTO DIFFERENT VARIABLES.

Check the results of this recoding in the following way:

ANALYZE
DESCRIPTIVE STATISTICS
FREQUENCIES
Q2new
Click OK.

Note: You should have subgroups of 70 (plan to re-enter MU), 46 (attending another school), and 25 (no plans).

One-Way ANOVA

Compare the sentiments for a football program (which MU does not currently have) across the three subgroups of Q2 regarding educational plans for the future.

(What are the H_0 and H_1 for your ANOVA analysis?)

ANALYZE
COMPARE MEANS
ONE-WAY ANOVA
ONE-WAY ANOVA window
DEPENDENT LIST
Q5n
FACTOR
Q2new
Click OK.

Epilogue

Download Musial Retention Report to get a glimpse of what was presented to the MU administrators in a PowerPoint presentation. The most illuminating finding for the MU administrators was that almost 50 percent of the nonreturning students declared an intention to return to MU before the end of the year. This was far more than any of the administrators had expected. (This result can be seen in the frequency distribution for Q2.)

EXCEL

Detailed Steps: One-Sample *t*-Test

The following are detailed steps for running a one-sample test on the data of Table 17.1. The corresponding screen captures for these steps can be downloaded from the Web site for this book. The null hypothesis is that the mean preference for sample one before entering the theme park is 5.0.

1. Add a column with the name **Dummy** beside PREF2, and fill the first 10 rows with **5**.
2. Select **Tools** (Alt + T).
3. Select **Data Analysis** under **Tools.**
4. Data Analysis Window pops up.

5. Select ***t*-Test: Paired Two Sample for Means** from Data Analysis window.
6. Click **OK.**
7. ***t*-Test: Paired Two Sample for Means** pop-up window appears on screen.
8. ***t*-Test: Paired Two Sample for Means** window has two portions:
   a. Input
   b. Output Options
9. Input portion asks for five inputs
   a. Click in the **Variable 1 Range** box. Select (highlight) the first 10 rows of data under PREF1. $C$2:$C$11 should appear on **Variable 1 Range.**
   b. Click in the **Variable 2 Range** box. Select (highlight) the first 10 rows of data under DUMMY. $E$2:$E$11 should appear on **Variable 2 Range.**
   c. Leave **Hypothesized Mean Difference** and **Labels** as blank.
   d. Default value of **Alpha 0.05** is seen on the Alpha box. Let the **Alpha** value be like that.
10. In the Output portion of pop-up window, select **New Workbook Options**.
11. Click **OK.**

Detailed Steps: Two-Independent-Samples *t*-Test

The following are detailed steps for running a two-independent-samples *t* test on the data of Table 17.1. The corresponding screen captures for these steps can be downloaded from the Web site for this book. The null hypothesis is that the mean preference for adults and teenagers before visiting Disney theme parks is the same.

1. Select **Tools** (Alt + T).
2. Select **Data Analysis** under **Tools.**
3. Data Analysis window pops up.
4. Select ***t*-Test: Two-Sample Assuming Equal Variances** from Data Analysis window.
5. Click **OK.**
6. ***t*-Test: Two-Sample Assuming Equal Variances** pop-up window appears on screen.
7. ***t*-Test: Two-Sample Assuming Equal Variances** window has two portions:
   a. Input
   b. Output Options
8. Input portion asks for two inputs.
   a. Click in the **Variable 1 Range** box. Select (highlight) the first 10 rows of data under PREF1. $C$2:$C$11 should appear on **Variable 1 Range.**
   b. Click in the **Variable 2 Range** box. Select (highlight) the last 10 rows of data under PREF1. $C$12:$C$21 should appear on **Variable 2 Range.**
   c. Leave **Hypothesized Mean Difference** and **Labels** as blank.
   d. Default value of **Alpha** 0.05 is seen on the Alpha box. Let the **Alpha** value be like that.
9. In the Output portion of pop-up window, select **New Workbook Options**.
10. Click **OK.**

Detailed Steps: Paired-Samples *t*-Test

The following are detailed steps for running a paired-samples *t*-test on the data of Table 17.1. The corresponding screen captures for these steps can be downloaded from the Web site for this book. The null hypothesis is that there is no difference in the mean preference of teenagers before and after visiting Disney theme parks.

1. Select **Tools** (Alt + T).
2. Select **Data Analysis** under **Tools.**
3. Data Analysis window pops up.
4. Select ***t*-Test: Paired Two Sample for Means** from Data Analysis window.
5. Click **OK.**
6. ***t*-Test: Paired Two Sample for Means** pop-up window appears on screen.

7. ***t*-Test: Paired Two Sample for Means** window has two portions:
   a. Input
   b. Output Options
8. Input portion asks for two inputs.
   a. Click in the **Variable 1 Range** box. Select (highlight) the first 10 rows of data under PREF1. $C$2:$C$11 should appear on **Variable 1 Range.**
   b. Click in the **Variable 2 Range** box. Select (highlight) the first 10 rows of data under PREF2. $E$2:$E$11 should appear on **Variable 2 Range.**
   c. Leave **Hypothesized Mean Difference** and **Labels** as blank.
   d. Default value of **Alpha** 0.05 is seen on the Alpha box. Let the **Alpha** value be like that.
9. In the Output portion of pop-up window, select **New Workbook Options**.
10. Click **OK.**

Detailed Steps: One-Way ANOVA

The following are the detailed steps for running a one-way ANOVA on the data of Table 17.6. The corresponding screen captures for these steps can be downloaded from the Web site for this book. The null hypothesis is that there is no difference in mean normalized sales for the three levels of in-store promotion.

1. Select **Tools** (Alt + T).
2. Select **Data Analysis** under **Tools.**
3. Data Analysis window pops up.
4. Select **Anova: Single Factor** from Data Analysis window.
5. Click **OK.**
6. **Anova: Single Factor** pop-up window appears on screen.
7. **Anova: Single Factor** window has two portions:
   a. Input
   b. Output Options
8. Input portion asks 2 inputs.
   a. Click in the **Input Range** box. Select (highlight) all the data under the columns High, Medium, Low at the same time. $B$2:$D$6 should appear in the Input Range.
   b. Click in **Columns** beside **Grouped by.**
   c. Labels in the First row/ Labels in the First Column are optional.
   d. Leave **Alpha** at the default value of 0.05.
9. In the Output portion of pop-up window, select **New Workbook Options**.
10. Click **OK.**

Summary

Hypotheses related to differences in the population means and proportions can be tested using the *t* distribution. Different forms of the *t*-test are suitable for testing hypotheses based on one sample, two independent samples, or paired samples.

One-way ANOVA involves a single metric dependent variable and a single independent categorical variable. Interest lies in testing the null hypothesis that the category means are equal in the population. The total variation in the dependent variable is decomposed into two components: variation related to the independent variable and variation related to error. The variation is measured in terms of the sums of squares corrected for the mean (*SS*). The mean square is obtained by dividing the *SS* by the corresponding degrees of freedom. The null hypothesis of equal means is tested by an *F* statistic, which is the ratio of the mean square related to the independent variable to the mean square related to error.

Key Terms and Concepts

Parametric tests, 463
***t*-test,** 464
***t* statistic,** 464
***t* distribution,** 464
***z*-test,** 466
Independent samples, 468
***F*-test,** 469
***F* statistic,** 469
***F* distribution,** 470
Paired samples, 473
Paired-samples *t*-test, 474
Analysis of variance, 476
One-way analysis of variance, 477
Factor, 477
Treatment, 477
Decomposition of the total variation, 477
SS_y, 477
$SS_{between}$ (SS_x), 477
SS_{within} (SS_{error}), 477
Eta^2 (η^2), 478
Mean square, 478
Significance of the overall effect, 479

Suggested Cases and Video Cases

Cases

3.1 Ford **3.2 Darden** **3.3 Microsoft** **3.4 Catalogs**
4.1 Boeing **4.2 Gucci**

Video Cases

3.1 AFLAC **3.2 Honest Tea** **4.1 Subaru** **4.2 Marriott**

Additional cases and video cases are available in the Instructor's Manual and on the instructor and student Web sites.

Live Research: Conducting a Marketing Research Project

1. Differences between groups are of interest in most projects. These can be examined by using independent-samples *t*-tests for two groups or one-way ANOVA for more than two groups.
2. Often each respondent evaluates many stimuli. For example, each respondent may evaluate different brands or provide importance ratings for different attributes. In such cases, differences between pairs of stimuli may be examined using the paired-samples *t*-test.

Acronyms

The major characteristics of *t*-tests can be summarized by the acronym *t*-TEST:

t distribution is similar to the normal distribution
T est of difference: means or proportions
E stimate of variance from the sample
S ingle sample
T wo samples: independent or paired

Review Questions

1. Present a classification of hypothesis testing procedures.
2. Describe the general procedure for conducting a *t*-test.
3. Give the formula for the *t* statistic when examining a hypothesis related to a single mean.
4. Give the formula for the *t* statistic when examining a hypothesis related to a single proportion.
5. Give the formula for the *t* statistic when examining a hypothesis related to means of two independent samples.
6. Give the formula for the *t* statistic when examining a hypothesis related to means of paired samples.
7. What is the relationship between analysis of variance and the *t*-test?
8. What is total variation? How is it decomposed in a one-way analysis of variance?
9. What is the null hypothesis in one-way ANOVA? What basic statistic is used to test the null hypothesis in one-way ANOVA? How is this statistic computed?

Applied Problems

1. In each of the following situations, indicate the statistical analysis you would conduct and the appropriate test or test statistic that should be used.
   a. Consumer preferences for Camay soap were obtained on an 11-point Likert scale. The same consumers were then shown a commercial about Camay. After the commercial, preferences for Camay were again measured. Has the commercial been successful in inducing a change in preferences?
   b. Respondents in a survey of 1,000 households were asked to indicate their frequency of domestic air travel on an interval scale. They were also classified as being in high-, medium-, or low-income categories. Is the frequency of domestic air travel related to income level?
   c. In a telephone survey using a representative sample of 3,000 households, the respondents were asked to indicate their preference for fast-food restaurants using a seven-point Likert-type scale. The sample was divided into small and large households based on a median split of the household size. Does preference for fast-food restaurants vary by household size?
2. The current advertising campaign for a major automobile brand would be changed if fewer than 70 percent of the consumers like it.
   a. Formulate the null and alternative hypotheses.
   b. Which statistical test would you use? Why?
   c. A random sample of 300 consumers was surveyed, and 204 respondents indicated that they liked the campaign. Should the campaign be changed? Why?
3. A major computer manufacturer is having an end-of-season sale on computers. The number of computers sold during this sale at a sample of 10 stores was 800 1,100 0 400 700 800 1,000 500 800 300
   a. Is there evidence that an average of more than 500 computers per store were sold during this sale? Use $\alpha = 0.05$.
   b. What assumption is necessary to perform this test?
4. After receiving complaints from readers, your campus newspaper decides to redesign its front page. Two new formats, B and C, are developed and tested against the current format, A. A total of 75 students are randomly selected, and 25 students are randomly assigned to each of three format conditions. The students are asked to evaluate the effectiveness of the format on an 11-point scale (1 = poor, 11 = excellent).
   a. State the null hypothesis.
   b. What statistical test should you use?
   c. What are the degrees of freedom that are associated with the test statistic?
5. A marketing researcher wants to test the hypothesis that, within the population, there is no difference in the importance attached to shopping by consumers living in the northern, southern, eastern, and western United States. A study is conducted and analysis of variance is used to analyze the data. The results obtained are presented in the following table.

Source	df	Sum of Squares	Mean Squares	*F* Ratio	*F* Probability
Between groups	3	70.212	23.404	1.12	0.3
Within groups	996	20812.416	20.896		

   a. Is there sufficient evidence to reject the null hypothesis?
   b. What conclusion can be drawn from the table?
   c. If the average importance was computed for each group, would you expect the sample means to be similar or different?
   d. What was the total sample size in this study?
6. In a pilot study examining the effectiveness of three commercials (A, B, and C), 10 consumers were assigned to view each commercial and rate it on a nine-point Likert scale. The data obtained are shown in the following table. These data should be analyzed by doing hand calculations (i.e., without using the computer).

Commercial		
A	B	C
4	7	8
5	4	7
3	6	7
4	5	6
3	4	8
4	6	7
4	5	8
3	5	8
5	4	5
5	4	6

   a. Calculate the category means and the grand mean.
   b. Calculate SS_y, SS_x, and SS_{error}.
   c. Calculate η^2.
   d. Calculate the value of *F*.
   e. Are the three commercials equally effective?
7. Conduct the following analyses for the Internet usage data given in Applied Problem number 6 in Chapter 16.
   a. Test the hypothesis that the mean familiarity with the Internet exceeds 4.0.
   b. Is the Internet usage different for males as compared to females? Formulate the null and alternative hypotheses, and conduct the test.
   c. Is the proportion of respondents using the Internet for shopping the same for males and females? Formulate the null and alternative hypotheses, and conduct the test.

d. Do the respondents differ in their attitude toward the Internet and attitude toward technology? Formulate the null and alternative hypotheses, and conduct the test.

8. In a pretest, respondents were asked to express their preference for an outdoor lifestyle (V1) using a seven-point scale (1 = not at all preferred, 7 = greatly preferred). They were also asked to indicate the importance of the following variables on a seven-point scale (1 = not at all important, 7 = very important).

   V2 = enjoying nature

   V3 = relating to the weather

   V4 = living in harmony with the environment

   V5 = exercising regularly

   V6 = meeting other people

   The sex of the respondent (V7) was coded as 1 = female and 2 = male. The location of residence (V8) was coded as 1 = midtown/downtown, 2 = suburbs, and 3 = countryside. The data obtained are given in the following table.

V1	V2	V3	V4	V5	V6	V7	V8
7.00	3.00	6.00	4.00	5.00	2.00	1.00	1.00
1.00	1.00	1.00	2.00	1.00	2.00	1.00	1.00
6.00	2.00	5.00	4.00	4.00	5.00	1.00	1.00
4.00	3.00	4.00	6.00	3.00	2.00	1.00	1.00
1.00	2.00	2.00	3.00	1.00	2.00	1.00	1.00
6.00	3.00	5.00	4.00	6.00	2.00	1.00	1.00
5.00	3.00	4.00	3.00	4.00	5.00	1.00	1.00
6.00	4.00	5.00	4.00	5.00	1.00	1.00	1.00
3.00	3.00	2.00	2.00	2.00	2.00	1.00	1.00
2.00	4.00	2.00	6.00	2.00	2.00	1.00	1.00
6.00	4.00	5.00	3.00	5.00	5.00	1.00	2.00
2.00	3.00	1.00	4.00	2.00	1.00	1.00	2.00
7.00	2.00	6.00	4.00	5.00	6.00	1.00	2.00
4.00	6.00	4.00	5.00	3.00	3.00	1.00	2.00
1.00	3.00	1.00	2.00	1.00	4.00	1.00	2.00
6.00	6.00	6.00	3.00	4.00	5.00	2.00	2.00
5.00	5.00	6.00	4.00	4.00	6.00	2.00	2.00
7.00	7.00	4.00	4.00	7.00	7.00	2.00	2.00
2.00	6.00	3.00	7.00	4.00	3.00	2.00	2.00
3.00	7.00	3.00	6.00	4.00	4.00	2.00	2.00
1.00	5.00	2.00	6.00	3.00	3.00	2.00	3.00
5.00	6.00	4.00	7.00	5.00	6.00	2.00	3.00
2.00	4.00	1.00	5.00	4.00	4.00	2.00	3.00
4.00	7.00	4.00	7.00	4.00	6.00	2.00	3.00
6.00	7.00	4.00	2.00	1.00	7.00	2.00	3.00
3.00	6.00	4.00	6.00	4.00	4.00	2.00	3.00
4.00	7.00	7.00	4.00	2.00	5.00	2.00	3.00
3.00	7.00	2.00	6.00	4.00	3.00	2.00	3.00
4.00	6.00	3.00	7.00	2.00	7.00	2.00	3.00
5.00	6.00	2.00	6.00	7.00	2.00	2.00	3.00

   Using a statistical package of your choice, answer the following questions. In each case, formulate the null and the alternative hypotheses and conduct the appropriate statistical test(s).

   a. Does the mean preference for an outdoor lifestyle exceed 3.0?
   b. Does the mean importance of enjoying nature exceed 3.5?
   c. Does the mean preference for an outdoor lifestyle differ for males and females?
   d. Does the importance attached to V2 through V6 differ for males and females?
   e. Do the respondents attach more importance to enjoying nature than they do to relating to the weather?
   f. Do the respondents attach more importance to relating to the weather than they do to meeting other people?
   g. Do the respondents attach more importance to living in harmony with the environment than they do to exercising regularly?

Group Discussion

1. "The *t*-tests are so simple to conduct that they should be used more often in analyzing marketing research data." Discuss as a small group.

2. Which procedure is more useful in marketing research—*t*-test or analysis of variance? Discuss as a small group.

CHAPTER

18 Data Analysis: Correlation and Regression

"As marketing research professionals, we continually examine the relationship between consumers' perceptions and ultimate purchase decisions. Consequently, correlation and regression techniques serve as the foundation for many of the most commonly used analytical tools in marketing research."

JAMIE BAKER-PREWITT, *Ph.D., Vice President, Marketing & Decision Support Sciences, Burke, Inc., Cincinnati, OH*

OPENING QUESTIONS

1. What is product moment correlation, and how does it provide a foundation for regression analysis?
2. What are the nature and methods of bivariate regression analysis, and how can you describe the general model?
3. How can you explain the estimation of parameters, standardized regression coefficient, significance testing, and prediction accuracy in bivariate regression?
4. How does multiple regression differ from bivariate regression?
5. What is the meaning of partial regression coefficients?

Regression Models Model the Marketing Strategy of Adidas

In 2002, Adidas parted ways with the Los Angeles Lakers basketball star Kobe Bryant and, instead, signed Tracy McGrady, Tim Duncan, and Kevin Garnett. The company wanted to be a leader in how they bring products to the markets, in what the products do for the athletes, and how they service them. Adidas is a sports-performance brand.

Adidas realized that preference for athletic shoes has strong positive correlations with sports-related variables, such as interest in sports, attitude toward sports personalities, attendance at sports events, and time spent watching sports on television. Research by the company revealed that consumers with a greater interest in sports, a more favorable attitude toward sports personalities, higher attendance at sports events, or those who spent more time watching sports on television exhibited a stronger preference for brand-name athletic shoes. A multiple regression model with preference for athletic shoes as the dependent variable, and interest in sports, attitude toward sports personalities, attendance at sports events, and time spent watching sports on television as the independent variables had a very good fit. The model fit was determined by strength of association (a measure of how strongly the dependent variable and the independent variables are related) and the accuracy of predicted values of the dependent variable. The coefficient (partial regression coefficient) associated with each independent variable was positive and significant, indicating that higher values on each independent variable were associated with stronger preference for athletic shoes. Thus, the model had the following form:

Estimated preference for athletic shoes = $a + b_1$ (interest in sports) + b_2 (attitude toward sports personalities) + b_3 (attendance at sports events) + b_4 (time spent watching sports on television)

Where a = constant, and b_1, b_2, b_3, and b_4 are positive partial regression coefficients.

Armed with such information, Adidas, the nation's fourth-ranked athletic footwear company, attempted to boost the visibility of its brand with

star athletes. As of 2004, Adidas featured Muhammad Ali; Ali's daughter, Laila, also a world champion boxer; soccer icons David Beckham and Zinedine Zidane; Thai tennis star Paradorn Srichaphan; long-distance runner Haile Gebrselassie; and NBA all-star Tracy McGrady. Thus, regression models have played a key role in modeling the marketing strategy of Adidas.[1] •

Overview

This chapter describes regression analysis, which is widely used for explaining variation in a dependent variable in terms of a set of independent variables. In marketing, the dependent variable could be market share, sales, or brand preference while the independent variables are marketing management variables, such as advertising, price, distribution, product quality, and demographic and lifestyles variables. This was illustrated in the opening vignette, where the regression model had preference for athletic shoes as the dependent variable, and sports-related lifestyle variables as the independent variables.

However, before discussing regression, we will describe the concept of the product moment correlation or the correlation coefficient, which lays the conceptual foundation for regression analysis. Figure 18.1 briefly explains the focus of the chapter, the relationship of this chapter to the previous ones, and the steps of the marketing research process on which this chapter concentrates.

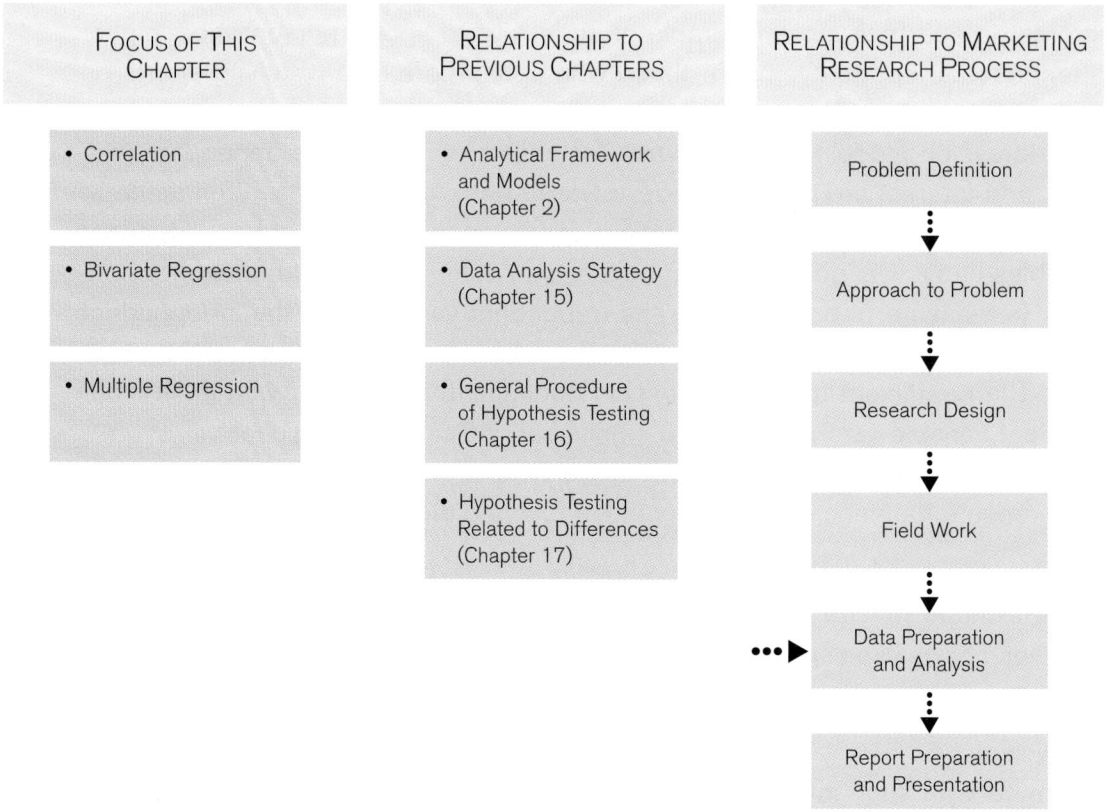

Figure 18.1

Relationship of Correlation and Regression to Previous Chapters and the Marketing Research Process

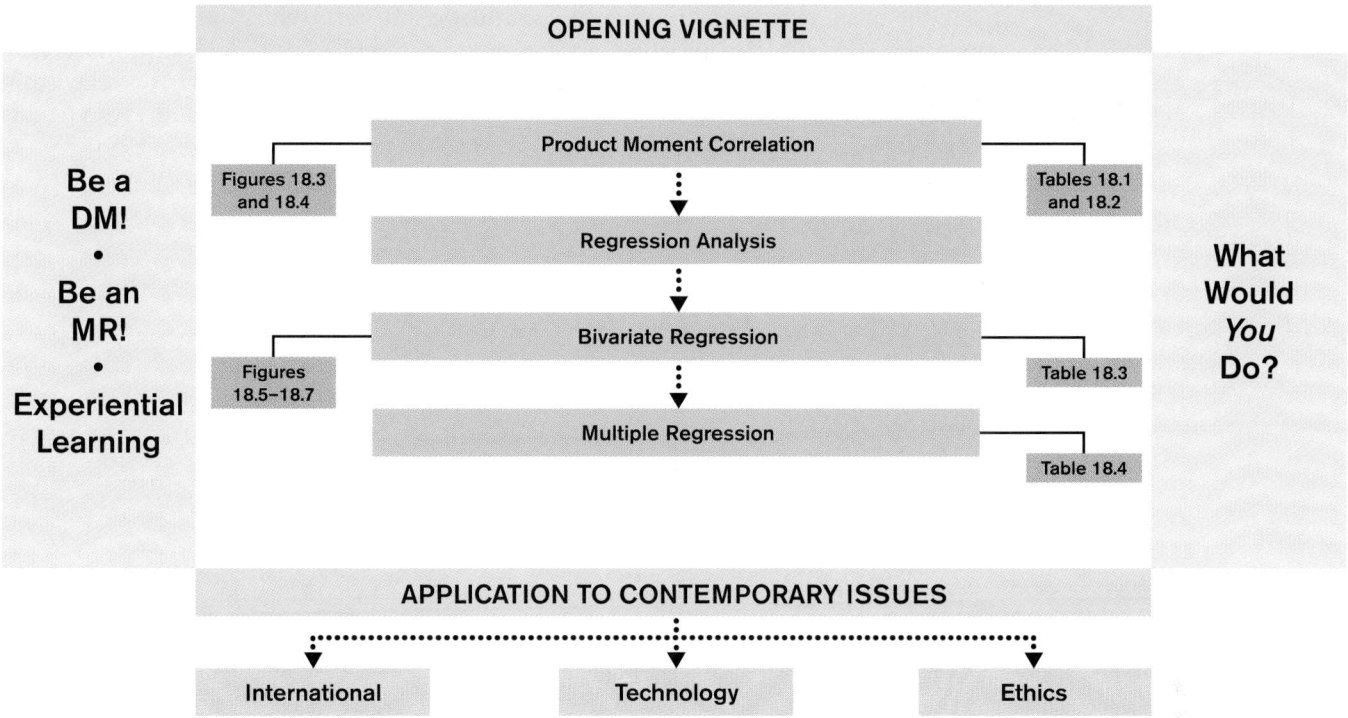

Figure 18.2

Correlation and Regression: An Overview

In introducing regression analysis, we discuss the simple bivariate case first. We describe estimation, standardization of the regression coefficients, testing and examination of the strength and significance of association between variables, prediction accuracy, and the assumptions underlying the regression model. Next, we discuss the multiple regression model, emphasizing the interpretation of parameters, strength of association, significance tests, and examination of residuals. Figure 18.2 gives an overview of the different topics discussed in this chapter and how they flow from one to the next.

Fundamental to regression analysis is an understanding of the product moment correlation.

Product Moment Correlation

In marketing research, we are often interested in summarizing the strength of association between two metric variables, as in the following situations:

- How strongly are sales related to advertising expenditures?
- Is there an association between market share and size of the sales force?
- Are consumers' perceptions of quality related to their perceptions of prices?

In situations like these, the **product moment correlation** is used. It is denoted by r. It is the most widely used statistic that summarizes the strength and direction of association between two metric (interval- or ratio-scaled) variables, say X and Y. It is an index used to determine whether a linear or straight-line relationship exists between X and Y. It indicates the degree to which the variation in one variable, X, is related to the variation in another variable, Y. Karl Pearson originally proposed it, so it is also known as the *Pearson correlation coefficient*. It is also referred to as *simple correlation*, *bivariate correlation*, or merely the *correlation coefficient*.

product moment correlation
A statistic summarizing the strength of association between two metric variables.

In the opening vignette, preference for athletic shoes showed strong positive correlations with sports-related variables, such as interest in sports, attitude toward sports personalities, attendance at sports events, and time spent watching sports on television. From a sample of n observations, X and Y, the product moment correlation, r, can be calculated as

$$r = \frac{\sum_{i=1}^{n}(X_i - \bar{X})(Y_i - \bar{Y})}{\sqrt{\sum_{i=1}^{n}(X_i - \bar{X})^2 \sum_{i=1}^{n}(Y_i - \bar{Y})^2}}$$

Division of the numerator and denominator by $(n - 1)$ gives

$$r = \frac{\sum_{i=1}^{n}\frac{(X_i - \bar{X})(Y_i - \bar{Y})}{n-1}}{\sqrt{\sum_{i=1}^{n}\frac{(X_i - \bar{X})^2}{n-1}\sum_{i=1}^{n}\frac{(Y_i - \bar{Y})^2}{n-1}}}$$

$$= \frac{COV_{xy}}{S_x S_y}$$

covariance
A systematic relationship between two variables in which a change in one implies a corresponding change in the other (COV_{xy}).

In these equations, $\bar{X}$ and $\bar{Y}$ denote the sample means and S_x and S_y the standard deviations. COV_{xy}, the **covariance** between X and Y, measures the extent to which X and Y are related. The covariance may be either positive or negative. Division by $S_x S_y$ achieves standardization, so that r varies between -1.0 and $+1.0$. Note that the correlation coefficient is an absolute number and is not expressed in any unit of measurement. The correlation coefficient between two variables will be the same regardless of their underlying units of measurement.

As an example, suppose a researcher wants to explain attitudes toward sports cars (attitude) in terms of the number of years the respondent has owned a car (duration). The attitude is measured on an 11-point scale (1 = do not like sports cars, 11 = very much like sports cars), and the duration of car ownership is measured in terms of the number of years the respondent has owned one or more cars. In a pretest of 12 respondents, the data shown in Table 18.1 were obtained. This table gives the data for only 12 respondents

Table 18.1
Explaining Attitude toward Sports Cars

Respondent Number	Attitude toward Sports Cars	Duration of Car Ownership	Importance Attached to Performance
1	6	10	3
2	9	12	11
3	8	12	4
4	3	4	1
5	10	12	11
6	4	6	1
7	5	8	7
8	2	2	4
9	11	18	8
10	9	9	10
11	10	17	8
12	2	2	5

because we want to show the calculations of the basic statistics by hand. We think that it is important to show these hand calculations so that you can get a better idea of the basic concepts. In practice, the sample size is much larger. We illustrate the analysis of such large datasets later in the chapter in an Experiential Learning exercise that analyzes the data for 146 respondents in a survey for Musial University.

The correlation coefficient between attitude and duration based on the data of Table 18.1 may be calculated as follows:

$$\bar{X} = (10+12+12+4+12+6+8+2+18+9+17+2)/12$$
$$= 9.333$$
$$\bar{Y} = (6+9+8+3+10+4+5+2+11+9+10+2)/12$$
$$= 6.583$$

$$\begin{aligned}\sum_{i=1}^{n}(X_i - \bar{X})(Y_i - \bar{Y}) &= (10-9.33)(6-6.58) + (12-9.33)(9-6.58)\\ &+ (12-9.33)(8-6.58) + (4-9.33)(3-6.58)\\ &+ (12-9.33)(10-6.58) + (6-9.33)(4-6.58)\\ &+ (8-9.33)(5-6.58) + (2-9.33)(2-6.58)\\ &+ (18-9.33)(11-6.58) + (9-9.33)(9-6.58)\\ &+ (17-9.33)(10-6.58) + (2-9.33)(2-6.58)\\ &= -0.3886 + 6.4614 + 3.7914 + 19.0814\\ &+ 9.1314 + 8.5914 + 2.1014 + 33.5714\\ &+ 38.3214 - 0.7986 + 26.2314 + 33.5714\\ &= 179.6668\end{aligned}$$

$$\begin{aligned}\sum_{i=1}^{n}(X_i - \bar{X})^2 &= (10-9.33)^2 + (12-9.33)^2 + (12-9.33)^2 + (4-9.33)^2\\ &+ (12-9.33)^2 + (6-9.33)^2 + (8-9.33)^2 + (2-9.33)^2\\ &+ (18-9.33)^2 + (9-9.33)^2 + (17-9.33)^2 + (2-9.33)^2\\ &= 0.4489 + 7.1289 + 7.1289 + 28.4089\\ &+ 7.1289 + 11.0889 + 1.7689 + 53.7289\\ &+ 75.1689 + 0.1089 + 58.8289 + 53.7289\\ &= 304.6668\end{aligned}$$

$$\begin{aligned}\sum_{i=1}^{n}(Y_i - \bar{Y})^2 &= (6-6.58)^2 + (9-6.58)^2 + (8-6.58)^2 + (3-6.58)^2\\ &+ (10-6.58)^2 + (4-6.58)^2 + (5-6.58)^2 + (2-6.58)^2\\ &+ (11-6.58)^2 + (9-6.58)^2 + (10-6.58)^2 + (2-6.58)^2\\ &= 0.3364 + 5.8564 + 2.0164 + 12.8164\\ &+ 11.6964 + 6.6564 + 2.4964 + 20.9764\\ &+ 19.5364 + 5.8564 + 11.6964 + 20.9764\\ &= 120.9168\end{aligned}$$

Thus,

$$r = \frac{179.6668}{\sqrt{(304.6668)(120.9168)}}$$

Table 18.2

Calculation of the Product Moment Correlation

Number	Attitude (Y)	Duration (X)	$X_i - \bar{X}$	$(X_1 - \bar{X})^2$	$(Y_1 - \bar{Y})$	$(Y_i - \bar{Y})^2$	$(X_1 - \bar{X})(Y_1 - \bar{Y})$
1	6	10	0.667	0.4489	−0.583	0.3364	−0.3886
2	9	12	2.667	7.1289	2.417	5.8564	6.4614
3	8	12	2.667	7.1289	1.417	2.0164	3.7914
4	3	4	−5.333	28.4089	−3.583	12.8164	19.0814
5	10	12	2.667	7.1289	3.417	11.6964	9.1314
6	4	6	−3.333	11.0889	−2.583	6.5664	8.5914
7	5	8	−1.333	1.7689	−1.583	2.4964	2.1014
8	2	2	−7.333	53.7289	−4.583	20.9764	3.5714
9	11	18	8.667	75.1689	7.417	19.5364	38.3214
10	9	9	−10.333	0.1089	2.417	5.8564	−0.7986
11	10	17	7.667	58.8289	3.417	11.6964	26.2314
12	2	2	-7.333	53.7289	−4.583	20.9764	33.5714
Mean	2.583	9.333					
Sum				304.668		120.9168	179.6668

Using the above values the product moment correlation can be calculated as

$$r = \frac{\sum_{i=1}^{n}(X_i - \bar{X})(Y_i - \bar{Y})}{\sqrt{\sum_{i=1}^{n}(X_i - \bar{X})^2 \sum_{i=1}^{n}(Y_i - \bar{Y})^2}}$$

or

$$r = \frac{179.6668}{\sqrt{(304.6668)\ (120.9168)}} = \frac{179.6668}{(17.4547)(10.9962)} = 0.9361$$

or

$$r = \frac{179.6668}{(17.4547)(10.9962)}$$

$$= 0.9361$$

These calculations are summarized in Table 18.2. The product moment correlation can also be calculated using SPSS and EXCEL, and the corresponding outputs can be downloaded from the Web site for this book. In this example, $r = 0.9361$, a value close to 1.0. This means that the number of years a respondent has owned a car is strongly associated with attitude toward sports cars. Thus, the length of time a person has owned a sports car is positively related to degree of favorableness of the attitude toward sports cars. Furthermore, the positive sign of r implies a positive relationship; the longer the duration of car ownership, the more favorable the attitude and vice versa. If John has owned a sports car much longer than Paul, John is likely to have a much more

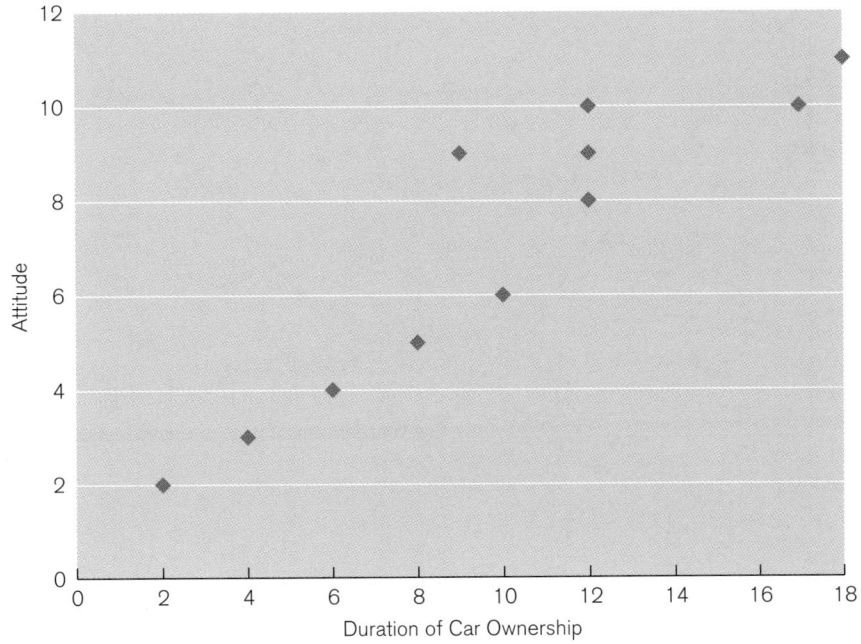

Figure 18.3

Plot of Attitude with Duration of Sports Car Ownership

favorable attitude toward sports cars than Paul. Over many years of ownership, John sees his sports car as a treasured possession. On the other hand, Paul has only recently purchased a sports car and is yet to develop such strong feelings toward it. This can be seen from a plot of Y (attitude toward sports cars) against X (duration of car ownership) given in Figure 18.3. The points seem to be arranged in a band running from the bottom left to the top right.

Since r indicates the degree to which variation in one variable is related to variation in another, it can also be expressed in terms of the decomposition of the total variation (see the explanation in Chapter 17). In other words,

$$
\begin{aligned}
r^2 &= \frac{\text{Explained variation}}{\text{Total variation}} \\
&= \frac{SS_x}{SS_y} \\
&= \frac{\text{Total variation} - \text{Error variation}}{\text{Total variation}} \\
&= \frac{SS_y - SS_{error}}{SS_y}
\end{aligned}
$$

Therefore, r^2 measures the proportion of variation in one variable that is explained by the other. Both r and r^2 are symmetric measures of association. In other words, the correlation of X with Y is the same as the correlation of Y with X. It does not matter which variable is considered the dependent variable and which the independent. The product moment coefficient measures the strength of the linear relationship and is not designed to measure nonlinear relationships. Thus $r = 0$ merely indicates that there is no linear relationship between X and Y. It does not mean that X and Y are unrelated. There could well be a nonlinear relationship between them, which would not be captured by r (Figure 18.4).

When it is computed for a population rather than a sample, the product moment correlation is denoted by ρ, the Greek letter rho. The coefficient r is an estimator of ρ. Note that the calculation of r assumes that X and Y are metric variables whose distributions have the same shape. If these assumptions are not met, r is deflated and underestimates ρ. In marketing research, data obtained by using rating scales with a small number of categories may not be strictly interval. This tends to deflate r, resulting in an underestimation of ρ.

Figure 18.4

A Nonlinear Relationship for Which $r = 0$

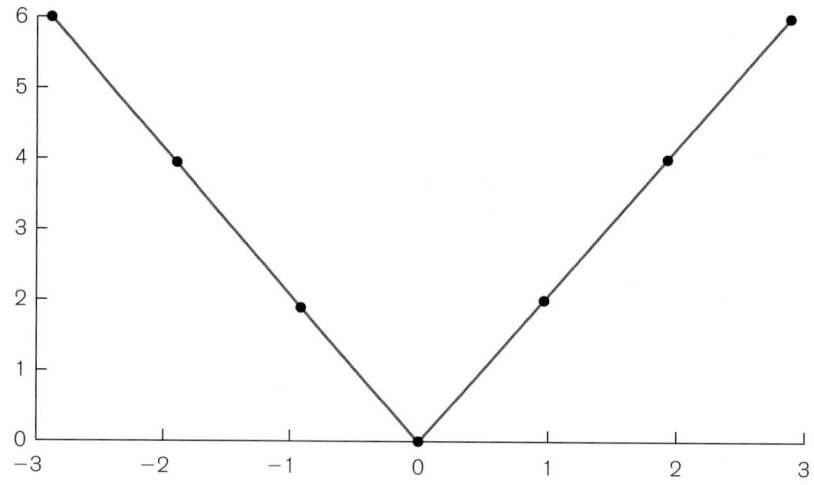

The statistical significance of the relationship between two variables measured by using r can be conveniently tested. The hypotheses are

$$H_0: \rho = 0$$
$$H_1: \rho \neq 0$$

The test statistic is

$$t = r\left[\frac{n-2}{1-r^2}\right]^{1/2}$$

which has a t distribution with $n - 2$ degrees of freedom. For the correlation coefficient calculated based on the data given in Table 18.1,

$$t = 0.9361\left[\frac{12-2}{1-(0.9361)^2}\right]^{1/2}$$

or

$$t = 0.9361\left[\frac{10}{0.1237}\right]^{1/2}$$

or

$$\begin{aligned} t &= 0.9381[80.8407]^{1/2} \\ &= 0.9361 \times 8.991 \\ &= 8.414 \end{aligned}$$

and the degrees of freedom = 12 − 2 = 10. From the t distribution table (Table 4 in the Appendix of Statistical Tables), the critical value of t for a two-tailed test and $\alpha = 0.05$ is 2.228. Hence, the null hypothesis of no relationship between X and Y is rejected. This, along with the positive sign of r, indicates that attitude toward sports cars is positively related to the duration of car ownership. Moreover, the high value of r indicates that this relationship is strong. The usefulness of the product moment correlation, r, in assessing relationships is illustrated by the example on the following page.

The product moment provides a conceptual foundation for bivariate as well as multiple regression analysis.

RESEARCH IN ACTION

It's a Small World

A recent study analyzed the ratings of 186 countries on seven dimensions of quality of life (QOL): favorable cost of living (COL), culture (CUL), economy (ECON), freedom (FREE), infrastructure (INFRA), health (HEA), and environment (ENV). The simple correlations between these dimensions are as follows:

	COL	CUL	ECON	FREE	INFRA	HEA	ENV
COL	1.0						
CUL	−.03	1.0					
ECON	.27*	.66*	1.0				
FREE	−.05	.57*	0.46*	1.0			
INFRA	−.26*	.76*	.85*	.55*	1.0		
HEA	−.03	.78*	.59*	.47*	.70*	1.0	
ENV	−.05	.04	−.02	.10	−.01	−.07	1.0

* Indicates correlation is statistically significant at $\alpha = .05$.

The magnitude of the correlation indicates the extent to which the two QOL dimensions are interrelated. The highest correlation of 0.85 is observed between INFRA and ECON, indicating that infrastructure and economic development are highly interrelated. In contrast, there is no relationship between infrastructure and environment ($r = -.01$). Based on ratings on the QOL dimensions, the 186 countries were classified into 12 clusters or groups. The 10th cluster, which consisted of 19 developed countries–including the United States, Canada, the United Kingdom, Japan, France, Germany, and the Scandinavian countries–represented the highest QOL.

Country policymakers can use this information to identify possible rival countries for direct investment, and to form alliances with countries having complementary resources, cultures, and economic development.[2]

Regression Analysis

Regression analysis is a powerful and flexible procedure for analyzing associative relationships between a metric-dependent variable and one or more independent variables. It can be used in the following ways:

regression analysis
A statistical procedure for analyzing associative relationships between a metric-dependent variable and one or more independent variables.

1. Determine whether the independent variables explain a significant variation in the dependent variable: whether a relationship exists.
2. Determine how much of the variation in the dependent variable can be explained by the independent variables: strength of the relationship.
3. Determine the structure or form of the relationship: the mathematical equation relating the independent and dependent variables.
4. Predict the values of the dependent variable.
5. Control for other independent variables when evaluating the contributions of a specific variable or set of variables.

Although the independent variables may explain the variation in the dependent variable, this does not necessarily imply causation. The use of the terms *dependent* or *criterion* variables, and *independent* or *predictor* variables in regression analysis arises from the mathematical relationship between the variables. These terms do not imply that the criterion variable is dependent on the independent variables in a causal sense, as at least two of the three criteria for causation discussed in Chapter 8 (time order of occurrence of variables and absence of other causal factors) may not be satisfied. Regression analysis is concerned with the nature and degree of association between variables and does not imply or assume any causality. We will discuss bivariate regression first, followed by multiple regression.

Bivariate Regression

bivariate regression
A procedure for deriving a mathematical relationship, in the form of an equation, between a single metric-dependent variable and a single metric-independent variable.

bivariate regression model
An equation used to explain regression analysis in which one independent variable is regressed onto a single dependent variable.

Bivariate regression is a procedure for deriving a mathematical relationship, in the form of an equation, between a single metric-dependent or criterion variable and a single metric-independent or predictor variable. The analysis is similar in many ways to determining the simple correlation between two variables. However, since an equation has to be derived, one variable must be identified as the dependent and the other as the independent variable. For example, the growth rate of the U.S. economy has a positive correlation with the level of consumer spending. Thus, a **bivariate regression model** could be constructed with growth rate of the U.S. economy as the dependent variable and the level of consumer spending as the independent variable. The examples of simple correlation given earlier can be translated into the regression context:

- Can variation in sales be explained in terms of variation in advertising expenditures? What is the structure and form of this relationship, and can it be modeled mathematically by an equation describing a straight line?
- Can the variation in market share be accounted for by the size of the sales force?
- Are consumers' perceptions of quality determined by their perceptions of price?

Conducting Bivariate Regression Analysis

The steps involved in conducting bivariate regression analysis are described in Figure 18.5. Suppose the researcher wants to explain attitudes toward sports cars in terms of the duration of car ownership (see Table 18.1). In deriving such relationships, it is often useful to first examine a scatter diagram.

Figure 18.5
Conducting Bivariate Regression Analysis

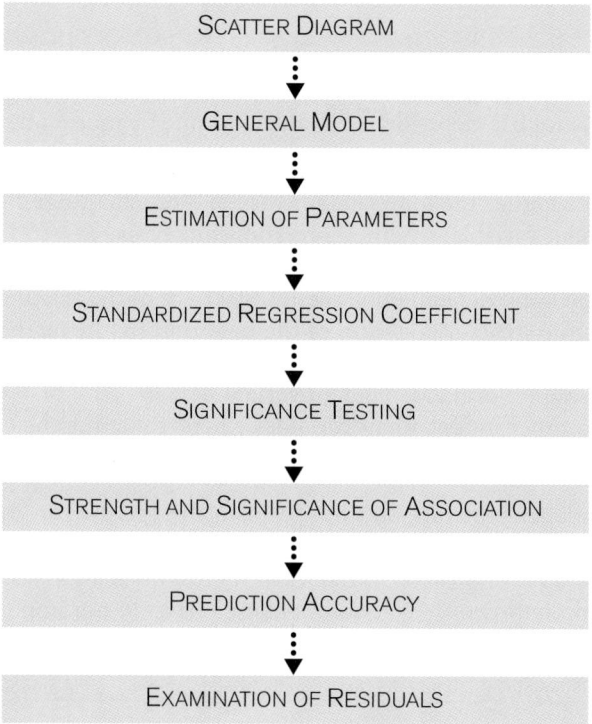

Scatter Diagram

A **scatter diagram,** or scattergram, is a plot of the values of two variables for all the cases or observations. It is customary to plot the dependent variable on the vertical axis and the independent variable on the horizontal axis. A scatter diagram is useful for determining the form of the relationship between the variables. A scatter plot can alert the researcher to any patterns or problems in the data. Any unusual combinations of the two variables can be easily identified. A plot of Y (attitude toward sports cars) against X (duration of car ownership) is given in Figure 18.3. The points seem to be arranged in a band running from the bottom left to the top right.

scatter diagram
A plot of the values of two variables for all the cases or observations.

One can see the pattern: as one variable increases, so does the other. It appears from this scattergram that the relationship between X and Y is linear and that it could be well described by a straight line. By fitting the best straight line to the data, the equation of the line gives the estimate of the underlying relationship in the data. How should the straight line be fitted to best describe the data?

The most commonly used technique for fitting a straight line to a scattergram is the **least-squares procedure.** This technique determines the best-fitting line by minimizing the vertical distances of all the points from the line. The best-fitting line is called the *regression line*. Any point that does not fall on the regression line is not fully accounted for. The vertical distance from the point to the line is the error, e_j (Figure 18.6). The distances of all the points from the line are squared and added together to arrive at the sum of the squared errors, which is a measure of total error, $\sum e_j^2$. In fitting the line, the least-squares procedure minimizes the **sum of squared errors.** If Y is plotted on the vertical axis and X on the horizontal axis, as in Figure 18.6, the best-fitting line is called the regression of Y on X since the vertical distances are minimized. The scatter diagram indicates whether the relationship between Y and X can be modeled as a straight line, and, consequently, whether the bivariate regression model is appropriate.

least-squares procedure
A technique for fitting a straight line to a scattergram by minimizing the vertical distances of all the points from the line.

sum of squared errors
The sum of the squared vertical differences between the actual data point and the predicted one on the regression line.

Bivariate Regression Model

In the bivariate regression model, the general form of a straight line is

$$Y = \beta_0 + \beta_1 X$$

Where

Y = dependent or criterion variable
β_0 = intercept of the line
β_1 = slope of the line
X = independent or predictor variable

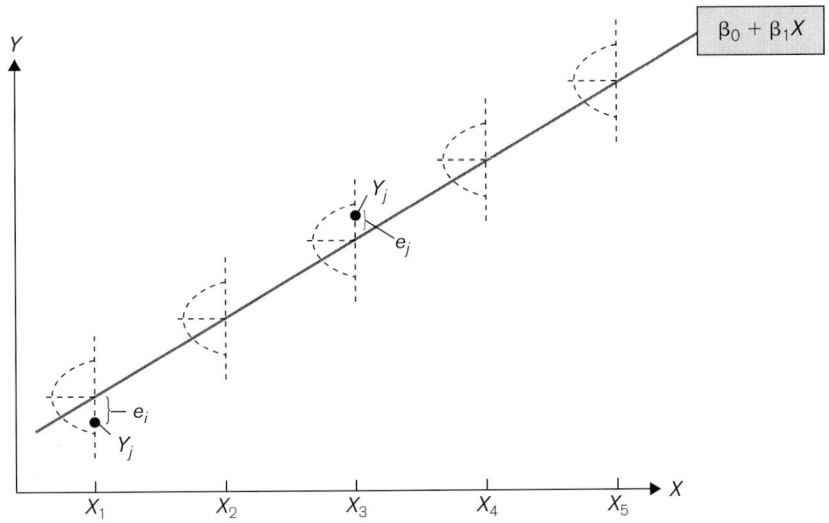

Figure 18.6
Bivariate Regression

This equation is very similar to the equation of a straight line with which you are familiar: $y = mx + b$, with $b = \beta_0$, and $m = \beta_1$. This model implies a deterministic relationship, in that Y is completely determined by X. The value of Y can be perfectly predicted if β_0 and β_1 are known. In marketing research, however, very few relationships are deterministic. So the regression procedure adds an error term to account for the probabilistic or stochastic nature of the relationship. It is assumed that the error terms are independent and normally distributed with a mean of zero and a constant variance. The basic regression equation becomes

$$Y_i = \beta_0 + \beta_1 X + e_i$$

where e_i is the error term associated with the ith observation.[3] Estimation of the regression parameters, β_0 and β_1, is relatively simple.

Estimation of Parameters

In most cases, β_0 and β_1 are unknown and are estimated from the sample observations using the equation

$$\hat{Y}_i = a + b\,x_i$$

estimated or predicted value
The value $\hat{Y}_i = a + b\,x_i$ where $\hat{Y}_i$ is the estimated or predicted value of Y_i, and a and b are estimators of β_0 and β_1, respectively.

nonstandardized regression coefficient
The weight or multiplier of the independent variable when it is regressed onto a single dependent variable.

where $\hat{Y}_i$ is the **estimated or predicted value** of Y_i, and a and b are estimators of β_0 and β_1, respectively. The constant b is usually referred to as the **nonstandardized regression coefficient.** It is the slope of the regression line, and it indicates the expected change in Y when X is changed by one unit. The formulas for calculating a and b are simple. The slope, b, may be computed in terms of the covariance between X and Y (COV_{xy}) and the variance of X as

$$b = \frac{COV_{xy}}{S_x^2}$$

$$= \frac{\sum_{i=1}^{n}(X_i - \bar{X})(Y_i - \bar{Y})}{\sum_{i=1}^{n}(X_i - \bar{X})^2}$$

$$= \frac{\sum_{i=1}^{n} X_i Y_i - n\bar{X}\bar{Y}}{\sum_{i=1}^{n} X_i^2 - n\bar{X}^2}$$

The intercept, a, may then be calculated using

$$a = \bar{Y} - b\bar{X}$$

For the data in Table 18.1, the estimation of parameters for the regression of attitude (Y) on duration (X) may be illustrated as follows:

$$\sum_{i=1}^{12} X_i Y_i = (10)(6) + (12)(9) + (12)(8) + (4)(3) + (12)(10) + (6)(4)$$
$$+ (8)(5) + (2)(2) + (18)(11) + (9)(9) + (17)(10) + (2)(2)$$
$$= 917$$

$$\sum_{i=1}^{12} X_i^2 = 10^2 + 12^2 + 12^2 + 4^2 + 12^2 + 6^2$$
$$+ 8^2 + 2^2 + 18^2 + 9^2 + 17^2 + 2^2$$
$$= 1350$$

It may be recalled from earlier calculations of the simple correlation that

$$\bar{X} = 9.333$$
$$\bar{Y} = 6.583$$

Given $n = 12$, b can be calculated as

$$b = \frac{917 - (12)(9.333)(6.583)}{1350 - (12)(9.333)^2}$$

or

$$b = \frac{917 - 737.370}{1350 - 1045.259}$$
$$= \frac{179.73}{304.741}$$
$$= 0.5897$$

$$a = \bar{Y} - b\bar{X}$$
$$= 6.583 - (0.5897)(9.333)$$
$$= 6.583 - 5.504$$
$$= 1.079$$

Note that these coefficients have been estimated on the raw (untransformed) data. Should standardization of the data be considered desirable, the calculation of the standardized coefficients is also straightforward.

Using a computer program, the regression of attitude on duration of car ownership, using the data shown in Table 18.1, yielded the results shown in Table 18.3. The corresponding SPSS and EXCEL outputs can be downloaded from the Web site for this book. The intercept, a, equals 1.0793, and the slope, b, equals 0.5897, as shown earlier by hand calculations. Therefore, the estimated equation is

$$\text{Attitude } (\hat{Y}) = 1.0793 + 0.5897 \text{ (Duration of car ownership)}$$

Table 18.3

Bivariate Regression

Multiple *R*	.9361				
R^2	.8762				
Adjusted R^2	.8639				
Standard Error	1.2233				

Analysis of Variance

	df	Sum of Squares	Mean Square
Regression	1	105.9522	105.9522
Residual	10	14.9644	1.4964
F = 70.8027		Significance of F = .0000	

Variables in the Equation

Variable	b	SE_b	Beta (B)	T	Sig. T
Duration	.5897	.0700	.9361	8.414	.0000
(Constant)	1.0793	.7434		1.452	.1772

Attitude toward sports cars can be explained by the duration of sports car ownership using bivariate regression.

Standardized Regression Coefficients

standardization
The process by which the raw data are transformed into new variables that have a mean of 0 and a variance of 1.

beta coefficient
Also known as *beta weight;* used to denote the standardized regression coefficient.

Standardization is the process by which the raw data are transformed into new variables that have a mean of 0 and a variance of 1. This process is similar to the calculation of z values discussed earlier (Chapters 13, 16, and 17). To standardize a variable, simply subtract the mean and divide the difference by the standard deviation. When the data are standardized, the intercept assumes a value of 0. The term **beta coefficient,** or *beta weight*, is used to denote the standardized regression coefficient. Standardization may be desirable because it is easier to compare the beta coefficients than it is to compare the raw coefficients. In this case, the slope obtained by the regression of Y on X, B_{yx}, is the same as the slope obtained by the regression of X on Y, B_{xy}. Moreover, each of these regression coefficients is equal to the simple correlation between X and Y.

$$B_{yx} = B_{xy} = r_{xy}$$

Thus, instead of running Pearson correlations in the opening vignette, we could have alternatively run four bivariate regressions with preference for athletic shoes as the dependent variable. Each of the independent variables in turn would serve as the independent or predictor variable: interest in sports, attitude toward sports personalities, attendance at sports events, and time spent watching sports on television.

There is also a simple relationship between the standardized and nonstandardized regression coefficients:

$$B_{yx} = b_{yx}\,(S_x/S_y)$$

To illustrate the calculation of the beta coefficient by hand for the bivariate regression of Table 18.1 recall from the hand calculations for the correlation coefficient that

$$\sum_{i=1}^{n}(Y_i - \bar{Y})^2 = 120.9168$$

Therefore,

$$S_y = \sqrt{\frac{120.9168}{(12-1)}}$$
$$= 3.3155$$

and,

$$\sum_{i=1}^{n}(X_i - \bar{X})^2 = 304.6668$$

Therefore,

$$S_x = \sqrt{\frac{304.6668}{(12-1)}}$$
$$= 5.2628$$

Therefore,

$$B_{yx} = (0.5897)(5.2628)/(3.3155)$$
$$= 0.9361$$

For the regression results given in Table 18.3, the value of the beta coefficient is also estimated as 0.9361. Note that this is also the value of r calculated earlier in this chapter.

Once the parameters have been estimated, they can be tested for significance.

Significance Testing

The statistical significance of the linear relationship between X and Y may be tested by examining the hypotheses:

$$H_0: \beta_1 = 0$$
$$H_1: \beta_1 \neq 0$$

The null hypothesis implies that there is no linear relationship between X and Y. The alternative hypothesis is that there is a relationship, positive or negative, between X and Y. For example, the relationship between income and the number of times people dine out in a month can be statistically tested via bivariate regression. The null hypothesis would be that income has no relationship with the number of times people dine out in a month. The alternative hypothesis would be that income has a positive relationship with the number of times people dine out in a month. If the null hypothesis is not rejected, then we conclude that there is no relationship between X and Y, even though the regression coefficient may not be exactly zero. Typically, a two-tailed test is done. A t statistic with $n - 2$ degrees of freedom can be used, where

$$t = \frac{b}{SE_b}$$

SE_b denotes the standard deviation of b and is called the **standard error.**[4] The t distribution was discussed in Chapter 17.

standard error
SE_b denotes the standard deviation of b and is called the standard error.

The standard error or standard deviation of b is estimated as 0.07008 and the value of the t statistic is $t = 0.5897/0.0700 = 8.414$, with $n - 2 = 10$ degrees of freedom (see Table 18.3). From Table 4 in the Appendix of Statistical Tables, we see that the critical value of t with 10 degrees of freedom and $\alpha = 0.05$ is 2.228 for a two-tailed test. Since the calculated value of t is larger than the critical value, the null hypothesis is rejected. Hence, there is a significant linear relationship between attitude toward sports cars and duration of car ownership. The positive sign of the slope coefficient indicates that this relationship is positive. In other words, those who have owned cars for a longer time have more favorable attitudes toward sports cars, indicating a stronger liking for these cars.

Strength and Significance of Association

A related inference involves determining the strength and significance of the association between Y and X. The strength of association is measured by the **coefficient of determination,** r^2. In bivariate regression, r^2 is the square of the simple correlation coefficient obtained by correlating the two variables. The coefficient r^2 varies between 0 and 1. It

coefficient of determination
The proportion of variance in one variable associated with the variability in a second variable.

Figure 18.7

Decomposition of the Total Variation in Bivariate Regression

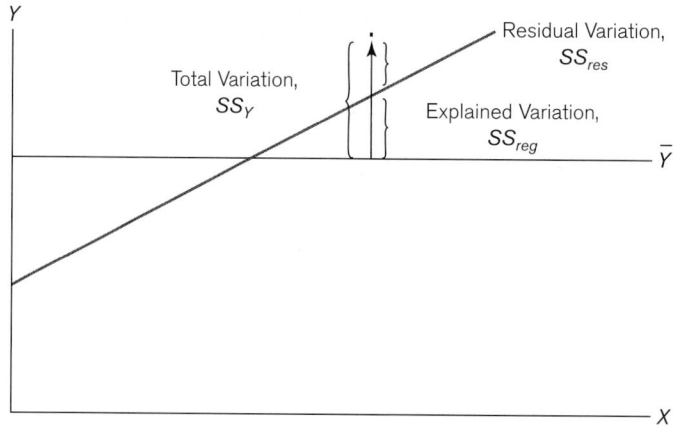

signifies the proportion of the total variation in Y that is accounted for by the variation in X. The decomposition of the total variation in Y is similar to that for analysis of variance (see Chapter 17). As shown in Figure 18.7, the total variation, SS_y, may be decomposed into the variation accounted for by the regression line, SS_{reg}, and the error or residual variation, SS_{error} or SS_{res}, as follows:

$$SS_y = SS_{reg} + SS_{res}$$

Where

$$SS_y = \sum_{i=1}^{n} (Y_i - \bar{Y})^2$$

$$SS_{reg} = \sum_{i=1}^{n} (\hat{Y}_i - \bar{Y})^2$$

$$SS_{res} = \sum_{i=1}^{n} (Y_i - \hat{Y}_i)^2$$

The strength of association may then be calculated as follows:

$$r^2 = \frac{SS_{reg}}{SS_y}$$

$$= \frac{SS_y - SS_{res}}{SS_y}$$

To illustrate the calculations of r^2, let us consider again the effect of the duration of car ownership on attitude toward sports cars. It may be recalled from earlier hand calculations of the simple correlation coefficient that

$$SS_y = \sum_{i=1}^{n} (Y_i - \bar{Y})^2$$

$$= 120.9166$$

The predicted values $(\hat{Y})$ can be calculated using the regression equation:

$$\text{Attitude } (\hat{Y}) = 1.0793 + 0.5897 \text{ (Duration of car ownership)}$$

For the first observation in Table 18.1, this value is

$$(\hat{Y}) = 1.0793 + 0.5897 \times 10 = 6.9763$$

For each successive observation, the predicted values are, in order, 8.1557, 8.1557, 3.4381, 8.1557, 4.6175, 5.7969, 2.2587, 11.6939, 6.3866, 11.1042, and 2.2587. Therefore,

$$
\begin{aligned}
SS_{reg} = \sum_{i=1}^{n} (\hat{Y}_i - \bar{Y})^2 &= (6.9763 - 6.5833)^2 + (8.1557 - 6.5833)^2 \\
&+ (8.1557 - 6.5833)^2 + (3.4381 - 6.5833)^2 \\
&+ (8.1557 - 6.5833)^2 + (4.6175 - 6.5833)^2 \\
&+ (5.7969 - 6.5833)^2 + (2.2587 - 6.5833)^2 \\
&+ (11.6939 - 6.5833)^2 + (6.3866 - 6.5833)^2 \\
&+ (11.1042 - 6.5833)^2 + (2.2587 - 6.5833)^2 \\
&= 0.1544 + 2.4724 + 2.4724 + 9.8922 + 2.4724 \\
&+ 3.8643 + 0.6184 + 18.7021 + 26.1182 \\
&+ 0.0387 + 20.4385 + 18.7021 \\
&= 105.9522
\end{aligned}
$$

$$
\begin{aligned}
SS_{res} = \sum_{i=1}^{n} (Y_i - \hat{Y}_i)^2 &= (6 - 6.9763)^2 + (9 - 8.1557)^2 + (8 - 8.1557)^2 \\
&+ (3 - 3.4381)^2 + (10 - 8.1557)^2 + (4 - 4.6175)^2 \\
&+ (5 - 5.7969)^2 + (2 - 2.2587)^2 + (11 - 11.6939)^2 \\
&+ (9 - 6.3866)^2 + (10 - 11.1042)^2 + (2 - 2.2587)^2 \\
&= 14.9644
\end{aligned}
$$

It can be seen that $SS_y = SS_{reg} + SS_{res.}$ Furthermore,

$$
\begin{aligned}
r^2 &= SS_{reg}/SS_y \\
&= 105.9524 / 120.9168 \\
&= 0.8762
\end{aligned}
$$

Another equivalent test for examining the significance of the linear relationship between X and Y (significance of b) is the test for the significance of the coefficient of determination. The hypotheses in this case are

$$H_0: R^2_{pop} = 0$$
$$H_1: R^2_{pop} > 0$$

The appropriate test statistic is the F statistic:

$$F = \frac{SS_{reg}}{SS_{res}/(n-2)}$$

which has an F distribution with 1 and $n - 2$ degrees of freedom. The F-test is a generalized form of the t-test (see Chapter 17). If a random variable is t distributed with n degrees of freedom, then t^2 is F distributed with 1 and n degrees of freedom. Hence, the F-test for testing the significance of the coefficient of determination is equivalent to testing the following hypotheses:

$$H_0: \beta_1 = 0$$
$$H_0: \beta_1 \neq 0$$

or

$$H_0: \rho = 0$$
$$H_0: \rho \neq 0$$

From Table 18.3, it can be seen that

$$
\begin{aligned}
r^2 &= 105.9522 / (105.9522 + 14.9644) \\
&= 0.8762
\end{aligned}
$$

Which is the same as the value calculated by hand earlier. The value of the F statistic is

$$F = 105.9522/(14.9644/10)$$
$$= 70.8027$$

with 1 and 10 degrees of freedom. The calculated F statistic exceeds the critical value of 4.96 determined from Table 5 in the Appendix of Statistical Tables. Therefore, the relationship is significant at $\alpha = 0.05$, corroborating the results of the t-test. If the relationship between X and Y is significant, it is meaningful to predict the values of Y based on the values of X and to estimate prediction accuracy.

Prediction Accuracy

standard error of estimate
The standard deviation of the actual Y values from the predicted $\hat{Y}$ values.

To estimate the accuracy of predicted values, $\hat{Y}$, it is useful to calculate the **standard error of estimate** (SEE). This statistic is the standard deviation of the actual Y values from the predicted $\hat{Y}$ values. The larger the SEE is, the poorer the fit of the regression. From Table 18.3, it can be seen that SEE is 1.2233. The SEE can be used for constructing confidence intervals around predicted values of Y (see Chapter 13).

Examination of Residuals

residual
The difference between the observed value of Y and the value predicted by the regression equation $\hat{Y}_i$.

A **residual** is the difference between the observed value of Y_i and the value predicted by the regression equation $\hat{Y}_i$. Residuals are used in the calculation of several statistics associated with regression. Scattergrams of the residuals, in which the residuals are plotted against the predicted values, $\hat{Y}_i$, time, or predictor variables, provide useful insights in examining the appropriateness of the underlying assumptions and regression model fitted. For example, the assumption of a normally distributed error term can be examined by constructing a histogram of the residuals. A visual check reveals whether the distribution is normal. Additionally, if the pattern of residuals is not random, then some of the underlying assumptions are being violated.

The following example illustrates how regression analysis can result in findings with great managerial relevance.

RESEARCH IN ACTION

Avoiding Dissatisfaction to Enhance Overall Satisfaction

A large health maintenance organization (HMO) collects data regularly as part of its ongoing patient satisfaction measurement program. In a recent study, data on patient satisfaction, quality of interaction, and related variables were obtained from 4,517 patients who subscribed to 501 primary care physicians (PCPs) affiliated with the HMO. The survey was conducted by telephone. To estimate the impact of the quality of interaction with the PCP on patient satisfaction, the researchers conducted regression analysis.

The dependent variable was patient satisfaction, and the independent variable was the quality of PCP interaction. Three regressions were run: for satisfied patients, for dissatisfied patients, and for all patients. The estimates of the regression coefficient for these three regressions were 1.04, 3.73, and 2.02, respectively. As can be seen, the value of the coefficient was the highest for dissatisfied patients, indicating that dissatisfied patients are differentially more sensitive to the quality of PCP interaction. The implication is that, in order to enhance overall patient satisfaction, health-care providers should accord greater attention to those aspects of PCP interaction that lead to dissatisfaction than to those that lead to satisfaction.[5]

BE an MR!

Visit Ford's Web site (www.ford.com) and conduct an Internet search using a search engine and your library's online database to obtain information on the relationship between advertising and sales for automobile manufacturers.

Formulate a bivariate regression model explaining the relationship between advertising and sales in the automobile industry.

BE a DM!

As the marketing director for Ford Motor Company, how would you determine your advertising expenditures for boosting awareness among NASCAR fans of the Ford Escape Hybrid–the most fuel-efficient SUV on the road?

Multiple Regression

Multiple regression involves a single dependent variable and two or more independent variables. Just as bivariate regression attempts to fit a best line to the data, regression with two independent variables tries to fit a best plane to the data. To extend the bivariate regression example considered earlier, the growth rate of the U.S. economy has a positive correlation with the level of consumer spending and the level of interest rates. Thus, a **multiple regression model** could be constructed with growth rate of the U.S. economy as the dependent variable and the level of consumer spending and the level of interest rates as the independent variables. The concept is similar in regression with more than two independent variables. The questions raised in the context of bivariate regression can also be answered via multiple regression by considering additional independent variables:

multiple regression
A statistical technique that simultaneously develops a mathematical relationship between two or more independent variables and an interval-scaled dependent variable.

multiple regression model
An equation used to explain the results of multiple regression analysis.

- Can variation in sales be explained in terms of variation in advertising expenditures, prices, and level of distribution?
- Can variation in market shares be accounted for by the size of the sales force, advertising expenditures, and sales promotion budgets?
- Are consumers' perceptions of quality determined by their perceptions of prices, brand image, and brand attributes?

Additional questions can also be answered by multiple regression:

- How much of the variation in sales can be explained by advertising expenditures, prices, and level of distribution?
- What is the contribution of advertising expenditures in explaining the variation in sales when the levels of prices and distribution are controlled?
- What levels of sales may be expected given the levels of advertising expenditures, prices, and level of distribution?

The general form of the multiple regression model is as follows:

$$Y = \beta_0 + \beta_1 X_1 + \beta_2 X_2 + \beta_3 X_3 + \ldots + \beta_k X_k + e$$

which is estimated by the following equation:

$$\hat{Y} = a + b_1 X_1 + b_2 X_2 + b_3 X_3 + \cdots + b_k X_k$$

As before, the coefficient a represents the intercept, but the b's are now the partial regression coefficients. The least-squares criterion estimates the parameters in such a way as to minimize the total error, SS_{res}. This process also maximizes the correlation between the actual values of Y and the predicted values $\hat{Y}$. All the assumptions made in bivariate regression also apply in multiple regression.

Conducting Multiple Regression Analysis

The steps involved in conducting multiple regression analysis are similar to those for bivariate regression analysis. The discussion focuses on partial regression coefficients, strength of association, and significance testing.

Partial Regression Coefficients

To understand the meaning of a partial regression coefficient, let us consider again the multiple regression model with growth rate of the U.S. economy as the dependent variable and the level of consumer spending and the level of interest rates as the independent variables. In this case, there are two independent variables, so that

$$\hat{Y} = a + b_1X_1 + b_2X_2$$

First, note that the relative magnitude of the partial regression coefficient of an independent variable is, in general, different from that of its bivariate regression coefficient. In other words, the partial regression coefficient, b_1, will be different from the regression coefficient, b, obtained by regressing Y on only X_1. This happens because X_1 and X_2 are usually correlated. In bivariate regression, X_2 was not considered, and any variation in Y that was shared by X_1 and X_2 was attributed to X_1. However, in the case of multiple independent variables, this is no longer true. Thus, in modeling the growth rate of the U.S. economy, the (partial) regression coefficient for the level of consumer spending in the multiple regression model will be different than that for bivariate regression.

partial regression coefficient
Also known as b_1, denotes the change in the predicted value of Y when X_1 is changed by one unit but the other independent variables, X_2 to X_k, are held constant.

The interpretation of the **partial regression coefficient**, b_1, is that it represents the expected change in Y when X_1 is changed by one unit but X_2 is held constant or otherwise controlled. Thus, the partial regression coefficient for the level of consumer spending will be different in multiple regression than the coefficient in bivariate regression. Likewise, b_2 represents the expected change in Y for a unit change in X_2, when X_1 is held constant. Thus, calling b_1 and b_2 partial regression coefficients is appropriate. It can also be seen that the combined effects of X_1 and X_2 on Y are additive. In other words, if X_1 and X_2 are each changed by one unit, the expected change in Y would be $(b_1 + b_2)$.

Extension to the case of k variables is straightforward. The partial regression coefficient, b_1, represents the expected change in Y when X_1 is changed by one unit and X_2 through X_k are held constant. It can also be interpreted as the bivariate regression coefficient, b, for the regression of Y on the residuals of X_1, when the effect of X_2 through X_k has been removed from X_1.

In the opening vignette, a multiple regression model was estimated with preference for athletic shoes as the dependent variable, and interest in sports, attitude toward sports personalities, attendance at sports events, and time spent watching sports on television as the independent variables. The partial regression coefficient associated with each independent variable was positive and significant, indicating that higher values on each independent variable were associated with stronger preference for athletic shoes. The partial regression coefficient for interest in sports would represent the expected change in preference for athletic shoes when interest in sports is changed by one unit and attitude toward sports personalities, attendance at sports events, and time spent watching sports on television are held constant.

The beta coefficients are the partial regression coefficients obtained when all the variables $(Y, X_1, X_2, \ldots X_k)$ have been standardized to a mean of 0 and a variance of 1 before estimating the regression equation. The relationship of the standardized to the nonstandardized coefficients remains the same as before:

$$B_1 = b_1\,(S_{x1}/S_y)$$

$$\cdot$$

$$\cdot$$

$$B_k = b_k\,(S_{xk}/S_y)$$

The intercept and the partial regression coefficients are estimated by solving a system of simultaneous equations derived by differentiating and equating the partial derivatives to 0. Since the various computer programs automatically estimate these coefficients, we will not present the details. However, it is worth noting that the equations cannot be solved if: (1) the sample size, n, is smaller than or equal to the number of independent variables, k; or (2) one independent variable is perfectly correlated with another.

Suppose that in explaining the attitude toward sports cars, we now introduce a second variable, the importance of performance. The data for the 12 pretest respondents on attitude toward sports cars, duration of car ownership, and importance attached to performance are given in Table 18.1. The results of multiple regression analysis are depicted in Table 18.4. The corresponding SPSS and EXCEL outputs can be downloaded from the Web site for this book. The partial regression coefficient for duration (X_1) is now 0.4811, which is different from what it was in the bivariate case. The corresponding beta coefficient is 0.7636. The partial regression coefficient for importance attached to performance (X_2) is 0.2887, with a beta coefficient of 0.3138. The estimated regression equation is

$$(\hat{Y}) = 0.3373 + 0.4811\,X_1 + 0.2887\,X_2$$

or

$$\text{Attitude} = 0.3373 + 0.4811\ (\text{Duration}) + 0.2887\ (\text{Importance})$$

This equation can be used for a variety of purposes, including predicting attitudes toward sports cars, given a knowledge of the respondents' duration of car ownership and the importance they attach to performance.

Strength of Association

The strength of the relationship stipulated by the regression equation can be determined by using the appropriate measures of association. The total variation is decomposed as in the bivariate case:

$$SS_y = SS_{reg} + SS_{res}$$

Table 18.4

Multiple Regression

Multiple *R*	.9721				
R^2	.9450				
Adjusted R^2	.9330				
Standard Error	.8597				

Analysis of Variance

	df	Sum of Squares	Mean Square
Regression	2	114.2643	57.1321
Residual	9	6.6524	.7392
***F* = 77.2936**		Significance of *F* = .0000	

Variables in the Equation

Variable	*b*	SE_b	Beta (*B*)	*T*	Sig. *T*
Importance	.2887	.08608	.3138	3.353	.0085
Duration	.4811	.05895	.7636	8.160	.0000
(Constant)	.3373	.56736		.595	.5668

Where

$$SS_y = \sum_{i=1}^{n} (Y_i - \bar{Y})^2$$

$$SS_{reg} = \sum_{i=1}^{n} (\hat{Y}_i - \bar{Y})^2$$

$$SS_{res} = \sum_{i=1}^{n} (Y_i - \hat{Y}_i)^2$$

The strength of association is measured by the square of the multiple correlation coefficient, R^2, which is also called the **coefficient of multiple determination.**

coefficient of multiple determination
In multiple regression, the strength of association is measured by the square of the multiple correlation coefficient, R^2, which is called the coefficient of multiple determination.

$$R^2 = \frac{SS_{reg}}{SS_y}$$

The multiple correlation coefficient, R, can also be viewed as the simple correlation coefficient, r, between Y and $\hat{Y}$. Several points about the characteristics of R^2 are worth noting. The coefficient of multiple determination, R^2, cannot be less than the highest bivariate, r^2, of any individual independent variable with the dependent variable. R^2 will be larger when the correlations between the independent variables are low. If the independent variables are statistically independent (uncorrelated), then R^2 will be the sum of the bivariate r^2 of each independent variable with the dependent variable. R^2 cannot decrease as more independent variables are added to the regression equation. However, diminishing returns do set in, so that after the first few variables, the additional independent variables do not make much of a contribution. For this reason, R^2 is adjusted for the number of independent variables and the sample size by using the following formula:

adjusted R^2
The value of R^2 adjusted for the number of independent variables and the sample size.

$$\textbf{Adjusted } R^2 = R^2 - \frac{k(1-R^2)}{n-k-1}$$

For the regression results given in Table 18.4, the value of R^2 is

$$\begin{aligned} R^2 &= 114.2643/(114.2643 + 6.6524) \\ &= 114.2643/120.9167 \\ &= 0.9450 \end{aligned}$$

This is higher than the r^2 value of 0.8762 obtained in the bivariate case. The r^2 in the bivariate case is the square of the simple (product moment) correlation between attitude toward sports cars and duration of car ownership. The R^2 obtained in multiple regression is also higher than the square of the simple correlation between attitude and importance attached to performance (which can be estimated as 0.5379). The adjusted R^2 is estimated as

$$\begin{aligned} \text{Adjusted } R^2 &= 0.9450 - 2\,(1.0 - 0.9450)/(12 - 2 - 1) \\ &= 0.9450 - 0.0122 \\ &= 0.9328 \end{aligned}$$

Note that the value of adjusted R^2 is close to R^2 and both are higher than r^2 for the bivariate case. This suggests that the addition of the second independent variable, importance attached to performance, makes a contribution in explaining the variation in attitude toward sports cars. Of course, R^2 should be significant and higher values of R^2 are more desirable than lower values. However, in commercial marketing research, values of R^2 as high as 0.9 or higher are uncommon. Values of R^2 in the 0.5 to 0.8 may be reasonable in many commercial marketing research projects.

Significance Testing

Significance testing involves testing the significance of the overall regression equation as well as specific partial regression coefficients. The null hypothesis for the overall test is that the coefficient of multiple determination in the population, R^2_{pop}, is zero.

$$H_0 : R^2_{pop} = 0$$

This is equivalent to the following null hypothesis:

$$H_0: \beta_1 = \beta_2 = \beta_3 = \ldots = \beta_k = 0$$

The overall test can be conducted by using an F statistic:

$$F = \frac{SS_{reg}/k}{SS_{res}/(n-k-1)}$$

$$= \frac{R^2/k}{(1-R^2)/(n-k-1)}$$

which has an F distribution with k and $(n - k - 1)$ degrees of freedom. For the multiple regression results given in Table 18.4,

$$F = \frac{114.2643/2}{6.6524/9} = 77.2936$$

which is significant at $\alpha = 0.05$.

If the overall null hypothesis is rejected, one or more population partial regression coefficients have a value different from 0. To determine which specific coefficients (b_i's) are nonzero, additional tests are necessary. Testing for the significance of the b_i's can be done in a manner similar to that in the bivariate case by using t-tests. The significance of the partial coefficient for importance attached to performance may be tested by the following equation:

$$t = \frac{b}{SE_b}$$

$$= 0.2887/0.08608$$

$$= 3.353$$

which has a t distribution with $(n - k - 1)$ degrees of freedom. This coefficient is significant at $\alpha = 0.05$. The significance of the coefficient for duration of car ownership is tested in a similar way and found to be significant. Therefore, both the duration of car ownership and the importance attached to performance are important in explaining attitude toward sports cars. However, if any of the regression coefficients are not significant, they should be treated as zero.

Some computer programs provide an equivalent F-test, often called the partial F-test. This involves a decomposition of the total regression sum of squares, SS_{reg}, into components related to each independent variable. We further illustrate the application of multiple regression with an example.

Because of complications with many multiple regression models with more than six independent variables (a condition when too much association exists between the independent variables called multicolinearity) discipline must be used in constructing multiple regression models. Although a powerful statistical tool, multiple regression must not be used in a mindless way as an exploratory method in which many variables are forced into the roles of independent variables. Wrong conclusions often result from such a misguided approach.

BE a DM!

As the marketing director for the IBM ThinkPad, how would you improve the image and competitive positioning of your brand among business students in the United States?

BE an MR!

Visit IBM's Web site (www.ibm.com) and conduct an Internet search using a search engine and your library's online database to obtain information on the factors consumers use to evaluate competing brands of laptop computers.

Formulate a multiple regression model explaining consumer preferences for laptop computer brands as a function of the brand evaluations on the consumer choice criteria factors used to evaluate competing brands.

RESEARCH IN ACTION

The New York Times Campaign Reflects Changing Times

A representative sample of 2,500 households was surveyed recently by telephone to determine their interest in reading daily newspapers. The survey found that the United States had become much more global or "world minded." One of the most important factors influencing interest in reading a newspaper was that it provides "sensitive insight into the world," regardless of whether it was a local or national newspaper. Other important factors that emerged were that a newspaper should reflect intelligence, quality, and trustworthiness.

A multiple regression model was estimated with interest in reading a daily newspaper as the dependent variable and insight into the world, intelligence, quality, and trustworthiness as the independent variables. This model had an excellent fit as determined by a high R^2, and the partial regression coefficient for each of the independent variables was positive and significant.

The New York Times built a campaign around these findings. The $20 million national image campaign had the tagline "Expect the World," and it reflected all four of the important factors that influence interest in a daily newspaper: insight into the world, intelligence, quality, and trustworthiness. TV spots appeared during the news magazine

and analysis shows, such as "Dateline," "Primetime Live," "20/20," and "Nightline," as well as during "The Today Show," "Good Morning America," and CNN's "Headline News." In addition, the commercials ran on the CNN airport network in 30 major metropolitan airports and on network and local radio. The campaign was successful, substantially increasing circulation in its very first year.[6]

Summary Illustration Using the Opening Vignette

The Pearson product moment correlation coefficient measures the linear association between two metric variables. In the opening vignette, preference for athletic shoes showed strong positive correlations with sports-related variables, such as interest in sports, attitude toward sports personalities, attendance at sports events, and time spent watching sports on television.

Bivariate regression derives a mathematical equation, in the form of a straight line between a single metric-criterion variable and a single metric-predictor variable. Instead of running Pearson correlations, we could have alternatively run four bivariate regressions with preference for athletic shoes as the dependent variable. Each of the independent variables in turn would serve as the predictor variable: interest in sports, attitude toward sports personalities, attendance at sports events, and time spent watching sports on television.

Multiple regression involves a single dependent variable and two or more independent variables. The partial regression coefficient represents the expected change in the dependent variable when one of the independent variables is changed by one unit and the other independent variables are held constant. A multiple regression model—with preference for athletic shoes as the dependent variable, and interest in sports, attitude toward sports personalities, attendance at sports events, and time spent watching sports on television as the independent variables—had very good strength of association. The partial regression coefficient associated with each independent variable was positive and significant, indicating that higher values on each independent variable were associated with stronger preference for athletic shoes. The partial regression coefficient for interest in sports would represent the expected change in preference for athletic shoes when interest in sports is changed by one unit and attitude toward sports personalities, attendance at sports events, and time spent watching sports on television are held constant.

WHAT WOULD *YOU* DO?

The West Michigan Whitecaps: Fanning Fan Loyalty

The Situation

The West Michigan Whitecaps (www.whitecaps-baseball.com), a minor league baseball team in Grand Rapids, wondered what they should do to develop fan loyalty. How could they best keep it, make it grow, and take advantage of it? So, General Manager Scott Lane got Message Factors (www.messagefactors.com), a Memphis, Tennessee-based research firm to help them determine how to effectively maintain fan loyalty on a limited budget. Message Factors developed a study that used a proprietary value analysis technique that would examine the relationship between the overall perceived value and specific satisfaction attributes in order to determine loyalty drivers. It helps determine the four things your customers want to tell you, which are: the basics–what customers expect of the company; value issues–what customers value about the company; irritations–what customers do not like about the company; and unimportants–what customers do not care about.

Qualitative research was conducted to identify a set of 71 attributes that influenced fan loyalty. Next, a questionnaire was designed that incorporated the 71 attributes and was administered to fans at Whitecaps games. The questionnaire was administered to 1,010 respondents. From this, the marketing research company was able to determine the information they were seeking. The basics were determined to be values such as stadium safety, restroom cleanliness, and variety in the food items available. The Whitecaps want to not only meet these basic expectations, but also to surpass them to guarantee fans will return and be loyal.

The value issues are the ones that can really help the team build loyalty. These included things like helpful box office personnel, convenience of purchasing tickets, convenience of parking, and providing the opportunity for autographs. Some irritations were determined as souvenir price, quality, and lack of variety. However, the research also showed that fans don't really expect to be pleased with these areas of sports attendance. It was also determined that there were no unimportant aspects in this survey.

The Marketing Research Decision

1. In order to determine the relative importance of value drivers, what type of data analysis should Message Factors conduct? Check as many as are applicable.
   a. Mean importance of helpful box office personnel, convenience of purchasing tickets, convenience of parking, and providing the opportunity for autographs.
   b. Cross-tabulation of overall value with helpful box office personnel, convenience of purchasing tickets, convenience of parking, and providing the opportunity for autographs.

   c. Product moment correlations of overall value with helpful box office personnel, convenience of purchasing tickets, convenience of parking, and providing the opportunity for autographs.
   d. Multiple regression with overall value as the dependent variable and helpful box office personnel, convenience of purchasing tickets, convenience of parking, and providing the opportunity for autographs as the independent variables.
   e. All of the above.
2. Discuss the role of the type of data analysis you recommend in enabling Scott Lane to determine the relative importance of the four value drivers.

The Marketing Management Decision

1. In order to enhance the value of Whitecaps games for the fans what should Scott Lane do? Check as many as are applicable.
   a. Train box office and other personnel to be helpful
   b. Increase the convenience of purchasing tickets
   c. Increase the convenience of parking
   d. Provide fans with opportunities for autographs
   e. All of the above
2. Discuss how the marketing management-decision action that you recommend to Scott Lane is influenced by the type of data analysis that you suggested earlier and by the findings of that analysis.

What Scott Lane Did

Data analysis revealed that the Whitecaps had performed well on the basics, so they were able to shift their focus to improving in the value areas. Analysis also showed that the personnel variable was a very high contributor to value perception. The Whitecaps were rated as average in this area, as were their competitors, so this is a key area that provides them with an opportunity to be better than and overtake the competition. Scott Lane also improved ease of ticket purchasing and provided fans with opportunities for autographs after the game. The next season, the Whitecaps raised ticket prices by 25 percent and still got a 100 percent renewal. Scott Lane had figured out how to enhance fan loyalty![7]

Software Applications

The computer programs available for conducting correlation analysis are described in Exhibit 18.1. In SPSS, CORRELATIONS can be used for computing Pearson product moment correlations, and in SAS, the corresponding program is CORR. In MINITAB, correlation can be computed using STAT>BASIC STATISTICS>CORRELATION function. It calculates Pearson's product moment. Correlations can be determined in EXCEL by using the TOOLS>DATA ANALYSIS>CORRELATION function. Use the Correlation Worksheet Function when a correlation coefficient for two cell ranges is needed.

As described in Exhibit 18.2, the statistical packages contain several programs for performing regression analysis, calculating the associated statistics, performing tests for significance, and plotting the residuals. In SPSS, the main program is REGRESSION. In SAS, the most general program is REG. Other specialized programs such as RSREG, ORTHOREG, GLM, and NLIN are also available; however, readers who are not familiar with the intricate aspects of regression analysis are advised to stick to REG when using SAS. In MINITAB, regression analysis, under the STATS>REGRESSION FUNCTION, can perform simple and multiple analysis. In EXCEL, regression can be assessed from the TOOLS>DATA ANALYSIS menu.

SPSS Windows

The CORRELATIONS program computes Pearson product moment correlations with significance levels. Univariate statistics, covariance, and cross-product deviations may also be requested. Significance levels are included in the output. To select this procedure using SPSS for Windows click

ANALYZE > CORRELATE > BIVARIATE ...

Scatterplots can be obtained by clicking

GRAPHS > SCATTER ...> SIMPLE > DEFINE ...

REGRESSION calculates bivariate and multiple regression equations, associated statistics, and plots. It allows for an easy examination of residuals. This procedure can be run by clicking

ANALYZE > REGRESSION > LINEAR ...

Detailed Steps: Correlation

The following are the detailed steps for running a correlation between attitude toward sports cars and duration of sports car ownership given in Table 18.1. The corresponding screen captures for these steps can be downloaded from the Web site for this book. A positive correlation is to be expected.

1. Select ANALYZE from the SPSS menu bar.
2. Click CORRELATE and then BIVARIATE.
3. Move "Attitude Towards Sports Cars and Duration of Car Ownership" into the VARIABLES box.
4. Check PEARSON under CORRELATION COEFFICIENTS.
5. Check ONE_TAILED under TEST OF SIGNIFICANCE.
6. Check FLAG SIGNIFICANT CORRELATIONS.
7. Click OK.

Detailed Steps: Bivariate and Multiple Regression

The following are the detailed steps for running a bivariate regression with attitude toward sports cars as the dependent variable and duration of sports car ownership as the independent variable using the data of Table 18.1. The corresponding screen captures for these steps can be downloaded from the Web site for this book.

1. Select ANALYZE from the SPSS menu bar.
2. Click REGRESSION and then LINEAR.
3. Move "Attitude Towards Sports Cars" into the DEPENDENT box.
4. Move "Duration of Car Ownership" into the INDEPENDENT(S) box.
5. Select ENTER in the METHOD box.
6. Click on STATISTICS and check ESTIMATES under REGRESSION COEFFICIENTS.
7. Check MODEL FIT.
8. Click CONTINUE.
9. Click OK.

The steps for running multiple regression are similar, except for Step 4. In Step 4, move "Duration of Car Ownership" and "Importance Attached to Performance" into the INDEPENDENT(S) box. The corresponding screen captures for these steps can be downloaded from the Web site for this book.

EXPERIENTIAL LEARNING

Correlation and Regression

Go to the textbook Web site and download the survey used in interviewing recently nonreturning students at Musial University (MU), a public urban university in the mid-sized city of Musial. The administrators at MU were interested in obtaining the perspectives of "drop-out" or "stop-out" students so that the administrators at MU could enhance the programs, facilities, and services at MU. While the actual name of the university has been disguised, the research project and the accompanying data are real. Download the actual survey used in this study, Musial Retention Survey, as well as the SPSS system file, Musial Retention Data.

- **Read Musial Retention Survey.**
- **Open SPSS and read-in your data from Musial Retention Data.**
- **Try to understand the associations for having no football program at MU.**

Focus upon question Q5n ("I would have very much enjoyed having a football team at MU.") and the correlations with this variable. (Try Q5k–good rec facilities, Q5l–great social environment, Q5o–attended many sporting events, Q5x–rich learning environment, Q5aa–felt my progress mattered to MU administrators, and Q5bb–felt I mattered to other students.)

Create a correlation table comprised of Pearson product moment correlations for the seven variables: Q5n, Q5k, Q5l, Q5o, Q5x, Q5aa, and Q5bb. Review the output.

(*What are the* H_0 *and* H_1 *for each of these binary relationships?)*

ANALYZE
  CORRELATE
    BIVARIATE
      BIVARIATE CORRELATIONS window
        Select Q5n, Q5k, Q5l, Q5o, Q5x, Q5aa, and Q5bb.
          Click OK.

- **Multiple Regression**

Using questions 5x as the dependent variable ("The MU learning environment is a rich one."), conduct a multiple regression analysis composed of five independent variables. (Try Q5k–good recreation facilities, Q5l–great social environment, Q5r–convenient location, Q5s–good advising center, and Q5bb–felt I mattered to other students.)

(*What are the* H_0 *and* H_1 *for your regression model?)*
ANALYZE
REGRESSION
LINEAR
DEPENDENT box of the LINEAR REGRESSION window
Enter Q5x ("...learning environment is a rich one.").
INDEPENDENT(S) box of the LINEAR REGRESSION window
Enter all five variables: Q5k, Q5l, Q5r, Q5s, and Q5bb.
Make sure the Method selected is ENTER.
Click the STATISTICS button.
Select DESCRIPTIVES in addition to the default selections.
Click CONTINUE.
Click the OPTIONS button.
Under MISSING VALUES select REPLACE WITH MEAN.
(In this way, you will make sure any missing values receive a mean value.)
Click CONTINUE.
Click OK.
Review your SPSS output.

- **Correlation**

Run the Correlation analysis for the five variables chosen for the previous regression analysis.
ANALYZE
CORRELATE
BIVARIATE
BIVARIATE CORRELATIONS window
Select Q5x, Q5k, Q5l, Q5r, Q5s, and Q5bb.
Click OK.

Compare the binary correlation coefficients of Q5x with Q5k, Q5l, Q5r, Q5s, and Q5bb in the Correlations portion with the Beta values under the Standardized Coefficients column of the Coefficients table for your multiple regression analysis. What did you find? Why is this so?

Extra

As you can sense, there are many analyses to conduct with this data set. Have fun doing cross-tabulations, *t*-tests, and other analyses.

Epilogue

Download Musial Retention Report to glimpse what was presented to the MU administrators in a formal presentation session.

EXCEL

Detailed Steps: Correlation

The following are the detailed steps for running a correlation between attitude toward sports cars and duration of sports car ownership given in Table 18.1. The corresponding screen captures for these steps can be downloaded from the Web site for this book.

1. Select **Tools** (Alt + T).
2. Select **Data Analysis** under Tools.
3. Data Analysis window pops up.
4. Select **Correlation** from Data Analysis window.
5. Click **OK.**
6. **Correlation** pop-up window appears on screen.
7. Correlation window has two portions:
   a. Input
   b. Output Options

8. Input portion asks for two inputs.
   a. Click in the **Input Range** box. Select (highlight) all the rows of data under Attitude and Duation. $B$2:$C$13 should appear on Input Range.
   b. Select **Group by Columns**.
   c. Leave Labels as blank.
9. In the Output portion of pop-up window, select **New Workbook Options.**
10. Click **OK.**

Detailed Steps: Bivariate and Multiple Regression

The following are the detailed steps for running a bivariate regression with attitude toward sports cars as the dependent variable and duration of sports car ownership as the independent variable using the data in Table 18.1. The corresponding screen captures for these steps can be downloaded from the Web site for this book.

1. Select **Tools** (Alt + T).
2. Select **Data Analysis** under Tools.
3. Data Analysis window pops up.
4. Select **Regression** from Data Analysis window.
5. Click **OK.**
6. **Regression** pop-up window appears on screen.
7. Regression window has four portions:
   a. Input
   b. Output Options
   c. Residuals
   d. Normal Probability
8. Input portion asks for four inputs.
   a. Click in the **Input Y Range** box. Select (highlight) all the rows of data under Attitude. $B$2:$B$13 should appear on Input Y Range.
   b. Click in the **Input X Range** box. Select (highlight) all the rows of data under Duration. $C$2:$C$13 should appear on Input X Range.
   c. Leave Labels, Constant is zero, and Confidence Level as blanks.
9. In the Output portion of pop-up window, select **New Workbook Options.**
10. Leave residuals and normal probability as it is.
11. Click **OK.**

The steps for running multiple regression are similar, except for Step 8b. In Step 8b: Click in the **Input X Range** box. Select (highlight) all the rows of data under **Duration** and **Importance**. $C$2:$D$13 should appear on **Input X Range**.

Summary

The product moment correlation coefficient, r, measures the linear association between two metric (interval- or ratio-scaled) variables. Its square, r^2, measures the proportion of variation in one variable explained by the other.

Bivariate regression derives a mathematical equation between a single metric-criterion variable and a single metric-predictor variable. The equation is derived in the form of a straight line by using the least-squares procedure. When the regression is run on standardized data, the intercept assumes a value of 0, and the regression coefficients are called beta weights. The strength of association is measured by the coefficient of determination, r^2, which is obtained by computing a ratio of SS_{reg} to SS_y. Scattergrams of the residuals are useful for examining the appropriateness of the underlying assumptions and the regression model fitted.

Multiple regression involves a single dependent variable and two or more independent variables. The partial regression coefficient, b_1, represents the expected change in Y when X_1 is changed by one unit and X_2 through X_k are held constant. The strength of association is measured by the coefficient of multiple determination, R^2. The significance of the overall regression equation may be tested by the overall F-test. Individual partial regression coefficients may be tested for significance using the t-test.

Key Terms and Concepts

Product moment correlation, 497
Covariance, 498
Regression analysis, 503
Bivariate regression, 504
Bivariate regression model, 504
Scatter diagram, 505
Least-squares procedure, 505
Sum of squared errors, 505
Estimated or predicted value, 506
Nonstandardized regression coefficient, 506
Standardization, 508
Beta coefficient, 508
Standard error, 509
Coefficient of determination, 509
Standard error of estimate, 512
Residual, 512
Multiple regression, 513
Multiple regression model, 513
Partial regression coefficient, 514
Coefficient of multiple determination, 516
Adjusted R^2, 516

Suggested Cases and Video Cases

Cases

3.1 Ford **3.2 Darden** **3.3 Microsoft** **3.5 Advertising**
4.1 Boeing **4.2 Gucci**

Video Cases

3.1 AFLAC **3.2 Honest Tea** **4.1 Subaru** **4.2 Marriott**

Additional cases and video cases are available in the Instructor's Manual and on the instructor and student Web sites.

Live Research: Conducting a Marketing Research Project

1. It is desirable to calculate product moment correlations between all interval-scaled variables. This gives an idea of the correlations between variables.
2. Students should also be encouraged to run several bivariate regressions and to compare these results with the corresponding product moment correlations.
3. Multiple regressions should be run when examining the association between a single dependent variable and several independent variables.

Acronyms

The main features of regression analysis may be summarized by the acronym REGRESSION:

R esidual analysis is useful
E stimation of parameters: solution of simultaneous equations
G eneral model is linear
R^2 strength of association
E rror terms are independent and $N(0, \sigma^2)$
S tandardized regression coefficients
S tandard error of estimate: prediction accuracy
I ndividual coefficients and overall *F*-tests
O ptimal: minimizes total error
N onstandardized regression coefficients

Review Questions

1. What is the product moment correlation coefficient? Does a product moment correlation of zero between two variables imply that the variables are not related to each other?
2. Give an example of a bivariate regression model and identify the dependent and the independent variables.
3. What are the main uses of regression analysis?
4. What is the least-squares procedure?
5. Explain the meaning of standardized regression coefficients.
6. How is the strength of association measured in bivariate regression? In multiple regression?

7. What is meant by prediction accuracy?
8. What is the standard error of estimate?
9. What assumptions underlie the error term?
10. What is multiple regression? How is it different from bivariate regression?
11. Explain the meaning of a partial regression coefficient. Why is it called such?
12. State the null hypothesis in testing the significance of the overall multiple regression equation. How is this null hypothesis tested?

Applied Problems

1. A major supermarket chain wants to determine the effect of promotion on relative competitiveness. Data were obtained from 15 states on the promotional expenses relative to a major competitor (competitor expenses = 100) and on sales relative to this competitor (competitor sales = 100).

State No.	Relative Promotional Expense	Relative Sales
1	95	98
2	92	94
3	103	110
4	115	125
5	77	82
6	79	84
7	105	112
8	94	99
9	85	93
10	101	107
11	106	114
12	120	132
13	118	129
14	75	79
15	99	105

You are assigned the task of telling the manager whether there is any relationship between relative promotional expense and relative sales.

a. Plot the relative sales (Y-axis) against the relative promotional expense (X-axis), and interpret this diagram.
b. Which measure would you use to determine whether there is a relationship between the two variables? Why?
c. Run a bivariate regression analysis of relative sales on relative promotional expense.
d. Interpret the regression coefficients.
e. Is the regression relationship significant?
f. If the company matched the competitor in terms of promotional expense (if the relative promotional expense was 100), what would the company's relative sales be?
g. Interpret the resulting r^2.

2. To understand the role of quality and price in influencing the patronage of drugstores, 14 major stores in a large metropolitan area were rated in terms of preference to shop, quality of merchandise, and fair pricing. All the ratings were obtained on an 11-point scale, with higher numbers indicating more positive ratings.

Store No.	Preference	Quality	Price
1	6	5	3
2	9	6	11
3	8	6	4
4	3	2	1
5	10	6	11
6	4	3	1
7	5	4	7
8	2	1	4
9	11	9	8
10	9	5	10
11	10	8	8
12	2	1	5
13	9	8	5
14	5	3	2

a. Run a multiple regression analysis explaining store preference in terms of quality of merchandise and pricing.
b. Interpret the partial regression coefficients.
c. Determine the significance of the overall regression.
d. Determine the significance of the partial regression coefficients.

3. Imagine that you've come across a magazine article reporting the following relationship between annual expenditure on prepared dinners (*PD*) and annual income (*INC*):

$$PD = 23.4 + 0.003\ INC$$

The coefficient of the *INC* variable is reported as significant.

a. Does this relationship seem plausible? Is it possible to have a coefficient that is small in magnitude and yet significant?
b. From the information given, can you tell how good the estimated model is?
c. What are the expected expenditures on *PD*s of a family earning $30,000?
d. If a family earning $40,000 spent $130 annually on *PD*s, what is the residual?
e. What is the meaning of a negative residual?

4. Conduct the following analyses for the Internet usage data given in Applied Problems, Exercise 6, in Chapter 16.

a. Find the simple correlations between the following sets of variables: Internet usage and attitude toward Internet, Internet usage and attitude toward technology, and attitude toward Internet and attitude toward technology. Interpret the results.

b. Run a bivariate regression with Internet usage as the dependent variable and attitude toward Internet as the independent variable. Interpret the results.

c. Run a bivariate regression with Internet usage as the dependent variable and attitude toward technology as the independent variable. Interpret the results.

d. Run a multiple regression with Internet usage as the dependent variable, and attitude toward Internet and attitude toward technology as the independent variables. Interpret the results.

5. Conduct the following analyses for the preference of the outdoor-lifestyle data given in Applied Problems, Exercise 8, of Chapter 17. Recall that

V1 = preference for an outdoor lifestyle

V2 = enjoying nature

V3 = relating to the weather

V4 = living in harmony with the environment

V5 = exercising regularly

V6 = meeting other people

a. Calculate the simple correlations between V1 to V6 and interpret the results.

b. Run a bivariate regression with preference for an outdoor lifestyle (V1) as the dependent variable and the importance of enjoying nature (V2) as the independent variable. Interpret the results.

c. Run a multiple regression with preference for an outdoor lifestyle as the dependent variable and V2 to V6 as the independent variables. Interpret the results. Compare the coefficients for V2 obtained in the bivariate and the multiple regressions.

6. In a pretest, data were obtained from 20 respondents on preferences for sneakers on a seven-point scale, 1 = not at all preferred, 7 = greatly preferred (V1). The respondents also provided their evaluations of the sneakers on comfort (V2), style (V3), and durability (V4), also on seven-point scales, 1 = poor, and 7 = excellent. The resulting data follow.

V1	V2	V3	V4
6.00	6.00	3.00	5.00
2.00	3.00	2.00	4.00
7.00	5.00	6.00	7.00
4.00	6.00	4.00	5.00
1.00	3.00	2.00	2.00
6.00	5.00	6.00	7.00
5.00	6.00	7.00	5.00
7.00	3.00	5.00	4.00
2.00	4.00	6.00	3.00
3.00	5.00	3.00	6.00
1.00	3.00	2.00	3.00
5.00	4.00	5.00	4.00
2.00	2.00	1.00	5.00
4.00	5.00	4.00	6.00
6.00	5.00	4.00	7.00
3.00	3.00	4.00	2.00
4.00	4.00	3.00	2.00
3.00	4.00	3.00	2.00
4.00	4.00	3.00	2.00
2.00	3.00	2.00	4.00

a. Calculate the simple correlations between V1 to V4 and interpret the results.

b. Run a bivariate regression with preference for sneakers (V1) as the dependent variable and evaluation on comfort (V2) as the independent variable. Interpret the results.

c. Run a bivariate regression with preference for sneakers (V1) as the dependent variable and evaluation on style (V3) as the independent variable. Interpret the results.

d. Run a bivariate regression with preference for sneakers (V1) as the dependent variable and evaluation on durability (V4) as the independent variable. Interpret the results.

e. Run a multiple regression with preference for sneakers (V1) as the dependent variable and V2 to V4 as the independent variables. Interpret the results. Compare the coefficients for V2, V3, and V4 obtained in the bivariate and the multiple regressions.

Group Discussion

1. As a small group, discuss the following statement: "Regression is such a basic technique that it should always be used in analyzing data."

2. As a small group, discuss the relationship between bivariate correlation, bivariate regression, and multiple regression.

EXHIBIT 18.1 Computer Programs for Correlations

SPSS

The CORRELATIONS program computes Pearson product moment correlations with significance levels. Univariate statistics, covariance, and cross-product deviations may also be requested. Significance levels are included in the output.

SAS

CORR produces metric and nonmetric correlations between variables, including Pearson's product moment correlation.

MINITAB

Correlation can be computed using STAT>BASIC STATISTICS>CORRELATION function. It calculates Pearson's product moment using all the columns.

EXCEL

Correlations can be determined in EXCEL by using the TOOLS> DATA ANALYSIS>CORRELATION function. Use the Correlation Worksheet function when a correlation coefficient for two cell ranges is needed.

EXHIBIT 18.2 Computer Programs for Regression

SPSS

REGRESSION calculates bivariate and multiple regression equations, associated statistics, and plots. It allows for an easy examination of residuals. Regression statistics can be requested with PLOT, which produces simple scattergrams and some other types of plots.

SAS

REG is a general-purpose regression procedure that fits bivariate and multiple regression models using the least-squares procedure. All the associated statistics are computed, and residuals can be plotted.

MINITAB

Regression analysis, under the STATS>REGRESSION function can perform simple and multiple analysis. The output includes a linear regression equation, table of coefficients, *R* square, *R* squared adjusted, analysis of variance table, and a table of fits and residuals that provide unusual observations. Other available features include fitted line plot and residual plots.

EXCEL

Regression can be assessed from the TOOLS>DATA ANALYSIS menu. Depending on the features selected, the output can consist of a summary output table, including an ANOVA table, a standard error of *y* estimate, coefficients, standard error of coefficients, R^2 values, and the number of observations. In addition, the function computes a residual output table, residual plot, line fit plot, normal probability plot, and a two-column probability data output table.

CHAPTER

19

Report Preparation and Presentation

"In any report or presentation, get right to the point in why these results matter to the firm. The tendency for beginners is to present all the answers and all the data, whether relevant or not. The role of the analyst is to boil, filter and distill, so the audience receives the pure distillation."

JERRY THOMAS, *President/CEO, Decision Analyst, Inc., Arlington, TX*

OPENING QUESTIONS

1. What process should be followed in preparing and presenting the final report?
2. Are any guidelines available for writing a report that includes graphs and tables?
3. How should an oral presentation be made, and what are some of the principles involved?
4. Why is the follow-up with the client important, and what assistance should be given to the client in implementing and evaluating the research project?
5. How is the report preparation and presentation process different in international marketing research?
6. How does technology facilitate report preparation and presentation?
7. What ethical issues are related to the interpretation and reporting of the research process and findings?

Research Reports Make United's Friendly Skies Even More Friendly

United Airlines EasyUpdate had more than 250,000 subscribers registered and delivered over 10 million messages in 2003. EasyUpdate is United's notification system, which delivers departure and arrival information, delays or cancellation updates, as well as rebooking and seat upgrade confirmations. Updates can be sent directly to mobile phones, pagers, personal data assistants, e-mail addresses, Microsoft .Net Alerts, or fax machines. The vice president of United Airline's customer satisfaction stated, "Our investment in this leading-edge technology further demonstrates United Airline's commitment to providing our customers with an airport experience that involves less hassle and a faster check-in experience."

United Airlines does indeed put a premium on customer satisfaction. For its in-flight customer satisfaction tracking program, United surveys passengers on some 900 flights per month using a four-page scannable questionnaire. It administers 192,000 questionnaires in nine languages to people traveling to 40 different countries. The survey covers passenger satisfaction with the entire air travel process: reservations, airport service, flight attendants, meal service, and the aircraft itself.

The marketing research department at United prepares a monthly report summarizing the customer satisfaction data for about 100 people worldwide, including airport, country, and regional managers, executive management, and others at United's headquarters. The report is very thorough and includes a title page, table of contents, executive summary, problem definition, approach, research design, data analysis, results, and conclusions and recommendations. Several tables and graphs are prepared to enhance the clarity of the findings. The report findings are also available online.

After issuing the monthly report, the marketing research department handles several requests from internal customers (i.e., various departments within United Airlines) for additional analysis. For example, the marketing department may request a breakdown of customer satisfaction rating by demographic characteristics for a specific route (city pair), such as Atlanta to Los Angeles. Since the data can be linked to operational data, such as arrival and departure times and number of passengers, United's researchers can dig deep to answer questions from internal customers. Alex Maggi, United's senior staff analyst for market research, says, "We have often used the data to identify the reasons why some ratings might differ from one airport to another or one segment to another, by looking at customer mix, by linking survey data to operational data. For example, we can take ratings for a given flight and link them to the on-time performance of the flight in that market and we can show that when on-time performance went down so did the ratings in specific categories."

This monthly report on customer satisfaction and the follow-up activities that it generates has helped United Airlines to become much more customer focused, thereby improving its competitive positioning in a very demanding industry and making its friendly skies even more friendly.[1] •

Overview

Report preparation and presentation constitutes the sixth and final step of the marketing research project. It follows problem definition, developing an approach, research design formulation, field work, and data preparation and analysis. This chapter describes the importance of this final step as well as a process for report preparation and presentation. Figure 19.1 briefly explains the focus of the chapter, the relation of this chapter to the

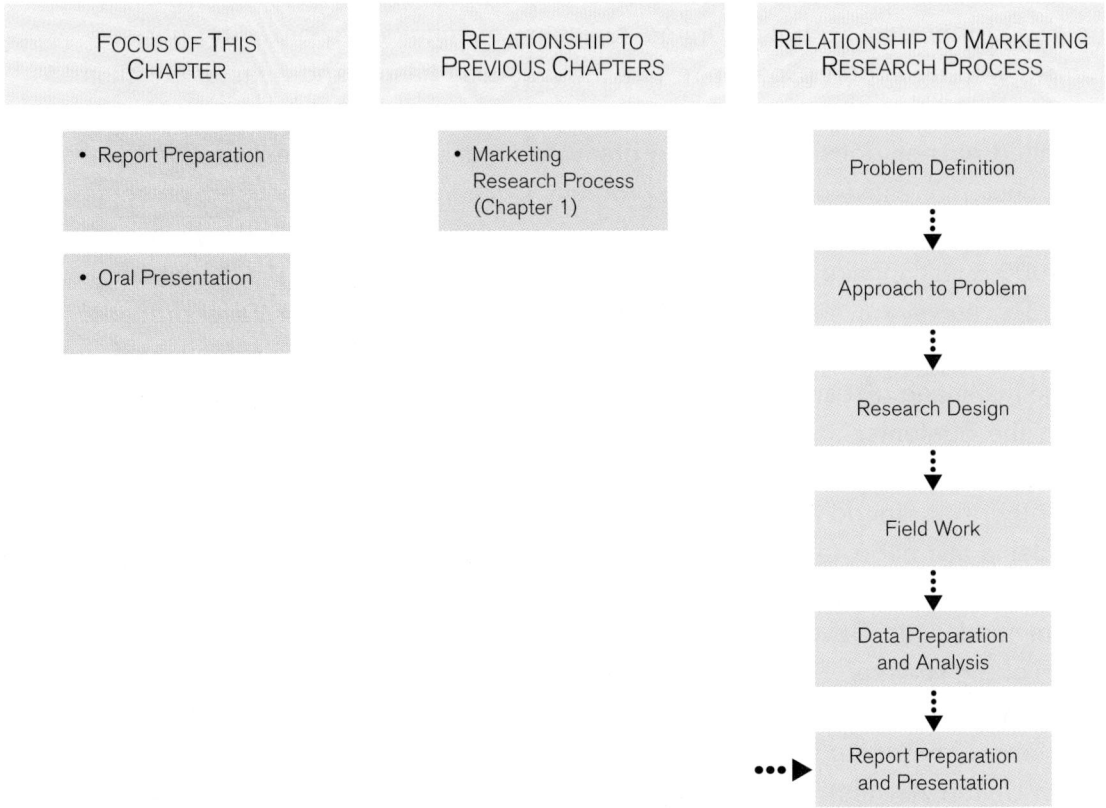

Figure 19.1

Relationship of Report Preparation and Presentation to Previous Chapters and the Marketing Research Process

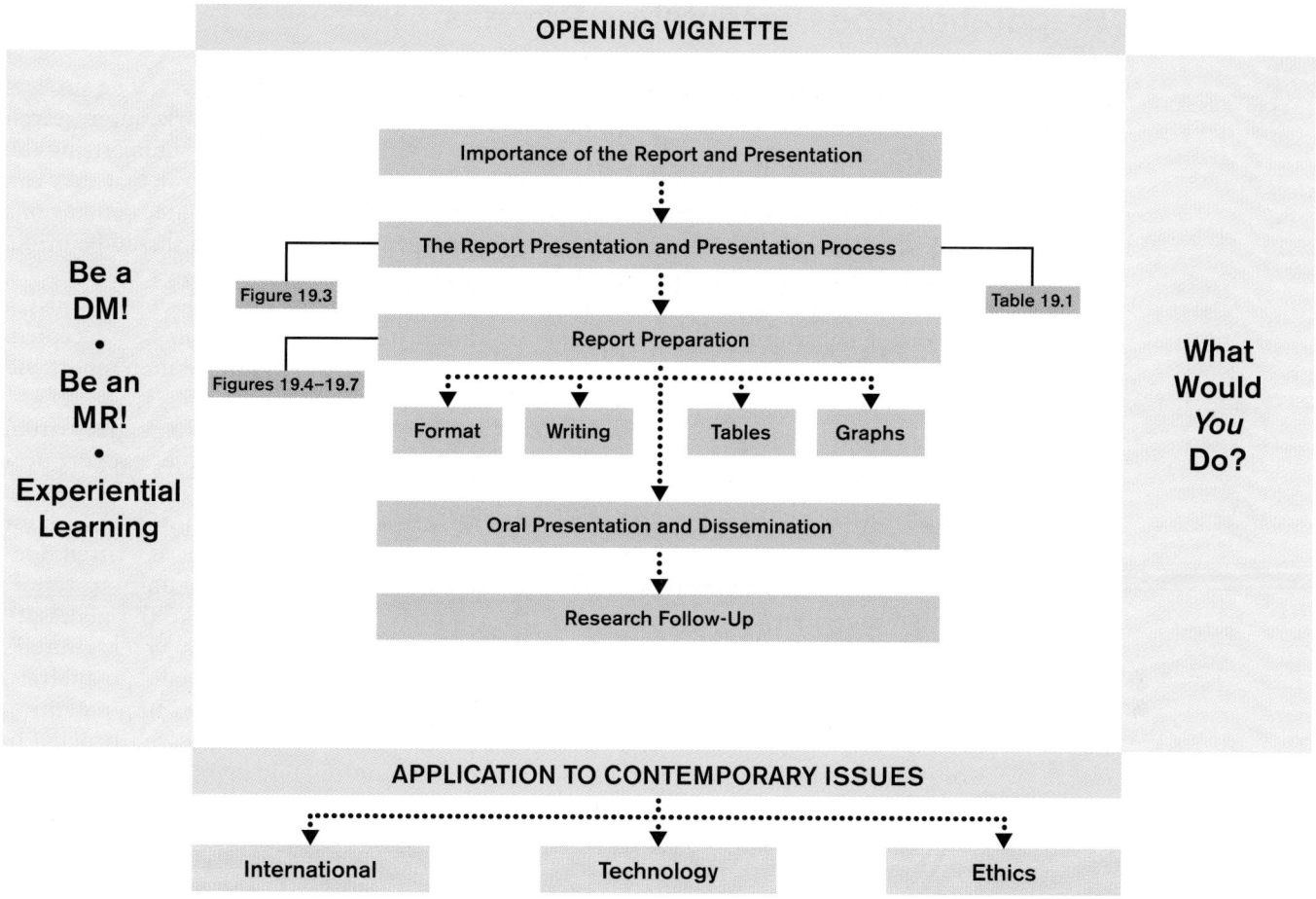

Figure 19.2

Report Preparation and Presentation: An Overview

previous ones, and the steps of the marketing research process on which this chapter concentrates. As illustrated in the opening vignette, well-prepared marketing research reports and associated follow-up activities add substantial value to the marketing research process.

In this chapter, we provide guidelines for report preparation, including report writing and preparing tables and graphs. We discuss oral presentation of the report. We describe research follow-up, including assisting the client and evaluating the research process. We discuss special considerations for report preparation and presentation in international marketing research and identify applications of technology and ethics. Figure 19.2 gives an overview of the topics discussed in this chapter and how they flow from one to the next.

Importance of the Report and Presentation

The report and its presentation are the tangible products of the research effort, and the report serves as a historical record of the project. If inadequate attention is paid to this step, the value of the project to management will be greatly diminished. The involvement of many marketing managers in the project is limited to the written report and the oral presentation. These managers evaluate the quality of the entire project based on the quality of the report and presentation. Management's decision to undertake marketing research in the future or to use the particular research supplier again will be influenced by the perceived usefulness of the report and the presentation. For these reasons, report preparation and presentation assume great importance.

The Report Preparation and Presentation Process

Figure 19.3 illustrates the report preparation and presentation process. The process begins with interpreting the results of data analysis in light of the marketing research problem, approach, research design, and field work. Instead of merely summarizing the statistical results, the researcher should present the findings in such a way that they can be used directly as input into decision making. Wherever appropriate, conclusions should be drawn and recommendations that management can act upon should be made. Before writing the report, the researcher should discuss the major findings, conclusions, and recommendations with the client's key decision makers. These discussions play a major role in ensuring that the report meets the client's needs and is ultimately accepted. These discussions should confirm specific dates for the delivery of the written report and other data.

The entire marketing research project should be summarized in a single written report or in several reports addressed to different readers. For example, a report prepared for top management should emphasize the strategic aspects of the research project rather than the operating details. The reverse is true for a report prepared for operating managers. Generally, an oral presentation supplements these written documents. After the presentation, the client should be given an opportunity to reflect on the report and the project. After that, the researcher should take the necessary follow-up actions. Such actions are found in the opening vignette, in which United's marketing research department handles several requests for additional data analysis. The researcher should assist the client in understanding the report, implementing the findings, undertaking further research, and evaluating the research process in retrospect. The importance of the researcher being intimately involved in the report preparation and presentation process is highlighted by the following Research in Action example.

Figure 19.3
The Report Preparation and Presentation Process

RESEARCH IN ACTION

Focus Group Moderators' Ghostwriters Can Shortchange Clients

Thomas Greenbaum, president of Groups Plus Inc. of Wilton, Connecticut, a market research company focusing on qualitative research, notes a disturbing trend in recent years in the focus-group service sector. Greenbaum asserts that some moderators of focus groups misrepresent their work to clients because their reports are actually written by ghostwriters who did not participate in the focus-group sessions.

According to Greenbaum, perhaps more than half of moderators use ghostwriters to develop their reports for clients. Often, junior researchers learning the business or part-time employees write these ghostwritten reports. Greenbaum criticizes such ghostwriting because those who merely listen to audiotapes or view videotapes of focus-group sessions cannot always accurately report the nonverbal reactions of focus-group participants. Greenbaum calls upon moderators to be forthright with clients about the authorship of focus-group reports. He also calls upon clients to be more demanding of their contracted research teams.

"Although some people in the industry defend ghostwriting by saying they always review the reports before they are sent to the client, or perhaps even write certain key sections, this practice must be looked at carefully by clients who use focus-group research," Greenbaum said. "If the clients know in advance that their reports will be written by someone else, it is clearly less of a problem, but they still do not get the best effort from their research consultants."[2]

Report Preparation

Researchers differ in the way they prepare a research report. The personality, background, expertise, and responsibility of the researcher, along with the decision maker (DM) to whom the report is addressed, interact to give each report a unique character. Nonetheless, there are guidelines for formatting and writing reports and designing tables and graphs.

Report Format

Report formats are likely to vary with the researcher or the marketing research firm conducting the project, the client for whom the project is being conducted, and the nature of the project itself. Hence, the following is intended as a guideline from which the researcher can develop a format for the research project at hand. Most research reports, as in the opening vignette, include most of the following elements.

I. Title page
II. Letter of transmittal
III. Letter of authorization
IV. Table of contents
V. List of tables
VI. List of graphs
VII. List of appendices
VIII. List of exhibits
IX. Executive summary
    a. Major findings
    b. Conclusions
    c. Recommendations
X. Problem definition
    a. Background to the problem
    b. Statement of the problem
XI. Approach to the problem
XII. Research design
    a. Type of research design
    b. Information needs
    c. Data collection from secondary sources

d. Data collection from primary sources
e. Scaling techniques
f. Questionnaire development and pretesting
g. Sampling techniques
h. Field work

XIII. Data analysis
a. Methodology
b. Plan of data analysis

XIV. Results

XV. Limitations and caveats

XVI. Conclusions and recommendations

XVII. Exhibits
a. Questionnaires and forms
b. Statistical output
c. Lists
d. Bibliography

Sections I to IX constitute the prefatory parts, sections X through XVI the main body, and section XVII the appended parts of the report. This format closely follows the earlier steps of the marketing research process. The format should be flexible, however, so that it can accommodate the unique features of a specific project. For instance, the results may be presented in several chapters of the report. For example, in a national survey, data analysis may be conducted for the overall sample, and the data for each geographic region may be analyzed separately. In this case, the results can be presented in five chapters instead of one.

Title Page The title page should include the title of the report, information (name, address, and telephone numbers) about the researcher or organization conducting the research, the name of the client for whom the report was prepared, and the date of release. The title should also indicate the nature of the project.

letter of transmittal
A letter that delivers the report to the client and summarizes the researcher's overall experience with the project without mentioning the findings.

Letter of Transmittal A formal report generally contains a **letter of transmittal** that delivers the report to the client and summarizes the researcher's overall experience with the project. The letter should also identify the need for further action on the part of the client, such as implementation of the findings or further research that should be undertaken.

Letter of Authorization The client writes a letter of authorization to the researcher before work on the project begins. It authorizes the researcher to proceed with the project and specifies its scope and the terms of the contract. Often, it is sufficient to refer to the letter of authorization in the letter of transmittal. Sometimes, however, it is necessary to include a copy of the letter of authorization in the report. The letter of transmittal and the letter of authorization may be eliminated in the case of recurring projects conducted internally by the marketing research department of the firm, as in the case of United Airlines in the opening vignette.

Table of Contents The table of contents should list the topics covered and the appropriate page numbers. In most reports, only the major headings and subheadings are included. A list of tables, list of graphs, list of appendices, and list of exhibits follow the table of contents.

Executive Summary The executive summary is an extremely important part of the report, as this is often the only portion of the report that executives read. The summary should concisely describe the problem, the approach, the research design, major results, conclusions, and recommendations. The executive summary should be written after the rest of the report because it is much easier for the writer to read through the body of the report and then summarize the most important points.

Problem Definition This section of the report provides background on the problem, highlights discussions with the decision makers and industry experts, and discusses the secondary data analysis, the qualitative research that was conducted, and the factors that were considered. It should contain a clear statement of the management-decision problem and the marketing research problem (see Chapter 2).

Approach to the Problem This section should discuss the broad approach that was adopted in addressing the problem. It should also contain a description of the theoretical foundations that guided the research, any analytical models formulated, research questions, and hypotheses.

Research Design The section on research design should specify the details of how the research was conducted (see Chapters 3 through 13). This should include the nature of the research design adopted, information needed, data collection from secondary and primary sources, scaling techniques, questionnaire development and pretesting, sampling techniques, and field work. These topics should be presented in a nontechnical, easy-to-understand manner. The technical details should be included in an appendix. This section of the report should justify the specific methods selected.

Data Analysis This section should describe the plan of data analysis and justify the data analysis strategy and techniques used. The techniques used for analysis should be described in simple, nontechnical terms.

Results This section is normally the longest part of the report and may comprise several chapters. Often, the results are presented not only at the aggregate level but also at the subgroup (market segment, geographical area, etc.) level. The results should be organized in a coherent and logical way. The presentation of the results should be geared directly to the components of the marketing research problem and the information needs that were identified. The details should be presented in tables and graphs and the main findings discussed in the text.

Limitations and Caveats All marketing research projects have limitations caused by time, budget, and other organizational constraints. Furthermore, the research design adopted may be limited in terms of the various types of errors (see Chapter 3) that may be serious enough to warrant discussion. This section should be written with great care and a balanced perspective. On one hand, the researcher must make sure that management does not overly rely on the results or use them for unintended purposes, such as projecting them to unintended populations. On the other hand, this section should not erode their confidence in the research or unduly minimize its importance.

Conclusions and Recommendations Presenting a mere summary of the statistical results is not sufficient. The researcher should interpret the results in light of the problem being addressed to arrive at major conclusions. Based on the results and conclusions, the researcher may make recommendations to the decision makers. Sometimes marketing researchers are not asked to make recommendations because they research only one area but do not understand the bigger picture at the client firm. If recommendations are made, they should be feasible, practical, actionable, and directly usable as inputs into managerial decision making. It is very important that the report of a conclusive research project (see Chapter 3) be written in such a way that the findings can be used as input into managerial decision making. Otherwise the report is unlikely to get undue attention from management, as illustrated by the following Research in Action example.

Report Writing

A report should be written for specific readers—the marketing managers who will use the results. The report should take into account the readers' technical sophistication and interest in the project, as well as the circumstances under which they will read the report and how they will use it.

Technical jargon should be avoided. The researcher is often required to cater to the needs of several audiences with different levels of technical sophistication and interest in the project. Such conflicting needs may be met by including different sections in the report for different readers or separate reports entirely.

The report should be easy to follow. It should be structured logically and written clearly. An excellent check on the clarity of a report is to have two or three people who are unfamiliar with the project read it and offer critical comments. Several revisions of the report may be needed before the final document emerges.

RESEARCH IN ACTION

Does Management Read Marketing Research Reports?

Every profession has its nagging doubts. Teachers sometimes wonder if their students are really learning anything; police officers occasionally question whether they're actually reducing crime. Once in a while, marketing researchers have a sneaking suspicion that no one is reading their reports.

Determined to resolve this doubt, one marketing researcher inserted a very undignified photo of himself from a recent office party in the middle of his report. Weeks went by as the report was passed through brand and category management with no response. Finally, the senior vice president of advertising called to ask if he needed a vacation. Evidently, this senior vice president was the only one who had read the report in detail.

Who is responsible when research reports are ignored–the research department or management? According to a study recently released by the Advertising Research Foundation and the American Marketing Association, most marketing managers truly believe that marketing research can be valuable. They also claim that most of what they see isn't delivering the kind of information they need to make business decisions. Thus, the responsibility of writing readable reports lies with marketing researchers.[3]

Objectivity is a virtue that should guide report writing. The report should accurately present the methodology, results, and conclusions of the project without slanting the findings to conform to the expectations of management.

It is important to reinforce key information in the text with tables, graphs, pictures, maps, and other visual devices. Visual aids can greatly facilitate communication and add to the clarity and impact of the report. The appearance of a report is also important. The report should be professionally reproduced with quality paper, typing, and binding. Guidelines for tabular and graphical presentation are discussed next.

BE an MR!

Visit Gallup's Web site (www.gallup.com) and search for the recent reports posted on this Web site. Many of these can be found as the lead story or a piece in *The Gallup Management Journal.* What can you learn about report writing from these reports?

Critically evaluate, from a researcher's perspective, the format of one of the reports posted at Gallup's Web site.

BE a DM!

As the marketing manager for whom the Gallup report was meant, how useful do you find the report you considered?

Guidelines for Tables

Statistical tables are a vital part of the report and deserve special attention (see opening vignette). We illustrate the guidelines for tables using the data for Hewlett-Packard sales reported in Table 19.1. The numbers in parentheses in the following paragraphs refer to the numbered sections of the table.

Title and Number Every table should have a number (1a) and title (1b). The title should be brief yet clearly describe the information provided. Arabic numbers are used to identify tables so that they can be referred to easily in the text.

Arrangement of Data Items Data should be arranged in a table to emphasize the most significant aspect of the data. For example, when the data pertain to time, the items should be arranged by appropriate time period. When order of magnitude is most

Table 19.1

Hewlett-Packard Revenues by Business Segment: 2003

Business Segment	PERCENTAGE REVENUE (%) 2003
Imaging and Printing Group	31
Personal Systems Group	29
Enterprise Systems Group	20
HP Services	17
Other*	3
Total	100

* Includes all other products

Source: The 2003 Annual Report, Hewlett-Packard Company.

important, the data items should be arranged in that order (2a). If ease of locating items is critical, an alphabetical arrangement is most appropriate.

Basis of Measurement The basis or unit of measurement should be clearly stated (3a).

Leaders, Rulings, Spaces **Leaders**—dots or hyphens used to lead the eye horizontally—impart uniformity and improve readability (4a). Instead of ruling the table horizontally or vertically, use white spaces (4b) to set off data items. Skipping lines after different sections of the data can also assist the eye. Horizontal rules (4c) are often used after the headings.

leaders
Dots or hyphens that are used in a table to lead the eye horizontally, impart uniformity, and improve readability.

Explanations and Comments: Headings, Stubs, and Footnotes Explanations and comments clarifying the table can be provided in the form of captions, stubs, and footnotes. Designations placed over the vertical columns are called *headings* (5a). Designations placed in the left-hand column are called **stubs** (5b). Information that cannot be incorporated into the table should be explained by footnotes (5c). Letters or symbols should be used for footnotes rather than numbers. The footnotes should come after the main table but before the source note.

stubs
Designations placed in the left-hand column of a table.

Sources of the Data If the data contained in the table are secondary, the source of data should be cited (6a).

Guidelines for Graphs

As a general rule, graphic aids should be used whenever practical, as in the opening vignette. Graphical display of information can effectively complement the text and tables to enhance clarity of communication and impact. As the saying goes, a picture is worth a thousand words. The guidelines for preparing graphs are similar to those for tables. Therefore, this section focuses on the different types of graphical aids. We illustrate several of these using the data from Table 19.1 and other data for Hewlett-Packard (HP) reported in Table 19.2.[4]

Table 19.2

Hewlett-Packard Sales: 1999–2003

Year	Net Revenues (Billions of Dollars)
1999	42.4
2000	48.8
2001	81.1*
2002	72.4*
2003	73.7*

*Combined company (HP and Compaq) results

Source: The 2003, 2002, 2000, and 1999 Annual Reports, Hewlett-Packard Company.

Graphs can be used to highlight the sales of Hewlett-Packard.

Geographic and Other Maps Geographic and other maps, such as product positioning maps, can communicate relative location and other comparative information. Geographic maps can pertain to countries, states, counties, sales territories, and other divisions. For example, suppose the researcher wanted to display the percentage of HP revenues by business segment for each state in the United States. This information could be effectively communicated in a map in which each state is divided into four areas, proportionate to the percentage sales for each of the major product lines of HP: imaging and printing, personal systems, enterprise systems, and services. Each area should be displayed in a different color or pattern.

pie chart
A round chart divided into sections.

Pie Charts In a **pie chart**, also called a *round chart*, the area of each section, as a percentage of the total area of the circle, reflects the percentage associated with the value of a specific variable. A pie chart is not useful for displaying relationships over time or relationships among several variables. As a general guideline, a pie chart should not require more than seven sections. Figure 19.4 shows a pie chart for HP revenues by business segment for 2003 as presented in Table 19.1.

line chart
A chart that connects a series of data points using continuous lines.

Line Charts A **line chart** connects a series of data points using continuous lines. This is an attractive way of illustrating trends and changes over time (Figure 19.5). Several

Figure 19.4

Pie Chart of 2003 Hewlett-Packard Revenues by Business Segment

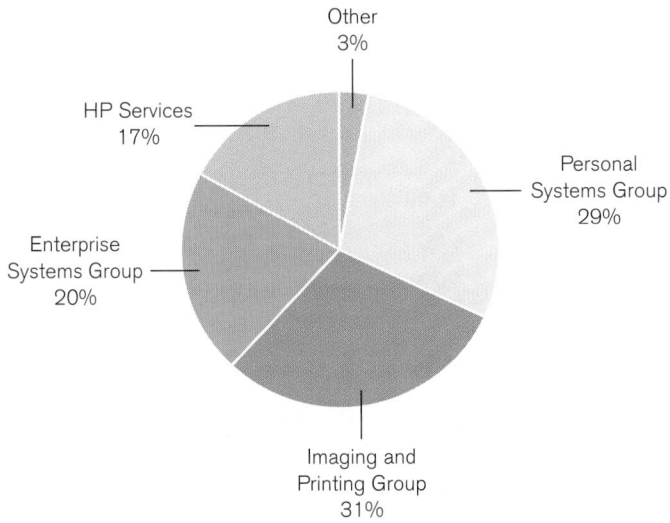

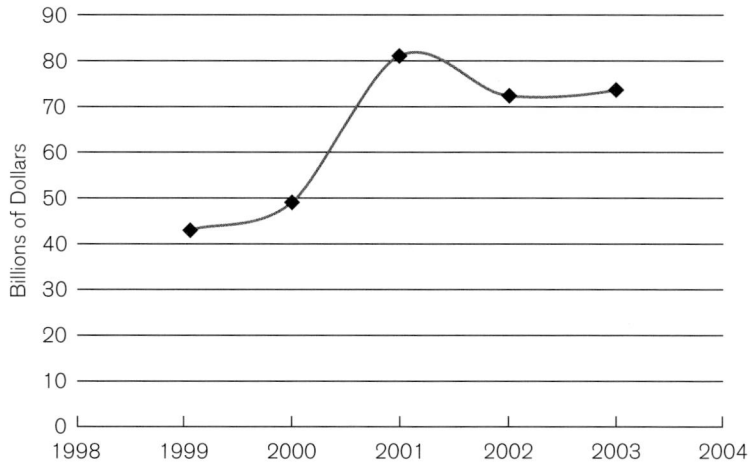

Figure 19.5
Line Chart of Total Hewlett-Packard Net Revenues

series can be compared on the same chart, and forecasts, interpolations, and extrapolations can be shown. If several series are displayed simultaneously, each line should have a distinctive color or form.

Pictographs A **pictograph** uses small pictures or symbols to display the data. As Figure 19.6 shows, pictographs do not depict results precisely. Therefore, caution should always be exercised when using them.

pictograph
A graphical depiction that makes use of small pictures or symbols to display the data.

Histograms and Bar Charts A **bar chart** displays data in various bars that may be positioned horizontally or vertically. Bar charts can be used to present absolute and relative magnitudes, differences, and changes. The **histogram** is a vertical bar chart where the height of the bars represents the relative or cumulative frequency of occurrence of a specific variable (Figure 19.7).

bar chart
A chart that displays data in bars positioned horizontally or vertically.

histogram
A vertical bar chart in which the height of the bars represents the relative or cumulative frequency of occurrence.

Schematic Figures and Flow Charts Schematic figures and flow charts take on a number of different forms. They can be used to display the steps or components of a process, as in Figure 19.3, or they can be used as classification diagrams. Examples of classification charts for classifying secondary data were provided in Chapter 4 (Figures 4.3 to 4.6).

BE an MR!

Visit Coca-Cola's Web site (www.cocacola.com) and search for the company's latest annual report.

Critically evaluate the use of graphs in Coca-Cola's latest annual report. What additional graphs would you construct?

BE a DM!

As the vice president of marketing, how useful do you find the graphs in Coca-Cola's latest annual report?

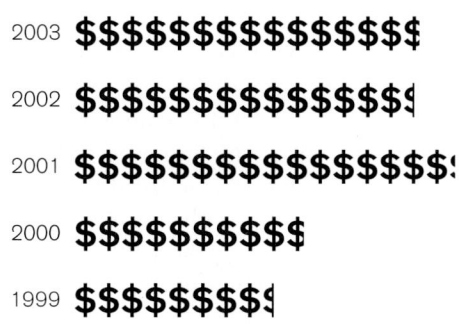

Figure 19.6
A Pictograph of Hewlett-Packard Sales

Figure 19.7

Histogram of Hewlett-Packard's Net Revenues

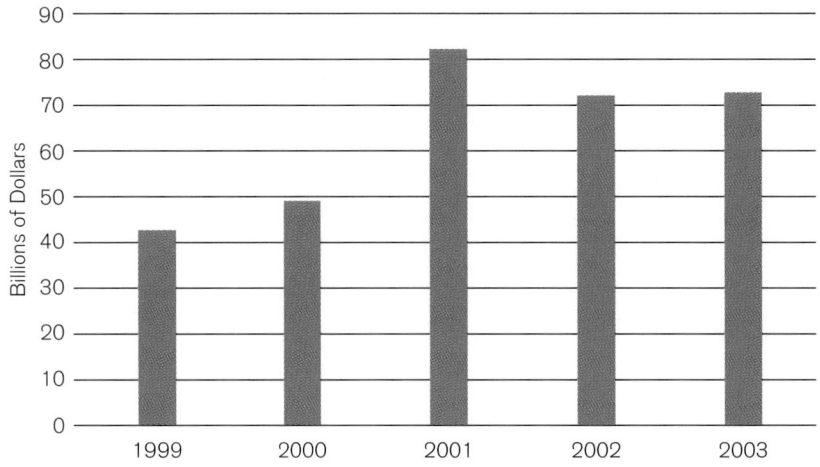

Oral Presentation and Dissemination

The researcher should present the entire marketing research project to the management of the client firm. This presentation will help management understand and accept the written report. Any preliminary questions that the management may have can be addressed in the presentation. Since many executives form their first and lasting impressions about the project based on the presentation, its importance cannot be overemphasized.

The key to an effective presentation is preparation. A written script or detailed outline should be prepared following the format of the written report. The presentation must be geared to the audience. For this purpose, the researcher should determine their backgrounds, interests, and involvement in the project, as well as the extent to which they are likely to be affected by it. For example, a presentation prepared for the advertising department should put more emphasis on advertising decisions, including budget, media, copy, and execution details. The presentation should be rehearsed several times before it is made to management.

Visual aids, such as tables and graphs, should be displayed with a variety of media. It is important to maintain eye contact and interact with the audience during the presentation. Sufficient opportunity should be provided for questions, both during and after the presentation. The presentation should be made interesting and convincing with the use of appropriate stories, examples, experiences, and quotations. Filler words like "uh, " "y'know," and "all right" should not be used.

"tell 'em" principle
An effective guideline for structuring a presentation. This principle states: (1) tell 'em what you're going to tell 'em, (2) tell 'em, and (3) tell 'em what you've told 'em.

"KISS 'em" principle
A principle of report presentation that states Keep It Simple and Straightforward.

The **"tell 'em" principle** is effective for structuring a presentation. This principle states: (1) tell 'em what you're going to tell 'em; (2) tell 'em; and (3) tell 'em what you've told 'em. Another useful guideline is the **"KISS 'em" principle**, which states: **K**eep **I**t **S**imple and **S**traightforward.

Body language is also important. It helps speakers to convey their ideas more emphatically. The body language can reinforce the issue or the point the speaker is trying to communicate to the audience. The speaker should vary the volume, pitch, voice quality, articulation, and rate while speaking. The presentation should terminate with a strong closing. To stress its importance, a top-level manager in the client's organization should sponsor the presentation.

TNS, a marketing research firm, conducted a research project to measure the relative effectiveness of television, print, and radio as advertising media for a client firm. They also assessed the effectiveness of 10 TV commercials, radio commercials, and print ads. Given the nature of the project, the oral presentation of the report was particularly important in communicating the findings. In addition to a PowerPoint presentation, TNS used a videocassette recorder (for playing TV commercials), a tape recorder (for playing radio commercials), and a story board (for showing print ads). The presentation was made to the client's top corporate officers, consisting of the president, all vice presidents, and all assistant vice presidents at one of their monthly meetings.[5]

RESEARCH IN ACTION

Important Presentation Realities

How many minutes would a research team that worked on a months-long consumer attitudes research project be given to brief the CEO of a Fortune 500 company, such as the Ford Motor Company? One hour? Thirty minutes? Both of these estimates are far above what is actually done. According to Mary Klupp, a veteran researcher with the Ford Motor Company and Director of Global Consumer Insights for Ford Financial, researchers would be allowed a maximum of 12 minutes. Other senior executives would give researchers a 15-minute time block.[6] The CEO's likely expectation from any research briefing is as follows:

- Remind me what this is about again.
- In our last communication, what did we agree you, the researcher, should do? What decision should I make based on these research results?
- How confident are you in making the recommendations based on this research?
- What will be the impact on sales/profits or our workforce?
- What were the most important numbers (results) I need to know? (Give them to me in percentages, so that I will be able to make comparisons with other information I have already in that form.)

To answer these questions effectively, the researcher needs to apply powerful thinking about how the results of extensive analysis can be linked to the issues facing the CEO. This will lead to the greatest benefit of research in that the CEO can greatly increase the likelihood of executing the right decisions or of capitalizing on valuable opportunities.

The dissemination of the research results should go beyond the oral presentation. The marketing research report, or at least sections of it, should be widely distributed to key executives within the client firm and be made available on demand, as by online distribution. This was illustrated in the opening vignette in which United Airlines makes the monthly customer satisfaction report available online. After dissemination, key executives in the client firm should be given time to read the report in detail before follow-up activities are initiated.

Research Follow-Up

The researcher's task does not end with the oral presentation. Two other tasks remain. First, the researcher should help the client understand and implement the findings and take any follow-up actions. Second, while it is still fresh in her or his mind, the researcher should evaluate the entire marketing research project.

Assisting the Client

After the client has read the report in detail, several questions may arise. The client may not understand parts of the report, particularly those dealing with technical matters. The researcher should provide any help that is needed, as routinely done by the marketing research department of United Airlines in the opening vignette. Sometimes the researcher helps implement the findings. Often, the client retains the researcher to help select a new product or advertising agency or to develop a pricing policy, a market segmentation, or other marketing actions. An important reason for client follow-up is to discuss further research projects. For example, the researcher and management may agree to repeat the study after two years. Finally, the researcher should help the client firm make the information generated in the marketing research project a part of the firm's marketing (management) information system (MIS) or decision-support system (DSS), as discussed in Chapter 1.

Evaluating the Research Project

While marketing research is scientific, it also involves creativity, intuition, and expertise. Hence, every marketing research project provides an opportunity for learning, and the researcher should critically evaluate the entire project to obtain new insights and knowledge. The key question to ask is as follows: Could this project have been conducted more

EXPERIENTIAL LEARNING

Brevity in Report Writing and Presentation

Ipsos Group SA is a leading global marketing research company. Go to Ipsos Group SA's Web site (www.ipsos-na.com/news/results.cfm), review the list of press releases in the archives, and choose a press release with data that can be rendered into a brief report including a set of charts using Excel. Import your charts into PowerPoint. Some of the press releases include PowerPoint slides already; others include charts that can be readily imported into PowerPoint.

Can you make a compelling business presentation in three minutes? Select a topic from among the press release archives of research agency Ipsos. Then, develop a three-minute presentation using no more than five PowerPoint slides to explain (1) why this research finding matters to a firm in an industry of your choosing and (2) what this firm can do to take advantage of this finding.

Alternatively, you can create your report and presentation by using your analysis skills and the SPSS program to include a set of Excel charts from one of the following sources:

- Chapter 10's McCann Erickson Experiential Learning Exercise
- Chapter 16's KitKat taste test
- Chapter 17's Musial University retention study results

Share your final presentation with a group of fellow students in a formal setting.

1. What was the most challenging part of preparing, rehearsing, and making this presentation?
2. What will you do differently in your next presentation as a result of what you have learned in this Experiential Learning exercise.

effectively or efficiently? This question, of course, raises several more specific questions. Could the problem have been defined differently so as to enhance the value of the project to the client or reduce the costs? Could a different approach have yielded better results? Was the research design the best? How about the mode of data collection? Should mall intercepts have been used instead of telephone interviews? Was the sampling plan the most appropriate? Were the sources of possible design error correctly anticipated and kept under control, at least in a qualitative sense? If not, what changes could have been made? How could the selection, training, and supervision of field workers be altered to improve data collection? Was the data analysis strategy effective in yielding information useful for decision making? Were the conclusions and recommendations appropriate and useful to the client? Was the report adequately written and presented? Was the project completed within the time and budget allocated? If not, what went wrong? The insights gained from such an evaluation will benefit the researcher and subsequent projects.

Summary Illustration Using the Opening Vignette

Report preparation and presentation is the last, but not the least, step in the marketing research project. A formal report should be prepared and an oral presentation made. As in the case of United Airlines' customer satisfaction survey, the report should be very thorough and include a table of contents, executive summary, problem definition, approach, research design, data analysis, results, and conclusions and recommendations. Several tables and graphs should be prepared to enhance the clarity of the findings. The report, or at least some portion of it, may need to be widely disseminated, for example by making the findings available online as United Airlines did. After management has read the report, the researcher should conduct a follow-up. The researcher should provide assistance to management and conduct a thorough evaluation of the marketing research project, as illustrated by the numerous requests that the marketing research department of United Airlines handles following each report.

International Marketing Research

The guidelines presented earlier in this chapter apply to international marketing research as well, although report preparation may be complicated by the need to prepare reports for management in different countries and in different languages. In such

RESEARCH IN ACTION

Camry Chicken Fries Ford

"Why did the chicken cross the road?" Toyota asked in a continuing series of TV commercials aired recently in Australia. The answer: "To sell more Toyota Camrys, of course." The spots, showing an animated chicken trying to cross the road and getting its feathers blown off by a passing Camry, were created by Saatchi & Saatchi Advertising. When Bob Miller, Toyota's general manager for marketing tried to explain the ad to their counterpart in Japan, they thought he was insane.

Maybe so, but the commercials did unbelievably well. Hoary old joke that it was, the gag helped Toyota topple Ford's dominance in Australia. As part of a continuing series, the next ad showed the featherless chicken sitting on a pile of eggs in the middle of the road and hatching chicks as the Camry sped past. While such use of humor would not have made sense to the Japanese, it solicited a favorable response from the Australians.[7]

a case, the researcher should prepare different versions of the report, each geared to specific readers. The reports should be comparable, although the formats may differ. The guidelines for oral presentation are also similar to those given earlier, with the added proviso that the presenter should be sensitive to cultural norms. For example, telling jokes, which is frequently done in the United States, is not appropriate in all cultures.

Most marketing decisions are made from facts and figures arising out of marketing research. But these figures have to pass the test and limits of logic, subjective experience, and gut feelings of decision makers. The subjective experience and gut feelings of managers could vary widely across countries, necessitating that different recommendations be made for implementing the research findings in different countries. This is particularly important when making innovative or creative recommendations, such as advertising campaigns, as illustrated by the Camry Chicken Fries Ford example.

Technology and Marketing Research

Marketing research reports can be published or posted directly to the Web. Normally, these reports are not located in publicly accessible areas but in locations that are protected by passwords or on corporate intranets. The various word-processing, spreadsheet, and presentation packages have the capability to produce material in a format that can be posted directly to the Web, thus facilitating the process.

There are a number of advantages to publishing marketing research reports on the Web. These reports can incorporate all kinds of multimedia presentations, including graphs, pictures, animation, audio, and full-motion video. The dissemination is immediate, and an authorized person anywhere in the world can access the reports online. These reports can be searched electronically to identify materials of specific interest. For example, a Coca-Cola manager in Brazil can electronically locate the portions of the report that pertain to South America. Storage and future retrieval is efficient and effortless. It is easy to integrate these reports to become a part of the decision-support system. The advantages of publishing marketing research reports on the Web are illustrated by The Gallup Organization.

RESEARCH IN ACTION

Gallup Is on a Gallop

The Gallup Organization is a world leader in the measurement and analysis of people's attitudes, opinions, and behavior. Although Gallup is best known for the Gallup Poll, which dates from 1935, Gallup also provides marketing and management research, consulting, and training. Its Web site (www.gallup.com) contains several reports presenting the detailed methodology and findings of surveys they have conducted. One of the reports posted on the Gallup Web site in October 2004 stated that teens considered war and terrorism as top problems. Most teens don't have mortgages or mouths to feed, so they were likely to tune out when they heard economy-related words that set many adults' teeth on edge, like *runaway deficit*, *higher taxes*, and *soaring energy prices*. But teens were clearly tuning in when they hear words like *terrorism* and *war*. The usefulness of such reports to marketers and the general public has made the Gallup site very popular.[8]

Ethics in Marketing Research

Several ethical issues also arise during report preparation and presentation. These issues include ignoring pertinent data when drawing conclusions or making recommendations, not reporting relevant information (such as low response rates), deliberately misusing statistics, falsifying figures, altering research results, and misinterpreting the results with the objective of supporting a personal or corporate viewpoint. These issues should be addressed in a satisfactory manner, and the researchers should prepare reports that accurately and fully document the details of all the procedures and findings.

Like researchers, clients also have the responsibility for full and accurate disclosure of the research findings and are obligated to employ these findings honorably. For example, a client who distorts the research findings to make a more favorable claim in advertising can negatively affect the public. Ethical issues also arise when client firms, such as tobacco companies, use marketing research findings to formulate questionable marketing programs.

Software Applications

The mainframe and microcomputer versions of the major statistical packages have reporting procedures. In SPSS, the program REPORT can be used to present results in the desired format. TABLE(S) is particularly suited for formatting data for a one-page presentation. In

RESEARCH IN ACTION

Tobacco Industry Is a "Smoking Gun"

It is well known that tobacco smoking is responsible for 30 percent of all cancer deaths in the United States, is a leading cause of heart disease, and is associated with colds, gastric ulcers, chronic bronchitis, emphysema, and other diseases. Should tobacco companies be ethically responsible for this situation? Is it ethical for these companies to employ marketing research to create glamorous images for cigarettes that have a strong appeal to the target market?

Based on the findings of extensive research, it is estimated that advertising by the tobacco industry plays a part in creating more than 3,000 teenage smokers each day in the United States. Advertising for Camel cigarettes through the Old Joe cartoon advertisements increased Camel's share of the illegal children's cigarette market segment from 0.5 percent to 32.8 percent, which represents sales estimated at $500 million per year.

These detrimental effects were not limited to the United States. Not only was the tobacco industry enticing children to smoke, it also targeted other less-informed populations, such as those living in Third World countries. This raises the question of whether tobacco companies employed these tactics in an effort to replace those U.S. smokers who quit or die.[9]

WHAT WOULD *YOU* DO?

Subaru of America, Inc.: A Report on Reporting

The Situation

Takao Saito, CEO of Subaru, knows that customer loyalty is a big part of the automotive industry today, and Subaru has long been aware of this fact. Subaru, in the past, has relied heavily on the traditional, paper-based customer response surveys. Short, follow-up Purchase Experience Surveys and Service Experience Surveys are mailed to customers within 7 to 14 days after purchase. These surveys entail both multiple-choice questions and open-ended questions. The response rates from the mailings range from 30 to 45 percent. After all the data are collected from the mailings, dealerships receive a Subaru Owner Loyalty Indicator (SOLI) rating quarterly report. These reports provide valuable information to the dealer, but they received this information only four times a year. Upon receipt of the comments from their customers it was usually too late to resolve any of their problems.

The solution for Saito was the Internet, which would provide faster, more flexible service and information to dealers, field staff, and the management team. Subaru hired the Data Recognition Corp. (DRC), based in Minneapolis, to set up the program design and provide the ongoing service. The process begins by scanning the responses from customer survey forms using optical character recognition. Customer comments are captured and categorized. Next, all survey information is electronically added to the appropriate dealer's database using a customized program developed by DRC. The entire process is managed by DRC; hence, Subaru may concentrate on selling cars.

The Web-based reports give field managers an opportunity to see what is happening at their assigned dealerships. They can access up-to-the-minute reports on a specified dealership before meeting with the dealer. This works well because the managers are able to access this information from anywhere as long as they can tap into the Internet.

Dealers are able to use the site to stay apprised of customer satisfaction. They can see their quality scores and check on a particular salesman's performance. Dealers are able to take immediate action because of this new technology. This allows for better management and, in the long run, better performance from all employees. As dealers became more comfortable with the Web format, they began to request more detailed and timely reports. Due to this request, Subaru has recently begun to develop a series of reports called Just in Time Reports. These reports provide immediate access to current performance rankings in addition to the quarterly rankings. This has become another tool to help Subaru boost their sales and performance. This new technology and refocused goals on customer measurement and loyalty will help propel Subaru ahead of their competition.

The Marketing Research Decision

1. While Subaru management finds the report very useful, the dealers have a slightly different opinion. To improve the usefulness of the report to the dealers, the report should be modified to (check as many as are applicable):
   a. Put more stress on the problem definition
   b. Describe the research design extensively
   c. Explain data analysis in more detail
   d. Emphasize the limitations and caveats
   e. Contain more graphs
2. Discuss the role of the type of report you recommend in enabling Tako Saito to make the dealer sales effort more effective.

The Marketing Management Decision

1. To make the dealer sales effort more effective, Tako Saito should (check as many as are applicable):
   a. Build closer online relationship with consumers
   b. Build closer online relationship with dealers
   c. Boost Internet leads for dealers
   d. Make greater use of the Internet for reporting research findings to dealers
   e. Boost dealers' online presence
2. Discuss how the marketing management-decision action that you recommend to Tako Saito is influenced by the type of report that you suggested earlier.

What Tako Saito Did

Subaru of America has launched an e-business program that the automaker hopes will build a closer online relationship with customers while providing Subaru dealers with enhanced e-business features for their own sites. The program, developed in partnership with

(continued)

The Cobalt Group, is designed to boost Internet leads and sales for dealers and to create a consistent online presence for Subaru's 500 dealers. This collaborative effort puts dealers at the center of the sales and value equation. The system includes features that let local dealers customize their sites from online pricing flexibility to interactive hours. Since the emergence of the new Subaru dealer Internet program, dealers have seen a boost in their online traffic and are receiving better leads with more informative quote requests.[10]

SAS, procedures such as PRINT, FORMS, CHARTS, PLOT, CALENDAR, and TIMEPLOT display information for reporting purposes. The tables and graphs produced from these packages can be directly incorporated into the report. MINITAB also has the capability to create graphs and charts and to edit them for use in reports or professional presentations. Graphs can be created using GRAPH > PLOT, or GRAPH > CHART, or GRAPH > HISTOGRAM. Editing can be done using EDIT > EDIT LAST COMMAND DIALOG. EXCEL has extensive charting capabilities and through Microsoft OFFICE provides a direct link to WORD, and POWERPOINT for report preparation and presentation.

SPSS Windows

While the normal graphs can be produced using the Base module of SPSS, for more extensive graphing, the DeltaGraph package can be used. This package has extensive graphing capabilities with more than 80 chart types and more than 200 chart styles.

Likewise, SPSS TABLES enables the researcher to create even complicated tables. For example, the results of multiple response tables can be condensed into a single table. The researcher can create a polished look by changing column width, adding boldface, drawing lines, or aligning.

SPSS OLAP cubes are interactive tables that enable you to slice your data in different ways for data exploration and presentation.

SMARTVIEWER enables the researcher to distribute reports, graphs, tables, even pivotal report cubes, over the Web. Company mangers can be empowered to interact with the results by putting a report cube on the Web, intranet, or extranet. Thus, they can answer their own questions by drilling down for more detail and creating new views of the data.

Summary

Report preparation and presentation is the final step in the marketing research project. This process begins with interpretation of data analysis results and leads to conclusions and recommendations. Next, the formal report is written and an oral presentation made. After management has read the report, the researcher should conduct a follow-up, assisting management and undertaking a thorough evaluation of the marketing research project.

In international marketing research, report preparation may be complicated by the need to prepare reports for management in different countries and in different languages. Available software can greatly facilitate report preparation and presentation. Several ethical issues are pertinent, particularly those related to the interpretation and reporting of the research process and findings to the client and to the subsequent ways the client uses these results.

Key Terms and Concepts

Letter of transmittal, 534
Leaders, 537
Stubs, 537
Pie chart, 538
Line chart, 538
Pictograph, 539
Bar chart, 539
Histogram, 539
"Tell 'em" principle, 540
"KISS 'em" principle, 540

Suggested Cases and Video Cases

Cases

3.2 Darden **4.1 Boeing** **4.2 Gucci**

Video Cases

4.1 Subaru **4.2 Marriott**

Additional cases and video cases are available in the Instructor's Manual and on the instructor and student Web sites.

Live Research: Conducting a Marketing Research Project

1. The individual parts of the report can be assigned to teams, with each team writing a specific part. Each team also prepares the PowerPoint slides for that part.
2. The project coordinators should be responsible for compiling the final report and the presentation.
3. Make liberal use of graphs.
4. A presentation of the project should be made to the client, with each team presenting its portion.
5. If each team has worked on the entire report, compile the final report by combining the best parts of the various team reports. This task can be handled by the project coordinators under the supervision of the instructor. The team to make the client presentation can be selected by the instructor based on class presentations by individual teams.

Acronyms

The guidelines for constructing tables may be described by the acronym TABLES:

T itle and number
A rrangement of data items
B asis of measurement
L eaders, rulings, spaces
E xplanations and comments: headings, stubs, and footnotes
S ources of data

GRAPHS can be used as an acronym for guidelines for constructing graphs:

G eographic and other maps
R ound or pie chart
A ssembly or line charts
P ictographs
H istograms and bar charts
S chematic figures and flow charts

The guidelines for making a presentation can be summarized by the acronym PRESENTATION:

P reparation
R ehearse your presentation
E ye contact
S tories, experiences, examples, and quotations
E quipment: multimedia
N o filler words
T ell 'em principle
A udience analysis
T erminate with a strong closing
I nteract with the audience
O utline or script should be prepared
N umber-one level manager should sponsor it

Review Questions

1. Describe the process of report preparation.
2. Describe a commonly used format for writing marketing research reports.
3. Describe the following parts of a report: title page, table of contents, executive summary, problem definition, research design, data analysis, and conclusions and recommendations.
4. Why is the "Limitations and Caveats" section included in the report?
5. Discuss the importance of objectivity in writing a marketing research report.
6. Describe the guidelines for report writing.
7. How should the data items be arranged in a table?
8. What is a pie chart? For what type of information is it suitable? For what type of information is it not suitable?
9. Describe a line chart. What kind of information is commonly displayed using this type of chart?
10. Describe the role of pictographs. What is the relationship between bar charts and histograms?
11. What is the purpose of an oral presentation? What guidelines should be followed in an oral presentation?
12. Describe the "tell 'em" and "KISS 'em" principles.
13. Describe the evaluation of a marketing research project in retrospect.

Applied Problems

1. The following passage is taken from a marketing research report prepared for a group of printers and lithographers without much formal business education who run a small family-owned business.

   > "To measure the image of the printing industry, two different scaling techniques were employed. The first was a series of semantic differential scales. The second consisted of a set of Likert scales. The use of two different techniques for measurement could be justified based on the need to assess the convergent validity of the findings. Data obtained using both these techniques were treated as interval-scaled. Pearson product moment correlations were computed between the sets of ratings. The resulting correlations were high, indicating a high level of convergent validity."

   Rewrite this paragraph so that it is suitable for inclusion in the report for this audience.

2. Graphically illustrate the consumer decision-making process described in the following paragraph:

   > The consumer first becomes aware of the need. Then the consumer simultaneously searches for information from several sources: retailers, advertising, word of mouth, independent publications, and the Internet. Next, the consumer develops a criterion for evaluating the available brands in the marketplace. Based on this evaluation, the consumer selects the most preferred brand.

3. For the data given in Table 19.1, use a graphics package or a spreadsheet, such as Excel, to construct the following graphs:
   a. Pie chart
   b. Line chart
   c. Bar chart
4. Visit Gallup's Web site (www.gallup.com) to identify a recent report prepared by this company. How does the format of this report compare to the one in the book?

Group Discussion

1. As a small group, discuss the following statement: "All the graphical aids are really very similar; it doesn't matter which ones you use."
2. "Writing a report that is concise yet complete is virtually impossible, as these two objectives are conflicting." Discuss.
3. "Writing, presenting, and reading reports is an acquired talent." Discuss as a small group.

CASES FOR PART 3A: CASES WITH EXTERNAL DATA

CASE 3.1

Ford Seeks a New Image

Ford Motor Company postponed the building of a new Greenfield, Georgia, assembly plant, thus, extending the production of its Ford Taurus and Sable through the 2009 model year. The Taurus and Sable lines were slated to shut down by mid-2005 had the construction of the assembly plant pushed through. A failure to conduct appropriate market research had hindered the Taurus from realizing its potential of becoming the best-selling American car, and it lost ground to the Toyota Camry and the Honda Accord.

Historically, the Taurus did much better with sales among the older segment of the U.S. population than with the younger baby boomers. As this latter group made up more of the auto-buyer market, sales of the domestic Taurus fell. Additionally, almost half of all Taurus sales were low-margin fleet buyers, such as automobile rental agencies and corporate-owned fleets. Ford wanted to reduce Taurus fleet sales to 40 percent of total sales, thereby increasing its overall profit margin.

Ford also felt compelled to upgrade the Taurus due to one of its major competitors, the Toyota Camry. The Camry was upgraded with many of the features of its luxury Lexus line, and Toyota's sales were increasing. Ford felt it had to beat the Camry in order to accomplish its goals. The Taurus was a key to Ford's plans to displace General Motors as the number-one auto manufacturer in the world, and to wrest the world-quality title away from Toyota.

One of the most difficult tasks was to change the look of the Taurus without changing its identity. Inspired by the familiar Taurus oval grille, designer Doug Gaffka and his team decided on an elliptical shape. The 2005 Taurus had an elongated oval shape, which was reflected in its headlights, rear window, door handles, control panel, airbag pad, and more. It did not have chrome trim or visible seams, but it did have a curving, dropped rear deck and a very steep, sloping windshield. "We tried to make it sleek, sleek, and sleeker," said Gaffka. "We wanted to suck the body molding right down over the mechanics as if it were carved out of a single piece of metal."

Despite the praise from designers and automotive critics, right from the beginning, many felt that the Taurus was just too expensive with the price increase for the new model, which had been intended to cover the high cost of bringing the car to the market. However, the higher cost resulted in lowered sales with Ford Taurus lagging behind the Toyota Camry. Ford knew it needed to improve the Taurus; however, it failed to determine the effect of the increased price on sales. Consumers constantly make trade-offs between benefits and costs. Consumers buy the level of benefits that they believe is worth the cost, and is within their means. Despite the increased benefits provided by the new Taurus, many consumers were not willing to pay the higher price Ford charged.

For future success and increased profits the Taurus must attract the yuppie crowd—the highly educated, affluent baby boomers—who tend to prefer imported vehicles. Since this group is one of the prime target groups for this car, Ford needed to ensure that it could compete in a market where the Toyota Camry and the Honda Accord offer stiff competition. Primary concerns for Ford were overcoming its conservative image with this group, determining if it should offer incentives on the Taurus, and the importance of styling and prestige when promoting to this market.

To address these concerns, 30 statements were constructed to measure attitudes toward these factors and to classify the respondents. The respondents used a nine-point Likert scale (ranging from 1 = definitely disagree, 9 = definitely agree). The respondents were obtained from the mailing lists of *Car and Driver*, *Business Week*, and *Inc.* magazines. They were telephoned at their homes by an independent surveying company. The statements used in the survey of 400 respondents are listed below:

1. I am in very good physical condition.
2. When I must choose between the two, I usually dress for fashion, not comfort.

3. I have more stylish clothes than most of my friends.
4. I want to look a little different from others.
5. Life is too short not to take some gambles.
6. I am not concerned about the ozone layer.
7. I think the government is doing too much to control pollution.
8. Basically, society today is fine.
9. I don't have time to volunteer for charities.
10. Our family is not too heavily in debt today.
11. I like to pay cash for everything I buy.
12. I pretty much spend for today and let tomorrow bring what it will.
13. I use credit cards because I can pay the bill off slowly.
14. I seldom use coupons when I shop.
15. Interest rates are low enough to allow me to buy what I want.
16. I have more self-confidence than most of my friends.
17. I like to be considered a leader.
18. Others often ask me to help them out of a jam.
19. Children are the most important aspect of a marriage.
20. I would rather spend a quiet evening at home than go out to a party.
21. American-made cars can't compare with foreign-made cars.
22. The government should restrict imports of products from Japan.
23. Americans should always try to buy American products.
24. I would like to take a trip around the world.
25. I wish I could leave my present life and do something entirely different.
26. I am usually among the first to try new products.
27. I like to work hard and play hard.
28. Skeptical predictions are usually wrong.
29. I can do anything I set my mind to.
30. Five years from now, my income will be a lot higher than it is now.

In addition, the criterion variable, attitude toward Taurus, was measured by asking each person to respond to the statement, "I would consider buying the Taurus made by Ford." This statement was measured on the same nine-point scale as the 30 predictor statements.

The data for the case are provided. In the enclosed data, the first variable represents attitude toward a Taurus automobile. The next 30 variables, in the order listed in the case, represent the ratings of the lifestyle statements. The data are available in SPSS, EXCEL, and text (tab delimited) format. In the text file, each field occupies three columns.

Questions

The director of marketing for Ford is interested in knowing the psychological characteristics of the yuppies to configure the Taurus program. You have been presented with the responses from the survey outlined above. Analyze the data according to the following guidelines:

1. Frequency distribution: Ensure that each variable is appropriate for analysis by running a frequency distribution for each variable.
2. Categorize the attitude toward Taurus and the 30 lifestyle statements as follows: 1 to 5 = 1, 6 to 9 = 2. Run cross-tabs with attitude toward Taurus as the dependent variable and each categorized lifestyle variable as the independent variable. Thus, you will run 30 cross-tabs in all.
3. Now recategorize the 30 lifestyle statements as follows: 1 to 3 = 1, 4 to 6 = 2, and 7 to 9 = 3. Run one-way analyses of variance with attitude as the dependent variable and each categorized lifestyle variable as the independent variable. Thus, you will run 30 analyses of variances in all.
4. Run product moment correlations between all possible pairs of lifestyle statements. Interpret the results.
5. Run a multiple regression with attitude toward Taurus as the dependent variable. The independent variables are those lifestyle statements which were significant at $\alpha = 0.05$ in the cross-tabs run in Question 2. Interpret the results.

Based on the analysis, prepare a report to management explaining the yuppie consumer and offering recommendations on the design of the Ford Taurus. Your recommendations should aid Ford in achieving what it seeks: an image for the Taurus that is attractive to the yuppie market and that helps them outperform the competition.

References

1. (www.ford.com).
2. "Ford Gives Taurus a Longer Life, " *Automotive News*, 77(6048), (July 14, 2003): 8.

Note: This case was prepared for class-discussion purposes only and does not represent the views of Ford or its affiliates. The problem scenario is hypothetical and the data provided are simulated.

CASE 3.2

A Breeze for Darden Restaurants

Bill Darden created the Red Lobster chain of restaurants in the late 1960s. At the time, the new chain was a much-appreciated casual dining concept geared toward families. Darden Restaurants' pioneering move led to a boom of new restaurants in the same segment throughout the 70s and 80s. The family restaurant boom continued to be fueled by changing demographics in the United States. More and more women were going back to work, divorce rates were on the rise, and the amount of dual income families were increasing. This translated into less home-prepared meals and more dining out.

As of 2005, Darden Restaurants, Inc. is the largest casual dining restaurant company in the world. It operates more than 1,300 restaurants in four chains: Red Lobster, Olive Garden, Bahama Breeze, Smokey Bones BBQ, and a Seasons 52 restaurant in North America. It has over $5 billion in sales. Darden's ability to keep its chains ahead of the competition is a result of being more in tune with its customers.

To accomplish this, Darden relied on a strong vision and a hefty amount of marketing research. Research became a key focus in the early 80s when Darden formed a development team to investigate the potential for creating an Italian restaurant in the casual-dining segment. During this development, Darden used a wide variety of research techniques, ranging from survey research, data analysis, reviewing social and demographic trends, and focus groups. The objective of the research was to find out what connections consumers made with Italian restaurants. The result: People expected a warm, homey place for family gatherings with lots of food.

Darden soon began making plans to unveil its new chain, the Olive Garden. The marketing strategy behind the rollout directly reflected the attitudes and demographic trends the development team uncovered based on marketing research. Olive Garden ads depicted large Italian families laughing and eating together at large tables overflowing with pasta and wine. The research and marketing efforts definitely paid off. Olive Garden is now patronized by over 150 million customers a year. By fine-tuning its already popular menu, Olive Garden succeeded in winning the Nation's Restaurant News 2004 MenuMasters Best Menu Revamp Award.

Shortly after the successful launch of the Olive Garden chain, Darden began a new initiative to save the Red Lobster chain, which had been experiencing lagging sales for quite some time. Again, Darden relied heavily on marketing research to gain a better understanding of what customers expected in a seafood restaurant. Revitalizing Red Lobster posed more of a challenge than developing Olive Garden in that it had to overcome an already tired image. Red Lobster was quick to change the menu, adding fresh catch-of-the-day specials and offering regional dishes, such as baked fish with a cracker-crumb crust in New England. Management also revamped the physical appearance of the restaurants: adding bars, changing the wardrobe of the staff to a more casual look, and even adding new colorful dinnerware instead of the traditional white. In Red Lobster's case, the research was not limited to just customers. Executives held "town hall" meetings and sent out surveys to employees. Some of the employee-input surveys led to the lifting of the ban on beards and earrings for staff and allowed chefs to test new recipes for a month in order to get real customer feedback. The result of the new efforts was an entirely new Red Lobster, and same store sales have slowly been recovering since.

Darden's subsequent experiment was the new chain of Bahama Breeze restaurants. These restaurants focus on creating a true Caribbean atmosphere. Each restaurant provides frozen drinks, tropical fruit, and a fun outdoor atmosphere. The rollout of the Bahama Breeze chain has been slow so that Darden managers can truly assess the performance of the new chain and determine if new marketing approaches need to be implemented. Marketing research has found that Bahama Breeze thrives well in high-quality, densely populated areas. Furthermore, with its higher priced checks (around $22 per person) the chain targets a higher-income customer than Red Lobster or Olive Garden. However, the chain has the issue of attracting repeat customers since many people do not frequent a restaurant for Caribbean food as often as for seafood or Italian.

The relaxed atmosphere and a great barbeque menu are an enticing combination at Darden's newest casual dining concept, Smokey Bones BBQ Sports Bar. Again, extensive marketing research in the form of secondary data analysis, focus groups, and surveys supported the launch of this chain. At each of Smokey Bones' locations, guests revel in the rustic mountain lodge ambience as they tune in to a wide range of sporting events—each table features an individual control box that allows diners to select which game they want to hear. Genuine hickory logs are used in the smokers. Pulled pork is slow roasted for 12 hours for peak flavor and tenderness. A secret sauce gives each dish that distinctive Smokey Bones signature taste. With high annual sales and several new restaurants in the works, Smokey Bones is truly smokin'!

In the increasingly competitive restaurant market, Darden is very concerned about positioning its four restaurant chains distinctively so that they do not cannibalize each other's sales. Darden's marketing department desires to formulate new approaches to marketing based on an understanding of the underlying restaurant preference and patronage process. To do so, 300 men and women who fell into Darden's target market were surveyed. Each was given a randomly selected brochure of one of the chains (either Olive Garden, Red Lobster, Bahama Breeze, or Smokey Bones) and asked to rate that restaurant on nine attributes and to give his/her overall preference for that restaurant. These ratings were obtained on seven-point Likert scales. The study was designed so that each of the four chains appeared 75 times. The goal of the study was to learn which attributes of restaurants were most important in influencing preference *(Y)*. The nine attributes used in the study were

Variable	Attribute	Marketing Options
X_1	Reputation	Promote a good name
X_2	Price	Charge a fair price
X_3	Quality of food	High-quality ingredients and preparation
X_4	Variety of food	A variety of menu options
X_5	Decor	Casual and inviting
X_6	Waiters and waitresses	Attentive and friendly
X_7	Waiting time to be served	12 minutes or less
X_8	Parking	Ample free parking
X_9	Location	Convenience

Data were collected using in-home personal interviewing and are enclosed. The first variable represents brand preference *(Y)*. The next nine variables represent the ratings of the brands on the nine attributes in the order listed in the case (X_1 to X_9). The data are available in SPSS, EXCEL, and text (tab delimited) format. In the text file, each field occupies three columns.

Questions

You must analyze the data and prepare a report for the marketing department. The one-page memo you received suggested that you use the following procedures:

1. Frequency distribution: Obtain a frequency distribution for each variable and show bar graphs of all variables.
2. Cross-tabs: Group brand preference as low, medium, and high under the formula low = 1 or 2, medium = 3 to 5, and high = 6 or 7. Group all independent variables as

either low = 1 to 3, medium = 4, and high = 5 to 7. Cross-tabulate brand preference with each independent variable. Interpret these results for management.

3. Do a paired *t*-test with price and decor as the two variables. Interpret the results for management.
4. Do a paired *t*-test with quality of food and variety of food as the two variables. Interpret the results for management.
5. One-way analysis of variance: Group all independent variables into low, medium, and high groups as you did for cross-tabs. Run a one-way analysis of variance on each independent variable with brand preference. Explain the results to management.
6. Regression: Find a regression equation for preference that includes all independent variables for the model and describe how meaningful the model is. Interpret the results for management.

Interpret the results of the survey and make recommendations based on your findings to the marketing department. They want your opinion about which of the nine attributes the consumers value most highly, as well as your ideas for specific actions that can increase market share for Darden in today's market. The marketing department is counting on your recommendations to provide them with ways to continue to improve Darden's patronage.

References

1. (www.darden.com), (www.redlobster.com), (www.olivegarden.com), (www.bahamabreeze.com), and (www.smokeybones.com).
2. Naomi R. Kooker, "Olive Garden," *Nation's Restaurant News*, 38(19) (May 10, 2004): 90.
3. Susan Spielberg, "Darden Takes Wind Out of Bahama Breeze's Sails," *Nation's Restaurant News*, 38(21), (May 24, 2004): 6, 208.

Note: This case was prepared for class-discussion purposes only and does not represent the views of the Darden Restaurants or its affiliates. The problem scenario is hypothetical and the data provided are simulated.

CASE 3.3

Should Microsoft "Soften" Up to Rescue Its Image?

For over a decade, Microsoft has enjoyed near monopoly power in the market for computer-operating systems. The Windows operating system has dominant control in both consumer and commercial computer systems. Microsoft was extremely successful in using its operating systems as a way to control and dominate other software markets. When it began its campaign in the Internet browser market (against Netscape), it started to draw attention from the Justice Department. Microsoft soon faced an antitrust lawsuit that greatly changed its environment.

In May 1998, the Justice Department filed a lawsuit against Microsoft because it felt that the company was using its monopoly power to act as a corporate predator by hindering competition and ultimately hurting the consumer. Microsoft settled its suit with the Justice Department in 2001. On June 30, 2004, the U.S. Court of Appeals for the District of Columbia endorsed the 2001 settlement and turned down appeals for stricter sanctions on the world's largest software maker. However, as of 2004, the company was still settling class-action suits in several states. Moreover, the European Union's antitrust case against the company was still pending. A company's image is one of its most valuable assets, and Microsoft scrambled to protect its own. Microsoft was concerned about what effect these legal actions had on the company's image. Microsoft decided to conduct a survey to analyze the image and perception of Microsoft. The polls were Microsoft's efforts to try to fight back against these legal allegations. Microsoft wanted to keep in touch with customer perceptions and make sure that the lawsuits did not irreparably damage its image.

Any time a company is in trouble, or what they think might be trouble, they'll track groups to figure out how the public perceives them. That is exactly what Microsoft did. It tried to avoid a potential marketing research problem by conducting surveys to tap into the environmental changes occurring. The legal environment wanted to destroy

Microsoft, but where did the customers stand? Microsoft needed to keep focusing a good portion of its marketing effort toward maintaining its image.

Accordingly, the marketing research department of Microsoft designed a survey for its new Office software. The company wished to determine executives' willingness to buy Microsoft Office. Management wanted information in three areas: the reactions of businesses of various sizes, the impact of familiarity with Microsoft Office on willingness to buy, and how American businesses were using PCs in the workplace. This led to the related question of whether sales of other Microsoft products to technically competent PC users could be increased.

To address these issues, 1,080 companies throughout the United States were selected from a list of subscribers to the magazine *PC Week*. They were sent a questionnaire designed to uncover executives' willingness to purchase Microsoft Office, assuming they were in the market for office-productivity software (the dependent variable). The companies were classified for research purposes along three variables—company size, familiarity with Microsoft Office, and business application of PCs (the independent variables). Each of these variables could assume one of three values as listed below.

Variable	Value
X_1 **Company Size**	
Small/entrepreneurial	1
Medium/private	2
Division of major corporation	3
X_2 **Familiarity with Microsoft Office**	
No experience	1
Has used Microsoft Office for 5 or less years	2
Has used Microsoft Office for more than 5 years	3
X_3 **Business Applications**	
Individual use (word processing and data analysis)	1
Departmental use (functional computing, networking)	2
Corporate use (enterprise integration)	3

Forty respondents were randomly assigned to each of the 27 possible combinations of variables (i.e., 40 respondents with low-low-low ratings, 40 with low-low-medium ratings, etc.). The respondents' stated willingness to purchase a Microsoft Office product was measured on an 11-point scale.

The data for this case are provided. In the enclosed data, the first variable represents the stated willingness to purchase a Microsoft Office product. The next three variables, in the order listed in the case, represent the variables used to classify the companies. The data are available in SPSS, EXCEL, and text (tab delimited) format. In the text file, each field occupies six columns. This design was chosen to allow for subsequent data analysis. Using SPSS, SAS, MINITAB, or EXCEL (or a similar statistical software package), you have been assigned to analyze the data using the following procedures.

1. Frequency distribution: Ensure that the frequency distributions of all variables are appropriate for further analysis.
2. Cross-tabs: Recode the dependent variable, willingness to buy, into three relatively equal groups (low, medium, and high). Run cross-tabs on the dependent variable with each of the independent variables (company size, familiarity, and business application). Interpret the results for management.
3. Do a two-group *t*-test with groups based on company size: small (coded as 1) versus division of major corporation (coded as 2). The dependent variable is willingness to purchase Microsoft Office.
4. One-way analysis of variance: Explain the variation in the dependent variable by running three ANOVAs of the dependent variable (willingness to purchase) with each of the predictor variables (company size, familiarity with Microsoft Office, and business application).

The principal consultant of your firm has asked you to analyze the data using a significance level of .05, and to prepare a thorough report detailing the results of the analysis and offering recommendations for Microsoft management on its promotional program for the Office software. Remember that American business executives are your target. Your mission, while not impossible, is a difficult one—help Microsoft retarget its market and regain its image.

References

1. Mark Jewell, "Microsoft Makes Proposed Suit Settlement," (www.forbes.com) (June 30, 2004).
2. Michael Paige, "E.U. Sanctions Versus Microsoft on Hold," (www.marketwatch.com) (June 28, 2004).

Note: This case was prepared for class-discussion purposes only and does not represent the views of Microsoft or its affiliates. The problem scenario is hypothetical and the data provided are simulated.

CASES FOR PART 3B: CASES WITHOUT EXTERNAL DATA

CASE 3.4

Are Catalogs Risky Business?

Shopping may be shifting to the Internet; however, plain old paper catalogs still have a place of pride as America's first—and still most popular—virtual retailers. Consumer spending on catalog purchases is expected to be about $100 billion in the year 2005. Much of that is spent on apparel. Computers and sporting goods are also catalog mainstays. The catalog shopping habits of America show that parents and couples are the two main groups that use catalogs as a means of shopping.

Why do people shop from catalogs as opposed to store shopping? The top reasons for catalog shopping are convenience, perceived value, unique merchandise, the right price, direct home delivery, and lack of time to store shop. However, some people do not shop from catalogs for reasons such as not trusting ordering procedures, wanting to see a product before buying it, not wanting to wait for delivery, and not seeing anything of interest to order. Many people feel that ordering from a catalog is very risky due to hidden taxes or service fees and possible problems with returning goods. In addition, many people would rather not deal with the hassle of paying for delivery costs when they can purchase the same item at a store without any extra charge.

Twelve product categories were examined to compare catalog to store shopping. For each product, respondents evaluated the degree of risk perceived in buying that product from a retail store and from a catalog. The null hypothesis, that there is no significant difference in the overall amount of risk perceived when buying products by catalog compared to buying the same products in a retail store, was tested by computing 12 (one for each product) paired *t*-tests. Mean scores for overall perceived risk for some of the products in both buying situations are presented in the following table, with higher scores indicating greater risk.

Mean Scores of Overall Perceived Risk for Products by Purchase Mode

	Overall Perceived Risk	
Product	**Catalog**	**Retail Store**
Stereo hi-fi	48.89	41.98*
Record albums	32.65	28.74*
Dress shoes	58.60	50.80*
13″ color TV	48.53	40.91*
Athletic socks	35.22	30.22*
Pocket calculator	49.62	42.00*
35mm camera	48.13	39.52*
Perfume	34.85	29.79*

* Significant at 0.01 level

Questions

1. Interpret the statistical results. Are catalogs risky business? What is your conclusion?
2. Are paired *t*-tests appropriate in this case? Why or why not?
3. Suppose we wanted to test the hypothesis that the perceived risk of buying dress shoes from a catalog exceeded 50. Formulate the null and alternative hypothesis. Assume that the population variance is known to be 25; test the null hypothesis.
4. Suppose the sample was split into two equal groups. One group evaluated the perceived risk of buying each product from a retail store and the other group evaluated the perceived risk of buying each product from a catalog. What would be the appropriate way of testing the null hypothesis?
5. Suppose the sample was split into three equal groups. One group evaluated the perceived risk of buying each product from a retail store, the second group evaluated the perceived risk of buying each product from a catalog, and the third group evaluated the perceived risk of buying each product on the Internet. What would be the appropriate way of testing the null hypothesis so that there is no significant difference in the overall amount of risk perceived when buying products from a catalog, retail store, or the Internet?

References

1. Margery Weinstein, "Bebe Stores Get Sporty with Catalog," *Catalog Age,* 20(7), (June 2003): 21.
2. Troy A. Festervand, Don R. Snyder, and John D. Tsalikis, "Influence of Catalog Versus Store Shopping and Prior Satisfaction on Perceived Risk," *Journal of the Academy of Marketing Science,* (Winter 1986): 28–36.

CASE 3.5

Does Advertising Subsidize the Price of Consumer Magazines?

For many magazine publishers, advertising growth is likely to pick up further in 2005 and 2006 compared to the economic slowdown of 2001–2003. TNS estimated that the summer Olympic games and the November presidential election helped ad spending grow by 7.8 percent in 2004 to $138.4 billion, with Spanish-language network TV the fastest growing, followed by the Internet. Large marketers led the charge. Total spending among the top-10 ad spenders rose 11.5 percent, led by Procter & Gamble Company, up 16.4 percent. Among the top 10, only DaimlerChrysler and Walt Disney Company were flat.

Many magazine companies rely heavily on advertising for revenue. The more magazines consumers buy, the more magazine companies can charge advertisers. It is widely believed that consumer magazines' prices are subsidized by the advertising carried within the magazines. A study examined the contribution of advertising to the price per copy of magazines. Multiple regression analysis was used to examine the relationships among price per copy, circulation, percentage of newsstand circulation, promotional expenditures, percentage of color pages, and per-copy advertising revenues. The form of the analysis was

$$PPC = b_0 + b_1\,(\text{Ed Pages}) + b_2\,(\text{Circ}) + b_3\,(\%\ \text{News Circ}) + b_4\,(\text{PE}) + b_5\,(\%\ \text{Color}) + b_6\,(\text{Ad Revs})$$

Where	PPC	= price per copy (in $)
	Ed Pages	= editorial pages per average issue
	Circ	= the log of average paid circulation (in 000s)
	% News Circ	= percentage newsstand circulation
	PE	= promotional expenditures (in $)
	% Color	= percentage of pages printed in color
	Ad Revs	= per-copy advertising revenues (in $)

Table 1

Zero-Order Correlation Matrix of Variables in Analyses

	Price per Copy	Circulation	Editorial Pages	Promotion Expenditures	% Color Pages	% Newsstand Circulation
Circulation	-.21*					
Editorial Pages	.52*	.29*				
Promotion Expenditures	-.22*	.42*	-.19			
% Color Pages	.01	.33*	.19	-.15		
% Newsstand Circulation	.46*	.09	.31*	.26*	.02	
Ad Revenues per Copy	.29*	-.25*	.30*	-.14	.15	.08

*p < .05

Table 1 shows the zero-order Pearson product moment correlations among the variables.

The results of the regression analysis using price per copy as the dependent variable are given in Table 2. Of the six independent variables, three were significant ($p < .05$): the number of editorial pages, average circulation, and percentage newsstand circulation. The three variables accounted for virtually all of the explained variance ($R^2 = .51$, adjusted $R^2 = .48$). The direction of the coefficients was consistent with prior expectations: The number of editorial pages was positive, circulation was negative, and percentage newsstand circulation was positive. This was expected because of the structure of the magazine-publishing industry, and confirmed the hypothesized relationship.

Promotional expenditures, use of color, and per-copy advertising revenues were found to have no relationship with price per copy, after the effects of circulation, percentage newsstand circulation, and editorial pages were controlled in the regression analysis.

Table 2

Regression Analysis Using Price per Copy as Dependent Variable

Dependent Variable: Price per Copy
Independent Variables:

	b	*SE*	*F*
Editorial Pages	.0084	.0017	23.04*
Circulation	-.4180	.1372	9.29*
Percentage Newsstand Circulation	.0067	.0016	18.46*
Promotional Expenditures	.13-04**	.0000	.59
Percentage Color Pages	.0227	.0092	.01
Per-Copy Ad Revenues	.1070	.0412	.07
Overall $R^2 = .51$	$df = 6.93$	Overall $F = 16.19$*	

*p < .05 **decimal moved in by four zeros

Questions

1. Interpret the correlations.
2. Interpret the results of the regression. Does advertising subsidize the price of consumer magazines? What is your conclusion?
3. What should be the nature of regression results for you to conclude that consumers who purchase magazines are, in fact, paying for the advertising in those magazines?

References

1. Mercedes M. Cardona, "Q1 Ad Spending Up 9.6%; Big Marketers Lead Charge," *Advertising Age* (Midwest Region Edition), 75(23), (June 7, 2004): 8.
2. Lawrence Soley and R. Krishnan, "Does Advertising Subsidize Consumer Magazine Prices?" *Journal of Advertising*, 16 (Spring, 1987): 4–9.

VIDEO CASES FOR PART 3

VIDEO CASE 3.1

AFLAC: Marketing Research Quacks a Duck

In 1989, the Columbus, Georgia-based company, American Family Life Assurance Company adopted the acronym AFLAC (www.aflac.com). At this point, the company had very little brand recognition, and the name AFLAC meant nothing to potential customers. In order to boost this brand recognition, AFLAC undertook extensive marketing research and emerged with the symbol of the duck. As of 2005, AFLAC boasts of 89 percent brand recognition. This is so high that it actually rivals Coke, the company with the highest brand recognition, at 95 percent. Even kids (ages 8 to 13) are familiar with the AFLAC name, as it ranked in the company of Pepsi, Old Navy, and M&Ms. This is important because as kids age and start to buy insurance, the AFLAC name will be at the front of their minds.

From the start of this campaign, marketing research was at the forefront. First, the decision was made to simply try to increase brand recognition in ads instead of actually trying to sell insurance in ads. This decision came from focus groups and survey research that found customers would usually think they didn't need whatever type of insurance was being advertised, whether it was life, health, home, and so forth. Instead, the research said that customers would respond to insurance ads better if they simply raised the recognition of the brand. Then, salespeople would do the job of educating the individual customer about the needs for different types of insurance.

After the decision was made to just raise brand awareness with ads, a specific campaign had to be created. Again, marketing research played a major role. The decision was made from the start that the ads that tested the best were going to be the ads that were used. The research said that test customers viewing the ads preferred the AFLAC duck much more than any other ad viewed. But where did the duck come from? During the ad development process, one of the ad agency (the Kaplan Thaler Group) researchers just began to say the word "AFLAC " over and over again. Eventually, it was noticed that this word, said the right way, sounded like a quacking duck. The risk in this was that AFLAC was making fun of the fact that no one knew about the brand name, and humor in advertising does not always appeal to people who want a more serious tone from their insurance company. What if viewers see the television commercial and think, "How stupid!" or "A life insurance company should be more serious than that." Therefore, the duck commercials were tested against alternatives in experimental design situations. The test audiences loved the duck commercials and ranked them the most memorable out of all the possibilities (AFLAC's main objective). Thus, the duck was born.

The campaign has been nothing but a success. Not only has the brand recognition soared, but the company's sales growth has as well. Before the duck campaign, AFLAC's sales were growing steady in the 10% to 15% range. Post duck, AFLAC's sales are growing at an annual rate of 24 percent. Surprisingly, the growth is not limited to the United States. In fact, 70 percent of AFLAC's profits are from clients in Japan. The duck is now a world phenomenon, and AFLAC has marketing research to thank.

Questions

1. AFLAC wants to test a duck TV commercial against a nonduck TV commercial to determine which generates more favorable attitudes toward AFLAC (measured using Likert scales). What type of experimental design would you recommend? Why would you recommend this type of design?
2. Given your design in Question 1, what type of statistical test would you conduct to determine which commercial is more effective?
3. If a duck commercial is tested against two nonduck commercials to determine which TV commercial generates more favorable attitudes toward AFLAC, what type of experimental design would you recommend?
4. Given your design in Question 3, what type of statistical test would you conduct to determine which commercial is more effective?
5. If a survey is to be conducted to determine attitude toward AFLAC, how should the sample size be determined? What is the minimum sample size you recommend?
6. If the goal is to explain attitude toward AFLAC in terms of familiarity with AFLAC, what statistical technique should be used if both variables are measured using standard Likert scales?
7. If the goal is to explain attitude toward AFLAC (measured as favorable or unfavorable) in terms of familiarity with AFLAC (measured as high, medium, or low), what statistical technique should be used?
8. If the goal is to explain attitude toward AFLAC in terms of familiarity with AFLAC and attitude toward insurance, what statistical technique should be used if all three variables are measured using standard Likert scales?
9. Would it be useful to run frequencies on attitude toward AFLAC, familiarity with AFLAC, and attitude toward insurance if all three variables are measured using standard Likert scales? Why?
10. About 13 percent of the respondents have missing values on one or more variables. How would you treat the missing values?

Reference

1. Tony Adams, "Sales in Japan Help AFLAC Raise First-Quarter Net Earning by Almost 33%," *Knight Ridder Tribune Business News*, (April 28, 2004): 1.

VIDEO CASE 3.2

Honest Tea: Honesty Is the Best Policy

Honest Tea started in 1997 when Seth Goldman took a run in Central Park, New York City, and wanted a drink afterwards. What he wanted, he couldn't find–a nonsweet, healthy, clean-tasting drink. He created a batch of tea in his home. Then, along with one of his past professors from Yale, he sold the idea to Whole Foods. Whole Foods signed up to buy 15,000 bottles and Honest Tea was born. Since then, Honest Tea's 11 varieties have grown to be sold in 4,000 stores across the country, and in 2003 grossed $5.6 million in sales. In 2004, Honest Tea was finally in the black and the market leader in the natural tea industry. The mission statement of the company is: "Honest Tea creates and promotes great tasting, truly healthy, organic beverages made the way their cultures of origin intended. We strive to grow our business with the same honesty and integrity we use to craft our products."

Research has shown what is responsible for this impressive growth over the last several years: Honest Tea is honest. Goldman has been committed to giving back to the community ever since the start of the company. One of the flavors of the tea, First Nation Peppermint, is brewed from the recipe and expertise of the Crow Indian Nation. Part of the profit is then filtered back to the reservation to help build more business and facilities where unemployment is rampant. The same type of organization is set up for Harlem, South Africa. Harlem Honeybush comes from the honeybush plants that are grown in Harlem, South Africa. Again, the local community receives substantial financial compensation for the plants, which is put into computers, fax machines, and other tools to help the community develop.

According to the marketing research conducted by the company, the public likes this type of community involvement and, if a choice has to be made between Honest Tea and a similar product, the customer is likely to choose Honest Tea. Honest Tea doesn't want to help the community to make money; it wants to make money in order to help the community. However, it realizes that they go hand in hand based on the research. Marketing research has found that in blind taste tests, most consumers cannot tell the differences between tea brands. However, consumers don't choose brands blindly. They buy in stores, and they make positive and negative associations with tea brands. If this tea and that tea pretty much taste alike, well, why not buy the one known to turn some of its profits into making the world a better place.

With this desire to help others instead of making a profit, and a world community that loves to hold onto something wholesome and "honest," all the research points to this tea maker continuing to create smiles around the globe. Honest Tea wants to succeed at quenching thirsts—physical thirst for liquid and humanity's thirst for helping one another. It wants to create "more than just a business." It wants to make a difference around the world. Honest Tea should continue to make a difference, guided by marketing research and a firm belief that honesty is the best policy.

Questions

1. What research design should be adopted to measure the image of Honest Tea?
2. Design an experiment to determine which of three television commercials communicates the most positive image of Honest Tea.
3. Which primary type of scale(s) should be used to measure the image of Honest Tea?
4. In a survey measuring the image of the Honest Tea brand, consumers are asked to express their degree of agreement with the statement, "Honest Tea is the most authentic brand of tea available," using a standard Likert scale (the dependent variable). They also expressed their evaluation of Honest Tea using five-point scales (1 = poor, 5 = excellent) with the following four variables selected as independent variables: taste, healthfulness, honesty, and community involvement. Which statistical technique(s) will you use to answer the following questions?
   a. Is the Honest Tea image associated individually with each of the four independent variables?
   b. Considered collectively, which independent variables best explain the ratings of the Honest Tea image?
   c. For the sample as a whole, do the ratings on taste differ significantly from the ratings on honesty?
   d. The sample is divided into two groups: those with a favorable rating (ratings of 4 or 5) and those with an unfavorable or neutral (ratings of 1, 2, or 3) response to the Honest Tea image. Do the two groups differ in their ratings of each of the four independent variables?

5. Consider again the survey mentioned in Question 1. However, suppose that the agreement with the Honest Tea image and the four independent variables was measured using a categorical scale consisting of three categories: disagree, neutral, and agree for image, and poor, fair, and excellent for the four independent variables. Which statistical technique(s) will you use to determine whether the Honest Tea image is associated individually with each of the four independent variables?
6. Consider again the survey mentioned in Question 1. However, suppose that the agreement with the Honest Tea image was measured using the standard Likert scale, but the four independent variables were measured using a categorical scale consisting of three categories: poor, fair, and excellent. Which statistical technique(s) will you use to determine whether the Honest Tea image is associated individually with each of the four independent variables?

References

1. (www.honesttea.com).
2. Robyn Lamb, "Honest Tea–The Marketing Is in the Product's Name," *The Daily Record*, (November 28, 2003): 1.

CASES FOR PART 4: CASES WITH EXTERNAL DATA

CASE 4.1

Boeing: Taking Flight

The Boeing Company, together with its subsidiaries, is an aerospace company that operates in six principal segments. The first five are collectively known as Integrated Defense Systems (IDS) and include Commercial Airplanes, Aircraft and Weapon Systems, Network Systems, Support Systems, and Launch and Orbital Systems. The sixth principal segment is Boeing Capital Corporation (BCC). The Commercial Airplanes operations principally involve development, production, and marketing of commercial jet aircraft and providing related support services, principally to the commercial airline industry worldwide. Harry Stonecipher took over as CEO in December 2003.

In April 2004, Boeing announced its first new plane in 10 years, the 7E7 (E as in efficient) Dreamliner, a powerful but fuel-stingy midsize aircraft. This aircraft is capable of transporting passengers on long-haul routes that now are the province of jumbo jets. With spacious interiors, large luggage cabinets, and huge windows, it promises to be a change maker.

The Dreamliner, which is expected to debut in 2008, should revivify Boeing's somewhat tired product line and stem Airbus's market-share depredations. More than 3,000 midsize aircraft, including Boeing 757 and 767 and Airbus A300, A310, and A330 models, will be reaching the end of their operating lives by 2025 or so, along with various Lockheed and Douglas models. The sales opportunity is huge. Yet, the Boeing salesforce must be more effective than ever before in the company's history.

Mr. Stonecipher wants to put a very strong marketing and sales organization in place to take advantage of the opportunities that lie ahead for the 7E7 Dreamliner. His years of experience have shown him that salesperson loyalty is a very important factor because of the long-term nature of contracts with the major air carriers of the world. Being driven by fundamentals, Mr. Stonecipher wants to understand what drives a salesperson's loyalty toward the place of work. He hopes that this research effort will inform him on how to develop his business-to-business salesforce in the future through improved selection, training, and leadership of Boeing salespersons. He commissioned TNS, one of the leading custom marketing research firms, to undertake the research. The research firm of TNS adopted the following methodology.

Methodology

The project began with an exploratory phase that involved a thorough analysis of secondary data. Both academic and trade sources were examined. This was followed by eight focus groups with B2B field salespersons from a variety of industries. The findings of the exploratory phase were used to design a descriptive survey. A telephone survey was administered to a cross section of business-to-business salespersons ages 18 to 65 in the United States and in the Canadian metropolitan areas of Toronto and Montreal using a list obtained from the Sales and Marketing Executives International (SMEI). This age qualification enabled the company to reach the population of potential adult workers in the specified regions, avoiding most retirees. A final sample size comprised 1,000 adults in the United States and Canada. This sample size ensured a sampling error of less than 3 points. Expecting a cooperation rate of 33.3 percent, the sample frame consisted of 3,000 people from the SMEI list.

All U.S. telephone interviews were handled from TNS's office in Atlanta, using trained interviewers and computer-assisted telephone interviewing (CATI). Interviewing of the

Montreal and Toronto metropolitan areas was conducted locally by a Canadian affiliate of the company to best facilitate regional French and English dialects.

In terms of the survey duration, TNS's experience has shown that a 30-minute telephone interview is not desirable. The completion rate suffers as people judge it to be too long a period of time to cooperate and either refuse to participate or to complete the full interview. Therefore, the duration of the telephone interview was limited to 10 minutes. The questionnaire used is presented at the end of the case. The data obtained were analyzed. A formal report was prepared and presented to Boeing.

Building a Loyal Salesforce

As Mr. Stonecipher pondered the report from TNS, he still wondered what would be the best way for him to build the loyalty of his current salesforce toward Boeing. He would also like to recruit a new breed of loyal salespeople. The potential for the 7E7 Dreamliner is high. Having a loyal salesforce would be a key to realizing it.

Questions

Chapter 1

1. Discuss the role that marketing research can play in helping Mr. Stonecipher build a strong salesforce.
2. Discuss the role that marketing research can play in enabling strong sales for the 7E7 Dreamliner.

Chapter 2

1. Mr. Stonecipher would like to see that the 7E7 Dreamliner is a strong success. Define the management-decision problem.
2. Define the corresponding marketing research problem.
3. Develop two research questions with two hypotheses corresponding to each.

Chapter 3

1. Do you think that the research design adopted by TNS was appropriate? Why or why not?

Chapters 4 and 5

1. Search the Internet to determine the demand by a major airline for new planes in the next five years.
2. Search the Internet to determine the total number of passengers that traveled by air in the past year.
3. What type of internal database will help Boeing in forecasting the demand for new planes by its customers?

Chapter 6

1. Discuss the role of qualitative research in helping Boeing develop and market the 7E7 Dreamliner.
2. Which qualitative research technique should be used to determine air passengers' attitudes and preferences for various types of aircraft?

Chapter 7

1. If a survey is to be conducted to determine air passengers' attitudes and preferences for various types of aircraft, which survey method should be used and why?
2. If a survey is to be conducted to determine commercial airlines' attitudes and preferences for various types of aircraft, which survey method should be used and why?
3. Was the telephone survey conducted by TNS the most appropriate method for determining the drivers of salesforce loyalty toward the place of work? If not, which survey method would you recommend?

Chapter 8

1. Discuss the role of causal research in developing an advertising campaign for the 7E7 Dreamliner.

Chapter 9

1. Develop ordinal and interval scales for measuring preference of commercial airlines for Boeing 757, 767, and 7E7 and Airbus A300, A310, and A330 models.

Chapter 10

1. Develop Likert, semantic differential, and Stapel scales for measuring the importance that commercial airlines attach to the fuel efficiency of a plane.
2. Which type of scale would you use for measuring commercial airlines' image of Boeing? Develop such a scale.

Chapter 11

1. Critically evaluate the questionnaire given in this case. What improvements do you suggest?

Chapter 12

1. Describe the sampling plan adopted in this case. Do you think it is appropriate?

Chapter 13

1. Do you think that the sample size was appropriate in this case? Present statistical reasoning to support your answer.

Chapter 14

1. This case made use of telephone surveys. How would you customize the field work process mentioned in the book to the case of telephone interviews?

Chapter 15

1. Carry out consistency checks for the data file for this case. Do you identify any problems with the data?
2. Develop a codebook for Questions D1 to D12 of the questionnaire for this case.

Chapter 16

1. Run a frequency distribution including descriptive statistics for all the variables. Interpret the results.
2. Recode Question 3 ("How loyal would you say that you are personally to the place you work?") into a new variable with two categories (1 to 6 = 1, low loyalty; 7 = 2, high loyalty). Recode Question 4 ("How much loyalty would you say the place you work for has to you?") into a new variable with three categories (1 to 3 = 1, no loyalty; 4 to 5 = 2, some loyalty; 6 to 7 = 3, high loyalty). Are these two categorical variables associated? Interpret your results.
3. Do salespeople who exhibit low or high loyalty to a place of work (recoded Question 3) differ in terms of each of the demographic characteristics, D1 to D12? In other words, is salesperson loyalty associated with any of the 12 demographic characteristics? Note that age (D10) is recorded as the year of birth. Instead of D10, use the age variable. Divide the sample into four roughly equal age groups based on age.
4. Sum all the items (a through o) of Question 2 to form an overall satisfaction scale. Obtain a frequency distribution and summary statistics for this overall satisfaction scale. Interpret the results.

Chapter 17

1. Do salespeople who exhibit low or high loyalty to a place of work (recoded Question 3) differ in terms of each of the items of Question 1 (a through h)?
2. Do salespeople who exhibit low or high loyalty to a place of work (recoded Question 3) differ in terms of each of the satisfaction items of Question 2 (a through o)? Identify the five items that exhibit the greatest difference between the two groups.
3. Do the no-loyalty, some-loyalty, or high-loyalty groups of Question 4 (recoded Question 4) differ in terms of each of the satisfaction items of Question 2 (a through o)?

Chapter 18

1. What is the correlation between the two original loyalty measures of Questions 3 and 4? What can be said of the causal relationship between the two original measures of loyalty?
2. Conduct a multiple regression using the loyalty to the place of work (original Question 3) as the dependent variable. The five independent variables will be the

five items of Question 2 that exhibited the greatest difference in the *t*-tests of Chapter 17. Interpret the results.

3. Conduct a multiple regression using the loyalty to the place of work (original Question 4) as the dependent variable and items a through f of Question 2 as the independent variables. Interpret the results.

Chapter 19

1. What do Mr. Stonecipher and his staff need to know about business-to-business salesperson loyalty? Create a one-page, single-spaced summary of these results.

References

1. (www.boeing.com).
2. Jonathan R. Laing, "Taking Flight: A No-Nonsense CEO and the Promise of 7E7 have Boeing Climbing Again," *Barron's,* (July 5, 2004): 17–19.

Note: This case was prepared for class-discussion purposes only and does not represent the views of Boeing, TNS, or their affiliates. The problem scenario is hypothetical. However, the data provided are real as collected in an actual survey.

Survey of North American B2B Salespersons

Hello, I am _____ from TNS, a national public opinion research firm. We are conducting a very important survey about job satisfaction for B2B salespersons. For your help today, we will send you an executive summary of the results of our study. This will allow you to understand how your perspectives compare with other B2B salespersons. This survey should take no more than 10 minutes.

Screener Questions

(CATI Programmer: Please note that all screener questions and responses must be included in the programming so that individual responses can be tabulated for respondents that qualify.)

S1. Are you currently employed full-time, employed part-time, or are you not employed?

a. Full-time	SKIP TO Q.1
b. Part-time	SKIP TO Q.1
c. Employed on a temporary basis	SKIP TO Q.1
d. Employed on a contract basis	SKIP TO Q.1
e. Not employed	CONTINUE
f. Retired	CONTINUE
g. Don't know/refused	DO NOT READ

S2. Do you plan to enter (or reenter) the workforce within the next year, the next 1 to 5 years, the next 5 to 10 years, longer than 10 years, or not at all?

a. Within the next year	CONTINUE
b. 1 to 5 years	CONTINUE
c. 5 to 10 years	CONTINUE
d. >10 years	CONTINUE
e. Not at all	THANK AND TERMINATE

(ASK EVERYONE)

1. I would like you to think about how work fits into your life personally, whether or not you are currently working. I am going to read you some statements about working and your career. Using a scale from 1 to 7–where 1 means *"completely disagree"* and 7 means *"completely agree,"* I'd like you to consider each statement. First (READ STATEMENT). (RANDOMIZE LIST)
   - **a.** I am just starting out in the work world.
   - **b.** I am moving up the ladder in my work, but I haven't reached my peak yet.
   - **c.** I am at the peak of my working potential.
   - **d.** I am in a holding pattern when it comes to work, not really moving ahead but not falling behind.
   - **e.** I am now past the peak of my work life and am slowing down.

f. I expect to retire from work in the next five years.
g. I am on a break from working at the moment but expect to return to work within the next twelve months.
h. I am not working at the moment and do not expect to return for at least a year.

(ASKED OF THOSE WHO ANSWERED "a," "b," "c," or "d" TO S1.)

2. Please rate each of the following aspects of your work in terms of how satisfied you feel with each. Please use a scale of 1 to 7, with 1 meaning you *"disagree very much"* with that aspect and 7 meaning you *"very much agree"* with that aspect of your work. (RANDOMIZE LIST)
a. Management really knows its job.
b. My customers are fair.
c. I'm really doing something worthwhile in my job.
d. My work is challenging.
e. I have plenty of freedom on my job to use my own judgment.
f. I'm satisfied with the way employee benefits are handled around here.
g. My opportunities for advancement are reasonable.
h. I am highly paid.
i. My job is interesting.
j. The workspace given is adequate.
k. Compared with other companies, employee benefits here are good.
l. The people I work with get along well together.
m. I'm allowed to work from home, if I desire.
n. Management here is really interested in the welfare of employees.
o. I have plenty of freedom on my job to use my own judgment.

(ASKED OF THOSE WHO ANSWERED "a," "b," "c," or "d" TO S1.)

3. We hear a lot these days about company loyalty or the degree to which employees feel loyal and committed to their employer. How loyal would you say that you are personally to the place you work using a scale of 1 to 7, where 1 means *"not at all loyal"* and 7 means *"extremely loyal"*?
1 2 3 4 5 6 7

(ASKED OF THOSE WHO ANSWERED "a," "b," "c," or "d" TO S1.)

4. Now using the same scale where 1 means *"not at all loyal"* and 7 means *"extremely loyal,"* how much loyalty would you say the place you work for has to *you*?
1 2 3 4 5 6 7

Demographics

D1. Gender
a. Male
b. Female

D2. What is the highest level of education you have completed?
a. Some high school or less
b. High school graduate
c. Some college
d. College graduate
e. Post-graduate degree
f. Don't know/refused DO NOT READ

D3. What is your current marital status?
a. Single
b. Married
c. Living with someone as if married
d. Separated
e. Divorced
f. Widowed
g. Don't know/refused DO NOT READ

D4. How would you classify yourself?
- **a.** American Indian or Alaskan Native
- **b.** Asian
- **c.** Black or African American
- **d.** White
- **e.** Other [specify: _____]
- **f.** Don't know/refused DO NOT READ

D5. Do you consider yourself to be of Hispanic origin?
- **a.** Yes
- **b.** No
- **c.** Don't know/refused DO NOT READ

D6. How many children under the age of 6 are currently living at home with you?
- **a.** Under age 6 _____

D7. How long have you been working in your current position?
- **a.** Less than 1 year
- **b.** 1 to less than 5 years
- **c.** 5 to less than 10 years
- **d.** 10 to less than 20 years
- **e.** 20 to less than 30 years
- **f.** 30 years or more
- **g.** Don't know/refused DO NOT READ

D8. Do you plan to change jobs in the next five years?
- **a.** Yes
- **b.** No
- **c.** Don't know/refused DO NOT READ

(ASK EVERYONE)

D9. How many jobs have you had in the past five years?
- **a.** 0
- **b.** 1
- **c.** 2
- **d.** 3
- **e.** 4
- **f.** 5
- **g.** Between 5 and 10
- **h.** 10 or more
- **i.** Don't know/refused DO NOT READ

D10. In what year were you born?
- **a.** _____
- **b.** Refused DO NOT READ

D11. How many people in your household contribute their income to the household?
- **a.** 0
- **b.** 1
- **c.** 2
- **d.** 3 or more
- **e.** Don't know/refused DO NOT READ

D12. I'm going to read to you a list of income categories. Please stop me when I get to the category that best describes the total combined household income before taxes of all members of your household.
- **a.** Under $25,000
- **b.** $25,000 to less than $40,000
- **c.** $40,000 to less than $50,000
- **d.** $50,000 to less than $60,000
- **e.** $60,000 to less than $75,000
- **f.** $75,000 to less than $100,000
- **g.** $100,000 to less than $150,000
- **h.** $150,000 or more
- **i.** Don't know/refused DO NOT READ

D13. State _____

Thank you for completing The Survey of North American B2B Salespersons. If you would like an e-mail copy of the executive summary, please provide your e-mail address now. You should receive your copy in the next 90 days from TNS.

CASE 4.2

Do Gucci Catalogs Stack Up in Direct Marketing?

Catalogs, one type of direct-mail merchandising, have been increasing in popularity as consumers look for convenience in their shopping. Catalog business has even been expanding on the international horizon. Harris Catalog Library has offered 1,250 domestic and international catalogs from which patrons can order. Catalog libraries can be found close to home, in U.S. libraries, and as far away as Japanese department stores. The Japanese have been especially fond of shopping by catalog because they save up to 30 or 40 percent over local retailers by ordering American products directly from catalogs.

Approximately 12 billion catalogs are produced each year in the United States. The largest catalogers were expected to generate 90 percent of the entire industry's revenues, which were projected to approach an estimated $125.1 billion in 2005. This projection came from the "Future of Catalogs" report, which was prepared by W. A. Dean & Associates. According to the study, larger players would sell a wider array of products in the future. This growth won't be realized through a return to the "big book" catalog it predicted, but through the distribution of specialized titles with a narrower product focus.

Closer to home, American catalog marketers have been striving to increase sales and promote catalog growth on the domestic horizon. The big dilemma facing these marketers is how to accomplish this goal—a difficult task since look-alike catalogs and merchandising is standard in the industry. The problem is only compounded by the fact that attempts to break out of this trend are unusual for catalog marketers, especially because the industry occupies one of the most conservative locations on the American marketing landscape.

A few catalog marketers have made attempts to break away from the traditional modes of catalog marketing. Gucci is one such company that employs innovative marketing techniques. Gucci's unorthodox style emerged in 1985 when the Gucci autumn/winter catalog took a new distribution route in the United States. For the first time, Gucci catalogs were made available in bookstores.

Gucci fell on bad times in the early 1980s, but revitalized itself by the 1990s primarily by the leadership of Maurizio Gucci, the company's owner and original designer. Despite the killing of Maurizio Gucci by his wife in March 1995, Gucci continued to expand its presence both globally and in the United States. A great deal of their strategy involved creating a unified image for Gucci worldwide and discontinuing products that did not fit that image. Gucci's CEO, Domenico De Sole, personally traveled the globe to visit Gucci's stores and closed several that did not present Gucci's products effectively. Part of the effort to revitalize Gucci's image has been with a catalog of very high standard. According to a company spokesperson, "the amount that Gucci spends on catalogs is unheard of in the industry."

Described as a product in itself, the Gucci catalog was predicted to generate interest that went beyond the typical catalog, even offering editorial appeal. Released in early September 2004, the Gucci catalog had a cover price of $5. Five thousand copies of the catalog were given to Crown Publishers for distribution, and Gucci began courting other booksellers such as Rizzoli, Endicott, Waldenbooks, and B. Dalton. Containing 96 color pages, the book was produced in-house at a very high budget.

Apart from bookstores, the Gucci catalog was also available in Gucci stores and was mailed out free of charge to 50,000 of Gucci's best customers. The merchandise shown in the catalog was available in the stores, by mail, by telephone, or on the Internet (www.gucci.com). Furthermore, this strategy allowed Gucci to determine where the customers got their catalogs. The order forms in each catalog were coded to indicate whether the catalog was distributed through bookstores, the Gucci stores, or through the mail.

While this campaign was not as successful as Gucci would have liked, the company did not give up on the idea of developing a new approach to generate growth and sales. In particular, Gucci hoped to gain a competitive advantage by capitalizing on the latest high-technology development for direct marketers—automated voice response.

Automated voice response (AVR), also known as audiotex, combines computer intelligence with telephone accessibility, a phenomenon with tremendous marketing applications. This technique has leapt to even greater heights with the introduction of interactive 900 numbers. Unlike an 800 number, for which the marketer pays the cost, the cost of the 900 number call is passed on to the consumer. This is done by billing callers on their monthly phone bill, and the marketer receives any money that is left after the telephone company deducts its charge.

The marketing department at Gucci thought that it might use AVR technology to build catalog readership. They felt confident that they could do this by working under the assumption that "...the more time people spend poring over the pages of a catalog, the more likely they are to find something in there that they can't live without." To gain readership, a game that required a touch-tone phone would be employed. On the cover of the catalog, the reader would be informed that there were lucky numbers scattered throughout the catalog. When lucky numbers were found, the person could dial the game phone number (which could be an 800 or 900 number) and punch in the lucky numbers along with their personal identification code (PIN). The person was instructed to try finding as many lucky numbers as possible, since the more lucky numbers a person had, the greater the discount on purchases made from the catalog. This game, therefore, not only benefited Gucci by stimulating readership (due to the consumer's increased scrutiny of the catalog for lucky numbers), but also served as an inducement for the customer to make a catalog purchase.

Unfortunately, while the marketing department felt that they had a winning strategy, top management was not so sure. Before authorizing the implementation of this plan, top management wanted a marketing researcher to assess if the plan was a viable one. Based on the researcher's report, management would decide whether or not to give marketing the green light. As the company looked to the future, Gucci management realized that reliance on marketing research was essential for continued success.

Questions

Chapter 1

1. Marketing research involves the identification, collection, analysis, and dissemination of information. Explain how each of these phases of marketing research applies to Gucci's problem.
2. Is the problem facing Gucci a case of problem identification research or problem solution research? Explain.
3. How can Gucci use MIS or DSS to assist them in their study?

Chapter 2

1. Before marketing research can effectively be carried out, a marketing research problem must be defined. However, to arrive at a problem definition, the first thing that must occur is the analysis of the environmental factors of the problem. In the Gucci catalog scenario, what information, relevant to the construction of a problem definition, can be obtained from the environmental factors and how might it be obtained?
2. What is the management-decision problem?
3. What is the marketing research problem?
4. The tasks undertaken to help define the problem (i.e., discussions with management, interviews with experts, secondary data analysis, and qualitative research) are also helpful in developing an approach to the marketing research problem. How can these tasks help in developing an approach?
5. Regardless of which techniques are used to develop the problem, the approach development process should produce several outputs. What output might result from the approach process applied to the Gucci scenario, in terms of
   a. Objective/theoretical foundations
   b. Research questions
   c. Hypotheses

Chapter 3

1. Can exploratory research be used in this case, and if so, how?
2. Can descriptive research be used in this case, and if so, how?
3. Can causal research be used in this case, and if so, how?

Chapters 4 and 5

1. What internal sources of secondary data can you identify which would be helpful to Gucci?
2. What published sources of secondary data can you identify that would be helpful?
3. Would you recommend using syndicate sources of secondary data? If so, which ones would you recommend?

Chapter 6

1. Which exploratory research techniques would you recommend and why?
2. Develop a moderator's outline for a focus group to assess consumer desires in catalog purchases with respect to Gucci.
3. Devise word association techniques to measure consumer associations that may affect attitudes towards catalogs.
4. Design sentence completion techniques to uncover underlying motives.

Chapter 7

1. Which of the criteria for selecting survey methods are most important in this case? Please explain your reasoning.
2. Which survey method would you recommend to Gucci for conducting descriptive research? Why? What are the limitations of this method?
3. Can observational methods be used to collect data? How? What are the limitations of your method?

Chapter 8

1. Is causal research necessary in this case? If so, which experimental designs would you recommend and why? If not, devise a scenario in which it would be.
2. If a mall intercept interview is used and Gucci conducts causal research without randomizing respondents, which preexperimental design would you recommend?
3. Can you think of any way in which the static group design above can be randomized to increase its validity?

Chapters 9 and 10

1. In constructing an item for a questionnaire, Gucci decides to use a noncomparative itemized rating scale to measure attitudes (i.e., like or dislike) toward Gucci catalogs. They ask you to construct a Likert scale for this item. Construct the scale.
2. What types of comparative scales can be used to gather the information needed on motivation, attitudes, and intentions? Design these scales.
3. What types of noncomparative scales can be used to gather the information needed on psychographics, motivation, attitudes, and intentions?
4. How would you determine the reliability of the scales?
5. How would you assess the validity of the scales?

Chapter 11

1. What challenges exist in this case in meeting the three objectives of a questionnaire?
2. Design a questionnaire to be used in a survey.

Chapter 12

Answer Questions 1 through 3 assuming that an in-home personal interview is being conducted.

1. What is the target population for this study?
2. What sampling frame can you use?
3. What sampling technique do you recommend for this study and why?

Chapter 13

1. Suppose Gucci conducts a preliminary market study of 12 respondents to determine the average discount respondents would like to receive from a promotional game. The mean response is calculated to be $5. If Gucci wants to be 90 percent sure that the true value lies within $0.50 of this figure, how large a sample do they

need to survey given that the sample standard deviation is $2? What is the confidence interval for the mean based on the preliminary market study?

2. Suppose after conducting the experiment in Exercise 1, Gucci learns that these observations generated a mean of $6.00 and sample standard deviation of $3. What is a better estimate of the 90 percent confidence interval than previously calculated?

Chapter 14

Answer the following questions assuming in-home personal interviews are being conducted.

1. What characteristics would you look for when hiring field workers for this survey?
2. What issues are most important in training your field workers for this survey?
3. What issues must you as the supervisor be most concerned with during the interviewing?
4. How would you validate the field work?
5. How would you evaluate the success of your field workers?

Chapter 15

1. Suppose the following responses appeared on completed questionnaires which you, as the project supervisor, are editing. What is the problem with the responses, and how would you treat them?
   a. How likely are you to participate in this promotional game?
   Not So Likely Maybe/Maybe Not Very Likely
   1 2 3 4 5 6 7
   Please explain why or why not.
   Games sometimes are fun.
   For the next two questions, assume that we can not recontact the respondent, only three unsatisfactory responses exist, and the sample size is 200.
   b. How likely are you to participate in this promotional game?
   Not So Likely Maybe/Maybe Not Very Likely
   1 2 3 4 5 6**X** 7
   Please explain why or why not.
   I don't like games. They bore me and really don't save any money when you buy something.
   c. How likely are you to participate in this promotional game?
   Not So Likely Maybe/Maybe Not Very Likely
   1 2 3 4 5 6 7
   Please explain why or why not.
   I probably wouldn't play the game since it takes too much time to look through the whole catalog. I usually know what I want and go right to it.
2. Develop a codebook for the first 10 questions in the questionnaire given at the end of the case.

Chapter 16

A survey was designed (see questionnaire given at the end of the case) and data were collected from 250 respondents. Run the following analyses on the data (provided for this case), and draw conclusions from the results obtained.

1. Run descriptive statistics and obtain frequency distributions for all variables. Interpret the results.
2. Determine if receiving catalogs (Q1), playing promotional games (Q4), awareness of Gucci (Q8), receiving Gucci catalogs (Q9), looking through Gucci catalogs (Q10), and purchasing from a Gucci catalog (Q11) are related to any of the demographic variables (Q14 to Q18, Q20).

Chapter 17

1. Conduct two-group *t*-tests to see if there is any difference in responses to the demonstration catalog shown (Q13) between those who are aware of Gucci and those who are not (Q8), between those who have received a Gucci catalog and those who have not (Q9), between those who have looked through a Gucci catalog and those who have not (Q10), and between those who have purchased from a Gucci catalog and those who have not (Q11).

2. Determine whether the respondents have greater agreement with "Games save me money" (Q6c) than with "I play games for enjoyment" (Q6d) in answering the Gucci questionnaire. Formulate the null and alternative hypotheses, and prescribe an appropriate statistical test.
3. Determine whether the respondents find promotional games in catalogs to be more fun (Q5a) than sophisticated (Q5b). Formulate the null and alternative hypotheses, and prescribe an appropriate statistical test.
4. Conduct a one-way analysis of variance to see if there is any difference in responses to the demonstration catalog shown (Q13) among those who receive Gucci catalogs, those who receive other catalogs, and those who receive no catalogs (Q2).
5. Conduct a one-way analysis of variance with each of the six statements of Q6 describing opinions about playing games in catalogs as the dependent variable. The independent variables will be the demographic variables (Q14 to Q18, Q20). Thus, you will run 36 different analyses ($6 \times 6 = 36$). Interpret the results.

Chapter 18

1. Regress each of the four dimensions of promotional games (Q5) on the respondents' attitudes toward playing promotional games (Q6). Thus, you will be running four separate regressions. Interpret the results.
2. Regress each of the six statements of Q13 describing Gucci catalog ratings against the four statements of Q12. Thus, you will be running six separate regressions. Interpret the results.

Chapter 19

1. Prepare an executive summary of the results from the study. Specifically, answer the research questions that were posed at the beginning of the study.

References

1. John Carreyrou and Cecilie Rohwedder, "Style & Substance: In Again at Gucci: Licensing; PPR Says It May Start to Sell Franchises, Product Rights for Smaller Designer Brands," *The Wall Street Journal,* (Eastern edition), (March 5, 2004): A9.
2. John Carreyrou and Alessandra Galloni, "Can Gucci Make Its Other Label Profitable?" *The Wall Street Journal,* (Eastern edition), (November 6, 2003): B1.

Note: This case was prepared for class-discussion purposes only and does not represent the views of Gucci or their affiliates. The problem scenario is hypothetical, and the data provided are simulated.

Gucci Questionnaire

Please answer ALL the questions whether or not your household currently receives a Gucci catalog.

Q1. Do you currently receive catalogs in the mail?

Yes _____
No _____

Q2. What catalogs are you currently receiving?

_____

_____

Q3. In the catalogs you have received in the past year, did any of them have a promotional game?

Yes _____
No _____

If YES, which catalogs had promotional games?

_____

_____

Q4. Did you play any of the promotional games in the catalogs?

Yes _____
No _____

(If NO, go to Question Q8)

Q5. Please mark the scale below in terms of what the statement means to you.
Promotional games in catalogs are

a. Fun |___|___|___|___|___|___|___| Dull
b. Sophisticated |___|___|___|___|___|___|___| Simplistic
c. Valuable |___|___|___|___|___|___|___| Not valuable
d. Worth my time |___|___|___|___|___|___|___| Not worth my time

Q6. Below are statements that describe different opinions about playing the games in catalogs which have been sent to you. Please indicate how strongly you agree or disagree with each statement by using the following scale:

1 = Strongly Disagree
2 = Disagree
3 = Somewhat Disagree
4 = Neither Agree nor Disagree
5 = Somewhat Agree
6 = Agree
7 = Strongly Agree

	Strongly Disagree			**Neither Agree nor Disagree**			**Strongly Agree**
a. Promotional games in magazines add to the image of the magazine.	1	2	3	4	5	6	7
b. I'm likely to buy something from a catalog which has a game in it.	1	2	3	4	5	6	7
c. Games save me money on my shopping.	1	2	3	4	5	6	7
d. I play games for the enjoyment.	1	2	3	4	5	6	7
e. I play games because I like to win.	1	2	3	4	5	6	7
f. It is important for a game to offer real savings on items in the catalog.	1	2	3	4	5	6	7

Q7. Please mark the scales below in terms of what the statement means to you.
Company catalogs I receive in the mail are

a. Helpful |___|___|___|___|___|___|___| A bother
b. Informative |___|___|___|___|___|___|___| Not informative

Shopping from a catalog is

c. Convenient |___|___|___|___|___|___|___| Not convenient
d. Inexpensive |___|___|___|___|___|___|___| Expensive
e. Easy |___|___|___|___|___|___|___| Difficult
f. Advisable |___|___|___|___|___|___|___| Not advisable

Q8. Have you ever heard of Gucci?
Yes _____
No _____

Q9. Have you ever received a Gucci catalog in the mail?
Yes _____
No _____

Q10. Have you ever looked through a Gucci catalog?
Yes _____
No _____

Q11. Have you ever purchased anything from a Gucci catalog?

Yes _____

No _____

Q12. Please mark the scales below in terms of what the statement means to you.

Gucci is

a. Expensive |__|__|__|__|__|__|__| Inexpensive

b. Sophisticated |__|__|__|__|__|__|__| Common

c. High status |__|__|__|__|__|__|__| Low status

d. Poor quality |__|__|__|__|__|__|__| Top quality

I am going to show you a Gucci catalog. I would like you to look through the catalog for a few minutes before answering the next question. (Give the respondent catalog.)

Q13. Please rate the catalog you have just seen on the following attributes. Use a 1 to 7 scale where 1 means Very Poor and 7 means Excellent.

	Very Poor						Excellent
a. Attention grabbing	1	2	3	4	5	6	7
b. Fun to look at	1	2	3	4	5	6	7
c. Matches the Gucci image	1	2	3	4	5	6	7
d. Shows quality products	1	2	3	4	5	6	7
e. Fashionable	1	2	3	4	5	6	7
f. Easy to place an order	1	2	3	4	5	6	7

Q14. Your gender?

a. _____ Male

b. _____ Female

Q15. Marital Status

a. _____ Married

b. _____ Never Married

c. _____ Divorced/Separated/Widowed

Q16. Family Size

a. _____ 1

b. _____ 2

c. _____ 3

d. _____ 4

e. _____ 5+

Q17. Your age?

a. _____ 18–24

b. _____ 25–40

c. _____ 41–60

d. _____ 60+

Q18. Your formal education?

a. Less Than High School _____

b. High School Graduate _____

c. Some College _____

d. College Graduate _____

Q19. What is your address?

_____

Q20. What is the approximate combined annual income of your household before taxes?

a. $10,000 or less _____

b. $10,001 to $30,000 _____

c. $30,001 to $50,000 _____

d. $50,001 to $90,000 _____

e. $90,001 to $150,000 _____

f. $150,001 and over _____

Thank you for your participation.

VideO CASES FOR PART 4

VIDEO CASE 4.1

Subaru: "Mr. Survey" Monitors Customer Satisfaction

Subaru is the automobile division of Fuji Heavy Industries (FHI). Subaru has been operating in the United States since 1968 when it began selling the 360 Minicar. Subaru has offered many different cars over the years but as of 2005 it sold five different brands in the United States. These brands each include a variety of different models that can be purchased. The five main brands are the Outback, Forester, Legacy, Impreza, and Baja. One of the unique things about Subaru is that 100 percent of its models come with all-wheel drive. The Outback and Forester fall into the sport-utility category, Baja combines the versatility of a pickup truck with the ride and handling of a passenger car, while the Legacy and Impreza fall into the more traditional four-door car category.

Subaru's strategy is apparent in one of its key players, Joe Barstys. Joe has been with Subaru for 18 years, and he spends his time there worrying about customer satisfaction. Joe and people like him are the backbone of Subaru. These people help Subaru focus on the customer and cater to the wants and needs of these customers by conducting marketing research. Joe has incorporated the use of customer surveys into his practice and for this he has gained the title of "Mr. Survey." Joe's goal is to develop a customer satisfaction level that will help to build a certain level of loyalty in Subaru's customers. This loyalty is extremely important in the car business because it has historically been much lower than in other industries. In fact, while approximately 90 percent of customers are pleased with their automobile purchase, only 40 percent are loyal enough to buy the same brand again. This is a result of the short-term approach that has been traditionally used by the auto industry. Subaru hopes to avoid this approach by making the entire experience of owning a Subaru an enjoyable one.

Surveys are a very valuable tool to Subaru in the quest for customer loyalty. The company mails a survey to each customer within 30 to 45 days of purchase to assess customer's feelings toward the newly purchased vehicle, to obtain information on the nature of the interaction with the dealer, and to learn about other elements of the car buying process. Subsequent to the initial contact, more surveys follow throughout the "lifetime" of the customer (that is, the duration of ownership of the car, on average six to seven years). The latter surveys assess the long-term satisfaction with the vehicle and the dealership. The mail surveys have a high 50 percent response rate. As of 2005, about 500,000 surveys are mailed each year. Additional surveys are conducted over the Internet. These surveys provide important feedback, allowing Subaru to adjust its approach to the demands of the consumer. An example of the importance of adjustments can be found in the case of the female consumer. Through surveying, Subaru learned that it needed to adjust its marketing to include female consumers, who are becoming an increasingly large part of the market. It was important for Subaru to understand what types of features would appeal to women in order to offer a more desirable product for them.

Another benefit of marketing and survey research is that Subaru has been able to identify what types of people are more likely to buy its automobiles. Subaru believes that the typical Subaru owner is different from the average consumer. The typical Subaru consumer is highly intelligent, highly independent, and somebody that is outside the mainstream crowd. Thus, Subaru tries to market automobiles to these types of people and attempts to distinguish itself from the larger, more mainstream competitors. Results of affinity for the company can be seen already as customers have felt motivated to send pictures of their cars to Subaru.

Subaru is ambitiously aiming for U.S. sales of more than 250,000 units in 2006 and hopes that with the help of marketing research, it will achieve this goal. It believes that listening to the customers and adapting its practices to meet their concerns will provide customers with a higher level of satisfaction and ultimately lead to a higher level of loyalty. Subaru's marketing research staff, like "Mr. Survey," will be critical to this endeavor.

Questions

1. Discuss the role that marketing research can play in helping Subaru understand the devotion of consumers to its brands.
2. To continue to grow, Subaru must foster and build the loyalty of its customers. Define the management-decision problem.
3. Define an appropriate marketing research problem based on the management-decision problem you have identified.
4. What type of research design should be adopted to investigate the marketing research problem you have identified?
5. In what way can Subaru make use of Census 2000 data? What are the limitations of these data? How can these limitations be overcome?
6. What type of data available from syndicate marketing research firms will be useful to Subaru?
7. Discuss the role of qualitative research in understanding the devotion of consumers to a particular automobile brand. Which qualitative research technique(s) should be used and why?
8. If a survey is to be conducted to understand consumer preferences for various automobile brands, which survey method should be used and why?
9. Design ordinal, interval, and ratio scales for measuring consumer preferences for various automobile brands.
10. Design a questionnaire to measure consumers' evaluation of Subaru brands.
11. Develop a sampling plan for the survey in Question 8.
12. How should the sample size be determined?
13. How would you supervise and evaluate the field workers conducting the survey in Question 8.
14. Qualitative research has indicated that the following factors influence the willingness of consumers to purchase an automobile brand (dependent variable): (1) reliability, (2) performance, (3) gas mileage, (4) repair and maintenance, (5) price, (6) image, and (7) features (independent variables). In a survey, consumers were asked to state their willingness to purchase an automobile brand by Subaru, Toyota, Honda, and Nissan using five-point scales ranging from 1 = not at all willing to 5 = very willing. The respondents were also asked to evaluate each of these four major brands on the seven independent variables, again using five-point scales ranging from 1 = Very Poor to 5 = Very Good. What statistical analyses will you perform to answer the following questions?
    a. Is the willingness to purchase an automobile brand related to each of the seven independent variables when the variables are considered individually?
    b. Is the willingness to purchase an automobile brand related to all the seven independent variables when the variables are considered simultaneously?
    c. Do the respondents rate Subaru brands higher on reliability than image?
    d. Are Toyota brands perceived as more reliable than Subaru brands?
    e. Do the evaluations of Subaru based on the seven independent variables differ for those who have purchased and those who have not purchased a Subaru brand?
    f. Are men more willing to purchase Subaru brands than women?
    g. Respondents were classified into four age groups: less than 25, 26 to 45, 46 to 65, and 66 or older. Do the four groups differ in their willingness to purchase Subaru brands?
    h. Willingness to purchase Toyota brands was classified into three categories: unwilling (ratings of 1 and 2), neutral (rating of 3), and willing (ratings of 4 and 5). Do the four age groups of Question (g) differ in their willingness to purchase Toyota brands?
    i. Do the never married, currently married, and divorced/separated/widowed groups differ in their willingness to purchase Subaru brands?

j. Do the never married, currently married, and divorced/separated/widowed groups differ in their willingness to purchase Toyota brands as classified in Question (h)?

15. Prepare an outline of an oral presentation to Subaru management.
16. If Subaru were to conduct marketing research to determine consumer willingness to purchase automobile brands in Germany, how would the research process be different?
17. Discuss the ethical issues involved in researching consumer willingness to purchase automobile brands.

References

1. (www.subaru.com).
2. Donald I. Hammonds, "Subaru Adds Upscale Looks to Its Durable Image," *Knight Ridder Tribune Business News,* (June 16, 2004): 1.

VIDEO CASE 4.2

Marriott: Marketing Research Leads to Expanded Offerings

With roots to back before the Great Depression, Marriott has come a long way from being founded by husband and wife John and Alice Marriott. Host Marriott (www.hostmarriott.com), the parent company, is responsible for 14 subsidiaries, including Marriott, Ritz Carlton, Courtyard by Marriott, Fairfield Inn and Suites, and Residence Inn. As of 2005, Marriott had a presence in 65 countries with more than 2,500 properties and more than $20 billion in annual sales.

This sustained vast expansion over the last several decades is due in large part to marketing research. Marriott began pioneering segmentation in the hospitality industry by expanding its product offering in the 1980s both upward and downward in quality relative to its flagship Marriott brand. Marriott found from its research that it could have many types of hotels serving different market segments and that these market segments would not be competing with each other although they all serve the same basic needs. Certain brands under the Marriott umbrella serve the business traveler. Courtyard by Marriott, with pricing and service levels scaled back compared to the big Marriott hotels, is targeted toward the price-sensitive frequent business traveler. Courtyard hotels, said to be designed for business travelers by business travelers, offer high-speed Internet access, ample workspace within the room, and other amenities that appeal to the business traveler. Fairfield Inns are priced still more modestly to appeal to travelers who are even more price sensitive. Other brands under the Marriott flag, such as the Ramada line, offer more of a family-style vacation with focus directed toward comfort and affordability.

Differentiation is not based on service and pricing alone, however. Marketing research has revealed other attributes that are important. For example, a family or a basic business traveler on a budget might be looking for a convenient location in addition to affordability. Hence, Marriott places Fairfield Inns along interstates and highways, because these targeted groups often travel by car. Convenient location becomes another attribute that adds value and enhances perception of the Marriott brand name.

When Marriott began its Fairfield Inn and Suites brand, it started as simply Fairfield Inn. Then, with marketing research (i.e., focus groups and surveys), Marriott found that its Fairfield Inn customers desired a luxury-class room within the value hotel of the Fairfield line. Responding to this, Marriott changed the name to Fairfield Inn and Suites and added these high-class rooms that contained amenities such as spas.

Analysis of internal secondary data identified a substantial number of travelers who stayed in Marriott hotels for more than a few nights. Focus groups and surveys revealed that these extended-stay travelers have different needs. They might need meeting space to conduct business, a kitchenette to dine in occasionally, or a suite space so they don't tire of seeing the same four walls around their beds when they come "home" in the evening after yet another day on the road. For these travelers, Marriott opened the Residence Inn line, a hotel line designed for an extended stay. Marriott found from subsequent marketing research that this segment had room to expand to a more value priced line as well. Again, responding to this research, Marriott introduced TownePlace Suites (a value priced extended-stay hotel line).

At the high end, Marriott offers even fuller service and higher prices with its Hotel Resorts & Suites and its renaissance upscale business properties. According to Marriott's research estimating potential demand, the size of this high-end segment is substantial.

With all of these hotel lines, Marriott continues the commitment to quality that began with its founders. Because research has taught them that all hotel residents, whether in a Ritz Carlton or a Courtyard by Marriott, still desire quality, Marriott strives to provide this in all facets of the hotel service. One way in which Marriott demonstrates this is by empowering its customer service representatives to address customer problems. From top to bottom, Marriott is a company that listens to its customers through marketing research and continues to succeed by expanding its offerings.

Questions

1. Discuss the role that marketing research can play in helping Marriott formulate sound marketing strategies.
2. Marriott would like to further penetrate the nonbusiness travelers segment in the United States. Define the management-decision problem.
3. Define an appropriate marketing research problem based on the management-decision problem you have identified.
4. Suggest an appropriate research design for investigating the marketing research problem that you have defined.
5. Use the Internet to determine the market shares of the major hotel chains for the last calendar year.
6. What types of internal secondary data will be useful to Marriott?
7. What types of syndicate data will be useful to Marriott?
8. Discuss the role of qualitative research in helping Marriott further penetrate the nonbusiness travelers segment in the United States.
9. Marriott has developed a new hotel package for families on vacation. It would like to determine consumers' responses to this package before introducing it in the marketplace. If a survey is to be conducted to determine consumer preferences, which survey method should be used and why?
10. Develop Likert, semantic differential, and Stapel scales for measuring consumer preferences for hotel chains.
11. Develop a questionnaire for assessing consumer preferences for hotels when on vacation.
12. What sampling plan should be adopted for the survey in Question 8?
13. How should the sample size be determined for the survey in Question 8?
14. How would you conduct the training and supervision of the field-workers for the survey in Question 8?
15. According to Marriott's vice president of marketing, quality, price, service, amenities, comfort, and convenience are all independent variables that affect the preference for a hotel chain. Assume that in a survey of hotel chains, each of the independent variables is measured on a seven-point scale ranging from 1 = poor to 7 = excellent. Preference for hotel chains is also measured on a seven-point scale ranging from 1 = not at all preferred to 7 = greatly preferred. Each respondent rates Marriott and three competing hotel chains on all the independent variables as well as preference for staying there on a vacation. What statistical technique(s) would you use to answer the following questions?
    a. Is preference related to each of the independent variables considered individually? What is the nature of the relationship you expect?
    b. Is preference related to all the independent variables considered simultaneously?

c. Do the respondents evaluate the hotel chains more favorably on quality than they do on price?
d. The sample is divided into two groups: regular patrons of Marriott and patrons of other hotels. Do these two groups differ in terms of their ratings of Marriott on quality?
e. The sample is divided into three groups: heavy, medium, and light users of hotels. Do the three groups differ in terms of preference for Marriott?
f. About 13 percent of the respondents have missing values on one or more variables. How would you treat the missing values?
g. A question asked the respondents to check as many of the seven hotels they had stayed in during the past three years. How should the data for this question be coded?

16. What charts and graphs would you use in preparing a report for Marriott?
17. If marketing research to determine consumer preferences for hotels was to be conducted in Latin America, how would the research process be different?
18. Discuss the ethical issues involved in researching consumer preferences for hotels.

References

1. (www.marriott.com), (www.hostmarriot.com), and (www.hoovers.com).
2. M. A. Baumann, "High-end Offerings the Result of In-depth Research," *Hotel and Motel Management*, 219(9), (May 17, 2004): 36.

APPENDIX

Statistical Tables

Table 1 Simple Random Numbers

Line/Col.	(1)	(2)	(3)	(4)	(5)	(6)	(7)	(8)	(9)	(10)	(11)	(12)	(13)	(14)
1	10480	15011	01536	02011	81647	91646	69179	14194	62590	36207	20969	99570	91291	90700
2	22368	46573	25595	85393	30995	89198	27982	53402	93965	34095	52666	19174	39615	99505
3	24130	48390	22527	97265	76393	64809	15179	24830	49340	32081	30680	19655	63348	58629
4	42167	93093	06243	61680	07856	16376	39440	53537	71341	57004	00849	74917	97758	16379
5	37570	39975	81837	16656	06121	91782	60468	81305	49684	60072	14110	06927	01263	54613
6	77921	06907	11008	42751	27756	53498	18602	70659	90655	15053	21916	81825	44394	42880
7	99562	72905	56420	69994	98872	31016	71194	18738	44013	48840	63213	21069	10634	12952
8	96301	91977	05463	07972	18876	20922	94595	56869	69014	60045	18425	84903	42508	32307
9	89579	14342	63661	10281	17453	18103	57740	84378	25331	12568	58678	44947	05585	56941
10	85475	36857	53342	53988	53060	59533	38867	62300	08158	17983	16439	11458	18593	64952
11	28918	69578	88231	33276	70997	79936	56865	05859	90106	31595	01547	85590	91610	78188
12	63553	40961	48235	03427	49626	69445	18663	72695	52180	20847	12234	90511	33703	90322
13	09429	93969	52636	92737	88974	33488	36320	17617	30015	08272	84115	27156	30613	74952
14	10365	61129	87529	85689	48237	52267	67689	93394	01511	26358	85104	20285	29975	89868
15	07119	97336	71048	08178	77233	13916	47564	81056	97735	85977	29372	74461	28551	90707
16	51085	12765	51821	51259	77452	16308	60756	92144	49442	53900	70960	63990	75601	40719
17	02368	21382	52404	60268	89368	19885	55322	44819	01188	65255	64835	44919	05944	55157
18	01011	54092	33362	94904	31273	04146	18594	29852	71685	85030	51132	01915	92747	64951
19	52162	53916	46369	58586	23216	14513	83149	98736	23495	64350	94738	17752	35156	35749
20	07056	97628	33787	09998	42698	06691	76988	13602	51851	46104	88916	19509	25625	58104
21	48663	91245	85828	14346	09172	30163	90229	04734	59193	22178	30421	61666	99904	32812
22	54164	58492	22421	74103	47070	25306	76468	26384	58151	06646	21524	15227	96909	44592
23	32639	32363	05597	24200	13363	38005	94342	28728	35806	06912	17012	64161	18296	22851
24	29334	27001	87637	87308	58731	00256	45834	15398	46557	41135	10307	07684	36188	18510
25	02488	33062	28834	07351	19731	92420	60952	61280	50001	67658	32586	86679	50720	94953
26	81525	72295	04839	96423	24878	82651	66566	14778	76797	14780	13300	87074	79666	95725
27	29676	20591	68086	26432	46901	20849	89768	81536	86645	12659	92259	57102	80428	25280
28	00742	57392	39064	66432	84673	40027	32832	61362	98947	96067	64760	64584	96096	98253
29	05366	04213	25669	26422	44407	44048	37937	63904	45766	66134	75470	66520	34693	90449
30	91921	26418	64117	94305	26766	25940	39972	22209	71500	64568	91402	42416	07844	69618
31	00582	04711	87917	77341	42206	35126	74087	99547	81817	42607	43808	76655	62028	76630
32	00725	69884	62797	56170	86324	88072	76222	36086	84637	93161	76038	65855	77919	88006
33	69011	65795	95876	55293	18988	27354	26575	08625	40801	59920	29841	80150	12777	48501
34	25976	57948	29888	88604	67917	48708	18912	82271	65424	69774	33611	54262	85963	03547
35	09763	83473	73577	12908	30883	18317	28290	35797	05998	41688	34952	37888	38917	88050
36	91567	42595	27958	30134	04024	86385	29880	99730	55536	84855	29088	09250	79656	73211
37	17955	56349	90999	49127	20044	59931	06115	20542	18059	02008	73708	83517	36103	42791
38	46503	18584	18845	49618	02304	51038	20655	58727	28168	15475	56942	53389	20562	87338
39	92157	89634	94824	78171	84610	82834	09922	25417	44137	48413	25555	21246	35509	20468
40	14577	62765	35605	81263	39667	47358	56873	56307	61607	49518	89656	20103	77490	18062
41	98427	07523	33362	64270	01638	92477	66969	98420	04880	45585	46565	04102	46880	45709
42	34914	63976	88720	82765	34476	17032	87589	40836	32427	70002	70663	88863	77775	69348
43	70060	28277	39475	46473	23219	53416	94970	25832	69975	94884	19661	72828	00102	66794

(continued)

Table 1 (continued)

Line/Col.	(1)	(2)	(3)	(4)	(5)	(6)	(7)	(8)	(9)	(10)	(11)	(12)	(13)	(14)
44	53976	54914	06990	67245	68350	82948	11398	42878	80287	88267	47363	46634	06541	97809
45	76072	29515	40980	07391	58745	25774	22987	80059	39911	96189	41151	14222	60697	59583
46	90725	52210	83974	29992	65831	38857	50490	83765	55657	14361	31720	57375	56228	41546
47	64364	67412	33339	31926	14883	24413	59744	92351	97473	89286	35931	04110	23726	51900
48	08962	00358	31662	25388	61642	34072	81249	35648	56891	69352	48373	45578	78547	81788
49	95012	68379	93526	70765	10592	04542	76463	54328	02349	17247	28865	14777	62730	92277
50	15664	10493	20492	38301	91132	21999	59516	81652	27195	48223	46751	22923	32261	85653
51	16408	81899	04153	53381	79401	21438	83035	92350	36693	31238	59649	91754	72772	02338
52	18629	81953	05520	91962	04739	13092	97662	24822	94730	06496	35090	04822	86774	98289
53	73115	35101	47498	87637	99016	71060	88824	71013	18735	20286	23153	72924	35165	43040
54	57491	16703	23167	49323	45021	33132	12544	41035	80780	45393	44812	12515	98931	91202
55	30405	83946	23792	14422	15059	45799	22716	19792	09983	74353	68668	30429	70735	25499
56	16631	35006	85900	98275	32388	52390	16815	69293	82732	38480	73817	32523	41961	44437
57	96773	20206	42559	78985	05300	22164	24369	54224	35083	19687	11052	91491	60383	19746
58	38935	64202	14349	82674	66523	44133	00697	35552	35970	19124	63318	29686	03387	59846
59	31624	76384	17403	53363	44167	64486	64758	75366	76554	31601	12614	33072	60332	92325
60	78919	19474	23632	27889	47914	02584	37680	20801	72152	39339	34806	08930	85001	87820
61	03931	33309	57047	74211	63445	17361	62825	39908	05607	91284	68833	25570	38818	46920
62	74426	33278	43972	10119	89917	15665	52872	73823	73144	88662	88970	74492	51805	99378
63	09066	00903	20795	95452	92648	45454	69552	88815	16553	51125	79375	97596	16296	66092
64	42238	12426	87025	14267	20979	04508	64535	31355	86064	29472	47689	05974	52468	16834
65	16153	08002	26504	41744	81959	65642	74240	56302	00033	67107	77510	70625	28725	34191
66	21457	40742	29820	96783	29400	21840	15035	34537	33310	06116	95240	15957	16572	06004
67	21581	57802	02050	89728	17937	37621	47075	42080	97403	48626	68995	43805	33386	21597
68	55612	78095	83197	33732	05810	24813	86902	60397	16489	03264	88525	42786	05269	92532
69	44657	66999	99324	51281	84463	60563	79312	93454	68876	25471	93911	25650	12682	73572
70	91340	84979	46949	81973	37949	61023	43997	15263	80644	43942	89203	71795	99533	50501
71	91227	21199	31935	27022	84067	05462	35216	14486	29891	68607	41867	14951	91696	85065
72	50001	38140	66321	19924	72163	09538	12151	06878	91903	18749	34405	56087	82790	70925
73	65390	05224	72958	28609	81406	39147	25549	48542	42627	45233	57202	94617	23772	07896
74	27504	96131	83944	41575	10573	03619	64482	73923	36152	05184	94142	25299	94387	34925
75	37169	94851	39117	89632	00959	16487	65536	49071	39782	17095	02330	74301	00275	48280
76	11508	70225	51111	38351	19444	66499	71945	05422	13442	78675	84031	66938	93654	59894
77	37449	30362	06694	54690	04052	53115	62757	95348	78662	11163	81651	50245	34971	52974
78	46515	70331	85922	38329	57015	15765	97161	17869	45349	61796	66345	81073	49106	79860
79	30986	81223	42416	58353	21532	30502	32305	86482	05174	07901	54339	58861	74818	46942
80	63798	64995	46583	09785	44160	78128	83991	42865	92520	83531	80377	35909	81250	54238
81	82486	84846	99254	67632	43218	50076	21361	64816	51202	88124	41870	52689	51275	83556
82	21885	32906	92431	09060	64297	51674	64126	62570	26123	05155	59194	52799	28225	85762
83	60336	98782	07408	53458	13564	59089	26445	29789	85205	41001	12535	12133	14645	23541
84	43937	46891	24010	25560	86355	33941	25786	54990	71899	15475	95434	98227	21824	19535
85	97656	63175	89303	16275	07100	92063	21942	18611	47348	20203	18534	03862	78095	50136
86	03299	01221	05418	38982	55758	92237	26759	86367	21216	98442	08303	56613	91511	75928
87	79626	06486	03574	17668	07785	76020	79924	25651	83325	88428	85076	72811	22717	50585
88	85636	68335	47539	03129	65651	11977	02510	26113	99447	68645	34327	15152	55230	93448
89	18039	14367	61337	06177	12143	46609	32989	74014	64708	00533	35398	58408	13261	47908
90	08362	15656	60627	36478	65648	16764	53412	09013	07832	41574	17639	82163	60859	75567
91	79556	29068	04142	16268	15387	12856	66227	38358	22478	73373	88732	09443	82558	05250
92	92608	82674	27072	32534	17075	27698	98204	63863	11951	34648	88022	56148	34925	57031
93	23982	25835	40055	67006	12293	02753	14827	23235	35071	99704	37543	11601	35503	85171
94	09915	96306	05908	97901	28395	14186	00821	80703	70426	75647	76310	88717	37890	40129

Table 1 (continued)

Line/Col.	(1)	(2)	(3)	(4)	(5)	(6)	(7)	(8)	(9)	(10)	(11)	(12)	(13)	(14)
95	59037	33300	26695	62247	69927	76123	50842	43834	86654	70959	79725	93872	28117	19233
96	42488	78077	69882	61657	34136	79180	97526	43092	04098	73571	80799	76536	71255	64239
97	46764	86273	63003	93017	31204	36692	40202	35275	57306	55543	53203	18098	47625	88684
98	03237	45430	55417	63282	90816	17349	88298	90183	36600	78406	06216	95787	42579	90730
99	86591	81482	52667	61582	14972	90053	89534	76036	49199	43716	97548	04379	46370	28672
100	38534	01715	94964	87288	65680	43772	39560	12918	80537	62738	19636	51132	25739	56947

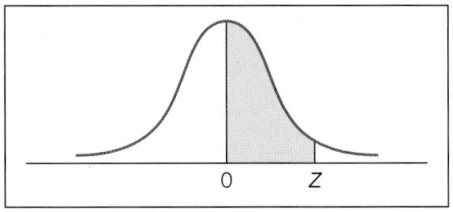

Table 2 Area Under the Normal Curve

Z	.00	.01	.02	.03	.04	.05	.06	.07	.08	.09
0.0	.0000	.0040	.0080	.0120	.0160	.0199	.0239	.0279	.0319	.0359
0.1	.0398	.0438	.0478	.0517	.0557	.0596	.0636	.0675	.0714	.0753
0.2	.0793	.0832	.0871	.0910	.0948	.0987	.1026	.1064	.1103	.1141
0.3	.1179	.1217	.1255	.1293	.1331	.1368	.1406	.1443	.1480	.1517
0.4	.1554	.1591	.1628	.1664	.1700	.1736	.1772	.1808	.1844	.1879
0.5	.1915	.1950	.1985	.2019	.2054	.2088	.2123	.2157	.2190	.2224
0.6	.2257	.2291	.2324	.2357	.2389	.2422	.2454	.2486	.2518	.2549
0.7	.2580	.2612	.2642	.2673	.2704	.2734	.2764	.2794	.2823	.2852
0.8	.2881	.2910	.2939	.2967	.2995	.3023	.3051	.3078	.3106	.3133
0.9	.3159	.3186	.3212	.3238	.3264	.3289	.3315	.3340	.3365	.3389
1.0	.3413	.3438	.3461	.3485	.3508	.3531	.3554	.3577	.3599	.3621
1.1	.3643	.3665	.3686	.3708	.3729	.3749	.3770	.3790	.3810	.3830
1.2	.3849	.3869	.3888	.3907	.3925	.3944	.3962	.3980	.3997	.4015
1.3	.4032	.4049	.4066	.4082	.4099	.4115	.4131	.4147	.4162	.4177
1.4	.4192	.4207	.4222	.4236	.4251	.4265	.4279	.4292	.4306	.4319
1.5	.4332	.4345	.4357	.4370	.4382	.4394	.4406	.4418	.4429	.4441
1.6	.4452	.4463	.4474	.4484	.4495	.4505	.4515	.4525	.4535	.4545
1.7	.4554	.4564	.4573	.4582	.4591	.4599	.4608	.4616	.4625	.4633
1.8	.4641	.4649	.4656	.4664	.4671	.4678	.4686	.4693	.4699	.4706
1.9	.4713	.4719	.4726	.4732	.4738	.4744	.4750	.4756	.4761	.4767
2.0	.4772	.4778	.4783	.4788	.4793	.4798	.4803	.4808	.4812	.4817
2.1	.4821	.4826	.4830	.4834	.4838	.4842	.4846	.4850	.4854	.4857
2.2	.4861	.4864	.4868	.4871	.4875	.4878	.4881	.4884	.4887	.4890
2.3	.4893	.4896	.4898	.4901	.4904	.4906	.4909	.4911	.4913	.4916
2.4	.4918	.4920	.4922	.4925	.4927	.4929	.4931	.4932	.4934	.4936
2.5	.4938	.4940	.4941	.4943	.4945	.4946	.4948	.4949	.4951	.4952
2.6	.4953	.4955	.4956	.4957	.4959	.4960	.4961	.4962	.4963	.4964
2.7	.4965	.4966	.4967	.4968	.4969	.4970	.4971	.4972	.4973	.4974
2.8	.4974	.4975	.4976	.4977	.4977	.4978	.4979	.4979	.4980	.4981
2.9	.4981	.4982	.4982	.4983	.4984	.4984	.4985	.4985	.4986	.4986
3.0	.49865	.49869	.49874	.49878	.49882	.49886	.49889	.49893	.49897	.49900
3.1	.49903	.49906	.49910	.49913	.49916	.49918	.49921	.49924	.49926	.49929
3.2	.49931	.49934	.49936	.49938	.49940	.49942	.49944	.49946	.49948	.49950
3.3	.49952	.49953	.49955	.49957	.49958	.49960	.49961	.49962	.49964	.49965
3.4	.49966	.49968	.49969	.49970	.49971	.49972	.49973	.49974	.49975	.49976
3.5	.49977	.49978	.49978	.49979	.49980	.49981	.49981	.49982	.49983	.49983
3.6	.49984	.49985	.49985	.49986	.49986	.49987	.49987	.49988	.49988	.49989
3.7	.49989	.49990	.49990	.49990	.49991	.49991	.49992	.49992	.49992	.49992
3.8	.49993	.49993	.49993	.49994	.49994	.49994	.49994	.49995	.49995	.49995
3.9	.49995	.49995	.49996	.49996	.49996	.49996	.49996	.49996	.49997	.49997

Entry represents area under the standard normal distribution from the mean to *Z*.

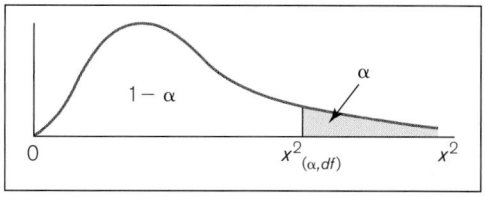

Table 3 Chi-Square Distribution

Degrees of Freedom	Upper-Tail Areas (α)											
	.995	.99	.975	.95	.90	.75	.25	.10	.05	.025	.01	.005
1			0.001	0.004	0.016	0.102	1.323	2.706	3.841	5.024	6.635	7.879
2	0.010	0.020	0.051	0.103	0.211	0.575	2.773	4.605	5.991	7.378	9.210	10.597
3	0.072	0.115	0.216	0.352	0.584	1.213	4.108	6.251	7.815	9.348	11.345	12.838
4	0.207	0.297	0.484	0.711	1.064	1.923	5.385	7.779	9.488	11.143	13.277	14.860
5	0.412	0.554	0.831	1.145	1.610	2.675	6.626	9.236	11.071	12.833	15.086	16.750
6	0.676	0.872	1.237	1.635	2.204	3.455	7.841	10.645	12.592	14.449	16.812	18.548
7	0.989	1.239	1.690	2.167	2.833	4.255	9.037	12.017	14.067	16.013	18.475	20.278
8	1.344	1.646	2.180	2.733	3.490	5.071	10.219	13.362	15.507	17.535	20.090	21.955
9	1.735	2.088	2.700	3.325	4.168	5.899	11.389	14.684	16.919	19.023	21.666	23.589
10	2.156	2.558	3.247	3.940	4.865	6.737	12.549	15.987	18.307	20.483	23.209	25.188
11	2.603	3.053	3.816	4.575	5.578	7.584	13.701	17.275	19.675	21.920	24.725	26.757
12	3.074	3.571	4.404	5.226	6.304	8.438	14.845	18.549	21.026	23.337	26.217	28.299
13	3.565	4.107	5.009	5.892	7.042	9.299	15.984	19.812	22.362	24.736	27.688	29.819
14	4.075	4.660	5.629	6.571	7.790	10.165	17.117	21.064	23.685	26.119	29.141	31.319
15	4.601	5.229	6.262	7.261	8.547	11.037	18.245	22.307	24.996	27.488	30.578	32.801
16	5.142	5.812	6.908	7.962	9.312	11.912	19.369	23.542	26.296	28.845	32.000	34.267
17	5.697	6.408	7.564	8.672	10.085	12.792	20.489	24.769	27.587	30.191	33.409	35.718
18	6.265	7.015	8.231	9.390	10.865	13.675	21.605	25.989	28.869	31.526	34.805	37.156
19	6.844	7.633	8.907	10.117	11.651	14.562	22.718	27.204	30.144	32.852	36.191	38.582
20	7.434	8.260	9.591	10.851	12.443	15.452	23.828	28.412	31.410	34.170	37.566	39.997
21	8.034	8.897	10.283	11.591	13.240	16.344	24.935	29.615	32.671	35.479	38.932	41.401
22	8.643	9.542	10.982	12.338	14.042	17.240	26.039	30.813	33.924	36.781	40.289	42.796
23	9.260	10.196	11.689	13.091	14.848	18.137	27.141	32.007	35.172	38.076	41.638	44.181
24	9.886	10.856	12.401	13.848	15.659	19.037	28.241	33.196	36.415	39.364	42.980	45.559
25	10.520	11.524	13.120	14.611	16.473	19.939	29.339	34.382	37.652	40.646	44.314	46.928
26	11.160	12.198	13.844	15.379	17.292	20.843	30.435	35.563	38.885	41.923	45.642	48.290
27	11.808	12.879	14.573	16.151	18.114	21.749	31.528	36.741	40.113	43.194	46.963	49.645
28	12.461	13.565	15.308	16.928	18.939	22.657	32.620	37.916	41.337	44.461	48.278	50.993
29	13.121	14.257	16.047	17.708	19.768	23.567	33.711	39.087	42.557	45.722	49.588	52.336
30	13.787	14.954	16.791	18.493	20.599	24.478	34.800	40.256	43.773	46.979	50.892	53.672
31	14.458	15.655	17.539	19.281	21.434	25.390	35.887	41.422	44.985	48.232	52.191	55.003
32	15.134	16.362	18.291	20.072	22.271	26.304	36.973	42.585	46.194	49.480	53.486	56.328
33	15.815	17.074	19.047	20.867	23.110	27.219	38.058	43.745	47.400	50.725	54.776	57.648
34	16.501	17.789	19.806	21.664	23.952	28.136	39.141	44.903	48.602	51.966	56.061	58.964
35	17.192	18.509	20.569	22.465	24.797	29.054	40.223	46.059	49.802	53.203	57.342	60.275
36	17.887	19.233	21.336	23.269	25.643	29.973	41.304	47.212	50.998	54.437	58.619	61.581
37	18.586	19.960	22.106	24.075	26.492	30.893	42.383	48.363	52.192	55.668	59.892	62.883
38	19.289	20.691	22.878	24.884	27.343	31.815	43.462	49.513	53.384	56.896	61.162	64.181
39	19.996	21.426	23.654	25.695	28.196	32.737	44.539	50.660	54.572	58.120	62.428	65.476
40	20.707	22.164	24.433	26.509	29.051	33.660	45.616	51.805	55.758	59.342	63.691	66.766
41	21.421	22.906	25.215	27.326	29.907	34.585	46.692	52.949	56.942	60.561	64.950	68.053
42	22.138	23.650	25.999	28.144	30.765	35.510	47.766	54.090	58.124	61.777	66.206	69.336
43	22.859	24.398	26.785	28.965	31.625	36.436	48.840	55.230	59.304	62.990	67.459	70.616

(continued)

Table 3 (continued)

Degrees of Freedom	Upper-Tail Areas (α)											
	.995	.99	.975	.95	.90	.75	.25	.10	.05	.025	.01	.005
44	23.584	25.148	27.575	29.787	32.487	37.363	49.913	56.369	60.481	64.201	68.710	71.893
45	24.311	25.901	28.366	30.612	33.350	38.291	50.985	57.505	61.656	65.410	69.957	73.166
46	25.041	26.657	29.160	31.439	34.215	39.220	52.056	58.641	62.830	66.617	71.201	74.437
47	25.775	27.416	29.956	32.268	35.081	40.149	53.127	59.774	64.001	67.821	72.443	75.704
48	26.511	28.177	30.755	33.098	35.949	41.079	54.196	60.907	65.171	69.023	73.683	76.969
49	27.249	28.941	31.555	33.930	36.818	42.010	55.265	62.038	66.339	70.222	74.919	78.231
50	27.991	29.707	32.357	34.764	37.689	42.942	56.334	63.167	67.505	71.420	76.154	79.490
51	28.735	30.475	33.162	35.600	38.560	43.874	57.401	64.295	68.669	72.616	77.386	80.747
52	29.481	31.246	33.968	36.437	39.433	44.808	58.468	65.422	69.832	73.810	78.616	82.001
53	30.230	32.018	34.776	37.276	40.308	45.741	59.534	66.548	70.993	75.002	79.843	83.253
54	30.981	32.793	35.586	38.116	41.183	46.676	60.600	67.673	72.153	76.192	81.069	84.502
55	31.735	33.570	36.398	38.958	42.060	47.610	61.665	68.796	73.311	77.380	82.292	85.749
56	32.490	34.350	37.212	39.801	42.937	48.546	62.729	69.919	74.468	78.567	83.513	86.994
57	33.248	35.131	38.027	40.646	43.816	49.482	63.793	71.040	75.624	79.752	84.733	88.236
58	34.008	35.913	38.844	41.492	44.696	50.419	64.857	72.160	76.778	80.936	85.950	89.477
59	34.770	36.698	39.662	42.339	45.577	51.356	65.919	73.279	77.931	82.117	87.166	90.715
60	35.534	37.485	40.482	43.188	46.459	52.294	66.981	74.397	79.082	83.298	88.379	91.952

For a particular number of degrees of freedom, entry represents the critical value of χ^2 corresponding to a specified upper-tail area, α.

For larger values of degrees of freedom (df) the expression $z = \sqrt{2\chi^2} - \sqrt{2(df) - 1}$ may be used and the resulting upper-tail area can be obtained from the table of the standardized normal distribution.

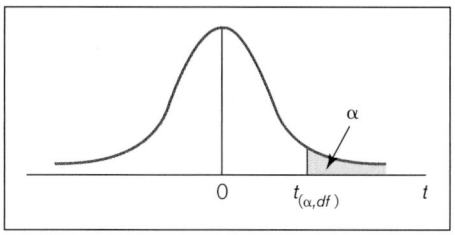

Table 4 *t* Distribution

Degrees of Freedom	Upper-Tail Areas (α)					
	.25	.10	.05	.025	.01	.005
1	1.0000	3.0777	6.3138	12.7062	31.8207	63.6574
2	0.8165	1.8856	2.9200	4.3027	6.9646	9.9248
3	0.7649	1.6377	2.3534	3.1824	4.5407	5.8409
4	0.7407	1.5332	2.1318	2.7764	3.7469	4.6041
5	0.7267	1.4759	2.0150	2.5706	3.3649	4.0322
6	0.7176	1.4398	1.9432	2.4469	3.1427	3.7074
7	0.7111	1.4149	1.8946	2.3646	2.9980	3.4995
8	0.7064	1.3968	1.8595	2.3060	2.8965	3.3554
9	0.7027	1.3830	1.8331	2.2622	2.8214	3.2498
10	0.6998	1.3722	1.8125	2.2281	2.7638	3.1693
11	0.6974	1.3634	1.7959	2.2010	2.7181	3.1058
12	0.6955	1.3562	1.7823	2.1788	2.6810	3.0545
13	0.6938	1.3502	1.7709	2.1604	2.6503	3.0123
14	0.6924	1.3450	1.7613	2.1448	2.6245	2.9768
15	0.6912	1.3406	1.7531	2.1315	2.6025	2.9467
16	0.6901	1.3368	1.7459	2.1199	2.5835	2.9208
17	0.6892	1.3334	1.7396	2.1098	2.5669	2.8982
18	0.6884	1.3304	1.7341	2.1009	2.5524	2.8784
19	0.6876	1.3277	1.7291	2.0930	2.5395	2.8609
20	0.6870	1.3253	1.7247	2.0860	2.5280	2.8453
21	0.6864	1.3232	1.7207	2.0796	2.5177	2.8314
22	0.6858	1.3212	1.7171	2.0739	2.5083	2.8188
23	0.6853	1.3195	1.7139	2.0687	2.4999	2.8073
24	0.6848	1.3178	1.7109	2.0639	2.4922	2.7969
25	0.6844	1.3163	1.7081	2.0595	2.4851	2.7874
26	0.6840	1.3150	1.7056	2.0555	2.4786	2.7787
27	0.6837	1.3137	1.7033	2.0518	2.4727	2.7707
28	0.6834	1.3125	1.7011	2.0484	2.4671	2.7633
29	0.6830	1.3114	1.6991	2.0452	2.4620	2.7564
30	0.6828	1.3104	1.6973	2.0423	2.4573	2.7500
31	0.6825	1.3095	1.6955	2.0395	2.4528	2.7440
32	0.6822	1.3086	1.6939	2.0369	2.4487	2.7385
33	0.6820	1.3077	1.6924	2.0345	2.4448	2.7333
34	0.6818	1.3070	1.6909	2.0322	2.4411	2.7284
35	0.6816	1.3062	1.6896	2.0301	2.4377	2.7238
36	0.6814	1.3055	1.6883	2.0281	2.4345	2.7195
37	0.6812	1.3049	1.6871	2.0262	2.4314	2.7154
38	0.6810	1.3042	1.6860	2.0244	2.4286	2.7116
39	0.6808	1.3036	1.6849	2.0227	2.4258	2.7079
40	0.6807	1.3031	1.6839	2.0211	2.4233	2.7045
41	0.6805	1.3025	1.6829	2.0195	2.4208	2.7012
42	0.6804	1.3020	1.6820	2.0181	2.4185	2.6981

(continued)

Table 4 (continued)

Degrees of Freedom	Upper-Tail Areas (α)					
	.25	.10	.05	.025	.01	.005
43	0.6802	1.3016	1.6811	2.0167	2.4163	2.6951
44	0.6801	1.3011	1.6802	2.0154	2.4141	2.6923
45	0.6800	1.3006	1.6794	2.0141	2.4121	2.6896
46	0.6799	1.3002	1.6787	2.0129	2.4102	2.6870
47	0.6797	1.2998	1.6779	2.0117	2.4083	2.6846
48	0.6796	1.2994	1.6772	2.0106	2.4066	2.6822
49	0.6795	1.2991	1.6766	2.0096	2.4049	2.6800
50	0.6794	1.2987	1.6759	2.0086	2.4033	2.6778
51	0.6793	1.2984	1.6753	2.0076	2.4017	2.6757
52	0.6792	1.2980	1.6747	2.0066	2.4002	2.6737
53	0.6791	1.2977	1.6741	2.0057	2.3988	2.6718
54	0.6791	1.2974	1.6736	2.0049	2.3974	2.6700
55	0.6790	1.2971	1.6730	2.0040	2.3961	2.6682
56	0.6789	1.2969	1.6725	2.0032	2.3948	2.6665
57	0.6788	1.2966	1.6720	2.0025	2.3936	2.6649
58	0.6787	1.2963	1.6716	2.0017	2.3924	2.6633
59	0.6787	1.2961	1.6711	2.0010	2.3912	2.6618
60	0.6786	1.2958	1.6706	2.0003	2.3901	2.6603
61	0.6785	1.2956	1.6702	1.9996	2.3890	2.6589
62	0.6785	1.2954	1.6698	1.9990	2.3880	2.6575
63	0.6784	1.2951	1.6694	1.9983	2.3870	2.6561
64	0.6783	1.2949	1.6690	1.9977	2.3860	2.6549
65	0.6783	1.2947	1.6686	1.9971	2.3851	2.6536
66	0.6782	1.2945	1.6683	1.9966	2.3842	2.6524
67	0.6782	1.2943	1.6679	1.9960	2.3833	2.6512
68	0.6781	1.2941	1.6676	1.9955	2.3824	2.6501
69	0.6781	1.2939	1.6672	1.9949	2.3816	2.6490
70	0.6780	1.2938	1.6669	1.9944	2.3808	2.6479
71	0.6780	1.2936	1.6666	1.9939	2.3800	2.6469
72	0.6779	1.2934	1.6663	1.9935	2.3793	2.6459
73	0.6779	1.2933	1.6660	1.9930	2.3785	2.6449
74	0.6778	1.2931	1.6657	1.9925	2.3778	2.6439
75	0.6778	1.2929	1.6654	1.9921	2.3771	2.6430
76	0.6777	1.2928	1.6652	1.9917	2.3764	2.6421
77	0.6777	1.2926	1.6649	1.9913	2.3758	2.6412
78	0.6776	1.2925	1.6646	1.9908	2.3751	2.6403
79	0.6776	1.2924	1.6644	1.9905	2.3745	2.6395
80	0.6776	1.2922	1.6641	1.9901	2.3739	2.6387
81	0.6775	1.2921	1.6639	1.9897	2.3733	2.6379
82	0.6775	1.2920	1.6636	1.9893	2.3727	2.6371
83	0.6775	1.2918	1.6634	1.9890	2.3721	2.6364
84	0.6774	1.2917	1.6632	1.9886	2.3716	2.6356
85	0.6774	1.2916	1.6630	1.9883	2.3710	2.6349
86	0.6774	1.2915	1.6628	1.9879	2.3705	2.6342
87	0.6773	1.2914	1.6626	1.9876	2.3700	2.6335
88	0.6773	1.2912	1.6624	1.9873	2.3695	2.6329
89	0.6773	1.2911	1.6622	1.9870	2.3690	2.6322
90	0.6772	1.2910	1.6620	1.9867	2.3685	2.6316
91	0.6772	1.2909	1.6618	1.9864	2.3680	2.6309
92	0.6772	1.2908	1.6616	1.9861	2.3676	2.6303

Table 4 (continued)

Degrees of Freedom	Upper-Tail Areas (α)					
	.25	.10	.05	.025	.01	.005
93	0.6771	1.2907	1.6614	1.9858	2.3671	2.6297
94	0.6771	1.2906	1.6612	1.9855	2.3667	2.6291
95	0.6771	1.2905	1.6611	1.9853	2.3662	2.6286
96	0.6771	1.2904	1.6609	1.9850	2.3658	2.6280
97	0.6770	1.2903	1.6607	1.9847	2.3654	2.6275
98	0.6770	1.2902	1.6606	1.9845	2.3650	2.6269
99	0.6770	1.2902	1.6604	1.9842	2.3646	2.6264
100	0.6770	1.2901	1.6602	1.9840	2.3642	2.6259
110	0.6767	1.2893	1.6588	1.9818	2.3607	2.6213
120	0.6765	1.2886	1.6577	1.9799	2.3578	2.6174
130	0.6764	1.2881	1.6567	1.9784	2.3554	2.6142
140	0.6762	1.2876	1.6558	1.9771	2.3533	2.6114
150	0.6761	1.2872	1.6551	1.9759	2.3515	2.6090
∞	0.6745	1.2816	1.6449	1.9600	2.3263	2.5758

For a particular number of degrees of freedom, entry represents the critical value of t corresponding to a specified upper-tail area, α.

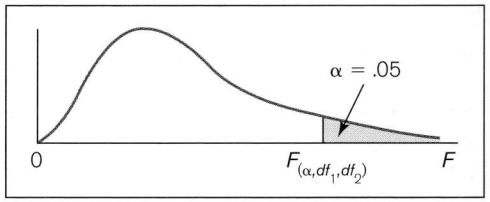

Table 5 *F* Distribution

Denominator df_2	Numerator df_1 1	2	3	4	5	6	7	8	9	10	12	15	20	24	30	40	60	120	∞
1	161.4	199.5	215.7	224.6	230.2	234.0	236.8	238.9	240.5	241.9	243.9	245.9	248.0	249.1	250.1	251.1	252.2	253.3	254.3
2	18.51	19.00	19.16	19.25	19.30	19.33	19.35	19.37	19.38	19.40	19.41	19.43	19.45	19.45	19.46	19.47	19.48	19.49	19.50
3	10.13	9.55	9.28	9.12	9.01	8.94	8.89	8.85	8.81	8.79	8.74	8.70	8.66	8.64	8.62	8.59	8.57	8.55	8.53
4	7.71	6.94	6.59	6.39	6.26	6.16	6.09	6.04	6.00	5.96	5.91	5.86	5.80	5.77	5.75	5.72	5.69	5.66	5.63
5	6.61	5.79	5.41	5.19	5.05	4.95	4.88	4.82	4.77	4.74	4.68	4.62	4.56	4.53	4.50	4.46	4.43	4.40	4.36
6	5.99	5.14	4.76	4.53	4.39	4.28	4.21	4.15	4.10	4.06	4.00	3.94	3.87	3.84	3.81	3.77	3.74	3.70	3.67
7	5.59	4.74	4.35	4.12	3.97	3.87	3.79	3.73	3.68	3.64	3.57	3.51	3.44	3.41	3.38	3.34	3.30	3.27	3.23
8	5.32	4.46	4.07	3.84	3.69	3.58	3.50	3.44	3.39	3.35	3.28	3.22	3.15	3.12	3.08	3.04	3.01	2.97	2.93
9	5.12	4.26	3.86	3.63	3.48	3.37	3.29	3.23	3.18	3.14	3.07	3.01	2.94	2.90	2.86	2.83	2.79	2.75	2.71
10	4.96	4.10	3.71	3.48	3.33	3.22	3.14	3.07	3.02	2.98	2.91	2.85	2.77	2.74	2.70	2.66	2.62	2.58	2.54
11	4.84	3.98	3.59	3.36	3.20	3.09	3.01	2.95	2.90	2.85	2.79	2.72	2.65	2.61	2.57	2.53	2.49	2.45	2.40
12	4.75	3.89	3.49	3.26	3.11	3.00	2.91	2.85	2.80	2.75	2.69	2.62	2.54	2.51	2.47	2.43	2.38	2.34	2.30
13	4.67	3.81	3.41	3.18	3.03	2.92	2.83	2.77	2.71	2.67	2.60	2.53	2.46	2.42	2.38	2.34	2.30	2.25	2.21
14	4.60	3.74	3.34	3.11	2.96	2.85	2.76	2.70	2.65	2.60	2.53	2.46	2.39	2.35	2.31	2.27	2.22	2.18	2.13
15	4.54	3.68	3.29	3.06	2.90	2.79	2.71	2.64	2.59	2.54	2.48	2.40	2.33	2.29	2.25	2.20	2.16	2.11	2.07
16	4.49	3.63	3.24	3.01	2.85	2.74	2.66	2.59	2.54	2.49	2.42	2.35	2.28	2.24	2.19	2.15	2.11	2.06	2.01
17	4.45	3.59	3.20	2.96	2.81	2.70	2.61	2.55	2.49	2.45	2.38	2.31	2.23	2.19	2.15	2.10	2.06	2.01	1.96
18	4.41	3.55	3.16	2.93	2.77	2.66	2.58	2.51	2.46	2.41	2.34	2.27	2.19	2.15	2.11	2.06	2.02	1.97	1.92
19	4.38	3.52	3.13	2.90	2.74	2.63	2.54	2.48	2.42	2.38	2.31	2.23	2.16	2.11	2.07	2.03	1.98	1.93	1.88
20	4.35	3.49	3.10	2.87	2.71	2.60	2.51	2.45	2.39	2.35	2.28	2.20	2.12	2.08	2.04	1.99	1.95	1.90	1.84
21	4.32	3.47	3.07	2.84	2.68	2.57	2.49	2.42	2.37	2.32	2.25	2.18	2.10	2.05	2.01	1.96	1.92	1.87	1.81
22	4.30	3.44	3.05	2.82	2.66	2.55	2.46	2.40	2.34	2.30	2.23	2.15	2.07	2.03	1.98	1.94	1.89	1.84	1.78
23	4.28	3.42	3.03	2.80	2.64	2.53	2.44	2.37	2.32	2.27	2.20	2.13	2.05	2.01	1.96	1.91	1.86	1.81	1.76
24	4.26	3.40	3.01	2.78	2.62	2.51	2.42	2.36	2.30	2.25	2.18	2.11	2.03	1.98	1.94	1.89	1.84	1.79	1.73
25	4.24	3.39	2.99	2.76	2.60	2.49	2.40	2.34	2.28	2.24	2.16	2.09	2.01	1.96	1.92	1.87	1.82	1.77	1.71
26	4.23	3.37	2.98	2.74	2.59	2.47	2.39	2.32	2.27	2.22	2.15	2.07	1.99	1.95	1.90	1.85	1.80	1.75	1.69
27	4.21	3.35	2.96	2.73	2.57	2.46	2.37	2.31	2.25	2.20	2.13	2.06	1.97	1.93	1.88	1.84	1.79	1.73	1.67
28	4.20	3.34	2.95	2.71	2.56	2.45	2.36	2.29	2.24	2.19	2.12	2.04	1.96	1.91	1.87	1.82	1.77	1.71	1.65
29	4.18	3.33	2.93	2.70	2.55	2.43	2.35	2.28	2.22	2.18	2.10	2.03	1.94	1.90	1.85	1.81	1.75	1.70	1.64
30	4.17	3.32	2.92	2.69	2.53	2.42	2.33	2.27	2.21	2.16	2.09	2.01	1.93	1.89	1.84	1.79	1.74	1.68	1.62
40	4.08	3.23	2.84	2.61	2.45	2.34	2.25	2.18	2.12	2.08	2.00	1.92	1.84	1.79	1.74	1.69	1.64	1.58	1.51
60	4.00	3.15	2.76	2.53	2.37	2.25	2.17	2.10	2.04	1.99	1.92	1.84	1.75	1.70	1.65	1.59	1.53	1.47	1.39
120	3.92	3.07	2.68	2.45	2.29	2.17	2.09	2.02	1.96	1.91	1.83	1.75	1.66	1.61	1.55	1.50	1.43	1.35	1.25
∞	3.84	3.00	2.60	2.37	2.21	2.10	2.01	1.94	1.88	1.83	1.75	1.67	1.57	1.52	1.46	1.39	1.32	1.22	1.00

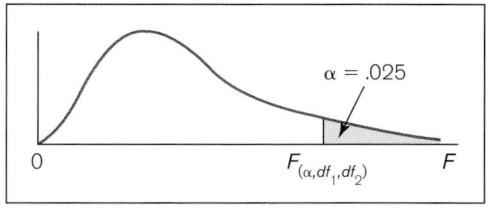

Table 5 (continued)

Denominator df_2	Numerator df_1																		
	1	2	3	4	5	6	7	8	9	10	12	15	20	24	30	40	60	120	∞
1	647.8	799.5	864.2	899.6	921.8	937.1	948.2	956.7	963.3	968.6	976.7	984.9	993.1	997.2	1001	1006	1010	1014	1018
2	38.51	39.00	39.17	39.25	39.30	39.33	39.36	39.37	39.39	39.40	39.41	39.43	39.45	39.46	39.46	39.47	39.48	39.49	39.50
3	17.44	16.04	15.44	15.10	14.88	14.73	14.62	14.54	14.47	14.42	14.34	14.25	14.17	14.12	14.08	14.04	13.99	13.95	13.90
4	12.22	10.65	9.98	9.60	9.36	9.20	9.07	8.98	8.90	8.84	8.75	8.66	8.56	8.51	8.46	8.41	8.36	8.31	8.26
5	10.01	8.43	7.76	7.39	7.15	6.98	6.85	6.76	6.68	6.62	6.52	6.43	6.33	6.28	6.23	6.18	6.12	6.07	6.02
6	8.81	7.26	6.60	6.23	5.99	5.82	5.70	5.60	5.52	5.46	5.37	5.27	5.17	5.12	5.07	5.01	4.96	4.90	4.85
7	8.07	6.54	5.89	5.52	5.29	5.12	4.99	4.90	4.82	4.76	4.67	4.57	4.47	4.42	4.36	4.31	4.25	4.20	4.14
8	7.57	6.06	5.42	5.05	4.82	4.65	4.53	4.43	4.36	4.30	4.20	4.10	4.00	3.95	3.89	3.84	3.78	3.73	3.67
9	7.21	5.71	5.08	4.72	4.48	4.32	4.20	4.10	4.03	3.96	3.87	3.77	3.67	3.61	3.56	3.51	3.45	3.39	3.33
10	6.94	5.46	4.83	4.47	4.24	4.07	3.95	3.85	3.78	3.72	3.62	3.52	3.42	3.37	3.31	3.26	3.20	3.14	3.08
11	6.72	5.26	4.63	4.28	4.04	3.88	3.76	3.66	3.59	3.53	3.43	3.33	3.23	3.17	3.12	3.06	3.00	2.94	2.88
12	6.55	5.10	4.47	4.12	3.89	3.73	3.61	3.51	3.44	3.37	3.28	3.18	3.07	3.02	2.96	2.91	2.85	2.79	2.72
13	6.41	4.97	4.35	4.00	3.77	3.60	3.48	3.39	3.31	3.25	3.15	3.05	2.95	2.89	2.84	2.78	2.72	2.66	2.60
14	6.30	4.86	4.24	3.89	3.66	3.50	3.38	3.29	3.21	3.15	3.05	2.95	2.84	2.79	2.73	2.67	2.61	2.55	2.49
15	6.20	4.77	4.15	3.80	3.58	3.41	3.29	3.20	3.12	3.06	2.96	2.86	2.76	2.70	2.64	2.59	2.52	2.46	2.40
16	6.12	4.69	4.08	3.73	3.50	3.34	3.22	3.12	3.05	2.99	2.89	2.79	2.68	2.63	2.57	2.51	2.45	2.38	2.32
17	6.04	4.62	4.01	3.66	3.44	3.28	3.16	3.06	2.98	2.92	2.82	2.72	2.62	2.56	2.50	2.44	2.38	2.32	2.25
18	5.98	4.56	3.95	3.61	3.38	3.22	3.10	3.01	2.93	2.87	2.77	2.67	2.56	2.50	2.44	2.38	2.32	2.26	2.19
19	5.92	4.51	3.90	3.56	3.33	3.17	3.05	2.96	2.88	2.82	2.72	2.62	2.51	2.45	2.39	2.33	2.27	2.20	2.13
20	5.87	4.46	3.86	3.51	3.29	3.13	3.01	2.91	2.84	2.77	2.68	2.57	2.46	2.41	2.35	2.29	2.22	2.16	2.09
21	5.83	4.42	3.82	3.48	3.25	3.09	2.97	2.87	2.80	2.73	2.64	2.53	2.42	2.37	2.31	2.25	2.18	2.11	2.04
22	5.79	4.38	3.78	3.44	3.22	3.05	2.93	2.84	2.76	2.70	2.60	2.50	2.39	2.33	2.27	2.21	2.14	2.08	2.00
23	5.75	4.35	3.75	3.41	3.18	3.02	2.90	2.81	2.73	2.67	2.57	2.47	2.36	2.30	2.24	2.18	2.11	2.04	1.97
24	5.72	4.32	3.72	3.38	3.15	2.99	2.87	2.78	2.70	2.64	2.54	2.44	2.33	2.27	2.21	2.15	2.08	2.01	1.94
25	5.69	4.29	3.69	3.35	3.13	2.97	2.85	2.75	2.68	2.61	2.51	2.41	2.30	2.24	2.18	2.12	2.05	1.98	1.91
26	5.66	4.27	3.67	3.33	3.10	2.94	2.82	2.73	2.65	2.59	2.49	2.39	2.28	2.22	2.16	2.09	2.03	1.95	1.88
27	5.63	4.24	3.65	3.31	3.08	2.92	2.80	2.71	2.63	2.57	2.47	2.36	2.25	2.19	2.13	2.07	2.00	1.93	1.85
28	5.61	4.22	3.63	3.29	3.06	2.90	2.78	2.69	2.61	2.55	2.45	2.34	2.23	2.17	2.11	2.05	1.98	1.91	1.83
29	5.59	4.20	3.61	3.27	3.04	2.88	2.76	2.67	2.59	2.53	2.43	2.32	2.21	2.15	2.09	2.03	1.96	1.89	1.81
30	5.57	4.18	3.59	3.25	3.03	2.87	2.75	2.65	2.57	2.51	2.41	2.31	2.20	2.14	2.07	2.01	1.94	1.87	1.79
40	5.42	4.05	3.46	3.13	2.90	2.74	2.62	2.53	2.45	2.39	2.29	2.18	2.07	2.01	1.94	1.88	1.80	1.72	1.64
60	5.29	3.93	3.34	3.01	2.79	2.63	2.51	2.41	2.33	2.27	2.17	2.06	1.94	1.88	1.82	1.74	1.67	1.58	1.48
120	5.15	3.80	3.23	2.89	2.67	2.52	2.39	2.30	2.22	2.16	2.05	1.94	1.82	1.76	1.69	1.61	1.53	1.43	1.31
∞	5.02	3.69	3.12	2.79	2.57	2.41	2.29	2.19	2.11	2.05	1.94	1.83	1.71	1.64	1.57	1.48	1.39	1.27	1.00

(continued)

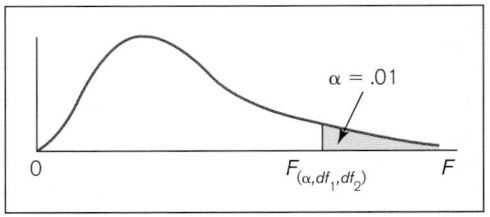

Table 5 (continued)

Denominator df_2	Numerator df_1: 1	2	3	4	5	6	7	8	9	10	12	15	20	24	30	40	60	120	∞
1	4052	4999.5	5403	5625	5764	5859	5928	5982	6022	6056	6106	6157	6209	6235	6261	6287	6313	6339	6366
2	98.50	99.00	99.17	99.25	99.30	99.33	99.36	99.37	99.39	99.40	99.42	99.43	99.45	99.46	99.47	99.47	99.48	99.49	99.50
3	34.12	30.82	29.46	28.71	28.24	27.91	27.67	27.49	27.35	27.23	27.05	26.87	26.69	26.60	26.50	26.41	26.32	26.22	26.13
4	21.20	18.00	16.69	15.98	15.52	15.21	14.98	14.80	14.66	14.55	14.37	14.20	14.02	13.93	13.84	13.75	13.65	13.56	13.46
5	16.26	13.27	12.06	11.39	10.97	10.67	10.46	10.29	10.16	10.05	9.89	9.72	9.55	9.47	9.38	9.29	9.20	9.11	9.02
6	13.75	10.92	9.78	9.15	8.75	8.47	8.26	8.10	7.98	7.87	7.72	7.56	7.40	7.31	7.23	7.14	7.06	6.97	6.88
7	12.25	9.55	8.45	7.85	7.46	7.19	6.99	6.84	6.72	6.62	6.47	6.31	6.16	6.07	5.99	5.91	5.82	5.74	5.65
8	11.26	8.65	7.59	7.01	6.63	6.37	6.18	6.03	5.91	5.81	5.67	5.52	5.36	5.28	5.20	5.12	5.03	4.95	4.86
9	10.56	8.02	6.99	6.42	6.06	5.80	5.61	5.47	5.35	5.26	5.11	4.96	4.81	4.73	4.65	4.57	4.48	4.40	4.31
10	10.04	7.56	6.55	5.99	5.64	5.39	5.20	5.06	4.94	4.85	4.71	4.56	4.41	4.33	4.25	4.17	4.08	4.00	3.91
11	9.65	7.21	6.22	5.67	5.32	5.07	4.89	4.74	4.63	4.54	4.40	4.25	4.10	4.02	3.94	3.86	3.78	3.69	3.60
12	9.33	6.93	5.95	5.41	5.06	4.82	4.64	4.50	4.39	4.30	4.16	4.01	3.86	3.78	3.70	3.62	3.54	3.45	3.36
13	9.07	6.70	5.74	5.21	4.86	4.62	4.44	4.30	4.19	4.10	3.96	3.82	3.66	3.59	3.51	3.43	3.34	3.25	3.17
14	8.86	6.51	5.56	5.04	4.69	4.46	4.28	4.14	4.03	3.94	3.80	3.66	3.51	3.43	3.35	3.27	3.18	3.09	3.00
15	8.68	6.36	5.42	4.89	4.56	4.32	4.14	4.00	3.89	3.80	3.67	3.52	3.37	3.29	3.21	3.13	3.05	2.96	2.87
16	8.53	6.23	5.29	4.77	4.44	4.20	4.03	3.89	3.78	3.69	3.55	3.41	3.26	3.18	3.10	3.02	2.93	2.84	2.75
17	8.40	6.11	5.18	4.67	4.34	4.10	3.93	3.79	3.68	3.59	3.46	3.31	3.16	3.08	3.00	2.92	2.83	2.75	2.65
18	8.29	6.01	5.09	4.58	4.25	4.01	3.84	3.71	3.60	3.51	3.37	3.23	3.08	3.00	2.92	2.84	2.75	2.66	2.57
19	8.18	5.93	5.01	4.50	4.17	3.94	3.77	3.63	3.52	3.43	3.30	3.15	3.00	2.92	2.84	2.76	2.67	2.58	2.49
20	8.10	5.85	4.94	4.43	4.10	3.87	3.70	3.56	3.46	3.37	3.23	3.09	2.94	2.86	2.78	2.69	2.61	2.52	2.42
21	8.02	5.78	4.87	4.37	4.04	3.81	3.64	3.51	3.40	3.31	3.17	3.03	2.88	2.80	2.72	2.64	2.55	2.46	2.36
22	7.95	5.72	4.82	4.31	3.99	3.76	3.59	3.45	3.35	3.26	3.12	2.98	2.83	2.75	2.67	2.58	2.50	2.40	2.31
23	7.88	5.66	4.76	4.26	3.94	3.71	3.54	3.41	3.30	3.21	3.07	2.93	2.78	2.70	2.62	2.54	2.45	2.35	2.26
24	7.82	5.61	4.72	4.22	3.90	3.67	3.50	3.36	3.26	3.17	3.03	2.89	2.74	2.66	2.58	2.49	2.40	2.31	2.21
25	7.77	5.57	4.68	4.18	3.85	3.63	3.46	3.32	3.22	3.13	2.99	2.85	2.70	2.62	2.54	2.45	2.36	2.27	2.17
26	7.72	5.53	4.64	4.14	3.82	3.59	3.42	3.29	3.18	3.09	2.96	2.81	2.66	2.58	2.50	2.42	2.33	2.23	2.13
27	7.68	5.49	4.60	4.11	3.78	3.56	3.39	3.26	3.15	3.06	2.93	2.78	2.63	2.55	2.47	2.38	2.29	2.20	2.10
28	7.64	5.45	4.57	4.07	3.75	3.53	3.36	3.23	3.12	3.03	2.90	2.75	2.60	2.52	2.44	2.35	2.26	2.17	2.06
29	7.60	5.42	4.54	4.04	3.73	3.50	3.33	3.20	3.09	3.00	2.87	2.73	2.57	2.49	2.41	2.33	2.23	2.14	2.03
30	7.56	5.39	4.51	4.02	3.70	3.47	3.30	3.17	3.07	2.98	2.84	2.70	2.55	2.47	2.39	2.30	2.21	2.11	2.01
40	7.31	5.18	4.31	3.83	3.51	3.29	3.12	2.99	2.89	2.80	2.66	2.52	2.37	2.29	2.20	2.11	2.02	1.92	1.80
60	7.08	4.98	4.13	3.65	3.34	3.12	2.95	2.82	2.72	2.63	2.50	2.35	2.20	2.12	2.03	1.94	1.84	1.73	1.60
120	6.85	4.79	3.95	3.48	3.17	2.96	2.79	2.66	2.56	2.47	2.34	2.19	2.03	1.95	1.86	1.76	1.66	1.53	1.38
∞	6.63	4.61	3.78	3.32	3.02	2.80	2.64	2.51	2.41	2.32	2.18	2.04	1.88	1.79	1.70	1.59	1.47	1.32	1.00

For a particular combination of numerator and denominator degrees of freedom, entry represents the critical values of F corresponding to a specified upper-tail area, α.

NOTES

CHAPTER 1

1. David Lipke, "Reebok Targets Men with New NYC Store," *DNR*, 33(43), (October 27, 2003): 14; Rich Thomaselli, "Reebok's Strategy: Play Up Vector Logo," *Advertising Age*, 74(34), (August 25, 2003): 6.
2. Robert Swanekamp, "Southern Company Emphasizes Employee Development," *Power*, 144(6), (November/December, 2000): 25; (www.southerncompany.com).
3. Kate MacArthur, "Fast-Food Rethinks Marketing," *Advertising Age,* (Midwest region edition), 74(26), (June 30, 2003): SR2.
4. Jean Halliday, "GM Seeks 'Redemption' with Quality Effort," *Advertising Age*, 74(18), (May 5, 2003): 1–2; Phil Frame, "GM's Design Chief: The Customer," *Automotive News*, 67(5528), (November 29, 1993): 3.
5. John W. Huppertz, "Passion vs. Dispassion," *Marketing Research: A Magazine of Management and Applications*, 15(2), (summer 2003):16; Naresh K. Malhotra, "Shifting Perspective on the Shifting Paradigm in Marketing Research," *Journal of the Academy of Marketing Science*, 20 (fall 1992): 379–387; William Perreault, "The Shifting Paradigm in Marketing Research," *Journal of the Academy of Marketing Science*, 20, (fall 1992): 367–375.
6. Deborah L. Vence, "Better! Faster! Cheaper! Pick Any Three. That's Not a Joke," *Marketing News*, (February 1, 2004): 1, 31–32.
7. Jack Honomichl, "Top 25 Global Research Organizations," *Marketing News*, 37(17), (August 15, 2004): H4.
8. Jane Simms, "How to Drive Business Success ... and Your Own Career," *Marketing,* (September 18, 2003): 22; Ralph W. Giacobbe and Madhav N. Segal, "Rethinking Marketing Research Education: A Conceptual, Analytical, and Empirical Investigation," *Journal of Marketing Education*, 16, (spring 1994): 43–58.
9. Jack Honomichl, "Top 25 Global Research Organizations," *Marketing News*, (August 15, 2004): H4.
10. Normandy Madden, "China Warms Up to P&G," *Advertising Age*, 74(14), (April 7, 2003): S5; "P&G Viewed China as a National Market and Is Conquering It," *The Wall Street Journal*, (September 12, 1995).
11. Steven Landberg, "Strategic Marketing Technology," *Best's Review*, 104(6), (October 2003): 114; Marydee Ojala, "Information Role Models in Market Research," *Online*, 24(2), (March/April 2000): 69–71; Matthew W. Green, Jr. and John A. Fugel, "Third Wave Has Ups and Downs," *Rural Telecommunications*, 15(1), (January/February 1996): 10; Donald E. Schmidt, " Third Wave of Marketing Research on the Horizon," *Marketing News*, 27(5), (March 1, 1993): 6.
12. Scott J. Vitell, Joseph G. P. Paolillo, and James L. Thomas, "The Perceived Role of Ethics and Social Responsibility: A Study of Marketing Professionals," *Business Ethics Quarterly,* 13(1), (January 2003): 63; Diane K. Bowers, "The Strategic Role of the Telemarketing Sales Rule in the Research Industry," *Marketing Research: A Magazine of Management and Applications*, 11(1), (spring 1999): 34–35.
13. (www.samsonite.com/global/history_90now.jsp).

CHAPTER 2

1. Based on Karl Greenberg, "Subaru Is Driven by New Marketing, New Direction, Lance Armstrong," *Brandweek*, 44(8), (February 24, 2003): 12.
2. Jonathan B. Cox, "Rising Competition Forces BellSouth to Redefine Business," *Knight Ridder Tribune Business News,* (September 20, 2003): 1; "Forget the Code–BellSouth," *Adweek*, (special planning section), (August 5, 1996): 13.
3. Anonymous, "Norwegian Cruise Line," *Incentive*, 177(11), (November 2003): 89; David Goetzl, "Luxury Cruise Lines Woo Boomers to Sea," *Advertising Age*, 70(11), (March 15, 1999): 26; "It's Different Out Here–Norwegian Cruises," *Adweek,* (special planning section), (August 5, 1996): 7.
4. Allison Sherry, "University of Colorado Hospital to Offer Luxury Suites Complete with Chef," *Knight Ridder Tribune Business News,* (September 15, 2003): 1; Rachel Zoll, "Hospitals Offer Hotel-Style Perks to Fill Maternity Beds," *Marketing News*, 31(10), (May 12, 1997): 11; "Hospital Puttin' on the Ritz to Target High-End Market," *Marketing News*, (January 17, 1986): 14.
5. Anonymous, "Gillette Passion for Shaving," *Retail World,* 56(15), (August 4–15, 2003): 30; "A Woman's Touch," *Discount Merchandiser*, 39(5), (May 1999): 104; Sean Mehegan, "Gillette Big on Body Wash," *Brandweek*, 38(5), (February 3, 1997): 5; *Marketing News*, 30(10), (May 6, 1996).
6. Wayne C. Booth, Gregory G. Colomb, and Joseph M. Williams (1995), *The Craft of Research*, Chicago: University of Chicago Press.
7. Patricia Sellers, "P&G: Teaching an Old Dog New Tricks," *Fortune*, (May 31, 2004): 167–180.
8. Sandra O'Loughlin, "Lee Jeans Launching One True Fit in Move to Extend Market Share," *Brandweek*, 44(2), (January 13, 2003): 4; Sandra O'Loughlin, "Buddy Lee Takes Show on the Road," *Brandweek,* 44(33), (September 15, 2003): 12.
9. Jeff Manning, "Got Milk? A Decade of Lessons Pours In," *Brandweek,* 44(22), (June 2, 2003): 24; Hillary Chura and Stephanie Thompson, "Bozell Moving Beyond Mustaches in Milk Ads," *Advertising Age*, 70(43), (October 18, 1999): 81.
10. Tania Mason, "Heinz Backs Its Best Varieties," *Marketing,* (March 27, 2003): 17; Judann Dagnoli, "Why Heinz Went Sour in Brazil," *Advertising Age*, (December 5, 1988).
11. Anonymous, "Closing the Gap Between the Ethical and Profitable," *Marketing Week,* (October 16, 2003): P32; Ishmael P. Akaah, "Influence of Deontological and Teleological Factors on Research Ethics Evaluations," *Journal of Business Research*, 39(2), (June 1997): 71–80; G. R. Laczniak and P. E. Murphy (1993), *Ethical Marketing Decisions, the Higher Road*, Boston: Allyn and Bacon.
12. (www.kelloggs.com).
13. Carlos Gutirrez became the U.S. Secretary of Commerce in 2005.

CHAPTER 3

1. Sandra O'Loughlin, "Struggling Spiegel Group Dresses Up Eddie Bauer," *Brandweek*, 44(31), (September 1, 2003): 10; Mercedes Cardona, "Eddie Bauer Banks on Basics for Season," *Advertising Age,* 74(47), (November 24, 2003): 10.

2. (www.bankofamerica.com).
3. Adapted from Don Mills, "Jergens Naturally Smooth Shave Minimizing Lotion" *Cosmetics,* 30(5), (September 2002); "Bath Boom Rah!", *Discount Merchandiser*, 39(6), (June 1999): 52; Rick Klein, "1995 Edison Best New Products Awards Winners," *Marketing News*, 30(10), (May 6, 1996): E4–E11.
4. Adapted from "Oral Care," *Progressive Grocer*, 79(8), (August 2000): 18; Christine Bittar, "Chesebrough, Colgate Stir Up Brush War," *Brandweek*, 40(14), (April 5, 1999): 4; "1995 Edison Best New Products Awards Winners," *Marketing News*, 30(10), (May 6, 1996): E4–E11.
5. Adapted from Kristi Heim, "Microsoft Branches Out Beyond Personal Computers to Maintain Success," *Knight Ridder Tribune Business News,* (August 4, 2003): 1; Danny Forinash, "New Microsoft Windows XP Draws Good Reviews from Computer Users," *The State Journal*, 17(50), (December 10, 2001): 6; "1995 Edison Best New Products Awards Winners," *Marketing News*, 30(10), (May 6, 1996): E4–E11.
6. Adapted from Pacific Research Consulting, "Renewed and Improved Treatment in Hair Shampoo with New Package," *Cosmetics & Toiletries & Household Products Marketing News in Japan*, 25(4), (April 25, 2003): 1; Catherine Becker, "Hair and Cosmetic Products in the Japanese Market," *Marketing and Research Today*, 25(1), (February 1997): 31–37.
7. Molly Prior, "New Gains in Toy Technology Limit Need for Bells and Whistles," *DSN Retailing Today,* 41(4), (Feburary 25, 2002): 4–5; Daniel Abelow, "Networking Subsystems: Products That Talk," *Data Communications* (March 21, 1993): 90.
8. Susan Bardi Kleiser, Eugene Sivadas, James J. Kellaris, Robert F. Dahlstrom, "Ethical Ideologies: Efficient Assessment and Influence on Ethical Judgments of Marketing Practices," *Psychology & Marketing,* 20(1), (January 2003): 1; Betsy Peterson, "Ethics Revisited," *Marketing Research: A Magazine of Management & Applications*, 8(4), (winter 1996): 47–48.
9. Leigh Somerville, "In the Driver's Seat: NASCAR Seeks Diversification," *The Business Journal,* 5(49), (August 08, 2003): 11; "NASCAR, Nextel Buckle Up as Partners for Top Racing Series," *Knight Ridder Tribune Business News,* (June 20, 2003): 1.

CHAPTER 4

1. Lucia Moses, "Papers Get Bigger Piece of Ad Pie," *Editor & Publisher*, 136(44), (December 8, 2003): 5; Anonymous, "Secondary Source Materials," *Database*, 21(5), (October/November 1998): 20; Joe Nicholson, "Report for the Vindicator," *Editor & Publisher*, 132(38), (September 18, 1999): 38.
2. Anuradha Raghunathan, "Changes May Come for Texas Banks; Market Stunted by Savings-and-Loan Crisis," *Knight Ridder Tribune Business News*, (October 30, 2003): 1; John F. Waldron, "Pat Frost Out to Build Stronger Connections South of the Border," *San Antonio Business Journal,* 16(30), (August 16, 2002): B25; Bill Stoneman, "Banking on Customers," *American Demographics*, 19(2), (February 1997): 36–41.
3. Joseph S. Rabianski, "Primary and Secondary Data: Concepts, Concerns, Errors, and Issues," *The Appraisal Journal*, 71(1), (January 2003): 43–55; John Chapman, "Cast a Critical Eye: Small Area Estimates and Projections Sometimes Can Be Dramatically Different," *American Demographics*, 9, (February 1987): 30.
4. Gary H. Anthes, "Portal Powers GE Sales," *Computerworld,* 37(22), (June 2, 2003): 31; Pamela L. Moore, "GE Catches Online Fever," *Business Week*, (3694), (August 14, 2000): 122; Andy Cohen, "General Electric," *Sales & Marketing Management,* 149(11), (October 1997): 57.
5. Stephen B. Castleberry, "Using Secondary Data in Marketing Research: A Project That Melds Web and Off-Web Sources," *Journal of Marketing Education,* 23(3), (December 2001): 195–203; Diane K. Bowers, "The New Research Tool," *Marketing Research: A Magazine of Management & Applications*, 10(3), (Fall 1998): 34, 38.
6. Anonymous, "State of Ohio Recognizes Lexis-Nexis U.S.," *Information Today,* 20(11), (December 2003): 3; Helen Jezzard, "Lexis-Nexis Responds to User Demands," *Information World Review*, 173, (October 2001): 2.
7. Society of Competitive Intelligence Professionals, "What Is Competitive Intelligence?"(www.scip.org/ci); Jim Underwood (2002), *Competitive Intelligence*, Oxford, UK: Capstone Publishing, pp. 56–59.
8. "2003 Top 10 Soft Drink Review," *Beverage World,* 122(1724), (March 15, 2003): 51–62; Peter J. DePaulo and Rick Weitzer, "Interactive Phone Technology Delivers Survey Data Quickly," *Marketing News*, (June 6, 1994): H33–34.
9. Melanie Payne, "California Agency Spreads Word to Retailers about Credit Card Privacy Law," *Knight Ridder Tribune Business News,* (January 13, 2004): 1; Carol Kroll, "Consumers Reach the Boiling Point Over Privacy Issues," *Advertising Age*, 70(13), (March 29, 1999): 22.
10. Tara Croft, "Tommy Hilfiger Seeks Targets," *The Daily Deal*, (May 9, 2003): (www.tommyhilfiger.com/info/press-release.jhtml?id=701245).

CHAPTER 5

1. Naomi Aoki, "From New England to Hawaii, Surfer-Inspired Clothing Styles Are Hot," *Knight Ridder Tribune Business News,* (August 28, 2003): 1; Sandra Dolbow, "Dockers Goes with Go Khaki," *Brandweek*, 43(16), (April 22, 2002): 5; Cyndee Miller, "A Casual Affair: Clothesmakers Respond to Dress-down Trend with New Lines, Consumer Education Programs," *Marketing News*, 29(6), (March 13, 1995): 1–2.
2. Barbara Correa, "Producers Scramble to Meet Demand for Low-Carbohydrate, Organic Foods," *Knight Ridder Tribune Business News*, (January 18, 2004): 1; Stephanie Thompson, "Oscar Mayer Hams It Up for New Lunch Meat Line," *Advertising Age*, 71(32), (July 31, 2000): 14; "1995 Edison Best New Products Awards Winners," *Marketing News*, 30(10), (May 6, 1996): E4–E11.
3. (www.gallup-robinson.com).
4. Scarborough PrimeNext, Release 2, 2001. NY: Scarborough Research.
5. Joe Mandese, "Sizing Up Audiences by Body Type," *TelevisionWeek*, 22(36), (September 8, 2003): 15; Rick Wartzman, "Nielsen Ratings Spark a Battle Over Just Who Speaks Spanish," *Wall Street Journal*, (February 25, 2000): B1; Megan Larson, "Nielsen Does Full Cable Book," *Mediaweek*, 9(15), (April 12, 1999): 16; Steve McClellan, "Nielsen's Digital Display," *Broadcasting & Cable*, 127(17), (April 21, 1997): 37–38.
6. (www.infores.com).
7. (www.acnielsen.com).
8. (www.nopworld.com).
9. Sonia Reyes, "Campbell's V8 Attempts to Juice Up Young Demo," *Brandweek*, 44(36), (October 6, 2003): 9; Stephanie Thompson, "Diet V8 Splash Carves Niche in

Juice Category for Adults," *Advertising Age*, 71(13), (March 27, 2000): 24; Judann Pollack, "V8, Tropicana Pump Spending for Juices," *Advertising Age*, 68(33), (August 18, 1997): 30; Joanne Lipman, "Single-Source Ad Research Heralds Detailed Look at Household Habits," *The Wall Street Journal*, (February 16, 1988): 39.

10. David Smith, "A Deficit of Consumer Loyalty," *Management Today*, (July 1996): 22; "Europeans More Active as Consumers," *Marketing News*, (October 6, 1991).
11. "iTV: Still Finding Its Place within the New Media Mix," *New Media Age,* (October 30, 2003): P16; Tim Greene, "Bell Atlantic Expands Beyond Local Data Market," *Network World*, 17(25), (June 19, 2000): 48; "Bell Atlantic TV, Mail Push Backs DirecTV," *Advertising Age*, 70(13), (March 29, 1999): 31; Richard Tedesco, "Bell Atlantic's iTV Scorecard," *Broadcasting & Cable*, 126(9), (February 26, 1996): 52; Debra Aho Williamson, "Two-Way, Interactive TV Panels," *Advertising Age*, (May 1, 1995): 26.
12. Anonymous, "Ratings Broken? Demand Better," *Advertising Age,* 74(49), (December 8, 2003): 22; Donna Petrozzello, "Arbitron Moves to Offer Audio Measuring," *Broadcasting & Cable*, 126(36), (August 26, 1996): 38; Steve McClellan, "New Nielsen System Is Turning Heads," *Broadcasting*, (May 18, 1992): 8.
13. Anonymous, "Jowell Brings MPs' Child Ad Complaints to ITC Attention," *Campaign*, (March 8, 2002): 2; Rob Gray, "Perils of Sending Brands to School," *Marketing*, (April 22, 1999): 30–31; Kevin Heubusch, "Is It Ok to Sell to Kids?" *American Demographics*, 19(1), (January 1997): 55.
14. (www.bostonmarket.com/newsroom/index.jsp?page=pressReleases&subPage=2003/060403;] (www.bostonmarket.com/newsroom/index.jsp?page=pressReleases&subPage=2003/012003).

CHAPTER 6

1. William Symonds, "Can Gillette Regain Its Edge?" *Business Week*, 3867, (January 26, 2004): 46; Charles Forelle, "Gillette to Launch Vibrating Razor," *The Wall Street Journal,* (Eastern edition), 243(11), (January 16, 2004): A8; Anonymous, "RB to Launch 'Bladeless' Female Razor," *Marketing Week*, (November 6, 2003): 9.
2. Judith Langer, "'On' and 'Offline' Focus Groups: Claims, Questions," *Marketing News*, 34(12), (June 5, 2000): H38; Richard Cook, "Focus Groups Have to Evolve If They Are to Survive," *Campaign-London*, (July 9, 1999): 14; Howard Furmansky, "Debunking the Myths about Focus Groups," *Marketing News*, 31(13), (June 23, 1997): 22.
3. Elizabeth Dinan, "Focus Group Firm Uses Web for Efficiency, Size," *Mass High Tech,* 21(51), (December 22, 2003): 3; Lynn Vincent, "7 Deadly Sins of Focus Groups," *Bank Marketing*, 31(5), (May 1999): 36–39; John M. Hess and R. L. King, eds. (1968), "Group Interviewing," *New Science of Planning*, Chicago: American Marketing Association, p. 4.
4. *Joe Flint*, "ABC Takes Risks with Fall Lineup," *The Wall Street Journal,* (Eastern edition), (May 15, 2002): B; T. L. Stanley, "Fate by Focus Group," *Mediaweek*, 6, (July 8, 1996): 22–23.
5. Mike Beirne, "Mars Gets Hot and Spicy for Hispanic Consumers," *Brandweek,* 44(21), (May 26, 2003): 10; Kennedy Carol, "The Chocolate Wars: Inside the Secret Worlds of Mars and Hershey," *Director*, 52(9), (April 1999): 80; Judann Pollack, "Mars Says Milky Way Lite Eating Up the Competition," *Advertising Age*, 67(40), (September 30, 1996): 28.
6. Alex Taylor III, "Porsche Risky Recipe," *Fortune,* 147(3), (February 17, 2003): 91; Chris Reiter, "Porsche to Offer Cheaper Version of Hot SUV," *The Wall Street Journal* (Eastern edition), 242(42), (August 28, 2003): D2; Alex Taylor III, "Porsche Slices Up Its Buyers," *Fortune*, 131(1), (January 16, 1995): 24.
7. Jill Dunning, "Fear of Flying: White-Knuckle Ride," *Director,* 57(4), (November 2003): 51; "Fear of Flying, *The Economist*, 339(7966), (May 18, 1996): 30.
8. Mark Beresford, "Trains, Low-Cost Airlines Likely to Put Squeeze on Iberia's Profit," *The Wall Street Journal,* (Eastern edition), (September 3, 2003): 1; Anonymous, "Airlines Brief: Iberia," *The Wall Street Journal,* (February 3, 2003): C11; John Pollack, "Iberia Eyes Americas," *Advertising Age* (International edition), (April 27, 1992).
9. Joan Obra, "Political Mudslinging Makes Money for Media Companies," *Knight Ridder Tribune Business News,* (August 20, 2003): 1; S. Banker, "The Ethics of Political Marketing Practices, The Rhetorical Perspective," *Journal of Business Ethics*, 11, (1992): 843–848.
10. Lotus Web site: (www.lotus.com); (www-3.ibm.com/software/swnews/swnews.nsf/n/jmae5n7sjh?OpenDocument&Site=default).

CHAPTER 7

1. Based on Anonymous, "Bernie Brookes . . . Three Reasons Behind EDLP," *Retail World*, 56(9), (May 12–23, 2003): 24; Anonymous, "Brand Extensions: Five Ways to Avoid a One-Way Ticket to Palookaville," *MIN's B-to-B*, 6(45), (November 24, 2003): 1; Mercedes Cardona, "P&G Ads Support Oil of Olay Brand Extension," *Advertising Age*, 70(10), (March 8, 1999): 22; "1993 Edison Best New Products Awards Winners," *Marketing News*, (April 25, 1994): E5.
2. Victor Godinez, "Pizza Hut President Reflects on Company's Lead Role in Business," *Knight Ridder Tribune Business News,* (December 24, 2003): 1; Gregg Cebrzynski, "Top 100: Pizza Chains Keep New Products Rolling, but Marketing Experts See Commodity Image Downside," *Nation's Restaurant News,* 37(26), (June 30, 2003): 94; Chad Ruben, "Pizza Hut Explores Customer Satisfaction," *Marketing News*, 30(7), (March 25, 1997): 15.
3. Based on Karyn Strauss, "New World Coffee–Manhattan Bagel Aims to Diversify, Adds Smoothies, Sandwiches," *Nation's Restaurant News*, 33(29), (July 19, 1999): 36; "1996 Saw Record Number of New Products," *Quirk's Marketing Research*, 11(2), (February 1997): 27–30.
4. Based on Stephanie Thompson, "Campbell Can Latest Soup Effort," *Advertising Age*, 71(32), (July 31, 2000): 1–2; "Campbell Soup's Stockpot Makes Appointments to Its Sales Teams," *Nation's Restaurant News*, 33(5), (February 1, 1999): 48; "1996 Saw Record Number of New Products," *Quirk's Marketing Research*, 11(2), (February 1997): 27–30.
5. Konstantinos Karagiannis, "Compaq Goes for Gamers," *PC Magazine*, 23(1), (January 20, 2004): 41; *Quirk's Marketing Research Review*, (April 1988): 20.
6. Lillian Chaney, "Making U.S. Teams Work," *SuperVision*, 61(1), (January 2000): 6–8; Anne Marie Moss, "The Challenges of the Future," *FDM, Furniture Design & Manufacturing*, 71(5), (April 1999): 108–115; Anne Marie Moss, "The Office of the Future," *FDM, Furniture Design & Manufacturing*, 69(8), (August 1997): 36–42; "Ignore Your Customers," *Fortune*, (May 1, 1995): 121–122, 124, 126.
7. Based on "1998 Edison Best New Product Winners," *Marketing News*, 33(7), (March 29, 1999): E4, E13+;

"1995 Edison Best New Products Awards Winners," *Marketing News,* 30(10), (May 6, 1996): E4–E11.

8. Barbara Benson, "Market Researcher Wins Clients with Documentaries," *Crain's New York Business*, 17(17), (April 23, 2001): 31.
9. Boaz Herzog, "Nike Is Catching Up with Adidas in Central European Market," *Knight Ridder Tribune Business News,* (November 23, 2003): 1; Stanley Holmes, "The Real Nike News Is Happening Abroad," *Business Week,* 3842, (July 21, 2003): 30; Terry Lefton, "Nike Bulls Ahead," *Brandweek*, 40(7), (February 15, 1999): 3; Roger Baird, "Game, Set and Match," *Marketing Week*, 20(22), (August 28, 1997): 28–31.
10. Nina M. Ray, and Sharon W. Tabor, "Cybersurveys Come of Age," *Marketing Research*, 15(1), (spring 2003): 32; Gordon A. Wyner, "Collaborative Filtering: Research or IT?" *Marketing Research: A Magazine of Management & Applications*, 10(3), (fall 1998): 35–37; Peter J. DePaulo and Rick Weitzer, "Interactive Phone Technology Delivers Survey Data Quickly," *Marketing News*, (June 6, 1994): H33–H34.
11. Thomas R. Shaw, "The Moral Intensity of Privacy: An Empirical Study of Webmasters' Attitudes," *Journal of Business Ethics,* 46(4), (September 2003): 301; Lou E. Pelton, Jhinuk Chowdhry, and Scott J. Vitell, Jr., "A Framework for the Examination of Relational Ethics: An Interactionist Perspective," *Journal of Business Ethics*, 19(3), (Part 2), (April 1999): 241–253; Marla Royne Stafford and Thomas F. Stafford, "Participant Observation and the Pursuit of Truth: Methodological and Ethical Considerations," *Journal of the Market Research Society*, 35, (January 1993): 63–76.
12. Based on Michael Bazeley, "Internet Users Have Ways to Reclaim Privacy," *Knight Ridder Tribune Business News,* (April 17, 2003): 1; Ellen Messmer, "ISP Software Tracks Customers' Every Move," *Network World*, 14(39), (September 29, 1997): 17.
13. Renee Boucher Ferguson, "Automating the Back Office: Netledger, Microsoft Aim Updates at Smaller Firms," *eWeek*, (August 4, 2003): 1.

CHAPTER 8

1. James J. Farrell, "Muzak" *Clergy Journal,* 79(4), (February 2003):14; James J. Farrell, "Merchandising Music," *Clergy Journal*, 79(4), (February 2003): 14; Colleen Bazdarich, "A Buying Mood? Maybe It's the Muzak," *Business 2.0*, 3(3), (March 2002): 100; (www.muzak.com).
2. Matthew Valentine, "And the Overall Winner Is . . . the P-O-P Sector," *In-Store Marketing,* (November 2003): 15; Rachel Miller, "In-Store Impact on Impulse Shoppers," *Marketing*, (November 21, 2002): 27–28; Ken Gofton, "POP Moves Up the Charts," *Marketing*, (POP & Field Marketing Supplement), (April 17, 1997): xi.
3. Susan K. Harmon, and C. Jeanne Hill, "Gender and Coupon Use," *The Journal of Product and Brand Management,* 12(2/3), (2003): 166; Robert W. Shoemaker and Vikas Tibrewala, "Relating Coupon Redemption Rates to Past Purchasing of the Brand," *Journal of Advertising Research*, 25, (October/November 1985): 40–47.
4. Laurel Wentz, "Pepsi Puts Interests Before Ethnicity," *Advertising Age*, 74(27), (July 7, 2003): S–4; Bruce Gilley, "Pepsi Gets Street Smart," *Far Eastern Economic Review*, 163(22), (June 1, 2000): 37; Bruce Crumley, "French Cola Wars," *Advertising Age*, 61(52), (December 17, 1990): 22.
5. "Business: Virtual Advertising," *The Economist*, 354(8153), (January 15, 2000): 68; Robyn Lawrence, "Virtual Advertising Becomes a Reality," *Campaign-London,* (July 2, 1999): 26; Laurence N. Gold, "Virtual Reality Now a Research Reality," *Marketing Research*, (fall 1993): 50–51; Howard Schlossberg, "Shoppers Virtually Stroll Through Store Aisles to Examine Packages," *Marketing News*, (June 7, 1993): 2.
6. Fara Warner, "Levi's Fashions a New Strategy," *Fast Company,* 64 (November 2002): 48, at (www.fastcompany.com/magazine/64/smartcompany.html).

CHAPTER 9

1. James P. Sterba, "Winter Olympics 2002: Annie and Wyatt, Where Are You?–Or Why the Gun-Happy U.S. Keeps Missing the Mark in the Olympic Biathlon," *The Wall Street Journal,* (February 14, 2002): A6; "Olympics Big with Teens around the World," *Quirk's Marketing Research*, (March 1996).
2. Teresa M. McAleavy, "Iraq Tops List of Worries of CEOs, Survey Shows," *Knight Ridder Tribune Business News*, (June 8, 2004): 1; Bill Atkinson, "Greenspan Says Protectionism Won't Cure Outsourcing of American Jobs," *Knight Ridder Tribune Business News*, (March 12, 2004): 1.
3. Sarah Hale Meitner, "Open-Air Centers Overtake Malls in Orlando, Fla., Area," *Knight Ridder Tribune Business News,* (January 12, 2004): 1; Warren Shoulberg, "Mall People," *Home Textiles Today*, 18(49), (August 18, 1997): 16; "The Malling of America," *Quirk's Marketing Research Review*, (May 1990): 15.
4. Tracey Boles, "Japanese Cars Move Up a Gear in Europe," *Knight Ridder Tribune Business News*, (August 12, 2003): 1; Michele Martin, "Why Nissan Cars Are Sporty in the U.S. But Sensible in Europe," *Campaign-London,* (July 4, 1997): 21.
5. James R. Heichelbech, "Ethics 101 Unabridged," *Marketing Research*, 15(1), (spring 2003): 45; Cheryl MacLellan and John Dobson, "Women, Ethics, and MBAs," *Journal of Business Ethics*, 16(11), (August 1997): 1201–1209; Ishmael Akaah, "Differences in Research Ethics Judgments Between Male and Female Marketing Professionals," *Journal of Business Ethics*, 8, (1989): 375–381.
6. Hilary Cassidy, "New Balance Ages Up; IMG Skates Off with Disson," *Brandweek*, 42(2), (January 8, 2001): 8.

CHAPTER 10

1. John Lippman, "Hollywood Research Official Resigns–Rivals Seen Seeking Turf in Movie-Tracking Surveys Long Controlled by NRG," *The Wall Street Journal* (September 23, 2002): B6; Shannon Dortch, "Going to the Movies," *American Demographics*, 18(12), (December 1996): 4–7; Joe Rapolla, "Music Finds an Audience If You Know How to Look," *Marketing News*, 29(18), (August 28, 1995): 17.
2. Kate Macarthur, "McD's Taps Timberlake for 'I'm Lovin' It' Tie-In," *Advertising Age,* 74(31), (August 4, 2003): 3; William Murphy and Sidney Tang, "Continuous Likability Measurement," *Marketing Research: A Magazine of Management & Applications*, 10(2), (summer 1998): 28–35; Ian Fenwick and Marshal D. Rice, "Reliability of Continuous Measurement Copy-Testing Methods," *Journal of Advertising Research*, 31(1), (February/March 1991): 23–29.
3. David Kiley, "Automobile Quality Surveys Disagree," *USA Today*, (June 4, 2003); (www.lexus.com).
4. Naresh K. Malhotra, "A Scale to Measure Self-Concepts, Person Concepts, and Product Concepts," *Journal of Marketing Research*, 18, (November 1981): 456–464.

See also Julie H. Yu, Gerald Albaum, and Michael Swenson, "Is a Central Tendency Error Inherent in the Use of Semantic Differential Scales in Different Cultures?" *International Journal of Market Research,* 45, (second quarter 2003): 213.

5. William M. Rogers, Neal Schmitt, and Morelle E. Mullins, "Correction of Unreliability of Multifactor Measures: Comparison of Alpha and Parallel Forms Approaches," *Organizational Research Methods*, 5(2), (April 2002): 184–199; Kevin E. Voss, Donald E. Stem, Jr., and Stergios Fotopoulos, "A Comment on the Relationship Between Coefficient Alpha and Scale Characteristics," *Marketing Letters*, 11(2), (May 2000): 177; Robert A. Peterson, "A Meta-Analysis of Chronbach's Coefficient Alpha," *Journal of Consumer Research*, 21, (September 1994): 381–391.
6. Mark Peterson, and Naresh K. Malhotra, "Measuring the Appraisal of Ad-Based Affect with Ad Promises," *Journal of Business Research*, 42, (1998), 227–239.
7. Larry Pace, and Eileen Kelly, "TQM at Xerox: Lessons Worth Duplicating," *International Journal of Technology Management*, 16(4–6), (1998): 326–335; Sam M. Malone, "The Baldrige Award: One Step in Xerox's Quest for Excellence," *Quality Progress*, 30(6), (June 1997): 39–42; Betsy McKay, "Xerox Fights Trademark Battle," *Advertising Age International,* (April 27, 1992).
8. Naresh K. Malhotra, (2004), *Marketing Research: An Applied Orientation*, fourth edition, Upper Saddle River, NJ: Prentice Hall.
9. Saul Klein, "Marketing Norms Measurement: An International Validation and Comparison," *Journal of Business Ethics*, 18(1), (January 1999): 65–72; Anusorn Singhapakdi, Scott J. Vitell, Kumar C. Rallapalli, and Kenneth L. Kraft, "The Perceived Role of Ethics and Social Responsibility: A Scale Development," *Journal of Business Ethics*, 15(11), (November 1996): 1131–1140; R. Eric Reidenbach and Donald P. Robin, "A Response to 'On Measuring Ethical Judgments;'" *Journal of Business Ethics*, 14, (February 1995): 159–162.
10. Andrea L. Stape, "Job-Search Site Monster Gets Ready to Make Noise," *Knight Ridder Tribune Business News*, (August 28, 2003): 1; John R. Rossiter, "The C-OAR-SE Procedure for Scale Development in Marketing," *International Journal of Research in Marketing,* 19(4), (December 2002): 305.

CHAPTER 11

1. Based on (www.worldvision.org), Maja Pawinska, "World Vision Raises Profile Among Scots," *PR Week*, (May 23, 2003): 13; Greg Gattuso, Elaine Santoro, and George R. Reis, "Notebooks Open Hearts of Sponsors," *Fund Raising Management*, 27(10), (December 1966): 10–11.
2. Based on Anonymous, "Toons' Study Finds Kids Call the Shots in Buying Decisions," *Businessline*, (February 12, 2003): 1; Paul Miller, "Tapping the Teen Market," *Catalog Age*, 20(8), (July 2003): 31; (www.justkid.com).
3. Based on Janet M. Kelly, and David Swindell, "The Case for the Inexperienced User: Rethinking Filter Questions in Citizen Satisfaction Surveys," *American Review of Public Administration*, 33(1), (March 2003): 91–109; Kenneth C. Schneider and James C. Johnson, "Link Between Response-Inducing Strategies and Uninformed Response," *Marketing Intelligence & Planning*, 12(1), (1994): 29–36; Del I. Hawkins and Kenneth A. Coney, "Uninformed Response Error in Survey Research," *Journal of Marketing Research*, (August 1981): 373.
4. Sonia Reyes, "Healthy Choice for Ice Cream," *Brandweek*, 44(1), (January 6, 2003): 3; "Edison, American Marketing Association, Best New Product Awards," *Marketing News*, 31(6), (March 17, 1997): E5.
5. Based on Sonia R. Reyes, "Kellogg's Goes Bananas for Healthier Corn Flakes," *Brandweek*, 45(1), (January 5, 2004): 4; Judann Pollack and Beth Snyder, "Kellogg's Shifts Two JWT Brands to Burnett in Rift," *Advertising Age*, 70(5), (February 1, 1999): 3, 44; "Edison, American Marketing Association, Best New Product Awards," *Marketing News*, 31(6), (March 17, 1997): E5.
6. Rating a brand on specific attributes early in a survey may affect responses to a later overall brand evaluation. For example, see Larry M. Bartels, "Question Order and Declining Faith in Elections," *Public Opinion Quarterly*, 66(1), (spring 2002): 67–79; Barbara A. Bickart, "Carryover and Backfire Effects in Marketing Research," *Journal of Marketing Research*, 30, (February 1993): 52–62.
7. Robert A. Peterson (2000), *Constructing Effective Questionnaires*, Thousand Oaks, CA: Sage Publications; Elizabeth Martin, and Anne E. Polivka, "Diagnostics for Redesigning Survey Questionnaires," *Public Opinion Quarterly*, 59(4), (winter 1995): 547–567; A. Diamantopoulos, Bodo B. Schlegelmilch, and Nina Reynolds, "Pretesting in Questionnaire Design: The Impact of Respondent Characteristics on Error Detection," *Journal of the Market Research Society*, 36, (October 1994): 295–314.
8. Based on David Cruise Malloy, and James Agarwal, "Factors Influencing Ethical Climate in a Nonprofit Organization: An Empirical Investigation," *International Journal of Nonprofit and Voluntary Sector Marketing,* 8(3), (August 2003): 224; Peter Coolsen, "Opinion Surveys Uncover Cultural Preferences," *Nonprofit World,* 17(2), (March/April 1999): 17–18; Edgar P. Hibbert and Jonathan Liu (1996), *International Market Research–A Financial Perspective*, Blackwell Publishers Inc.
9. Howard J. Gershon, and Gary E. Buerstatte, "The E in Marketing: Ethics in the Age of Misbehavior," *Journal of Healthcare Management*, 48(5), (September/October 2003): 292; Thomas Donalson and Thomas Dunfee, "When Ethics Travel: The Promise and Peril of Global Business Ethics," *California Management Review*, 41(4), (summer 1999): 45–63; R. W. Armstrong, "An Empirical Investigation of International Marketing Ethics: Problems Encountered by Australian Firms," *Journal of Business Ethics*, 11, (1992): 161–171.
10. Trebor Banstetter, "Delta Flights from Dallas/Fort Worth Airport Will Pilot Food Sales," *Knight Ridder Tribune Business News,* (July 9, 2003): 1; Joseph Rydholm, "A Global Perspective," *Quirks Marketing Research Review*, (November 2000) at (www.quirks.com/articles/article.asp?arg_ArticleId=623).

CHAPTER 12

1. Based on "Gillette and Lever Faberge Prepare for Deodorant 'War,'" *Marketing Week,* (January 22, 2004): 9; Alice Naude, "Men's Toiletries in a New Age," *Chemical Market Reporter*, 257(19), (May 8, 2000): FR20–21; Martin Croft, "Men's Toiletries Come of Age," *Marketing Week*, 22(16), (May 20, 1999): 40–41; "Edison, American Marketing Association, Best New Product Awards," *Marketing News*, 31(6), (March 17, 1997): E5.
2. Anonymous, "Gearing Up for 2010," *Forecast,* 23(2), (Feb 2003): 11; Carol O. Rogers, "Census 2000 Update," *Indiana Business Review*, 75(1), (spring 2000): 12; "Just a

Traditional Census," *U.S. News & World Report*, (July 29, 1991): 10.

3. For the effect of sample frame error on research results see Gregory B. Murphy, "The Effects of Organizational Sampling Frame Selection," *Journal of Business Venturing*, 17(3), (May 2002): 237; Seymour Sudman and Edward Blair, "Sampling in the Twenty-First Century," *Journal of the Academy of Marketing Science*, 27(2), (spring 1999): 269–277.
4. Todd Pack, "Orlando, Fla., Survey Finds Only a Quarter of Tourists Changing Plans," *Knight Ridder Tribune Business News,* (April 1, 2003): 1; Donn Tilson and Don Stacks, "To Know Us Is to Love Us: The Public Relations Campaign to Sell a 'Business-Tourist-Friendly' Miami," *Public Relations Review*, 23(2), (summer 1997): 95–115; and "Florida Travel Habits Subject of Phone Survey," *Quirk's Marketing Research Review*, (May 1987): 10, 11, 31, 56, 60.
5. Based on Anonymous, "Coffee News: An Anniversary Promo; Two Cold Coffee Concoctions; A New," *BusinessWorld*, (July 10, 2003): 1; "Edison, American Marketing Association, Best New Product Awards," *Marketing News*, 31(6), (March 17, 1997): E11.
6. Penny Maher, Peter Higgs, Nick Crofts, "Risk Behaviours of Young Indo-Chinese Injecting Drug Users in Sydney and Melbourne," *Australian and New Zealand Journal of Public Health,* 25(1), (February 2001): 50–54; Raymond F. Barker, "A Demographic Profile of Marketing Research Interviewers," *Journal of the Market Research Society*, (July 1987): 279–292.
7. When the sampling interval, *i*, is not a whole number, the easiest solution is to use as the interval the nearest whole number below or above *i*. If rounding has too great an effect on the sample size, add or delete the extra cases.
8. Lisa Granatstein, "Tennis Moves to Net Readers," *Mediaweek*, 8(44), (November 23, 1998): 32; "Readership Survey Serves Tennis Magazine's Marketing Needs," *Quirk's Marketing Research Review*, (May 1988): 75–76.
9. Based on David Chris Reiter, "BMW Reports Increase in Net, Driven by New 5 Series Sedan," *The Wall Street Journal,* (November 7, 2003): B2; "Edison, American Marketing Association, Best New Product Awards," *Marketing News*, 31(6), (March 17, 1997): E4.
10. Based on Laurel Wentz, and Emma Hall, "Kidman to Appear in Chanel No. 5 Ads," *Advertising Age*, 75(3), (January 19, 2004): 17; Barbara Busch, "The Scent of Advertising," *Global Cosmetic Industry*, 171(6), (June 2003): 24; "Edison, American Marketing Association, Best New Product Awards," *Marketing News*, 31(6), (March 17, 1997): E4.
11. Trudy Harpham, Sharon Huttly, Ian Wilson, and Thea De Wet, "Linking Public Issues with Private Troubles: Panel Studies in Developing Countries," *Journal of International Development,* 15(3), (April 2003): 353; B. J. Verhage, U. Yavas, R. T. Green, and E. Borak, "The Perceived Risk Brand Loyalty Relationship: An International Perspective," *Journal of Global Marketing*, 3(3), (1990): 7–22.
12. For the use of different nonprobability and probability sampling techniques in cross-cultural research, see N. L. Reynolds, A. C. Simintiras, and A. Diamantopoulos, "Theoretical Justification of Sampling Choices in International Marketing Research: Key Issues and Guidelines for Researchers," *Journal of International Business Studies*, 34(1), (January 2003): 80–89; Humphrey Taylor, "The Very Different Methods Used to Conduct Telephone Surveys of the Public," *Journal of the Market Research Society*, 39(3), (July 1997): 421–432; Saeed Samiee and Insik Jeong, "Cross-Cultural Research in Advertising: An Assessment of Methodologies," *Journal of the Academy of Marketing Science*, 22, (summer 1994): 205–215.
13. Wendy Zellner, "Lessons from a Faded Levi Strauss; It Has One of the World's Best-Known Brands, But It's Not Hip. And Sales Are Dismal," *Business Week,* 3862, (December 15, 2003): 44; Alice Z. Cuneo, "Levi's 501 Stephen Wilkie," *Advertising Age*, 67, (June 1996): 36.
14. Daulatram B. Lund, "An Empirical Examination of Marketing Professional's Ethical Behavior in Differing Situations," *Journal of Business Ethics*, 24(4), (April 2000): 331–342; William A. Weeks, Carlos W. Moore, Joseph A. McKinney, and Justin G. Longenecker, "The Effects of Gender and Career Stage on Ethical Judgment," *Journal of Business Ethics*, 20(4), (Part 2), (July 1999): 301–313; Marshall Schminke and Maureen L. Ambrose, "Asymmetric Perceptions of Ethical Frameworks of Men and Women in Business and Nonbusiness Settings," *Journal of Business Ethics*, 16(7), (May 1997): 719–729; I. P. Akaah, "Differences in Research Ethics Judgments Between Male and Female Marketing Professionals," *Journal of Business Ethics*, 8, (1989): 375–381.
15. Catherine Belton, Brian Bremner, Kerry Capell, Manjeet Kripalani, Tom Lowry, Dexter Roberts, "MTV's World," *Business Week*, 3770, (February 18, 2002): 81; Gordon Masson, "MTV Availability Reaches 100 Million Mark in Europe," *Billboard*, 113(29), (July 21, 2001): 10–11.

CHAPTER 13

1. Based on Suzanne Vranica, and Charles Goldsmith, "Nielsen Adapts Its Methods as TV Evolves," *The Wall Street Journal* (September 29, 2003): B1; Phillip E. Pfeifer, "The Economic Selection of Sample Sizes for List Testing," *Journal of Interactive Marketing*, 12(3), (summer 1998): 5–20; "The 'Infocritical' Eye," *Marketing Research: A Magazine of Management & Applications*, 9(1), (spring 1997): 37–39.
2. A discussion of the sampling distribution may be found in any basic statistics textbook. For example, see Mark L. Berenson, David M. Levine, and Timothy Krehbiel (2004), *Basic Business Statistics: Concepts and Applications*, ninth edition, Upper Saddle River, NJ: Prentice Hall.
3. Anonymous, "ACSI Government Agency Scores Drop Slightly," *Quality Progress*, 36(2), (February 2003): 18; Barbara Everitt Bryant and Jaesung Cha, "Crossing the Threshold: Some Customers Are Harder to Please Than Others, So Analyze Satisfaction Scores Carefully," *Marketing Research: A Magazine of Management & Applications*, 8(4), (winter 1996): 21–28.
4. Based on Alexandra Jardine, "L'Oreal Puts Brands Under One Roof," *Marketing*, (May 27, 1999): 4; "Edison, American Marketing Association, Best New Product Awards," *Marketing News*, 31(6), (March 17, 1997): E6.
5. "Chinese Airline on a High," *BRW*, 25(29), (July 31, 2003): 13; Kristin S. Krause, "China Airlines' Big Buy," *Traffic World*, 259(7), (August 16, 1999): 37; "Another Chinese Take-Off," *The Economist,* (December 19, 1992).
6. Donna L. Gillin, "Political Poll Disclosure," *Marketing Research*, 15(2), (summer 2003): 8; Nick Panagakis and Warren Mitofsky, "The Polls–Response: Response to 'Was 1996 a Worse Year for Polls than 1948?'" *Public Opinion Quarterly*, 63(2), (summer 1999): 276–284; Vicki G. Morwitz and Carol Pluzinski, "Do Polls Reflect Opinions or Do Opinions Reflect Polls? The Impact of Political Polling on Voters' Expectations, Preferences, and Behavior," *Journal of Consumer Research*, 23(1), (June 1996): 53–67.

7. Based on Jack Neff, "P&G Brings Potty to Parties," *Advertising Age,* (Midwest region edition), 74(7), (February 17, 2003): 22.

CHAPTER 14

1. Based on Leah Nathans Spiro, "Gallup, the Pollster, Wants to Be Known for Its Consulting," *The New York Times*, (July 21, 2003); Gale D. Muller and Jane Miller, "Interviewers Make the Difference," *Marketing Research: A Magazine of Management & Applications*, 8(1), (spring 1996): 8–9.
2. Ted Samson, "Interviewing 101–For Managers," *InfoWorld*, 22(13), (March 27, 2000): 101; Peggy Lawless, "Empathic Interviewing Equals Insightful Results," *Marketing News*, 33(1), (January 4, 1999): 20; Bud Phillips, "The Four Faces of Interviewers," *Journal of Data Collection*, 23, (winter 1983): 35–40.
3. Based on Christine Bittar, "Unilever Brushes Up Mentadent," *Brandweek*, 44(21), (May 26, 2003): 8; "Edison, American Marketing Association, Best New Product Awards," *Marketing News*, 31(6), (March 17, 1997): E6.
4. Based on Mary Carmichael, "Lite Version of Mars Launched in Australia," *Grocer*, 225(7573), (September 28, 2002): 66; "Edison, American Marketing Association, Best New Product Awards," *Marketing News*, 31(6), (March 17, 1997): E6.
5. Janet Guyon, "Brand America," *Fortune*, 148(9), (October 27, 2003): 179; Laurel Wentz, "Poll: Europe Favors U.S. Products," *Advertising Age*, (September 23, 1991).
6. Michael McCarthy, Nissan Xterra Discover Extra Success," *USA Today Online*, (February 26, 2001) at (www.usatoday.com/money/index/2001-02-26-ad-track-nissan.htm#more).

CHAPTER 15

1. Deena M. Amato-McCoy, "Sears Combines Retail Reporting and Customer Databases on a Single Platform," *Stores*, 84(11), (November 2002): 26; Cyndee Miller, "Redux Deluxe: Sears Comeback an Event Most Marketers Would Kill For," *Marketing News*, 30(15), (July 15, 1996): 1, 14.
2. Debbie Thorne McAlister, and Robert C. Erffmeyer, "A Content Analysis of Outcomes and Responsibilities for Consumer Complaints to Third-Party Organizations," *Journal of Business Research,* 56(4), (April 2003): 341; Gordon A. Wyner, "Anticipating Customer Priorities," *Marketing Research: A Magazine of Management & Applications*, 11(1), (spring 1999): 36–38; Jagdip Singh and Robert E. Wilkes, "When Consumers Complain: A Path Analysis of the Key Antecedents of Consumer Complaint Response Estimates," *Journal of the Academy of Marketing Science*, 24, (fall 1996): 350–365.
3. See the SPSS, Excel, SAS, and MINITAB manuals available for microcomputers and mainframes.
4. Vincent Coppola, "Cancer Society Pays Its Way," *Adweek*, 21(14), (April 3, 2000): 3; Don Heinz and Richard K. Robinson, "Nonprofits Need Surveys in Order to Serve Better," *Marketing News*, 33(12), (June 7, 1999): H36; "American Cancer Society Initiative," *Fund Raising Management*, 29(2), (April 1998): 7.
5. Based on Anonymous, "Acer New Notebook Extensa Favors More," *SinoCast China Business Daily News*, (January 5, 2004): 1; Geoffrey James, "U.S. Computer Market: Where East Meets West," *Upside*, 8(12), (December 1996): 78–81.
6. Jim Kanzler, "Business Intelligence Integration," 22(12), (December 2002): 22; " New Data Capture System from NCS," *Quirk's Marketing Research*, (April, 1996).
7. Daniel P. Lorence, "The Perils of Data Misreporting," *Association for Computing Machinery. Communications of the ACM*, 46(11), (November 2003): 85; Barbara Libby, "Ethical Decision Making and the Law," *Journal of Business Ethics,* 26(3), (August 2000): 223–232; Frederick Greenman and John Sherman, "Business School Ethics: An Overlooked Topic," *Business & Society Review,* 104(2), (summer 1999): 171–177; Cheryl MacLellan and John Dobson, "Women, Ethics, and MBAs," *Journal of Business Ethics*, 16(11), (August 1997): 1201–1209; G. M. Zinkhan, M. Bisesi, M. J. Saxton, "MBAs' Changing Attitudes toward Marketing Dilemmas: 1981–1987," *Journal of Business Ethics*, 8 (1989): 963–974.
8. Based on Alice Z. Cuneo, "Calhoun Takes Up Challenge to Revamp Banana Republic," *Advertising Age*, 74(24), (June 16, 2003): 22.

CHAPTER 16

1. Based on Susan K. Harmon, and C. Jeanne Hill, "Gender and Coupon Use," *The Journal of Product and Brand Management*, 12(2/3), (2003): 166; Jack Neff, "Internet Enabling Coupon Fraud Biz," *Advertising Age*, 74(42), (October 20, 2003): 3–4; "Coupons, In-Store Promotions Motivate Consumer Purchasing," *Marketing News*, (October 9, 1995).
2. Avery M. Abernethy, and David N. Laband, "The Customer Pulling Power of Different-Sized Yellow Pages Advertisements," *Journal of Advertising Research*, 42(3), (May/June 2002): 66–72; Sandra Yin, "The Reach of the Yellow Pages," *American Demographics*, 24(10), (November 2002): 24–28; Daniel D. Butler and Avery M. Abernethy, "Yellow Pages Advertising by Physicians," *Journal of Health Care Marketing*, 16, (spring 1996): 45–50.
3. For our purposes, no distinction will be made between formal hypothesis testing and statistical inference by means of confidence intervals.
4. Technically, a null hypothesis cannot be accepted. It can be either rejected or not rejected. This distinction, however, is inconsequential in applied research.
5. Sandra O'Loughlin, "Celebs Fill Holiday Campaign from Gap," *Brandweek*, 44(41), (November 10, 2003): 4; Robin T. Peterson and Douglas T. Ross, "A Content Analysis of the Portrayal of Mature Individuals in Television Commercials," *Journal of Business Ethics*, 16 (1997): 425–433.
6. "General Mills Introduces Harmony–Nutritional Women's Cereal Now Available Nationally," General Mills Web site (January 17, 2001) at (www.generalmills.com/corporate/media/news/story.asp?storyID=706).

CHAPTER 17

1. Mercedes M. Cardona, "Affluent Shoppers Like Their Luxe Goods Cheap," *Advertising Age,* 74(48), (December 1, 2003): 6; Constance L. Hays, "One-Word Shoppers' Lexicon: Price," *The New York Times,* (December 26, 2002, late edition, final), (Section C): 1; Peter J. McGoldrick and Elisabeth Andre, "Consumer Misbehavior: Promiscuity or Loyalty in Grocery Shopping," *Journal of Retailing and Consumer Services*, 4(2), (1997): 73–81.
2. Technically, a null hypothesis cannot be accepted. It can be either rejected or not rejected. This distinction, however, is inconsequential in applied research.

3. The condition when the variances cannot be assumed to be equal is known as the "Behrens-Fisher problem." There is some controversy over the best procedure in this case.
4. Robert Weisman, "Harvard Business School Introduces Mandatory Ethics Course," *Knight Ridder Tribune Business News*, (December 30, 2003): 1; Lori T. Martens and Kristen Day, "Five Common Mistakes in Designing and Implementing a Business Ethics Program," *Business & Society Review*, 104(2), (summer 1999): 163–170; Richard J. Shannon and Robert L. Berl, "Are We Teaching Ethics in Marketing?: A Survey of Students' Attitudes and Perceptions," *Journal of Business Ethics*, 16, (1997): 1059–1075.
5. Based on Sandra O'Loughlin, "Rockport Prints All the New Shoes That Fit," *Brandweek*, 45(24), (June 14, 2004): 11; Carol Krol, "Rockport Updates Image with Comfort Philosophy," *Advertising Age*, (August 11, 1997): 6.
6. The *F*-test is a generalized form of the *t*-test. If a random variable is *t* distributed with *n* degrees of freedom, then t^2 is *F* distributed with 1 and *n* degrees of freedom. Where there are two factor levels or treatments, ANOVA is equivalent to the two-sided *t*-test.
7. Based on Sandra O'Loughlin, "Levi Strauss, Sears Have It Their Way at Burger King," *Brandweek*, 45(25), (June 21, 2004): 5; Soo Youn Soo, "Levi's New Signature Jeans Brand Seeks to Cure Company's Blues," *Knight Ridder Tribune Business News*, (May 20, 2004): 1.
8. Glenn Haussman, "Desks Become Important Aspect in Laptop Culture" (June 18, 1999) online at (www.hotelinteractive.com/news/articleView.asp?articleID=46).

CHAPTER 18

1. Based on Alfred Hille, "Sporting Heritage to Boost Adidas Profile," *Media*, (February 27, 2004): 5; "Adidas: Earning Its Stripes in the U.S." *Business Week Online*, (October 13, 2003).
2. Mark Peterson, and Naresh K. Malhotra, "Comparative Marketing Measures of Societal Quality of Life: Substantive Dimensions in 186 Countries," *Journal of Macromarketing*, 17(1), (spring 1997): 25–38. See also Caroline Fisher, "How Cities Are Ranked for Quality of Life: International," *Benefits*, 32(9), (May 2003): 25.
3. In a strict sense, the regression model requires that errors of measurement be associated only with the criterion variable and that the predictor variables be measured without error.
4. Technically, the numerator is $b - \beta$. However, because it has been hypothesized that $\beta = 0.0$, it can be omitted from the formula.
5. Based on Jean M. Appleby, "Top 25 HMOs with High Satisfaction Ratings," *Managed Healthcare Executive*, 13(1), (January 2003): 47; Vikas Mittal, William T. Ross, Jr., and Patrick M. Baldasare, "The Asymmetric Impact of Negative and Positive Attribute-Level Performance on Overall Satisfaction and Repurchase Intentions," *Journal of Marketing*, 62(1), (January 1998): 33–47; Vikas Mittal and Patrick M. Baldasare, "Eliminate the Negative: Managers Should Optimize Rather Than Maximize Performance to Enhance Patient Satisfaction," *Journal of Health Care Marketing*, 16(3), (fall 1996): 24–31.
6. Based on James T. Madore, "New York Times Looks to Boost Circulation, Sales in Home Market," *Knight Ridder Tribune Business News,* (June 26, 2003): 1; Kelly Shermach, "Times Campaigns to Strengthen Brand Image," *Marketing News*, 31(6), (March 17, 1997): 2.
7. Tom Logue, "Minor League, Major Loyalty: Michigan Baseball Team Surveys Its Fans," *Quirk's Marketing Research Review*, (October 2000) online at (www.quirks.com/articles/article.asp?arg_ArticleId=616).

CHAPTER 19

1. "United Airlines Enhances Easy Check-In Self-Service Units," *Airline Industry Information,* (December 5, 2003): 1; Steve Raabe, "United Airlines Passengers Report Improvement in Customer Service," *Knight Ridder Tribune Business News,* (December 20, 2002): 1; Joseph Rydholm, "Surveying the Friendly Skies," *Quirk's Marketing Research Review*, (May 1996): 11, 33–35.
2. Michele D. Newhouse, "Writing Robust Reports," *Association Management,* 55(3), (March 2003): 83; Thomas L. Greenbaum, "Note to Clients: Hands Off Moderator Report," *Marketing News*, 31(13), (June 23, 1997): 22; Thomas L. Greenbaum, "Using 'Ghosts' to Write Reports Hurts Viability of Focus Group," *Marketing News*, 27(19), (September 13, 1993): 25.
3. Naomi R. Henderson, "In Defense of Clients," *Marketing Research: A Magazine of Management and Applications*, 15(2), (summer 2003): 38; Joop van der Vegt, "We Are Drowning in Data but We Want Information," *Marketing & Research Today*, 26(2), (May 1998): 73–79; Jeannine Bergers Everett, "Value-Added Research Begins Where the Marketplace Meets Management," *Marketing Research: A Magazine of Management and Applications*, 9(1), (spring 1997): 33–36.
4. Paul McDougall, "HP Expands Initiatives for Open Storage," *Information Week*, 795, (July 17, 2000): 36; Lee Gomes, "Hewlett-Packard Sets Its PC Bar Higher and Higher," *The Wall Street Journal*, (September 8, 1997): B4.
5. Information provided by TNS.
6. Personal communication from Mary Klupp.
7. "Toyota Grabs Biggest Market Share in Australia in February," *Jiji Press English News Service*, (March 6, 2003): 1; "Business Briefing," *Far Eastern Economic Review*, 160(35), (August 28, 1997): 65; Lee Geoffrey, "Aussies Chicken Fries Ford," *Advertising Age*, (January 18, 1993).
8. Julie Ray, "Teens Zero in on War, Terrorism as Top Problems," (October 19, 2004) at (www.gallup.com).
9. Lindsey Tanner, "Tobacco Firms Put on Pressure," *Marketing News*, 36(19), (September 16, 2002): 44; Elise Truly Sautter and Nancy A. Oretskin, "Tobacco Targeting: The Ethical Complexity of Marketing to Minorities," *Journal of Business Ethics*, 16(10), (July 1997): 1011–1017; Kenman L. Wong, "Tobacco Advertising and Children: The Limits of First Amendment Protection," *Journal of Business Ethics*, 15(10), (October 1996): 1051–1064; S. Rapp, "Cigarettes: a Question of Ethics," *Marketing*, (November 5, 1992): 17.
10. Terry Box, "Subaru's Expansion Route Includes Solo Dealerships, Sporty Vehicles," *Knight Ridder Tribune Business News*, (August 16, 2003): 1.

PHOTO CREDITS

Chapter 1
Pages 2/3: Corbis Royalty Free. Page 8: AP Wide World Photos. Page 13: Jeff Haynes/Getty Images, Inc.–Agence France Presse. Page 24: Henry Westheim Photography. Page 26: Daniel Acker/Landov LLC.

Chapter 2
Pages 30/31: John Zich/Landov LLC. Page 45: The Gillette Co. Page 52: National Fluid Milk Processor Promotion Board. Page 54: AP Wide World Photos. Page 56: Frank LaBua/Pearson Education/PH College.

Chapter 3
Pages 68/69: Spiegel Catalog New York. Page 78: © Teri Stratford. All rights reserved. Page 81: Sean Gallup/Getty Images. Page 88: AP Wide World Photos. Page 90: AP Wide World Photos.

Chapter 4
Pages 94/95: The *Vindicator*. Page 105: Corbis Royalty Free. Page 115: U.S. Census Bureau. Page 117: The Terry Wild Studio, Inc. Page 119: [Prakash Singh]/Agence France Presse/Getty Images.

Chapter 5
Pages 122/123: Gerhard Steiner/CORBIS-NY. Page 130: © Teri Stratford. All rights reserved. Page 132: AP Wide World Photos. Page 141: Frank LaBua/Pearson Education/PH College. Page 143: Dennis Brack/Landov LLC.

Chapter 6
Pages 146/147: © Teri Stratford. All rights reserved. Page 156: Scott Olson/CORBIS–NY. Page 164: © Teri Stratford. All rights reserved. Page 167: AP Wide World Photos. Page 171: AP Wide World Photos.

Chapter 7
Pages 178/179: © Teri Stratford. All rights reserved. Page 186: Don Smetzer/PhotoEdit. Page 195: Bicycle Magazine. December 2004 issue. Page 199: David Parket/Omni-Photo Communications, Inc. Page 204: Microsoft Corporation.

Chapter 8
Pages 208/209: Myrleen F. Cate/PhotoEdit. Page 215: David Young Wolff/PhotoEdit. Page 220: Pepsi-Cola North America. Page 230: Jean Claude Moschetti/REA Agency/Corbis/SABA Press Photos, Inc. Page 232: © Teri Stratford. All rights reserved.

Chapter 9
Pages 236/237: Nigel Marple/CORBIS–NY. Page 241: Leo Dennis/CORBIS–NY. Page 250: Tim Page/CORBIS–NY. Page 253: Thomas Lohnes/Getty Images, Inc.–Agence France Presse. Page 255: AP Wide World Photos.

Chapter 10
Pages 258/259: Stephanie Cardinale/CORBIS–NY. Page 263: © 2002 MSInteractive LLC. Page 265: Toyota Motor Sales, USA. Inc. Page 277: Xerox Corporation. Page 280: Eric Neurath/Stock Boston.

Chapter 11
Pages 284/285: David Turnley/CORBIS–NY. Page 292: Tom Boyle/Getty Images. Page 300: Henry T. Kaiser/Index Stock Imagery, Inc. Page 301: Jeff Greenberg/PhotoEdit. Page 314: George Hall/Corbis/Bettmann.

Chapter 12
Pages 320/321: © Teri Stratford. All rights reserved. Page 332: Tony Freeman Photographs. Page 337: *Tennis* Magazine. Page 338: AP Wide World Photos. Page 347: AP Wide World Photos.

Chapter 13
Pages 352/353: Cale Merege/Landov LLC. Page 364 (top): Brian A. Vikander/CORBIS-NY. Page 364 (bottom): Getty Images, Inc.–Thinkstock. Page 366: Frank LaBua/Pearson Education/PH College. Page 367: Chuck Nacke/Woodfin Camp & Associates. Page 369: STR/Getty Images, Inc.–Agence France Presse. Page 370: © Teri Stratford. All rights reserved.

Chapter 14
Pages 386/387: Michael Newman/PhotoEdit. Page 391: Ryan McVay/Getty Images, Inc. Photodisc. Page 393: © Teri Stratford. All rights reserved. Page 394: Felicia Martinez/PhotoEdit.

Chapter 15
Pages 402/403: Scott Olson/Getty Images. Page 408: Michael Newman/PhotoEdit. Page 410: LWA Stephen Welstead/CORBIS–NY. Page 416: Acer America. Page 418: James Leynse/CORBIS–NY.

Chapter 16
Pages 426/427: Scott Olson/Getty Images. Page 427: David Young Wolff/Photo Edit. Page 432: Liu Jin/Getty Images, Inc.–Agence France Presse. Page 433: © Teri Stratford. All rights reserved. Page 442: David Cumming/Corbis/Bettmann. Page 451: Peter Mason/Getty Images Inc.–Stone Allstock.

Chapter 17
Pages 460/461: AP Wide World Photos. Page 472: Mike Lovett/Brandeis University Photography Department. Page 476: Frank LaBua/Pearson Education/PH College. Page 481: The Terry Wild Studio, Inc. Page 483: Jay Mallin Photos.

Chapter 18
Pages 494/495: Getty Images. Page 508: Pascal Le Segretain/Getty Images. Page 512: Larry Williams/CORBIS–NY. Page 518: Rudy Von Briel/PhotoEdit. Page 519: Mark Newman.

Chapter 19
Pages 528/529: AP Wide World Photos. Page 536: Tom McCarthy/PhotoEdit. Page 538: Hewlett-Packard Co. Page 543: Toyota Motor Corporation. Page 545: Susan Van Etten/PhotoEdit.

SUBJECT INDEX

A

Accuracy of the data, evaluating the, 100–101
Adjusted R^2, 516
Advertising evaluation, 130–131
Advertising Research Foundation, 536
Alternative-form reliability, 273
Alternative hypothesis, 438
American Demographics, 107
American Marketing Association, 7, 20, 25, 536
American Statistics Index (ASI), 111
Analysis of variance (ANOVA)
  dependent and independent variables, 477
  eta^2, 478
  factors, 477
  illustrative applications, 479–480
  mean square, 478
  measurement of effects, 478
  one-way analysis of variance, 477
  proportions for more than two samples, 480
  significance of the overall effect, 479
  significance testing, 478
  $SS_{between}$, 477
  SS_{error}, 477
  SS_{within}, 477
  SS_y, 477
  treatment conditions, 477
Analytical model, 49–50
ANOVA. *See* Analysis of variance (ANOVA)
Approach to the problem
  analytical framework and models, 49–50
  graphical models, 50
  mathematical models, 50
  objective evidence, 49
  research questions and hypotheses, 50–51
  specification of information needed, 51–53
  theory, 49
  verbal models, 50
Area sampling, 339
ASI. *See* American Statistics Index (ASI)
Association techniques, 165
Audilogs, 133
Audiotex, 569
Audit services, 128, 137–138
Authorization, letter of, 534
Automated voice response, 569
Average value, 434

B

Balanced *versus* unbalanced scale, 268–269
Bar charts, 539
Basic information, 303
Beta coefficient, 508
Beta weight, 508
Bibliographic databases, 111
Bibliographies, 106–107
Bivariate correlation, 497–502
Bivariate cross-tabulation, 443
Bivariate regression, 504, 505–506, 507
Branching questions, 304
Brand Strategy, 232
Broad statement, 48
Budgeting and scheduling the project, 85
Business America, 109
Business Conditions Digest, 109
Business Index, 106
Business Information Sources, 106
Business Periodical Index, 106
Business Statistics, 109
Business Week, 549
Buyer behavior, 43–44
Buying Power Index, 114

C

CAPI. *See* computer-assisted personal interviewing (CAPI)
Cartoon tests, 166
CASRO. *See* Council of American Survey Research Organizations (CASRO)
Categorical data analysis, 453
CATI. *See* computer-assisted telephone interviewing (CATI)
CATS. *See* Completely Automated Telephone Surveys (CATS)
Causal design, 80–82
Causal research, 74, 80–82
Causal research design
  absence of other possible causal factors, 213
  causality, concept of, 210, 212
  concomitant variation, 212
  conditions for causality, 212–213
  control group, 215
  controlling extraneous variables, 218–219
  demand artifacts, 226
  dependent variables, 214
  design control, 219
  evidence, role of, 213
  experimental design, 215
  experimental group, 215
  experimentation, role of, 211, 214
  external validity, 216–217
  extraneous variables, 214, 217–218
  factorial design, 225
  field environment, 227
  history (*H*), 217
  independent variables, 214
  instrumentation (*I*), 217
  interactive testing effects, 223
  internal validity, 216
  laboratory environments, 226
  laboratory *versus* field experiments, 226–227
  limitations of experimentation, 227–228
  matching, 219
  maturation (*MA*), 217
  mortality (*MO*), 218
  multiple time series design, 224
  one-group pretest/posttest design, 221
  one-shot case study, 220–221
  posttest-only control group design, 223–224
  preexperimental designs, 219, 220–222
  pretest/posttest control group design, 222–223
  quasi-experimental designs, 219, 224
  random assignment, 215
  randomization, 218
  selecting an experimental design, 226
  selection bias (*SB*), 218
  static group, 221, 222
  statistical control, 219
  statistical design, 219, 225
  statistical regression (*SR*), 218
  symbols, definition of, 216
  test marketing, 228
  test units, 214
  testing effects, 217
  time order of occurrence of variables, 212–213
  time series design, 224
  true experimental designs, 219, 222–223
  validity in experimentation, 216–217
Causality, concept of, 210, 212
Census, 321, 323
Census data, 108
Central limit theorem, 356
Chi-square distribution, 446, 585–586
Chi-square statistic, 445–447
Classical conditioning, 230
Classification information, 303
Classification of market research designs, 72
Cluster sampling, 335, 338–339, 340
CMOR. *See* Council for Marketing and Opinion (CMOR)
Codebook, 407–409
Coding, 407–410
Coding and data entry services, 18
Coefficient alpha, 274
Coefficient of determination, 509–510
Coefficient of multiple determination, 516
Combined adjustment, 366–367
Comparative scales, 246
Completely Automated Telephone Surveys (CATS), 202, 203, 398
Completion rate, 366
Completion techniques, 165
Computer-assisted personal interviewing (CAPI), 187–188, 411
Computer-assisted telephone interviewing (CATI), 184, 411, 562
Computer mapping, 114
Computerized databases, 109–112
Conceptual map, 46
Conclusive research, 73, 82–83
Concomitant variation, 212
Confidence interval approach, 358–360
Confidence intervals, 356
Confidence level, 356
Consistency checks, 412–413
Constant sum scaling, 249–250
Construct, 271–272
Construct validity, 274
Construction techniques, 166
Consultants and Consulting Organizations Directory, 107

Consumer Reports, 382
Content of questions, determination of, 292–293
Content of the data, evaluating the, 102
Content validity, 274
Contingency coefficient, 447–448
Contingency tables, 443
Continuous rating scale, 260–261, 263
Control group, 215
Convenience sampling, 330–331, 340
Convergent validity, 274
Correlation coefficient, 497–502
Council for Marketing and Opinion (CMOR), 26
Council of American Survey Research Organizations (CASRO), 26, 183, 284, 397
Country Business Patterns, 109
County and City Data Book, 109
Covariance (COV_{xy}), 498
COV_{xy}. *See* Council of American Survey Research Organizations (COV_{xy})
Cramer's *V,* 448
Criterion validity, 274
Critical value, determining and comparing the, 440–441
Critical value of the test statistic (TS_{CR}), 471
Cronbach's alpha, 274
Cross-sectional design, 78
Cross-sectional *versus* longitudinal designs, 79, 80
Cross-tabulations, 442–445, 448–449
Currency of data, evaluating, 102
Customer databases, 104
Customer-relationship management (CRM) systems, 104
Customized services, 18

D

Data analysis
  alternative hypothesis, 438
  average value, 434
  bivariate cross-tabulation, 443
  chi-square distribution, 446
  chi-square statistic, 445–447
  contingency coefficient, 447–448
  contingency tables, 443
  Cramer's *V,* 448
  critical value, comparing the, 441
  critical value, determining the, 440–441
  cross-tabulations, 442–445, 448–449
  data collection, 439
  formulating the hypothesis, 438
  frequency distribution, 429–432
  frequency histogram, 433
  goodness-of-fit tests, 447
  hypothesis testing, 436–441, 481
  hypothesis testing related to differences (*See* Hypothesis testing related to differences)
  level of significance, choosing a, 439
  marketing research conclusion, 441
  mean, 434
  measures of location, 433
  median, 434
  mode, 434
  null hypothesis, 438
  one-tailed test, 438
  outliers, presence of, 430
  phi coefficient, 447
  power of a statistical test, 439
  power of a test, 439
  probability, determining the, 440–441
  range, 435
  selecting an appropriate test, 438–439
  skewed distribution, 435
  standard deviation, 435
  symmetric distribution, 435
  test statistic, 438–439
  two-tailed test, 438
  type-I error, 439, 440
  type-II error, 439
  variability, measures of, 435
  variance, 435
Data analysis services, 18
Data analysis strategy, selecting a, 414–415
Data cleaning, 412–413
Data collection, 439. *See* Field work/data collection
Data conversion and preparation, 421–423
Data mining, 104
Data preparation and analysis strategy
  codebook, 407–409
  coding, 407–410
  consistency checks, 412–413
  data analysis strategy, selecting a, 414–415
  data cleaning, 412–413
  data preparation process, 405–406
  editing, 406–407
  fixed field codes, 409
  missing responses, treatment of, 413–414
  multivariate techniques, 415
  open-ended question responses, coding, 410–411
  questionnaire checking, 406
  structured questions, coding, 409
  transcribing, 411–412
  univariate techniques, 415
  unstructured questions, coding, 409
  variable respecification, 414–415
Data warehouse, 104
Database marketing, 104, 105
Debriefing, 231
Decision-support systems (DSS), 21, 22
Decomposition of the total variation, 477, 510
Demand artifacts, 226
Dependability of the data, 103
Dependent and independent variables, 477
Dependent variables, 214
Descriptive research, 74, 76–77, 82–83
Design checklist, 308–309
Design process, 288–289, 290, 325–329
Dichotomous question, 298
Direct approach, 152
Direct Marketing Association, 117
Directories, 107
Directories in Print, 107
Directories of databases, 112
Directory databases, 111
Discriminant validity, 275
Discussion guide, preparing the, 154
Dissemination, 539–540
Double-barreled question, 292–293
Dual statements, 302

E

E-mail surveys, 191
Economic environment, 44
Editing, 406–407
Electronic scanner data, 134–135
Element, 322
Encyclopedia of Associations, 107
Encyclopedia of Business Information Sources, 106
Environment, designing the proper, 153
Environmental context of the problem, 42
ESOMAR. *See* European Society for Opinion and Marketing Research (ESOMAR)
Estimated value, 506
Estimation of parameters, 506–507
Eta^2, 478
Ethnographic research, 200
European Society for Opinion and Marketing Research (ESOMAR), 26
Evaluation, scale, 273–276
Evidence, role of, 213
Executive summary, 534
Experience survey, conducting an, 39
Experimental design, 215, 226
Experimental group, 215
Experimentation, role of, 211, 214
Exploratory research, 72, 74–75, 82–83
Exploratory research and conclusive research, differences between, 73
Expressive techniques, 166–168
External data, 103
External secondary data, 106–109
External supplier, 15
External validity, 216–217
Extraneous variables, 214, 217–218, 218–219

F

F distribution, 470, 590–592
F statistic, 469
F-test, 469, 517
Factorial design, 225
Factors, 477
FAST search, 12
Fax surveys, 189
Federal Trade Commission, 19
Field environment, 227
Field services, 18
Field work/data collection
  evaluating field workers, 395
  Internet, using the, 396
  nature of, 390
  probing, 392
  process of, 390
  psychographic breakdown of interviewers, 391
  sampling control, 394
  selecting field workers, 390–391
  supervising field workers, 392–393
  training of field workers, 391–392
  validating field work, 394–395
Filter questions, 293
FIND/SVP, 107
FINDEX: The Directory of Market Research Reports, 107
Fixed field codes, 409
Flow charts, 539

Focus-group discussion guide for pocket PCs, 155
Focus-group interviews, 152
Focus groups. *See* Qualitative research
Follow-up methods, 194, 541–542
Forced or nonforced choice, 269
Format, report, 533–535
Formulating a research design, 72, 84
Fortune 500 Directory, 107
Frequency distribution, 429–432
Frequency histogram, 433
Full-service suppliers, 16
Full-text databases, 111
Funnel approach to ordering questions, 304

G

General business data, 106–107
General Business File, 106–107
General surveys, 131
Geo-demographic coding, 113
Geo-visual databases, 113–114
Geographic maps, 538
Goodness-of-fit tests, 447
Government publications, 108, 109
Government sources, 107–108
Graphic rating scales, 261
Graphical models, 50
Graphs, guidelines for, 537–540
Group interview, conducting the, 154
Guide to Consumer Markets, 107
Guides, 106

H

Headings, 537
Histogram, 539
Historical Market Data Center, 111
History (*H*), 217
Humanistic inquiry, 196
Hypothesis
  formulating the, 438
  testing the, 436–441, 481
Hypothesis testing related to differences
  analysis of variance (ANOVA), 476–481 (*See also* Analysis of variance (ANOVA))
  critical value of the test statistic (TS_{CR}), 471
  F distribution, 470
  F statistic, 469
  F-test, 469
  independent samples, two, 468
  means, 468, 474
  one-sample *t*-tests, 465–468
  one-tailed test, 471–472
  paired samples, 473–475
  paired-samples *t*-test, 474–475
  parametric tests, 463
  proportions, 472–473, 475
  t distribution, 464
  t statistic, 464
  t-test, 464–465, 471
  test for a single mean, 465–467
  test for a single proportion, 467–468
  two-sample *t*-tests, 468–475
  two-tailed test, 471–472
  z-test, 466

I

Identification information, 303
IFOP-CMR, 230
IMRO. *See* Interactive Marketing Research Organization (IMRO)
In-depth interviews, 161–163
In-home interviews, personal, 186
Inability to answer, overcoming respondent's, 293–294
Incentives, using, 193–194
Incidence rate, 365
Independent samples, 468
Independent variables, 214, 477
Index to Publications, 109
Indexes, 106–107
Indirect approach, 152
Industrial product syndicated services, 128
Industry experts, interviews with, 39
Industry services, 138–139
Information required, specification of, 289–290
Information value chain, 14–15
Instrumentation (*I*), 217
Interactive testing effects, 223
Interactive voice-response (IVR), 202
Internal and external data, merging, 112–114
Internal-consistency reliability, 274
Internal data, 103–104
Internal supplier, 15
Internal validity, 216
International Council of Shopping Centers, 101
International marketing research, 23, 54
Internet databases, 110
Internet surveys, 191–192
Interval scale, 243–245
Interviewer bias, 187
Interviewing method, specification of, 290–291
Itemized rating scales, 263–267
IVR. *See* Interactive voice-response (IVR)

J

Judgmental sampling, 331–332, 340

K

"KISS 'em" principle, 540
Known probabilities, finding values corresponding to, 374–375
Known values, finding probabilities corresponding to, 373–374

L

Laboratory environments, 226
Laboratory *versus* field experiments, 226–227
Leaders, 537
Least-squares procedure, 505
Legal environment, 44
Level of significance, choosing a, 439
Lifestyle, 130
Likert scale, 263–265
Limited-service suppliers, 18
Line chart, 538–539
Longitudinal data, 134
Longitudinal design, 78–79

M

Mail interviews, 188–190
Mail methods, 188–189
Mail panels, 190
Mall intercept personal interviews, 187
Management-decision problem, 45–46
Marketing decision making, 11–13
Marketing information systems (MIS), 21–22
Marketing research
  career opportunities, 19–20
  definition of, 5–6
  DSS, role in, 21–22
  ethics, role of, 25, 55
  evolution of, 62–63
  international, 54
  Internet, role of the, 6
  MIS, role in, 20–22
  overview of, 5
  problem identification research, 7–8
  problem-solving research, 8
  stakeholders in, 25
  technology and, 24–25, 54
Marketing Research Association, 25, 399
Marketing research conclusion, 441
Marketing research industry
  coding and data entry services, 18
  customized services, 18
  data analysis services, 18
  external supplier, 15
  field services, 18
  full-service suppliers, 16
  internal supplier, 15
  Internet services, 18
  limited-service suppliers, 18
  syndicated services, 16
Marketing research problem
  analytical framework and models, 49–50
  broad statement, 48
  defining the, 47–48
  errors in defining the problem, 48
  graphical models, 50
  mathematical models, 50
  objective evidence, 49
  research questions and hypotheses, 50–51
  specific components of the problem, 48
  specification of information needed, 51–53
  theory, 49
  verbal models, 50
Marketing research process, 9–11
Marketing research proposal, 86–87
Marketing Tools, 107
Matching, 219
Mathematical models, 50
Maturation (*MA*), 217
Mean square, 478
Means, 434, 468, 474
Means and proportions, sample size determination for, 360–362
Measurement, definition of, 238
Measurement and scaling
  alternative-form reliability, 273
  balanced *versus* unbalanced scale, 268–269
  classification of scaling techniques, 246–247
  coefficient alpha, 274
  comparative scales, 246
  components of, 238–239
  constant sum scaling, 249–250
  construct, 271–272
  construct validity, 274
  content validity, 274
  continuous rating scale, 260–261, 263
  convergent validity, 274
  criterion validity, 274

Cronbach's alpha, 274
discriminant validity, 275
evaluation, scale, 273–276
forced or nonforced choice, 269
graphic rating scales, 261
internal-consistency reliability, 274
interval scale, 243–245
itemized rating scales, 263–267
Likert scale, 263–265
marketing research process, relationship of, 251
measurement, definition of, 238
monadic scales, 260
multi-item scales, 271–272
nominal scale, 240–242
nomological validity, 275
noncomparative itemized rating-scale decisions, 268–271
noncomparative scales, 246
noncomparative scaling techniques, 260–263
number of scale categories, 268
odd or even numbers of categories, 269
ordinal scale, 242–243
paired comparison scaling, 247–248
physical form or configuration, 270
primary scales, 240–241, 246
random error, 273
rank order scaling, 248–249
ratio scale, 244–245
reliability, 273
reliability and validity, relationship between, 276
scaling, definition of, 239
selecting a level of measurement, 245
selecting a scaling technique, 276
semantic differential, 263
semantic differential scale, 265–267
sensitivity of a scale, 268
split-half reliability, 274
Stapel scale, 263, 267
systematic error, 273
test–retest reliability, 273
validity of scale, 274
verbal description, nature and degree of, 269–270
Measurement of effects, 478
Measures of location, 433
Mechanical observation, 196–198
Media panels, 128, 132–134
Median, 434
Methodology used for data collection, examination of, 100
Million Dollar Directory: Leading Public and Private Companies, 107
Missing responses, treatment of, 413–414
MO. See Mortality (*MO*)
Mode, 434
Moderator, selecting a, 154
Monadic scales, 260
Monthly Catalog of United States Government Publications, 106
Mortality (*MO*), 218
Multi-item scales, 271–272
Multiple-choice questions, 297–298
Multiple regression analysis, 513–517
Multiple time series design, 224
Multivariate techniques, 415

N

NAICS. *See* North American Industry Classification System (NAICS)
National Newspaper Index, 107
Nominal scale, 240–242
Nomological validity, 275
Nongovernmental statistical data, 107
Noncomparative itemized rating-scale decisions, 268–271
Noncomparative scales, 246
Noncomparative scaling techniques, 260–263
Nonprobability sampling, 327, 330–334, 339–341
Nonresponse bias, 190
Nonsampling errors, 85
Normal distribution, 373–375
North American Industry Classification System (NAICS), 109
Null hypothesis, 438
Number of scale categories, 268
Numeric databases, 111

O

Objective evidence, 49
Objective of the data, evaluating the, 102
Observation, definition of, 195
Observation methods
advantages of observation methods, 196, 198–199
disadvantages of observation methods, 199
humanistic inquiry, 196
mechanical observation, 196–198
observation, definition of, 195
on-site observation, 196
personal observation, 196
Observational forms, 307, 309
Odd or even numbers of categories, 269
Offline databases, 110–111
Omnibus panels, 128
On-site observation, 196
One-group pretest/posttest design, 221
One-sample *t*-tests, 465–468
One-shot case study, 220–221
One-stage cluster sampling, 338
One-tailed test, 438, 471–472
One-way analysis of variance, 477
Online databases, 110
Online focus groups, 158–159
Online sampling, 341–344
Online sampling adjustments, 367–368
Online *versus* traditional focus groups, 160
Open-ended question responses, coding, 410–411
Opening questions, 302
Oral presentation, 539–540
Order or position bias, 298
Ordinal scale, 242–243
Organization of questions, 302–305
Outliers, presence of, 430

P

Paired comparison scaling, 247–248
Paired samples, 473–475
Paired-samples *t*-test, 474–475
Panel, 79
Panel surveys, 127–129
Parameter, 355
Parametric tests, 463
Partial *F*-test, 517
Partial regression coefficients, 514–515
Past information and forecasts, 42
Pearson correlation coefficient, 497–502
Periodic surveys, 127
Personal methods, 186–188
Personal observation, 196
Phi coefficient, 447
Physical form or configuration, 270
Pictographs, 539
Picture-response techniques, 166
Pie charts, 538
Pilot surveys, 41
PIMS. *See* Profit Impact of Market Strategies (PIMS)
Point-of-purchase (POP), 213
Population, 322
Posttest-only control group design, 223–224
Power of a statistical test, 439
Power of a test, 439
Preexperimental designs, 219–222
Precision level, 355
Precision of sample results, 327–328
Precoding, 305–306
Predicasts Basebook, 107
Predicasts Forecasts, 107
Predicted value, 506
Prediction accuracy, 512
Prepaid incentive, 193–194
Preparing the focus-group report, 154, 156
Pretest/posttest control group design, 222–223
Pretesting the questionnaire, 307
Primary data, 40, 97
Primary scales, 240–241, 246
Primary *versus* secondary data, 99
Prior notification, 193
PRIZM (Potential Rating Index for Zip Markets), 113
Probability, determining the, 440–441
Probability sampling, 328, 334–339
Probing, 392
Problem audit, conducting a, 36–37
Problem definition process
buyer behavior, 43–44
case studies, 41
conducting discussions with decision makers, 36–37
economic environment, 44
environmental context of the problem, 42
experience survey, conducting an, 39
industry experts, interviews with, 39
Internet, role of the, 37–38
legal environment, 44
past information and forecasts, 42
pilot surveys, 41
primary data, 40
problem audit, conducting a, 36–37
qualitative research, 40–41
resource constraints and objectives, 43
secondary data analysis, 39–40
Problem identification research, 7–8
Product moment correlation, 497–502
Projective techniques, 164–169
Promised incentive, 193–194
Proportions, 472–473, 475
Proportions, sample size determination for, 362–365

Proportions for more than two samples, 480
Psychographic breakdown of interviewers, 391
Psychographics, 104, 130
Purchase panels, 128, 132–134

Q

Qualitative research
  advantages of focus groups, 157
  analysis of qualitative data, 169
  applications of focus groups, 159
  association techniques, 165
  cartoon tests, 166
  classification of qualitative research procedures, 152
  completion techniques, 165
  conducting a focus group, 152–153
  construction techniques, 166
  direct approach, 152
  disadvantages of focus groups, 157
  discussion guide, preparing the, 154
  environment, designing the proper, 153
  expressive techniques, 166–168
  focus-group discussion guide for pocket PCs, 155
  focus-group interviews, 152
  focus groups *versus* in-depth interviews, 163
  group interview, conducting the, 154
  in-depth interviews, 161–163
  indirect approach, 152
  moderator, selecting a, 154
  online focus groups, 158–159
  online *versus* traditional focus groups, 160
  picture-response techniques, 166
  preparing the focus-group report, 154, 156
  projective techniques, 164–169
  qualitative research *versus* quantitative research, 150–151
  recruiting and selecting focus-group participants, 153–154
  role playing, 166
  sentence completion, 165
  software, 172
  story completion, 165
  third-person technique, 167–168
  word association, 165
Qualitative research *versus* quantitative research, 150–151
Quasi-experimental designs, 219, 224
Questionnaire and form design
  basic information, 303
  branching questions, 304
  classification information, 303
  content of questions, determination of, 292–293
  definition of questionnaire, 288
  design checklist, 308–309
  design process, 288–290
  dichotomous question, 298
  double-barreled question, 292–293
  dual statements, 302
  filter questions, 293
  form and layout, selecting, 305–306
  funnel approach to ordering questions, 304
  identification information, 303
  importance of the questionnaire, 288
  inability to answer, overcoming respondent's, 293–294
  information required, specification of, 289–290
  interviewing method, specification of, 290–291
  multiple-choice questions, 297–298
  observational forms, 307, 309
  opening questions, 302
  order or position bias, 298
  organization of questions, 302–305
  precoding, 305–306
  pretesting the questionnaire, 307
  reproducing the questionnaire, 306
  scales, 298–299
  structure, determination of question, 296–299
  structured questions, 296–297
  unstructured questions, 296–297
  unwillingness to answer, overcoming respondent's, 294–295
  wording, determination of question, 299–302
Questionnaire checking, 406
Quirk's Marketing Research Review, 117
Quota sampling, 331–333, 340

R

Random assignment, 215
Random-digit dialing (RDD), 336, 347
Random error, 273
Random sampling error, 85, 356
Randomization, 218
Range, 435
Rank order scaling, 248–249
Ratio scale, 244–245
RDD. *See* Random-digit dialing (RDD)
Regression analysis
  adjusted R^2, 516
  applications of, 503–504
  beta coefficient, 508
  beta weight, 508
  bivariate correlation, 497–502
  bivariate regression, 504–507
  coefficient of determination, 509–510
  coefficient of multiple determination, 516
  correlation coefficient, 497–502
  covariance (COV_{xy}), 498
  decomposition of the total variation in bivariate regression, 510
  estimated value, 506
  estimation of parameters, 506–507
  F-test, 517
  least-squares procedure, 505
  multiple regression analysis, 514–517
  multiple regression model, 513
  partial *F*-test, 517
  partial regression coefficients, 514–515
  Pearson correlation coefficient, 497–502
  predicted value, 506
  prediction accuracy, 512
  product moment correlation, 497–502
  regression line, 505
  residuals, examination of, 512
  scatter diagram, 505–512
  scattergram, 505–512
  significance testing, 509, 517
  simple correlation, 497–502
  SS_{error}, 510
  SS_{reg}, 510–511
  SS_{res}, 510–511
  SS_y, 510–511
  standard error, 509
  standard error of estimate (SEE), 512
  standardization, 508
  standardized regression coefficients, 508–509
  strength and significance of association, 509–512, 515–516
  sum of squared errors, 505
  t-statistic, 509
Regression coefficient, 495
Regression line, 505
Reliability, 273
Reliability and validity, relationship between, 276
Report preparation and presentation
  approach to the problem, 535
  assisting the client after the research report, 541
  authorization, letter of, 534
  bar charts, 539
  conclusions and recommendations, 535
  data analysis, 535
  dissemination, 539–540
  evaluation of the research project, 541–542
  executive summary, 534
  flow charts, 539
  follow-up actions, 541–542
  format, report, 533–535
  geographic maps, 538
  graphs, guidelines for, 537–540
  headings, 537
  histogram, 539
  importance of, 531
  "KISS 'em" principle, 540
  leaders, 537
  limitations and caveats, 535
  line chart, 538–539
  oral presentation, 539–540
  pictographs, 539
  pie charts, 538
  problem definition, 534–535
  process of, 532
  research design, 535
  results, 535
  round chart, 538
  schematic figures, use of, 539
  stubs, 537
  table of contents, 534
  tables, guidelines for, 536–537
  "tell 'em" principle, 540
  title page, 534
  transmittal, letter of, 534
  writing the report, 535–536
Reproducing the questionnaire, 306
Research design
  basic research designs, 72–73
  causal design, 80–82
  causal research, 74, 80–82
  classification of market research designs, 72
  conclusive research, 73, 82–83
  cross-sectional design, 78
  cross-sectional *versus* longitudinal designs, 79–80
  definition of, 71–72
  descriptive research, 74, 76–77, 82–83
  exploratory research, 72, 74–75, 82–83

exploratory research and conclusive research, differences between, 73
formulating a research design, 72, 84
longitudinal design, 78–79
marketing research, and the importance of, 85
nonsampling errors, 85
panel, 79
random sampling error, 85
selecting research designs, 82–83
surveys, 77
Research supplier, selecting a, 18–19
Residuals, examination of, 512
Resource constraints and objectives, 43
Response rates, 184, 193–194, 366
Results, 535
Role playing, 166
Round chart, 538

S

Sales and Marketing Management Survey of Buying Power, 107
Sample, 322–323
Sample control, role of, 184
Sample size determination, final and initial
adjusting the statistically determined sample size, 365–366
central limit theorem, 356
combined adjustment, 366–367
completion rate, 366
confidence interval approach, 358–360
confidence intervals, 356
confidence level, 356
incidence rate, 365
means and proportions, sample size determination for, 360–362
online sampling adjustments, 367–368
parameter, 355
precision level, 355
proportions, sample size determination for, 362–365
random sampling error, 356
response rate, 366
sampling distribution, 356–358
standard error, 357
statistic, 355
statistical approach to determining sample size, 358
statistical inference, 356
symbols for population and sample variables, 356
z value, 357
Sample *versus* census, 324–325
Sampling control, 394
Sampling design and procedures. *See also* Sample size determination, final and initial
area sampling, 339
census, 323
classification of sampling techniques, 330
cluster sampling, 335, 338–340
convenience sampling, 330–331, 340
design process, 325–329
element, 322
judgmental sampling, 331–332, 340
nonprobability sampling, 327, 330–334
nonprobability sampling *versus* probability sampling, 339–341
one-stage cluster sampling, 338
online sampling, 341–344
population, 322
precision of sample results, 327–328
probability sampling, 328, 334–339
quota sampling, 331–333, 340
sample, 322–323
sample size, determining, 328–329
sample *versus* census, 324–325
sampling efficiency, 334
sampling error, 323
sampling frame, determining the, 326–327
sampling interval, 336
sampling process, executing the, 329
sampling technique, selecting a, 327–328
sampling unit, 326
simple random sampling (SRS), 335–336, 340
single-stage area sampling, 339
snowball sampling, 331, 333–334, 340
stratified sampling, 335, 337–340
systematic sampling, 335–336, 340
target population, defining the, 326
two-stage area sampling, 339
two-stage cluster sampling, 338
Sampling distribution, 356–358
Sampling efficiency, 334
Sampling error, 323
Sampling frame, determining the, 326–327
Sampling interval, 336
Sampling process, executing the, 329
Sampling techniques, 327–328, 330
Sampling unit, 326
SB. See Selection bias (*SB*)
Scales, 298–299
Scaling. *See* Measurement and scaling
Scaling, definition of, 239
Scanner data, 136–137
Scanner panels with cable TV, 128, 135–136
Scanner-volume tracking data, 128
Scatter diagram, 505–512
Scattergram, 505–512
Schematic figures, use of, 539
Secondary data
accuracy of the data, evaluating the, 100–101
advantages of, 99
applications of, 99–100
bibliographic databases, 111
bibliographies, 106–107
Buying Power Index, 114
census data, 108
classification of, 103–105
computer mapping, 114
computerized databases, 109–112
content of the data, evaluating the, 102
criteria for evaluation, 100–103
currency of data, evaluating, 102
customer databases, 104
data mining, 104
data warehouse, 104
database marketing, 104–105
dependability of the data, 103
directories, 107
directories of databases, 112
directory databases, 111
disadvantages of, 100
external data, 103
external secondary data, 106–109
full-text databases, 111
general business data, 106–107
geo-demographic coding, 113
geo-visual databases, 113–114
government publications, 108–109
government sources, 107–108
guides, 106
indexes, 106–107
internal and external data, merging, 112–114
internal data, 103–104
Internet databases, 110
methodology used for data collection, examination of, 100
nongovernmental statistical data, 107
North American Industry Classification System (NAICS), 109
numeric databases, 111
objective of the data, evaluating the, 102
offline databases, 110–111
online databases, 110
versus primary data, 99
psychographics, 104
special-purpose databases, 112
Standard Industrial Classification Code (SIC), 108
syndicated services, 113
Secondary data analysis, 39–40
SEE. *See* Standard error of estimate (SEE)
Selection bias (*SB*), 218
Semantic differential, 263
Semantic differential scale, 265–267
Sensitivity of a scale, 268
Sentence completion, 165
Shared surveys, 129
SIC. *See* Standard Industrial Classification Code (SIC)
Significance testing, 478, 509, 516
Simmons Marketing Research Bureau, 113
Simmons National Consumer Survey (NCS), 134
Simple correlation, 497–502
Simple random sampling (SRS), 335–336, 340
Single-source data, 140
Single-stage area sampling, 339
Skewed distribution, 435
Snowball sampling, 331, 333–334, 340
Social desirability, 187
Social Sciences Citation Index, 107
Software, 172
Special-purpose databases, 112
Split-half reliability, 274
SR. See Statistical regression (*SR*)
SRS. See Simple random sampling (*SRS*)
$SS_{between}$, 477
SS_{error}, 477, 510
SS_{reg}, 510–511
SS_{res}, 510–511
SS_{within}, 477
SS_y, 477, 510–511
Standard & Poor's Statistical Service, 107
Standard deviation, 435
Standard Directory of Advertisers, 107
Standard error, 357, 509
Standard error of estimate (SEE), 512
Standard Industrial Classification Code (SIC), 108
Standard Rate and Data Service, 107
Standardization, 508

Standardized regression coefficients, 508–509
Stapel scale, 263, 267
Static group, 221–222
Statistic, 355
Statistical Abstract of the United States, 109
Statistical approach to determining sample size, 358
Statistical control, 219
Statistical design, 219, 225
Statistical inference, 356
Statistical regression (*SR*), 218
Story completion, 165
Stratified sampling, 335, 337–340
Strength and significance of association, 509–512, 515–516
Structure, determination of question, 296–299
Structured data collection, 182
Structured questions, 296–297, 409
Stubs, 537
Sum of squared errors, 505
Survey methods
  advantages of, 181–182, 185
  classification of, 183
  computer-assisted personal interviewing (CAPI), 187–188
  computer-assisted telephone interviewing (CATI), 184
  definition of, 181
  disadvantages of, 181–182
  e-mail surveys, 191
  electronic methods, 190–192
  fax surveys, 189
  follow-up methods, 194
  in-home interviews, personal, 186
  incentives, using, 193–194
  Internet surveys, 191, 192
  interviewer bias, 187
  mail interviews, 188–190
  mail methods, 188–189
  mail panels, 190
  mall intercept personal interviews, 187
  nonresponse bias, 190
  personal methods, 186–188
  prepaid incentive, 193–194
  prior notification, 193
  promised incentive, 193–194
  response rate, 184
  response rates, improving, 193–194
  sample control, role of, 184
  selecting a survey method, 193
  social desirability, 187
  structured data collection, 182
  telephone interviews, 183–185
Survey of Buying Power, 114
Survey of Current Business, 109
Surveys, 77, 127–128, 131–132
Symbols for population and sample variables, 356
Symmetric distribution, 435
Syndicated data
  advertising evaluation, 130–131
  audit services, 128, 137–138
  classification of syndicated services, 127–132
  electronic scanner data, 134–135
  general surveys, 131
  industrial product syndicated services, 128
  industry services, 138–139
  lifestyle, 130
  media panels, 128, 132–134
  nature of, 125
  omnibus panels, 128
  panel surveys, 127–129
  periodic surveys, 127
  psychographics, 130
  purchase panels, 128, 132–134
  scanner data, 136–137
  scanner panels with cable TV, 128, 135–136
  scanner-volume tracking data, 128
  shared surveys, 129
  single-source data, 140
  surveys, 127–128
  syndicated services, 125
  syndicated sources, 125
  syndicated survey research, classification of, 129
  volume-tracking data, 135
Syndicated services, 16, 113, 125
Syndicated sources, 125
Syndicated survey research, classification of, 129
Systematic error, 273
Systematic sampling, 335–336, 340

T

t distribution, 464, 587–589
t statistic, 464
t-test, 464–465, 471
Table of contents, 534
Tables, guidelines for, 536–537
Target population, 321, 326
Telephone interviews, 183–185
"Tell 'em" principle, 540
Test for a single mean, 465–467
Test for a single proportion, 467–468
Test marketing, 228
Test–retest reliability, 273
Test statistic, 438–439
Test units, 214
Testing effects, 217
Theory, 49
Third-person technique, 167–168
Third wave, 24
Thomas Register of American Manufacturers, 107
Time order of occurrence of variables, 212–213
Time series design, 224
"Time-use" research, 3
Title page, 534
Transcribing, 411–412
Transmittal, letter of, 534
Treatment conditions, 477
True experimental designs, 219, 222–223
TS_{CR}. *See* Critical value of the test statistic (TS_{CR})
Two-sample *t*-tests, 468–475
Two-stage area sampling, 339
Two-stage cluster sampling, 338
Two-tailed test, 438, 471–472
Type-I error, 439–440
Type-II error, 439

U

Univariate techniques, 415
Universal product code (UPC), 134, 196
Unstructured questions, 296–297, 409
Unwillingness to answer, overcoming respondent's, 294–295

V

Validity in experimentation, 216–217
Validity of scale, 274
Variability, measures of, 435
Variable respecification, 414–415
Variance, 435
Verbal description, nature and degree of, 269–270
Verbal models, 50
Virtual reality (VR), 230
Volume-tracking data, 135
VR. *See* Virtual reality (VR)

W

Wall Street Journal Index, 107
Word association, 165
Wording, determination of question, 299–302
Writing the report, 535–536

Z

z-test, 466
z value, 357

COMPANY AND PRODUCT INDEX

A
ABC, 161
ABI/Inform Global, 111
Abt Associates Inc., 17
Accenture, 65–67, 123
Acer, 253, 416
ACNielsen Company, 16, 19, 111, 122, 134, 136, 138, 144, 179, 196, 384
Adam Opel AG, 377
Adidas, 74, 202, 495–496
Advanced Micro Devices (AMD), 271
Advertising Research Foundation, 536
AFLAC (American Family Life Assurance Company), 558–559
AGB Group, 17
Aim toothpaste, 215
Airbus, 369
Allstate, 104
Allure, 341
Alta Vista, 12
America Online, Inc., 12, 353
American Airlines, 131, 369
American Cancer Society, 413
American Marketing Association, 7, 20, 25, 536
American Statistics Index (ASI), 111
American Tourister, 26
Andersen Consulting, 66
Andrew Jergens Company, 78
Apple, 253
Arbitron Inc., 17, 113
Arby's, 40
Arizona jeans, 232
Arnold Worldwide of Boston, 144
Arthur Andersen, 66
Ask Jeeves, 12
AT&T, 38, 133, 141, 159
Atra Plus, 60
AutoPacific Group, 13

B
B. Dalton, 568
Bahama Breeze, 551–552
Banana Republic, 418
Bank of America (BOA), 75
BBDO International, 19
BellSouth, 37–38
Berrier Associates, 386
Bloomingdales, 379–381
BMW, 81, 159, 338, 377
Boeing Company, 369, 562–568
Bon-Macy's, 379
Boston Market Corp., 144
Brain Waves Group, 237
Brand Strategy, 232
Brisk Iced Tea, 200
Bugle Boy, 243
Buick, 377
Burdines-Macy's, 379
Burger King, 381–382
Burke, Inc., 16, 18–20, 62–65, 494

C
Cadillac, 159, 376–378
Cadillac Catera, 377
Cadillac Cimarron, 377
Calvin Klein, 232, 243, 245, 481
Camay bath soap, 88
Camel cigarettes, 544
Campbell Soup Company, 140–141, 191
Canon, 224, 277
Cap'n Crunch, 85, 230
Carnival Cruise Lines, 41
Century City Hospital, 41
Chanel No. 5, 341
Chanel, Inc., 341
Charles of the Ritz, 44
Charmin, 370–371
Cheer, 159
Cheerios, 159, 230
Chesebrough-Pond's, 79
Cingular Wireless, 47
CIT Group/Commercial Services, 119
Citibank, 345
Citigroup, 16
Citrosuco Paulista, 54
Claritas, Inc., 101, 113
Clear Stick deodorant, 321–322, 344
Coach, 244
Cobalt Group, 546
Coca-Cola, 16, 19, 61, 90, 117, 123, 125, 133, 151, 168, 197, 230, 247–248, 288, 325, 467
Cold Brew Blend, 200
Colgate, 247, 442
Colgate Palmolive, 16, 138
Columbia-HCA Healthcare Corp., 378
Comcast, 113
Compaq, 194, 253
Computers for Marketing Corp. (CfMC), 278
ComScore Networks, 134
ConAgra Frozen Foods, 44, 297
Congressional Information Service, Inc., 112
Courtyard by Marriott, 577–578
Crest, 179, 192, 247
Crown Publishers, 568
Cuadra Associates, Inc., 112
CustomerSat, 271

D
DaimlerChrysler, 556
Darden Restaurants, Inc., 551–553
Data Recognition Corp. (DRC), 545
Data World Research Inc., 368
Decision Analyst, Inc., 528
Del Monte International, 442
Dell Computers, 89, 253
Delta Airlines, 90, 197, 200, 314
Dentsu Research Inc., 17
Designory Team, 399
Dial, 261
Dialog Corp., 111
Diesel, 232, 243
Diet V8 Splash, 141
Direct Marketing Association, 117
Dockers, 124, 347
Dockers Individual Fit, 124
Donnelley Marketing Information Services, 101
Dooney and Bourke, 244
Doritos, 332
DoubleClick, 197
Dow Jones News Retrieval, 111
DSS Research, 313
Dun & Bradstreet (D&B), 111
Duracell brand, 60, 321

E
E*TRADE, 160
E-Valuations.com, 83–84
Eastman Kodak, 14, 159
eCareers, 280
eJobs, 280
Encyclopedia Britannica, 107
Endicott, 568
Enron, 124
Equifax, 118
Eric Marder and Associates, 208
ESPN, 4
European Opel Omega MV6, 377
European Society for Opinion and Marketing Research (ESOMAR), 26
EXCEL, 420
Experian, 104

F
Fairfield Inn and Suites, 577
Federated Department Stores, Inc., 165, 379
Field Facts, Inc., 18
Field Work Chicago, Inc., 18
FIND/SVP, 107
First Nation Peppermint, 560
Fisher-Price, 43
Florida Department of Tourism, 329
Ford Motor Company, 15, 90, 123, 129, 146, 549–551
Ford Sable, 549
Ford Taurus, 129, 549
Frappuccino, 383
Frito-Lay, 332
Frost Bank, 99–100
Frosted Flakes, 230
Fuji Heavy Industries, 575

G
Gale Research Company, 112
Gallup and Robinson Magazine Impact Studies, 131
Gallup Organization, The, 80, 249, 387–388, 395–396, 544
Gap, Inc., 232, 243, 245, 418, 481
Gateway, 253
Gatorade, 158

General Electric, 105, 141
General Hospital, 141
General Mills, 136, 159, 451
General Motors, 11–13, 15, 131, 196, 376–378, 549
GfK Group, 17, 23
Gillette Company, 45, 60–61, 147–148, 150–151, 321–322, 325, 329, 340, 344
Global Mapping International, 402
Goldsmith's-Macy's, 379
Goody, Silverstein & Partners, 123
Google, 12
Greenfield Consulting Group, 18
Greenfield Online Research Center Inc., 18
Groups Plus Inc., 533
Gucci, 131, 244, 568–574
Guess?, 242–243, 481
Guiding Light, 141

H
H Hilfiger, 165
Haggar Apparel, 123–125
Haggar's Comfort Fit, 124
Harris InfoSource, 107
Harris Interactive Inc., 17
HCA-Healthcare Corp., 378–379
Head & Shoulders, 179
Healthy Choice, 44, 297
Hefty OneZip, 199
Heinz, 54
Hewlett-Packard, 16, 194, 197, 253, 537–540
Holiday Inn, 74
Home Depot, 102
Honda, 200, 549
Honda Accord, 129, 549
Honest Tea, 559–561
Honomichl Global Top 25, 17
Host Marriott, 577
HotJobs, 280
Hotwired, 204
Huggies, 47

I
Iberia, 171
IBM, 253
IFOP-CMR, 230
IMS Health Inc., 17, 23
IncrediBagel Stuffed Bagels, 188
Infiniti, 159
Information Resources Inc., 17, 23, 135, 140, 332
Inland Research Corp., 95–96, 100, 108, 114
IntegralGIS, 197
INTGATE Inc., 17
Ipsos Group, S.A., 17, 542
Ivory, 73

J
J. Walter Thompson, 19
JC Penney, 44, 133, 142, 232, 247, 481
J.D. Power and Associates, 17, 265, 377
J.P. Morgan, 123
Jergens Body Shampoo, 78
Jobtrack, 280
Jordache, 242–243
JP Morgan Chase, 16
Just Kid, Inc., 289

K
Kantar Group, 17, 23
Kaplan Thaler Group, 558
Kellogg Company, 56, 133, 136, 215, 303
Kellogg's Corn Flakes, 215
Kellogg's Honey Crunch Corn Flakes, 303
Kellogg's Product 19, 247
Kellogg's Smart Start, 451
Kenmore, 61
Kforce, 280
Kimberly-Clark, 47
KitKat, 248, 453
Kraft, 130
Kroger, 83, 427

L
Lancôme, Paris, 366
Lands' End, 61, 142
Lays, 332
Lazarus-Macy's, 379
Lee jeans, 50–51, 243
Leo Burnett USA, 418
Levi Strauss & Company, 44, 124–125, 232, 237, 243, 252, 347, 481
LexisNexis, 111–112
Lexus, 159, 265, 377, 549
Lieberman Research Worldwide, 17
Lipton, 200
Lotus Development Corporation, 175
Lycos, 12

M
M3Power, 60
Mach III, 60
Macy's, 165, 379
Macy's Home Store, 379
Maritz Research, 17–18, 23, 346
Market & Opinion Research Int'l, 17
Market Strategies, Inc., 178
Marriott International, Inc., 55, 197, 483, 577–579
Mars, Inc., 36–37, 163–164, 394, 558
Marshall Field's, 124–125
Maxfli, 375–376
Maytag, 61
McCann Erickson Worldwide Advertising, 275
McDonald's, 8, 144, 197, 309–310, 381–382
McDonnell Douglas, 369
MCI, 38, 159
McKinsey & Company, 144
Mediamark, 113
Mentadent, 79
Mentadent Inter-Sweep, 393
Mentadent Oral Care toothbrush, 393
Mercedes, 102, 159, 377
Message Factors, 519
Meteor Motorcycle Company, 87, 307
Micra, 253
Microrebate Investing, 461
Microsoft Corp., 76, 81, 89, 205, 553–555
Milky Way, 164
Milky Way Lite Bar, 394
Minolta Camera Company, 277
Mintel International, 255
Mitsubishi Electric Corp., 277
Modern Media, 117
Moist Mates, 370–371
Monster.com, 280
Motorola, 141, 197
Mr. Potato Head, 381
MSInteractive, 263
MSN Search, 13
MTV Networks, 348
Musial University, 486–487, 499, 522–523
Muzak, 209–210, 214–216, 223, 229

N
N.Y. Yankees, 330
National Association of Stock Car Auto Racing (NASCAR), 90–91
National Purchase Diary, 79
NationsBank, 75
NEC, 253
Neiman Marcus, 406
Nestlé, 453
Netscape Search, 13
New Balance Athletic Shoe, Inc., 255
New York Times, 365, 518
NFO WorldGroup Inc., 17, 133
Nike, 3, 49, 74, 184, 202, 255, 384–385, 430–432, 443–444
Nikkei Research Inc., 17
Nissan Motor Company, 142, 253, 399–400
NOP World, 17
Nordstrom, 142
Norwegian Cruise Lines, 41
NPD Group Inc., 17–18, 79, 123, 125, 144
NRC Data Systems, 18

O
Ogilvy & Mather, 19
Olay, 179–180, 187, 193, 201
Old Navy, 242–243, 418, 558
Old Spice, 46
Olestra, 332
Olive Garden, 551–552
Opinion Research Corporation, 17, 236
Option Technologies, 278
Oral-B, 60
Osbourne, 220
Oscar Mayer, 130
Oshkosh B'Gosh, 44
Oxy-Gen.com, 246

P
P. Robert and Partners, 314
Pampers, 47, 88, 179
Pearson NCS, 416
Pearson Research, 258
Pep Boys, 139
Pepperidge Farms, 297
PepsiCo, 117, 125, 159, 219–225, 227, 230–231, 247–248, 266, 288, 558
Philippe Starck, 26
Pillsbury, 133
Pink Passion Venus, 147–148
Pizza Hut, 42, 186
Polo, 8, 481
Pontiac, 377
Porsche, 167
PortiCo Research, 200
Procter & Gamble, 15, 19, 23–24, 47, 61–62, 73, 88, 105, 179–180, 187, 190, 193, 196–197, 200–201, 229, 370–371, 556
Progress Energy, Inc., 320

ProQuest Information & Learning, 111
Puma, 202

R
R.L. Polk, 104
R.R. Bowker, 112
R.R. Donnelley, 104
Ralph Lauren, 8, 481
Ramada, 577
RC Cola, 247
RCA, 141
Red Lobster, 551–552
Reebok International, 3, 4, 6, 10–11, 16, 19, 22–23
Renaissance, 578
Renault, SA, 253
Research International, 398
Residence Inn, 577
Revlon, 48
Rich's-Macy's, 379
Ricoh Company, 277
Ritz Carlton, 577–578
Rizzoli, 568
Rockport, 476
Roper Reports, 129
RoperASW, 129–130, 221
Rouge Attraction, 366
Royal Caribbean Cruises, 41

S
Saatchi & Saatchi Advertising, 543
Saks Fifth Avenue, 406
Samsonite, 26
Sara Lee, 144
SaveRite Grocery Warehouses, 461
SBC, Inc., 115
Scarborough Research, 132
SDR Consulting, 18, 426
Sears, Roebuck and Company, 39, 61–62, 247, 403, 413, 481
Seasons 52, 551
Sensor, 60
Sensor Excel, 60
Sensor for Women, 147–148, 165
Smokey Bones BBQ, 551–552
Southern Company, 7
Southwestern Bell, 115
Spiegel, 69–70, 75, 78, 81, 87
Sprint, 159
Sprite, 288
SRI Consulting, 130
Standard & Poor's, 111
Starbucks Corporation, 332, 383–384
Starbucks International Coffee, 383
State Fair Foods, 188
Steelcase, 197–198
Stockpot Soups, 191
Subaru of America, Inc., 31–32, 34, 53, 545–546, 575–577
Survey Samples, Inc. (SSI), 344
Swatch, 77
Synovate, 17–18, 129, 376, 427

T
Target, 165, 166, 232, 257, 264–267, 271, 274, 302, 414
Taylor Nelson Sofres plc, 17
TaylorMade-Adidas Golf, 375
TeleNation, 129
Tenet Healthcare Corporation, 41
Tide, 179, 215
TNS, 18–19, 23, 190, 540, 562–563
Tommy Hilfiger Corp., 8, 119, 165, 232, 481
Total cereal, 247, 451
Toyota, 129, 543, 549
Tracker Marine Group, 352
Tracy-Locke Direct, 117
Travelocity, 204

U
U.S. Census Bureau, 19, 40–41
U.S. Department of Transportation, 342
U.S. Postal Service, 164
Unilever USA, 133, 393
United Airlines, 529
UPS (United Parcel Service), 188
USAData.com, 107

V
V8 juice, 141
V8 Splash, 141
V8 Splash Smoothies, 141
Vanderbilt perfume, 159
Vende, 244
Venus, 60
Verizon, 142
Verizon Information Services, 460
Vick's, 179
Video Research Ltd., 17
Visa International, 102, 142, 166
VNU N.V., 17

W
W.A. Dean & Associates, 568
Wal-Mart, 39, 61, 132, 135, 232
Waldenbooks, 568
Walt Disney, 418, 467, 471, 556
WardsAuto.com, 377
WebCrawler, 13
Wendy's, 382
West Interactive, 117
West Michigan Whitecaps, 519
Westat Inc., 17
Whirlpool, 61
Whole Foods, 559
Winn-Dixie, 461
Wirthlin Worldwide, 17
World Vision (WV), 285–286
WorldCom, 124
WorldOpinion, 21
Wrangler, 243, 245

X
Xerox, 277
Xterra, 399

Y
Yahoo!, 13
Yankelovich Research and Consulting Services, 130
Yellow Pages, 433
Young & Rubicam, 19

NAME INDEX

A
Ali, Laila, 496
Ali, Muhammad, 496
Andres, Michel, 144

B
Bacik, Roger, 30
Baker, Kris, 122
Baker-Prewitt, Jamie, 494
Ballmer, Steve, 205
Barberena, Manuel, 258
Barstys, Joe, 575
Beckham, David, 496
Berrier, Robert J., 386
Blythe, Bruce, 253
Bonbright, Chris, 352
Bowers, Diane, 284
Branson, Jeff, 87
Bryant, Kobe, 495
Burke, Alberta, 62–65
Bush, George, 174, 249, 370

C
Calhoun, Jack, 418
Cedergren, Chris, 13
Charles, Ray, 117, 220
Clinton, William, 174
Close, Glenn, 260
Crystal, Billy, 220

D
Davis, Jim, 255
De Sole, Domenico, 568
Drexler, Millard, 418
Dukakis, Michael, 174
Duncan, Tim, 495
Duyff, Roberta, 451

E
Eisenberg, Hallie, 220
Estefan, Gloria, 230

F
Fink, James C., 236
Flickinger, Burt, 418
Fox, Michael J., 220
Franklin, Allen, 7
Freston, Tom, 348
Fruend, David, 320

G
Gaffka, Doug, 549
Garber, Amy, 382
Garnett, Kevin, 495
Garvey, Jennifer, 460
Ghosn, Carlos, 399–400
Gibson, Larry, 208
Goldman, Seth, 559–560
Gore, Al, 174
Green, Tom, 220
Greenbaum, Thomas, 533
Grinstein, Gerald, 314
Gucci, Maurizio, 568
Gutierrez, Carlos, 56

H
Hammer, M.C., 230
Hansen, Mark, 418
Helton, Mike, 90–91
Hilfiger, Tommy, 119
Hodapp, Susan, 483
Hogan, Paul, 32
Horowitz, Joel J., 119
Howell, John, 378

I
Iglesias, Enrique, 220

J
Jackson, Michael, 219
Johnson, Don, 220
Jung, Helen, 385

K
Kennedy, Joe, 377
Kennon, Kevin, 380
Kerry, John, 370
Klupp, Mary, 146, 541
Knowles, Beyonce, 220
Kroll, Bob, 442

L
Lacy, Alan, 62
Lafley, A.G., 370–371
Lai, Paul, 314
Lane, Scott, 519
Linnane, Fran, 14

M
Marineau, Philip, 232
Mariott, John, 577
Marriott, Alice S., 483, 577
McGee, Jim, 402
McGrady, Tracy, 495–496
Miller, Bob, 543
Moses, Elissa, 237

N
Neal, William, 426
Nevel, Luc Van, 26

P
Paslick, Marty, 379
Pearson, Kar, 497
Pressler, Paul, 418

R
Randall, Wayne, 370
Richie, Lionel, 220
Romer, Richard, 119
Rooke, Dennis, 376
Roy, Surjya, 178

S
Saito, Takao, 545
Salaam, Eric, 398
Sanger, Stephen W., 451
Schultz, Howard, 383
Shakira, 220
Shurtleff, Jill, 147–148
Spears, Britney, 231
Srichaphan, Paradorn, 496
Stapel, Jan, 267
Stewart, Rod, 230
Stonecipher, Harry, 562–563
Szorek, Jerry, 96

T
Taylor, Jeff, 280
Thomas, Jerry, 528
Toffler, Alvin, 24
Turner, Tina, 230

W
Wallace, Chris, 68
Ward, Leah Beth, 385
Wilkins, Michael, 380
Willard, J., 483
Winter, Jerry, 117

Z
Zidane, Zinedine, 496
Zollar, Al, 175

CLASS NOTES

CLASS NOTES

CLASS NOTES

CLASS NOTES

CLASS NOTES

CLASS NOTES

CLASS NOTES

CLASS NOTES

CLASS NOTES

THIS LICENSE AGREEMENT IS YOUR PROOF OF LICENSE.

To license the software, you must be a currently enrolled student or an instructor at a university or college, and using the software for educational purposes only. **THIS IS A LEGAL AGREEMENT FOR A SINGLE-USER LICENSE OF THE SOFTWARE BETWEEN YOU (Student or Instructor) AND SPSS INC.** If you do not agree to the terms of this License Agreement or you are not a student or an instructor at college or university using the software for educational purposes, immediately return the package.

This software is protected by both United States copyright law and international copyright treaty provisions.

LICENSE

SPSS Inc. grants you a non-exclusive license to use the software in accordance with the following terms. SPSS Inc. retains title and all ownership rights to the software.

SPSS Inc. grants you a single-user license which allows one (1) designated individual, and only one (1) individual, the right to install and use the software on up to two (2) computers.

SPSS Inc. grants you the right to make one (1) archival copy of the software for the sole purpose of backing up the software and protecting your investment from loss.

TERM AND TERMINATION

Failure to comply with any of these terms will terminate this agreement and your right to use the software. Upon termination of this agreement, you must immediately destroy the software and all copies of it.

LIMITED WARRANTY

The media the software is furnished is warranted to be free of defects in workmanship and material under normal use for a period of sixty (60) days from the date of purchase by you. SPSS Inc. and its suppliers' sole responsibility and your exclusive remedy under this warranty will be to receive a replacement of the media or a full refund if SPSS Inc. or its suppliers are unable to deliver media free from defects in workmanship and materials.

You alone are responsible for determining which software best meets your particular needs for installing software and for the results obtained.

THIS SOFTWARE IS LICENSED "AS IS" WITHOUT WARRANTY AS TO ITS PERFORMANCE. EXCEPT FOR THE MEDIA WARRANTY PROVIDED ABOVE, THERE ARE NO WARRANTIES EXPRESSED OR IMPLIED, INCLUDING BUT NOT LIMITED TO IMPLIED WARRANTIES OF MERCHANTABILITY OR FITNESS FOR A PARTICULAR PURPOSE, AND ALL SUCH WARRANTIES ARE EXPRESSLY DISCLAIMED. IN NO EVENT SHALL SPSS INC. OR ITS SUPPLIERS BE RESPONSIBLE FOR ANY INDIRECT OR CONSEQUENTIAL DAMAGES OR LOST PROFITS, EVEN IF SPSS INC. AND ITS SUPPLIERS HAD BEEN ADVISED OF THE POSSIBILITY OF SUCH DAMAGE. SOME STATES DO NOT ALLOW THE EXCLUSION OR LIMITATION OF IMPLIED WARRANTIES OR LIABILITY FOR INCIDENTAL OR CONSEQUENTIAL DAMAGES, SO THE ABOVE LIMITATION MAY NOT APPLY TO YOU.

GENERAL

The software and this agreement cannot be transferred without the express written consent of SPSS.

This agreement will be governed by the laws of the State of Illinois.

You acknowledge that this agreement supersedes all prior agreements, proposals, representations and communications between the parties relating to the subject matter herein. In the case of conflict between this agreement and purchase orders issued for the software, the terms of this agreement shall prevail.

You may return the software only in accordance with the return policy of SPSS Inc. Contact your SPSS representative for the proper procedure.

U.S. GOVERNMENT RESTRICTED RIGHTS

The Software and documentation are provided with Restricted Rights. Use, duplication, or disclosure by the Government is subject to restrictions as set forth in subparagraph (c)(1) of the Rights in Technical Data and Computer Software clause at DFARS 252.227-7013 or subparagraphs (c)(1)(ii) and (2) of Commercial Computer Software-Restricted Rights at 48 CFR 52.227-19, as applicable. Contractor/manufacturer is SPSS Inc., 233 S. Wacker, 11th Floor, Chicago, IL 60606-6307.

This product includes software developed by the Apache Software Foundation (http://www.apache.org/).

This software consists of voluntary contributions made by many individuals on behalf of the Apache Software Foundation and was originally based on software copyright © 1999, International Business Machines, Inc., <http://www.ibm.com>. For more information on the Apache Software Foundation, please see <http://www.apache.org/>.

The following warranty applies for Xerces and ICU:

Copyright © 1999,2000,2001 Compaq Computer Corporation
Copyright © 1999,2000,2001 Hewlett-Packard Company
Copyright © 1999,2000,2001 IBM Corporation
Copyright © 1999,2000,2001 Hummingbird Communications Ltd.
Copyright © 1999,2000,2001 Silicon Graphics, Inc.
Copyright © 1999,2000,2001 Sun Microsystems, Inc.
Copyright © 1999,2000,2001 The Open Group

All rights reserved.

THE SOFTWARE IS PROVIDED "AS IS", WITHOUT WARRANTY OF ANY KIND, EXPRESS OR IMPLIED, INCLUDING BUT NOT LIMITED TO THE WARRANTIES OF MERCHANTABILITY, FITNESS FOR A PARTICULAR PURPOSE AND NONINFRINGEMENT OF THIRD PARTY RIGHTS. IN NO EVENT SHALL THE COPYRIGHT HOLDER OR HOLDERS INCLUDED IN THIS NOTICE BE LIABLE FOR ANY CLAIM, OR ANY SPECIAL INDIRECT OR CONSEQUENTIAL DAMAGES, OR ANY DAMAGES WHATSOEVER RESULTING FROM LOSS OF USE, DATA OR PROFITS, WHETHER IN AN ACTION OF CONTRACT, NEGLIGENCE OR OTHER TORTIOUS ACTION, ARISING OUT OF OR IN CONNECTION WITH THE USE OR PERFORMANCE.